THIS COPY OF

BRITISH MOTORCYCLES

IS SIGNED BY THE AUTHOR

RINSEY MILLS

H&S

BRITISH MOTORCYCLES 1945-1965

from Aberdale to Wooler

By Rinsey Mills

Herridge & Sons

British Motorcycles 1945-1965 is published with the support of the Michael Sedgwick Memorial Trust. The M.S.M.T. was founded in memory of the motoring historian and author Michael C. Sedgwick (1926–1983) to encourage the publication of new motoring research, and the recording of Road Transport History. Support by the Trust does not imply any involvement in the editorial process, which remains the responsibility of the editor and publisher. The Trust is a Registered Charity, No 290841, and a full list of the Trustees and an overview of the functions of the M.S.M.T. can be found on: www.michaelsedgwicktrust.co.uk

CONTENTS

Published 2018 by
Herridge & Sons Ltd
Lower Forda, Shebbear
Beaworthy, Devon EX21 5SY

Designed by Ray Leaning
MUSE Fine Art & Design

ISBN 978-1-906133-61-0

Printed in China

INTRODUCTION

Heartened by the reception given to my book on *British Lorries*, and then to its sequel *British Vans and Pick-ups*, my publisher suggested that as I had a soft spot for elderly British motorcycles, and perhaps more importantly had amassed a fair amount of relevant sales literature, the formula could be repeated with these as the subject.

Easier said than done as, quite apart from the writing of such a work, with over 35 makes to cover they totalled more than the other two books put together. This coupled with a multiplicity of models and, often, yearly changes along with the necessity to feature illustrations of a sufficient size to show details of cycle and other parts made us consider two volumes before deciding upon a single larger one.

In common with my other two books of the same format this one is not intended to be encyclopaedic: but I hope you will find the majority of makes and different models well represented. A word of warning however – autocycle and moped manufacturers are not included unless their primary products were motorcycles and neither are scooters unless produced by motorcycle manufacturers, and then only in passing.

The material that I have drawn upon in the compilation of this work ranges from glossy, informative and well illustrated brochures published by the larger manufacturers to folders, or even simply flyers, produced by jobbing printers for the lesser makers. Their content at times features gloriously fanciful covers, which I'm afraid to say that, in some cases, I couldn't resist inventing little scenarios for: but in the main the content is informative: whether it be photographic, diagrammatic, table or artwork – with just the occasional smidgen of artistic licence that veers from the truth.

The vast majority of it is drawn from my own collection but Robert, son of Triumph's southern England sales manager George Wheeler, very kindly let me have his father's brochures and photos; whilst Jacqueline Bickerstaff, who is a fount of Vincent knowledge, assisted with relevant material; as did Benjamin Gradler over in Ohio who sought out American publicity which enabled me to fill some gaps in its coverage.

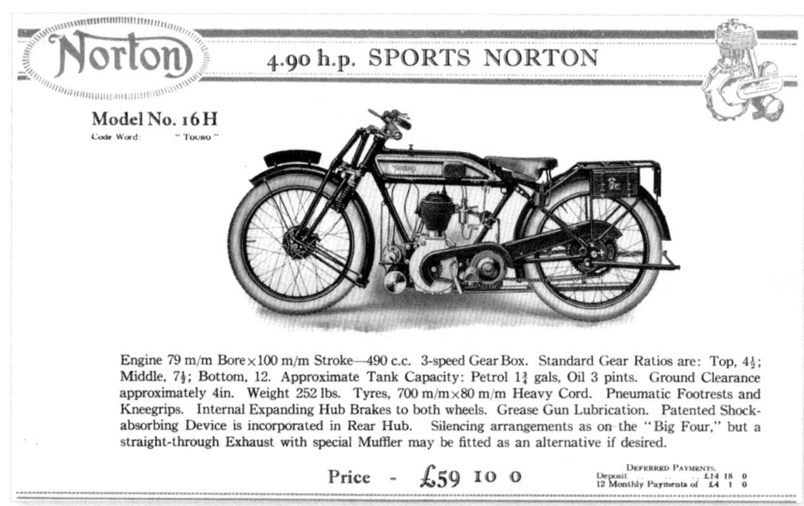

Long, lean and light, Norton's 16H of 1926 is the epitome of a good vintage motorcycle.

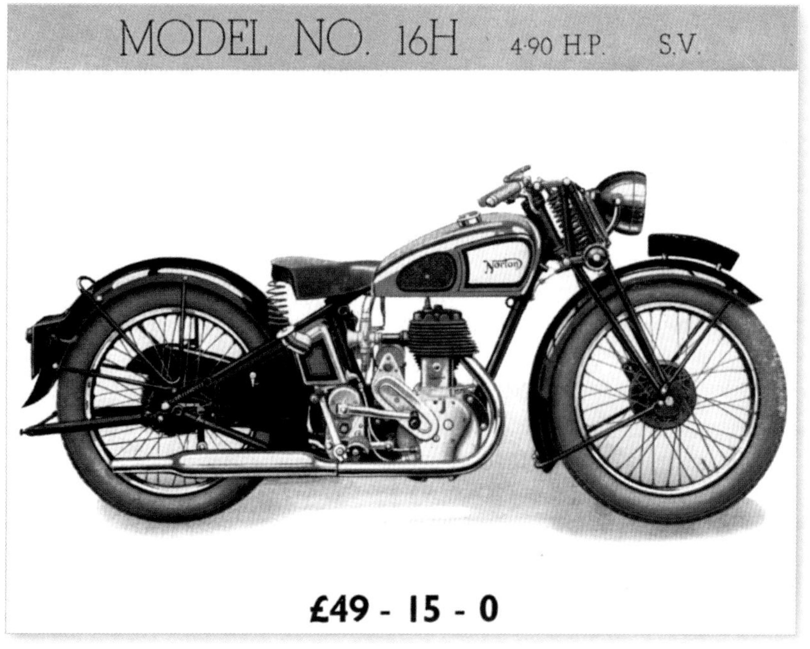

The 1930s ushered in an altogether stockier look and although valve-in-head motors were now prevalent there was still a healthy market for the slogging abilities of a good side-valve – this one effectively now in its twenty-fifth year: but, in those inflation free days, cheaper than it had been a decade earlier.

Come WW2 the War Department selected Norton 16Hs and Big Fours over other models in their range and some 100,000 military versions were turned out by 1945.

Two-strokes played their part too, and whilst the diminutive folding Welbike was next to useless in the field both James and Royal Enfield produced thoroughly worthwhile lightweights.

Twenty years, the period covered here, is but a short time unless you are young - when the time passes slowly.

This double decade however saw Britain's famed motorcycle industry's post-war emergence, often with hastily re-introduced pre-war models, amidst a shortage of raw materials coupled with the edict to "export".

Even when desirable new machines began to be ushered in during the late '40s this all too often dictated that foreign markets took preference whilst enthusiasts at home had to wait a year or two before they had the chance to get their hands on what had been dangled tantalisingly under their noses at the yearly Motor Cycle Show.

Outwardly the '50s were the glory years of British motorcycles as the country rode high on the post war economic boom – epitomised perhaps by its then Prime Minister Harold Macmillan's infamous "you've never had it so good" speech in the summer of 1957. Underlying this however was complacency along with stagnation when the need for modernisation and its attendant investment were neglected.

The situation was little different at the dawn of the '60s, by which time the Japanese had got into their stride and their motorcycles were flooding onto world markets – their technology, productivity and pricing a force majeure that would change the face of motorcycling for ever. Continuing very much as they had been, whilst consoling themselves that, if nothing else, their market for large-capacity machines was secure, allowed the British industry to survive for some

BSA offered a military derivative of their 350cc o.h.v Silver Sports as well as their 500 s.v M20 to the War Department but it was the latter that won the day and around 125,000 of them saw service in all theatres of the war.

years, selling to an ever-shrinking niche market.

Even as late as 1965 doyens of the industry such as Edward Turner were reportedly of the opinion that as Honda, Suzuki et al were primarily concerned with the manufacture of small-capacity machines they were not in direct competition: and that those who acquired a taste for motorcycling via their products would be likely to move up to the ownership of a larger British machine.

Up to that point there could have been some truth in this but the Japanese were already planning to move into the big bike field – and when they did it was with machines of such sophistication and speed that they would prove irresistible.

From then on it was only a matter of time and by the early 1970s it was all but over – with just a pitiful few of the legendary names to continue as best as they were able after being subjected to a mauling by venture capitalists, takeover bids and government intervention.

Better by far that we recall the times before those dark days and hopefully this book will enable its readers to do that very thing.

Rinsey Mills, June 2018

From TRIUMPH to Yugoslavia

"The bravery and successes of your patriot Army are admired by the free peoples of the world and their achievements will be an important factor in the final liberation of the Balkans and will form the foundation of the future prosperity of your country. We look forward to the day when we can be associated with you and other countries in successful commerce to the benefit of mankind."

ZAGREB FIUME OSIJEK BIHAC BROD NOVISAD KARLOBAG DOBOJ BANJALUKA BELGRADE ZARA SARAJEVO SPLIT ADRIATIC SEA GRUZ CETINJE SKOPLJE ITALY FOGGIA

SPEED TWIN 500 c.c. O.H.V.
PAT. Nos. 474963, 475860 and 469635

TRIUMPH ENGINEERING COMPANY LIMITED COVENTRY

Triumph had developed a lightweight 350 vertical twin especially for military use but the virtual destruction of their Coventry factory in the Blitz put paid to it and when they got going again they produced both sidevalve (below) and overhead-valve singles for the armed forces. Anxious that their Speed Twin should stay in the forefront of enthusiasts' minds they ran this rather ironic advertisement towards the end of the war with the Balkans as a backdrop. Some liberation! Poor Yugoslavia was destined to endure many years of Communist government with its wartime patriot leader, Josip Tito, as president. Worse still, after his death in 1980, increasing ethnic unrest spilled over into the bloody Yugoslav wars of the 1990s.

By no means all dispatch riders were men and here's a Wren, gas mask slung over her left shoulder and dispatch bag over her right, on one of Royal Enfield's ohv 350s.

ABERDALE

Initially, in 1947 pressed-steel engine shields were incorporated in the design but once production got under way they were dispensed with. Lightweight pressed-steel girder forks were by Webb and finish was in black with gold coach lines.

In the aftermath of the First World War, during which the armed forces returned to civilian life and sought employment, there grew a demand for economical transport in the form of cheap bicycles; to take advantage, the Aberdale Cycle Company was founded by the Levy family during 1919. By the early 1930s the business had prospered to such an extent that modernistic premises on Bridport Road, Edmonton, North London were built and became the firm's headquarters in 1934. Further expansion came with the acquisition of the small-scale specialist cycle and motorcycle manufacturer Bown, but by the end of the decade Great Britain was at war with Germany once more and Aberdale spent the duration manufacturing equipment such as small generating sets.

The 1945 return to peace once again saw a call for economy transportation and again Aberdale, by now a subsidiary of Raleigh Cycles, sought to satisfy the demand – this time with a Bown-designed Autocycle. Powered by a 98cc Villiers two-stroke motor the Auto-roadster was in production by 1947. Updated models with the latest 2F Villiers were shown at the 1948 Motor Cycle Show but in the event they would not become available until 1950, and under another name to boot. Taking advantage of the Labour government's Advanced Factory Scheme, Aberdale had relocated the manufacture of its motor-powered cycles to Llwynypia in the Rhonda Valley, Wales and henceforth they would be marketed under the name of Bown.

The following year the Bown Autocycle was supplemented by a small motorcycle of the same capacity but with a two-speed gearbox: and then for the 1952 season a 122cc three-speed Villiers-powered version completed the range. The latter was inappropriately named the Tourist Trophy model: it will come as no surprise that none made it to the Isle of Man, other than any that happened to be used by residents or holidaymakers. The TT turned out to be the least successful of the firm's not outstandingly successful wares, with production probably totalling less than 200; but a few thousand of the others were manufactured before sales tailed off to such an extent that the factory closed at the end of 1954.

Rising phoenix-like, however, the Bown name reappeared at the 1955 Earls Court Show attached to an Anglicised version of the German company Fichtel & Sachs's 50cc moped. Assembled at Aberdale's Edmonton factory, with a sprinkling of home-market components in order to be eligible for the Commonwealth Preferential Tariff, it was initially christened the Bown Bambi but soon renamed the Bown 50.

At first, in true moped tradition, there was no rear suspension but a plunger rear end had been introduced a year or so before production ceased in 1958.

Shortly prior to the Welsh factory's demise the parent company Aberdale had been acquired by Tube Investments and consequently became part of its subsidiary the British Cycle Corporation. What remained of the cycle manufacturing business transferred to BCC's Britannia Works at Handsworth, Birmingham early in 1959.

Although that marked the end of the Aberdale name the Levys, along with some ex-employees

ANNOUNCING THE MAGNIFICENT NEW

Bown

AUTOCYCLE

B.1950

Specification

ENGINE Villiers Mark 2.F. 98 c.c. engine. Two-plate cork insert clutch. Final drive to rear wheel is by roller chain running in an oil bath case. Ignition and lighting current by Villiers flywheel magneto. Headlamp carries 6 volt 12-watt bulb.

FRAME Hand-built throughout, incorporating perfect design twin-tube cradle frame, giving 3-point suspension for the engine unit. Angle of frame designed to give light steering and perfect control in all conditions.

FORKS Front fork spring type — link action, giving greater comfort to the rider.

SADDLE Large, well-sprung mattress saddle.

HANDLEBARS Chromium-plated comfort pattern.

TANK Welded steel, capacity approximately 1½ gallons. Push type—on/off—petrol tap, situated in convenient position.

WHEELS Built with heavy gauge spokes, Dunlop 2/25-21 depressed rims, heavily chromium-plated, fitted with Dunlop tyres and internal expanding hub brakes.

FINISH All enamel parts bonderised, followed by a coat of anti-rust primer, and finished with maroon enamel and heavy gold lines. All bright parts chrome-plated.

EQUIPMENT Complete Tool-Kit comprising:—Brooks Tool Bag, with complete set of good quality spanners and grease gun. Bluemel pump, front and rear number plates. Tubular rear carrier and stand.

BOWN CYCLE COMPANY LTD., LLWYNYPIA, TONYPANDY, GLAM.

The 1955 Bown was a good example of its type and could approach a speed of 40mph or so under favourable conditions. Throughout this book you will find references to Bonderising. This was an anti-corrosion solution developed and manufactured by Pyrene, which was applied to the steel components of many British motorcycles during manufacture.

One of the post-war Labour government's all-but-forgotten and short-lived contributions to the economy of South Wales was the Rhonda Valley-made 98cc Bown.

including Mr Bown, turned to the manufacture of children's cycles under the brand name Trusty at fresh premises on the Angel Factory Colony in Edmonton. The mid '70s saw Trusty buy the ailing but futuristic Lambert sports/racing bike business, with production continuing but known as Viscount. Marketed as having aerospace technology, some components – most notably the cast-aluminium front forks – were prone to breakage but this didn't stop a takeover by Yamaha in 1978. Faced with mounting instances of fork failures the Japanese corporation announced a recall on these components in 1981, and a few years later let the brand lapse – the Levys et al being long gone by this time.

Colourfully finished in maroon with gold-lined, grey-blue tank panels and gold-lined wheel rims, the TT Bown was thoroughly approved of by Motor Cycling *when tested in July 1952. With a top speed of 49mph and a cruising speed of over 40 it averaged 35mph and 90mpg on a trip from Somerset to Brighton – its cornering and braking abilities giving "absolute confidence". Despite* Motor Cycling*'s appraisal of its "above average performance" for a lightweight, it failed to sell in significant numbers.*

AJS

During Queen Victoria's Diamond Jubilee year the Stevens Screw Company of Wednesfield near Wolverhampton put together a motorcycle using a bicycle frame and an American-made Mitchell single-cylinder engine. Encouraged by this but reluctant to go into the manufacture of complete machines, the company developed an improved version of the Mitchell before becoming a maker and supplier of various single-cylinder and V-twin engines of its own design to other firms.

In 1909, inspired by their showing in reliability and speed trials, riding Wolf and other motorcycles powered by their own engines, the Stevens brothers finally became manufacturers on their own account, founding AJ Stevens and Company Ltd, with premises in Retreat Street, Wolverhampton. Their aim was to take part in the Tourist Trophy races on the Isle of Man but it would be two years before they got there; although they didn't win, an AJS-mounted privateer came fifteenth in the Junior race followed by Jack Stevens in sixteenth place.

Too busy with the day-to-day running of their business to compete the following year, they were back for 1913 with two entries; just one made it to the finish, in tenth position. With ample prior warning of a hike in the capacity limit of the 1914 Junior event from 300 to 350cc, special machines were built with four-speed transmissions and engines that would approach an almost unheard-of 5000rpm. Over on the island their meticulous build and exhaustive testing reaped a thoroughly just reward, and all five entries completed the course – with the best of them in first, second, fourth and sixth places.

This success brought orders flooding in but hardly had there been time to capitalise on the dramatic increase in sales before Britain was at war with Germany. The company had outgrown its present building, however, and in order to raise capital for expansion through shares it became AJ Stevens (1914) Ltd. A large house in its own grounds was acquired on nearby Graisley Hill – this giving the space for a new factory, which was completed and moved into during 1915.

AJ Stevens was not amongst those who were initially called upon to supply machines for the armed forces, and production of any for sale to the public was prohibited during 1916. But the new factory was kept more than busy on all manner of engineering work, including much specialised material for the aircraft industry. Later in the war, however, the firm was awarded part of a government contract for the supply of vehicles to Russia and made something over 1000 of its V-twin Model Ds to help fulfil it – the upshot of this being rapid expansion in the immediate post-armistice period, with the factory buildings quadrupled in size during 1919.

With racing in mind the development of overhead valve engines was now under way, and with them AJS won the Junior TT in 1920, both Junior and Senior (with a 350) in 1921 and the Junior in 1922

Two years after the war, and AMC's 350cc 16M was little different from its Teledraulic-forked Matchless G3/L that was supplied to the forces. You can always tell the difference between the two, however, as AJS singles had their magneto in front of the motor whilst the equivalent Matchless models had it behind – the timing case thus sloping forward on an AJS and to the rear on a Matchless.

SPECIFICATION

MODELS 16M & 18

ENGINE	Bore	Stroke	Capacity
Model 16M ...	69 m.m.	93 m.m.	347 c.c.
Model 18	82.5 m.m.	93 m.m.	498 c.c.

Both engines are of the single port O.H.V. type and incorporate the latest features of design. All moving parts are totally enclosed and lubricated from the main engine pump, and the valve gear is readily accessible for adjustment by the removal of the cover plate provided.

Of exceptionally rigid construction the flywheel assembly is supported on the drive side by two large diameter ball races, and on the timing side by a caged roller and plain phosphor bronze bearing. The big end bearing is of particular interest and comprises a two piece crankpin, Duralumin cage and triple row roller bearing.

LUBRICATION. Full dry sump system with large capacity rotary reciprocating plunger pump and separate oil tank. Pressure feed to big end, main bearings, valve gear, piston and camshaft bearings.

GEARBOX. Four speed heavyweight, with enclosed foot gear-change mechanism, and handlebar controlled clutch.

TRANSMISSION. Primary chain enclosed in oil bath chaincase. Rear chain protected by efficient deep section guard. Smooth running ensured by efficient spring loaded cam type shock absorber.

CARBURETTOR. Semi-automatic Amal. Quick action twist grip and lever air control.

FRAME. Heavy gauge steel tube duplex cradle, with single straight front down member. Integral pillion footrest lugs and forged rear fork ends.

FORKS. Patented "Teledraulic" with improved three rate springs and controlled by hydraulic damping. Self lubricating and no maintenance required.

STANDS. Central prop stand, tubular front and spring-up rear.

HANDLEBARS. Chromium plated, fully adjustable semi-sports.

TANKS. Welded steel 3 gall. petrol tank with twin cork seated filter taps. 3 pint oil tank of same construction incorporating detachable fabric filter.

BRAKES. Large diameter internal expanding with finger adjustment.

SADDLE. Large Lycett spring seat.

WHEELS. 19" front and rear with 26" × 3.25" Dunlop cord Tyres.

MUDGUARDS. Portion of rear guard quickly detachable for wheel accessibility. Both guards of special efficient section and design.

ELECTRICAL EQUIPMENT. Separate magneto and dynamo independently driven by roller chains in oil bath cases. Large diameter headlamp, handlebar dipper switch, electric horn, centrally mounted battery and constant voltage control.

FINISH. Three coats of finest quality black stove enamel on Bonderized surface. Wheel rims, handlebars, headlamp rim, filler caps and exhaust system chromium plated. Petrol tank and wheel rims hand-lined in gold.

EQUIPMENT. Full set of tools, including grease gun and tyre pump. Ninety Page Instruction Manual.

– production versions coming to the market in 1922. TT victories then passed to other makes but the 'big port' overhead valve AJSs are still considered amongst the ablest sporting machines of the 1920s – during which period the company continued to cater for the more pedestrian market with single-cylinder and V-twin side-valve models. Seeking to regain racing laurels AJS introduced sports models with chain-driven overhead camshaft engines of either 350 or 500cc in 1927, but outright victory in the Isle of Man was to elude a 'camshaft Ajay' until the '50s, apart from a surprise win for Jimmie Guthrie on a special 250 in 1930's lightweight TT.

In spite of the post-war boom, the marque's racing successes and the quality of its products, by the mid '20s its financial state was on the decline and by 1927 it had reached a point were shareholders received no dividends. Motorcycle sales were falling, largely due to cheap two-, three- or four-wheeled competition, and the subsidiary AJS Wireless and Scientific Instruments Company was also suffering from increasingly cheap radios flooding the market.

A year later, however, although the wireless concern was wound up and remaining stock sold to the Symphonic Gramophone & Radio Company, things were looking better for the motor vehicle side of the business. A contract to build bodies for Clyno cars was under way and AJS Commercial Vehicles had been formed. It didn't last. In February 1929 the first commercial, in the shape of the 24-seat Pilot coach, was launched at almost the same moment as Clyno cars went under. In an attempt to offset the latter the decision to become a car manufacturer was taken and within a few months the AJS Nine car took to the roads. But neither this nor the Pilot and subsequent larger models, nor the firm's motorcycles, could avert the downslide, and in the autumn of 1931 AJ Stevens & Company went bankrupt.

BSA showed interest in the motorcycle side of the business but it ended up being acquired by Matchless. Production was transferred to London, while the motorcar side went to Crossley Motors.

During 1932 the Stevens brothers recommenced manufacturing at their old Retreat Street factory, where they began by building three-wheeler delivery vans. Two years later there were motorcycles as well – starting with a 250 OHV and adding 350s and 500s later. Lacking sufficient finance and equipment the new firm was very much a hand-to-mouth operation, however, and the last machines were built in 1938,

Despite having the same cycle parts, the 1947 500cc Model 18 was immediately distinguishable by its chunkier head and barrel along with horizontally-mounted Amal 1³⁄₃₂in carburettor, as opposed to the inclined inlet port of the current 16M. Described as 'large diameter' by the manufacturer, the front brake was in fact only a 6in and its efficiency marginal.

after which the company carried out engineering work.

Meanwhile, down at the Plumstead, Woolwich, AJS motorcycles had become, with few exceptions, little more than Matchless under another name. But in recognition of the marque's racing and sporting heritage the OHC machines had been re-introduced, and at the 1935 Olympia show a prototype OHV 500cc V4 was unveiled. Although it never made it into production, supercharged racing versions – firstly air- then water-cooled, did – and one of the latter made the first 100mph lap of the Ulster Grand Prix course in 1939. They were magnificent machines, with a top speed of 135-plus but sadly no match for the supercharged BMWs that were then all but omnipotent.

During 1937 Matchless's owners, the Collier brothers, created Amalgamated Motor Cycles out of the Matchless/AJS duo, as well as adding Sunbeam to their portfolio. Then, the year before the Second World War, the combine became Associated Motor Cycles (AMC), during which the Plumstead factory produced Matchless motorcycles for the armed forces alongside large quantities of aircraft components.

After the war and throughout the period covered by this book AJS machines were in most respects identical to those carrying the Matchless name – the two notable exceptions both being racing machines.

One was a 68x68.5mm 500cc twin with twin OHC, mounted in a duplex swinging arm frame, that would have been supercharged had not a ban on forced induction for international events dictated a switch to twin carburettors. Unlike other OHC AJSs the camshafts were driven by a chain of spur gears, and for some reason it was designed to run backwards, an idiosyncrasy that necessitated gear- rather than chain-drive to the four-speed gearbox. Dubbed Porcupines on account of the quill-like cylinder head finning, a pair were taken to the Isle of Man for the first post-war TT and entrusted to Jock West and Les Graham. In between bouts of misfiring and cutting out due to their mica spark plugs not being up to the job they were very fast, but at the finish they were ninth and fourteenth in the Senior – West's average speed being over 20mph slower than the winning Norton.

This catchphrase was certainly accurate during the 1920s but the new 7R racer pictured had yet to win its spurs. But it read well and conjured up a sporting image for the road machines – in part fulfilled in the '48 Junior Clubmans TT when a Model 16 was narrowly beaten into second place.

The following year three 'Porcs' raced on the island but all retired in spite of Lodge having developed special ceramic plug insulation for them. In '49 they were back but their bad luck persisted when, with victory in sight, Les Graham's mount expired, leaving him to push in tenth – recompense manifesting itself with wins in the Swiss and Ulster GPs, and overall victory in the 500cc World Championship. Their apogee was 1949, however, and thereafter one was runner-up to Geoff Duke in the 1951 Senior and,

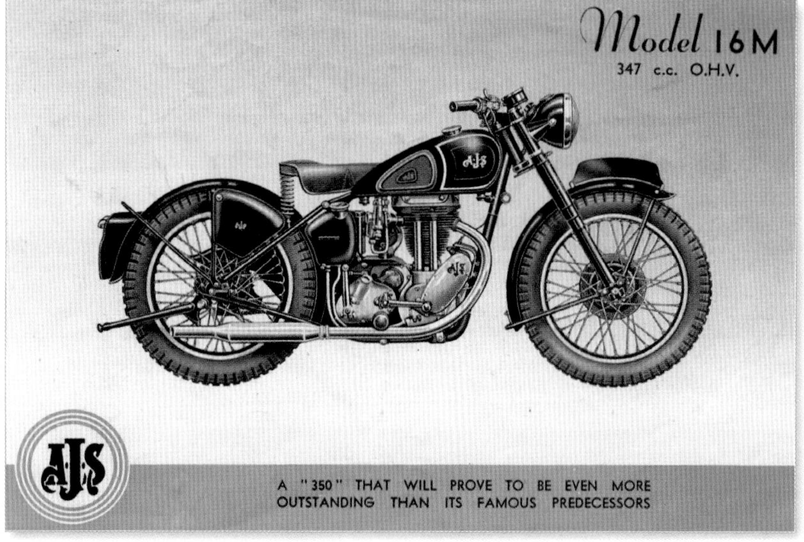

At a quick glance the 1949 16M is very much the same as in the mid '40s but many improvements and alterations had been effected the previous year – notably, and clearly visible here, a larger and more powerful 7in front brake. Visible too is the different oil tank filler cap and neck, as well as the more modern headlamp with its mountings integral with the top shrouds. Not so immediately obvious, though, is the completely redesigned cylinder head, which incorporated hairpin valve springs, and the adjustable saddle. All frames, with the exception of the 7R, now incorporated sidecar lugs.

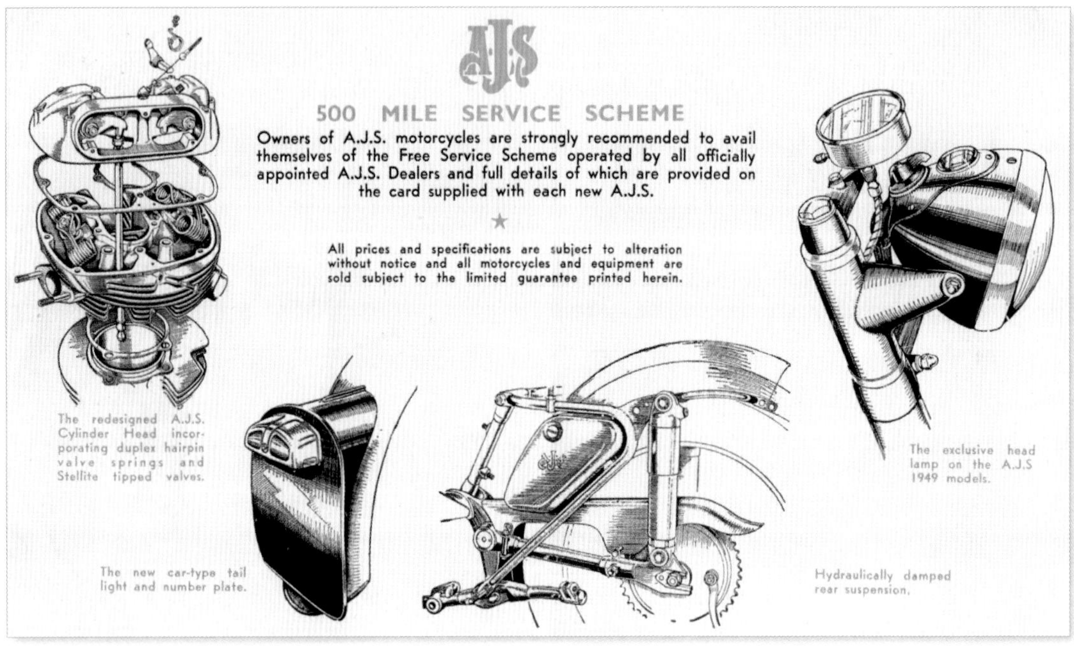

Relatively trivial details regarding lighting took equal precedence in the brochure to the big news for 1949 – the introduction of rear suspension.

Here's the 1949 500cc 18S with the brand-new swinging-arm frame. To help justify a higher basic retail price of £138 as opposed to £122 for the regular rigid rear-end machine this and its 350cc sibling, the 16MS (£128, or £112 for the 16), had chromium-plated petrol tanks with painted panels.

after an extensive revamp Rod Coleman managed a fourth in '53. Lacking nothing in speed, it was all too often dogged by unreliability but did on occasion shine, taking a number of records at Montlhéry in 1948 as well as that championship for Les Graham.

The second machine was the pre-war AJS overhead camshaft 350cc 7R, which was revived in 1948 – a pukka racer that would be for sale to the public, with a basic engine design based upon that of its predecessors but in every other respect completely up-to-the-minute. From the outset there was no shortage of customers and that year's Junior TT saw over 20 take the start with Maurice Cann finishing fifth behind a brace apiece of KTT Velocettes and Manx Nortons – more telling, however, was that another 15 finished the course, thus beginning what would become the little machine's legendary reputation for reliability.

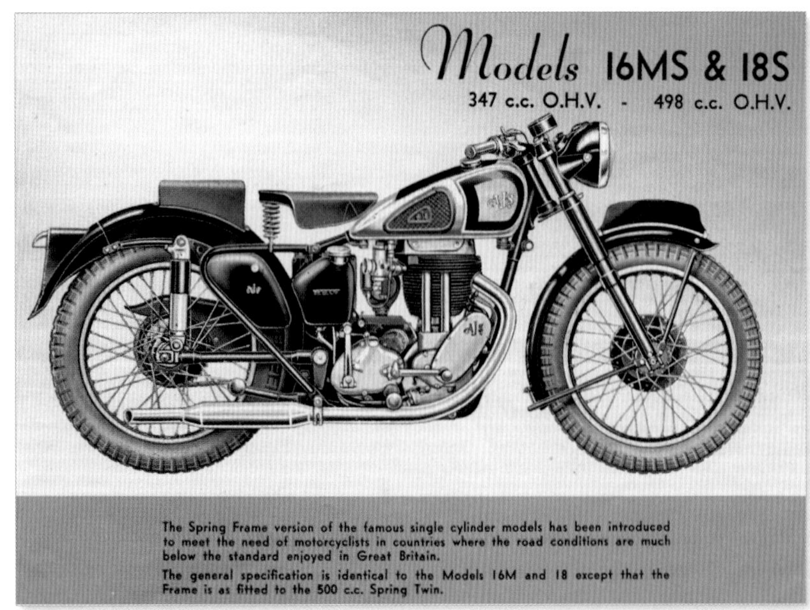

The following year 32 of them finished out of 41 starters with, once again, a fifth behind two Velocettes and two Nortons.

All the while 7Rs had been notching up success after success on the Continent but victory in the Junior TT eluded them until Rod Coleman's win in the1954 event – albeit with a special Ike Hatch-designed triple OHC version. It would be the 350 AJS's sole Junior victory, and at the end of the season the factory retired from racing – continuing to manufacture the 7R as an over-the-counter racer until the early '60s. In the face of increasingly stiff opposition from Italian machinery, Derek Ennet's second place in 1956 was a brave effort; but for many years, along with the 350 Manx Norton, the 7R would be the mainstay of the 350 class for non-works riders in Britain and abroad.

Of greater relevance to the ordinary motorcyclist were the single-cylinder factory Trials machines, almost exclusively based upon the road-going 350cc Model 16. The Scottish Six Days Trial was the single most important event of this nature in the British Isles, and between 1947 and 1961 AJS's Hugh Viney and Gordon Jackson took works machines to victory on no less than eight occasions (Viney in 1947-to-'49 and '53; Jackson in 1956, '58, '60 and '61), with the manufacturer's award also falling to AJS four times from 1953 to '56. Customer versions of these competition machines were catalogued and available to the general public throughout this period – a period that, did AMC and other British makers but know it, would precede the onset of their inexorable fall from grace and in almost all cases extinction.

AJS and Matchless had for years been virtually the same machines, identifiable in the main by badging and colour schemes, but by the mid '60s AMC's other big bike, Norton, had been thrown into the melting pot of mix and match – all three marques being represented by just a single brochure in 1965.

A year later what had become a house of cards collapsed and the now-bankrupt AMC organisation was acquired by Dennis Poore's Manganese Bronze Holdings. Aside from his business interests Poore had long been associated with, as well as successfully competing in, motorsport and was keen to salvage what he could of the motorcycle brands that had come his way. The formation of Norton-Villiers was an early move, as was the decision to eventually create a fresh manufacturing base at Andover in Hampshire. But what to do with AJS?

Its four-stroke singles were axed but twins continued with Norton engines whilst an entirely new competition two-stroke with 250cc Villiers Starmaker engine was developed. Unveiled as the Y4 Scrambler towards the end of 1967, it was manufactured in Wolverhampton and went on to take the British Motocross Championship in 1968. From 1969 to 1974 it was marketed as the Stormer and made with 250, 370 and 410cc engines; once the new Andover factory had been built it was assembled there.

It came to an end when the finances of Norton-Villiers took a nosedive and the rights to AJS were sold to Fluff Brown, who then made and sold the Stormer as the FB-AJS until 1980.

The marque sadly lives on to this day, in name only, and is in the hands of Brown's son, from whom can be bought spares for Stormers and a range of Chinese-made small-capacity motorcycles.

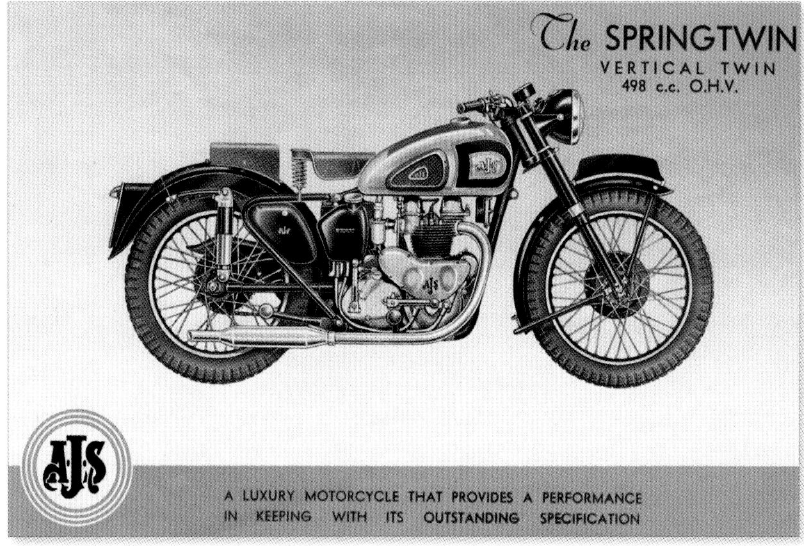

Very conscious of the popularity of Triumph's vertical twins, which had been introduced before the war, AMC had come up with one of its own for the 1949 season and what's more stole a march on them by having one with the latest suspension whilst the Meriden concern's Speed Twins and Tiger 100s had their rear springing contained within the rear hub. The slender in-house Teledraulic rear suspension units (often referred to as the candlestick type) were prone to bottoming, even if each was kept filled with its correct 50cc quota of SAE 20 oil, and all too often leaked.

THE 498 c.c. "SPRINGTWIN" Specification

ENGINE. High efficiency vertical twin with robust three bearing crankshaft, separate deeply spigoted cylinders and heavily finned Light Alloy cylinder heads. Stellite tipped valves, eccentric rocker spindle adjustment, forged Light Alloy connecting rods, wire wound pistons, shrunk in valve seats, crankshaft supported on roller outer races, Vandervell centre main and big end bearings.

Bore 66 m.m. Stroke 72.8 m.m. Capacity 498 c.c.

LUBRICATION. Full dry sump with separate oil tank. Circulation 26 gallons per hour by twin gear pumps. Pressure lubrication to all moving parts without external pipes.

GEAR BOX. Pivot mounted heavyweight 4 speed with adjustable positive stop foot gear-change lever. Multi plate five stud clutch, enclosed operation and handlebar control.

CARBURETTOR. Semi automatic Amal with separate air lever and twist grip throttle control.

ELECTRICAL EQUIPMENT. Separate gear driven flange mounted generator and magneto. Voltage control, central battery, electric horn, large diameter domed glass headlamp and specially designed chromium plated rear light.

FRAME. Swinging arm Duplex cradle spring frame with twin oil damped rubber bushed Teledraulic units. Rear frame pivots from continuously lubricated bearings of large dimensions in Light Alloy bridge casting. Integral three point fully adjustable saddle mounting, pillion footrest lugs and twin large capacity tool boxes.

STANDS. Spring up forged steel centre with "up" clip, tubular front and quick action foot operated prop stand.

TANKS. Four gallon Chromium plated fuel tank and ½ gallon oil tank of pressed steel-welded construction. Quick action filler caps, twin petrol taps with reserve position and detachable fabric oil filter.

MUDGUARDS. Valanced rear guard hinged, to permit easy wheel removal. Deep section front.

TRANSMISSION. ½" x 5/16" primary chain operating in oil bath case with cam type lubricated shock absorber. ⅝" x ⅜" rear chain protected by deep section guard of efficient design.

FORKS. Patented Teledraulic. Telescopic, hydraulically damped with three rate springs and integral headlamp brackets.

SADDLE. Spring top Lycett with semi roll back.

HANDLEBARS. Fully adjustable semi sports with all controls mounted on straight portion.

BRAKES. Large diameter internal expanding, cast aluminium shoes with special independent shim adjustment. Cast chromidium drums with rain excluders.

WHEELS. Fabricated steel hubs with caged taper roller bearings. 3.25" x 19" front tyre. 3.50" x 19" rear tyre.

FINISH. All enamelled parts Bonderised and finished with three thicknesses of finest black stoved enamel. Exhaust system, handlebars wheel rims, battery strap, front brake cover plate, saddle springs and many other parts chromium plated.

EQUIPMENT. High grade tool kit in canvas roll, large capacity tyre pump, grease gun and Instruction Book.

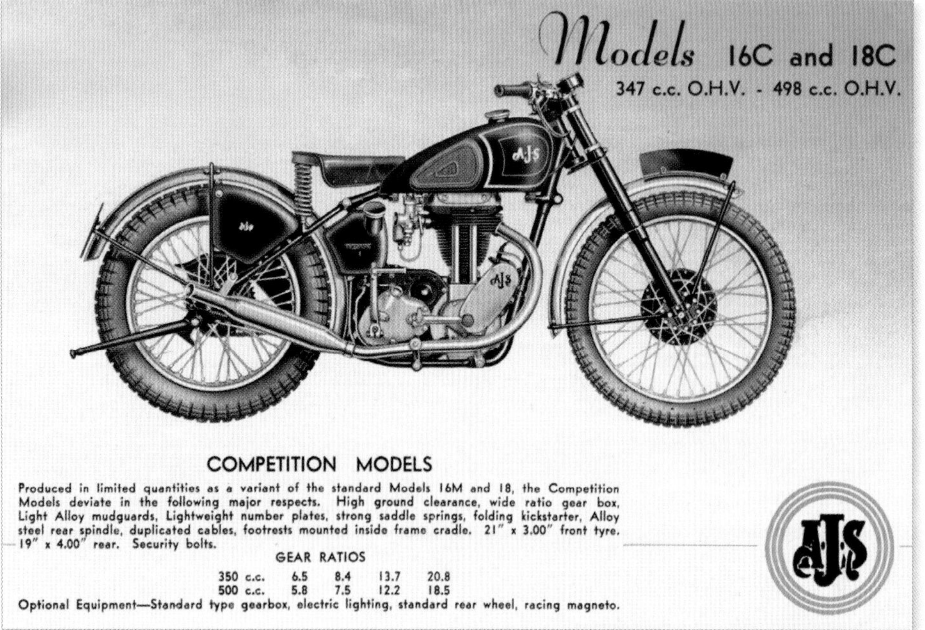

Highly specialised off-road machinery was still in the future, and in common with the majority of its competitors the AJS versions had no rear suspension. Hugh Viney won the Scottish Six Days Trial on one for the third time in a row in 1949, and would go on to win it for a fourth time in 1953, as well as becoming the firm's competition manager.

The 7R had existed in the late 1930s but, apart from the basic engine design, this one was entirely new and before long had been dubbed the 'Boy Racer'. What is not apparent here is the enormous width of the early model's oil tank. As the oil heated up so did your calves – something I well remember from my ownership of a similar example, 40 or so years ago.

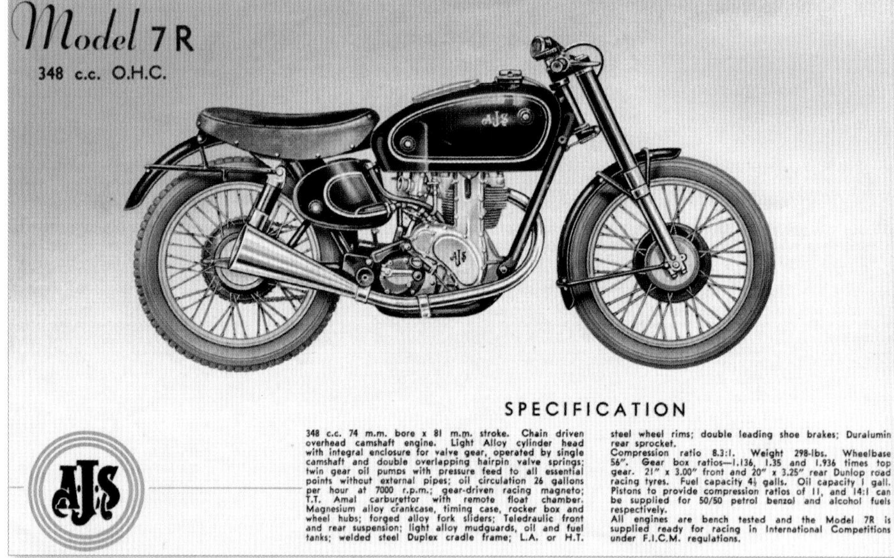

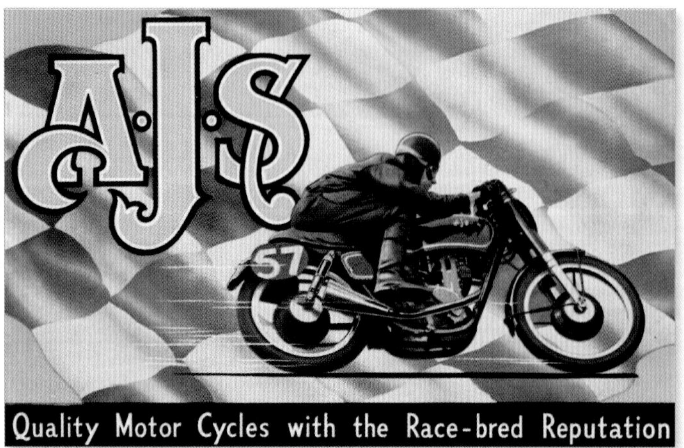

Good quality AMC's machines most certainly were; and yes, thanks to AJS advertising copy and mounting successes by the 7R they were truthfully race-bred by reputation as claimed on the 1951 brochure cover – even though the 7R shared few parts with the firm's other machinery.

This is a 16M but the 1951 18 (not to be confused with Norton's Model 18 that had been around since the 1920s) shared the same new features such as an aluminium cylinder head, repositioned tool box of slightly differing shape, and ribbed mudguards. The three-gallon petrol tank was still enamelled black but oval badges now carried the AJS logo rather than transfers.

The 1951 'springers' now had improved Teledraulic rear suspension units with greater oil capacity; damping on the Teledraulic front forks fitted to all models had also been improved. The former became known as jampots, and to this day the AJS and Matchless Owners' Club magazine carries the same name. This is the 500cc single (18S) and has a chromium-plated petrol tank that was catalogued as an optional export extra.

The 500cc Springtwin, in line with other AJS models, in 1951 had been assigned a number – becoming the Model 20.

Scrambles riders welcomed the new sprung frame in 1951 but for trials work the short wheelbase rigid rear end set-up was preferred. Aluminium heads and barrels meant considerable weight saving. On the rigid trials models there was a cylindrical tool container with chromium quick-action filler cap as a lid above the oil tank.

By 1951 development of the Boy Racer had resulted in a less bulky oil tank and re-routed exhaust system amongst other things, but the handlebars were still the swan-neck variety that precluded the rider from really getting down to it.

In Europe as well as further afield the 7R had rapidly come to enjoy considerable success, but for the while a win in the Isle of Man eluded it.

Back to race-bred for the '52 brochure but if one included scrambles and similar events then it was especially true. Besides, AJ's little racer looked so good on the cover.

Tank badging was changed once again for the 1952 season. Some materials used in the chrome plating process were in short supply at this time, so wheel rims and a few other minor parts were given a matt-aluminium Argenised finish.

A stronger, lighter and more compact Burman gearbox was introduced for the road bikes at this juncture. Named the B52 (but perversely stamped GB) it was described in the brochure as 'racing type'; this was not too far-fetched. as it had been developed directly from the box that Burman made for the 7R. These boxes featured a rotary lift for the clutch, which necessitated a small plate in the primary chain case to access the clutch adjustment screw.

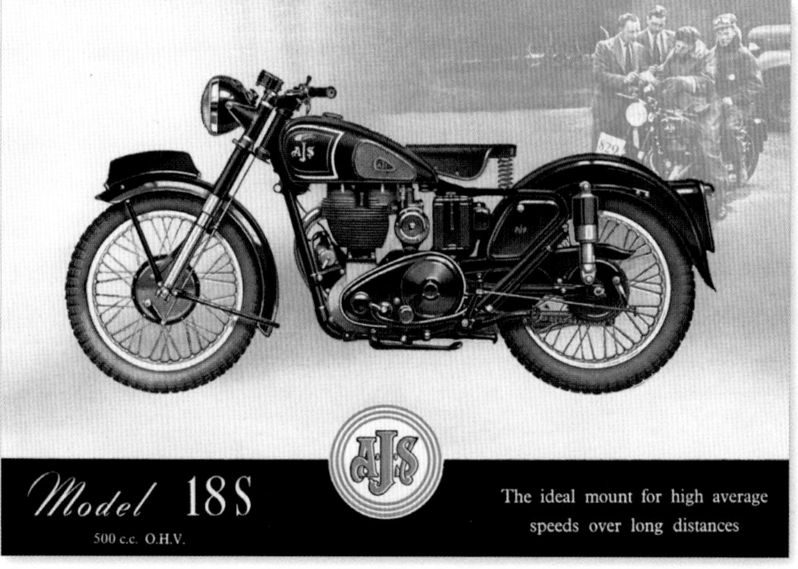

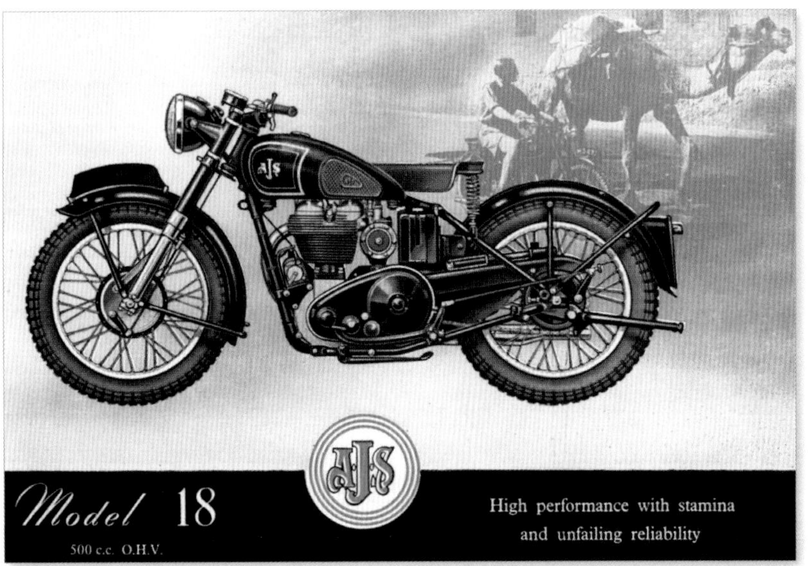

Other manufacturers of heavyweight motorcycles were phasing out their rigid frame models by 1952 but AMC saw no reason to do so, as they kept selling. Front brakes on all models now had a cast aluminium back plate with, of course, the exception of the 7R, which had entirely different brakes made mainly of magnesium alloy.

1952's finish was, the brochure proclaimed, three thicknesses of best quality black stoved enamel for the frame, tanks and mudguards. With chromium in short supply, just the exhaust system, handlebars etc. were chromed whilst wheel rims were finished in aluminium. Nuts and bolts were cadmium plated or Parkerised.

Unusual amongst vertical twins in their use of three crankshaft bearings, AMC's aim was to reduce vibration, but in practice the additional shell centre main did little to alleviate this type of engine's inherent characteristic. They would rev freely but high crankshaft speeds induced the one-piece crank to transmit any roughness caused by its restricted attempts to flex through the engine casings and hence the frame.

The facility to carry tools was unnecessary on a scrambles machine so this season it had been done away with for the 16MCS and 18CS models.

When a Scrambles machine such as this was supplied with a centre stand it would almost invariably be removed before use on the grounds of safety and weight saving.

By 1952 the 7R stood on 19in wheels and a good one was putting out up to 34hp at around 7,200 rpm, but the factory's reluctance to commit to definite specifications in print was because a much-improved version was in the offing. This would have a completely new and narrower cradle frame, a stronger bottom end as well as roller rockers for the motor, a larger tank secured by a spring strap rather than through bolts, and a hump-backed seat amongst other features.

As was customary the new season's models would be shown at the Motorcycle Show in November where potential customers and any number of eager schoolboys could pick up a brochure for the following year – often printed well in advance like this example dated August 1952. Dual seats were introduced on springer models at this time and the show publicity flyer depicted a model 18S thus equipped.

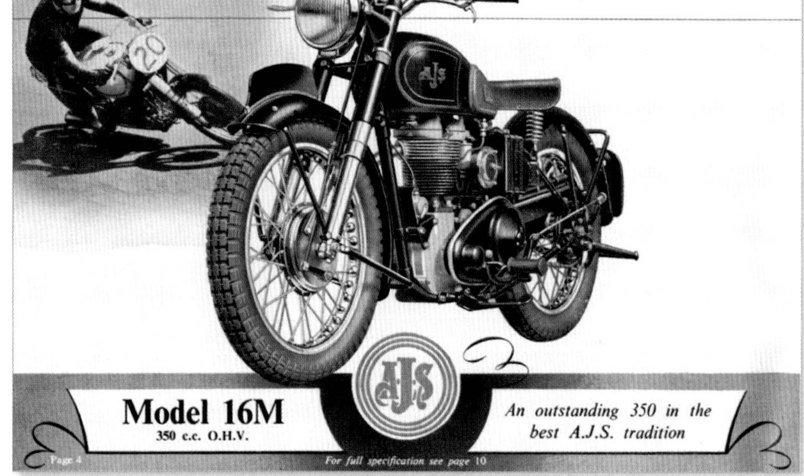

Chromium wheel rims were back for 1953 export models and headlights with an underslung sidelight made an appearance for this season only.

Specification

With the exception of the "Springtwin" engine and the size of the petrol tank fitted to this model, the specifications of the Single-cylinder and Twin-cylinder models are almost identical. A general specification has therefore been provided, except for the Twin-cylinder engine which is dealt with separately :

ENGINE—Single Cylinder

Capacity	*Bore*		*Stroke*
347 c.c.	69 m.m.	×	93 m.m.
498 c.c.	82.5 m.m.	×	93 m.m.

Exceptionally robust crankshaft assembly, twin ball race drive side main bearing, bronze timing side oil distribution main bearing, triple row caged roller big end bearing with two-piece crankpin, racing type single port die cast light alloy cylinder head with cast in valve seats, duplex hairpin valve springs and Stellite tipped valves operated by tubular Duralumin push rods, all moving parts totally enclosed and positively lubricated by comprehensive dry sump lubrication system circulated by double acting rotary reciprocating plunger pump, low clearance wirewound piston, twin gear-driven cam wheels, chain-driven Lucas magneto and semi-automatic Amal carburettor with twist grip throttle control.

ENGINE—Twin Cylinder

Capacity 498 c.c. Bore 66 m.m. Stroke 72.8 m.m.

Spherical die-cast crankcase, twin caged roller outer main bearings, three bearing statically and dynamically balanced crankshaft. Vandervell centre main and big end bearings, forged light alloy connecting rods, full dry sump lubrication, gear oil pumps driven by twin camshafts and even oil distribution to all moving parts without external pipes by initial delivery to centre crankshaft bearing, light alloy single port cylinder heads, cast in valve seats, forged rockers, eccentric rocker spindle valve adjustment and Duralumin pushrods. Flange mounted gear-driven 45 watt dynamo and magneto and semi-automatic twist grip operated Amal carburettor.

GEAR BOX

Designed and developed for the Racing Model 7R, the 4-speed gear box combines exceptional strength with ease of operation. Dry multi-plate clutch, enclosed positive stop foot-operated gear change and internal ratios of 2.6 : 1.7 and 1.3 times top gear.

TRANSMISSION

Chain throughout. Primary chain and engine shaft shock absorber enclosed in oil bath case. Rear chain protected by efficient deep section guard.

FRAME—Rigid and Spring

The Rigid frame is of the duplex cradle type of brazed construction, incorporating sidecar and pillion footrest lugs.
The front portion of the Spring frame is similar to the above, but the rear portion incorporates a robust swinging arm, self-lubricating bronze bushes, integral pillion footrest lugs and flexibly mounted oil damped Teledraulic spring units.
Front and side stands are fitted to both frames : the Rigid frame is additionally fitted with a rear stand and the Spring frame with a centre stand.

FORKS

Self-lubricating oil-damped Teledraulic.

MUDGUARDS

Deep section with centre rib and supported by tubular steel stays. Valanced rear guard on all standard Spring frame models.

SEAT

Combined seat of registered design for rider and passenger on all standard spring frame models. Spring top saddle with adjustable three-point mounting on Rigid and Competition Models.

TANKS

Fitted with quick-action filler caps and twin filter petrol taps, the welded steel tanks provide the following capacity :

Petrol : 3 gallons ; "Springtwin" : 4 gallons. Oil : 4 pints.

WHEELS AND BRAKES

Robust steel hubs of A.J.S. design and manufacture, mounted on adjustable taper roller bearings. Fully and quickly adjustable 7" dia. internal expanding brakes incorporating cast drums and Ferodo lined aluminium shoes.

3.25" × 19" Dunlop tyres on 350 c.c. Models.
3.25" × 19" front and 3.50" × 19" rear on 500 c.c. Models.

ELECTRICAL EQUIPMENT

Eccentrically mounted 32 watt chain-driven dynamo, 7" dia. headlamp with finger-controlled dipper switch, new rear light of greatly improved design, flexibly mounted voltage control unit and electric horn.

FINISH

Traditional A.J.S. black and gold on Bonderised surface. Exhaust system, handlebars, etc., chromium-plated, fork sliders and front brake plate polished aluminium. Chromium-plated wheel rims on export models.

EQUIPMENT

Tool kit to cover all normal requirements, tyre pump, grease gun, comprehensive maintenance manual and illuminated speedometer.
(For details of extra and optional equipment see Page 11 and Spares List.)

1953 bought a well padded and distinctive dual seat as standard on all sprung frame models. Finish was still in black enamel with gold lining to the tank. Not always mentioned in their brochures was that steel components were Bonderised before painting. Use of chromium remained restricted so, somewhat unfairly some might have maintained, it was applied to the wheel rims of export machines only. A tool kit, tyre pump, grease gun, maintenance manual and an illuminated speedometer were standard, but if you wanted a brake light, air cleaner, pillion footrests, a luggage rack or panniers they were all extras.

One of the top scrambles riders of the day was Geoff Ward, who gave AJS many wins and much publicity. He later owned a garage in North Devon and, when I got to know him in the early '70s, he still had some of his old bikes that we'd occasionally exercise around his fields. Foolishly, when he decided to sell them, I passed up the opportunity.

You'd have had to have known the likes of Charlie Plummer or Wally Wyatt, who were in charge of the building and preparation of the competition machines, to know all the small changes that were made during their constant process of improvement. Just one in 1953 was the re-positioning of the front brake cable and activating lever to forward of the forks.

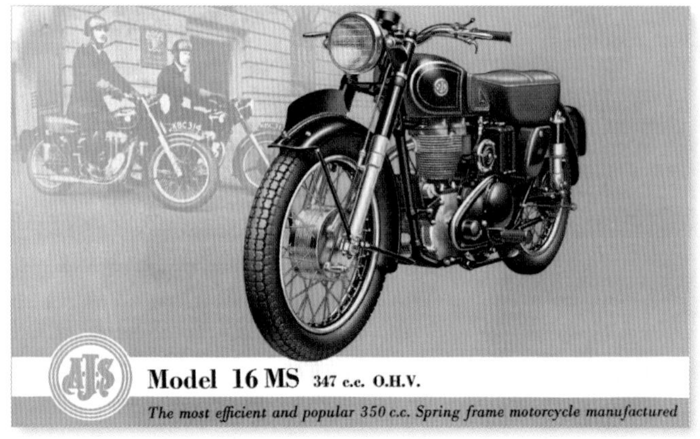

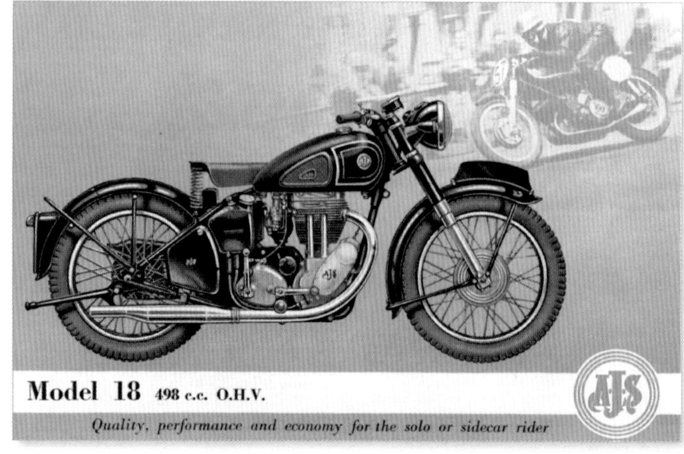

For the 1954 model year there was an aluminium full-width front hub (still with 7in brake) for all road bikes, slightly flared mudguards and round plastic tank badges. A pair of sidelights now straddled the headlight as a supposed improvement over the lamp with underslung sidelight of the previous season. Gone too was the small circular plate for clutch adjustment and, instead, the whole assembly could be accessed by removing the large domed clutch cover.

The twin and other spring frame models had twin pannier toolboxes.

The Model 18 now had a larger (3¾ gallon) petrol tank and bigger (1⁵⁄₃₂-inch) carburettor as well as a rotating magnet magneto with automatic advance, which necessitated a different timing cover to accommodate the mechanism. The 16s were also given a larger (1¹⁄₁₆-inch) carburettor.

ITEM	16M	16MS	16MC	16MCS	18	18S	18C	18CS	20
Engine	347 c.c. O.H.V. SINGLE				498 c.c. O.H.V. SINGLE				498 c.c. O.H.V. Twin
Bore and Stroke	69 mm. × 93 mm.				82.5 mm. × 93 mm.				66 × 72.8mm.
Power	18 b.h.p. @ 5750 rpm			24 at 6000	24.4 b.h.p. @ 5500 rpm			30 at 5600	29@6800 rpm
Comp. Ratio	6.5 or 7.5	6.5 or 7.5	6.5 or 7.5	7.5	6.3 or 7.3	6.3 or 7.3	6.3 or 7.3	7.3	7.0 or 8.0
Carburettor	1 1/16"	1 1/16"	1 1/16"	1 1/16"	1 5/32"	1 5/32"	1 5/32"	1 5/32"	1"
Main Jet	150	150	150	150	180	180	180	180	180
Throttle Slide	6/4	6/4	6/4	6/4	29/4	29/4	29/4	29/4	6/4
Ignition Advance	37° or 7/16"	37° or 7/16"	37° or 7/16"	37° or 7/16"	37° or 7/16"	37° or 7/16"	37° or 7/16"	37° or 7/16"	39° or 3/8"
Engine Sprocket	18	18	16	16	21	21	18	18	20
Generator	6v 32w	6v 32w	—	—	6v 32w	6v 32w	—	—	6v 45w
Petrol	3G 13.6Lt.	3G 13.6Lt.	2G 9Lt.	2G 9Lt.	3¾G 16.9Lt.	3¾G 16.9Lt.	2G 9Lt.	2G 9Lt.	3¾G 16.9Lt.
Consumption	90 m.p.g.	90 m.p.g.	80 m.p.g.	80 m.p.g.	85 m.p.g.	85 m.p.g.	75 m.p.g.	75 m.p.g.	75 m.p.g.
Gear Ratios	5.8 7.6 9.9 & 15.4:1	5.8 7.6 9.9 & 15.4:1	6.6 10.4 16.1 & 21.1:1	6.6 8.6 11.2 & 17.3:1	5.0 6.5 8.5 & 13.3:1	5.0 6.5 8.5 & 13.3:1	5.8 9.1 14.1 & 18.9:1	5.8 7.6 9.9 & 15.4:1	5.3 6.9 8.9 & 13.9:1
Fork Oil	185 c.c. S.A.E. 20 OIL EACH LEG								
Suspension Oil	85 c.c. S.A.E. 20 OIL PER UNIT ALL SPRING FRAME MODELS								
Primary Chain	½" × 5/16" ALL MODELS								
Rear Chain	5/8" × 3/8" ALL MODELS								
Dyno. & Mag. Chain	3/8" × .225 ALL MODELS								
Wheelbase	54"	55½"	53"	55¼"	54"	55¼"	53"	55¼"	55¼"
Length	85"	86½"	82"	85½"	85	86½"	82"	85½"	86½"
Seat Height	30"	31½"	32½"	32½"	30"	31½"	32½"	32½"	31½"
Ground Clearance	5½"	5½"	6½"	6½"	5½"	5½"	6½"	6½"	5½"
Weight	344 lbs.	375 lbs.	293 lbs.	321 lbs.	354 lbs.	387 lbs.	296 lbs.	324 lbs.	394 lbs.

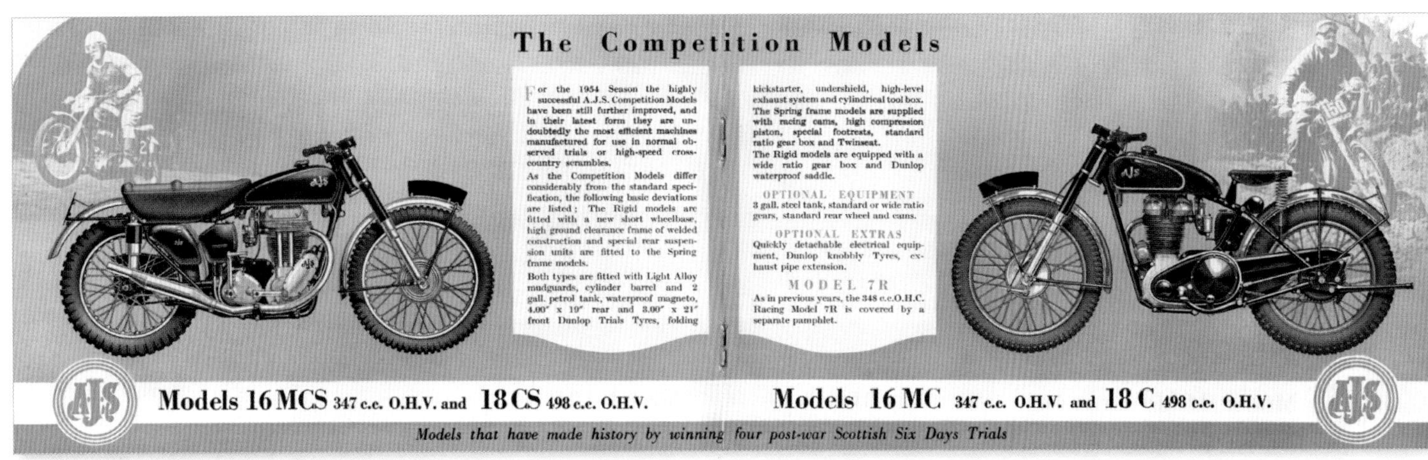

A significant alteration to the factory's competition bikes for 1953 was a new all-welded high ground clearance frame for the 16MC and 18C.

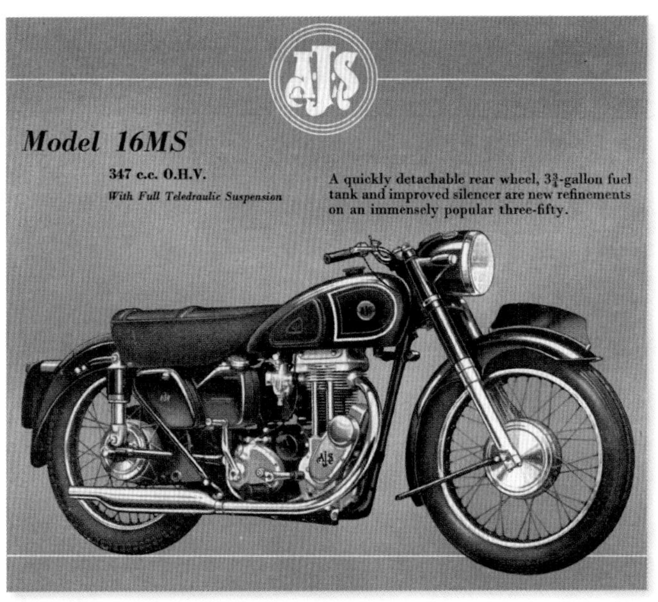

With the Plumstead factory in the midst of an expensive re-tooling phase, the micrometer is perhaps an apt feature of the 1955 brochure cover, whilst the bike is the 7R that at last managed to win the Junior TT in 1954. It took this very special triple camshaft version to do so, however, with New Zealander Rod Coleman setting a race average of 91.51mph.

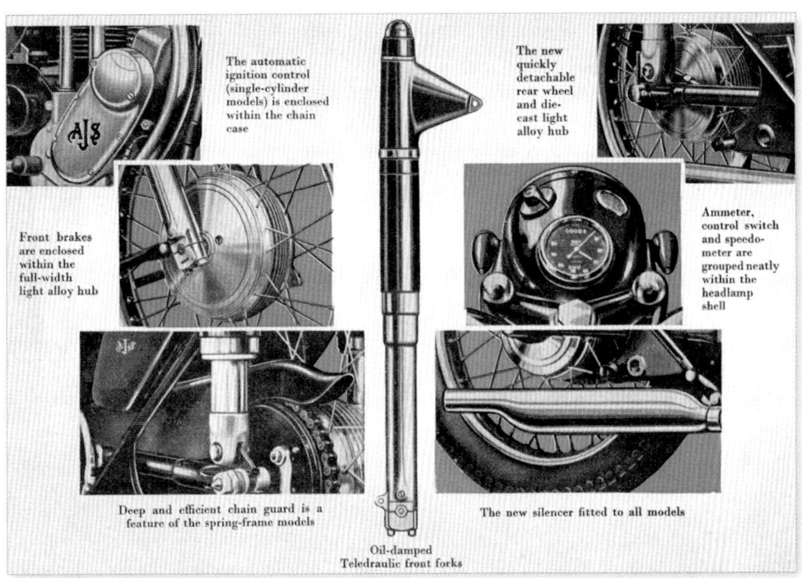

With a new design of front mudguard that eliminated the front stay by employing the side valances as attachment points, as well as the speedo now mounted within the headlamp shell, a more modern look was achieved. The 16s were also given the larger petrol tank and auto advance magneto that had been introduced on the 500 a year earlier.

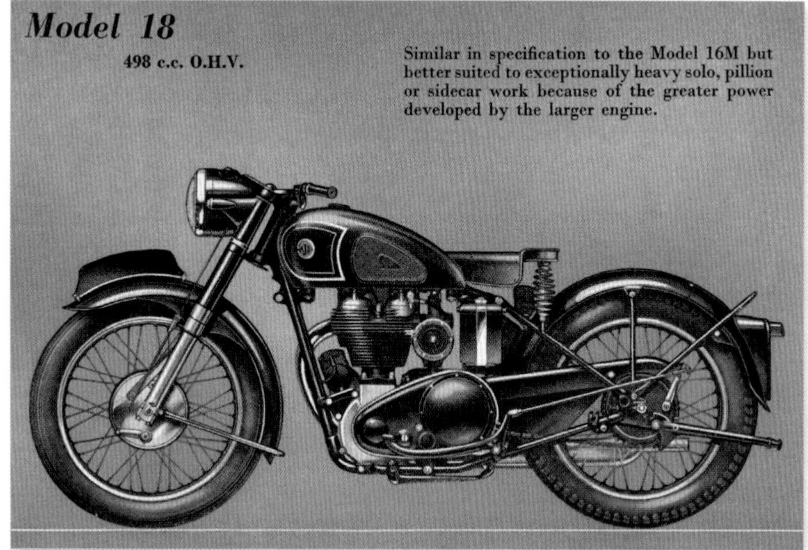

One last facelift for the trusty rigid singles for 1955, their final season; but I'm not sure the public would have agreed that the 500 would be ideal for pillion work. The average working man could only aspire to £10 a week in the mid '50s but for a few shillings more than £25 extra they could have had a springer 18S already fitted with a comfy dual seat. Until the advent of the dual seat and then the almost universal adoption for road going machines its owner could choose a proprietary mudguard-top second seat or cobble up something for themselves if passenger accommodation was required.

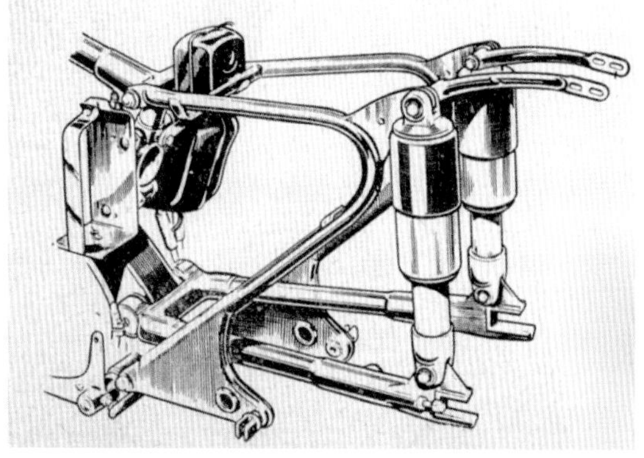

From the 1955 season onwards this type of extension to mount pillion footrests was a feature on AMC swinging-arm frames. For some reason I find it a rather unattractive feature and prefer the rather more workmanlike mounting of the necessary lugs on tubular loops. Voltage control regulators, on both swinging-arm and rigid bikes, had lived under the seat since the previous model year.

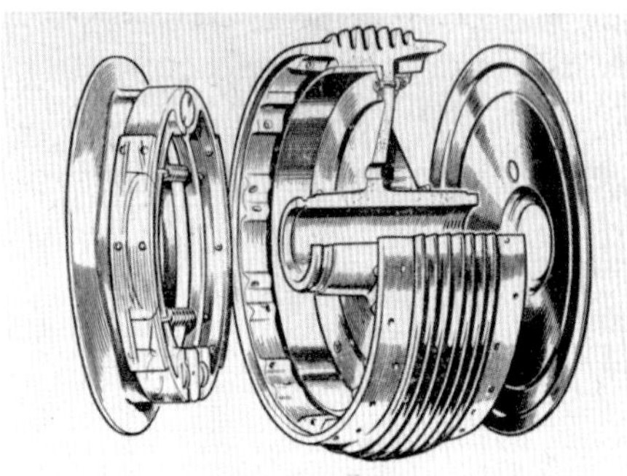

This was the 1955 replacement for the first type of full width front hub that had been introduced for 1954.

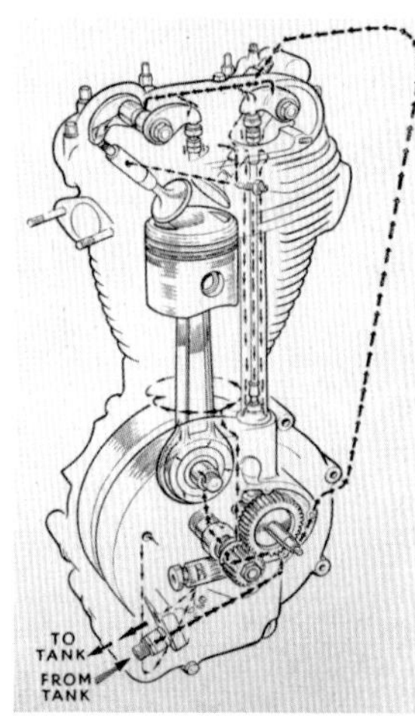

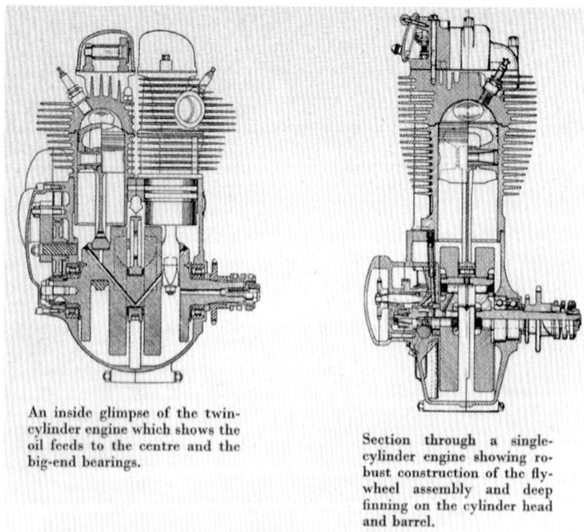

The 1955 Model 20 boasted all the facelift features of the singles plus a chromium tank with black enamelled panels to further set it apart from the rest of the range, which had all-black tinware.

Full-width hubs for the 1955 competition models too; and in line with the road machines the 16MCs and 18Cs were fitted with the new Amal monobloc carburettor. Scramblers 16MCSs and 18CSs, on the other hand, boasted Amal TT.10 carbs for this year, whilst all four eschewed automatic ignition advance in favour of manual control via a handlebar lever. Dunlop rubber saddles were now standard for the rigid trials bikes and the scramblers had what was described as a 'competition Twinseat'. The latter, with their uprated suspension and tuned motors (24bhp at 6,000 rpm for the 350, and 30bhp at 5,600 for the 500) made them amongst the most capable off-the-peg scramblers you could buy.

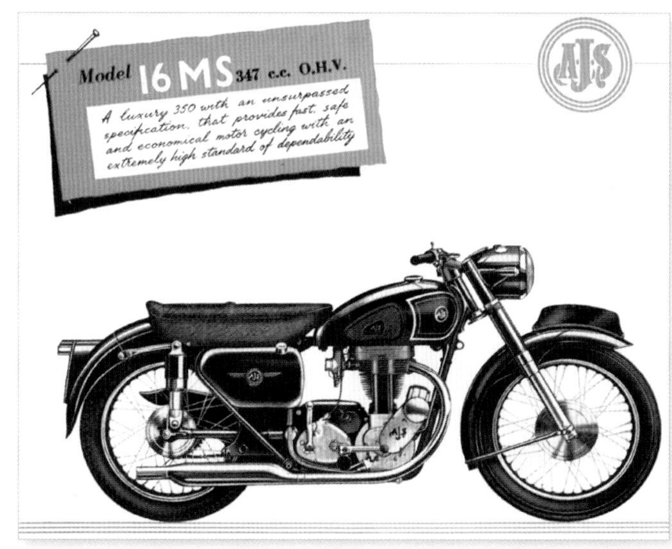

Oil tank, toolboxes and battery mounting were tidied up for 1956 with the last now mounted within a single toolbox – it and the oil tank neatly filling the rear frame loop. The resulting cleaner look was enhanced by the aperture between being closed by a vertical panel whilst another pressing covered the engine/gearbox plates-cum-dynamo housing. Both 350 and 500 singles had a redesigned cylinder head casting that resulted in shorter pushrod tubes.

The Model 20 acquired a larger brother in 1956, in the form of the 600cc Model 30 that the manufacturer – you will notice – claimed to have 'performance only limited by road conditions'. In pre-motorway and pre-litigious Great Britain an innocent enough assertion but perhaps it should have ended with 'and rider's prudence'. A couple of easy-to-miss differences between this and other road models from the previous year were that the lower front mudguard stay no longer doubled as a front stand, and the front brake operating lever was now located above and a little behind the wheel spindle. Both this and the 500 twin had chromed tanks but the latter had coach-lining surrounding the badges of a similar pattern to that applied to the road-going singles.

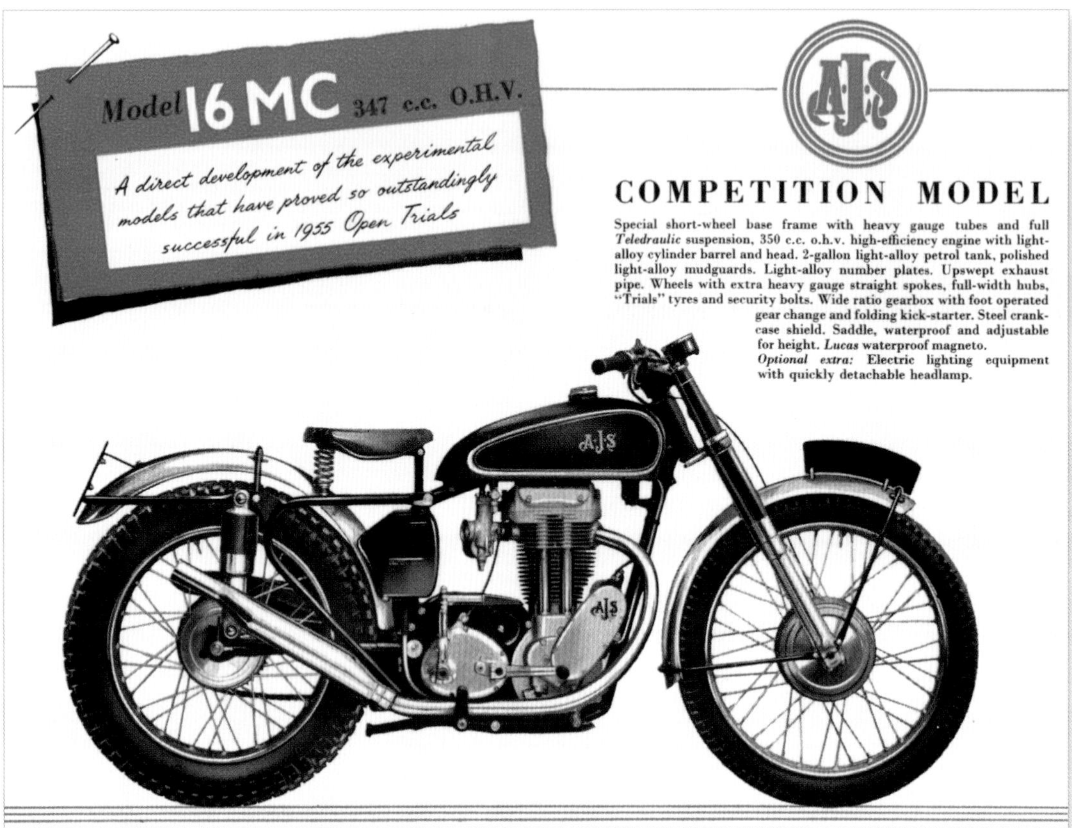

The only competition model to be listed in the 1956 brochure was this 350 trials version with swinging-arm frame.

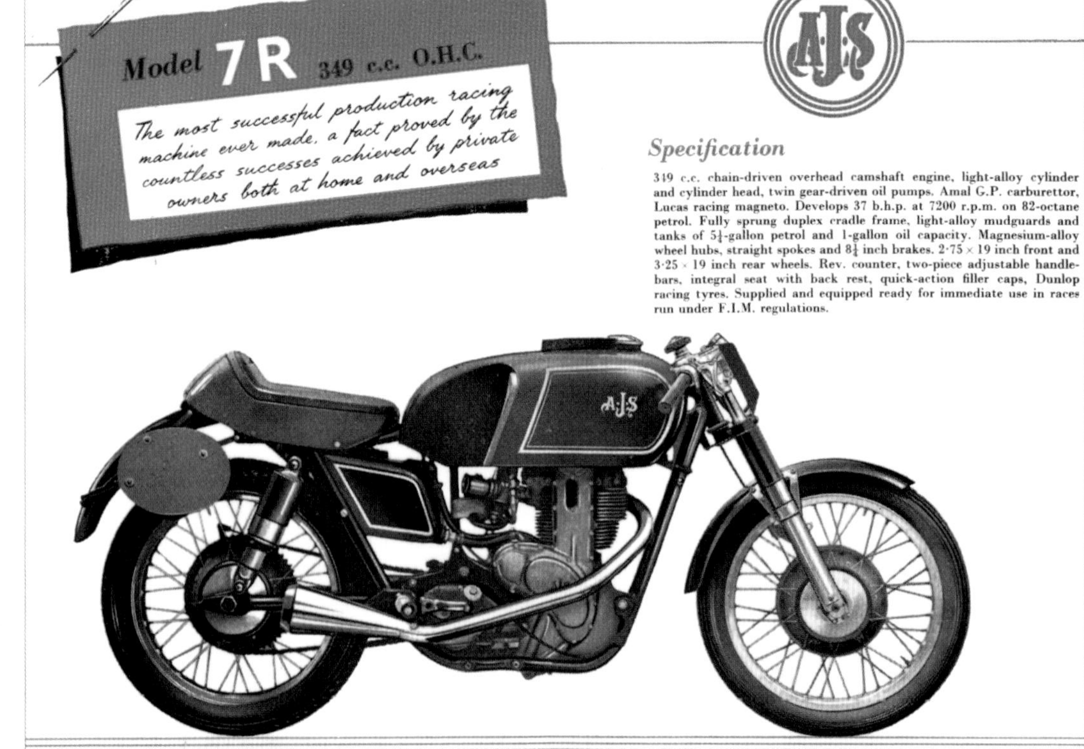

In search of more power and even greater reliability the 1956 Boy Racer's motor had now been reconfigured with oversquare dimensions of 75.5x78mm, which resulted in a capacity increase of 1cc to 349cc over the original's 74x81mm 348cc measurements. Its overall appearance was considerably changed since it last appeared in the general brochure four years earlier, having been given a new frame and different tanks and seat in the interim.

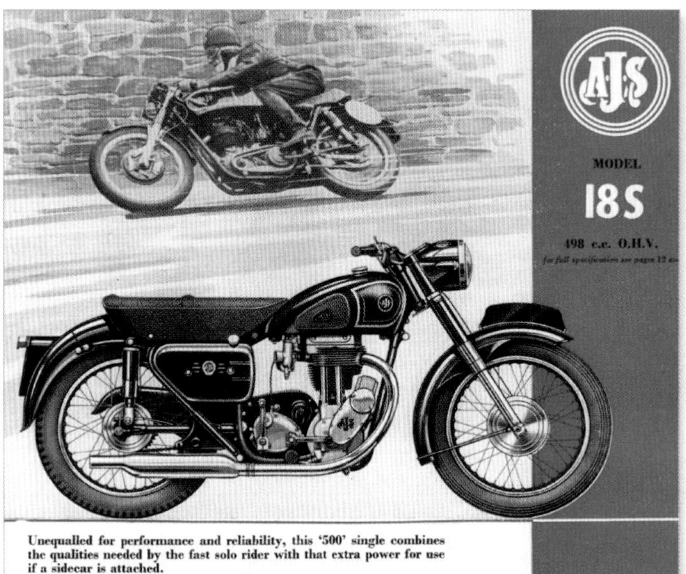

Looking very much the same as last year's models but there were alterations such as the change from jampots to Girling rear suspension units for 1957 and, although not staring you in the face in this brochure picture, a brand-new gearbox developed and manufactured by AMC.

Here's the '57 twin sporting a petrol tank with chrome side panels and, in common with its 1957 stablemates, the oil tank had acquired a few diminutive ribs. The 600cc Model 30 was visually all but identical and it would take an eagle-eyed enthusiast to spot the slight dfferences, such as its larger 1¹⁄16-inch carb against the 20's 1-inch unit.

MODEL	16MS	18S	20	30	16MCS	18CS	16MC
Engine: Type	O.H.V.	O.H.V.	O.H.V.	O.H.V.	O.H.V.	O.H.V.	O.H.V.
No. of cylinders	1	1	2	2	1	1	1
Bore/Stroke mm.	69 × 93	82·5 × 93	66 × 72·8	72 × 72·8	72 × 85·5	86 × 85·5	69 × 93
Capacity c.c.	347	498	498	592	348	497	347
Compression ratio	7·5 or 6·5	7·3 or 6·3	8·0 or 7·0	7·4 or 6·75	9·9	8·7	6·5
Gear ratios: Top	5·8	5·0	5·25	5·0	6·5	5·8	6·5
Third	7·8	6·8	7·1	6·8	8·8	7·8	9·6
Second ...	10·3	8·9	9·3	8·9	11·5	10·3	15·5
First	15·5	13·4	14·0	13·4	17·4	15·5	21·3
Carburettor: Amal	Monobloc 376/5	Monobloc 389/1	Monobloc 376/6	Monobloc 376/78	Monobloc 389/18	Monobloc 389/12	Monobloc 376/5
Choke size	1 1/16"	1 5/32"	1"	1 1/16"	1 1/8"	1 3/16"	1 1/16"
Main Jet No.	210	260	220	300	270	440	210
Throttle Slide No.	3½		4		3		3
Rear chain	⅝" Pitch × 0·380" Width		⅝" Pitch × 0·380" Width		⅝" Pitch × 0·380" Width		⅝" Pitch × 0·380" Width
Front chain	½" Pitch × 0·305" Width		½" Pitch × 0·305" Width		½" Pitch × 0·305" Width		½" Pitch × 0·305" Width
Tyres: Front	3·25" × 19"		3·25" × 19"		3·00" × 21"		2·75" × 21"
Rear	3·25" × 19"	3·50" × 19"	3·50" × 19"		4·00" × 19"		4·00" × 19"
Brakes: Front and Rear ...	7" diam. × ⅞" wide		7" diam. × ⅞" wide		7" diam. × ⅞" wide		7" diam. × ⅞" wide
Seat Height	31½"		31½"		32½"		32½"
Wheelbase	55¼"		55¼"		55¼"		54"
Length	86¼"		86¼"		85¼"		83"
Width	28"		28"		28"		28"
Height	41½"		41½"		43"		43"
Clearance	5½"		5½"		6½"		10"
Weight lbs.	375	387	394	396	326	329	320
Petrol tank capacity galls. ...	3¾		3¾		2		2
Oil tank capacity pints ...	4		4		4		4

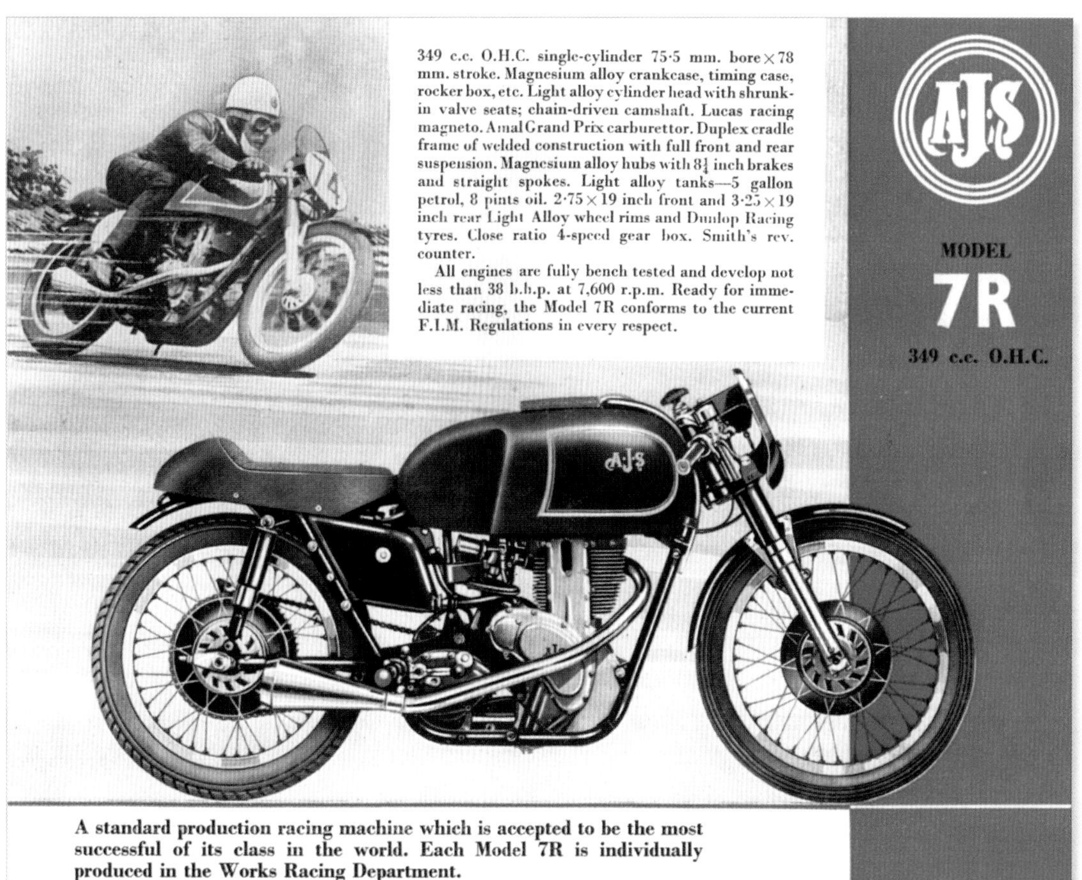

349 c.c. O.H.C. single-cylinder 75·5 mm. bore × 78 mm. stroke. Magnesium alloy crankcase, timing case, rocker box, etc. Light alloy cylinder head with shrunk-in valve seats; chain-driven camshaft. Lucas racing magneto. Amal Grand Prix carburettor. Duplex cradle frame of welded construction with full front and rear suspension. Magnesium alloy hubs with $8\frac{1}{4}$ inch brakes and straight spokes. Light alloy tanks—5 gallon petrol, 8 pints oil. 2·75 × 19 inch front and 3·25 × 19 inch rear Light Alloy wheel rims and Dunlop Racing tyres. Close ratio 4-speed gear box. Smith's rev. counter.

All engines are fully bench tested and develop not less than 38 b.h.p. at 7,600 r.p.m. Ready for immediate racing, the Model 7R conforms to the current F.I.M. Regulations in every respect.

A·J·S

MODEL

7R

349 c.c. O.H.C.

A standard production racing machine which is accepted to be the most successful of its class in the world. Each Model 7R is individually produced in the Works Racing Department.

In the majority of races, bikes were still ridden 'naked' and as the years passed the 7R gained an ever more purposeful stance. Clip-on bars had been a standard fitment for a while but in 1957 the abbreviated rear mudguard, latest slimmer rear suspension units and 'turbo-finned' aluminium plates to aid brake cooling all added to the look. More importantly they went enormously well and kept on doing so whilst more exotic machines often fell by the wayside. In the mid '70s I rode many miles on a slightly earlier example than this, which was road registered but illegally noisy. It never missed a beat and was more chuckable and more tractable than my Gold Star Clubmans. For no good reason I sold it and have regretted it ever since.

Special Features of the 1957 A·J·S Quality Range

The new quickly detachable rear wheel eliminates metal to metal contact with large diameter rubber sleeved driving pins.

Redesigned chainguard affords even greater protection to both top and bottom runs of the chain.

Completely new gear box of A·J·S design and manufacture. Robust construction. 4-speed with positive foot control and dry multi-plate clutch.

Petrol tanks featuring chromium plated side panels have enhanced the appearance of the twin cylinder models.

The rubber shock absorber incorporated in the clutch eliminates transmission shocks and improves tractability.

Full width light alloy hubs with racing type straight spokes.

Compare this '57 model to the one at the top left of page 29 of the '56 machine and you will see the difference in the frame and other evolutionary cycle parts.

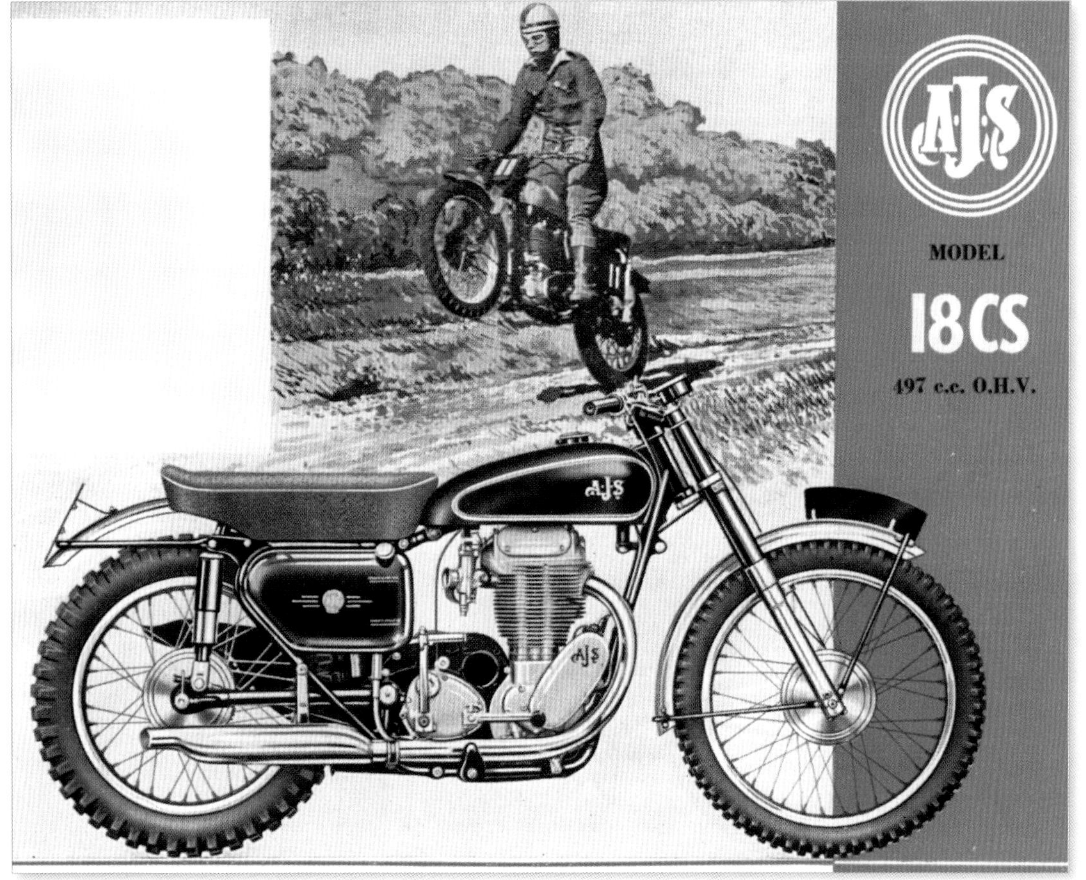

For 1957 the over-the-counter scramblers had special, highly developed, short-stroke (85.5mm) motors. The 18C's was oversquare with an 86mm bore whilst its smaller relation's was 72mm. With no need for a battery, a considerably smaller '53-to-'55-type toolbox was mounted on the left instead of the current road machine variety that would have matched the oil tank.

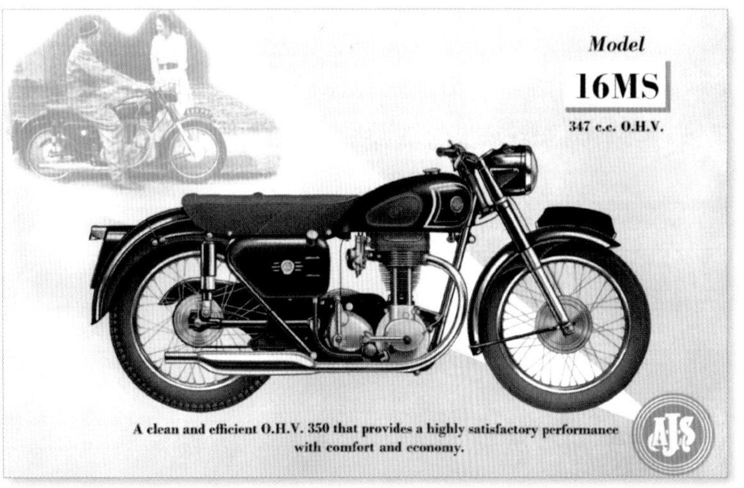

PRICE LIST FOR 1958

MODEL	BASIC PRICE £ s. d.	PURCHASE TAX £ s. d.	TOTAL PRICE £ s. d.
MODEL 16MS 350 c.c. O.H.V. Single	187 10 0	46 8 2	233 18 2
MODEL 16MC 350 c.c. O.H.V. Trials	195 0 0	48 5 3	243 5 3
MODEL 16MCS 350 c.c. O.H.V. Scrambles	201 0 0	49 14 11	250 14 11
MODEL 18S 500 c.c. O.H.V. Single	198 10 0	49 2 7	247 12 7
MODEL 18CS 500 c.c. O.H.V. Scrambles	218 0 0	53 19 1	271 19 1
MODEL 20 500 c.c. O.H.V. Vertical Twin	225 10 0	55 16 3	281 6 3
MODEL 30 600 c.c. O.H.V. Vertical Twin	231 10 0	57 5 11	288 15 11
MODEL 30CS 600 c.c. O.H.V. Sports Twin	240 0 0	59 8 0	299 8 0
MODEL 7R 350 c.c. O.H.C. Racing	335 0 0	82 18 3	417 18 3
Electric Lighting on Trials and Scrambles Models	8 17 6	2 4 0	11 1 6

A change from magneto ignition to coil and from dynamo to alternator for 1958 gave the singles' motor a much altered appearance – points were to be found within the elliptical aluminium cover at the base of the pushrod tunnels whilst the coil lived up under the petrol tank. The alternator was mounted on the (left) primary drive side of the crankshaft, so the opportunity was taken to do away with the steel chain case, which was prone to leakage, and replace it with one of cast aluminium that would accommodate the assembly. The necessary rectifier was located under the seat. At last the stylish but feeble twin sidelights had been done away with and the obligatory side or pilot light made integral with the headlamp reflector.

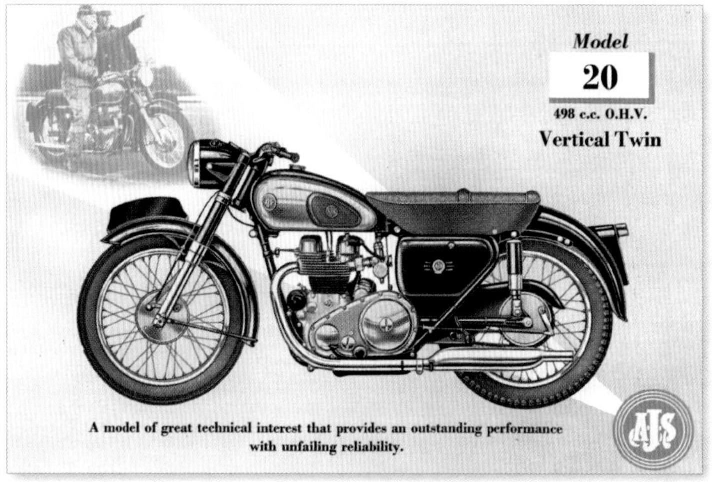

Both 500 and 600 twins retained magneto ignition and a dynamo so the new cast aluminium case with which they were fitted was less bulky and had a much smaller domed protrusion in the vicinity of the primary drive sprocket. Both varieties had a pair of large slotted screw caps – the lower one for oil replenishment and the other to access the clutch centre for adjustment.

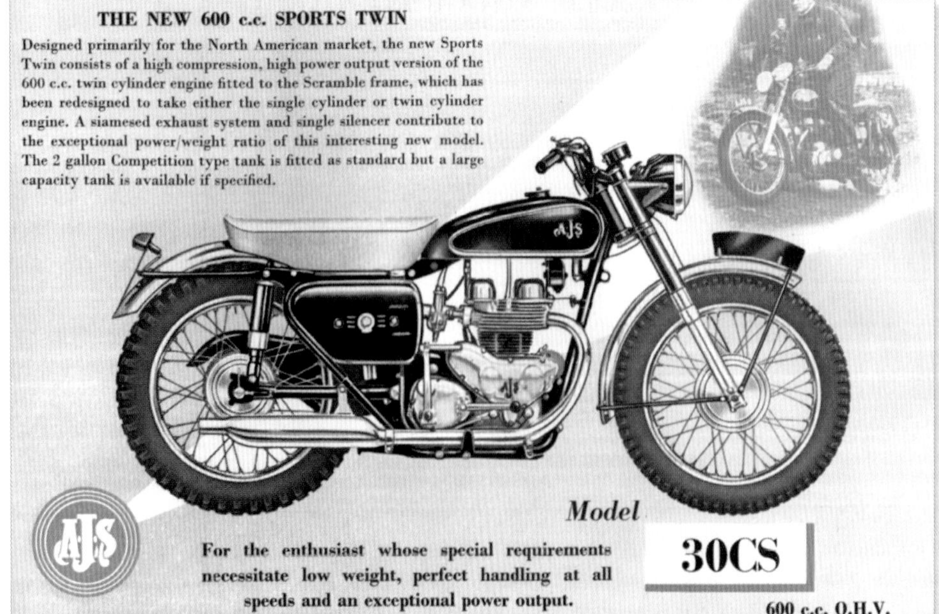

For a number of years the single-cylinder scrambles models had been earning export dollars due to the immense popularity of major off-road endurance events in the United States – particularly in California. Allied to this was the American cult of the street scrambler – a machine that would normally be ridden daily on the road but had the looks and capability to go 'off piste' if and when. It was solely to cater for these markets that lighting sets were catalogued as an optional extra. By this time other English manufacturers, notably Triumph and BSA, were producing big twins especially for this market, so AMC decided it had better get in on the act.

Something completely different, in the form of a brand-new 250, featured on the marque's 1959 brochure cover. The unit-construction Model 14 was the first post-war AJS of this capacity and the first with integral gearbox.

To complement the Model 14 and to give the make a foothold in the up-to-250cc scrambles class – for so long the province of other, in many cases, smaller manufacturers – the CS version was introduced at the same time. It had 19in wheels rather than a 21 at the front as normally employed on this type of machine. The road-going 14, on the other hand, had 17s front and rear. A lighting set was an optional extra.

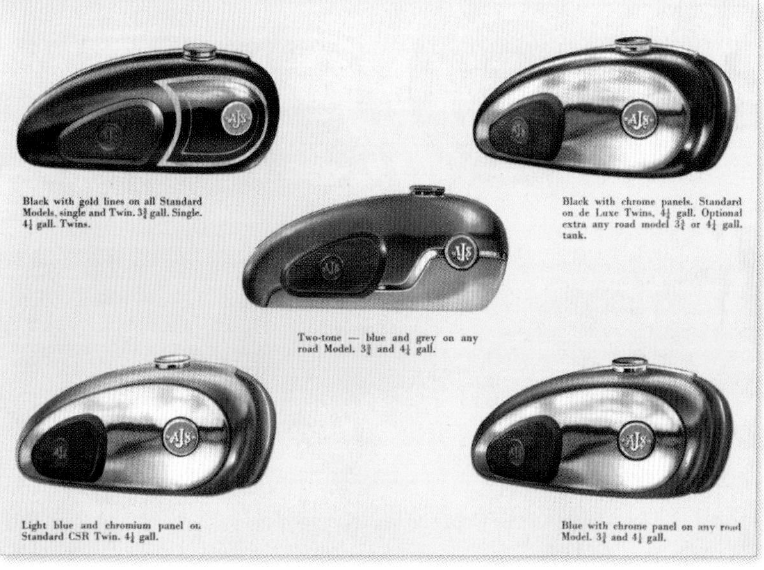
Black with gold lines on all Standard Models, single and Twin. 3¾ gall. Single. 4¼ gall. Twins.

Black with chrome panels. Standard on de Luxe Twins, 4¼ gall. Optional extra any road model 3¾ or 4¼ gall. tank.

Two-tone — blue and grey on any road Model. 3¾ and 4¼ gall.

Light blue and chromium panel on Standard CSR Twin. 4¼ gall.

Blue with chrome panel on any road Model. 3¾ and 4¼ gall.

For the 1959 road-going singles and twins there was a large choice of tanks and finishes. These also had deeply valanced steel mudguards finished in either AJS blue or black. C, CS and CSR models had polished aluminium guards and light Mediterranean blue petrol tanks (excepting for the 16C, which was black) and, according to model, either light Mediterranean blue or black oil tanks.

AMC's 600 twins had been somewhat out on a limb so in 1959 they were made up to 650s in line with other manufacturers. The CSR version was intended as direct competition for Triumph's Bonneville and BSA's Rockets. There was also a 500 CSR – both had the new larger 4¼-gallon petrol tank and were, to all intents and purposes, visually indistinguishable from each other.

FOR THE TECHNICALLY MINDED

<table>
<tr><th>MODEL</th><th>16</th><th>16C</th><th>16CS</th><th>18</th><th>18CS</th><th>20</th><th>20 de Luxe</th><th>20CS</th><th>20CSR</th><th>31</th><th>31 de Luxe</th><th>31CS</th><th>31CSR</th><th>7R</th><th>14</th><th>14CS</th></tr>
<tr><td>CYLINDERS</td><td>1</td><td>1</td><td>1</td><td>1</td><td>1</td><td>2</td><td>2</td><td>2</td><td>2</td><td>2</td><td>2</td><td>2</td><td>2</td><td>1</td><td>1</td><td>1</td></tr>
<tr><td>BORE x STROKE</td><td colspan="2">69 x 93</td><td>72 x 85·5</td><td>82·5 x 93</td><td>86 x 85·5</td><td colspan="4">66 x 72·5</td><td colspan="4">72 x 79·3</td><td>75·5 x 78</td><td colspan="2">70 x 65</td></tr>
<tr><td>CAPACITY</td><td colspan="2">347</td><td>348</td><td>498</td><td>497</td><td colspan="4">498</td><td colspan="4">646</td><td>349</td><td colspan="2">248</td></tr>
<tr><td>COMPRESSION RATIO</td><td>7·5 or 6·5</td><td>6·5</td><td>9·9</td><td>7·3 or 6·5</td><td>8·7</td><td colspan="2">8 or 7</td><td colspan="2">8·5</td><td colspan="2">7·5</td><td colspan="2">8·5</td><td>10·5</td><td>7·8</td><td>10</td></tr>
<tr><td>IGNITION</td><td>COIL</td><td>MAG</td><td>MAG</td><td>COIL</td><td>MAG</td><td>COIL</td><td>MAG</td><td colspan="2">MAG</td><td>COIL</td><td colspan="3">MAG</td><td>MAG</td><td colspan="2">COIL</td></tr>
<tr><td>GENERATOR</td><td>ALT</td><td>—</td><td>—</td><td>ALT</td><td>—</td><td>ALT</td><td colspan="3">DYNAMO</td><td>ALT</td><td colspan="3">DYNAMO</td><td>—</td><td colspan="2">ALT</td></tr>
<tr><td>AMAL CARBURETTOR</td><td colspan="2">1 1/16"</td><td>1 1/8"</td><td>1 3/16"</td><td>1 3/16"</td><td colspan="4">1"</td><td colspan="4">1 1/8"</td><td>1 3/8"</td><td colspan="2">1 1/16"</td></tr>
<tr><td>TYRE FRONT</td><td>3·25 x 19</td><td>2·75 x 21</td><td>3·00 x 21</td><td>3·25 x 19</td><td>3·00 x 21</td><td colspan="2">3·25 x 19</td><td>3.00 x 21</td><td colspan="3">3·25 x 19</td><td>3·00 x 21</td><td>3·25 x 19</td><td>2·75 x 19</td><td>3·25 x 17</td><td>3·00 x 19</td></tr>
<tr><td>TYRE REAR</td><td>3·25 x 19</td><td>4·00 x 19</td><td>4·00 x 19</td><td>3·50 x 19</td><td>4·00 x 19</td><td colspan="2">3·50 x 19</td><td>4·00 x 19</td><td colspan="3">3·50 x 19</td><td>4·00 x 19</td><td>3·50 x 19</td><td>3·25 x 19</td><td>3·25 x 17</td><td>3·50 x 19</td></tr>
<tr><td>BRAKE SIZE</td><td>7"</td><td>5·5"</td><td colspan="11">7"</td><td>8"</td><td colspan="2">6"</td></tr>
<tr><td>GEAR RATIO 1st
2nd
3rd
4th</td><td>15·5
10·3
7·8
5·8</td><td>21
15·8
10·1
6·5</td><td>17·9
11·5
8·8
6·5</td><td>13·4
8·9
6·8
5·0</td><td>15·5
10·3
7·8
5·8</td><td colspan="2">14·0
9·3
7·1
5·3</td><td>15·5
10·3
7·8
5·8</td><td>14·0
9·3
7·1
5·3</td><td colspan="2">12·8
8·5
6·5
4·8</td><td>14·0
9·3
7·1
5·25</td><td>12·8
8·5
6·5
4·8</td><td>8·67
6·48
5·36
4·87</td><td>20·1
12·6
8·9
6·9</td><td>23·4
14·8
10·4
8·0</td></tr>
<tr><td>ENGINE SPROCKET</td><td>19</td><td colspan="2">17</td><td>22</td><td>19</td><td colspan="2">21</td><td>19</td><td>21</td><td colspan="2">23</td><td>21</td><td>23</td><td>23</td><td>21</td><td>17</td></tr>
<tr><td>PETROL GALLONS</td><td>3·75</td><td colspan="2">2</td><td>3·75</td><td>2</td><td colspan="2">4·25</td><td>2</td><td colspan="3">4·25</td><td>2</td><td>4·25</td><td>5·25</td><td colspan="2">2·75</td></tr>
<tr><td>OIL PINTS</td><td>4</td><td>2·75</td><td colspan="5">4</td><td colspan="2">5</td><td colspan="2">4</td><td colspan="2">5</td><td>5·25</td><td colspan="2">2·75</td></tr>
<tr><td>IGNITION TIMING</td><td colspan="2">39°</td><td>41°</td><td colspan="2">39°</td><td colspan="4">35°</td><td colspan="4">35°</td><td>34°</td><td colspan="2">36°</td></tr>
<tr><td>LENGTH</td><td>86·25"</td><td>83"</td><td>85·25"</td><td>86·25"</td><td>85·25"</td><td colspan="2">86·25"</td><td colspan="2">85·25"</td><td colspan="2">86·25"</td><td colspan="2">85·25"</td><td>80"</td><td>82"</td><td>82·5"</td></tr>
<tr><td>WIDTH</td><td>29"</td><td colspan="2">32·5"</td><td>29"</td><td>32·5"</td><td colspan="2">29"</td><td colspan="2">32·5"</td><td colspan="2">29"</td><td colspan="2">32·5"</td><td>24"</td><td colspan="2">28"</td></tr>
<tr><td>WEIGHT (LBS)</td><td>375</td><td>306</td><td>326</td><td>387</td><td>329</td><td>392</td><td>394</td><td>377</td><td>379</td><td>396</td><td>398</td><td>379</td><td>381</td><td>285</td><td>325</td><td>321</td></tr>
<tr><td>SEAT HEIGHT</td><td>31·5"</td><td colspan="2">32·5"</td><td>31·5"</td><td>32·5"</td><td colspan="2">31·5"</td><td>32·5"</td><td colspan="3">31·5"</td><td>32·5"</td><td>31·5"</td><td>31"</td><td>30"</td><td>32"</td></tr>
<tr><td>WHEEL BASE</td><td>55·25"</td><td>53·75"</td><td colspan="3">55·25"</td><td colspan="4">55·25"</td><td colspan="4">55·25"</td><td>55"</td><td>53"</td><td>53·75"</td></tr>
<tr><td>GROUND CLEARANCE</td><td>5·5"</td><td>10"</td><td>6·5"</td><td>5·5"</td><td>6·5"</td><td colspan="2">5·5"</td><td>6·5"</td><td colspan="3">5·5"</td><td>6·5"</td><td>5·5"</td><td>6·75"</td><td>5·5"</td><td>7·25"</td></tr>
</table>

MODEL 16C 350 c.c. O.H.V.

The model that has won the 'Scottish Six Days Trial', the most difficult and strenuous trial in the world, on six postwar occasions and again in 1958, requires no introduction. Lighter and much improved as a result of experience gained during the past season, the Model 16C is without doubt the finest Trials machine produced.

Standard finish

A smaller (5½in) front brake for the over-the-counter 16C was introduced for 1959 to save weight, as braking from speed was not a factor. At 306lb the Trials 350 was a full 20lb lighter than the 18CS Scrambles version – a good deal of which was accounted for by the new special shorter lightweight rear tubular frame, as it did not have to withstand the punishment meted out by motocross. Scrambles and Trials single-cylinder machines were still fitted with steel primary chain cases as on this 18CS. Catalogued extras for these, as well as the sports twins, were in the main aimed at the US market and included lighting, quickly detachable rear wheel, Western bars and (for the 18CS only) a 'special single cylinder speed kit for normal racing'.

Looks should be the least consideration when evaluating a racing machine but there would be few who would disagree that the 7R's improved with the years. The seat and tank combination introduced for 1959, as well as being practical, imparted a more flowing, unified, line to its already business-like appearance.

'Universally recognised as the fastest and best looking standard '250' ever produced', read the 1960 brochure blurb for the Model 14, which was materially unaltered except for different tank lining. The Scrambles 14C was treated to the same plus a black seat with piping. A newcomer, however, was the 350cc Model 8 – in many respects a scaled-up carbon copy of the 250 Model 14 with heavyweight forks and 18in wheels.

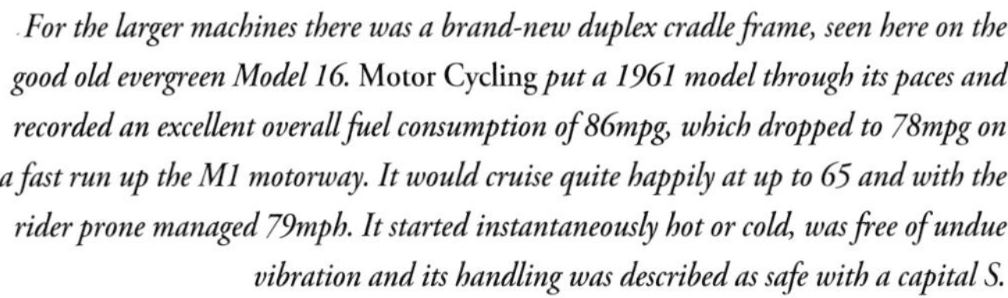

For the larger machines there was a brand-new duplex cradle frame, seen here on the good old evergreen Model 16. Motor Cycling *put a 1961 model through its paces and recorded an excellent overall fuel consumption of 86mpg, which dropped to 78mpg on a fast run up the M1 motorway. It would cruise quite happily at up to 65 and with the rider prone managed 79mph. It started instantaneously hot or cold, was free of undue vibration and its handling was described as safe with a capital S.*

In 1960 the Model 20 was now the sole 500 twin as the CS and CSR variants had been dropped after just the one year.

The printer's colours have gone a bit awry with this 31CS but you'll be able to see some of the changes over the previous year's model such as upswept exhaust, different seat and tank lining. Both it and the CSR had the new twin-tube frame, of course, but I'm not certain that the former had more power than before as claimed in the brochure.

Definitely more power for the 18CS, as it had a reworked cylinder head and an Amal GP carb. You will see that it now had an aluminium primary chain case and that the oil tank was mounted on the left-hand side – of necessity due to the big racing carburettor. Optional extras included quickly-detachable lighting equipment and rear wheel, rev counter and a three-gallon tank.

	MODEL	14	14CS	8	16	16C	7R	18	18CS	20	31	31DL	31CS	31CSR
		SINGLE CYLINDER								TWIN CYLINDER				
			SCRAMBLES			TRIALS	RACING		SCRAMBLES			DE LUXE	SCRAMBLES	SPORTS
ENGINE	Capacity	248	248	348	347	347	349	498	498	498	646	646	646	646
	Bore and Stroke, m.m.	70×65	70×65	72×85·5	69×93	69×93	75·5×78	82·5×93	86×85·5	66×72·5	72×79·3	72×79·3	72×79·3	72×79·3
	Tappet Clearance (Cold) Inlet	Nil	Nil	Nil	Nil	Nil	·008"	Nil	Nil	·008"	·008"	·008"	·008"	·008"
	Tappet Clearance (Cold) Exhaust	Nil	Nil	Nil	Nil	Nil	·012"	Nil	·005"	·008"	·008"	·008"	·008"	·008"
	Valve Timing, Inlet Opens	35°	35°	35°	36°	26°	55°	18°	67°	37°	37°	37°	37°	37°
	Valve Timing, Inlet Closes	77°	77°	77°	51°	53°	78°	69°	81°	77°	77°	77°	77°	77°
	Valve Timing, Exhaust Opens	77°	77°	77°	50°	64°	78°	50°	69°	73°	73°	73°	73°	73°
	Valve Timing, Exhaust Closes	38°	38°	38°	30°	25°	44°	30°	48°	43°	43°	43°	43°	43°
	Compression Ratio	7·8	10	7·4	6·5 or 7·5	6·5	11·6	6·5 or 7·3	8·7	7·0 or 8·0	7·5	7·5	8·5	8·5
IGNITION	Magneto	—	—	—	—	N.C.1	2 M.T.T.	—	N.C.1	—	—	K.2.F.	K.2.F.	K.2.F.
	Coil	Wipac 06500	Wipac 08413	Wipac 06500	Lucas M.A.6	—	—	Lucas M.A.6	—	Lucas MA6	Lucas MA6	—	—	—
	Ignition Timing	36°	32°	34°	39°	39°	33·5°	39°	37°	35°	35°	35°	34°	34°
	Sparking Plug, Long Reach K.L.G.	FE80	FE220	FE80	FE80	FE80	E/258/2	FE80	FE220	FE80	FE80	FE80	FE220	FE220
	Sparking Plug Gap, inch	·020–·022	·020–·022	·020–·022	·020–·022	·020–·022	·013	·020–·022	·020–·022	·020–·022	·020–·022	·020–·022	·020–·022	·020–·022
	Contact Breaker Gap, inch	·012–·015	·018	·012–·015	·014–·016	·012	·012	·014–·016	·012	·014–·016	·014–·016	·012	·012	·012
CARBURETTOR	Carburettor	376/99	376/99	389/42	376/5	376/59T	T5GP	389/1	T5GP	376/6	389/18	389/18	389/22	389/22
	Choke Diameter, inches	1 1/16	1 1/16	1 1/8	1 1/16	1 1/16	1 3/8	1 1/32	1 3/8	1	1 1/8	1 1/8	1 1/8	1 1/8
	Main Jet No.	180	190	220	210	210	330	260	350	220	400	400	430	430
	Main Jet No. with Air Cleaner	180	190	220	200	—	—	250	320	210	330	330	340	340
	Pilot Jet No.	25	25	25	30	30	—	30	Air Jet ·125"	25	20	20	20	20
	Slide No.	3·5	3·5	3	3·5	3	5	3·5	7	4	3·5	3·5	3·5	3·5
	Needle Position	Centre	Centre	3	Centre	Centre	3	Centre	2	Centre	4	4	4	4
LIGHTING	Alternator	Wipac S114	Wipac S114	Wipac S114	Lucas RM15	—	—	Lucas RM15	Lucas RM15	Lucas RM15	Lucas RM15	—	—	—
	Dynamo, 6-volt Lucas	—	—	—	—	E3N	—	—	—	—	—	E3L	E3L	E3L
	Battery	Exide 3ER7L	Exide 3ER7L	Exide 3ER7L	Lucas MLZ9E	Lucas PUZ7E/11	—	Lucas MLZ9E	Lucas MLZ9E	Lucas MLZ9E	Lucas MLZ9E	Lucas MLZ9E	Lucas MLZ9E	Lucas MLZ9E
	Headlamp Bulb, Double Filament watts	30 & 24	30 & 24	30 & 24	30 & 24	30 & 24	—	30 & 24	30 & 24	30 & 24	30 & 24	30 & 24	30 & 24	30 & 24
	Tail Lamp Bulb, Double Filament watts	Separate bulbs 3 & 18	Separate bulbs 3 & 18	Separate bulbs 3 & 18	6 & 18	6 & 18	—	6 & 18	6 & 18	6 & 18	6 & 18	6 & 18	6 & 18	6 & 18
	Pilot Bulb, watts	3	3	3	3	3	—	3	3	3	3	3	3	3
	Speedo Bulb, watts	3	3	3	1·8	1·8	—	1·8	1·8	1·8	1·8	1·8	1·8	1·8
	Magneto Chain Size, inch	—	—	—	—	·375×·225	·375×·225	—	·375×·225	—	—	—	—	—
	Dynamo Chain Size, inch	—	—	—	—	·375×·225		—	—	—	—	—	—	—
TRANSMISSION	Primary Chain Size, inch	3·75×·225	·5×·205	·375×·225 Duplex	·5×·305	·5×·305	·5×·305	·5×·305	·5×·305	·5×·305	·5×·305	·5×·305	·5×·305	·5×·305
	Rear Chain Size, inch	·5×·305	·5×·305	·5×·305	·625×·380	·625×·380	·625×·380	·625×·380	·625×·380	·625×·380	·625×·380	·625×·380	·625×·380	·625×·380
	Engine Sprocket (teeth)	21	17	22	19	17	23	22	19	21	23	23	21	23
	Clutch Sprocket (teeth)	50	37	46	42	42	42	42	42	42	42	42	42	42
	Gearbox Sprocket (teeth)	19	17	18	16	16	21	16	16	16	16	16	16	16
	Rear Wheel Sprocket (teeth)	55	70	55	42	42	56	42	42	42	42	42	42	42
	Gearbox Ratio 1st	2·92	2·42	2·92	2·56	3·24	1·78	2·56	2·56	2·56	2·56	2·56	2·56	2·56
	Gearbox Ratio 2nd	1·85	1·85	1·85	1·70	2·44	1·33	1·70	1·70	1·70	1·70	1·70	1·70	1·70
	Gearbox Ratio 3rd	1·30	1·30	1·30	1·22	1·56	1·10	1·22	1·22	1·22	1·22	1·22	1·22	1·22
	Gearbox Ratio Top	1·00	1·00	1·00	1·00	1·00	1·00	1·00	1·00	1·00	1·00	1·00	1·00	1·00
	Gear Ratios (overall) 1st	20·12	21·62	18·66	14·85	21·00	8·68	12·86	14·85	13·42	12·23	12·23	13·42	12·23
	Gear Ratios (overall) 2nd	12·75	16·55	11·82	9·85	15·80	6·48	8·53	9·85	8·93	8·13	8·13	8·93	8·13
	Gear Ratios (overall) 3rd	8·95	11·63	8·30	7·08	10·10	5·36	6·13	7·08	6·40	5·83	5·83	6·40	5·83
	Gear Ratios (overall) Top	6·89	8·95	6·39	5·80	6·48	4·87	5·02	5·80	5·25	4·78	4·78	5·25	4·78
WHEELS	Tyre, Front	3·25×17	3·00×19	3·25×18	3·25×19	2·75×21	2·75×19	3·25×19	3·00×21	3·25×19	3·25×19	3·25×19	3·00×21	3·25×19
	Tyre, Rear	3·25×17	3·50×19	3·25×18	3·25×19	4·00×19	3·25×19	3·50×19	4·00×19	3·50×19	3·50×19	3·50×19	4·00×19	3·50×19
	Tyre Pressure, lb/sq. inch, Front	22	As required	21	20	As required	21	21	As required	22	22	22	As required	22
	Tyre Pressure, lb/sq. inch, Rear	22	As required	22	22	As required	23	24	As required	25	25	25	As required	25
	Rim, Front	W.M.2.17	W.M.1.19	W.M.2.18	W.M.2. 19	W.M.1. 21	Dural W.M.1. 19	W.M.2. 19	W.M.1. 21	W.M.2. 19	W.M.2. 19	W.M.2. 19	W.M.1. 21	W.M.2. 19
	Rim, Rear	W.M.2.17	W.M.2.19	W.M.2.18	W.M.2. 19	W.M.3. 19	Dural W.M.2. 19	W.M.2. 19	W.M.3. 19	W.M.2. 19	W.M.2. 19	W.M.2. 19	W.M.3. 19	W.M.2. 19
	Brake Dia. and Width, Front, inches	6×1	7×·875	6×1	7×·875	7×·875	8×1·75	7×·875	7×·875	7×·875	7×·875	7×·875	7×·875	7×·875
	Brake Dia. and Width, Rear, inches	6×1	5·5×·75	6×1	7×·875	7×·875	8×1·25	7×·875	7×·875	7×·875	7×·875	7×·875	7×·875	7×·875
LUBRICATION	Engine Oil, above 50°F.	SAE50	SAE50	SAE50	SAE50	SAE50	Castor	SAE50	SAE50	SAE50	SAE50	SAE50	SAE50	SAE50
	Engine Oil, 32°–50°F.	SAE30	SAE30	SAE30	SAE30	SAE30	Castor	SAE30	SAE30	SAE30	SAE30	SAE30	SAE30	SAE30
	Engine Oil, below 32°F.	SAE20	SAE20	SAE20	SAE20	SAE20	Castor	SAE20	SAE20	SAE20	SAE20	SAE20	SAE20	SAE20
	Gearbox Oil, above 50°F.	SAE50	SAE50	SAE50	SAE50	SAE50	Castor	SAE50	SAE50	SAE50	SAE50	SAE50	SAE50	SAE50
	Gearbox Oil, 32°–50°F.	SAE50	SAE50	SAE50	SAE50	SAE50	Castor	SAE50	SAE50	SAE50	SAE50	SAE50	SAE50	SAE50
	Gearbox Oil, below 32°F.	SAE30	SAE30	SAE30	SAE30	SAE50	Castor	SAE30	SAE30	SAE30	SAE30	SAE30	SAE30	SAE30
	Suspension Oil per Leg, Front	70 c.c. SAE30	185 c.c. SAE20	185 c.c. SAE20	185 c.c. SAE20	185 c.c. SAE20	200 c.c. SAE5	185 c.c. SAE20	185 c.c. SAE20	185 c.c. SAE2i	185 c.c. SAE20	185 c.c. SAE20	185 c.c. SAE20	185 c.c. SAE20
	Petrol Tank Capacity, Imp. galls.	3·25	2·75	3·25	4·25	2	5·25	4·25	2	4·25	4·25	4·25	2	4·25
	Oil Tank Capacity, pints	2·5	2·5	2·5	4	2·75	5·25	4	4·5	4	4	4	4·5	4·5
	Gearbox Capacity, pints	3	3	3	1	1	1	1	1	1	1	1	1	1
DIMENSIONS	Overall Length, inches	82	81·5	83	86	83	80	86	85	86	86	86	85	85
	Overall Height, inches	40·5	42	41·5	41·5	44	37	41·5	44	41·5	41·5	41·5	44	41·5
	Overall Width, inches	27	32·5	27	27	32·5	24	27	32·5	27	27	27	32·5	27
	Wheelbase, inches	53	53·75	53·75	55·25	53·75	55	55·25	55·25	55·25	55·25	55·25	55·25	55·25
	Seat Height, inches	29	32	29·5	31	32·5	31	31	32·5	31	31	31	32·5	31
	Ground Clearance, inches	5·5	7·25	6	5·5	10	6·75	5·5	6·5	5·5	5·5	5·5	6·5	5·5
	Weight, lbs.	325	321	340	382	306	285	394	336	398	403	405	386	388

AJS really did have something to boast about when they depicted the Monty and Ward-entered 31CSR that had won the 1960 Thruxton 500, ridden by Don Chapman and Ron Langston, on the cover of their '61 brochure. Optional extras included a QD rear wheel and rev counter and, as the 31CS was no longer catalogued, two- or three-gallon competition tanks.

The unit-construction Model 8 that had been introduced for 1960 is probably the least loved, then and now, of the machines to bear the initials AJS during the period covered by this book. It lasted for one more year, during which it was known as the Senator, and was quietly dropped at the end of the 1962 season.

1961's standard finish for both the 20 and 31 was black with tank lined in gold but you could pay a little extra and have this colour scheme of grey and blue (shown on a Model 20) or, in my opinion, the rather smarter but seldom seen all-grey with chrome tank panels (as shown on a Model 31). Both were standard models (denoted by the alternator type primary chain case) in spite of the more expensive optional paint finish.

Gordon Jackson 347 c.c. A.J.S. Winner of the 1956, 1958 and 1960 Scottish 6 Days Trials.

Single-cylinder competition bikes were still very competitive, and although both Hugh Viney and Gordon Jackson had been on the successful factory ISDT team, the latter had now become the man to fly the flag in the Scottish, firstly with a 16MC and then a 16C – he would win it again this year too. The 18CS had very much the same specification but its two-gallon fuel tank was specified as pressed steel as opposed to the 16C's aluminium tank of the same capacity.

For its penultimate year of production (1961) the 7R had just about reached the end of its factory development but improvements were still being made, such as a revised rear brake operating system, which in turn necessitated a repositioned back plate. By this time they were running an 11.9:1 piston (for 1962 it would be 12:1) and straight from the factory made some 42hp at 7,800 rpm. With specialist attention they could realise more: a privately-entered machine ridden by the one and only Mike Hailwood would have given the Boy Racer a magnificent swan song in the 1961 Junior TT had not a broken gudgeon pin sidelined him on his last lap.

The owner of this 1962 250 Sapphire has stopped to take a snapshot but I doubt he'll find he's included both cottages unless he's got a wide-angle lens. The entire range had all been given names, apart from the 7R – which, after all, already had its long-standing nickname.

To capture the L-plate café racer there was a new sports version of the 250 for 1962 but I'm sorry to say that, search as I might amongst its specifications, I could find absolutely nothing that would impart extra performance over the regular 250. Compression ratio (7.8:1), carb (1 1/16in monobloc), timing, gear ratios – all identical. Just the weight, mysteriously, differed, with the S catalogued at 322lb – 3lb less than its more staid stablemate! Still, the chromed guards and semi-dropped bars looked good.

The unlovely Senator (Model 8) had just this season left to run so we don't need to have a picture of it but AJS's hardy perennial, the 16, had gained momentum for 1962 with a new name and a modernised version of its engine. The long-stroke (69x93mm) that had been around since pre-war days was retained for the Experts, as the trials 16C was now known, but reconfigured to 74x81mm and a heady 8.5:1 compression ratio for the road 16. Sorry to say, however, that AMC pulled the same stunt on the revamped 16 as it had with the Sapphire. The Sceptre, as the Model 16 was now called, differed in no mechanical way from the 16S Sceptre Sports – just the semi-dropped bars, chromed guards, blue tanks and toolbox of the latter to differentiate it from its all-black Model 16 stablemate. At extra cost either could be had in blue (including the frame), in which case one told them apart by the Sceptre's white guards and the Sports's chrome versions. The road 18, by the way, still had its 93mm stroke motor and went by the name of the Statesman, with the same optional finishes as the Sceptre.

To continue with model names having no apparent common theme in 1962, other than beginning with S, the 31 could even have been given its name in memory of the junior version of the Eagle *comic (the two had recently been merged – retaining the raptor's title rather than that of the sprightly little* Swift*). Standard trim was a coil and alternator but you could spend a bit more if you preferred a magneto and dynamo as well as a siamesed exhaust, high- or low-compression pistons and sidecar gearing but no colour options or QD rear wheel. The CSR spec and nomenclature were unaltered for the meanwhile.*

In contrast to the way young motorcyclists were often portrayed by the press these youngsters look quite innocent in their sweaters and slacks. The chap on the left is holding on tight to his new Sapphire Super Sports whilst the others are gathered around a Swift fitted with colour-matched Watsonian Monza sidecar, and the 'cooking' Sapphire has been left to fend for itself.

During my first motorcycle test, in 1964 (ouch, that's upwards of 50 years ago!), I embarrassingly performed the not-unheard-of idiot trick of nearly running down the examiner when he leapt out from behind a parked car to evaluate my reactions. My reactions were fine but the brakes on my sorely-abused 1956 James Commando were not – I failed. A few weeks later I turned up on a kindly-lent circa-'62 Sapphire Sports, which whisked me through the whole procedure with no trouble.

This year, to justify its elevation to CSR status, the sporting 250 had been given a marginally higher compression of 8:1 against the standard Sapphire's 7.8:1, as well as a larger carb (up from 1 1/16 to 1 1/8in) and slightly higher gearing on all four speeds.

The nonsense of the Sceptre and Sceptre Sports must have dawned on someone who made decisions, so for 1963 there was now just the former. It and the 500 Statesman, along with the 650 Swift, had been endowed with more shapely oil tanks and toolboxes, modern silencers and 18in wheels. Standard finish for all three was black but blue tanks, as on this Swift, were an option – as were a fully-enclosed chain case, air cleaner, steering damper, steering lock, safety bars and luggage carrier. The single alone could have chromed guards too, whilst the Swift buyer could still plump for a magneto/dynamo, siamesed exhausts and/or sidecar gearing.

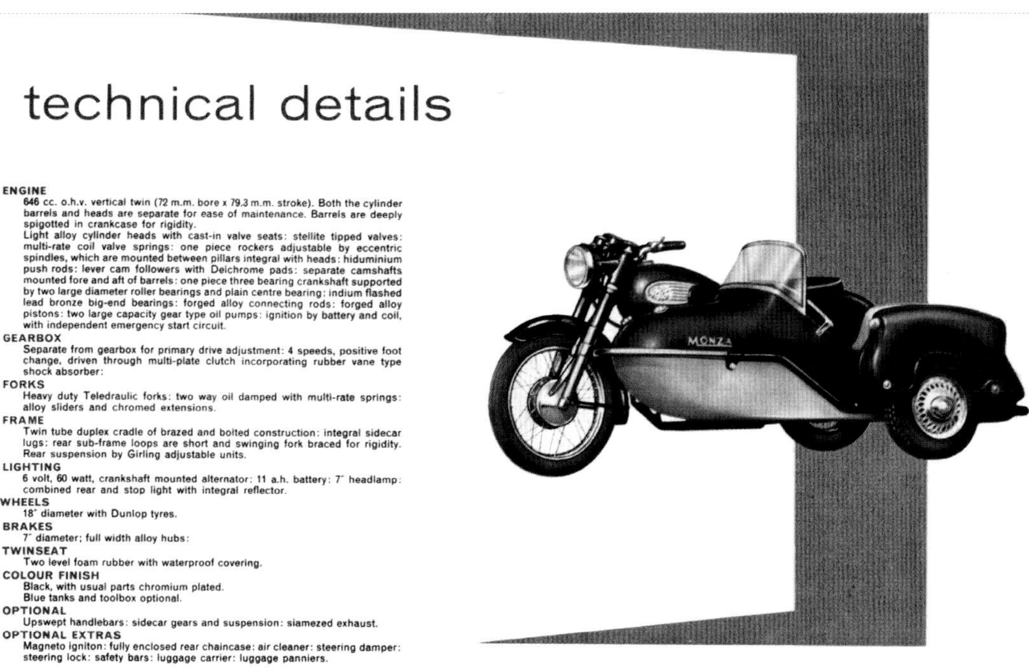

technical details

ENGINE
646 cc. o.h.v. vertical twin (72 m.m. bore x 79.3 m.m. stroke). Both the cylinder barrels and heads are separate for ease of maintenance. Barrels are deeply spigotted in crankcase for rigidity.
Light alloy cylinder heads with cast-in valve seats: stellite tipped valves: multi-rate coil valve springs: one piece rockers adjustable by eccentric spindles, which are mounted between pillars integral with heads: hiduminium push rods: lever cam followers with Deichrome pads: separate camshafts mounted fore and aft of barrels: one piece three bearing crankshaft supported by two large diameter roller bearings and plain centre bearing: indium flashed lead bronze big-end bearings: forged alloy connecting rods: forged alloy pistons: two large capacity gear type oil pumps: ignition by battery and coil, with independent emergency start circuit.

GEARBOX
Separate from gearbox for primary drive adjustment: 4 speeds, positive foot change, driven through multi-plate clutch incorporating rubber vane type shock absorber:

FORKS
Heavy duty Teledraulic forks: two way oil damped with multi-rate springs: alloy sliders and chromed extensions.

FRAME
Twin tube duplex cradle of brazed and bolted construction: integral sidecar lugs: rear sub-frame loops are short and swinging fork braced for rigidity. Rear suspension by Girling adjustable units.

LIGHTING
6 volt, 60 watt, crankshaft mounted alternator: 11 a.h. battery: 7˝ headlamp: combined rear and stop light with integral reflector.

WHEELS
18˝ diameter with Dunlop tyres.

BRAKES
7˝ diameter; full width alloy hubs:

TWINSEAT
Two level foam rubber with waterproof covering.

COLOUR FINISH
Black, with usual parts chromium plated.
Blue tanks and toolbox optional.

OPTIONAL
Upswept handlebars: sidecar gears and suspension: siamezed exhaust.

OPTIONAL EXTRAS
Magneto igniton: fully enclosed rear chaincase: air cleaner: steering damper: steering lock: safety bars: luggage carrier: luggage panniers.

If sidecar gearing had been chosen then for around £120 extra a suitably finished Watsonian Monza made a smart outfit.

With its new title AMC's 1963 sporting 650 pre-empted the name given to Triumph's triple six years later. The Motor Cycle *tested an early example and although they summed it up as a 'tireless high-speed road burner' with 'excellent road-holding' the text contained one or two less complimentary passages. Tireless? "Vibration became noticeable through the handlebar at 75mph in top gear and gradually increased through the footrests and seat as well, right up to the maximum speed." Talking about maximum speed, they did manage 104mph one way but with a gusty wind it obstinately refuse to break the 100 barrier both ways – even though over 90mph was possible in third and the standing-start quarter-mile was covered in 14.8 seconds. Brakes were judged to be 'adequately powerful' providing one applied a good deal of effort and, as far as economy went, it returned 51mpg at a steady 60mph. For those in search of greater performance the speed kit (brochure rendition Speedkit) would have been a tempting way to spend a few extra pounds, as would a QD wheel. How many went for the optional sidecar gearing and suspension on this model, I wonder?*

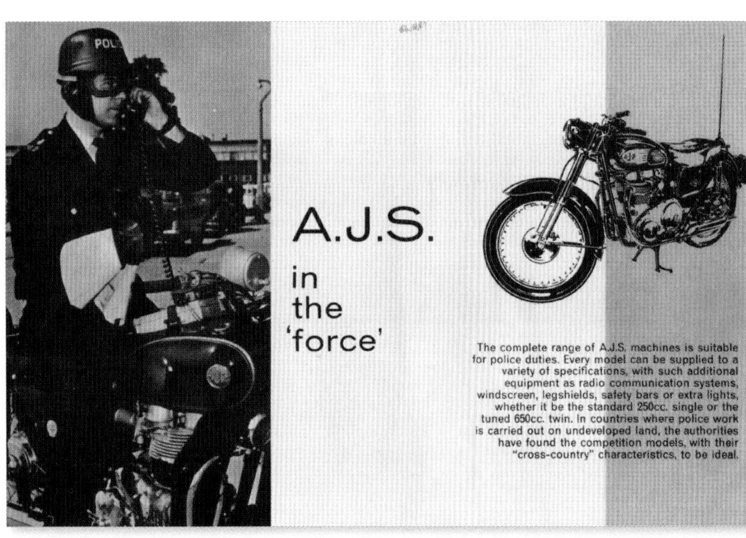

Funny – I have no recollection of AJS police bikes in the '60s. Perhaps I was more law-abiding than I remember or any destined for police use were in fact sent abroad as remarked upon here. The thought of 'natives' let loose on 40-or-so horsepower of 18CS Southerner scramblers over 'undeveloped land' – or almost any terrain at all, come to that – is food for thought.

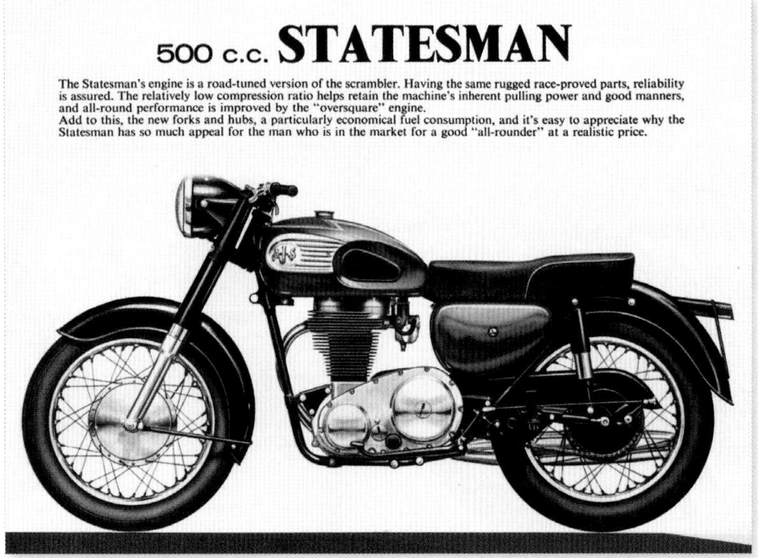

Continuing the attempt to promote a squeaky-clean image, but now in a kind of avant-garde fashion, the '64 brochure's cover slightly missed the mark with its choice of the rather-too-homely young couple – but thinking about it, was it so wrong? After all, 1963 had seen the launch of Great Britain's very own Sindy as a far more wholesome alternative to America's outrageously raunchy Barbie. The bike, by the way, is a Sapphire Super Sports.

At a quick glance the 1964 Statesman, and the 350 Sceptre, look very similar to the previous year but look again and you will see they have Norton Roadholder forks and their 18in wheels have Norton hub and brake assemblies. The Statesman, as the brochure points out, now has the 86x85.5mm engine that had been developed for the18CS and incorporated in customer machines since the winter of 1956. The Sceptre has the same engine but with a reduced bore of 72mm to give it 348cc against the Statesman's 497cc.

The big twins were also fitted with Norton forks and brakes but the Hurricane was losing the look of the production racer with this new style of chrome mudguard – similar in appearance but slighter briefer than those fitted to the Sceptre. As well as the optional Speedkit introduced the previous season you could have a racing magneto and twin exhausts but for some reason only if you'd specified the rest as original equipment. The 650 Swift's colour schemes were as before – all black or black with blue tanks and toolbox.

As for competition singles, the trials 350, known as the Expert since '62, now had a magneto fired version of the short-stroke (72x85.5mm) motor for 1964. For 1964 the rolling chassis was essentially the same but cycle parts such as the shorter petrol tank and unsprung vestigial vinyl-covered seat were noticeably different. The scrambles 500, marketed as the Southerner from '62, had outlived other big-banger scramblers such as the Gold Star but was virtually in its final form by this time.

500 c.c.

SOUTHERNER

Powered by what is probably motor cycling's most potent push-rod single, only detail mods are made this year. A new gear-type oil-pump, and modified feeds to the big-end and rockers, improved oil circulation and thereby increased reliability.
Detailed specifications of both models available on request.

AJS 14CSR
SAPPHIRE NINETY

A first-place win by A.J.S.—9 laps ahead of its nearest rival—in the 250cc class of the Thruxton 500 mile Race for Production Machines—proof indeed of the speed, handling and reliability contained in these tough little machines.

Additional tuning of the engine includes an increase in compression ratio, modification of the piston and fitment of coil valve springs. The exhaust system alterations take in the larger and more efficient silencer already fitted to the larger capacity machines. Gear ratios are higher and closer to make more practical use of the extra power available.

SPECIFICATION

Engine. 248cc o.h.v. single (70mm. bore x 65mm. stroke). Alloy cylinder head: stellite tipped valves: coil valve springs: built-up rockers: hiduminium push-rods: lever type cam followers: both cams on single shaft: steel connecting rod: caged roller big-end bearings: built-up crankshaft supported by roller, ball and plain bearings: rotary reciprocating plunger oil pump: ignition by battery and coil with independent, emergency start circuit.
Gearbox. Separate from engine, but polished side covers give appearance of unit construction with engine. 4 speeds; multi-plate clutch; duplex primary chain adjusted by rotation of gearbox shell.
Forks. Teledraulic, two way oil damped, with multirate springs.
Frame of brazed and bolted construction: pressed steel engine under-channel: short triangulated rear sub-frame: pivoted fork rear suspension controlled by Girling adjustable units.
Lighting 6 volt, 54 watt, crankshaft mounted alternator: 11 a.h. battery: 6" headlamp: combined rear and stop-light with integral reflector.
Wheels. 17" diameter with 3.25" Dunlop tyres.
Brakes. 6" diameter at front and rear: full width hubs.
Twinseat Two level foam rubber with waterproof coverings.
Colour finish. Primarily black, with blue and chrome tank (for A.J.S.) cherry red and chrome (for Matchless), and black accessory covers; usual parts are chrome plated . . . and most of the light alloy components are highly polished.
Optional Extra. Range of dolphin fairings.

As a reminder of its class win in the '64 Thruxton 500-mile race AMC popped this full-page action shot into the 1965 brochure.

The 1965 14CSR Sapphire Ninety, to give it its full name, was rather different, however. Immediately recognisable by its larger-capacity silencer, changes had been effected to the engine and gearbox too – the former having its compression ratio raised from 8:1 to 9.5:1, and coil instead of hairpin valve springs were now fitted; for the gearbox there was a set of closer ratios. When The Motor Cycle *put one through its paces they were full of praise for the 'rock steady adhesion to line' with 'predictable handling when flicking the machine through a right-left-right series of bends'. It went pretty well for a British 250 too, with two-way speeds of 70mph in third and 82mph in top, and the standing quarter-mile coming up in 19.4 seconds. If you were prepared to tootle about at a steady 30 then it would give you 112mpg, but double your speed and you'd get only 58.*

Circa 1974 I ended up running one of these 1965 CSRs (with their less-ostentatious tank badging) for a month or so, but paying heed to the stories of big AMC twins being 'crank breakers' I never went far or fast on it. Shame, really, as I have no lasting impressions of it either way – especially as I was told much later that it was only the 1961 versions that broke, apparently due to a foundry supplying a large batch of what, once they were in use, proved to be faulty castings. Mine was a bog-standard version devoid of any of the speed goodies that its first owner could have opted for.

AJS 750cc. Model 33

Get the best of both worlds with these racy 750's. Although new to many, they in fact embody features which have been proved through years of use. The most outstanding qualities of the Matchless and A.J.S. machines are blended powerfully with the potent Atlas engine, resulting in incredible speed vitality coupled with superb roadholding and braking.

Just look at the specification — exceptionally powerful engine, twin carburettors with air cleaner, magneto ignition, 12-volt electrics, duplex cradle frame, Roadholder forks, [illegible] inch front brake, four gallon tank, [illegible] mudguards, alloy chaincase, quality finish.

These machines merit a personal trial now. Visit your dealer today and let your own skill prove just how exciting they are.

SPECIFICATION

Engine. 750cc o.h.v. vertical twin [illegible] alloy cylinder head [illegible] forged steel rockers [illegible] carburation by twin Amal Monoblocs [illegible]

Transmission. [illegible]

Frame. [illegible]

Forks. Roadholder forks with built in [illegible]

Wheels. [illegible]

Lighting. 12 volt crankshaft mounted alternator [illegible] headlamp [illegible] combined rear and stop light with integral reflector.

Tanks. 4 gallon petrol tank [illegible] mounted, single two level tap, 4 pint oil tank.

Colours. All black and chrome.

A good friend of mine once had a 1965 AJS 750 and remembers it as a fabulous machine, but personally I'd have thought the big Norton engine was better off in its own frame.

AMBASSADOR

To anyone with a lust for speed, on two wheels or four, Brooklands track in Surrey had become a natural Mecca once racing resumed after the First World War. And it was there, in 1920, that a Dublin-born ex-RFC Lieutenant named Kaye Don (real name Donsky, as he was of Polish extraction) began his racing career. Cutting his teeth with motorcycles, he enjoyed success early on by riding a single-speed Norton to second place early in the season and then won with a 350 AJS later in the year.

Unlike many of his Brooklands contemporaries he was not a man of private means or even wealthy, having taken a junior position with the Avon tyre company in order to support his mother and sister after his father had died when he was a teenager. Notwithstanding, he had found enough money to run a motorcycle and time to take part in a few trials before the war curtailed pursuits of that nature. Having served his country, including a stint flying on the Western Front, he had returned to Avon and in time was promoted to head of sales. Although continuing to compete on two wheels, cars increas-

This is the Series Five with 'easy-ride' telescopic forks featured on the cover of the 1949 brochure. Finish was all black with Ambassador Grey tank lined in black and red. Chain guard was chrome.

The first of the Ambassadors featured the Villiers 5E, which had been introduced in 1946 as a replacement for the pre-war 3E. Featuring twin exhausts in conjunction with four transfer ports this 197cc was not, I believe I am right in saying, employed by any other manufacturer.

Bargain-basement Ambassador for 1949 was the Popular. A small dry battery housed in the headlamp served for night-time parking, whilst on the move headlight brightness depended on engine speed.
It shared Webb's pressed steel girder forks with Ambassador's slightly more sophisticated Series Three, however.

ingly took precedence after he had taken a number of track records in the autumn of 1921 in a 1½-litre AC, including the flying kilometre at just over 100mph.

Over the next few seasons he competed in a variety of vehicles, from the aero-engined Wolseley Viper to the little Avon-JAP, but really came into his own racing Sunbeams during the 1928 season. In May of that year he became the first person the take the coveted 130mph badge when he won the Gold Star Handicap, recording a lap of over 131mph in a four-litre V12. Later on in the year his reputation was further enhanced when he won the inaugural Ards TT at the wheel of a Lea Francis; and March 1929 saw him over at Daytona Beach in the US with the Silver Bullet land-speed record contender that Sunbeam built for him to drive.

Two years earlier, with Henry Seagrave driving, Sunbeam's previous contender had been the first car to break the 200mph barrier – but since then the record had been broken twice more, and the company wanted it back. Through no fault of Don's the Silver Bullet was doomed to failure and struggled to pass the 180 mark whilst Seagrave, who was also there with his Golden Arrow, pushed the record to over 231mph.

The newly knighted Sir Henry next turned his attentions to the water-speed record with Lord Wakefield's Miss England II; but in 1930 he was killed when, just a few minutes after capturing the record on Lake Windermere, the boat struck some flotsam and capsized during a further run. Salvaged and completely rebuilt, Miss England was turned over to Kaye Don, and during 1931 he reclaimed the record from the American Gar Wood who had recently passed the 100mph barrier. In 1932 their duel intensified with Gar Wood once again the fastest, then Don in a new Miss England III at a fraction under 120mph. But when the American got close to 125mph in the latest Miss America they both called it a day.

Kaye Don returned to the track with a fearsome Type 54 Bugatti but although fast it proved unreliable, and second place in the 1933 British Empire Trophy was probably its best result.

Two years later his racing career came to an end as a result of some unauthorised late evening practice in the K3 MG he was to drive in the 1934 Mannin Beg race on the Isle of Man. He and a mechanic who had been making some adjustments to the car set out in the half-light with the roads open to the public, and whilst rounding a corner struck an oncoming vehicle a glancing blow, which tore the wheel off the MG before it rolled over. Both men were injured and taken

GENERAL SPECIFICATION FOR ALL MODELS

ENGINE—The famous Villiers 6E 197 c.c. two-stroke. (See overleaf.)

GEARBOX—Villiers, unit construction with engine, 3-speed, foot operated, ratios (engine to rear wheel) 5.86 to 1, 8.14 to 1, and 15.58 to 1, oil level dip stick, double plate cork clutch, with quick adjustments for clutch and cable.

SILENCER—Burgess, large capacity, chromium plated.

TRANSMISSION—Renold chains, ½in. by $\frac{3}{16}$in., primary chain pre-stretched and enclosed in aluminium oil bath case.

FRAME—The famous Ambassador cradle frame, constructed of first quality steel tubing brazed into machined malleable iron lugs, giving extreme strength and rigidity.

WHEELS — Dunlop rims WM.1-19, rustless steel 10-gauge spokes, plated brass nipples.

TYRES—Dunlop 3.00 × 19, front and rear.

BRAKES—Front and rear drums both 5in. diameter, with quick adjustments.

MUDGUARDS—Ample width with streamlined steel stays. Rear guard provided with detachable part, to facilitate wheel removal.

HANDLEBAR—Chromium plated, ⅞in. diameter, adjustable for height and reach. Standard equipment includes twist grip throttle, separate mixture control, compression release, clutch and front brake controls.

TANK—All steel, welded, streamlined, four point mounting on rubber buffers, chromium plated quick action positive locking filler cap incorporating ¼-pint oil measure, capacity 2 gallons, twin fuel pipes providing reserve.

SPEEDOMETER—Smiths, illuminated dial, calibrated 65 m.p.h. or 110 k.p.h.

TOOLS—Tool kit in roll, including tyre lever and grease gun. Tyre inflator mounted on chainguard.

WHEELBASE—46in., giving exceptional controllability.

CONSUMPTION—Minimum 110 m.p.g. under normal conditions.

The Manufacturers reserve the right to deviate from all specifications at any time, with or without notice

to hospital, where Don's passenger died a few hours later. The Manx authorities decided that his death was due to Kaye Don's negligence and the court, which found him guilty of manslaughter, imposed a four-month prison sentence that was upheld despite his own injuries and appeals.

Still suffering from back pain he nevertheless put his business acumen to good use in 1935 when negotiations with Pontiac resulted in his company Sole Concessionaires Ltd becoming the distributor for Great Britain and Northern Ireland. In short time this became US Concessionaires Ltd and henceforth would have a sizeable stand at the London Motor Show. Initially based solely in London, by the war a depot had been established in Berkshire and it undertook work for the ministry of supply for the duration.

Post-war, with potential sales of large American cars for the meanwhile obviously limited, Don embarked upon additional activities – firstly motorcycle manufacture and then Latil-licenced four-wheel-drive/steering tractors with emergent African and Indian markets in mind.

What would become the Ambassador motorcycle was initially planned to be a sizeable machine powered by a 500cc JAP side-valve parallel twin motor. But by the time the production stage was reached early in 1947 the motorcycles would be altogether smaller and powered by Villiers two-strokes. Initially intended for export they became available on the home market by the late spring of 1948. Offering nothing radical in the way of design, Ambassadors stood slightly apart from their rivals with a choice of brightly-coloured finishes; they were, however, early in offering a model with electric starting. Firstly manufactured by US Concessionaires Ltd, a separate company Ambassador Motorcycles Ltd (but still operating from the same Pontiac Works, at Ascot) was formed during 1951.

As the '50s drew to a close it was all too obvious that the firm, perhaps Kaye Don himself, had drawn upon some of the less memorable aspects of American styling for inspiration. He was, after all, still the Pontiac importer and surely it is no coincidence that the Ambassador 3 Star Special was adorned with chrome stars in the same manner as the Star Chief's bodywork. He was also importing Zundapp two-wheelers, which included the Trophy 250 two-stroke – a direct competitor to his own Ambassadors.

Shortly after his 70th birthday Don decided to wind down his business operations, and with sales diminishing was happy to pass Ambassador Motorcycles over to DMW – the marque continuing in badge-engineered form until 1965. Kaye Don died in 1981, aged 90.

Ever the salesman, Don must surely have written this blurb for the 1949 Series Three himself: "Tested on the roughest going in all parts of the world it has come through with flying colours." But was it really true? You could choose it in some nice colours besides the traditional black frame with grey tank: maroon with crimson-lined silver tank, blue with blue-lined silver tank or green with light green tank lined in dark green, and all with a chromium-plated chain guard.

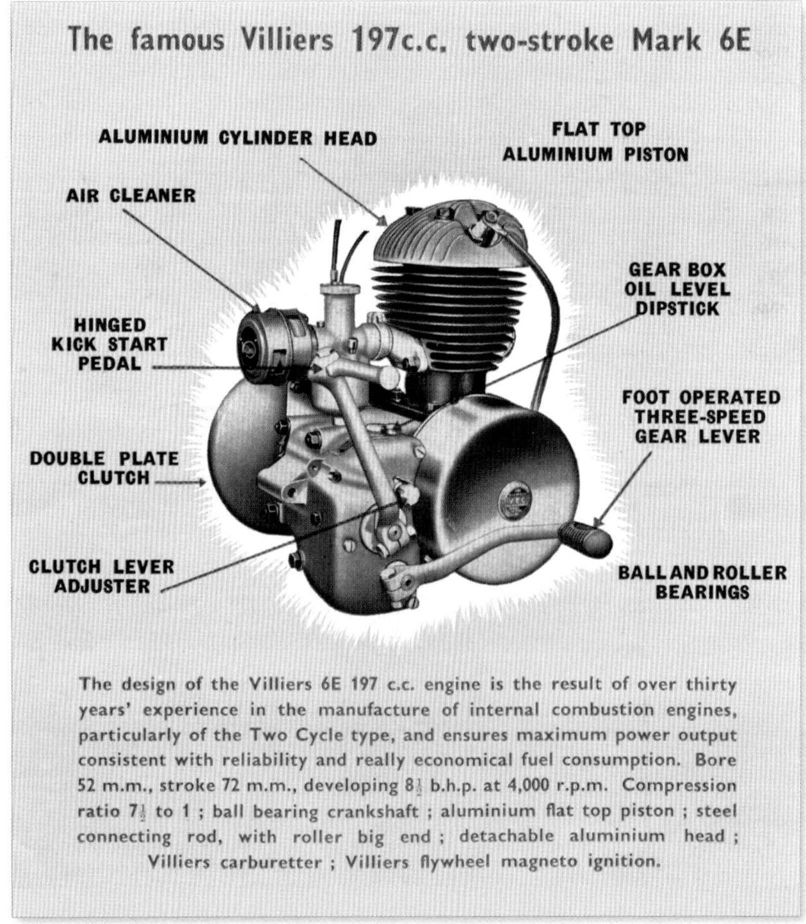

The introduction of this engine as a replacement for the 5E meant a change of power unit for the 197 Ambassadors for the 1949 season.

Never afraid of superlatives, the 1954 publicity invited you to 'Ride an Aristocratic Ambassador – the machine for the Connoisseur'. The Supreme had been introduced in 1951, the year that the company's identity changed and model names replaced Series. With plunger rear suspension it had been the first Ambassador to be so equipped – for 1953 its brakes were increased from 5 to 6in whilst other models retained the former. Motor Cycling *managed to squeeze 58mph out of one whilst petroil consumption ranged from 94 to an excellent 132mpg.*

For the brochure, Ambassador illustrated the Self Starter from the offside. Viewed from this side the machine did not look its best, or even good, with a large cowling to cover the starter drive. I can also imagine the possibility of acid leaking from the batteries carried in the panniers and the resultant damage to metalwork, clothing or even skin.

GENERAL SPECIFICATION

Supreme. — Engine : Villiers, Mark IH.225 c.c., two stroke. Gear Box : Villiers unit construction, four speed, foot change. Transmission : Renold chain, primary in oilbath. Lighting : 6 volt, operated by fly-wheel generator with accumulator. Dipper switch to headlamp. Frame : Swinging-arm rear suspension, adjustable to load. Telescopic front forks. Brakes : Front and rear, 6 in. diameter. Mudguards : Deeply valanced, with rigid-fix stays. Tyres : 3.25 x 18 standard, front and rear. Seat : Dual, 2½ in. Dunlopillo section. Petrol Tank : 2⅓ gal. with rubber knee grips. Wheelbase : 48¾ in. Weight 238 lbs. Finish : Grey, with chrome fittings, tank, silver grey.

Envoy. — Engine, gearbox and transmission as Embassy. Lighting and frame as Supreme. Hubs 5 in. diameter. Rims Dunlop NM1-19 Tyres 3.00 x 19. Seat dual construction as Supreme. Finish black with chromium-plated components. Wheel base 48¾ in. Weight 230 lbs.

Embassy.—Engine : Villiers, Mark 8E, 200 c.c., two stroke. Gear Box : Villiers unit construction, three speeds, foot change (also 4-speed model). Transmission : Renold chain. Lighting : As Supreme. Frame : Plunger action rear springing, telescopic front forks. Brakes : Front and rear 5 in. diameter. Mudguards : As Supreme. Tyres : 3.00 x 19 standard, front and rear. Saddle : Lycetts, extra large. Petrol Tank : As Supreme. Wheelbase : 47 in. Weight 215 lbs. Finish : Black, with chrome fittings, tank silver grey.

Popular. — General Specifications as Embassy but rigid frame at rear. Direct lighting with dry battery for parking. Unvalanced mudguards. Weight 181 lbs.

Self Starter. — General Specification as Embassy, but with press-button self starter, powered by batteries carried in panniers. Battery : 6 volt 47 amp. Starter Motor : 6 volt. Weight 240 lbs.

Sidecar. — General Specification as Embassy, but with strengthened rigid frame and heavy girder-type front forks. Sidecar : Steel frame, aluminium panels. Saloon type hood. Weight 324 lbs. This model is sold only as a complete unit.

ENVOY

Especially designed for today's fashion- and comfort-conscious rider. This handsome machine is finished in black and chrome with petrol tank in Dimenso double-tone grey. Prominent features are the dual saddle, valanced mudguards, swinging-arm rear suspension. Outstanding performance and appearance.

POPULAR

For sterling service with ultra-economy the Popular is very hard to beat. Now considerably improved by the introduction of telescopic forks, rider comfort is equal to many far more expensive machines. If you are looking for fine performance at low initial cost the Popular must be your choice.

The 197cc Envoy was new for 1955 and shared the Supreme's cycle parts whilst the Popular was very much as it had been since its introduction. The Supreme had Grey, Black or Bella Red listed as colour options.

POPULAR. 150 c.c. Villiers Inclined Engine with enclosed Flywheel Magneto. Bore 59 mm. Stroke 58 mm. 6·3 b.h.p. at 5000 r.p.m. Compression ratio 7·75: I. Three-speed gearbox, welded tubular frame, deep valanced front and rear mudguards. Telescopic front fork with 4 in. movement and fully damped swinging arm rear suspension. Direct lighting with 5½ in. headlamp incorporating speedometer. Petrol tank finished Black. Dunlop tyres 3·00 × 18 front and rear fitted on chromium plated rims. Full-width Hubs. Foam rubber padded dual seat. Complete to normal specification and with all usual tools and equipment.
Colour: Black or Maroon. **Weight** 212 lbs.

Basic Price **£100** *Purchase Tax* **£24 15 0**

POPULAR. As above with Four-speed gearbox.
Weight: 214 lbs.

Basic Price **£105** *Purchase Tax* **£25 19 9**

STATESMAN. 175 c.c. Villiers Inclined Engine with enclosed Flywheel Magneto. Bore 59 mm Stroke 63·5 mm. Compression ratio 7·4: I Developing 7·4 b.h.p. at 5000 r.p.m. Constant Mesh Three-speed gearbox, welded tubular frame, deep valanced front and rear mudguards. Telescopic front fork with 4 in. movement, fully damped swinging arm rear suspension. Direct lighting with 5½ in. headlamp incorporating speedometer. Petrol tank finished Black and Chrome. Dunlop 3·00 × 18 tyres front and rear, fitted on chromium-plated rims. Full width hubs. Foam rubber padded dual seat. Complete to normal specifications and with all usual tools and equipment.
Colour: Black and Chrome. **Weight:** 216 lbs.

Basic Price **£110** *Purchase Tax* **£27 4 6**

STATESMAN. As above with Four-speed gearbox.
Weight: 218 lbs.

Basic Price **£115** *Purchase Tax* **£28 9 3**

ENVOY. Villiers 200 c.c. Inclined Engine with enclosed Flywheel Magneto. Bore 59.mm Stroke 72.mm Compression Ratio 7·25: I. Developing 8·4 b.h.p. at 4000 r.p.m. Constant Mesh Three-speed gearbox, heavy duty tubular frame, oversize Metalastic bearings for swinging arm with fully damped rear suspension. Telescopic front fork with 4 in. movement. Extra deep valanced front and rear mudguards. Rectifier lighting with 5½ in. headlamp incorporating speedometer. Dunlop tyres 3·25 × 17 front and rear, chromium-plated rims, full width hubs. Super comfort dual seat—2¾ gallon petrol tank Black and Chrome finish. Complete to normal specification and with all usual tools and equipment.
Colour: Black and Chrome. **Weight:** 251 lbs.

Basic Price **£123** *Purchase Tax* **£30 8 10**

ENVOY. As above with Four-speed gearbox.
Weight: 253 lbs.

Basic Price **£128** *Purchase Tax* **£31 13 7**

SUPREME. Villiers 250 c.c. *Twin* Cylinder Inclined Engine incorporating the latest design in two-stroke development. Bore 50 mm. Stroke 63·5 mm. Compression Ratio 8·2: I developing 15 b.h.p. at 5500 r.p.m. Constant Mesh four-speed gearbox. Extra heavy duty tubular frame with swinging arm on oversize Metalastic bearings, incorporating fully damped rear suspension. Cruiserweight telescopic front fork allowing 4 in. movement. Extra deep valanced front and rear mudguards. Rectifier lighting with 72 in. long beam, 7 in. headlamp with 3½ in. trip speedometer mounted in shell. Speedometer driven from gearbox, full width light alloy hubs with cast-in liners. Brake drum diameter 6 in., brake and shoe width I in. Dunlop tyres 3·25 × 17 front and rear, wheels constructed with extra heavy gauge spoke on chromium-plated rims. Super comfort dual seat, rubber mounted 2¾ gallon capacity petrol tank in Black and Chrome finish, fitted with plated carrier. Complete to normal specification and with all usual tools and equipment.
Colour: Black and Chrome. **Weight:** 283 lbs.

Basic Price **£155** *Purchase Tax* **£38 7 3**

SUPREME. Latest Villiers 250 c.c. *Single* Cylinder Inclined Engine with enclosed Flywheel Magneto. Bore 66. Stroke 72. Compression Ratio 7·25: I developing 11·5 b.h.p. at 4750 r.p.m. Constant Mesh Four-speed gearbox. Further details as above.
Colour: Black and Chrome. **Weight:** 275 lbs.

Basic Price **£147** *Purchase Tax* **£36 7 8**

By 1957 the entire range had swinging-arm rear suspension and electric self-starting had been abandoned.

Motor Cycling *tested the Supreme twin and praised its handling, particularly on soaking wet roads, at the same time managing to extract 72mph from it. Economy wasn't too bad either for a two-stroke, with 84mpg at a steady 40mph or 70mpg at 50.*

This was announced as the replacement for the Supreme in the autumn of 1958.

"Battery, tool kit, rectifier, ignition coils and tyre pump neatly housed inside the casing, and reached by merely lifting the dual seat".

AMBASSADOR SUPER "S"

GENERAL SPECIFICATION

Engine.	250 c.c. Villiers parallel twin two-stroke; bore 50 mm. by stroke 63·5 mm.; cast-iron cylinders, alloy head. Compression ratio 8·2 : 1. Power output 15 brake horse power at 5,500 r.p.m. Exhaust pipes 1½" diameter.
Carburettor.	Villiers Type S22/3. Handlebar air control.
Transmission.	Four speed gear box in unit with engine. Positive stop footchange; ratios 5·8, 7·6, 10·9 and 17·6 : 1. Primary drive by fully enclosed chain in oilbath, final drive by chain with large guard enclosing top half. Chromium plated gear lever, kick start pedal and engine side plates.
Frame.	Brazed and welded tubular steel construction with malleable iron lugs. Rear frame fully enclosed by side panels.
Wheels.	Plated rims, fitted with Dunlop tyres; 3·25 in by 17 in., ribbed front; 3·25 in. by 17 in. studded rear. Full width hubs incorporate 7 in. brake at front and rear.
Lubrication.	Petroil. First 500 miles 1 : 16 and subsequently 1 : 20.
Electrical Equipment.	7 in. diameter headlamp incorporating ammeter, switch and 85 m.p.h. speedometer with trip; stoplamp; twin reflectors; twin horns with dual tone.
Suspension.	Telescopic front forks of AMBASSADOR design, adjustable to individual requirements. Rear springing by swinging forks, movement controlled by hydraulic adjustable dampers.
Tank.	Steel fuel tank of 3½ gallons capacity of AMBASSADOR design, fully rubber mounted. Extra large petrol filler cap.
Seat.	Foam cushioned dual seat, secured by two plated screws.
Handlebars.	1 in. diameter fitted with large clutch and brake levers.
Weight.	312 lbs.
Finish.	Black and Tartan red and Grey and Tartan red, stove enamelled.
General Equipment.	Tool kit, tyre pump and pillion footrest.
Overall Length.	6 ft. 9 in.
Handlebar Width.	26½ in.
Dual Seat Height.	31 in.
Ground Clearance.	6 in.
Petrol Consumption.	85 M.P.G.
Maximum Speed.	Approximately 72 M.P.H.
Manufacturers.	Ambassador Motor Cycles Ltd., Pontiac Works, Fernbank Road, ASCOT, Berks.

I will refrain from making any comment and will instead allow the manufacturer to speak for itself: "A spectacular new Cruiser-weight machine of colourful lines and extraordinary elegance." Motor Cycling *liked it too, opening the road test by remarking that, "It could reasonably be claimed that the 1959 'Super S' is one of the prettiest machines on the road". Performance-wise they timed it at 70½mph (rider crouched) and around 75mpg.*

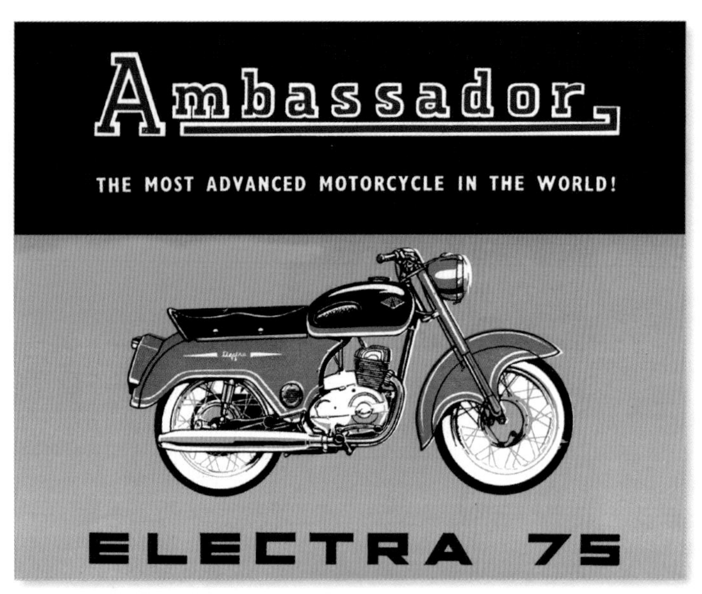

"Dropped handlebars, light alloy front mudguard and cutaway rear enclosure give it a trim 'racy' appearance". Possibly. "The specially tuned, high-compression Villiers engine with large-bore carburettor provides that extra speed whenever it's needed for racing and competition work." Racing against what, for goodness' sake? Utter nonsense.

"Why didn't somebody think of this before?" was the question posed within the autumn 1960 brochure of the Electra. The answer was that they had with the Self Starter a few years previously, at the time the only production British motorcycle to have electric starting. Motor Cycling *borrowed one in September, which proved to have a top speed of 74mph and an overall fuel consumption of 68mpg. The tester noted that it had a more highly-tuned (larger carb and greater compression) version of the Villiers 2T engine in order to overcome drag from the Dynastart, which was obviously successful as he noted its top speed was some 4mph higher than most other machines engined with the standard 2T.*

	ELECTRA 75	SUPER S	THREE STAR SPECIAL
engine gear box unit	Special 250cc Villiers parallel twin two stroke with integral gear box and Siba electric starter-generator. Bore 50mm Stroke 63.5mm Compression Ratio 10:1 Max. B.H.P. 17 at 5750 R.P.M. Carburetter Villiers S25 Gear Ratios 5·8, 7·6, 10·9, 17·6	250 cc Villiers parallel twin two-stroke with integral gear box Bore 50 mm Stroke 63·5 mm Compression Ratio 8·2:1 Max. B.H.P. 15 at 5500 R.P.M. Carburetter Villiers S22/2 Gear Ratios 5·8, 7·6, 10·9, 17·6	200cc Villiers inclined single cylinder two-stroke with integral gearbox Bore 59 mm Stroke 72 mm Compression Ratio 7·25:1 Max. B.H.P. 8·4 at 4000 R.P.M. Carburetter Villiers S.25 Gear Ratios— 3 Speed 6·2, 8·15, 15·55 4 Speed 6·2, 7·4, 10·85, 17·9
wheels	7in. Dia. Brakes front and rear Front Tyre 3·25×17 Ribbed Whitewall Rear Tyre 3·25×17 Studded Whitewall	7 in. Dia. Brakes front and rear Front Tyre 3·25×17 Ribbed Rear Tyre 3·25×17 Studded	6 in. Dia. Brakes front and rear Front and Rear Tyres 3·25×17
fuel tank	3½ Galls. with reserve supply	3½ Galls. with reserve supply	3½ Galls. with reserve supply
electrical system	12 Volt, Siba Dynastart Combined ignition and starter switch. Ignition warning light. Twin Batteries. 7 in. Headlamp with switch and speedometer. Stop and Tail lamps. Twin Dual-tone Horns.	6 Volt A.C. with rectifier. 7 in. Headlamp with ammeter switch and speedometer. Combined stop and tail lamp. Twin Dual-tone Horns.	6 Volt A.C. with rectifier. 6 in. Headlamp with ammeter switch and speedometer. Combined stop and tail lamp. Twin Dual-tone Horns.
dry weight	318 lbs.	312 lbs.	262 lbs.
overall length	81 in.	81 in.	81 in.
handlebar width	26.5 in.	26.5 in.	26.5 in.
finish	Royal Gold, Black and Chromium Plate	Grey Stone White/Raven Black and Chromium Plate or Tartan Red / Raven Black and Chromium Plate	Grey Stone White/Raven Black and Chromium Plate or Tartan Red / Raven Black and Chromium Plate

Pontiac inspired? The Three Star Special.

ARIEL

Ariel Motors emanated from a business formed at the beginning of the 1870s by William Hillman and James Starley to manufacture ordinary bicycles, naming them Ariels on account of their lightweight frames and then-revolutionary wire spoke wheels. The two soon went their separate ways (Hillman much later becoming a motorcar manufacturer) but Starley continued with the Ariels, as well making his own design of sewing machine, the Europa, before licencing his cycles to be made by another Coventry firm of Haynes and Jefferis. These were made until the company's bankruptcy in 1879, which resulted in the assets and Ariel name being acquired by a local solicitor named George Woodcock, who shortly afterwards acquired Dan Rudge's Wolverhampton cycle business from his widow – amalgamating it with another bicycle company and relocating the two to the Ariel works in Coventry. The small combine then traded as D Rudge and Co, producing bicycles but with no mention of the name Ariel.

A while later, and by a circuitous route, the Dunlop name entered the story when the Dunlop Cycle Co (an offshoot of the rubber concern that had operated a chain of depots selling bicycles and accessories) was liquidated after being taken over by an Irish company in 1893. Come 1896 Dunlop decided to re-form the Dunlop Cycle Co, this time to actually manufacture bicycles; but after some dissent from other cycle makers, who all used Dunlop tyres, changed this to the Ariel Cycle Co – the lapsed name having been acquired some time before. The following year this business was acquired by the Cycle Components Manufacturing Co, which continued to produce Ariel cycles, but now under the direction of CCM's Charles Sangster and at Selly Oak, Birmingham.

By the late 1890s the cycling boom had passed its peak and in 1898 the Ariel Cycle Co brought out a Sangster-designed motorised tricycle, which drew heavily on the French de Dion he had imported and been using. The tricycles were well received and during the first years of the 20th century the factory grew and was producing two-, three- and four-wheelers, with

Since its introduction in 1933 the Red Hunter had been a highly regarded and popular mount for the motorcyclist of a sporting bent so, although the company had been part of the BSA group since 1944, it was back in production by 1946, all but unaltered and complete with now-old-fashioned girder forks...

The following year, however, a change to telescopics took place for the company's entire range.

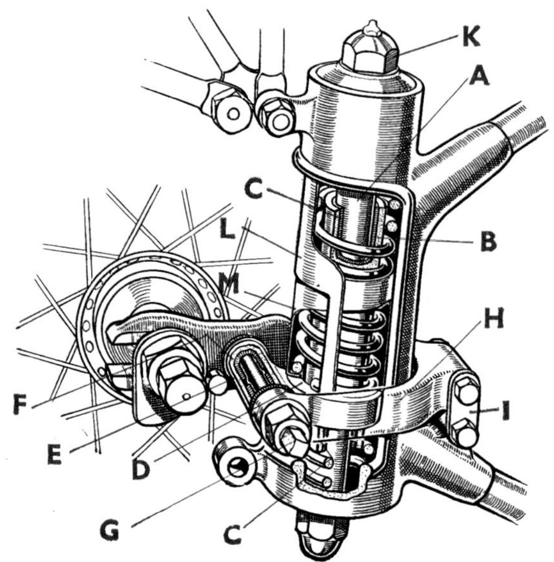

- Exceptional riding comfort.
- Increased stability, road holding and braking.
- Longer life of tyres, battery, etc.
- Minimum unsprung weight.
- Complete lateral rigidity.
- Constant chain tension.
- Total enclosure of working parts.

The frame is a completely brazed unit to provide maximum rigidity. Fitted through the centre of each rear fork end is a hardened guide tube A, which is clamped to the lug by a substantial bolt K. On this tube is mounted the slider B with bushes C at each end. The spring abutment collar D is forged integral with the slider and extended rearwards to form a horizontal pivot boss E, fitted with bushes F. The pin G passing through this pivot supports each side of the stirrup H, which surrounds the fork lug. The closed end of the stirrup is anchored to the chain stays by short links I, and one arm is extended to carry the wheel spindle. Renewable bushes are fitted to all bearings and the slider mechanism is completely enclosed against mud and dust by tubes L and M.

Ariel's flagship continued after the war, very much as it had left off, with girder forks at the front and Frank Anstey's somewhat quirky spring system at the rear. The 600cc version had been quietly dropped. Despite the firm's publicity the 1000 was no racehorse due to its weight, and the 600 had been slower. Although these illustrations are taken from the 1939 catalogue they show Ariel's rear suspension that in practice proved to be wear-prone, which led to movement in directions other than those intended by its designer. The four-cylinder engine in its ultimate pre-war 1000cc form was carried on until 1948.

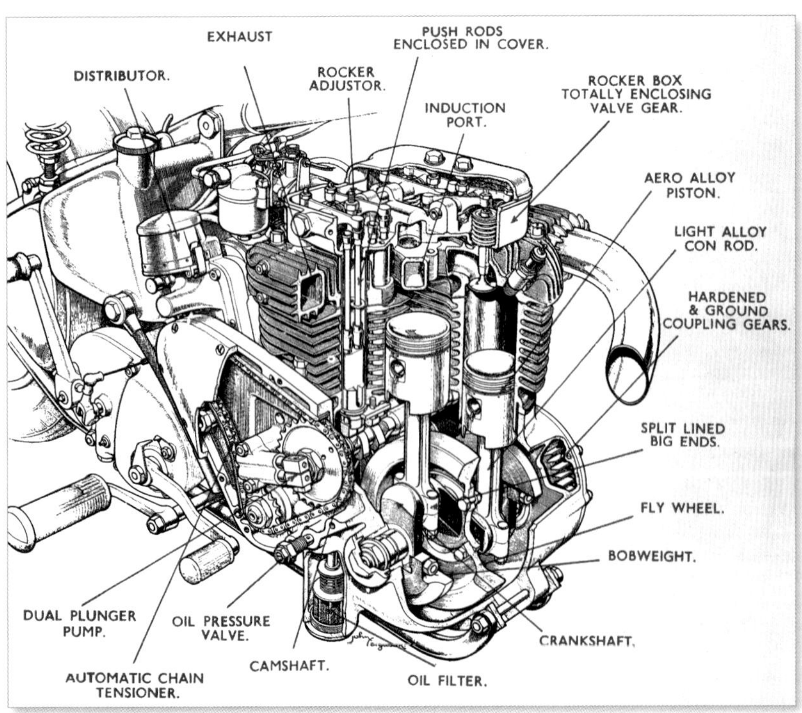

sales being handled by the Ariel Motor Company of Long Acre, London.

From there on things took many a twist and turn in the dozen-or-so years leading up to the First World War, with Ariel Motors (1906) being floated on the stock exchange to take over the manufacture of motorcars including the recently-introduced Mercedes-influenced (and up to 60hp) Ariel-Simplex. Before too long Simplex had been dropped and from thereon the cars were once more simply Ariels; but teetering finances prompted what would prove to be a short-lived financial tie-up whereby British versions of the French Lorraine-Dietrich would be built at the Selly Oak factory.

Rocky finances and a multiplicity of models notwithstanding, Ariel Motors managed, just, to survive until the war – the last being a 1.3-litre light car. The fortunes of Ariel motorcycles, on the other hand, had been far less hectic and settled down to a small range of singles and V-twins almost exclusively powered by four-stroke White and Poppe engines; a few even made it over to the Isle of Man to contest the

Tourist Trophy races.

Although the 1914-to-18 war failed to bring large contracts for these machines some did see active service; other government work stood them in good stead once peace was restored – motorcycle production being stepped up but motorcars, for the meanwhile, left well alone. Offering nothing extraordinary in the way of design, and still with White and Poppe engines, Ariels were nevertheless well-made and sturdy, unlike some of the hastily put-together horrors that tried to cash in on the ex-servicemen market.

The marque was given a fillip in 1923 when Charles Sangster's son Jack joined the company and set about embracing alternative engine suppliers, starting with a lightweight 250cc Blackburn in 1924. The following year he effected a major coup by persuading the hugely-talented designer Valentine Page to forsake JA Prestwich and join Ariel, where his first brief was to come up with something to replace the ageing White and Poppes. This he did to such good effect that, benefitting over the years from updates and modifications, various configurations of his singles remained in production right up until the end of 1958 when Ariel axed four-strokes in favour of sub-250cc two-strokes.

Next to receive his attentions were the remainder of the machines, and in 1927 new-look all-black Ariels were introduced with saddle tanks and substantial drum brakes, along with a prancing horse motif – Ariels had become what their new logo claimed, 'The Modern Motorcycle'. Around this time a young man named Edward Turner, at the same time as running a South London motorcycle shop, was beginning to look around for someone who would be interested in building a four-cylinder OHC engine he had designed for motorcycle use. After knocking on BSA's door in vain he was welcomed by Jack Sangster and joined Page, along with his protégé Bert Hopwood who had joined the company's drawing office fresh from school.

The following year, despite the economic slump, his designs had been translated into metal, and what would be the first of Ariel's Square Fours made a sensational debut at the 1930 Olympia Show. Its initial capacity was 500cc but for 1932 this was enlarged to 597cc to improve its somewhat disappointing performance, something that had been in the manufacturer's mind when it also brought out the first of what would be its long-running Red Hunter singles – the super sports version of Page's original OHV design. Hardly had there been time to distribute the latest models to dealers than Ariel's long-time parent company Components Ltd was taken down by the recession; had it not have been for its managing director Charles Sangster's son and fellow director Jack's purchase of tools, tooling, stock and other assets from the receivers, that could have been the end of the story. As it was the whole lot was transported to fresh premises nearby and, with Edward Turner in charge of design (Val Page having gone to Triumph), Ariel Motors Ltd (as it was retitled) regained its feet and proceeded with a reduced range that nevertheless continued with Square Fours and Hunters.

Having successfully completed Ariel's change of ownership, Jack Sangster took on yet another challenge when financial difficulties persuaded the Triumph Motor Company to sell off the motorcycle and cycle part of its business. He jumped in, changed its name to the Triumph Engineering Co Ltd and put some his best men in to run it, with Edward Turner, assisted by Bert Hopwood, to head up the design team (Page had recently moved yet again – this time to BSA).

In search of more power and to effect a cure for the overheating that had plagued it from the outset, the 1937 Squariel's engine was considerably altered and now had a longer stroke as well as pushrod valve actuation. It was also now produced with a choice of engine capacity – 599cc or 997cc. Never intended to be out-and-out racers, Red Hunters were one of the better genuinely-sporting road machines of the period

Although Ariel made no Isle of Man racers the Square Four was just the sort of machine that the luxury touring-minded enthusiast might ride to attend the TT week; such was the island's fame amongst motorcyclists that such advertising was of universal appeal.

From a distance the black tank panels distinguished a 'cooking' 1949 350 NG from the sportier NH Red Hunter but the latter also had a 20in front wheel and slightly skimpier mudguard to go with it.

Engine: 72×85 mm. (347 c.c.) High efficiency engine. Completely enclosed valve and rocker gear. Double roller bearing big end. Aluminium alloy piston. **Lubrication:** Dry sump system. ½-gallon capacity separate oil tank. **Gearbox:** Four speed. Foot control. **Speedometer:** Smith 80 m.p.h. trip speedometer. **Transmission:** Engine shaft shock absorber. Polished aluminium oilbath chaincase. Rear chain fully protected. **Exhaust System:** Two port. Low level exhaust pipes. Single port optional. **Wheels:** Dunlop tyres, 3.25×19. **Tank:** 2½-gallon capacity. Superbly finished chromium and black, lined gold.

Engine: 72×85 mm. (347 c.c.) O.H.V. Specially bench tested. Ground and highly polished ports. Polished forged steel flywheels. Ball bearings on both sides of mainshaft. Double roller bearing big end. Aluminium alloy piston. **Lubrication:** Dry sump system, employing dual plunger pumps and ½-gallon capacity separate oil tank. **Gearbox:** Four speed. Foot control. **Speedometer:** Smith 80 m.p.h. trip speedometer. **Transmission:** Engine shaft shock absorber. Polished aluminium oilbath chaincase. Rear chain fully protected. **Exhaust System:** Two port low level exhaust pipes. Single port optional. Upswept pipes with leg guard to special order. **Wheels:** Dunlop tyres, 3.25×19 rear, 3.00×20 ribbed front. Chromium rims, red centres. **Tank:** 2½-gallon capacity. Superbly finished chromium and red, lined gold.

and also proved to be more than capable of ending in the money at important events such as the Scottish Six Days and ISDT. By 1939 the 500 RH was claimed, with a little tuning, to be capable of 100mph, all OHV machines had enclosed rocker gear, and all models except for 250s could be bought with Ariel's own Anstey link plunger rear suspension.

Shortly before the outbreak of World War Two Ariel had submitted a lightened 500 side-valve machine to the war department for tests, but in the meantime decided that a militarised version of the 350 OHV NG would be more suitable. Designated the W/NG, and in production by the spring of 1940, it was given a cool reception by the War Department on account of its lighter build than the normal fare such as BSA's M20; but needs must, and contracts for its supply were forthcoming. Devoid of such niceties as the civilian models' tank-top dashboard and reminiscent of Ariel's successful trials machines, it proved to be nimble in difficult conditions and was well liked by the service personnel who used it.

With the end of the war in sight work had

For the 1949 season Ariel could boast of being the only manufacturer from which one could obtain a single-, twin- or four-cylinder motorcycle. The Anstey link rear suspension had been around since just before the war but was still an extra, as was a speedo – its space in the tank-top dashboard filled by a chromium disc if you didn't want to fork out an extra five quid.

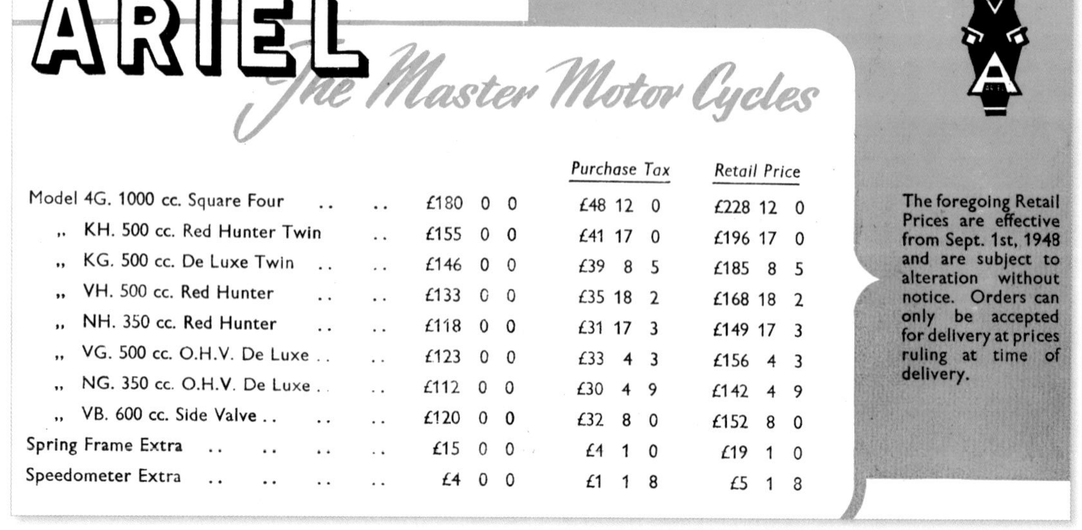
ARIEL The Master Motor Cycles

		Purchase Tax	Retail Price
Model 4G. 1000 cc. Square Four	£180 0 0	£48 12 0	£228 12 0
,, KH. 500 cc. Red Hunter Twin ..	£155 0 0	£41 17 0	£196 17 0
,, KG. 500 cc. De Luxe Twin	£146 0 0	£39 8 5	£185 8 5
,, VH. 500 cc. Red Hunter	£133 0 0	£35 18 2	£168 18 2
,, NH. 350 cc. Red Hunter	£118 0 0	£31 17 3	£149 17 3
,, VG. 500 cc. O.H.V. De Luxe	£123 0 0	£33 4 3	£156 4 3
,, NG. 350 cc. O.H.V. De Luxe	£112 0 0	£30 4 9	£142 4 9
,, VB. 600 cc. Side Valve	£120 0 0	£32 8 0	£152 8 0
Spring Frame Extra	£15 0 0	£4 1 0	£19 1 0
Speedometer Extra	£4 0 0	£1 1 8	£5 1 8

The foregoing Retail Prices are effective from Sept. 1st, 1948 and are subject to alteration without notice. Orders can only be accepted for delivery at prices ruling at time of delivery.

Engine: 81.8×95 mm. (497 c.c.) High efficiency engine. Completely enclosed valve and rocker gear automatically lubricated under pressure. High tensile steel connecting rod. Aluminium alloy piston, 6 to 1 compression. **Lubrication:** Dry sump system. ¾-gallon capacity separate oil tank. **Gearbox:** Four speed. Foot control. **Speedometer:** Smith 80 m.p.h. trip speedometer. **Transmission:** Engine shaft shock absorber. Polished aluminium oilbath chaincase. Rear chain fully protected. **Exhaust System:** Single port low level exhaust pipe. **Wheels:** Dunlop tyres, 3.25×19. **Tank:** 3¼-gallon capacity. Superbly finished chromium and black, lined gold.

No twin port option for the 1949 overhead valve 500s but, like the 350s, black tank panels for the regular VG and red for the VH Red Hunter, along with a 20in front wheel and sports mudguard. Both had a large three-quarter-gallon oil tank.

Engine: 81.8×95 mm. (497 c.c.) O.H.V. Specially bench tested. Ground and highly polished ports. Polished forged steel flywheels. Large diameter mainshafts mounted on two heavy duty roller bearings and one ball bearing. Extra large double roller bearing big end with duralumin cage. Aluminium alloy piston. **Lubrication:** Dry sump system employing dual plunger pumps and ¾-gallon capacity separate oil tank. **Gearbox:** Four speed. Foot control. **Speedometer:** Smith 100 m.p.h. trip speedometer. **Transmission:** Engine shaft shock absorber. Polished aluminium oilbath chaincase. Rear chain fully protected. **Exhaust System:** Single port low level exhaust pipe. (Upswept pipe with leg guard to special order.) **Wheels:** Dunlop tyres, 3.25×19 rear, 3.00×20 front. Chromium rims, red centres. **Tank:** 3¼-gallon capacity. Superbly finished chromium and red, lined gold.

commenced on a vertical twin along the lines of Triumph's Speed Twin. But, more importantly, Ariel was now owned by BSA – Jack Sangster having sold the company in 1944. Immediate post-war production consisted of a portion of the 1939 range with modernisation in the form of telescopic forks introduced for the 1947 season, and a year later the 500 twin was at last brought to the market.

Under BSA's ownership it was inevitable that some cross-pollination would take place and the Huntmaster of 1954, with its reworked A10 engine, was an example, as was the adoption of Ariel's brakes for two seasons a couple of years later. By this time Jack Sang-

Engine: 86.4×102 mm. (598 c.c.) Totally enclosed valve springs. Double roller bearing big end. Aluminium alloy piston, 5 to 1 compression. **Lubrication:** Dry sump system. ¾-gallon capacity separate oil tank. **Gearbox:** Four speed. Foot control. **Speedometer:** Smith 80 m.p.h. trip speedometer. **Transmission:** Engine shaft shock absorber. Polished aluminium oilbath chaincase. Rear chain fully protected. **Exhaust system:** Large diameter exhaust pipe with streamlined silencer. **Wheels:** Dunlop tyres, 3.25×19. **Tank:** 3¼-gallon capacity. Superbly finished chromium and black, lined gold.

Some traditionalists still favoured a side-valve engine for sidecar work and a few even for a solo, so for them Ariel's VB, which had first seen the light of day in 1926, was an alternative to the ubiquitous BSAs and Nortons. Its valanced mudguard was shared with the 500 OHV VG. The Motor Cycle *tested a de luxe version hitched to a Watsonian single seat sidecar in the late summer of 1947 and managed to get it up to a creditable 61mph. Fuel consumption at a steady 50mph proved to be 42mpg and they described the brakes as 'good but not outstanding' – a kind of backhanded compliment considering the sidecar, even devoid of a passenger.*

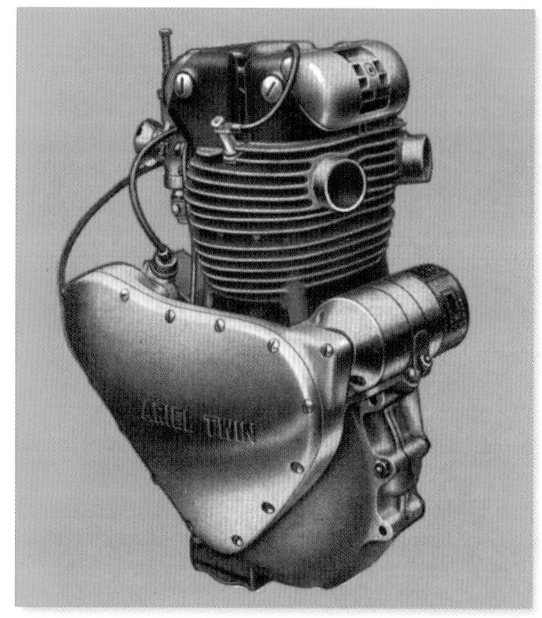

The RED HUNTER TWIN 500 c.c. MODEL KH

Engine: 63×80 mm. vertical O.H.V. cylinder heads and rocker boxes in one casting. Balanced crankshaft forged in one piece. Light alloy connecting rods with replaceable white metal liners. Light alloy pistons 6.8 compression ratio. Twin camshafts driven by duplex chain. Magneto with automatic ignition control. 56 watt dynamo. Each engine has polished ports and cylinder heads and is specially bench tested and tuned. 7.5 compression ratio pistons can be supplied to order for use with 80 octane fuel. **Lubrication:** Circulation by double gear pump. 40 lbs. oil pressure to main bearings and rockers. ¾-gallon separate oil tank. **Carburettor:** Large bore Amal, single control by twist grip. Petroflex pipe. **Gearbox:** Four speed, foot control. **Wheels:** Dunlop tyres, 3.50×19 rear, 3.00×20 ribbed front. Chrome rims, red centres, lined gold. **Frame and Forks:** Telescopic front forks. Rigid frame with integral sidecar lugs (rear springing optional extra). Front, rear, and prop stands. **Tank:** 3¼-gallon capacity. Superbly finished in chrome and red, lined gold. Incorporating 100 m.p.h. trip speedometer, oil gauge and inspection lamp.

The DE LUXE TWIN 500 c.c. MODEL KG

Engine: 63×80 mm. vertical O.H.V. cylinder heads and rocker boxes in one casting. Balanced crankshaft forged in one piece, carried on a large roller bearing on drive side and plain white metal bearing on timing side. Light alloy connecting rods with replaceable white metal liners. Light alloy pistons 6.8 compression ratio. Twin camshafts driven by automatically adjusted duplex chain. Magneto with automatic ignition control. 56 watt dynamo. **Lubrication:** Circulation by double gear pump. 40 lbs. oil pressure to main bearings and rockers. ¾-gallon separate oil tank. **Carburettor:** Amal, single control by twist grip. **Gearbox:** Four speed, foot control. **Wheels:** Dunlop tyres, 3.50×19 rear, 3.25×19 front. Chrome rims, black centres, lined gold. **Frame and Forks:** Telescopic front forks. Rigid frame with integral sidecar lugs (rear springing optional extra). Front, rear, and prop stands. **Tank:** 3¼-gallon capacity. Superbly finished in chrome and black, lined gold. Incorporating 100 m.p.h. trip speedometer, oil gauge and inspection lamp.

Vertical twins were all the rage in 1948 at Earls Court's first post-war motorcycle show and Ariel, whether the sports Red Hunter or KG, considered its machines to be of noble breeding – the engine from the drawing board of Val Page..

ster was once again in charge, but now as chairman of BSA, having sold Triumph to the company in 1951 and joined the board at more or less the same time, taking the chair upon the removal of the notorious Bernard Docker.

In 1953 the Square Four had what would be its last makeover, which featured a redesigned cylinder head with quadruple exhausts, this mainly in the continuing quest to dissipate heat; but it retained its by-that-time-antediluvian pre-war rear suspension until its last gasp in 1958.

The end of the Square Four, and all of Ariel's other four-strokes for that matter, was perhaps ironically brought about by the introduction of a completely new machine masterminded by Val Page, who had also designed a good deal of what was being replaced more than 30 years before.

Like nothing else produced by the British motorcycle industry up to that time – and following a great deal of research as to the type of motorcycle Mr Everyman (if he existed) would buy – the Leader represented a big risk for its makers. The gamble paid off, however, and after kindly treatment by the press, as well as a successful Motor Cycle Show debut in November 1958, its sales surpassed expectations. Joined by a sports version, the Arrow, for the 1960 season both sold well in the face of increasing opposition from the East. But by 1965 they'd had their day and were terminated.

During their lifetime BSA closed the Selly Oak factory and transferred production to Small Heath, as well as foisting a kind of undersized Beagle upon the firm and attempting to do the same to the public; marketed as the Pixie it is best forgotten and was also (thankfully) killed of at the same time. Even more forgettable is the early '70s attempt by a floundering BSA to reintroduce the name with the Ariel 3 – a truly ghastly moped device with tiny two-stroke Dutch motor and a swivelling front end so the rider could pretend it was a proper machine and lean into corners whilst the two rear wheels (hopefully) stayed firmly planted on terra firma. It would have been better by far to spare the name Ariel that last indignity, but justice was served with the hastening of BSA's own demise.

Aluminium Engine of the model 4G showing robust construction and clean lines of this outstanding power unit.

In an effort to lose avoirdupois and cure overheated cylinder heads the Square Four's engine had received some attention. Henceforth its top end, from barrels upwards, was of aluminium – this shedding getting on for 40lbs and going some way towards alleviating the hot spots

Was there a clairvoyant in the house? The next coronation, that of our present Queen Elizabeth, would not be for more than three years hence, in June 1953, whilst this 1950 season brochure cover was printed in the autumn of 1949. Fanciful too, as I doubt if the occupants of the coronation coach would have taken too kindly to a Squariel-mounted police outrider droning past.

The SQUARE 4 DE LUXE **1,000 c.c. MODEL 4G with aluminium engine and coil ignition**

The light cool running engine has cylinder head incorporating twin rocker boxes, inlet and exhaust manifolds and push rod tunnels in one casting. The cylinder barrel finning ensures complete circulation of air. The car type distributor and coil provides a positive, well tried ignition system.

The SQUARE 4 DE LUXE

1,000 c.c. MODEL 4G

Engine: 65×75 mm.=997 c.c. capacity (2.56×2.95=60.8 cubic inches). Aluminium alloy cylinders are cast "en bloc" in square formation. Fitted with wear resisting detachable sleeves. Aluminium alloy cylinder heads with valve seat inserts. Spark plug holes are bronze bushed. Enclosed and automatically lubricated overhead valves. Twin counterbalanced alloy steel crankshafts interconnected by hardened and ground gears. Aluminium alloy con rods with replaceable white metal liners. **Lubrication:** Dry sump with dual plunger pump; feeds oil to bearings under pressure. Scavenger pump returns filtered oil to separate ¾-gallon tank. **Electrical Equipment:** 70 watt voltage controlled dynamo, incorporating distributor with automatic ignition timing. Large 6 volt coil. Headlamp with 36 watt bulb. **Gearbox:** Four speed, foot control. **Wheels:** Dunlop tyres, 4.00×18 rear, 3.25×19 front. Chrome rims with red centres (black centres optional). **Frame and Forks:** Telescopic front forks. Rigid frame with integral sidecar lugs (rear springing optional extra). Front, rear, and prop stands. **Tank:** 3½-gallon capacity. Superbly finished in chrome and red, lined gold. (Chrome and black, lined gold, optional.) Incorporating 100 m.p.h. trip speedometer, oil gauge and inspection lamp.

Depicted here is the 1950 350cc NG, which of course had the smaller, half-gallon, oil tank than its larger-capacity brother as well as the option of a twin-port head with twin low-level exhausts. This would be the final year for these models.

Engine VG: 81.8 × 95 mm. = 497 c.c. (3.22 × 3.74 = 30.4 cubic inches). High efficiency engine, completely enclosed valve and rocker gear. Automatically lubricated under pressure. High tensile steel connecting rod. Aluminium alloy piston 6.8 compression ratio.

Engine NG: 72 × 85 mm. = 347 c.c. (2.835 × 3.346 = 21.2 cubic inches). High efficiency engine, completely enclosed valve and rocker gear. Double roller bearing big end. Aluminium alloy piston 6.2 compression ratio.

Lubrication: Dry sump system employing dual plunger pump. VG—¾ gallon (3.4 litres), NG—½ gallon (2.3 litres) capacity. Separate oil tank.

Exhaust System: VG—Single port low level pipe. NG—Single or double port low level pipes.

Wheels: Dunlop tyres 3.25 × 19. Chrome rims, black centres, lined gold. (Ariel green centres, optional.)

Tank: VG—3¼ gallon (14.8 litres) capacity. NG—2½ gallons (11.4 litres) capacity. Superbly finished in chrome and black, lined gold. (Chrome and Ariel green, lined gold, optional.)

The 1950 Red Hunters' extra zip came by way of their hand-finished components and careful assembly rather than high compression ratios, as these were identical to their more touring 350 and 500cc stablemates.

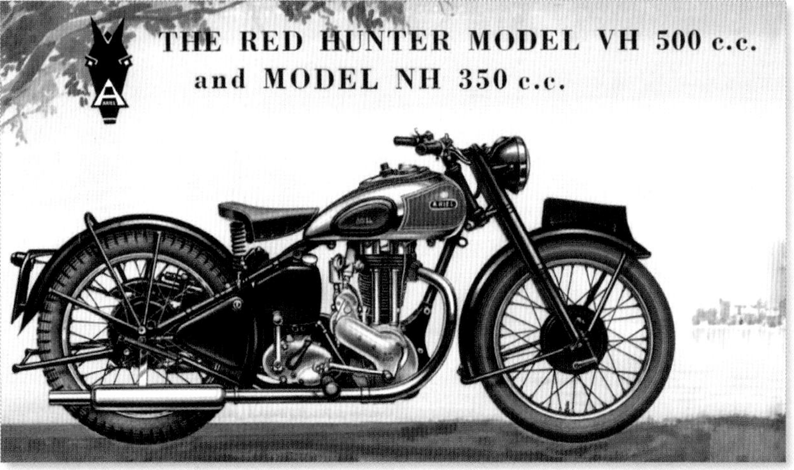

Engine VH: 81.8 × 95 mm. = 497 c.c. (3.22 × 3.74 = 30.4 cubic inches) O.H.V. Specially bench tested and tuned. Ground and highly polished ports and cylinder head. Polished forged steel flywheels. Large diameter mainshafts mounted on two heavy duty roller bearings and one ball bearing. Extra large double roller bearing big end with duralumin cage. Aluminium alloy piston 6.8 compression ratio.

Engine NH: 72 × 85 mm. = 347 c.c. (2.835 × 3.346 = 21.2 cubic inches) O.H.V. Specially bench tested and tuned. Ground and highly polished ports and cylinder head. Polished forged steel flywheels. Ball bearings on both sides of mainshaft. Double roller bearing big end. Aluminium alloy piston 6.2 compression ratio.

Lubrication: Dry sump system employing dual plunger pump. VH—¾ gallon (3.4 litres), NH—½ gallon (2.3 litres) capacity. Separate oil tank.

Exhaust System: VH—Single port low level pipe. NH—Single or double port, low level pipes.

Wheels: Dunlop tyres 3.25 × 19 rear, 3.00 × 20 ribbed front. Chrome rims, red centres, lined gold.

Prop Stand: Fitted on near side of machine.

Tank: VH—3¼ gallon (14.8 litres) capacity. NH—2½ gallon (11.4 litres) capacity. Superbly finished in chrome and red, lined gold.

Engine: 86.4 × 102 mm. = 598 c.c. (3.4 × 4.01 = 36.5 cubic inches). Totally enclosed valve springs. Double roller bearing big end. Aluminium alloy piston 5.0 compression ratio.

Lubrication: Dry sump system ¾ gallon (3.4 litres) capacity. Separate oil Tank.

Exhaust System: Large diameter pipe with streamlined silencer.

Wheels: Dunlop tyres 3.25 × 19. Chrome rims, black centres, lined gold. (Ariel green centres optional.)

Tank: 3¼ gallon (14.8 litres) capacity. Superbly finished in chrome and black, lined gold. (Chrome and Ariel green, lined gold, optional.)

A strange analogy in this 1950 brochure. I would have thought something akin to the architecture of a medieval castle more in keeping with the aura of the good old side-valve VB that had been around since it left Val Page's drawing board in the '20s.

Engine KG : 63 × 80 mm. = 498 c.c. (2.48 × 3.15 = 30.4 cubic inches). Vertical O.H.V., cylinder heads and rocker boxes in one casting. Balanced crankshafts forged in one piece, carried on a large roller bearing on drive side and plain white metal bearing on timing side. Light alloy connecting rods with replaceable white metal liners. Light alloy pistons 6.8 compression ratio. Twin camshafts driven by automatically adjusted Duplex chain. Oil circulates by double gear pump. 25-35 lb. oil pressure to main bearings and rockers. ¾ gallon (3.4 litres) separate oil Tank. Magneto with automatic ignition control. 56 watt dynamo. **Engine KH :** Specification as model KG, but has polished ports and cylinder heads and is specially bench tested and tuned. 7.5 compression ratio pistons can be supplied to order for use with 80 octane fuel. **Carburettor :** Amal single control by twist grip. Large bore Amal on Model KH with Petroflex pipe. **Wheels :** KG—Dunlop tyres 3.50 × 19 rear, 3.25 × 19 front. Chrome rims, black centres, lined gold (Ariel green centres optional). KH-Dunlop tyres 3.50 × 19 rear, 3.00 × 20 ribbed front. Chrome rims, red centres, lined gold. **Prop Stand :** Fitted on near side of machine. **Tank :** 3¾ gallon (17.0 litres) capacity. KG—Superbly finished in chrome and black, lined gold. (Chrome and Ariel green, lined gold, optional.) KH—Superbly finished in chrome and red, lined gold.

The possibilities offered by a full colour brochure for 1950, its first since 1939, seem to have gone to Ariel's head with a trip to the Canadian Rockies for its vertical twins. But why show the standard rigid frame rather than the one with optional rear suspension when the latter could induce potential purchasers to part with some extra cash?

They run in the family

Did the Surman family coincidentally own this across-the-board range of Ariels or was it a carefully orchestrated publicity exercise? The four is the obsolete (since the autumn of 1948) model and the Red Hunter, with its single upswept exhaust, of similar vintage.

SPECIFICATION OF THE SQUARE FOUR 1000 c.c. MODEL 4G

Engine : 65 × 75 mm. = 997 c.c. (2.56 × 2.95 = 60.8 cubic inches). Aluminium alloy cylinders are cast "*en bloc*" in square formation. Fitted with wear resisting detachable sleeves. Aluminium alloy cylinder heads with valve seat inserts. Sparking plug holes are bronze bushed. Enclosed and automatically lubricated overhead valves. Twin counterbalanced alloy steel crankshafts interconnected by hardened and ground gears. Aluminium alloy con rods with replaceable white metal liners. Pistons 6.0 compression ratio (6.8 compression ratio can be supplied to order for use with 80 octane fuel).

Lubrication : Dry sump with dual plunger pump, feeds oil to bearings under pressure. Scavenger pump returns filtered oil to separate ¾ gallon (3.4 litres) tank.

Electrical Equipment : 70 watt voltage controlled dynamo, incorporating distributor with automatic ignition timing. Large 6 volt coil. Headlamp with 30 watt bulb.

Wheels : Dunlop studded tyres 4.00 × 18 rear, 3.25 × 19 front. Ribbed front tyre optional. Chrome rims, red centres, lined gold. (Black centres optional). Quickly detachable rear wheel.

Prop Stand : Fitted on near side of machine.

Tank : 3½ gallon (16 litres) capacity. Superbly finished in chrome and red, lined gold. (Chrome and black, lined gold, optional.)

Standard on the Square Four from 1950 on was a QD rear wheel but you had to pay a bit more to have this facility on the vertical twins or singles. The speedo, on this and the vertical twin, had migrated from the tank mounting to a light-alloy casting bridging the top of the front fork legs.

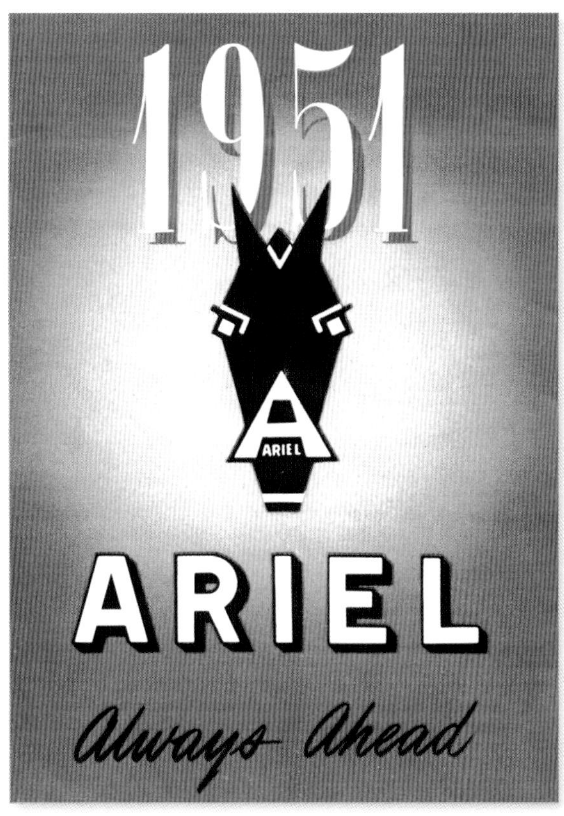

TECHNICAL DATA

Description	NH	VH	VB	KG	KH	4G
Wheelbase—inches ..	56	56	56	56	55	56
Overall length—inches ..	86	86	86	86	86	86
Handlebar width—inches	27	27	27	27	27	27
Saddle height—inches ..	30	30	30	30	30	30
Ground clearance—inches ..	5	5	5	5	5	5
*Weight fully equipped—lbs.	348	375	365	384	384	412
Petrol consumption—m.p.g.	75—80	75—80	70—75	75—80	75—80	65—70
Oil consumption—m.p.g. ..	2000	2000	2000	2000	2000	1800
Petrol Tank capacity—galls.	2¾	3½	3½	4	4	4
Oil Tank capacity—pints ..	4	6	6	6	6	6
Solo Gear Ratio —Top ..	5.7	4.7	4.7	5.20	5.20	4.5
,, ,, ,, —Third ..	7.3	6.0	6.0	6.65	6.65	5.7
,, ,, ,, —Second	10.1	8.0	8.0	9.15	9.15	7.7
,, ,, ,, —First ..	15.3	12.6	12.6	13.85	13.85	12.1
Sidecar Gear ratio—Top ..	—	5.7	5.7	5.75	5.75	4.9
,, ,, ,, —Third	—	7.2	7.2	7.40	7.40	6.2
,, ,, ,, —Second	—	9.7	9.7	10.15	10.15	8.4
,, ,, ,, —First ..	—	15.3	15.3	15.40	15.40	13.2
Engine Sprocket—Solo ..	20T	23T	23T	21T	21T	24T
,, ,, —Sidecar	—	19T	19T	19T	19T	22T
Chain, Front, ½″ Pitch						
No. of Links—Solo ..	80	81	81	81	81	72
Chain, Rear, ⅝″ Pitch						
No. of Links—Solo ..	95	95	95	95	95	91
Cylinder Bore	72 mm.	81.8 mm.	86.4 mm.	63 mm.	63 mm.	65 mm.
Engine Stroke	85 mm.	95.0 mm.	102.0 mm.	80 mm.	80 mm.	75 mm.
Engine b.h.p. at	19.4	24.6	15.5	24.0	26.0	34.5
,, r.p.m.	5600	6000	4400	6000	6500	5400
Cubic capacity—actual ..	347 c.c.	497 c.c.	598 c.c.	498 c.c.	498 c.c.	997 c.c.
Compression ratio ..	6.2	6.8	5.0	6.8	6.8	6.0
Approx. max. speed—m.p.h. —Solo	74	85	65	85	90	95

*Spring frame machines 22 lb. heavier.

Petrol consumption at 45 m.p.h. steady speed.

B.H.P. is the average figure for low compression engines.

Maximum speeds, under average conditions on the level.

Engine sprockets for other gear ratios supplied to special order, except Models KG-KH.

Speed, Petrol and Oil consumption figures cannot be applied to new machines that have covered less than 2,000 miles.

THE RED HUNTER SINGLE CYLINDER 350c.c. Model NH

Engine : 72×85 mm.=347 c.c. (2.835×3.346=21.2 cubic inches). OHV. Specially bench tested and tuned. Ground and polished ports and cylinder head. Polished forged steel flywheels. Ball bearings on both sides of mainshaft. Double roller bearing big end. High efficiency cam gear. Aluminium alloy piston 6.2 compression ratio. **Lubrication :** Dry sump system employing dual plunger pump. Separate oil tank, ½ gallon (2.3 litres) capacity. **Exhaust System :** Single port low level pipe and sound absorbing silencer. **Wheels :** Dunlop studded tyre 3.25×19 rear, 3.00×20 ribbed front. Chrome rims, red centres, lined gold. **Prop Stand:** Fitted on near side of machine. **Tank :** Approx. 2¾ gallon (12.5 litres) capacity. Superbly finished in chrome and red, lined gold.

Price £127 0 0 plus Purchase Tax £34 5 10

It may have made a catchy slogan but was Ariel really ahead of the opposition in 1951? True, it was still the only manufacturer to offer fours, twins and singles but what else had been going on? Well, the tank-top dashboard had gone, leaving just the oil gauge in its place, thus increasing the capacity. Speedometers were by now a standard fitment on all models and mounted atop the fork legs, whilst ammeter and switchgear (the four and twins had a separate one for the ignition) was integral with the headlamp. As far as this data sheet is concerned, when The Motor Cycle *tested a springer 500cc Red Hunter in the summer of 1951 their top speed exactly concurred with Ariel's and a gallon of fuel carried them 84 miles at 40mph and 67 miles at 50mph.*

Little visible change for any of the range apart from the speedo position but all fuel capacities were greater – eg the Hunters were up by quarter of a gallon. Although the 'cooking' 350 and 500 singles were no more, the Hunter motors had been improved and now featured a single cam and appropriate rockers rather than the two previously employed. A competition version of the 500 had been introduced in 1949 and this, the VCH, featured an alloy engine and special frame – it was produced only in small numbers. The 500 twins had been endowed with deeper finning on both barrels and head whilst, in search of smoother running, the flywheels were 20 per cent heavier.

No new models at Earls Court in November but a national shortage of chromium dictated a good deal less of it in evidence amongst the exhibitors – especially as far as petrol tank finishes were concerned. A rigid-framed twin is shown on the left and a Square Four on the right.

The four-pipe Square Four made its debut at the '52 show. In yet another and final effort to expunge its hot running characteristics a larger and more extensively finned cylinder head was combined with separate bolt-on exhaust manifolds and individual exhausts. Power was up but the increase in performance accentuated the shortcomings of the chassis, whilst the engine would happily demonstrate that it too could overheat. One was put through its paces by The Motor Cycle *in the spring of 1953; although they managed a one-way best speed of 107mph (97mph mean two-way) no mention was made of any untoward heat. In the handling department, however, although generally impressed, passing mention was made of pitching (on surfaces that were not smooth) at ultra high speeds and weaving (on bad surfaces) at high velocities. Nice – or better slow down! And you really would have to if you wanted to try and emulate the factory's published fuel consumption figures of 65-to-70mpg at 45mph. The very best the magazine could squeeze out was 57mpg and that was at a steady 30! All that aside, when did you last see a blue Ariel? It was a suggested alternative to the traditional combinations of Red, Red and Black or Black, but for 1953 alone. An even less likely sighting would be one of the aluminium-engined KHA Red Hunters in that colour, as fewer than 500 were made, and only during the 1953 season.*

The 1954 brochure, and long-overdue modernisation meant the company could, with some justification, entitle its range 'modern'. The girls looked up for a bit of motorcycle fun as well. This was, of course, years away from helmet laws but perversely, providing there's a helmet on your head, there is nothing to stop you or your girl dressing just like this today. Arthur Wheeler had opened his motorcycle shop in the late '30s and its post-war success had enabled him to finance riding, as a privateer, to Grand Prix level – this culminating with third place in the world 250cc championship of 1961 on a Moto Guzzi, when he was in his mid-40s.

Entirely new for 1954 – or nearly so, as it was in reality a downsized variant of parent BSA's C11 to give a machine with the under-200cc classification. Although never destined for glory, Ariel's Colt was a better machine than history records it as being.

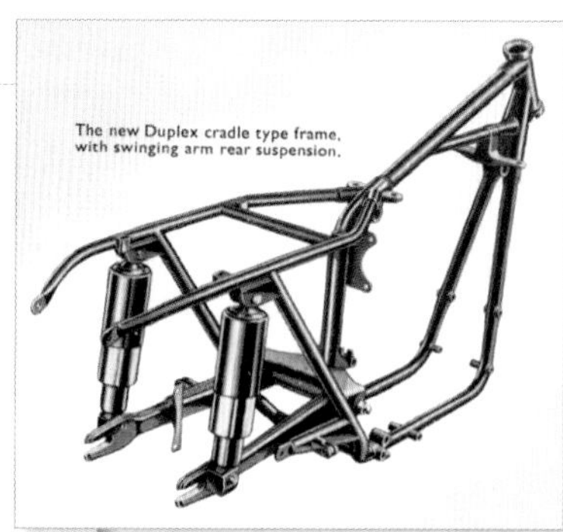

MODEL NH

350 c.c. HUNTER SINGLE

ENGINE: Vertical O.H.V. 72 × 85 mm. = 347 c.c. (2.83 × 3.34 = 21.2 cubic inches). Cast iron cylinder and head. Heavy duty ball bearings on both sides of mainshaft. Double row roller big end bearing. Amal carburetter with air cleaner. Dual plunger oil pump. Lucas manual ignition control.

FRAME: Duplex cradle type, fully triangulated, ensuring great strength and rigidity, with lugs for sidecar attachment either side. Swinging arm rear suspension with hydraulic damping. 3½ inch wheel movement. All pivot points rubber bushed.

MUDGUARDS: Wide D section with tubular stays. Back end of rear guard detachable for easy wheel removal.

BRAKES: Ariel design of great power, ensuring positive and progressive action. 7 inch diameter front and rear. Car type fulcrum adjustment.

LIGHTING EQUIPMENT: 7½ inch headlamp incorporating lighting switch and ammeter. 56 watt voltage controlled magdyno. 6 volt battery. Stop and tail lamp. Electric horn.

FINISH: Superbly finished throughout in best quality Deep Claret enamel.

With the styling of Ariel's new petrol tanks the uninitiated might be excused for thinking BSA had disposed of the company to GM's Vauxhall Motors – which had in the dim and distant past dallied with a motorcycle of its own. Circa 1922, prior to its American takeover, Vauxhall had made half-a-dozen prototypes of a luxury machine with Ricardo-designed 1000cc straight-four motor; but that was as far as it went, and the similarly-styled Ariel tank was just a coincidence. That aside, the 1954 season's new swinging-arm frame and associated cycle parts had done much to make believe that this 350 Red Hunter was a total departure from the old – unless one looked at its engine.

MODEL VH

500 c.c. HUNTER SINGLE

ENGINE: Vertical O.H.V. 81.8 × 95 mm. = 497 c.c. (3.22 × 3.74 = 30.4 cubic inches). Cast iron cylinder and polished aluminium alloy cylinder head with valve seat inserts. Large diameter mainshafts mounted on two heavy duty roller bearings and one ball bearing. Double row roller big end bearing. Amal carburetter with air cleaner. Dual plunger oil pump. Lucas manual ignition control.

FRAME: Duplex cradle type, fully triangulated, ensuring great strength and rigidity, with lugs for sidecar attachment either side. Swinging arm rear suspension with hydraulic damping. 3½ inch wheel movement. All pivot points rubber bushed. Easy-lift spring-up central and strong tubular front stands, also prop stand.

MUDGUARDS: Wide D section with tubular stays. Back end of rear guard detachable for easy wheel removal.

BRAKES: Ariel design of great power, ensuring positive and progressive action. 7 inch diameter front and rear. Car type fulcrum adjustment.

LIGHTING EQUIPMENT: 7½ inch headlamp incorporating lighting switch and ammeter. 56 watt voltage controlled magdyno. 6 volt battery. Stop and tail lamp. Electric horn.

FINISH: Superbly finished throughout in best quality Deep Claret enamel.

The standard road 500 Red Hunter's engine now looked very much like that of the alloy VHA versions, with pushrod tunnels all but totally enclosed within the finning. The latter are not to be confused with true competition motors which were designated VCH. The first of these, from the late '40s, were very special in that they had magnesium alloy crankcases that mate to a circular flange to the base of the sparsely finned barrel and head, secured with six studs. Later editions had no magnesium components, were more fully finned and the barrel had a rectangular four-stud flange as on other single-cylinder Ariels.

For 1954 the KH 500 twin now had an aluminium cylinder head on its iron barrel whilst the short-lived all-alloy KHA had been discontinued. I wonder why? It had been more expensive (£184 against £174), so it wasn't being given away for nothing – unduly noisy perhaps, or for no good reason at all?

MODEL KH

500 c.c. HUNTER TWIN

ENGINE: Vertical O.H.V. 63 × 80 mm. = 498 c.c. (2.40 × 3.15 = 30.4 cubic inches). Cast iron twin cylinder and polished aluminium alloy cylinder head, with valve seat inserts. Forged steel crankshaft with counterbalanced weights, carried on a large roller bearing on drive side, white metal lined bearing on timing side. Light alloy connecting rods with white metal liners. Twin camshafts driven by adjustable Duplex roller chain. Amal carburetter with air cleaner. Double gear oil pump. Lucas magneto with automatic ignition control.

FRAME: Duplex cradle type, fully triangulated, ensuring great strength and rigidity, with lugs for sidecar attachment either side. Swinging arm rear suspension with hydraulic damping. $3\frac{1}{2}$ inch wheel movement. All pivot points rubber bushed. Easy-lift spring-up central and strong tubular front stands, also prop stand.

MUDGUARDS: Wide D section with tubular stays. Back end of rear guard detachable for easy wheel removal.

BRAKES: Ariel design of great power, ensuring positive and progressive action. 7 inch diameter front and rear. Car type fulcrum adjustment.

LIGHTING EQUIPMENT: $7\frac{1}{2}$ inch headlamp incorporating lighting switch and ammeter. 56 watt voltage controlled dynamo. 6 volt battery. Stop and tail lamp. Electric horn.

FINISH: Superbly finished throughout in best quality Deep Claret enamel.

It was no coincidence that Ariel's new Huntmaster shared the same bore and stroke dimensions as that of BSA's Golden Flash, as it was a reworked version of the Bert Hopwood design.

MODEL FH

650 c.c. HUNTMASTER TWIN

ENGINE: Vertical O.H.V. 70 × 84 mm. = 646 c.c. (2.76 × 3.30 = 39.3 cubic inches). Cast iron twin cylinders and heads. Forged steel crankshaft with counter-balanced weights, carried on a large roller bearing on drive side, white metal lined bearing on timing side. Light alloy connecting rods with lead-bronze liners. Camshaft gear driven from engine shaft operates O.H.V. rockers by means of tappets and push rods. Mechanical crankcase breather. Amal carburetter with air cleaner. Double gear oil pump. Lucas magneto with automatic ignition control.

FRAME: Duplex cradle type, fully triangulated, ensuring great strength and rigidity, with lugs for sidecar attachment either side. Swinging arm rear suspension with hydraulic damping. $3\frac{1}{2}$ inch wheel movement. All pivot points rubber bushed. Easy-lift spring-up central and strong tubular front stands, also prop stand.

MUDGUARDS: Wide D section with tubular stays. Back end of rear guard detachable for easy wheel removal

BRAKES: Ariel design of great power, ensuring positive and progressive action. 7 inch diameter front and rear. Car type fulcrum adjustment.

LIGHTING EQUIPMENT: $7\frac{1}{2}$ inch headlamp incorporating lighting switch and ammeter. 56 watt voltage controlled dynamo. 6 volt battery. Stop and tail lamp. Electric horn.

FINISH: Superbly finished throughout in best quality Deep Claret enamel.

MODEL VB

600 c.c. SIDE VALVE

ENGINE: Specially designed for solo or heavy duty sidecar work. 86.4 × 102 mm. = 598 c.c. (3.4 × 4.01 = 36.5 cubic inches). Cast iron cylinder barrel with polished aluminium alloy cylinder head. Heavy duty ball bearings on both sides of mainshaft. Totally enclosed valve gear. Double row roller connecting rod big end bearing. Amal carburetter. Dual plunger oil pump. Lucas manual ignition control.

FRAME: Full cradle type, rigid, with lugs for sidecar attachment either side. (Ariel patented plunger rear suspension at extra.) Forged steel girder spring-up rear and strong tubular front stands.

MUDGUARDS: Wide D section with tubular stays. Rear guard can be lifted for easy wheel removal.

BRAKES: Ariel design of great power, ensuring positive and progressive action. 7 inch diameter front and rear Car type fulcrum adjustment.

LIGHTING EQUIPMENT: 7½ inch headlamp incorporating lighting switch and ammeter. 56 watt voltage controlled magdyno. 6 volt battery. Stop and tail lamp. Electric horn.

FINISH: Superbly finished throughout in best quality black enamel.

The geriatric 600 side-valve still soldiered on but it too had been given an aluminium cylinder head for 1954. Stonehenge, I think you'll agree, is a rather fitting backdrop.

In common with Triumph's Thunderbird of that period the MkII Square Four motor was fitted with an SU carburettor – this necessitating a dogleg in the frame to give clearance.

MODEL 4G

1000 c.c. SQUARE FOUR

ENGINE: Four cylinder O.H.V. 65 × 75 mm. = 997 c.c. (2.56 × 2.95 = 60.8 cubic inches). Aluminium alloy cylinder with wear resisting detachable sleeves. Aluminium alloy cylinder head with valve seat inserts. Twin counterbalanced alloy steel crankshafts coupled by hardened and ground gears. Light alloy connecting rods with white metal liners. S.U. variable choke carburetter with air cleaner. Double gear oil pump. Lucas coil ignition incorporating 70 watt voltage controlled dynamo with built-in distributor and automatic ignition control. 6 volt 20 amp. hour battery.

FRAME: Full cradle type with lugs for sidecar attachment either side. Ariel patented plunger rear suspension. Forged steel girder spring-up rear and strong tubular front stands, also prop stand.

MUDGUARDS: Wide D section with tubular stays. Rear guard can be lifted for easy wheel removal.

BRAKES: Ariel design of great power, ensuring positive and progressive action. 8 inch diameter rear, 7 inch diameter front. Car type fulcrum adjustment.

LIGHTING EQUIPMENT: 7½ inch headlamp incorporating lighting switch and ammeter. 6 volt battery. Stop and tail lamp. Electric horn.

FINISH: Superbly finished throughout in best quality black enamel.

POWER UNIT OF THE WORLD-FAMOUS SQUARE FOUR

For the latest Square Four the improved engine was still housed in a slightly modified version of the same old frame with quirky rear suspension

MODEL	4G	FH	KH	VH	NH	LH	VB
TYPE	O.H.V.	O.H.V.	O.H.V.	O.H.V.	O.H.V.	O.H.V.	S.V.
Number of Cylinders	4	2	2	1	1	1	1
Bore and Stroke	65×75	70×84	63×80	81.8×95	72×85	60×70	86.4×102
Cylinder Capacity	997	646	498	497	347	197	598
Compression Ratio	7.2	6.5	6.8	6.8	6.2	7.5	5
Engine B.H.P.	42	35	28	26	18	10	18
Engine R.P.M.	5,800	5,600	6,200	6,000	5,600	5,600	4,400
Engine Sprocket: No. of Teeth—Solo	26	24	21	23	19	17	23
Sidecar	23	22	19	19	—	—	19
Solo Gear Ratio—Top	4.18	4.35	5.18	4.74	5.72	7.0	4.74
Third	5.46	5.70	6.77	6.20	7.50	8.5	6.20
Second	7.1	7.40	8.81	8.05	9.72	11.6	8.05
First	11.07	11.55	13.72	12.55	15.15	17.5	12.55
Sidecar Gear Ratio—Top	4.74	4.73	5.72	5.72	—	—	5.72
Third	6.20	6.19	7.50	7.50	—	—	7.50
Second	8.05	8.04	9.72	9.72	—	—	9.72
First	12.55	12.35	15.15	15.15	—	—	15.15
Tyre Size: Dunlop—Front	3.25×19	3.00×20	3.00×20	3.00×20	3.00×20	2.75×19	3.25×19
Rear	4.00×18	3.50×19	3.50×19	3.25×19	3.25×19	2.75×19	3.25×19
Wheelbase (inches)	56	56	56	56	56	51½	56
Overall Length (inches)	86	86	86	86	86	80	86
Handlebar Width (inches)	27	27	27	27	27	27	27
Dual Seat Height (inches)	31	31	31	31	31	29½	*30
Ground Clearance (inches)	5½	5½	5½	5½	5½	5½	5½
Weight: fully equipped (lbs.)	435	410	390	375	365	270	362
Petrol Tank Capacity (gallons)	5	4	4	4	4	2½	4
Oil Tank Capacity (pints)	6	6	6	6	6	4	6
Petrol Consumption (M.P.G.)	65 – 70	65 – 70	75 – 80	75 – 80	80 – 85	120 – 130	65 – 70
Approximate Maximum Speed (M.P.H.)	95 – 100	90 – 95	85 – 90	80 – 85	70 – 75	60	65

*Saddle

NOTE. Speed and petrol consumption figures do not apply to new machines that have covered less than 2,000 miles. Petrol consumption figures are based on a maintained speed of 45 m.p.h.

1954 model year specifications.

What a surprise! The VB 600 in a swinging-arm frame but you could still opt for the old-style frame, with single sprung saddle if you found modernity totally abhorrent.

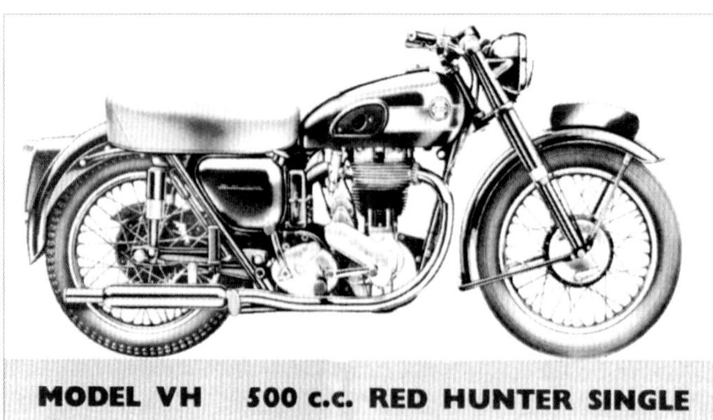

Only minor changes, such as the oil tank filler repositioned to avoid the rider's right leg. Although these illustrations are not in colour I think I'm right in telling you that 1955 was the year Ariel began to use tan vinyl to cover the dual seats on some models.

The Square Four, 'new look' or otherwise, was definitely not the kind of machine to traverse shingle or the kind of slippery surface one finds on the tideline, so I do hope he didn't make a fool of himself by trying to show off in front of the two popsies when it came time to leave.

I don't know whether others will agree but I have always found Ariel's hooded headlamp nacelle particularly unattractive. For some reason I'm also not keen on the look of the firm's alloy full-width brakes either, and to my mind BSA's short-lived adoption of the same did its machines no favours – especially as, at the front, they replaced the existing and very excellent 8in versions.

I've never really liked the appearance of a fully-enclosed rear transmission but there's no denying its practicality on all counts. Motor Cycling *liked it too when they tested one of these Red Hunters. They were impressed with the positive handling and described the latest full-width brakes as 'remarkable' and capable of bringing the bike to a halt in 29ft from 30mph. Its best speed turned out to be just over 86mph, with 70 available in third gear, and at a steady 50mph a gallon of fuel was consumed every 72 miles.*

When Ariel publicised its 1957 competition machinery it was by way of a separate leaflet.

It was with a much-modified version of a swinging-arm HT5 that Sammy Miller enjoyed unparalleled success for so many years. Its famous registration number GOV 132 had started life on one of three (rigid framed) works trials machines (GOV 130-132) registered by the factory in 1949. All were retained and used on subsequent team bikes but Miller's victories in literally hundreds of events with GOV, before he finally switched to Bultaco in 1965, are truly legendary.

The scrambles Hunter was a popular and not uncompetitive alternative to BSA's Gold Star or Matchless's G80CS in the United States and for that market it was available with QD lighting, a dynamo and battery. A MkII version with alternative front forks never reached production but a MkIII with slightly softer engine tune did. Prior to this the HS had single-sided brakes in line with then-current road Hunters but all switched to alloy full-width hubs in 1956.

Built-in instrument panel containing lighting switch, illuminated speedometer and ammeter.

"A lively lightweight from the Selly Oak stable," wrote Motor Cycling *of the Colt in the summer 1957 test. It'd cruise all day at 50 to 55 but when its 197cc was asked to cope with a pillion passenger the speed dropped to 40mph or a bit more, with a lot more gear changing to boot. Solo it would do just over 110 miles to a gallon if you stuck to 40mph, and just under 90 miles to a gallon if you did 50. Sounds like they gave it some stick in the intermediate gears when trying for performance, however: 62mph in top and 52 in third. "Valve float was imminent and the incipient jangle from the valve mechanism was accompanied by an immediate fall-off of power." Ouch!*

Classed as accessories for the British market, the chrome safety bars were standard in the US on Red Hunters, Huntmasters and Square Fours. The windshield was an extra in any country.

Features of Interest

Headlamp hood and fork cover.

New single bolt fixing petrol tank for all swinging arm models.

Quickly detachable rear wheel for all swinging arm models. All enclosed rear chain case as illustrated available for all swinging arm models at extra charge.

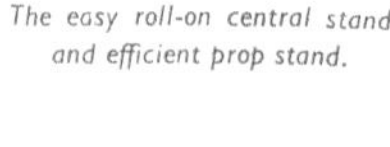

The easy roll-on central stand and efficient prop stand.

More economical to simply stick a label on the cover of this 1957 home-market brochure than to produce one especially for the United States, but surely US dealerships and customers alike would have appreciated factory sales material all of their own? It should be said, however, that Ariel wasn't alone amongst the larger manufacturers in its neglect to address this issue.

By 1957 the long-running Red Hunters had reached the end of the road development-wise and here they are in their final form – the 350 NH viewed from the timing side and the 500 VH from the drive side.

The 500 KH Fieldmaster had never proved popular and sales figures bore this out so it was discontinued at the end of the summer of '57.

"Swiftness, safety and docility characterise this model," was the header of Motor Cycling*'s summertime test of a 1957 Huntmaster. Since the advent of its swinging-arm frames Ariel had employed Burman C-type gearboxes (recognisable by the screw cap to gain access to and adjust the internal clutch lever) but the testers did have a small gripe concerning the occasional difficulty in engaging gears – particularly bottom. Otherwise, however, they liked the machine's 'reassuring' handling and reliable brakes, with the front being 'particularly good'. On several occasions, over 100mph was seen on the speedo but the timed maximum turned out to be 97mph at 5800rpm whilst (an unkind?) 1100rpm more gave them 91 in third gear. Throttled back to a steady 50mph they found that a gallon of fuel equated to 75 miles.*

The Square Four's oil tank had been enlarged as part of the continuing quest to alleviate borderline running temperatures and now held a full gallon.

What a dapper chappie: but what a twit too! A Squariel was more than capable of – and many would say more suitable for – sidecar use, so why didn't he turn up with it hitched to a smart single-seater Watsonian, or even better a Steib, if he was serious about a date with the young lady and her poodle? He gives the appearance of being sufficiently well heeled; or was he just window shopping?

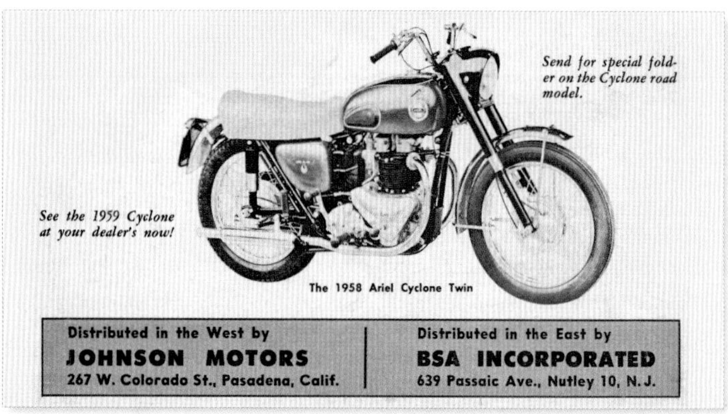

It was May 1958 and things were going well for him and his friends so the three, all keen motorcyclists, took a trip to Dallas to buy a new 'cycle' apiece. He was the oldest at 21, but barely looked it, and the youngest of them was only 17. Nevertheless, they didn't expect the cool reception they got from uptown dealerships, so they took a cab out to Oak Cliff and West Davis St where Ray Miller sold Triumphs and Ariels. It didn't take Ray too long to figure out who the youngsters were and that their money would be good. It was and they paid cash. The two teenagers had chosen Triumphs, a Trophy and a Thunderbird, but the eldest – how about him? His name was Buddy Holly, and he went for an Ariel Cyclone. Search the internet for 'Buddy Holly home movie footage' and you'll see the three of them fooling around with their bikes – wonderful stuff!

He's changed his jacket, followed the lady and her dog down to the beach, and is eyeing her up lasciviously. Looks like she's been to the hairdresser but I can't believe it was for his benefit, so let's hope little Alphonse (the poodle) gave him a nip that sent him on his way, or better still into the sea. Goodness knows what foreign prospects thought of these banal illustrations other than viewing them as being rather charmingly old-fashioned and very English. However, I doubt that a certain young man from Lubbock, Texas, Buddy Holly, ever saw them before he made up his mind to buy an Ariel…

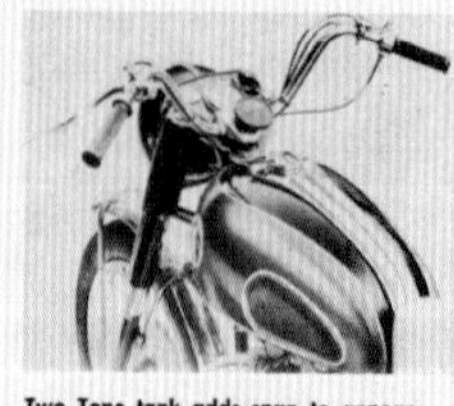

Two Tone tank adds snap to appearance on the new Cyclone Twin.

NEW — Super-performance engine—highest compression power unit ever produced by Ariel!
BRIGHT — Red and Black Two Tone finish, chrome fenders, lots of chrome and polished alloy!
BRAWNY — Big rugged 40 inch engine with heavy duty crankshaft, Burman heavy duty clutch and gearbox, sturdy double tube frame.
POWERFUL — Full width hubs and husky brakes for powerful braking action and freedom from fade.
BIG — A Big motorcycle with plenty of room for two — power to flatten the steepest hill.
GREAT — Great buy for any motorcycle enthusiast!

ARIEL HUNTMASTER TWIN: Ariel Huntmaster Twin in Touring trim also available

The BSA Road Rocket inspired Cyclone was definitely for the US market alone, and back in the UK, whoever you were, if you wanted an Ariel twin it was a Huntmaster and that was it. Some say there were less than fifty Cyclones made; but others have it that production was more like two hundred – either way it was a rarity and today rarer still.

Although for '58 the entire range could be had in Deep Claret or Black, most customers chose the former.

The last year for Ariel's flathead was 1958. The remainder of the lacklustre range would soldier on but only for a while, as something was afoot.

After a good deal of research into the type of machine that the majority of the motorcycling public would consider their ideal, Ariel's designers, headed by Val Page, came up with this – the revolutionary Leader that was revealed at the 1958 Motor Cycle Show. Would I be presumptuous to suggest its general outline was not dissimilar to that of the fully-enclosed Vincents that had been that firm's swansong?

At the beginning of October 1958 The Motor Cycle *published their findings on the new Ariel, which they described as a 'sprightly two-stroke twin with excellent road holding and steering'. Cold, hard facts recorded a best one-way speed of 69mph, with 57 attained in third and a petroil consumption of 82 miles to a gallon at a steady 40mph, or 73 at 50mph. Unlike the firm's vertical twins, and those of others come to that, the 250 two-stroke twin was 'delightfully smooth'. Its host of practical features, from thief-proofing to the adjustable (for height) headlamp beam, came in for praise too.*

The most advanced thought in motor cycle design—

Most attractive front panel fitted with the usual instruments, and in addition an Eight-day clock, Two-way parking lamp and switch, Flasher and Neutral indicator lamps. The handlebar and cables are completely enclosed and there is a spacious locker for parcels.

The Petrol Tank Filler Cap, Battery, Tyre Inflator and Tool Kit are neatly arranged under the Dualseat, which can be locked in the closed position.

The metal panniers and rear carrier blend perfectly with the general styling of the machine and provide ample luggage space. The plastic holdalls can be pre-packed, fitted into the Pannier, the lid replaced and locked. Front and rear Flashers with handlebar switch can be fitted as an aid to safe driving.

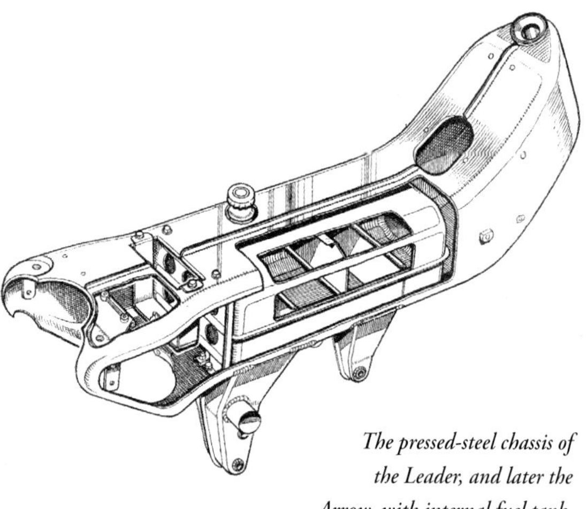

The pressed-steel chassis of the Leader, and later the Arrow, with internal fuel tank.

Engine	Twin cylinder two stroke
Bore and stroke .	54 x 54 mm. (2⅛″ x 2⅛″)
Capacity . .	249 c.c. (15.2 cu. in.)
Compression ratio	8.25 - 1
Engine B.H.P. .	16
Engine R.P.M. .	6400
Gear ratios—top .	5.9
,, ,, —third	8.5
,, ,, —second	11.0
,, ,, —first .	19.0
Engine revs. top gear .	1000=11 m.p.h. (17.7 k.p.h.)
Tyre—front . .	Ribbed, white wall 16 x 3.25″
,, —rear . .	Studded, white wall 16 x 3.25″
Wheelbase . .	51″ (130 cm.)
Overall length .	73½″ (187 cm.)
Overall width .	24½″ (62.5 cm.)
Dualseat height .	30″ (76.2 cm.)
Ground clearance	5″ (12.7 cm.)
Weight standard spec. .	300 lb. (136 kilogm.)
Petrol tank capacity	2½ gallons, reserve ½ gallon (11.4 litre)
Petrol consumption	80/90 m.p.g. (28/32 k.p.l.)
Approx. maximum speed	70 m.p.h. (113 k.p.h.)

NOTE

Speed and petrol consumption figures apply to machines that have been run in for 1,000 miles (1609 km.)

Petrol consumption figures are based on a steady speed of 40 m.p.h. (64.5 k.p.h.).

The 250 c.c. Twin Cylinder Two-Stroke engine of Ariel design and manufacture has been developed to give high maximum power consistent with durability, economy, easy starting and to require maintenance only after long periods of service. Cruising at, say, 50/55 m.p.h., the Turbine-like smoothness of the well-balanced twin engine is at once apparent. There is ample power to climb main road hills in top gear, and when 3rd or 2nd gear is engaged the high revving engine immediately responds to give thrilling acceleration or a brisk climb of the steepest hill. Engine and gearbox are of unit construction. The gearbox has four well-chosen gear ratios, foot operated and all components have a large margin of safety. For general maintenance the design is such that the whole of the engine or gearbox can be dismantled while the unit is in the frame.

Steel pressings of high quality have been extensively used in the construction of the "Leader". The outer shell, side panels, front shield, etc., which constitute the external form or enclosure have been attractively styled and beautifully finished, while the internal or stressed parts are extremely strong yet light in weight. The frame, for example, consists of two deep steel pressings welded together to form a long hollow member. The front end carries the steering head and the rear end the suspension dampers. The petrol tank, battery and ignition coils are housed inside the frame.

Full weather protection is provided by a large curved front shield which extends downwards to form legshields. A large swept back Perspex windscreen is affixed to the top of the shield and extends at the side to handlebar width so that the rider's hands and body have complete weather protection. It is so shaped that the handlebars will turn to full lock within the screen. There is an attractively styled instrument panel furnished with all necessary instruments with provision for extra fittings when required. The headlamp beam can be adjusted to the correct height by moving a simple lever. This is an additional refinement to normal headlamp dipping device.

The front forks of unique design, have a pair of trailing links and two-way hydraulic damping. The two tubular stanchions are of immense strength and in conjunction with the general design, the forks impart a new high standard of precision control to the steering and adds considerably to road safety and improved tyre wear.

The Dualseat hinges to give access to the battery, tool kit, tyre inflator and petrol filler cap. The tail member hinges upwards for tyre inspection or wheel removal. At the forward part of the outer shell is a spacious parcel locker. A thief-proof steering lock and Dualseat lock are made secure from inside the locker by locking the lid. The machine is then immobilised and proofed against petty theft.

The two side panels which give complete engine unit enclosure are readily detachable by undoing five captive screws on each panel. Most of the running adjustments can be made from the near side of the machine but if it is necessary to remove the offside panel, the kickstarter and gear pedal have also to be removed by unscrewing one pinch bolt on each.

The brakes are powerful yet smooth in action and the stop light is operated by both front and rear brake controls. Full width light alloy hubs are fitted front and rear, and light alloy brake shoes have adequate area of non-fade linings. Large section white wall tyres on 16″ diameter rims ensure comfort, good wheel grip and long life.

Clean handlebars with concealed cables have the usual controls of twist grip, clutch and brake levers, horn push and dipper switch.

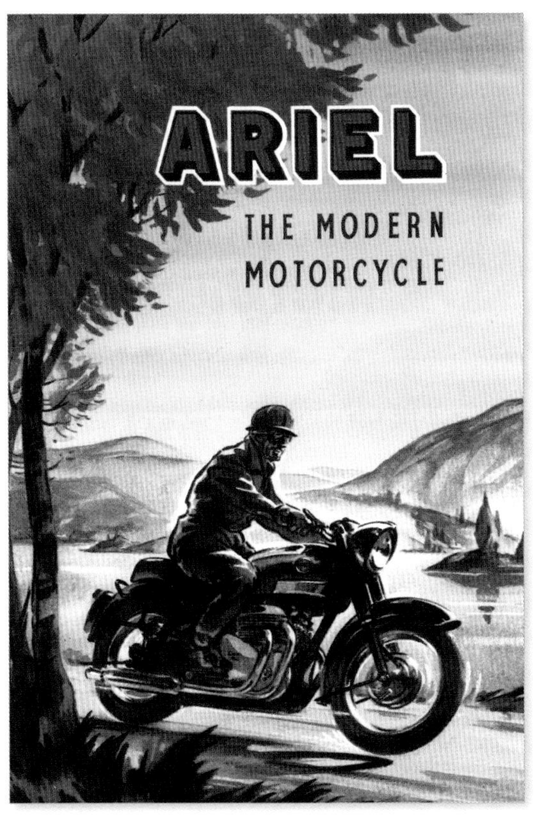

The cover of the main 1959 brochure saw a Square Four scurrying across a slightly surreal landscape on its last date – the one with oblivion. The end of its road, and the rest of old stagers too for that matter, would come at the end of the season.

ENGINE: Vertical O.H.V. 70×84 mm.=646 c.c. (2·76×3·30=39·3 cubic inches). Cast iron cylinders and heads. Vachrome top piston rings. Forged steel crankshaft mounted on heavy duty roller and white metal lined bearing. Light alloy connecting rods with lead-bronze liners. Gear driven camshaft. Magneto with automatic advance. Amal 'Monobloc' carburetter with air cleaner.

FRAME: Duplex cradle type. Swinging arm rear suspension. Hydraulic damping. Lugs for sidecar attachment either side. Stands: easy-lift spring-up central and strong tubular front, also foot operated prop stand.

FRONT FORKS: Telescopic with hydraulic damping.

HUBS: Full width polished light alloy, fitted with heavy duty ball bearings front and rear. Powerful central brakes with non-fade linings. Car type fulcrum adjustment. Quickly detachable rear wheel.

TRANSMISSION: Four-speed gearbox, foot control. Three-plate dry clutch. Engine shaft shock absorber. Polished aluminium oil bath primary chain case.

EQUIPMENT: Basic price includes air cleaner; prop stand; thief-proof steering lock; quickly detachable rear wheel; pillion footrests; trip speedometer, 120 m.p.h. (180 km.p.h.); 7½ in. headlamp; 56 watt dynamo; 12 amp. battery; stop and tail lamp incorporating reflector; electric horn; tool box and tools; tyre inflator.

FINISH: Superbly finished in Deep Claret, Glamour Red, or all Black.

For some reason the Huntmaster had a publicity flyer all of its own for its last year of production.

MODEL	4G	VH	NH	LH
TYPE	O.H.V.	O.H.V.	O.H.V.	O.H.V.
Number of Cylinders	4	1	1	1
Bore and Stroke	65×75	81.8×95	72×85	60×70
Cylinder Capacity	997	497	347	197
Compression Ratio	7.2	7	7	7.5
Engine B.H.P.	42	26	19	10
Engine R.P.M.	5,800	6,000	5,600	5,600
Engine Sprocket: No. of Teeth—Solo	25	23	19	17
Sidecar	22	19	17	—
Solo Gear Ratio— Top	4.36	4.74	5.72	7.0
Third	5.70	6.20	7.50	8.5
Second	7.40	8.05	9.72	11.6
First	11.55	12.55	15.15	17.5
Sidecar Gear Ratio—Top	4.95	5.72	6.4	—
Third	6.50	7.50	8.37	—
Second	8.42	9.72	10.88	—
First	13.10	15.15	16.96	—
Tyre Size— Front	3.25×19	3.25×19	3.25×19	3.00×19
Rear	4.00×18	3.25×19	3.25×19	3.00×19
Wheelbase (inches)	56	56	56	51½
Overall Length (inches)	86	86	86	80
Handlebar Width (inches)	27	27	27	27
Dualseat Height (inches)	31	31	31	29½
Ground Clearance (inches)	5½	5½	5½	5½
Weight Fully Equipped (lbs.)	435	375	365	270
Petrol Tank Capacity (gallons)	5	4½	4½	2½
Oil Tank Capacity (pints)	8	6	6	4
Petrol Consumption (M.P.G.)	70–75	75–80	85–90	100–110
Approx. Mean and Max. Speeds (M.P.H.)	100–105	80–85	75–80	55–60

NOTE. Speed and petrol consumption figures do not apply to new machines that have covered less than 2,000 miles. Petrol consumption figures are based on a maintained speed of 45 m.p.h.; Model LH at 35 m.p.h. With child-adult sidecar fitted, reduce above m.p.g. figures approximately by 20.

Vital statistics of the very much-reduced 1959 range of four-strokes showed few changes from those of several seasons before. Glamour Red and Black, as used for the Cyclone, had now been added to the existing colours of Deep Claret or all Black, however.

With the Leader a little over a year old a sporting version was introduced in the autumn of 1959. In truth, apart from its lighter weight (275lb against 315lb) and looks, it was no more sporting than the Leader due to their mechanical specification being identical – the manufacturer's sales material even suggesting the same approximate top speed of 70mph. Arrows were however ridden, often as not, in a much more sporting manner than their siblings and on twisty going proved to be something of an unlikely giant-killer.

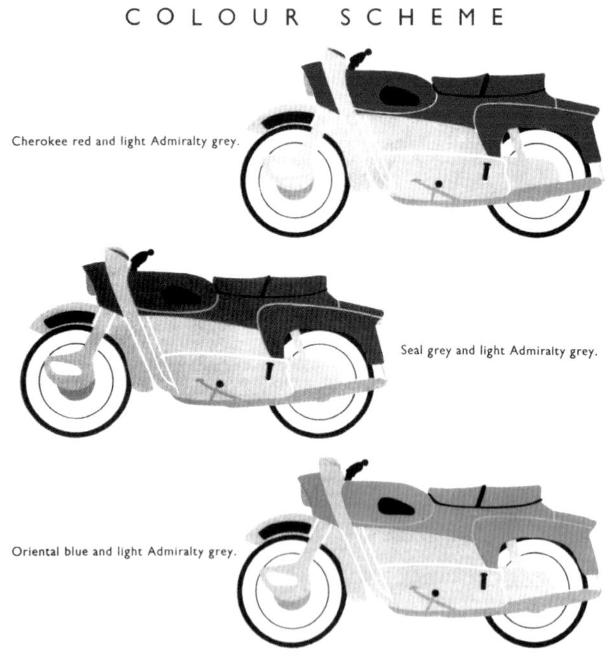

Cherokee red and light Admiralty grey.

Seal grey and light Admiralty grey.

Oriental blue and light Admiralty grey.

Engine
Robust 250 c.c. (15.2 cu. in.) twin cylinder two-stroke of Ariel design and manufacture, operating on the loop scavenging principle, has separate ported cast iron cylinders and alloy heads, with deep directional finning arranged for maximum cooling, each pair secured to the crankcase by four studs and high tensile steel sleeve nuts; built up crankshaft of exceptional rigidity mounted on three heavy duty ball bearings; there is a taper and key coupling in the middle of the shaft secured by a bolt, which is easily accessible through the hollow main shaft for easy servicing; the crankcase pressure is held by four self-adjusting rubber oil seals; the crankcase gearbox unit is of light alloy; the Lucas 50 watt A.C. generator is spigot mounted on the offside of the crankcase with a twin contact breaker assembly on the nearside; the primary drive is by $\frac{3}{8}$" pitch endless chain fitted with a rubber-covered spring steel adjuster for silent running, it has external adjustment; each big end has a double row roller bearing; the Amal Monobloc carburetter has a cold starting device and lubrication is by the petroil system.

Gearbox and Transmission
Four speed with foot control; the Ariel patented clutch incorporates a rubber cush drive and is of the three-plate wet type; the $\frac{1}{2}$" pitch rear chain is totally enclosed and automatically lubricated from the primary chaincase.

Frame and Fittings
Engine is secured to underslung extension of the frame by three long bolts, the lower high tensile bolt also carries the swinging arm of the rear suspension which is pivoted on rubber bushes. By unscrewing these three bolts the engine–gearbox unit, with rear wheel and chaincase, can be withdrawn, the box type rear frame extension forms an air intake silencer having the carburetter connection at the front and a large efficient air filter with easily replaceable element on the offside.

Front Forks
These are of the trailing link type with long coil suspension springs, supporting two-way hydraulic dampers they are contained within the two large diameter stanchion tubes; the patented link motion gives a constant wheelbase, the action eliminating uneven tyre wear; all swivelling points have anti-friction nylon bushes.

Full Width Hubs
The hubs are fitted with heavy duty ball bearings, whilst the wheels are quickly detachable. The brakes are 6" diameter and are genuine full width.

Mudguards
The front guard has a deep valance with concealed fixing to the fork stanchion tubes. The rear tail section forms the rear guard, this is also of deep section.

Dualseat
Scientifically designed sponge rubber interior, shaped for maximum comfort and trimmed with best quality waterproof material.

Standard Equipment
Easy lift central stand, 100 m.p.h. speedometer, ammeter, ignition and lighting switch, lightweight 13 amp. hour 6 volt Lucas heavy duty battery, A.C. generator and rectifier, 6" diameter pre-focus headlamp with double filament and pilot bulbs, electric horn, folding pillion footrests, licence holder, knee grips, set of tools and tyre inflator.

Finish
The machine has a remarkably fine finish in best quality stove enamel, colour two-tone light grey and seal grey. Wheel rims, silencers, levers and other bright parts heavily chromium plated.

Optional Extras (See separate price list)
Prop stand; detachable front stand; carrier (pressed steel); dualseat waterproof cover; windscreen; white wall tyres; dualseat strap; three gallon fuel tank (fitted ex Works only).

The Motor Cycle*'s ace tester, as well as experienced road racer, Vic Willoughby tried out an early example and if someone such as he wrote that it had 'magnificent steering and road holding' it really meant something. Its surefootedness under all conditions was attributed to the torsional stiffness of the pressed-steel beam-type frame. So impressed was he, in fact, that he omitted to mention that he had been victim to the Arrow's 'sting in the stand' and had the sole of his boot perforated. Owners will know what I mean by this, and would-be owners watch out! Note that the artist omitted to show the seam just forward of the grab handle and rear suspension unit, thus giving the false impression that frame and rear mudguard were in one piece.*

That's a map in her hand but surely she's not even thinking of jumping on the pillion of her boyfriend's Arrow dressed like this? No – she's the boatyard owner's rather glam wife who's simply giving the errand boy directions whilst another, similarly mounted, waits his turn. By the time that Motor Cycling *tested one of these in the autumn of 1960 the improved '61 model was put at their disposal. Ariel's two-stroke twins now had oval, as opposed to H-section, connecting roads, squish-type heads with central sparking plugs and a compression ratio of 10:1. Nevertheless the best they could get out of it was just under 73mph with the rider flat on the tank, but fuel consumption was better than the manufacturer claimed, working out at 84mpg overall. Acceleration, steering and road holding were, however, the Arrow's forte rather than top speed and brakes, which were never the two-stroke Ariel's strong point.*

The Leader's number plate on the cover of the 1960 brochure is a trifle misleading as by that time the model was well-established and had in fact recently been the winner of the newly-inaugurated Motor Cycle News *motorcycle of the year award. This year it would be the turn of the Arrow to garner what its manufacturer was proud to term the Blue Riband of the motorcycle industry; the Leader was runner up.*

She's hardly dressed for motorcycling but they look like overnight bags, so if they're not going to get changed before setting out they will at least have excellent weather protection on their Leader.

The Pixie, introduced in 1963, with its scaled-down BSA Beagle motor, was one of the British motorcycle industry's unsuccessful attempts to retaliate against the large numbers of Japanese featherweights that were proving so popular.

Engine: Single cylinder O.H.V., bore 38.9 mm.; stroke 42 mm., Capacity 50 c.c. Aluminium alloy cylinder head. Ignition by flywheel magneto. Totally enclosed and lubricated valve gear.

Gearbox & Transmission: Four-speed foot-operated gearbox integral with engine. Final chain drive with effective guard.

Body Shell: Comprises two deep steel pressings welded together to form an attractively styled body of great strength. The head-lamp is enclosed in the front section, the centre section houses the fuel tank and the rear section carries the seat.

Sub-frame: A unique design feature which carries the engine-gearbox unit, pivoted fork rear suspension and the rear wheel and chainguard, all of which can be removed instantly from the body shell for servicing.

Suspension: Front forks of proven Ariel design for precise steering and comfort. Patented link motion with rubber-in-compression units, used also for the pivoted fork rear suspension. All bearings incorporate Nylon bushes, grease packed "for life" during assembly and require no further attention.

Wheels & Brakes: Strongly spoked wheels with 2.50 × 15 in. studded tyres front and rear. Powerful, smooth acting 4 in. diameter brakes on each wheel mounted in full width hubs. Efficient mudguarding for both wheels.

Seat & Tool Container: Seat has scientifically designed sponge interior which is upholstered in contrasting waterproof plastic. The seat hinges rearward to reveal tyre inflator, petrol filler cap, and large tool compartment.

Controls: Pressed steel handlebar, adjustable for height, carries twistgrip throttle, clutch and brake levers and horn push. Provision for central speedometer mounting.

Electrical Equipment: Crankshaft mounted magneto/alternator with separate ignition and lighting coils. 18 watt 6 volt headlamp with main and dipped beams. Electric horn, tail lamp and reflector.

Finish: Best quality Ivory stove enamel with choice of two-tone finish for handlebar unit, rear pivoted fork and chainguard. Wheel rims, silencer and other bright parts heavily chrome plated.

Optional Extras: Windscreen, Leg Shields, Rear Panniers, Rear Carrier, Speedometer, Rear Fender, Driving Mirrors, Shopping Basket.

Dimensions:
Wheelbase - - - 42 ins.
Overall Length - - 64 ins.
Seat Height - - 26½ ins. (Rider seated)
Width - - - 22½ ins. (Over handlebar)
Minimum Ground Clearance - - 4 ins.
Petrol Capacity - 1⅛ gallons
Oil Capacity - - 1¼ pints
Weight - - - 115 lbs.
Performance — speed up to 45 m.p.h.

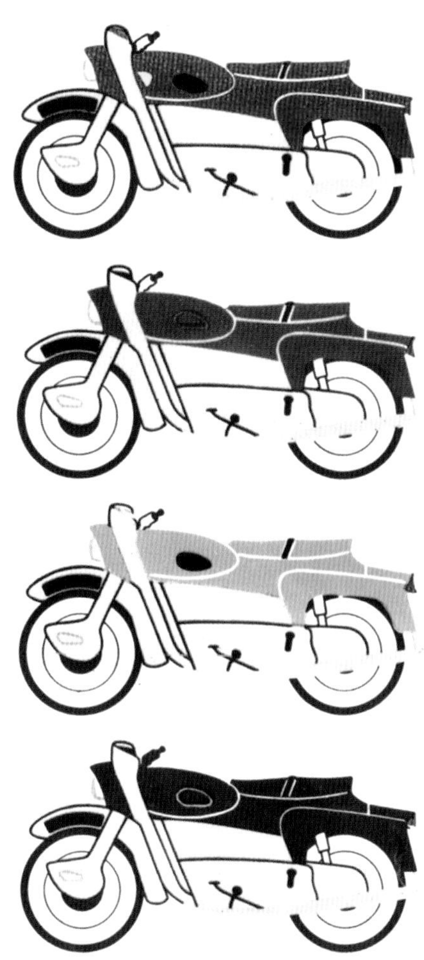

Technical improvements for the 1962 model year meant improved electrics such as uprated alternator, key-operated ignition switch and new high-frequency Lucas 8H horn. Brakes had come in for attention also, with car-type anti-squeal springs now fitted and the back plates redesigned to cut down ingress of water. Who amongst you have noticed that the kneepads now had a polished aluminium surround?

Visually the range had been, the maker said, spruced up with a fresh base colour of Ivory, instead of the previous Admiralty Grey. For the Leader there was a choice of Cherokee Red, Oriental Blue, Seal Grey or Black to go over the Ivory but the Arrow was only in Black over Ivory.

Big news for Arrow enthusiasts had been the Super Sports or Golden Arrow at the beginning of 1961. In line with its stablemates it had the same Admiralty Grey base colour but with gold tank – the former changing to Ivory for '62. Ritzy colour scheme, polished chain case, low bars and canted screen apart it had a full 20hp against its siblings' 17.5. The manufacturer's published data, however, tells us that it achieved this at 500rpm less than its more pedestrian chums (6,500 against 7,000rpm). Compression ratio was the same but the carb was a throatier 1$\frac{1}{16}$in Amal monobloc against the $\frac{7}{8}$in instrument employed on regular Arrows and Leaders. When The Motor Cycle *got around to testing one early in 1962 they managed a scorching (for a 250) quarter-mile time of 17.6 seconds and an absolute maximum speed of 81mph.*

SPECIFICATION:

ENGINE: Robust 250 c.c. (15.2 cu. in.) twin cylinder, two-stroke of Ariel design and manufacture. Separate ported cast-iron cylinders and alloy heads, built-up crankshaft mounted on three heavy-duty ball bearings. The crankcase gearbox unit is of light alloy. Lucas 55 watt A.C. generator. The primary drive is by $\frac{3}{8}$" pitch endless chain. Each big end has a double row roller bearing. Large bore Amal Monobloc carburetter with cold starting device.
GEARBOX: Four-speed with foot control.
FRAME: Engine is secured to frame by three long bolts, the lower high tensile bolt carrying the swinging arm of the rear suspension.
FRONT FORKS: These are of the trailing link type with long coil suspension springs supporting two-way hydraulic dampers. Constant wheelbase.
FULL WIDTH HUBS: Fitted with heavy-duty ball bearings. Quickly detachable wheels, 6" dia. Brakes, incorporating water excluders.
STANDARD EQUIPMENT: Easy lift central stand, prop stand, 100 m.p.h. speedometer, ammeter, combined key ignition and emergency start switch, lighting switch, lightweight 13 amp/hour 6 volt Lucas heavy duty battery, A.C. generator and rectifier, 6" diameter pre-focus headlamp with double filament and pilot bulb, electric horn, folding pillion footrests, folding kickstarter, special sports pattern handlebars with sports windscreen and ball ended control levers, reserve type petrol tap, licence holder, knee grips, set of tools and inflator.
FINISH: The machine has a super finish in best quality stove enamel. Colour: two-tone Gold and Ivory. Engine cover, fork cover plate, toolbox lid, lifting handles, wheel rims, silencers, levers and other decorative trim are heavily chromed. The alloy chaincase of this model is highly polished.

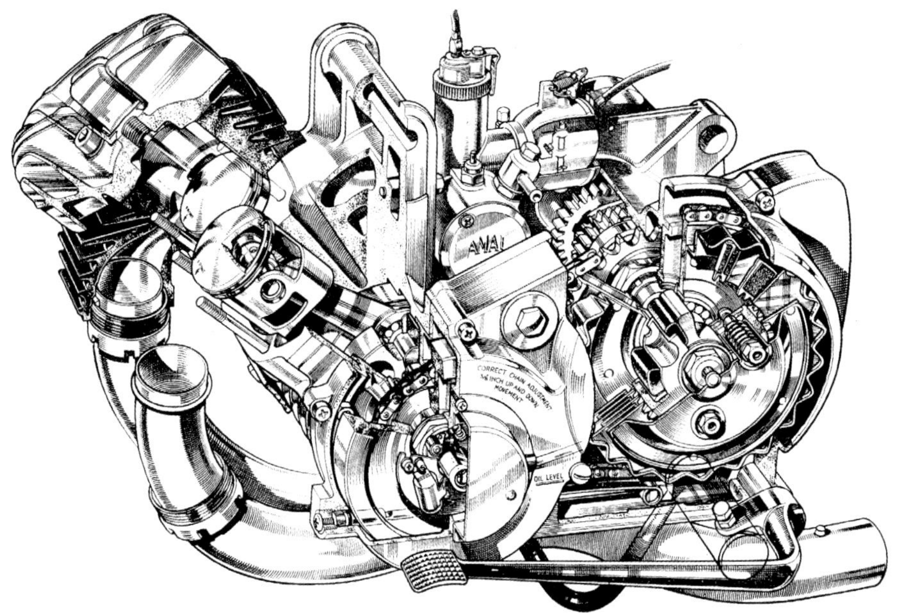

Ariel's 54x54mm 249cc two-stroke in in its final form. For inspiration Val Page had looked closely at the German Adler MB twin.

October, 1962.

ARIEL BSA TRIUMPH

The Birmingham Small Arms Motor Cycle and Scooter Policy

Underwritten by The Minster Insurance Co. Ltd.

THE BIRMINGHAM SMALL ARMS Co., Ltd. ARMOURY ROAD, BIRMINGHAM 11.

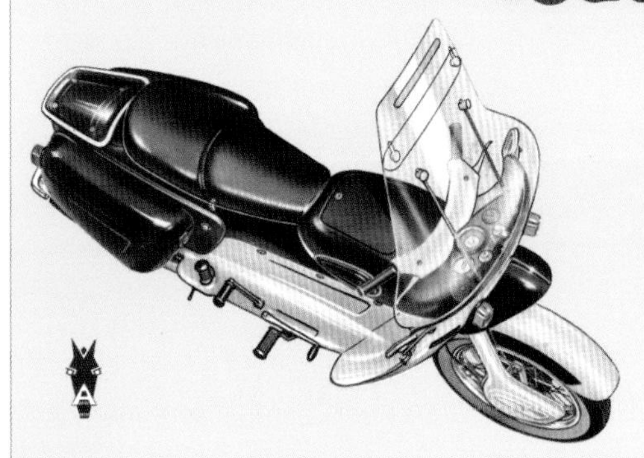

The Leader on the cover of the 1963 brochure had been dressed up with quite a number of optional extras, including the flashing indicator set, windscreen extension, rear fender with reflectors, carrier, pannier cases and mirrors fitted to the front shield. Can you spot any more?

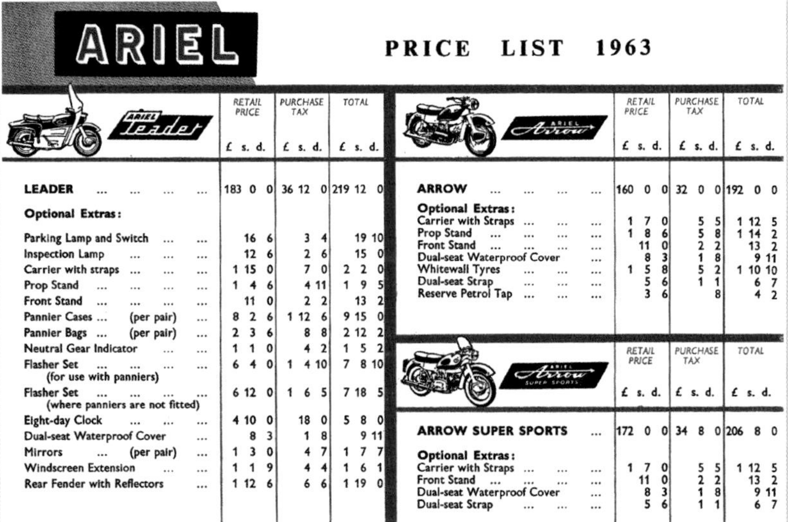

ARIEL — PRICE LIST 1963

Ariel Leader	RETAIL PRICE £ s. d.	PURCHASE TAX £ s. d.	TOTAL £ s. d.
LEADER	183 0 0	36 12 0	219 12 0
Optional Extras:			
Parking Lamp and Switch	16 6	3 4	19 10
Inspection Lamp	12 6	2 6	15 0
Carrier with straps	1 15 0	7 0	2 2 0
Prop Stand	1 4 6	4 11	1 9 5
Front Stand	11 0	2 2	13 2
Pannier Cases ... (per pair) ...	8 2 6	1 12 6	9 15 0
Pannier Bags ... (per pair) ...	2 3 6	8 8	2 12 2
Neutral Gear Indicator	1 1 0	4 2	1 5 2
Flasher Set ... ... (for use with panniers)	6 4 0	1 4 10	7 8 10
Flasher Set ... ... (where panniers are not fitted)	6 12 0	1 6 5	7 18 5
Eight-day Clock	4 10 0	18 0	5 8 0
Dual-seat Waterproof Cover ...	8 3	1 8	9 11
Mirrors ... (per pair) ...	1 3 0	4 7	1 7 7
Windscreen Extension	1 1 9	4 4	1 6 1
Rear Fender with Reflectors ...	1 12 6	6 6	1 19 0

Ariel Arrow	RETAIL PRICE £ s. d.	PURCHASE TAX £ s. d.	TOTAL £ s. d.
ARROW	160 0 0	32 0 0	192 0 0
Optional Extras:			
Carrier with Straps	1 7 0	5 5	1 12 5
Prop Stand	1 8 6	5 8	1 14 2
Front Stand	11 0	2 2	13 2
Dual-seat Waterproof Cover ...	8 3	1 8	9 11
Whitewall Tyres	1 5 8	5 2	1 10 10
Dual-seat Strap	5 6	1 1	6 7
Reserve Petrol Tap	3 6	8	4 2

Ariel Arrow Super Sports	RETAIL PRICE £ s. d.	PURCHASE TAX £ s. d.	TOTAL £ s. d.
ARROW SUPER SPORTS ...	172 0 0	34 8 0	206 8 0
Optional Extras:			
Carrier with Straps	1 7 0	5 5	1 12 5
Front Stand	11 0	2 2	13 2
Dual-seat Waterproof Cover ...	8 3	1 8	9 11
Dual-seat Strap	5 6	1 1	6 7

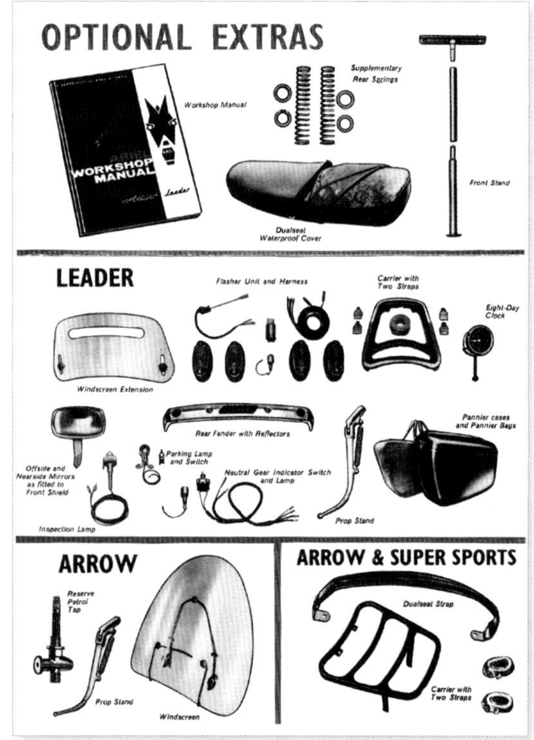

BAC

It beggars belief how someone who had worked in the design department of an aircraft manufacturer and then held government contracts to produce aircraft components could even imagine that this flimsy strip-steel arrangement was suitable for motorcycle front forks (illustrated here in pre-production advertising). True, Lawrie Bond soon came partially to his senses regarding that aspect of his design but the fact that he thought it sound engineering in the first place raises a question mark over the structural integrity of the rest of what, on the face of it, appears to be akin to aeronautical construction – albeit ugly with a capital U.

A sibling of the Bond three-wheeler car by designer rather than manufacturer, the BAC was one of Lawrence 'Lawrie' Bond's many brainchildren.

After serving an apprenticeship with the steam lorry manufacturer Atkinson he worked in the drawing office of Henry Meadows's Wolverhampton engineering works during the 1930s, moving on to Blackburn Aircraft's design department where he spent the early years of World War Two. Latterly, however, he established the Bond Aircraft and Engineering Company (Blackpool) Ltd, to take advantage of government contracts that were available to suppliers of aircraft components.

The going was good as long as the war lasted, but when it ended the work did also.

The name Blackpool was dropped from the company's name after a move of 20-or-so miles to Longridge and it was there that he set about his next ventures.

The Bond Minicar was amongst the first of these and, once proven that it had possibilities beyond the prototypical stage, the manufacturing rights were sold to Sharp's Commercials of nearby Preston.

Whilst Bond's three-wheeler car had been under development he'd been planning an unconventional lightweight motorcycle, and this then took precedence. It was to be powered by a 98cc Villiers Mk1F – the staple unit for Britain's smallest motorcycles at that time – but there any similarity to other makes ended, apart from the fact it had two wheels. Constructed largely of aluminium around a tapered oval tube, it really was an extraordinary looking device and was devoid of either front or rear suspension, other than the cushioning effect of relatively large-section low-pressure tyres. This proved insufficient, however, and after persistent fracturing of the tubular front forks that had replaced Mr Bond's initial and misguided ideas as to how that part of the machine should be put together, the design was modified to incorporate telescopic dampers.

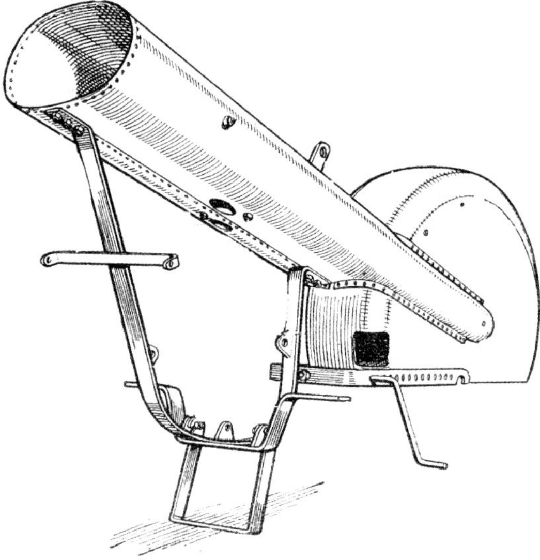

Space heater? Potato gun? Leaf blower? No – it's the basic structure of Mr Bond's mini motorcycle.

Production commenced at the beginning of 1950, and quite how many Minibykes were made by Bond's firm are, as far as I know, unrecorded. But by midsummer the manufacturing rights had been sold to John Ellis of Leeds.

Either having learnt from his first foray into two-wheeled transport, or happy to distance himself from it, Laurie Bond's next motorcycle was quite a conventional, if diminutive, machine. This motorcycle was named the Lilliput on account of its size and – unintentionally, as its originator was soon to find out – its sales potential too. For it to compete with other identically-engined 98cc tiddlers from such established makers as James or Sun it had to offer something extra – or less, in the form of a cheaper price. But it did neither, and was discontinued sometime in 1952 after just a couple of hundred-or-so had been made.

Concurrently with the Lilliput, Bond was involved making a scooter that he named the Gazelle but it (probably deservedly on account of sharing its front forks and suspensionless rear with the Minibyke) proved to be less popular than his little motorcycle. With the luck of the devil he managed to persuade Projects and Developments of Blackburn to give him some money for the latest of his white elephants. Completely rehashed and now powered by a 197 Villiers with electric starting, it was renamed the Oscar and appeared at the 1953 Show. But that was the last we heard of it.

In the mid '50s Bond had yet another go and came up with a scooter he called the Sherpa – it too went nowhere.

Lest it be thought that I am too unkind about Laurie Bond's undeniably inventive mind it should be mentioned that he built and competed in a number of single-seater racing cars; the first being his tiny 500cc Rudge-engined Doodlebug of 1947, with which he demonstrated his predilection for no suspension other than that imparted by the tyres. It is to his credit that he won his class with it at Bouley Bay hillclimb, before finding out the reason cars are fitted with suspension when he left the course with a bounce, skip and a roll at Shelsley Walsh. His next 500 did have suspension but with front-wheel drive via chain as well as wire-and-bobbin steering. Production was planned.

Later he collaborated with caravan manufacturer Berkeley, the outcome of which were the fibreglass-monocoque Berkeley three- and four-wheeler sports cars. By 1960 he was running Lawrence Bond Cars at Loxwood in Essex, where a pair of Formula Junior single-seaters were built to advanced specification. Just one had been completed and raced a couple of times before the company folded, however, and Lawrie Bond took himself off to the north of England to run a pub.

BOND MINIBYKE

FOR BUSINESS OR PLEASURE IN ANY WEATHER

The "BOND MINIBYKE" with its 98c.c. Villiers engine and 2-speed gearbox, will take you anywhere in comfort, and keep you clean. It is the most economical form of transport possible and yet has a performance only previously associated with much larger motor cycles. It will cruise comfortably and silently at 35-40 m.p.h., and has a maximum speed of over 45 m.p.h., and a petrol consumption of over 200 miles per gallon.

£55-0-0 plus **£14-17-0** purchase tax

BOND AIRCRAFT & ENG. CO. LTD.
TOWNELEY WORKS, LONGRIDGE, LANC'S

By early 1950, when the Minibyke went into production, the front forks were tubular but they were initially still devoid of any form of springing.

SPECIFICATION

ENGINE. Villiers 98 c.c. Mark I.F. with two-speed Gearbox in unit construction. The engine has a bore and stroke of 47mm. x 57mm., and exclusive features are detachable aluminium alloy cylinder head, flat-top aluminium alloy piston, ball-bearing crankshaft and roller-bearing big end.

GEARBOX. (Two-speed.) This is in unit construction with the engine and is operated by finger-tip control lever mounted on the handlebars—all gears are constant mesh with sliding dog. The overall gear ratios are 8.75 low gear and 5.65 top gear. The drive is taken through a cork insert two-plate clutch, running in oil. The gearbox is fitted with a kick starter with folding pedal.

CARBURETTER. Villiers single lever with air cleaning and strangler, throttle controlled by lever on handlebars.

IGNITION AND LIGHTING. Is by Villiers flywheel magneto generator which, in addition to producing H.T. current for ignition, also provides L.T. current for lighting. This is used in conjunction with a 5½in. headlamp containing parking battery. A dipping switch is mounted on the handlebars.

LUBRICATION. Petroil, I part of oil to 16 parts of petrol. The gearbox and primary chain drive are lubricated through an easily accessible filler plug, and a special level plug is provided to ensure correct oil level.

FRAME. An exclusive B.A.C. design incorporating an unusual system of welded tubes and cradle plate giving immense strength with incredible lightness. Special telescopic forks of B.A.C. design are fitted with compression and rebound springs. Mattress-type saddle with three-point suspension. Central stand with automatic return. Tank capacity I½ gallons.

WHEELS. Special B.A.C. design taking 20in. x 2in. tyres. Deep section mud-guards. 3½in. internal expanding hub brakes, front operated by handlebar lever, rear by pedal.

TRANSMISSION. Is by roller chain throughout. The primary chain runs in an oil bath, and the driving chain is enclosed in an efficient deep chain guard.

EQUIPMENT AND FINISH. Tool kit, tyre pump and horn. The whole machine is finished in polychromatic bronze and maroon, with chromium-plated handle-bars, exhaust pipe, silencer, etc.

GENERAL DETAILS. Weight 92lb.; wheelbase 45in.; saddle height 25½in.

NOTICE.—This specification may be altered without notice.

BOND

John Ellis had many varied and successful business interests in and around Leeds, amongst which was Motor Distributors (Leeds) Ltd – a sizable dealership that supplied motorcycles, cars and commercial vehicles, as well as housing Ellis's growing collection of vintage vehicles. As if he didn't already have enough to occupy him he had ambition to become a manufacturer, and a conversation with Ewatt Bradshaw (brother of aero and motorcycle engine designer as well as co-founder of ABC motorcycles Granville) is reputed to have set him on the path to become one. Bradshaw, too, had many strings to his bow and amongst these was the Loxhams Group that owned Sharp's Commercials, the manufacturer of the Bond three-wheeler. Its originator had also, Ellis learnt, begun to produce his own design of small motorcycle, the 98cc Minibyke, but would be more than happy to turn it over to someone else in the same way as he had with his car to Sharps. With the Minibyke seemingly proven, Ellis came to a financial agreement regarding the rights with Laurie Bond and became the manufacturer.

Within a short time an additional 125cc De-Luxe version was catalogued; but once numbers of both types had been in service for a while, some elements of the machine's design and construction began to show shortcomings – primarily failure of the pop-riveted frame structure. To his credit, Ellis had already done away with the length of steel strip (cut from the same material as the Minibyke's original forks?) that Bond had seen fit to use as a front frame tube-cum-engine cradle in favour of tubing. He would also experiment with rear suspension, as well as steel instead of aluminium mudguards, but to little avail because the overall design was compromised.

Nevertheless the things continued to be made and, perhaps more surprisingly, enough customers came forward to warrant the production of around 500 of them before Ellis called it a day in the late summer of 1953. Somewhat poignantly, when he retired to Ireland a few years later, amongst the vast collection of vehicles that he took with him were a small number of unsold Minibykes as a kind of memento.

Poor John Ellis, landing himself with this contraption – even in this 'improved' format. His desire to become a motorcycle manufacturer must have temporarily deprived him of all reason, or maybe Mr Bond was simply a very smooth talker, as the Minibyke must surely be a strong contender for, if not the winner of, the Beastliest 1950s' British Motorcycle Award. I'm not at all sure that one of these was ever submitted for a full road test but I cannot imagine that its designer's initial claims of 50mph and 200mpg would have been realised. Still, they were finished in an attractive shade of blue.

BOWN (SEE ABERDALE)

BROCKHOUSE

(ALSO SEE CORGI)

During the 1880s John Brockhouse started a small firm specialising in forging of components such as springs for vehicles, and by the turn of the century had prospered to such a degree that the company carrying his name had gone public. There followed a period of further expansion, which included the acquisition of other firms engaged in allied iron and steel trades, so that by the First World War the company was well placed to reap enormous profits.

The inter-war years saw a continued policy of takeovers and absorptions – the post-depression '30s in particular adding firms such as Bell's, which produced AGA cookers, and the long-troubled commercial vehicle manufacturer Vulcan. Vulcan's large Southport factory site had been the main aim of the latter manoeuvre, and it became Brockhouse Engineering (Southport) whilst the vehicle rights and associated assets were disposed of to Tilling Stevens.

With the increasing prospect of another conflict with Germany, the Southport site (and others that were part of the conglomerate) commenced armaments work well before hostilities commenced in September 1939 – their heavy engineering, steel founding and other metalworking facilities fortuitously being indispensible to what became the war effort.

At this time, on the other side of the Atlantic, what had once been the largest motorcycle manufacturer in the world was not in too good a shape. Having suffered gradual decline post-World War One, with its rival Harley Davidson becoming increasingly dominant, the Springfield, Massachusetts firm of Indian had come under the control of Du Pont Motors in 1930. With sales of his limited-production, expensive high-end motorcars almost non-existent, its owner E Paul du Pont, a member of the enormously wealthy industrialist family of the same name, had decided to change tack. Car manufacture was thus curtailed and he put his energies into Indian motorcycles. For a while it appeared as though he had been the marque's saviour and its

Brave words and not strictly true but they had to talk it up somehow. Even if, as claimed, the machine set a new standard of performance and quality in its class, it was but a pale shadow of its forebears.

future was secured; but come America's entry into the Second World War it was Harley Davidson, with its WLAs, that secured the bulk of government contracts.

Another change of ownership took place just after the war's end when a consortium led by Ralph Rogers gained financial control, ousting du Pont. Breaking with the tradition of medium-to-large capacity V-twins, the new owner brought out a 220cc single and 440cc vertical twins. In some ways they were ahead of their time, and could well have been better than history records, but were not well received and this, along with countless problems due to insufficient development, brought the firm to its knees – which is where Brockhouse came in.

As the new owner of the Indian name, which it seems made the purchase merely to take control of the dealerships, Brockhouse began to wind down production of singles, vertical twins and what V-twins were still made – eventually closing the Springfield plant. At the same time the company began to produce a 250cc motorcycle fitted with an in-house single-cylinder side-valve engine, and proceeded to market this most un-American machine in the US as the Indian Brave during 1950. By 1953 it was available in Great Britain – and how the likes of BSA must have quaked in their shoes, as it was over 10 per cent more expensive than its own infinitely better side-valve 250!

Performance of the 1953 Brave outfit was not mentioned but it would have appeared veritably scintillating compared with a sidecar-equipped Corgi.

The following year the same mechanicals were put into a completely new swinging-arm frame and in April one was tested by *The Motor Cycle* who were, in the circumstances, surprisingly complimentary. After they had covered 1000 miles the engine became sufficiently noisy for them to investigate the cause and this turned out to be a fractured crankpin, whereupon the maker fitted a new engine so the test could continue. We'll never know, but if their 'bulkily clad' tester carried out the speed tests that recorded a heady 62mph (one way) prior to the mechanical mishap or if it occurred during them, a twinge of guilt might have stayed the hand of criticism.

With its British-made motorcycles failing to set the world alight and the American operation losing money, Brockhouse's next wheeze was to kill off the puny 250 Brave, close down the Southport factory, and come to an arrangement with Royal Enfield whereby Americanised/Indian-badged Enfields would be imported and sold in the States. This lasted until 1959 when Brockhouse sold Indian to AMC, which henceforth used the Indian dealerships to peddle its own wares – a second time around, in fact, as Brockhouse had marketed AJS and Matchless when Brave was faltering prior to the Royal Enfield involvement.

A moustachioed gent pretends to circle one of the first of the swinging-arm Braves, registered locally to the Southport factory at the end of summer '53 – the evidence of this deception consisting of his left foot planted firmly on the ground and the ignition key in the off position.

BSA

At one point the largest motorcycle manufacturer in the world, BSA, itself by that time part of a huge combine, became extinct over 40 years ago.

Its roots, however, stretched back over 100 years to a company formed in 1861 by a number of gun makers who had supplied armaments to the British Government at the time of the Crimean War. Concerned by the Royal Small Arms Factory's increasing employment of American-made machinery for mass-production, they managed to come to an agreement whereby they received the same knowhow and facilities. This done, the newly-formed Birmingham Small Arms Trade Association purchased a sizeable parcel of land at Small Heath, to the south east of Birmingham, upon which a factory was built – the road leading to it at the same time being named Armoury Road.

Early orders came from the governments of such countries as Turkey, Russia and Portugal, with the first from the British Government being a contract for the supply of Enfield muzzle-loading rifles – this leading to another for Sniders when the army was re-equipping with breech loaders. As these used ammunition with brass cartridges a nearby metal works was acquired in 1873 to facilitate their manufacture, with a change of name to the Birmingham Small Arms and Metal Company taking place at the same time.

By the late 1870s, despite the onset of the Anglo-Zulu War of 1879, business had slackened off to such a degree that the factory was underused and so the prospects of alternative manufacturing activities were explored. At that time cycling was experiencing something of a boom, and having the wherewithal to produce components or even complete machines the firm accordingly began to do so – firstly by undertaking the manufacture of a strange device known as the Dicycle for its designer, a Mr Otto. By its very nature it could not be a success, and so the company soon moved on to other designs with two wheels and three for various firms – eventually coming to the conclusion, as had other cycle manufacturers, that the so-called 'safety' was the way forward.

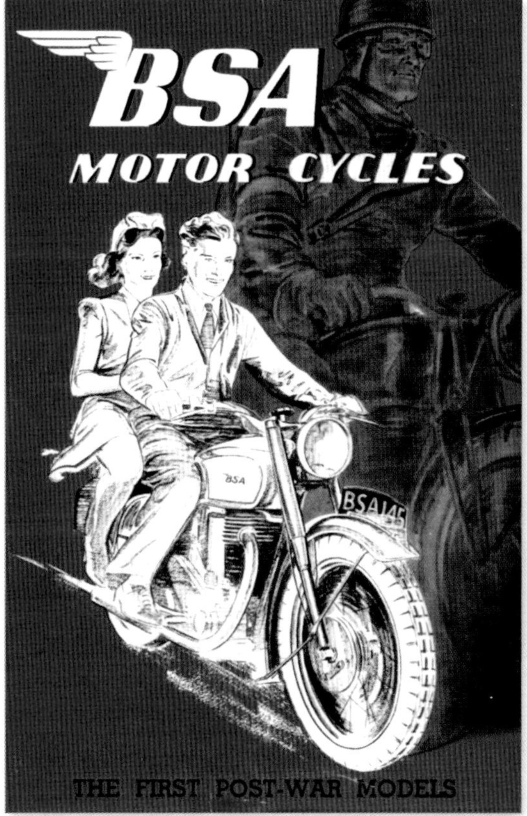

No sooner had the war in the Pacific come to an end, in August 1945, than BSA rushed out this sales material with a sketch of one of its new B31s on the cover – wind whipping at the girl's skirt as the carefree young couple enjoy some peacetime riding on a new machine. Sadly to remain a dream for all but a very lucky few for a good while.

There then followed a surge in demand for both rifles and light-to-medium quick-firing field gun cartridges, so government work took precedence over the firm's cycle and component output – this enforced sabbatical lasting for six years. By 1893 the demand had at last diminished sufficiently for the company to recommence the manufacture of cycles, along with its precision cycle fittings and components – the parts reaching such demand that the factory was soon outgrown. It was enlarged in 1896 and in the same year the firm's ammunition factory at Adderley Park was sold to the Nobel-Dynamite Trust Ltd – subsequent to which the company reverted to its original name. As this denoted, the company's main business was the manufacture of light arms; but, although it was yet to market machines in its own name, the cycle trade was

Of the four models catalogued in 1945 three were mildly revamped 1939 machines – the B31 alone being a new model. It too had pre-war origins, however, in that its motor owed quite a bit to the old Silver Star. But it was the first BSA to feature telescopic forks.

also very important and it was a natural progression to encompass motorised versions when they came into vogue. Consequently, in 1902 the company began to make frames and fittings suitable for small engines, and then in 1905 spring frames that would accept engines of up to 4hp.

The following year the appointment of the avaricious and highly successful businessman Frank Docker as a director heralded a period of expansion and acquisitions for the company, the first of which was the purchase of the nearby Royal Small Arms factory at Sparkbrook from the government, on the understanding that large contracts for rifles would be forthcoming – something that failed to be honoured. The resulting financial setback did not stop BSA's amalgamation with the Eadie Manufacturing Co, of Redditch, in 1907, however – enlarging production capacity as well as adding Eadie hub gears and other specialities to the firm's repertoire. So much so that in 1908 the company decided to come out in the open: rather than supplying complete bicycles that would carry a badge other than its own, as had hitherto been the practice, in future they would be marketed and sold as BSAs.

Shortly before this the company had begun the manufacture of BSA cars at the Sparkbrook complex, part of which was already the home of the (at that time) unconnected Lanchester automobile company. Brought into being as something of a side-line to make fuller use of the large ordnance premises, BSA cars were made until the mid 1930s, by which time Lanchester was owned (from 1931) by the group.

Of far greater importance, however, was the purchase of the prestigious Daimler Company, after complex negotiations by Docker who was by then vice chairman, in 1910. Acquired with company shares rather than cash (a surplus of which BSA was deficient of at the time), it could have proved to be one step too far, as this was the year that the company also moved into motorcycle manufacture; but bank loans and share issues saved the day.

By no means innovative when it was unveiled in 1910, BSA's single-speed, belt-drive 3½hp side-valve single was nevertheless a well-built and workmanlike machine that sold readily; and with the company's considerable expertise in hub gears it was a natural progression for a two-speed model to follow. The way forward was with a separate gearbox, and by 1913 BSA catalogued an all-chain-drive two-speed model. Then followed three-speed countershaft gearbox models with either enclosed chain drive (the Model H) or the, at that time, more widely accepted belt-drive rear (the Model K).

Both of these continued to be manufactured into and after World War One, seeing service both at home and abroad, but it is the special military folding bicycles that were supplied to the forces that are perhaps better remembered. Armaments were the main contribution to the war effort, however, and out of Small Heath poured hundreds of thousands of Lee-Enfield rifles, around 150,000 Lewis machine guns and other ordnance, whilst brother company Daimler, as well as continuing to make motor cars and lorries for military use, manufactured gun tractors, the engines that were used in the new-fangled tanks, radial, V8 and V12 aero engines, as well as hundreds of complete aircraft; and if that were not sufficient, it turned out vast amounts of 12in shell casings.

The return to peace saw the motorcycle arm of BSA introduce a 770cc V-twin, predominantly intended as a sidecar machine, with three-speed 'box, cast aluminium chain cases and quickly-detachable wheels.

However, in 1920 the group dissipated a large portion of the monies that had been accrued through war work and came close to putting itself into penury when a branch of Daimler bought Airco, which by the end of the War professed to be the world's largest aircraft manufacturer. Unfortunately its principal, George Holt Thomas, had completely misled BSA as to the financial state of his companies and within a short while, upon full realisation of the deception, the large part of the acquisition was put into the hands of the liquidators, and Thomas was ejected from the board. An organisation of lesser financial standing would have been taken down by something of this nature but as it was shareholders would be deprived of their dividends for several years.

A lesser but more lastingly influential setback at this period was BSA's bid for Senior TT honours on the Isle of Man in 1921. Encouraged by the success of one of its 3½s, with which the factory tester Kenneth Holden had unexpectedly won a race at Brooklands over Easter 1913, seven similar machines had been entered for the TT in June. Only one lasted the course, finishing 17th, but undismayed, four were taken to Fontainebleau in France for the Motorcycle Grand Prix shortly after; one ridden by Archie Fenn finished third.

In 1914, nine BSAs took to the Island and on this occasion the best of them came home 12th, with just two retirements. Full of immediate post-war euphoria, a serious team assault on the 1920 Senior had been planned; but the prototype, with its special four-valve aluminium-head engine, performed so badly in trials that the design was scrapped and something less radical formulated for the following year. Alas the new machine had various faults that failed to come to light in the all-too-brief tests that were carried out before the team left for the Island. Once there, poor handling led to last-minute experimentation with wheel sizes, and although the all-iron engine had but two overhead valves its rocker gear's design, amongst other details, was flawed and engine troubles began even in practice. The race was a debacle and not one of the six BSAs managed to complete even the second lap. Never again would the company run the risk of such humiliation, vowed its directors – in future its competition activities would be confined to events such as trials and long-distance events, with absolutely no racing.

In truth the company's TT disappointment most probably set it back on the path that it was most comfortable following – the manufacture of good-quality, well-engineered, robust motorcycles that carried a none-too-exorbitant price and had few sporting pretensions.

Along these lines was a larger 985cc version of the V-twin: introduced in 1922 the two ran side by side until the smaller 770 was dropped at the close of the 1931 season. At the other end of the scale, in 1924, to take advantage of the economy market, BSA brought out its diminutive workhorse the 250 'round tank'; at first it was turned out with only a rear brake, but a change in the law demanded two independent brakes, which BSA neatly sidestepped by providing two rears on the little machine!

No racer, perhaps, but 1924 also saw the first of BSA's sporty singles, a 350 OHV that paved the way for the 493cc 'sloper' two years later – much of the design work for these more up-to-date machines being carried out by Harold Briggs, who had transferred from Daimler in the early '20s.

Despite these advancements the firm was in some respects reluctant to move with the times, as exemplified by leaving it until 1927 to do away with dummy belt rim brakes throughout the range and standardise drums. With a degree of clairvoyance the company did, however, see the possibilities for still-cheaper transport than the little 250 and to this end brought out a 174cc two-stroke in 1928; but unlike the Bantam of 20 years later, even with the onset of the depression, it was not a resounding success and was discontinued after barely three years.

The little two-stroke's lack of success aside, BSA's continuing policy of workmanlike no-nonsense machines at a fair price had elevated the company to the position of Great Britain's premier motorcycle manufacturer, and in the best position possible to weather the lean times that brought so many firms financial ruin.

Thus BSA entered the 1930s with no less than 15 different models in its brochure – unloved 'stroker' apart, these ran from side- and overhead-valve 250s to the largest of the V-twins, in normal and 'world tour' (colonial) spec. Additionally available were tuned versions of 350 and 500 OHV slopers, a simple red star adorning their timing covers making them the first in what would be a long line of BSA's top-of-the-range and most sporting singles – the next of which would be the vertical-engined 350 and 500 Blue Stars of 1932.

By that time the frame in general use (excepting the smaller basic singles and V-twins) was based around a hefty forged steel backbone, which had first seen the light of day on the slopers of 1930. Fuel tank-mounted instrument panels were de rigueur too, after a brief dalliance with them atop the handlebars for some models in '31. The Stars gained a Junior 250 version in 1933 and there was an even more highly-tuned 500 Special complete with Amal TT carb – BSA may not have been in the business of racing but was edging somewhat closer.

Displayed on the company's stand at that year's Show were three completely new models: two – an economy 149cc overhead-valve single and a good-looking 499 OHV V-twin – would go into production but the third would not. At a quick glance there was nothing too extraordinary about it – just another 500 OHV single – but the unusual timing and primary drive castings contained a fluid flywheel with chain drive to a three-speed pre-selector gearbox and kick starter operating through separate gears on the timing side. Whatever possessed this normally conservative manufacturer to come up with such a device I cannot imagine, but for sure it must have been connected with the Daimler alliance, whose cars employed a similar system. Had it gone on the market I can just imagine riders juggling with the hand and foot controls of the gearbox and brakes whilst trying to arrest pre-select creep when stationary.

To celebrate King George V's Silver Jubilee the Empire Star was introduced as a top-of-the-range replacement for the Specials (there'd been a 350 version too in 1935 only), although the 350 and 500 Blue Stars remained current. This would be the last year of overhead-valve engines with twin pushrod tubes and a bulky oil reservoir incorporated in the crankcase for Stars and some other singles, and the fashion for twin-port heads and upswept exhaust was due to end too, except for pukka off-road competition machines that had single pipes in any case. Also new for '36 was a larger 750 OHV V-twin – another good-looking machine but in common with its smaller sibling, which had been developed for the military, it lacked the kind of performance its looks hinted at.

A major coup was effected by BSA at around this time when Valentine Page came over from the ailing Triumph concern. Ready for the 1937 season, he had carried out a thorough redesign of the company's singles.

Gone were the heavy bolt-up frames with massive upper member that had characterised many of the firm's machines for several years, lighter-weight fully tubular structures with a single front down-tube taking their place. Engines of the 250s, 350s and 500s, although retaining existing bore and stroke dimensions (63x80mm, 71x88mm and 82x94mm) and whether side- or overhead-valve, were of lighter construction, with the latter all featuring a single ovoid section pushrod tube, with tappets accessed by a removable plate in its base on the 350s and 500s. All were dry-sump lubrication with a separate oil tank, and four-speed gearboxes were employed throughout the entire range, even though some more basic models clung on to a by-now-antiquated hand change.

Empire Stars naturally had all the latest features and there was now a 250 version. But it was the performance of a 500 at a relatively unimportant Brooklands meeting that proved to be a seminal moment. Specially put together by the factory's competition department, this methanol-burning Empire Star, with a heady compression ratio and numerous other mods, was intended to steal a little thunder from Ariel, whose Red Hunters were gaining a reputation at track events. Run by Bert Perrigo, a very successful trials rider himself and who oversaw BSA's participation in such events, the department had been instructed to 'see what they could do' with what they had rather than engage in a full race programme.

With three-times TT winner Walter Handley, who had been persuaded to come out of retirement to ride it, the Star won its first race at over 102mph, with a fastest lap of over 107, but it was written off later on in the day when it was baulked by a slower machine in another race, and Handley took a tumble. With little more than his pride hurt he was rewarded (automatically) for those 100mph laps with a coveted Brooklands Gold Star – nothing too extraordinary for a 500 at that time but it got the hierarchy at Small Heath thinking. They still had no desire to manufacture out-and-out race machinery but did have an idea, and it now had a name.

Debuted at the Motor Cycle Show that autumn in prototype form, the Gold Star went on sale in 1938. Despite its aluminium engine and electron-cased gearbox (paradoxically with wide ratios) being housed in a special frame of Reynolds 531 tubing, and the fact that both 'competition' and 'track racing' models were catalogued, it was marketed as a sports tourer in the same way as the still-current Empire Stars. Even Shropshire clubman Roy Evans's unexpected fifth place in that year's Ulster GP did nothing to sway BSA management and the 1939 Gold Star was if anything emasculated, despite a set of close-ratio gears in a plain aluminium casing.

The Royal Tank Corps trials team was given the use of Gold Stars by the factory, however, and with them won the *Motor Cycling* trophy in the 1938 ISDT whilst one of their number, future BSA works rider Fred Rist, earned a gold medal. Rist was also a member of the British Army BSA team in the following year's ISDT,

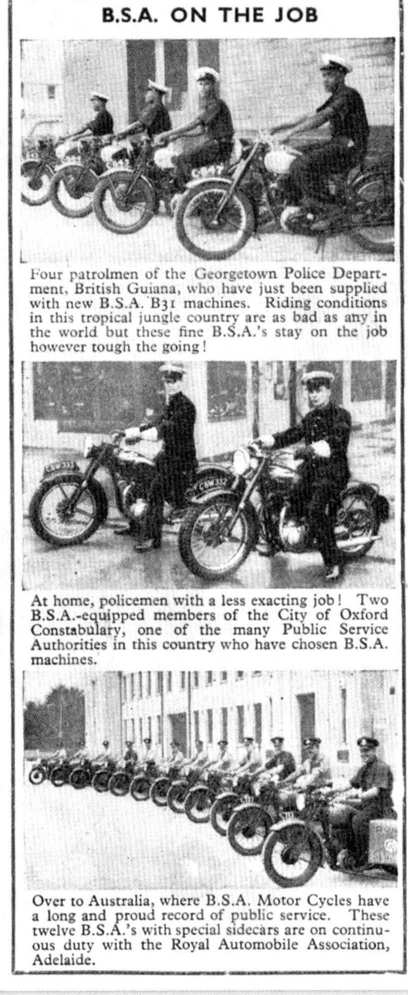

During the immediate post-war years export markets received priority, so much of BSA's output ended up in foreign parts. The US market was the province of English-born expatriate Rich Child, who held the distribution rights. But in 1949, realising the whole country was too much for him, he hived off 11 western states to Hap Alzina, who later negotiated for an additional eight. In 1954 Child sold the remainder to BSA, which then founded BSA Inc to handle distribution in those states.

which took place in Austria in late August – an event in which they might have shone if things hadn't turned nasty. With the situation in Europe fast deteriorating, British civilian competitors were instructed to head for home after just four days of competition, but service personnel and a handful of others elected to stay on. At the close of the fifth day, with the Army BSAs as yet unpenalised, the remaining British contingent were told to head posthaste for the Swiss border, accompanied by an officer of the Luftwaffe to ensure their safe passage – the majority finally arriving back in the UK via Calais on 30 August.

Two days later Germany invaded Poland and on 3 September, Britain and France's ultimatum unheeded, Europe was once again at war – an eventually that had been foreseen as far back as 1935 by James Leek, now BSA's managing director, upon his return from a trade fair in Leipzig. Accordingly the group's management had implemented the revivification of its arms manufacturing capability – and to such good effect that from the outset of hostilities BSA, unlike the Royal Ordnance Factories, was in a position to produce and supply all manner of ordnance including large quantities of Lee-Enfield rifles and Browning machine guns. With its enormous manufacturing capability and robust motorcycles that had proved themselves in long distance reliability trials it was a foregone conclusion that BSA would be called upon to provide them. Small Heath didn't see the recently-introduced coil-ignition 250s as likely contenders but did submit a military version of the brand-new 350 Silver Sports (the machine that was intended to replace the Gold Star in 1940) for evaluation, as well as the side-valve 500 M20 that had been around since 1937. All were Val Page designs but in the event it was the M20 that won the day, and by the war's end they made up the bulk of over 125,000 BSAs turned out for the armed forces.

Motorcycles, along with folding military cycles and light weaponry, were by no means all that poured out of the group's factories. Bombing raids in August and November 1940 resulted in the destruction of buildings and machinery as well as the death of over

50 employees. Production faltered and then resumed.

Over at Coventry, Daimler made scout and armoured cars, aircraft engines and gun turrets, gearboxes for tanks, Bren guns and much more. Its main factory was destroyed during the catastrophic air raid on the city during the night of 14 November 1940. Again, production was compromised; but it recommenced in a time and manner that would be unimaginable today, made possible by the creation of shadow factories and a resolute dedicated workforce. In the main located in what were considered safer areas of the country, out of hundreds operated by Great Britain's larger manufacturers, BSA alone ended up running 67 such establishments during the war.

In addition to this vast undertaking the group added two more famous marques to its portfolio during these years – buying the moribund Sunbeam name from AMC in 1943 and then the very much alive Ariel concern from Jack Sangster a year later (to anyone interested in learning more about the group's work during World War Two the publication *The Other Battle* is essential reading).

The Earls Court Motor Cycle Show of 1948 was the first chance in ten years for the British public to see the industry's products under one roof. Not everything on display was new to the market, however, and BSA's answer to the Triumph Speed Twin, the A7, had been unveiled two years earlier at the Paris Salon. In fact, had not the war intervened it would have first seen the light of day, with girder forks, in 1940. Designed by Herbert Perkins, with input from Val Page, the 62x82mm 495cc twin was similar in some respects to the early-'30s Triumph twin designed by the latter, with semi-unit-construction engine/gearbox and a rear camshaft. Thermal efficiency was not its strongest point and, particularly on the low octane petrol of the day, it had a propensity for running awfully hot.

Despite experiments with side- and overhead-valve vertical twins in the early '40s, some being carried out by Edward Turner when he had forsaken Triumph for BSA in 1942-to-1943, the firm's first post-war machines were all singles – three essentially pre-war and one new, if based upon the Silver Star – the 350cc B31.

By 1946 they had been joined by the re-introduced M21 and a competition version of the B31, the B32. The same year saw the unveiling of a 500 vertical twin at the Paris Salon – this having been mooted in 1939 by Val Page and brought to fruition in the interim by BSA's chief designer Herbert Perkins. The public would have to wait a while to get their hands on one, however, despite BSA devoting the entire Small Heath factory to motorcycles in order to cater for a boom in sales.

A larger alternative to the B31, the 500cc B33, was introduced in 1947, but by 1948 BSA was well and truly back in its stride and brought out three very different new machines. There was an economy 125 two-stroke, the first of what would be the company's long-running little maid of all work, the Bantam series; then at the Motor Cycle Show the 500 twin had its UK launch, as did an alloy-engined 350 that re-introduced the Gold Star title – the lineage traceable back to the stillborn B29 Silver Sports rather than the pre-war Gold Stars.

During its 15-year lifespan the post-war Goldie

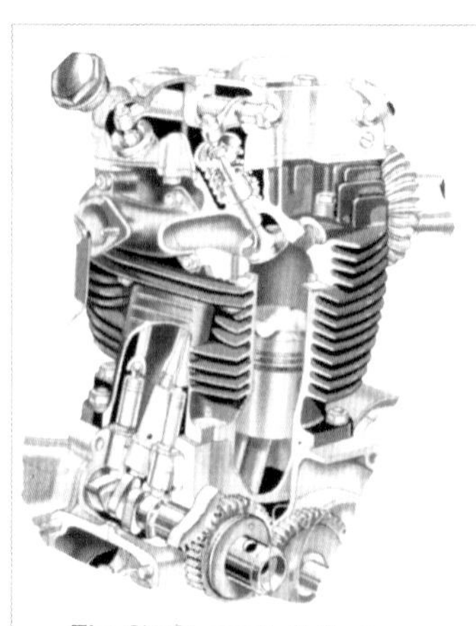

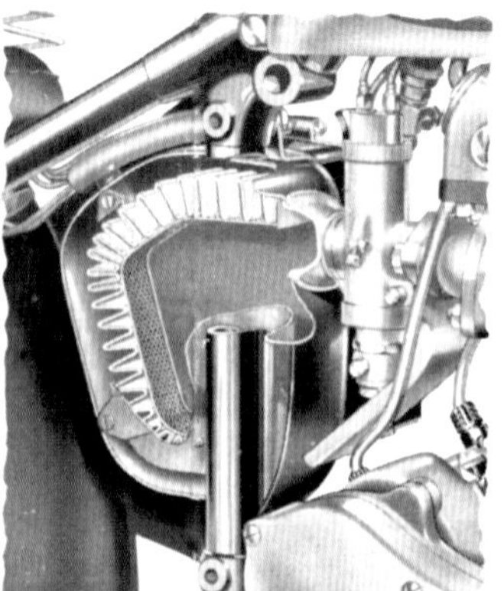

became, almost without a doubt, the most effective multipurpose road-based competition motorcycle ever produced by a British manufacturer. BSA brought out a 500 version in 1949 but it was the 350 that was initially the more successful, winning the Junior Clubmans TT that year and then, with eight consecutive victories, going on to totally dominate the event. The 500, however, at first unable to match the fleet and well-ridden Norton Internationals and Triumph Tiger 100s that made the running in the Senior Clubmans, gained the advantage with the advent of the 'big fin' models in 1954 and from then on they too were unbeatable. In what would be the final Senior, in 1956, they took the first six places with 20 out of the 28 finishers being on BSA's big single; in the Junior no less than 48 out of the 50 machines that completed the course were BSA 350s. Legend has it that the Gold Star's omnipotence led to the demise of the Clubmans races, and there is some truth in it; but apart from the reluctance of other manufacturers to have their machines humiliated year after year, other factors such as falling spectator numbers, finance and logistics played a larger part in their curtailment.

Whatever the reasons, BSA had proved a point, and although the Gold Star in Clubmans trim continued to be sold until the early '60s it was developed no further and saw out its twilight years as a fabulous, if impractical, road burner – ownership of a DBD 34 Clubman garnering something akin to awe from both reserved enthusiast and coffee bar cowboy.

The beauty of the Gold Star package was, however, its sheer diversity; and with little other than a set of different gear ratios, footrests and suitable handlebars it could succeed in many branches of motorcycle sport and on every continent, with any kind of off-road competition its particular forte. Other BSAs from Bantam to the twins were successful too, BSA being particularly proud of the performance of its Star Twins in the 1952 ISDT, which also brought home the coveted Maudes Trophy at the same time.

Competition, however, despite good results leading to good publicity and a veneer of glamour, was still far removed from the group's main modus operandi, which was the manufacture and sale of large quantities of well-engineered motorcycles that would serve the errand boy, family man or sportsman alike. From the little Bantam to the new flagship – the Hopwood-designed 650cc Golden Flash that was brought out for the 1950 season – BSA had the market well covered.

Having for some time laid claim to having the world's finest range of motorcycles and being accepted as one of the largest manufacturers, the BSA group ascended to simply the largest in 1951 when it bought Triumph from Jack Sangster. Unlike AMC, which had a habit of melding its acquisitions (and not always to their betterment), BSA left Triumph very much to its own devices and in the very capable hands of Edward Turner – so much so that the vast majority of the motorcycling public would have been unaware that a change of ownership had taken place.

With its riders as if frozen in time, a Birmingham-registered A7 ambles though a village in middle England, on the cover of the autumn 1948 brochure. This is the standard A7 with rigid frame – plunger suspension was an optional extra.

Part of Sangster's deal with BSA ensured him a seat on the board, which for some time had been chaired by Frank Docker's son Bernard who, in cahoots with his second wife Norah, enjoyed a profligate lifestyle that saw them both (particularly her) frequently featured in the press. Docker was also chairman of Daimler, and what with the fabulously ostentatious show cars that he and publicity-seeking Norah instigated and were seen out and about in, their 850-ton yacht Shemara, a Welsh castle as well as her predilection for mink and diamonds, it was only a matter of time before the public – and, perhaps more importantly, shareholders and fellow directors of the various companies with which Docker was involved – tired of the couple's antics. As a result, and in spite of being a long-time incumbent, he was given the push from the Midland Bank's board early in 1953 (although he retained his position at BSA until 1956). At that point Docker's ongoing use of company money for expenses gave his fellow board members the reason and excuse to send him packing, Jack Sangster thereupon taking his place. Ill health brought about the retirement of James Leek in the same year, and Sangster took this opportunity to promote Edward Turner to oversee BSA's entire car and motorcycle interests.

Up until 1953 BSA bicycles and motorcycles had been made by BSA Cycles Ltd but from then on manufacture of the latter was undertaken by a newly-created part of the group, BSA Motorcycles Ltd, and in 1957 the entire bicycle operation was disposed of to rival Raleigh Industries. With a range that encompassed machines from 125 to 650cc (or from 35 to 1000cc if you included BSA's own diminutive Winged Wheel cycle attachment and Ariel's Square Four), combined with the group's well-established worldwide network of importers and dealerships, this era, some would avow, were the marque's golden years.

These years brought what in retrospect might appear to have been complacency, however, as little attempt was made to move with the times, which were on the eve of great change. True, there was the 250cc C15 of 1958, followed by its 350cc derivative the B40 two years later; and then a brace of twins, the 500cc A50 and 650cc A65, in 1962 – all unit-construction machines but nevertheless on traditional lines.

The burgeoning Japanese motorcycle industry had prompted Edward Turner to undertake a fact-finding trip to the land of the rising sun during 1960. And although he returned with some foreboding it would appear to have been insufficient to have much effect on the way things were done at Small Heath. Even though the company's modern small-capacity and ultra lightweights were appearing in increasing numbers on the roads of the UK and US, the market for larger British singles and twins remained buoyant.

The following year marked BSA's centenary and Jack Sangster, who turned 65 in May, saw it as an opportune time to retire. There was talk of Edward Turner doing the same, but although loss-making Daimler, along with its new V8 engines he'd designed, had been disposed of to Jaguar the year before, he still felt he had work to do – which included the awful little 75cc Beagle that he'd instigated. Intended to compete with the popular tiddlers from the Far East and Italy, it would turn out to be a dismal failure and a sad footnote to Turner's long and enviable career as a designer.

That aside, what would be a highly successful development of the unit-construction singles was coming to fruition when his time as CEO of the automotive division finally came to an end in 1963 – BSA's 441cc Victor winning the World Motor Cross Championship in both 1964 and '65. To take Turner's place the company had selected another from its own ranks and chose Harry Sturgeon who, in search of greater efficiency, set about plant modernisation to increase production, as well as integrating the policymaking and running of BSA with that of Triumph. Meanwhile Turner, despite becoming increasingly unhappy with the general state of affairs, stayed on as a director of BSA until finally bowing out in 1967.

Shortly before this, however, Sturgeon had died unexpectedly and BSA's chairman Eric Turner (no relation to Edward) brought in Lionel Jofeh from the aircraft instrument industry to take his place.

At the time of his accession there was still a healthy demand for BSA's twins, particularly in the US, whilst roadster versions of the Victor were on the verge of introduction and would become best-sellers towards the end of the decade.

This was in relative terms only, however, as BSA had long since lost its place as the world's number one in overall sales to manufacturers from the East, which less than ten years previously had been all but unknown in the UK and US. Yet BSA won the Queen's Award to Industry for Export in 1967 and '68.

Having conquered the small-to-medium capacity markets the Japanese turned their attentions to ever-larger machines in the late '60s, but the British conglomerate was ready for them, or at least it thought so. The 750cc Rocket 3 of 1968 had been developed expressly for the US market but Honda's almost simultaneously introduced CB 750 four, although arguably an inferior motorcycle, was greeted voraciously by the buying public and outsold the British machine by many to one. Even the racing successes enjoyed by BSA's triple, which peaked with a one, two, three at Daytona in 1971, or the Craig Vetter-designed custom version, which would eventually see the light of day as a Triumph, did little to woo customers away from the often poor-handling but blindingly fast first generation of Nipponese superbikes.

The triples' disappointing sales were an almost insignificant part of BSA's woes, however, as under Jofeh's control things had been going badly wrong, and it is with good reason that history cites him as one of the villains of BSA's final years. Partially to blame, also, was the research and development facility based at Umberslade Hall, Warwickshire, which had been instigated by his predecessor but set up by Jofeh in 1967. During its four-year existence, although it undertook work for other industries within the group, it concentrated on motorcycles, with the overhaul, restyling and development of both BSA and Triumph ranges for 1971 remembered as its most memorable debacle.

This, however, paled into insignificance when the catastrophic state of BSA's finances became public knowledge during the spring of that year. Jofeh's stance was to blame anything and anyone but himself – production problems, bank borrowing, anything. The board had heard enough, however, and his resignation, announced at the beginning of July, was followed by drastic action over the following weeks.

First to go, despite its ongoing successes, was

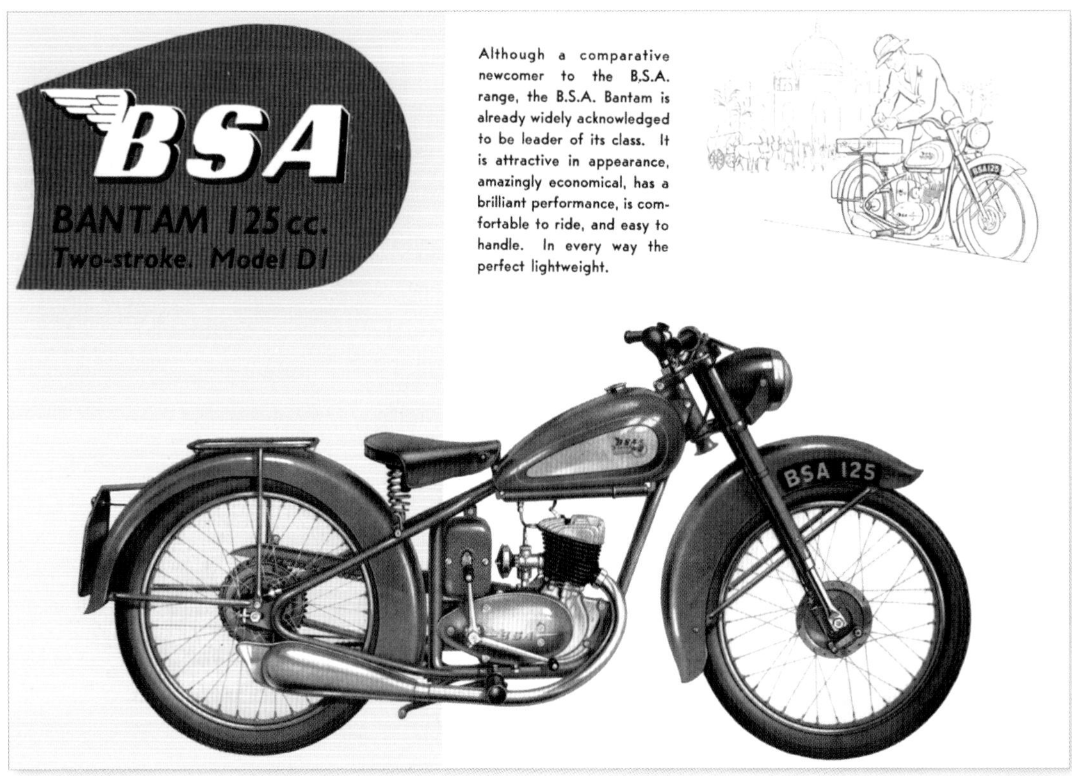

The little green Bantam, correctly referred to as Pastel Green, had been introduced earlier in the year (1948). Its motor/gearbox was a mirror copy of DKW's two-stroke which had been passed around as war reparations, with Harley Davidson doing a Model 125 version and MMZ its own in the USSR. A Wico-Pacy flywheel magneto-generator took care of sparks and lighting, whilst 5in brakes checked its speed. Originally it was an export-only commodity, but Motor Cycling *got hold of an early home-market example in the autumn. Their tester was 'convinced that he had seldom ridden such a really nice lightweight' and described the aforementioned brakes as having 'big-machine' capabilities. At 54mph, if one accepts the accuracy of the Smiths speedo, it was also the fastest 125 Bantam to be tested (others were timed at between 47 and 49mph), and frugal too, using a gallon of petroil every 120 miles or so.*

Small Heath's competition shop; then price increases were made throughout the BSA and Triumph ranges. Possible salvation appeared in the form of a bid from venture capitalists Vision Enterprises but disappeared almost as quickly once they learnt the true state of affairs.

Henceforth 1971 became a sad procession of sell-offs of subsidiaries, premises (including the old Redditch factory to Quinton Hazell) and the group's interest in machine tool manufacturer Alfred Herbert. Axed too was what was to have been the group's brand-new 350cc twin-OHC twin – in BSA-form the Fury. Autumn brought more bad news when accountants Coopers stipulated that, in order for BSA to remain solvent, motorcycle production at Small Heath should be terminated, the majority of the complex sold, and manufacture of BSAs transferred to Triumph's Meriden factory with an abbreviated range for 1972. This activated the large-scale redundancies that had been feared and by mid-November over 2,000 jobs had gone.

Remarkably, shipments to BSA Incorporated in the US had continued, if sporadically, throughout; but the recently restructured organisation's president Peter Thornton had been ousted, even before Jofeh in the UK, and his place taken by the British-born ex-chief of Tri-Cor, Denis McCormack. For all his faults Thornton's extravagant use of funds for publicity and racing had produced results, however; whilst his successor, who favoured the Triumph brand, indulged in underhand and disloyal actions that turned the knife in BSA Inc's UK parent, which was fighting for its life.

For a while production was split between Meriden and Small Heath, with 500 singles and 750 triples continuing to be made at the latter until the spring of '72. By that time Lord Shawcross had replaced Eric Turner as chairman, and towards the end of 1972, with the company sliding irrevocably further into the red, government assistance was sought. Talks with the Department of Trade and Industry, as well as Norton-Villiers, ensued – during which it was made clear that for BSA to receive government financial aid its four remaining profit-making non-motorcycle companies had to be sold to N-V's parent company Manganese Bronze Holdings for a knock-down price: a derisory £3.5 million. Furthermore, despite noises made by the DTI about an up-to-the-minute factory and plant to secure the future, it was becoming increasingly obvious that with the government's insistence on N-V's involvement, BSA's days as a manufacturer were likely numbered whatever the outcome. Finally, in March 1973 Dennis Poore's MBH combine made a bid for BSA that, if accepted, would create an enlarged N-V named Norton Villiers Triumph, with Poore himself as chairman.

Before Shawcross had time to put these proposals to his board some extraordinary and suspect machinations on the stock market sent BSA shares plummeting, so

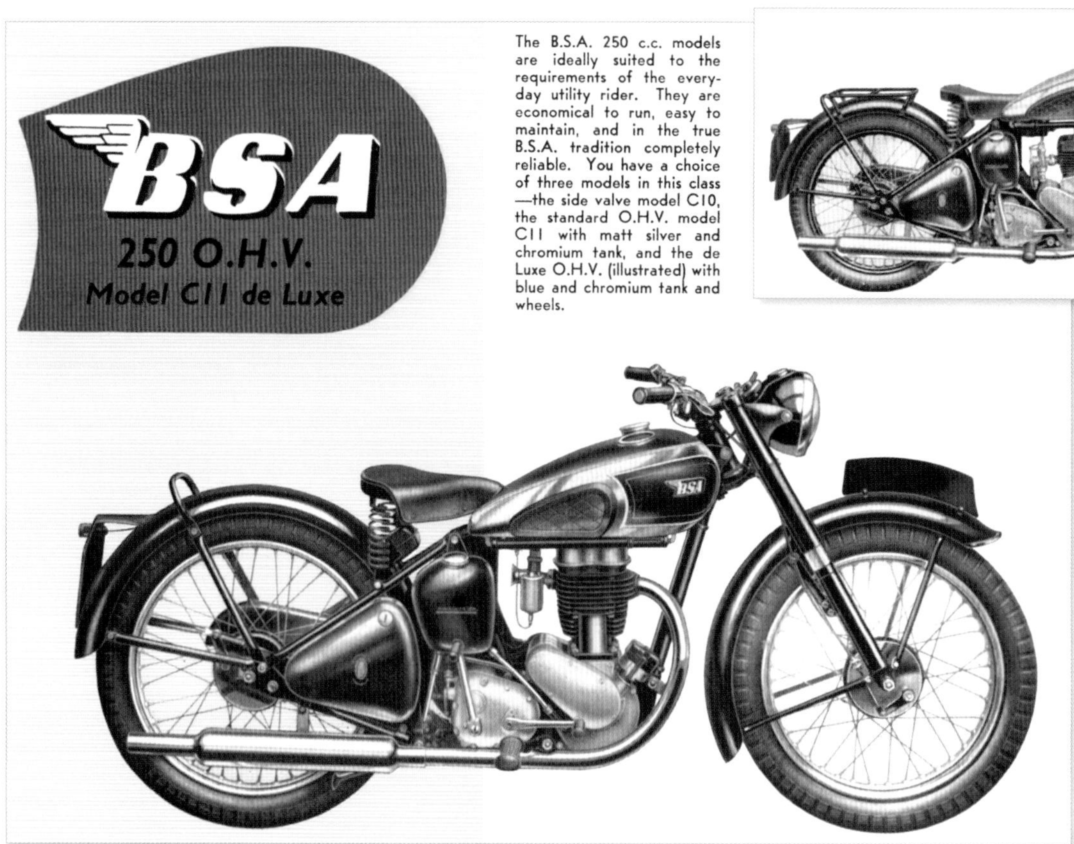

Both 250s had telescopic forks by 1949 and the speedo was mounted in the fuel tank to the right of the filler cap. Designed by BSA's chief engineer David Munro shortly before the war, the overhead-valve C11 had cross-over pushrods for an optimum angle of attack to the rockers, and coil ignition with automatic advance – unusual features for the time.

The 500cc B33 (upper) was identical apart from its engine dimensions and the colour of the petrol tank. Its 85x88mm bore and stroke gave it a cubic capacity of 499cc whilst the B31 had the same stroke combined with a bore of 71mm, which resulted in a capacity of 348cc. The B31 tank had green panels on chrome whilst the B33 had red – both lined in gold. Either model could be had with a spring (plunger) frame for just under £16 extra, whilst for an A7 twin the same luxury cost under £13. A 1948 test carried out by The Motor Cycle *showed the B31 to be capable of 73mph and fuel consumption of just under 80 miles to a gallon of fuel at a steady 50mph. Road-holding was 'well above average for a solid-frame machine', but brakes were 'adequate' on account of a below-par front.*

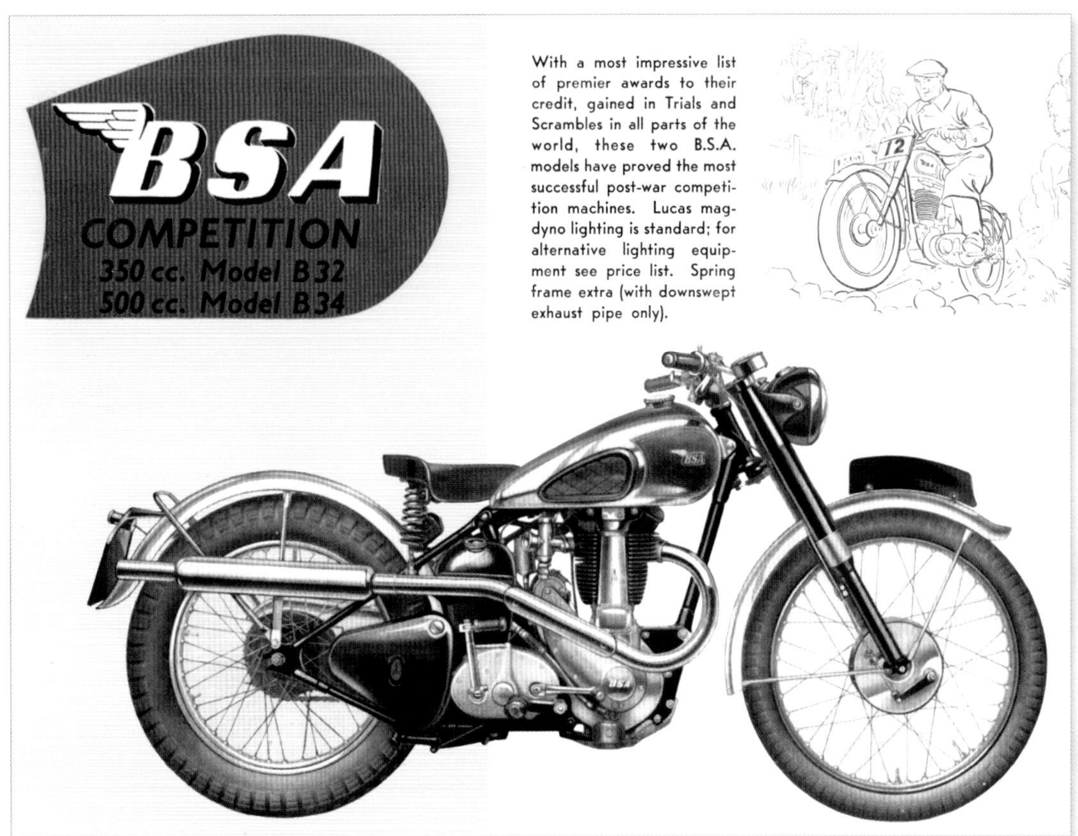

Back in those days trials machines were less specialised, but in 1949 a B32 would still cost you a bit over £157 as opposed to about £142 for a stock B31. These were over-the-counter machines whereas the B32s and 34s that had been so successful in the hands of the likes of Bill Nicholson were, in truth, a little more 'trick'. Like the 31s and 33s a spring frame was an optional extra but at the time many riders, cost notwithstanding, preferred the standard set-up.

The artist has shown the oil tank cut out to allow the high-level exhaust to be tucked well in but omitted to include the oil return pipe and union on the lower outer face of said recess. B32s had green tank panels and B34s red, both lined in gold. From 1949, for £10 extra, an aluminium head and barrel could be specified. These were the same castings as the ZB Gold Star, but an engine originally supplied with these had an A in its engine number (eg ZB.A.3223) and is not to be confused with a Gold Star, which would have GS (eg ZB.GS.268). Motor Cycling *had tried out a brand-new B34 during 1947 to find out how suitable one might be as a dual-purpose mount and their conclusion was, providing the owner was prepared to alternate between available engine sprockets, 'admirably'. Standard competition gearing gave a cruising speed of 45-to-50mph whilst the substitution of an 18-tooth sprocket and suitable primary chain allowed 55-to-60 mph to be easily maintained.*

when the meeting was convened there were but two choices – acceptance or bankruptcy.

As had been feared, the takeover that had been all but forced upon it did spell the end, and by late summer 1973 the days when you could buy a BSA made by BSA were gone.

Ironically, a matter of weeks after MBH had done the deal Dennis Poore announced that Meriden would cease motorcycle manufacture early the following year and this would be transferred to Small Heath. Thus was eventually born the Meriden Co-operative, which would supply Triumphs to NVT, which would market them.

With the liquidation of NVT in 1978 its management bought the rights to the BSA motorcycle brand and formed the BSA Company. For the next decade or so, Rotax-powered military machines, as well as Yamaha-engined lightweights with names such as Beaver, Brigand and Boxer, were made as BSAs.

In 1991 a merger took place with Andover Norton International Ltd, out of which arose the BSA Group. This was taken over by the Regal Group in 1994 which, three years later brought out the Gold SR, a single-cylinder parody of the Gold Star of the '50s and '60s. Ironically attracting something of a following in Japan, several hundred were built before falling sales brought about its termination in 2003. There was to have been a 1,000cc Tempest but it went no further than being prototypical.

Since then there have been no BSA motorcycles manufactured but the name has, through various machinations, been passed around. As of today it rests with the Mahindra Group of India, which purchased BSA Co Ltd in 2016. Already a maker of small two-wheelers, the company apparently intends to reintroduce the BSA name and add it to its range of products.

By 1949, the old M20 that had performed such sterling service in the war now had telescopic forks as well as a bigger-capacity brother. Hard to see the reason for the M33 as an alternative to a B33 but it was primarily intended as a sidecar bike and shared the same, longer, wheelbase with the M20 and M21s. An M20 (KOP 298, in case it's still out there somewhere) was put through its paces by Motor Cycling *in 1951 and, maybe helped by its post-war-type alloy head, managed a flying quarter-mile at just over 64mph. Side-valve motors are generally not renowned for thrifty fuel consumption but this one returned around 70mpg.*

The bog-standard A7 was BSA's direct competition to Triumph's well-established Speed Twin.

ENGINE: 495 c.c. O.H.V. twin (62 x 82 mm.); forged steel crankshaft; Indium flashed lead bronze big-end bearings; high compression pistons; sports camshaft; Lucas magneto with automatic ignition advance; twin Amal carburetters; efficient exhaust system.

LUBRICATION: Dry sump lubrication for engine with double-gear type pump; main oil supply to timing side plain bearing and big-ends; by-pass oil feed to overhead rocker spindles and rocker gear; capacity of oil tank under saddle, 5 pints; separate supply for oil bath and gearbox, other parts by grease gun.

TRANSMISSION: Engine shaft cush drive; gearbox and engine in bolted-up unit construction with fixed front chain centre distance; $\frac{3}{8}$ in. pitch duplex front chain with adjustable slipper type tensioner in cast aluminium oil bath; chain tensioner adjustable from outside; B.S.A. five plate clutch fitted with oil resisting fabric inserts; rear chain $\frac{5}{8}$ in. x $\frac{3}{8}$ in. pitch; gear ratios—solo: 5.1, 6.2, 9.0, 13.2; sidecar: 5.4, 6.6, 9.5, 14.0; B.S.A. four-speed gear with positive stop foot-change.

FRAME: Duplex cradle with integral sidecar lugs; steering damper; central and front stand; pillion footrest lugs; petrol tank, $3\frac{1}{2}$ gallons; flexible petrol pipes with reserve taps.

SUSPENSION: Front suspension by B.S.A. telescopic forks with automatic hydraulic damping; rear suspension by totally enclosed plunger and rebound springs.

WHEELS: Both instantly detachable and fitted with Dunlop Universal tyres; front—3.25-19, rear—3.50-19; 7 in. diameter brakes with finger adjustment.

CONTROLS: Adjustable handlebar; twist grip throttle, front brake, air lever and horn button on right bar; clutch and headlamp dip switch control on left.

EQUIPMENT: Lucas 6-volt C.V.C. dynamo; sealed beam headlamp; electric horn; spring seat saddle; rubber kneegrips; tool kit; tyre inflator; licence holder.

FINISH: Black enamel with bright parts chromium plated; tank finished in matt silver and chromium with maroon lining and special badge.

Price £160 plus £43. 4s. P.T.

Speedometer **£4** extra, plus **£1. 1. 8.** P.T.

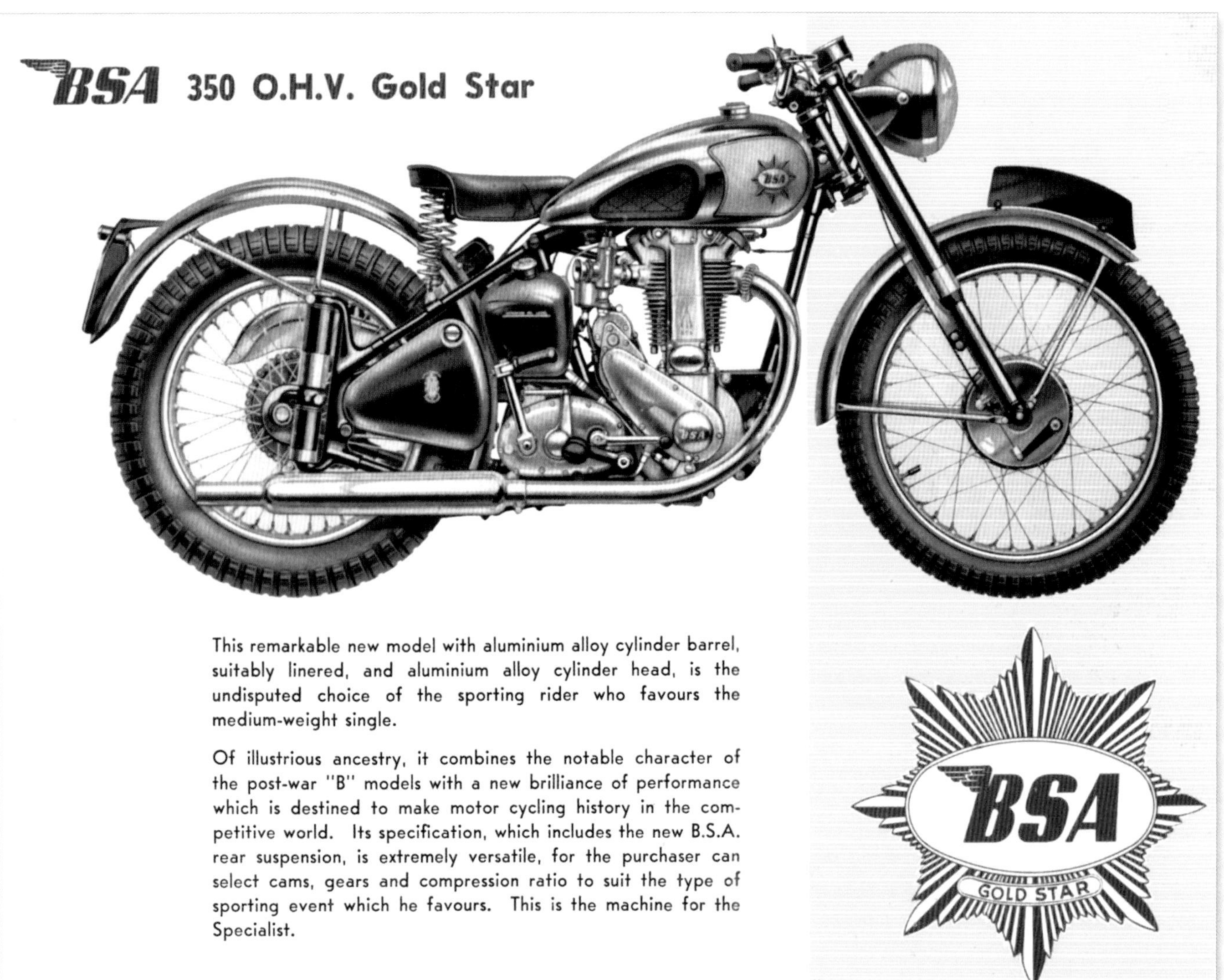

Whoever foretold the new Gold Star of 1949 would make motorcycling history could have had little idea of how right he would prove to be. Since the debacle of the BSA entries in the 1921 Senior TT the factory had never returned to the Island and nor had one of its machines ever won a race there. That all changed with the 350 Gold Star, which fulfilled its manufacturer's claims in its very first season when Harold Clark won the Junior Clubmans TT from a couple of Inter Nortons, with Ray Hallett fourth on another Goldie.

ENGINE: 71 x 88 mm. bore and stroke; aluminium alloy cylinder barrel with wear-resisting alloy iron liner; aluminium alloy cylinder head with valve seat inserts; polished flywheels and connecting rod; high duty crankpin; high, low or medium compression ratio piston to order; port sizes, cams, valve springs, carburetter, etc., to suit specified compression ratio; (T.T. carburetter of suitable size, optional); Stellite tipped G2 valves, racing magneto (see Equipment below); engine specially tuned and bench tested.

LUBRICATION: Dry sump lubrication with double-gear pump; oil tank under saddle, capacity—5 pints; separate supply for oil bath and gearbox, other parts by grease gun.

TRANSMISSION: Engine shaft cush drive; front chain $\frac{1}{2}$ in. x .305 in. in oil bath; rear chain $\frac{5}{8}$ in. x $\frac{1}{4}$ in.; B.S.A. multi dry-plate clutch with oil-resisting fabric inserts; B.S.A. heavy four-speed gearbox with enclosed clutch operation and speedometer drive; positive stop foot gear-change; gear ratios: standard, close or extra close ratios with engine shaft sprocket to suit requirements.

FRAME: Tubular frame of great strength with forged steel lugs; central stand; steering damper; pillion footrest lugs; 3 gallon petrol tank (2 gallon tank optional).

SUSPENSION: Front suspension by B.S.A. telescopic forks with automatic hydraulic damping; rear suspension by totally enclosed plunger and rebound springs.

WHEELS: Fitted with Dunlop Universal tyres; front: quickly detachable, 2.75-21; rear: quickly detachable, 4.00-19 (optional tyre sizes to suit requirements); 7 in. diameter brakes with finger adjustment.

CONTROLS: Adjustable handlebar; twist grip control; front brake, air lever and horn button (if fitted) on right bar; clutch, ignition, exhaust lifter and headlamp dip switch (if fitted) on left.

EQUIPMENT: Lucas Racing magneto with battery lighting set and electric horn standard (Lucas Magdyno lighting set optional); spring seat saddle; rubber kneegrips; tool kit; tyre inflator; licence holder; rev. counter extra.

FINISH: Mudguards with stays, front chain-case and rear chain guard, brake cover plates, handlebars, exhaust system and other bright parts chromium plated; frame finished in black enamel; matt silver and chromium tank with maroon lining and special Gold Star badge.

Price **£166. 10s.** plus **£44. 19. 1. P.T.**

Speedometer **£4** extra, plus **£1. 1. 8.** P.T.

Technical Data

Model	D1	C10	C11	B31	B32	B32 Gold Star	B33	B34	M20	M21	M33	A7	A7 S.T.
Valve Arrangement	2-stroke	S.V.	O.H.V.	O.H.V.	O.H.V.	O.H.V.	O.H.V.	O.H.V.	S.V.	S.V.	O.H.V.	O.H.V.	O.H.V.
No. of Cylinders	1	1	1	1	1	1	1	1	1	1	1	2	2
Bore (mm.)	52	63	63	71	71	71	85	85	82	82	85	62	62
Stroke (mm.)	58	80	80	88	88	88	88	88	94	112	88	82	82
Capacity (c.c.)	123	249	249	348	348	348	499	499	496	591	499	495	495
Compression Ratio	—	5–1	6.5–1	6.5–1	6.5–1	†	6.8–1	6.8–1	4.9–1	5–1	6.8–1	7–1	7.5–1
Gear Ratios (Solo)—													
Top	—	—	—	5.6	7.1	‡	5.0	5.6	5.3	4.8	4.8	5.1	5.1
Third	7.0	6.6	6.6	7.4	9.3		6.6	7.4	7.0	6.3	6.3	6.2	6.2
Second	11.7	9.8	9.8	11.5	14.5		10.3	11.6	10.9	9.8	9.8	9.0	9.0
First	22.0	14.5	14.5	16.7	21.1		14.9	16.8	15.8	14.2	14.2	13.2	13.2
Gear Ratios (Sidecar)													
Top	—	—	—	—	—		—	—	5.9	5.9	5.6	5.4	5.4
Third	—	—	—	—	—		—	—	7.8	7.8	7.4	6.6	6.6
Second	—	—	—	—	—		—	—	12.2	12.2	11.5	9.5	9.5
First	—	—	—	—	—		—	—	17.7	17.7	16.7	14.0	14.0
Front Tyre	2.75–19	3.00–19	3.00–20	3.25–19	2.75–21	2.75–21	3.25–19	2.75–21	3.25–19	3.25–19	3.25–19	3.25–19	3.25–19
Rear Tyre	2.75–19	3.00–19	3.00–20	3.25–19	4.00–19	4.00–19	3.50–19	4.00–19	3.25–19	3.50–19	3.50–19	3.50–19	3.50–19
Front Chain (ins.)	⅜ x .250	½ x .305	½ x .305	½ x .305	½ x .305	½ x .305	½ x .305	½ x .305	½ x .305	½ x .305	½ x .305	⅜ Duplex	⅜ Duplex
Rear Chain (ins.)	½ x .305	½ x .305	½ x .305	⅝ x ¼	⅝ x ¼	⅝ x ¼	⅝ x ¼	⅝ x ¼	⅝ x ¼	⅝ x ¼	⅝ x ¼	⅝ x ⅜	⅝ x ⅜
Brake Diameters (ins.)	5	5½	5½	7	7	7	7	7	7	7	7	7	7
§Saddle Height (ins.)	27	28	28½	30½	31½	31½	30½	31½	30½	30½	30½	30	30
§Overall Length (ins.)	77	80½	80½	82	82	83½	82	82	85	85	85	83	84
§Overall Height (ins.)	38¾	39	39½	40	41	41	40	41	39¼	39¼	39¼	40½	40½
§Overall Width (ins.)	26½	28	28	28	28	28	28	28	28	28	28	28	28
§Ground Clearance (ins.)	4¾	4½	5	5	6¼	6¼	5	6¼	5½	5½	5½	4½	4½
§Weight (lbs.)	153	270	284	343	*320	*325	354	*330	369	370	372	369	382
§Petrol Tank Capacity (galls.)	1¾	2½	2½	3	3	3	3	3	3	3	3	3	3½
§Oil Tank Capacity (pints)	—	4	4	4	4	4	4	4	5	5	5	4	4

† Optional Compression Ratios for B32 Gold Star:—6.5, 7.5, 8.8, 12.5 to 1.

* Weights stripped for trials, etc.

‡ Gear Ratios:—	Touring	Trials	Scrambles	Road Racing
Top	5.6	7.06	7.06	5.3
Third	7.4	9.30	9.30	5.8
Second	11.5	14.5	12.15	6.9
First	16.7	21.1	17.44	9.9

A choice of engine and gearbox sprockets is available giving a wide range of overall ratios to suit requirements.

§ Figures for these are approximate.

In common with many manufacturers, BSA's brochures included comprehensive data on their entire range. This covers the 1949 season's models and was published in the autumn of 1948.

Two new BSAs made their debut at Earls Court in October 1949.

Anyone for tennis? The summer of 1950 would see Budge Patty of the USA take the Wimbledon men's singles from Australian Frank Sedgman – and with an over-generous helping of artistic licence this might be one of them on the Bantam. At the time Birmingham Small Arms was the most prolific of global motorcycle makers and proud to announce the fact – in its heyday turning out some 75,000 machines annually.

A 500 version of the Gold Star was introduced to the UK market for the 1950 season but in fact they had been leaving the factory for export since May 1949.

Lightweight two-strokes were becoming a popular mount for some trials riders so BSA brought out a mildly-modified version of the best-selling Bantam. There was little or no chance of an outright victory but works tester George Pickering won six class cups in national trials over the winter of 1949/50.

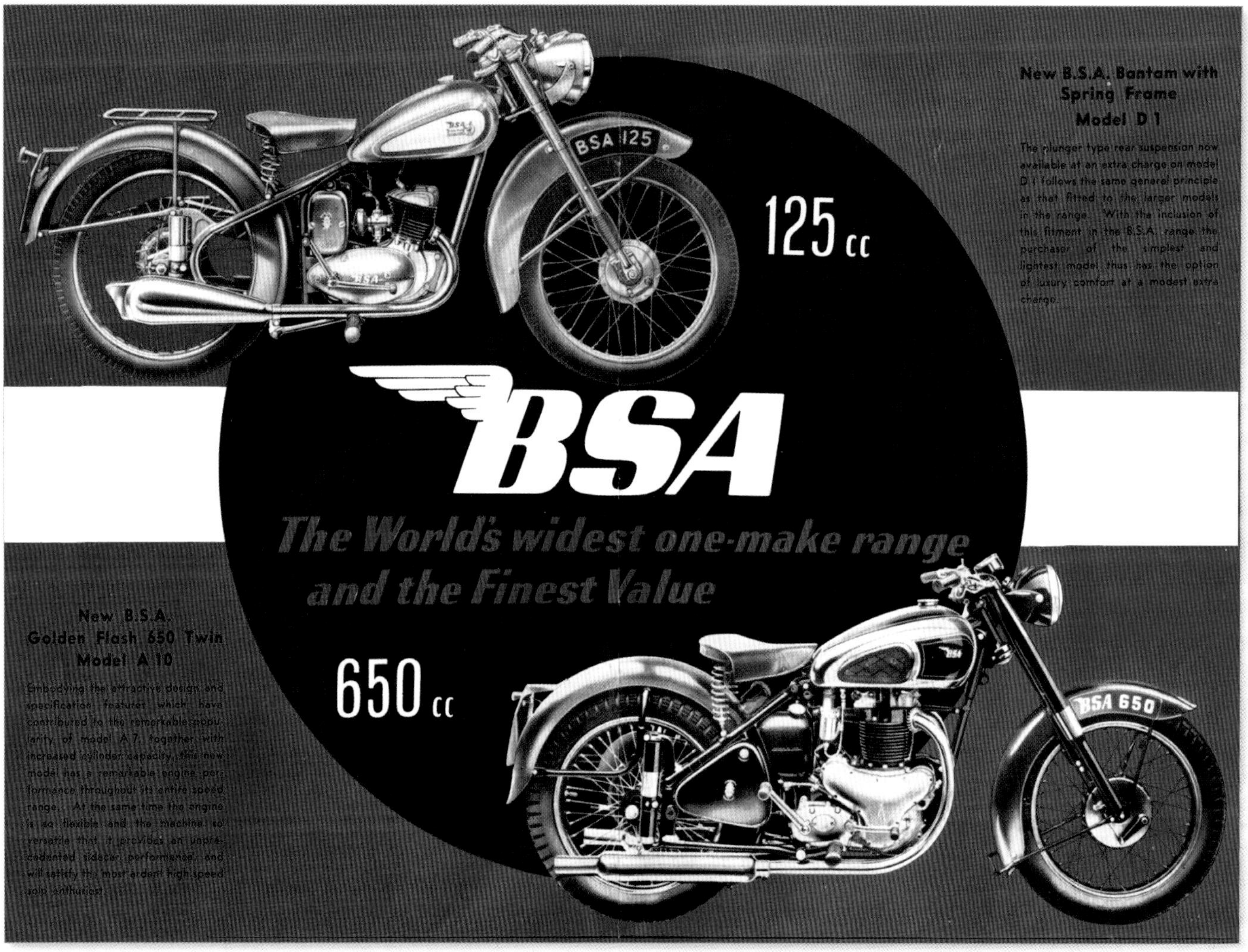
New B.S.A. Bantam with Spring Frame Model D 1
The plunger type rear suspension now available at an extra charge on model D 1 follows the same general principle as that fitted to the larger models in the range. With the inclusion of this fitment in the B.S.A. range the purchaser of the simplest and lightest model thus has the option of luxury comfort at a modest extra charge.
BSA 125
125 cc
BSA
The World's widest one-make range
and the Finest Value
New B.S.A. Golden Flash 650 Twin Model A 10
Embodying the attractive design and specification features which have contributed to the remarkable popularity of model A 7, together with increased cylinder capacity, this new model has a remarkable engine performance throughout its entire speed range. At the same time the engine is so flexible and the machine so versatile that it provides an unprecedented sidecar performance, and will satisfy the most ardent high speed solo enthusiast.
650 cc
BSA 650

New for the 1950 season was the Bert Hopwood-designed Golden Flash – having worked with Edward Turner on Triumph's pre-war Speed Twin and then formulated Norton's twin post-war, Hopwood's experience of the vertical twin was considerable. Nevertheless, although it was not simply an enlarged version of the Val Page-designed A7 it was a derivation. Initially, plunger Bantams had the same rear mudguard as the rigid-frame model but before long they were given one with a deeper valence.

VIC
31-359
BSA
The Worlds Largest
Motorcycle Manufacturers.

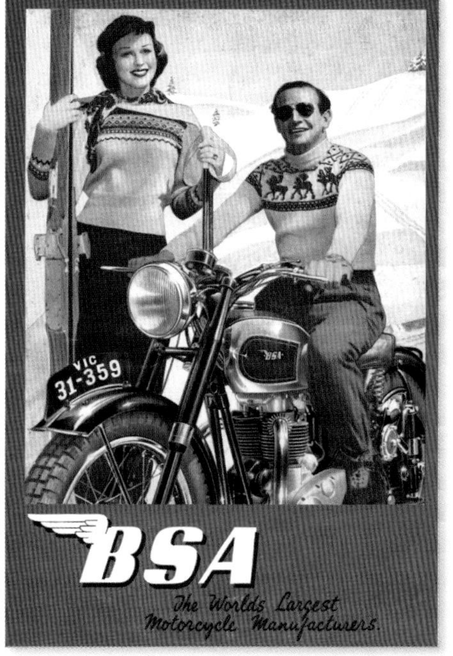

With their Victoria, New South Wales-registered A7 our skiers could be at Kiandra, Kosciusko or another of the state's skiing areas, but the fir trees suggest another continent.

The October 1951 brochure was printed in more than one language but the cover of this Danish edition proclaimed BSA's slogan in its mother tongue.

Cutaway twin engine

This illustration from the same publication is especially for Danish readers but I'm sure that the rest of you will get the gist of it.

From India to Australia, London to South Africa, BSAs were bought by governments the world over – and also by customers of JA Hansen, the Danish importer.

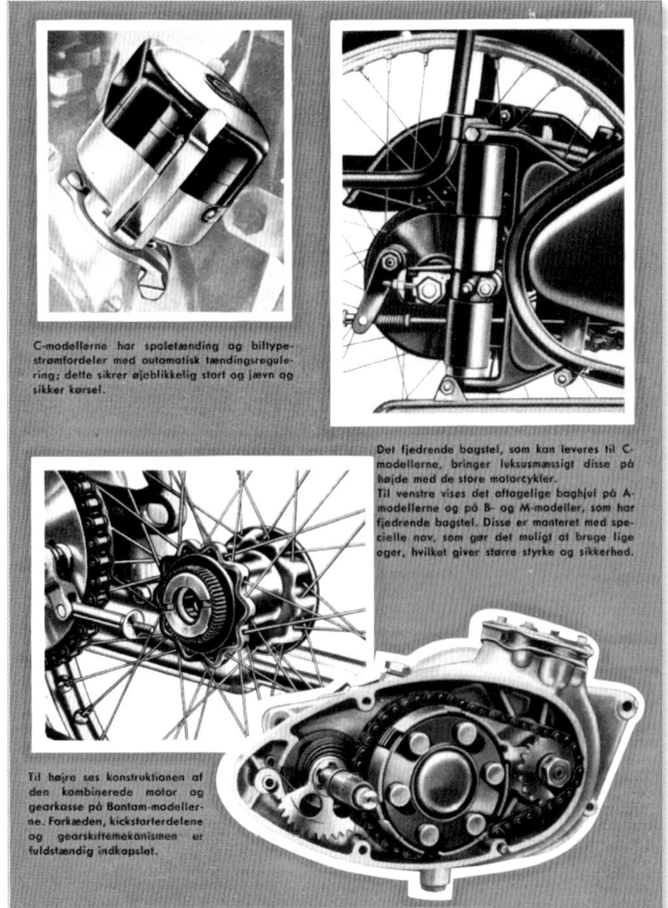

BSA's most sumptuous brochure for 1952 had a leather-grained card cover with gold lettering, and inside a dramatic illustration of the Golden Flash.

BSA GOLDEN FLASH 650 Twin Model A 10

The B.S.A. Golden Flash embodies a number of attractive design features which make it the Leader of the Twins. The engine has a remarkable performance throughout its entire speed range. At the same time it is so flexible and the machine so versatile that it provides an unprecedented sidecar performance, and will satisfy the most ardent high-speed solo enthusiast.

ENGINE. Vertical Twin O.H.V. 70 mm. bore by 84 mm. stroke; 646 c.c. Forged steel crankshaft with integral bobweights and bolted-on central flywheel. Roller journal bearing on drive-side mainshaft. Plain bearing big-ends with indium-flashed lead-bronze liners. Plain bearing for mainshaft timing side. Forged light alloy connecting rods; low expansion aluminium silicon alloy split skirt pistons. Twin cylinders cast in single unit with specially cored air passages. Unit cylinder head-casting with narrow angle valves, two per cylinder, operating in shallow combustion chambers specially developed for maximum efficiency. Overhead rockers operated by push rods from single camshaft at rear with large car-type tappets. Camshaft gear-driven from engine-shaft through idler pinion, and incorporating timed mechanical breather. Absorption type silencers.

LUBRICATION SYSTEM. Engine lubricated by dry-sump system with twin gear-type pump, driven by skew gear from engine shaft; pressure feed to timing-side main bearing and big-ends, timing gears and specially-designed camshaft trough, with by-pass oil pressure release. Pressure feed to overhead rocker spindles. Capacity of oil-tank—four Imperial pints.

INDUCTION SYSTEM. Bifurcated inlet manifold cast in cylinder head; Amal carburetter; large capacity built-in air cleaner, mounted on seat tube between oil tank and battery.

IGNITION. Lucas magneto, gear driven from camshaft with automatic advance.

TRANSMISSION. Primary drive from engine by $\frac{3}{8}$" duplex roller chain, running in cast aluminium oil-bath chaincase. Chain tension correctly maintained by adjustable slipper-type tensioner with hard-chrome bearing surface and external adjustment. Engine shaft cush drive. Rear chain $\frac{5}{8}$" x $\frac{3}{8}$" roller, lubricated by breather-pipe from oil-tank. Five-plate clutch with oil-proof fabric inserts.

GEARBOX. B.S.A. four-speed constant mesh gearbox with built-in positive stop foot change.

FRAME. Duplex triangulated cradle of ample strength for solo or sidecar work. Plunger type rear suspension. B.S.A. telescopic front forks with automatic progressive hydraulic damping. Wheels quickly detachable, front with 8" brake, rear of straight spoke type with 7" brake; Dunlop tyres, front 3.25-19, rear 3.50-19. Petrol tank, capacity $4\frac{1}{4}$ Imperial gallons; adjustable handlebar; generous mudguards; tail portion of rear guard detachable for easy wheel removal; spring-up central stand; adjustable footrests.

EQUIPMENT. Adjustable spring-seat saddle; B.S.A. Dual Seat extra. Lucas 6-volt c.v.c. lighting set with sealed-beam headlamp and high frequency electric horn; metal toolbox under seat tube with complete toolkit; tyre pump; rubber knee-grips.

CONTROLS. On left handlebar, clutch lever, ignition cut-out button, and headlamp dip-switch; on right handlebar, front brake, air lever and horn button; rear brake operated by left toe pedal; kickstarter and gear-change pedals on right. Twin petrol taps at rear of tank, one for reserve. Finger adjustment for brakes and clutch controls.

FINISH. All bright parts including the exhaust system heavily chromium plated; frame, mudguards, etc., lustrous black enamel; petrol tank, black with distinctive motif; wheel rims chrome with black centres; polished front chain case, gearbox cover, timing cover. Finished in beige extra.

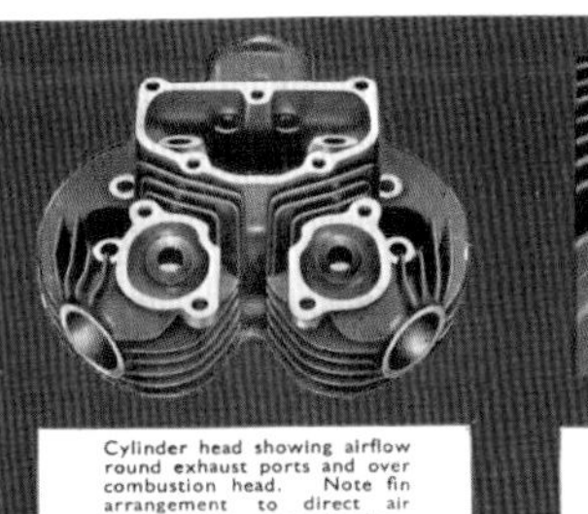

Cylinder head showing airflow round exhaust ports and over combustion head. Note fin arrangement to direct air round valve spring chambers.

The car-type tappets with greatly increased bearing area, and "siamesed" in pairs to ensure perfect constant alignment.

The pistons have split skirts, a feature which in conjunction with the low-expansion alloy used, permits of accurately-controlled clearances, with consequent freedom from slap and the risk of seizure.

The new 8-in. front brake with super-ribbed shoes for smooth, efficient, straightline stops.

The engine of the latest Star Twin, in common with that of the standard A7, had undergone considerable redesign work and was now virtually a scaled-down version of the Bert Hopwood-designed A10. It also had but a single carb in place of the previous Star Twin's two – the fresh engine giving better results with just the one. "Zestful acceleration, excellent road holding and the ability to devour the miles in unobtrusive fashion," began The Motor Cycle*'s appraisal when they tested one in early 1952. A standing-start quarter-mile in 16.8 seconds was not to be sneezed at, and nor were the two-way maximum speeds of 92mph in top and 86 in third. Vibration, the bugbear of vertical twins, was described as 'negligible' with cruising speeds in the neighbourhood of 75-plus talked about – provided you didn't mind the wind pressure.*

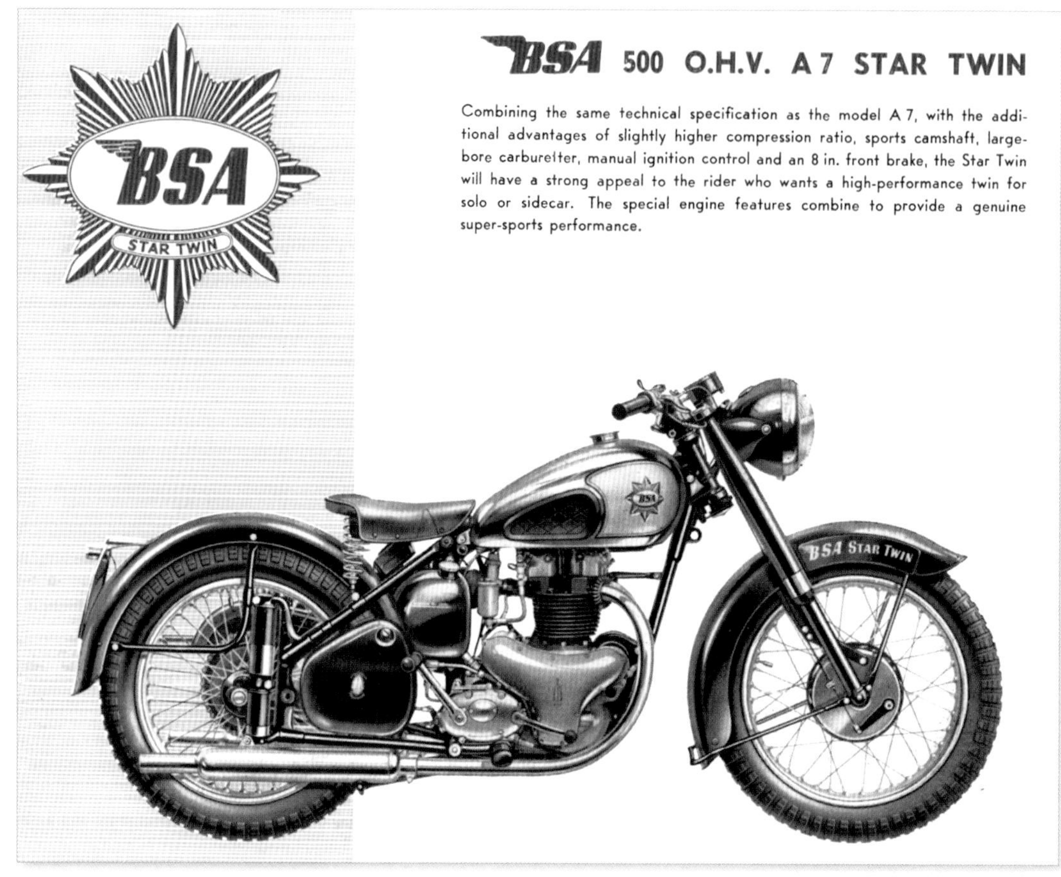

The Gold Star depicted in the 1952 brochure was something of a transitional model in that it had the last of the ZB 32 or 34 motors which had the appearance of a BB, with raised rather than incised piled arms on the pushrod tunnel and vestigial finning to the cylinder head above. The rocker box was no longer integral with the head and this, along with cylinder barrel and head itself, was die cast rather than sand-cast as they had been previously.

Model (Standard Specification)	D1	D1 Comp.	C10	C11	B31	B32 Comp.	B32 Gold Star	B33	B34 Comp.	B34 Gold Star	M20	M21	M33	A7	A7 Star Twin	A10 Golden Flash
Valve Arrangement	2-stroke	2-stroke	S.V.	O.H.V.	O.H.V.	O.H.V.	O.H.V.	O.H.V.	O.H.V.	O.H.V	S.V.	S.V.	O.H.V.	O.H.V.	O.H.V.	O.H.V.
No. of Cylinders	1	1	1	1	1	1	1	1	1	1	1	1	1	2	2	2
Bore (mm.)	52	52	63	63	71	71	71	85	85	85	82	82	85	66	66	70
Stroke (mm.)	58	58	80	80	88	88	88	88	88	88	94	112	88	72.6	72.6	84
Capacity (c.c.)	123	123	249	249	348	348	348	499	499	499	496	591	499	497	497	646
Compression Ratio	—	—	5–1	6.5–1	6.5–1	6.5–1	†	6.8–1	6.8–1	†	4.9–1	5–1	6.8-1	††6.6–1	7.2–1	††6.5–1
Gear Ratios (Solo)—																
Top	—	—	§	§	5.6	7.1	×	5.0	5.6	×	5.3	4.8	4.8	††5.1	††5.0	††4.4
Third	7.0	8.65	6.6	6.6	7.4	9.3		6.6	7.4		7.0	6.3	6.3	6.2	6.05	5.4
Second	11.7	14.5	9.8	9.8	11.5	14.5		10.3	11.6		10.9	9.8	9.8	9.0	8.8	7.8
First	22.0	27.1	14.5	14.5	16.7	21.1		14.9	16.8		15.8	14.2	14.2	13.2	12.9	11.4
Gear Ratios (Sidecar)—																
Top	—	—	—	—	—	—		—	—		5.9	5.9	5.6	††5.4	††5.4	††5.2
Third	—	—	—	—	—	—		—	—		7.8	7.8	7.4	6.6	6.6	6.3
Second	—	—	—	—	—	—		—	—		12.2	12.2	11.5	9.5	9.5	9.1
First	—	—	—	—	—	—		—	—		17.7	17.7	16.7	14.0	14.0	13.3
Front Tyre	2.75–19	2.75–19	3.00–19	3.00–19	2.75–19	2.75–21	2.75–21	3.25–19	2.75–21	2.75–21	3.25–19	3.25–19	3.25–19	3.25–19	3.25–19	3.25–19
Rear Tyre	2.75–19	3.25–19	3.00–19	3.00–19	3.25–19	4 00–19	4.00–19	3.50–19	4.00–19	4.00–19	3.25–19	3.50–19	3.50–19	3.50–19	3.50–19	3.50–19
Front Chain (ins.)	⅜ Pitch	⅜ Pitch	½ × .305	½ × .305	½ × .305	½ × .305	½ × .305	½ × .305	½ × .305	½ × .305	½ × .305	½ × .305	½ × .305	⅜ Duplex	⅜ Duplex	⅜ Duplex
Rear Chain (ins.)	½ Pitch	½ Pitch	½ × .305	½ × .305	⅝ × ¼	⅝ × ¼	⅝ × ¼	⅝ × ¼	⅝ × ¼	⅝ × ¼	⅝ × ¼	⅝ × ¼	⅝ × ¼	⅝ × ⅜	⅝ × ⅜	⅝ × ⅜
Brake Diameters (ins.)	5	5	5½	5½	7	7	F8.R7***	7	7	F8.R7***	7	7	7	7	F8.R7	F8.R7
Saddle Height (ins.) approx.	27	29	28	28	30½	31½	31½	30½	31½	31½	30½	30½	30½	30	30	30
Overall Length (ins.) approx.	77	77	80½	80½	82	82	83½	82	82	83½	85	85	85	84	84	84
Overall Height (ins.) approx.	38¾	38¾	39	39	40	41	41	40	41	41	39¼	39¼	39¼	40½	40½	40½
Overall Width (ins.) approx.	26½	26½	28	28	28	28	28	28	28	28	28	28	28	28	28	28
Ground Clearance (ins.) approx.	4¾	4¾	4½	4½	5	6¼	6¼	5	6¼	6¼	5½	5½	5½	4½	4½	4½
Weight (lbs.) approx.	**153	**165	**270	**285	345	*325	*340	355	*335	350	365	370	365	395	395	400
Petrol Tank Capacity (galls) approx.	1¾	1¾	2½	2½	3	3	3	3	3	3	3	3	3	3½	3½	4½
Oil Tank Capacity (pints) approx.	—	—	4	4	4	4	5	4	4	5	5	5	5	4	4	4

† Optional Compression Ratios for B32 Gold Star:—6.5, 7.5, 8.0, 9.0, 12.5 to 1; B34 Gold Star:—6.8, 7.5, 8.0, 9.0, 11.1 to 1.

†† Optional Compression Ratios, A7 and A10:—7.25 to 1.

× Gear Ratios:—

	B32 Gold Star Top	Third	Second	First	B34 Gold Star Top	Third	Second	First
Touring	5.6	7.4	11.5	16.7	5.0	6.6	10.3	14.9
Trials	7.06	9.3	14.5	21.1	5.64	7.44	11.6	16.8
Scrambles	7.06	9.3	12.15	17.44	6.63	8.74	11.4	16.4
Road Racing	5.3	5.8	6.9	9.9	4.75	5.2	6.2	8.9

Wide gear ratios:—	Top	Third	Second	First
A7				
Solo	5.1	7.4	10.8	16.2
Sidecar	5.4	7.9	11.6	17.2
A7 Star Twin				
Solo	5.0	7.3	10.6	15.8
Sidecar	5.4	7.9	11.6	17.2
A10 Golden Flash				
Solo	4.4	6.45	9.37	13.45
Sidecar	5.16	7.25	10.46	16.35

A choice of engine and gearbox sprockets is available giving a wide range of overall ratios to suit requirements.

* Weights with magneto only.

** Lucas equipment 10 lb. extra; Spring Frame 15 lb. extra. 20 lb. extra on C, B, and M. C models with 4-speed gearbox 4 lb. extra.

*** 7-in. front brake fitted for Trials and Scrambles.

§ Gear Ratios with 4-speed gear box: Top 6.5, Third 8.06, Second 11.7, First 17.15.

Specifications of the full 1952 range.

"The Machines you might have bought"

The story of an A·C·U–CERTIFIED TEST

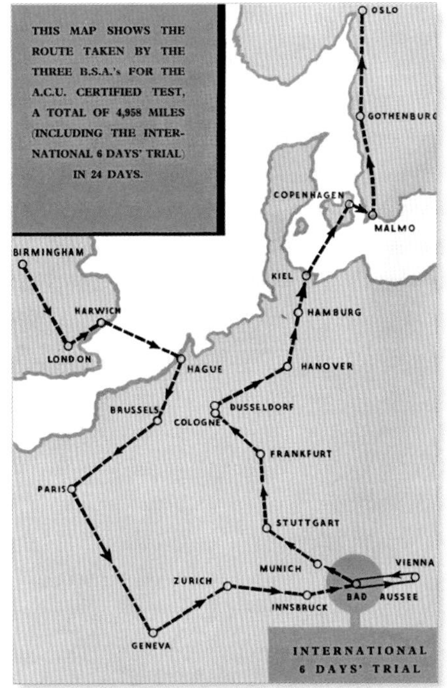

On 30 August 1952 three Star Twins were selected from a batch that had just come off the production line and, with no special preparation whatsoever, ridden by Fred Rist, Norman Vanhouse and Brian Martin, they left Small Heath a week later. From there, and the entire time under strict ACU observation, they travelled to London and thence Harwich for a ferry to Holland, then onwards via various capital cities to Austria where all three machines took part in the international Six Days Trial centred on Bad Aussee. In this they finished without the loss of a single mark – the only British team to do so – and won three Gold Medals. From there they struck out north through Germany and into Scandinavia, finishing in Oslo where high-speed tests were undertaken. The entire journey, including the ISDT, extended to 4,958 miles and occupied 22 days.

This booklet was published to celebrate their achievement and the award of the coveted Maudes Trophy – a perpetual trophy for, in the opinion of the ACU, the most meritorious performance in any one year. Last won by BSA in 1938, this was the first time it had been awarded since 1939.

Aimed firmly at the sidecar market, the M20s and M21 had sales material all of their own in 1953. A couple of years later Motor Cycling *got hold of an M21 hitched to a Gladiator two-seater sidecar. By then the M series models were fitted with Amal's Monobloc carbs but were otherwise much the same. Performance tests were taken with an adult passenger in the sidecar and top speed worked out at 55mph, with a gallon of fuel being consumed every 46 miles at a steady 50mph. The following, however, I do find impressive: "With two passengers in the chair and one on the pillion, performance was not noticeably impaired."*

M20. Rigid Frame	**£132.**	Tax	£36.	13.	4.	Total	**£168.**	**13.**	**4.**
M20. Spring Frame	**£141.**	Tax	£39.	3.	4.	Total	**£180.**	**3.**	**4.**
M21. Rigid Frame	**£135.**	Tax	£37.	10.	0.	Total	**£172.**	**10.**	**0.**
M21. Spring Frame	**£144.**	Tax	£40.	0.	0.	Total	**£184.**	**0.**	**0.**

B.S.A. 500 S.V. Model M 20 and 600 S.V. Model M 21

BSA BANTAM COMPETITION

125 c.c. Model D.1. Competition

150 c.c. Model D.3. Competition

ENGINE: Single cylinder two-stroke; D.1., 52 mm. bore × 58 mm. stroke, 123 c.c.; D.3., 57 mm. bore × 58 mm. stroke, 148 c.c.; deflectorless piston head with twin transfer ports giving efficient scavenging; aluminium alloy piston; improved roller bearing big-end; detachable aluminium alloy cylinder head with decompressor; Amal carburetter incorporating air cleaner; mainshaft on ball journal bearings with spring-loaded crankcase compression seals; combined flywheel magneto and dynamo; petroil lubrication; upswept exhaust system with efficient silencer. TRANSMISSION: Crankcase and gearbox in unit construction, with fixed-centres; primary chain drive from engine shaft to clutch on gearbox mainshaft; three-speed constant mesh gearbox, positive foot change and folding kick-starter, both pedals on right; gear ratios 8.64, 14.45 and 27.14 to 1; front chain .375 in. pitch; rear chain ½ in. pitch × .335 in. roller diameter. FRAME: Of tubular welded construction; 1¾ gallons petrol tank; front forks of new pattern; front wheel fitted with taper roller bearings; 5½ in. front brake, 5 in. rear brake, both of weatherproof design with finger adjustment; spring-up central stand; spring seat saddle, in raised position; adjustable footrests; unvalanced mudguards. CONTROLS: Twist grip throttle and front brake lever on right handlebar; clutch lever and dipper switch on left handlebar; rear brake operation by left toe pedal. EQUIPMENT: Dunlop tyres (Trials Universal), 2.75—19 front, 3.25—19 rear; Wico-Pacy flywheel dynamo direct lighting with headlamp switch operation; parking battery in headlamp; bulb horn built into steering stem; metal toolbox with complete tool kit; tyre inflator; licence holder. FINISH: D.1.—Frame, Tank, Forks, Wheels, etc. attractive pastel green; bright parts including wheel rims chromium plated. D.3—Frame, Tank, Forks, Wheels etc. in pastel grey; bright parts including wheel rims chromium plated.

D.1. 125 Comp. Rigid frame **£73** Tax £14 12s.

D.1. 125 Comp. Spring frame **£78** Tax £15 12s.

D.3. 150 Comp. Rigid frame **£78** Tax £15 12s.

D.3. 150 Comp. Spring frame **£83** Tax £16 12s.

With the introduction of the 150cc Bantam Major there were now four varieties of BSA's little competition two-stroke catalogued for 1954, which in common with the normal road-going 125 and 150cc versions had increased head and barrel finning over the original D1.

BSA GOLD STAR Models

To give an international flavour the cover of this brochure featured 1953 French 350cc motocross champion Paul Godey on his BB32. My first Gold Star was one of these. It was about ten years old and had had a hard life, starting out in the hands of John Tribble, but I was more than happy to give the £15-or-so asked for it. A couple of friends had big-fin Clubman Goldies but I was more interested in attempting to emulate the likes of Burly John Burton and other well-known scrambles riders – some hopes on a clapped-out 350 BB, not to mention rider inexperience and inability. Remarkably, it still retained a battered dull-chrome two-gallon tank and good SC gearbox but the original TT carb had long gone in favour of a Monobloc, although such niceties were lost on me back then.

Gold Stars were the first BSAs to feature the company's duplex swinging-arm frame as standard – the BB32 and BB34s, so equipped, being introduced at the 1952 show. Any owners, please take note – the BB Clubmans had what the factory referred to as fork outer sleeves with integral headlamp brackets and semi-drop handlebars mounted on the top yoke. In common with some other manufacturers at this time, a headlight with underslung side-lamp was fitted. The manufacturer's standard spiral-baffle barrel silencer was employed but for racing a plain extension pipe giving the optimum exhaust length was available – the swept-back exhaust and tapered silencer were in the future.

Derek Powell ran away with the 1953 Junior Clubmans TT on one of these at an average speed of 80.17mph in spite of fuel seeping from a split tank and reaching the rear tyre from the second lap on. He'd been given a specially prepared engine by BSA but it blew in practice so his own was refitted for the race. As for the rest of the bike it had the optional GP carb and, as the regulations allowed for the headlight and dynamo to be removed, this had been done and a suitable spacer clamped in place of the latter.

Alternative Specifications B.S.A. Gold Star Models

The B.S.A. Gold Star enjoys the highest reputation in sporting circles all over the world, and its outstanding successes in competitive events have made it supreme in its class. Available in two capacities, 350 c.c. and 500 c.c., it is offered with a wide diversity of specifications as detailed below. The purchaser of a B.S.A. Gold Star can thus obtain a specification exactly suited to his needs, and can alter the specification by selecting suitable items from the range of pistons, cams, gears, etc., which are available.

SPEC.	TOURING		SCRAMBLES		ROAD RACING		CLUBMANS	
MODEL	B. 32	B. 34	B. 32	B. 34	B. 32	B. 34	B. 32	B. 34
Frame	Swinging Arm		Swinging Arm		Swinging Arm		Swinging Arm	
Piston	65–1616 with .010 plate	65–1467	65–1674	65–1532	65–1674 with .012 plate	65–1532 with $\frac{1}{16}''$ plate	65–1674 with .012 plate	65–1285
Comp. Ratio	7.8 : 1	7.5 : 1	9 : 1	8.75 : 1	9 : 1	8.4 : 1	8.75 : 1	8 : 1
Carburetter	Amal $1\frac{3}{32}''$ TT 10	Amal $1\frac{5}{32}''$ TT 10	Amal $1\frac{3}{32}''$ TT 10	Amal $1\frac{5}{32}''$ TT 10	Amal $1\frac{3}{32}''$ R.N. or G.P.	Amal $1\frac{3}{16}''$ R.N. or G.P.	Amal $1\frac{3}{32}''$ R.N. or G.P.	Amal $1\frac{3}{16}''$ R.N. or G.P.
Ignition	Magdyno		Magneto		Magneto		Magdyno	
Oil	Mineral		Mineral		Castor Base		Castor Base	
Oil Tank Capacity	6 pints		6 pints		6 pints		6 pints	
Instruments	Speedometer		Speedometer		Rev. Counter		Rev. Counter	
Exhaust System	Downswept with silencer		Downswept straight through with extension piece		Downswept with megaphone		Downswept with silencer and extension piece	
Gear Ratios	5.6, 6.77, 9.86, 14.42	5.0, 6.05, 8.79, 12.9	7.72, 10.19, 13.54, 18.08	7.26, 9.62, 12.73, 17.0	5.28, 5.8, 7.0, 10.15	4.52, 4.96, 5.99, 8.71	5.28, 5.8, 7.0, 10.15	4.52, 4.96, 5.99, 8.71
Eng. Sprocket	17 teeth	19 teeth	16 teeth	17 teeth	18 teeth	21 teeth	18 teeth	21 teeth
Gearbox Sprocket	19 teeth		16 teeth		19 teeth		19 teeth	
Brakes	8″ Front 7″ rear		7″ Front 7″ Rear		8″ Front 7″ Rear		8″ Front 7″ Rear	
Tyres	Dunlop Universal Front : 3.00 × 21 or 3.00 × 19 Rear : 3.25 × 19 or 3.50 × 19		Dunlop Sports Front : 3.00 × 21 Rear : 4.00 × 19		Dunlop Racing Front : 3.00 × 21 or 3.00 × 19 Rear : 3.25 × 19	Rear : 3.50 × 19	Dunlop Racing Front : 3.00 × 21 or 3.00 × 19 Rear : 3.25 × 19	Rear : 3.50 × 19
Petrol Tank	4 gallons		2 gallons		4 gallons		4 gallons	
Saddle or Dualseat	Dualseat		Dualseat		Dualseat		Dualseat	
Footrest and Brake Pedal	Standard		Scramble Pattern		Racing Pattern		Racing Pattern	
Handlebars	Standard		Standard		Racing		Racing	
Lighting	Magdyno		Not fitted		Not fitted		Magdyno	

Extras: On Road Racing and Clubman Models, speedometers, alloy rims and G.P. Carburetters can be fitted at extra charge.
On Touring and Scramble Models, Rev. Counter can be fitted at extra charge.

Note: On Road Racing and Clubman Models, remote mounted float chambers are fitted without extra charge.
On those models without Magdyno, Lucas or B.T.H. Magnetos are optional.

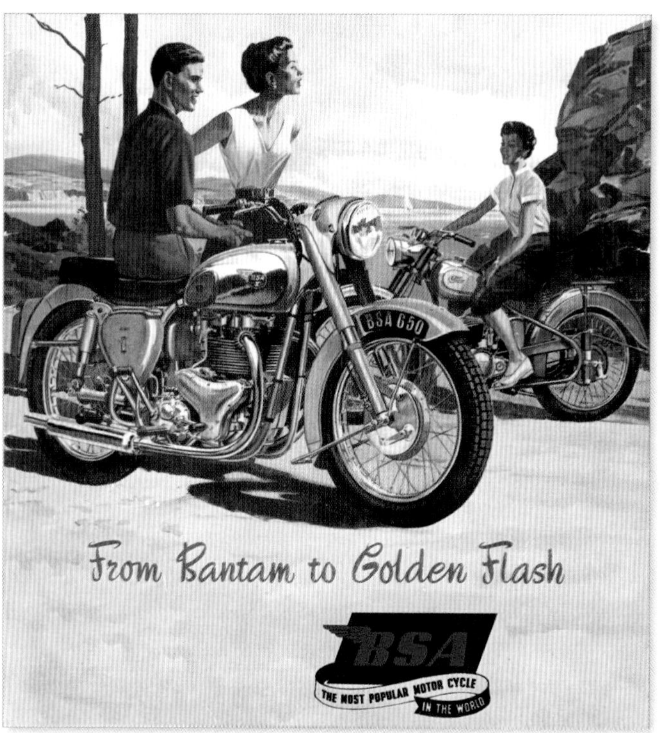

As well as giving Sally a hand getting to know her new 125cc Bantam D1, Miles was also keen to show off his Golden Flash and perhaps give her a ride. They'd arranged to meet near the beach but his girlfriend Wanda had got wind of what was going on and was waiting for them… He'd read about the swinging-arm version of BSA's 650 when it had been introduced in the autumn of 1953 but had only recently managed to save up for the hire purchase deposit on the basic price of £201 plus purchase tax and a bit extra for pillion footrests and a prop stand. One in black would have been £3 cheaper but it had to be Beige; and was he thinking of Sally or Wanda when he spent an extra £3 12s on those additional footrests?

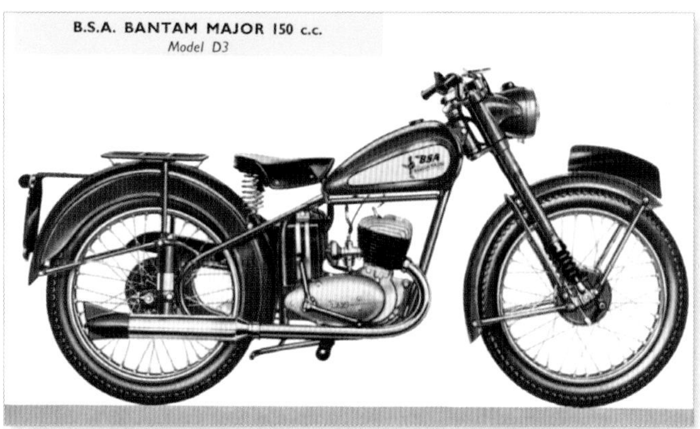

The D3 had been introduced in the autumn of 1953 as a supplement to the enormously popular D1. Although no faster it did have a little more grunt on hills at the expense of a cupful of extra fuel being used every hundred miles or so.

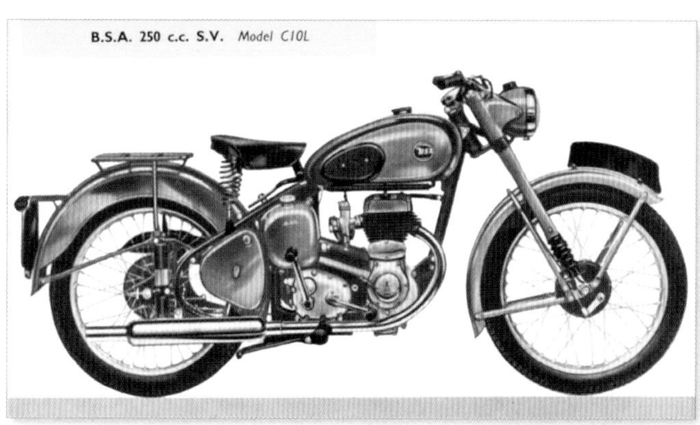

With the demise of the more expensive Indian Brave and OEC's Apollo, the C10 had no competitors for the diminishing side-valve 250 market.

The C11G had superseded the C11 in 1953 and could be had with either rigid or plunger frame and three- or four-speed gearbox. For 1955 it had been given a larger front brake and the rigid frame option dropped, although there was still a choice of gearboxes. As The Motor Cycle *pointed out when they had one on test it made no pretensions to being a sports machine, rather 'an excellent example of an average 250'. They loved its instantaneous starting under any conditions, hot or cold, maybe due to the model now being equipped with an Amal Monobloc carb. It had average 250 performance to boot, with a 62/63mph top whack and just under 80mpg if you kept to 50 and no more.*

The 500cc B33 was identical in most respects and also could be had with swinging-arm or plunger frame. It was fitted with higher overall gear ratios, however, as well as an 8in front brake.

Some individual details showcased in the 1955 brochure.

B.S.A. Tipon colour enamel tube with "pencil" nylon brush for touching-up.

Dual Seat and rubber-covered Pillion Footrests standard equipment on swinging arm models. Battery concealed but accessibly mounted under dual seat on swinging arm models.

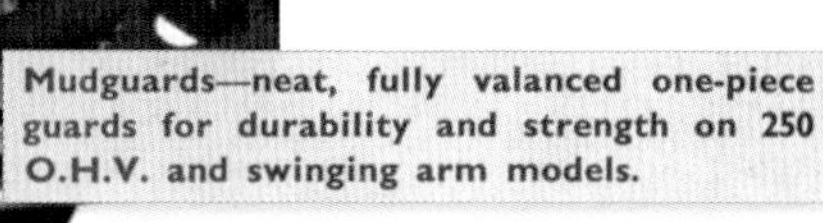

Mudguards—neat, fully valanced one-piece guards for durability and strength on 250 O.H.V. and swinging arm models.

Quickly-detachable Rear Wheel of patented design with straight spokes for strength, fitted to B, M spring frame and A models.

Front Brake. Powerful 8 in. front brake on model B33 and A models, as illustrated. New front wheel with 7 in. brake on 250 O.H.V. model.

A.C. Generator ensures easy starting independent of battery. Rubber Cush Drive in clutch assembly gives flexibility at low speed and smooth acceleration. On 250 c.c. models.

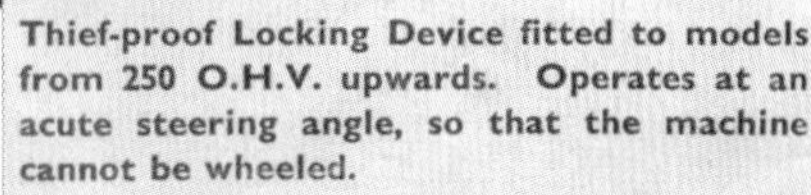

Thief-proof Locking Device fitted to models from 250 O.H.V. upwards. Operates at an acute steering angle, so that the machine cannot be wheeled.

Petrol Tank in attractive chrome and colour finish, 100% rubber mounted, single bolt fixing for easy engine accessibility, on swinging arm models. Duplex Cradle Frame for maximum stability and rock-steady steering. On B group swinging arm and A group models.

Whilst other manufacturers had turned to swinging-arm suspension for their trials machines, BSA adhered to rigid frames until the end of the 1955 model year – although a swinging-arm version was available as an optional extra from 1954. This duplex-framed model with either BB32 or BB34 aluminium motor had replaced the single down-tube B32 and 34 competition models towards the end of 1953 but, unlike them, an alloy head and barrel were standard. Aluminium petrol tanks had been introduced for 1955 and until this point they had been steel, normally painted polychromatic silver with chromium side panels.

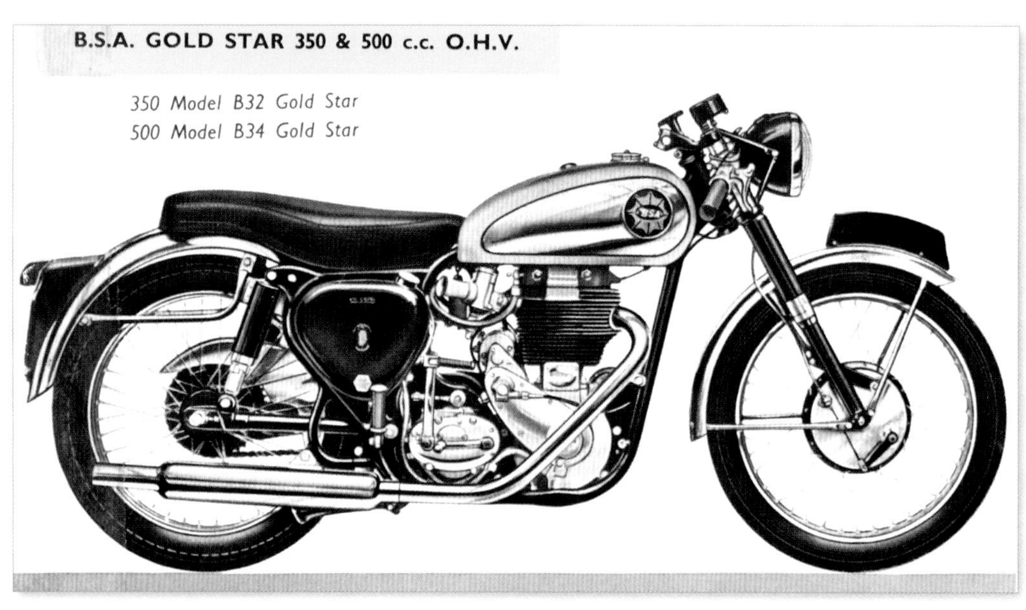

First of the 'big fin' Gold Stars were the CB32 and CB34. Apart from obvious differences in the external appearance their motors were much developed within, including a shorter connecting rod than the BB which, in the case of the CB34, necessitated oval flywheels in order to allow for a reasonable length of piston skirt. This was the first Gold Star that, when in Clubmans trim, was equipped with clip-on handlebars – the headlamp then being mounted on brackets consisting of four individual steel tubes.Alistair King won the 1954 Senior Clubmans with one of these and was followed home by two others – all three averaging over 85mph. A measure of the 350 Gold Star's standing amongst riders was that no less than 42 took the start out of a field of 49, so it was almost a case of who rather than which make. Geoff Tanner on an International Norton, which coincidentally was once owned by a friend of mine, made a brave challenge but could do no better than fifth, with the next best Norton ninth. Other than them it was BSAs right down to 22nd place, with Phil Palmer winning and the first six all averaging over 81mph.

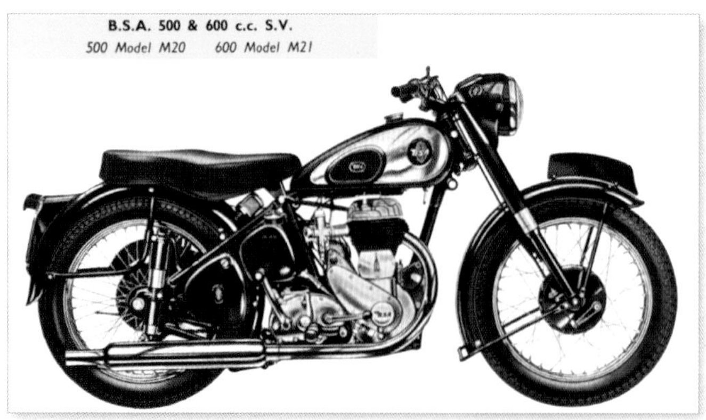

"For sheer dogged dependability there's nothing to touch the BSA M20 and M21," read the sales blurb; and here is the 1955 plunger version of the two hardy perennials, which would be reduced to one at the end of the season with the passing of the M20. If you wanted to save a tenner-or-so you could still opt for the rigid model but either way you got the latest Amal monobloc carb that was now fitted to the entire range other than the Clubmans Gold Stars.

"This is the motorcycle for the rider who needs a dual purpose machine. It is robust, with a lively performance solo or sidecar." Like the big side-valve machines it too could be had with rigid frame and there was also the option of solo or sidecar gearing.

BSA's 500 twins are often dismissed as second-best to the 650s, but the sports versions such as the 1955 Shooting Star are surprisingly fleet of foot. Developed from the Star Twin and making its first appearance at the 1953 show, it had high-compression pistons and a sports camshaft, an aluminium cylinder head and manual ignition control. The Pale Polychromatic Green front forks, mudguards, tanks and toolbox were set off against a Dark Green frame. All this for £200 plus £40 purchase tax.

The updated A7, featuring a separate gearbox, had been introduced in the autumn of 1954 with plunger rear suspension and BSA's new duplex swinging-arm frame as an optional extra. This year it was standard.

In case you didn't fancy a swinging-arm Flash, or resented the £8-or-so extra that one cost, there was still the plunger-framed version, which also offered a set of gear ratios to suit the sidecar man.

Additional Equipment for your BSA

Legshields and bumper bars as fitted to B.S.A. D group models.

		£	s.	d.	
Electric Horn	Model D1	1	2	3	incl. p.t.
Safety Bars	Model D1		19	3	,,
Legshields	C and D Models . .	1	16	0	,,
Legshields	A, B and M models . .	3	0	0	,,
Carrier	All models except D1, D3, C10L and models fitted with Dual Seat . .	1	5	3	,,
B.S.A. Dual Seat and Pillion Footrests	When not standard . .	3	12	0	,,
Prop Stand	Except D1, D3 and C10L .		18	0	,,
Air Cleaner	C and B models . .		15	0	,,
Air Cleaner	M models and A7 Shooting Star		19	3	,,

The 1956 brochure cover depicts Miles and Wanda relaxing in the grass beside their new Shooting Star, as a couple on one of the latest Ariel-braked Golden Flashes speed by with Sally in hot pursuit on her Bantam.

The US brochure only specified Maroon for the D1 whilst the UK version offered it in the traditional Pastel Green or Black as well. The cheaper rigid-framed model was no longer available in the UK, whilst at home and abroad the D3 Major now had a swinging-arm frame and also a choice of Pastel Grey, Maroon or Black.

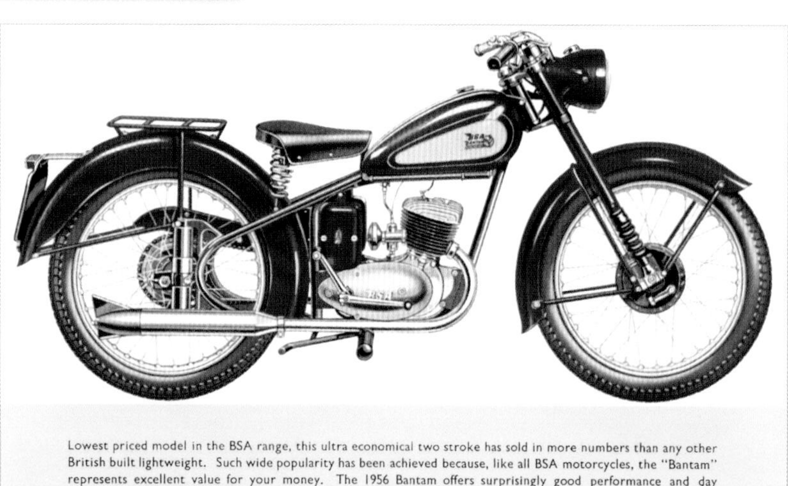

Although no contenders for the land speed record, Bantams were willing little beasts and around town and on minor country roads they were surprisingly nippy, point to point. The Motor Cycle *put a swinging arm Major to the test in 1956 and found it had "ample power for touring" as well as "docility in traffic". It would do 50 flat out and returned around 100mpg overall, or 165mpg if you stuck to 20mph. Top speed of a D1 was only a little less, say 47mph, but it was , understandably, a little less quick off the mark and lost momentum more readily when faced with a gradient.*

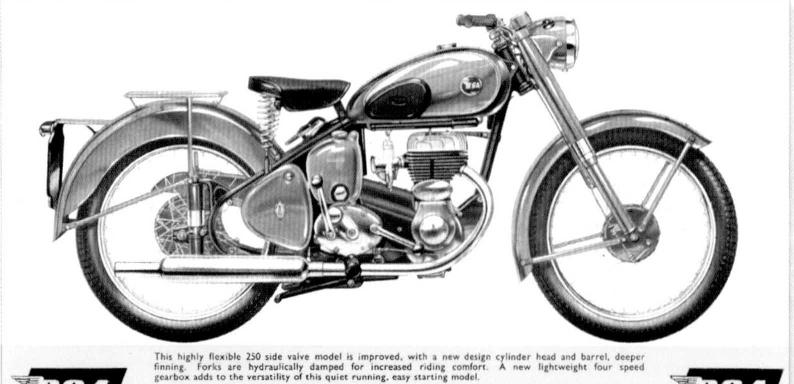

The C10 was perhaps an even more unlikely machine than the Bantam for the North American market; nevertheless a few made their way over the Atlantic. Both home and export models now featured the heavier pattern forks. Home and export models alike were finished in two-tone green with chromium tank panels as an optional extra.

With an entirely new frame and hydraulically controlled swinging arm rear suspension, the BSA C12 offers sparkling performance with minimum investment, low upkeep costs. Full width type hubs and cowl-mounted headlight add to smart new appearance. Finish is in lustrous maroon with chrome tank panels, chrome wheel rims and exhaust system and many other parts in chrome plate or polished alloy. Plenty of snap and speed for highway traffic—ideal around town mount.

The final flowering of BSA's C type 250, as illustrated in its 1956 transatlantic catalogue. US laws did not require a front number plate, so they were omitted from illustrations of individual machines in specially produced publicity material. UK versions had cream tank panels but chrome was available for a little extra.

When BSA's 1956 range was introduced in the autumn of '55 its 350cc-and-over machines now featured Ariel's full-width alloy brakes. Here's the Americanised version of the 500cc B33. Home-market bikes were Maroon.

The famous B33 "Iron Single"—one of the most reliable and trouble free motorcycles ever built—now, for 1956, in a new and handsome finish which brings it into the winner's circle for sparkle and good looks. Here's an attractively priced big single, with an excellent turn of speed and snappy acceleration—the choice of many thousands of experienced motorcycle riders the world over. Featuring the same type of frame and suspension as the larger BSA twins, the 1956 B33 also includes all new season improvements. Full width alloy hubs with cast-in alloy iron brake drums are standard equipment. Finish, handsome Ebony Black frame, Rocket fire red tank with gleaming chrome tank panels. Full chrome mudguards.

PERFORMANCE: "Cycle Magazine" in independent road test reports: "One of the B33's many accomplishments is a healthy 90 m.p.h. speed,—this standard model with full equipment clocked an honest 90"

Smooth, quiet, and dependable power coupled with superior road holding and comfortable riding qualities have made this BSA model a favorite among motorcyclists everywhere. Except for the difference in engine capacity this is basically the same motor cycle as the "Golden Flash", and, as the lowest priced twin in the BSA range, is an excellent buy for a large group of motorcycle riders. For 1956, the "500 Flash" will be fitted with the new, full width alloy hubs with centrally positioned cast-in alloy iron brake drums, dual seat, and other improvements. Full rear chain enclosure is optional at extra cost.

In American-speak the A7 became the 500 Flash but apart from the US-style handlebars and passenger grab rail it was to the same specification as for the home market, with the exception of an all-Maroon finish for those sold in the UK or Europe.

For the 1956 season US brochure the Shooting Star had been given the American treatment too but survived with the same name. Note the blanking plate for a rev counter driving on the timing cover – a feature not incorporated in home-market versions.

Somehow, 40 cubic inches sounds more impressive than 650cc, don't you think? Despite it retaining its British title a beige (gold) version was not mentioned, but one was still available in its home country.

BSA 40 cubic inch Twin Model A10
"GOLDEN FLASH"

Flexible, outstandingly dependable yet capable of the high speeds necessary to stay with modern American highway traffic. The "Golden Flash" has established itself as a popular model in all world markets as an easy starting, sweet running motorcycle with outstanding performance characteristics. Finish is very appealing, with "Rocket-fire" red tank with chrome panels, full chrome wheel rims and exhaust system, glossy black baked enamel fenders, and many other parts in full chrome or polished alloy. 1956 features include the new full width alloy hubs with centrally disposed brakes, dual seat, and many other improvements. Full rear chain enclosure is optional, at extra cost.

PERFORMANCE: "Cycle Magazine" reports in independent road test: "Golden Flash top speed 103.5 m.p.h." "The Motor Cycle" reports: "Open road cruising at 80-85 m.p.h. delightful and comfortable"

BSA 40 cubic inch Twin Model A10
"ROAD ROCKET"

Thrilling high speed performance—smashing acceleration and extremely handsome appearance are combined in the spectacular 1956 "Road Rocket". This popular tuned-at-the-factory special comes equipped with Amal T.T. racing carburetor, high compression pistons, high compression alloy cylinder head, special hi-speed camshaft, and 8000 r.p.m. tachometer on twin mount with speedometer. Finish is highly attractive, with "Rocket-fire" red tank with chrome panels, fully chromed fenders and many other parts in heavy chrome and polished alloy. Features for 1956 include the new alloy full width hubs with centrally disposed brakes, dual seat, and other improvements. Full rear chain enclosure is optional at extra cost.

PERFORMANCE: "Motorcyclist Magazine" reports: "An honest 110 m.p.h. motorcycle" "Cycle Magazine" in independent road test reports "110.76 m.p.h. through the measured mile with *all road equipment*"

The Road Rocket had been an export-only model for the US market since 1954 but finally became available in the United Kingdom during the latter part of 1956. This, however, is the US model complete with front fender-mounted rocket motif. Home-market models did not have this or the grab handle at the rear of the dual seat. The British description of the fuel tank's paintwork was bright scarlet but for those with subtler taste silver was an option. A rev counter was an optional extra, however, although the timing cover was machined to accept its drive.

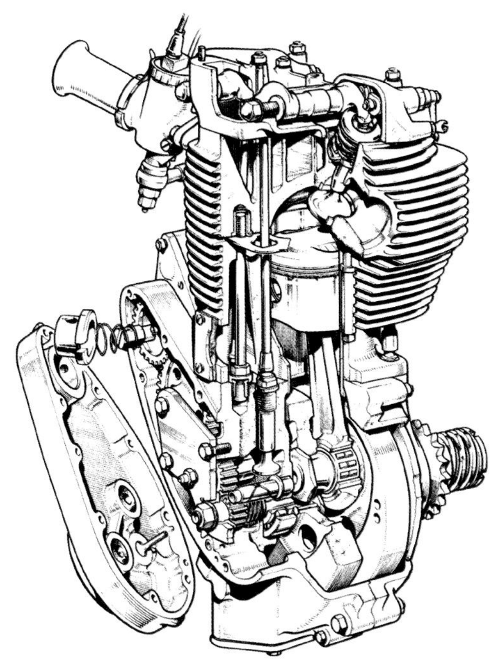

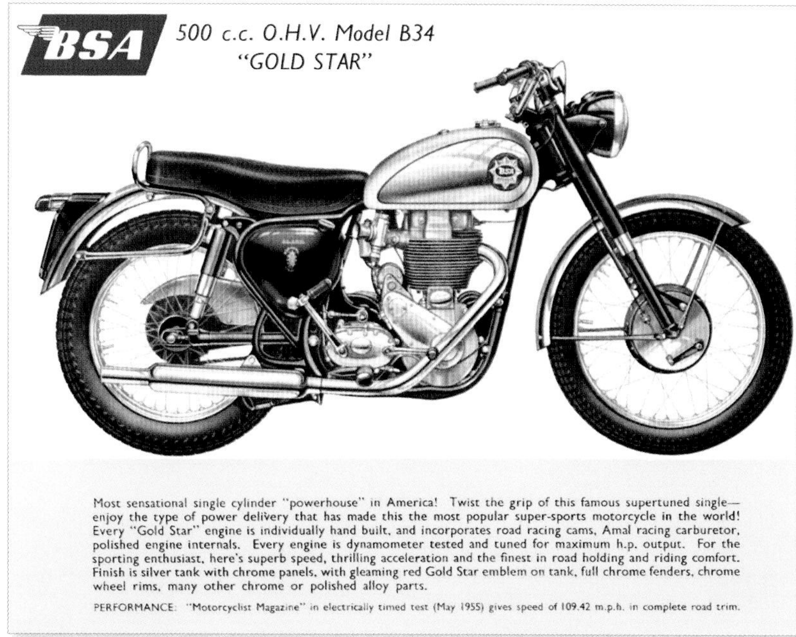

WINDSCREENS

The PHOENIX range

	Retail Price
The Royal Twin, as on A.A. Patrols	147/- each
The Royal, the same as A.A. but without metal apron	105/- each
The Telefork 3/16"x24"x16" Perspex } both with plastic transparent aprons	70/6 each
The Universal 3/16"x18"x16" Perspex }	65/6 each
The Standard 3/16"x16"x14½" Perspex	52/6 each
The Bantam Major ⅛"x16"x14½" Perspex, P.V.C. Apron	49/6 each

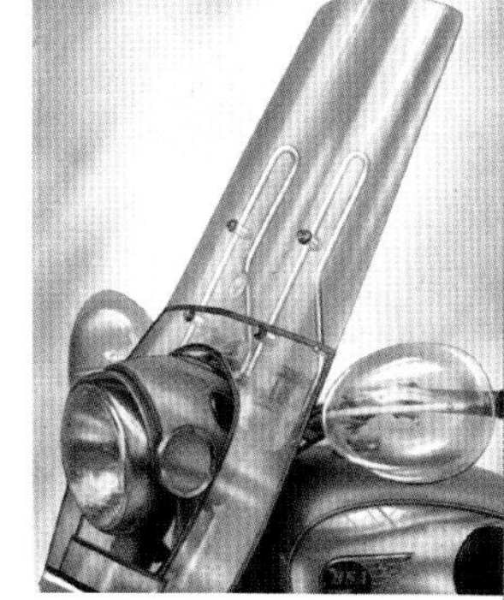

The MONSOON range

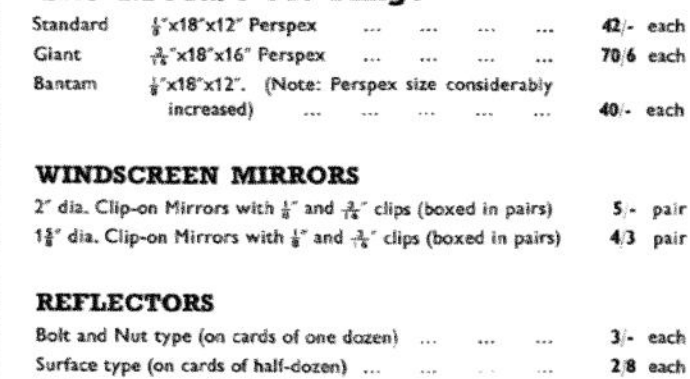

Standard	⅛"x18"x12" Perspex	42/- each
Giant	3/16"x18"x16" Perspex	70/6 each
Bantam	⅛"x18"x12". (Note: Perspex size considerably increased)	40/- each

WINDSCREEN MIRRORS

2" dia. Clip-on Mirrors with ⅛" and 3/16" clips (boxed in pairs)	5/- pair
1⅝" dia. Clip-on Mirrors with ⅛" and 3/16" clips (boxed in pairs)	4/3 pair

REFLECTORS

Bolt and Nut type (on cards of one dozen)	3/- each
Surface type (on cards of half-dozen)	2/8 each
Self-tapping type with white background (on cards of half-dozen)	2/8 each

FRONT AND REAR SAFETY BARS

		Retail Price £ s. d.
A Group	67–4919. (Front)	3 15 4
	67–4937. (Rear, complete with Pillion Footrests, Spring Frame Models, up to 1952)	4 8 0
	67–4938. (Rear, complete with Pillion Footrests, 1953 Spring Frame Models) ...	4 8 0
	66–4832. (Rear, when no Pillion Footrests are required, all Spring Frame Models)	3 19 2
B Group	65–4794. (Front)	3 15 4
D Group	90–7203. (Front)	1 1 1
M Group	66–7366. (Front)	3 6 6
	Rear — as for A Group.	

TRANSPARENT PLASTIC HANDGUARDS ... 29/11 pair

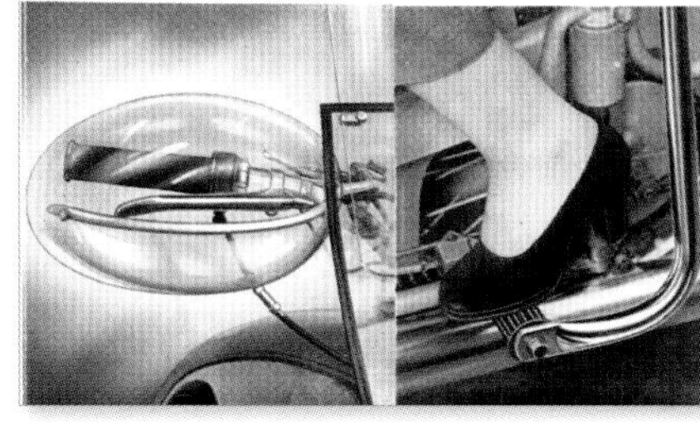

DUAL SEATS

Model	Assembly Part No.		Retail Price £ s. d.
A Group	17–9104	...	4 12 6
B.31, B.33, Rigid Frame	65–9252	...	4 12 6
B.31, B.33, Spring Frame	65–9254	...	4 12 6
B.32, B.34, Rigid Frame	65–9253	...	4 12 6
B.32, B.34, Spring Frame	65–9255	...	4 12 6
C Group, Rigid Frame	29–9375	...	4 12 6
C Group, Spring Frame	29–9376	...	4 12 6
D Group, Rigid Frame	90–9110	...	4 12 6
D Group, Spring Frame	90–9111	...	4 12 6
M Group, Rigid Frame	66–9246	...	4 12 6
M Group, Spring Frame	66–9247	...	4 12 6

Available in the following Colours:
Black, Blue, Maroon, Beige and Bantam Green.

ORDER FROM YOUR LOCAL B.S.A. DEALER

Gold Stars went by various titles at different times in the United States but as BSA chose not to name this version neither shall I. However, I can tell you that it is a 1956 DB34 in sports road-going trim as produced for the American market. Factory despatch records don't help us much either, as DB34s bound for the US were almost without exception recorded as Scramblers, American Spec or Clubmans – the latter confusingly being, normally, quite different from home-market Clubmans. Call it what you will but it's a handsome and, even in today's traffic conditions, much more usable machine – especially as it will have been supplied with a standard rather than close-ratio gearbox.

For Europe and the United Kingdom there was often a black-and-white brochure dedicated to the single-cylinder sports machines, such as this 1956 edition printed in October 1955.

First off, just look at this DB Clubmans's rear hub! (above right) The artist had given the unfortunate machine one of the Ariel type as fitted to other big BSAs, complete with cable operation. To the best of my knowledge the manufacturer never even thought of equipping Gold Stars with such things and at this time the rear brake was a special version of the rod-activated 7in single-sided unit with six ventilation holes and three Alfin-type aluminium cooling fins. He has also omitted the 'oil level' transfer on the oil tank but, on the other hand, correctly depicted the new optional 190mm front brake that would shortly be available. At this time an uprated version of the RRT gearbox was introduced with a needle roller bearing incorporated in the mainshaft assembly and a higher bottom gear; it was designated the RRT2.

Alternative Specifications B.S.A. Gold Star Models

The B.S.A. Gold Star enjoys the highest reputation in sporting circles all over the world, and its outstanding successes in competitive events have made it supreme in its class. Available in two capacities, 350 c.c. and 500 c.c., it is offered with a wide diversity of specifications as detailed below.

SPEC.	TOURING		SCRAMBLES		ROAD RACING		CLUBMANS	
MODEL	B. 32	B. 34	B. 32	B. 34	B. 32	B. 34	B. 32	B. 34
Frame	Swinging Arm		Swinging Arm		Swinging Arm		Swinging Arm	
Piston	65-1921	65-1930	65-2287	65-2300	65-2554	65-2307	65-2554	65-2307
Comp. Ratio	7.25 : 1	7.25 : 1	9 : 1	9 : 1	8 : 1	8 : 1	8 : 1	8 : 1
Carburetter	Amal 1 3/32"	Amal 1 5/32"	Amal 1 1/16"	Amal 1 1/8"	Amal 1 3/32"	Amal 1 1/2"	Amal 1 3/32"	Amal 1 1/2"
Ignition	Magdyno		Magneto		Magneto		Magdyno	
Oil	Mineral		Mineral		Castor Base		Castor Base	
Oil Tank Capacity	6 pints		6 pints		6 pints		6 pints	
Instruments	Speedometer				Rev. Counter		Rev. Counter	
Exhaust System	Downswept with silencer		Downswept straight through		Downswept with megaphone		Downswept with silencer and extension piece	
Gear Ratios	5.6, 6.77, 9.86, 14.42	5.0, 6.05, 8.79, 12.9	7.73, 10.24, 13.56, 18.11	7.26, 9.62, 12.73, 17.0	5.28, 5.8, 7.0, 9.24	4.52, 4.96, 5.99, 7.92	5.28, 5.8, 7.0, 9.24	4.52, 4.96, 5.99, 7.92
Eng. Sprocket	17 teeth	19 teeth	16 teeth	17 teeth	18 teeth	21 teeth	18 teeth	21 teeth
Gearbox Sprocket	19 teeth		16 teeth		19 teeth		19 teeth	
Tyres	Dunlop Universal Front: 3.00×21 or 3.00×19 Rear: 3.25×19 or 3.50×19		Dunlop Sports Front: 3.00×21 Rear: 4.00×19		Dunlop Racing Front: 3.00×21 or 3.00×19 Rear: 3.25×19	Rear: 3.50×19	Dunlop Racing Front: 3.00×21 or 3.00×19 Rear: 3.25×19	Rear: 3.50×19
Petrol Tank	4 gallons		2 gallons		4 gallons		4 gallons	
Saddle or Dualseat	Dualseat		Dualseat		Dualseat		Dualseat	
Footrest and Brake Pedal	Standard		Scramble Pattern		Racing Pattern		Racing Pattern	
Handlebars	Standard		Standard		Racing		Racing	
Lighting	Magdyno		Not fitted		Not fitted		Magdyno	

Extras: On Scrambles Models, 2 Gal. Alloy Tank can be supplied at extra charge.
5 Gal. Alloy Tank can be supplied at extra charge.
On Road Racing and Clubman Models, speedometers, alloy rims can be fitted at extra charge.

Note: On Road Racing and Clubman Models, remote mounted float chambers are fitted without extra charge.
On those models without Magdyno, Lucas or B.T.H. Magnetos are optional.

In real terms it was the scrambles version of the Gold Star that earned it true universal appeal, with large numbers shipped to BSA Inc in New Jersey and Hap Alzina in California, particularly the latter. On mainland Europe the French were probably the biggest buyers but numbers were also sent to Belgium, Switzerland, Holland, Sweden, Denmark, Finland and even tiny Lichtenstein. The timing cover had provision for a rev counter drive, although I've never heard of one being hooked up for scrambles use. Riders who preferred to stick with the standard pannier oil tank, rather than opting for the central one that allowed fitting of the factory air filter box, often rigged up their own filtration system to the carb inlet.

500 cc OHV model B34 SCRAMBLES

ENGINE. 85 × 88 mm. bore and stroke (499 c.c.) 350 c.c. engine optional to order; specially designed to give optimum connecting rod/crank ratio; strengthened crankcase and heavy duty main bearings; aluminium alloy cylinder barrel with wear-resisting alloy iron liner; aluminium alloy cylinder head with valve seat inserts and stellite tipped high duty valves; specially adjusted lightweight valve actuating mechanism; polished fly-wheels and connecting rod; reinforced crankpin; cams, valve springs, etc., to suit compression ratio; Amal Monobloc carburetter, special air filter extra, only fitted with central oil tank; engine specially tuned and bench tested.

LUBRICATION. Dry sump lubrication with double gear pump; large bore oil pipes; oil tank capacity 5½ pints and fitted with a specially-designed breather; central oil tank extra; primary chain oil bath; gearbox lubrication by oil and other parts by grease gun.

TRANSMISSION. Engine shaft cush drive; front chain ½ in. × .305 in. in oil bath; rear chain ⅝ in. × ⅜ in.; B.S.A. multi plate dry clutch with oil resisting fabric surfaces; B.S.A. four-speed gearbox with special needle roller bearings; enclosed clutch operation; positive-stop foot gear-change; wide ratio scrambles gears; alternative gear ratios to suit requirements; engine shaft sprocket to suit requirements.

FRAME. Tubular frame of all welded construction; central stand; steering damper; additional rear footrest position; crankcase shield optional; 2-gallon tank, 2-gallon alloy tank extra; tank breather.

SUSPENSION. Front suspension by B.S.A. telescopic forks with automatic hydraulic damping; rear suspension by totally enclosed hydraulically damped main and rebound spring units in conjunction with swinging arm rear wheel cradle.

WHEELS. Fitted with Dunlop Tyres, front 3.00—21; rear, 4.00—19, both sports type. Highly efficient brakes; front 7 in.; rear 7 in.

CONTROLS. Twist grip throttle control, front brake and air lever on right bar; clutch, ignition and exhaust lifter on left bar.

EQUIPMENT. Lucas racing magneto; B.S.A. Dualseat; shortened leather dualseat extra; tool kit; tyre inflator.

FINISH. Handlebars, stays, exhaust system, wheel rims, mudguards, etc., chromium-plated; frame finished in black enamel; silver tank with chromium panels and special Gold Star badge.

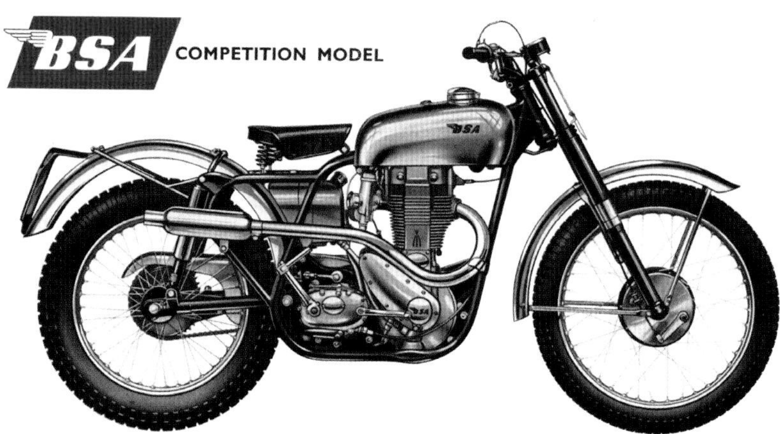

A swinging-arm frame and two-gallon aluminium fuel tank were standardised for the B32 and B34 Competition by the 1956 season. Although much more of a specialised machine than the B31 and B33-derived originals from the late '40s, they enjoyed less success in British trials than their predecessors. Large numbers were sold in the United States, however, where they became known as Clippers.

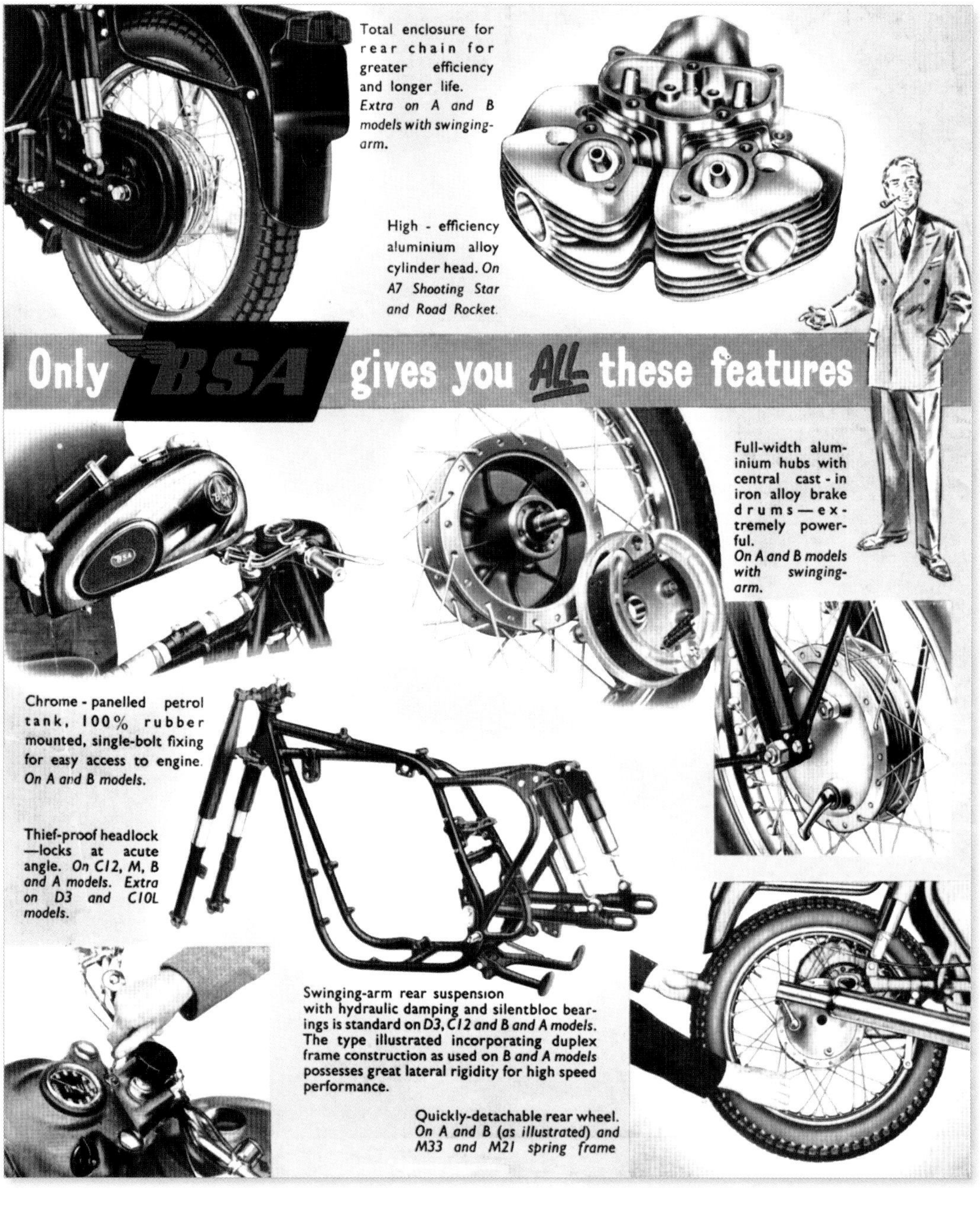

Total enclosure for rear chain for greater efficiency and longer life. *Extra on A and B models with swinging-arm.*

High - efficiency aluminium alloy cylinder head. *On A7 Shooting Star and Road Rocket.*

Only BSA gives you ALL these features

Full-width aluminium hubs with central cast - in iron alloy brake drums—extremely powerful. *On A and B models with swinging-arm.*

Chrome - panelled petrol tank, 100% rubber mounted, single-bolt fixing for easy access to engine. *On A and B models.*

Thief-proof headlock —locks at acute angle. *On C12, M, B and A models. Extra on D3 and C10L models.*

Swinging-arm rear suspension with hydraulic damping and silentbloc bearings is standard on *D3, C12 and B and A models.* The type illustrated incorporating duplex frame construction as used on *B and A models* possesses great lateral rigidity for high speed performance.

Quickly-detachable rear wheel. *On A and B (as illustrated) and M33 and M21 spring frame*

None of this was new for 1957 so was aimed at those who were unfamiliar with the marque.

(Chaincase £3. 2s. extra, including p.t.)

BSA 350 c.c. O.H.V. B31
£162 (p.t. £38. 17s. 8d. total £200. 17s. 8d.)

(Dual seat and pillion footrests £3. 14s. 5d. extra, including p.t.)

BSA 500 c.c. O.H.V. M33
£161 (p.t. £38. 12s. 10d. total £199. 12s. 10d.)

(Dual seat and pillion footrests £3. 14s. 5d. extra, including p.t.)

BSA 600 c.c. S.V. M21
£147 (p.t. £35. 5s. 8d. total £182. 5s. 8d.)
(With spring frame as illustrated £156 (p.t. £37. 8s. 10d. total £193. 8s. 10d.))

(Chaincase £3. 2s. extra, including p.t.)

BSA 500 c.c. O.H.V. TWIN A7
£192. 10s. (p.t. £46. 4s. total £238. 14s.)

MODELS	ENGINE	TRANSMISSION	IGNITION AND LIGHTING	FUEL CAPACITY
BSA Bantam and Bantam Major D models	D1 — 123 c.c. (52 x 58 mm.), D3 — 148 c.c. (57 x 58 mm.), single cylinder two-stroke; roller bearing big ends; timing side supported by ball race, drive-side by two ball races; petroil lubrication; **silencer with detachable baffle unit.**	B.S.A. three-speed gearbox with positive-stop foot control, built in unit construction with engine; gear ratios, 7.0, 11.7, 22.1; multi-plate cork insert clutch; primary chain $\frac{3}{8}$ x .250" in oil-bath case; rear chain $\frac{1}{2}$ x .335" with guard over top run.	Wico-Pacy flywheel generator with direct lighting; 6" diameter cowl-mounted headlamp; bulb horn; illuminated speedometer. **Battery lighting set with stop and tail lamp, rear reflector, electric horn and 8 amp. hr. battery extra.**	$1\frac{3}{4}$ gallons.
BSA 250 S.V. 250 O.H.V. C models	249 c.c. (63 x 80 mm.) single cylinder four-stroke with fully enclosed valve gear operation, S.V. on C10L, and O.H.V. on C12 with pressure oil feed to overhead rocker gear; ball race for drive-side mainshaft, and plain bearing on timing side; roller big end; dry sump lubrication with double gear type oil pump; oil tank 4 pints.	**New B.S.A. four-speed gearbox** with layshaft running on needle roller bearings; positive-stop foot control; gear ratios C10L, 6.6, 8.0, 11.7, 17.1; C12, 6.26, 7.64, 11.1, 16.15; Multi-plate cork insert clutch incorporating a **rubber cush drive;** primary chain $\frac{1}{2}$ x .305"; rear chain $\frac{1}{2}$ x .335" on C10L, and $\frac{1}{2}$ x .305" on C12; primary chain running in oil bath and guard over top run of the rear chain.	**Coil ignition incorporating A.C. generator with rectifier for D.C. battery lighting;** contact breaker and automatic advance and retard unit on timing side; special switch position for emergency starting. **Stop and tail lamp incorporating rear reflector;** electric horn; illuminated speedometer. C10L: Wico-Pacy equipment with 6" diameter headlamp. C12: Lucas equipment with $7\frac{1}{2}$" diameter headlamp, mounted in cowl. and 12 amp. hr. battery.	$2\frac{3}{4}$ gallons.
BSA 350 O.H.V. 500 O.H.V. B models	B31 — 348 c.c. (71 x 88 mm.), B33 — 499 c.c. (85 x 88 mm.), single cylinder four-stroke with fully enclosed valve gear; ball and roller bearings support drive-side mainshaft, roller bearing and plain outrigger bearing on timing side; double row roller big end bearings; gear driven magdyno; dry sump lubrication with double gear type oil pump; tank capacity $5\frac{1}{2}$ pints; absorption silencer.	B.S.A. four-speed gearbox with positive-stop foot control; gear ratios B31, 5.6, 6.77, 9.86, 14.42; B33, 5.0, 6.05, 8.79, 12.9; Multi-plate fabric insert clutch plates with cork insert chain wheel on B31: all fabric inserts on B33; primary chain $\frac{1}{2}$ x .305" in oil-bath; double cam cush drive on engine shaft; rear chain $\frac{5}{8}$ x $\frac{1}{4}$" with guard over top run.	Lucas 6-volt C.V.C. magdyno with manual ignition control (pull to retard) on handlebar; $7\frac{1}{2}$" diameter cowl-mounted headlamp with prefocus light unit and incorporating pilot light; **stop and tail lamp incorporating rear reflector;** electric horn; 12 amp. hr. battery; illuminated speedometer.	4 gallons.
BSA 600 S.V. 500 O.H.V. M models	M21 — 591 c.c. (82 x 112 mm.), four-stroke single cylinder side valve; ball and roller bearings support drive-side mainshaft, ball and roller bearings and a plain outrigger bearing support on timing side mainshaft; double row roller big end bearing; gear driven magdyno; dry sump lubrication with double gear type oil pump; oil tank capacity 5 pints. M33 engine is identical to model B33.	B.S.A. four-speed gearbox with positive-stop foot control; solo gear ratios 4.75, 6.25, 9.77, 14.15; side-car ratios: M21, 5.94, 7.82, 12.2, 17.7; M33 5.59, 7.37, 11.5, 16.72; primary chain $\frac{1}{2}$ x .305" running in oil-bath case; double cam cush drive on engine shaft; rear chain $\frac{5}{8}$ x $\frac{1}{4}$" with guard over top run; multi-plate fabric insert clutch with fabric lined chain-wheel.	Lucas 6-volt C.V.C. magdyno with manual ignition control (pull to retard) on handlebar; $7\frac{1}{2}$" diameter cowl-mounted headlamp with prefocus light unit and incorporating pilot light; **stop and tail lamp incorporating rear reflector;** electric horn; 12 amp. hr. battery; illuminated speedometer.	3 gallons.
BSA 500 O.H.V. Twins 650 O.H.V. Twins A models All models are equipped with a toolkit, tyre inflator and licence holder. Note.—Alternative strengths of spring available to suit requirements on A and B swinging arm models.	A7 — 497 c.c. (66 x 72.6 mm.), A10 — 646 c.c. (70 x 84 mm.), O.H.V. four-stroke with fully enclosed valve gear; **aluminium alloy cylinder head on A7 Shooting Star and A10 Road Rocket;** crankshaft drive-side supported by roller bearing, timing side by white metal bush; indium flashed lead bronze big end bearings; single camshaft at rear, with gear drive to magneto; dry sump lubrication with double gear type oil pump; oil tank $5\frac{1}{2}$ pints; $4\frac{1}{2}$ pints on A10 Golden Flash with plunger suspension; twin absorption silencers.	B.S.A. four-speed gearbox with positive-stop foot control; gear ratios A7 and A7 Shooting Star 5.28, 6.38, 9.28, 13.62; A10 Golden Flash and A10 Road Rocket swinging arm model 4.53, 5.48, 7.96, 11.68; Golden Flash plunger model solo 4.42, 5.36, 7.77, 11.41; sidecar 5.16, 6.26, 9.06, 13.3; multiplate fabric insert clutch and a fabric lined chain-wheel on swinging arm models; primary chain $\frac{1}{2}$ x .305" with double-cam cush drive on engine shaft; $\frac{3}{8}$" duplex on Golden Flash plunger model; chain running in an oil-bath case; rear chain $\frac{5}{8}$ x $\frac{3}{8}$" with a guard over the top run	Lucas magneto with automatic advance and retard (manual control on Shooting Star) and separate chain driven 6-volt C.V.C. dynamo; $7\frac{1}{2}$" diameter cowl-mounted headlamp with prefocus light unit and incorporating pilot light (except Road Rocket); **stop and tail lamp incorporating rear reflector;** electric horn; 12 amp. hr. battery; illuminated speedometer.	4 gallons. A10 Plunger model $4\frac{1}{4}$ gallons.

500 c.c. O.H.V. TWIN A7 SHOOTING STAR
£202. 10s. (p.t. £48. 12s. total £251. 2s.)

650 c.c. O.H.V. TWIN A10 ROAD ROCKET
£217. 10s. (p.t. £52. 4s. total £269. 14s.)

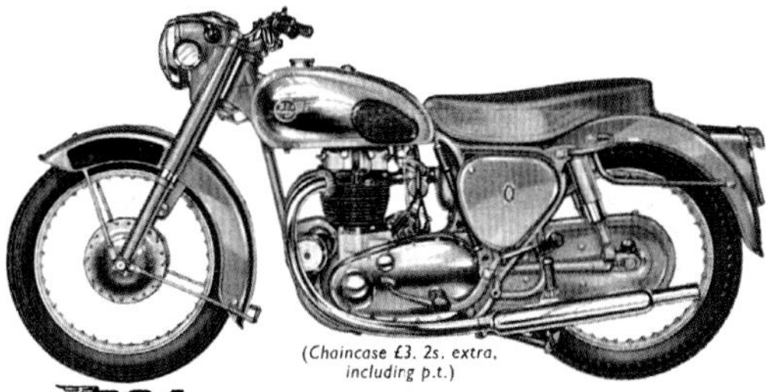

BSA 650 c.c. O.H.V. TWIN A10 GOLDEN FLASH
Black: £200. 10s. (p.t. £48. 2s. 5d. total £248. 12s. 5d.)
Beige: £203. 10s. (p.t. £48. 16s. 10d. total £252. 6s. 10d.)

Vital statistics of the entire 1957 range with some illustrated. Best to take no notice of the colour-coded dual seats on B31, A7, A7SS and A10 Golden Flash as, to the best of my knowledge, BSA never offered dual seats to match the paintwork.

BRAKES	SUSPENSION	FRAME	EXTRA FITTINGS (Prices include P.T.)	FINISH (Prices include P.T.)	GENERAL DIMENSIONS
5″ diameter with finger operated adjusters.	B.S.A. telescopic forks with flexible gaiters. Plunger rear suspension on D1; **hydraulically damped swinging arm rear suspension on D3.**	Tubular cradle type; all welded on D1; of brazed and welded construction on D3. Spring-up central stand; B.S.A. dual seat and pillion footrests on D3.	Legshields £1. 17s. 3d. Safety bars 19s. 10d. On D1: B.S.A. dual seat and pillion footrests £3. 14s. 5d. **On D3: Key operated steering head lock 12s. 5d.**	Pastel green D1, pastel grey D3; alternative colours maroon or black; cream panels on petrol tank; chrome wheel rims; all other bright parts chromed.	Wheel base, D1 50″, D3 51″; ground clearance, D1 4¾″, D3 5″; overall length, D1 77″, D3 78½″; dry weight, D1 180 lb.; D3 216 lb.
5½″ diam. front and 5″ rear on C10L. **New full width style on C12: 7″ diam. front, 5½″ diam. rear;** finger operated adjusters.	B.S.A. hydraulically damped telescopic front forks. Plunger rear suspension on C10L; **hydraulically damped swinging arm rear suspension on C12.**	All welded tubular construction on C10L; brazed and welded construction for C12. **Spring-up central stand. Key operated steering head lock on C12.** B.S.A. dual seat and pillion footrests on C12.	Legshields £1. 17s. 3d. Safety bars £1. 14s. 2d. Air cleaner 15s. 6d. On C10L: B.S.A. dual seat and pillion footrests £3. 14s. 5d. **Key operated steering head lock 12s. 5d.** On C12: Prop stand 18s. 8d.	C10L, two tone green with gold lined petrol tank. C12 maroon or black with **cream panels on petrol tank; chrome strips on petrol tank; chrome wheel rims; polished gearbox, and contact breaker cover**; all other bright parts chromed. Chrome panels on tank (or green on C10L) £1. 17s. 3d. extra.	C10L, wheelbase 52½″; ground clearance 5″; overall length 81″; dry weight 260 lb. C12 wheelbase 54″; ground clearance 4″; overall length 82″; dry weight 312 lb.
New full width aluminium alloy hubs with centrally disposed cast-in alloy iron drums; 7″ diameter x 1½″ wide; fulcrum point adjustment.	B.S.A. hydraulically damped telescopic front forks; **hydraulically damped swinging arm rear suspension, adjustable for weight in three positions.**	All welded duplex tubular cradle; spring-up central stand; front stand; **key operated steering head lock; quickly detachable rear wheel; B.S.A. dual seat and pillion footrests.**	Legshields £3. 2s. Safety bars £4. 0s. 8d. **Air cleaner 15s. 6d.** Prop stand 18s. 8d. **Rear chaincase giving total enclosure £3. 2s.**	Maroon; **petrol tank chrome and maroon** (alternative colour black); **chrome wheel rims; polished primary chaincase, gearbox and timing covers;** all other bright parts chromed.	Wheelbase 56″; ground clearance 5″; overall length 85″; dry weight B31, 410 lb.; B33, 421 lb.
Front brake 8″ diameter; rear brake 7″ diameter, both with finger adjustment.	B.S.A. hydraulically damped telescopic front forks; plunger rear suspension on M33. Extra on M21.	Brazed triangular tubular cradle with integral sidecar lugs; spring-up central stand; (rear on M21 rigid) front stand; **key operated steering head lock; quickly detachable rear wheel on M33 and M21 spring frame.**	Legshields £3. 2s. Safety bars £4. 0s. 8d. **Air cleaner 19s. 10d.** B.S.A. dual seat and pillion footrests £3. 14s. 5d. Prop stand 18s. 8d. Carrier £1. 6s. 1d.	Black; **petrol tank maroon with cream panels; chrome wheel rims; polished gearbox and timing cover;** all other bright parts chromed. Chrome panels on tank £1. 17s. 3d. extra.	Wheelbase 54″; ground clearance 5½″; overall length 85″; dry weight M21, spring frame, 396 lb.; M33, 406 lb.
New full width aluminium hubs with centrally disposed cast-in alloy iron drums; 7″ diameter x 1½″ wide; fulcrum point adjustment. Steel hubs with 8″ diameter front brake and 7″ diameter rear brake, both with finger adjustment, on A10 Golden Flash with plunger rear suspension.	Hydraulically damped telescopic front forks; **hydraulically damped swinging arm rear suspension, adjustable for weight in three positions;** plunger rear suspension available on A10 only.	All welded duplex tubular cradle; spring-up central stand; front stand; key operated steering head lock; **quickly detachable rear wheel; B.S.A. dual seat and pillion footrests.** Plunger rear suspension A10 frame when fitted is of brazed tubular construction, with standard saddle.	Legshields £3. 2s. Safety bars £4. 0s. 8d. Prop stand 18s. 8d. On swinging arm models: **rear chaincase** giving total enclosure £3. 2s. Carrier, to special order. On A7 Shooting Star: air cleaner 19s. 10d. On A10 with plunger rear suspension: B.S.A. dual seat and pillion footrests £3. 14s. 5d. Carrier £1. 6s. 1d.	A7 maroon; **petrol tank chrome and maroon** (alternative colour black); A7 Shooting Star duo-green; **petrol tank chrome and green;** A10 Golden Flash black; **petrol tank chrome panelled** (alternative colour beige); A10 Road Rocket black, chrome and silver tank, (or bright red instead of silver); **chrome mudguards;** all models **chrome wheel rims; polished primary chaincase, gearbox and timing covers;** other bright parts chromed.	Wheelbase 56″; ground clearance 6″; overall length 85″; dry weight A7 425 lb.; A7 Shooting Star 416 lb.; A10 Swinging Arm 430 lb.; A10 Golden Flash plunger model wheelbase 54¾″; ground clearance 4½″; overall length 84″; dry weight 415 lb.

BSA **SIDECARS**

B.S.A. FAMILY SIDECAR MODEL 23/51

Here's the sidecar for the family man. It provides saloon car comfort for an adult and child. It is completely weatherproof. The top of the body hinges towards the machine for easy access. Leg room: Front seat 51"; Rear seat 21"; seat width at elbows 21"; height inside 32".

Black or Maroon £67. 10s. (p.t. £15. 13s. 11d. total £83. 3s. 11d.)

Beige (Body and chassis) £69. (p.t. £16. 0s. 11d. total £85. 0s. 11d.)

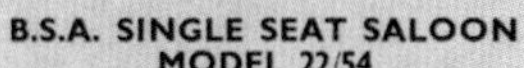

B.S.A. SINGLE SEAT SALOON MODEL 22/54

The comfort, smart appearance and many practical features of this single seat saloon sidecar makes it ideal for year round transport. The luggage compartment is fitted with a lock and the lid at the rear hinges down to form a platform. Leg room 51"; seat width at elbows 21½"; height inside 30"; luggage compartment 22" x 20" x 18".

Black or Maroon £64. (p.t. £14. 17s. 8d. total £78. 17s. 8d.)

Beige (Body and chassis) £65. 10s. (p.t. £15. 4s. 7d. total £80. 14s. 7d.)

B.S.A. DE LUXE TOURER SIDECAR MODEL 22/47

The light weight of this handsome touring sidecar, its useful luggage accommodation and the superb comfort of its springing and seating make this sidecar very suitable for fast, long distance touring. Leg room 51"; seat width at elbows 21½"; height inside 30"; luggage compartment 25" x 17" x 12½".

Black or Maroon £61. 10s. (p.t. £14. 6s. total £75. 16s.)

Beige (Body and chassis) £63. (p.t. £14. 13s. total £77. 13s.)

A range of sidecars had long been a traditional offering of BSA's but, with the plethora of affordable micro and small cars on the market, interest was waning amongst diehard sidecarists. There was little interest amongst the younger generation either, who might start off with a bike but then switch to a car when they could – seeing sidecars as rather old-hat and plodding. The last year they featured in the company's brochures would be 1957.

The Shooting Star on the cover of the 1958 brochure shows off the new full-width hub with 8in brake that it shared with the A10 Golden Flash and Super Rockets. B-series singles and the A7 had the hubs of the same design but incorporating a smaller 7in brake – all having the advantage of straight-pull spokes. The Sharam family had started their motorcycle business during the 1920s and by this time had showrooms in the centre of Torquay that were South Devon's largest dealership, holding agencies for BSA and Triumph.

New for 1958 was the 175 Bantam. Shame the British public were never offered the US version of the D5 – who knows, they too might have liked the lined mudguards. The (52x58mm) 125 Bantam's bore had been increased to 57mm for the now-defunct D3 150 but as the cylinder wall thickness did not allow any further increase new castings were made and bored to 61.5mm to create the 175 (actually 173cc) – thus giving its motor modern oversquare (61.5x58mm) dimensions. The British version was maroon with black as an option and the brochure talked in terms of 'long distance tours' – facilitated no doubt, whether at home or abroad, by the larger two-gallon tank than its forebears.

The curtain call for the long running C-series was 1958, and most distinguished it looked in jet black. UK models had cream tank panels, whether in maroon or as here, but for America nothing but the best – chrome!

Coil ignition and an alternator for the B-series, along with the new full-width hubs enclosing 7in brakes. Almond Green with black frame for the B31 and Gunmetal Grey and Grey for the B33 with Black as an option for either.

They didn't bother with the B31 for the US market but my, was the transatlantic B33 flashy in a Sapphire Blue tank with enlarged chrome panels picked out in red lining and Ivory fenders with double red and blue striping! In the event that you've noticed the strange (to British eyes) mounting for the rear light, this was because in certain US states the law stipulated that it must constitute the rearmost extremity of the vehicle.

The home-market A7 looked rather distinguished in Princess Grey and Grey in comparison with its US counterpart, the A7 500 Flash with Sapphire Blue tank and blue mudguards (fenders) with double gold striping. The seat looked comfy, though, and I know those bars were. US versions of the Golden Flash were turned out in the same colour scheme.

MODELS	EXTRA FITTINGS (Prices Include P.T.)	FINISH (Prices Include P.T.)
BSA Bantam 125 and Bantam Super 175 D models	Legshields £2. 1s. 2d. Safety bars £1. 1s. 10d. On D1: B.S.A. dual seat and pillion footrests £4. 2s. 4d. On D5: Key operated steering head-lock 10s.	Pastel green D1, maroon D5; alternative colours maroon D1 or black both models. Cream panels and chrome strip on petrol tank; chrome wheel rims; all other bright parts chromed.
BSA 250 O.H.V. C model	Legshields £2. 1s. 2d. Safety bars £1. 17s. 9d. Air cleaner 17s. 2d. Prop stand £1. 0s. 7d.	Maroon or black with cream panels on petrol tank; chrome strips on petrol tank; chrome wheel rims; polished gearbox and contact breaker cover; all other bright parts chromed. Chrome panels on tank £2 1s. 3d. extra.
BSA 350 O.H.V. 500 O.H.V. B models	Legshields £3. 18s. Safety bars £4. 9s. 3d. Air cleaner 17s. 2d. Prop stand £1. 0s. 7d. Rear chaincase giving total enclosure £3. 4s. Steering Damper B33. Desirable for use with sidecar, 8s. 9d.	Almond green, green and chrome petrol tank, black frame, 350 model; gunmetal grey, grey and chrome-plated tank, black frame, 500 model. Alternative colour, black. Chrome wheel rims; polished primary chain-case, gearbox and timing covers; all other bright parts chromed.
BSA 600 S.V. M21 model	Legshields £3. 18s. Safety bars £4. 9s. 3d. Air cleaner £1. 1s. 10d. B.S.A. dual seat and pillion footrests £4. 2s. 4d. Prop stand £1. 0s. 7d. Carrier £1. 8s. 9d. Plunger rear suspension with detachable rear wheel and spring-up central stand £11. 4s. 7d.	Black; petrol tank maroon with cream panels; chrome wheel rims; polished gearbox and timing cover; all other bright parts chromed. Chrome panels on tank £2 1s. 3d. extra.
BSA 500 O.H.V. Twins 650 O.H.V. Twins A models All models are equipped with a toolkit, tyre inflator and licence holder. Note.—Alternative strengths of suspension springs available to suit requirements on A and B solo and/or sidecar models.	Legshields £3. 18s. Safety bars £4. 9s. 3d. Prop stand £1. 0s. 7d. Rear chaincase giving total enclosure £3. 4s. Carrier, to special order. On A7 Shooting Star: air cleaner £1. 1s. 10d. On Super Rocket: rev-counter (headlamp cowl not fitted) £8. 2s. 2d. extra.	A7 Princess grey, grey and chrome petrol tank; Shooting Star polychromatic green, polychromatic green and chrome petrol tank; A10 Golden Flash beige, beige and chrome petrol tank. Super Rocket black with red mudguards, red and chrome petrol tank; or silver sheen mudguards, oil tank and toolbox with silver sheen and chrome petrol tank. All frames black. Alternative colour all models black except Shooting Star. All models chrome wheel rims; polished primary chain-case, gearbox and timing covers; other bright parts chromed.

This year home- and European-market Shooting Stars were finished in Polychromatic Green with black frame and forks – including the fuller, more attractive, headlamp cowl that was now a feature of both B- and A-series machines. The large Star badges referred to in this US publicity were in fact fitted to all Shooting Stars from their inception. They also had a briefer front mudguard than the regular A7 or US A7 Flash. Provision for a rev counter drive on the timing cover remained a feature of American-spec Shooting Stars, as well as high-rise bars, this dual seat and, of course, double gold stripes on the fenders.

Some of the 1958 range, for both US and UK markets, with extras and colour schemes available for the latter.

For 1958 the Road Rocket had been replaced with the Super Rocket and here's the UK version. In common with the Shooting Star, Rockets had the large 8in brake version of the new full-width hub. An improved design of crankshaft was now employed in all A10 motors but otherwise it was very much as its predecessor, even down to the same gear ratios. On British and European versions, in common with other B- and A-series BSAs (some Gold Stars excepted) an Amal Monobloc carburettor was now fitted as standard; if you wanted your Rocket with a TT you could but it would cost you an extra £6 11s. You could have a rev counter too, for £8 2s 2d, but that meant headlamp and instrumentation US-style.

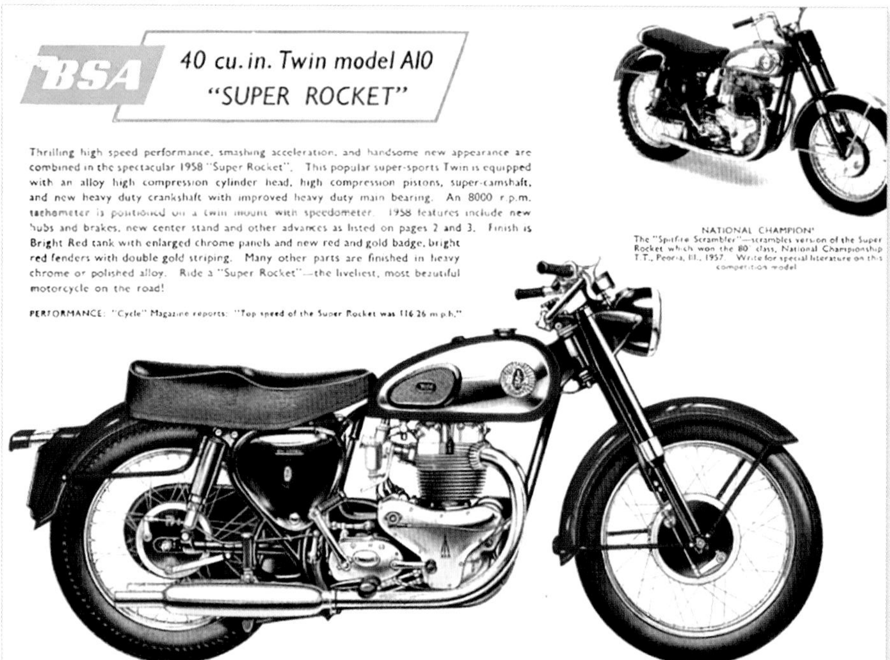

The Super Rocket for North America may have had the plush seat and higher bars along with 'pansy' gold striping on its fenders, but with headlamp cowling deleted, rev counter and TT carb as standard it was altogether a more sporting package than you could buy in the UK. For off-road racing or simply antisocial cruising (they came with open pipes) Americans could also buy a 'scrambler' version of the Rocket – the Spitfire.

With the availability of the 500 Gold Star Scrambler, and now the Catalina, it is hard to imagine that there was a worthwhile market for these in the States; but there was and they sold pretty well. Softer BB (than a DB) motor and lighter frame with some different geometry made these more of a 'go anywhere over all terrain machine' than one won races with – despite what this page from BSA's brochure might imply.

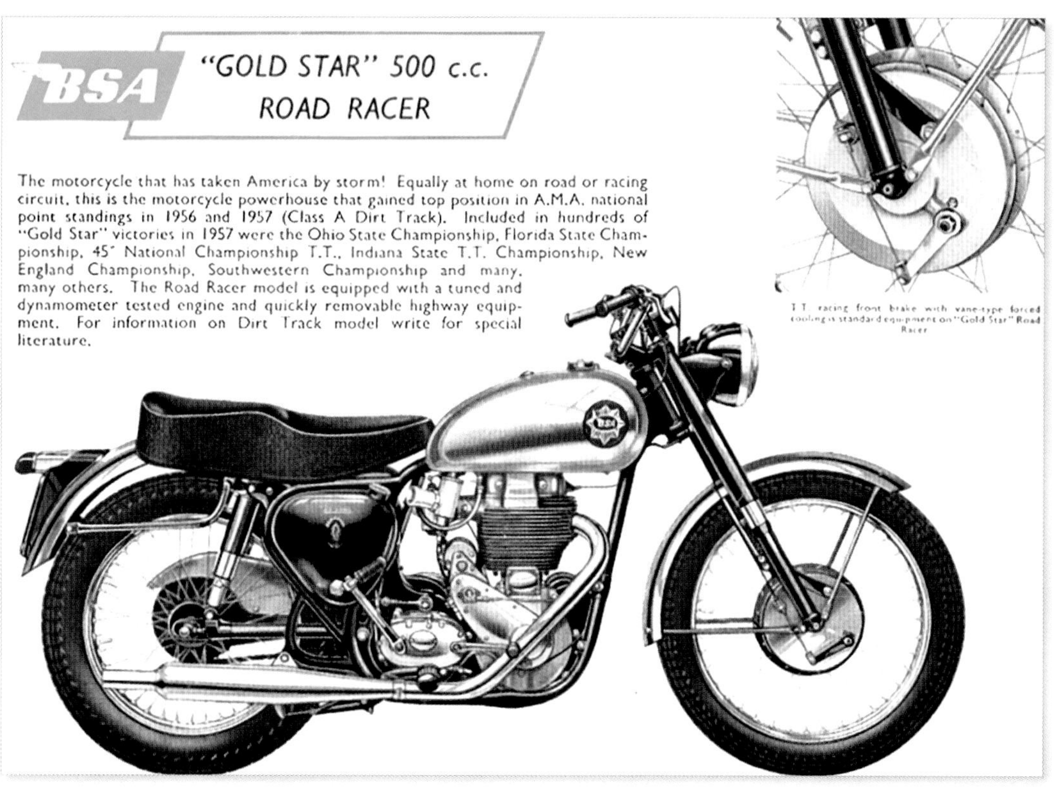

Road Racer by name but not, in this guise, by nature; and anyhow it was the Dirt Track variant of the Gold Star that was responsible for the multitude of victories cited here. It had a rigid frame, was devoid of brakes and only around 200 were made to order. A small point: why depict the Road Racer with single-sided 8in brake whilst asserting that the (illustrated) 190mm front brake was standard on this 1958 model?

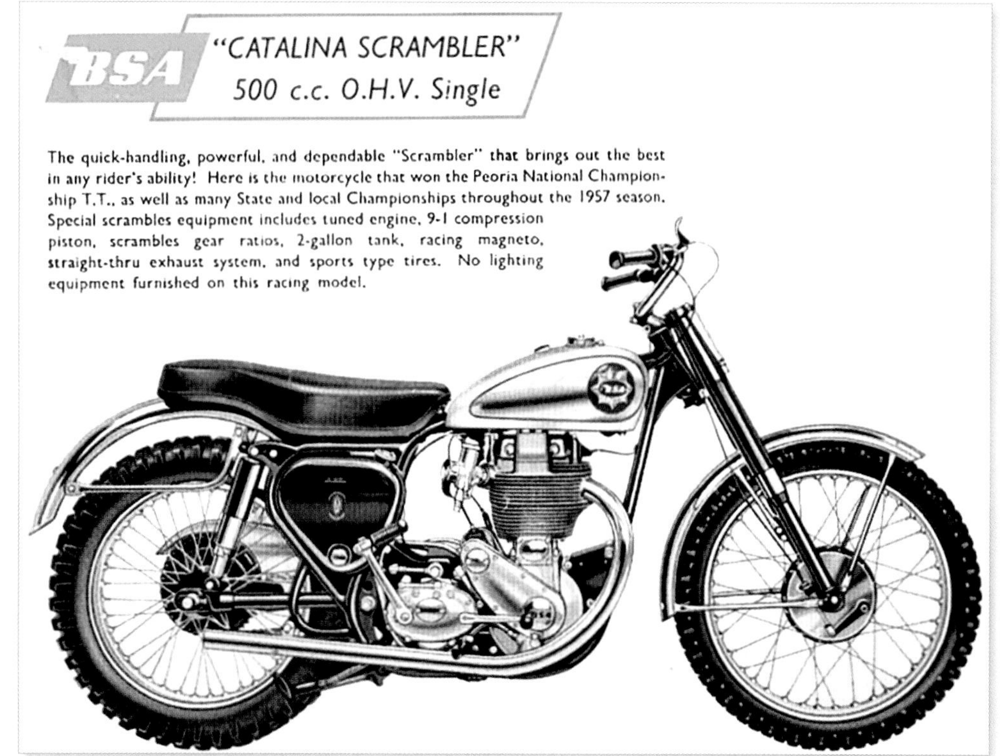

Somewhat surprisingly Chuck Minert's victory in the 1956 Catalina Grand Prix was not mentioned, as it was this that prompted West Coast importer Hap Alzina to request that BSA make and market a machine that would cash in on the kudos attached to the races held on the Pacific island a little over 20 miles south-west of Los Angeles. British bikes often did well there and in '56 BSA particularly so – with Minert's mildly-modified DB scrambler victorious in the main 100-miler, and a couple of 650 Rockets that had been given similar treatment in second and third. A Beeza also took the up-to-350 section and in the 60-mile Lightweight race a pair of C-types, normally not thought of as suitable for competition work, headed the 250cc class. In the 125 class, however, the best-placed Bantam was fifth behind four NSUs. For a machine mainly intended for off-road use in the hot, dry and dusty climate of the Western states the omission of an air cleaner was extraordinary – this would later be attended to.

Despite being printed in England the 1959 US brochure's cover depicted blue skies and a carefree lifestyle with a Shooting Star as an accessory. The British version, on the other hand, had a somewhat staid couple gazing wistfully into the distance – the picturesque landscape in the background ever-elusive except on rare occasions, and thanks to their Golden Flash.

With the demise of the Clubmans TT races in 1956 the demand for 350cc Gold Stars had lessened to such an extent that they were no longer included in this October 1958 brochure, although they were still available.

500 cc OHV model B34 CLUBMAN'S

ENGINE. 85 × 88 mm. bore and stroke (499 c.c.) 350 c.c. engine optional to order; specially designed to give optimum connecting rod/crank ratio; strengthened crankcase and heavy duty main bearings; aluminium alloy cylinder barrel with wear-resisting alloy iron liner; aluminium alloy cylinder head with valve seat inserts and stellite tipped high duty valves; specially adjusted lightweight valve actuating mechanism; polished fly-wheels and connecting rod; reinforced crankpin; cams, valve springs, etc., to suit compression ratio; Amal G.P. carburetter; engine specially tuned and bench tested.

LUBRICATION. Dry sump lubrication with double gear pump; large bore oil pipes; oil tank capacity 5½ pints and fitted with a specially-designed breather; primary chain oil bath; gearbox lubrication by oil and other parts by grease gun.

TRANSMISSION. Engine shaft cush drive; front chain ½ in. × .305 in. in oil bath; rear chain ⅝ in. × ⅜ in.; B.S.A. multi plate dry clutch with oil resisting fabric surfaces; B.S.A. four-speed gearbox with special needle roller bearings; enclosed clutch operation; positive-stop foot gear-change; close ratio gears; alternative gear ratios to suit requirements; gear-change pedal can be fitted in the rearward position with internal mechanism modified to give the standard movement; engine shaft sprocket to suit requirements.

FRAME. Tubular frame of all welded construction; central stand; steering damper; additional rear footrest position; crankcase shield optional; 2 or 4 gallon petrol tank; 5-gallon alloy tank extra; tank breather.

SUSPENSION. Front suspension by B.S.A. telescopic forks with automatic hydraulic damping; rear suspension by totally enclosed hydraulically damped main and rebound spring units in conjunction with swinging arm rear wheel cradle.

WHEELS. Fitted with Dunlop Tyres, front 3.00—19 or 21 ribbed racing; rear, 3.50—19 Directional Pattern; alloy rims extra. Highly efficient brakes; front 8 in., rear 7 in., 190 mm. front brake with iron rubbing surfaces featuring light alloy subsidiary construction extra.

CONTROLS. Racing type handlebars, twist grip throttle control, front brake and air lever on right bar; clutch, ignition and exhaust lifter on left bar.

EQUIPMENT. Lucas Magdyno lighting set; B.S.A. Dualseat; tool kit; tyre inflator; speedometer; rev-counter extra. Special racing seat extra.

FINISH. Handlebars, stays, exhaust system, wheel rims, mudguards, etc., chromium-plated; frame finished in black enamel; silver tank with chromium panels and special Gold Star badge.

Perhaps BSA considered it irrelevant but if you were not familiar with Gold Stars, or even if you were, it was not immediately apparent as to which big-fin model you were looking due to the policy of referring to any as just B32 or B34, rather than CB32, CB34, DB32, DB34 or DBD34 (there was no DBD32). In this case the fact that this brochure deals with 1959 models tells us that this is a DBD34 – for most people the ultimate Goldie when in Clubmans form. Some purists might argue, however, that the DB32s and DB34s of 1955 and '56 – manufactured whilst the Isle of Man Clubmans races still took place – are of greater interest because meaningful development ceased thereafter.

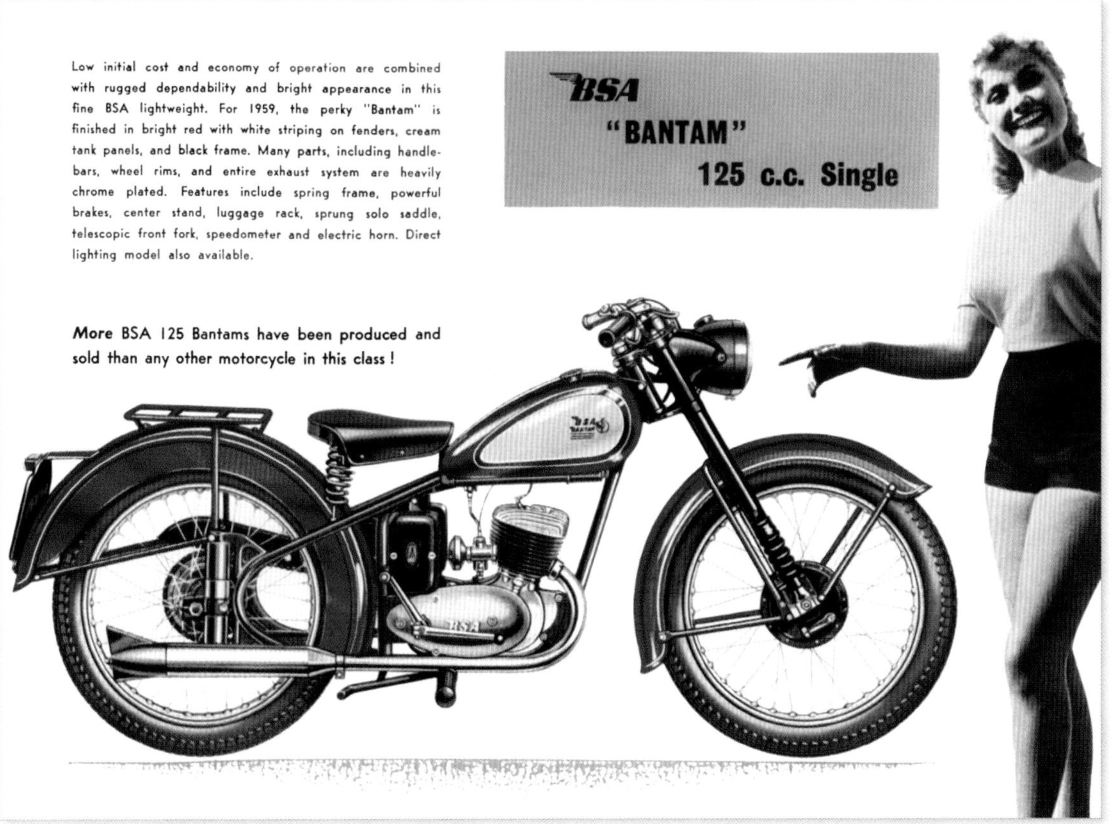

Stateside dealers told BSA that pin-striping was popular, so the maker obliged – even with the bargain-basement 125 Bantam that was consigned to the US. Sporty looking blondes featured on most of the pages of the '59 US brochure featuring on the next few pages.

After just one year the 175 D5 was replaced by the 175 D7. Whilst the US brochure confined itself to this description the British version was more enlightening: "The D7 Bantam Super simply bristles with new features including redesigned frame with cradle-mounted dual seat, hydraulically damped front forks, larger and wider brakes, new style mudguards and other items." You'll have noticed the headlamp cowl with inset speedo and enlarged toolbox now enveloping the frame's down-tube too, of course. Home-market D7s came in Black as well as Royal Red.

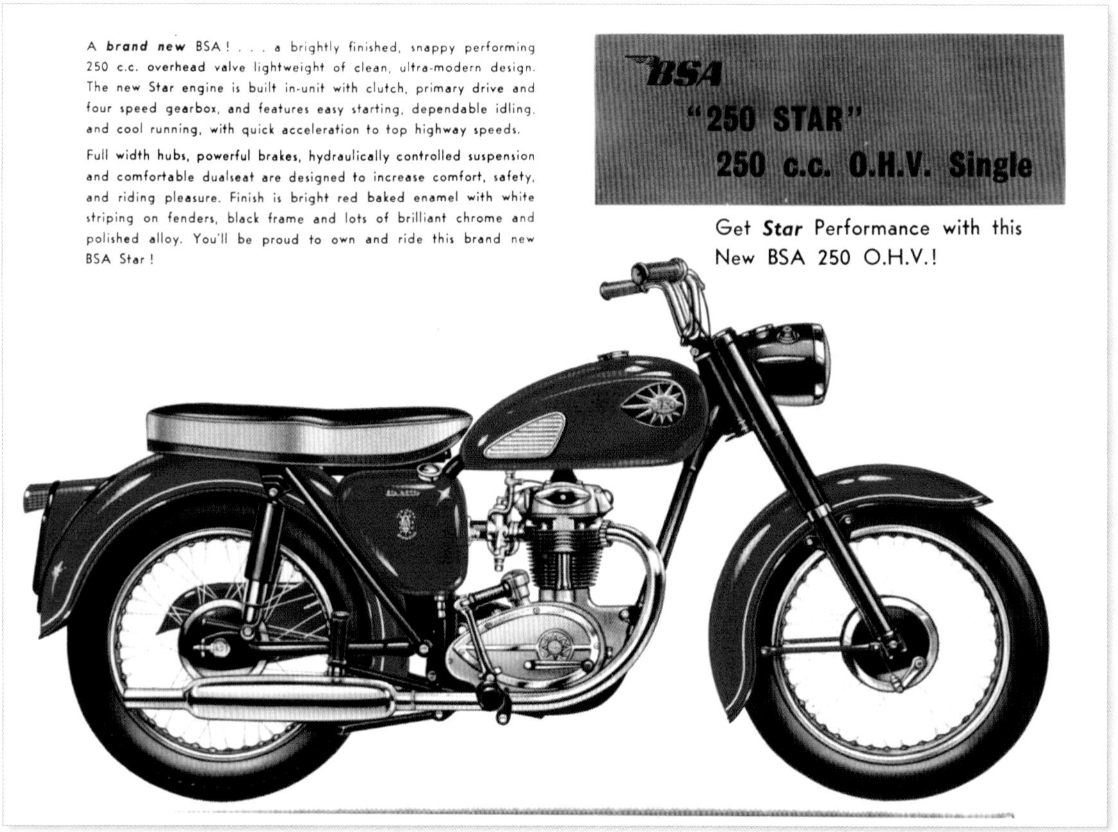

BSA's new short-stroke (67x70mm) 250 was based upon Triumph's Edward Turner-designed Terrier/Cub motors but heralded a new line as well as being the manufacturer's first unit-construction four-stroke. Marketed as the Star it would be more commonly known as the C15, its model designation. With the exception of the lack of white lining on the mudguards UK models had the same paint finish as this US model – 17in road wheels were a feature of both.

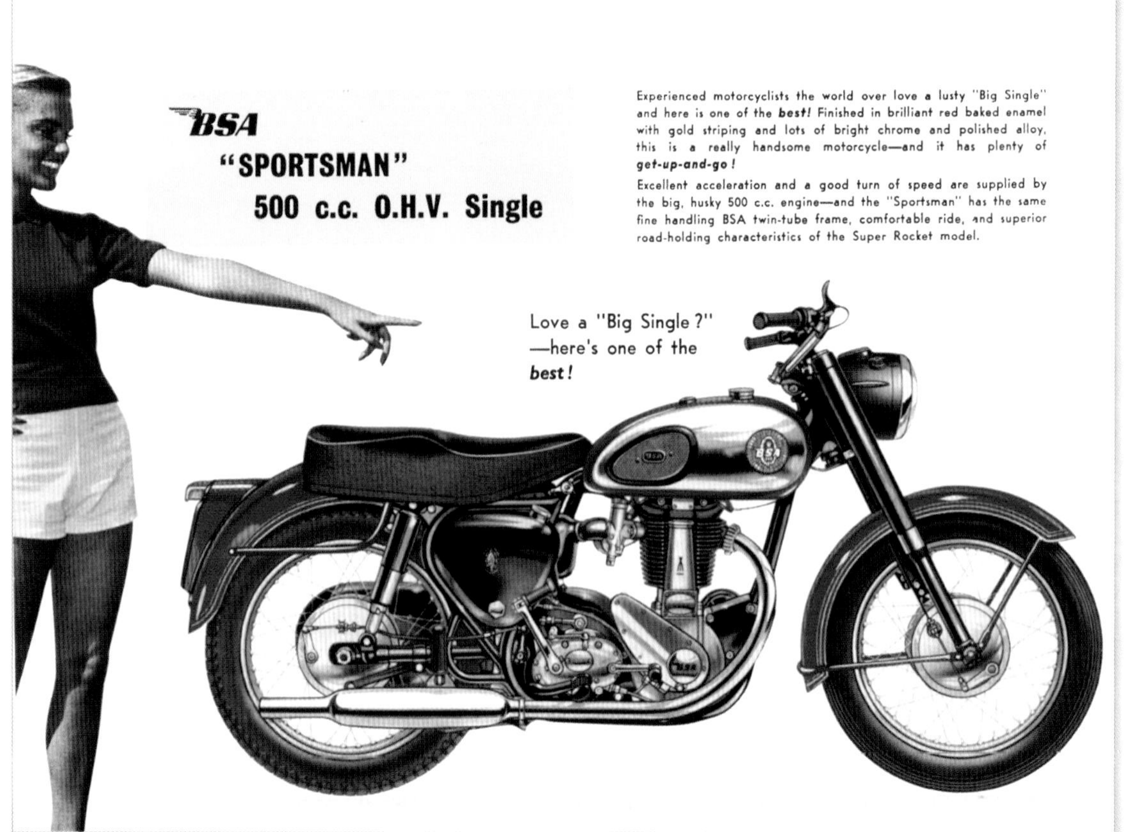

For Britain and Europe both B31s and B33s were unchanged from 1958 but the 1959 US-spec B33 was now turned out thus. Transatlantic-market B- and A-series brake plates were polished but the B33, A7 and Super Rocket also had chromium spokes.

BSA Inc and Hap Alzina also had brochures printed in the United States. So different, and special, was the new US version of the Super Rocket that it was showcased on the cover and with a centre-page spread. The championship events referred to were largely, if not all, won with Gold Stars and also included several state scrambles championships, including Indiana and Illinois as well as the entire East Coast.

Home and European-market A7s were still in Princess Grey with black brake plates, and the US Flash Twin versions remained Sapphire Blue – but now with polished brake plates and chrome spokes.

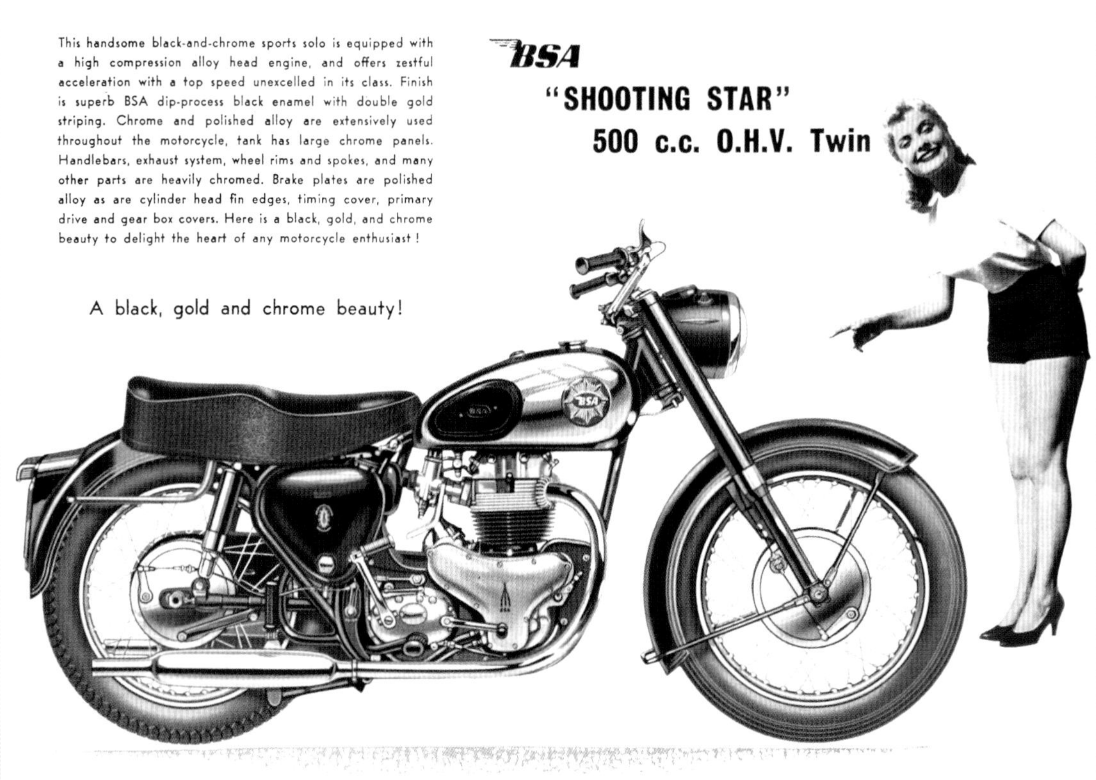

Colour schemes for UK and US Shooting Stars were unchanged for '59 but the latter no longer had provision for a rev counter drive on the timing cover, and apparently a rear light extension was no longer required.

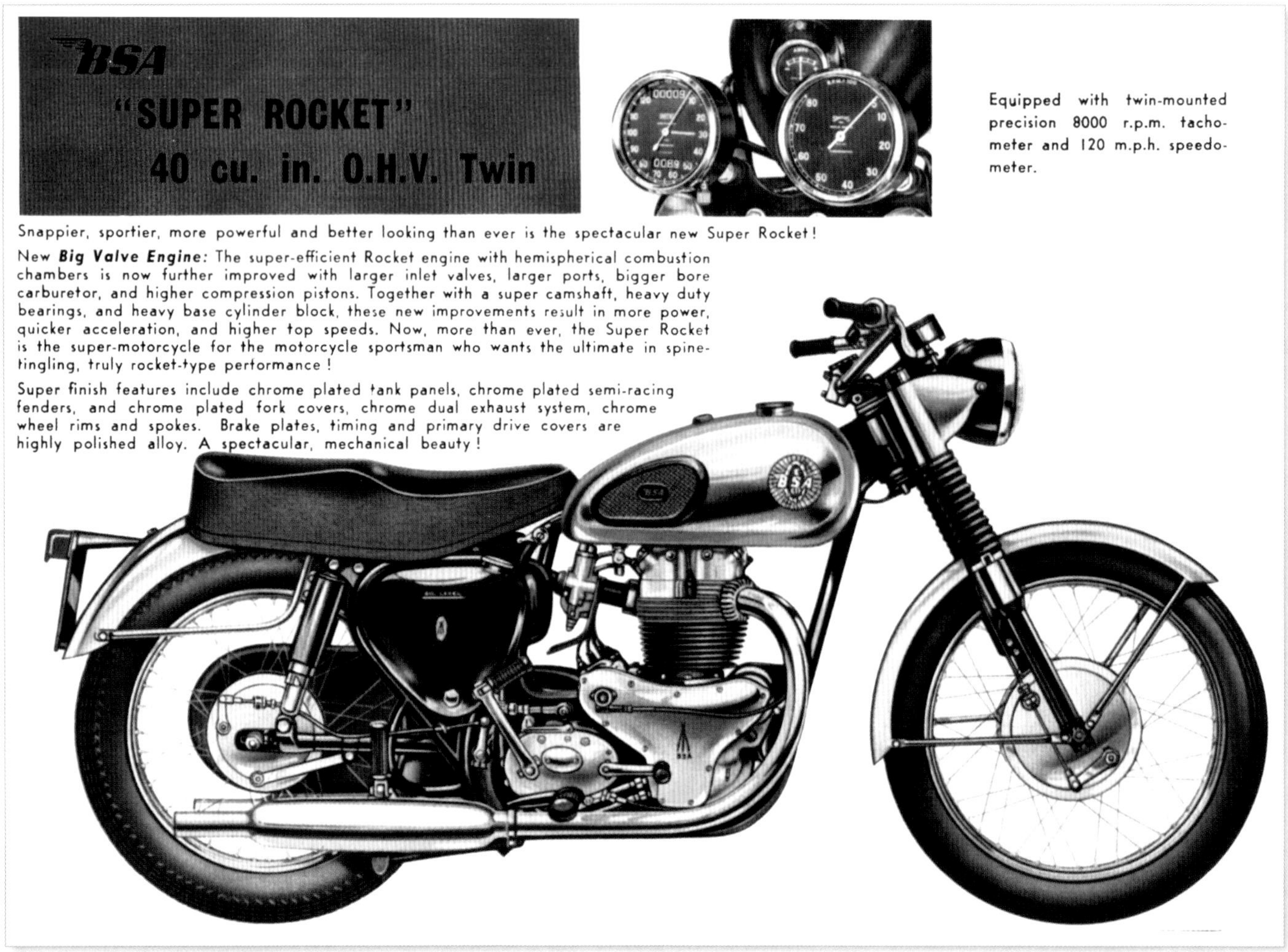
BSA
"SUPER ROCKET"
40 cu. in. O.H.V. Twin
Equipped with twin-mounted precision 8000 r.p.m. tachometer and 120 m.p.h. speedometer.
Snappier, sportier, more powerful and better looking than ever is the spectacular new Super Rocket!
New Big Valve Engine: The super-efficient Rocket engine with hemispherical combustion chambers is now further improved with larger inlet valves, larger ports, bigger bore carburetor, and higher compression pistons. Together with a super camshaft, heavy duty bearings, and heavy base cylinder block, these new improvements result in more power, quicker acceleration, and higher top speeds. Now, more than ever, the Super Rocket is the super-motorcycle for the motorcycle sportsman who wants the ultimate in spine-tingling, truly rocket-type performance!
Super finish features include chrome plated tank panels, chrome plated semi-racing fenders, and chrome plated fork covers, chrome dual exhaust system, chrome wheel rims and spokes. Brake plates, timing and primary drive covers are highly polished alloy. A spectacular, mechanical beauty!

Gold Stars aside this had to be the ultimate sports BSA from the '50s both for looks and go, with an even more exciting specification than '58 – excepting that the TT carb had been replaced by a Monobloc. From its Sapphire Blue and chrome tank to its chrome 'semi-racing fenders' it was for the North American market only, however – the UK version remaining all but unaltered from 1958, even to the optional extra of a TT carb.

BSA
"SPITFIRE SCRAMBLER"
40 cu. in. Twin
Dynamic power—
superb handling—
the top choice of
Scrambles Champions!
9-1 compression pistons
"Big Valve" engine with full race camshaft
Scrambles gear ratios
Dual cross-over straight-through exhaust pipes
Racing dualseat—scrambles type tires.
Polished brake plates—
Chrome tank panels—chrome fenders
Lightweight frame
Sensational Performance!
For full information on this model
send for special literature.

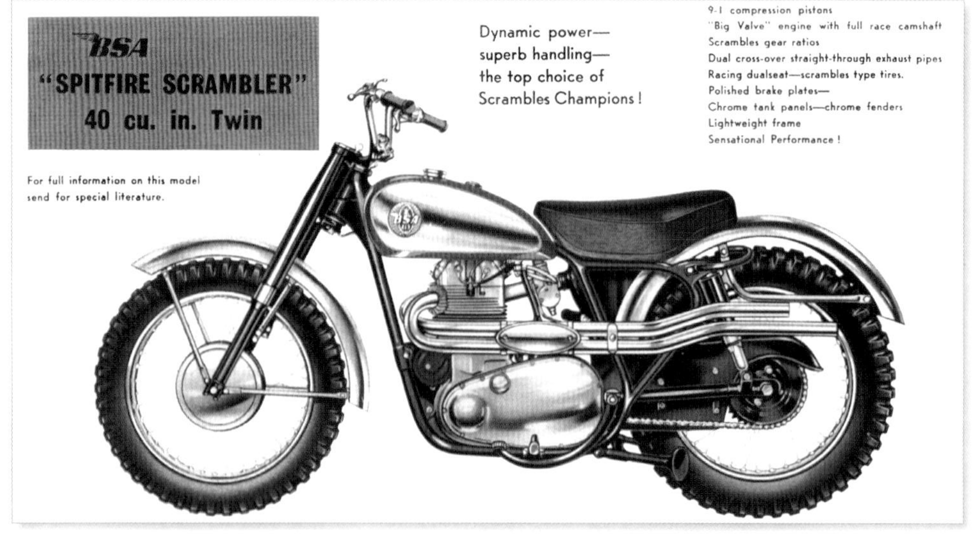

Much as I like BSAs, and I'll probably upset not a few people by saying this, the Spitfire almost certainly found a bigger following with weekenders than serious competition riders. That is not to say it wasn't raced, and successfully too, as one came second to Bob Sandgren's Triumph TR6 in the last, 1958, running of the Catalina GP. The Gold Star was, however, as they say, a hard act to follow. The gearbox had lower 'scrambles' ratios than other A10s, of 15.3:1, 10.2, 8.7 and 6.5:1.

Since its introduction the Catalina had been refined to this 1959 spec with 8in front brake (despite the fact that the brochure listed it as a 7in) laced into a 19in rim, essential large-capacity air cleaner, central oil tank and Twin-Solo dual seat. Frames were peculiar to the Catalina and were stamped CB32C whilst all other Gold Star swinging-arm frames from 1954 (with the exception of a very few produced for racing in US) were CB32. In common with UK and European Scrambles Gold Stars they had a gearbox with scrambles ratios (stamped SC) of 17:1, 12.73, 9.62 and 7.26:1, along with substantial footrests that were clamped to both frame side and cross tube, a centre stand (almost without exception removed before use by any serious competition rider) and a timing cover machined to accept a rev counter. Ironically, a Catalina was never to win the event it was named after.

BSA

"GOLD STAR"
ROAD RACER

1958 GOLD STAR VICTORIES
include:
10 Mile National Championship
15 Mile National Championship
25 Mile National Championship
Dodge City Grand Prix
Tobacco Trail Classic
Ohio State Championship
Minnesota State Championship
many, many others

A superb high speed road cruiser, the famous Gold Star is equipped with a super-tuned engine of racing characteristics—***exactly the same*** engine that BSA competition stars use in road racing and track racing events. Can be quickly converted to road racing trim. Dirt track racing equipment also available.

Equipment includes 8000 r.p.m. tachometer on twin mount with speedometer, racing cams, 1½" racing carburetor, racing type fenders, racing 190 mm. positive-cooled front brake, and ventilated racing rear brake. Brilliantly finished dark blue tank with chrome panels, chrome fenders, and many other chrome plated parts

The US brochure credited the Road Racer with a compression ratio of 8.6:1 and the Catalina with one of 9:1 – the latter the same as a home-market DBD34 Clubmans.

A few months after the introduction of the C15, in June 1959, this brochure for competition versions was published.

ENGINE: 249 c.c. (67 x 70 mm.); single cylinder four-stroke; die cast light alloy head; fully enclosed valve gear with pressure oil feed to overhead rocker mechanism; ball race on drive side mainshaft; copper-lead bearings on timing-side mainshaft and connecting rod big-end; dry sump lubrication with double gear type oil pump; oil tank capacity four pints; crankcase shield.

CARBURETTER: Amal Monobloc type with twist grip throttle control and enclosed air cleaner.

TRANSMISSION: B.S.A. four-speed gearbox in unit construction with engine; positive stop foot control; multi-plate clutch with resilient facings and incorporating a synthetic rubber cush drive; ⅜″ duplex primary chain; rear chain ½″ x .305″ rollers; rear chain guide, primary chain oil bath and guard over top run of rear chain; folding kick-starter.

IGNITION: Direct ignition from flywheel magneto; automatic advance and retard unit mounted on crankcase.

FUEL CAPACITY: 2 gallons.

BRAKES: Full width hubs; 6″ diameter brakes front and rear with finger adjustment; straight spokes.

SUSPENSION: B.S.A. hydraulically-damped telescopic front forks with rubber gaiters. Hydraulically-damped swinging-arm rear suspension.

FRAME: Cradle type, of brazed construction with duplex tubes for engine mounting. Plain blade mudguards. Raised footrests. Spring-up prop stand; B.S.A. short dual seat.

FINISH: Frame, etc., enamelled Black. Mudguards Blue; Petrol tank Blue enamel and chrome; chrome wheel rims; polished primary chain cover; timing cover, and rims on brake cover plates. All other bright parts chromium plated.

General specification as above together with the following features:—

	Scrambles C15 S.	Trials C15 T.
Piston	High compression (9.0).	Medium compression (7.5).
Camshaft ...	Scrambles type.	Trials type.
Carburetter ...	Large bore.	Standard.
Exhaust System ...	Plain upswept pipe.	Upswept pipe with silencer.
Direct Lighting Set	Not supplied.	Extra.
Tyres	Dunlop Sports. Front 3.00 x 20. Rear 3.50 x 19.	Dunlop Trials Universal. Front 3.00 x 20. Rear 4.00 x 18.
Handlebar Levers	With ball ends.	Standard.
Gear Ratios ...	7.92; 10.13; 13.93; 21.13.	7.92; 12.9, 19.4, 25.0.
Ground Clearance	6½ inches.	6½ inches.
Weight	265 lbs.	275 lbs.

Model C15 S.	£176 . 19s. including £30 . 5 . 2d. purchase tax
Extra for horn and speedometer	£4 . 16 . 8d. including 16/7d. purchase tax
Model C15 T. (including horn and speedometer)	£181 . 15s. 8d. including £31 . 1 . 8d. purchase tax
Extra for direct lighting	£4 . 7s. including 14/11d. purchase tax
Extra for chromium plated mudguards on both models ...	£3 . 0 . 5d. including 10/4d. purchase tax

Looks like our blonde bathing belle, whom we shall name Frances, is awaiting the owner of one of the yachts to come and collect her – for lunch perhaps. Or has she just perched herself on a conveniently-parked C15? An improbable scene courtesy of an unknown, to me, commercial artist for the 1960 brochure.

Wonderful! So these two couples have ridden, on their Bantam 175 Super D7 and Star C15, to Shirley Park, Warwickshire with the girls clinging onto their chaps as well as their picnic hampers. More likely don't you think, as the 'picnic site' was just a little way down the A34 from the factory, that a couple of demo models were delivered to the waiting 'picnickers' and ready-laid-out picnic?

BSA 250 OHV STAR model C15

Reinforced glass fibre legshields £5. 19s. 6d. extra.

£168
including £28. 14s. 7d. purchase tax

This is the already famous B.S.A. 250 Star with many fine features—Unit construction of engine and gearbox; styled petrol tank; nacelled headlamp; two-tone dual seat; oil tank and toolbox unit enclosing battery and air cleaner; absorption silencer; dome section guards, the rear guard without stays; 17" wheels with full width hubs; folding kickstarter; low weight of 280 lb.—giving a most favourable power-weight ratio and outstanding performance.

ENGINE
249 cc (67 × 70 mm.); single cylinder four-stroke; die-cast light alloy head, fully enclosed valve gear with pressure oil feed to overhead rocker mechanism; ball race on drive-side mainshaft; copper-lead bearings on timing side mainshaft and connecting rod big-end; dry sump lubrication with double-gear type oil pump; oil tank capacity 4 pints.

CARBURETTER
Amal Monobloc type with twist grip throttle control and enclosed air cleaner.

TRANSMISSION
B.S.A. 4-speed gearbox in unit construction with engine; positive-stop foot control; gear ratios 5.98 — 7.65 — 10.54 — 15.96; multi-plate clutch with bonded resilient facings and incorporating a synthetic rubber cush drive; cable adjustment by knurled thumbscrew on handlebar; ⅜" duplex primary chain; rear chain ½ × .335" rollers; primary chain oil-bath, and guard over top run of rear chain. Optional internal gear ratios available.

IGNITION AND LIGHTING
Coil ignition incorporating A.C. generator with rectifier for D.C. battery lighting; automatic advance and retard unit mounted on crankcase; special switch position for emergency starting; folding kick-starter. Lucas electrical equipment; 6" diameter nacelle-mounted headlamp with ammeter, lighting switch, and built-in illuminated speedometer; stop and tail lamp incorporating rear reflector; electric horn; 12 amp. hr. battery housed in a special compartment.

FUEL CAPACITY
2½ gallon petrol tank.

TYRES
Dunlop 3.25—17 ribbed front, Universal rear. Whitewall tyres, see extra fittings.

BRAKES
Full width hubs; 6" diameter

The last of BSA's 'iron' big singles. The B33 with a modicum of restyling, meaning the fuel tank and badge, for the 1960 season. "For the rider who enjoys the lusty and zestful qualities of a well-tuned big single," read the caption, and that still holds true today if you could find a nice original example.

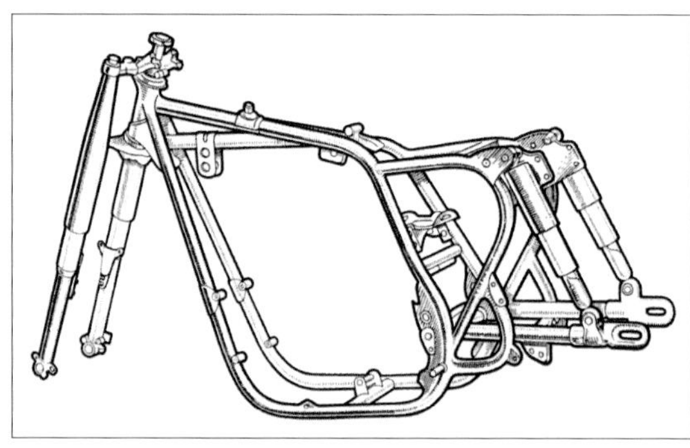

The well-designed and extremely robust cradle frame, complete with its pivoted rear fork and suspension units, which formed the basis for BSA's A-series twins. The variety utilised for B-series singles can very easily be told apart from these on account of the lower right-hand tube being flattened and slightly kinked outward in order to clear the bulge in the corresponding crankcase that houses the oil pump.

The Shooting Star 1960 edition. "Flashing acceleration, high averages, rock steady at speed, docile in traffic" enthused The Motor Cycle *when they tested one. Highest one way speed was 98mph, with an average of 95 and a snorting 92 in third.*

All the twins had been given something of a facelift with fresh tank styling and badges. There were other minor alterations too – such as the rerouted rear brake cable, which now fell away under the right rear fork, and revised position for the brake arm to suit.

The 1960 Golden Flash came in Sapphire Blue, the traditional Beige or even Black but, horror of horrors, for an extra £1 16s you could opt for whitewall tyres – on any of the other twins, too, come to that.

A re-designed drive is now provided for the rev-counter which is available on the Super Rocket. Neater, more compact and less vulnerable than the previous design, the new drive is taken from the front of the timing case and is directly coupled through a dog drive to the oil pump spindle which has been modified for this purpose.

All Super Rocket engines are fitted with the modified pump in readiness to receive the rev-counter drive.

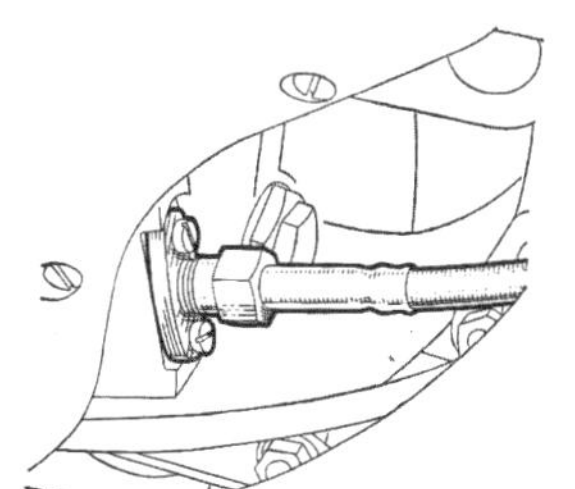

Super Rockets were almost invariably red but you could have one in black. TT carb was still an option, as was a rev counter – the latter, as on previous home-market Rockets, necessitating headlamp and instrument arrangements as on US versions.

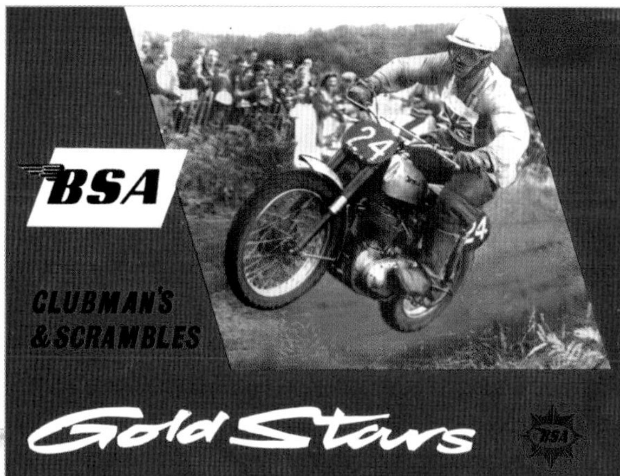

Clubmans and Scrambles Gold Stars offered in the April 1960 brochure were essentially unchanged as the seasons passed, but for the Scrambler there was now the option, at extra cost, of an Amal GP carburettor. Although not original equipment, aluminium fuel tanks and mudguards as seen here were popular.

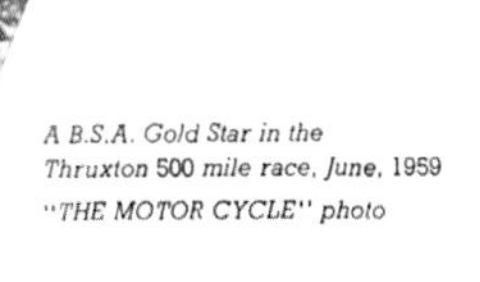

A B.S.A. Gold Star in the Thruxton 500 mile race, June, 1959 "THE MOTOR CYCLE" photo

BSA 500 Gold Stars had won the first three (1955-to-57) Thruxton 500s outright whilst 350s were first in their class from 1955 to '59, in which year the 500s were third and sixth overall. The machine pictured here was fitted with the optional Lyta aluminium fuel tank and, like many other Gold Stars that were raced, the 8in single-sided front brake was fitted in preference to the much-vaunted 190mm.

BSA Factory engineered and built speed parts are now available for 1959-60 250 Road Star and Starfire Scrambler models. Installation of complete speed kits "A" (for road model) or "B" for scrambler as listed below together with correct tuning procedures should result in a very substantial boost in horsepower for racing or road use.

RACING CYLINDER HEAD

For racing and improved road performance. Has larger inlet bore and port for improved cylinder-charging. Required in kits A and B.

No. 40-338 $41.04

HIGH COMPRESSION 10 TO 1 PISTON

Top quality high-tensile-strength alloy piston complete with pin and rings. Use with racing cylinder head above. Required in kits A and B.

Standard: No. 40-444 $12.51
(Also available in +.020 and +.040)

RACING CAMSHAFT

Quick-opening high lift camshaft for more acceleration and top speed. Replaces standard camshaft without alteration. Required in kit A (already installed in Scrambler).

No. 40-335 $9.00

RACING KIT "A" FOR 250 STAR ROAD MODEL

Contains all items required for full-horsepower motor as listed below.

Racing cylinder head — Oversize inlet valve
Racing camshaft — Racing valve springs
Racing 10 to 1 ratio piston — 1-1/16" bore carburetor

Racing kit "A" No. B612 $92.71

RACING KIT "B" FOR 250 STARFIRE SCRAMBLER

Contains all items required for full horsepower motor as listed below. Other items listed in kit "A" are already in the Starfire engine.

Racing cylinder head — Racing valve springs
Racing 10 to 1 ratio piston — 1-1/16" bore carburetor

Racing kit "B" No. B613 $80.15

BSA Inc published this very comprehensive 24-page catalogue for the 1960 season.

RACING GAS TANK

As used on Gold Star model. Fits any BSA Twin or big single. 3 gallon capacity. Finished in silver with large chrome panels.

No. 42-8056/19
$84.00

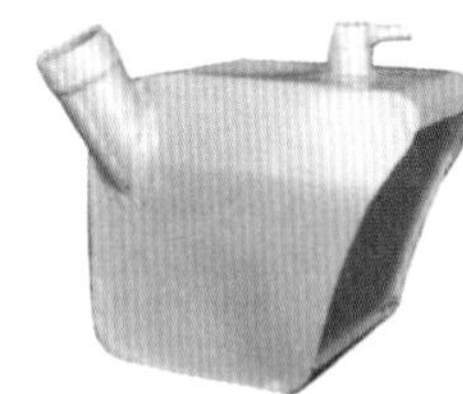

RACING OIL TANK

As supplied on 1959-60 Catalina Scrambler. Has anti-froth tower. Mounts under saddle.

No. 42-8391
$48.00

CROSS-OVER EXHAUST PIPES

As supplied on 1959-60 Spitfire model. Fits all BSA 650 Twins. Crosses over to left hand side of machine. Straight-thru pipes—not for road use. Finished in brilliant chrome, complete with all brackets, and polished chrome leg guard.

No. B170 $44.27

TWIN CARB. CONVERSION HEAD: for 650 c.c. twins

Fits Super Rocket or Golden Flash 1956-60. Permits installation of twin carburetors. **No. 67-1105 $112.60**

TWIN CARB. CONVERSION HEAD: for 500 c.c. twins

Same type head as above, fits BSA 500 c.c. twins 1956-60.
No. 67-1101 $112.60

ALLOY MANIFOLD FOR TWIN CARBURETOR INSTALLATION

Special alloy manifolds for mounting right and left hand carburetors on twin port heads above.

Right manifold, No. 67-1330 **$5.67**
Left manifold, No. 67-1331 **5.67**

TWIN CONTROL CABLES FOR TWIN CARBURETORS

For throttle or air control. Set includes cables and junction box. **2 sets required** for complete twin carb. installation. **No. 67-8571 $5.79**

"DAYTONA" CONNECTING RODS

BSA 500 twin connecting rods with large big ends to fit heavy duty racing crankshaft or standard 650 c.c. shaft as fitted to Super Rocket and Golden Flash 1958-60. Orders accepted subject to possible waiting period on this special production item. **No. 67-1207 $19.47 each**

To fill the gap left by the demise of the trusty B31, BSA's new 350 was, dimensionally, a much over-bored C15 but the engine/gearbox unit had all manner of dissimilarities including a more substantial bottom end. The B40's frame appeared identical but if laid bare would be found to have a larger-diameter top tube. More obvious were the 18- as opposed to 17-inch wheels and the 7-inch front brake hitherto found on the standard A7 and recently discontinued B33. Motorcycle Mechanics *tried one and were very impressed with the handling and, in fact, all aspects of the machine, including its top speed of 75. However, their assertion that "it goes like a 500!'" was too generous for 1960, I feel.*

Engine. 343 cc (79 × 70 mm.); single cylinder four-stroke; die cast light alloy head, fully enclosed valve gear with pressure oil feed to overhead rocker mechanism; ball race on drive side mainshaft; copper-lead bearings on timing side mainshaft and connecting rod big-end; dry sump lubrication with double gear type oil pump; oil tank capacity four pints.

Carburettor. Amal Monobloc type with twist grip throttle control and enclosed air cleaner.

Transmission. B.S.A. four-speed gearbox in unit construction with engine; positive stop foot control; gear ratios 5.22—6.78—9.4—14.25; multi-plate clutch with bonded resilient facings and incorporating a synthetic rubber cush drive; cable adjustment by knurled thumbscrew on handlebar; ⅜" duplex primary chain; rear chain ½" × .335" rollers; primary chain oil-bath and guard over top run of rear chain.

Ignition and Lighting. Coil ignition incorporating A.C. generator with rectifier for D.C. battery lighting; automatic advance and retard unit mounted on crankcase; special switch position for emergency starting; folding kick starter; Lucas electrical equipment; 6" diameter nacelle mounted headlamp with ammeter, lighting switch, and built-in illuminated speedometer; stop and tail lamp incorporating rear reflector; electric horn; 12 amp. hr. battery housed in a special compartment.

Fuel Capacity. 3 gallons.

Tyres. Dunlop 3.25 × 18" ribbed front and 3.50 × 18" Universal rear.

Brakes. Full width hubs; 7" diameter front brake and 6" rear, both with finger adjustment, front by knurled thumbscrew on handlebar; straight spokes.

Suspension. B.S.A. hydraulically-damped telescopic front forks. Hydraulically-damped swinging arm rear suspension.

Frame. Cradle type, of brazed construction with Duplex tubes for engine mounting. Rigid rear mudguard without stays. Spring-up central stand; B.S.A. dual seat and pillion footrests. Special lug on steering head for fitting padlock.

Finish. Royal red or Black; black frame and forks; styled petrol tank with chrome strips and side panels; hubs and brake cover plates silver sheen; chrome wheel rims; polished primary chain cover, timing cover, and rims on brake cover plates. Bright parts chromed. Attractive plastic tank badges.

General Dimensions. Wheelbase 54"; ground clearance 7"; overall length 80"; dry weight 300 lbs.

Extra Fittings. (Prices include P.T.). Safety bars £3. 18s. 5d.; Prop stand £1. 0s. 6d.

For the 1961 brochure cover photo-shoot the advertising entourage travelled further down the A34 to Stratford where they arranged machines and riders by the riverside. The red bike is a C15 and the blue one a Golden Flash but there's an impostor in the form the Edward Turner-designed 250cc twin-cylinder BSA-Sunbeam scooter. It's not in the brochure but they slipped it into this scene for good measure. They didn't think of everything, however: this year black enamelled brake plates had given way to polished ones for the Super Rocket, as they had on the majority of US versions a couple of seasons earlier, and silver sheen on the others; but here they've pictured older models. It has been noticed and an attempt made to rectify the error by re-touching the front brakes but the C15's rear brake has been overlooked – thus giving the game away.

There certainly was! And included amongst them was the new B40 – named the 350 Star Sportsman and very fetching in jet black with gold stripes edging its fenders. The regular A10 had become the Royal Tourist whilst the Super Rocket now had a 140mph speedo and full-race 357 camshaft. Competition C15s equipped with lighting were marketed as the Starfire Scrambler and Starfire Roadster.

There were two editions (October 1961 and April 1962) of the 1962 brochure and the covers of both took us to Worcestershire; but what has happened? The long-standing slogan of 'The most popular Motor Cycle in the World' has gone – the booklet now entitled 'Guide to Better Motorcycling'. Well, if this is the first lesson, the two girls are shortly going to learn it. They're more suitably attired for the dance hall than an invigorating ride in the countryside.

250 STAR SCRAMBLES
250 STAR TRIALS

Scrambles Special C15S
H.C. piston (10.0), special camshaft, large bore carburettor, upswept exhaust pipe with expansion box, Dunlop Sports tyres front 3.00—20, rear 3.50—19, handlebar levers with ball ends, gear ratios 9.0—11.8—14.94—19.0, optional internal gear ratios available, polished alloy mudguards, clearance 7", weight 265 lb.

Trials Special C15T
L.C. piston (6.4), special camshaft; upswept pipe with silencer, Dunlop Trials Universal tyres front 3.00—20, rear 4.00—18, lighting set extra, gear ratios 9.0—14.67—22.05—28.53, optional internal gear ratios available, polished alloy mudguards, clearance 7¾", weight 275 lb.

B.S.A. STAR SCRAMBLES SPECIAL model C15S

250 SPORT STAR
model C15SS 80

Specification as model C15 except for the following:—

Engine. Die-cast light alloy head with polished fins. 8.75 compression ratio; high-duty valve springs and special large diameter inlet valve; sports camshaft; roller bearing big-end; steel flywheels.

Carburettor. 1" bore Amal Monobloc type.

Transmission. B.S.A. 4-speed close-ratio gearbox in unit construction with the engine; gear ratios 5.98—7.19—9.91—12.63, optional internal gear ratios available; primary chain with slipper type adjuster.

Fuel Capacity. 3 gallons.

Frame. Sports type handlebar, with combined front brake and air control lever.

Finish. Black or Flamboyant blue; petrol tank with chrome panels and gold linings; chrome plated mudguards £4. 4s. 1d. extra.

The competition versions of the C15 became a little more specialised too – as you can see by the aluminium fuel tank and single-sided front brake.

Little new in the October edition other than the announcement of the 250 Sport Star C15SS accompanied by a black-and-white illustration. But by April not only had it gone up in price from roughly £194 to £201 (basic – in both cases chromium mudguards were extra), it had become the Sport Star C15SS 80.

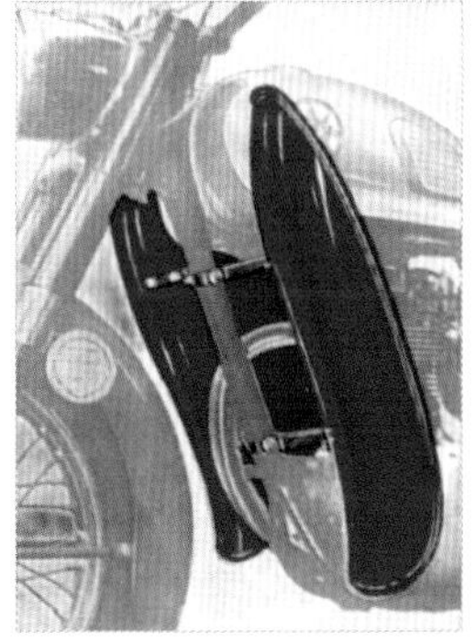

The standard C15 now had the option of Sapphire Blue finish added to Fuschia Red. A chromium-plated tank, safety bars and a prop stand were optional extras; but if keeping your legs dry was more important than your bike's looks you could pay extra for a pair of fibreglass leg shields similar to these as fitted to a B40.

"BSA Goes Everywhere," announced the centre spread of the April 1962 brochure, and so they did.

I thought for a minute, a Spitfire Scrambler for the Japanese police! Nice thought, but upon closer inspection it's a couple of civilians chatting up what look like nurses. It shows import of motorcycles wasn't all one way by this time, however.

The October 1961 brochure had presented A7s, and very nearly A10s, for the last time, with just the Super Rocket in the April '62 edition. Available in Royal Red or Princess Grey (introduced the previous season) this one was fitted with the optional-extra siamesed exhaust pipes. Other extras such as TT carb, rev counter, enclosed rear chain case and prop stand were still listed.

Engine. Twin cylinders A50—65.5 mm. bore × 74 mm. stroke (499 cc); A65—75 mm. bore × 74 mm. stroke (654 cc). Overhead valve four-stroke; cast-iron cylinder block; die-cast light alloy cylinder head with cast-in valve seats and down-draught divided inlet port for single carburettor. Compression ratio 7.5 to 1 on both models. Pressure oil feed to rocker mechanism mounted direct on cylinder head; crankshaft drive-side mounted on ball-race, timing side mounted on heavy duty bi-metal plain bearing in steel housing. Centrifugal oil filter carried in crankpin journals. Single gear-driven camshaft, incorporating timed breather; light alloy connecting rods; micro-babbit steel-backed big end liners; dry sump lubrication with double-gear type oil pump.

Carburettor. Amal Monobloc enclosed within quickly detachable fairing, accessible tickler; A50—1" bore, A65—1⅛" bore, twist grip throttle control; lever-operated air slide; both controls with cable adjusters. Large diameter felt air cleaner.

Transmission. B.S.A. four-speed gearbox, built-in unit construction with engine; positive stop foot control. Gear ratios A50—5.12, 6.04, 8.44, 13.1; A65—4.35, 5.13, 7.18, 11.1, optional gear ratios available. Lower ratios for sidecar available. Multi-plate clutch running on roller bearings and incorporating a synthetic rubber cush drive—bonded resilient facings. Triple-row ⅜" pitch primary chain with tensioner, running in oil-bath case. Rear chain ⅜" wide × ⅝" pitch.

Ignition and Lighting. Lucas electrical equipment; twin-coil ignition incorporating engine-shaft A.C. generator with rectifier for D.C. battery lighting. Gear-driven contact breaker and automatic advance and retard mechanism mounted on crankcase; provision for emergency starting independent of the battery; headlamp with pre-focus light unit, pilot light, ammeter, ignition and lighting switches and illuminated speedometer housed in styled nacelle; electric horn; stop-tail light incorporating rear reflector; 13 amp. hr. battery with polystyrene body enclosed within quickly detachable fairing.

Fuel Tank. 4-gallon capacity, including reserve. Rubber mounted and single point fixing.

Oil Tank. 6 pint capacity.

Wheels and Tyres. Dunlop tyres, front 3.25 × 18 ribbed; rear 3.50 × 18 Universal. Quickly detachable rear wheel; straight spokes to both wheels. Full width hubs of close grained cast-iron.

Brakes. A50—7" diam. front and rear; A65—8" diam. front. Floating brake shoes with adjustable fulcrum pins for easy centralisation. Both brakes cable operated with finger adjustment.

Suspension. B.S.A. telescopic front forks hydraulically damped and sealed. Swinging arm rear suspension pivoted on rubber bonded bushes with self-contained hydraulic damper units and fully enclosed springs, adjustable for weight in three positions.

They should have been front-page news, but instead they were centre-spread on pages 8 and 9: "The brilliant NEW 650 and 500 STAR twin cylinder models."

Frame. B.S.A. duplex cradle type incorporating sidecar lugs. Easily operated spring-up central stand; B.S.A. dual seat and pillion footrests; key-operated steering headlock; attractively styled front and rear mudguards; provision for rear chaincase; large capacity twin high-efficiency absorption type silencers. Siamesed exhaust pipes and single silencer optional.

Finish. A50—Polychromatic green and black; A65—Polychromatic blue and black. Flamboyant red £2. 16s. 10d. extra on A65. Alternative colour, black. Petrol tank panels, wheel rims and usual bright parts chromium plated. Polished primary chaincase, timing cover, rocker box cover. Silver sheen hubs and brake plates with polished rims.

General Dimensions. Wheelbase 54⅛"; ground clearance 7"; overall length 81"; handlebar width 28"; seat height 31½" (unladen); dry weight A50—385 lb., A65—390 lb.

Extra Fittings. (Prices include P.T.). Legshields £4. 10s. 11d.; Rear chaincase giving total enclosure £3. 6s. 10d.; Safety bars £6. 0s. 4d.; Whitewall tyres £1. 17s. 10d.; Handrail £1. 19s. 4d.; Prop stand £1. 5s. 4d.; Folding kickstart 14s. 6d.

At less than £5 more than the 500 Star the 650 Star did indeed represent value for money but ever since their introduction there have been those, and amongst Triumph aficionados too, who maintain that 'proper' machines pre-date unit construction.

A 1959 Thruxton photo, previously used on the rear cover of Gold Star brochures, was an odd way to publicise the final and ultimate incarnation of the long-lived A10 – this time around including the Triumph that's tailing the Goldie, and each with fictitious race numbers. They'd got a photographer and willing models, so why didn't they head over to Shirley Park or down to Stratford-upon-Avon, Worcester with the subject of this publicity material?

If one wanted to be unkind about the Rocket Gold Star it could be termed as a 'parts bin special', but for those who wanted a factory-produced café racer twin, rather going to the trouble of making one, this was just about the ultimate. Technology's advances would preclude it from winning its spurs on the track, thus contradicting Motorcycle Sport*'s quotation that it was 'destined for an unassailable position in the world of Motor Sport'; but that was not the reason for its existence. What's more, the glory days of the A10 in competition had been in the early '50s with Fred Rist's alcohol-burning 140mph machine on the sands of Pendine and elsewhere.*

BSA 650 ROCKET GOLD STAR

The superlative Gold Star now goes one better! With a Super Rocket engine the acceleration, speed, and flexibility set a new high standard in performance. This, combined with all the near-perfect characteristics of the winner of numerous Clubman TT races, provides a machine which is destined for an unassailable position in the world of motor cycle sport.

To the discerning eye of the expert the Rocket Gold Star has everything including the wide range of accessories which make it adaptable for various types of competitive events at a minimum outlay.

The quotations in this folder are from the road test report which was published in "Motor Cycle Sport", February 7th, 1962.

REVISED PRICES FROM APRIL 10th, 1962

£309 . 13 . 6

Including £52 · 19 · 0 purchase tax

BSA 650 ROCKET GOLD STAR
model A10 RGS

ENGINE:
70 mm. bore x 84 mm. stroke — 646 c.c. O.H.V. four-stroke with fully enclosed valve gear and high performance camshaft; aluminium alloy cylinder head with pistons giving a compression ratio of 9 to 1; crankshaft drive-side supported by roller bearing; timing side by a lead-bronze bush; crankshaft of immense strength; light alloy connecting rods with micro-babbit big-end liners; single camshaft at rear with gear drive to magneto; dry sump lubrication and double gear-type oil pump; oil tank $5\frac{1}{2}$ pints; siamesed exhaust pipe and absorption silencer; track silencer extra; engine specially bench tested.

CARBURETTER:
Amal Monobloc 1.5/32 in. bore, large capacity air cleaner to order; twist-grip throttle, air slide operated by lever on handlebar.

TRANSMISSION:
Double-cam cush drive on engine shaft; front chain $\frac{1}{2}$-in. x .305 in oil bath case with inspection cap for rapid clutch spring adjustment; rear chain $\frac{5}{8}$ x $\frac{3}{8}$-in. with guard over the top run; multi-plate clutch, with oil resistant friction surfaces and finger adjustment; B.S.A. 4-speed gearbox with special needle roller bearings; positive stop foot gearchange with pedal mounted in either forward or rearward position and internal mechanism modified to suit; extra close ratio gears, internal ratios 1.0, 1.10, 1.32 and 1.75; engine shaft sprocket to suit requirements; alternative gear ratios available, folding kickstarter pedal.

IGNITION AND LIGHTING:
Lucas magneto, manually controlled advance mechanism and separate chain driven 6-volt C.V.C. dynamo; quickly detachable headlamp with socket connections, pre-focus light unit and pilot light. Speedometer, rev. counter extra, rubber mounted on fork yoke, stop and tail light incorporating rear reflector; 13 amp./hr. battery. Standard models can be supplied less lighting and dynamo to order.

FUEL:
Four gallon capacity; special breather, 2 gallon and 5 gallon alloy tanks extra.

WHEELS:
Dunlop tyres, front 3.25–19 ribbed, rear 3.50–19 Universal; 18-in. rim available for rear wheel only; alloy rims extra; 8-in. dia. front brake; light alloy 190 mm. brake with cast-iron braking surface extra; 7-in. dia. rear brake, rod operated; quickly detachable wheels with single bolt fixing; finger adjustment to both brakes.

SUSPENSION:
B.S.A. hydraulically-damped telescopic front forks with rubber dust sleeves; swinging arm rear suspension with hydraulically-damped spring units adjustable for weight in three positions. Alternative spring strength available.

FRAME:
Cradle type of all-welded construction; central stand; steering damper; forward or rear footrest position to suit gear-change; B.S.A. dual seat; pillion footrests; blade type mudguards.

CONTROLS:
Handlebar adjustable and invertible; clip-on low level handlebars extra; clutch and ignition levers on left of bar, front brake and air lever on right of bar; ball-ends to clutch and front brake levers.

EQUIPMENT:
Tool kit; tyre inflator; speedometer; rev. counter extra.

FINISH:
Handlebar, exhaust system, wheel rims, mudguards, fork sleeves etc, chromium-plated, silver tank with chromium panels and special Gold Star badge; polished primary chaincase, gearbox and timing covers; frame, oil tank, tool box etc., black.

EXTRA FITTINGS (Prices include P.T.):
Alternative gear ratios; air cleaner £1 . 4 . 9; prop-**stand £1 . 5 . 4;** 190 mm. front brake **£5 . 14 . 7;** **2 gallon tank** (alloy) **£8 . 3 . 1;** alloy rim and 3.25–19 **tyre can be supplied with** 190 mm. brake only; 3.00–19 **ribbed racing** front tyre, and 3.50–19 directional road **racing** tyre **£3.16.8;** alloy rims **£11 . 12 . 9;** clip-on handlebars **£1 . 18 . 5;** rev. counter **£8 . 11 . 0;** **track silencer 11/6d.;** twin pipes and standard **silencers** (forward footrests only fitted) **£2 . 10 . 0;**

Some anomalies in the listed extras, such as the two-gallon aluminium fuel tank and the possible combinations of tyres and rims, but that's what was listed. Almost invariably Rocket Gold Star publicity depicted a machine fitted with a selection of racing goodies, and this brochure is no exception. One image-changing extra that would have been a must for the aspiring racer, road or track, has been left off, however – clip-on handlebars a la Gold Star Clubmans. These of course necessitated the removal of the upper fork sleeves and mounting the headlamp on the latter's three-piece tubular bracketry.

As he set off for Brighton with Megan on the pillion Graeme congratulated himself for spending the extra £2 19s 5d to have his new 650 Star in Flamboyant Red. She'd told him the standard Polychromatic Blue was too sissy and the alternative of Black was just plain morbid – if she meant anything to him it had to be red.

The sole fresh arrival for '63 was the sporting version of the B40.

"I ride the new SS90—you can't beat that extra punch of power".

350 SPORTS STAR

MODEL B40 SS90

£231
including **£38. 10s.** purchase tax

Light and easy to handle yet powered by a husky large-capacity engine. Attractively styled and handsomely finished, the SS90 will give you zestful acceleration and top cruising speeds for modern highway travel.

Specification as Model B40 except for the following:—

Engine. Die-cast alloy head with polished profile; 8.75 compression ratio; high duty valve springs and special large diameter inlet valve; sports camshaft.

Carburettor. $1\frac{1}{8}$" bore Amal Monobloc type.

Transmission. B.S.A. 4-speed close ratio gearbox in unit construction with engine; gear ratios 5.78—6.93—9.6—12.3; optional internal ratios available.

Frame. Sports type handlebar with combined front brake and air control lever.

Finish. Flamboyant red or black; chromium-plated mudguards.

The Rocket Gold Star was included in the main colour brochure for this season – decked out as usual with most of the available goodies. The price had gone up a bit and by the looks of things someone had been doing their sums, which would have added up to nearer £430 if they'd included the purchase tax. Purchase tax then, VAT now – governments get their percentage somehow or other!

"This time B.S.A. have hit the jackpot—really hard. The new Rocket Gold Star is a jet-age genius!"

650 ROCKET GOLD STAR

MODEL A10RGS

£323. 8s.
including **£53. 18s.** purchase tax

Track silencer, rev. counter, 190 mm. front brake, alloy rims and rearward footrests as illustrated, to order.

During its 15 years of existence BSA's equivalent of the Austin Seven had introduced multitudes to motorcycling, proved a willing and faithful little workhorse, and occasionally attracted ridicule (but far more friends). But its time was now up. It still came with a single sprung saddle and carrier over the mudguard as standard, but this one had the optional-extra dual seat and pillion footrests (£4 10s). The basic, direct lighting, model was now priced at £117 9s plus purchase tax but if battery lighting was wanted the price rose to £122 14s. Colours for the D1's final year were Fuschia Red, Pastel Green or Black.

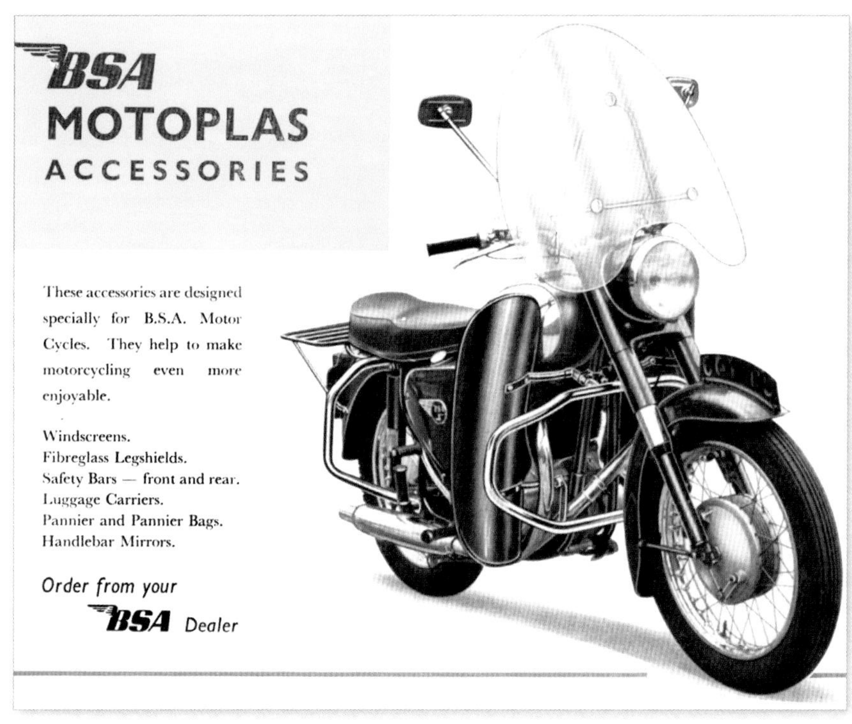

BIGGEST NEWS IN MOTORCYCLING for 1963!

EXCITING! NEW!

THE GOLD STAR TWIN by BSA

DETAILS OF COMPLETE 1963 RANGE INSIDE

From the beauty to the beastly. Very practical, I've no doubt, but somewhere underneath that lot lurks an A65.

As usual, the brochure printed in the US carried this rider: "Specifications between Eastern and Western models may vary." Fortunately in this instance it went on to explain that all pictured machines were to Eastern specification. The Rocket Gold Star on the cover, you will notice, had a small tank – one that looks very much like the two-gallon type fitted to Catalinas. Illustrated within was another identical RGS, excepting the tank, which was the standard four-gallon variety. To complicate matters further a three-gallon sport tank was offered (for either Royal Star or RGS), whilst the two-gallon was not; but common sense dictates that in fact the customer could choose from any of them. Both bikes had twin exhausts and the same 'new road-track mufflers' – yes, that's how they referred to them. They also noted that Western-type bars were standard but the 'racing type' handlebars shown were available from BSA dealers. Frames were black, and tanks and toolbox were finished in brilliant metallic red.

In addition to such fare as the 175 Bantam, complete with pin-striped fenders, of course, and C15s, here are some of the other machines available in the areas served by BSA Inc in 1963. North America remained the last overt stronghold of the Gold Star, having all but disappeared from showrooms in the UK a year or more previously. Legend has it that they continued to be manufactured for the US market alone but factory records tell a different tale – both Clubmans and Scrambles machines continuing to be delivered to destinations in the UK and as far flung as Sweden, Switzerland, Finland or Canada into the summer of 1963, after which their manufacture ceased.

The artwork on 1964's brochure cover is a little more trendy, both in its execution and depiction of some make-believe adventures. I'll give the participants' names and you can supply the storyline. That's Richard talking to Angie, whilst Jeannie makes ready with the rope. The bike, just like last year's cover, is an A65 in Flamboyant Red. The Motor Cycle *found that top whack for one of these was around 100mph. Third gear was good for 87mph and the standing quarter mile could be covered in 15.7 seconds. A steady 40mph meant 78mpg, while holding 60mph gave you 66mpg.*

With the smallest Bantam gone and in answer to the increasingly popular Italian and Japanese ultra-lightweights, BSA unleashed its Beagle (sorry, the pun was written before I realised). Its Turner family motor, looking for all the world like a diminutive wet-sump Triumph Cub unit, was plagued by marginal lubrication, leading to failure of its plain big end. But that wasn't the whole story – it just didn't catch on.

The BSA Beagle is an ultra-modern ultra-lightweight—and livelier than the rest too, thanks to its potent little 75 cc o.h.v. engine. Combined with a four speed gearbox this gives a first rate performance with phenomenally low petrol consumption. Well sprung, well braked, it is light and easy to handle and completely dependable.

BSA

Dimensions

Bore, mm.	47·6 (1·87 ins.)
Stroke, mm.	42 (1·65 ins.)
Capacity, cc	74·8 (4·56 cu.ins.)
Comp ratio	9·5
Valves	O.H.
Lubrication	Wet sump
Ignition	Fixed
Top gear	11·52
Third gear	15·1
Second gear	23·8
First gear	34·4
Generator	23W
Battery	Dry, parking
Secondary chain	½ pitch × ·305
Tyre size, front	2·25—19
Tyre size, rear	2·25—19
Tyre type, front	Gold Seal
Tyre type, rear	Gold Seal
Brake diam ins.(cms.)	Front, 4½ (11·4) Rear, 5 (12·7)
Front suspension	Leading link
Fuel, galls. (litres)	2 (9)
Oil, pints (litres)	1¼ (·71)
Seat height, ins. (cms.)	29 (73·7)
Length, ins. (cms.)	72½ (184)
Width, ins. (cms.)	23½ (59·7)
Clearance ins. (cms.)	7½ (19)
Weight, lbs. (kilos)	140 (63·5)
Colour scheme	Mist Green/Ivory

Gear drive on the ***Beagle*** *means complete freedom from maintenance. There is no necessity for adjustment and lubrication is automatically provided from the engine.*

Specification

ENGINE Completely new high efficiency engine of 75 cc with push rod operated overhead valves. Light alloy cylinder head. The lubricating system is of the wet sump type, a plunger pump supplying oil under pressure to the big end. Amal carburetter with twist grip throttle control and air filter.

TRANSMISSION Four-speed gearbox in unit with the engine, and with gear primary drive. The secondary gear teeth are formed on the periphery of the clutch plates on which the friction pads are bonded. The whole of the primary drive runs in an oil bath its level being automatically maintained from the engine.

IGNITION AND LIGHTING An engine shaft alternator provides ignition and direct lighting. Four-inch diameter headlamp, electric horn, tail lamp and reflector.

BRAKES 4½ in. diameter front and 5 in. diameter rear, both with finger adjustment.

SUSPENSION Front suspension is by leading links mounted in steel pressings which conceal the springs. Pressed steel rear swinging fork pivoted on rubber bonded bearings. Hydraulically damped suspension units.

FRAME Cantilever (or spine) type, of box section, and its design allows the engine an unobstructed air flow. It is braced internally at strategic points and carries the tools within the hollow main section. Spring-up central stand. Dual seat is standard but a single seat with a rear carrier can be supplied as an alternative.

FINISH Ivory with contrasting colour. Chromium plated wheel rims. Bright parts chromium plated

EXTRAS Pillion footrests, Windscreen, Legshields, Pannier Carriers and Bags, Speedometer.

350 Star

Model B40

Designed to the same general specification as the popular C15 model, the B40 with its 350 cc engine gives that additional performance so useful with a passenger or under adverse conditions. The robust engine-gearbox unit is smooth, quiet and economical.

350 Sport Star

Model B40 SS90

The high performance sports version of the B40—special piston, cams and large bore carburetter give this model some real "edge" to its performance. Other special features include plated guards, sports handlebar and striking flamboyant red finish.

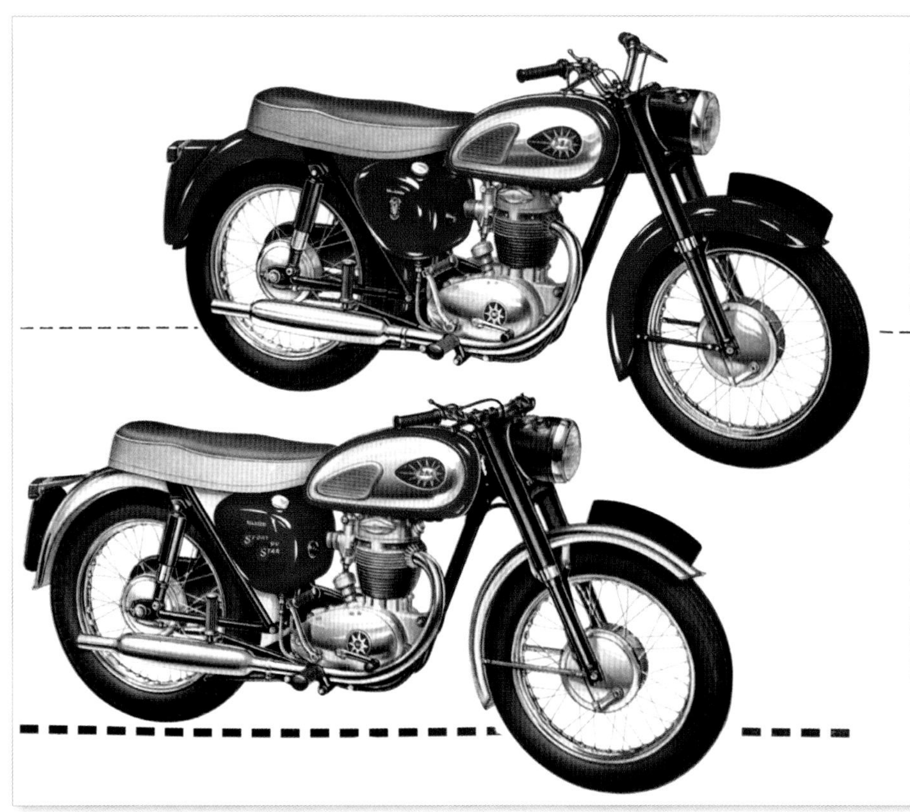

BSA had always prided itself on sound and precision engineering, as well as excellent quality control. Both 250 and 350 Stars had roller-bearing big ends and here's the equipment that was used to measure the bearing surface of their connecting rods. The little Beagle could have benefitted from a similar bottom end.

Robust primary transmission of the 250/350 Star and Sport Star models. A duplex chain with tensioner ensures long life and minimum of attention. Note accessibility of AC/DC generator and clutch.

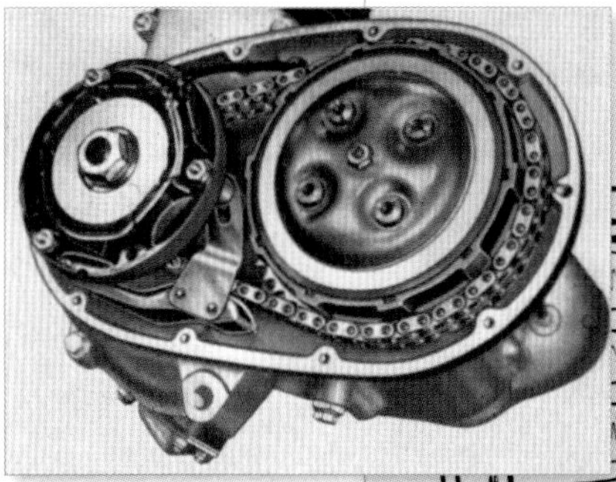

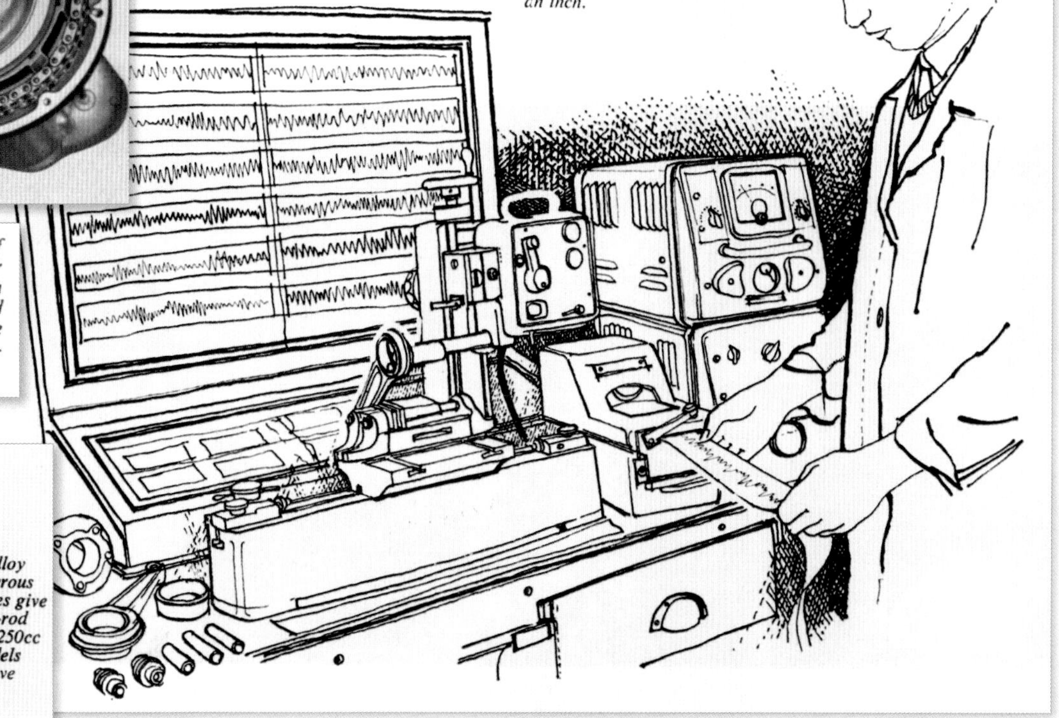

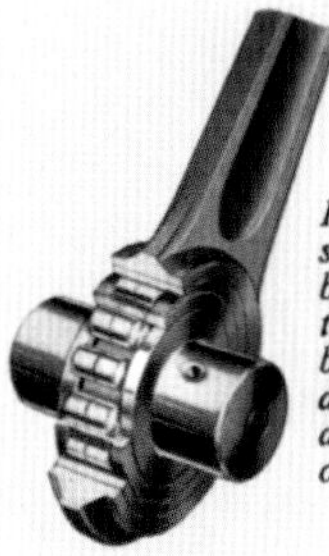

High duty alloy steels and generous bearing surfaces give the connecting-rod big-end of the 250cc and 350cc models an ample reserve of strength.

Typical of the many precision instruments used for checking BSA motorcycle components is this one which measures the quality of surface finish in millionths of an inch.

To replace the now-defunct sports A10 for 1964 was the A65R with a higher compression (9:1) engine than either the A65 (7.5:1) or even the smaller A50 (8.5:1). All had 18in wheels front and rear but a rev counter was an optional extra for the A65R (Rocket) alone. The Motor Cycle *put one of the latter through its paces and clocked 97mph in third before cogging up to top, which took them to a one-way best of 108 – at which speed, unusually, the speedo recorded about 10mph slow. Lighter than its A10 predecessor by some 40lb, mainly above the waistline, it was easier to manoeuvre in traffic at low speeds as well as more forgiving in the negotiation of high-speed twisty sections. The weight advantage was not translated to the braking, however – the front was pronounced somewhat short of 'bite' and a 30-to-zero distance of 34ft unexceptional. At a constant 60mph they managed to return 62mpg. An A50 Star tested by the same magazine a little later in the year recorded 88mph in third gear, with a highest one-way speed of 96mph, 68mpg at a steady 60mph, and braking from 30 to zero in 32ft.*

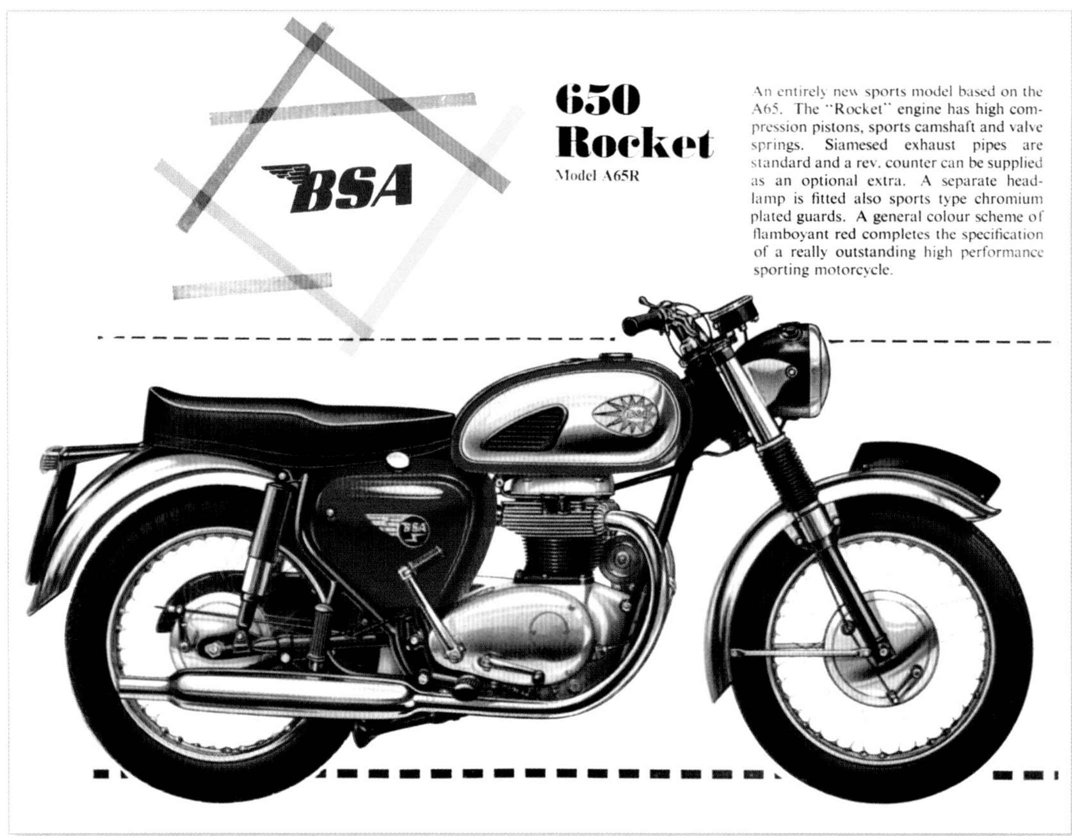

175 Bantam	250 Star	250 Sport Star	350 Star	350 Sport Star	◀ MODEL ▶	500 Star	650 Star	650 Rocket
SINGLE CYLINDER MODELS						TWIN CYLINDER MODELS		
					ENGINE			
61·5 (2·42)	67 (2·64)	67 (2·64)	79 (3·11)	79 (3·11)	Bore, mm. (ins.)	65·5 (2·58)	75 (2·95)	75 (2·95)
58 (2·28)	70 (2·75)	70 (2·75)	70 (2·75)	70 (2·75)	Stroke, mm. (ins.)	74 (2·91)	74 (2·91)	74 (2·91)
173 (10·55)	249 (15·19)	249 (15·19)	343 (20·93)	343 (20·93)	Capacity, cc (cu.ins.)	499 (30·45)	654 (39·91)	654 (39·91)
7·4	8·0	8·75	7·0	8·75	Compression ratio	8·5	7·5	9·0
None	O.H.	O.H.	O.H.	O.H.	Valves	O.H.	O.H.	O.H.
Petroil	Dry sump	Dry sump	Dry sump	Dry sump	Lubrication	Dry sump	Dry sump	Dry sump
Fixed	Variable (Auto.)	Variable (Auto.)	Variable (Auto.)	Variable (Auto.)	Ignition	Variable (Auto.)	Variable (Auto.)	Variable (Auto.)
					TRANSMISSION Sprockets;			
17	23	23	23	23	Engine	28	28	28
38	52	52	52	52	Clutch	58	58	58
16	17	17	19	18	Gearbox (solo)	17	20	20
—	16	—	17	—	Gearbox (sidecar)	16	17	17
47	45	45	46	46	Rear wheel (solo)	42	42	42
—	46	—	46	—	Rear wheel (sidecar)	43	42	42
6·58	5·98	5·98	5·48	5·78	Top gear (solo)	5·11	4·35	4·35
—	7·66	7·19	7·0	6·93	Third gear (solo)	5·85	4·98	4·98
11·0	10·53	9·91	9·63	9·6	Second gear (solo)	8·18	6·96	6·96
20·65	15·98	12·63	14·6	12·3	First gear (solo)	12·82	10·92	10·92
½" × ·250	⅜" (duplex)	⅜" (duplex)	⅜" (duplex)	⅜" (duplex)	Chain, front	⅜" (triple)	⅜" (triple)	⅜" (triple)
½" × ·335	½ × ·335	½" × ·335	½" × ·335	½" × ·335	Chain, rear	⅝" × ⅜"	⅝" × ⅜"	⅝" × ⅜"
					BRAKES			
5½ (13·97)	6 (15·24)	6 (15·24)	7 (17·78)	7 (17·78)	Diam., front, ins. (cms.)	7 (17·78)	8 (20·32)	8 (20.32)
5½ (13·97)	6 (15·24)	6 (15·24)	6 (15·24)	6 (15·24)	Diam., rear, ins. (cms.)	7 (17·78)	7 (17·78)	7 (17·78)
					DUNLOP TYRES			
3·00—18	3·25—17	3·25—17	3·25—18	3·25—18	Size, front	3·25—18	3·25—18	3·25—18
3·00—18	3·25—17	3·25—17	3·50—18	3·50—18	Size, rear	3·50—18	3·50—18	3·50—18
Reinforced	Ribbed	Ribbed	Ribbed	Ribbed	Type, front	Ribbed	Ribbed	Ribbed
Reinforced	Gold Seal	Gold Seal	Gold Seal	Gold Seal	Type, rear	Gold Seal	Gold Seal	Gold Seal
					ELECTRICAL			
30w.	60w.	60w.	60w.	60w.	Generator	60w.	60w.	60w.
8 a.h.	13 a.h.	13 a.h.	13 a.h.	13 a.h.	Battery	13 a.h.	13 a.h. (12v. 26 a.h.)	13 a.h.
					Headlamp size, ins. (cms.)			
					MISCELLANEOUS			
2 (9)	3 (13·5)	3 (13·5)	3 (13·5)	3 (13·5)	Fuel, galls. (litres)	4 (18)	4 (18)	4 (18)
—	4 (2·27)	4 (2·27)	4 (2·27)	4 (2·27)	Oil, pints (litres)	5½ (3·1)	5½ (3·1)	5½ (3·1)
29 (73·7)	30 (76)	30 (76)	31 (79)	31 (79)	Seat height, ins. (cms.)	30½ (77·5)	30½ (77·5)	30½ (77·5)
79½ (202)	78 (198)	78 (198)	80 (203)	80 (203)	Length, ins. (cms.)	81 (206)	81 (206)	81 (206)
27¾ (70·5)	26 (66)	27 (68·6)	26 (66)	27 (68·6)	Width, ins. (cms.)	28 (71)	28 (71)	28 (71)
5½ (14)	5 (12·7)	5 (12·7)	7 (17·8)	7 (17·8)	Clearance, ins. (cms.)	7 (17·8)	7 (17·8)	7 (17·8)
210 (95)	275 (125)	275 (125)	293 (134)	293 (134)	Weight, lbs. (kilos)	385 (175)	390 (177)	390 (177)

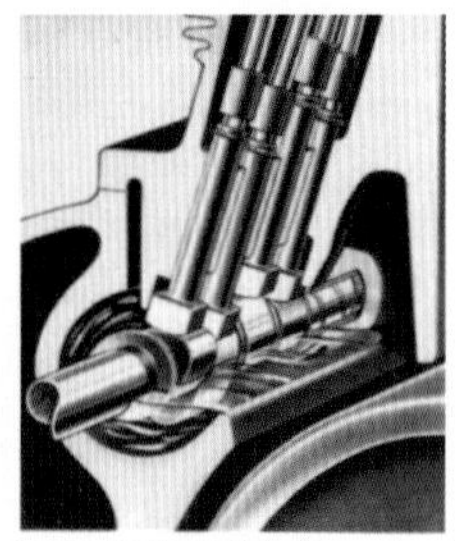

Oiling arrangements for A50, A65 and A65R engines.

There was also a Cyclone Competition with a full-race camshaft, straight-through high-level exhaust and without lighting equipment. Both were turned out in Mandarin Red and chrome.

Brand new super-performance 500 with twin-carburetor cylinder head, sports camshaft, high-compression pistons, and many other equipment items designed for maximum horsepower, brilliant acceleration and flashing top speeds.

Some of the machines featured in Hap Alzina and BSA Inc's 1964 catalogue, like the Lightning, preempted their availability in the UK whilst some models were made for the US alone – the ridiculous Bantam Trail Bronc, with its vast rear sprocket, for one.

New!

LIGHTNING ROCKET 650 TWIN

WITH TWO CARBURETORS

All New Sports Twin, **Super-powered** to produce absolute maximum acceleration and top-speed performance!

TWIN CARBURETORS are mounted on new two-port high compression cylinder head, make for highest efficiency and power.

FULL-RACE CAMSHAFT of entirely new design gives dynamic performance through a wide r.p.m. range.

HEAVY-BASE CYLINDER BARREL—adds rigidity, handles high horsepower output of new Lightning engine.

NEW GEAR RATIOS are designed for flash-performance through the gears and at top speed. Transmission is improved with new high-alloy gears.

ROAD-RACING BRAKES, powerful, quick-cooling make for fast, straight-line stops. Rear wheel is racing, single-bolt, quick-detachable type.

NEW MAGNETIC SPEEDOMETER and 10,000 rpm tachometer are mounted on twin bracket.

BRILLIANT FINISH: Lightning is finished in new Mandarin Red, with chrome tank panels, chrome sport fenders, many other parts in bright chrome. Engine cases are highly polished. A dazzlingly beautiful motorcycle!

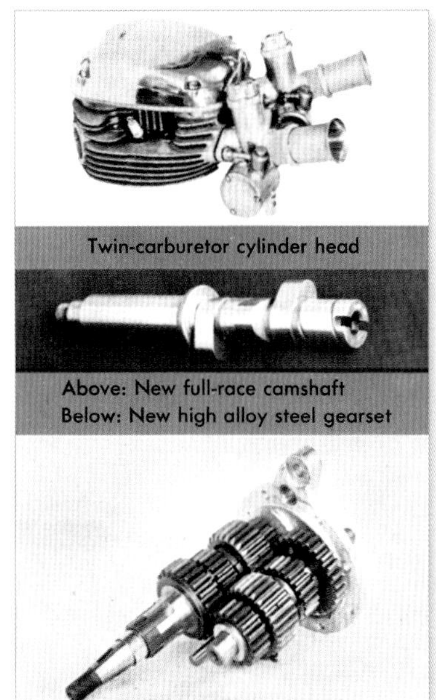

BSA 650cc TWINS

LIGHTNING Rocket Twin Carburetor fast Super-Sport road model.
THUNDERBOLT Rocket 650 Twin—powerful high speed road cruiser for those who prefer a single carburetor model. Has full-race camshaft, full power equipment, super-chrome finish.
SPITFIRE HORNET Twin Carburetor—Fast Scrambles-Sports Model.
ROYAL STAR 650 DeLuxe Twin for the highway tourist.

STARLITE 75

New 75cc ultra-light motorcycle.

BSA 500cc TWINS

CYCLONE with twin carburetors—Fast Super Sports Road Model.
CYCLONE COMPETITION with twin carburetors—Special for racing, competition.
ROYAL STAR 500 Highway Cruiser—Quiet, capable road model.

BSA 350cc MODELS

350cc SPORTSMAN o.h.v. Single—Powerful Road-Sports Lightweight.
350 ENDURO-STAR o.h.v. Single—Specially equipped for Enduro work.

BSA 250cc MODELS

250 STAR Road Model—Peppy road performer. Lowest priced BSA 250.
SS80 Sport Star—Powerful roadster. Has special equipment, super finish.
STARFIRE Scrambler—High-powered scrambles racing model.
STARFIRE Roadster—Scrambler with road equipment.
STARFIRE Trial-Cat— Special for Trials, Enduro, Cross-Country.

BSA 175cc MODELS

SUPER BANTAM—Reliable, snappy, two stroke roadster.
TRAIL BRONC—Rugged, specially equipped trail bike.

BSA Victor Grand Prix Model B44 GP. Price £349 (including £56.16.0 PT)

Manufacturers recommended retail price

Polished alloy guards

Fibre-glass air cleaner with double paper element

Light alloy cylinder with hard chrome plated bore

Oil filler

Light alloy petrol tank

Chrome molybdenum fork shafts

Hydraulically-damped suspension units, adjustable for load

Frame of Reynolds 531 tubing with reinforced head-lug. Oil carried in frame tubes and integral header tank

7 in. rear brake

New internal damping units

Q.D. wheels, front and rear

7 in. front brake

Upswept exhaust system with megaphone

Oil header tank

Ground clearance 7 in. (laden)

Contact breaker with automatic ignition control mounted in timing case and driven from camshaft

Specially strengthened crankcase with heavy-duty roller bearings drive side and ball bearings on timing side

BSA's long-overdue replacement for the DBD Gold Star scrambler fully justified its brochure cover blurb by going on to win the World Motocross Championship in 1964 and '65 in Jeff Smith's hands. On the surface the motor could be taken for little more than a 79mm-bore B40 Star with its stroke increased from 70 to 90mm, but it was in reality the result of a great deal of development.

Specification

ENGINE 441 c.c. (79 x 90 mm.); single cylinder four stroke; light alloy cylinder barrel with hardchrome plated bore; die cast light alloy head; compression ratio 11.4; high performance camshaft; pressure oil feed to overhead rocker mechanism; strengthened crankcase with heavy duty ball bearings drive side and timing side; roller bearing big-end; dry sump lubrication with double gear type oil pump; crankcase shield; upswept exhaust system with megaphone.

CARBURETTER Amal Monobloc type of $1\frac{5}{32}$ in. bore with twist-grip throttle control. Readily-accessible large capacity fibre-glass air cleaner with double paper element. Quick-action twist-grip with nylon body.

TRANSMISSION BSA four-speed unit construction gearbox; ratios 6.97, 8.65, 11.42, 15.4; positive-stop foot control; multi-plate clutch with resilient facings and a synthetic rubber cush drive; $\frac{3}{8}$ in. duplex primary chain with tensioner; rear chain $\frac{1}{2}$ in. x .305 in. rollers; rear chain guide, primary chain oil bath, folding starter pedal.

IGNITION Direct ignition from high output generator; contact breaker with automatic ignition control mounted in timing case and driven from camshaft; capsulated coil.

The double-paper element air cleaner in fibre-glass case with the quickly-detachable cover removed. Note oil header tank immediately below air cleaner casing.

FUEL TANK Light alloy, capacity $1\frac{1}{2}$ gallons.

BRAKES & TYRES 7 in. dia. front and rear brakes, both with finger adjustment. Quickly detachable wheels front and rear. Dunlop Sports tyres 3.00—20 front and 4.00—18 rear.

SUSPENSION BSA hydraulically-damped telescopic front forks with chrome molybdenum shafts and specially-developed internal damping units. Heavy-duty pivoted fork rear suspension hydraulically-damped and adjustable for load.

FRAME Cradle type of Reynolds 531 tubing, with duplex seat tubes and engine mounting; specially reinforced head-lug; all-brazed construction, with oil carried in tubes and integral header tank. Oil capacity $4\frac{1}{4}$ pints. Plain blade alloy mudguards. Raised footrests. BSA single seat. Reinforced handlebar with ball ends to levers.

FINISH Frame, etc. enamelled black. Fuel tank deep ivory and polished alloy; chrome wheel rims and front brake cover plate. Polished primary chain cover, timing cover rim, mudguards, and rim on rear brake cover plate. All other bright parts chromium-plated.

GENERAL DIMENSIONS Ground clearance 7 in. (laden); seat height 32 in.; wheel-base $52\frac{3}{4}$ in.; overall length $81\frac{1}{2}$ in.; weight 255 lbs.

A thoroughly uninspiring cover for the 1965 brochure – which, were it not for the A65 Star, could well have been for a railway timetable. Why ever didn't BSA make more of a song and dance about the exciting Lightning that was brand-new to the UK? It would seem, however, that the publicity department was not too worldly-wise; otherwise they would have been aware that National Benzole had claimed the 'Get Away' slogan a couple of years earlier: "Pale sunrise and purple evening…getaway hours! Sleek, beckoning roads and away-from-it places… getaway playgrounds. Put your right foot down! Relish the power of Super National. Getaway people get Super National."

The beastly little Beagle now came in Ivory with Royal Red frame and fuel tank. This would be its last year and few would mourn its passing.

KEEPING THE OIL MOVING

All single and twin cylinder four stroke models with the exception of the Beagle have dry sump lubrication, and the heart of the system is this robust gear type pump which guarantees the reliable functioning of the vital lubricating system.

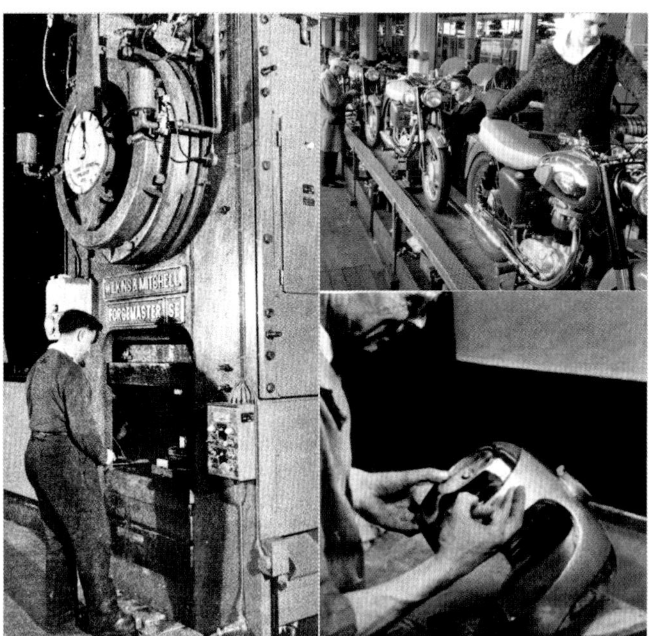

Mass production 1965-style by BSA. This 500-ton forging press turned out components such as sprockets and connecting rods. For petrol tanks, however, there was yet a machine to be invented, so they said, that could equal the superb skill of the man with a brush in his hand.

EFFICIENT ACCESSIBILITY

The ignition contact breaker on all 250 and 350 cc. models is enclosed in the timing case where it is readily accessible by the removal of the cover plate. This new drive arrangement ensures ultra accurate ignition setting and a contact breaker working under ideal conditions

Having read all about them and patiently waited, British enthusiasts were at last able to get their hands on what their American cousins had been riding around on for the past year.

500 Cyclone 650 Lightning

New two carburetter high performance twins

Fresh from a successful conquest of the American market come these sparkling new twins. We've even retained the American names—Lightning for the 650, Cyclone for the 500. High compression pistons, special camshaft, two monobloc carburetters with cylindrical air cleaners, twin-mounted speedometer and tachometer, chromium plated headlamp, fork covers, mudguards and fuel tank are just some of the features to make these models the undoubted leaders in their class. As for performance, it's breathtaking—coupled of course with the traditional BSA standards of braking, steering and handling.

Speed . Sparkle . Stamina

CYCLONE CLUBMAN
LIGHTNING CLUBMAN

For production sports model racing both the Lightning and Cyclone may be specified (at a small additional charge) with rear mounted footrests, brake pedal and gearchange, racing seat, special silencer and downswept handlebars, as shown in this photograph.

Model A65L

Mike Hailwood won the Hutchison 100 in the pouring rain at Silverstone with one of these in 1965, and another – unless it was a standard Lightning with gold tank and side panels à la Clubman – was equipped with missile launchers for Fiona Volpe (alias Italian actress Luciana Paluzzi, or Bill Ivy with blonde wig for the stunts) to ride in the James Bond film Thunderball. *These performances, plus the fact that only around 200 were made in its single season of production (autumn 1964 to '65) should give it a status above its spiritual predecessor the Rocket Gold Star – deserved or not, that day has yet to come.*

BSA MOTOR CYCLES

PRICE LIST *from* **14th NOV., 1964**

Prices are subject to alteration without notice.

Prices charged will be those ruling at date of despatch.

Model		Price £ s. d.	Purchase Tax £ s. d.	Total £ s. d.
75 Beagle	K1	82 3 6	15 19 6	98 3 0
175 Bantam (Direct Lighting) ...	D7	105 18 3	20 11 9	126 10 0
175 Bantam (Battery Lighting) ...	D7	108 8 6	21 1 6	129 10 0
173 Bantam D/L (Battery Lighting)	D7	118 1 0	22 19 0	141 0 0
250 Star	C15	166 10 0	32 7 4	198 17 4
250 Sport Star	C15 SS80	182 15 0	35 10 6	218 5 6
250 Star Trials Special	C15T	180 5 0	35 0 9	215 5 9
250 Star Scrambles Special ...	C15S	181 0 0	35 3 8	216 3 8
350 Star	B40	185 17 6	36 2 7	222 0 1
350 Sports Star	B40 SS90	195 2 6	37 18 7	233 1 1
500 Star	A50	246 2 6	47 16 10	293 19 4
500 Cyclone	A50C	277 16 0	54 0 0	331 16 0
500 Cyclone Clubman	A50CC	281 3 0	54 13 0	335 16 0
650 Star — 6-volt ... ... 12-volt (extra) ...	A65 A65	255 2 6 3 10 4	49 11 10 13 8	304 14 4 4 4 0
650 Rocket	A65R	268 10 0	52 3 10	320 13 10
650 Lightning	A65L	286 3 6	55 12 6	341 16 0
650 Lightning Clubman	A65LC	289 10 6	56 5 6	345 16 0

This 1966 model year brochure's attempt at trendiness fails miserably due to its inept artwork and lurid colour scheme. It and the machines it features are included, however, because of the changes introduced, to wit the amalgamation of the British and US ranges, which came into being for the autumn of 1965.

All twins, even these two basic models (the equivalent to the previous year's standard A50 and A65s), were now equipped with the Lightning-type frame, as well as forks with two-way damping that had been developed for the Victor scrambler. For the transmission there was a new six-plate clutch, and cylinder heads featured larger inlet valves. Another common feature was a rear wheel-driven speedometer, where one was fitted, to avoid the necessity of changing the gearbox take-off pinions when overall gearing is altered. Royal Stars were finished in Flamboyant Red with White lining, and the Thunderbolts were flamboyant Blue with White lining.

For this season the Lightning's carbs were a pair of handed 1⅛in Amal Monoblocs – up from the previous year's 1$\frac{5}{32}$in instruments. Rear hump of the racing-style dual seat had embossed BSA badge on the rear and was squashable to allow easier two-up riding. Front brake on these and the firm's other twins was of Gold Star 8in diameter type but easily recognisable from the desirable earlier variety on account of its 25 per cent-greater width. Speedo and rev counter were carried on a cast alloy bracket, and finish was Flamboyant Red with chrome-plated mudguards.

Both Wasp and Hornet were wholly American in concept and, although they shared the multinational brochure, few if any will have remained in the British Isles. Definitely more street scramblers than out-and-out competition machines, at least in the form they left the factory, they did however have the same heady compression ratio (10.5:1) as the A65 Spitfire, twin Amal Monoblocs (the Wasp 1$\frac{5}{32}$in and the Hornet 1⅛in) as well as a two- gallon (US) fibreglass fuel tank and crankcase undershield. Although the Wasp depicted here had matched speedo and rev counter, either model came with just a rev counter as standard. Both had energy transfer ignition and although no lights were fitted the alternator stator incorporated two coils, which could be used to hook up a direct lighting set if so desired. The Wasp was turned out in Sapphire Blue and the Hornet in Mandarin Red – mudguards and fork shrouds being chrome plated.

Confusingly titled the MkII, unless you remember that BSA's first Spitfire was the US-market A10 scrambler introduced getting on for ten years earlier, this was BSA's final answer to Triumph Bonnevilles, Norton 650SSs et al and as such was the fastest road-burner the firm had yet turned out, with a tested one-way speed of 123mph and a two-way mean of 119mph. The twin 1 5/32-inch Amal GP carbs looked business-like and were in part responsible, along with Hornet head and 10.5:1 pistons, for the manufacturer's claim of getting on for 55hp; but coupled with the 10.5 compression some owners complained of difficult starting, so they were ditched in favour of Amal's Concentrics (and a lower 9:1 compression ratio) on the subsequent MkIII version. Borrani wheel rims were standard but there was a choice of fibreglass fuel tanks – US customers normally favouring a two-gallon (US) over the five-gallon Lyta lookalike shown here – both part-finished in Flamboyant red along with the side panels.

TECHNICAL DATA

MODEL	175 Bantams	250 Star	250 Sports-man	500 Royal Star	500 Wasp	650 Lightning	650 Thunder-bolt	650 Hornet	650 Spitfire Mk. II Special
	SINGLE CYLINDER MODELS			TWIN CYLINDER MODELS					
ENGINE									
Bore, mm. (ins.)	61.5 (2.42)	67 (2.64)	67 (2.64)	65.5 (2.58)	65.5 (2.58)	75 (2.95)	75 (2.95)	75 (2.95)	75 (2.95)
Stroke, mm. (ins.)	58 (2.28)	70 (2.75)	70 (2.75)	74 (2.91)	74 (2.91)	74 (2.91)	74 (2.91)	74 (2.91)	74 (2.91)
Capacity, cc (cu. ins.)	173 (10.55)	249 (15.19)	249 (15.19)	499 (30.45)	499 (30.45)	654 (39.91)	654 (39.91)	654 (39.91)	654 (39.91)
Compression ratio	7.4:1	8.0:1	8.75:1	9.0:1	10.5:1	9.0:1	9.0:1	10.5:1	10.5:1
Valves	None	O.H.	O.H.	O.H.	O.H.	O.H.	O.H.	O.H.	O.H.
Lubrication	Petroil	Dry Sump	Dry Sump	Dry Sump	Dry Sump	Dry Sump	Dry Sump	Dry Sump	Dry Sump
Ignition	Fixed	Variable (Auto.)	Variable (Auto.)	Variable (Auto.)	Variable (Auto.)	Variable (Auto.)	Variable (Auto.)	Variable (Auto.)	Variable (Auto.)
TRANSMISSION Sprockets:									
Engine	17	23	23	28	28	28	28	28	28
Clutch	38	52	52	58	58	58	58	58	58
Gearbox	16	17	16	18	18	20	20	20	21
Rear wheel	47	45	46	47	47	47	47	47	47
Top gear	6.58	5.98	6.36	5.41	5.41	4.87	4.87	4.87	4 64
Third gear	—	7.66	8.14	6.2	6.2	5.58	5.58	5.58	5.32
Second gear	9.26	10.53	11.19	8.67	8.67	7.8	7.8	7.8	7.43
First gear	17.4	15.98	16.98	13.6	13.6	12.27	12.27	12.27	11.69
Chain (front)	⅜" × .250	⅜" (duplex)	⅜" (duplex)	⅜" (triplex)	⅜" (triplex)	⅜" (triplex)	⅜ (triplex)	⅜" (triplex)	⅜" (triplex)
Chain (rear)	½" × .335	½" × .335	½" × .335	⅝" × ⅜"	⅝" × ⅜"	⅝" × ⅜"	⅝" × ⅜"	⅝" × ⅜"	⅝" × ⅜"
BRAKES									
Diam., front, ins. (cms.)	5½ (13.97)	6 (15.24)	6 (15.24)	8 (20.32)	8 (20.32)	8 (20.32)	8 (20.32)	8 (20.32)	190 mm.
Diam., rear, ins. (cms.)	5½ (13.97)	6 (15.24)	6 (15.24)	7 (17.78)	7 (17.78)	7 (17.78)	7 (17.78)	7 (17.78)	7 (17.78)
DUNLOP TYRES									
Size, front	3.00 × 18	3.25 × 17	3.25 × 17	3.25 × 19	3.50 × 19	3.25 × 19	3.25 × 19	3.50 × 19	3.25 × 19
Size, rear	3.00 × 18	3.25 × 17	3.25 × 17	3.50 × 19	4.00 × 18	3.50 × 19	3.50 × 19	4.00 × 18	4.00 × 18
Type, front	Reinforced	Ribbed	Ribbed	Ribbed	K70	Ribbed	Ribbed	K70	Ribbed
Type, rear	Reinforced	K70	K70	K70	K70	K70	K70	K70	K70
ELECTRICAL									
Battery	10 a.h.	13 a.h.	13 a.h.	8 a.h. (2)	—	8 a.h. (2)	8 a.h. (2)	—	8 a.h. (2)
Headlamp size, ins. (cms.)	5 (12.7)	5½ (14)	5½ (14)	7 (18)	—	7 (18)	7 (18)	—	7 (18)
Voltage	6	6	6	12	6	12	12	6	12
MISCELLANEOUS									
Fuel, galls. (litres)	2 (9)	3 (13.5)	3 (13.5)	4 (18)	2 (9)	4 (18)	4 (18)	2 (9)	5 (22.5)
Oil, pints (litres)	—	4 (2.27)	4 (2.27)	5 (3)	5 (3)	5 (3)	5 (3)	5 (3)	5 (3)
Seat height, ins. (cms.)	31 (78.7)	30½ (78)	30½ (78)	31½ (80)	31½ (80)	31½ (80)	31½ (80)	31½ (80)	31½ (80)
Length, ins. (cms.)	78 (198)	78 (198)	78 (198)	85¼ (216)	85 (215)	85¼ (216)	85¼ (216)	85 (215)	85¼ (216)
Width, ins. (cms.)	27 (70)	26 (66)	26½ (68)	28 (71)	28 (71)	28 (71)	28 (71)	28 (71)	28 (71)
Clearance, unladen, ins (cms.)	6½ (15.5)	5½ (14)	5½ (14)	8 (20)	7½ (19)	8 (20)	8 (20)	7½ (19)	8 (20)
Weight, lbs. (kilos)	214 (100)	275 (125)	275 (125)	391 (178)	386 (175)	391 (178)	391 (178)	386 (175)	382 (172)
FINISH Frame and forks / Petrol tank	Black Chrome, Flam. Red	Black Chrome, Royal Red or Sapphire Blue	Black Chrome, Flam. Blue	Black Chrome, Flam. Red	Black Sapphire Blue	Black Chrome, Flam. Red	Black Chrome, Flam. Blue	Black Mandarin Red	Black Ivory, Flam. Red
SILVER BANTAM Frame and forks	Black	—	—	—	—	—	—	—	—
Mudguards	Silver,	—	—	—	—	—	—	—	—
Petrol tank	Sapphire Blue } Silver	—	—	—	—	—	—	—	—
Side covers	Sapphire Blue	—	—	—	—	—	—	—	—

BSA's bargain-basement Bantam at £120 all in, against £135 for the De Luxe – identical to each other apart from their finish.

250 SPORTSMAN. Only 250 cc. yet feels like a million! Made for the man who wants big bike "bite" with economy riding. High compression piston, sports-type camshaft and many other special features combine in this rugged all-rounder.

Sports-type handlebars incorporating combined brake/air levers; plated guards front and rear; large inlet valve, large bore carburettor, special high-duty valve springs; chromium plated tank panels, chromium plated separate headlamp, flamboyant blue finish.

250 STAR. The ideal run-around cum get-around. Handles and brakes like the thoroughbred it is, gives pleasurable performance under all conditions. A "good looker" that's also a good buy.

4-speed gearbox, rack and pinion clutch mechanism; contact breaker enclosed in timing case; roller bearing big-end; dry sump lubrication; hydraulically damped suspension; full width hubs. Royal red or Sapphire Blue finish.

500 ROYAL STAR. Silk-smooth performance, mile-eating power, commendable economy — with the Royal Star you get the best of everything. Stablemate of the bigger 650's — has the same superb steering, suspension and braking.

1" monobloc carburettor; twin downswept exhaust pipes; ribbed front tyre, 8" front brake, 7" rear; blade-type front guard, valanced rear; speedometer, sports-type headlamp with ammeter. Flamboyant red petrol tank with chrome panels.

500 WASP. Scaled-down equivalent of the "Hornet". Capable of speeds high enough for competitive events.

Twin downswept exhaust pipes with silencers; energy transfer ignition; fibre glass petrol tank with quick-release filler; blade-type guards; speedometer, tachometer, two 1⅛ monobloc carburettors.

650 LIGHTNING. The motorcycle that conquered America! Acclaimed in the U.S.A. for it's easy-flowing power laced with "mule-kick" acceleration . . . has to be ridden to be believed. It's the model on which Mike Hailwood won the 1965 Hutchinson 100 Production Machine Race at Silverstone.

Chrome headlamp, 8" front brake, chrome plated blade-type guards, racing pattern dual seat, speedometer, tachometer. Flamboyant red tank with chrome panels.

650 THUNDERBOLT. Lives up to its name — goes like a Thunderbolt out of the blue! Surging power, vivid acceleration, 100% certain BSA braking. Solo or two-up, Thunderbolt is the all-action machine that sets an all-time standard. Sidecar specification available to special order.

Chrome headlamp, twin downswept pipes, ribbed front tyre, 8" front brake, 7" rear; blade-type front guard, valanced rear. Speedometer.

650 HORNET. Keen on closed-circuit racing? — then the Hornet is the machine for you. Record-breaking power and performance coupled to superb suspension, steering and handling. Twin upswept straight-through exhaust pipes; energy transfer ignition; 2-gallon fibre-glass petrol tank; GS K70 tyres; tachometer. Hornet is for use on closed circuits only.

650 Spitfire Mk. II Special. It's the road racing version of the Hornet — it's the one with the built-in get up and go, go, GO!

Superbly equipped: Lights, racing pattern dual seat, 5 Gallon petrol tank, 190 mm. front brake; twin Grand Prix carburettors, downswept pipes and silencers; ribbed front tyre, alloy rims, speedometer and tachometer. Front and top of tank and side panels finished flamboyant red.

COMMANDER

A motorcycle of extraordinarily futuristic appearance made its debut at the November 1952 Motor Cycle Show, and what's more it was the product of an extremely unlikely manufacturer.

Tucked away behind the Avon and Goodyear

A new British Leader:

the

Commander

3 revolutionary machines powered by

Villiers

Modern low-cost motoring in armchair comfort

8 **reasons for Commander superiority: construction progress, design distinction built into all models**

1 Square-tube patented Beam Frames: for strength and stability
2 Motorcar front and rear suspensions: complete riding comfort on foam rubber saddles
3 Patented bonnets, easily removable: protect engine, rider, passenger
4 Powerful brakes: encased cable controls
5 Ultra-modern safety lighting: increased front-rear visibility
6 Low centre of gravity ensures stability at all speeds
7 Easy to clean cowlings: streamlined for unique riding protection
8 Car-body beauty: two colour metallic finish

Commander I

Auto-cycle—***Economy:*** pedal start. Villiers Mk. 2F engine. Brake h.p. 2.05 at 3,750 r.p.m. 160 miles per gallon! 40 m.p.h. **£74.19.6**

Commander II

Ultra lightweight motor cycle—***Versatility:*** two-speed gear box. Villiers Mk. 1F engine. Brake h.p. 2.08 at 4,000 r.p.m. 160 miles per gallon! 45 m.p.h. **£84.19.6**

Commander III

Lightweight motor cycle—***Power:*** three-speed gearbox. Villiers 10D engine. Brake h.p. 4.8 at 4,000 r.p.m. 120 miles per gallon! 55 m.p.h. **£95.16.8**

All prices include Purchase Tax

This is the 98cc Commander 2. The 1 was of the same capacity and looks but was pedal-assisted ,whilst the 122cc Commander 3 had a dual seat, curvaceous leg shields and footboards. As well as being brightly coloured all had lashings of chrome including the front and rear hubs.

tyre stands was 108A, which had been taken by the General Steel and Iron Company of Hayes in Middlesex to display its Commander range. Unlikely? Because, as far as I am aware, the firm had no previous experience in the manufacturing of motorcycles so this represented a bold venture indeed.

In their show review *Motor Cycling* magazine described what they found on the first-time exhibitor's stand thus: "A small but impressive display of three models is featured on the Commander stand. The mounts on view are shown with the main member of the frame cream enamelled with a chrome motif, the rest of the machine being coloured in light blue, dark blue or red and the biggest model displays a combined leg-shield and two-stage footboard fitting designed specially for pillion passenger use." Apart from listing the models and their engine capacities, technical details were confined to noting that they had a 'beam type frame'. This would suggest they may have been unaware that the cream-enamelled 'main member of the frame' was in fact simply a part of the pressed-steel panelwork that enclosed the actual frame, which was fabricated from a series of square-section tubes. These formed a V as they emanated from the steering head – a pair, one above the other, on either side – and swept down in a very shallow S to converge and terminate just forward of the rear wheel spindle. Forward of this there was a substantial bridge, which housed a novel single spring cantilever suspension system that gave over 4in of travel to the rear forks; the engine cradle and seat supports also formed part of the frame and were of the same section tubing. Front forks were of heavy square tubing with leading-link suspension controlled by thick rubber bands.

The 122cc Commander 3 was claimed to be capable of 55mph but what it, or its smaller brethren, were like to ride must remain a mystery, as journalists were never given the opportunity to find out – presuming, of course, that they were rideable. This, however, seems a virtual certainty, as when the show was over they found a home in the Edgware Road showrooms of Marble Arch Motor Supplies. What became of them I have no idea, nor whether any more were made. There was talk of a Commander 4 in the spring 1953 buyers' guides but after that nothing – almost as though they had been but a dream.

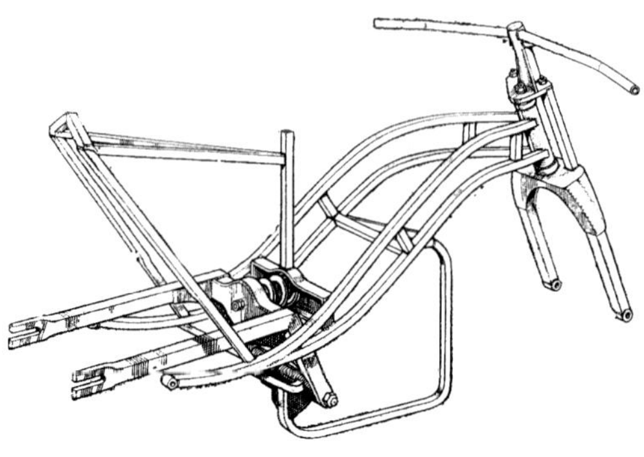

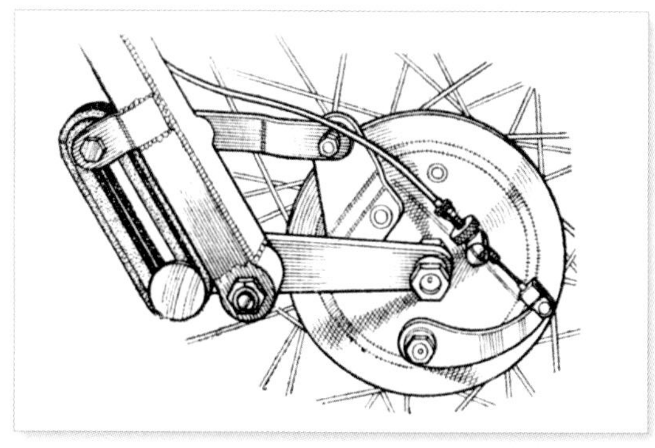

The rubber band-controlled leading-link forks.

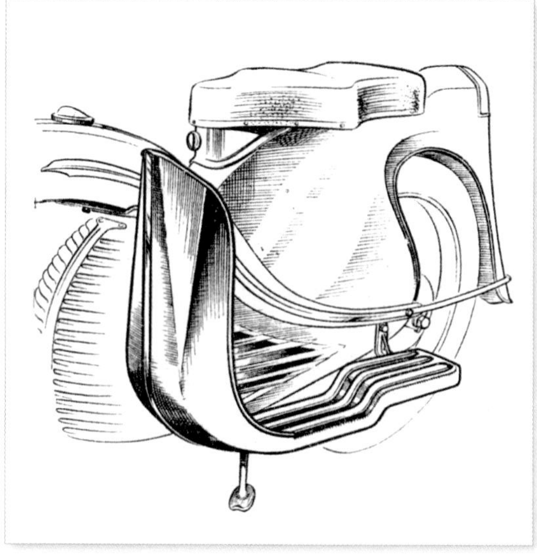

The Commanders had some very practical features, like this on the 3, but were perhaps too weird and must go down as one of motorcycling's oddest and least-remembered white elephants.

CORGI

During the Second World War, just off the A1 to the north of London and near to the small town of Welwyn, was located a secret establishment – the mysteriously-named Station IX. Run by the SOE (Special Operations Executive), and based around a Victorian mansion, all manner of military equipment for clandestine and commando use was developed, with anything that reached 'production' being given the prefix Wel. Amongst these treasures were two varieties of midget submarines going by the name of Welman and Welfreight, whilst specialised firearms were christened Welrod and Welgun, and a small folding motorcycle the Welbike.

The Welbike was the brainchild of inventor and keen motorcyclist John Dolphin, a hostilities-only Lieutenant Colonel who was the unit's commanding officer.

Once past the prototype stage its manufacture was put in the hands of Excelsior Motorcycles, which went on to produce almost 4,000 of them by the end of the war.

Designed to be used in conjunction with paratroopers, and paradropped in a special container, the Welbike, like many brainwave inventions, proved to be of limited suitability for its intended function. Having landed under fire the last thing a paratrooper would want to do would be to unpack, unfold and start up the Welbike. In the event that he persevered rather than abandoning it, and did manage to get mobile, it was next to useless on rough terrain due to its instability as well as a tendency to trip over itself due to the small wheels and ground clearance.

Seeing peacetime possibilities for his diminutive folding motorcycle, Dolphin got together with Brockhouse Engineering in the immediate post-war years and as a result they put a civilianised version of the Welbike into production as the Corgi during 1947. Apart from the petrol tank, which was now in the conventional position twixt handlebars and seat – albeit very low-slung – and rudimentary road equipment the first Corgis looked to be little changed from their forebears. The general construction was, however, somewhat more robust, although a single speed and push start sufficed until a kick-start was introduced for the Mk2.

The first of the Corgis made no secret of its military forebears, in fact quite the reverse, but it was still quite primitive with run-and-jump or paddle-off starting and a single speed. I remember my father, at the time of the Suez Crisis, getting hold of an early model such as this – his rationale being that the Isle of Wight, where we then lived, was a small place and he could do short trips economically on the little beast despite the fact that he had no motorcycling experience whatsoever. He was not a small man, and my abiding memory of his trial (and only) run is of the run-and-jump technique being adopted; after which things got rather out-of-hand on the bumpy lane that passed our house, and the tiny machine took itself and him into a bramble-filled ditch. I never saw it again.

Remarkably, in my view, the little creatures endeared themselves to certain souls who, further encouraged by Brockhouse's sponsorship of an International Corgi Club from 1952, would meet with their Corgis – some embarking on domestic holidays, with the hardiest amongst them even venturing abroad. Sales material suggested all manner of uses – district nurse, for goodness' sake! In addition more than one firm began to produce sidecars for the Corgi – surely KVP Motors of Acton's banking version being the most outlandish.

Brockhouse's American Indian venture resulted in the Corgi reaching what had once been our colonies

The Mk2 had a clutch and kick-starter. Disc wheels were also introduced due to problems with spoke breakage on the wires.

I remember district nurses on bicycles and then later driving Morris Minors or Minis, but not on these. Do you?

and beyond, when one was, I'm told, ridden coast to coast for publicity. Certainly it was marketed in the US as the Indian Papoose and circumstantially found popularity amongst service personnel as run-arounds on army camps and air bases – even seeing service out in Korea. I don't recall seeing one on my favourite 1970s TV series, so the nurses and staff at Mobile Army Surgical Hospital 4077 can't have got hold of one, although legend has it that several found their way onto aircraft carriers and were used for getting about the flight deck.

Back in the United Kingdom, Brockhouse continued to produce Corgis in further improved form until the end of 1954, when the imminent closure of the Southport factory and an almost innumerable amount of more-roadworthy competitors brought about their euthanasia after some 27,000 had been made.

By the early '50s it had grown up and now boasted a two-speed gearbox to go with its little Spryt motor. Due to its manufacturer now owning the Indian name it was marketed in the United States alongside the Brave as the Indian Papoose.

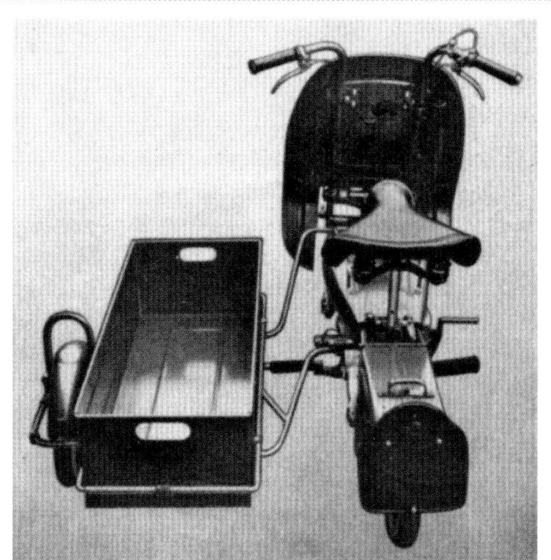

THE CORGI SIDE-CAR

Transforms the CORGI into a handy light goods carrier, at small additional cost. Easily attached, the side-car is complete, right down to electric side-light, and has a strong tubular steel frame, with quickly detachable pressed-steel container body, and sprung wheel. Ideal for tradesmen or carrying that heavy shopping load! Available in the same colours as the CORGI Mk. IV.

I've never seen one of these in the flesh. Have you?

Specification (ABRIDGED)

Engine : 98 c.c. 2-stroke SPRYT.

Gearbox : 2-speed ALBION.

Ignition : Flywheel magneto, incorporating dyno for lighting (battery for parking lights).

Lighting : Supplied with headlamp, rear lamp, electric horn.

Fuel System : Petroil mixture (25 parts petrol to 1 oil).

Tank Capacity : 10 pints.

Clutch : Single plate cork insert, controlled by handlebar lever.

Brakes : Front brake controlled from right handlebar, rear brake from foot pedal.

Wheels : Disc type, cup and cone with steel balls ; rims $8\frac{3}{4}$" x $1\frac{3}{4}$" for $12\frac{1}{2}$" x $2\frac{1}{4}$" Dunlop tyres.

Carburettor : AMAL.

Dimensions : Overall length—56". Height to top of handlebars 38". Width—19". When folded, the height is reduced to 25".

The makers reserve the right to alter the specification at any time.

Still fully folding it was available in Polychromatic Bronze, Polychromatic Blue, high-gloss Black or Indian Red.

COTTON

In 1957 Motor Cycling *tested one of the 322cc Anzani Cottons fitted with Metal Profiles front forks and adjustable Girling rear dampers, rather than the optional Armstrong leading-link forks and rear dampers, during the summer of 1956. Their machine was finished in Maroon but alternative factory finishes were Golden Brown, Black or Rich Red. Described as having 'good all-round characteristics' they liked its Albion gearbox and, despite some reservations, noted its brakes as giving 'not an unsatisfactory performance'. Its top speed, however, fell short of expectations, based on their experience with similarly-powered machines, by some 5mph – with just 65 attained flat out. A siamesed exhaust of unsuitable diameters was cited as a likely cause for this discrepancy. Fuel consumption worked out at 60mpg at 50mph or 80 at 40mph.*

Driving between Hereford and Worcester on the A4103 you will come across a steep incline known as Fromes Hill where, during the early years of the 20th century, there was held a motor speed event that drew competitors from all over the country and spectators from surrounding towns and villages. One of the latter was a teenager named Frank Willoughby Cotton, who had been born and lived at Ledbury a few miles to the south, and so enthralled was he by the spectacle that just as soon as he was able he acquired a motorcycle and became a competitor himself. Not at his local hillclimb, however, as the last had been held in 1907, but at other trials and speed events that were within his reach.

Having abandoned a nascent career in the legal profession as less attractive than one concerned with motorcycles, the years leading up to the First World War found him working for Butterfields in Birmingham, which in 1911 had begun to manufacture Levis two-strokes. Finding that the handling of much of the machinery he rode left much to be desired, and already having definite ideas of his own, he designed a novel straight-tube triangulated frame. No sooner had he taken out a patent on it, however, and a few experimental examples had been built by his employees, than the onset of war dictated that other matters took precedence for the time being.

The next we hear of Frank Cotton is that he had moved down to Gloucester where he had set up as a manufacturer in his own right, and in 1920 the Cotton Motorcycle Company, of Bristol Road, went into small-scale production – becoming another of a number of makers using Villiers's 269cc two-stroke. Anxious to put the road-holding qualities of his machines to one of the ultimate tests and mindful of the kudos that would be achieved if they were successful, his thoughts quite soon turned to the Isle of Man; and in June 1922 three Blackburne-engined Cottons awaited the start of the Junior TT. Astride one was a teenaged lad from Dublin who had talked his way into the team and what would be his first appearance on the Island. A little less than four hours later, having suffered a fire during refuelling, fractured exhaust, two tumbles and completing his last lap with no brakes, Stanley Woods brought his Cotton home in fifth place – the other two finishing 11th and 15th.

Twelve months later Cotton was back with three machines for the Junior and four for the Ultra Lightweight, with Woods (who was still not yet 20) to ride in both. Had not Le Vack's New Imperial had to pull out he most probably wouldn't have won the Junior but win he did – riding for a good part of the race with bent forks after hitting a wall in Parliament Square. He was not so lucky with the smaller machine and retired, leaving his teammates to finish second, third and fourth, but these successes heralded what transpired to be golden years for the marque.

With demand at times outstripping production capacity a move was made to larger premises at the Vulcan Works, Quay Street, in 1927. But Cottons are perhaps better remembered for their many successes on the racetrack than for the number seen on the road – the former reaching its pinnacle in 1926 with a one-two-three in the Junior TT.

With the depression came the inevitable downturn but machines powered by Villiers, Blackburne and JAP continued to be manufactured, with Rudge Python-powered 350s and 500s joining the ranks in 1931.

Through the '30s machines still appeared at the Isle of Man but further meaningful competition success eluded them except for some records taken at Brooklands during 1935. By the final years of the decade

Engine—Villiers 197 c.c. 9E motor complete to Specification 544B. Bore and stroke 59 mm. × 72 mm. with three-speed gearbox, kick starter, foot operated gear change, fully enclosed flywheel magneto, carburetter with single lever control, and fitted with suppressor.

Frame—Jig-built strongly constructed in "A" quality cold-drawn tubing 1⅛″ . . . 14g. bronze welded. Swinging-arm portion as above, hinged on bronze or steel bushes. Scientifically designed to ensure even load distribution and eliminate stress concentration at all critical points.

Wheels—Front. Full width, British Motoloy Hub. W.M. 1 . . . 19. Rim chrome plated. 300 × 19″ ribbed tyre. 6″ brake cable operated. Rear. Full width, British Motoloy Hub. W.M. 2 . . 19. Rim chrome plated, 325 × 19″ deep section tyre. 6″ brake, rod operated.

Lighting—Miller lighting equipment. Harness designed to fit straight onto pick-up points. 6″ headlamp with combined dip and horn push. Rear light" stop and tail. Stop switch operated by brake rod.

Speedo Set—Smith's 80 m.p.h. round type head, fitted into headlamp, driven from gearbox.

£132 10 0 P.T. £27 6 7 Total £159 16 7

Two-tone colours extra £1·6·2 including P.T.

the range had shrunk to Villiers- and JAP-powered bikes and the business was in serious decline – this ending with creditors filing for bankruptcy at the beginning of the war. With small factories needed to produce material and undertake engineering for the war effort Cotton was allowed to continue in business but his firm emerged from the war in, if anything, an even worse state and with a miniscule workforce. For the next few years, although a tiny amount of motorcycles were made, the company kept its head just about above water with engineering work, so effectively the marque had all but ceased to exist.

Things came to a head around the time that Frank Cotton reached retirement age, at which point the firm passed into the ownership of Monty Denley and Pat Onions, and would henceforth be known as E Cotton (Motorcycles) Ltd. By using existing stocks of components and the now-dated rigid frames a few machines were produced whilst preparations were made to recommence as a motorcycle manufacturer in the accepted sense. By 1955 this was well under way and a 197 Villiers Vulcan was listed, along with a 197 trials bike. There was also a brace of Anzani-powered two-stroke twins – the Cotanza 242cc and a larger 322cc version. All had spring frames and telescopic forks, although Armstrong leading-link were soon offered as an option.

Cotton was not alone amongst manufacturers in finding Anzani's rotary-valve two-strokes less than entirely satisfactory, and so a 249cc Villiers twin derivation of the Vulcan was added to the range for 1957. Up until 1958 there was a choice between telescopic or Armstrong leading-link forks but the latter then became standard, and the following year the Villiers twin, now known as the Herald, was joined by the 325cc Messenger – the adoption of a second and larger Villiers twin signalling the end of the Cotanzas.

By now the workforce numbered around 25,

At the risk of appearing snarky I have to say that Cotton's rear enclosure looked distinctly home-made. Optional two-tone colours (£1 6s 2d) were two-tone blue, two-tone green, black and red or black and cream – this price making the 1961 Vulcan the cheapest of the range by 1d!

The far better looking Vulcan Sports cost exactly the same as the Vulcan ordinaire unless you went for the two-tone paint job, in which case it cost you a penny more. How on earth did they arrive at these costings?

The COTTON Vulcan SPORTS

Engine—Villiers 197 c.c. 9E motor complete to Specification 544B. Bore and stroke 59 mm. x 72 mm. with three-speed gearbox kick starter, foot operated gear change, fully enclosed flywheel magneto, carburetter with single lever control, and fitted with suppressor.

Frame—Jig-built strongly constructed in "A" quality cold-drawn tubing 1⅛″ . . . 14g. bronze welded. Swinging-arm portion as above, hinged on silent bloc bushes. Scientifically designed to ensure even load distribution and eliminate stress concentration at all critical points.

Wheels—Front. Full width, British Motoloy Hub. W.M. 1 . . .19. Rim chrome plated. 300 x 19″ ribbed tyre. 6″ brake cable operated. Rear. Full width, British Motoloy Hub. W.M. 2 . . 19. Rim chrome plated. 325 x 19″ deep section tyre. 6″ brake, rod operated.

Lighting—Miller lighting equipment. Harness designed to fit straight onto pick-up points. 6″ headlamp with combined dip and horn push. Rear light: stop and tail. Stop switch operated by brake rod.

Speedo Set—Smith's 80 m.p.h. round type head, fitted into headlamp, driven from gearbox.

£132 10 0 P.T. £27 6 7 Total £159 16 7

Two-tone colours extra £1·6·3 including P.T.

Engine—250 c.c. Villiers Twin complete to Specification 950A, with foot controlled four-speed gearbox. Compression ratio 8.2: 1. Gear ratios: top 6.2, third 8.2, second 11.78, bottom 18.97: 1. Road test by Roger Maughfling, 80 m.p.h.

Frame—Jig-built strongly constructed in "A" quality cold-drawn tubing 1⅛"...14g. bronze welded. Swinging-arm portion as above, hinged on bronze or steel bushes. Scientifically designed to ensure even load distribution and eliminate stress concentration at all critical points.

Wheels—Front. Full width 6", British Motoloy Hub. W.M. 1 ...19. Rim chrome plated. 300 x 19" ribbed tyre. Brake cable operated. Rear. Full width 6", British Motoloy Hub. W.M. 2...19. Rim chrome plated. 325W19; deep section tyre. Brake rod operated.

The COTTON Herald Twin

In the 1961 brochure there was a choice of Heralds – this one no more than a Vulcan with 250 twin motor, but retaining that delightful rear fabricated from 'strong gauge steel'. How reassuring... and reassuring too to learn that a Mr Maughfling had taken it up to 80mph – a feat that I doubt his fellow testers at Motor Cycling *could have duplicated, despite very often managing greater speeds than their rivals at* The Motor Cycle.

and although the firm was still small, and with no presence at the annual Earls Court Show, it was selling all it could produce. Thus moves towards some more ambitious competition machinery began in the form of scramblers and the engagement of Fluff Brown to oversee their development.

Before too long the distinctive Cottons with their brass-badged maroon-and-black tanks and Armstrong forks were increasingly seen in both trials and scrambles – with John Draper and Badger Goss riding for the factory. In search of more power for the scramblers the firm dallied with Cross alloy barrels and special pistons for the 34a engine, but Villiers was not too keen and was anyway busy with developments of its own. These culminated in the 247cc Starmaker of 1963, which Cotton used for an improved version of the existing Cougar scrambler, called the Cobra. Trendily naming it after communications satellites and a hit record, Cotton also, adventurously, entered the over-the-counter racer market with the Starmaker-powered Telstar; one of these, ridden by Derek Minter, went on to win the 1964 British 250 championship.

That year also saw the introduction of the Conquest, which by virtue of its Starmaker engine was very likely the fastest British road-going 250 sports bike of the time; Minter and Peter Inchley won their class of the Southampton Club's Castle Combe 500 on two occasions with such a machine.

These were high spots, however, and failed to affect declining sales of an increasingly small range of road bikes. Cotton's plight worsened when the situation at Villiers resulted in engine supplies from that source terminating, along with the death of Monty Denley and the forced move to smaller premises. From then on the firm's bikes were powered by engines from the Italian firm of Minarelli; extra income was generated by the manufacture of a little three-wheeler factory truck named the Sturdy.

Pat Onions held out for as long as he could but, with hopes of a ministry contract, the business was bought by Terry Wilson who disposed of Onions and relocated to Bolton. After a few false starts, including a Rotax-powered EM34 road racer, the official receiver was called in and the company ended up absorbed by Armstrong Industries, which ironically went on to successfully develop the aforesaid racer under its own name.

So ended Cotton motorcycles, other than a number of replicas of 1960s' competition bikes built under the aegis of the indomitable Fluff Brown in the early '90s.

The COTTON Herald Twin

Lighting—Miller lighting equipment. Harness designed to fit straight on to pick-up points. 6" front headlamp with combined dip and horn push. Rear light: Stop and Tail. Stop switch operated by brake rod.

Speedo Set—Smith's 80 m.p.h. round type head, fitted into headlamp, driven from gear-box.

The New Herald Twin can now offer alternative trim design. If required a one piece cowl can be fitted.

£160 0 0 P.T. £33 0 0
Total £193 0 0

Two-tone colours extra £1.6.3 including P.T.

The alternative Herald was a slight improvement, but what of its top speed without any endorsement by ace tester Maughfling? This shared the same colour schemes as the Vulcan.

THE COTTON DOUBLE GLOSTER

Engine—250 c.c. Villiers Twin complete to Specification 039D, with foot controlled four-speed gearbox. Compression ratio 8.1 : 1. Gear ratios: top 6.2, third 8.2, second 11.78, bottom 18.97 : 1.

Frame—Jig-built strongly constructed in "A" quality cold-drawn tubing 1⅛" . . 14g. bronze welded. Swinging-arm portion as above, hinged on silent bloc bushes. Scientifically designed to ensure even load distribution and eliminate stress concentration at all critical points.

Wheels—Front. Full width 6", British Motoloy Hub. W.M. 1 . . 19. Rim chrome plated. 300 x 19" ribbed tyre. Brake cable operated. Rear. Full width 6", British Motoloy Hub. W.M.2 . . 19. Rim chrome plated. 325 x 19" deep section tyre. Brake rod operated.

Lighting—Miller lighting equipment. Harness designed to fit straight onto pickup points 6" front headlamp with combined dip and horn push. Rear light: Stop and Tail. Stop switch operated by brake rod.

Speedo Set—Smith's 80 m.p.h. round type head, fitted into headlamp, driven from gear-box.

£160 0 0 P.T. £33 0 0 Total £193 0 0

Two-tone colours extra £1·6·3 including P.T.

By the look of it, if the touring '61 Herald twin was capable of 80mph, this one should do 90 or more easily – but you'd have to attain some extraordinarily high revs, as it had exactly the same gear ratios. The ace bars, sports mudguard and race cowl look good though.

The COTTON Messenger Twin

Engine—325 c.c. Villiers Twin complete to specification, 054D with foot controlled four-speed gearbox. Compression ratio 7.25 : 1. Gear ratios: top 6.2, third 8.2, second 11.78, bottom 18.97 : 1.

Frame—Jig-built, strongly constructed in "A" quality cold-drawn tubing 1⅛" . . . 14g. bronze welded. Swinging-arm portion as above, hinged on bronze or steel bushes. Scientifically designed to ensure even load distribution and eliminate stress concentration at all critical points.

Wheels—Front. Full width 7". British Motoloy Hub. W.M. 1, 21. Rim chrome plated. 300 x 21" ribbed tyre. Brake cable operated. Rear. 7" British Hub. W.M. 2, 19. Rim chrome plated. 325 x 19" deep section tyre. Brake rod operated.

Lighting—Miller lighting equipment. Harness designed to fit straight onto pick-up points. 7½" front headlamp with combined dip and horn push. Rear light: Stop and Tail. Stop switch operated by brake rod.

Speedo Set—Smith's 120 m.p.h. round type head, fitted into headlamp, driven from gear-box.

£169 10 0 P.T. £34 19 2 Total £204 9 2

The 120mph speedo and knowledge that you'd got an extra 75cc over an otherwise similar machine that had been proven to do 80mph must have been an exciting prospect. You'd also got larger brakes to haul you down from those eye-watering speeds, as well as a 21in front wheel – more normally found on off-road competition machines.

The COTTON Trials Model

Engine—Villiers 9E Trials, 197 c.c., complete to Specification 478B with four-speed gearbox.

Frame—Strongly constructed in "A" quality tubing, cold drawn, 1⅛" . . 14 g. bronze welded, giving ground clearance of 9". Swinging-arm "A" quality 1⅛" . . 10g. hinged on bronze bushes or steel.

Wheels—Front. Full width 6", British Motoloy Hub. W.M. 1 . . . 21" Rim. 2.75 x 21" Trials cover and tube with security bolt.
Rear. Full width 6", British Motoloy Hub. W.M. 3 . . 19" Rim. 400 x 19" Trials cover and tube with security bolts.
Front—cable operated. Rear—rod operated.

Lights—Direct lighting complete with headlamp and tail light. Extra.

Speedo Set—"D" type speedo head. Inner and outer cable, gearbox, pinion and gear ring.

£140 0 0 P.T. £28 17 6 Total £168 17 6

In '61 somewhat ungainly-looking road machines were still the firm's mainstay; but before long the emphasis would be on competition or sports.

The COTTON ***CONTINENTAL***

Two-stroke sports twins were all the rage and although Cotton already had their Double Gloster to compete with similar offerings from the other manufacturers such as Norman and Greeves, it went one better with the Continental. Special duplex frame it may have had, as well as an impressive 180mm front brake, but sorry to say it had the same gear ratios and 52T rear sprocket as Cotton's less-exciting roadsters.

The specification table describes both trials and scrambles models as having mudguards of 'strong gauge steel – chrome plated'. The previous year there had been a choice of steel or aluminium (the preferable option). The Scrambler's handlebars were also said to be 'heavy gauge', whilst road machines' were merely 'strong gauge'! The Scrambler's wheelbase was 53½in as opposed to 52in for other Cottons. Weight was 245lb.

THE 250cc Corsair

Engine—250 c.c. Villiers Specification 400 D/31A. Single cylinder. Foot-controlled four-speed gearbox. Gear ratios: top 6·2, third 7·9, second 11·0, bottom 18·2.

Wheels—Front. 180 mm. in full width cast alloy hub. Fitted with a floating sideplate. W.M.1 19" chrome plated rim, 300 × 19" ribbed tyre. Cable operated brake. Rear. 160 mm. brake in full width cast alloy hub. Housing a sprocket shock absorber plate giving maximum smoothness at all speeds, and minimum chain wear. W.M.2 19" chrome plated rim 325 × 19" deep section tyre. Cable operated brake.

Frame—Jig-built strongly constructed in "A" quality cold-drawn tubing $1\frac{1}{8}$" . . 14g. bronze welded. Swinging arm strongly constructed in $1\frac{1}{8}$" tubing. Great rigidity at the Pivot point hinged on silent bloc bushes is assured by a width of 8".

With its fancy brakes from the Continental, tank that would also find its way onto the following year's Vulcan Sports, and Villiers 31A engine that was seldom used in two-wheelers, this was a bit of an oddball but it was quite good looking and was far cheaper than the 250 twins.

THE COTTON DUPLEX FRAME

Designed specifically for the *CONTINENTAL* model

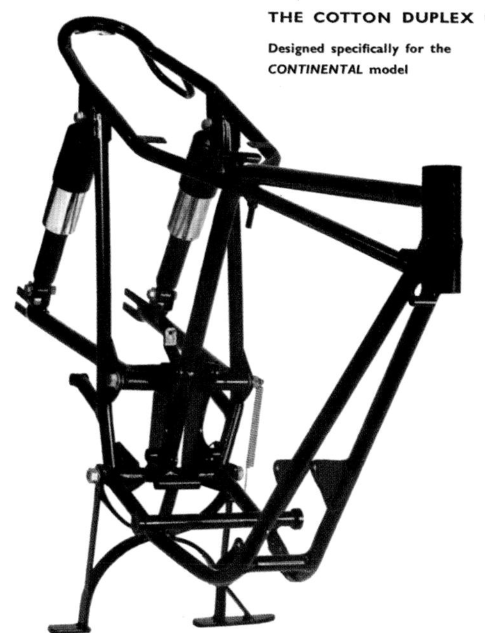

ENGINE

250 c.c. Villiers Sports Twin, with high compression heads. Foot-controlled four-speed gear box. Gear ratios: Top, 6.2, Third 8.2, Second 11.78, Bottom 18.97:1.

FRAME

Jig Built—Top portion strongly constructed in "A" quality cold drawn tubing, $1\frac{1}{8}$" × 14g. The Duplex cradle $\frac{7}{8}$". The Swinging Arm $1\frac{1}{8}$" × 10g, hinged on widely separated silent bloc bushes, also being anchored on the outside to gusset plates welded to the outer down tubes of the rear portion of the Duplex frame. Giving hair line steering with absolute minimum of whip.

WHEELS

Front—180-mm. brake in full width cast alloy hub, with Air Scoops which can be opened if required. W.M.1, 19" chrome plated rim, 300 × 19" ribbed tyre. Brake cable operated.

Rear—160-mm. brake in full width cast alloy hub. Housing a sprocket shock absorber plate giving maximum smoothness at all speeds, and minimum chain wear. W.M.2, 19" chrome plated rim. 325 × 19" deep section tyre. Brake cable operated.

SPEEDO

Smith's 80 m.p.h. round type head, fitted into headlamp, driven from gear-box.

The few brochures that Cotton produced were all too often poorly put together and with little attention to detail – eg the 1963 spec for the Herald Twin and Vulcan describes (correctly) the fibreglass cowling at the rear but also the 'deep valance carried well to the rear in strong gauge steel', which had been discontinued. There is also no clue as to how the Messenger in Sports Trim might differ from the norm, although both must have had the duplex Continental-type frame. Colours for all models were said to be Black/Red, Black/Scarlet, Black/Bronze and Black/Dark Blue.

The COTTON Messenger Twin

★ *Also available in Sports trim*

Engine—325 c.c. Villiers Twin complete to specification 054D, with foot controlled four-speed gearbox. Compression ratio 7.25 : 1. Gear ratios: top 6.2, third, 8.2, second 11.78, bottom 18.97 : 1.

Frame—Jig-built. Top portion strongly constructed in "A" quality cold drawn tubing $1\frac{1}{8}$" . . 14g. The Duplex cradle $\frac{7}{8}$". The Swinging arm $1\frac{1}{8}$" . . 10g., hinged on widely separated silent bloc bushes, also being anchored on the outside to gusset plates welded to the outer down tubes of the rear portion of the Duplex frame. Giving hair line steering with absolute minimum of whip.

Wheels—Front. Full width, British alloy hub. W.M.1 . . 19. Rim chrome plated. 300 × 19" ribbed tyre. 6" brake, cable operated.
Rear. Full width, British alloy hub.
W.M.2 . . 19. Rim chrome plated. 325 × 19" deep section tyre. 6" brake, rod operated.

Lighting—Miller lighting equipment. Harness designed to fit straight onto pick-up points. $7\frac{1}{2}$" front headlamp with combined dip and horn push. Rear light: Stop and Tail. Stop switch operated by brake rod.

Speedo Set—Smith's 120 m.p.h. round type head, fitted into headlamp, driven from gearbox.

The COTTON Trials Model "SPECIAL"

Frame—*Re-designed.* Top tube and down tube $1\frac{1}{8}$" cold drawn. Rear portion $\frac{7}{8}$" Duplex cradle. Swinging arm $1\frac{1}{8}$" . . 10g. cold drawn. The Swinging Arm $1\frac{1}{8}$" x 10g, hinged on widely separated silent bloc bushes, also being anchored on the outside to gusset plates welded to the outer down tubes of the rear portion of the Duplex frame giving maximum rigidity. Prop stand pivoting on swinging arm.

Wheels—New British alloy Hubs. Chrome rims. Front W.M.1 × 21. Rear, with shock absorber, W.M.3 × 18.

Engine—Villiers 32A. 250c.c. with alloy square barrel and head.

Exhaust—Chrome plated pipe with Cotton designed silencer.

Trials model continued with single down-tube frame and either 9E or 32A Villiers motors but for 1963 here is the considerably more expensive Special with duplex cradle frame, and engine with Parkinson alloy barrel and head. Cotton told us it was on a 32A bottom end but other sources suggest it was in fact on a 36A. Customers could choose between a standard 2¾-gallon road tank or smaller-capacity trials type. Towards the end of 1964 a supplementary, and dearer, Trials bike with Starmaker engine would be added to the range.

The name Cougar had first been applied to the firm's scramblers when Cross-modified engines had been fitted a couple of years earlier but was carried on for this one, which had an entirely new frame. For 1963 there was also an 'Exciting new model' – the Cobra Scrambler – a Cougar equipped with twin-carburettor variant of the Villiers Starmaker engine. To take advantage of a loophole in purchase tax regulations, Trials and Scrambles machines were available in kit form – this saving the customer up to £40. Added to these in 1964 was a bare frame kit to take a Triumph Tiger 100 engine developed from the machine that Arthur Lampkin was riding in large-capacity classes.

The Cotton Cougar

Frame—Duplex of all bronze welded construction, it is mainly made out of $\frac{7}{8}$" diameter tubing. The two top members are of $1\frac{1}{8}$" tubing. The engine is fitted into a welded section which completely cradles the crank case and gear box. In this way all loads are distributed evenly to the engine and gear box. Timken tapered bearings are used in the steering head. The Swinging arm is hinged on two plain bearings $9\frac{1}{4}$" apart also being anchored on the outside to gusset plates welded to the outer down tubes of the rear portion of the Duplex frame thus giving maximum rigidity.

Wheels—Front. Full width 6" light alloy hub with floating side plate and using $1\frac{1}{8}$" brake shoes. Air scoop is also provided which is left closed for normal use. W.M.1 21" rim, chrome plated, cable operated.

Rear. Full width 6" light alloy hub, housing a sprocket shock absorber alleviating shock load to gear box thus minimising potential gear breakage. Rod operated brake.

Engine—Villiers two-stroke Mark 34A. four-speed gearbox, 250 c.c. to Specification 016D, with alloy barrel and head.

DMW

During the 1930s successful grass-track and road-racer Leslie Dawson would occasionally build machines for fellow enthusiasts in the garage he ran at Heswall on the Wirral (Merseyside). These were little more than an assemblage of components from well-known makers, but just under a year before the commencement of World War Two, in October 1938, he patented a swinging-arm rear suspension system – precursor to the type universally used to this day.

During the war, although ineligible for the armed forces due to old racing injuries, he was employed by the RAF to train aircraft mechanics, as well as running his own motorcycle workshop behind a pub in Wolverhampton, near to where he now lived. There he designed and patented his own version of the telescopic front fork, which he named the Telematic. He also further developed his own ideas on rear suspension and henceforth undertook conversions of customers' machines, or made and supplied them with kits, at what was by then called Dawson's Motor Works.

Next, with hostilities at an end, he embarked upon the construction of a small number of complete motorcycles in the form of JAP-engined grass-track racing machines carrying the DMW name, which stood for Dawson's Motorcycles Wolverhampton. With demand growing and keen to expand, he entered into a partnership with Harold Nock, who owned a company named Metal Profiles; but before too long the partners began to disagree on the direction the company should take. Nock favoured a range of lightweight two-strokes whilst Dawson's abiding interest was in competition-orientated machinery. Sadly the outcome was a foregone conclusion and Nock (who held the purse strings) prevailed, so Leslie Dawson left the company he had started and emigrated to Canada.

Although Harold Nock had previously worked within the motorcycle industry he felt the need for someone with a sound technical grounding, so with Dawson gone he employed the services of an ex-BSA development engineer named Michael Riley. The Wolverhampton premises had by this time become too cramped and, with future manufacturing operations in mind, a move was made to the Metal Profiles factory, just down the road at Sedgeley.

With an all-in price of £99 the 122cc Coronation model was introduced as a successor to the Standard 122 at the 1952 Motor Cycle Show. Despite being the cheapest in the range it featured the DMW's own Metal Profiles leading-link front forks with some 4in of suspension travel – this 'contributing to the high standard of steering excellence' commented by The Motor Cycle *when they had one on test. Top speed proved to be 47mph, with 39 available in its intermediate gear and a not-particularly-noteworthy 90mpg at a constant 40mph.*

By the end of 1950 preparations were complete and the first of a range of Villiers-powered DMWs went into production using 122 and 197cc versions of the Wolverhampton maker's two-strokes. All had Metal Profiles-made telescopic front forks and, as an alternative to a conventional tubular rigid frame, the customer could have one with square-section tubes and plunger rear suspension as an optional extra. As well as Standard and De Luxe versions there were also Competition models of both capacities. Extraordinarily, at around this time ambitious plans were made to build a small number of twin-cylinder machines with rotary valve heads to contest the lightweight TT. Apparently impetus for this stemmed from Riley but even so it is strange that Nock, who had shortly before taken a stand against competition, condoned such activities up to the point he did. Supposedly frames and running gear were built and there was a prototype engine running under test by the time the plug was pulled.

Next, during 1953, Nock came to an arrangement with the French engine manufacturer AMC (Ateliers de Mécanique du Centre), which had been started by the Chartoire brothers and had a factory at Clermont-Ferrand. As result DMW announced three new machines featuring AMC four-stroke power units at the November show – the 175P had a pushrod OHV of 170cc, the Dolomite a 249cc OHC, and there was

DMW was not much given to producing publicity material, and its 1955 brochure is possibly the most comprehensive. Featured on the cover was the 224cc Cortina – pre-empting Ford's family saloon that also took its name from the Italian ski resort by a good few years. The DMW was so called on account of it being Harold Nock's favourite winter holiday destination. Its frame was the company's P-series, fabricated from squared-section tube with pressed-steel rear subframe that incorporated the swinging arm suspension bush as well as enclosing a compartment for battery and tools. Both pivoted rear fork and front forks were of course by Metal Profiles. Motor was the four-speed Villiers 1H with flywheel ignition and rectified lighting. On test with The Motor Cycle *one proved capable of some 60mph, with petroil disappearing at a rate of around a gallon every 70 miles whilst cruising at 50.*

The optional square-tube frame with plunger suspension available as an extra during the early manufacturing years. The Motor Cycle *published a test of a 197, finished in Turquoise Blue and Silver, with this frame and MP telescopic forks, in January 1952 and were impressed with its handling and brakes on roads that were in places icy. Top speed was 58mph, with 51 possible in second gear and about 100 miles covered for every gallon of petroil at 40mph.*

the Hornet 125cc double-OHC racer. All this from a man who had all but railroaded out the firm's founder due to his own predilection for nothing much else than utility two-strokes!

The latest models, as well as another with the latest Villiers 1H 225cc single, were built around a frame with square-section tubing and pressed-steel rear – a method of construction that would be used on the majority of subsequent DMWs.

By the 1956 season AMC-powered exotica had been discontinued (the French firm itself going out of business within a year or so) and DMWs were once more powered exclusively by Villiers; including a little 98cc scooter charmingly named the Bambi.

Competition machinery for trials and scrambles continued to be produced alongside road-going bikes but the swingeingly-priced 125 racer that had come to nothing discouraged further endeavours of that nature until, in 1963, its name was resurrected for a 247cc Starmaker-powered Hornet. It would never attain great heights but as an over-the-counter club racer it was capable of picking up places if the opposition wasn't too fierce – probably its finest hour being Jack Findlay's tenth position in the 1965 Lightweight TT. The firm also experimented with a racing 500 twin consisting of coupled 250s based on the Starmaker: named the Typhoon it proved to be one step too far for DMW's research and development facilities.

Prior to all this, and reinforcing Nock's apparent affinity for Walt Disney, a scooter-cum-motorcycle named the Dumbo had been publicised but never listed; it was shelved until a similar concept was brought to the market as the Deemster in 1962. Powered by a 249cc Villiers twin, De Luxe versions even had an electric starter. Unloved by the buying public they did, however, gain acceptance with the police and remained in production for several years, latterly being fitted with Velocette Viceroy running gear.

In 1962 Ambassador Motor Cycles was purchased and henceforth manufactured at Sedgley until 1965 – the majority in fact being DMW Dolomite IIs marketed as Ambassadors. DMWs themselves ranged through the Mk9 197cc, 249cc twins, Trials and Scrambles machines to the Hornet racer, which shared a similar frame to the Mk18 scrambler.

As the decade wore on motorcycles continued to be manufactured, but in decreasing numbers, until Harold Nock retired to the Isle of Man around 1970. By this time, however, having acquired a large amount of spares, patterns and tooling from Villiers, the company had become the main source of parts as well as undertaking rebuilds. This included a lucrative contract with the government for maintaining the Villiers 11E power units that were fitted in invalid cars.

In 1975 Nock sold the company to two of its directors, Graham Beddall who owned a local engineering business and Ivan Dyke, who was also the company's accountant. From then on the emphasis turned increasingly to engineering and a wide range of associated products but the Villiers side of the business was continued. This included the manufacture of complete Villiers-type engines for other manufacturers such as Cotton, as well as putting them into the occasional competition machine of DMW's own – one of these, in the hands of Mike Parkes, winning the Midland Centre Trials Championship in 1976 and '77.

The very last DMW was almost certainly made the following year but the engineering, Metal Profiles, and Villiers sides of the business continued and were sold upon the partners' retirement in 1995. The DMW name, however, remained current but unused until it was finally put to rest a little over five years later.

"200 P"

This is a smaller edition of the Cortina, and is fitted with the Villiers 197 c.c. 8E engine, three or four speed gearbox optional. The famous "P" series frame with M.P. telescopic or MP–Earles front fork. M.P. pivot fork rear suspension with oil damped spring units. 3.25 Dunlop tyres. Large capacity petrol tank. Other features include battery lighting, electric horn, 6½" headlamp enclosed in a streamlined nacelle, and journal bearing hubs fully sealed and not requiring adjustment.

Available in Dark Blue or Paris Grey.

The P-type frame and its subsequent variants' method of construction was unique to DMW. They also featured snail cam rear chain adjustment at the swinging-arm pivot point.

Cortina and 200P could be told apart at a glance on account of the pressed-aluminium 'saucepan' cover for the latter's flywheel magneto on the offside; also its exposed, rather than cowled-in, carburettor. DMWs this season were normally finished in the company's own shade of DMW (Turquoise) Blue (with beige seat) with Paris Grey or even Black (with maroon seating) as options (despite this brochure offering Dark Blue or Paris Grey).

"DOLOMITE"

Fitted with 250 c.c. overhead camshaft. A.M.C. engine. Alloy cylinder and head. Hair pin valve springs. Four-speed gearbox. Rev. counter and/or speedometer. "P" series frame with MP cruiser weight telescopic fork, and MP Pivot fork rear suspension, with oil damped spring units. 3.25 x 18 Dunlop tyres. Large capacity petrol tank.

Available in Dark Blue or Paris Grey.

Again taking its name from the Italian mountains, but pre-empted by Triumph with its 1930s Dolomite cars, this was unique amongst smaller British motorcycles in its use of an OHC motor. This came about as a result of a liaison between DMW and Ateliers de Mécanique du Centre (AMC) of Clermont-Ferrand, which manufactured engines for several French motorcycle makers. I have never seen one or spoken to anyone who has, so I wonder how many were made in the two years it was listed.

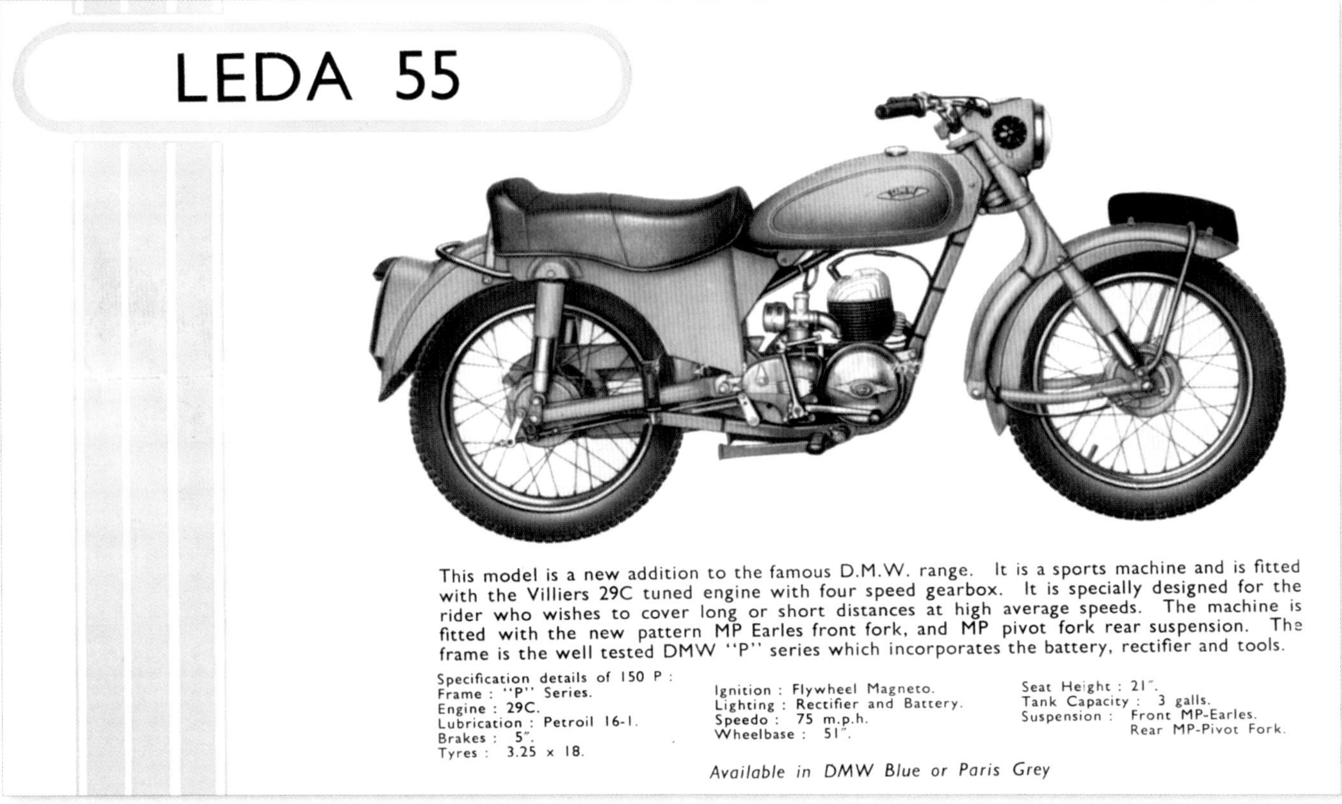

In 1955, one might have thought DMW would have gone for a larger engine than the 147cc Villiers 29C to justify the claim that it was a 'sports machine' capable of 'high average speeds'; but Motor Cycling*'s seasoned tester Bernal Osborne endorsed the decision by describing it as a 'high petrformance lightweight'. 'Finger light steering', smooth braking' and 'first class handling characteristics' were amongst other observations and its top speed, by design or coincidence, was almost bang on its model number at 56mph, with an overall consumption of 90mpg.*

Shortly after I turned 16 my first legal road miles, as well as my first trial, were at the helm of a three-speed 197 DMW Trials bike. Registered in 1954 (with the number POD 228, in case it's still around) it had a round-tube rigid frame and rather curvaceous upswept exhaust with similar silencer to the machine pictured here. Years ago someone who might have been expected to know, ex-DMW dealer Ron Lake, told me that at that time the works machines had frames of this material rather than rectangular tubing. In retrospect I think he may well have been wrong but, either way, this is the next-generation model with plunger suspension.

MOTO CROSS

This machine is designed specially for the enthusiastic scrambler. MP–Earles front forks and pivot fork rear suspension units are used. The handlebars are braced, specially streamlined tank, Latex foam cushion seat designed to give an ideal riding position. Extra strong footrests. Fitted with the Villiers 7E tuned engine, three or four speed gearbox optional. 3.00 x 19 front, 3.25 x 19 rear, Dunlop Sports Tyres. Should this machine be required for road use, it must be ordered with stand, exhaust pipe, silencer, number plates and horn.

International 6-Day Trials.
Two entries: Two Gold Medals.

The same Ron Lake, whose shop was in Bideford, North Devon, sponsored South Devon farmer John Tribble to ride one of these, or one very like it, and the combination enjoyed a good deal of success in West Country events. The short open exhaust shows that the principles of efficient two-stroke exhaust systems were not understood by all manufacturers at this time!

"Hornet"

What a fantastic little machine, in spite of an eye-watering price tag of over £360 – but did it ever make it into production? Its appeal, it has to be said, stems mainly from the power unit – and how about the large-diameter brakes with MP logo? Certainly none made it to start line of the Island's Ultra Lightweight TT, and I suspect that no more than one or two were assembled – to be but glorious little white elephants. If so, its brochure appearance must serve as both expectancy announcement and epitaph.

"HORNET" ROAD RACING MODEL

This machine has been designed specially for the rider who wants the opportunity of competing on equal terms with machines from any part of the world. It is powered by a 125 c.c. double o.h.c. alloy engine, manufactured by the famous French firm A.M.C. This engine is the last word in design, incorporating all the latest refinements such as: Double o.h.c. bi-metal alloy cylinder, three bearing cam shaft, engine gearbox unit, oil radiator, Amal G.P. carburettor, racing magneto ignition. A limited quantity of these machines will be available to riders interested in serious competitions, the machines will be capable of extremely high speeds and further technical details will be available upon request. The frame is the well tested DMW "P" Series, giving a very low riding position, petrol tanks for long or short distance racing will be available. Streamlining will be incorporated on the front of the machine. Alloy rims and Dunlop 2.50 racing tyres fitted as standard. Adjustable clip-on handlebars. MP racing fork and rear suspension units. Rev. Counter. Latex cushion seat.

"Motor Cycles of advanced design," read the cover of DMW's 1960 sales folder – in spite of the by-now rather dated MP front forks. Be that as it may they were certainly mildly individualistic despite being powered by the ubiquitous Villiers in one form and another – in this case a 9E/4. Some items proudly listed as standard were what people had come to expect but also included QD wheels and enclosure for the rear chain. Extras such as windscreen, panniers and leg shields could be bought to dress up any machine but the option of MP/Earles forks was more meaningful and also necessitated differing patterns of front mudguard.

Both publicity illustrations for 1960 depicted machines in the optional-extra two-tone finish of Maroon and Old Gold but as standard the customer could choose from Turquoise Blue, Paris Grey or Black. In an attempt to cash in on the trend for lightweight sports machines in the early '60s there would later be the Sports Twin with Italianesque tank in red and chrome mudguards. Like many of its peers, however, it promised more than it delivered, with a top speed that wouldn't quite reach 70mph – rather a sad state of affairs when you consider that a bog standard Dolomite II had been persuaded to reach 71mph by Motor Cycling's *staff back in 1956.*

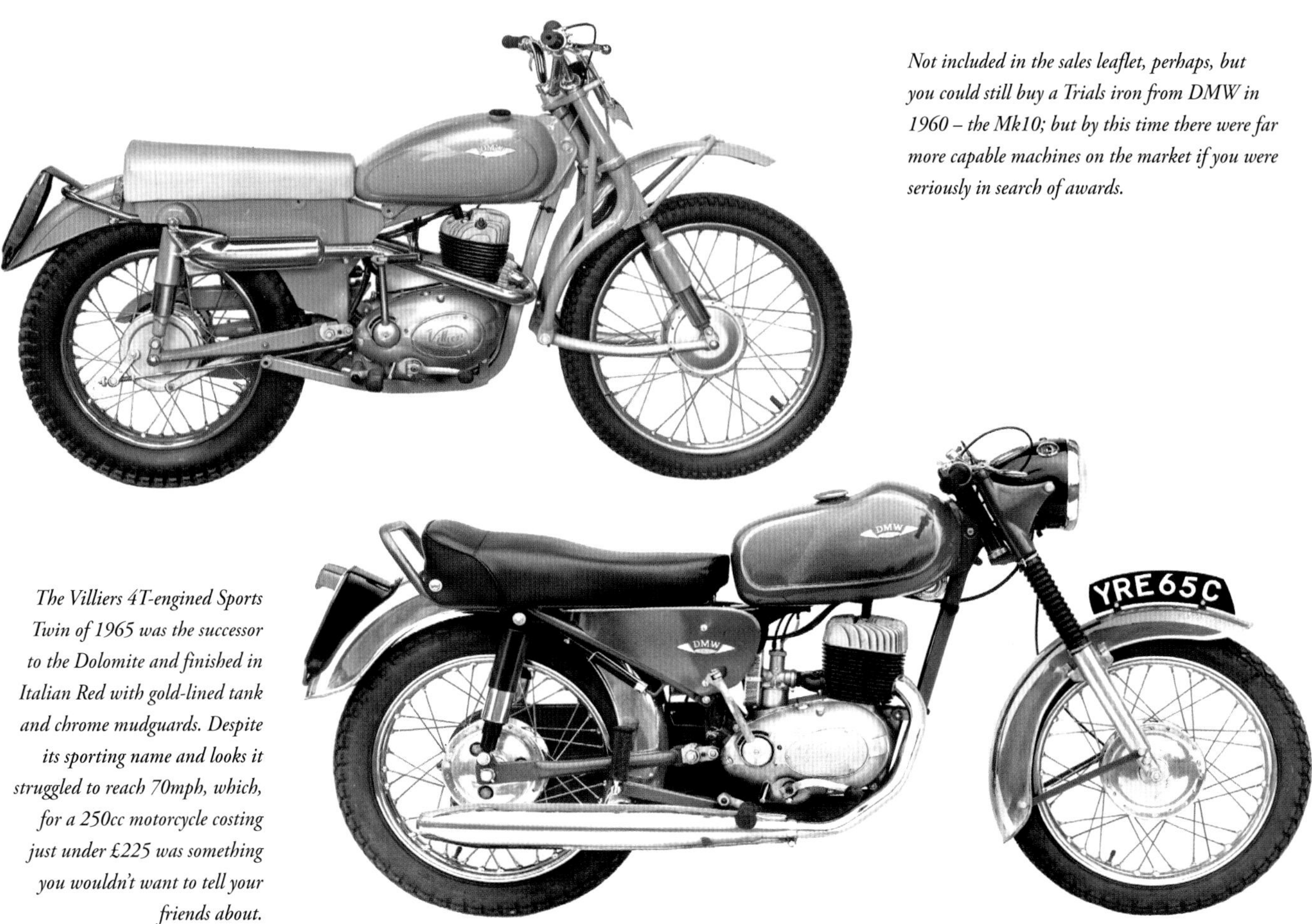

Not included in the sales leaflet, perhaps, but you could still buy a Trials iron from DMW in 1960 – the Mk10; but by this time there were far more capable machines on the market if you were seriously in search of awards.

The Villiers 4T-engined Sports Twin of 1965 was the successor to the Dolomite and finished in Italian Red with gold-lined tank and chrome mudguards. Despite its sporting name and looks it struggled to reach 70mph, which, for a 250cc motorcycle costing just under £225 was something you wouldn't want to tell your friends about.

SPECIFICATIONS (K SERIES)

Frame of welded construction with square tubes and pressed steel rear portion neatly enclosing the battery and tool compartments.

Front Fork M.P. Cruiserweight telescopic (or M.P./Earles at extra cost).

Rear Fork Pivot type mounted on rubber bearings and incorporating cam adjusters for the rear chain—the wheel being automatically kept in line.

Fuel Tank $3\frac{1}{2}$ galls. with off-main-reserve tap and two filters in fuel line.

Silencers detachable for cleaning.

Rear Suspension Springs. Quickly adjustable to the load being carried by means of the C Spanner provided.

Brakes. D.M.W./Girling 6" dia. x $1\frac{1}{4}$" wide with cast iron braking surfaces. Floating shoes with fulcrum adjustment.

Hubs. Light alloy on journal bearings.

Rear Wheel. Quickly detachable leaving brake and chain in position.

Rear Chain. Totally enclosed.
The moving parts of the rear suspension (and of the Earles type front suspension) are mounted on rubber bearings not requiring lubrication. In fact the only grease nipples on D.M.W. Motor cycles are on the front forks of telescopic fork models.

STANDARD COLOURS :—Paris Grey, Turquoise Blue, Black. EXTRA :—Two tone finish in maroon and old gold.

MODEL	ENGINE UNIT	TRANSMISSION	ELECTRICAL	EQUIPMENT	TYRES	DIMENSIONS
MARK 9 DE LUXE **200 cc. SINGLE**	Villiers 9E/4 (59 x 72 mm. single cylinder two-stroke) Compression ratio 7.25/1 B.H.P. 8.4 at 4,000 r.p.m. Petroil Lubrication. Flywheel magneto. Carburetter type S.25 with air cleaner and strangler.	$\frac{3}{8}$" pitch primary chain and 4-plate clutch running in oil. 4-speed gearbox in unit with engine. Positive foot change. Ratios 6.3, 8.0, 11.2, 18.5. Final drive by $\frac{1}{2}$" pitch x .305" chain fully enclosed. Sprockets 15/44T. Speedometer driven from gear-box.	Headlamp nacelle with $5\frac{1}{2}$" prefocus light unit. 24/24 watt main bulb. A.C. Horn. Stop light. Exide 3ET5 battery 12 a.h. charged through rectifier. Switch for direct lighting.	Dual-seat. Pillion footrests. Centre stand. 70 m.p.h. D-shaped speedometer. Toolkit. Inflator.	Dunlop. Front— 3.25 x 18 ribbed. Rear— 3.25 x 18. Universal.	Wheelbase 51" Ground clearance $7\frac{1}{2}$" Seat Height 30" Weight 266 lbs. Fuel Capacity $3\frac{1}{2}$ gallons.
DOLOMITE II DE LUXE **250 cc. TWIN**	Villiers 2T (50 x $63\frac{1}{2}$ mm. twin cylinder two-stroke) Compression ratio 8.2/1 B.H.P. 15 at 5,500 r.p.m. Petroil Lubrication. Flywheel generator with two external ignition coils. Enclosed carburetter type S.22/2 with air cleaner and strangler.	$\frac{3}{8}$" pitch primary chain and 4-plate clutch running in oil. 4-speed gearbox in unit with engine. Positive foot change. Ratios 6.3, 8.3, 12.0, 19.3. Final drive by $\frac{1}{2}$" pitch x .305" chain fully enclosed. Sprockets 15/44T. Speedometer driven from gear-box.	Headlamp nacelle with $5\frac{1}{2}$" prefocus light unit. 30/24 watt main bulb. D.C. Horn. Stop light. Exide 3ENA5 battery 8 a.h. charged through rectifier with half charge switch.	Dual-seat. Pillion footrests. Extra wide roll-on centre stand. 80 m.p.h. trip speedo. Toolkit. Inflator.	Dunlop. Front— 3.25 x 18 ribbed. Rear— 3.25 x 18 Universal.	Wheelbase 52" Ground clearance 5" Seat Height 30" Weight 296 lbs. Fuel capacity $3\frac{1}{2}$ gallons.
DOLOMITE IIA DE LUXE **324 cc. TWIN**	Villiers 3T (57 x $63\frac{1}{2}$ mm. twin cylinder two-stroke) Compression ratio 7.25/1 B.H.P. 16.5 at 5,000 r.p.m. Petroil Lubrication. Flywheel generator with two external ignition coils. Enclosed carburetter type S.22/3 with air cleaner and cable operated strangler.	$\frac{3}{8}$" pitch primary chain and 4-plate clutch running in oil. 4-speed gearbox in unit with engine. Positive foot change. Ratios 5.9, 7.8, 11.2, 18.0. Final drive by $\frac{1}{2}$" pitch x .305" chain fully enclosed. Sprockets 16/44T. Speedometer driven from gear-box.	Headlamp nacelle with $5\frac{1}{2}$" prefocus light unit. 30/24 watt main bulb. D.C. Horn. Stop light. Exide 3ENA5 battery 8 a.h. charged through rectifier with half charge switch.	Dual-seat. Pillion footrests. Extra wide roll-on centre stand. 80 m.p.h. trip speedo. Toolkit. Inflator.	Dunlop. Front— 3.25 x 18 ribbed. Rear— 3.25 x 18 Universal.	Wheelbase 52" Ground clearance 5" Seat Height 30" Weight 300 lbs. Fuel capacity $3\frac{1}{2}$ gallons.

DOT

DOT marked its return to motorcycle manufacture with a stand at the 1949 show, where examples of this 200RS as well as the economy direct-lighting 200DS and several versions of its three-wheeler trucks. The pressed-steel Webb-forked two-wheelers with Villiers 6E motors were finished in black with cream mudguards and chromium-plated 2¾-gallon tank.

Manufacturers who rode their own machines in races are few and far between but those who won important events with them are a real rarity – the Collier brothers of Matchless being probably the most well known. Their racing careers occupied a few short years prior to World War One, however, whilst a scarcely remembered rider named Harry Reed's lasted from 1908 until 1925; and like Charlie Collier he not only won the first TT he entered but on a machine of his own.

Reed had established a cycle business in Salford, Manchester during 1903 and by 1907 had moved to larger premises in nearby Hulme, where he was making motorcycles fitted with Peugeot's proprietary 3½hp V-twin motor. The previous year he'd successfully run a similarly-powered machine at Blackpool's Speed Trials, and when he heard that a Peugeot-engined Norton had won the twin-cylinder class of the Isle of Man's inaugural motorcycle Tourist Trophy races it was sufficient inspiration to ready one of his DOTs for the 1908 event. The name DOT, incidentally, was happened upon when Reed was casting around for a moniker with desirable characteristics: Devoid Of Trouble very definitely being one.

So it was that towards the end of the following September Harry, along with 20 other competitors (including last year's winner Rem Fowler, once again Norton/Peugeot mounted), set off on ten laps of the St John's course. Fowler was an early retirement; but just over four hours and 158 miles later ten survivors trailed in with Harry Reed, his DOT living up to its name, emerging the winner. Although neither Harry nor his motorcycles would ever repeat this performance both returned to the Island on many occasions, and in 1924 he was second in the sidecar TT, whilst prior to 1930 DOTs ridden by others placed as high as second or third in the Lightweight and Junior TTs.

Racing aside, by the outset of the First World War DOT had settled upon JAP as its main engine supplier; this state of affairs lasted into the early 1920s, when machines with engines by Bradshaw and Blackburne, then Anzani, were introduced as a supplement to single-cylinder and V-twin JAPs.

In 1925 not only did Harry Reed retire from racing but also from the firm that he had started, henceforth it being run by Thomas Sawyer who had joined DOT shortly after the war. Under his tenure machines of larger capacity than 350cc were phased out and a range of smaller two-strokes introduced in their place, but soon the Great Depression was upon them and the market dwindled, bringing about firstly a reduced range and then cessation of production in 1932 – the firm passing to BS Wade and R Johnson during the same year.

For the remainder of the '30s DOT's workforce turned out a range of pedal-powered three-wheeler delivery vehicles on the lines of those popular with ice-cream vendors and those that had been made since the 1920s by Warrick. Fortunately the government even found uses for them during the war, by which time Johnson had gone to Rolls-Royce, leaving Burnard Scott Wade in sole charge. Production continued and motorised versions powered by small Villiers two-strokes were developed – an unlikely contribution to the war effort being a contract from the Ministry of Food to produce milk floats for export to India.

As soon as was practicable after hostilities had ended, the little Villiers-engined three-wheelers were put into regular production, and being the smallest,

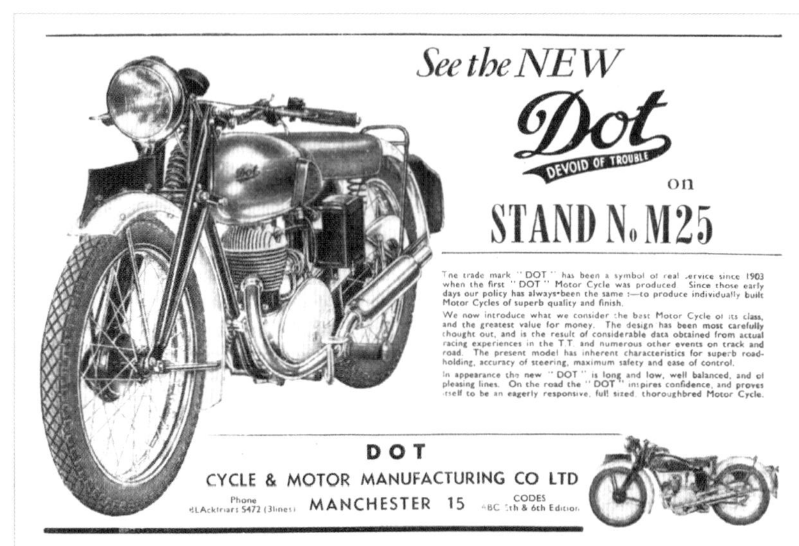

lightest motor commercial available, DOT's light delivery truck, at a purchase tax-free price of about £125, enjoyed ready sales at home and abroad. Sweden was a particularly popular destination and reputedly it was the agent in that country who suggested a light motorcycle would also be a good seller.

From that basis a return to motorcycle manufacture was a logical step, and in 1949 two 197 Villiers-powered models were introduced – DOT taking a stand at Earls Court that November.

The following year they were joined by a scrambler, the first of many off-road competition machines that in the future would constitute a speciality of the marque and the bulk of its output.

Meanwhile DOT embarked on what would prove to be something of a red herring by building a small number of machines to contest the 1951 Ultra Lightweight TT. With swinging-arm frames constructed of special light square-section tubing by Talbot Stead, an angular fuel tank mounted beneath the top tube and a Villiers engine canted forward almost to the horizontal, they were somewhat unorthodox-looking. They also proved to be hopelessly slow compared with the all-conquering Mondials but all finished – thereby winning the manufacturers' team prize as well as the kudos of the first British machine home, in seventh place.

A second herring, shortly after, took the form of a four-stroke 250 with Indian Brave motor, and then yet another departure from the 197cc norm was made when DOT announced what was described as a trials/scrambler with 224cc Villiers 1H engine in the autumn of '53 for the export market. By this time the firm was offering its own unique front forks as an alternative to Metal Profiles versions, and until the introduction of the 197 Mancunian roadster in 1955, would manufacture nothing but competition machinery.

Another road machine, in the form of the DOT-Vivi moped, was marketed from 1957 until 1962 but this was merely a bit of badge engineering, as it was nothing much more than a copy of the German Victoria manufactured in Italy by Fiat subsidiary Viberti. The Mancunian remained current until the end of 1958, and the 1959 season saw what was now a truly bewildering range of competition bikes catalogued – 14 in all if one counted the trials/road models, and ranging from 197 to 349cc, the latter featuring an RCA two-stroke twin that was also fitted to the newly-announced Sportsman's Roadster.

By the early '60s road machines had been discontinued and the stranglehold that manufacturers such as Greeves now had on the two-stroke off-road market, and hence newsworthy results, made it very difficult for small firms such as DOT to make any headway. There were those who swore by their capabilities over the rough stuff, however, and it was their custom that kept the firm going even during the period that saw the demise of its engine supplier Villiers.

For some this didn't matter and I can well remember a local scrambler who had already replaced his with a full-house alloy Tiger 100 motor – its power coupled with the machine's short wheelbase making for an exciting ride. Conversions of this type were the exception rather than the rule, though, and by the end of the decade demand had dwindled to such an extent that DOTs were available in kit form only, to special order – this state of affairs lasting through the '70s and latterly with Minarelli as the suggested engine option.

In 1978 one last attempt was made to revivify the brand, when a freshly-designed prototype featuring a DMW-built Villiers 250 motor was made. But times and allegiances had moved on, so there was little interest – and that was the end of that.

Metal Profiles forks were standardised during 1950 and this short-wheelbase scrambler was added to the range. Silencer and tailpipe were removable, as was the headlight, and the outer half of the expansion chamber (just in front of the cylinder) and remaining exhaust could be rotated so it pointed downwards.

To supplement the range of 197cc two-strokes this 250 with Brockhouse-built side-valve engine was introduced in 1951 and remained current for just over a year. During the 1920s DOT had favoured a flamboyant finish of cerise and silver. Attention-grabbing back then it was equally so when used in the early '50s – which is more than can be said for the DOT 250's performance when tested by Motor Cycling. *A flat-out maximum of 53mph with very nearly 40 seconds required to reach this velocity was none too rapid even then; but British motorcyclists didn't have to worry, as it was tagged 'for export only'. If you stuck rigorously to 30mph it would return you nearly 130mpg, however.*

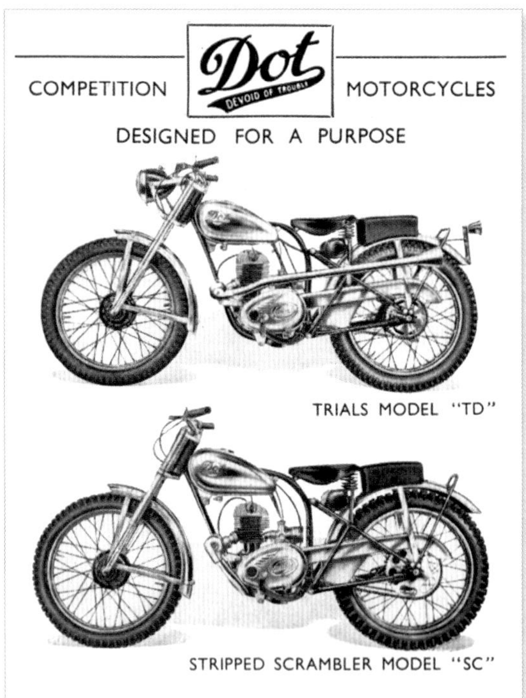

From the construction of frames to the firm's own ideas on exhaust systems, DOT's 1952 Villiers 197-engined competition machines would be hard to confuse with any other make.

By the end of 1953 DOT had perfected its own unique front forks as an alternative to MP telescopics – the little 197 scramblers, already having gained a reputation as giant-killers, becoming even more capable over rough ground when fitted with these. This is the SCH Stripped Scrambler.

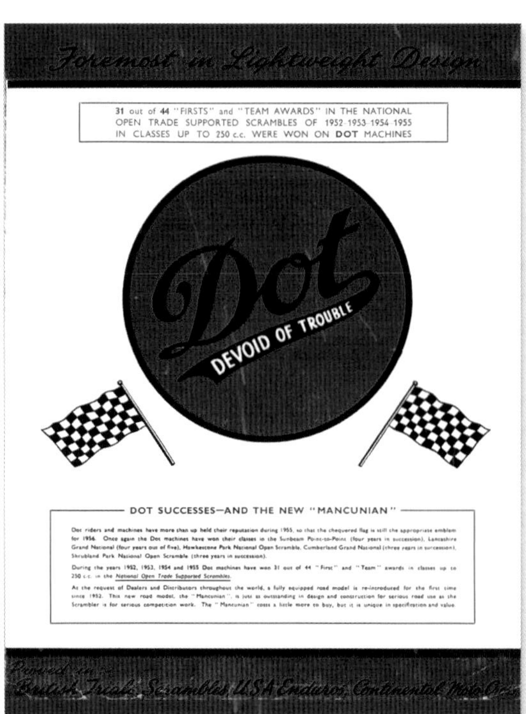

Trials machines could be had with full road equipment.

The "MANCUNIAN"

The "MANCUNIAN" is supplied at an INCLUSIVE PRICE, fully equipped, as illustrated. The full equipment includes:. Rectified Accumulator Lighting, Illuminated 80 m.p.h. "Trip" Speedometer, four speed 9E Engine Unit, Dual Seat and Pillion, Foot Rests and, of course, the new "DOT" Bottom Link Forks incorporating Oscillating 6″ diameter DUAL Brakes. Full width, steel reinforced aluminium alloy Hubs, front and rear.

There are NO extras. INCLUSIVE PRICE.

List Price	Purchase Tax	Total Price
£137 0 0	**£32 17 0**	**£169 17 0**

In the autumn of 1955 DOT's first road model for three years was unveiled and could be had in either British Racing Green or Continental Red – cerise having been consigned once more to the firm's past with the last of the previous roadsters. The Mancunian's patented front forks could be fitted to their competition machines if required and stocks were available.

Code	Specification	List Price	Purchase Tax	Total Price
TDH	Trials Rear Springing Model with 19″ × 3.00″ Front and 19″ × 3.25″ Rear Dunlop Trials Universal Tyres. (Touring or Road Racing Tyres on request). Full road equipment.	124 0 0	29 15 2	153 15 2
THX	Trials SPECIAL Springer Model. Footrests are 2″ further back than the TH Model. 21″ × 2.75″ Front and 19″ × 3.50″ Rear Dunlop Trials Universal Tyres. Full road equipment. NO LIGHTING.	121 0 0	29 0 10	150 0 10
TDH-X	Same specification as THX but with DIRECT LIGHTING EQUIPMENT.	126 0 0	30 4 10	156 4 10
SH	Scrambler Springer Model with 19″ × 3.00″ Front and 19″ × 3.25″ Rear Dunlop Sports Tyres. Full road equipment. NO LIGHTING.	121 0 0	29 0 10	150 0 10
SDH	Same specification as SH but with DIRECT LIGHTING EQUIPMENT.	126 0 0	30 4 10	156 4 10
SCH	Scrambler Springer Track Model, stripped for racing events. Fitted with 19″ × 3.00″ Front and 19″ × 3.25″ Rear Dunlop Sports Tyres. The following parts are NOT supplied with this model: Lighting, Speedometer, Number Plates, Long Exhaust, Silencer.	117 0 0	28 1 7	145 1 7
	Extra for Four Speed Gear Box	6 10 0	1 11 2	8 1 2
	Extra for Pivoting Front Fork Suspension. including the 6″ dia. Brake with Oscillating Back Plate and Long Torque Arm, allowing maximum braking application without interference of the suspension. (Dot Patents 27351-27352).	5 0 0	1 4 0	6 4 0
	Extra for "TRIALS TUNING" the engine	2 15 0	13 2	3 8 2
	Extra for "SCRAMBLE TUNING" the engine	4 0 0	19 2	4 19 2

DOT was unusual in that it offered scrambles and trials bikes for the road with 19in front wheels and fully road-equipped – the serious competition man, or woman, would go for either the THX or SCH.

The TDHX was the 'proper' trials model but with direct lighting – here fitted with Mancunian-type front forks.

1958 SEASON  MANCUNIAN

The MANCUNIAN is supplied fully equipped as illustrated.

The specification includes :

The latest Villiers 9E Engine with 3 or 4 speeds and with wide or close ratios, built to **Dot** requisition incorporating High Capacity Coil and Special Cam ; Rectified Accumulator Lighting ; Electric Horn ; Stop Light ; Adjustable Head Lamp ; Illuminated 80-m.p.h. TRIP Speedometer ; Wide Chain and Sprockets ; Ribbed Front Tyre and Studded Rear in DUNLOP STANDARD QUALITY (not lightweight quality) ; Dual Seat and Pillion Footrests ; Full width, steel reinforced aluminium alloy Hubs ; 6-in. dia. Rear Brake and 6-in. dia. DUAL FRONT BRAKE, with dual torque arms and oscillating anchorage ; Swinging Arm rear suspension ; Bottom Leading Link front suspension ; Hydraulically controlled spring units of Armstrong and Girling manufacture, the rear adjustable for load. Finished in Black or Green, with the Petrol Tank, Wheel Rims, Chain Guard, Handle Bars, Fittings and Accessories all Chrome Plated. Centre Stand, also Prop Stand, Full Kit of Tools and Tyre Inflator.

THERE ARE NO EXTRAS TO THESE INCLUSIVE PRICES

MODEL	List Price	Purchase Tax	Total Price
MANCUNIAN 3 SPEED	**£139 0 0**	**£34 8 0**	**£173 8 0**
MANCUNIAN 4 SPEED	**£144 0 0**	**£35 12 10**	**£179 12 10**

This would be the last season for the Mancunian and it was little changed apart from revised colours.

Bereft of decorative or even well-illustrated sales material, but long on a bewilderingly complex range of models.

1959 SEASON. SPECIFICATIONS AND PRICES

Model	*Supplementary Specification*
TRIALS MODELS THX TDHX	**Trials or Sports Road Model.** Full road equipment, upswept exhaust system, 70 m.p.h. Speedo. Dunlop TRIALS Universal tyres 21″ × 2·75″ front and 19″ × 3·25″ rear. Fitted with security bolts. 4-speed gear box with wide ratio 524W. 7·45, 10·00, 17·90, 26·83. Alternative gear ratios fitted on request ; 484W. 484C. 524C. 564W. 574C. THX (No Lighting) 200cc. £145 10s. 0d. *P.T. :* £36 0s. 2d. *Total :* £181 10s. 2d. THX (No Lighting) 250cc. £158 0s. 0d. *P.T. :* £39 2s. 0d. *Total :* £197 2s. 0d. TDHX (With Lights) 200cc. £150 10s. 0d. *P.T. :* £37 5s. 0d. *Total :* £187 15s. 0d. TDHX (With Lights) 250cc. £163 0s. 0d. *P.T. :* £40 6s. 10d. *Total :* £203 6s. 10d.
TRIALS MODEL "WR" (Works Replica)	**This is a THX specially prepared for exclusive TRIALS work.** The footrests are positioned 3″ further back to give ease of balance in a most difficult Trials section. This necessitates a modification in the exhaust pipe bend and silencer positioning. A 4″ section rear tyre is fitted on a wider WM3 rim. Dunlop TRIALS Universal tyres 21″ × 2·75 front and 18″ × 4·00″ rear, with security bolts, NO LIGHTING, 4-speed gear box with specially recommended Trials wide ratio gears 564W, 8·03, 10·76, 19·28, 28·90. Alternative gear ratios fitted on request. 524W. 200cc. £148 0s. 0d. *P.T. :* £36 12s. 7d. *Total :* £184 12s. 7d. 250cc. £160 0s. 0d. *P.T. :* £39 12s. 0d. *Total :* £199 12s. 0d.
SCRAMBLER (Works Replica) SCH	**Stripped Scrambler Model for Track Use Only (Works Replica).** Dunlop SPORTS tyres 21″ × 2·75″ front and 19″ × 3·25″ rear, fitted with security bolts. This is a model designed exclusively for Scramble events and the following parts are NOT fitted ; Lighting equipment, speedometer, registration plates, long exhaust pipe and silencer (the short open exhaust pipe is fitted). Normally recommended 4-speed ratios most suitable for Scramble events 564C, 8·03, 10·20, 14·30, 23·61. Alternative gear ratios fitted on request : 524C. SCH 200cc. £142 10s. 0d. *P.T. :* £35 5s. 5d. *Total :* £177 15s. 5d. SCH 250cc. £155 0s. 0d. *P.T. :* £38 7s. 3d. *Total :* £193 7s. 3d.
SCRAMBLER (WITH ROAD EQUIPMENT) SH & SDH	**Scrambler Model With Road Equipment.** Primarily designed for Scramble events, but fitted with equipment for road use ; upswept exhaust and silencer system, 70 m.p.h. Speedo. (Silencer and exhaust system should be removed for Scramble events and the DOT short open pipe fitted). Dunlop Sports tyres 21″ × 2·75″ front and 19″ × 3·25″ rear. Fitted with security bolts. 4-speed gear box. Ratios most suitable for Scramble events, 564C, 8·03, 10·20, 14·30, 23·61. Alternative gear ratios fitted on request ; 524C. SH (No Lighting) 200cc. £146 10s. 0d. *P.T. :* £36 5s. 2d. *Total :* £182 15s. 2d. SH (No Lighting) 250cc. £159 0s. 0d. *P.T. :* £39 7s. 0d. *Total :* £198 7s. 0d. SDH (With Lights) 200cc. £151 10s. 0d. *P.T. :* £37 10s. 0d. *Total :* £189 0s. 0d. SDH (With Lights) 250cc. £164 0s. 0d. *P.T. :* £40 11s. 10d. *Total :* £204 11s. 10d.
SCRAMBLER TWINS 250 c.c. and 350 c.c. Works Replicas	**Stripped Scrambler Models for Track Use Only (Works Replicas).** Dunlop SPORTS tyres 21″ × 2·75″ front and 19″ × 3·50″ rear. (18″ × 4·00″ on the 350 cc model). These models are designed exclusively for Scramble events and the following parts are NOT fitted : Lighting equipment, speedo, registration plates, long exhaust pipe, silencer. The engines fitted to these models, including the carburettors and the ignition system, are specially tuned for high torque and develop their full power within 5,500 r.p.m. The gears are made of special material and are chosen so that all four ratios can be made full use of in any Scramble event. There is also a wide range of sprocket sizes available for the enthusiast. SCH-Twin 250cc. £176 0s. 0d. *P.T. :* £43 11s. 2d. *Total :* £219 11s. 2d. SCH-Twin 350cc. £184 0s. 0d. *P.T. :* £45 10s. 10d. *Total :* £229 10s. 10d.
SPORTSMAN'S ROADSTER 350 c.c.	The " **Sportsman's Roadster** " has been designed for the sporting enthusiast who likes to own a motor-cycle that is " different," and for the man who appreciates the joy of driving a twin cylinder two-stroke. Such engines have the power impulses of a four cylinder four-stroke, but in addition to this, the particular engine fitted in the DOT Sportsman's model has a truly amazing spread of torque which gives to the model fantastic acceleration right through the power range up to 80 m.p.h. (A specially tuned version of the same engine can give a road speed approaching 90 m.p.h., details on request). The sportsman enthusiast will notice several desirable features on this model which distinguish it from the commonplace : For instance there is the HAND MADE polished aluminium petrol tank which is truly the work of craftsmen. The polished aluminium front and rear mudguards combine to save further unnecessary weight. A fast machine requires good brakes; the front brake on the "Sportsman's Roadster" is more than just a full width hub, it is actually a DUAL BRAKE 6″ in diameter with dual cables and compensating mechanism. Note also the oscillating brake plate (covered by DOT patent) which allows maximum braking efficiency without interference of the suspension. Take a look at the front forks, they are a one-piece solid unit, not just two legs clamped to a bracket. The method of construction and the steering adjustment is covered by DOT patents. And now for the frame construction : the renowned DOT cradle loop frame, with all stressed members in manganese molybdenum alloy steel tubes. Truly a mount you can be proud of. There are no extras : a long dual seat and pillion footrests are included in the standard specification. 350cc. £189 0s. 0d. *P.T. :* £46 15s. 8d. *Total :* £235 15s. 8d.

On display at the '58 Show was the 350 RCA-engined Works Replica scrambler but how many, if any, were sold? If nothing else the din from the twin exhausts would have frightened the opposition.

The short-lived Sportsman's Roadster had polished-aluminium fuel tank and mudguards as well as a dual front brake, and featured the Peter Hogan-designed RCA 349cc (63x56mm) two-stroke twin manufactured by R Christoforides and Associates of Harlesden, North London – later makers of Dolphin Marine engines. A prototype of this engine, which employed twin Amal carbs and an Albion gearbox, had been fitted to a Greeves and tested by Vic Willoughby of The Motor Cycle, *who recorded a mean top speed of 75mph but, as far as I aware, Greeves showed no interest in incorporating it into one of its production machines – this honour falling to DOT. Below it is the Villiers 250 THX that, like all 250 DOT singles of the time, was either fitted with a Villiers 9E equipped with Vale-Onslow head, barrel and piston or with a Villiers 31A.*

SPECIFICATION DATA

Model	SCH Scrambler	SCH Scrambler	Trials Works Rep.	Trials Works Rep.	Trials Marshall	Trials Marshall	Californian
Capacity	200 cc.	250 cc.	200 cc.	250 cc.	200 cc.	250 cc.	250 cc.
Engine Type	9E 455B	34A	9E 342B	32A	9E 342B	32A	34A
Bore and Stroke ...	59 × 72 mm.	66 × 72 mm.	59 × 72 mm.	66 × 72 mm.	59 × 72 mm.	66 × 72 mm.	66 × 72 mm.
B.H.P.	13 b.h.p. at 6,000 r.p.m.	19 b.h.p. at 6,000 r.p.m.	9·2 b.h.p. at 4,000 r.p.m.	13 b.h.p. at 5,600 r.p.m.	9·2 b.h.p. at 4,000 r.p.m.	13 b.h.p. at 6,000 r.p.m.	19 b.h.p. at 6,000 r.p.m.
Compression Ratio ...	10: 1	12: 1	8·25: 1	8: 1	8·25: 1	8: 1	12: 1
Carburettor	Villiers	Amal Monobloc	Villiers	Villiers	Villiers	Villiers	Amal Monobloc
Air Cleaner	Villiers V1100	6″ Vokes	Villiers V1100	Villiers V1100	Villiers V1100	Villiers V1100	6″ Vokes
Tank Capacity	2½ gal.	2½ gal.	2½ gal.	2½ gal.	2½ gal.	2½ gal.	4½ gal.
Optional Tank	← 1¾ GALLON ALLOY TANK IS AVAILABLE AS OPTIONAL EXTRA →						
Front Tyre Size ...	2·75″ × 21″	2·75″ × 21″	2·75″ × 21″	2·75″ × 21″	2·75″ × 21″	2·75″ × 21″	3·50″ × 19″
Rear Tyre Size	3·25″ × 19″	3·50″ × 19″	4·00″ × 18″	4·00″ × 18″	3·25″ × 19″	3·50″ × 19″	4·00″ × 18″
Optional Rear Tyre ...	3·50″ × 19″	4·00″ × 18″	3·50″ × 19″	3·50″ × 19″	3·50″ × 19″	—	3·50″ × 19″
Ground Clearance ...	9½″	9½″	9½″	9½″	9½″	9½″	9½″
Footrest Width ...	19″	19″	16″	16″	19″	19″	19″

GEAR RATIOS

Sprocket Size	Scrambler 200 9E 455B				Scrambler 250 34A				Trials 200 9E 342B				Trials 250 32A			
48 Tooth	6·88	8·74	12·25	20·24	6·88	8·74	12·25	17·54	6·88	9·22	16·52	24·77	6·88	9·22	16·52	24·77
52 Tooth	7·45	9·47	13·18	21·92	7·45	9·47	13·27	19·00	7·45	10·00	17·90	26·83	7·45	10·00	17·90	26·83
56 Tooth	8·03	10·20	14·20	23·61	8·03	10·20	14·29	20·47	8·03	10·76	19·28	28·90	8·03	10·76	19·28	28·90
60 Tooth	8·60	10·93	15·21	25·30	8·60	10·93	15·31	21·93	8·60	11·53	20·66	30·96	8·60	11·53	20·66	30·96
64 Tooth	9·18	11·66	16·22	26·98	9·18	11·66	16·33	23·40	9·18	12·30	22·04	33·02	9·18	12·30	22·04	33·02
70 Tooth	10·03	12·75	17·75	29·52	10·03	12·75	17·87	25·59	10·03	13·45	24·10	36·12	10·03	13·45	24·10	36·12

By 1960/61 the firm had once more ceased to catalogue road bikes and the range of competition machines had shrunk. There was now, however, the Californian, which was aimed at the US enduro market.

This machine has the standard single sided brakes – all DOTs fitted with their pivoted link forks had an oscillating front brake plate in order to maximise braking efficiency under all conditions. Mudguards, on most models, could be had in either polished aluminium or chromium-plated steel.

WORKS REPLICA TRIALS

SCRAMBLER

Racing two-strokes have always been raucous and DOT's scramblers fitted with this exhaust were particularly so. The publicity materials claimed it gave a wide power band from 4,500 up to 6,800rpm, with power throughout this entire range being not less than 94 per cent of maximum. The nearside tubular frame member was oil-filled and had an adjustable drip feed to lubricate the chain on all models. An optional extra, seen here, was a pair of light alloy full-width hubs incorporating an 8in front brake and 6½in rear.

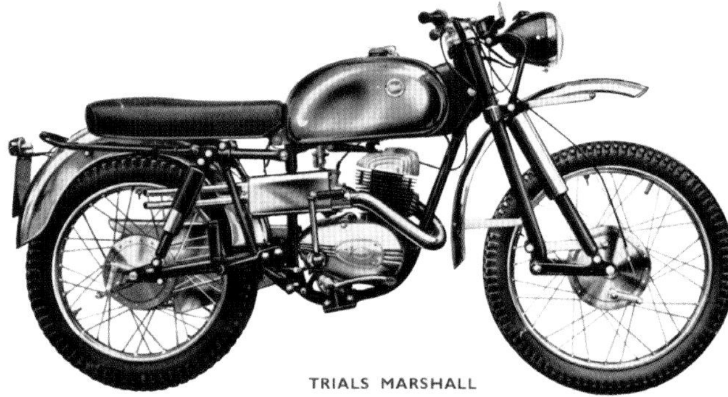
TRIALS MARSHALL

This 250 Trials Marshall has the optional-extra large alloy hubs and brakes. Mudguards were chromed steel and the deeply-valanced rear was to protect the pillion passenger; front stays and bridges on all models were in polished aluminium. Direct lighting and pillion rests were included but an optional extra was a rearward-mounted footrest and brake pedal set to convert the Marshall for more serious trails work. Colour schemes for the entire range were white with black fittings, red with black fittings or all black – supplemented, they clearly pointed out, by an abundance of chrome and polished aluminium.

The 1964 Demon, with its square-section tube frame, was a robust and very capable machine but its maker faced an uphill struggle against the likes of Greeves in British events; often the runners-up but never champions.

DOUGLAS

By the beginning of the 20th century the Douglas Engineering Company, founded by Edward and William Douglas some 20 years earlier, had progressed from little more than jobbing blacksmiths to foundry and engineering work. One of its customers was Joseph Barter, who ran a small company named Light Motors concerned with the manufacture of small engines for mounting in modified bicycles. Starting with a single-cylinder, he had moved onto designing one of some 200cc with horizontally-opposed cylinders in search of smooth running. This he named the Fee, and with castings and other components supplied by Douglas a larger version (now Anglicised to Fairy) soon went into complete machines, with much of its construction carried out by the local (Bedminster) firm of Humpage, Jacques and Pederson.

Supposedly a good number of Light Motors's motorcycles found customers but before long the firm was in financial trouble and Douglas Engineering ended up acquiring various manufacturing rights, along with Joseph Barter himself, who later went on to become the works manager as well as carrying out much design work.

Some details had not been finalised when the advance leaflet for the brand-new 1946 model was printed. A rigid frame version was listed but didn't appear until a competition trial model was made a few seasons later.

The rest, as they say, is history and when Douglas Engineering made its first motorcycle in 1907, the motor that powered it was a horizontally-opposed side-valve flat twin of 340cc. Five years later, only the second time that the make had appeared there, a pair of its twins would beat all-comers by finishing first and second in the Junior TT on the Isle of Man. The marque would remain faithful to this engine configuration for its entire life, which would span very nearly 50 years.

Come the First World War the company secured lucrative government contracts for the supply of many thousands of its 2¾ (348cc) motorcycles to the armed forces; and at its end their hard-earned reputation for reliability and longevity ensured ready sales throughout the post-war boom. OHV engines were introduced for sports models in 1921.

Two more Tourist Trophy victories came the company's way in the summer of 1923, when Manxman Tom Sheard won the Senior and the innovative, hard-riding Freddie Dixon took the Sidecar TT on a Douglas equipped with a banking sidecar of his own design. Fearless Freddie came near to making it a double the following year, leading the Sidecar race for three laps before retiring, then the Senior for four, as well as making the fastest lap, until he slowed and at the finish was third behind a Norton and a Scott.

In 1925 Fred didn't finish the Senior but pushed the lap record for sidecars up to over 57mph before retiring, leaving another Douglas ridden by Len Parker to win. This was to be the last running of the Sidecar race for nearly 30 years and the last Isle of Man victory for the Bristol firm. Dixon rode for them just one more year, managing a fourth in the Junior, but finally achieved his goal of winning a solo TT in 1927 after he had forsaken flat-twins for a single-cylinder HRD.

During the '20s Douglas also made machines especially for dirt-track racing, which was enjoying enormous popularity, and a large number were sold. Most successful were the 500 and 600cc (DT5 and DT6) models, which pretty much dominated the sport towards the end of the decade. That was the firm's high point, however, and from then on there was a downward slide with a succession of mediocre models and financial difficulties, which resulted in Douglas Motors (1932) being formed when the family had had to relinquish financial control. After going into liquidation the company ended up being bought by the British Pacific Trust in 1935. The trust's intention was to axe motorcycles and expand the aero engine manufacturing arm of the business that had since the early 1920s been a sideline; and to this end the company became Aero Engines Ltd. Things didn't quite work out as planned, however, and although a good deal of aero engine development took place it was never on the scale envisaged, and motorcycle manufacture continued, albeit on a reduced scale, with the Aero range until the Second World War.

With what motorcycles they made unsuitable for military use, a repeat of the First War couldn't happen but instead the company was contracted to manufacture flat-twin engines by the thousand. The majority were built into generator sets but they also powered the little industrial trucks that had been yet another sideline for many years – suddenly very much in demand for moving materials within the many establishments around the country engaged in war work.

With peace came an end to an era and a need for fresh capital to finance new projects, which resulted in Aero Engines becoming Douglas (Kingswood) Ltd. This in turn brought about a brand-new motorcycle with torsion-bar rear suspension and a modernised overhead-valve flat-twin engine as well as the Douglas ACM Electric commercial. Up until 1935 all Douglas motorcycles had longitudinally-mounted engines but the shaft-drive 500cc side-valve Endeavour's was transverse and this was continued for the T35, which went on sale in 1947. The T35, however, reverted to traditional chain drive, and its 350cc square engine, with a bore of 60.8mm and stroke of 60mm, was an evolution of the wartime generator motor. More adventurous models were planned during the late '40s but yet again the company was in trouble financially, as well as the hands of the official receiver before long, so these were scrapped and the 350 continued in improved and updated form for the remainder of Douglas's motorcycle-manufacturing days. The MkIII followed on from the T35 (there was no MkII) and then the MkIV and V appeared, along with various sports or competition variants until what proved to be the last of the line, which was unveiled as the Dragonfly at the 1954 Motor Cycle Show.

Why the well-equipped and well-placed business should be unable to get itself on a firm footing is hard to understand considering that it had so many other interests. In addition to motorcycles, and the electric commercials, which had been discontinued in 1952, there was also a good deal of subcontract work for the Bristol Aeroplane Company, not to mention the building of Vespa scooters under a licence granted by the Italian parent firm of Piaggio on very favourable terms, as well as distribution rights for the United Kingdom and the entire Commonwealth.

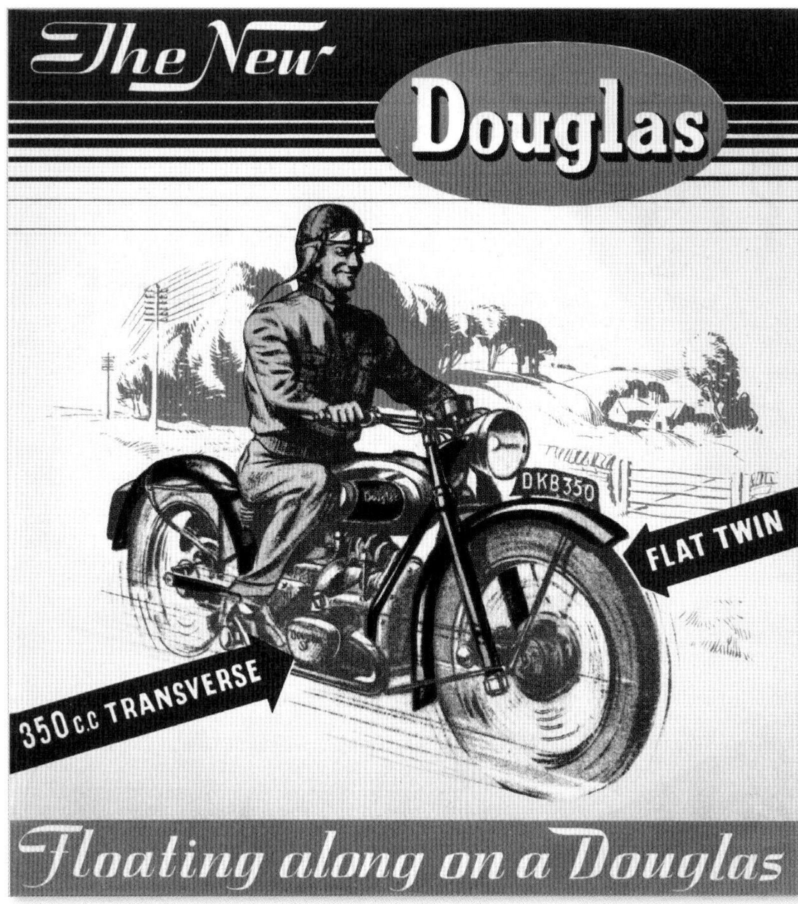

Great minds think alike? "Sixty was a delightful cruising gait at which the fore-and-aft springing smoothed out slightly uneven main-road surfaces and produced a pleasant floating sensation," pronounced Motor Cycling *after an extended test of one of the first off the production line in the summer of '47. The earliest machines were in fact a little too softly sprung and the factory soon stiffened up the suspension. Top speed was a very respectable 76mph and fuel was consumed at a rate of some 65mpg.*

Douglas had pinned hopes of stability upon the Dragonfly but the public fought shy of its styling, so sales were disappointing, and in 1956 the company was still in receivership when it was taken over by Westinghouse Brake and Signal of Chippenham.

Henceforth the majority of the extensive premises was given over to the new owner's products and

Douglas
DKB 350
BALANCED COOLING
QUICK STARTING
EASY RUNNING

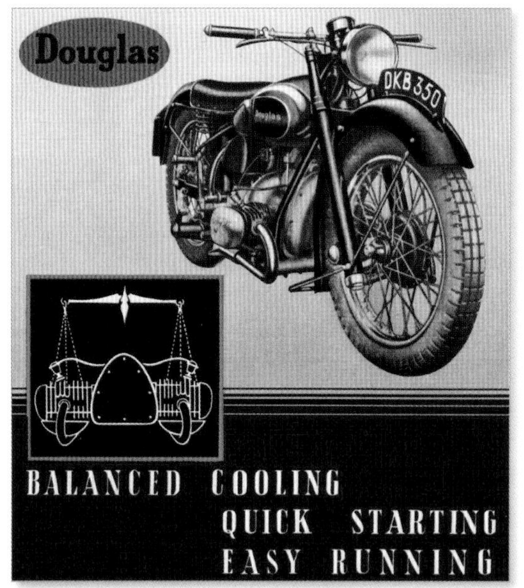

the Dragonfly was terminated, but Douglas Vespa scooters continued to be produced until well into the 1960s, by which time Hawker Siddeley had acquired Westinghouse. They in turn were merged with Bendix in 1971 and in 1977 Hawker Siddeley Aviation and Dynamics was nationalised whilst what was left became the Hawker Siddeley Group. The latter was bought by BTR in the early '90s and at the end of the decade merged with Siebe and renamed Invensys – by which time the remaining links to Douglas motorcycles were tenuous to say the least.

The benefits of cylinders poking out into the airstream were quick to be pointed out in spite of the fact that, with the exception of the late 1930s Endeavour, they'd been fore-and-aft since the very beginning. True the old system could lead to problems, not the least of which being an over-warm rear cylinder, but it had done them well.

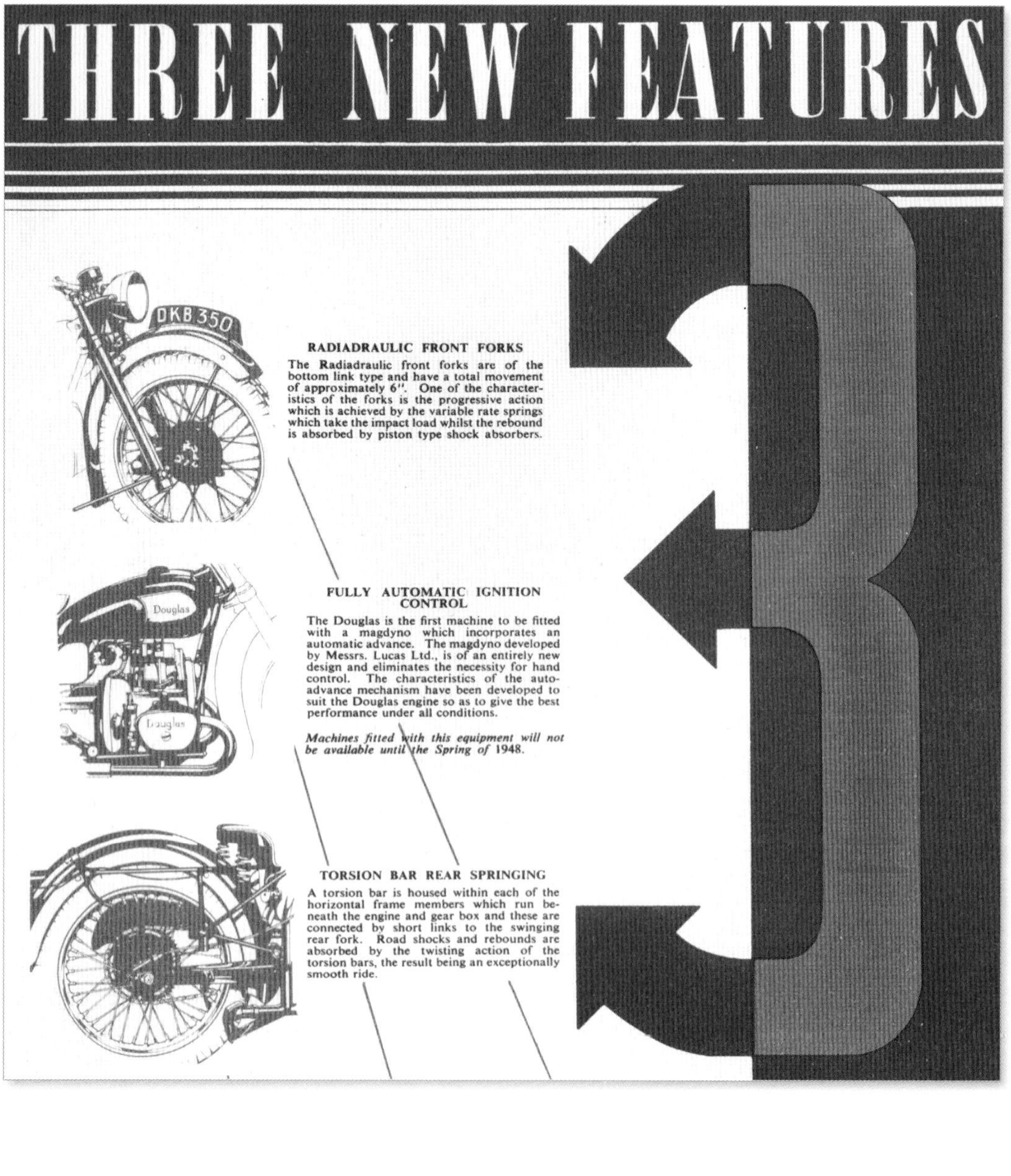
THREE NEW FEATURES
DKB 350
RADIADRAULIC FRONT FORKS
The Radiadraulic front forks are of the bottom link type and have a total movement of approximately 6". One of the characteristics of the forks is the progressive action which is achieved by the variable rate springs which take the impact load whilst the rebound is absorbed by piston type shock absorbers.
Douglas
FULLY AUTOMATIC IGNITION CONTROL
The Douglas is the first machine to be fitted with a magdyno which incorporates an automatic advance. The magdyno developed by Messrs. Lucas Ltd., is of an entirely new design and eliminates the necessity for hand control. The characteristics of the auto-advance mechanism have been developed to suit the Douglas engine so as to give the best performance under all conditions.
Machines fitted with this equipment will not be available until the Spring of 1948.
TORSION BAR REAR SPRINGING
A torsion bar is housed within each of the horizontal frame members which run beneath the engine and gear box and these are connected by short links to the swinging rear fork. Road shocks and rebounds are absorbed by the twisting action of the torsion bars, the result being an exceptionally smooth ride.
3

The determined-looking rider and machine on the cover of the 1949 MkIII brochure were portrayed by George Bishop, one of the best of the British commercial artists specialising in transport at this time. Sadly, in later years he had an accident with a camping stove, which burnt his hands and severely curtailed his work.

This is the De Luxe Sports model. It was to the same specification as the MkIII De Luxe other than having 'special light section mudguards finished in metallic silver' and twin upswept chromium exhausts with guards and silencers. Motor Cycling *put an early example though its paces and pronounced it to be 'the fastest in its class yet tested' by them – with a top speed of 78mph and 69 attainable in third. Overall fuel consumption worked out at 60mpg.*

Douglas 350 cc De LUXE MODEL MK III

Specification

Engine. Horizontally opposed Twin set transversely in frame. Bore 60·8 *mm.* Stroke 60 *mm.* Capacity 348 *cc.* Compression ratio 7·25 to 1. Built up crankshaft, mounted at flywheel end on double row ball bearings and on large plain bearing at timing gear end. High tensile steel connecting rods fitted with plain bearing in small end and double row roller bearings at the crank pin. Aluminium alloy pistons. Twin camshafts located below the crankshaft, valve mechanism is totally enclosed, the rockers being mounted in long plain bearings. Twin AMAL carburettors mounted directly on to cylinders. Gear driven Lucas Magdyno. Air filter is available as an extra.

Lubrication. Car type sump lubrication with vane type oil pump. Sump capacity ½ gallon (2·27 *litres*).

Clutch. Single plate, dry clutch. 6¾" diameter (171 *mm.*). Ferodo linings. Easily adjustable through inspection cover.

Gearbox. Unit construction with engine. Four speeds, operated by totally enclosed foot-change. The gearbox mainshaft is in line with the crankshaft bevel gearing transfers the drive from the mainshaft to the final drive chain sprocket through a shock absorber.

Gear Ratios. Top 5·86, Third 7·42, Second 10·1, First 16·3.

Transmission. Chain to rear wheel. Deep channel section guards over chain span.

Frame. Duplex cradle type. Swinging fork Torsion Bar rear springing. (DOUGLAS Patent No. 558,387).

Stand. Cast aluminium centre stand enables machine to be raised by foot pressure.

Footrests. Fully adjustable.

Tank. Welded steel saddle type finished in blue, chrome and metallic silver.

Front Forks. DOUGLAS "Radiadraulic" bottom link forks (DOUGLAS Patent No. 645,565).

Wheels. 19" (48 *cm.*) rim fitted with 9-gauge spokes and 19" × 3¼" diameter tyres (480 *mm.* × 80 *mm.*).

Brakes. DOUGLAS Shoe type 7" diameter × 1¼" wide (17·78 *cm.* × 3·17 *cm*). Steel drum bolted to hub. Light alloy back plates.

Lighting. 7" (17·78 *cm.*) diameter head lamp fitted with domed glass and incorporating switch and ammeter. The following combinations of lights are provided :
(*a*) Headlamp and tail lamp.
(*b*) Marker headlamp and tail lamp.

Mudguards. Deep section, giving adequate protection, finished in black with silver lining.

Controls. Twist grip throttle, hand operated clutch and front brake. Left foot operated rear brake pedal.

Saddle. Terry sprung top, height, loaded 28½" (72·4 *cm.*) ; unloaded 29½" (74·9 *cm.*). Saddle springs chromium plated.

Exhaust. Twin exhaust pipes to single cast aluminium silencer.

Dry Weight. 350 lb. (158·9 *kg.*) with accessories.

Dimensions.
Wheelbase, 54½" (138·4 *cm.*).
Overall Length, 84¼" (214 *cm.*).
Overall Width (handlebars), 29¼" (74·3 *cm.*)
Overall Height. Loaded, 38¼" (97·2 *cm.*) ;
Unloaded, 39¼" (99·7 *cm.*).
Ground Clearance. Loaded 5¼" (13·4 *cm.*) ;
Unloaded, 6¼" (15·8 *cm.*).

Finish. High quality finish throughout. All sheet metal and frame work is "Bonderised" before application of fine black stove enamel finish. Tank top in metallic silver. Crankcase and gearbox are lightly polished.

The underlying reasons for Douglas superiority

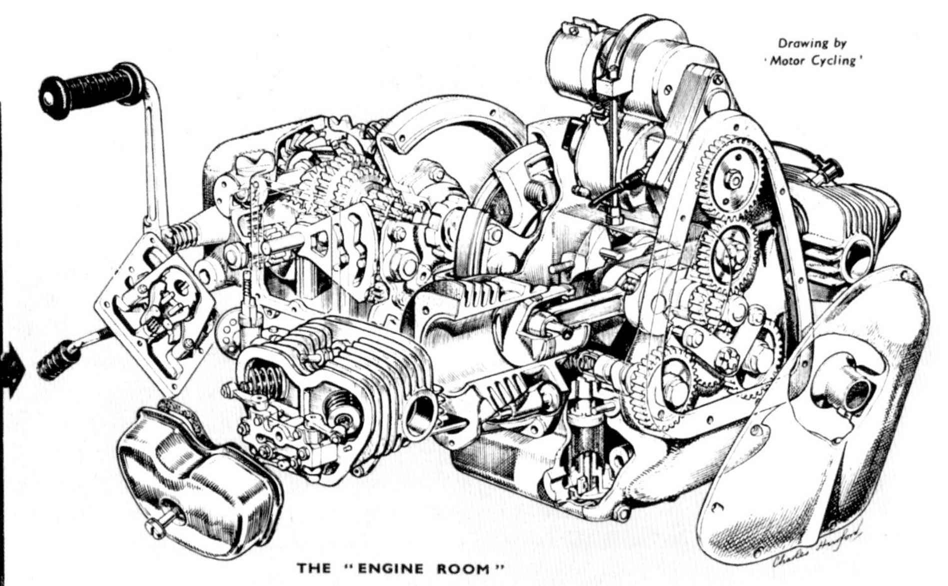

THE "ENGINE ROOM"

This Sectional View of the Douglas Power Unit shows Timing Mechanism, Cylinder-Head Accessibility, Gear Box and general solidarity of construction

Transverse Twin. The reliability of the DOUGLAS engine has been conclusively proved by service in two world wars. The new T.35 Model has this famous 180° opposed-twin power unit mounted transversely in the Frame. Engine and gear box are of unit construction combining lightness with great strength.

Car-type Oiling. External pipes are completely eliminated by the car-type pressure oiling system. Absence of oil leakage ensures that the machine is as clean to handle as it is clean in design.

Twin Carburettors. Each cylinder has its own carburettor securing easy starting, sparkling performance and economical petrol consumption.

Torsion Bar Rear Springing. A torsion bar is housed within each of the horizontal frame members which run beneath the engine and these are connected by short links to the swinging rear fork. Road shocks and rebounds are absorbed by the twisting action of the torsion bars.

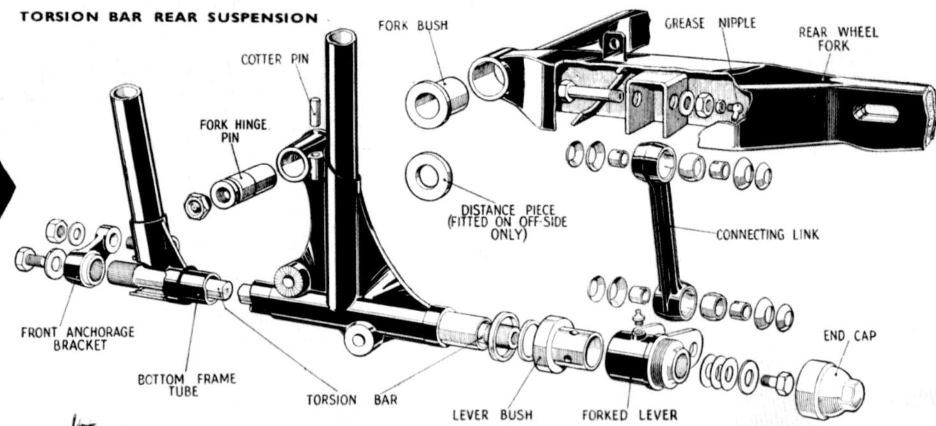

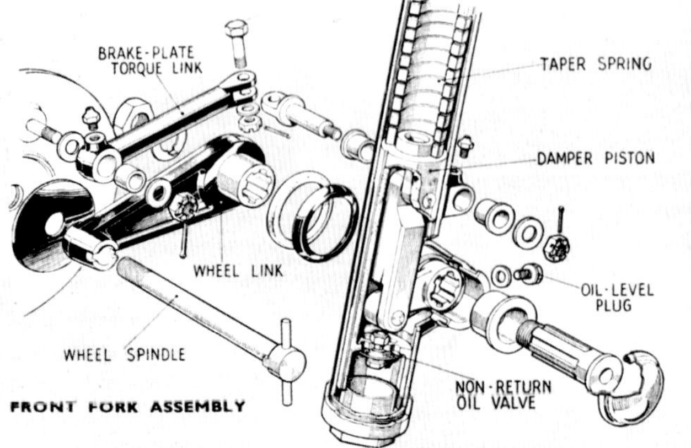

Radiadraulic Front Forks. The Radiadraulic front forks are of the bottom link type and have a total movement of approximately 6". One of the characteristics of the forks is the progressive action which is achieved by the variable rate springs which take the impact load whilst the rebound is absorbed by piston type shock absorbers.

Low C.G. The Duplex cradle frame of great strength, lightness and rigidity enables the engine to be mounted well down in the frame, gives a low C.G. and greatly improved stability and road-holding qualities.

You certainly wouldn't have thought Douglas was hard up from the quality of the sumptuous folio brochure of October 1950. This version of the MkV has the same mechanical specifications as the machine with the sportier bars and briefer exhaust but does differ in a number of respects – the front mudguard for instance. Artistic licence?

Douglas Mark 'V'

(Fitted with cast alloy silencer and semi-straight handlebars)

The popular model in the specialist range of 350 c.c. machines, the Mark 'V' represents one of the most highly developed models in the Industry and has no rival for the motor-cyclist who needs efficiency, comfort, reliability and perfect road-holding.

The technical specification comprises:—

POWER UNIT

Horizontally opposed twin cylinder O.H.V. engine set transversely in the frame forming a single unit with the 'in-line' gearbox.

The layout provides a low centre of gravity giving faultless steering and cornering exclusive to DOUGLAS. Cooling is perfectly balanced as both cylinders have equal air frontage, and are not cast 'en bloc' but are two separate independent units. The 180° cylinder disposition also assures a power curve free from vibration—the crankshaft accepting a power impulse for every revolution.

DATA

Bore, 60.8 m.m. Stroke, 60 m.m. 348 c.c.

O.H. Valves set at 58° in cylinder heads, operated by push rods.

Compression ratio, 7.25 : 1.

Lubrication. Vane type submerged pump, circulation of oil through drillings—no exterior oil pipes.

Crankshaft. Made entirely from high grade steel forgings, built up by end and centre sections pressed on to massive crankpins.

Connecting rods. Of alloy steel forgings, balanced in pairs, big-ends ground to accept the bearings direct.

Valve operation. By two camshafts, gear driven, one for each cylinder allowing the use of short and light push rods through lever type rockers carried in well-proportioned bronze bearings.

Bearings.	Crankshaft.	Drive end. Large double row ball bearing.
	Crankshaft.	Timing end. Phosphor Bronze bush.
	Camshafts.	Phosphor Bronze both ends.
	Big-ends.	20 Caged ¼" diam. × ¼" Steel rollers.
	Small-ends.	Bronze bushes for ⅝" diam. gudgeon pins.
	Ancillaries.	Ground spindles working in bronze bushes.

Carburation by twin AMAL Carburettors.

Ignition by Lucas Magdyno. Gear driven unit, well protected, on top of crankcase.

Clutch. Car type, single dry plate 'Ferodo' lined 6¾" diam. (171 m.m.) Totally enclosed in the bell-housing of the crankcase, light in operation and capable of a great reserve in torque transmission.

GEARBOX

The four speed gearbox of unit construction is operated by a positive footchange and is quiet in operation. Alloy steel gears run in constant mesh on large main and layshafts supported by ball and roller bearings. Final drive is by roller chain (½" × 5/16") through a conventional type shock absorber.

Gear ratios: 5.86 : 1, 7.42 : 1, 10.1 : 1, and 16.3 : 1.

FRAME

The DOUGLAS frame is of duplex cradle type, developed to withstand the most arduous conditions in any part of the world. Patent and exclusive torsion bar rear suspension, operating through swinging rear forks provides a spring frame which sets a new standard of comfort.

FRONT FORKS

The patent DOUGLAS 'Radiadraulic' forks are a worthy counterpart for the rear springing and provide some 5½" (139.7 m.m.) movement by *variable rate* springs. Oil damping is contained within the forks and the design has several features worthy of special note. The action is through swinging links which maintain equal wheel base throughout the entire travel. Unsprung weight is reduced to the minimum.

WHEELS and BRAKES

Large and totally enclosed journal ball bearing hubs carry WM 2 × 19" Rims. The shoe type brakes are 7" diam. × 1¼", giving 17½ sq. ins. of frictional contact area. 3.25 × 19" (480 m.m. × 80 m.m.) Firestone Tyres are fitted as Standard, the front being of the ribbed pattern.

PETROL TANK

Of welded steel, rust-proofed inside, and of pleasing design, adjustable for height, carrying well-shaped knee-pads.

FOOTRESTS

Correctly stationed in relation to the saddle, and adjustable through a wide arc.

ELECTRICAL EQUIPMENT

LUCAS Magdyno with output of 48 watts at 6 volts, includes the Automatic Voltage control system. The accumulator is housed low in the frame and is well protected from accidental damage. The switchgear is integral with the headlamp and the head-light dipper control is on the handlebar.

MUDGUARDS

Steel, light in weight but affording ample protection. The front mudguard follows the movement of the wheel through a specially designed light but strong stay assembly. The rear guard is sprung with the frame.

SADDLE

Terry, spring mattress type, adjustable for height.

HANDLEBARS

Attached to the forks by links, adjustable for rake and reach, to give perfect positioning for every rider.

CONTROLS

Every Control is adjustable. Handlebar twist grip throttle and lever operated front brake, clutch and ignition. Horn push and magneto cut-out buttons mounted on handlebars. Rear brake controlled by a forged steel pedal, so adjustable that it follows any positioning of the footrest. The footchange pedal is serrated for individual location.

STAND

Single centre stand, so arranged that the machine can be rolled to the raised position without effort.

EXHAUST SYSTEM

Large diameter dual chromium plated exhaust pipes fitted with barrel type silencers of pleasing appearance and high efficiency.

TOOL BOXES

The streamlined cast light alloy tool boxes carried each side of the rear sub-frame, are spacious and detachable.

EQUIPMENT

Includes high frequency electric horn, **Smiths 80 m.p.h. Chronometric illuminated trip type** speedometer. Footrest, kickstart and **footchange rubbers**, etc. The tool kit is comprehensive for running adjustments and includes tyre levers and grease gun. Pillion footrests are fitted as standard.

FINISH

All bright steel parts are heavily chromium plated and polished. Aluminium castings are highly polished. All parts are rust-proofed, enamelled parts being in distinctive DOUGLAS polychromatic blue, with special lacquer final finish. An alternative choice of colour is black and silver to order.

DIMENSIONS, WEIGHTS, CAPACITIES, ETC.

Capacity Petrol	3 gallons, main	15.3 litres
Capacity Petrol	3 pints, reserve	
Capacity Oil in sump	4 pints	2.27 litres
Weight (dry)	350 lbs.	158.9 kg.
Wheel base	54½ ins.	138.4 c.m.
Overall length	84 ins.	214 c.m.
Overall width	27½ ins.	69.8 c.m.
Overall height (loaded)	38¼ ins.	97.2 c.m.
Overall height (light)	39¼ ins.	99.7 c.m.
Min. ground clearance loaded	5¼ ins.	13.4 c.m.
Min. ground clearance light	6¼ ins.	15.8 c.m.

The machine illustrated is equipped with the following extras:—semi-straight handlebars with internal grip (19/- extra when fitted as initial equipment), and exhaust pipes with cast alloy silencer (£3/3/6 extra when fitted as initial equipment).

A comprehensive range of extras is available and is shown on a separate sheet.

This is the '80' Plus – poor relation of the '90' Plus and said to be virtually a road-equipped version of the latter using engines that didn't quite come up to the '90' mark on the factory dynamometer. They still had the same 8.25:1 compression and rev limit of 7,500, however. Official records tell us that 268 were built.

Hailed as the smartest outfit at the 1951 show was this Polychromatic Green 500 Douglas twin with Watsonian Avon sidecar. The large cast-aluminium ribbed cover atop the motor housed nothing more exciting than the magdyno and other components but along with other features such as the '90' Plus front brake conspired to give it presence. Destined to go nowhere except as a crowd puller on the stand, it had been developed at a time when the company could ill afford it and would never go into production.

Douglas '90' Plus

Basically similar to the '80' Plus DOUGLAS present the now famous '90' Plus model for the most discriminating sporting rider. It can be used with confidence either on the road or in competitive Club events. Made distinctive by its polychromatic gold finish, the engines in these machines are individually assembled and tested for a standard of horse power, torque and consumption. A very wide alternate specification schedule is set out on a separate sheet; the parts are interchangeable with the '80' and '90' Plus, and may be purchased as spares or supplied as original equipment at extra cost.

The technical specification comprises the following brilliant details:—

POWER UNIT

The world famous DOUGLAS transversely set horizontally opposed twin cylinder engine is retained together with the unit construction 'in-line' gearbox. In detail, the power unit is re-designed to provide not only very high power output but extreme acceleration and reliability. The most advanced technical character is reflected in this push-rod operated overhead valve engine.

DATA

Bore, 60.8 m.m. Stroke, 60 m.m. 348 c.c.
Compression ratio, 8.25 : 1. (Flat top pistons)
Safe operational crankshaft speed, 7,500 r.p.m.

CYLINDER HEADS

The new design allows straight-line inlet port efficiency. The large diameter valves set at 58° in the heads, of finest quality austanitic steel, working in semi-steel guides incorporate stem lubrication. Triple valve springs are employed. Forged steel rockers carried in long bearings are operated by short strong light push-rods. The spring effort has ample control in reserve to cater for the reciprocating weights.

CYLINDERS

High grade close grain alloy cast iron cylinders are ground and honed to fine limits and heavily flanged at either end.

CRANKSHAFT

The built up assembly comprises two end webs and centre section pressed on to massive drilled crankpins. The whole unit polished all over is strictly balanced to very fine limits.

CAMSHAFTS

Two gear driven camshafts are used, situated close to the outside of the crankcase under the cylinders, making for very light operation details. The cam form is harmonic, giving high lift to valves, economical petrol consumption, and quiet valve operation.

LUBRICATION

Vane type submerged pump circulating oil through drillings to crankshaft big-end bearings. No exterior oil pipes. The pump carries a well proportioned gauze filter, easily detachable.

ENGINE BEARINGS

Are all of ample size to withstand the high torque and crankshaft speeds.

Crankshaft: Double row ball bearing, drive end, single row ball bearing and bronze bush, timing end.
Big-ends: Twenty caged $\frac{1}{4}$" diameter rollers to each big-end bearing, running direct on to the crankpins and hardened tracks in the conrods.
Small-ends: Phosphor Bronze small-end bushes pressed in to the connecting rods to accept $\frac{5}{8}$" diam. gudgeon pins.
Ancillaries: All Phosphor Bronze bushes running in or on ground hardened steel spindles or bores, well lubricated.

CARBURATION

Standard equipment comprises two large choke diameter AMAL carburettors mounted on suitably shaped induction stub-pipes.

IGNITION and LIGHTING

By Lucas Magdyno. Gear driven unit, well protected, on top of crankcase. The quickly detachable 48 w. dynamo is of the A.V.C. type.

CLUTCH

Car type, single plate of large diameter, with air vent, the unit is totally enclosed, linking the engine with the gearbox in a direct line. The driven plate is made of light alloy carrying cork inserts providing ample reserve torque capacity, ensuring minimum self inertia and ease in gear changing.

GEARBOX

Unit construction with the engine but easily detachable, all gears being in constant mesh and carried upon short stiff shafts. The main components run in needle roller bearings to eliminate friction and provide utmost reliability. The patent footchange ensures positive action with the minimum pedal movement. Final ratios may be varied through a wide selection of sprockets. Final drive by heavy roller chain ($\frac{5}{8}$" × $\frac{1}{4}$") is transmitted through a conventional shock absorber.

Standard ratios: 5.7 : 1, 6.67 : 1, 7.87 : 1, 11.44 : 1. Alternative special close ratio 3rd 6.17 : 1.

FRAME

An immensely robust frame developed by competition experience, includes the DOUGLAS patent and exclusive torsion bar rear suspension, of the swinging fork type, the envy of the motorcycle industry.

FRONT FORKS

The patent DOUGLAS 'Radiadraulic' forks are a worthy counterpart for the rear springing providing some $5\frac{1}{2}$" (139.7 m.m.) movement by *variable rate* springs. Oil Damping is contained within the forks, the design has several features worthy of special note. The action is through swinging links which maintain equal wheel base throughout the entire travel. Unsprung weight is reduced to the minimum. Steering damper fitted, as standard.

WHEELS and BRAKES

Large totally enclosed journal ball bearing hubs incorporate shoe type brakes, the front being 9" diameter, heavily finned. The rear brake drum 7" diameter, carries the removable sprocket. The front wheel has rim size WM1-21 carrying a 3.00 ribbed tyre and the rear is 3.25 on a WM2 × 19" Rim, carrying a studded tyre.

PETROL TANK

Welded steel construction, of pleasing design, rust-proofed inside, and adjustable for height.

FOOTRESTS

Correctly stationed in relation to the saddle position.

MUDGUARDS

Steel, light in weight, affording ample protection, the front mudguard follows the movement of the wheel through a specially designed light but strong stay assembly. The rear guard is sprung with the frame.

CONTROLS

Every Control is adjustable. Handlebar twist grip throttle and lever operated front brake, clutch and ignition. Horn push and magneto cut-out buttons mounted on handlebars. Rear brake controlled by a forged steel pedal, so adjustable that it follows any positioning of the footrest without the necessity of adjusting the brake cable. The footchange pedal is serrated for individual location. Folding kickstarter.

SADDLE

Terry, spring mattress type, adjustable for height.

HANDLEBARS

Attached to the forks by links, adjustable for rake and reach, to give perfect positioning for every rider. They may be inverted to provide low swept position.

STAND

Easily detachable single centre stand so arranged that the machine can be rolled to the raised position without effort.

EXHAUST SYSTEM

Twin exhaust pipes are of the correct length when the efficient silencers of pleasing appearance are removed.

EQUIPMENT

The standard equipment includes high frequency electric horn, Smiths 120 m.p.h. Chronometric illuminated dial speedometer, rubbers for footrests, kickstart and footchange, pillion footrests. A comprehensive tool kit includes tyre levers, grease gun and inflator.

FINISH

All bright parts are heavily chromium plated and highly polished. The enamelled parts are rust-proofed and enamelled with hard wearing and distinctive DOUGLAS polychromatic gold, with special lacquer final finish.

DIMENSIONS, WEIGHTS, CAPACITIES

Petrol		3 gallons, main 3 pints, reserve	15.3 litres
Oil		4 ,, in sump	2.27 ,,
Weight in road trim, dry	Approx:	350 lbs.	158.75 kg.
Wheel base		$54\frac{1}{2}$ ins.	138.4 c.m.
O/A length		$84\frac{1}{2}$,,	214.5 ,,
,, width		$27\frac{1}{2}$,,	69.8 ,,
,, height (loaded)		40 ,,	101.6 ,,
,, ,, (unloaded)		$40\frac{1}{2}$,,	102.9 ,,
Min. ground clearance		$5\frac{1}{4}$,,	13.4 ,, loaded

The '90' Plus illustrated is equipped with the alternative specification, which includes revolution counter, road racing tyres, racing magneto, racing seat and light alloy guards, in place of the speedometer, standard tyres, magdyno lighting set, steel mudguards, tool boxes and saddle, without extra cost. A further wide range of extras is available. It is essential when ordering to state 'alternative specification' required.

If you're a sporting man then this is the ultimate post-war Douglas. It was said at the time that if the BSA Gold Star hadn't been around it would have mopped up the Junior Clubmans TT and they could have been right – if it were not for the Norton International. The 1950 race had 43 Gold Stars entered, 14 Inters and 21 of the Kingswood flyers, of which most (if not all) must surely have been '90's. The result? BSA first and second, Norton third and sixth, and Douglas in fourth and fifth. The following year BSA won again followed by three Nortons, a BSA and a Norton, with a Douglas seventh. However, by 1952 Douglas entries numbered just four against 69 BSAs and a dozen Nortons. The result was a foregone conclusion and the highest placed Douglas was 39th. They were handsome bikes, however, apart from that seat; just 218 were built.

In line with most other trials bikes of the time the Douglas had a rigid frame. Despite securing the services of some good riders such as Norman Vanhouse and David Tye they weren't consistently successful, however, and were dropped after 1951.

Douglas Competition Model

Developed from the world famous basic DOUGLAS design, the trials model has a rigid cradle duplex frame of great strength with special "Radiadraulic" front forks, giving perfect control under adverse conditions.

The engine unit is developed to provide high torque at low speeds and is mounted high in the frame to allow ample ground clearance. Special attention has been given to provide a wide steering lock. Development tests and subsequent trial results are convincing proof that this machine is a worthy addition to the competition world of motor cycles.

The technical specification comprises:—

ENGINE
Horizontally opposed Twin set transversely in frame. Bore 60.8 m.m. Stroke 60 m.m. Capacity 348 c.c. Compression ratio 6.5 : 1. Built up crankshaft, mounted at flywheel end in double row ball bearing and in large plain bearings at timing gear end. High tensile steel connecting rods fitted with plain bearing in small end and double row roller bearings at the crank pin. Aluminium alloy pistons. Twin camshafts located below the crankshaft. Valve mechanism is totally enclosed, the rockers being mounted on long plain bearings. Twin Amal carburettors. Gear driven Lucas magdyno or magneto, both with handlebar control. Ignition cut-out button mounted on handlebar.

LUBRICATION
Car type sump lubrication with vane type oil pump. Sump capacity ½ gallon (2.27 litres).

CLUTCH
Single plate, dry clutch. 6¾" diameter (171 m.m.). Ferodo linings. Totally enclosed.

GEARBOX
Unit construction with engine. Four speeds, operated by totally enclosed foot-change. The gearbox mainshaft is in line with the crankshaft. Bevel gearing transfers the drive from the mainshaft to the final drive chain sprocket through a shock absorber. Folding kick-start lever.

GEAR RATIOS
Standard trials gear ratios of 6.6, 8.35, 14.3 (optional 10.5) and 21.7 can be varied through a wide range by optional extra final drive and rear wheel sprockets.

TRANSMISSION
⅝" × ¼" chain to rear wheel adequately shielded from mud.

FRAME
Cradle duplex unsprung frame specially designed for competition use.

STAND
Prop stand fitted to the near side of the machine.

FOOTRESTS
Of steel, flat pad type. Adjustable.

TANK
Welded steel saddle tank reduced in width to assist rider's control when out of saddle. 2½ gallon capacity. Finished in stove enamel black with silver lining.

FRONT FORKS
DOUGLAS "Radiadraulic" bottom link forks of special design for competition work giving adequate springing and wide steering lock.

WHEELS and BRAKES
Both wheels have 7" diameter brakes of normal DOUGLAS design fitted to W.M. 3-19 rim for rear and W.M. 1-21 front. Rear tyre 400 × 19, front tyre 275 × 21.

MUDGUARDS
"D" section polished aluminium mudguards, giving ample tyre clearance. 5" wide rear, 4" front. Rear lifting handle.

CONTROLS
Twist grip throttle, hand operated clutch and front brake. Left foot operated rear brake pedal, rod operated.

SADDLE
Trials pattern 49-150 Dunlop saddle. 11" wide. Adjustable.

HANDLEBARS
Upswept, giving perfect control. Fully adjustable. Chromium plated.

EXHAUST SYSTEM
Upswept, both pipes leading into common expansion chamber mounted high on offside of machine.

FINISH
Black stove enamel on rust proofed surface, ensuring maximum durability Normal bright parts heavily chromium plated.

DIMENSIONS
Wheel base 54".
Ground clearance 8".
Weight (dry) 300 lb. approx.
Weight with magdyno lighting set. (dry) 320 lb.

EQUIPMENT
Single tool box mounted on nearside, carrying well furnished tool kit.
Inflator.
Solid "skid pan" undershield.
"Sports" type bulb horn (or electric lighting equipment).
Front trials number plate.
Speedometer.

A wide range of optional alternatives and extras is available and is set out on a separate schedule.

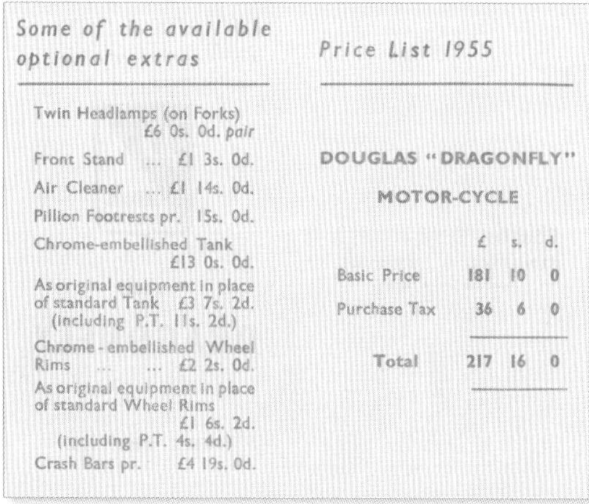

Some of the available optional extras

Twin Headlamps (on Forks)	£6 0s. 0d. *pair*
Front Stand ...	£1 3s. 0d.
Air Cleaner ...	£1 14s. 0d.
Pillion Footrests pr.	15s. 0d.
Chrome-embellished Tank	£13 0s. 0d.
As original equipment in place of standard Tank (including P.T. 11s. 2d.)	£3 7s. 2d.
Chrome-embellished Wheel Rims	£2 2s. 0d.
As original equipment in place of standard Wheel Rims (including P.T. 4s. 4d.)	£1 6s. 2d.
Crash Bars pr.	£4 19s. 0d.

Price List 1955

DOUGLAS "DRAGONFLY" MOTOR-CYCLE

	£	s.	d.
Basic Price	181	10	0
Purchase Tax	36	6	0
Total	217	16	0

The final fling – firstly proposed as the Dart, but I think you'll agree that the Dragonfly when overlaid thus makes perfect sense.

Unfortunately not the prettiest of machines in spite of its more conventional pivoted fork suspension, and production delays did little to help the public's enthusiasm for it. The Motor Cycle *finally got their hands on one in late summer '55 and reported mixed impressions. "Steering and road-holding were first class… Corners could be negotiated stylishly at speed and changes of direction (in winding country lanes) executed with the minimum of effort on the part of the rider… The machine displayed a high degree of inherent stability." The brakes, however, they found 'very poor' and the motor 'rough' when pulling hard at low- and medium-rpm. It thrived on high revolutions, however, and then 'turned out its power with satisfying smoothness'. The highest recorded speed was 75mph.*

POWER UNIT. Horizontally opposed twin cylinder engine, set transversely in the frame, unit constructed with the clutch and gearbox.

DATA

Bore	60.8 m.m.
Stroke	60 m.m.
Capacity	348
Overhead Valves operated by push rods.	
Compression Ratio	7.25 to 1

LUBRICATION. Vane type, totally submerged pump. All oilways drilled in Crankcase with a felt sack filter incorporated in oil pressure line. Gravity return to oil sump in crankcase.

CRANKSHAFT. Pressed up steel forgings.

CONNECTING RODS. Steel Forgings.

VALVE OPERATION. Twin Camshafts (one per Cylinder) gear driven operate the rocker mechanism through the medium of short light push rods.

BEARINGS. Crankshaft. (Drive End) Large Double row Ball Bearings.
Crankshaft. (Timing End) Plain Bearing.
Camshaft. Plain Bearings.
Big End. 32 caged rollers $\frac{3}{16}$" x $\frac{3}{16}$".
Small End. Plain on $\frac{5}{8}$" dia. Gudgeon Pin.

CARBURATION. Single Amal " Monobloc " carburettor with Induction Pipe cast integrally with engine gearbox unit.

IGNITION. A Miller Generator is crankshaft mounted on the timing end, supplying A.C. current to a Rectifier for Coil Ignition and Lighting. Distributor mounted high in Crankcase with Coil and Rectifier mounted under Petrol Tank. " Emergency Ignition " switch for easement of starting when battery is flat.

CLUTCH. Single dry plate " Ferodo " lined $6\frac{3}{4}$" dia., 171 m.m.

GEARBOX. Four speed constant mesh box. Final drive by $\frac{5}{8}$" x $\frac{1}{4}$" chain through a conventional type shock absorber giving the following ratios: 5.57, 7.05, 9.60, 15.54.

FRAME. All welded Duplex cradle.

FRONT FORK. "Reynolds-Earles" Patent swinging arm with Girling suspension units.

REAR FORKS. Swinging arm with Girling suspension units.

WHEELS AND BRAKES. Large and totally enclosed journal Ball Bearing Hubs carry W.M. 2 x 19" Rims. The shoe type Brakes are 7" x $1\frac{1}{4}$" wide. 3.25 x 19 (480 x 80 m.m.) Tyres fitted as Standard.

PETROL TANK. Of welded steel it has a capacity of $5\frac{1}{2}$ gallons.

FOOT RESTS. Well positioned and adjustable.

ELECTRICAL EQUIPMENT Varley Dry battery, Miller 30 watt x 24 watt " sealed beam " Headlamp. Separate Tail Lamp and Reflector. High frequency Clear Hooter horn.

MUDGUARDS. Wide, deep valanced steel, yet light in weight. Front Mudguard moves with the Wheel.

Rear guard sprung with Frame positioned such that the rear wheel may be removed without dismantling guard. Generous lifting handles provided each side.

TWINSEAT. Follows the latest lines for comfort and appearance.

HANDLEBARS. Adjustable for height, and attached to the fork by sturdy links.

CONTROLS. Fully adjustable to suit every individual rider. Handlebar twist grip throttle and lever operated front brake and clutch. Air lever for cold starting, and horn button combined with dip switch. A footchange pedal serrated for individual location.

CENTRE STAND. A strong tubular steel structure, spring loaded for safety return. Spring clip to lock in a raised position.

EXHAUST SYSTEM. Large diameter twin chromium plated exhaust pipes, fitted with absorption silencers of a pleasing design and high efficiency. Securely attached to frame.

TOOL BOX. Large capacity single box.

DIMENSIONS, WEIGHTS, CAPACITIES, ETC.

Capacity Petrol	$4\frac{1}{2}$ gallons Main	—	20.5 litres
Capacity Petrol	1 gallon reserve	—	4.54 litres
Capacity oil in sump	5 Pints	...	2.84 litres
Weight (Dry)	365 lbs.	...	165.6 kg.
Wheel Base	$56\frac{1}{2}$" ...	...	142.6 c.m.
Overall Length	86" ...	...	218.4 c.m.
Overall Width ...	27" ...	...	68.6 c.m.
Overall Height	42" ...	...	106.7 c.m.
Ground clearance	7" ...	...	17.8 c.m.

DUNKLEY

Amongst the bicycle manufacturers that abounded in Britain's industrial heartland, many expanded into motorised transport as the 19th century drew to a close. But to my knowledge, only one maker of children's perambulators took the same step – Dunkley.

Founded in the 1870s, its inventive owner, William Henry Dunkley, made his first foray into motor vehicles that might carry adults with a strange device having a diamond-pattern wheel plan and powered by a coal gas motor. Even stranger was the system of steering – by either of the smaller front or rear wheels, the choice depending on which was in contact with the ground due to the occupants shifting their weight. You won't be surprised when I tell you that it went no further but his next vehicle, on the face of it, sounded promising – in fact something akin to modern thinking. This was a relatively conventional four-wheeler and again powered by a coal gas motor – temptingly marketed as the Self Charging Gas Motor Car, the idea being that you hooked into a convenient municipal supply such as that for street lighting. How many were sold, how their owners paid for refuelling or how much trouble they got into if they didn't I have no idea, but it was catalogued for a year or two.

By 1910 William Henry had turned his talents to cycle cars and motorcycles. To realise the former he created the Alvechurch Light Car Co, and into his Alvechurch he put a Matchless V-twin engine – two, in fact, as there were two of these belt-driven devices made before the project was abandoned. Motorcycles did rather better, and there was even a 499cc Precision-engined Dunkley entered for the 1914 Tourist Trophy; what's more, it managed three laps of the mountain course before its rider, one-time competitor SR Norris, or the machine itself called it a day.

Prior to Mr Dunkley's motor-manufacturing adventures his products had ranged far beyond prams alone – rocking horses, roundabouts, tricycles and seesaws being just a few of his catalogued wares, so I'm sure his work was put to good use during the 1914-to-18 war.

It certainly didn't dampen his imagination or enthusiasm for the unusual or impractical, and by the early '20s he announced his pièce de résistance – his perambulator par excellence – the Pramotor. No mere figment of his imagination either, I assure you, as space was allotted to this fabulous product at the 1922 Motor Show. During its lifespan, which would seem to be until 1925, several different models were said to be available – from one that resembled a normal pram to the eye-wateringly-expensive Model 20 with ovular town carriage-cum-coupé bodywork at 135 guineas (not far short of the price of an Austin Seven, which, by 1925 was down to £149!). Initially a somewhat feeble Premier two-stroke provided power, but there are tales of a monster 750cc version with two speeds later on. Common sense tells me that this wasn't so, but if it's true what on earth was Mr Dunkley thinking of?

Whatever it was, fortunately for the general public, no more eccentricities left the Birmingham factory and by the mid-1930s the company boasted a showroom in the West End of London trading as the Kensington Baby Carriage Co.

The perambulator par excellence, but goodness knows how the constabulary viewed Mr Dunkley's fiendish device, or other road users come to that. Even back in those days I should have thought the nanny was way outside the law with, just for starters, no registration plates and no means of audible warning – unless the latter was taken care of by the infant's screams of terror at impending disaster. The outrigged springs and suspension straps were, by the way, patented by old William Henry Dunkley back in the 19th century and later adopted by many manufacturers.

Not entirely British, perhaps, but with its own motor and two-speed transmission, design by long-time Hounslow resident Bruno Fargion, British Hub brakes and Dunlop rims, we can forgive the Italian-sourced pressings that made up its frame.

WHIPPET

The WHIPPET is a Winner !

Low in price and amazingly cheap to run, it provides the lusty power output of a machine of twice its capacity. The tremendous acceleration of the high efficiency O.H.V. engine enables the proud owner to negotiate traffic with exhilarating ease. High cruising speeds can be maintained with economical petrol consumption.

The Whippet is perfect in its smooth running at low speed, thanks to the positive action of the four-stroke engine, free from disadvantages applicable to two-strokes and petroil systems.

Designed for long life and greater dependability, a high safety factor is built into the Whippet with the welded pressed steel frame and a low centre of gravity. Braking power, with 4" drums front and rear, matches the sparkling performance. Telescopic front forks, swinging arm rear suspension and luxurious dual seating all ensure comfort. Starting is easy, by kick-starter. Parking lights front and rear are standard fittings.

The owner of a British Whippet has the advantage of knowing that when eventually parts need renewing, they are readily available through authorised Dunkley dealers throughout the country.

The Whippet combines the economy of a Moped with the passenger-carrying capacity and comfort of a scooter.

ALL THIS—AT A PRICE LESS THAN A MOPED!

Motor manufacturers, in fact almost all manufacturers, can be accused of varying degrees of exaggeration but Dunkley took one of the proverbial biscuits! "Tremendous acceleration." "High cruising speeds." Please!

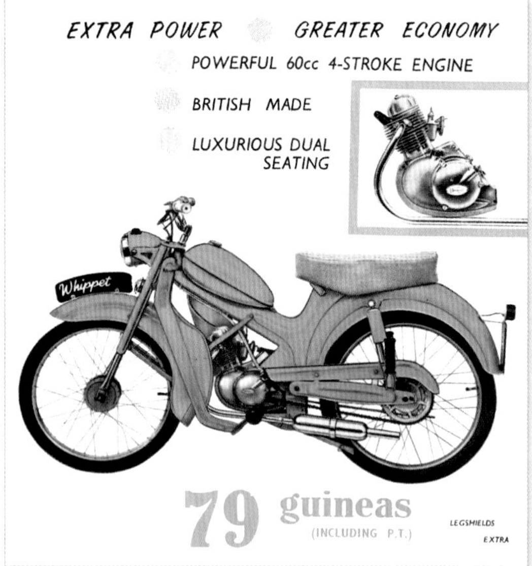

The next happening of note was during 1937 when the firm was suffering from one of its periodic bouts of financial difficulty and Airwork General Trading Ltd (AGT) acquired an interest in Dunkley. AGT was an offshoot of Airwork, which in less than ten years of existence had become a very large organisation that specialised in all things aviation, from the sale of aeroplanes to rebuilds, as well as providing hangars, flying training and even running airfields – first based at Heston, it had by this time moved to Gatwick and was securing an increasing amount of Air Ministry contracts. The reasoning behind this acquisition was that AGT was looking to diversify beyond aviation alone and that some of Dunkley's manufacturing processes involved materials not dissimilar those used in AGT's aeroplane manufacture and rebuilding departments. To take full advantage, a proportion of Dunkley's manufacturing, including prams, was henceforth undertaken at AGT's National Works, Bath Road, Hounslow. With the pressures of government and other contracts in the lead up to and during the Second World War, prams increasingly took a back seat but as far as I can establish they were still being produced at Bath Road up until the mid to late '50s, so the name Dunkley lived on although the Midlands factory was now history.

Anyone looking around the Mercury Industries stand at the 1956 Earls Court Show and paying particular attention to the brand-new Mercury Whippet 60 couldn't have failed to notice the name Dunkley on the left-hand side of its motor. A cycle manufacturer since shortly after the war, Mercury had recently branched out into mopeds and light motorcycles, the largest of which was the Villiers 98cc-powered Grey Streak. The firm's motorcycle manufacturing, or rather assembling, days were destined to be brief and it went into liquidation in 1958. The previous year, however, Dunkley had snatched the little Whippet from oblivion, renamed it the Dunkley Whippet 60 and added another model, the Whippet Sports.

Lightweight scooters joined the range the following year but early in 1959 Dunkley Products was taken over by MG Holdings Ltd, which shortly afterwards added Dayton Cycles (manufacturer of the Dayton Albatross scooter) to its portfolio. Having done so, Dunkley production was transferred to Dayton's Park Royal (NW London) factory and the old National Works became a distribution centre for imported scooters and mopeds. That MG's role had simply been that of an asset stripper became clear at the end of 1959 when Dunkleys were dropped, then Dayton in 1960, after which all remaining stock was sold off.

WORLD-BEATER BY DUNKLEY

WHIPPET SPORTS

British ultra-lightweight with a unique car-type 4-stroke engine and an absolutely outstanding performance.

Take a good look at the Whippet Sports. From the tail-light to the tip of the front tyre it's every inch a world-beater.

Look at the engine for a start. A minor miracle of British engineering. An overhead valve, four-stroke engine of 65 c.c. capacity, it gives the Whippet Sports a smooth flow of power, tremendous acceleration and a dogged dependability that no other engine of equal capacity can match.

Road-holding is rock-steady, cornering clam-like. The hand-controlled gear change is simple and silent, the headlight big and powerful and the hub brakes full-width for extra stopping power. But that's only a start. If you know what's what with light-weights study the specification overleaf. Or better still, take one out on the road. You'll soon see that nothing comes near the Whippet Sports at anything like the price.

It's a world-beater. And it's British!

A THOROUGHBRED FOR ONLY

£89 - 19 - 4 *inc.* £17-17-0 *p.t.*

or £13-19-4 *down and 24 instalments of* £3-16-2

Much more of this and we'd all be believing the Whippets – regular or sports – were real flyers. So it's a good thing Motor Cycling *wrote a brief report on one of the latter upon its introduction to the market. It was picked up from the Hounslow factory and made an immediate impression with its Italian looks; enhanced when its motor burst into life with a single prod of the kick-start and ticked over like a large single. Gear selection by means of the twist-grip control was simple and although the Whippet was brand-new power was 'quite good' – top being selected, easily, at something less than 20mph. It would 'cruise quite happily in the thirties' but respecting its newness no attempt to find its absolute maximum was made and the testers were quite prepared to accept its makers claim of around 45. Fuel consumption wasn't measured either, so the maker's claim of 160mpg at 30mph was quoted.*

ENGINE	Four stroke o.h.v. Bore 44 mm. Compression ratio 6.5 : 1, output 2.4 b.h.p. at 5,200 r.p.m.
CYLINDER	Aluminium alloy centrifugally cast-in liner. Detachable cylinder head.
PISTON	" Heplex " split skirt alloy piston. 1 compression ring, 1 step compression ring, 1 oil control ring.
BEARINGS	Heavy duty ball race bearings. Roller big end bearing.
LUBRICATION	Sump lubrication, o.h.v. lubrication by oil mist.
CLUTCH	Single dry plate Ferodo non-slip, incorporating rubber cushion drive.
TRANSMISSION	Two-speed unit construction. Final drive ½" x 3/16th" chain. Heavy Duty.
IGNITION	Flywheel magneto, incorporating lighting coil.
CARBURETTOR	Amal with easy starting choke control.
CONTROLS	Twist grip throttle control and front brake lever combined. Gear change twist grip and clutch lever combined. Foot pedal operating rear brake. Kick start.
PETROL TANK	One gallon capacity.
FRAME	Reinforced pressed steel welded frame specially designed to carry two people.
SUSPENSION	Telescopic front suspension specially designed to give maximum smooth road-holding conditions. Swinging arm rear suspension.
SEATING	Specially designed dual seat, foam rubber top.
MUDGUARDS	Fully valanced.
TYRES	Dunlop 23" x 2".
BRAKES	Internal expanding front and rear; full width 4" diameter hubs.
STAND	Quick release, foot operated.
EQUIPMENT	Electric horn, large headlamp, rear light incorporating reflector, number plates, battery " stand-by " parking light, front and rear.
FINISH	High lustre on rust-proof base.
PRICE	£66. 9s. 11d. Purchase Tax £16. 9s. 1d. Total £82. 19s. 0d.
EXTRAS	Dunkley Legshields £3. 3s. 0d. Chrome Luggage Carrier £1. 15s. 0d. Pillion Footrests 15/- per pair. Speedometer. Whippet Windscreen.

BRIEF SPECIFICATION

Engine: 65 c.c. single-cylinder four-stroke; bore 44 mm. by stroke 42 mm.; light-alloy cylinder and cylinder head; over-head valves; push-rod operated; C.R., 7.2 : 1; Amal carburetter, type 362/6.

Transmission: Two-speed gearbox in unit with engine; positive-stop handlebar change; ratios, 19.6 and 11.7 : 1; primary drive by gear; final drive by chain.

Frame: Pressed-steel beam-type welded up.

Wheels: Steel rims, carrying Dunlop tyres; 23 in. by 2.25 in. front and rear; hubs incorporate 4-in. brakes at front and rear.

Lubrication: Wet-sump lubrication with integral reservoir of ¾ pt. capacity.

Electrical Equipment: Wipac flywheel mag-generator, head and tail lamp with quickly detachable wiring harness.

Suspension: Telescopic front forks of Dunkley design, controlled by coil springs; rear springing by swinging fork, movement controlled by coil springs; spindle adjust-ment by means of draw-bolts.

Tank: Steel fuel tank, of 2¼ gal. capacity.

Dimensions: Wheelbase, 45 in.; ground clearance, 6 in.; unladen seat height, 30 in.; dry weight, 112 lb.

Finish: Dark green stove enamel, usual parts polished and plated.

General Equipment: Full kit of tools; pillion footrests.

Price: £72 2s. 4d. plus £17 17s. P.T.= £89 19s. 4d.

Annual Tax: 17s. 6d.

Makers: Dunkley Motors, Bath Road, Houns-low, Middx.

The Whippet's spec sheet omitted the stroke, which was 40mm – combining with the 44mm bore to give a capacity of 61cc. The Whippet Sports was assigned a stroke of 42mm, however, making it 64cc.

EMC

Reality was woefully at odds with Herr Ehrlich's advertising, with a fuel consumption of over 60mpg a rarity and attempts to cruise at much above the same figure accompanied by excessive vibration.

The annexation of Austria by Germany in March 1938 brought about an exodus by citizens from all walks of life, by no means all of whom were even part Jewish, who could not countenance life under the Nazi regime. For many, with what proved to be uncannily accurate foresight, to even remain on the European mainland was unthinkable so the United States and to a lesser extent Britain became their host.

Amongst those who chose to live in England was a 24-year-old engineer named Dr Joseph Ehrlich. In his native Austria he had been involved with two-stroke engines and, once settled in England, being of independent means, he carried on this work, which was heavily influenced by continental designs such as DKW and Puch. By the outbreak of World War Two he had built a twin piston split single two-stroke engine, and its possible use in a military motorcycle and similar projects occupied him during the war years.

In 1946 he took premises on the huge Park Royal industrial estate in NW London where the Ehrlich Motor Company would henceforth build EMC two-stroke motorcycles.

Prior to announcing the machine that would go on

Sven Kallin's Adelaide, South Australia dealership already had the agency for Vincent so taking on the unknown EMC seems a strange choice, unless it was EMC's crib of Vincent's double back-to-back front brake that attracted him. Anyway, keen to promote the make he sponsored Bill Thomas on one in the 1948 Adelaide Advertiser *24-hour Trial, and here he is after finishing joint first. By the way, although it might appear so, the large absorption silencer is not mounted upside down.*

sale to the general public he carried out a good deal of testing by entering prototype EMCs in grass-track and scramble meetings, as well as at least one race. Various (two-stroke) engine configurations were tried – blown and unblown, water-cooled and air-cooled, as well as various combinations of internal components – but by and large they were either slow or blew up.

By the spring of 1947, however, he considered that he had ironed out the gremlins and was confident enough to invite *Motor Cycling* to have a test run on the final pre-production prototype that, apart from having a greater density of finning on the cylinder barrel, was the same as the machines he hoped would soon be in the hands of his first customers. No figures were taken but the testers were cautiously complimentary when they wrote that the acceleration was good and performance up to its designer's claims, with special mention being made of the 'phenomenally slow' tick-over. Comments regarding its appearance were most certainly not negative but do I read a caveat into them? "Finished in black enamel with a great deal of polished aluminium in its components, the EMC is a handsome if unusual-looking mount."

The frame was certainly unusual in that a manganese-bronze alloy forging incorporating the steering head formed a backbone, to which was bolted the mainframe consisting of a pair of one-piece tubes forming a duplex loop construction. As this beam was hidden by the fuel tank the ensemble of rigid frame, Dowty Oleomatic forks, Burman gearbox as well as BSA/Matchlesslike tool box and oil tank appeared quite English. The 350cc engine, however, looked like a cross between a pre-war four-stroke and a mid-60s square-barrel two-stroke. Its bottom end had a cast-aluminium timing cover housing a pilgrim pump, whilst the square-barrel had (on all production models) large widely-spaced fins, each interspersed with a smaller one. To complete the unorthodox appearance the carb was horizontally mounted and set low down with considerable downdraught, whilst the exhaust exited towards the rear of the barrel, midway up and on the left side.

Whether it lost out because it was simply the wrong product at the wrong time, or because of its looks combined with a 'funny big two-stroke', or because post-war Britain felt more comfortable with brand names it knew, or any other reason, it went down something akin to a damp squib. Best estimate is that something around 200 were made and of those a goodly proportion went overseas – Swedish and Australian motorcyclists in particular proving to be more adventurous.

During the later part of 1947 one of Ehrlich's 250cc racers had been fast and reliable enough to enjoy brief

Shortly before he called it a day as a manufacturer Ehrlich was offering a 500cc Condor beside his 350T, 350S and 350SS road machines but what was it? There was no sign of one on his 1952 show stand, nor did it feature in price lists. The 125cc racer referred to is the EMC-Puch that he had developed and several competed at the Isle of Man; their only result of any note being in 1952 when they came 6th, 9th, 11th and 12th in the Ultra lightweight TT.

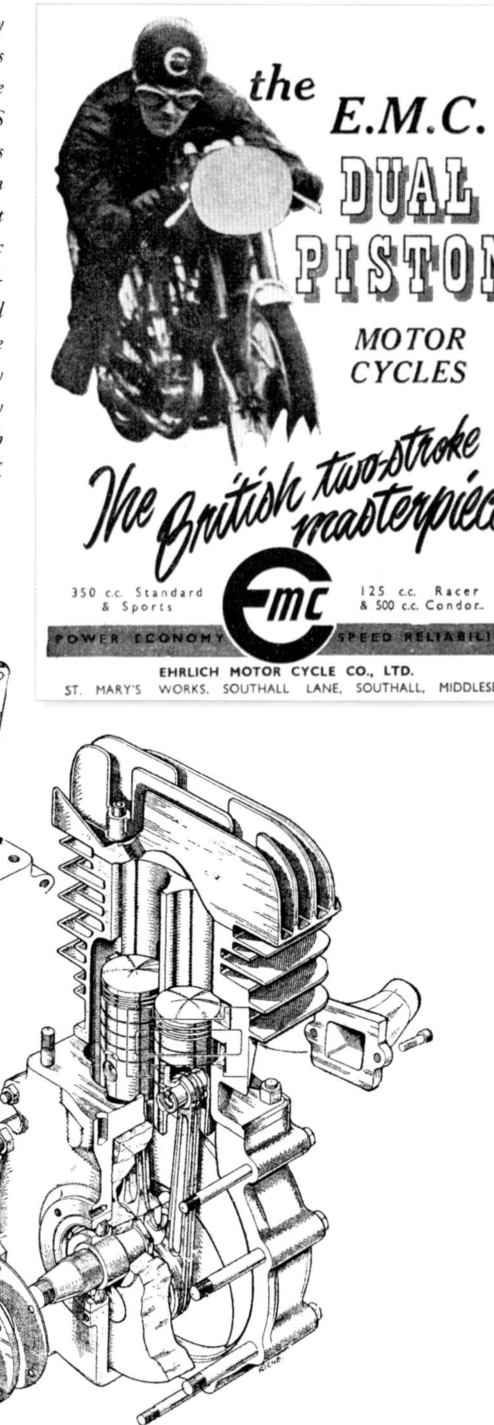

The internals of Josef Ehrlich's split twin two-stroke revealed. Note the articulated secondary connecting rod and exceptionally deep pistons. Inlet and exhaust ports are in the rear cylinder whilst the front has three radially-disposed transfer ports and the sparking plug above in the common combustion chamber. The motor's capacity of 348cc was arrived at with a bore and stroke of 50x88mm – rather antiquated dimensions if it had been a normal two-stroke. Crankcase sealing was taken care of by a combination of machined surfaces, including the mainshaft nut, and spring steel shims, so great care was essential during assembly.

success in the hands of a teenage Les Archer. At the Manx GP in September, after making fastest practice time, the bike had been banned on a technicality. But the following month he won the Hutchison 100, then a race at Scarborough early in '48, before moving on to race Velocettes and Nortons prior to his long and successful association with the latter in scrambles.

His racers may have been speedy but the reverse was true of the 350 road machine, with owners unimpressed by its sluggish acceleration and top speed the wrong side of 70, so Ehrlich developed a sporting model with optional sprung frame and conical light alloy hubs. Its engine retained the split-single layout but had throttle-controlled lubrication and a close-finned aluminium cylinder barrel amongst other features. There was one on his stand at Earls Court in 1952 alongside the new 125 EMC – a 125 JAP-powered machine with a novel, but in practice rather foolishly conceived, sprung frame. A 1¾in-diameter curved tubular backbone ran from the steering head down to a pivot housing, about which was pivoted a combined rear fork and engine bearer tubes that doubled as mini fishtail exhausts; the whole was controlled by a telescopic spring unit that took the place of a conventional front down-tube. As you can imagine, one's progress along anything but a smooth surface would have been accompanied by the little motor jiggling up and down in tune to the undulations with an occasional pothole-induced hiccup.

I'm not sure how many of either the sports 350 or the 125 were made or whether many, or even any, were sold, but by 1953 Dr Josef had become disenchanted with the manufacture of road-going motorcycles and for the next few years worked as a consultant for Austin. By the end of the 1950s he had become involved with the De Havilland Engine Company (small engine division) – the De Havilland-built EMC 125cc racer of 1960 resulting from this liaison. A water-cooled twin followed this and in 1962 Mike Hailwood was fifth in the lightweight World Championship on one behind the omnipotent works Hondas.

Turning to four wheels a few years later, the late 1960s to 1980 were his formula racing years and a number of Formula 3 cars bearing the EMC name were built by various constructors and competed with mixed success. The '80s saw him returning to motorcycles, and a Waddon with Rotax twin two-stroke engine he developed won the Junior TT. Soon after, Ehrlich revived the EMC name when Waddon folded, and in conjunction with George Beale Rotax-engined racers were built – winning the Lightweight TT in 1983-84 and '87.

Later on in life he worked on developing a revolutionary engine known as the EE (Environmental Engine) and although at the time of his death in 2003 it was dubbed 'the engine of the future' it has yet to fulfil its hoped-for potential.

At a quick glance the little 1952 JAP-engined 125 looked little different from many other lightweights of the period but Herr Ehrlich had endowed it with his own design of frame and suspension.

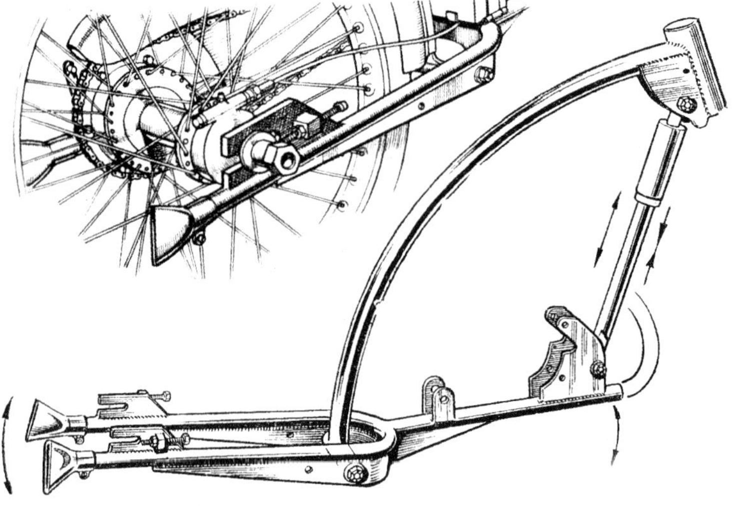

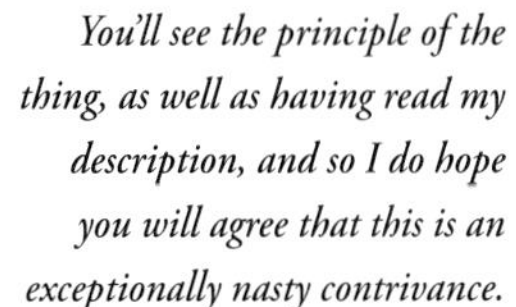

You'll see the principle of the thing, as well as having read my description, and so I do hope you will agree that this is an exceptionally nasty contrivance.

EXCELSIOR

One of the companies responsible for the city of Coventry becoming the epicentre of the English cycle industry during the 19th century was the firm of Bayliss, Thomas and Slaughter, who set up in business there in 1874. Under the brand name Excelsior rather than its own, which in any case soon became simply Bayliss, Thomas & Co, the company produced ordinary bicycles, tricycles and other machines before turning to the safety cycle in the mid-1880s. All were of exceptional quality.

There is a possibility that Bayliss, Thomas & Co was in fact the city's first manufacturer of ordinaries (also known as penny-farthings) but certainly, in 1896, it became the first company in Great Britain to go into the production of motorcycles. These motor-bicycles were sufficiently well received for the company to expand to the extent that at the 1902 Olympia show it exhibited no less that 35 machines. Ranging in size from 2hp to 2.75hp, with proprietary engines by MMC and Minerva, they were also enjoying success in speed trials and other competition. By 1904 a tricycle fore-carriage had been added to the range but before long trading conditions caused a lapse in motorcycle production for a while. They were back in production by 1910, however, and from thereon the firm would trade as the Excelsior Motor Co.

During the First World War a large contract was secured from the Russian government for the supply of V-twin JAP-engined machines; but before this could be completed the Bolshevik revolution intervened and Excelsior was left with the remainder of the order that had yet to be delivered. For a while it appeared as though the whole business might be in jeopardy but the excess stock was eventually sold and financial equilibrium regained by the time that the surviving original partners, John Thomas and Thomas Bayliss, made the decision to retire. Thus in 1919, R Walker & Son, primarily known as a manufacturer of ships' lamps, became the new owner of the company. Walker had done a good deal of subcontract work for Excelsior, as well as making some motorcycles and light cars of its own, so the acquisition was logical. Within a short while the company had been retitled as the Excelsior Motor Company Ltd, its old factory sold to the emergent motorcycle maker Francis and Barnett, and its operations relocated to Walker's headquarters at Tyseley on the outskirts of Birmingham.

These two machines comprised the initial post-war range. Pressed-steel girder forks were the norm for the 125 until telescopics were fitted to the 125 Universal, along with the new 197 Roadmaster for the 1949 season.

There, once the production of Excelsior motorcycles was up and running, preparations were made to become a car manufacturer too. However, due to there already being a Belgian luxury car maker of the same name, an alternative title was necessary, so the subsidiary Bayliss, Thomas & Company was set up. The Bayliss Thomas light car was made from 1922 to 1929, never in any great numbers, with various proprietary engines.

The motorcycle side of the business, on the other hand, was more of a success and during the '20s turned out machines ranging from small singles to large V-twins. Excelsiors were raced too, and by the time of the Depression had enjoyed a good deal of success at Brooklands track, as well having won the 1929 Lightweight TT with JAP-powered machines.

Having survived the slump, Excelsior sensibly

"Please wait for me!" calls Janet as Jeremy powers up the track from the beach on his 125cc Universal, leaving her frantically pedalling a De Luxe Autobyk in his wake. Rotter – he could have bought her a Super Autobyk with two-speed gears.

Excelsior unveiled the Talisman Twin at the 1949 show, with its in-house two-stroke motor. With this machine Excelsior pre-empted the adoption of the smooth two-stroke-twin format by other manufacturers.

offered basic fodder in the form of small economy two-strokes, but this did not stop the firm from liaising with Blackburne's Ike Hatch on the design of a complex two-cam, four-valve, twin-carb 250cc single. The Mechanical Marvel, as the resulting motorcycle was soon nicknamed, gave Excelsior its second Lightweight victory on the Isle of Man in 1933. The intention had been to put it into production, but realising that to do so would be fraught the management asked the same team to come up with something less complicated that would capitalise on this race success. This they did in a masterful manner and the OHC Manxman, carrying the three legs of Man on its cam box, went on to be made up until World War Two in 250, 350 and 500cc guises. Never a TT winner, though a phalanx of them placed second to seventh behind an indecently fast DKW in '38, it won numerous other events at home and abroad, becoming famed for its speed and reliability on road and track.

When the bulk of civilian motorcycle production was halted during 1940 Walker's Tyseley works was well suited to be able to carry out more essential work as a good proportion of its output was already applicable, or easily adapted, to the war effort. Later on in the war it was called upon to manufacture the Station IX-designed and developed Welbike, and some 4,000 of the diminutive folding devices left the King's Road factory.

As soon as was feasible peacetime production was recommenced, and by 1946 the 98cc Autobyk, which had first seen the light of day in 1937, along with a basic 125, became available on a limited basis – both were Villiers powered. Things had improved by the first post-war show and there were 14 machines on the Excelsior stand to introduce the '49 season, ranging from four versions of the Autobyk, two of which had their own engine, to various lightweights from 98 to 197cc and even a JAP 500-powered speedway

On the cover of the 1952 brochure Excelsior came up with an even less likely match, with Ian on his Talisman Twin touring in company with Denice on an Autobyk – even though it's a two-speed version.

In the summer of 1946 Motor Cycling *tested a two-speed Autobyk and were most impressed. The Goblin engine was good for nigh on 6,000 rpm – with 31mph coming up in bottom at 5,894rpm (what exactitude!) – but the poor little thing could only pull 4,250-or-so in top, which worked out at a whisker over 39mph. Not bad though, and with over 125mpg when thrashed they estimated that 200mpg was achievable.*

THE 125 c.c. " UNIVERSAL " (U.1 & U.2)
& 197 c.c. " ROADMASTER " (R.1 & R.2)

ENGINE AND GEAR UNIT (Models U.1 and U.2). 125cc. Two-stroke Villiers single port engine, 50 m/m. bore x 62 m/m stroke. Petroil lubrication. 3 Speed Foot Change Gear. Villiers Carburetter with twist grip control.
ENGINE AND GEAR UNIT (Models R.1 and R.2). 197 cc. Two-stroke Villiers single port engine, 59 m/m. bore x 72 m/m stroke. 3 Speed Foot Change Gear. Petroil lubrication. Villiers carburetter with twist grip control.
IGNITION AND LIGHTING. Villiers flywheel magneto ignition with 30-watt direct lighting. Large Headlamp with parking light and Dipper.
FRAME. Excelsior SPRING FRAME of exceptional strength, incorporating Coil Spring Suspension. Built with weldless steel tubing. Spring-up Central Stand.
FRONT FORKS. Excelsior TELESCOPIC. Built with heavy gauge alloy steel tubing. Dual Double Action coil springs. Phosphor bronze bushes support the sliding members.
TANK. Saddle tank, finished in maroon with cream side panels. Capacity 2½ gallons.
WHEELS AND TYRES. Chrome-plated rims and 5-in. diameter front and rear brakes. Dunlop tyres, 19-in. x 2.75-in. to Models U.1 and U.2, and 19-in. x 3-in. to Models R.1 and R.2.
TOOLBOX AND EQUIPMENT. Triangular Tool box. Full set of tools with Inflator, Bulb Horn and Licence Holder.
SPEEDOMETER. Smith's non-trip speedometer.
FINISH. Stove enamelled in maroon. All chromium plated parts heavily plated.
WEIGHTS. Models U.1—182-lbs.; U.2—194-lbs.; R.1—193-lbs.; R.2—205-lbs.
MODELS U.2 AND R.2. FITTED WITH RECTIFIED LIGHTING AND CHARGING SET, INCLUDING ACCUMULATOR AND ELECTRIC HORN.

A brace of Villiers-powered singles from the 1952 catalogue.

My goodness! The Motor Cycle *were ecstatic about the Talisman in their 1951 test! "The Talisman offers four-cylinder torque at a price within the range of many." Sadly, however, today's bikers would find its performance somewhat disappointing: "Even from 50mph the machine would perceptibly accelerate if the throttle were snapped open." But over 60 years ago expectations were lower, with talk of the 'Talisman's zooming acceleration'. They liked the road-holding but found that the 'top corners of the tank pads were too sharp and caused discomfort on even the briefest of journeys'. Their best speed was 61, and cruising at about 5mph less it'd return over 80mpg.*

THE 250 c.c. "TALISMAN TWIN" (TT.1.)

ENGINE AND GEAR UNIT. 250 cc. Two stroke EXCELSIOR Vertical Twin Engine. 50 m/m. Bore x 62 m/m. Stroke each cylinder — 246 cc. Petroil lubrication. Ball bearing Mainshaft, roller bearing big ends. 4-SPEED footchange gearbox. Amal Carburetter with Twist Grip Control.

IGNITION AND LIGHTING. Wico-Pacy flywheel magneto ignition with 30-watt rectified lighting and charging set. Large Headlamp with parking light and Dipper.

FRAME. Excelsior SPRING FRAME of exceptional strength, incorporating Coil Spring Suspension. Built with weldless steel tubing. Spring-up Central Stand.

FRONT FORKS. Excelsior TELESCOPIC. Built with alloy steel tubing. Dual Double Action coil springs. Phosphor bronze bushes support the sliding members.

TANK. Saddle Tank. Finished in maroon enamel with cream side panels. Capacity 2⅝ galls.

WHEELS AND TYRES. Chrome plated rims. 5-in. front and 6-in. rear brakes. Dunlop "Universal" tyres. 19-in. x 3-in.

TOOLBOX AND EQUIPMENT. Triangular Tool box fitted on each side of machine. Full kit of tools with Tyre Inflator, Electric Horn and Licence Holder.

FINISH. Frame stove enamelled in maroon. All chromium plated parts are heavily plated.

WEIGHT. 230-lb. approx.

SPEEDOMETER. Smith's non-trip speedometer.

bike. Big news came at the following show, however, with the announcement of the 250cc Talisman Twin featuring Excelsior's own two-stroke motor, as well as spring frames on everything bar the Autobyks.

From then on, through the '50s and into the '60s, the company's machines attempted to keep pace with the general trends, with a range of economy and mildly-sporting lightweights, and just a larger 328cc version of the Talisman later on to go over the 250 barrier. The range at times was bewildering in its complexity and the reasoning difficult to fathom – especially since most of their bikes lacked, as they say, a certain something.

In the autumn of 1955 the company became the importer for Heinkel scooters but this arrangement lasted no more than a year. Attempts were made to boost flagging sales with purchase-tax-free machines in kit form in the early '60s – it might have worked in earlier times but not then. By 1963 just two models were catalogued, and two years later it was all over. The car seat belt manufacturer Britax became the owner of whatever was left.

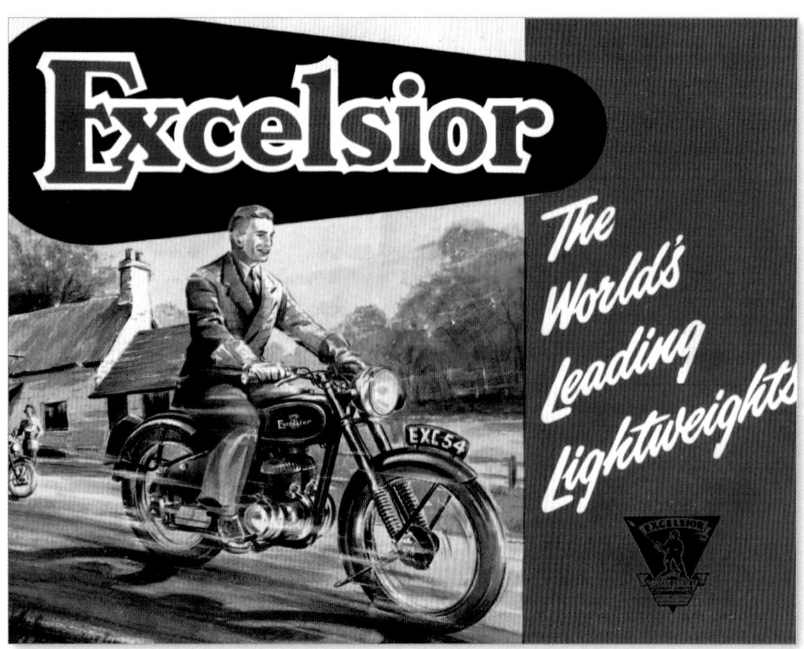

Please excuse the pun but they really excelled themselves for 1954 with no less than 14 models on offer – plus optional subdivisions! This is the TT1, the most basic of the four Talismen, with plunger frame and ridden by Bob. The TT2 was the same spec and colour (black) but had a swinging-arm frame.

Excelsior

The Consort 98 c.c. MODEL F4 AND *The Condor* 125 c.c. MODEL D12

MODELS F.4 and D.12

ENGINE AND GEAR UNIT (Model F.4). Two stroke "Villiers" 4.F engine unit. 47 mm. bore x 57 mm. stroke = 98 cc. Petroil lubrication. 2-speed constant mesh gears with handlebar control. "Villiers" carburetter with combined air filter and strangler. Twist grip control.

ENGINE AND GEAR UNIT (Model D.12). Two stroke "Villiers" 12.D engine unit. 50 mm. bore x 62 mm. stroke = 122 cc. Petroil lubrication. 3-speed gearbox unit with adjustable foot control. "Villiers" S.19 carburetter with combined air strangler and air filter. Twist grip control.

IGNITION AND LIGHTING. "Villiers" flywheel magneto ignition with direct lighting set. Large head lamp with dipper switch and parking light.

FRAME. Excelsior design semi-cradle type with 3-point suspension, constructed of high quality steel tubiing, giving both strength and rigidity. Spring-up central stand.

FRONT FORKS. Built with high quality steel taper tubing incorporating centre spring, link action. Adjustable spindles.

TANK. Pressed steel, welded saddle tank finished black enamel with heavy gold lining. Capacity 1¾ gallons. Tank fitted with oil measure.

WHEELS AND TYRES. Dunlop 19in. x 2.25in. tyres fitted to heavy gauge aluminised finish rims.

BRAKES. Internal expanding hub brakes, 4in. diameter front, handlebar operated, and 4⅝in. diameter rear, foot operated, both instantly adjusted.

HANDLEBARS. Semi-raised, chromium plated, adjustable, with twist grip control.

EQUIPMENT. Full set of tools, inflator, bulb horn, licence holder.

FINISH. Frame and other parts enamelled in brilliant black with gold lining to tank. Handlebar, exhaust pipe and other parts chromium plated.

WEIGHT. Model F.4, 130 lbs.; Model D.12, 140 lbs.; approx.

SPEEDOMETER. Model D.12 only—Smith's non-trip.

N.B.—A speedometer is not compulsory or supplied with any motor cycle under 100 cc. If required a speedometer can be supplied at an extra cost.

Why ever did they use different frames for these two in 1954?

The Courier 150 could be had as the C1 or C2 (with Excelsior's own 148cc motor). This is the latter with rectified lighting and charging set, accumulator and electric horn, whilst the C1 was the cheaper version with direct lighting. Either could also be fitted with a 122cc Villiers, in which case they became the U1 or U2. A C2 was tested by Motor Cycling *in the summer of '54 and they got 100mpg overall and managed to wind it up to almost 50mph.*

Here's the swinging-arm Roadmaster R4; and just to confuse any potential purchaser they could also go for an R1, and R2 or an R3. The 1 and 2 had plunger frames whilst the 3 had the same as the 4. However, the 1 and 3 had direct lighting whereas the 2 and 4 had the more comprehensive electrics. All had the 59x72mm Villiers 197cc with three-speed 'box but for £6 12 s extra you could have a four-speed. The R4, as you can see, had a dual seat but on any of the other three it was £3 12s extra. The R1 was the cheapest at £97 10s basic, whilst the dearest was the R4 at £108.

Even the flagship Sports Talisman Twin came in two guises – the STT1 with plunger (they called it spring) frame and the STT2 with swinging arm (£132 or £142 before tax). Both were beige whilst the entire rest of the range was in black – apart from the Autobyks, which had cream panels to tank and engine shields. The Motor Cycle *put one of the first twin-carb Talismen through its paces in the summer of '52, and its 64mph top whack (3mph more than the single-carb version) was obtained at the expense of 60mpg at around 55mph instead of 80.*

Two notes in ink show that someone was at least considering fitting a Watsonian Windsor to a 197 Roadmaster. These sidecars were offered with the current Indian Braves, so the idea was not as far fetched as it might appear.

MODELS and PRICES **SEASON 1954** Applicable from 1st NOVEMBER, 1953

"Excelsior" MOTOR CYCLES AND THE "AUTOBYK"

THE EXCELSIOR MOTOR CO. LTD., KINGS ROAD, TYSELEY, BIRMINGHAM 11

Model	Description	Cash Price £ s. d.	Purchase Tax £ s. d.	Total Price £ s. d.
	98 c.c. AUTOBYK			
54/S1	" De Luxe " Single Speed ...	49 10 0	9 18 0	59 8 0
54/G2	" Super " Two Speed ...	59 0 0	11 16 0	70 16 0
	98 c.c. CONSORT MOTOR CYCLE			
54/F4	Two Speed ...	55 0 0	11 0 0	66 0 0
	SPEEDOMETER is not compulsory or supplied, with any AUTOBYK or MOTOR CYCLE under 100 c.c. If required later it can be supplied and fitted by any EXCELSIOR Dealer.			
	125 cc. CONDEX Complete with Speedometer			
54/D12	Three Speed. Direct Lighting. Rigid Frame ...	67 0 0	13 8 0	80 8 0
	150 c.c. COURIER Complete with Speedometer			
54/C1	Spring Frame. Direct Lighting ...	89 0 0	17 16 0	106 16 0
54/C2	Spring Frame. Rectifier Lighting and Charging Set ...	94 0 0	18 16 0	112 16 0
	197 c.c. ROADMASTER Complete with Speedometer			
54/R1	Spring Frame. Direct Lighting ...	97 10 0	19 10 0	117 0 0
54/R2	Spring Frame. Rectifier Lighting and Charging Set ...	102 10 0	20 10 0	123 0 0
54/R3	Swinging Arm Rear Suspension. Direct Lighting. Twin Seat ...	103 0 0	20 12 0	123 12 0
54/R4	Swinging Arm Rear Suspension. Rectifier Lighting and Charging Set. Twin Seat ...	108 0 0	21 12 0	129 12 0
	250 c.c. TALISMAN TWIN Complete with 65/70 m.p.h. Speedometer			
54/TT1	Four Speed. Spring Frame. Rectifier Lighting and Charging Set ...	120 0 0	24 0 0	144 0 0
54/TT2	Four Speed. Swinging Arm Rear Suspension. Rectifier Lighting and Charging Set. Twin Seat ...	130 0 0	26 0 0	156 0 0
	250 c.c. SPORTS TALISMAN TWIN Complete with 80 m.p.h. Speedometer			
54/STT1	Four Speed. Spring Frame. Rectifier Lighting and Charging Set. Twin Seat. Twin Amal Carburetters ...	132 0 0	26 8 0	158 8 0
54/STT2	Four Speed. Swinging Arm Rear Suspension. Rectifier Lighting and Charging Set. Twin Seat. Twin Amal Carburetters ...	142 0 0	28 8 0	170 8 0

A 'works outing' to a yodelling contest in Austria for Brian – one of many that took place in 1955 to celebrate the end of ten years' occupation since World War Two. They've let him loose on one of the twin-carb Talismen too; but is it an STT2 or an SE STT2?

Just the one Courier for 1955, thank goodness. In common with many other makes, headlamps with underslung sidelight were fitted to all Excelsiors at this period. In true nonsensical Excelsior fashion, the following year the company retained the C3, which was now finished in Cactus Green and reintroduced the C1, now with the rather unfortunate title of Condex and fitted with a Villiers 147 in a duplex plunger frame.

The Roadmaster was cut back to three models. Plunger frames were gone but why two types of swinging-arm frame? The R4 duplex swinging-arm carried on from the previous year with the R5 and R6 having this swinging-arm loop frame.

MODEL & No.	ENGINE & GEAR UNIT	FRAME	FRONT FORKS	WHEELS & TYRES
TALISMAN TWINS TT2 TT3 STT2 SE STT2	250 c.c. two-stroke EXCELSIOR vertical twin engine, 50 mm. bore x 62 mm. stroke each cylinder (246 c.c.). Petroil lubrication. Ball and roller bearing mainshaft, roller bearing big ends. 4-speed footchange gear-box. Amal carburetter with twist grip control on Models TT2, TT3 and twin Amal car-buretters with special induction manifolds on Models STT2 and SE STT2.	Excelsior Swinging Arm rear suspension duplex cradle frames to Models TT2, STT2 and SE STT2 and loop frames to Model TT3 only.	Excelsior Telescopic built with alloy steel tubing. Double action coil springs. Phos-phor bronze bushes support.	Chrome plated rims, 5in. front and 6in. rear brakes. Dunlop "Universal" tyres, 19in. x 3in. Model SE STT2 fitted with 6in. front and rear brakes and ribbed front tyre.
ROADMASTER R4 R5 R6	197 c.c. two-stroke "Villiers" single port engine, 59 mm. bore x 72 mm. stroke. Petroil lubrication. 3-speed footchange gear. "Villiers" carburetter with twist grip control.	Excelsior Swinging Arm rear suspension duplex cradle frame to Model R4 and loop frames to Models R5 and R6.	Excelsior Telescopic built with alloy steel tubing. Double action coil springs. Phos-phor bronze bushes support.	Chrome plated rims, 5in. front and rear brakes. Dunlop tyres, 19in. x 3in.
COURIER C3	150 c.c. two-stroke EXCELSIOR single port engine, 55 mm. bore x 62 mm. stroke (148 c.c.). Petroil lubrication. 3-speed foot-change gear. Amal carburetter with twist grip control.	Excelsior Swinging Arm rear suspension with single loop frame.	Excelsior Telescopic built with alloy steel tubing. Double action coil springs. Phos-phor bronze bushes support.	Chrome plated rims, 5in. front and rear brakes. Dunlop tyres, 19in. x 3in.
CONSORT F4	98 c.c. two-stroke Villiers engine, 47 mm. bore x 57 mm. stroke. Petroil lubrication. 2-speed gear with handlebar control. Villiers carburetter with twist grip control.	Excelsior semi-cradle with 3 point suspen-sion robustly built.	Built with high grade steel tapered tubing incorporating centre spring and link action.	Aluminised finish rims, 4⅝in. diameter brakes. Fully adjust-able controls.

MODEL & No.	IGNITION & LIGHTING	TANK	FINISH	SPEEDOMETER	WEIGHT
TALISMAN TWINS TT2 TT3 STT2 SE STT2	Wico-Pacy flywheel magneto with 30 watt rectified lighting and battery. Large headlamp with park-ing light and dipper.	Saddle tank, capacity 3 gallons. Finished bright black with gold linings to Models TT2 and TT3. Beige with red linings to Models STT2 and SE STT2.	Frame and other parts stove enamelled bright black on Models TT2 and TT3. Beige colour on Models STT2 and SE STT2. Chromium parts heavily plated.	Smith's non-trip 70 m.p.h. on Models TT2 and TT3. 80 m.p.h. on Models STT2 and SE STT2.	TT2 .. 260 lbs. TT3 .. 250 lbs. STT2 .. 268 lbs. SE STT2 270 lbs.
ROADMASTER R4 R5 R6	Villiers flywheel magneto with 30 watt rectified lighting and battery. Head-lamp with parking light and dipper.	Saddle tank, capacity 2¾ galls. Finished bright black with gold linings.	Frame and other parts stove enamelled bright black. Chro-mium parts heavily plated.	Smith's non-trip 65/70 m.p.h.	R4 .. 210 lbs. R5 .. 200 lbs. R6 .. 203 lbs.
COURIER C3	Wico-Pacy flywheel magneto ignition with 30 watt rectified lighting and battery. Headlamp with park-ing light and dipper.	Saddle tank, capacity 2¾ galls. Finished bright black with gold linings.	Frame and other parts stove enamelled bright black. Chro-mium parts heavily plated.	Smith's non-trip 65/70 m.p.h.	C3 .. 198 lbs.
CONSORT F4	Villiers flywheel magneto with direct lighting. Headlamp with parking light and dipper.	Saddle tank, capacity 1¾ galls. Finished bright black with gold linings.	Frame and other parts stove enamelled bright black. Chro-mium parts heavily plated.	Supplied as an extra if required.	F4 .. 130 lbs.

Out of the three Talismen just the STT2 and SE STT2 had twin carbs but only the latter had full-width hubs with 6in brakes front and rear. Both were in beige. The TT3 was in black.

Excelsior
The World's Leading Lightweights
EXC 57

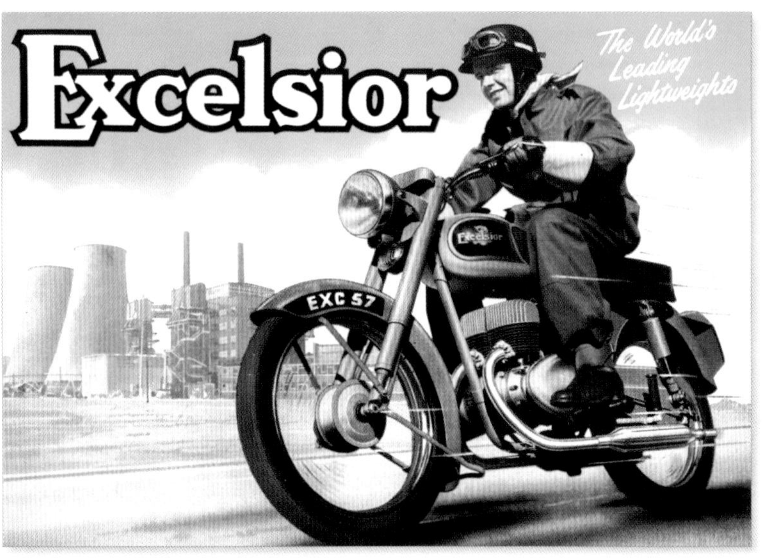

By the look on Steve's face this is most likely the 1957 twin-carb Talisman STT5 but you can tell for certain because it has the specially-tuned Excelsior MkV engine with deeper head finning. The single-carb TT3 used the older motor with less generous finning. Both were Cactus Green with Olive tank panels. Excelsior apparently couldn't quite decide where the horn lived this year, as elsewhere in the brochure only the TT3 had it beneath the headlight, but here it's mounted thus on the STT5 as well.

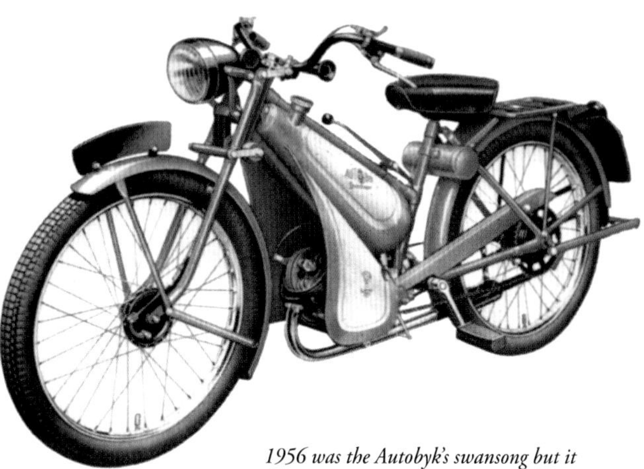

1956 was the Autobyk's swansong but it went out in a blaze of colour with both the S1 (single-speed) and G2 (two-speed) finished in Pearl Grey with cream panels. This is instantly recognisable as the latter, of course, on account of its gear lever above the tank.

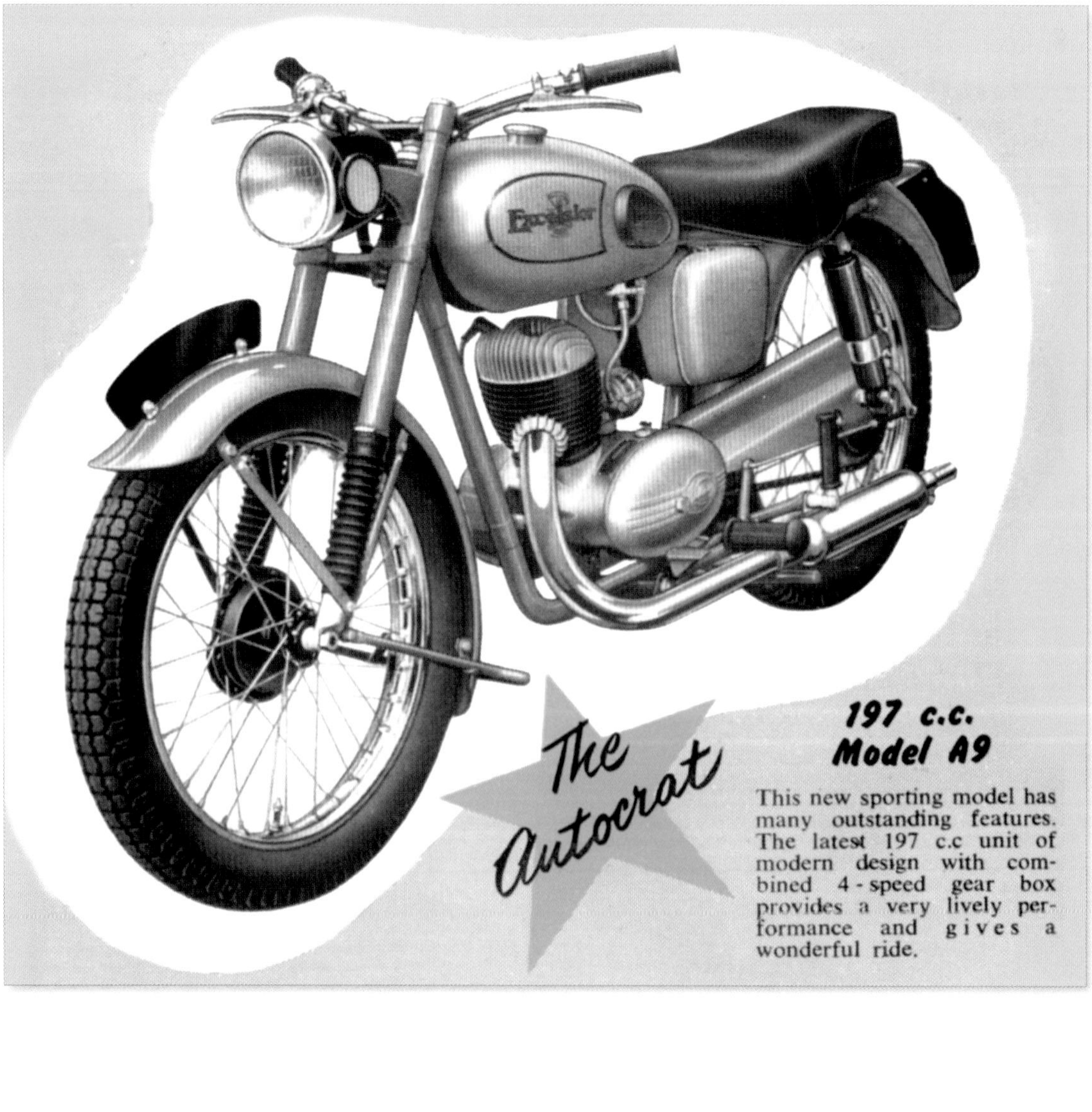
The Autocrat
197 c.c.
Model A9
This new sporting model has many outstanding features. The latest 197 c.c unit of modern design with combined 4-speed gear box provides a very lively performance and gives a wonderful ride.

Gosh, they did make things confusing: new for 1956 was the A9 sporting (the firm's word) Autocrat but it was nothing more than an R6 with new Villiers 9E (197cc) and four-speed box. The R6 (Roadmaster) itself, with older Villiers 197 and three speed, was still listed. The A9 was Pearl Grey and the R6 remained black.

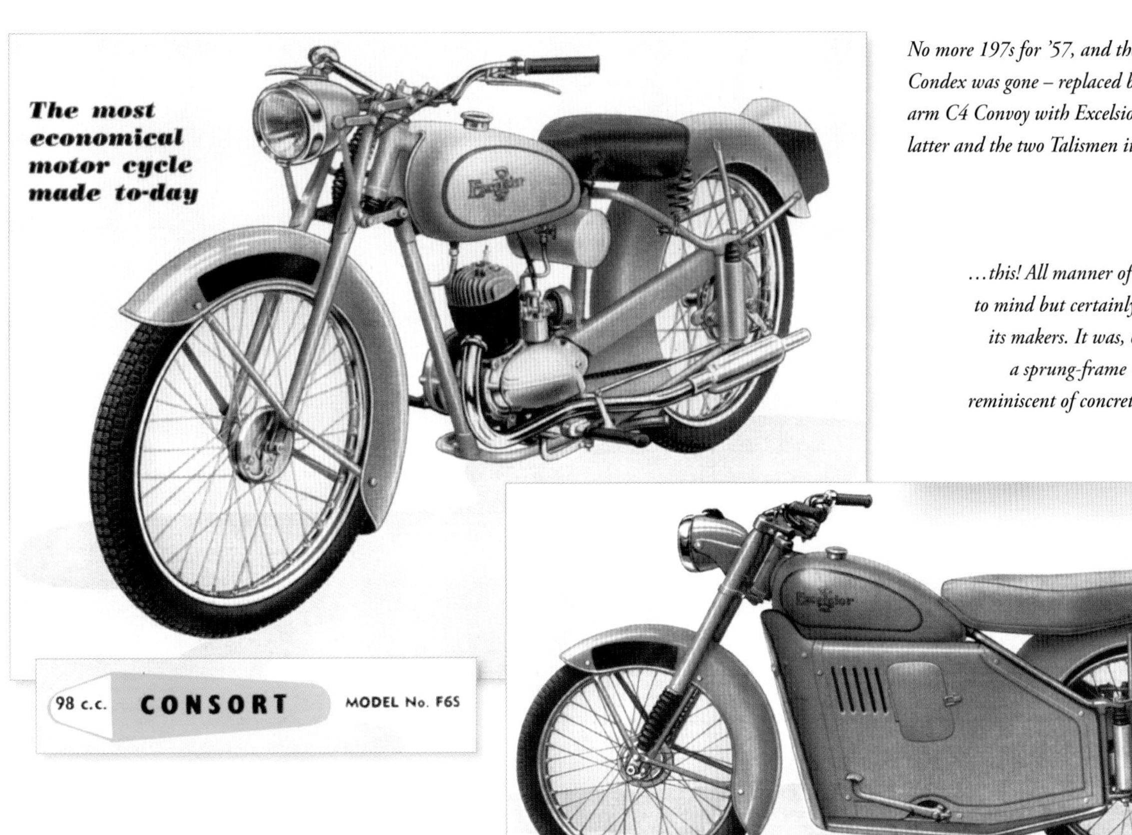

No more 197s for '57, and the Villiers 147-engined C1 Condex was gone – replaced by the loop-framed swinging-arm C4 Convoy with Excelsior 148 power. So besides the latter and the two Talismen it was just this 98 and…

…this! All manner of apt descriptions are brought to mind but certainly not 'elegant' as suggested by its makers. It was, of course, nothing more than a sprung-frame Consort with some panelling reminiscent of concrete mixer cowlings, leg shields, footboards and a dual seat.

	TALISMAN TWINS TT3 & STT5	CONVOY C4	SKUTABYKE SB1 & CONSORTS F4 & F6S
ENGINE AND GEAR UNIT	250 c.c. Two-stroke **EXCELSIOR** vertical twin engine 50 mm. bore x 62 mm. stroke each cylinder (246 c.c.) Petroil lubrication. Ball and roller bearing main-shaft. Roller bearing big end. 4-speed footchange gearbox with multi plate cork insert clutch. Twin exhaust pipes and silencers, Amal Monobloc car-buretter. The Sports Model STT5 has a Mark V specially tuned engine with twin carburetters.	150 c.c. Two-stroke **EXCELSIOR** single port engine 55 mm. bore x 62 mm. stroke (148 c.c.). Petroil lubrication. Ball bearing crankshaft and double row roller big end. 3-speed foot operated gearbox with multi plate cork insert clutch. Amal Monobloc carburetter.	98 c.c. Two-stroke "Villiers" engine gear unit 47 mm. bore x 57 mm. stroke. Petroil lubrication. Ball bearing mainshaft and roller bearing big end, 2-speed gear. Mark 4F with handchange gear control fitted to Model F4, and Mark 6F with footchange gear control to Models SB1 and F6S. Villiers Junior carburetter with air filter and twist grip control.
FRAME AND FRONT FORKS	Heavy gauge tubular loop frame on Model TT3 and duplex cradle frame with prop stand on Model STT5. Swinging fork pivoted on self-lubricated bushes and telescopic oil damped suspension units adjustable for varying loads. Telescopic front forks with multiple rate double action springs giving 4" movement, rock steady steering and safe cornering.	Loop type frame built with heavy gauge tube. Swinging fork pivoted on self lubri-cated bushes and telescopic oil damped suspension units adjustable for varying loads. Telescopic front forks with multiple rate double action springs giving 4" movement, rock steady steering and safe cornering.	Semi-cradle frame robustly built with 3-point suspen-sion. Rigid frame on Model F4 and spring frame with plunger rear suspension on Models SB1 and F6S. Tubular steel front forks with central spring on Models F4 and F6S. Telescopic front forks with multiple rate double action springs and flexible gaiters fitted to Model SB1. Quickly detachable side shields with efficient leg-guards and rigidly mounted wide com-fortable footboards are fitted to Model SB1.
WHEELS & TYRES	Full width alloy hubs with journal bearings and powerful front and rear brakes. Wheel rims chromium plated. Dunlop 19" x 3" studded tyres. Ribbed front tyre on Model STT5 only.	Journal bearing hubs with 5" front and rear brakes. Dunlop 19" x 3" studded tyres. Aluminised finish on wheel rims, hubs and silencer.	Front and rear wheels of 19" dia. fitted with 4⅜" brakes and Dunlop 19" x 2.25" tyres. Aluminised finish on wheel rims and hubs.
IGNITION AND LIGHTING	Flywheel magneto ignition with 30 watt generator. Lucas 7" headlamp with pre-focussed bulb and pilot light. 12 a.h. battery housed in closed case. Dipper switch on handlebar. Wide angle rear light and reflector. Instrument panel houses the speedometer, ammeter and light switch.	Flywheel magneto ignition with 30 watt generator. Lucas 6" headlamp with pre-focussed bulb and pilot light. 12 a.h. battery housed in closed case. Dipper switch on handlebar. Wide angle rear light and reflector. Speedometer, ammeter and light switch neatly mounted in headlamp shell.	Flywheel magneto ignition with Villiers direct A.C. lighting. 5" headlamp with parking light. Dipper switch mounted on handlebars. Large tail lamp and reflector.
TANK AND FINISH	All steel welded tank, 3 gallons capacity, enamelled cactus green with olive green side panels, hand lined, and rubber knee grips. Frame and other parts stove enamelled cactus green on rust proofed base. Handlebars, rims and exhaust system are chromium plated.	All steel welded tank 2¾ gallons capacity enamelled cactus green with olive green side panels, hand lined, and rubber knee grips. Frame and other parts stove enamelled cactus green on rust proofed base. Chromium plated handlebars and aluminised finish on wheel rims and silencer.	All steel welded tank 1¾ gallons capacity enamelled cactus green and attractively lined. Frame and other parts (including side panels and legshields on Model SB1) stove enamelled cactus green on rust proofed base. Wheel rims and hubs aluminised finish.
EQUIPMENT	Smith's illuminated chronometric speedometer. Luxurious twinseat with foam rubber interior. Electric horn. Inflator. Full kit of tools.	Smith's illuminated magnetic Speedo-meter. Luxurious twinseat with foam rubber interior. Electric horn. Inflator. Full kit of tools.	Large comfortable saddle on Models F4 and F6S. Luxurious twinseat with foam rubber interior on Model SB1. Bulb horn. Inflator. Full kit of tools. (Speedometer can be supplied at extra charge.)
WEIGHT	TT3 - 250 lbs. STT5 - 275 lbs.	C4 - 198 lbs.	F4 - 130 lbs. F6S - 140 lbs. SB1 - 160 lbs.

Looks like the 1958 annual get-together of the Excelsior Owners' Club, all two of them. That's Jeff Luff on the left with his brand-new Talisman S8 in Bronze Green. Ryan and Rosie turned up on his Pearl Grey Skutabyke but, although he's putting a brave face on, it looks as though she's more interested in going home with Mr Smoothie on the twin.

Excelsior's 328cc engine found an unlikely additional home in the little Berkeley sports cars manufactured by the people who made Berkeley caravans, with input from Mr Lawrence Bond, whom you will have come across earlier in this book. The first 150 or so of these (the SE322s) had British Anzani two-stroke twins but thereafter over 1250 SE328s were made with Excelsior's largest motor. Until, that is, it was stretched to a three-cylinder 492cc unit with triple carbs. This was done by the (relatively) simple expedient of modifying the centrally-split crankcase and inserting a different crankshaft and extra central cylinder. Not quite as easy as that but you'll get the general principle. The resulting engine was used in the Berkeley SE492. The little beggars were reputed to do 80mph, and just over 650 were made.

The Exciting NEW 328cc VERTICAL TWIN ENGINE

- Effortless Power
- Snappy Acceleration
- Smooth Performance
- Economical Running
- Fully Proved Efficient Unit

The Excelsior Engine

This new 328 c.c. Talisman Twin Engine is a development of the fully proved Sports Talisman Unit and embodies many features of advanced design with a B.H.P. figure considerably above the average standard. Acceleration is positively amazing and the exceptionally smooth quiet running of this high performance Twin Two-stroke is a joy to experience.

Excelsior's attempt at a trendy rear enclosure for the sportiest model did the poor thing no favours whatsoever. For all models a wide range of colours was now available – Bronze Green, Cherry Red or two-tone Pearl Grey and Cherry Red.

It's 1959 and Excelsior has pitted its crack rider Ed on a Cherry Red 328 TTS against what I take to be, allowing for artistic licence, an English Electric train. But where did this contest take place? Abroad somewhere, on account of the headlight; and the V-flash running back from its nose suggests that it could be somewhere like Bombay.

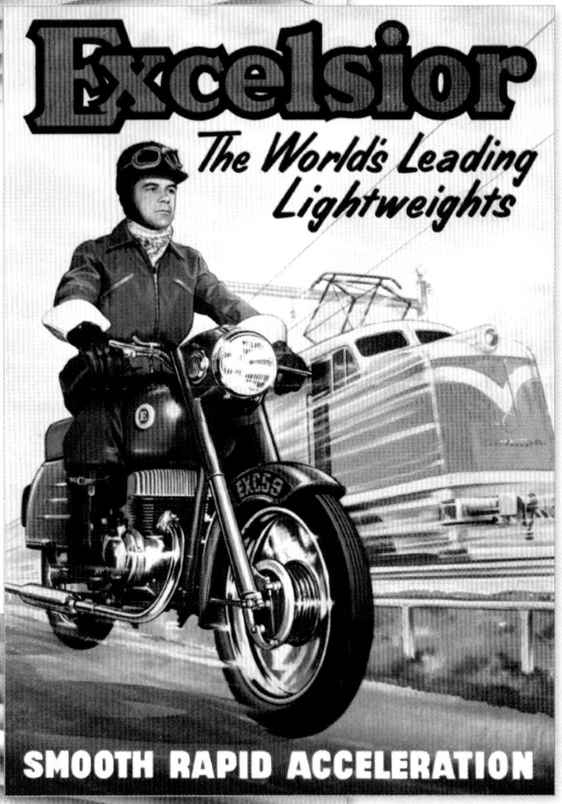

Swinging arm for the Consort had been an option with the CA8 the previous year and this was the latest version with additional tinware.

Excelsior
Consort
98c.c. Model CA9
Dependable economical transport is provided at all times by this fully proved very popular Lightweight. Low in initial cost, easy to ride and maintain, the Consort will give you years of reliable efficient service.

Paul's wife-to-be Sue would insist on wearing sandals when she rode pillion on his 1960 Talisman Twin Special – even on the new motorway. He did warn her but she was lucky to get away with just a broken strap when he clipped the pavement in Melksham one afternoon.

The round badge and plain tank finish that had first appeared in '59 on the 328 S9 was now found on all Excelsiors other than the Consorts.

MODEL & No.	ENGINE & GEAR UNIT	FRAME	FRONT FORKS	WHEELS & TYRES	IGNITION & LIGHTING	TANK & FINISH	EQUIPMENT	WEIGHT
TALISMAN TWINS 250c.c. STANDARD Model TT4 328c.c. SUPER Model S8 328c.c. SPECIAL Model S9	Two-stroke EXCELSIOR vertical twin engine. 50 m/m bore × 62 m/m stroke each cylinder = 246 c.c. (Model TT4) 58 m/m bore × 62 m/m stroke each cylinder = 328 c.c. (Models S8 and S9). Petroil lubrication. Ball and roller bearing mainshaft. Roller bearing big ends. Deeply finned cylinders and alloy cylinder heads. 4-speed footchange gearbox, with positive stop foot control and multi plate cork insert clutch. Twin exhaust pipes and silencers. Amal Monobloc carburetter. The Super S8 Model is fitted with twin carburetters. The Special Model S9 has a tuned engine and is also fitted with twin carburetters giving outstanding acceleration and high performance.	Heavy gauge steel tubular frame with Swinging Arm rear suspension, oil damped, adjustable and pivoting on self-lubricated bushes. Single loop on Model TT4, and braced duplex cradle frame on Super S8 and Special S9 Models.	Excelsior new type telescopic pattern automatically lubricated and hydraulically damped giving rock steady steering and safe cornering.	Full width alloy hubs with journal bearings and powerful front and rear brakes. Chromium plated rims. Dunlop tyres 19" × 3" on Model TT4, 19" × 3" ribbed front and 3.25" rear studded tyres on Model S8 and 18" × 3.25" Universal on Model S9.	Wico-Pacey magneto ignition with flywheel generator and on Models TT4 and S8. Miller ignition with 60 watt flywheel alternator on Model S9. Large headlamp with prefocussed bulb and pilot light. 12 a.h. battery neatly housed in container. Handlebar dipper switch. Wide angle rear light and reflector. Stop light on Model S9. The speedometer, ammeter and light switches are neatly housed in the headlamp shell or attractive headlamp cowl on Model S9.	All steel welded tank 3 gallons capacity on models TT4 and S8 and 3¼ gallons on Model S9, rubber insulated, enamelled to match the machine colour with hand lined side panels and plated motif or plastic badge. All enamelled parts are fully rust-proofed and triple coated with enamel, with a colour choice of bronze green, cherry red or (two-tone) pearl grey/cherry red.	Smith's illuminated chronometric speedometer. Luxurious twin seat with foam interior. Centre stand and prop stand on Model S9. Pillion foot rests. Electric horn. Inflator. Full kit of tools.	TT4 250 lbs. S8 285 lbs. S9 295 lbs.
UNIVERSAL 150c.c. Models U9 & U9R	Two-stroke Villiers single port Mark 30C engine. 55 m/m bore × 62 m/m stroke = 147c.c. Petroil lubrication. Ball bearing crankshaft, roller bearing big end. 3-speed positive-stop foot operated gearbox with multi plate cork insert clutch. Villiers type S19 carburetter.	Single loop tubular type of heavy gauge steel with Swinging Arm rear suspension. The telescopic oil damped suspension units pivot on self-lubricated bushes, and are adjustable for varying loads.	Telescopic pattern, equipped with protective shields and multi-springs giving a multi-rate double action movement, and absorbing all road shocks.	Full width journal bearing hubs in light alloy. Equipped with 5" front and rear brakes. Aluminised wheel rims on Model U9 and chrome-finish or enamelled plated rims on Model U9R. Dunlop 19" × 3" tyres front and rear.	Villiers flywheel magneto ignition with direct lighting on Model U9 and AC/DC lighting set with rectifier and 10 a.h. battery on Model U9R. 5" headlamp with pilot light. Dipper switch on handlebar. Wide angle rear light and reflector. The Speedometer, ammeter and light switches are neatly mounted in the headlamp shell on Model U9R.	All steel welded tank, 2¼ gallons capacity, enamelled to match colour of machine, with hand lined side panels. All enamelled parts are rust proofed and triple coated with enamel with a colour choice of bronze green, cherry red, or pearl grey/cherry red (two-tone). Bright parts are chromed or cadmium plated.	Smith's illuminated chronometric speedometer. Large twin-seat with foam interior. Bulb horn on Model U9 and electric horn with battery on Model U9R. Centre stand. Inflator. Full kit of tools.	U9 195 lbs. U9R 200 lbs.
CONSORT 98c.c. Model CA9 **SKUTABYKE** 98c.c. Model SB1	Two-stroke Villiers Mark 6F engine gear unit 47 m/m bore × 57 m/m stroke = 98c.c. Petroil lubrication. Ball bearing mainshaft and roller bearing big end, 2-speed foot change gear. Villiers type S/12 carburetter.	Semi-cradle tubular type, incorporating plunger action rear spring suspension on Model SB1 and Swinging Arm oil damped rear suspension on Model CA9. The Model SB1 is equipped with quickly detachable side shields, efficient leg guards, and rigidly mounted wide comfortable footboards.	Telescopic type with multi-rate double action springs with a 4" movement to absorb all road shocks.	Front and rear wheels of 19" dia. fitted with 4½" brakes and Dunlop 19" × 2.25" tyres. Aluminised or enamel finish on wheel rims and hubs. Full width alloy front hubs.	Villiers flywheel magneto ignition with direct AC lighting. 5" headlamp with parking light. Dipper switch mounted on handlebar. Large tail lamp and reflector.	All steel welded tank 1¾ gallon capacity enamelled to match the colour of the machine. Attractively lined. The enamelled parts are rust proofed & triple coated with a colour choice of bronze green, cherry red or pearl grey/cherry red (two-tone). Bright parts chrome or cadmium plated. Wheel rims and hubs aluminised finish. Model SB1 (inc side panels and legshields) stove enamelled pearl grey/cherry red (two-tone).	Large comfortable saddle on Model F6S and twin-seat with foam interior on Models CA8 & SB1. Centre stand. Bulb horn. Inflator. Full kit of tools. (Speedo meter can be supplied at extra charge.)	SB1 160 lbs. CA9 150 lbs.

98c.c.
Model F10
Low Priced Basic Transport for Everyone. For absolute economy the F.10 is unapproachable. Exceptionally low initial cost and a petrol consumption of approximately 150 miles per gallon are features of the outstanding value of this model.

Okay this consort was cheap at £93 13s 2d all-in against £116 19s 4d for the C10 De Luxe version, but anyone on a really tight budget would have been far better off to go for a good second-hand BSA Bantam. From a dealer such as George Clarke they'd have got a ten-year-old rigid 125 for about £14 10s or a three-year-old swing-arm 150 for £47 10s.

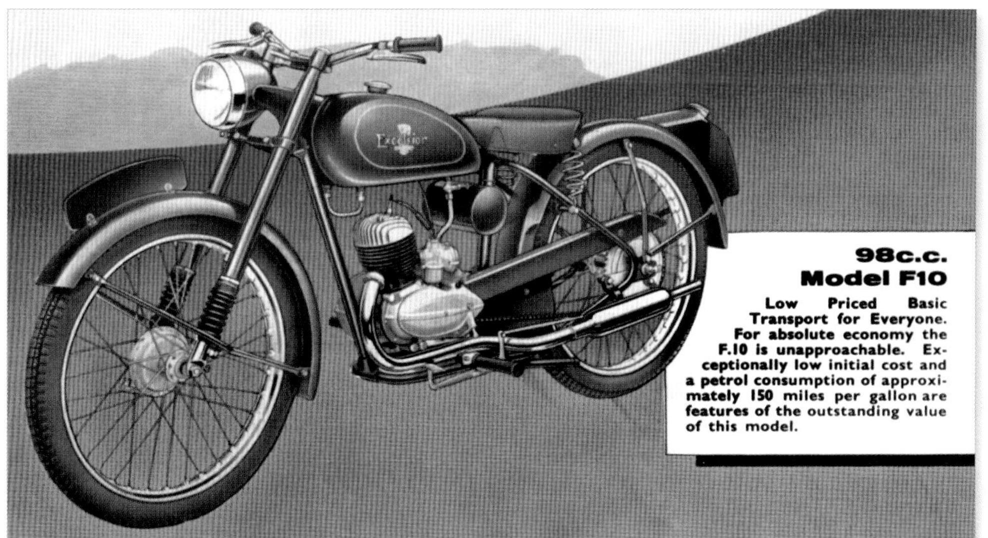

Further and fairly fruitless attempts to generate sales. Fully assembled at the factory and ready to go, the same machine was £124 14s 10d, £20 15s 10d of which was purchase tax, so on the face of it a factory build was less than a fiver.

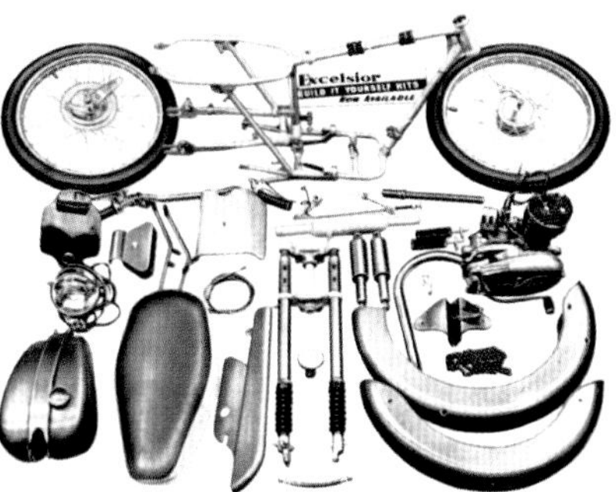

The Consort-de-luxe was offered in kit form for 85 guineas – or £106 14s 5d including tax, ready to go.

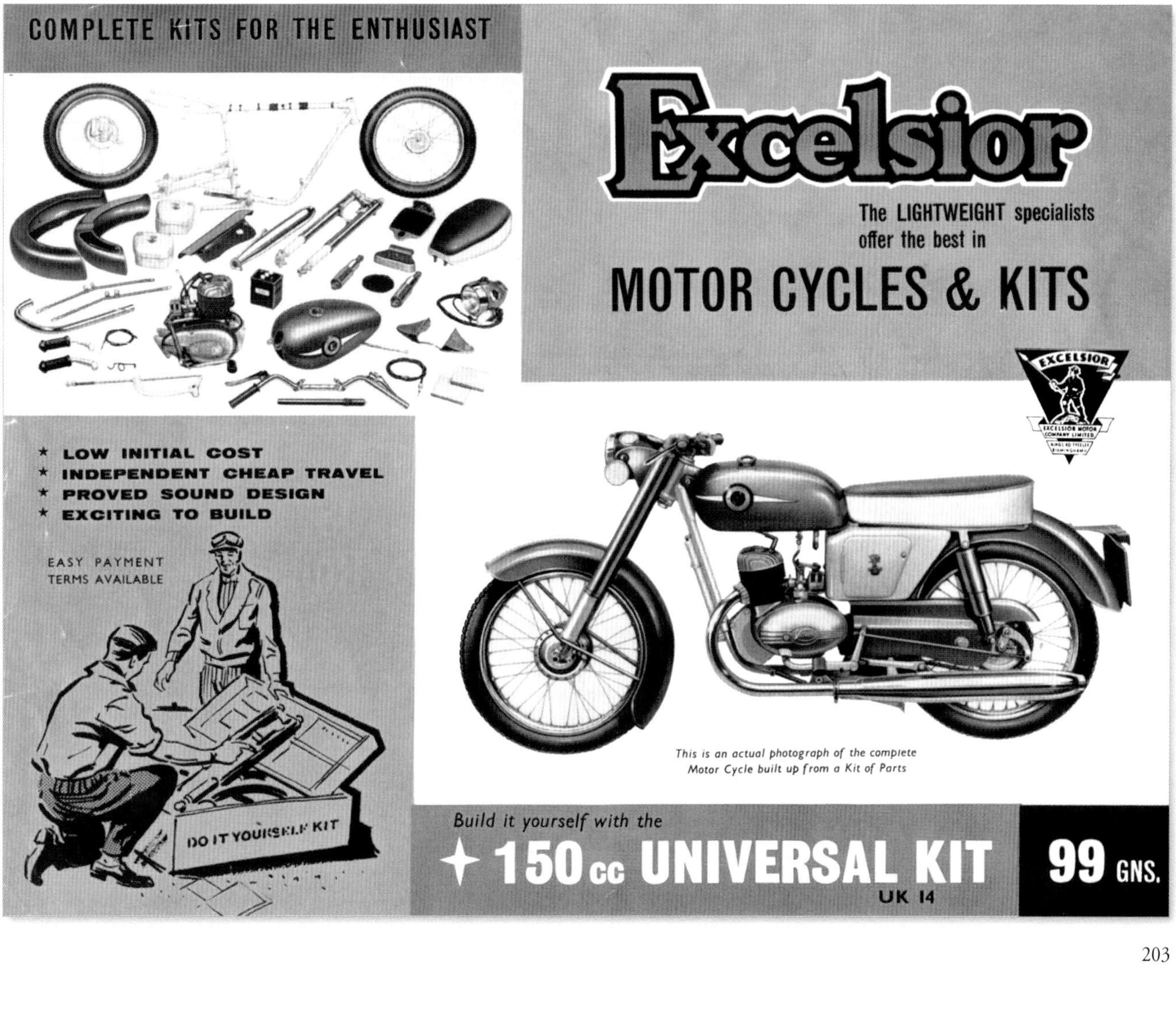

COMPLETE KITS FOR THE ENTHUSIAST
Excelsior
The LIGHTWEIGHT specialists offer the best in
MOTOR CYCLES & KITS
EXCELSIOR
★ LOW INITIAL COST
★ INDEPENDENT CHEAP TRAVEL
★ PROVED SOUND DESIGN
★ EXCITING TO BUILD
EASY PAYMENT TERMS AVAILABLE
DO IT YOURSELF KIT
This is an actual photograph of the complete Motor Cycle built up from a Kit of Parts
Build it yourself with the
✦ 150cc UNIVERSAL KIT
UK 14
99 GNS.

FLM

The FLM had a channel-section frame and a novel method of swinging-arm rear suspension controlled by a large open coil spring mounted beneath the motor.

After a spell working with Panther (Phelon & Moore) Motorcycles at its Cleckheaton factory, Frank Leach had opened a garage in Leeds that specialised in the marque and in the late 1930s was a vociferous advocate of the brand – his advertising copy often as not containing some doggerel.

His sales tactics must have worked because he was still up and running post-war, and soon with further premises, but had cooled off Panthers and become an agent for AMC's products amongst others. Although the majority of his business was in sales and repairs he took a stab at becoming a maker in his own right with the FLM motorcycle that was produced from 1951 to 1953. Was it local rivalry and eagerness to prove that he could make and market a more worthwhile machine than John Ellis's Minibyke that encouraged him to become a manufacturer? If it was, he was pretty safe on that count, as he'd have been hard pushed to come up with something more ridiculous. But whatever the reason his own brand had a marginally shorter life.

Next he tried his hand with another locally-made vehicle and became an agent for the Scootacar – the few sales that he made a testimony to his farsightedness and fickle public. They didn't want those things then, so why ever do they want Smart cars now? His forte by that time, however, was three-wheelers, and he became the self-avowed northern Bond, and other, mini-car specialist. As late as the mid '60s you'd go to Leach of Leeds for a Reliant three-wheeler if you lived in that part of the world.

FRANCIS-BARNETT

Francis-Barnett motorcycles came into being in 1919 when Gordon Francis, son of one of the originators of Lea Francis cars, and Arthur Barnett, his father-in-law and manufacturer of Invicta motorcycles, set up shop at Lower Ford Street in Coventry – naming their company Francis & Barnett Ltd. Aiming to capitalise on the post-war demand for economical motorised transport, their first efforts were conventional medium-capacity machines fitted with proprietary engines by both JAP and Villiers, but were not especially cheap. However, Francis was soon to come up with a novel idea that would take to the road in 1923.

Mindful of the need for strength but anxious to combine it with simplicity of manufacture and assembly, he designed a bolt-together triangulated frame. With six pairs of straight tubes and another specially-formed pair it achieved all he had set out to do and more, and a 147cc Villiers-engined Francis-Barnett for less than £30 was soon on the market. Compared with its contemporaries it looked somewhat spidery but this was an illusion – the company was quick to coin the phrase 'built like a bridge' and warranty the frame against breakage. They even held together to such good effect on the notoriously bumpy Brooklands track that the riders such as Tommy Meeten had a good deal of success, winning races and breaking records, with machines equipped with Villiers' state-of-the-art 172cc sports two-stroke. A factory publicity film extolling the virtues of the ease and speed with which a Frances-Barnett could be dismantled backfired slightly, however, when the firm received a number of complaints from members of the public who had tried to emulate factory fitters.

Nevertheless, various models, with engines of up to 350cc, utilising this type of frame were made until well into the 1930s. But before it was lapsed the firm brought out what was to be its most popular machine of the decade: the 250 Cruiser of 1933 was aimed at the man who wanted his own cheap independent transport, but without the grime and grit associated with motorcycling. It was based around a brand-new part-steel channel, part-tube, frame that was in any case largely hidden by a plethora of pressed-steel cowlings that largely enclosed the Villiers engine and the rest of the mechanicals. They were to keep the rider free of muck from that quarter whilst leg shields and a pair of very fully valanced mudguards would protect him, or her, from road filth. Not as unattractive as it might sound, it was at the same time totally unexciting – but it sold. So this, along with other two-strokes, not to forget the Blackburne engined four-stroke Stag, carried the firm through the '30s.

During this decade a penchant for naming its various wares after our feathered friends had developed in the form of Merlins, Seagulls, Plovers and Snipes – some of which, along with the Cruiser and recently-introduced 98cc Powerbike, made up the firm's range at the outbreak of the Second World War.

Either Snipes or Plovers might have ended up

The first of the post-war Merlins had the pre-war-type six-port, twin-exhaust Villiers engine, and telescopic forks were yet to be introduced. Petrol availability rather than price led to advertising such as this. What appears to be a tool box at the rear between chain stays was in fact a three-pint oil tank for use when refuelling – a draw-off tap in the bottom being used to fill a measure in the base of its filler cap. A matching toolbox was fitted on the offside. The pre-war pedal-assisted 98cc Powerbike, which had been updated with link-action spring forks, was the company's sole other listing in the immediate post-war years.

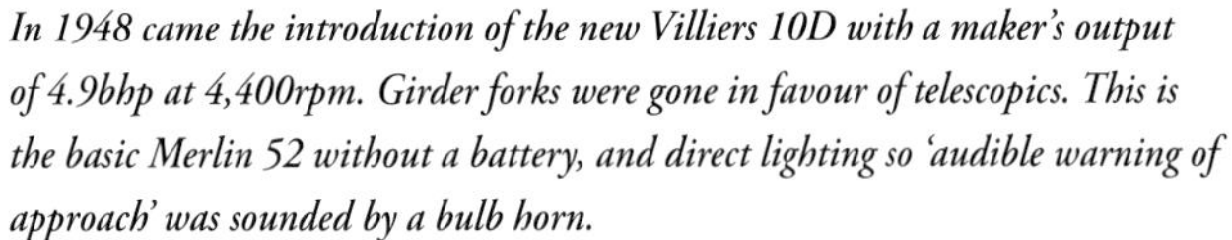
In 1948 came the introduction of the new Villiers 10D with a maker's output of 4.9bhp at 4,400rpm. Girder forks were gone in favour of telescopics. This is the basic Merlin 52 without a battery, and direct lighting so 'audible warning of approach' was sounded by a bulb horn.

First introduced in 1938 but shelved until now, the Villiers 197cc was supplied to Frances-Barnett for the top-of-the-range Falcons. Catalogued output was 7.5bhp at 4,000rpm. No protruding black rubber bulb on this bike as it's the model 55 with battery lighting and electric horn that set you back an extra fiver or so.

THE MERLIN AND FALCON RANGE OF MODELS

MERLIN 52 (as illustrated) : 122c.c. Villiers 10D engine unit, 50 mm. bore, 62 mm. stroke ; deflectorless piston ; 3-speed, gear ratios 7.2, 10 and 19.1 to 1 ; foot gear change. Direct lighting from flywheel dynamo magneto, with 7 inch headlamp, parking battery and dipper switch. Bulb horn fitted.

MERLIN 53 : As above, but equipped with **Battery Lighting Set** and **Electric Horn.**

FALCON 54 : 197 c.c. Villiers 6E engine unit, 59 mm. bore, 72 mm. stroke ; deflectorless piston ; 3-speed, gear ratios 5.9, 8.2 and 15.6 to 1 ; foot gear change. Direct lighting from flywheel magneto, with 7 inch headlamp, parking battery and dipper switch. Bulb horn fitted.

FALCON 55 (as illustrated) : As above, but equipped with **Battery Lighting Set** and **Electric Horn.**

GENERAL SPECIFICATION : ALL MODELS

IGNITION : Villiers flywheel magneto.

CARBURETTOR : Villiers: twist-grip throttle control.

LUBRICATION : Petroil system, half pint oil to one gallon petrol. **Separate oil tank to carry up to three pints of oil.**

TRANSMISSION : Renold chains; front chain enclosed in aluminium oil bath case.

TANK : Welded steel. Capacity 2¼ gallons. Anti-splash filler cap. Two-level tap fitted.

TYRES : 3.00″ × 19″ Dunlop Universal on rear wheel ; **ribbed** on front wheel.

BRAKES : 5 inch diameter internal expanding, front and rear. Finger adjustment for rear.

FRAME : Tubular, welded and brazed construction.

FORK : Telescopic, with 20 inch three rate springs which permit of a movement of over 5 inches for the inner slider tubes : providing exceptional comfort even under the worst conditions.

STANDS : Front and rear. Rear stand spring-up pattern.

MUDGUARDS : 5 inches wide. **Rear guard designed for easy wheel removal.**

SADDLE : Large Lycett spring top : adjustable for height and tilt.

EQUIPMENT : Horn, licence holder, inflator, grease gun and complete tool kit.

FINISH : Best quality black enamel. Tank, gold lined. Handlebar, exhaust system and other bright parts chromium plated.

PRICES

MERLIN 52, with Smiths Lightweight Speedometer	**£70 3s. 6d.**	plus Purchase Tax	**£18 19s. 0d.**
MERLIN 53, ,, ,, ,, ,,	**£74 3s. 6d.**	,, ,, ,,	**£20 0s. 7d.**
FALCON 54, with Smiths Trip Speedometer	**£77 0s. 0d.**	,, ,, ,,	**£20 15s. 10d.**
FALCON 55, ,, ,, ,, ,,	**£81 0s. 0d.**	,, ,, ,,	**£21 17s. 5d.**
LEGSHIELDS (for any Model) extra	**£2 0s. 0d.**	plus P. Tax	**10/10d.**

doing military service but whilst they were under consideration by the War Office the Lower Ford Street factory was put out of action by enemy bombing. The firm still had the Clarendon Pressing and Welding Co's nearby Earlsdon works, which it had owned for some years and had carried out much of their fabrication and sheet-steel work, but it was turned over to other essential work for the duration.

Post-war production commenced with the Powerbike and Merlin, then, during 1947 Francis-Barnett along with Clarendon Pressing and Welding became part of the expanding AMC group. On the surface nothing much changed, however, other than gentle evolution – the Villiers 125 powered Merlin was joined by the 197 Falcon and both were modernised with swinging-arm frames for 1952, by which time the

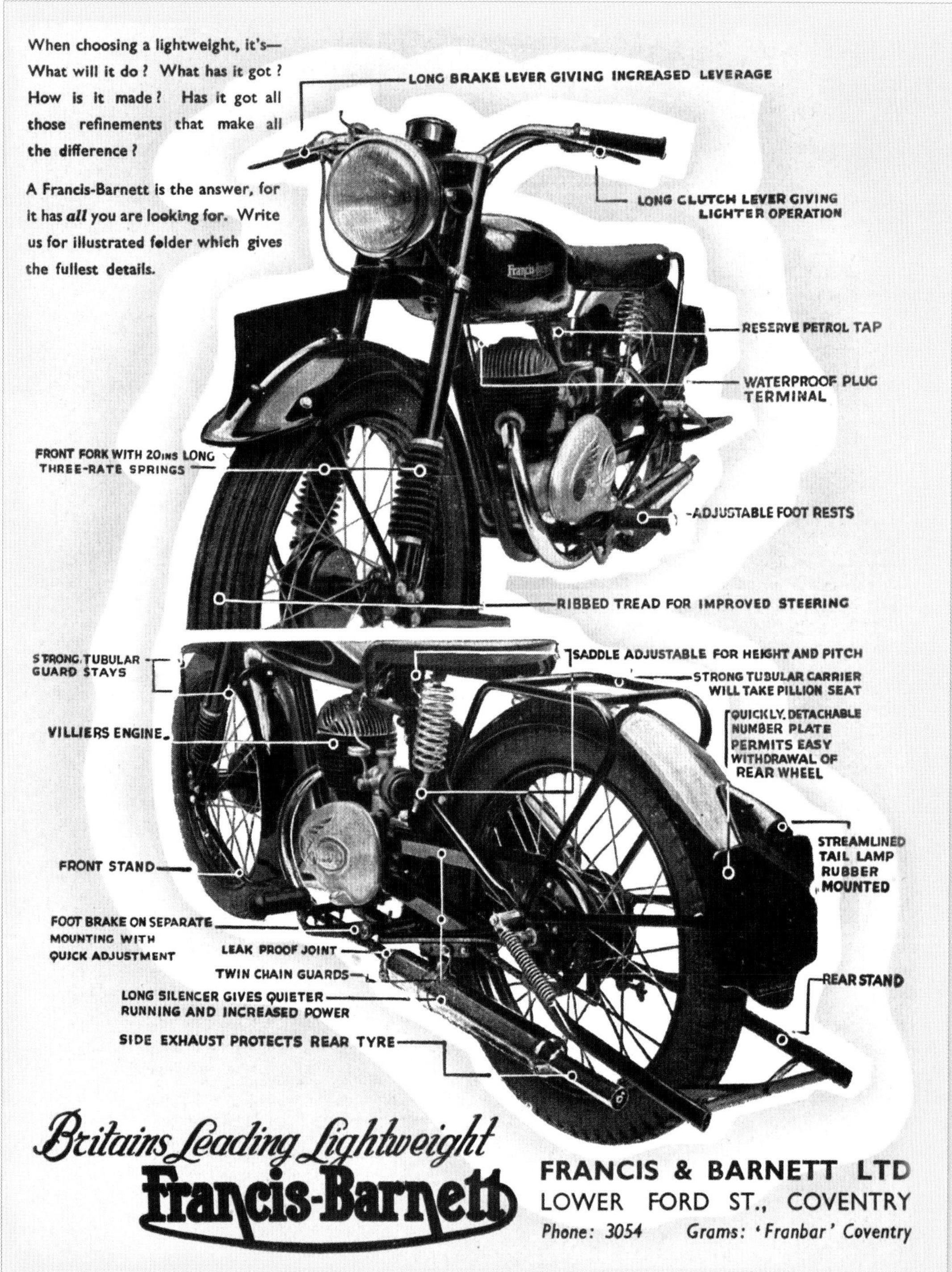

The quickly detachable number plate was indeed a Francis-Barnett refinement but to claim that the side exhaust, common to virtually all makes of motorcycle, was a special feature was a bit much!

Powerbike had been discontinued.

The Cruiser was back for 1954, now with a 225cc Villiers, but the Merlin had been ousted by the 150cc Plover and the Falcon could be had in road, trials or scrambles trim. Avian titles, allied to model numbers, would continue to be applied to some Francis-Barnetts as long as the marque existed but a break with tradition came when AMC's own two-stroke engines replaced the far better Villiers in the majority of machines.

The beginning of the end came during 1963 with the closing of the Lower Ford Street factory and relocation of some staff to the James factory in Birmingham – itself part of AMC since 1951. From then on the two makes were distinguishable by badge alone, and during 1966 the parent group's worsening situation dictated that both should die.

When Motor Cycling *tested the three-speed 58 in 1952 they extracted 57mph in top with 50 available in second, and found it would return from 83-to-112mpg depending on conditions. A special export version, the Overseas Falcon 65, was brought out for 1953 with high-clearance mudguards, competition forks, trial universal tyres, optional four-speed gearbox and other departures from standard.*

The Merlin 52 and 53 remained as before but this is the brand-new swinging-arm-framed 57 with the 53's luxuries of battery lighting and electric horn. On all models the lower front mudguard stay doubled as a front stand. Whilst a tubular rear carrier was standard on rigid-framed models it was an extra for your swinging-arm machine; but if you wanted a pillion seat it went straight onto the rear mudguard.

EASY REAR WHEEL REMOVAL

The patented rear guard construction greatly facilitates rear wheel removal. The number plate is detached by slackening two bolts, and the wheel may then be withdrawn through the arch in the guard. The built-in tail lamp remains undisturbed.

The 1952-season brochure cover heralded a new era for rider comfort – if you were prepared to fork out an extra tenner for a sprung frame.

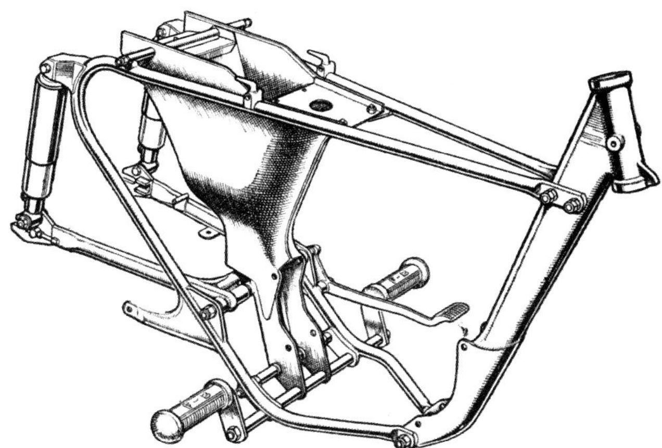

ENGINE UNIT :	225 c.c. Villiers Mk. IH ; 4-speed gearbox with gear indicator ; fully-enclosed carburettor ; flywheel magneto with external coil and cut-out switch, incorporating lock.
FRAME :	Oval section forward member and bolt-on duplex loop tubes ; pressed centre section housing 6V., 12 a.h. battery, coil, rectifier and main cables ; spring-up centre stand.
SUSPENSION :	Swinging rear fork with fully hydraulic damped spring units ; telescopic oil-damped front fork with self-lubricating bushes.
LIGHTING :	(AC and DC) 6" dia. headlamp with pre-focussed bulb and incorporating speedometer ; large wide-angle tail lamp with provision for stop light ; combined dipper and horn switch on handlebar. AC/DC switch on headlamp.
WHEELS :	6" dia. brakes accommodated in full-width hubs ; journal bearings ; rod operated rear brake ; spokes 10G. front and rear.
FINISH :	Rich deep green enamelled on 'phosphated' coating ; dualseat in matching green ; tank gold lined ; rims chromium plated, lined green and gold ; chromium and cadmium plating.
EQUIPMENT :	Smiths speedometer, electric horn, inflator and toolkit.

Somehow the frame used for the Cruiser, which had been introduced in the autumn of 1953, never looked right to me with its oval 'streamlined' front down-tube, pressed-steel centre section and those AMC pillion lugs. It was a heavyweight lightweight too, at over 280lb. Motor Cycling's *testers wound it up to 62mph in top and 52 in third but its extra capacity, oomph and weight made no difference to its fuel consumption (82-to-112mpg) over the Falcon they tested three years earlier.*

CRUISER 71 : The Villiers Mk. IH engine unit — power and flexibility coupled with handsome lines.

FALCON 70 : Showing electric horn mounting in the front of battery and tool-box compartment.

CRUISER 71 : View showing clean handlebar layout and new design headlamp incorporating instruments.

FALCON 70 : Compartment adjoining toolbox, containing battery, rectifier and horn.

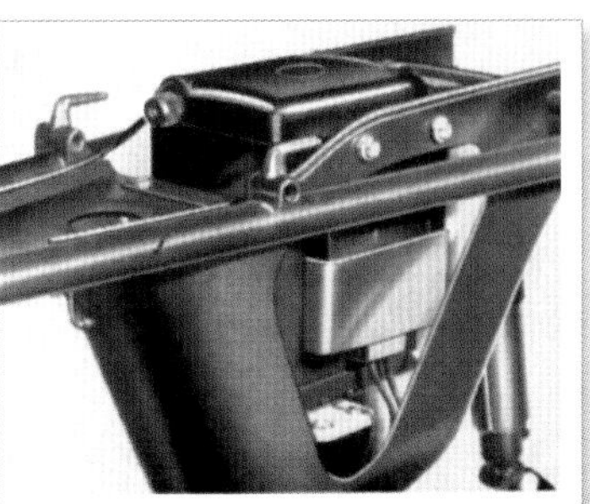

CRUISER 71 : Cut-away centre section of frame, showing neat housing of battery, rectifier and coil.

CRUISER 71 : Showing full-width hub and suspension units.

New features for the 1955 season.

The same bird of prey but now it's the much-improved 70 with three- or four-speed 8E Villiers, full-width hubs and new frame and forks, to say nothing of a much more modern appearance that included a dual seat – pillion rests were extra though.

ENGINE UNIT :	197 c.c. Villiers Mk. 8E ; 3-speed gearbox (4-speed optional extra) ; flywheel magneto ignition.
FRAME :	Brazed and welded tubular main frame with bolt-on duplex cradle-type loop tubes forming rear stays ; spring-up centre stand.
SUSPENSION :	Swinging rear fork with fully hydraulic damped spring units ; telescopic oil-damped front fork with self-lubricating bushes.
LIGHTING :	(AC and DC) 6" dia. headlamp with pre-focussed bulb and incorporating speedometer , large wide-angle tail lamp with provision for stop light ; 6V., 12 a.h. battery, rectifier and electric horn enclosed in streamlined compartment of toolbox unit ; combined dipper and horn switch on handlebar ; AC/DC switch on headlamp.
WHEELS :	5" dia. brakes accommodated in full-width hubs ; journal bearings ; rod operated rear brake ; spokes 10G. front and rear.
FINISH :	Black enamelled on ' phosphated ' coating ; tank gold lined ; rims chromium plated, lined gold and black ; chromium and cadmium plating.
EQUIPMENT :	Smiths speedometer, electric horn, inflator and toolkit.

You could also have a Falcon Scrambler or Trials mount. Both the swinging-arm and rigid frames were utterly different from those made for F-B's road machines.

Scrambles "Falcon" 72

ENGINE UNIT : 197 c.c. Villiers high compression Mk. 7E ; 4-speed gearbox (close ratio) ; ignition from special waterproofed flywheel magneto ; Amal carburettor with Vokes air filter.

FRAME : Specially reinforced, brazed and welded loop tube type ; detachable triangulated rear stays ; centre stand with quick release fixing.

SUSPENSION : Telescopic, oil-damped front fork with stiffened three-rate springs for heavy duty loading swinging rear arm with fully damped hydraulic spring units.

TANKS : 2¼ gals. petroil capacity ; recessed at front to allow ample steering lock.

WHEELS : 5" dia. brake hubs with journal bearings ; 10-12 G butted spokes ; Dunlop Sports tyres.

FINISH : Black enamelled on ' phosphated ' coating ; chromium plated rims ; tank gold lined ; chromium and cadmium plating.

EQUIPMENT : Smiths lightweight speedometer, H.M.F. raised back seat, inflator.

Quickly detachable direct lighting set and 50, 52, 54 and 56T rear wheel sprockets available as extras.

Trials "Falcon" 62

ENGINE UNIT : 197 c.c. Villiers high compression Mk. 7E ; 4-speed gearbox (wide ratio) ; ignition from special waterproofed flywheel magneto ; Amal carburettor with Vokes air filter.

FRAME : Rigid, specially reinforced ; brazed and welded loop tube type ; centre stand with quick release fixing.

FORK : Telescopic, oil damped with stiffened three-rate springs for heavy duty loading.

TANK : 2¼ gals. petroil capacity ; recessed at front to allow ample steering lock.

WHEELS : 5" dia. brake hubs with journal bearings 10-12 G. butted spokes ; Dunlop Trials Universal tyres.

FINISH : Black enamelled on ' phosphated ' coating chromium plated rims ; tank gold lined ; chromium and cadmium plating.

EQUIPMENT : Smiths trip speedometer ; Dunlop rubber trials saddle, comprehensive toolkit and inflator.

Note the high riding position which is adjustable and affords perfect control and balance. Quickly detachable direct lighting set and 48, 50, 54 and 56T rear wheel sprockets available as extras.

ENGINE UNIT :	147 c.c. Villiers Mk. 30C ; 3-speed gearbox ; flywheel magneto ignition ; Villiers lightweight carburettor.
FRAME :	Sturdy orthodox tubular type, brazed and welded ; spring-up centre stand.
SUSPENSION :	Telescopic front fork and plunger type rear units affording maximum comfort and accurate steering.
LIGHTING :	Direct from flywheel magneto ; 6″ dia. headlamp with pre-focussed bulb and incorporating speedometer ; large wide-angle tail lamp with provision for stop light ; easily accessible parking battery in roomy toolbox ; dipper switch on handlebar. (Electric horn with battery lighting via. rectifier optional extra).
WHEELS :	12G. spokes front, 10G. rear. Full-width hubs with 5 in. rear and 4 in. front brakes ; finger adjustment for rear.
FINISH :	Black enamelled on ' phosphated ' coating ; tank gold lined : chromium and cadmium plating.
EQUIPMENT :	Smiths speedometer, inflator, toolkit and bulb horn.

The baby of the range was now the Kestrel but plunger suspension coupled with the older-type front forks was a retrogressive step, even if the firm described the system as 'offering maximum comfort and accurate steering'. In that case, why did F-B bother with swinging-arm frames, one might ask.

Vital statistics of the entire 1955 range.

MODEL	69	70	71	62	72
ENG. BORE AND STROKE	55mm. × 62mm.	59mm. × 72mm.	63mm. × 72mm.	59mm. × 72mm.	59mm. × 72mm.
MAX. B.H.P.	5.5 at 4,250 r.p.m.	8.4 at 4,000 r.p.m.	10 at 4,500 r.p.m.	9.5 at 4,200 r.p.m.	9.5 at 4,200 r.p.m.
CARBURETTOR	Villiers L/Weight	Villiers S.24	Villiers S.25	Amal 276	Amal 276
PLUG : LODGE	H.14	HH.14	HH.14	R.49 *	R.49 *
GEAR RATIOS : TOP THIRD SECOND FIRST	6.5 — 8.7 16.6	5.75 or 5.75 — or 7.75 8.0 or 10.38 15.3 or 16.65	6.23 8.25 11.84 19.05	6.25 8.45 14.40 21.70	6.25 8.45 11.25 18.10
LUBRICATION	Petroil	Petroil	Petroil	Petroil	Petroil
SPRINGING : FRONT REAR	4¾″ Movement 2″ Movement	4¾″ Movement 4″ Movement	4¾″ Movement 4″ Movement	5″ Movement Nil.	5″ Movement 4″ Movement
TYRES, Dunlop, FRONT REAR	2.75″ × 19″ 2.75″ × 19″	3.00″ × 19″ 3.00″ × 19″	3.00″ × 19″ 3.25″ × 19″	2.75″ × 21″ 4.00″ × 19″	2.75″ × 21″ 3.50″ × 19″
RIM SIZES : FRONT REAR	WMO—19 WMO—19	WM1—19 WM1—19	WM1—19 WM2—19	WM1—21 WM2—19	WM1—21 WM2—19
BRAKE DRUM DIAMETER	4″ Front, 5″ Rear	5″	6″	5″	5″
REAR WHEEL SPROCKET	44 Tooth	44 Tooth	52 Tooth	52 Tooth	48 Tooth
TANK CAPACITY	2¼ gals. (10 Litres)	2¾ gals. (12.5 Litres)	3½ gals. (16 litres)	2¼ gals. (10 litres)	2¼ gals. (10 litres)
WHEELBASE	49″ (124.5 cm.)	49¾″ (126.5 cm.)	51″ (129.5 cm.)	49½″ (125.7 cm.)	50¼″ (127.6 cm.)
GROUND CLEARANCE	5″ (12.7 cm.)	6″ (15.24 cm.)	6½″ (16.5 cm.)	7½″ (19 cm.)	7½″ (19 cm.)
OVERALL WIDTH	28¼″ (72 cm.)	28¼″ (72 cm.)	28¼″ (72 cm.)	26½″ (67 cm.)	26½″ (67 cm.)
OVERALL LENGTH	78″ (198 cm.)	78″ (198 cm.)	80″ (203 cm.)	77″ (195.5 cm.)	77¾″ (197 cm.)
OVERALL HEIGHT	36¾″ (93.5 cm.)	38¼″ (97 cm.)	38¼″ (97 cm.)	41″ (104 cm.)	41″ (104 cm.)
SEAT HEIGHT	28″ (71 cm.)	31″ (78.5 cm.)	31½″ (80 cm.)	30½″ (77.5 cm.)	31″ (78.5 cm.)
WEIGHT	170 lbs. (76 kg.)	243 lbs. (109.5 kg.)	282 lbs. (128 kg.)	200 lbs. (91 kg.)	212 lbs. (96 kg.)

* Additional Lodge HH.14 Plug supplied for ordinary road work.

For 1956 the marque's flagship model was still the Cruiser, now the 75, and like its 197cc sibling there were few changes; but note the revised tank lining on both models. You could have one in chrome too, but that was an extra £3 plus tax. The 75, however, had acquired an 18in wheel at the front whilst sticking to a 19 at the rear – a strange mix.

He's lashed out on a pair of accessory panniers for his '56 Falcon 74 but completely forgotten about pillion rests, so his lady friend will be getting a toasted left foot and nowhere to put her right one – or perhaps he's a travelling salesman and she a prospect. Not a lot of difference between this and the previous model but both the wheels were now 18s, which give it a slightly cobbier appearance. Three speeds were the norm, so if you wanted four it would cost you an extra 6 guineas plus tax.

To replace the plunger Kestrel, F-B alighted on the less aggressive title of Plover (73), which was given a brand-new swinging-arm frame with 2in top tube and pressed-steel centre section, as well as updated front forks. The single cushion seat was standard but an accessory pillion seat in matching fabric could be fitted on the rear mudguard – the semi-enclosing shape of which gave a hint of styling trends to come. If you wanted battery lighting and an electric horn they, like the pillion, were extras, however. Also added to the machine tested by The Motor Cycle *had been leg shields and a windscreen, which rendered it true workaday utilitarian transport. Nevertheless it managed to record a pretty reasonable 50mph and returned 120mpg at a steady 40mph.*

MODEL	PLOVER 73	FALCON 74	CRUISER 75
Engine Bore and Stroke	55 mm. × 62 mm.	59 mm. × 72 mm.	63 mm. × 72 mm.
Max. B.H.P. ..	5.5 at 4,250 r.p.m.	8.4 at 4,000 r.p.m.	10 at 4,500 r.p.m.
Carburettor	Villiers S.19	Villiers S.25	Villiers S.25
Plug: Lodge ..	H.14	HH.14	HH.14
Gear Ratios: Top	6.5	6.27 6.27	6.23
Third	—	— or 8.45	8.25
Second	8.7	8.40 11.32	11.84
First ..	16.6	15.91 18.16	19.05
Lubrication	Petroil	Petroil	Petroil
Springing: Front ..	4¼" Movement	4¾" Movement	4¾" Movement
Rear ..	3½" Movement	4" Movement	4" Movement
Tyres: Dunlop, Front	3.00" × 18"	3.25" × 18"	3.25" × 18"
Rear	3.00" × 18"	3.25" × 18"	3.25" × 19"
Rim Sizes: Front ..	WMO-19	WM2-18	WM2-18
Rear ..	WMO-19	WM2-18	WM2-19
Brake Drum Dia. ..	4" Front, 5" Rear	5"	6"
Rear Wheel Sprocket	45 Tooth	48 Tooth	52 Tooth
Tank Capacity ..	2¼ gals. (10 litres)	2¾ gals. (12.5 litres)	3½ gals. (16 litres)
Wheelbase	49½" (125.7 cm.)	49¾" (126.5 cm.)	51" (129.5 cm.)
Ground Clearance ..	6" (15.24 cm.)	6" (15.24 cm.)	6½" (16.5 cm.)
Overall Width ..	26" (65.7 cm.)	28" (71 cm.)	28" (71. cm)
Overall Length ..	76½" (194 cm.)	78" (198 cm.)	80" (203 cm.)
Overall Height ..	37½" (95.5 cm.)	38¼" (97 cm.)	38¼" (97 cm.)
Seat Height	29½" (75 cm.)	30½" (77 cm.)	31" (78.5 cm.)
Weight	190lbs. (86.5 kg.)	243 lbs. (109.5 kg.)	282 lbs. (128 kg.)

Competition Falcons had their own separate sales leaflet for now. Both were very different machines from the 62 and 72 of a couple of years earlier but still had the Villiers 7E that was rated at 9.5bhp at 4,200rpm.

The F-B Arden Green frame was set off with a dull chrome tank lined in green on both the 76 and 77. In common with its forebear the 62 it had a Dunlop rubber saddle with cylindrical tool box beneath. A detachable direct lighting set was available with either model for an extra 5 guineas plus purchase tax.

TRIALS 76

Gearbox. 4 speed positive foot-change ; wide radios 6.52, 8.75, 15.0 and 22.5 to 1.

50 T sprocket fitted as standard.

Seat. Dunlop rubber trials saddle.

Wheels & Tyres :
Front : Dunlop Trials Universal 2.75" × 21" on WM1-21 rim.

Rear : Dunlop Trials Universal 4.00" × 18" on WM2-18 rim.

2 tyre security bolts per wheel.

Wheelbase	51¾"
Ground Clearance	8¼"
Overall Width	28½"
,, Length	78¾"
,, Height	44"
Seat Height	31"
Weight	230 lbs.

Price :— £129 0s. 0d. P.T.:— £30 19s. 3d.

SCRAMBLES 77

Gearbox. 4 speed positive foot-change ; close ratios' 6.52, 8.75, 11.73 and 18.9 to 1.

50 T sprocket fitted as standard.

Seat. Foam rubber twin seat.

Wheels & Tyres :
Front : Dunlop Sports 2.75" × 21" on WM1-21 rim.

Rear : Dunlop Sports 3.50" × 19" on WM2-19 rim.

2 tyre security bolts per wheel.

Wheelbase	51¾"
Ground Clearance	8¼"
Overall Width	28½"
,, Length	78¾"
,, Height	44"
Seat Height	31½"
Weight	233 lbs.

Price :—£131 0s. 0d. P.T. :— £31 8s. 10d.

The autumn 1957 brochure described the next season's models, and on its cover was the Cruiser 80 with AMC's own 25/T two-stroke 249cc motor. Both Plover and Falcon were all but unchanged, other than the latter switching to a Villiers 10E engine that was specially produced for Francis-Barnett/ James, but they were now the 78 and 81 respectively.

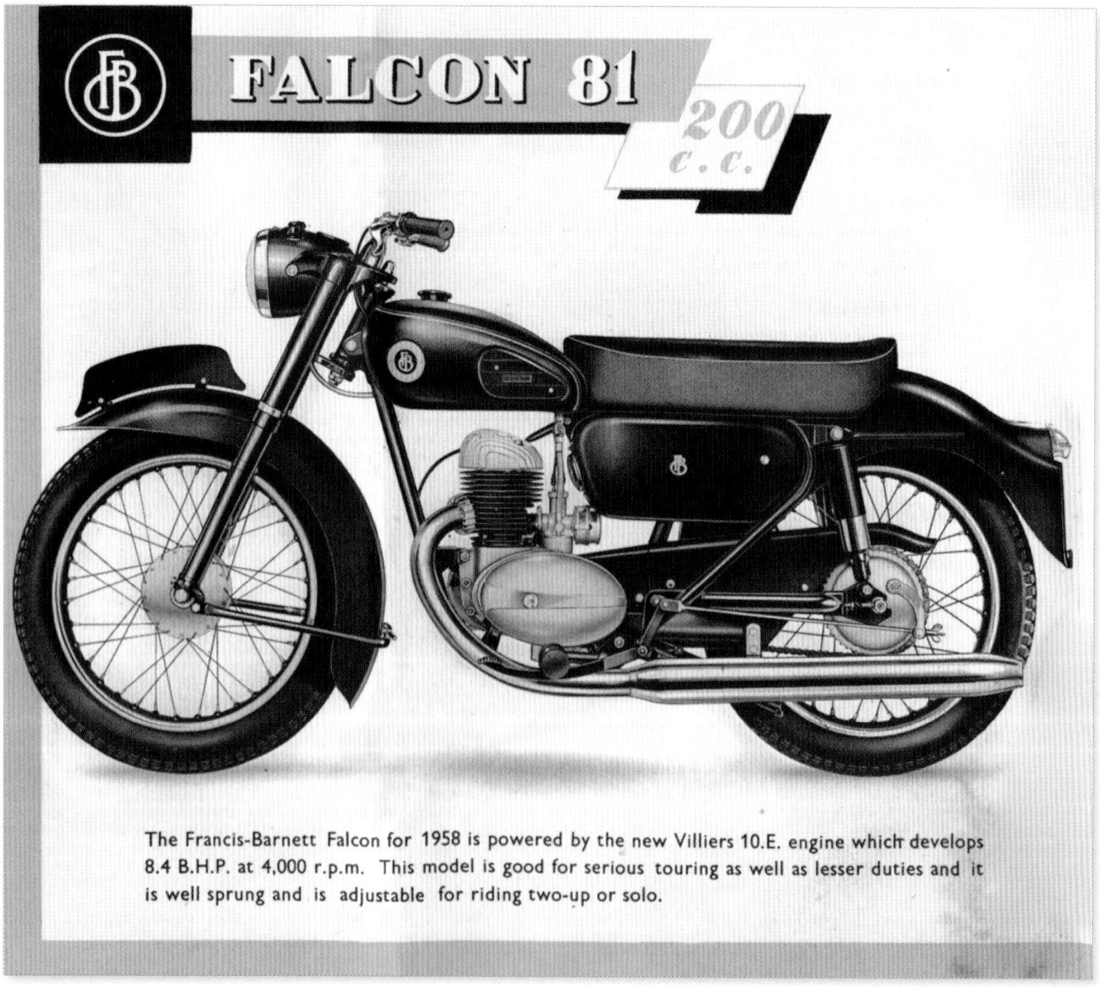

FB

FALCON 81

200 c.c.

The Francis-Barnett Falcon for 1958 is powered by the new Villiers 10.E. engine which develops 8.4 B.H.P. at 4,000 r.p.m. This model is good for serious touring as well as lesser duties and it is well sprung and is adjustable for riding two-up or solo.

The 1959 brochure's cover showed the Light Cruiser in its alternative livery of Dover White and Arden Green. It featured a smaller version of the Piatti/AMC motor. The 197 Villiers-engined Falcon 81 followed through virtually unchanged from the previous year but could now also be bought with Dover White mudguards, tank and toolbox covers as an alternative to its traditional Arden Green livery.

We are proud to fit our new 175 c.c. engine, into this clean-cut workmanlike frame specially designed and built for hard usage and a good long life.

SPECIFICATION

ENGINE UNIT:
Mk. 17/T ; 171 c.c. ; 4-speed gearbox with indicator ; Amal carburettor with strangler controlled by lever on handlebar ; coil ignition with special emergency circuit to give good spark irrespective of battery condition ; exhaust silencer quickly detachable for cleaning.

FRAME AND SUSPENSION:
Welded box-section forward member to which duplex loop tubes are bolted ; centre frame member bridges loop tubes for additional rigidity and carrying 6v., 9 a.h. battery, coil, rectifier and tool box ; all these and the carburettor totally enclosed by quickly detachable side covers.
Swinging rear fork pivoted on centre member and loop tubes ; fully damped hydraulic spring units adjustable for two-up or solo use ; telescopic oil-damped front fork with self-lubricating bushes ; wheels on journal bearings.
Centre stand ; front stand ; pillion footrests ; quick action non-spill filler cap on fuel tank.

LIGHTING:
Lucas A.C. generator giving full amperage at low engine speeds. 6″ dia. headlamp with pre-focused bulb and incorporating speedometer, ignition warning light and ammeter ; large wide angle tail lamp with provision for stop light ; combined dipper and horn switch on handlebar.

FINISH:
Stove enamelled on rust proofed base either in Arden Green throughout with transfers on tank and side covers or with Arden Green frame, forks etc. and Dover White guards, tank and two side covers. Rims and bright parts heavily chromium plated. The Arden Green finish is illustrated above and the Green and White finish is shown on the cover. Two-tone twin seat.

EQUIPMENT:
Smiths speedometer, Lucas electric horn, inflator and tool-kit.
For extras and specially designed all-weather equipment please see separate lists.

Ignition, carburettor and tools are readily accessible on removal of quickly detachable covers.

PLOVER 78

150 C.C.

SPECIFICATION

ENGINE UNIT:
147 c.c. Villiers Mk. 30 C ; 3-speed gearbox ; flywheel magneto ignition ; Villiers lightweight carburettor ; $1\frac{1}{2}$″ pipe exhausting into free expansion chamber and then on through quickly detachable silencer, with side exit. This ensures minimum noise and maximum power.

FRAME AND SUSPENSION:
2″ dia. main tube cantilevered from top of pressed steel centre section which houses battery, main cables and toolbox and also provides mountings for swinging rear fork and springs, rear engine mounting and footrests. Telescopic oil-damped front fork with self-lubricating bushes ; spring-up centre stand.
A rear friction damper is available as an extra for use on very bad roads.

LIGHTING:
Direct from flywheel magneto ; 6″ dia. headlamp with pre-focused bulb and incorporating speedometer ; large wide-angle tail lamp ; combined dipper and horn switch on handlebar. Battery and rectifier lighting, with or without stop light, available as an extra.

FINISH:
Stove enamelled on rust proofed base in Arden Green with tank panels in Dover White. Bright parts heavily chromium plated.

EQUIPMENT:
Smiths speedometer, electric horn, inflator and tool-kit.
For specially designed all-weather equipment, please see separate lists.

The Plover is easy to start and ride and requires minimum maintenance.
Specially designed legshields and windscreen can be added tax free at any time. With these fitted the Plover offers the protection and simplicity of a scooter at a very modest price.

The styling trends that were hinted at two years earlier with the Plover finally arrived for the '59 season.

The 25/T was the largest version of the unloved, Italian-designed, two-stroke motor that AMC manufactured for their Francis-Barnett and James ranges. It was the work of Vincenzo Piatti, who had previosly designed a hideous scooter that took his surname. His scooter was lacking in development and quality, the two conspiring ensure it gained a deserved reputation for unreliability.

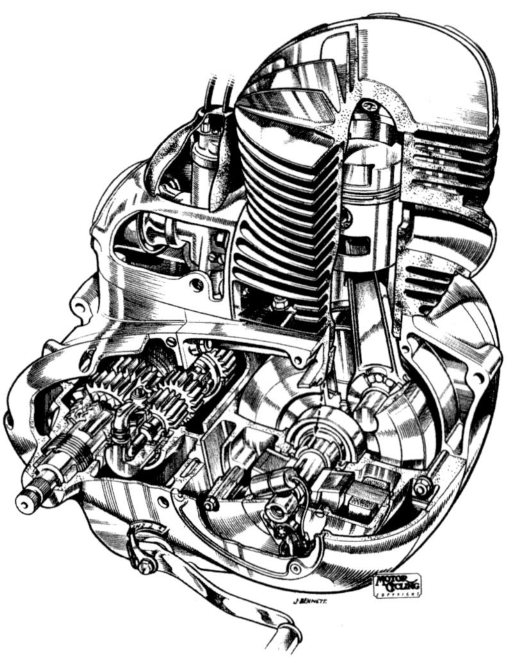

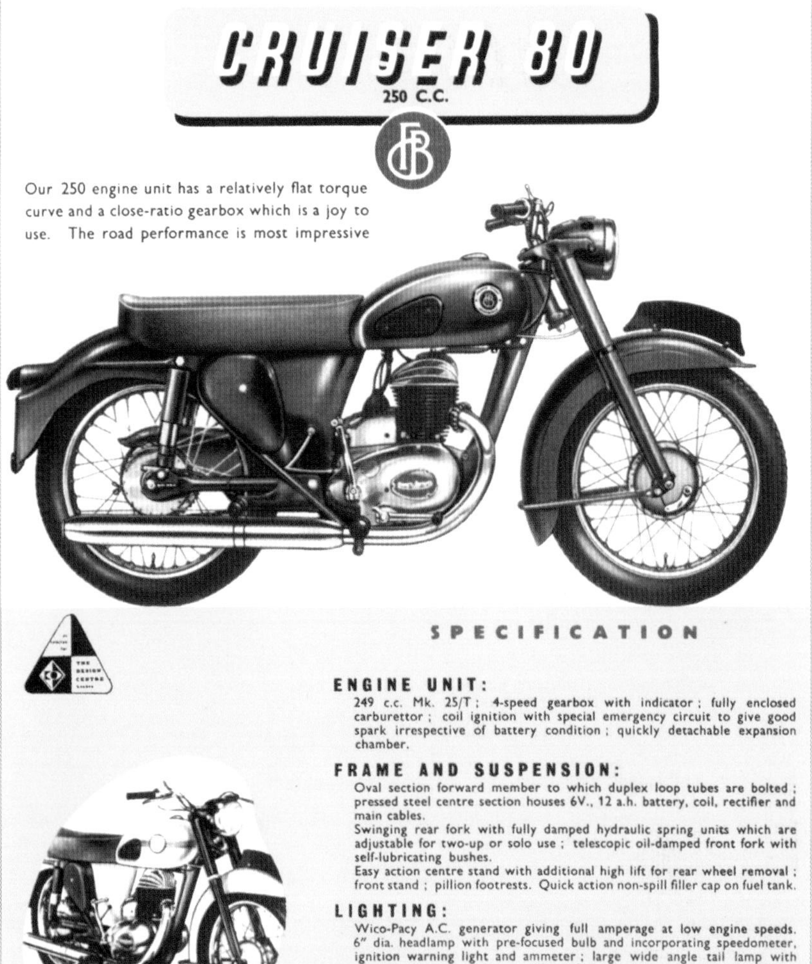

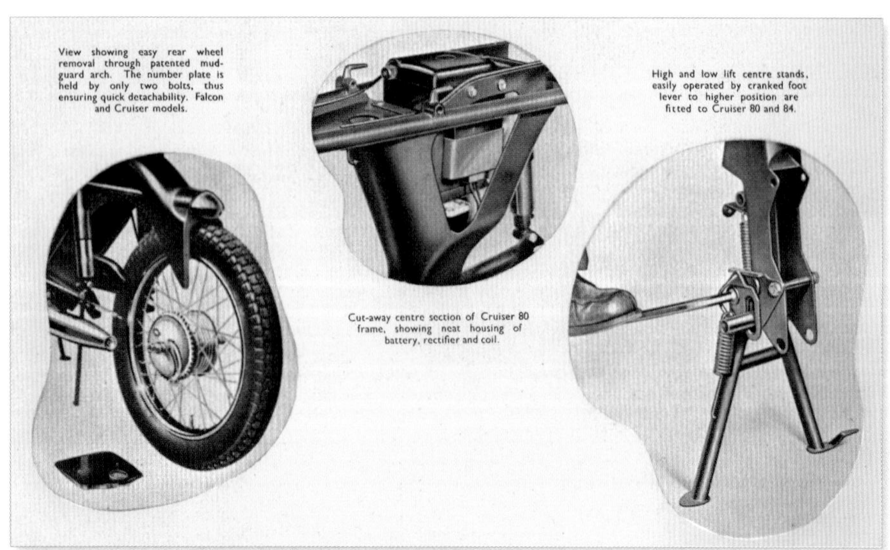

Francis-Barnett were never shy of pointing out what they considered indispensable features of their frankly utilitarian mounts.

The rear styling that was considered oh-so-chic in the late '50s. In the autumn of 1959 Bernal Osborne of Motor Cycling *took one of these, equipped with panniers filled with his typewriter and other impedimenta, across Belgium to report on the Moto-cross des Nations at Namur. Despite having the full optional screen, or perhaps on account of, it returned some 85mpg and proved capable of an indicated 60-65mph, giving this seasoned journalist an enjoyable and trouble-free journey.*

And here is the F-B Cruiser styled in the modern manner and finished in Dover White and Arden Green. The front down member carries legshields and a chromium plated safety bar. The rear portion of the model is enclosed in light but tough shields moulded in fibre glass ; these sweep back to a combined stop and rear lamp. Moulded containers to carry baggage and a "dolphin" fairing to give complete rider protection are in course of development.

Production will start early in 1959.

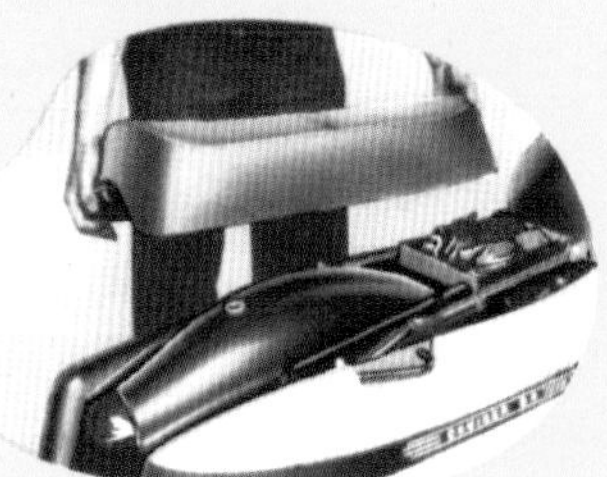

Capacious under-seat tool container with ready access to battery.

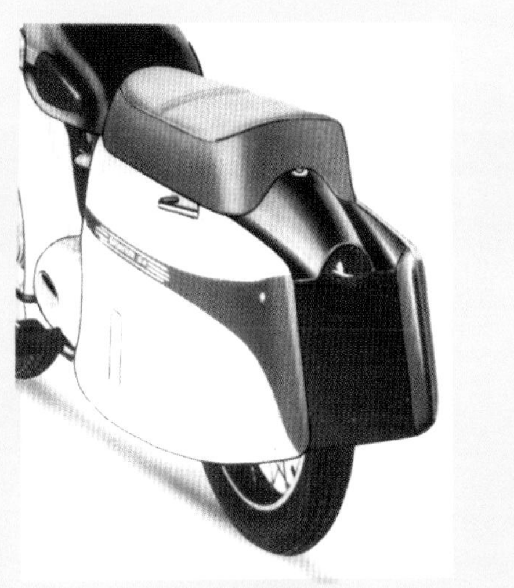

Distinctive and practical rear enclosure.

SPECIFICATION

ENGINE UNIT:

249 c.c. Special series Mk.25/C designed to operate on premium petrols ; compression ratio 9·25 : 1. Amal Monobloc single lever carburettor with large fabric filter. A.C. generator with lighting coils. Sparking plug mounted centrally ; release valve mounted in side of cylinder head. High level exhaust system calibrated for maximum extractor effect at low speeds. 4 speed positive foot change. Wide ratio gearbox.

FRAME AND SUSPENSION:

Main frame heavy gauge loop, brazed and welded ; $1\frac{1}{2}$" section down tube ; bolt-on top and bottom rear stays, top one extended forward to give reinforcement to main frame ; centre stand quickly released or detached ; chainguard on upper and lower chain runs with chain guide. Braced handlebars. 6" front, 5" rear brakes in full width hubs running on journal bearings. Polished alloy mudguards.

Special heavy duty two-way hydraulically damped front fork having polished alloy sliders and quickly detachable front spindle. Girling rear spring units.

FINISH:

Arden green stove enamel on rustproofed base. Fuel tank dull chromium plated to resist special fuels and lined green. Rims and bright parts chromium plated and polished.

EQUIPMENT:

Dunlop Trials saddle. Ball ended clutch and hand brake levers. Competition number plate, toolbox, toolkit, inflator bulb horn. Smiths Chronometric speedometer. Direct lighting set and 58T and 60T rear sprockets are available as extras.

A friend had one of these but my '56 Villiers 197-engined James Commando would run rings around it once one went cross-country. It was a heavy, unwieldy old thing for a 250 two-stroke trials bike and its reliability left much to be desired.

As I remember these AMC 250 two-strokes they had reasonable low-down power but if you thrashed them, road or cross-country versions alike, they were prone to piston and cylinder problems. Something to do with an over-heavy and inherently out-of-balance piston. The scrambles version had a heady 10.5:1 compression too.

	PLOVER 78	LIGHT CRUISER 79	CRUISER 80	FALCON 81	SCRAMBLER 82	TRIALS 83	CRUISER 84
ENGINE BORE AND STROKE	55 mm. × 62 mm.	59 mm. × 62·68 mm.	66 mm. × 73 mm.	59 mm. × 72 mm.	66 mm. × 73 mm.	66 mm. × 73 mm.	66 mm. × 73 mm.
CARBURETTOR	Villiers S.19	Amal 370	Amal Monobloc 389	Villiers S.25	Amal Monobloc 389/28	Amal Monobloc 376/138	Amal Monobloc 389
PLUG : LODGE	H.14	CCL.14	CCL.14	HH.14	RL.49	2.H.L.N.	CCL.14
GEAR RATIOS : TOP	6·64	6·9	5·9	6·1	8·0	8·0	5·9
,, ,, THIRD	—	8·96	7·7	—	10·4	11·5	7·7
,, ,, SECOND	8·91	12·77	10·9	8·2	14·9	19·4	10·9
,, ,, FIRST	16·94	20·15	17·4	15·6	23·4	28·6	17·4
LUBRICATION	Petroil	Petroil	Petroil	Petroil	Petroil	Petroil	Petroil
SPRINGING, FRONT	4¼" Movement	4¾" Movement	4¾" Movement	4¾" Movement	5¾" Movement	5¾" Movement	4¾" Movement
SPRINGING, REAR	3½" Movement	3¼" Movement	3¼" Movement	3¼" Movement	3¼" Movement	3¼" Movement	3¼" Movement
RIMS	WM1.18	WM1.18	WM2.18	WM2.18	Front WM1.21 Rear WM2.19	Front WM1..21 Rear WM219	WM2.18
SPOKES	Front 12 SWG. Rear 10 SWG.	10 SWG.	10 G.	10 G.	10 G.	10 G.	10 G.
BRAKES	Front 4" Rear 5"	5"	6"	5"	Front 6" Rear 5"	Front 6" Rear 5"	6"
TYRES	3·00" × 18"	3·00" × 18"	3·25" × 18"	3·25" × 18"	Front 2·75" × 21" Rear 3·50" × 19"	Front 2·75" × 21" Rear 4·00" × 19"	3·25" × 1l
REAR WHEEL SPROCKET	48 Tooth	52 Tooth	52 Tooth	48 Tooth	56 Tooth	56 Tooth	52 Tooth
TANK CAPACTIY	2¼ Gals. (10 Litres)	3¾ Gals. (17 Litres)	3¾ Gals. (17 Litres)	2¾ Gals. (12·5 Litres)	2¼ Gals. (10 Litres)	2¼ Gals. (10 Litres)	3¾ Gals. (17 Litres)
WHEELBASE	49½" (125·7 cm.)	51" (129·5 cm.)	51½" (131 cm.)	49¾" (126·5 cm.)	52¾" (134 cm.)	52¾" (134 cm.)	52¼" (132·7 cm)
GROUND CLEARANCE	5" (12·7 cm.)	5½" (14 cm.)	5½" (14 cm.)	6" (15·24 cm.)	8½" (21·6 cm.)	8½" (21·6 cm.)	6" (15·24 cm.)
OVERALL WIDTH	27¾" (70·5 cm.)	26" (66 cm.)	26" (66 cm.)	26" (66 cm.)	29½" (75 cm.)	29½" (75 cm.)	26" (66 cm.)
OVERALL LENGTH	76½" (194 cm.)	78" (198 cm.)	80" (203 cm.)	78" (198 cm.)	80½" (204·5 cm.)	80½" (204·5 cm.)	81" (205·75 cm.)
OVERALL HEIGHT	37½" (95·25 cm.)	39" (99 cm.)	39" (99 cm.)	39" (99 cm.)	43" (109 cm.)	43" (109 cm.)	39" (99 cm.)
SEAT HEIGHT	29½" (75 cm.)	29½" (75 cm.)	30" (76 cm.)	30½" (77·5 cm.)	31" (78·75 cm.)	32¾" (83 cm.)	30" (76 cm.)
WEIGHT	185 lbs. (84 kg.)	247 lbs. (112 kg.)	290 lbs. (131·5 kg.)	244 lbs. (111 kg.)	263 lbs. (119·5 kg.)	273 lbs. (124 kg.)	307 lbs. (139·5 kg.)

New for 1960 was Burma Red and Dover White for the Plover 86 – and that's the then-new Coventry Cathedral under construction in the background.

These are some of the catalogued accessories for 1960.

The switch from Villiers to their own power units was completed for the 1961 season and the Plover (86) now had the 15/T (149cc) AMC motor.

ENGINE UNIT :
Mk. 20/T ; 199 c.c. 4-speed gearbox with indicator ; Amal 376 monobloc carburettor with large air filter and handlebar operated air control ; coil ignition with special emergency circuit for easy starting irrespective of battery condition ; exhaust silencer quickly detachable for cleaning.

FRAME AND SUSPENSION :
Brazed and welded tubular loop main frame with bolt-on duplex cradle-type loop tubes forming rear stays.
6V., 11 a.h. battery, rectifier and carburettor air filter enclosed within covers of tool box compartment.
Swinging rear fork with fully damped hydraulic spring units which are adjustable for two-up or solo use ; telescopic oil-damped front fork with self-lubricating bushes ; wheels on journal bearings ; knock-out spindle on front wheel.
Centre stand ; front stand ; pillion footrests. Quick action non-spill filler cap.

LIGHTING :
Wico-Pacy A.C. generator giving full amperage at low engine speeds. 6" dia. headlamp with pre-focused bulb and incorporating speedometer, ignition warning light and ammeter ; large wide angle tail lamp incorporating a stop light ; combined dipper and horn switch on handlebar.

FINISH :
Stove enamelled on rust proofed base. Colour schemes available :— Arden Green throughout with white motifs. Arden Green frame, tank, etc., with Dover White guards and tool box covers. Black frame, tank, etc., with Dover White guards and tool box covers. Rims and bright parts heavily chromium plated.

EQUIPMENT :
Smiths speedometer, Lucas electric horn, inflator and tool-kit. For extras and specially designed all-weather equipment, please see separate lists.

The poor old Falcon was now an 87 and it too had been engined by AMC.

A more commodious seat for the Trials 250 and 5in brakes all round changed it into an 85, whilst the Scrambler was unchanged and remained an 82. I just had the word 'ignition' come to me – I'm pretty certain that AMC-engined off-roaders could give trouble in that department too.

	PLOVER 86	FALCON 87	CRUISER 80	CRUISER 84	TRIALS 85	SCRAMBLER 82
ENGINE BORE AND STROKE	55 mm. × 62 mm.	59 mm. × 72 mm.	66 mm. × 73 mm.	66 mm. × 73 mm.	66 mm. × 73 mm.	66 mm. × 73 mm.
PLUG : LODGE	H.L.N.	CCL.14	CCL.14	CCL.14	2.H.L.N.	RL.49
GEAR RATIOS : TOP	6·9	6·5	6·2	6·2	8·0	8·0
,, ,, THIRD	—	8·6	8·1	8·1	11·5	10·4
,, ,, SECOND	10·1	12·0	11·5	11·5	19·4	14·9
,, ,, FIRST	17·7	19·1	18·3	18·3	28·6	23·4
SPRINGING, FRONT MOVEMENT	4¼"	4¾"	4¾"	4¾"	5¾"	5¾"
REAR SPRING MOVEMENT	3½"	3"	3"	3"	3"	3"
RIMS	WM1.18	WM2.18	WM2.18	WM2.18	Front WM1.21 Rear WM2.19	Front WM1.21 Rear WM2.19
TYRES	3·00" × 18"	3·25" × 18"	3·25" × 18"	3·25" × 18"	Front2·75" × 21" Rear 4·00" × 19"	Front2·75" × 21" Rear 3·50" × 19"
BRAKES	Front 4" Rear 5"	5"	6"	6"	5"	Front 6" Rear 5"
REAR WHEEL SPROCKET	46 Tooth	50 Tooth	52 Tooth	52 Tooth	56 Tooth	56 Tooth
TANK CAPACITY	2¼ Gals. (10 Litres)	3¼ Gals. (14·7 Litres)	3¾ Gals. (17 Litres)	3¾ Gals. (17 Litres)	2¼ Gals. (10 Litres)	2¼ Gals. (10 Litres)
WHEELBASE	49½" (125·7 cm.)	49¾" (126·5 cm.)	51½" (131 cm.)	52¼" (132·7 cm.)	52¾" (134 cm.)	52¾" (134 cm.)
GROUND CLEARANCE	5" (12·7 cm.)	6" (15·24 cm.)	5½" (14 cm.)	6" (15·24 cm.)	8½" (21·6 cm.)	8½" (21·6 cm.)
OVERALL WIDTH	26½" (67 cm.)	26" (66 cm.)	26" (66 cm.)	26" (66 cm.)	29½" (75 cm.)	29½" (75 cm.)
OVERALL LENGTH	76½" (194 cm.)	78" (198 cm.)	80" (203 cm.)	81" (205·75 cm.)	80½" (204·5 cm.)	80½" (204·5 cm.)
OVERALL HEIGHT	37½" (95·25 cm.)	39" (99 cm.)	39" (99 cm.)	39" (99 cm.)	43" (109 cm.)	43" (109 cm.)
SEAT HEIGHT	29½" (75 cm.)	30½" (77·5 cm.)	30" (76 cm.)	30" (76 cm.)	31" (78·75 cm.)	31" (78·75 cm.)
WEIGHT	171 lb. (78 kg.)	267½ lb. (121·5 kg.)	290 lb. (131·5 kg.)	307 lb. (139·5 kg.)	271 lb. (123 kg.)	263 lb. (119·5 kg.)

'And now for something completely different,' or, 'We thought you might like something that looked a bit like an Ariel Arrow,' could have been the title of the 1962 brochure.

For all its futuristic looks, the Fulmar 88 was no different mechanically from the still-current Plover 86; and its space-age shape hid a fuel tank that was more lawnmower than motorcycle. It was also 8lb heavier than its more conventional sibling. I'm not too sure about the choice of name Fulmar either, as the seabird from whence it came is so called on account of a rather vile substance that is generated in the stomach and can be brought up to either repel enemies or feed its own chicks.

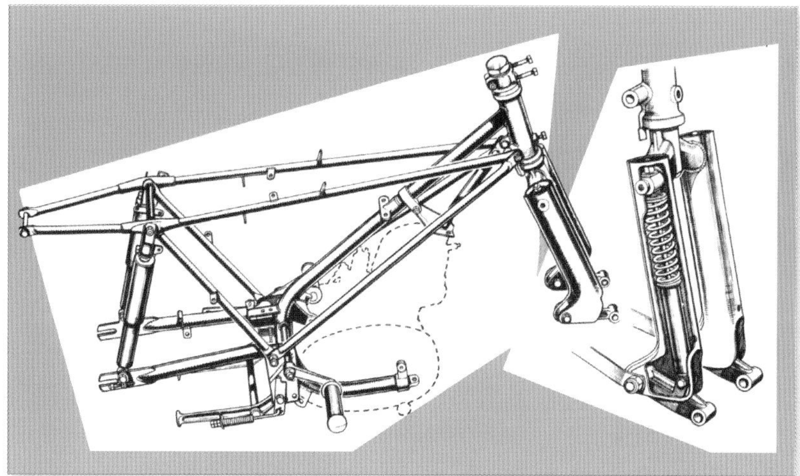

The Fulmar's frame design was quite nifty for the time and almost harked back to the firm's 1920s straight-tube contrivances. It could have handled something with a bit more poke than the 15/T, but the Armstrong leading-link forks would have let it down.

FRAME: An unorthodox frame is used. The engine and gearbox are located in a forward position and are easily accessible. The fuel tank is mounted low in the centre of the frame and has a reserve of 30 miles. Pressed steel streamlining sweeps rearward from the 6" headlamp to the rear guard and encloses a toolbox in front of the rider.
ENGINE/GEARBOX: The 149 c.c. 15/T. two-stroke engine has a built-up crankshaft substantially mounted on a pair of R.L.S.6 ball journal bearings on the drive side and a Torrington needle roller bearing on the timing side. The transfer system allows free access of incoming gases to the plug and this reduces whiskering and keeps the plug cool. Vertical slotting of the cylinder fins is used to minimise feed-back of heat from the exhaust port area. A down-draft Amal carburettor is fitted complete with air filter. The sturdy 3-speed gearbox is bolted to the crankcase and incorporates plain bronze and ball journal bearings.
FORKS: The new forks are of the leading link type. The dampers are neatly enclosed in pressed steel fairing and wide use has been made of nylon bushes to minimise maintenance. The 5" brake in a full width hub has a linkage specially designed to prevent interference with the fork movement on braking, thus ensuring rock steady retardation.
FUEL TANK The 2¼ gall. tank is positioned beneath the twin top tubes of the frame and is fitted with a quick action filler cap.
TWIN SEAT: The twin seat is hinged at the rear and has a trigger release, giving instant access to fuel tank. battery, etc.

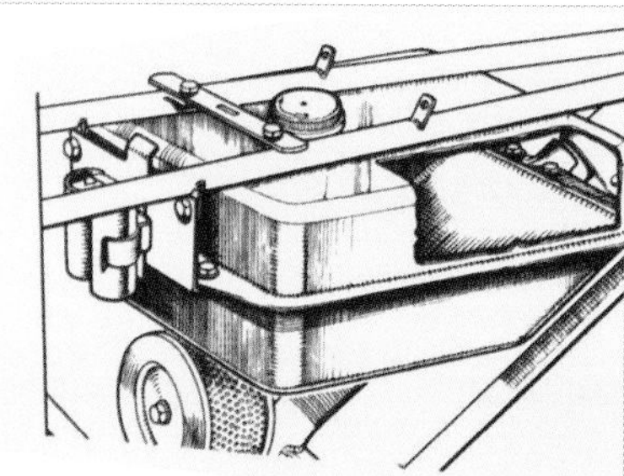

The Falcon 87 had been given some minimal restyling but, in addition to the previous season's colour schemes, could be had in Tartan Red and Black. A chromium tank was still an additional option, but now – horror of horrors – you could really waste your money and opt for some white-wall tyres. Fortunately the manufacturer spared us from them with this brochure illustration.

In addition to the still-catalogued Cruiser 80 and 84, F-B came up with the Cruiser Twin (89) and looked to Villiers once again to provide its power source.

The Cruiser Twin 89 is fitted with a Villiers Mark 2T twin cylinder two-stroke unit giving turbine smooth power and exhilarating acceleration. It is capable of serious continental touring and can be cruised all day at 55—60 m.p.h. without loss of tune.

The clean businesslike frame has an oval front down member to which are attached duplex looped tubes. Housing the battery, coil, rectifier and main cables the smooth pressed steel centre section gives rigidity to the whole assembly, resulting in positive road holding and neat appearance. Hydraulically dampened suspension front and rear, adjustable handlebars, footrests, gear and brake pedals provide both rider and passenger with a high degree of control and comfort.

Equipment includes front stand, centre stand, folding pillion footrests, 6″ brakes in full width hubs, knock-out front wheel spindle and Q-D. rear number plate for easy removal of the rear wheel.

Colours: Black and White. Arden Green and White. Extras. Chromium plated tank. White wall tyres.

For specially designed all-weather and luggage equipment please see separate lists.

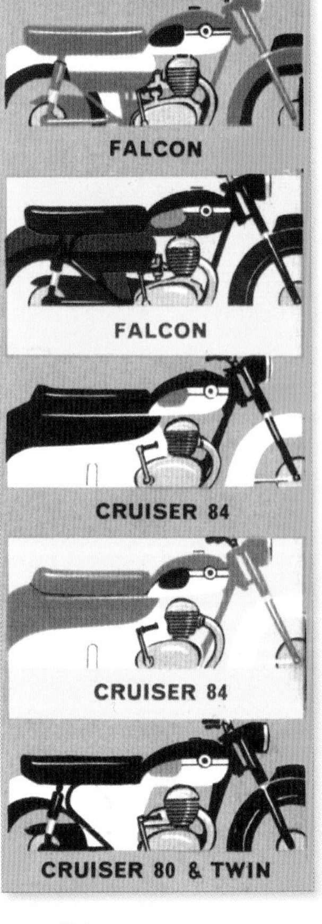

Sketches show alternative colour arrangements

So how much sportier was the Fulmar Sports 90? Well, it had a four-speed gearbox courtesy of Villiers, which specially (and kindly?) adapted one to go with the AMC engine. Other than that it was purely cosmetic in the form of a fly screen, inappropriate polished-aluminium mudguards, sportier handlebars and an abbreviated chrome chain guard. The manufacturer very kindly also equipped the little machine with a braking light; and lest you find my mention of this strange I must tell you that it was an optional extra on the regular Fulmar 88!

Francis-Barnett
motor cycles
1963

CRUISER 91 SPORTS

This is a machine for the rider who wishes to travel at above average speeds with maximum comfort and safety. It makes full use of a high compression and tuned version of the Villiers Twin engine.

Equipment includes hydraulically dampened suspension front and rear, low handlebars, rear set foot rest, gear, and brake pedals. The machine is to full "sports" specification and is ready for the road or track.

Another racy offering for '63 was the sports version of the Cruiser and this did go quite well for the time but, in common with all other full-width hub-braked Fanny Bs, the British Hub Company components were just about adequate rather than good – always tending to be on the spongy side.

1964
MOTOR-CYCLE
CATALOGUE

DISTINCTIVE... THAT'S **Francis-Barnett**

I would call that a slightly lascivious look – so what's he given her to drink?

The Plover was reintroduced for '64 with new frame and styling as a 150 capacity alternative to the Fulmar. I cannot remember anyone I knew having one – or a Fulmar, come to that – as by that time if you, or your father, were in the market for a new bike, providing you were happy to go Japanese you'd have been unlikely to go for either.

The ultimate Falcon – honest and faithful (with the exception of its AMC engine) right up to the end.

THE FALCON 87

Take the imagination of Francis-Barnett designers and add a 200 c.c. A.M.C. Villiers engine to give you all the power you need right through the rev range and you get the man-size Falcon! Safe, inexpensive (to buy, insure and run) but deceptively powerful, the Falcon with its 4-speed close-ratio gear box, cruises effortlessly between 45 and 55 m.p.h. and has enough power for a pillion rider, too. Main features include adjustable handlebars, number plates on either side of front mudguard and self-adjusting rear Girling dampers. Colours: Arden Green and White. Extras: Chrome tank.

WITH A SPECIAL ACCENT ON SPORT

THE TRIALS 92

A virtually identical machine to this standard production model ridden by Mick Ransom won the 250 c.c. Cup and made the best two-stroke performance in the Scottish 6-day trial the year it was introduced. Today the full Trials specification includes a Villiers 32A engine, a wide ratio 4-speed gearbox, 'Roadholder' folks, Girling adjustable rear suspension dampers, alloy mudguards with tubular steel stays, special light-weight wheel hubs with 5" brakes, steel petrol tank with quick action cap, wide handlebars, ball ended control levers. Colour: Arden Green and Silver. Extras: direct lighting set.

Sensibly the competition machinery returned to using Villiers engines.

THE SCRAMBLER 93

Powered by the Villiers 36A engine, with high performance alloy conversion unit, this machine is designed to the highest Moto-cross standards and one of the fastest 250 c.c. production Scramblers manufactured today. Similar to the Trials machine in frame and suspension specification, as well as in handling performance, the Scambler is made for the sportsman who wants to win! And win consistently! Colour: Arden Green, and Silver:

	Plover 95	Fulmar 88	Fulmar Sports 90	Falcon 87	Cruiser Twin 89	Sports Twin 91	Trials 92	Scram-bler 93
Bore and Stroke mm.	55 x 62	55x 62	55 x 62	59 x 73	50 x 63	50 x 63	66 x 72	66 x 72
Carburettor	Amal 375/37	Amal 375	Amal 375	Amal 376	Villiers S.22/2	Villiers S/25	Villiers S.25/5	Amal 389/34
Ignition	Flywheel Mag	Flywheel Mag	Flywheel Mag	Coil	Flywheel Mag	Flywheel Mag	Flywheel Mag	Flywheel Mag
Lighting	Flywheel Gen'tor	Flywheel Gen'tor	Flywheel Gen'tor	AC Gen'tor	Flywheel Gen'tor	Flywheel Gen'tor	—	—
Stoplight	Fitted on Btry. Ltg. Mdl. only	Fitted on Btry. Ltg. Mdl. only	Fitted on Btry. Ltg. Mdl. only	Fitted	Fitted	Fitted	—	—
Battery	Dry Cell (dir't ltg.) 10 A.H. type bat'ry ltg.	Dry Cell (dir't ltg.) 10 A.H. type bat'ry ltg.	Dry Cell (dir't ltg.) 10 A.H. type bat'ry ltg.	11 A.H.	11 A.H.	11 A.H.	—	—
Gear Ratios Top	6·7	6·7	6·87	6·5	6·2	6·21	6·88	6·6
Gear Ratios Third	—	—	8·72	8·6	8·2	8·3	9·35	10·9
Gear Ratios Sec'd	10·2	10·2	12·23	12·0	11·8	11·79	16·5	15·3
Gear Ratios First	17·2	17·2	20·20	19·1	19·0	19·0	24·8	25·3
Sprng. Mvmt. Front	4¼″	4½″	4½″	4¾″	4¾″	4¾″	6″	6″
Sprng. Mvmt. Rear	3″	2¾″	2¾″	3″	3″	3″	3⅞″	3″
Rims Front	WM 1·18	WM 1·18	WM 1·18	WM 2·18	WM 2·18	WM1·19	WM1x21″	WM1x21″
Rims Rear						WM2·18	WM3x19″	WM2x18″
Tyres Front	3.00″ x 18″	3.00″ x 18″	3.00″ x 18″	3.25″ x 18″	3.25″ x 18″	2.75″ x 19″	2.75″ x 21″	2.75″ x 21″
Tyres Rear						3.25″ x 18″	4.00″ x 19″	4.00″ x 18″
Brakes Front	5″	5″	5″	5″	6″	6″	5″	6″
Brakes Rear	5″	5″	5″	5″	6″	6″	6″	6″
Rear Wheel Sprocket		46 tooth	46 tooth	50 tooth	52 tooth	52 tooth	60 tooth	75 tooth
Tank Cap. Gl.	2¾	2¼	2¼	3¼	3¾	2¾	2¼	1½
Wheel base	49½″	49½″	49½″	49¾″	51½″	51¼″	52½″	52½″
Width Overall	24″	23½″	23½″	26″	26″	26″	25½″	
Length Ovrall	76½″	76″	73″	78″	80″	79″	80″	80″
Height Ovrall		36½″	42″	39″	39″	45″		
Seat Height	29½″	29″	29″	30½″	30″	30″	31″	31″
Grnd. Clrnce.	6½″	5″	5″	6″	5½″	5″	8½″	8″
Weight lbs.	165	225	223	267½	299	295	248	237

GREEVES

Until Bert Greeves turned his mind to constructing a specialised vehicle, the best form of transport that the physically disabled could look forward to was, as often as not, the somewhat quaint Argson – in petrol or battery electric-driven form.

Born in France of English parents, Greeves had served an engineering apprenticeship with the Austin Motor Company at Longbridge during the nascent days of the Austin Seven. From there he went into the motor trade on his own account and ended up running a garage in London where, as a spare-time project, he built what might best be described as a motorised buggy for his paraplegic cousin Derry Preston-Cobb. In truth it was not so very far removed from the Argson but from this sprang the idea for the two of them to start a business manufacturing such vehicles for others – many of them disabled as a result of World War Two.

Naming their venture Invacar they set up in business at Westcliff-on-Sea in Essex, and in 1947 began production, as well as negotiations with the Ministry of Health to secure contracts. Before long the contracts were forthcoming and by the early 1950s a move had been made to a larger site at nearby Thundersleigh.

Greeves's real love was for motorcycling, however, and he had definite views upon how he might improve upon some aspects of traditional designs – in particular frames and forks with off-road use in mind, as trials riding was his hobby.

He had already developed torsional rubber suspension units for the firm's Invacars and they were applied to a Villiers-powered prototype machine. Encouraged by the initial results, but seeking to build a frame that would withstand particularly rough usage, he and Preston-Cobb next devised a unique method of construction. A substantial cast-aluminium beam would take the place of a conventional down-tube with the (steel) top tube incorporated during the casting process, which could be done in-house, as by this time Invacar had its own foundry.

By mid-1953, after extended tests that particularly focused on cross-country work, a small range of machines was put into production for the 1954 season and a stand taken at the Motor Cycle Show.

The following year, due to an amount of customer resistance to the unorthodox, alternative road machines were introduced with conventional tubular frames and swinging-arm rear suspension, albeit retaining the Greeves forks. They remained in the catalogue for a couple of years until confidence in the composite frames translated into sufficient sales for them to be dropped, as the marque's trials and scrambles in particular found an increased following. The latter really took off with the arrival of Brian Stonebridge, however, and his work as the company's development engineer and competition manager – to say nothing of his successes as a rider – put Greeves on another plane. Tales of his amazing David-and-Goliath performances on a 197 against the best of the opposition's 500 riders went down in 1950s scrambles folklore.

It was the little Greeves's giant-killing capabilities that saw exports to the United States soar too, and in years to come the little two-strokes would frequently show the heavy BSA and Triumph 'desert sleds' the way home in off-road racing – their light weight, nimbleness and stamina often outweighing sheer power, and their simplicity less prone to mechanical failure.

In 1959 Stonebridge came close to winning the European 250 Motocross Championship but during October he was killed when Bert Greeves's car, in which he was a passenger, was in an accident with a lorry.

Tragedy was to turn to triumph, however, and the former junior team rider Dave Bickers, who'd previously been in his mentor's shadow, found his true form. An incredible sense of balance and his fluid riding style suited the softly-sprung Hawkstone scrambler (with powerful Greeves-developed square-barrel motor) perfectly; and four months after winning the season's opener in Switzerland he became the 1960 250cc champion.

At that year's Motor Cycle Show replicas of the championship machine with Greeves's own pricey in-house head and barrel conversions were a sell out and Bickers repeated his performance in 1961 – bringing the championship home for a second time. The future couldn't appear anything but bright –

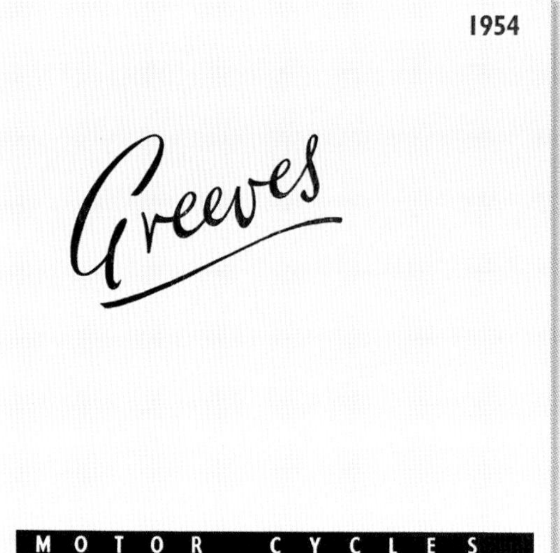

FRAME — Patented construction of revolutionary design, giving immense strength and reliability without increase of weight. Main frame member and dual engine cradles of shock resisting aluminium Alloy to B.S.S. 1490, cast under full control in our own foundry. Fully scramble tested.

FRONT & REAR SUSPENSION — Patented construction. All bearings on front and rear components of ULTRA DUTY bonded rubber bushes suspension units by rubber in torsion. NO parts in metallic contact, therefore NO wear, NO lubrication, NO adjustment, completely unaffected by water, dust or grit.
Total movement front 4"
Total movement rear 4½"
Finger adjusted dampers are provided to meet all load and road conditions; long life resin bonded friction discs unaffected by water.

FRONT FORK — Grade A taper tube to special temper. Full cantilever legs, load scientifically spread by patent crown plate construction. Greatest possible strength with controlled resilience.

REAR FORK — Grade A taper tube to special temper. Pivot bearings on bonded rubber bush. Pivot bolt straddle mounted for maximum stiffness. Both front and rear fork fully tested under arduous Scramble Conditions.

DE-LUXE — *Model 20 D*

As General Specifications with additions.

ENGINE — As General Specifications.

GEAR BOX — Villiers 4 speed foot change.
Overall ratios: Top 1 : 6.3
3rd 1 : 8.5
2nd 1 : 11.3
1st 1 : 18.2

LIGHTING — Villiers rectifier lighting set with 6" head lamp, fitted with 24/24 watt bulbs. Large tail and stop light.

HUBS — Standard design with journal bearings, requiring little maintenance. HIGH DUTY hubs as fitted to the Scrambler model, can be supplied as an extra.

TYRES — Front 2.75 × 19 Avon Ribbed Heavy Duty. Rear 3.25 × 19 Avon Supreme Heavy Duty.

FINISH — Stove enamelled in an attractive shade of Quaker Blue.

WHEEL BASE — 52 inches.

STAND — Rigid, centre type, accurately placed to raise either wheel.

WEIGHT — 240 lbs.

After a considerable period of development and testing, Greeves motorcycles, with their unique frame, suspension and front forks, were introduced to the public thus. There was also a Standard (20R) model with three-speed gearbox and finished in black. Both these and the competition versions were fitted with Villiers 8E/4 motors. The Motor Cycle *were given one of the first to try out in September 1953. They found the unfamiliar suspension to their liking and at its most comfortable on irregular surfaces if the friction dampers were just biting, some occasional pitch being rectified by adjusting the rear dampers whilst on the move! Best recorded speed was 57mph.*

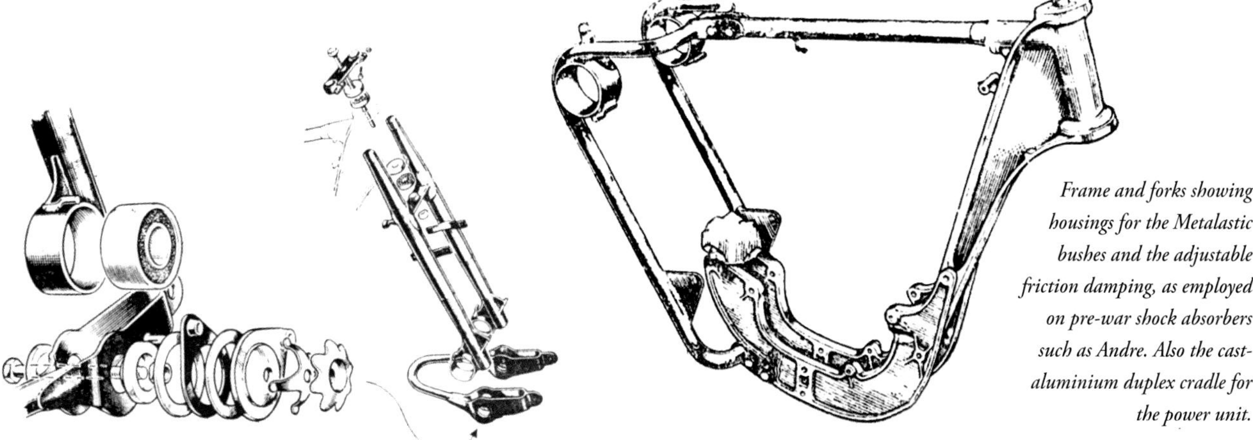

Frame and forks showing housings for the Metalastic bushes and the adjustable friction damping, as employed on pre-war shock absorbers such as Andre. Also the cast-aluminium duplex cradle for the power unit.

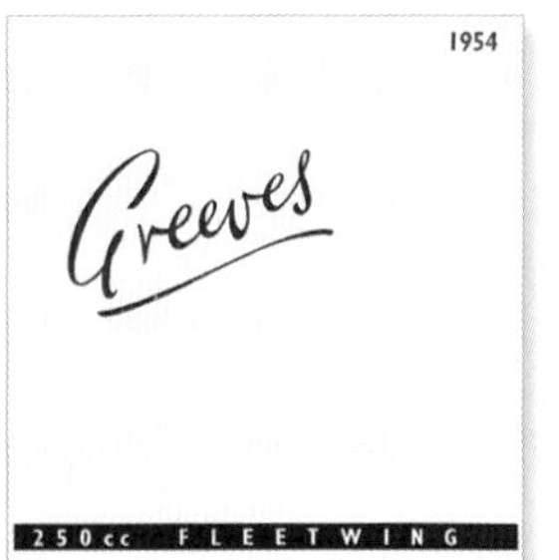

The Fleetwing 25D, announced a little while after the singles, was powered by British Anzani's twin-cylinder, 52x57mm, 242cc two-stroke – developed from the Unitwin outboard motor. "Bringing high performance with four cylinder smoothness," and, "from 10 to 60 in top gear in one smooth surge," said the brochure of its 10bhp at 4,800rpm. Motor Cycling*'s early-'54 test concurred with this exactly but the 'surge' couldn't be persuaded to carry it even a fraction past that mile a minute. Steering was found to be 'average' with a 'sluggish response' and if care was not taken to equalise the damper hand-wheel settings, side-to-side and front and rear, the road-holding 'deteriorated' – I should think so! They liked the way the quickly-detachable rear mudguard and seat gave access to the rear wheel, however. All machines, singles and twins, had whatever steel parts to be painted Jenolised in heated baths before finishing in Quaker Blue.*

SCRAMBLER — *Model 20 S*

As General Specifications with additions.

ENGINE — As General Specifications. A specially tuned engine can be supplied at extra cost.

GEAR BOX — Villiers 4 speed foot control. Overall ratios: Top 1 : 7.3; 3rd 1 : 9.9; 2nd 1 : 13.2; 1st 1 : 21.2

HUBS — These HIGH DUTY hubs are the result of two years extensive development work to produce a hub that would withstand the heavy load imposed upon it in scramble competitions.

Main hub body cast in aluminium alloy with steel brake drum and spoke flange. ⅞" diameter hardened and precision ground, spindle running in high density porous bronze bearings. Oil seals at each end and a final cork washer to eliminate the possibility of any dust or water entering the hub. Both hubs have pull out spindle bolts, which simplifies wheel removal. No routine attention required.

SADDLE — Dual seat pattern, specially strengthened for Scramble Competitions.

TYRES — Front 3.00 × 19 Avon Gripster. Rear 3.25 × 19 Avon Gripster.

FINISH — Quaker Blue or Black stove enamel, as desired.

MUDGUARDS — Aluminium competition type of adequate strength.

EXHAUST PIPE — Chromium plated. Short stub, length designed for optimum performance.

This model is supplied only in a stripped condition and it does not include speedometer or lighting set, but plain black racing number plates are supplied.

TRIALS — *Model 20 T*

As General Specifications with additions.

ENGINE — As General Specifications, a tuned engine can be supplied at extra cost.

GEAR BOX — Villiers 4 speed, wide ratio, foot control. Overall ratios: Top 1 : 6.78, 3rd 1 : 9.15, 2nd 1 : 15.6, 1st 1 : 26.4.

HUBS — High-Duty Hubs as on Model 20S.

TYRES — Front, 2.75 × 21 Dunlop Trials Universal. Rear, 3.50 × 19 Dunlop Trials Universal. Two Security Bolts to rear tyre, one to front.

FINISH — Quaker Blue stove enamel. Rims stoved silver.

MUDGUARDS — "D" Section polished Aluminium.

SILENCER — Special pattern, giving high outlet.

STAND — Designed to give clearing run to underside of Machine.

GROUND CLEARANCE — 8". Seating height 32".

This model is supplied in Competition trim and includes competition front number plate, 65 mph Speedometer, Bulb Horn, etc. No lighting is fitted, but Direct Lighting Set can be supplied as an extra.

especially as Villiers had begun the development of a purpose-built racing engine, with the first promised to Greeves towards the end of 1962.

An unlikely spin-off from the scrambles programme at about this time was the Silverstone road racer. Taking inspiration from a privately-built Hawkstone-based machine that had competed with success, the factory exhibited its own version at the '62 show with deliveries to begin in time for the next season. With the total dominance of Japanese machinery in the 250 class it would never be a contender for a world championship, but during its four-year lifespan it provided an affordable club racer that would not disgrace itself with a talented rider aboard.

Greeves's most talented rider, however, was becoming increasingly disenchanted with the machinery he was provided with, and in the late summer of '63 had bought himself, and started to compete on, a Husqvarna.

For its part Greeves felt similarly about Villiers's new Starmaker engine and was making one of its own, using an Alpha bottom end, which would go into a brand-new scrambler for 1964 – the Challenger. The redoubtable Derry Preston-Cobb, who some

Greeves's sales material was never colourful but, starting with the 1955 brochure, often as not had a really pretty lady to complement the products – in this case the new 32D Fleetmaster twin with the oversquare (60x57mm) 325cc British Anzani. New too was the Twin-Six front brake for this and the 25D Fleetwing – a coupled pair of the single-sided 6in brakes employed for other models back-to-back. The new model's additional 80cc (over the Fleetwing) translated to an extra 13mph when Motor Cycling *were lent a factory demonstrator; but fuel consumption rose from the 250's 90-ish to 60 miles, or a bit less, to the gallon. They must have remembered how to deal with the individually-adjustable dampers as they weren't mentioned, but did remark on an awkward riding position due to the handlebars fitted.*

A cheaper 250 twin, the 25R, was added to the range. It retained the Greeves cantilever front forks but had a conventional tubular swinging-arm frame with Armstrong hydraulic suspension units. Paint finish for all models this year, after Jenolising, was Moorland Blue.

would say was the real force behind what went on at Thundersleigh, managed to bring Bickers back into the fold but, did they but know it, Greeves was past its apogee. It was not that the Challenger was bad – in fact it was very good – but others, in particular Husqvarna and CZ, were forging ahead. Bickers hung on for two years and had a good deal of success on the domestic circuit, including the then popular TV scrambles, but another Championship remained elusive. At first the '65 season looked promising, with two straight wins in Europe, but his bid petered out with just his victory in the British GP to cheer his fans –and at the end of the season he moved on to CZ. Greeves would never again win a Grand Prix.

The following year marked the end of the line for road machines from the Thundersleigh factory but the Challenger continued to be updated and in production, as well as the Anglian trials version from '66, until 1968. This was also the final year for the Silverstone, which was joined by a larger 350cc Oulton version for its last season. Things had moved on in trials as well by the late '60s, with first Bultaco and then Ossa taking the honours punctuated, it must be said, by a swansong win for Bill Wilkinson on an Anglian in

Cheaper versions of the Villiers 8E-powered singles with a conventional frame were introduced as well, and Motor Cycling *tested one at the beginning of 1955; their findings were an overall fuel consumption of about 90mpg with a top speed of 60mph. Interestingly, their machine was fitted with an engine steady from head to frame, of which they made mention, whilst you will see that the brochure's example was not.*

1969. Griffons (250s and 380s) for scrambling, and Pathfinders for trials, came along in 1969. Then the QUBs (so called on account of the engine wizard who managed to increase the 380 Griffon's horsepower from 38 to 44 working at Queens University Belfast) but the company's fortunes continued to decline. The end came after Ministry of Health/Invacar contracts ceased to be renewed due to changes in the law for that class of vehicle – followed by a fire at the factory in 1977.

The name was acquired in the late '90s and since 1999 Greeves Motorcycles Ltd, based in Essex like its forebear, has specialised in restoration, manufacture of parts and even complete new machines.

The scrambler was given a conventional swinging-arm frame whilst the trials 20T remained very much as before with the exception of the rear wheel, which was now an 18in shod with 4.00-section tyre.

With a Bristol Freighter as a backdrop one of Freddie Laker's Air Bridge hostesses enhances the De Luxe Fleetstar (20D) on the cover of Greeves's October 1955 (1956 season) brochure. This and the competition machines were fitted with Villiers's 9E motor but if you wanted a cheaper Greeves the Standard Single 20R3 with Villiers 8E and three-speed 'box was still catalogued. Not sure that I like the 'ear muff' nacelle that doubled as a headlamp bracket and speedo mounting – how about you?

Models 32D Fleetmaster 325 c.c. Twin & 20D Fleetstar 200 c.c. Single

FRAME—Well proven revolutionary patented design having a strength/weight ratio unequalled by any other design. Girder section of highest quality LM6 cast aluminium alloy main frame member. Scientifically stressed design, produced under strict control from virgin ingot in our own foundry. Rear frame, tubular steel with bronze welded steel lugs.

FRONT & REAR FORKS—Grade A steel tube, tapered and tempered specially to our own requirements. Built up with steel pressings by bronze welding. Front forks of patented cantilever design giving maximum performance and even loading on special heavy duty steering head bearings. Bottom links relieving wheel spindles of aligning loads—lowest unsprung weight for best road holding.

SUSPENSION—Front: By METALASTIK Ultra-Duty bonded rubber bushes. The rubber is in torsion and there is no scuffing, rubbing, wear or metallic contact, therefore nothing to adjust or lubricate. Movement is controlled by hand adjusted friction dampers with "click" action. Maximum deflection limited by additional rubber buffers. Rear: Fork pivots on METALASTIK rubber bush. Suspension by ARMSTRONG telescopic units. Multi-rate springs for good response to light loads, retaining ability to deal with heavy shock. Hydraulically damped on both shock and rebound, fully sealed for retention of fluid. Rubber buffer stops to limit maximum travel.

SILENCER—Improved tubular pattern, body 15" long x 3" diameter heavy gauge steel. Heavily chrome plated and polished. NO small holes to choke up. Very much quieter than previous pattern but giving 5% more power from engine.

TRANSMISSION—Primary: Pre-stretched, endless, running in oil bath, ⅜" pitch Model **20D**, single; **32D**, duplex chain. Final Drive: RENOLD, ½" x 5/16". Chainguard fully valanced over top run and between chain and tyre.

PETROL TANK—4 gallon capacity, pressed steel, all welded construction. Two taps are provided giving a reserve. Large chrome plated quick release filler cap. The tank motif is an attractive cast aluminium badge.

HANDLEBARS—⅞" diameter heavily chrome plated, of our own design and manufacture. Readily adjustable in clamps. Controls are of the clip on pattern and are easily adjusted.

FOOT RESTS—Correctly placed for comfort and are fitted with large ribbed cylindrical rubbers.

SEAT—Pressed steel Dual Seat of our own design and manufacture. Full size for two adults, 25" long by 11½" wide. Dunlopillo cushion covered in long wearing plastic leathercloth.

TYRES—Front: AVON SPEEDMASTER, heavy-duty, interrupted rib, 3.00 x 19 Model **32D**; 2.75 x 19 Model **20D**. Rear: AVON "SM" studded 3.25 x 19. Studs offset to prevent heel and toe wear. Both treads with knife cuts and supporting pattern for maximum safety.

RIMS—DUNLOP WM2, heavy section, chrome plated with polished edges and matt centres.

SPOKES—10 gauge, high quality rustproof finish. 9 gauge spokes to brake side of rear wheel.

HUBS—Ball-journal bearings with protective covers, requiring no adjustment. Heavy-duty special high tensile steel spindles, 9/16" diameter. Safety retaining plates to front hub.

BRAKES—Internal expanding **20D**, 6" diameter by 1" wide both front and rear. **32D**, "Twin-six" dual 6" diameter by 1" wide front; 7" x 1⅛" rear.

MUDGUARDS—Heavy gauge steel. Special deep section with valances formed integrally. Fitted with concealed stays.

ELECTRICAL EQUIPMENT—MILLER Head Lamp, 7½" diameter, sealed beam light unit with ammeter. Stop/tail lamp, electric horn, etc. Sentercel full-wave rectifier with VARLEY 9 amp. hour semi-dry battery. Combined horn and dipper-switch on handlebar.

STAND—Centre fitting to lift either front or rear wheel, spring return, dual toe pegs.

ACCESSORIES—Speedometer, **32D**, 85 m.p.h.; **20D**, 75 m.p.h. "D" pattern. Tool box of ample size, immediately detachable, fitted under near side of dual seat, containing basic tools. 14" Dunlop pump fitted under offside of seat. Pillion footrests as Standard equipment.

DIMENSIONS—Wheel base 52". Width over handlebars 27". Ground clearance unladen 6¾". Seat height unladen 31". Weight, **32D**, 280 lbs; **20D**, 248 lbs.

FINISH—All steel parts treated in heated Jenolite bath which prevents the spread of rust in the event of damage to paintwork. This also provides a good key for the top quality stoving primer and finishing coats in our Moorland Blue. Handlebars, control levers, wheel rims, exhaust pipes and silencers, etc., chrome plated and polished. Other steel parts cadmium plated.

AIRCRAFT TYPE LOCK NUTS ARE USED THROUGHOUT THE MACHINE.

Models—20T Competition Trials and 20S Competition Scrambler

FRAME ETC.—Frame, forks, suspension, transmission, brakes, finish, etc. as Model **20D**, except that seat stays are fitted to frame.

PETROL TANK—2½ gallon capacity, pressed steel, all welded.

HANDLEBARS— ⅞" diameter, special heavy gauge of our design and manufacture.

FOOT RESTS— ⅝" solid steel bar, bolted direct to rear frame.

SEAT — *Trials Model* **20T** — Special sub-frame to take DUNLOP Trials rubber covered saddle with chrome plated springs. Dual seat available at no extra cost, if specified when ordering.

Scrambler Model **20S** —Fitted with Dual seat.

TYRES—20T—Front, 2.75 x 21 DUNLOP Trials Universal.
Rear, 4.00 x 18 ,, ,, ,,

20S—Front, 3.00 x 19 AVON GRIPSTER.
Rear, 3.25 x 19 ,, ,,

HUBS—Fitted with sealed ball-journal bearings for full protection.

MUDGUARDS — "D" section competition guards, heavy gauge polished aluminium.

STAND—Prop type, spring return to near side foot rest.

DIMENSIONS — Wheelbase 52". Width over handlebars 30¾". Ground clearance unladen: **20T**, 8½"; **20S**, 8". Seat height unladen 31½". Weight: **20T**, 228 lbs.; **20S**, 218 lbs.

ACCESSORIES—20T, 75 m.p.h. speedometer, bulb horn, etc. Front and rear number plates. Cylindrical tool box fitted on seat stay when saddle is supplied. **20S**, supplied in stripped condition but racing number plates are fitted and tool box is incorporated in dual seat as on Model **20D**.

BRITISH ANZANI

ENGINE—Twin cylinder two stroke. Bore and Stroke 60mm. x 57mm. = 325 c.c. **(32D)**: 52mm. x 57mm.= 242 c.c. **(25R).** Monoblock cylinders with greatly increased finning and new cast aluminium cylinder head. Solid skirt aluminium pistons with two high duty rings are fitted. Built up type crankshaft, hardened and ground to close limits. Roller bearing big ends and main bearing on drive side. Ball journals on magneto side and outrigger bearings. Large central bearing, hardened steel on bronze, both carrying ports for integral rotary valve ensuring even distribution etc.,

CARBURETTER—Amal monoblock pattern, designed for maximum performance with minimum fuel consumption. 250 c.c. type 375/8: 325 c.c. type 376/38.

MAGNETO—Wico-Pacy flywheel alternator providing ignition and ample current for lighting, etc.

LUBRICATION—Petroil mixture 16 to 1, for light duty 20 to 1.

VILLIERS Mk. 9E

ENGINE—Single cylinder two stroke. Bore and Stroke 59mm. x 72mm. = 197 c.c. Compression ratio 7·25—1. Close grained grey iron cylinder with increased fin area, with single exhaust port. The cylinder head is an aluminium alloy die casting generously finned. Aluminium alloy piston diamond turned. Gudgeon pin on bronze bushes. The crankshaft is mounted in four robust ball journal bearings.

CARBURETTER—Latest pattern Villiers type S.25 fitted with air cleaner incorporating starting choke.

IGNITION—Flywheel magneto with separate lighting coils. Fully accessible cam and contact points under quickly removable streamlined cover. Lighting current (Model **20D**) 36 watts rectified A.C. at 4,500 r.p.m.

LUBRICATION—Petroil mixture 16 to 1, for light duty 20 to 1.

COMPETITION SCRAMBLER—*Model 20S*

ENGINE—197cc. Villiers Mark 9E. Specially tuned by us for high performance on branded petrols.

GEARS—4-speed, close ratio, foot change. Overall ratios: Tc 7.1, 3rd 9.0, 2nd 12.6, 1st 20.8.

EXHAUST SYSTEM—Short racing stub, chrome plated, correct length for optimum performance.

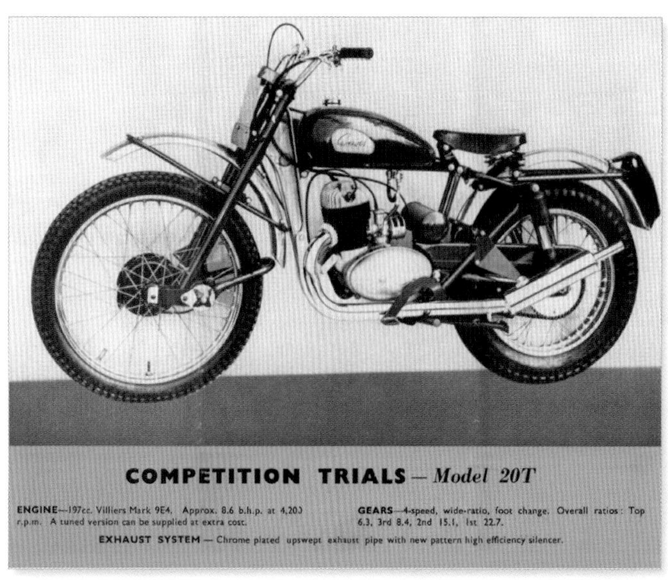

COMPETITION TRIALS—*Model 20T*

ENGINE—197cc. Villiers Mark 9E4. Approx. 8.6 b.h.p. at 4,200 r.p.m. A tuned version can be supplied at extra cost.

GEARS—4-speed, wide-ratio, foot change. Overall ratios: Top 6.3, 3rd 8.4, 2nd 15.1, 1st 22.7.

EXHAUST SYSTEM—Chrome plated upswept exhaust pipe with new pattern high efficiency silencer.

Conventional swinging-arm rear suspension with Armstrong units for the trials bike now, but in common with all models it still had adjustable damping at the front. The majority of trials riders preferred a small seat so the 20T had been equipped with a Dunlop rubber saddle.

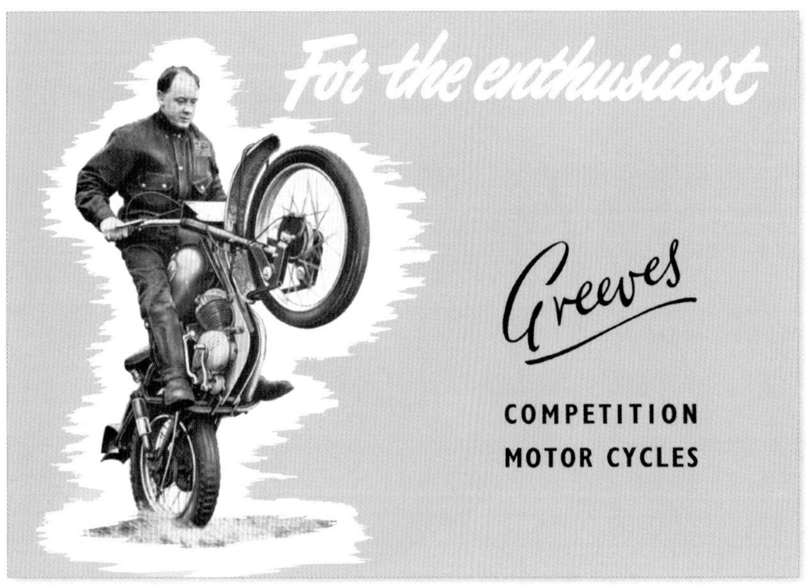

Competition bikes were given their own sales leaflet for '56 and both had the new-type front forks. Both had also been endowed with lower ratios in their four-speed 'boxes this year. The 20T's wide ratios went from 26.83:1 in bottom to 7.45:1 in top (previously 22.7:1 and 6.3:1). Wheelies are commonplace nowadays but it was only the likes of trials bikes such as this that could pull them with ease back then.

The 20S Scrambler's close-ratio 'box now encompassed a 25.28:1 bottom gear to an 8.6:1 top (previously 20.8:1 and 7.1:1). Competition frames were Moorland Blue and the steel tanks light grey. As standard it had a stub exhaust, but an exhaust pipe and silencer, along with 75mph speedo and number plates, could be specified at extra cost.

The 1957 brochure cover was a bit of a 'not' year, with a lady playing second fiddle to a rather rough-looking bloke lighting his fag. From her expression I can't be sure whether she thoroughly disapproves or wants one herself. The bike is one of the reintroduced Fleetwings with new Villiers twin that took the place of the Anzani unit employed previously for this model. The Motor Cycle *put one of the first through its paces and summed it up as 'an unconventional lightweight with zooming acceleration and smooth torque'. Flat out it would do 70 and was happiest cruising at around 55 – at which speed it returned about 65mpg.*

The British Anzani-powered Fleetmaster was still designated a 32D but had been updated with the new type of forks with Girling hydraulic dampers contained in the down-tubes. Style-wise there was a plaid pattern for the dual seat covering and a 'streamlined' battery casing that, along with the fuel tank, was finished in light grey, with the frame and cycle parts in Moorland Blue.

DE LUXE SINGLE "FLEETSTAR"

Model 20D

ENGINE: 197 c.c. Villiers Mk. 9E, 4 speed gearbox, Villiers carburettor with air cleaner. Flywheel magneto incorporating lighting coils etc. Petroil lubrication. **FRAME:** Cast aluminium alloy as 32D. **SUSPENSION:** Front: METALASTIK Bonded rubber in torsion bushes with adjustable friction dampers. Rear: ARMSTRONG hydraulic shock absorbers. **BRAKES ETC.:** 6″ front and rear WM2 heavy section rims chrome plated. **ELECTRICAL EQUIPMENT:** Rectifier lighting, 7½″ MILLER headlamp and stop/tail lamp, electric horn, Varley battery. **DUAL SEAT:** as Model 32D. **ACCESSORIES:** 75 m.p.h. speedo, tool box, pillion footrests, pump.

STANDARD SINGLE

Model 20R3

ENGINE: 197 c.c. Villiers Mk. 8E three speed gearbox. Villiers carburettor with air cleaner. Flywheel magneto incorporating lighting coils. Petroil lubrication. **FRAME:** Steel Tube as Model 25R. **SUSPENSION:** Front: METALASTIK bonded rubber in torsion bushes with adjustable friction dampers. Rear: ARMSTRONG Hydraulic shock absorbers. **BRAKES:** 5″ front and rear. Dunlop rims, chrome plated. **ELECTRICAL EQUIPMENT:** Rectifier lighting, 6″ MILLER headlamp and tail lamp, electric horn, VARLEY BATTERY. **DUAL SEAT:** As 20D. **ACCESSORIES:** 75 m.p.h. speedo, tool box, pump etc.

Road-going singles had yet to make the change to the new forks fitted to the twins and competition bikes.

Model	FLEETMASTER 32D	FLEETWING 25D	STANDARD TWIN 25R	FLEETSTAR 20D	20 R/3	TRIALS 20T	SCRAMBLER 20S
Engine	Anzani 322 c.c.	Villiers 2T 250c.c.	Anzani 242 c.c.	Villiers 9E 197 c.c.	Villiers 8E/3 197 c.c.	Villiers 9E 197 c.c.	Villiers 9E 197 c.c.
,, Bore	60 mm.	50 mm.	52 mm.	59 mm.	59 mm.	59 mm.	59 mm.
,, Stroke	57 mm.	63·5 mm.	57 mm.	72 mm.	72 mm.	72 mm.	72 mm.
Compression Ratio	8·5 : 1	8·2 : 1	8.5 : 1	7·25 : 1	7·25 : 1	7·25 : 1	
B.H.P. @ R.P.M.	16·5 @ 5250	15 @ 5500	10 @ 4500	8·6 @ 4200	8·4 @ 4000	8·6 @ 4200	
Ignition	Wico-Pacy	Villiers	Wico-Pacy	Villiers	Villiers	Villiers	Villiers
Carburettor	Amal 1″ Monobloc	Villiers S22/2	Amal 25/32″ Monobloc	Villiers S25/1	Villiers S25/1	Villiers S25/2	Villiers S25/2
Battery	Varley 9A/HR	Varley 9A/HR	Varley 9A/HR	Varley 9A/HR	Varley 9A/HR		
Lighting	Miller 7½″	Miller 7½″	Miller 6″	Miller 7½″	Miller 6″		
Petrol Tank Capacity	4 Gallons	4 Gallons	2⅝ Gallons	4 Gallons	2⅝ Gallons	2⅝ Gallons	2⅝ Gallons
Gear Ratios 1st	15·7 : 1	19·1 : 1	17·2 : 1	19·3 : 1	16·0 : 1	26·83 : 1	25·28 : 1
2nd	9·8 : 1	11·8 : 1	10·7 : 1	11·7 : 1	8·4 : 1	17·89 : 1	15·31 : 1
3rd	7·3 : 1	8·22 : 1	7·9 : 1	8·3 : 1	6·3 : 1	9·99 : 1	10·92 : 1
4th	5·4 : 1	6·2 : 1	5·9 : 1	6·5 : 1	—	7·45 : 1	8·6 : 1
Primary Chain	⅜″x7/32″ Duplex 70 Rollers	⅜″ x 7/32″ 60 Rollers	⅜″x7/32″ Duplex 70 Rollers	⅜″ x 7/32″ 58 Rollers	⅜″ x 7/32″ 66 Rollers	⅜″ x 7/32″ 58 Rollers	⅜″ x 7/32″ 58 Rollers
Secondary Chain	½″x5/16″ 122 Rollers	½″ x 5/16″ 126 Rollers	½″ x 5/16″ 124 Rollers	½″ x 5/16″ 123 Rollers	½″ x 3/16″ 124 Rollers	½″ x 5/16″ 122 Rollers	½″ x 5/16″ 126 Rollers
Front Tyre	Avon 3·00″ x 20″	Avon 3·00″ x 20″	Dunlop 3·00″ x 19″	Avon 2·75″ x 19″	Dunlop 3·00″ x 19″	Dunlop 2·75″ x 21″	Avon 3·00″ x 21″
Rear Tyre	Avon 3·25″ x 19″	Avon 3·25″ x 19″	Dunlop 3·00″ x 19″	Avon 3.25″ x 19″	Dunlop 3·00″ x 19″	Dunlop 4·00″ x 18″	Avon 3·25″ x 19″
Front Brake	Twin 6″ dia.	Twin 6″ dia.	6″ dia.	6″ dia.	5″ dia.	6″ dia.	6″ dia.
Rear Brake	7″ dia.	6″ dia.	6″ dia.	6″ dia.	5″ dia.	6″ dia.	6″ dia.
Ground Clearance	6¾″	6¾″	6¾″	6¾″	6¾″	8½″	8½″
Handlebar Width	24″	24″	27″	27″	27″	30¾″	30¾″
Seat Height	31½″ Dual seat	31½″ Dual seat	31″ Dual seat	31″ Dual seat	31″ Dual seat	31½″ Saddle	31½″ Dual Seat
Wheelbase	52″	52″	52″	52″	52″	52″	52″
Rear Wheel Sprocket	44T	52T	48T	52T	48T	52T	60T
Weight (Dry)	292 lbs.	294 lbs.	260 lbs.	254 lbs	230 lbs.	233 lbs.	223 lbs.

1957 model range and specifications.

It's the 1958 season and here are last year's couple once more, and on the same Fleetwing. They're looking a lot happier and are off somewhere, despite their clothing, so perhaps we caught them in a bad moment before. This year's road bike range comprised just the Villiers 2T-powered 25D and the 9E-powered 20D Fleetstar. The light grey used for tanks and battery casing was now referred to as Essex Grey, whilst the blue remained Moorland.

Securing the services of Brian Stonebridge to ride for Greeves had been a major coup, and to take advantage of the demand created by his successes the company introduced an additional machine up to the capacity limit as a stopgap for one season only. The 2T was not considered a competition engine but for this purpose its compression was upped by 0.3 to 1, which gave it an extra 1.5bhp. The standard 2T fitted to Fleetwings gave 15bhp on a compression of 8.2:1.

Greeves

the amazing 'Comp' bike

25SA 'Hawkstone Twin' SCRAMBLER

(For general specifications, see Competition Catalogue.)

ENGINE : Villiers Mark 2T 249 c.c. Bore and Stroke 50mm. x 63.5 mm. Compression ratio 8.5 to 1. Separate cylinder barrels, pistons fitted with chrome-plated top rings. Villiers carburettor, totally enclosed. Basic Tuning for premium petrols is carried on all engines. Develops 16.5 at 5,500 rpm.

GEAR BOX : 4-speed, foot change, close-ratio. Overall ratios; Top 7.16, 3rd 9.49, 2nd 13.6, 1st 21.91.

EXHAUST SYSTEM : Twin short racing stubs, correctly designed for optimum power.

FRAME : Well proven scientifically stressed design. Main beam of girder section cast from aluminium alloy in our own Foundry.

SEAT : Short narrow Dual Seat 19" long by 10" wide. Pressed steel construction, covered in hard wearing black plastic leathercloth.

PETROL TANK : 1¾ gall. capacity, narrow pattern pressed steel all welded construction, stove enamelled in Essex Grey.

TYRES : AVON, new pattern. Front 3.00 x 21. Rear 3.25 x 19.

DIMENSIONS : Wheelbase 52". Handlebar width 30¾". Seat Height 31½". Ground Clearance 8½". Weight 249 lbs.

ACCESSORIES : Supplied in stripped form with exhaust stubs and racing number plates.

EXTRAS : Road equipment can be supplied and consists of high-level exhaust system. 80 m.p.h. speedometer and front and rear number plates. Prices on application.

Greeves Scramble Successes 1957

EXPERTS GRAND NATIONAL
Brian Stonebridge **1st** 250 c.c. Class

SHRUBLAND PARK SCRAMBLE
Brian Stonebridge **1st** 250 c.c Class

SUNBEAM POINT TO POINT
Brian Stonebridge **1st** Lightweight Class

COTSWOLD SCRAMBLE
John Avery **1st** Ultra Lightweight

GREEVES MOTORCYCLES
CHURCH ROAD · THUNDERSLEY · ESSEX
Telephone: South Benfleet 2761 (3 lines)

The 1957 20S was little altered for '58 but had become the 20SA Hawkstone – named after the Shropshire scrambles track Hawkstone Park. As well as being the star rider Stonebridge had also become Greeves's competitions manager and chief development engineer. His expertise in tuning Villiers singles was second to none – the power developed by his works scrambler would be very different from the 13hp of the catalogued Hawkstone.

20SA 'Hawkstone' Scrambler

FRAME : Incorporating steering lockstops.

ENGINE : Villiers Competition Mark 9E 197 c.c. built to our own specifications (Basic tuning for premium petrols is carried out on all engines).

GEAR BOX : 4-speed, close ratio, foot change. Overall ratios : Top 8·6 3rd 10·92, 2nd 15·31, 1st 25·28 to 1. (Alternative overall ratios can be supplied to special order. Details on request).

EXHAUST SYSTEM : Model 20SA is fitted with a short racing stub, correct length for optimum power.

SEAT : Short narrow Dual Seat, 19″ long by 10″ wide. Pressed steel, covered in long wearing black plastic leathercloth.

TYRES : Avon. Front: 2·75″x 21″ Rear: 3·25″x 19″

DIMENSIONS : Wheel base 52″. Handlebar width 30¾″. Seat Height 31½″. Ground Clearance 8½″. Weight 223 lbs.

ACCESSORIES : Supplied in stripped form with racing number plates and short exhaust stub.

EXTRAS : Road equipment can be supplied and consists of high level exhaust system (as 20TA) 80 m.p.h. speedo and front and rear number plates. For cost see Price List.

20TA 'Scottish' Trials

FRAME: Specially modified to give a turning circle of ONLY 11′8″.

ENGINE : Villiers Mk. 9E. 197 c.c. built to our own specifications. (A special Engine is available in limited numbers at extra cost).

GEARBOX : 4-speed, foot change, wide ratio. Overall ratios Top 7·75, 3rd 10·4, 2nd 18·4, 1st 27·9 to 1. (Alternative overall ratios can be supplied to special order. Details on request).

EXHAUST SYSTEM : Chrome plated high level exhaust pipe with high efficiency Villiers silencer made from heavy gauge steel, heavily plated. This exhaust system has been developed after considerable testing and definitely gives added performance.

SEAT : Special sub frame to take DUNLOP rubber covered saddle with chrome plated springs. Short competition dual seat as fitted to 20 SA is available at no extra cost, if specified when ordering.

TYRES : DUNLOP TRIALS UNIVERSAL. Front: 2·75″ x 21″ Rear: 4·00″ x 18″.

DIMENSIONS : Wheel base 52″. Handlebar width 30¾″. Seat height 31½″. Ground clearance 9½″. Weight 233 lbs.

ACCESSORIES : 80 m.p.h. speedo, bulb horn, front and rear number plates and licence holder.

OPTIONAL EXTRA : A larger capacity (2⅝ gallon) petrol tank is available at no extra cost.

SPECIAL ENGINE : Individually built from selected components and fitted with heavy flywheel, special cylinder with modified porting and high compression head. Each engine is then thoroughly bench tested, stripped and examined before final assembly.

Stonebridge also had a large part in the development of the 20TA Scottish and took a modified version out to Germany for the 1958 International Six Days Trial where, as a member of the British Vase B team, he was unpenalised and won a Gold Medal.

What a lothario! Our unlikely-looking bloke has dumped last year's model and has his latest conquest posing on his 1959 25DB Sports Twin.

The new Sports Single 24DB with new Villiers 31A 66x72mm motor. Turbo-finned brakes were another of this year's innovations on this, the Sports Twin and the Hawkstone Special scrambler. Cycle parts were as ever Moorland Blue but the fuel tank on road sports bikes was two-tone blue and grey.

250 cc. HAWKSTONE SPECIAL SCRAMBLER MODEL 24SAS

ENGINE/GEARBOX: 246 cc. Villiers Mark 31A single cylinder two-stroke prepared in our Works and fitted with special racing piston with chrome-plated top ring. 4 speed close-ratio gearbox. (for overall ratios see data panel.) **CARBURETTOR:** AMAL Monobloc type 389 with large double element Air Filter. Flywheel Magneto with high voltage coil. **EXHAUST SYSTEM:** Short exhaust stub, chromium plated. **PETROL TANK:** 1¾ gallon capacity, narrow pattern. **SEAT:** Short narrow competition dual seat covered in real HIDE. **BRAKES:** 6" front and rear, fitted with special cast light alloy radial cooling fins to obviate brake fade and improve efficiency. **TYRES:** DUNLOP "SPORTS" Front 2.75 x 21. Rear 3.50 x 19. **ACCESSORIES:** Supplied stripped, with racing No. plates, quick-action racing twist grip and handlebars fitted with P.V.C. comp. grips. **FINISH:** Frame parts in Moorland Blue, Petrol tank, dull chrome plated.

Greeves **1959**

PRICE LIST

(As from October 30th, 1958)

	Model		TOTAL PRICE including Purchase Tax	Purchase Tax
249 cc.	**25DB**	**Sports Twin**	**£199.15. 0**	£39.12. 7
246 cc.	**24DB**	**Sports Single**	**£179.15. 0**	£35.13. 3
197 cc.	**20TA**	**Scottish Trials**	**£175. 0. 0**	£34.14. 5
197 cc.	**20TAS**	**Scottish Trials Special**	**£184. 0. 0**	£36.10. 1
246 cc.	**24TAS**	**Scottish Trials Special**	**£192. 0. 0**	£38. 1.10
197 cc.	**20SAS**	**Hawkstone Special**	**£187. 0. 0**	£37. 2. 0
246 cc.	**24SAS**	**Hawkstone Special**	**£199.15. 0**	£39.12. 7
EXTRA EQUIPMENT *(if specified when ordering)*				
	Direct lighting sets on Comp. models		**£ 6.17. 3**	£ 1. 7. 3
	Road Equipment on Hawkstone (Exhaust system, Number plates, speedometer, horn)		**£ 8. 2. 2**	£ 1.12. 2
	Alloy Finned Brakes (fitted as standard on model 24SAS)		**£ 4.10. 0**	17.10
	2½ Gallon Tank on Competition Models		**£ 1.10. 0**	6. 0
	Competition dual seat on Trials models		**£ 2.10. 0**	9.11
	"Dope" Conversion Kit on Scramblers		**£ 4. 4. 0**	

GREEVES MOTOR CYCLES · CHURCH ROAD · THUNDERSLEY · ESSEX

Largely due to Brian Stonebridge's input the Greeves range now consisted of no less than five competition machines and just two road bikes. This was the direct replacement for the short-lived Hawkstone Twin but if 250ccs were too many for you there was still the Hawkstone 197. There was also a 250 Scottish trials and two 197s but neither they nor the smaller-capacity scrambler had the aluminium turbo-finned (sometimes known as 'paddle') brakes. An example of his attention to detail that can be seen was the provision of a rear chain oiler on all competition bikes, using the nearside swinging-arm leg as a reservoir, with needle valve delivery for the lubricant.

1959 Competition Results

We are proud that Brian Stonebridge gained an overall position of **2nd** in the

250 cc. EUROPEAN MOTO CROSS CHAMPIONSHIP

1st—Swiss *Grand Prix* **1st**—Belgium *G.P.* **1st**—Italian *G.P.* **2nd**—French *G.P.* **2nd**—Luxembourg *G.P.*

SUNBEAM POINT TO POINT
Lightweight —
Manufacturer's Team Award
M. Jackson
B. G. Stonebridge
D. Bickers

COTSWOLD SCRAMBLE
Ultra Lightweight — **1st** D. Bickers

EXPERTS GRAND NATIONAL
Lightweight —
Manufacturer's Team Award
D. Bickers
W. Gwynne
T. Sharp

SHRUBLANDS PARK SCRAMBLE
Lightweight Class —
1st D. Bickers
2nd B. G. Stonebridge

Manufacturer's Team Award
D. Bickers, B. G. Stonebridge, T. Sharp

LANCS. GRAND NATIONAL
Lightweight
1st B. G. Stonebridge
3rd D. Bickers 4th G. Ward
5th B. Sharp 6th T. Sharp

Junior 350 cc.
1st B. G. Stonebridge
2nd B. Sharp 3rd T. Sharp
5th N. Crooks 6th G. Ward

SCOTT TRIAL — 150 Cup — D. C. Clegg Best Newcomer — D. Bickers

Past Trials Successes include :

SCOTTISH SIX DAYS TRIAL — (Class Winners 3 Years in Succession) • **MANVILLE CUP TRIAL** Premier Award
WELSH 3 DAYS TRIAL — Premier Award • **INTERNATIONAL SIX DAYS TRIAL** — 1 Gold Medal · 2 Bronze Medals

Relief – the avid photographer had been given the push for the 1960 brochure. Otherwise the cover remained the same to signify that the 24DB Sports Single and 25DB Sports Twin continued unchanged into the new season.

Had Brian Stonebridge not lost his life in a road accident he could well have gone on to even greater things; but as it was Greeves's up-and-coming star Dave Bickers went on to carry the torch for the firm in 1960 and make a bid for the championship.

A replica of Dave Bickers's 1960 European Championship machine was displayed at that year's Earls Court Show where it proved an instant hit. Named the Moto Cross Special it featured Greeves's own square-barrel conversion and plans for a production run of 200 had to be quickly revised in an upward direction.

Model	20DB	24DB	25DC	32DC	20TD	24TDS	24SCS
Engine	Villiers 9E 197 cc.	Villiers 32A 246 cc.	Villiers 2T 249 cc.	Villiers 3T 324 cc.	Villiers 9E 197 cc.	Villiers 32A 246 cc.	Villiers 34A 246 cc.
,, Bore	59 mm.	66 mm.	50 mm.	57 mm.	59 mm.	66 mm.	66 mm.
,, Stroke	72 mm.	72 mm.	63·5 mm.	63·5 mm.	72 mm.	72 mm.	72 mm.
Compression Ratio	7·25 : 1	7·4 : 1	10 :1	8·68 : 1	7·25 : 1	7·9 : 1	12 : 1
B.H.P. @ R.P.M.	8·6 @ 4500	12 @ 4500	17 @ 5750		8·6 @ 4500	12 @ 4500	19 @ 6000
Ignition	Villiers	Villiers	Villiers	Villiers	Villiers	Villiers	Villiers
Carburettor	Villiers S25/2	Villiers S25/6	Villiers S25/2	Villiers S25/2	Villiers S25/2	Villiers S25/6	Amal 389 1 3/16″
Battery	Exide 9 A.H.	Exide 9 A.H.	Exide 9 A.H.	Exide 9 A.H.			
Lighting	Miller 6″	Miller 6″	Miller 6″	Miller 6″			
Petrol Tank Capacity	2½ Gallons	2½ Gallons	2½ Gallons	2½ Gallons	2 Gallons	2 Gallons	2 Gallons
Gear Ratios 1st	19·35 : 1	18·17 : 1	17·54 : 1	17·54 : 1	27·9 : 1	27·9 : 1	21·92 : 1
2nd	11·74 : 1	11·0 : 1	10·9 : 1	10·9 : 1	18·6 : 1	18·6 : 1	15·31 : 1
3rd	8·36 : 1	7·85 : 1	7·6 : 1	7·6 : 1	10·4 : 1	10·4 : 1	10·92 : 1
4th	6·6 : 1	6·18 : 1	5·73 : 1	5·73 : 1	7·75 : 1	7·75 : 1	8·6 : 1
Primary Chain	3/8″ x 7/32″ 58 Rollers	3/8″ x 7/32″ 58 Rollers	3/8″ x 7/32″ 60 Rollers	3/8″ x 7/32″ 60 Rollers	3/8″ x 7/32″ 58 Rollers	3/8″ x 7/32″ 58 Rollers	3/8″ x 7/32″ 58 Rollers
Secondary Chain	1/2″ x 5/16″ 119 Rollers	1/2″ x 5/16″ 119 Rollers	1/2″ x 5/16″ 123 Rollers	1/2″ x 5/16″ 123 Rollers	1/2″ x 5/16″ 126 Rollers	1/2″ x 5/16″ 126 Rollers	1/2″ x 5/16″ 126 Rollers
Front Tyre	Avon 2·75″ x 19″	Avon 2·75″ x 19″	Avon 2·75″ x 19″	Avon 2·75″ x 19″	Dunlop 2·75″ x 21″	Dunlop 2·75″ x 21″	Dunlop 2·75″ x 21″
Rear Tyre	Avon 3·25″ x 18″	Avon 3·25″ x 18″	Avon 3·25″ x 18″	Avon 3·25″ x 18″	Dunlop 4·00″ x 18″	Dunlop 4·00″ x 18″	Dunlop 3·50″ x 19″
Front Brake	6″ dia.	6″ dia.	6″ dia.	6″ dia.	6″ dia.	6″ dia.	6″ dia.
Rear Brake	6″ dia.	6″ dia.	6″ dia.	6″ dia.	6″ dia.	6″ dia.	6″ dia.
Ground Clearance	6½″	6½″	6½″	6½″	9½″	9½″	8½″
Handlebar Width	27″	27″	27″	27″	30¾″	30¾″	30¾″
Seat Height	31½″	31½″	31½″	31½″	32½″	32½″	31½″
Wheelbase	52″	52″	51″	51″	51½″	51½″	52″
Rear Wheel Sprocket	46T	46T	48T	48T	54T	54T	60T
Gearbox Sprocket	15T	16T	18T	18T	15T	15T	15T
Weight (Dry)	238 lbs.	245 lbs.	270 lbs.	270 lbs.	233 lbs.	240 lbs.	230 lbs.

EXTRA EQUIPMENT Direct lighting sets on all competition models. Alloy finned brakes on all models except Scrambler Model 24 SCS. Road equipment on Scrambler including Speedo, complete exhaust system, horn, number plate etc. Dope Conversion kit for Scrambler including high compression cylinder head etc. Rock guard on Trials Models. For prices see current price list.

The 197 Scottish Special had been dropped whilst the other two had become the 24TAS and 20TA – having new frame main-beam castings with modified head angle to improve low-speed steering. The front forks too were altered to give greater lock, and from now on were made of the same Reynolds 531 tubing as the scramblers. The Hawkstone 250 became the 24SCS with a Villiers Mk34A motor and stronger gearbox to cope with increased power, whilst the 197 version became the 20SCS.

A greater choice of road bikes for 1961, at the forefront of which was the 32DC Sports Twin with 324cc Villiers Mk3T engine – shown here with our girl of the year. This was finished in the ubiquitous Moorland Blue with blue-and-silver tank, whilst its smaller sister the 25DC (249cc Villiers Mk2T) had one in two-tone blue. There were also a brace of Sports Singles – the 246cc 24DB and the 20DB. All had two-tone seats. Scottish trials bikes were still catalogued in 197 or 250 form but the 197 Hawkstone was now available to special order only.

Model	20DB	24DB	25DC	32DC	20TD	24TDS	24SCS
Engine	Villiers 9E 197 cc.	Villiers 32A 246 cc.	Villiers 2T 249 cc.	Villiers 3T 324 cc.	Villiers 9E 197 cc.	Villiers 32A 246 cc.	Villiers 34A 246 cc.
,, Bore	59 mm.	66 mm.	50 mm.	57 mm.	59 mm.	66 mm.	66 mm.
,, Stroke	72 mm.	72 mm.	63·5 mm.	63·5 mm.	72 mm.	72 mm.	72 mm.
Compression Ratio	7·25 : 1	7·4 : 1	10 :1	8·68 : 1	7·25 : 1	7·9 : 1	12 : 1
B.H.P. @ R.P.M.	8·6 @ 4500	12 @ 4500	17 @ 5750		8·6 @ 4500	12 @ 4500	19 @ 6000
Ignition	Villiers	Villiers	Villiers	Villiers	Villiers	Villiers	Villiers
Carburettor	Villiers S25/2	Villiers S25/6	Villiers S25/2	Villiers S25/2	Villiers S25/2	Villiers S25/6	Amal 389 $1\frac{3}{16}$″
Battery	Exide 9 A.H.	Exide 9 A.H.	Exide 9 A.H.	Exide 9 A.H.			
Lighting	Miller 6″	Miller 6″	Miller 6″	Miller 6″			
Petrol Tank Capacity	$2\frac{1}{2}$ Gallons	$2\frac{1}{2}$ Gallons	$2\frac{1}{2}$ Gallons	$2\frac{1}{2}$ Gallons	2 Gallons	2 Gallons	2 Gallons
Gear Ratios 1st	19·35 : 1	18·17 : 1	17·54 : 1	17·54 : 1	27·9 : 1	27·9 : 1	21·92 : 1
2nd	11·74 : 1	11·0 : 1	10·9 : 1	10·9 : 1	18·6 : 1	18·6 : 1	15·31 : 1
3rd	8·36 : 1	7·85 : 1	7·6 : 1	7·6 : 1	10·4 : 1	10·4 : 1	10·92 : 1
4th	6·6 : 1	6·18 : 1	5·73 : 1	5·73 : 1	7·75 : 1	7·75 : 1	8·6 : 1
Primary Chain	$\frac{3}{8}$″ x $\frac{7}{32}$″ 58 Rollers	$\frac{3}{8}$″ x $\frac{7}{32}$″ 58 Rollers	$\frac{3}{8}$″ x $\frac{7}{32}$″ 60 Rollers	$\frac{3}{8}$″ x $\frac{7}{32}$″ 60 Rollers	$\frac{3}{8}$″ x $\frac{7}{32}$″ 58 Rollers	$\frac{3}{8}$″ x $\frac{7}{32}$″ 58 Rollers	$\frac{3}{8}$″ x $\frac{7}{32}$″ 58 Rollers
Secondary Chain	$\frac{1}{2}$″ x $\frac{5}{16}$″ 119 Rollers	$\frac{1}{2}$″ x $\frac{5}{16}$″ 119 Rollers	$\frac{1}{2}$″ x $\frac{5}{16}$″ 123 Rollers	$\frac{1}{2}$″ x $\frac{5}{16}$″ 123 Rollers	$\frac{1}{2}$″ x $\frac{5}{16}$″ 126 Rollers	$\frac{1}{2}$″ x $\frac{5}{16}$″ 126 Rollers	$\frac{1}{2}$″ x $\frac{5}{16}$″ 126 Rollers
Front Tyre	Avon 2·75″ x 19″	Avon 2·75″ x 19″	Avon 2·75″ x 19″	Avon 2·75″ x 19″	Dunlop 2·75″ x 21″	Dunlop 2·75″ x 21″	Dunlop 2·75″ x 21″
Rear Tyre	Avon 3·25″ x 18″	Avon 3·25″ x 18″	Avon 3·25″ x 18″	Avon 3·25″ x 18″	Dunlop 4·00″ x 18″	Dunlop 4·00″ x 18″	Dunlop 3·50″ x 19″
Front Brake	6″ dia.	6″ dia.	6″ dia.	6″ dia.	6″ dia.	6″ dia.	6″ dia.
Rear Brake	6″ dia.	6″ dia.	6″ dia.	6″ dia.	6″ dia.	6″ dia.	6″ dia.
Ground Clearance	$6\frac{1}{2}$″	$6\frac{1}{2}$″	$6\frac{1}{2}$″	$6\frac{1}{2}$″	$9\frac{1}{2}$″	$9\frac{1}{2}$″	$8\frac{1}{2}$″
Handlebar Width	27″	27″	27″	27″	$30\frac{3}{4}$″	$30\frac{3}{4}$″	$30\frac{3}{4}$″
Seat Height	$31\frac{1}{2}$″	$31\frac{1}{2}$″	$31\frac{1}{2}$″	$31\frac{1}{2}$″	$32\frac{1}{2}$″	$32\frac{1}{2}$″	$31\frac{1}{2}$″
Wheelbase	52″	52″	51″	51″	$51\frac{1}{2}$″	$51\frac{1}{2}$″	52″
Rear Wheel Sprocket	46T	46T	48T	48T	54T	54T	60T
Gearbox Sprocket	15T	16T	18T	18T	15T	15T	15T
Weight (Dry)	238 lbs.	245 lbs.	270 lbs.	270 lbs.	233 lbs.	240 lbs.	230 lbs.

EXTRA EQUIPMENT Direct lighting sets on all competition models. Alloy finned brakes on all models except Scrambler Model 24 SCS. Road equipment on Scrambler including Speedo, complete exhaust system, horn, number plate etc. Dope Conversion kit for Scrambler including high compression cylinder head etc. Rock guard on Trials Models. For prices see current price list.

The 24TE and its square-barrel counterpart the 24TES were the direct result of prototypes developed and successfully campaigned by the factory in trials and motocross. Both had an improved frame with full-loop top-tube combined with box-section engine plates and the motor sited a little further forward. The TE retained the 12bhp 32A engine whilst the manufacturer coyly admitted to 'ample power' for the jointly-developed derivative of the same motor that went into the TES.

Competition machinery aside, the Essex concern came out with what it saw as an up-to-the-minute and attractive sportster to cater for the growing demand for such things. The Sportsman's forks were unaltered beneath space-age fairings, by the way; but even worse was the colour scheme – Mountain Blue and yellow with a red seat! If these two were not to your liking, however, the more staid 325, 250 and 200 sports were still catalogued as the 32DC, 25DC and 20DC in good old Moorland Blue.

SPORTS ROADSTERS

PERFORMANCE
COMFORT
ECONOMY

Just a few minor changes for the 1963 24TE such as a new seat with fibreglass base, revised exhaust and deletion of cylindrical toolbox. The TES, on the other hand, had more radical alterations such as trepanned engine plates, full-width alloy hubs, fibreglass mudguards and left-hand exhaust; it also had an aluminium fuel tank that had been a feature of the model since its introduction the previous year.

ENGINE (24TES)
246 cc. Greeves / Villiers. Bore and stroke 66 mm. x 72 mm. Special aluminium alloy Cylinder and Head designed to give ample power at low and middle engine r.p.m. ideally suitable for trials work. Carburettor : Amal Monobloc 1" bore. Heavy flywheel magneto with high voltage coil. Gearbox : 4 speed wide ratio, clutch fitted with NeoLangite inserts. Overall ratios : 1st 27.9 : 1, 2nd 18.6 : 1, 3rd 10.4 : 1, Top 7.75 : 1.

As the direct result of the success enjoyed by a little-known club racer named Reg Everett, who had built and circuit-raced a machine based largely on a Greeves scrambler, the factory decided to go into production on its own account. Unveiled at the 1962 Motor Cycle Show as the 24 RAS, deliveries during the following year were sporadic and its performance generally disappointing. Subsequent models, starting with the RBS, were more successful, however, and one won the Lightweight Manx GP in '64, with an RCS winning the same race in '65. Production ran on with the RDS and finally ended with the RES of 1967.

FRAME: This has been specially designed and developed for racing incorporating the GREEVES patented cast aluminium beam resulting in a rigid light assembly. The main beam is die cast from LM6 aluminium alloy to British Standards specification. The steering head is fitted with Timken taper roller races.
Electrically welded box section steel cradle plates carry the engine unit.

SUSPENSION: Front: unique GREEVES design providing extreme rigidity and really positive steering. METALASTIK bonded rubber bushes are used and hydraulic damping is provided by GIRLING units concealed within the REYNOLDS '531' chrome molybdenum steel fork down tubes. These fork tubes have been lengthened to improve ground clearance. Rear: GIRLING multi-rate springs with hydraulic damping. Square section swinging arm.

ENGINE: This is believed to be the most powerful standard production engine in the world for its size and weight. 246 c.c. GREEVES/VILLIERS Mark 36A specially developed by us for racing. Bore and stroke 66mm x 72mm Compression ratio 12.7:1. Power output approx. 31 bhp at 7,400 rpm. Exclusive GREEVES light alloy cylinder and head fitted with a cast-in iron liner with precision machined ports for consistent high power output. Special racing piston with narrow chrome plated rings. Cut away crankcase and latest pattern chain case for maximum cooling.

CARBURETTOR: 1⅛" AMAL Type 5GP2 racing pattern with remote float chamber. Spare jets supplied.

IGNITION: Flywheel magneto with high voltage coil.

EXHAUST SYSTEM: Specially developed with "tuned" expansion chamber giving an extremely wide power spread over the entire speed range.

PETROL TANK: Readily detachable glass fibre reinforced plastic with quick release cap. 2 gallon capacity (Imp.).

TRANSMISSION: Primary: Pre-stretched endless chain, running in oil bath. Final drive: Renold's ½" x 5/16" chain.

CONTROLS: Clamp-on handlebars providing adjustments both vertically and horizontally. Light alloy racing control levers with finger operated cable adjusters.

HUBS: High-duty full width 6" diameter aluminium alloy hubs fitted with cast iron brake liner. Front hub fitted with floating brake back plate with nylon bushed torque arm. Air scoop to provide cooling. Rear hub fitted with knock out spindle. Vane type shock absorber to smooth out transmission loads. Brakes size, 6" x 1⅛".

RIMS and TYRES: Racing pattern aluminium alloy. AVON 'Cling' racing tyre. Front: 2.75 x 18. Rear: 3.00 x 18.

SEAT: Slim streamlined racing seat, made in glass fibre reinforced plastic trimmed high-duty PVC cloth.

GEAR BOX: 4-speed, close ratio, high-duty gears. Overall ratios (with 50 tooth rear wheel sprocket as supplied) 1st: 15.2-1, 2nd: 10.6-1, 3rd: 7.56-1 and 4th: 5.96-1.

FAIRING: Small streamlined racing pattern carefully designed not to impair engine cooling, etc.

EQUIPMENT: Latest pattern Smith's rev. counter, 0-10,000 r.p.m. fitted into an anti-vibration mounting. Glass fibre racing number plates. Two alternative rear wheel sprockets. Additional main jets. Comprehensive handbook with engine performance graphs.

FINISH: Frame parts, etc., bonderised for rust protection, providing excellent key for high quality stove enamel. Steel parts, other than chrome, are cadmium plated. Aircraft type locknuts are used throughout.

DIMENSIONS ETC.
Seat height 28½"
Wheelbase 50¾"
Handlebar width 23"
Weight 189 lbs.

Development had lifted the prototype's power from 24bhp to over 30 but weight saving had also been a priority – for instance, the original machine's frame tubes were of 14 gauge whilst for production they were reduced to 16.

The machine that Greeves pinned its hopes on for 1964. Successful on the home circuits but all too often outclassed abroad.

The improved Mk2 Challenger looked as though it might bring its maker the European championship with two early season wins for Dave Bickers but thereafter there was just one more victory and he finished in third place behind Victor Arbekov and Joel Robert on CZs.

Greeves always referred, naturally I suppose, to its road bikes as Roadsters and for 1964 there were three – with this as the flagship. Supporting cast was made up of the 250cc 25DC Mk2 Sports Twin (both twins had the Villiers Mk4T) and the 200cc 20DC Sports Single powered by the evergreen Villiers 9E. The Motor Cycle *tested a 250 Essex in the spring of '63 and managed to get it up to 75mph. If you cruised it at 60, however, the petroil consumption was less than 55mpg.*

HJH

To the best of my knowledge HJH produced only one sales brochure, depicting the 1956 range, to be handed out and available at the time of the firm's one-and-only appearance at Earls Court in November 1955. Motor Cycling, *however, tested a plunger-framed Dragon a few months earlier, and very impressed with it they were too – going into raptures about both its standard of finish and its handling: "On the open road it could be heeled far over on corners and steered as though on rails." The middle gear of its three-speed 'box would take it within a whisker of 50 and top to 58mph, whilst at a steady 40mph it used a gallon of petroil every 100 miles.*

Alongside the River Neath, in the Welsh town of the same name, lies Canal Road, and it was there that Harry Hulsman's Canalside Works manufactured motorcycles from 1954 until 1956.

Reputedly starting with just £1000 lent him by friends, Hulsman sensibly refrained from attempting to design, develop and manufacture his own brand from scratch and instead looked to other manufacturers for his component parts. The choice of an engine/gearbox assembly was both easy and almost inevitable – Villiers. But it was DMW, or rather Metal Profiles, that he called upon for his frames and forks.

Being little more than a cottage industry staffed by local motorcycle enthusiasts, and in more than one case by a wife too, allowed a certain amount of latitude in interpreting model specifications. Great pride was also taken in the finish, and although assembled from humble components HJHs often featured metallic paint finishes as well as a good deal more chromium plate than their direct competitors.

By the autumn of 1955 business was such that one of the less expensive stands, tucked away in a corner at the top of the exhibition hall, was taken at Earls Court. Out of the seven models on display, four were roadsters and three were competition machines – a particular speciality of the makers.

Harry Hulsman had something of a reputation as a salesman but even so I find the story that he

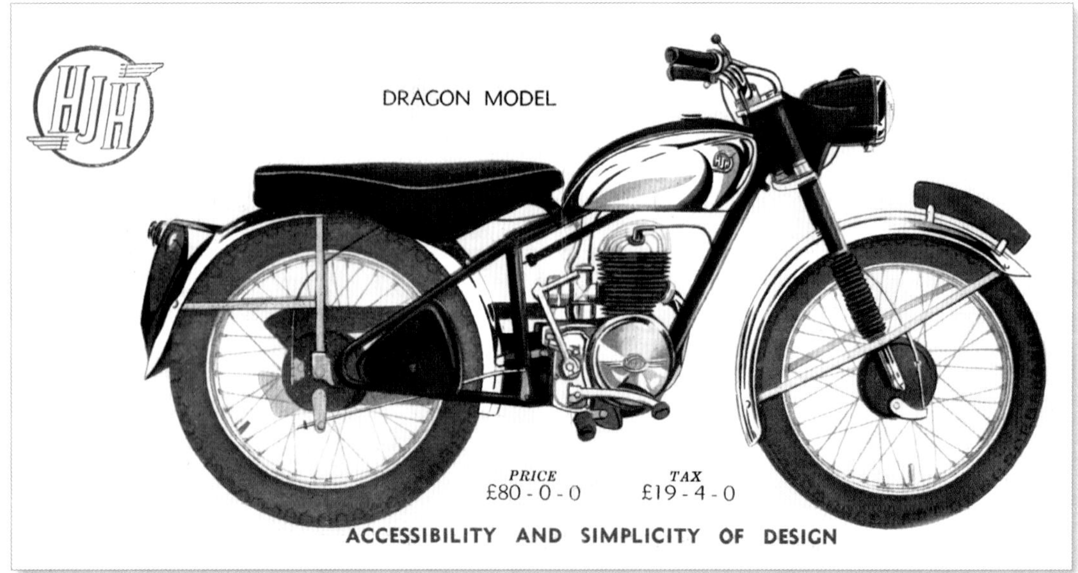

With an all-in price including purchase tax of a fraction under the magic £100, the Dragon was around £40 cheaper than any other Villiers 197-engined machine on the market. The catch was that you'd have to put up with a rigid frame whilst all the rest had swinging-arm by this stage. A 147cc version, the Dragonette, was also listed at just under £90, or £124 for a Sports Dragonette with swinging-arm frame, but neither appeared in the brochure.

The swinging-arm Sports Dragon, although understandably pricier than the (very) basic Dragon, was still a little cheaper than something like the Frances-Barnett Falcon 74 at just over £137 but both were pretty basic and for £154-odd you could get one of the more sophisticated new four-speed DMW 200Ps.

took orders for something around 1,000 machines during the course of the show a little hard to swallow. Nevertheless, he returned to South Wales brimming with confidence, plans for a new model and more orders than he and his existing workforce could realistically cope with – which became apparent over the ensuing months. Although a good number of machines were turned out it was well nigh impossible to source additional suitably-skilled labour locally. The business also lacked the funding to undertake enlargement, and what was tantamount to a hand-to-mouth existence led to sporadic deliveries from suppliers and a resultant shortfall in output.

It was none of these factors directly that spelt the end for HJH, however, but Harry's somewhat cavalier attitude to purchase tax and the necessity to pay it rather than plough it back into the business. With an accrued debt of something over £4,000 leading to a court appearance that resulted in a choice between a fine or six months in prison, he was able to escape the latter when friends had a whip-round. But the inevitable had to be faced and it was the end of his two-year adventure, the premises henceforth being used for light engineering and motorcycle repairs.

I do believe old Harry was being a bit fanciful with this one. With the same compression ratio, same power output (8.4bhp at 4,000rpm) and same set of ratios in its three-speed 'box, whatever was so super sporting? Surely not the Earles forks, which nudged the weight up from the Sports Dragon's 204lb to 206lb.

If you really wanted to push the boat out you could save up £149 8s 5d and get yourself an SSD with enhanced mechanical specification that gave it very nearly another whole horsepower and a four-speed gearbox. You also got a dinky little pair of sidelights along with rectifier/battery lighting instead of direct, and a triangular toolbox rather than a cylindrical one slung under the saddle. On all models except the scrambler that's the tyre pump mounted beneath the top frame tube, by the way.

SPECIFICATION

Model	Engine	Frame	Forks	Petrol Tank	Lighting	Tyres	Wheel Base	Ground Clearance	Brakes	Weight	Finish
Dragon	8 E	Rigid	Telescopic	2½ gall.	Direct	F 275 x 19 / R 275 x 19	46″	9″	5″	185 lbs.	Maroon, Beige, Jade Green, Electric Green
S.	8 E	Swinging Arm	Telescopic	2½ gall.	Direct	F 300 x 19 / R 325 x 19	47″	9″	5″	194 lbs.	
S.S.	8 E	Swinging Arm	Earls	2½ gall.	Direct	F 300 x 19 / R 325 x 19	47½″	9″	5″	206 lbs.	
S.S.D.	8 E	Swinging Arm	Earls	2½ gall.	Rectifier Battery	F 300 x 19 / R 300 x 19	47½″	9″	6″	208 lbs.	
Trials	7 E	Swinging Arm	Earls	1¼ gall.	—	F 275 x 21 / R 400 x 19	46″	10½″	6″	190 lbs.	Silver-Chrome
Scrambler	7 E	Swinging Arm	Earls	1¼ gall.	—	F 300 x 19 / R 350 x 19	47″	9½″	6″	196 lbs.	Silver-Chrome

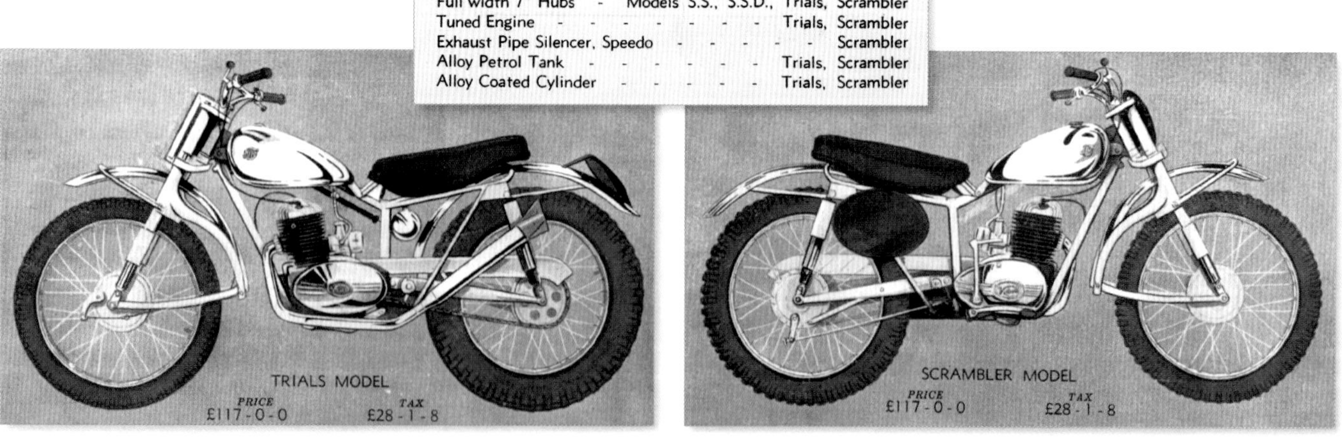

EXTRAS

Engine 9 E	Models S.S., S.S.D., Trials, Scrambler
Full width 7″ Hubs	Models S.S., S.S.D., Trials, Scrambler
Tuned Engine	Trials, Scrambler
Exhaust Pipe Silencer, Speedo	Scrambler
Alloy Petrol Tank	Trials, Scrambler
Alloy Coated Cylinder	Trials, Scrambler

Many trials riders preferred plain telescopic forks, maintaining that they gave more precise steering, but for those who were happy with alternative front ends and a 197 Villiers the HJH was bracketed by the DOT at about £140 and a Cotton at nearly £149, with the increasingly popular Greeves at £161.

HJH's own production manager Tom Wheeler doubled as the competition manager and works rider in both trials and scrambles. Before joining the firm he had been Welsh scrambles champion with a BSA in 1953 and the following year on an Ariel; but his build suited larger machines, so few successes came his way with the little home-grown 197s, and after the business folded he returned to bigger bikes for scrambling.

JAMES

When young Harry James set up his small factory in Birmingham's Constitution Hill around 1880 to build ordinary cycles he was but one of dozens, if not hundreds, of hopefuls eager to make their way in the world through this relatively new mode of transportation. Through hard work and determination he was one of those that succeeded, and by 1890 had been able to expand into a largish factory in Sampson Road North, Sparkbrook, by which time his firm had begun to manufacture the latest safety bicycles.

The advent of the pneumatic tyre at around this time was really putting cycling on the map, and in addition to touring machines for both gentlemen and ladies the company would produce specialist racing cycles to cater for this burgeoning sport – its wares much in evidence at the major exhibitions of the day such as the Stanley Cycle Show.

Royal Enfield had the Flea and James had its Clockwork Mouse, as the ML 125 was nicknamed. Thousands saw action with the armed forces, including a large number that were paradropped into France to aid communications and troop movements in the aftermath of D-Day. With the war at an end, this barely civilianised version was marketed just as soon as was practicable.

Whilst his business was flourishing Harry's health was in decline, however, and the year before he stepped down from its day-to-day running the James Cycle Co. was incorporated as a public company and his works manager Charles Hyde took over as managing director.

Not long after, like numerous other cycle manufacturers, James became interested in the concept of powered machines, and with the assistance of a newly-employed engineer named Frank Kimberley had the first of these running by 1902. By the following year machines that were little more than bicycles fitted with a proprietary Belgian Minerva engine were listed, but in 1904 the company introduced what it claimed was the first loop-frame motorcycle, its power unit also being Belgian but by FN. Seemingly this was soon discontinued while a new factory was being built at nearby Greet, and from there James launched its extraordinary Safety model in 1909 to supplement more conventional fare.

The brainchild of a sometime member of the Cycle Engineers Institute named Renouf, the Safety had a great many unconventional (some would say eccentric) features such as its road wheels being carried on live axles out-rigged to the right of the frame, hub-centre steering and a front mudguard that doubled as its fuel tank to name a few. Remarkably, this something-over-500cc oddity, subject to various modifications, remained on the firm's books until 1912, at which point it became one of the earliest manufacturers to introduce all-chain drive. This was a 3½hp machine, produced in addition to the existing chain-cum-belt models that by the following year were to include two-strokes and a small four-stroke V-twin of the firm's own construction.

Production continued throughout the First World War and although some machines saw active service the bulk of the work that they carried out for the Ministry was for varying types of munitions.

Post-war the company continued with two-strokes as well as both single and V-twin four-strokes – the latter having had a capacity hike to 750cc by the early '20s. For a while in mid-decade two-strokes were discontinued but they reappeared in lightweight form and powered by a 172cc Villiers for 1928, along with a larger 247cc Villiers; this year also saw the first of James's saddle tank machines with redesigned frames. Although the firm was little interested in racing it did produce a number of OHV sports models, including an OHV version of the V-twin with four speeds for

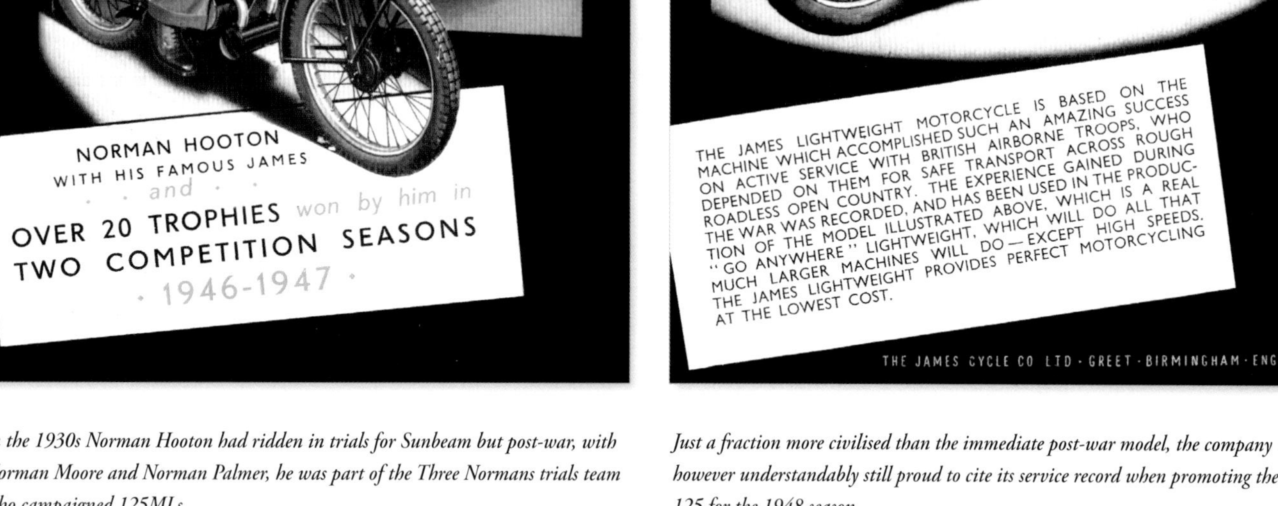

In the 1930s Norman Hooton had ridden in trials for Sunbeam but post-war, with Norman Moore and Norman Palmer, he was part of the Three Normans trials team who campaigned 125MLs.

Just a fraction more civilised than the immediate post-war model, the company was however understandably still proud to cite its service record when promoting their 125 for the 1948 season.

1929, and a single-gear speedway version was also catalogued.

The financial slump was soon upon James, however, and although the flagship V-twins were still produced the emphasis became increasingly upon more utilitarian fodder such as the two- and four-stroke singles of just under 250cc.

Another result of the times was the firm's purchase of the small Baker motorcycle concern, which produced a range of lightweights with bolt-up duplex frames and Villiers engines. It was also then that James ventured into the realms of small commercial vehicles, with the introduction of the 'Handyvan' – a quaint three-wheeled device featuring motorcycle-type girder front forks and wheel steering; it was powered at first by a 250 single and then a side-valve V-twin. It was made throughout the 1930s and, whether in pick-up or van form, was advertised to be able to cope with loads of up to 12cwt – this capability doubtless encouraging its makers to title it the Samson.

Although single-cylinder four-strokes lasted beyond the V-twin's eventual demise in 1935 it was increasingly two-strokes that made up the bulk of production, and one of these was approved by the War Department come World War Two. Affectionately known as the Clockwork Mouse, James's little Villiers 122cc-engined military lightweight was built in large numbers and saw service in many theatres of war, its small size belying its capabilities and usefulness. Post-war these same attributes applied and, apart from an Autocycle, the Mouse (now turned out in the company's maroon rather than khaki) represented the firm's entire range until a Villiers-engined 197 augmented the small group for 1949.

The last year of the old order proved to be 1950, and customers could choose between an Autocycle or a real motorcycle of 98cc, whilst there were various 125s and 197s including competition versions, as well as a choice of front forks and even rear springing on the 197.

By the end of the following year James had been taken over by the AMC group, which already owned (since 1947) one of its direct main rivals Francis-Barnett. Initially the two firms were more or less allowed to pursue their separate paths but from the 1956 show onwards, where both marques displayed a new 250 fitted with AMC's own two-stroke single, they become ever more intertwined – so much so that by 1960 the little 98cc Comet alone had a Villiers engine.

The decision by AMC to manufacture its own range of two stroke motors when it could call on Villiers' far superior products is one of the enigmas of the British motorcycle industry, but suffice to say they are remembered with little affection.

AMC partially came to its senses in the early '60s, however, by incorporating some Villiers know-how in its own motors and once again employing pure Villiers' powerplants for James's competition machines and 250 twin. By this time, Francis-Barnett production, along with what remained of the workforce, had been transferred to James's Greet factory but there was a general air of despondency about the place despite outward appearances. "James are made by the AMC Group – first and foremost makers of motorcycles," read the slogan on the rear of the 1964 brochure. Not for long, it would transpire: by the end of 1966 the once-proud Associated Motor Cycles was not going to be making anything ever again, and James was no more.

This is a 1948 125ML fitted with the optional speedo with exposed drive – pre-war fashion – from the front hub. But what jubilee is being referred to? The 50th (Golden) anniversary of the firm's foundation in 1897? Or, less likely, the 40th (Ruby) anniversary of their recommencement of motorcycle manufacture in 1908, following a lapse?

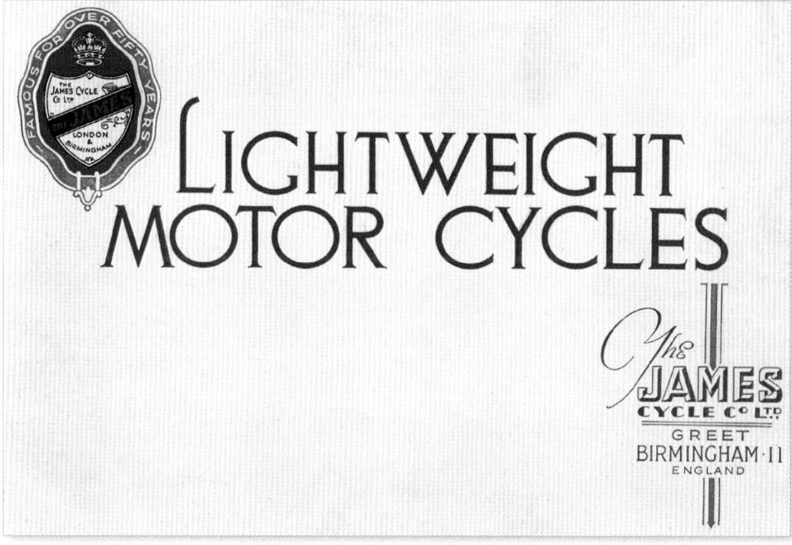

For the 1950 season the company published a rather splendid brochure complete with embossed cover.

98 c.c. "SUPERLUX" AUTOCYCLE

SPECIFICATION

Frame James' patented and registered design, all steel unit construction, made of high grade steel tubing. Specially low-built design, with perfect steering angle.

Forks James' registered design, made of high grade weldless steel taper tubes, reinforced by liners at essential points. Central compression spring, long bearings to shafts, adjustable fork links to compensate for wear.

Wheels Built on specially designed James' hubs with Dunlop rims and 2.25-in. x 21-in. tyres.

Brakes Powerful 4-in. internal expanding hub brakes operated by handlebar levers.

Saddle Multi-spring soft top adjustable for height from 31½-in. to 35½-in.

Handlebars "Comfort" type, fully adjustable for height and reach, chromium plated.

Mudguards Deep section steel with strong half round supporting stays.

Toolbox Made of pressed steel, rigidly mounted in convenient position.

Chain Guards Half round section fitted over rear driving chain and pedal chain.

Engine Shields Provide efficient protection to the rider against mud or water.

Rear Stand Secured by efficient spring clip to rear mudguard when not in use.

Tank 1½ gallon capacity, finished attractively in maroon enamel with blue side panels suitably lined.

Transmission Primary and final drive by heavy roller chain throughout and ½-in. x ⅛-in. pedal chain.

Equipment Comprises a full kit of tools, inflator, bulb horn, and rear carrier.

Finish The whole machine is attractively finished in brilliant maroon enamel on special bonderized rust-proof surface, wheels "Argenized" finish.

Power Unit The Villiers 2-Stroke Engine fitted to this Model is an entirely new design, the bore and stroke being 47 m.m. x 57 m.m. and the exclusive features include a light alloy detachable cylinder head, flat top aluminium alloy piston, ball bearing main shaft and roller bearing big end.

Clutch Two plate cork insert clutch running in oil with normal handlebar control and actuated by Bowden cable.

Lubrication *Engine :* Lubrication is effected by the Petroil System, whereby oil is added to the petrol in the tank by means of the measure incorporated in the filler cap, and thus all parts of the engine are automatically and efficiently lubricated when running. *Primary Chain Case :* Is filled at the easily accessible filler cap to level controlled by oil level plug.

Carburetter Villiers special Lightweight needle jet type operated by simple thumb lever. A strangler is fitted for easy starting.

Air Cleaner A fine mesh gauze is fitted over the carburetter choke tube.

Ignition By Villiers flywheel magneto.

Lighting Also provided by the Villiers flywheel magneto which produces ample current for powerful head and tail lights while the engine is running. A parking light may be provided by fitting a dry battery inside the headlamp.

Extra Smith's Lightweight Speedometer, and Electric (Battery) Horn, may be supplied extra to the above specification.

PERFORMANCE DATA : Speed 30-35 m.p.h., fuel consumption 160 m.p.g.
Measurements : Length 6-ft. 7-in. Width 2-ft. 1-in. Weight 126 lbs.

The 1950 98cc Comet De Luxe Lightweight differed from the Standard version in that it had 19in wheels with 2.50-section tyres, a carrier, triangular toolbox on the rear frame as opposed to smaller cylindrical one beneath the saddle, and most importantly battery-powered lighting that was charged via a rectifier by the flywheel magneto, which allowed for an electric horn and braking light. Gear changing was effected by means of a handlebar-mounted trigger connected by cable to the two-speed gearbox.

98 c. c. "COMET" STANDARD LIGHTWEIGHT

SPECIFICATION

Frame	James' patented and registered design, all steel unit construction, made of high grade steel tubing. Specially low-built design, with perfect steering angle.
Forks	James' registered design, made of high grade weldless steel taper tubes, reinforced by liners at essential points. Central compression spring, long bearings to shafts, adjustable fork links to compensate for wear.
Wheels	Built on specially designed James' hubs with Dunlop rims and 225 x 21 tyres.
Brakes	4-inch internal expanding hub brakes, front operated by handlebar lever, and rear operated by foot pedal.
Saddle	Multi-spring soft top with three point suspension.
Handlebars	Fully adjustable for height and reach, chromium plated.
Mudguards	Deep section steel with strong half round supporting stays.
Toolbox	Made of pressed steel, rigidly mounted in convenient position.
Chain Guard	Fitted over rear driving chain (front chain runs in oilbath).
Stand	Central prop stand with automatic return to riding position, effective for front and rear wheels.
Tank	1¾ gallon capacity, finished attractively in maroon enamel with blue side panels suitably lined.
Transmission	Primary and final drive by heavy roller chain.
Finish	The whole machine is attractively finished in brilliant maroon enamel on special bonderized rust-proof surface, wheels "Argenized" finish.
Equipment	Comprises a full kit of tools, inflator, and bulb horn.
Power Unit	The Villiers 2-stroke Engine fitted to this Model is an entirely new design, the bore and stroke being 47 m.m. x 57 m.m., and the exclusive features include a light alloy detachable cylinder head, flat top aluminium alloy piston, ball bearing main shaft and roller bearing big end.
Gearbox	Two speed incorporated in the engine unit and operated by a simple thumb lever on handlebar.
Clutch	Two plate cork insert clutch running in oil with normal handle-bar control and actuated by Bowden cable.
Lubrication	*Engine :* Lubrication is effected by the Petroil System, whereby oil is added to the petrol in the tank by means of the measure incorporated in the filler cap, and thus all parts of the engine are automatically and efficiently lubricated when running. *Gearbox and Primary Chaincase* are filled at the easily accessible filler cap to level controlled by oil level plug.
Carburetter	Villiers special Lightweight needle jet type operated by twist grip control. A strangler is fitted for easy starting.
Air Cleaner	A fine mesh gauze is fitted over the carburetter choke tube.
Ignition	By Villiers flywheel magneto.
Lighting	Provided by the Villiers flywheel magneto which produces ample current for powerful head and tail lights while the engine is running. A parking light may be provided by fitting a dry battery inside the headlamp.
Extras	Smith's lightweight non-trip Speedometer, James' design combined crash bar and legshield, Heavy Duty Rear Carrier. Electric (Battery) Horn.

PERFORMANCE DATA : 40 m.p.h. maximum speed, 160 m.p.g. fuel consumption.

Measurements : Length 6-ft. 1-in. Width 2-ft. 3¾-in. Weight 128½ lbs.

De Luxe version of the 122cc Lightweight had slightly larger 3.00-section tyres as well as the same luxuries as the 98cc De Luxe – from larger triangular toolbox to battery lighting with electric horn and braking light, the whole lot adding an extra 24lb to the weight. I wonder if you've noticed another feature that elevated De Luxe owners above other mere mortals – a chromium tip for the front mudguard!

122 c.c. "CADET" STANDARD LIGHTWEIGHT

SPECIFICATION

Frame James' patented and registered design, all steel unit construction, made of high grade steel tubing. Specially low-built design, with perfect steering angle.

Forks James' Telescopic Cushion Fork, fitted with Rubber Suspension by Dunlop Rubber Co. Limited. Patents applied for.

Wheels Built on specially designed James' hubs with WMO rims and Dunlop 2.75 x 19 tyres.

Brakes 5-inch internal expanding hub brakes, front operated by handlebar lever, and rear operated by foot pedal.

Saddle Multi-spring with three point suspension and large size soft top.

Handlebars Fully adjustable for height and reach, chromium plated.

Mudguards Deep section steel with strong half round supporting stays.

Toolbox Made of pressed steel, rigidly mounted in convenient position.

Chain Guard Half round section, fitted over rear driving chain (front chain runs in oilbath).

Stand Central prop stand with automatic return to riding position, effective for front and rear wheels.

Tank 1¾ gallon capacity, finished attractively in maroon enamel with blue side panels suitably lined.

Transmission Primary and final drive by heavy roller chain.

Finish The whole machine is attractively finished in brilliant maroon enamel on special bonderized rust-proof surface, wheels "Argenized" finish.

Equipment Comprises a full kit of tools, inflator, and bulb horn.

Speedometer Smith's non-trip type, driven by internal gear in rear hub.

Power Unit The 2-stroke Engine fitted to this Model is an entirely new Villiers Unit, the bore and stroke are 50 m.m. x 62 m.m. The cooling is improved over previous types by the extra large fins on both the cylinder head and barrel, and this together with a light alloy cylinder head, flat top aluminium alloy piston, ball bearing main shaft and roller bearing big end have combined to form a compact powerful unit which develops 4.9 brake h.p. at 4000 r.p.m.

Gearbox Three speed positive stop foot change, bolted direct to the engine crankcase.

Clutch Two plate cork-insert clutch running in oil with normal handlebar control and actuated by easily adjustable Bowden cable.

Lubrication *Engine :* Lubrication is effected by the Petroil System, whereby oil is added to the petrol in the tank by means of the measure incorporated in the filler cap, and thus all parts of the engine are automatically and efficiently lubricated when running.
Gearbox : Is filled at the accessible filler cap, and a dip stick is provided to check level.
Primary Chaincase : Is filled by filler cap low down on outer cover which acts as automatic check on oil level.

Carburetter Villiers Lightweight needle jet type operated by twist grip control. A strangler is fitted to the air cleaner for easy starting.

Air Cleaner An efficient fine mesh cleaner is fitted to the carburetter air intake, to prevent the ingress of dust to the engine.

Ignition By flywheel magneto which is incorporated in the engine unit.

Lighting Provided by the Villiers flywheel magneto which produces ample current for powerful head and tail lights while the engine is running. A parking light may be provided by fitting a dry battery inside the headlamp.

Extras James' design combined crash bar and legshield, Heavy Duty Rear Carrier, Electric (Battery) Horn.

PERFORMANCE DATA : 48 m.p.h. maximum speed, 120 m.p.g. fuel consumption.

Measurements : Length 6-ft. 7-in. Width 2-ft. 3¼-in. Weight 166 lbs.

The ultimate James for 1950 – unless you wanted one of the Competition models, that is.

The 197cc Captain De Luxe was almost the top of the range at £104 15s 6d – but not quite, because a little over £6 more was required to reach that pinnacle. However, if you wanted to save money rather than spend it there was a girder-fork option for Cadets and Captains that reduced the price by nearly £4.

197 c. c. "CAPTAIN" REAR SPRUNG LIGHTWEIGHT

SPECIFICATION

Frame James' registered design, all steel unit construction, made of high grade weldless steel tubing. Specially low-built design, with perfect steering angle. Rear portion arranged for sturdily designed rear suspension.

Forks James' Telescopic Cushion Fork, fitted with Rubber Suspension system by Dunlop Rubber Co. Limited. Patents applied for.

Wheels Built on specially designed James' hubs with heavy section WMI rims and Dunlop 300 x 19 tyres,.

Brakes 5-inch internal expanding hub brakes, front, operated by handle-bar lever, and rear operated by foot pedal.

Saddle Multi-spring with three point suspension and large size soft top.

Handlebars Fully adjustable for height and reach, chromium plated.

Mudguards Deep section steel with strong half round supporting stays and decorative motif.

Toolbox Triangular shape in pressed steel, fitting neatly into offside rear frame triangle.

Chain Guard Half round section fitted over rear driving chain (front chain runs in oilbath).

Stand Central prop stand with automatic return to riding position.

Tank 2¼ gallon capacity, finished attractively in maroon enamel with blue side panels suitably lined, and top strip chromium plated.

Transmission Primary and final drive by heavy roller chain.

Finish The whole machine is attractively finished in brilliant maroon enamel on special bonderized rust-proofed surface, wheels "Argenized" finish, and bright parts heavily chromium plated.

Equipment Comprises a full kit of tools, inflator, electric horn, ammeter, and a heavy-duty rear carrier.

Speedometer Smiths' non-trip driven by internal gear in rear hub.

Power Unit The 2-stroke Engine fitted to this Model is an entirely new Villiers Unit, the bore and stroke are 59 m.m. x 72 m.m. and the engine has been developed to produce 7.5 brake h.p. at 4000 r.p.m., and its efficiency is enhanced by the detachable light alloy cylinder head, flat top aluminium alloy piston, ball bearing main shaft and roller bearing big end.

Gearbox Three speed positive stop foot change, bolted direct to the engine crankcase.

Clutch Two plate cork-insert clutch running in oil with normal handle-bar control and actuated by easily adjustable Bowden cable.

Lubrication *Engine :* Lubrication is effected by the Petroil System, whereby oil is added to the petrol in the tank by means of the measure incorporated in the filler cap, and thus all parts of the engine are automatically and efficiently lubricated when running.
Gearbox : Is filled at the easily accessible filler cap, and a dip stick is provided to check level.
Primary Chaincase : Is filled by filler cap low down on outer cover which acts as automatic check on oil level.

Carburetter Villiers middleweight needle jet type operated by twist grip control. Rich mixture for easy starting is provided by thumb lever on Handlebar through Bowden cable to carburetter needle.

Air Cleaner An efficient fine mesh cleaner is fitted to the carburetter air intake, to prevent the ingress of dust to the engine.

Ignition By flywheel magneto, which is incorporated in the engine unit.

Lighting Is provided by an accumulator charged through a rectifier from the Villiers flywheel magneto to give full lighting at all times whether the engine is running or not. A rear stop light is operated by application of the rear brake.

Extra The James' design combined crash bar and legshield and Smiths' TRIP speedometer may be supplied extra to the above specification.

PERFORMANCE DATA : 58 m.p.h. maximum speed, 100 m.p.g. fuel consumption.

Measurements : Length 6-ft. 7-in. Width 2-ft. 3¼-in. Weight 215 lbs.

This gives the general idea but is not strictly accurate as, for instance, all Cadets and Captains were fitted with speedos. What is more, every single James had a clutch lever and to suggest that such a thing was an 'exclusive feature' is nothing short of ridiculous!

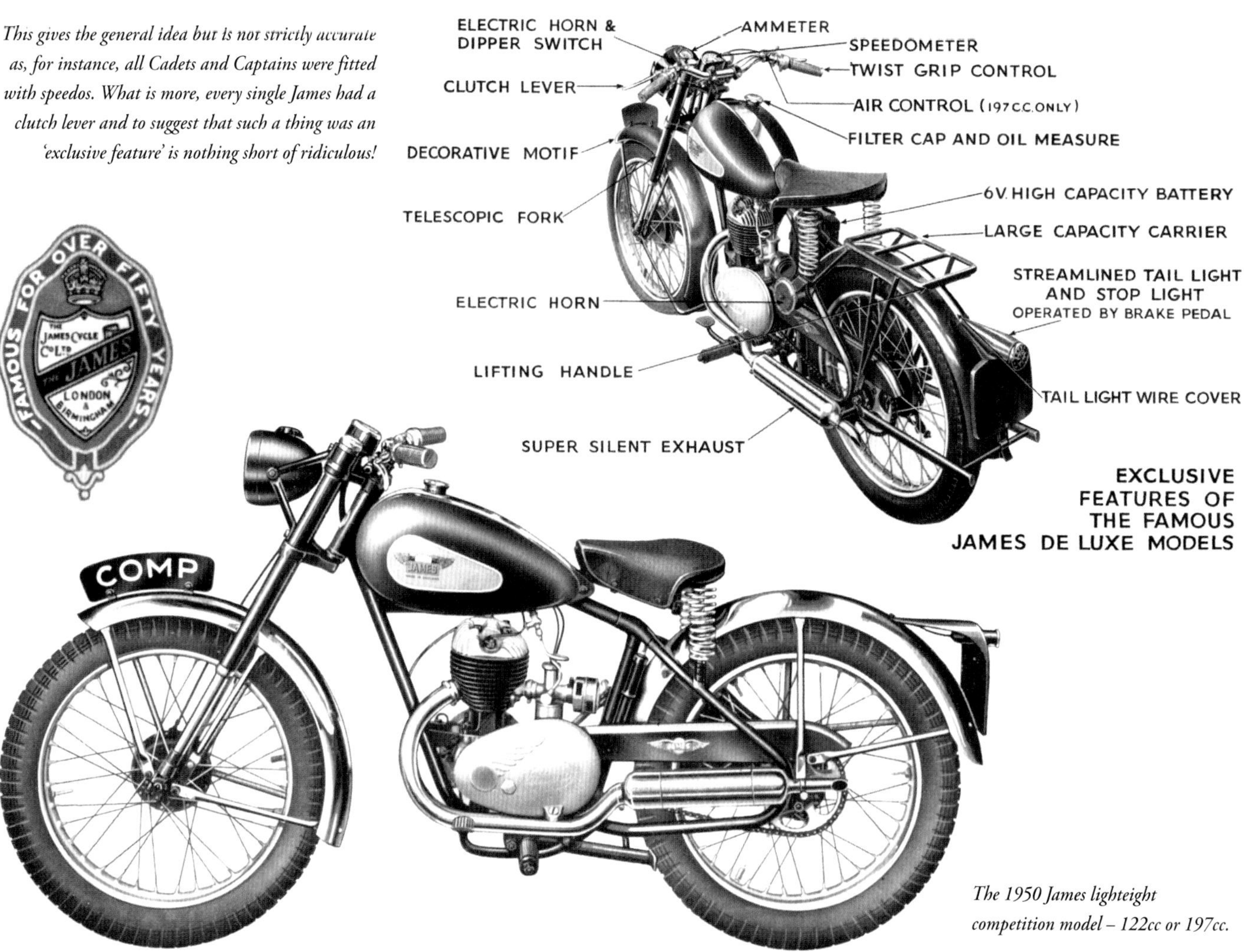

The 1950 James lighteight competition model – 122cc or 197cc.

LIGHTWEIGHT COMPETITION MODEL

AS SUCCESSFULLY PROVED IN THE INTERNATIONAL SIX DAYS RELIABILITY TRIAL

SPECIFICATION

Frame Special Competition type giving higher saddle position than normal.

Forks James' Dunlop Telescopic cushion forks adapted for Competition usage.

Wheels Built on specially designed James' hubs with heavy section WMI rims, heavy spokes and nipples and Dunlop Universal Tyres, rear 3.25″ x 19″ and front 2.75″ x 19″, both fitted with security bolts.

Brakes Powerful action. 5″ diameter front and rear.

Saddle Multi-spring with large size soft top.

Handlebars Competition Type. Fully adjustable for height and reach.

Mudguards Polished alloy with extra long stays giving adequate clearance.

Ground Clearance 6¼″ with stand, 8″ without.

Tank 2¼ gallon capacity.

Power Unit Either the Villiers latest design engine Series 10.D. 122 c.c. with bore and stroke of 50 m.m. x 62 m.m. which develops 4.9 b.h.p. at 4400 r.p.m., or Series 6E. 197 c.c. with bore and stroke of 59 m.m. x 72 m.m. which develops 7.5 b.h.p. at 4000 r.p.m.

Gearbox Three speed positive stop foot change bolted direct to crankcase.

Standard Gear Ratios 122 c.c. model—1st 30.68, 2nd 16.0, Top 9.44.
197 c.c. model—1st 21.64, 2nd 11.33, Top 6.66.

Clutch Two plate cork-insert clutch running in oil.

Air Cleaner An efficient fine mesh cleaner is fitted to the carburetter air intake, to prevent the ingress of dust to the engine.

Ignition By flywheel magneto incorporated in the engine unit.

Lighting Direct from the Villiers flywheel magneto. 5½″ head-lamp detachable for Competition work.

Equipment Comprises a full kit of tools, inflator and speedometer.

Extra The rear sprung frame as illustrated on page 16.

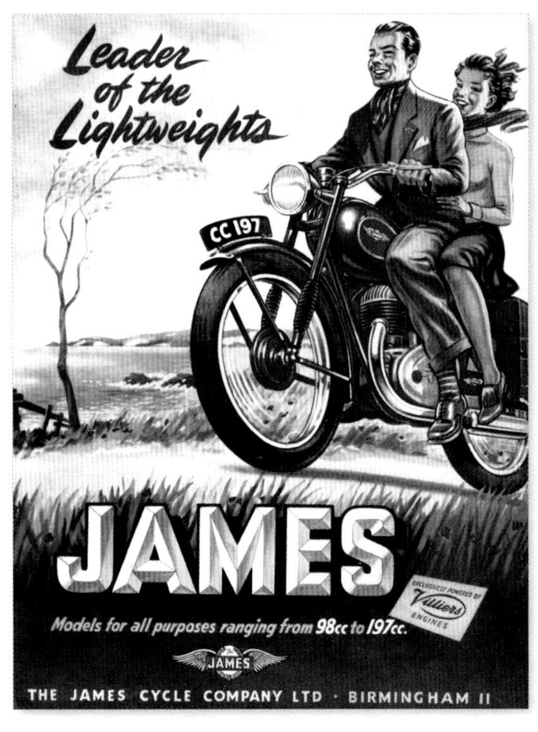

Francis-Barnett and BSA, with the Bantam, were up there but I do believe that James truly was the leader of the lightweights at that time.

"They won't mind," Joyce reassures Stuart as he plucks up the courage to ask the locals whether they'd allow him to park his new James Colonel on the quayside. James was now part of AMC but continued to produce its own distinctive maroon machines.

The Comet was fitted with a Villiers Mk4F with integral two-speed gearbox. Being a basic model, ignition and lighting were taken care of by a flywheel generator, whilst a small dry battery contained within the headlamp shell provided enough juice for a parking light.

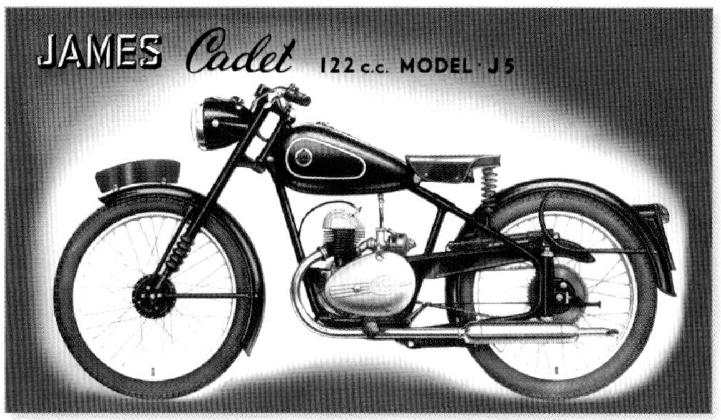

Like its smaller relation the 1954 Cadet relied on a flywheel generator for ignition and lighting, with a dry battery for a parking light. Like all the firm's machines it was powered by Villiers – in this case a Mk13D with three-speed gearbox. For 1955 the Cadet's capacity would be upped to 150cc. The Motor Cycle'*s 1953 test of one recorded a top speed of 46mph, with exactly a gallon of petroil being consumed every hundred miles at a steady 40mph, or one every 128 miles at 30.*

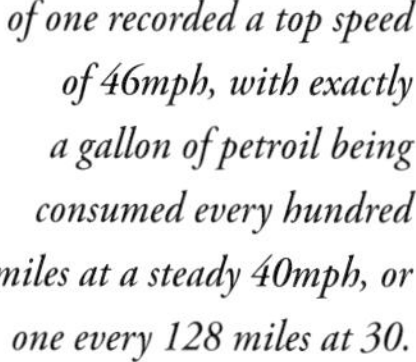

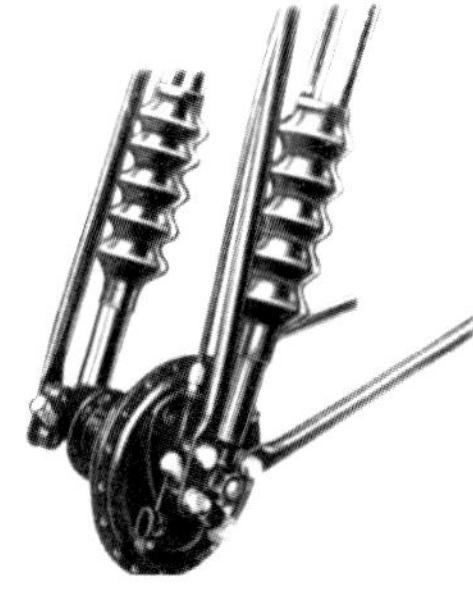

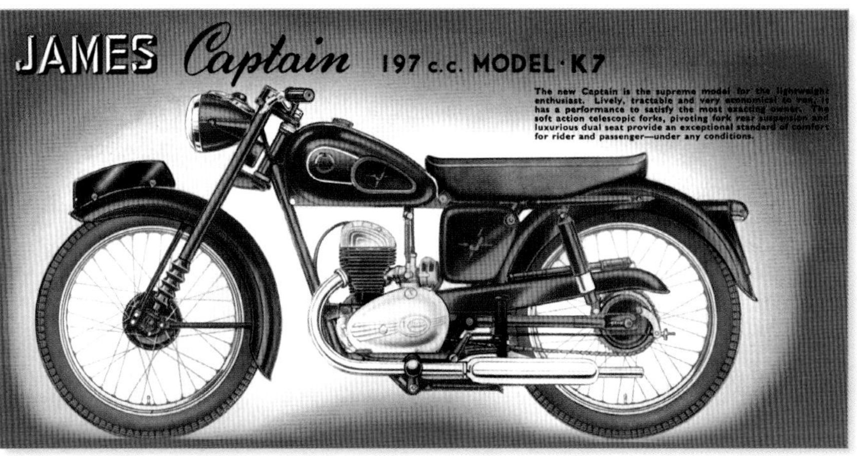

The first of, in my opinion, James's best all-round road bikes.

SPECIFICATION

FRAME and FORKS—James cantilever frame of brazed construction with malleable lugs. Pivoting fork, oil damped, rear suspension. Tubular centre stand. Drop forged, adjustable, rubber covered footrests. Soft action 3 rate spring telescopic forks with plastic gaiters protecting sliding members. Maroon stove enamel finish on " Bonderized " rust proofed surface.

ENGINE and GEARBOX—225 c.c. Villiers Mk 1H two-stroke engine/gearbox unit. Heavily finned grey iron cylinder and aluminium alloy head. Large diameter main-shafts mounted on 4 heavy duty ball races. Roller bearing connecting rod big end. Light alloy piston. Petroil lubrication. Single lever carburetter enclosed in streamlined aluminium cover with air filter and easy starting shutter. 4 speed gearbox with visual neutral and gear indicator, adjustable foot change and kick start pedals. Multiplate clutch and primary drive in oil bath.

ELECTRICAL EQUIPMENT—Ignition by flywheel generator enclosed in streamlined cover. Lodge sparking plug fitted with waterproof cover and suppressor. A.C. and D.C. lighting equipment incorporating rectifier and Lucas 6 volt 12 amp/hrs. battery. Pre-focussed head-lamp. Wide angle Diacon tail light. Electric horn.

WHEELS and BRAKES—Chromed WM1-19 rims with journal bearing hubs. 6" malleable cast iron brake drums with liners bonded to light alloy brake shoes. Rod operated rear brake with adjustable pedal position. Dunlop Universal 3.00×19 tyres.

EQUIPMENT—Deeply valanced mudguards and chainguard. 2½ gallon fuel tank, stove enamelled maroon with rubber knee grips. Plastic fuel pipe. Vynide covered sorbo rubber dualseat on pressed steel base. Chromed handlebars, control levers and exhaust system. Large capacity toolbox with comprehensive toolkit. Smiths chronometric 80 m.p.h. (140 k.p.h.) speedometer. Tyre pump.

SPECIFICATION

FRAME and FORKS—James loop-type rigid frame, reinforced by liners in top tube and strut between top and front down tubes. Detachable rear frame, side prop stand, adjustable forged steel footrests. Oil damped telescopic forks with plastic gaiters protecting sliding members. Maroon stove enamel finish on " Bonderized " rust proofed surface.

ENGINE and GEARBOX—197 c.c. Villiers Mk 7E competition two-stroke engine/gearbox unit. Heavily finned grey iron cylinder and light alloy head fitted with compression release valve. Large diameter mainshaft on 3 heavy duty ball races. Two rows of ¼"×¼" rollers at connecting rod big end bearing. Light alloy piston. Petroil lubrication. Single lever carburetter with air filter and choke. Wide ratio 4 speed gearbox with adjustable foot change and kick start pedals. Clutch and primary drive in oil bath.

ELECTRICAL EQUIPMENT—Ignition by watertight flywheel generator incorporating coil for optional A.C. lighting set. Lodge sparking plug with waterproof rubber cover.

WHEELS and BRAKES—Chromed wheel rims—front WM1-21 with 2.75×21 tyre, rear WM3-19 with 4.00×19 tyre. Dunlop Trials Universal tyres fitted with security bolts. Fabricated steel brake drums, liners bonded to light alloy shoes. Journal bearings.

EQUIPMENT—Polished alloy mudguards with robust tubular stays. Front and rear competition number plates. 2½ gallon fuel tank, stove enamelled maroon. Plastic fuel pipe. Adjustable, rubber trials saddle. Chromed handlebars, control levers and exhaust system. Smiths non trip speedometer. Toolbox with comprehensive toolkit. Tyre pump.

SPECIFICATION

FRAME and FORKS—James cantilever frame of brazed construction with malleable lugs. Pivoting fork, oil damped, rear suspension. Tubular centre stand. Drop forged adjustable footrests. Oil damped telescopic forks with plastic gaiters protecting sliding members. Maroon stove enamel finish on "Bonderized" rust proofed surface.

ENGINE and GEARBOX—197 c.c. Villiers Mk 7E competition two-stroke engine/gearbox unit. Heavily finned grey iron cylinder and light alloy head fitted with compression release valve. Large diameter mainshaft on 3 heavy duty ball races. Two rows ¼"×¼" rollers at connecting rod big end bearing. Light alloy piston. Petroil lubrication. Single lever carburetter with air filter and choke. Close ratio 4 speed gearbox with adjustable foot change and kick start pedals. Clutch and primary drive in oil bath.

ELECTRICAL EQUIPMENT—Ignition by watertight flywheel generator incorporating coils for optional A.C. lighting set. Lodge sparking plug with waterproof cover.

WHEELS and BRAKES—Chromed rims—front WM1-21 with 21×2.75 tyre, rear WM3-19 with 3.50×19 tyre. Dunlop Sports tyres fitted with security bolts. Journal bearing hubs with oilseals. 5" fabricated steel brake drums, liners bonded to light alloy shoes. Rod operated rear brake with adjustable pedal position.

EQUIPMENT—Polished alloy mudguards with robust tubular stays. Front and rear competition number plates. 2¼ gallon fuel tank, stove enamelled maroon. Plastic fuel pipe. Vynide covered sorbo rubber dualseat on pressed steel base. Chromed handlebars, control levers and exhaust system. Smiths non trip 65 m.p.h. (110 k.p.h.) speedometer. Toolbox and comprehensive toolkit. Tyre pump.

Model	J11 Comet	J5 Cadet	K7 Captain	K12 Colonel	J9 Commando	K7C Cotswold
Bore and Stroke	47×57 m.m.	50×62 m.m.	59×72 m.m.	63×72 m.m.	59×72 m.m.	59×72 m.m.
Cylinder Capacity	98 c.c. = 6 cu. ins.	122 c.c. = 7.4 cu. ins.	197 c.c. = 11.71 cu. ins.	225 c.c. = 13.66 cu. ins.	197 c.c. = 11.71 cu. ins.	197 c.c. = 11.71 cu. ins.
Compression Ratio	8 to 1	8 to 1	7.25 to 1	7 to 1	8.25 to 1	8.25 to 1
Gear Ratios. Top	8.5	7.33	5.74	6.21	6.54	6.27
„ Third	—	—	—	8.2	8.83	8.48
„ Second	—	10.19	7.7	11.8	15.0	11.3
„ First	13.1	19.5	14.7	19.05	22.6	18.2
Front Chain Size	⅜"×¼"×.225"	⅜"×¼"×.225"	⅜"×¼"×.225"	⅜"×¼"×.225"	⅜"×¼"×.225"	⅜"×¼"×.225"
Rear Chain Size	½"×.335"×.192"	½"×.335"×.205"	½"×.335"×.205"	½"×.335"×.305"	½"×.335"×.205"	½"×.335"×.205"
Brake Drum Diameter. Front ...	4" (10.15 cm.)	4" (10.15 cm.)	5" (12.7 cm.)	6" (15.25 cm.)	5" (12.7 cm.)	5" (12.7 cm.)
„ Rear ...	5" (12.7 cm.)	5" (12.7 cm.)	5" (12.7 cm.)	6" (15.25 cm.)	5" (12.7 cm.)	5" (12.7 cm.)
Brake Lining Area	11¾ sq. in. (76 cm.^{2})	11¾ sq. in. (76 cm.^{2})	13 sq. ins. (83.9 cm.^{2})	22 sq. in. (142 cm.^{2})	13 sq. ins. (83.9 cm.^{2})	13 sq. ins. (83.9 cm.^{2})
Tyres, Dunlop. Front	2.25×19	2.75×19	3.00×19	3.00×19	2.75×21	2.75×21
„ Rear	2.25×19	2.75×19	3.00×19	3.00×19	4.00×19	3.50×19
Wheel Base—(Static)	49" (124.5 cm.)	49" (124.5 cm.)	50" (127 cm.)	50" (127 cm.)	49" (124.5 cm.)	50" (127 cm.)
Overall Length	78" (198 cm.)	78" (198 cm.)	78" (198 cm.)	78" (198 cm.)	78" (198 cm.)	76½" (194 cm.)
Handlebar Width	25½" (65 cm.)	25½" (65 cm.)	25½" (65 cm.)	25½" (65 cm.)	27" (70 cm.)	27" (70 cm.)
Saddle Height	27½" (70 cm.)	28" (73.7 cm.)	30" (76.2 cm.)	30" (76.2 cm.)	31" (78.7 cm.)	30" (76.2 cm.)
Ground Clearance	4½" (12 cm.)	5" (12.7 cm.)	5½" (14 cm.)	5½" (14 cm.)	8½" (21.6 cm.)	6½" (16 cm.)
Weight (Approx.)	128 lbs. (58 kgms.)	166 lbs. (75.3 kgms.)	220 lbs. (100 kgms.)	275 lbs. (124 kgms.)	196 lbs. (89 kgms.)	208 lbs. (95 kgms.)
Fuel Tank Capacity	2 galls. (9 litres)	2 galls. (9 litres)	2¼ galls. (10 litres)	2¼ galls. (10 litres)	2¼ galls. (10 litres)	2¼ galls. (10 litres)
Approximate Top Speed	42 m.p.h. (67.5 k.p.h.)	48 m.p.h. (77.25 k.p.h.)	58 m.p.h. (93.5 k.p.h.)	62 m.p.h. (100 k.p.h.)	—	—
Average Fuel Consumption (Approx.)	165m.p.g. (1.7L/100k.m.)	135 m.p.g. (2L/100 km.)	110 m.p.g.(2.5L/100km.)	90 m.p.g. (2L/100 km.)	—	—

NOTE.—Model K7 can be supplied with 4-speed gearbox as alternative equipment with the following overall ratios: 5.74, 7.75, 10.34 and 16.65.

Full specifications for the 1954 James range.

Two Brilliant Newcomers

COMPLETELY RE-DESIGNED LIGHTWEIGHTS WITH THE ACCENT ON COMFORT, ECONOMY AND SILENCE

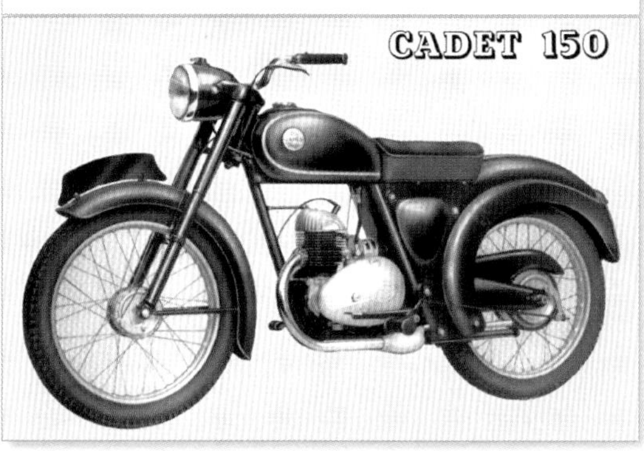

In fact there were three 'brilliant newcomers' if you counted Francis-Barnett's little Plover that shared everything except badge and colour. You could always tell them apart at that time, even from a distance – James bikes were maroon and Francis-Barnetts were dark green.

The James gang always made sure they had the best mounts, and here they are 1956 style. So, from left to right, that's Jesse on a Commando, Cole Younger with his girl on a Captain and Frank on a Cadet – ready to go, 80 years after their namesakes' disastrous foray to rob the First National Bank in Northfield, Minnesota. Since the previous season the entire range had been fitted with full light-alloy hubs courtesy of the British Hub Co and Commandos, Cotswolds, Captains and Colonels had oil-damped front forks.

POWER UNIT — COMET 100. Compact two stroke 98 cc. Mk. 4F Villiers engine-gear unit. Deeply finned cylinder and alloy head. Ball race mainshaft bearings. Roller connecting rod big end bearings. Flat top piston. Petroil lubrication. Villiers Junior carburetter with air filter and choke.

Two speed gearbox operated by handlebar lever. Gear ratios: First 13·1, top 8·5 to 1. Totally enclosed clutch and primary chain transmission. Folding kick-start pedal. Ignition and lighting current supplied by flywheel generator enclosed in streamlined alloy casing.

POWER UNIT — CADET 150. Robust two stroke 147 cc. Mk. 30C Villiers engine with cast iron cylinder and light alloy head. Mainshaft supported by 3 ball races. Roller big end bearings. Flat top piston. Petroil lubrication. Villiers S19 carburetter with air filter and choke.

Three speed gearbox bolted to engine. Overall ratios: First 15·9 to 1, second 8·36 to 1, top 6·24 to 1. Adjustable foot change and kick-starter pedals. Cork insert two plate clutch and primary drive running in oil bath alloy chaincase. Ignition and 6 volt lighting current provided by flywheel generator.

FRAME. Heavy gauge 2″ diameter tubular dorsal beam bolted to pressed steel centre section by two transverse members. Pivoted fork rear suspension controlled by coil springs, adjustable for load. Total movement 3½″. Adjustable footrests and brake pedal. Light action centre stand.

FRONT FORK. Self-lubricating hydraulically damped telescopic fork with tension springs. Overall movement 4½″.

WHEELS. Full width ribbed hubs. Powerful 4″ front and 5″ rear brakes. Journal bearings to rear wheel. Rust proof spokes. Tyre sizes — Comet 100: 2·25 × 19″. Cadet 150: 3·00 × 18″.

MUDGUARDS AND TANK. Very deep and efficient rear mudguard bolted to centre section and incorporating the rear number plate. Wide "D" section front guard and tubular stays. Welded steel 2¼ gallon tank, finished in maroon stove enamel with attractive name badge and silver lining. Self-sealing push-pull plastic filler cap with oil measure for fuel mixture.

EQUIPMENT. Direct AC lighting. 6″ pre-focussed headlamp incorporating 6 volt magnetic speedometer on Cadet 150. 5″ headlamp on Comet 100. Large tail light and reflector. Very efficient cast aluminium silencer with detachable plate for cleaning purposes. Ball joint handlebar adjusters. Luxurious foam rubber seat covered in hard wearing black and red leather cloth. Large toolbox in centre section houses comprehensive tool kit. Pump fitted under tank. Deep rear chainguard. *Accessories specially designed for these models include passenger seat and footrests, safety bar and legshield, windscreen, rear carrier and pannier equipment. Ask for James Accessory Leaflet.*

FINISH. High lustre maroon enamel on rust proofed base. Aluminium stove enamel on hubs and wheel rims. Chrome plated handlebars, control levers, exhaust pipes, etc.

Beneath the curvaceous tinwork lurked this bolt-up structure.

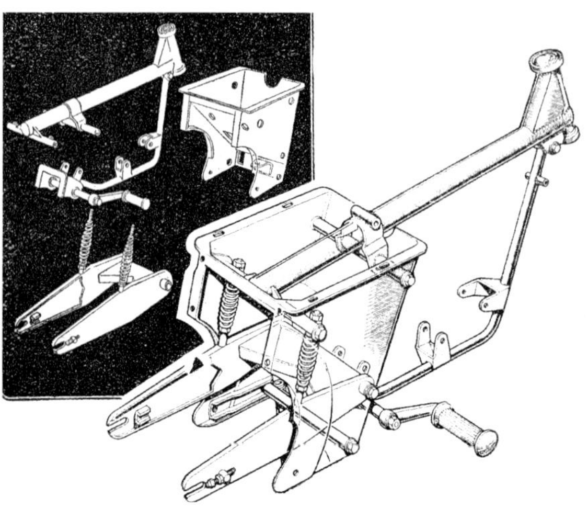

"Smartly styled, easy to clean lightweight two-stroke: lively performance enhanced by good handling and excellent brakes," summed up The Motor Cycle *after testing a Captain in the summer of 1956. They managed to obtain 61mph flat out with 51 in the middle of its three gears, with a standing-start quarter-mile in 22.8 seconds. At a steady 40mph it would return 106mpg but at 50 this dropped to 72.*

POWER UNIT — CAPTAIN 200. Two stroke 197 cc. Villiers Mk. 8E engine. Heavily finned cast iron cylinder with alloy head. Three ball races to mainshaft. Roller bearing big end. Flat top piston. Petroil lubrication. Villiers S.25 carburetter with air filter and choke. Ignition and lighting current supplied by flywheel generator.

Three speed gearbox. Overall ratios: First 14·5, second 7·43 top 5·54 to 1. Adjustable foot control and kick-starter pedals. Two plate cork insert clutch and primary transmission in alloy oil bath case.

POWER UNIT — COLONEL 225. Exceptionally smooth running 224 cc. Villiers two stroke engine and gearbox unit. Deeply finned barrel and alloy head. Mainshaft and flywheels supported by four bearings. Ignition and lighting generator enclosed in streamlined cover. Villiers S.25 carburetter housed in detachable alloy cowling. Anti-theft key operated ignition earthing switch.

Four speed gearbox with visual indicator. Overall ratios: First 19·05, second 11·8, third 8·2, top 6·21 to 1. Adjustable kick-starter and gear change pedals. Multiplate clutch. Gearbox speedometer drive.

FRAME. Tubular loop frame combines clean design and great strength. Swinging fork rear suspension pivoted on rubber torsion bushes and controlled by coil spring oleo units allowing 4″ total movement. Adjustable footrests, forged steel pillion footrest brackets, light action centre stand.

FRONT FORK. Self-lubricating spring controlled telescopic fork with hydraulic damping. Total fork movement $4\frac{3}{4}$″.

WHEELS. Full width ribbed hubs with journal ball bearings. Rust proof spokes. 5″ diameter brakes, argenised rims and 3·00 × 18″ tyres on Captain 200. 6″ brakes, chromed rims and 3·25 × 18″ tyres on Colonel 225.

MUDGUARDS AND TANK. Deeply valanced guards. Tubular front mudguard stays act as locking cotters for wheel spindle nuts. Rear number plate faired into mudguard. Welded steel $2\frac{3}{4}$ gallon tank, stove enamelled maroon with attractive silver lining and plastic name badge. Rubber knee grips. Push-pull plastic filler cap with oil measure for fuel mixture. Plastic fuel pipe.

EQUIPMENT. 6 volt AC/DC lighting enables the use of either rectifier battery lighting or direct current from generator. Pre-focussed 6″ headlamp with built in-Smiths 80 m.p.h. magnetic speedometer, ammeter and four position light switch. Combined dipswitch and horn button on handlebar. Large plastic tail light.

Ball joint handlebar adjusters. Luxurious foam rubber twin seat with leathercloth covering, red sides and black top. Comprehensive tool kit and inflator. Electric horn, concealed in tank channel. Deep rear chainguard. Rear reflector. Tool kit and battery housed in twin cases under seat. *Specially designed accessories for these models include pillion footrests, pannier equipment, safety bar and legshield, windscreen, etc. Ask for James Accessory Leaflet.*

FINISH. High lustre maroon stove enamel on rust proofed base. Aluminium finish on hubs. Chromium plated bars, controls, exhaust system, etc.

Afternoons were stolen away from boarding school at the local motorcycle shop, where head mechanic Brian Trott, having virtually given me a wreck of a '56 Commando, kindly allowed me to piece it together at the back of the workshop. Miraculously the finished result passed one of their MoTs, allowing me to dispose of my rigid DMW trials to a waiting school friend. I have nothing but happy memories of this game little James (STT 355) and even when its top frame tube fractured just behind the steering head the fault was mine.

ENGINE. Villiers Mk. 7E 197 cc. two stroke developing 9·3 b.h.p. at 4,300 r.p.m. Deeply finned cast iron cylinder. Alloy head fitted with compression release valve. Mainshaft supported by three heavy duty ball race bearings. Roller bearing big end. Flat top piston. Compression ratio: 8·25 to 1. Petroil lubrication. Villiers S.25 carburetter with air filter and choke. Waterproofed flywheel magneto includes coils and cables for optional 6 volt direct lighting set.

TRANSMISSION AND GEARBOX. Primary chain and two plate cork insert clutch running in alloy oil bath case. Villiers four speed gearbox. Wide ratios on trials Commando 200: First 22·6, second 15·0, third 8·83, top 6·54 to 1 with 50 tooth rear sprocket. Close ratios on scrambles Cotswold 200: First 18·2, second 11·3, third 8·48, top 6·27 to 1 with 48 tooth rear sprocket. Alternative gear ratios can be provided — details available upon application to Competition Department.

FRAME. Reinforced tubular loop frame linered and strutted at major stress points, malleable lug construction. Exceptionally strong pivoted fork rear suspension with hydraulically damped heavy duty coil spring units. Total movement 4″. Rigid footrest assembly mounted on dual cross members. Rear chain guide. Spring loaded side prop stand.

FRONT FORK. Robust telescopic fork with long progressive coil springs and hydraulic damping on both impact and rebound strokes. Total movement $4\frac{3}{4}$″. Fork top plate carries fully adjustable handlebar with ball ended control levers.

WHEELS. Full width hubs with powerful 5″ diameter brakes. Sealed journal ball bearings. Chromed rims with rust proof 10 swg. spokes. Security bolts on both wheels. Dunlop Trials Universal tyres on Commando 200: front 2·75 × 21″, rear 4·00 × 19″. Dunlop Sports tyres on Cotswold 200: front 2·75 × 21″, rear 3·50 × 19″.

MUDGUARDS AND TANK. Polished alloy mudguards with robust tubular stays. Front stays act as locking cotters for wheel spindle nuts. Deep rear chain guard. Slim welded steel $2\frac{1}{4}$ gallon tank permitting maximum steering lock. Push-pull plastic filler cap incorporates 20 to 1 oil measure for petroil mixture.

EQUIPMENT. High level exhaust system and silencer. Adjustable rubber trials saddle on Commando 200. Foam rubber seat with hard wearing leather cloth cover on Cotswold 200. Comprehensive tool kit in cylindrical toolbox. Competition number plates. Smiths non-trip speedometer. Tyre Pump. Bulb horn.

FINISH. James maroon stove enamel on rust proofed base. Tank lined silver with plastic name badge. Chromium plated handlebars, levers, rims, exhaust system, etc.

JAMES

+ MOTOR CYCLES FOR 1957 +

I fail to see the significance of the arrows but this somewhat lacklustre cover featured the brand-new Commodore, with 6in British Hub Co brakes, on the left, and reintroduced the Captain, which had 5in versions, on the right.

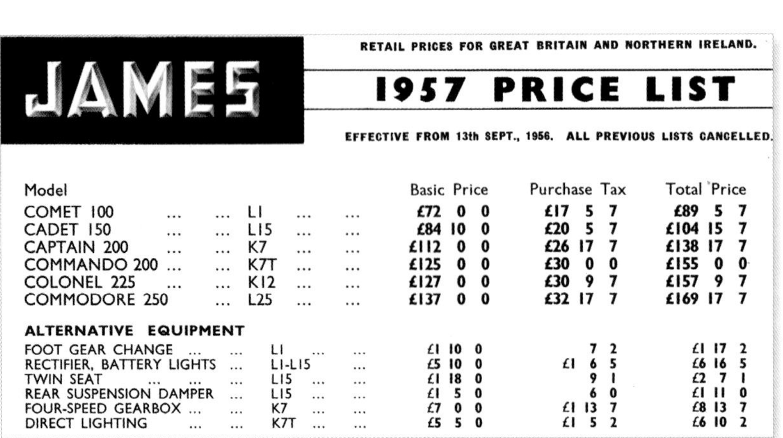

JAMES

RETAIL PRICES FOR GREAT BRITAIN AND NORTHERN IRELAND.

1957 PRICE LIST

EFFECTIVE FROM 13th SEPT., 1956. ALL PREVIOUS LISTS CANCELLED.

Model		Basic Price	Purchase Tax	Total Price
COMET 100	L1	£72 0 0	£17 5 7	£89 5 7
CADET 150	L15	£84 10 0	£20 5 7	£104 15 7
CAPTAIN 200	K7	£112 0 0	£26 17 7	£138 17 7
COMMANDO 200	K7T	£125 0 0	£30 0 0	£155 0 0
COLONEL 225	K12	£127 0 0	£30 9 7	£157 9 7
COMMODORE 250	L25	£137 0 0	£32 17 7	£169 17 7
ALTERNATIVE EQUIPMENT				
FOOT GEAR CHANGE	L1	£1 10 0	7 2	£1 17 2
RECTIFIER, BATTERY LIGHTS	L1-L15	£5 10 0	£1 6 5	£6 16 5
TWIN SEAT	L15	£1 18 0	9 1	£2 7 1
REAR SUSPENSION DAMPER	L15	£1 5 0	6 0	£1 11 0
FOUR-SPEED GEARBOX	K7	£7 0 0	£1 13 7	£8 13 7
DIRECT LIGHTING	K7T	£5 5 0	£1 5 2	£6 10 2

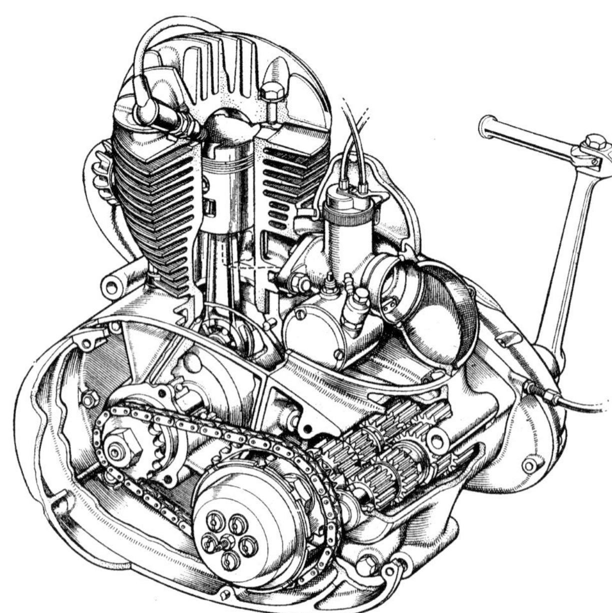

The Commodore featured AMC's new Piatti-designed 249cc two-stroke engine that was equipped with an Amal Monobloc carburettor and Wico-Pacy alternator.

Undoubtedly the finest lightweight trials model on the market, this superbly functional mount will successfully tackle any kind of going. Villiers 197 c.c. high compression motor with wide ratio 4-speed gearbox. Amal Monobloc carburettor with air filter. Steel shield for flywheel magneto. Cross-over exhaust. Reinforced frame, 8" ground clearance. Adjustable Girling rear suspension units. Two-way hydraulic damping on front fork. Dunlop Trials Universal tyres (2.75x21 front; 4.00x19 rear), chromed rims, 6" front brake, special rear chain guide. Trials saddle, ball ended control levers, bulb horn, competition number plates, light alloy guards, tools and inflator. Martial grey with royal blue tank panels. Scrambles specification and lighting equipment to special order.

The latest Commando incorporated features from the previous year's factory machines, in that the exhaust now crossed from left to right; this in turn dictated that the prop stand be repositioned from the right to left side and a curved sheet-steel plate now protected the vulnerable pressed-aluminium flywheel magneto cover. Performance-enhancing mods included an Amal Monobloc carb and larger 6in front brake.

Cadet
150

Powered by a Villiers 147 c.c. two-stroke engine, this exceptionally quiet lightweight offers a fine performance plus a standard of comfort worthy of a much more costly machine. A 2" diameter tube forms the backbone of the frame to which are attached the engine loop and pressed steel body with built-in swinging fork rear suspension. Flywheel magneto ignition and 6 volt direct lighting—AC/DC battery-rectifier lights extra. Pre-focussed headlamp. Hydraulically damped front fork. 3.00x18 tyres. Deep mudguards and chain cover. Foam rubber seat—twinseat available as extra. Smith's speedometer, electric horn, toolkit and pump. Maroon enamel with tropical grey tank panels or martial grey with royal blue panels. All parts rust-proofed.

A facelift for the Cadet with optional colour schemes, a new exhaust system with more efficient silencer, and a Villiers 30C motor. The Comet too had got away from James's traditional all-maroon and was finished in Martial Grey with Royal Blue tank panels. It was now powered by either a Villiers 4F (as before) or 6F. The former had cable and handlebar trigger gear-change and the latter by foot.

Partially, but not entirely due to AMC's own vibratory, gutless 25T two-stroke engine, James's Commodore was not one of their more memorable models.

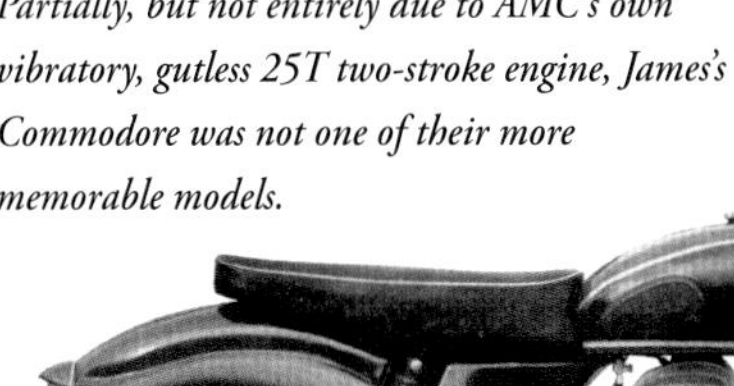

Captains and Colonels had also departed from the strict maroon-only regime with a choice of either Maroon/Tropical Grey or Martial Grey/Royal Blue – otherwise they were much as before. The factory also produced at least one machine in Seagull Grey with Pastel Grey tank panels but this may not have been translated into production. This is a Colonel, by the way.

an exciting new

JAMES ... the Commodore 250

NEW 249 c.c. TWO-STROKE MOTOR. Unit construction single cylinder engine and 4-speed gearbox. Petroil lubrication (24 to 1 ratio). Deeply finned cylinder and head for efficient cooling. Special 'squish' combustion chamber has projections mating with cut-outs in the piston crown, allowing maximum charge and creating near-perfect turbulence and combustion. Amal Monobloc carburettor in detachable alloy cover with filter and choke. Caged roller big end bearing positively lubricated through grooves in the crankcase to trap oil separated by swirl. Full disc balanced flywheels on ⅞" crankshaft supported by roller bearing on timing side and two ball races on drive side. Wico-Pacy generator for ignition and lighting. Special ignition circuit with emergency position ensures easy starting whether battery is fully charged or flat. Multiplate clutch with Klinger inserts. Four-speed gearbox with foot change, gear indicator and folding K/S pedal.
NEW COMPOSITE FRAME. All the centre frame components, rear swinging fork, etc., are built of steel pressings, the top and engine loop tubes being the only tubular members in the design. Electical wiring, battery, H.T. coil and rectifier are housed in the centre section and a surrounding platform accommodates the toolkit. Access is provided by two spring-loaded covers. Front and rear suspension have hydraulic damping; the front fork has 5" overall movement and the Girling R/S units allow 4½" rear wheel deflection.
LUXURIOUS DETAIL AND FINISH. The rear transmission is totally enclosed in a streamlined chain-case with a hinged cover for access to the rear brake and for chain lubrication. Exhaust noise is reduced to a pleasing note by the special long silencer. AC/DC 6 volt lighting, pre-focussed headlamp, quickly detachable plugs for wiring cables. Special twin bulb tail-lamp with reflector. Foam rubber twinseat. Chromed rims with 6" brakes and 3.25x18 tyres. Deeply valanced mudguards. Protective cover for inflator. Electric horn, toolkit. Choice of martial grey enamel with royal blue tank panels and black seat; or maroon with tropical grey tank panels and seat. Attractive tank badges. Bright parts heavily chromed or cadmium plated.

JAMES

Motor Cycles

for

1958

A Commodore in Maroon with Tropical Grey tank panels and seat was chosen for the brochure's cover – alternatively it could have been finished in Martial Grey with Royal Blue tank panels and black dual seat.

JAMES

1958 Models incorporate many excellent features:

1 Quick action filler cap and oil measure with special synthetic rubber seal ensuring immunity from fuel leaks.

Handlebars with concealed dome adjusters and hooded control levers.

Speedometer, ammeter and switch flush-mounted in headlamp.

2 Rear transmission on the Commodore is totally enclosed in a streamlined chaincase with hinged cover for access to rear brake, and for chain lubrication.

Pivoted fork rear springing all models.

3 James 172 c.c. and 249 c.c. power units feature a patented laminar-flow scavenging system, ported piston and open transfer ports. Full disc flywheels. Caged roller big end bearing.

4 Battery and toolkit in separate compartments under twinseat of Captain.

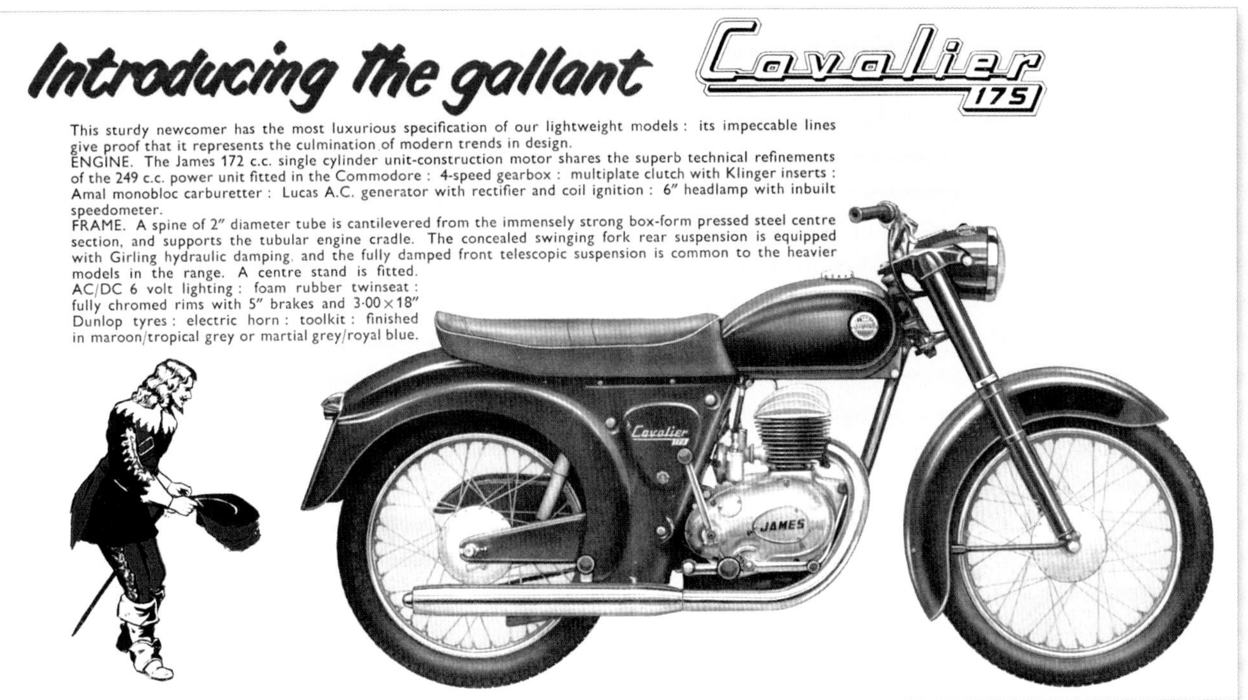

Certainly more modern looking than its direct competitor, BSA's new 175 Bantam, but was it as good? I know which one I'd sooner have – in spite of the James having four speeds to the Bantam's three. It would be no contest, not only on account of the Cavalier's engine being one from the house of AMC.

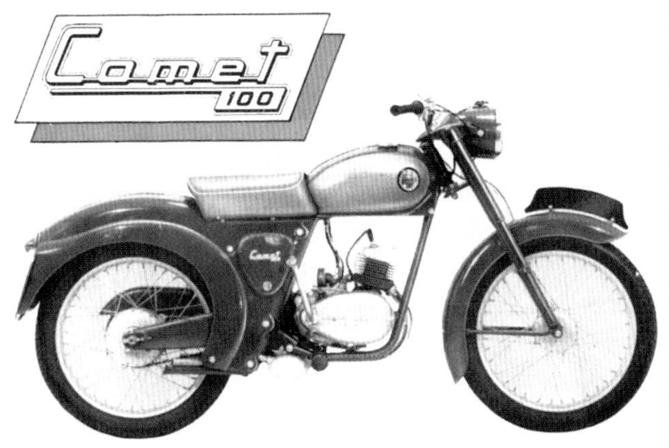

Not normally the type of machine one would associate with military use but nevertheless James's tiddler was, as the publicity material proudly pointed out, 'extensively used by the RAF'. Still equipped with a mere two speeds in its gearbox, it however returned to more traditional Maroon livery this year with Tropical Grey tank panels, the latter colour extending to the seat covering and handlebar finish.

Capable of pushing the speedometer needle to 60 m.p.h. and of averaging 90 to 110 m.p.g., the Captain has a lively and entirely redesigned Villiers 197 c.c. Mk. 10E enclosed engine with 3-speed gearbox. The well proved tubular frame with hydraulically damped front and rear suspension efficiently insulates rider and passenger from road shocks. Primary transmission and clutch in oilbath. Flywheel magneto ignition. Six volt direct and rectifier battery lighting. Deeply valanced mudguards and chain cover. 18″ chromed rims with 3·00 front and 3·25 rear tyres. Domed hub covers front and rear. Twin cases for battery and tools. Electric horn. Maroon and tropical grey or martial grey and royal blue with 3D tank badges. Bright parts chromed or cadmium plated.

James's best bike of the period had been updated with a new engine but no longer had the more expensive option of four speeds in the gearbox; otherwise it soldiered on unchanged.

1958 specifications.

MODEL	COMET 100 L 1	CADET 150 L 15	CAVALIER 175 L 17	CAPTAIN 200 K 7	COMMODORE 250 L 25
ENGINE TYPE	Villiers 4F or 6F	Villiers 30C	James 17T	Villiers 10E	James 25T
BORE AND STROKE	47×57 m.m.	55×62 m.m.	59×63 m.m.	59×72 m.m.	66×73 m.m.
CAPACITY	98 c.c.	147 c.c.	172 c.c.	197 c.c.	249 c.c.
COMPRESSION RATIO	8 to 1	8·3 to 1	8·5 to 1	7·25 to 1	8·1 to 1
CARBURETTER	Villiers S12	Villiers S/19	Amal 370	Villiers S/25	Amal Monobloc 389/17
PETROL-OIL MIXTURE	20 to 1	20 to 1	24 to 1	20 to 1	24 to 1
OVERALL GEAR RATIOS					
1.	13·1	16·9	20·37	16·10	17·3
2.	—	8·9	12·77	8·47	10·8
3.	—	—	8·96	—	7·6
Top.	8·5	6·6	6·9	6·32	5·8
CHAINS—Front	⅜″×¼″×·225″	⅜″×¼″×·225″	⅜″×¼″×·225″	⅜″×¼″×·225″	⅜″×¼″×·225″
Rear	½″×·305″×·192″	½″×·335″×·205″	½″×·335″×·205″	½″×·335″×·205″	½″×·335″×·305″
BRAKE DRUM dia.—Front	4″	4″	5″	5″	6″
Rear	5″	5″	5″	5″	6″
BRAKE LINING AREA	11¼ sq. ins.	11¼ sq. ins.	13 sq. ins.	13 sq. ins.	22 sq. ins.
TYRES—Front	2·25×19	3·00×18	3·00×18	3·00×18	3·25×18
Rear	2·25×19	3·00×18	3·00×18	3·25×18	3·25×18
WHEELBASE STATIC	49½″	49½″	49½″	50″	52″
OVERALL LENGTH	76½″	76½″	76½″	79″	79½″
HANDLEBAR WIDTH	26″	26″	26″	26″	26″
SEAT HEIGHT	29″	29″	29″	29″	30″
GROUND CLEARANCE	5″	5″	5″	5″	5½″
WEIGHT	165 lbs.	188 lbs.	240 lbs.	245 lbs.	295 lbs.
TANK CAPACITY	2¼ galls.	2¼ galls.	2¼ galls.	2¾ galls.	2¾ galls.

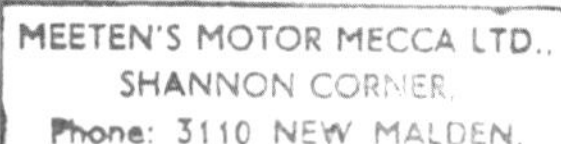

Well, at least AMC was pleased with the Commodore, as here it is again on the cover of the 1959 brochure – even though the young lady's body language doesn't suggest to me that she's too impressed by her would-be consort's mount. Of more interest is the brochure's source, however. In the 1920s Tommy Meeten had been a well-known competition rider with Francis-Barnetts, finishing sixth in the 1924 Ultra Lightweight TT on one in his sole Island ride. Always a champion of two-stroke machines, he had cannily encouraged a specialist club to be based at his Dorking motorcycle business and relocate with him when he moved to larger premises at New Malden – not surprising, then, that a club member had picked up this literature from there.

As well as the RAF the Comet was now being extensively used by police forces, the full caption to this picture tells us. Policeman or not, Virginia's new James Comet had caught Richard's eye but it was her he wanted – on the pretext of enquiring how many miles to the gallon she was getting, he got into conversation. Almost before she'd had a chance to reply that it averaged about 135mpg he had his special cigarettes out and was suggesting she might like to try one… By the time it was finished she'd had a chance to tell him that like all Comets, and Cadets too up to 1956, it had a cast-aluminium silencer with twin tail pipes, and you could clean it out too. He also learnt that it had a compression ratio of 8:1 and that it was easy to get the petrol/oil mixture of 20:1 right by using the measure in the filler cap. It'd do about 40 miles an hour but she didn't know exactly because she hadn't paid the extra to have a speedo, as it wasn't compulsory for machines under 100cc. "She's a really good little starter too, and thank you so much for the cigarette," she said as she engaged bottom gear before riding off.

Looks a bit on the purple side to me but here's a Martial Grey Cadet with Royal Blue tank panels and a Cavalier in Maroon with Tropical Grey tank panels. Below them is a Martial Grey/Blue Captain, which, you will notice, now has a front mudguard with provision for the machine's registration number. Any of these three could be had in either colour, although Maroon was more popular.

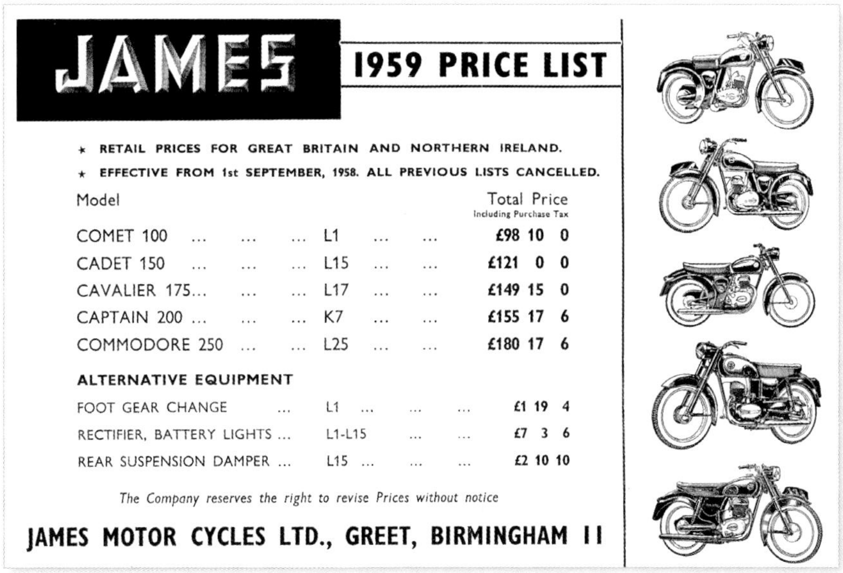

JAMES **1959 PRICE LIST**

★ RETAIL PRICES FOR GREAT BRITAIN AND NORTHERN IRELAND.
★ EFFECTIVE FROM 1st SEPTEMBER, 1958. ALL PREVIOUS LISTS CANCELLED.

Model		Total Price Including Purchase Tax
COMET 100	L1	**£98 10 0**
CADET 150	L15	**£121 0 0**
CAVALIER 175	L17	**£149 15 0**
CAPTAIN 200	K7	**£155 17 6**
COMMODORE 250	L25	**£180 17 6**

ALTERNATIVE EQUIPMENT

FOOT GEAR CHANGE	L1	**£1 19 4**
RECTIFIER, BATTERY LIGHTS	L1-L15	**£7 3 6**
REAR SUSPENSION DAMPER	L15	**£2 10 10**

The Company reserves the right to revise Prices without notice

JAMES MOTOR CYCLES LTD., GREET, BIRMINGHAM 11

FLYING Cadet 150

Equipped with flywheel magneto ignition and 6-volt direct lighting — AC/DC battery-rectifier lights extra. Pre-focussed headlamp. Deep mudguards and chain cover. 3.00 × 18" Dunlop tyres. Smiths illuminated speedometer. Electric horn. Tool kit and pump. Finished in Maroon and Tropical Grey.

107 GNS INCLUDING PURCHASE TAX

A LIVELY NEW POWER UNIT

This lion-hearted James power unit is engineered for long life: all stressed components are massively constructed to meet the exacting requirements of its high performance, yet cunning design methods have eliminated all unwanted weight.

Crisply styled, it features a flat-top piston with loop scavenging large diameter exhaust port with interrupted cylinder finning, integral three-speed foot-change gearbox, multiplate clutch with Ferodo inserts, Amal monobloc carburetter with plunger operated choke, and honeycomb air filter with replaceable element.

MODEL	CADET 150 L15A	BRAKE DRUM dia.—Front	4"
ENGINE TYPE	JAMES 15T	Rear	5"
BORE AND STROKE	55 mm × 62 mm	BRAKE LINING AREA	11¼" sq. ins.
CAPACITY	149 cc	TYRES—Front	3.00 × 18
COMPRESSION RATIO	7 to 1	Rear	3.00 × 18
CARBURETTER	AMAL 375/37	WHEELBASE STATIC	49½"
PETROL-OIL MIXTURE	20 : 1	OVERALL LENGTH	76½"
OVERALL GEAR RATIOS 1.	17.2	HANDLEBAR WIDTH	26"
2.	8.9	SEAT HEIGHT	29"
Top	6.7	GROUND CLEARANCE	5"
CHAINS—Front	⅜" × ¼" × .225"	WEIGHT	171 lb
Rear	½" × .335 × .205"	TANK CAPACITY	2¼ gallons

The Flying Cadet, featuring the new and smallest AMC two-stroke engine, was launched too late to be included in the initial 1959 brochure so it had a folder all of its own. Bob Currie of The Motor Cycle *was lent one of the first off the line and spent some time, as it was promoted as an economy model, evaluating its petroil consumption. At a steady 30mph he extracted a bit over 140mpg but on 'ride to work' runs 128. It would cruise happily at 50 and, although not checked electronically, he reckoned the top speed to be a bit over 55. On really steep hills a four-speed gearbox would have been an advantage as there was a considerable gap between bottom and second; but what could you expect for the price, he commented. Although only equipped with direct lighting he found it 'really good' but 'of the electric horn we will not speak'.*

JAMES
Money Saving Motor Cycles....
XOK 250
for 1960

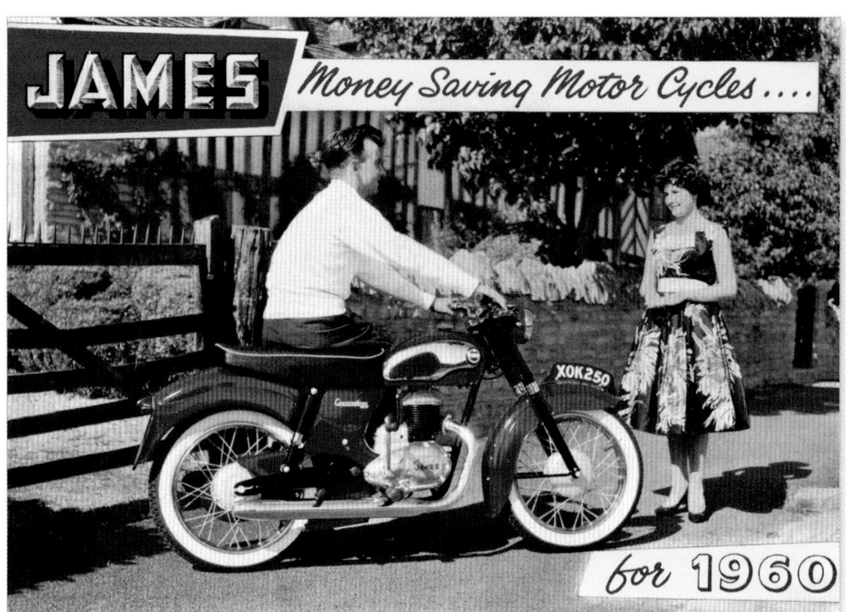

"Yes, very nice I'm sure, but can you please park it somewhere else." And can you blame her? I'll hand you over to James's publicity department to describe the firm's fresh rendition of the Commodore. "Pride of the range, this exceptionally sleek long-distance luxury tourer offers speed, comfort, economy, a high degree of manoeuvrability and considerable eye appeal."

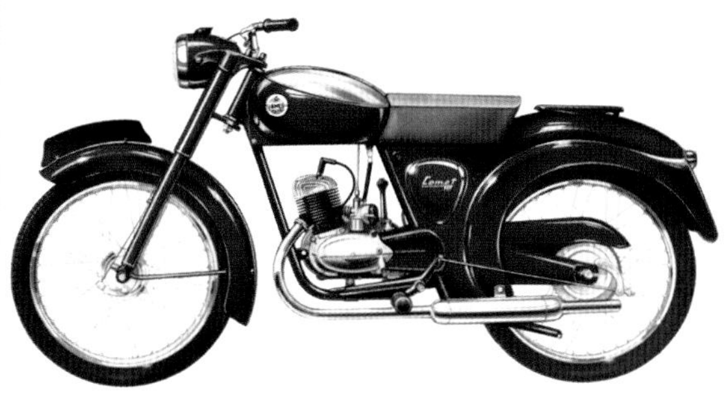

The Comet's fuel tank was now finished in the style of the Flying Cadet (below) and it been given a new exhaust system.

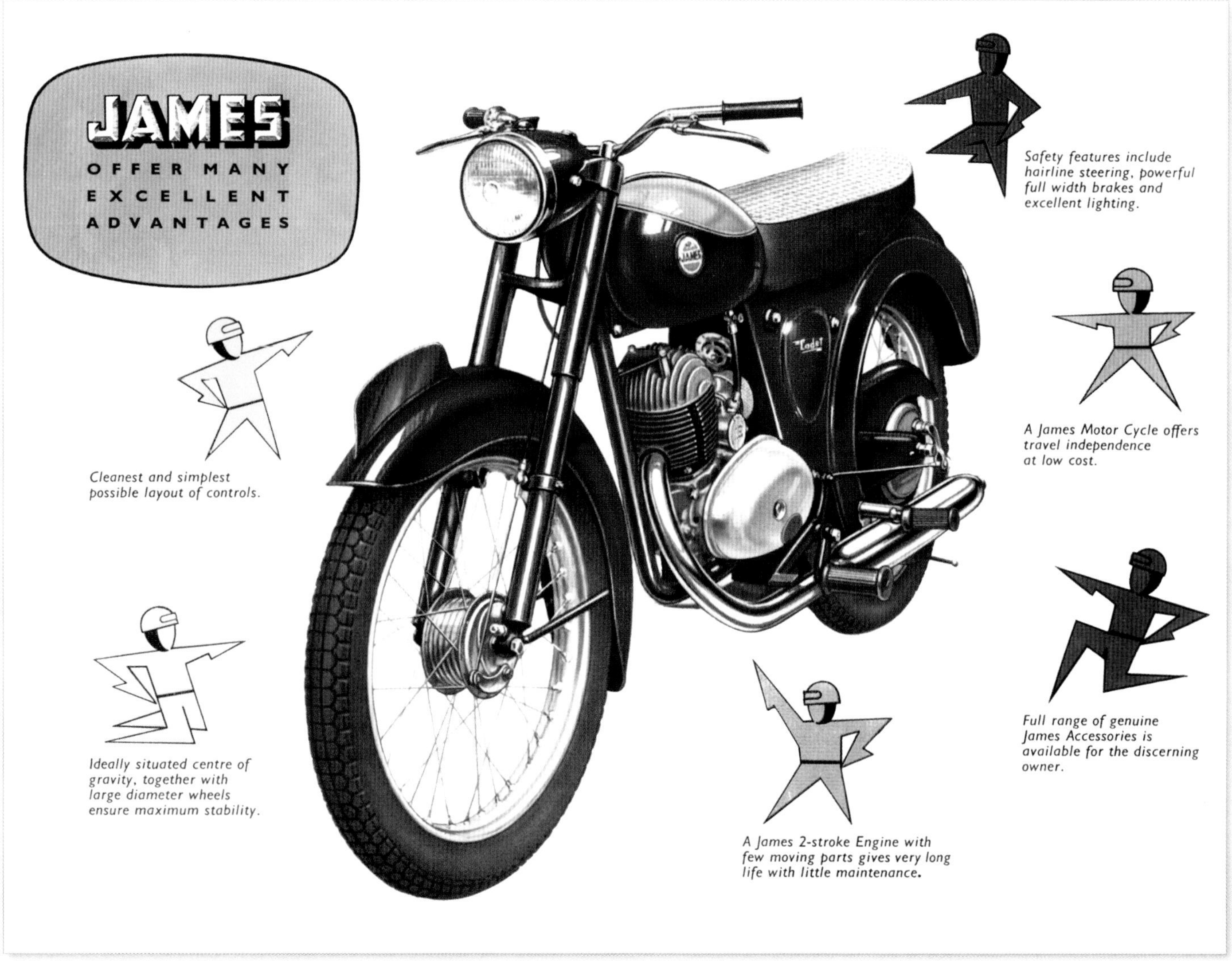
JAMES
OFFER MANY EXCELLENT ADVANTAGES
Safety features include hairline steering, powerful full width brakes and excellent lighting.
Cleanest and simplest possible layout of controls.
A James Motor Cycle offers travel independence at low cost.
Full range of genuine James Accessories is available for the discerning owner.
Ideally situated centre of gravity, together with large diameter wheels ensure maximum stability.
A James 2-stroke Engine with few moving parts gives very long life with little maintenance.

Captain 200

Boasting a luxurious specification, the Captain is designed to carry two persons comfortably, quickly, economically and with the utmost safety. Mounted in a well proved tubular frame, the snappy 4-speed 199 c.c. two-stroke power unit combines pleasing performance with low fuel consumption. Large capacity fuel tank with chrome panels and leak proof filler cap. Hydraulically damped front and rear suspension efficiently insulates rider and passenger from road shocks. AC generator with rectifier and coil ignition : 6-volt direct and rectifier battery lighting. Deep mudguards and chain cover : The rubber-cushioned " spring on " twin seat covers tool compartment, battery and rectifier. Electric horn. Finished in Caribean blue, high gloss black and chrome.

What a shame! The dear old Captain's been got at, restyled and re-engined. What's more, its new AMC-manufactured power plant was yet another from the drawing board of Vincenzo Piatti, the man who designed and gave his name to a 1950s scooter of extreme ugliness.

MODEL	COMET 100 L 1	FLYING CADET 150 L 15A	CAPTAIN 200 L 20	COMMODORE 250 L 25
ENGINE TYPE	Villiers 4F or 6F	James 15T	James 20T	James 25T
BORE AND STROKE	47×57 m.m.	55×62 m.m.	59×73 m.m.	66×73 m.m.
CAPACITY	98 c.c.	149 c.c.	199 c.c.	249 c.c.
COMPRESSION RATIO	8 to 1	7 to 1	8·5 to 1	8·1 to 1
CARBURETTER	Villiers S12	Amal S/19 375/31	Amal Monobloc 376	Amal Monobloc 389/17
OVERALL GEAR RATIOS				
1.	13·1	17·2	19·37	18·1
2.	—	8·9	12·27	11·5
3.	—	—	8·62	8
Top.	8·5	6·7	6·63	6·2
CHAINS—Front	⅜″×¼″×·225″	⅜″×¼″×·225″	⅜″×¼″×·225″	⅜″×¼″×·225″
Rear	½″×·305″×·192″	½″×·335″×·205″	½″×·335″×·305″	½″×·335″×·305″
BRAKE DRUM dia.—Front	4″	4″	5″	6″
Rear	5″	5″	5″	6″
BRAKE LINING AREA	11¼ sq. ins.	11¼ sq. ins.	13 sq. ins.	22 sq. ins.
TYRES—Front	2·25×19	3·00×18	3·00×18	3·25×18
Rear	2·25×19	3·00×18	3·25×18	3·25×18
WHEELBASE STATIC	49½″	49½″	51¼″	52″
OVERALL LENGTH	76½″	76½″	79″	79½″
HANDLEBAR WIDTH	26″	26″	26″	26″
SEAT HEIGHT	30″	30″	30″	32″
GROUND CLEARANCE	5″	5″	5″	5½″
WEIGHT	165 lbs.	171 lbs.	262 lbs.	295 lbs.
TANK CAPACITY	2¼ galls.	2¼ galls.	2¾ galls.	2¾ galls.

JAMES 1960 PRICE LIST

★ RETAIL PRICES FOR GREAT BRITAIN AND NORTHERN IRELAND.

★ EFFECTIVE FROM APRIL 20, 1960, ALL PREVIOUS LISTS CANCELLED.

Model		Basic Price	Purchase Tax	Total Price Including P. Tax
L1	COMET	£85 3 7	£17 11 5	**£102 15 0**
L15A	FLYING CADET	£106 12 8	£21 19 10	**£128 12 6**
L20	CAPTAIN	£141 15 3	£29 4 9	**£171 0 0**
L25	COMMODORE	£158 6 10	£32 13 2	**£191 0 0**
L25T	COMMANDO	£157 2 3	£32 8 1	**£189 10 4**
L25S	COTSWOLD	£157 2 3	£32 8 1	**£189 10 4**

ALTERNATIVE EQUIPMENT

FOOT GEAR CHANGE	L1	£1 13 2	6 10	**£2 0 0**
RECTIFIER BATTERY LIGHTING	L1	£5 15 0	£1 3 9	**£6 18 9**
RECTIFIER BATTERY LIGHTING	L15A	£4 9 0	18 4	**£5 7 4**
REAR SUSPENSION DAMPER	L15A	£2 3 6	8 11	**£2 12 5**
WHITE SIDEWALL TYRES	L20	£1 6 3	5 5	**£1 11 8**
TWIN SEAT	L1	£2 2 0	8 8	**£2 10 8**

The Company reserves the right to revise prices without notice

JAMES MOTOR CYCLES LIMITED
GREET :: BIRMINGHAM 11

Another brochure cover like last year's and the firm would have been out of business! Seriously, the Captain that I was so critical of doesn't look too bad - mind you, whether by accident or design, the rider's leg is all but hiding its worst feature. The 1961 range remained unchanged except that Comets and Cadets were now finished in Stromboli Red. A little bit garish perhaps, but it suited them better than their larger relation, the Commodore, that introduced Stromboli to the range – being cast away on the volcanic island of the same name might be a better fate than being compelled to ride around on one of those. Speaking of which, and just to remind you what I mean, here it is again.

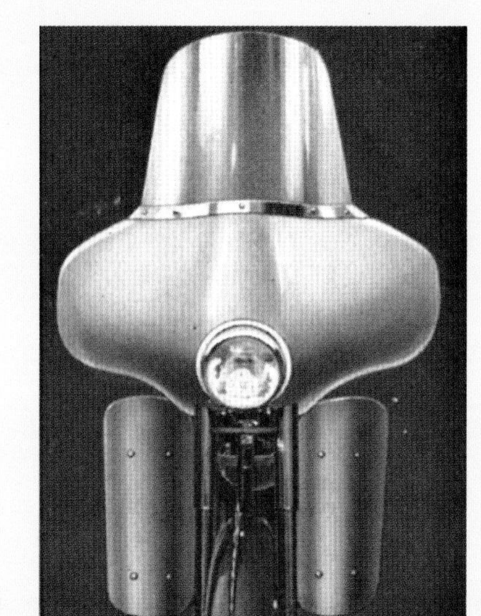

The streamlined windscreen and fairing and the wrap-round legshields provide all-weather protection.

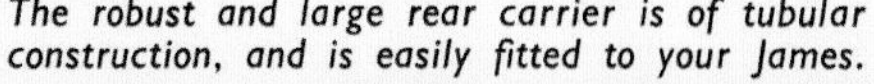
The robust and large rear carrier is of tubular construction, and is easily fitted to your James.

They'd do nothing for the lines of your machine but the brochure insisted that, "Even James motor cycling can be vastly improved by the fitting of accessories which have been specially tailored for James machines."

Since 1959 James's works and privateer trials riders alike were forced to persevere with the unlovely in-house motor but a favoured mod was to substitute AMC heavyweight front forks.

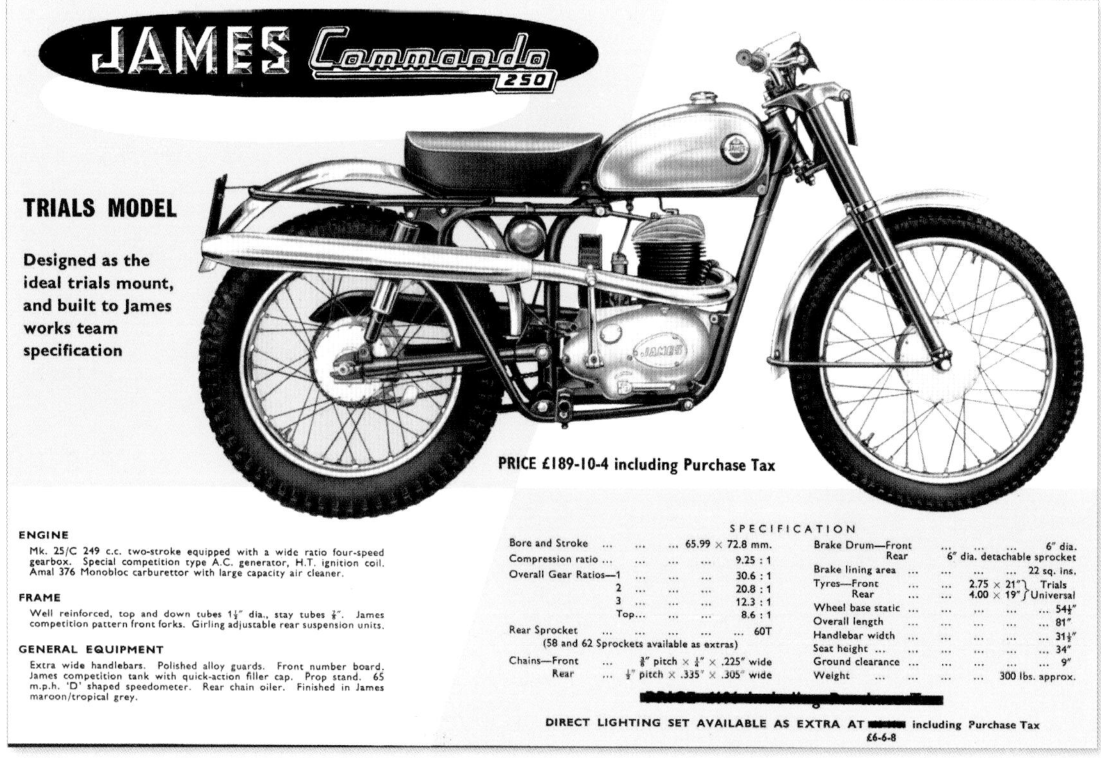

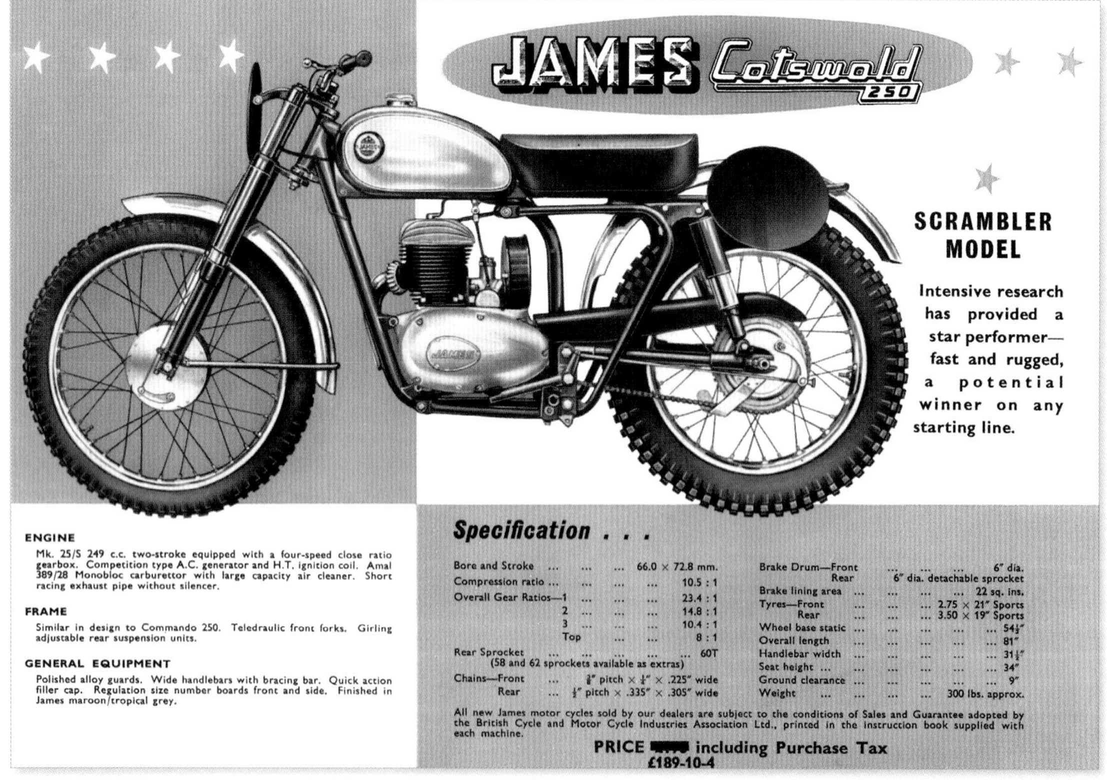

I don't remember the early '60s Cotswolds enjoying much success and when you consider James hadn't bothered to equip this example with scrambles tyres you have to call into question whether the firm, or anyone else, really did see it as 'a potential winner on any starting line'.

With its abbreviated light-alloy mudguards, chromed side panels and chain guard, rear-set footrests and reversed gear pedal, 6in front brake, humpy fuel tank and semi-dropped bars the Sports Captain certainly looked the part – hence his anticipatory grin. Unfortunately he would very shortly find out, if he didn't already know, it was nothing more than a sheep in wolf's clothing.

The Comet had retained a Villiers engine and two speeds throughout but was now finished in Arden Green – less confusing when I remind you that Francis-Barnett's all-but-identical-looking Plover had been discontinued a year earlier. Latterly all Comets had foot gear-change due to the discontinuation of Villiers's 4F cable gear-change unit.

The Captain was now enveloped in Carribean Blue – frame and all.

CADET 150

A distinctive-looking lightweight with an exhilarating performance backed by complete reliability—that's the Cadet! The power unit—a brisk 150 c.c. engine—is sufficiently versatile for lively open-road touring or for negotiating dense town traffic. Single tube backbone frame, telescopic front forks, swinging arm rear suspension, large capacity petrol tank, thick foam rubber twinseat... these are some of the features that help to make this comfortable, safe machine, gaily finished in Stromboli Red, top value in lightweight motor cycles.

The Cadet 150, in Stromboli Red, had no Francis-Barnett equivalent as its 150s were the entirely different Fulmars.

Sensibly, James had binned the awful 25T motor and returned to Villiers for the supply of its 250cc needs – in this case the latest of the twins.

SPORTS SUPERSWIFT 250

Take all the design features that have made the Sports Captain so popular. Add the new high powered Villiers 4T engine to a full 'Sports' specification—and you get the James Sports Twin. A machine destined to go places—fast! High cruising speeds, brisk acceleration, comfort, safety, roadholding—the Sports Superswift's got the lot . . . even a 6″ front brake for top stopping power. There's no mistaking that sleek, racy line, flamboyantly finished in Riviera Blue and Silver with polished alloy and chrome trim.

Model	Engine Type	Bore & Stroke Capacity	Comp. Ratio	Carburettor	Gear Ratios 1	2	3	top
Comet 100	Villiers 6F	47 x 57 98 c.c.	8:1	Villiers S12	13.1	–	–	8.5
Cadet 150	Villiers A.M.C. 15T	55 x 62 149 c.c.	7:1	Amal Monobloc 375/37	17.2	10.2	–	6.7
Captain 200	Villiers A.M.C. 20T	59 x 73 199 c.c.	8.5:1	Amal Monobloc 376/231	19.37	12.27	8.62	6.63
Sports Captain	Villiers A.M.C. 20S	59 x 73 199 c.c.	8.5:1	Amal Monobloc 376/231	19.37	12.27	8.62	6.62
Sports Superswift	Villiers 4T	50 x 63.5 250 c.c.	8.75:1	Villiers S/256	19.0	11.79	8.23	6.21
Trials Commando	Villiers 32A	66 x 72 246 c.c.	7.9:1	Villiers S25/5	24.8	16.5	9.35	6.88
Cotswold Scrambler	Villiers Parkinson 36A	66 x 72 246 c.c.	11.2:1	Amal 389/39	25.3	15.3	10.9	8.6

The entire 1964 range, including prices, would remain unchanged for the following season.

The Commando was by then altogether a much more serious machine with heavyweight Norton forks and Villiers 32A motor.

TRIALS COMMANDO 250

A machine for the real enthusiast—powered by a Villiers 32A engine and built to a specification identical to the cup winning bikes used by our works team. A cross braced tubular steel frame, famous "Roadholder" forks and Girling adjustable rear suspension dampers and lightweight wheel hubs make the Commando easy to handle in mud or bouncing over the rocks. A direct lighting set provides a useful optional extra. Finished in Stromboli Red with Chromium plate and polished alloy.

COTSWOLD SCRAMBLER 250

The new Cotswold Scrambler is the machine that's been hitting the headlines time and time again since its introduction last season, and no wonder! James development engineers have carefully tuned and matched Villiers engines to the well proved Cotswold Scrambler. The specially lined and reinforced tubular frame, famous Norton "Roadholder" forks and special high performance brakes are only some of the features that have helped the works riders achieve a notable run of sucess this season. Their machines are identical to the one you will want to buy!

Tyres Front	Tyres Rear	Wheel-base	length O'all	Width H'bar	Seat Height	Ground Clear-ance	Approx. weight lbs.	Tank. Capa-city Galls.
2.25 x 19	2.25 x 19	49½	76½″	26″	29″	5″	165	2¼
3.00 x 18	3.00 x 18	49½	76½″	24″	29½″	6½″	200	2¾
3.00 x 18	3.25 x 18	51¼	79″	26″	30′	5″	262	2¾
2.75 x 19	3.25 x 18	51¼	79″	25½″	30″	5″	260	2¾
2.75 x 19	3.25 x 18	51¼	79″	25½″	30′	5″	295	2¾
2.75 x 21	4.00 x 19	52½	81″	31″	31″	8½″	248	2¼
2.75 x 21	4.00 x 18	52½	81″	31″	31″	8″	237	1½

The Starmaker-engined Cotswold was a quick machine but early examples didn't handle as well as contemporary BSAs and Greeves bikes, as works rider Chris Horsefield found out at when vying for the lead with Jeff Smith at Hawkstone Park in 1962 – their duel ending with Smith the winner and Horsefield spending several weeks in hospital. Overall, however, they were amongst the best of their class and many were sold in the US – each Cotswold coming, somewhat ironically, with the cachet that it had been personally tested and okayed by Horsefield or another factory rider.

MATCHLESS

Like a great many other early motorcycles Matchless's roots lay in a cycle manufacturing business – in this case one started by Henry Collier in the South East London district of Plumstead during the late 1870s.

Some 20 years later his young sons, Henry born in 1883 and Charles in 1885, began working with him, and before long the boys were investigating the possibilities of incorporating an engine with one of the firm's bicycles. Their first efforts placed a small engine forward of the steering head, with direct belt-drive down to the front wheel – this device seeing the light of day in 1899. Thereon alternative configurations were toyed with until, in 1902, production commenced of a machine with 2¾hp MMC engine situated just forward of the pedals and in what would become the normal position for motorcycles.

Over the next couple of years or so, not only were alternative and larger-capacity engines introduced but also a Matchless version of the then-popular fore-cars. The latter was dropped in 1906, however, as two-wheeler developments (which included Belgian Antoine-engined V-twins) and the Collier brothers' competition activities took precedence.

After some success in the International Cup events their efforts came to impressive fruition when the first Tourist Trophy race was held on the Isle of Man the following year, where both rode JAP-powered Matchless singles – Charles leading the race from start to finish with Henry (or Harry, as he was known) running second until a broken valve put him out towards the end. The Matchless's 38mph average eclipsed that of the Norton that won the V-twin race by a handsome margin.

In 1908 it was a Triumph that took the honours but Charles was second and once again Harry retired, having run out of fuel. Single and twin classes were combined for 1909 and, remaining faithful to JAP power, the brothers had the latest magneto ignition V-twins for the island. On this occasion Charles was forced to retire when the failure of a drive-belt clip disabled his rear brake but Harry managed to see off Lee Evans's all-chain-drive Indian twin with a winning speed of just over 49mph. The apogee of the indomitable Colliers' Isle of Man appearances was 1910, with Charles winning his second TT and brother Harry runner-up – both machines outrunning the field that featured Triumphs as their main opposition. The Matchless bikes took the race average past 50mph for the first time but Charles easily eclipsed it a few weeks later at Brooklands when he took a sidecar record at better than 80 – just one of the marque's many successes at the Surrey track during its early years.

Although further TT victories were to elude the brothers (whose racing careers would end in 1914), and any Matchless in the future come to that, racing had contributed enormously to the make's popularity, even if the majority of its products were touring machines with V-twins, such as the well-respected 7hp MAG-engined Model 8B with three-speed countershaft gearbox and all-chain drive taking precedence in the years leading

up to the Great War. As it was well up to hefty sidecar duties, specially-adapted versions were employed by various branches of the services, as well as being supplied to the Russian government. A revised edition known as the Victory model was put on the market when peace returned – this leading to the sprung-frame Model H sidecar outfit that would be made until 1927.

In 1923 the company had re-entered the single-cylinder field with a Blackburn-engined 350 before bringing one out with a motor of its own a year later, followed shortly after by an OHC sports model. Having gained confidence in their own engine design and building capabilities, Matchless started to manufacture in-house V-twins in 1925 and by 1928, two years after the firm's founder Henry Collier had died, its products encompassed a varied range. Side-valve 250s, 350s and 500s, OHV 350s, 500s and 600s, a 350 OHC, touring and sports 990cc side-valve V-twins, as well as a choice of sidecar outfits including Matchless Motorcycle Vans, were all featured in that year's catalogue. It was at this stage, and doubtless with further expansion in mind, that the firm was floated as a public company and renamed Matchless Motorcycles (Colliers) Ltd.

With their coffers freshly boosted, Charlie and Harry Collier came up with a relatively unorthodox machine having a monobloc narrow-angle V-twin side-valve motor of 400cc, housed in a spring frame and with coupled brakes. Named the Silver Arrow it was unveiled at the 1929 show – just days after the disastrous Wall Street crash that heralded the depression years. Also under development, however, was the more exotic, and expensive, Silver Hawk, a luxury tourer that boasted a narrow-angle V4 motor with upstairs camshaft; it was launched with some bravado at the following show, with the slump in full swing. Neither Arrow nor Hawk were big sellers as, trading conditions aside, motorcyclists have ever been reluctant to embrace the unconventional. The Hawk lasted until 1935.

By that time, having acquired the bankrupt AJS concern in 1931 and transferred manufacture to Matchless's South East London base, the Colliers were on their way to assembling the conglomerate that they would soon preside over. In certain instances, such as the 500cc transverse V-twin S3 or reintroduced camshaft 350, AJS remained individualistic, but both it and Matchless followed the then-current fashion for sloper singles and would inexorably become even more closely intertwined. In 1935 came the introduction of the 350cc Clubman or G3 Matchless and then within a year the 250cc G2 and the 500cc G80 – a range of OHV machines with sporting pretensions that, in the case of the larger two, would go on to last the life of their manufacturer, be developed for a variety of uses and also be available as an AJS.

An exceedingly dog-eared brochure's cover depicts the winged M presiding over Europe, now at peace, from a lofty Arctic perch.

During 1937 the Collier brothers bought Sunbeam from Imperial Chemical Industries and together with the Matchless/AJS combine created Amalgamated Motor Cycles – Sunbeam production moving south to its new owner's factory henceforth. Matchless engines, which were by now all vertical with the exception of V-twins of course, were well regarded within the trade and thus had become available to other manufacturers, so the singles were fitted to certain Calthorpes, Coventry Eagles, OECs and OK Supremes. The 990cc (85.5x85.5) V-twins were also in demand, as no less a person than George Brough was happy to equip nearly 500 of his SS80s with the big side-valve unit from the X model; and since 1933 it had supplied the Morgan Motor Company, ranging from the side-valve MX to splendid OHV air-cooled MX2 and water-cooled MX4 units.

In 1938 there was a minor change in the name of the combine and so by the time Europe became engulfed in the Second World War, AMC stood for Associated Motor Cycles. For a while civilian production continued and for 1940 the duplex down-tube frame fitted to all singles was replaced by one with a single down-tube, so it was this type that was employed on the very excellent Matchless G3/L, which was supplied in large numbers to the armed forces. Not as well-known, perhaps, as BSA's M20 or Norton's 16H it was a lighter, more athletic machine that, from the summer of 1941, boasted a pair of newfangled telescopic forks and was the envy of the squaddies who were issued with more cumbersome mounts.

With other motorcycle production put on hold for the duration of the war the remainder of the large factory's manufacturing capacity was taken up with

AT LAST! THE FAMOUS MATCHLESS 'CLUBMAN'

THE World-famous Matchless "Clubman" Model re-appears in Civilian form after six years' strenuous service with the forces in every theatre of war. First in France and Belgium in 1939, then to Egypt, Libya, Algeria, Morocco, Sicily, Italy, India, Burma, again into France, Belgium, Holland and Germany—in fact, everywhere where there was a real tough job of work to be done—there was the Matchless "Clubman" in Service rig-out. The first British Military Matchless was the well-known '350' "Clubman" Model G3, which was superseded in August, 1941, by the now famous Teledraulic equipped G3/L, a machine which has been lauded and praised by British and Allied Servicemen in every place and clime.

The '500' "Clubman" G80 also re-appears, but Teledraulic equipped, of course. Here is a choice of two "Clubman" Models which we can, with the backing of our Fifty Years' experience in the industry, recommend to the Public with a confidence savoured with pride

government contracts for engineering work, as well as the manufacture of aircraft components. As the future of Sunbeam was uncertain the brand was disposed of to BSA – the marque's tenure by the Colliers had been short but its legacy was the expertise in quality paint finishes that had been learnt and would endure with AMC.

Post-war, Matchless was in the enviable position of having the very capable G3/L with its well-proven telescopic front forks already in production, so it was a simple procedure to civilianise it and reintroduce the G80 to the same specification in order to give an immediate two-model range. This state of affairs lasted until the first post-war Motor Cycle Show, where the singles were supplemented by a brand-new 500 twin, the Super Clubman G9, with 'Teledraulic rear suspension' for 1949 – AMC, like the other big British manufacturers, all seemed to decide at the same time that Triumphs had had vertical twins to themselves for far too long. At the same time swinging-arm frames were introduced as an optional extra for the G3L and G80, with competition versions of both now also available in limited numbers and only with rigid frame until a sprung-frame scrambles model was added to the range for 1951.

The proven and popular 350 and 500 singles saw Matchless through the immediate post-war years and beyond; but at the long-awaited 1948 Motor Cycle Show the firm would be unveiling not only modernised versions but an entirely new machine.

That same year AMC's competition shop put together a 500 racer, which consisted of a developed version of the G9 motor, replete with generously-finned aluminium barrels and heads, fitted into an AJS 7R rolling chassis. Entered for the 1951 Manx GP this prototype went well enough for Robin Sherry to bring it home fourth, and the following year it was a winner in the hands of Derek Farant. Having demonstrated distinct promise it was put into production as the G45 for 1953, and although its best result in the TT was Derek Ennett's sixth place in 1955 it was, despite the motor's reputation for fragility, raced internationally with some success. Around 100 were produced, including a handful that, dressed as AJSs and given the identity 10R, were exported to the marque's Venezuelan importer.

More successful, but in a different branch of motorcycle sport, during this period and right through until the 1960s, in the UK, the Continent and the USA, was the G80CS scrambler – both in its original long-stroke and, from 1956 on, short-stroke forms. Riders of the ilk of Brian Stonebridge and Dave Curtis were probably the most successful Britishers to campaign these 500s at home and abroad; but it was Belgian Auguste Mingels who used one (in conjunction with an FN) to take the European Motocross Championship in 1953. Although of similar performance to BSA's Gold Star scrambler, and some would say a comparable or even better machine, the G80CS was more often than not in its shadow. For Americans who wanted something more powerful there was the G80/TCS or

Typhoon, a bored and stroked version that approached 600cc and was made as demand dictated between 1959 and '61.

In 1958 a rather more formidable circuit racer than the discontinued G45 was introduced by Matchless. Named the G50 on account of its approximate horsepower, it represented a thoroughly sensible bit of badge engineering by AMC in that it was AJS's good old 7R 'boy racer' come of age, with its internal dimensions stretched to 90x78mm to give it 496cc (a procedure that necessitated the repositioning of the head and barrel through bolts in the crankcase). Trouble was that the maker should have come up with it at the same time as the 7R ten years earlier – or even instead of the G45 – as by now it was down on power from the latest Manx Nortons, to say nothing of Continental multis. In its favour, however, was that maintenance and repairs, like its smaller sibling, were cheaper than a twin-cam Manx and it kept its tune for longer, so it was popular amongst privateers and when well ridden, if not a world beater, could give a good account of itself – or better.

Over in the USA Dick Mann used them for AMA events from 1962 to '64 – winning the Grand National Championship in '63 in spite of being banned from running at Daytona due to controversy over the eligibility of a G50 in a competition that was open only to machines based around over-the-counter road bikes. A year earlier this had prompted AMC to equip upwards of 25 G80CS rolling chassis with G50 motors as homologation specials and send them to the States – often robbed of their motors early in life, original survivors are tantamount to the proverbial hens' teeth.

Despite its late start, the real G50 was destined to outlast its rivals in that, after AMC's race shop closed, it was picked up by Colin Seeley who carried on its development with frames of his own – and even to this day it is made by others.

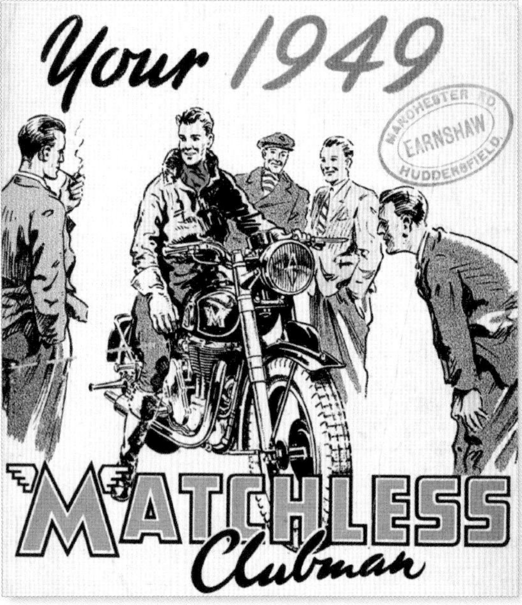

Confining itself simply to rigid-framed models, this leaflet was picked up from what is very likely the longest-running British motorcycle dealership. Established in 1906, Earnshaws are now long past their centenary and are still doing business in Huddersfield.

It was Matchless's road machinery, along with that of the group's other allied marques, that dictated the fortunes of AMC, however, and despite the introduction of cheaper-to-produce Matchless/AJS 250s and 350s at the end of the '50s things were not looking good – which predated the onslaught from the East that was soon to materialise. A combination of outmoded labour-intensive working conditions along with the failure to replace aged plant and machine tools saw profitability seep away, with around a quarter of a million pounds 'in the black' for 1960 plunging into a deficit of getting on for half as much again the following year. Economies such as the closing of the race department in 1962 made little or no difference to finances but brought to an end some honorable and long-standing traditions – in particular those of Norton, whose fortunes were linked to AMC since it had become part of the group some years earlier.

Despite this and other rationalisation, such as

SPECIFICATION

ENGINE

	Bore	*Stroke*	*Capacity*
MODEL G3/L	69 m.m.	93 m.m.	347 c.c.
MODEL G80	82.5 m.m.	93 m.m.	498 c.c.

Single port O.H.V., all moving parts totally enclosed and pressure lubricated, 3-row caged roller big end bearing, Duplex hairpin valve springs, Stellite tipped valves, individually balanced flywheels, low clearance wire wound piston, down draught inlet port, heavily finned cylinder and cylinder head.

LUBRICATION
Full dry sump system with large capacity Duplex rotary reciprocating plunger pump driven from timing side mainshaft and separate oil tank.

CARBURETTOR
Semi-automatic Amal with adjustable pilot jet for slow running.

GEAR BOX
Heavyweight 4 speed with positive type footgear change.
Multi-plate clutch with handlebar control.

TRANSMISSION
Primary chain enclosed in oil bath case. Lubricated cam type shock absorber. Rear chain protected by efficient deep section guard.

TANKS
3 Gallon welded steel petrol tank and 4 pint oil tank of similar construction incorporating detachable fabric filter.

FRAME
Duplex cradle with integral sidecar lugs and forged rear fork ends.

FORKS
Self lubricating, hydraulically damped "Teledraulic."

BRAKES
Highly efficient large diameter internal expanding with chromidium drums and finger adjustment.

SADDLE
Large Lycett spring seat with adjustable front and rear mounting.

TYRES
G3/L ... 3.25" x 19" Front and Rear.
G80 ... 3.25" x 19" Front and 3.50" x 19" Rear.

MUDGUARDS
Deep section steel guards, portion of rear guard quickly detachable for wheel accessibility.

ELECTRICAL EQUIPMENT
Magneto and dynamo driven by roller chains in oil bath cases. Large diameter headlamp with fluted domed glass and new type chromium-plated rear lamp of exclusive design. High frequency horn, constant voltage control, central battery and handlebar mounted dipper switch and horn button.

FINISH
Three thicknesses of best quality black stove enamel on Bonderised surface. Exhaust pipe, handlebars, wheel rims, saddle springs, etc., heavily chromium plated. Fuel tank and wheel rims silver lined.

EQUIPMENT
Complete set of high quality tools, grease gun, tyre pump and comprehensive Instructional Manual.

Apparently little difference between these and the immediate post-war models but in fact there were many alterations and improvements. The cradle frame had been redesigned and its seat tube repositioned further back in order to give more clearance for the carburettor and allow the employment of a Vokes filter if required. This also made provision for a larger, half-gallon oil tank. In addition the engine was set slightly lower and additional clearance at the rear allowed the fitting of a 4.00-section rear tyre. Cylinder head and rocker box had been redesigned and now featured hairpin valve springs – this applied to all Matchless motorcycles, as well as AJS singles. The headlamp (with convex glass) was now attached by brackets incorporated in the fork's top sleeves.

further melding of the marques, the downward slide was inexorable and by 1965, a little over ten years after the death of Charlie Collier, the end of the empire that had been started by him and his brother was nigh. That season a mix-and-match of Matchless, AJS and Norton were shoehorned into just one brochure for all models, and the following year AMC was bankrupt and had been acquired by Manganese Bronze Holdings.

Out of this arose Norton-Villiers, but as Matchless and AJS were surplus to requirements both makes were irreverently killed off within a short while – Matchless being catalogued until 1968 as a rebadged Norton P11 Ranger.

The name was resurrected for a while by South Devon businessman Les Harris, whose company LF Harris International of Newton Abbott went into

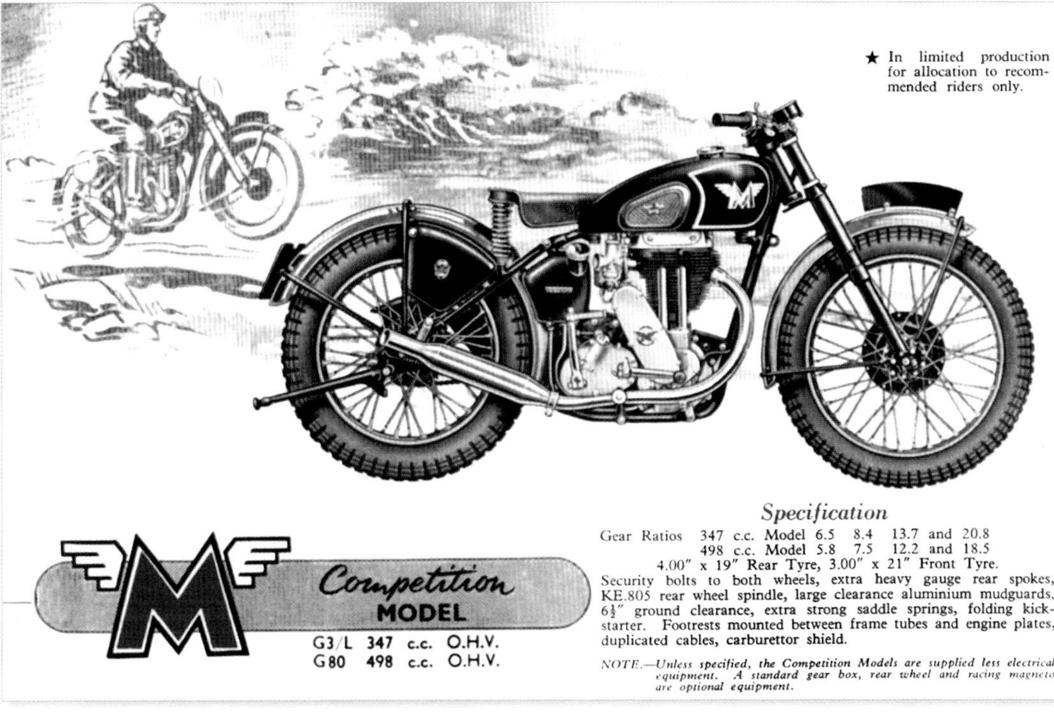

In common with other manufacturers' trials machines of the time, such as BSA's B32s and B34s, those for sale to the public were based closely on standard road models and still retained their heavy iron engines. Matchless did, however, fit aluminium mudguards whilst the competition BSAs were happy to incur a slight weight penalty with flashier chromium-plated steel. As the brochure states, these machines were produced in strictly limited numbers.

Matchless and its AMC twin AJS, along with unconnected Royal Enfield, stole a march on the other large-scale manufacturers, namely Triumph, BSA and Norton, with their introduction of optional swinging-arm, or pivoted-fork, frames for the 1949 season. They were not the first to come up with the system, of course, as Vincent had been using a variety of this type of suspension since the 1920s.

production with a completely new Matchless G80 powered by a 494cc Rotax single in the late 1980s.

Currently the Matchless brand has reappeared yet again – this time under the ownership of the Italian Malenotti family. Having enjoyed spectacular success with the reinvention of Belstaff clothing they turned their attentions to the Matchless name in 2012. Launched initially as Matchless London with a range of designer leather and other wear, a concept motorcycle named Model X Reloaded, powered by a 1.9-litre V-twin made by S & S of Illinois, was debuted in 2014 at the Milan Motorcycle Show with production said to be planned to follow.

1949 MATCHLESS PROGRAMME

HOME PRICES

		£	s.	d.	Purchase Tax £	s.	d.
Model 49/G3L	350 c.c. O.H.V. Single - -	112	0	0	30	4	10
Model 49/G3LS	As above with Teledraulic rear suspension - - - -	128	0	0	34	11	2
Model 49/G3LC	350 c.c. Competition Model -	117	0	0	31	11	10
	Lighting Extra - - -	7	10	0	2	0	6
Model 49/G80	500 c.c. O.H.V. Single - -	122	0	0	32	18	10
Model 49/G80S	As above with Teledraulic rear suspension - - - -	138	0	0	37	5	2
Model 49/G80C	500 c.c. Competition Model -	127	0	0	34	5	10
	Lighting extra - - -	7	10	0	2	0	6
Model 49/G9	500 c.c. Twin with Teledraulic rear suspension - - -	167	0	0	45	1	10

Illuminated Trip Speedometer, £4 0s. 0d. Purchase Tax £1 1s. 8d.

27/10/48

If for nothing else the first post-war show will be remembered as the moment that AMC (Matchless and AJS) along with BSA and Norton publicly threw down the gauntlet to Triumph – deciding that it had had the 500cc twin market to itself for quite long enough. Did it really have a dual seat that looked more akin to an old-fashioned vaulting horse?

A simple but striking piece of artwork to usher in the fifties. Convex glass of this pattern would be correct for the vast majority of British motorcycles fitted with Lucas headlamps at this time.

Just detail changes for the rigid-framed 350s and 500s once again – a new pattern of silencer, repositioned toolbox and ribbed mudguards, for instance.

SPECIFICATION

Models

G3/L *G80* *G3/LS* *G80S*

FRAME. G3/L and G80. Duplex cradle of brazed construction with forged fork ends and integral sidecar and pillion rest lugs. Rear, front and prop stands.
G3/LS and G80S. Duplex cradle with full Teledraulic oil-damped rear suspension. Swinging arm of massive construction pivoting in self-lubricating bush in light alloy casting. Centre, front and prop stands.
FORKS. Matchless Patented Teledraulic.
BRAKES. Quickly adjustable internal expanding of extra large diameter.

SADDLE. Fully adjustable spring seat of large dimensions.
CARBURETTOR. Amal semi-automatic with twist grip throttle control and air lever.
TRANSMISSION. Chain throughout with primary oil bath case and deep section rear guard.
TANKS. 3-gallon petrol tank of welded construction with twin filter taps and chromium plated winged Matchless emblems. 4-pint welded steel oil tank with easily cleaned fabric filter. Quick action filler caps.

ENGINE.	CAPACITY	BORE	STROKE
	350 cc.	69 mm.	93 mm.
	500 cc.	82.5 mm.	93 mm.

O.H.V. Single Cylinder, Single Port, all moving parts totally enclosed and pressure lubricated by large capacity Duplex rotary reciprocating oil pump; full dry sump lubrication system; triple row Duralumin caged big end bearing and two-piece crankpin; Stellite tipped valves; Duplex hairpin valve springs; wire-wound piston, individually balanced fly-wheels and lubricated cam type engine shaft shock absorber.
GEAR BOX. Oil lubricated heavyweight 4 speed with enclosed positive stop foot gear-change and kick-starter. Multi plate clutch with Bowden operated handlebar control.

MUDGUARDS. New deep section with central rib and tubular stays. Valanced rear guard on G3/LS and G80S.
TYRES. G3/L and G3/LS, 19" x 3.25" Triple Stud Dunlop front and rear. G/80 and G80S, 19" x 3.25" front, 19" x 3.50" rear, Dunlop Triple Stud.
ELECTRICAL EQUIPMENT. Chain-driven Lucas magneto and separate dynamo, central battery, constant voltage control, electric horn, large diameter headlamp, chromium plated rear lamp, handlebar dipper switch and horn button.
FINISH. High quality stoved black enamel of great depth on Bonderised finish. Exhaust system, wheel rims, handlebars, etc., heavily chromium plated. Petrol tank and wheel rims hand lined.
EQUIPMENT. Comprehensive tool kit, grease gun, tyre pump, speedometer and 90-page Instruction Manual.

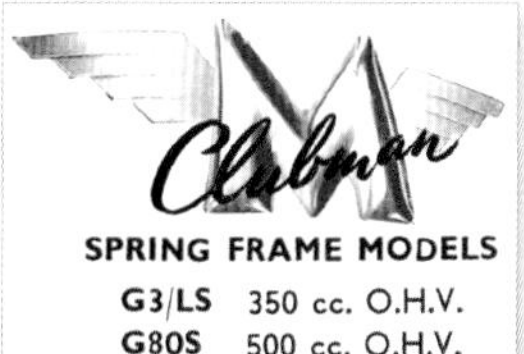

The fresh pattern of silencer was also fitted to the swinging-arm singles.

The SUPER CLUBMAN Model G9

500 cc. O.H.V.

VERTICAL TWIN

SPRING FRAME

The Outstanding Motorcycle of the 1950 Season

S P E C I F I C A T I O N

ENGINE. 500 cc. Vertical Twin. Bore 66 mm. Stroke 72.8 mm. Designed to provide an exceptional performance without any of the disadvantages usually associated with ultra efficient power units, the following outstanding specification has been provided:
Three bearing crankshaft of exceptional strength, incorporating twin flywheels of generous proportions, separate cylinders deeply spigotted into the die cast spherical crankcase, heavily finned light alloy cylinder heads with integral rocker posts and eccentric spindle rocker adjustment. Stellite tipped valves, cast in valve seats, forged light alloy connecting rods, wire-wound pistons, roller outer main bearings with Vandervell centre main and big end bearings, full dry sump lubrication with pressure feed to all moving parts by high output twin gear pumps.
GEAR BOX. Oil lubricated heavyweight 4 speed with enclosed positive stop foot gear-change and kick-starter. Multi plate clutch with Bowden operated handlebar control.
FRAME. Duplex cradle with full Teledraulic oil damped rear suspension, swinging arm of massive construction, pivoting in self lubricating bush in light alloy casting. Centre front and prop stands.
FORKS. Matchless Patented Teledraulic.
BRAKES. Quickly adjustable, internal expanding of extra large diameter.
SADDLE. Integral Dunlopillo leather covered upholstery provides unprecedented comfort for both rider and pillion passenger.
CARBURETTOR. Amal semi-automatic with twist grip throttle control and air lever.
TRANSMISSION. Chain throughout with primary oil bath case and deep section rear guard.
TANKS. 3-gallon petrol tank of welded construction with twin filter taps and chromium plated winged Matchless emblems. 4-pint welded steel oil tank with easily cleaned fabric filter. Quick action filler caps.
MUDGUARDS. New deep section with central rib and tubular stays. Valanced rear guard.
TYRES. 19″ x 3.25″ front, 19″ x 3.50″ rear, Dunlop Triple Stud.
ELECTRICAL EQUIPMENT. Gear driven flange mounted magneto and 45 watt dynamo, both instruments highly accessible for inspection or removal.
PILLION EQUIPMENT. As the Super Clubman provides seating for two people, pillion rests are included without extra charge.
EQUIPMENT. Comprehensive tool kit, grease gun, tyre pump, speedometer and 90-page Instruction Manual.

FOR the 1950 season the Competition Models have been entirely redesigned, and in their latest form they provide the enthusiastic Clubman with the ideal mount for every type of cross country competition. The following major deviations from the standard single cylinder models should be noted:

Light alloy cylinder head and barrel with cast in centrifugally cast iron liner and long retaining bolts. Short wheelbase frame with high ground clearance and undershield, wide ratio gear box, 21″ x 3.00″ front and 19″ x 4.00″ rear tyre, 4-pint oil tank with repositioned filler neck, small competition saddle and internally mounted foot rests positioned to give ideal Competition riding position. Light alloy polished mudguards with tubular stays, folding kick-starter, twin throttle and clutch cables. 2¼-gallon fuel tank, special alloy steel rear wheel spindle, security bolts, racing type magneto.

OPTIONAL EQUIPMENT. 3-gallon Fuel Tank, standard gear ratios, standard rear wheel, electric lighting.

1950 was the year that AMC's competition machines began to become more serious and increasingly veer away from their road brethren. It was also the year that aluminium engines became available to the public.

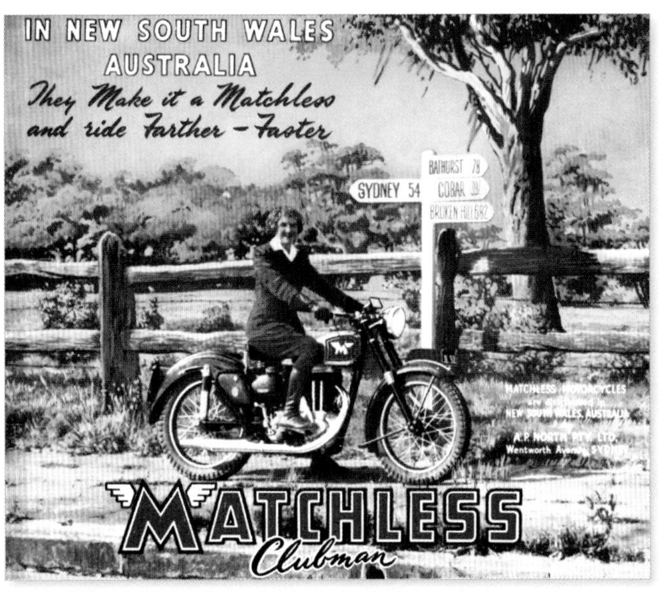

She looks as though she enjoys a long ride, so is she just heading for Bathurst or going the whole 682 miles to Broken Hill on her G80S?

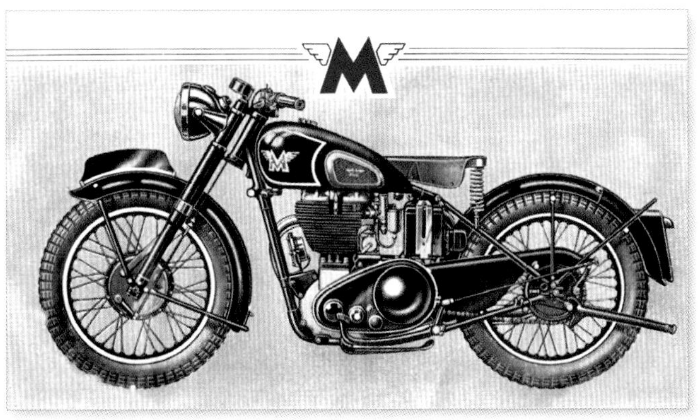

The drive side of the G80. At a glance it was all but unchanged since 1946.

Teledraulic forks now had improved damping, and larger-capacity Teledraulic rear suspension units were now employed on all swinging-arm machines – these giving rise to the 'jampot' nickname attached to both Matchless and AJS bikes so fitted.

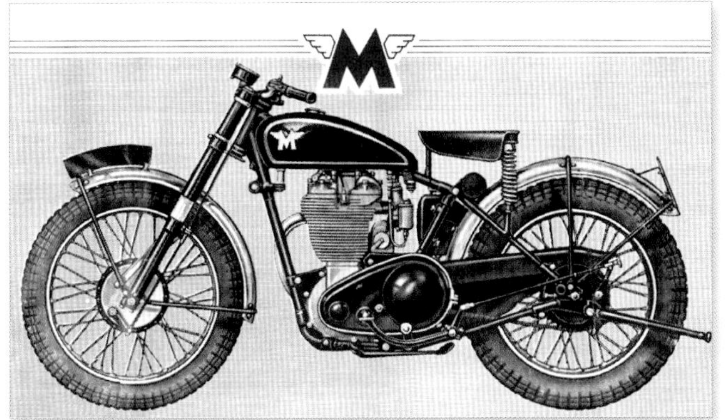

The 350cc G3/LC and 500cc G80C (this is the latter) were now fitted with aluminium cylinder heads and barrels, as well a slenderer 2¼-gallon fuel tank, and a small cylindrical tool carrier below the seat. Artie Ratcliffe won the 1950 Scottish Six Days Trial on a G3/LC.

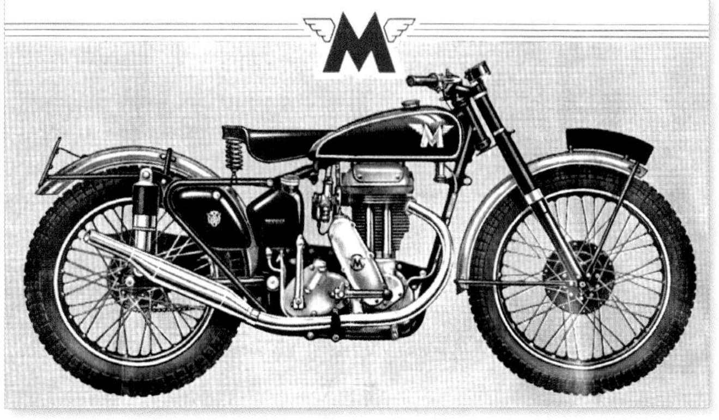

There was now a specialised machine with swinging-arm frame for scrambles and other high-speed off-road events such as were becoming popular in the United States. It could be had as the 350cc G3/LCS (as here) – both versions featured the lightweight engine with aluminium cylinder head and barrel.

As well as the latest models the 1952 brochure shows some of the processes involved in their making. Commencing with this model year, Matchless singles had their magneto mounted forward of the motor with a forward-sloping timing cover to suit – separate dynamo being located in the engine/gearbox plate and easily accessible. I have a rig for building wheels somewhat similar to the one shown but I'm sure this gentleman would have built ten to my one! Due to restrictions placed on chrome plating at this time wheel rims were Argenised (finished in baked matt-aluminium). By mid-1953 chrome was reintroduced on export models and then a year later for the home market.

The bike is a G80, the rider looks 'services' and the background smacks of Sicily, or maybe Southern Italy to me – so what was in the advertising department's mind?

Health and safety would have a fit if they came upon goings-on such as this, but I bet the operator of this press retired with all his limbs intact and lived to a good old age.

Until and during the 1920s motorcycle petrol tanks were assembled using solder but by the 1930s gas welding was almost universal.

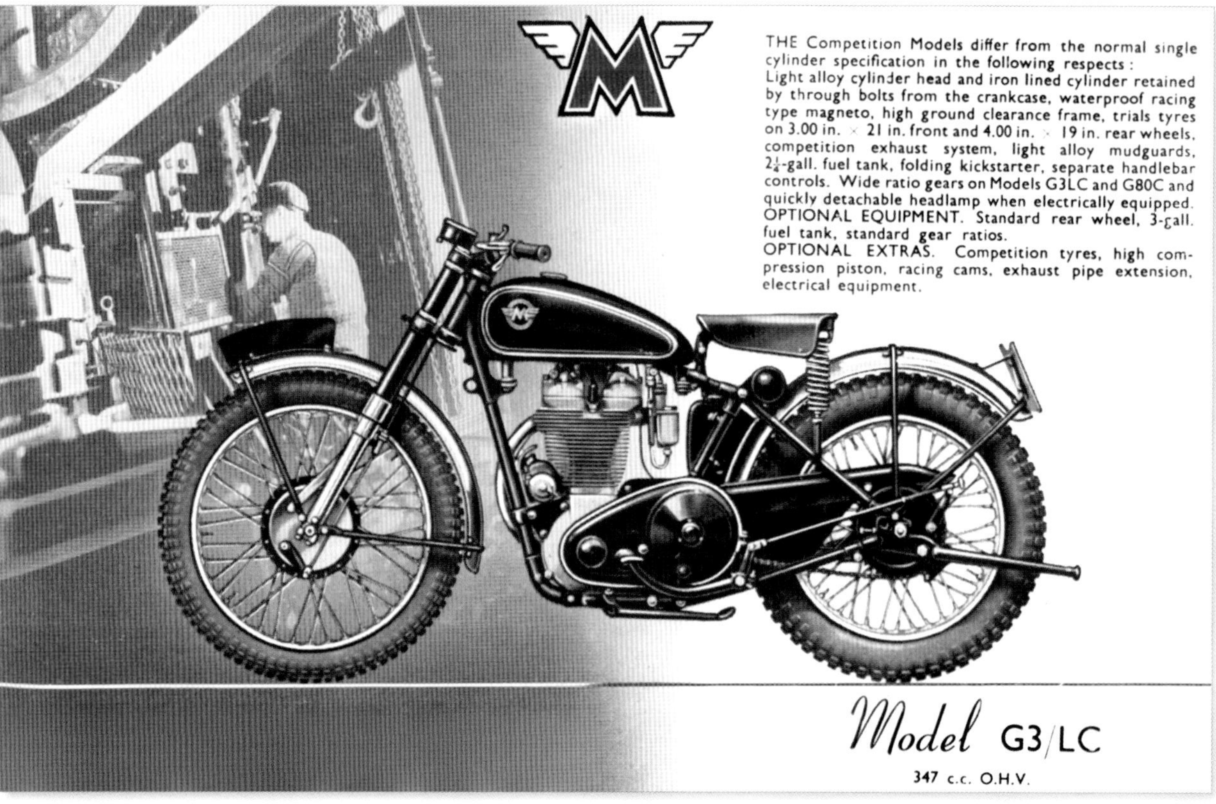

For the most part trials riders still had not made the conversion to sprung-framed machines, so Matchless's 350 had yet to make the change. Scrambles riders, on the other hand, couldn't get their hands on bikes with a sprung rear end quick enough and the G80CS was one of the best.

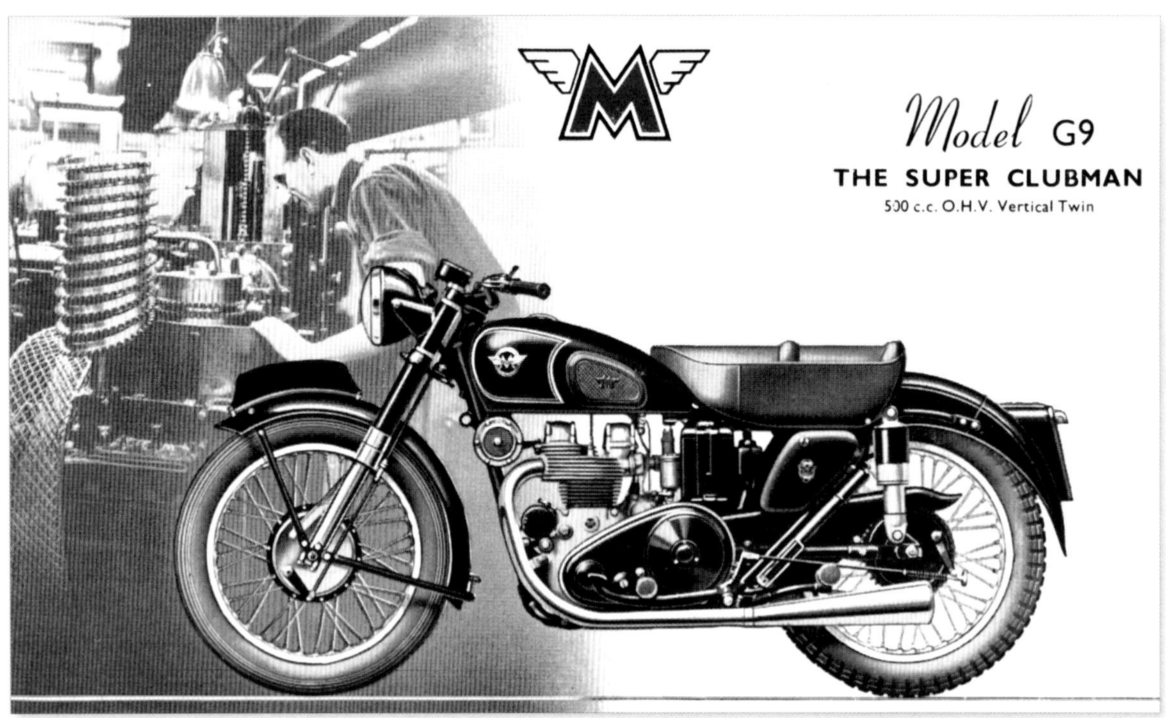

Model range and specs for 1952.

Poking fun at the way old English motorcycles were put together has long been a popular pastime but the quality of components, such as these clutch chain wheels being machined, is evidenced by the number of machines still running around with their originals to this day.

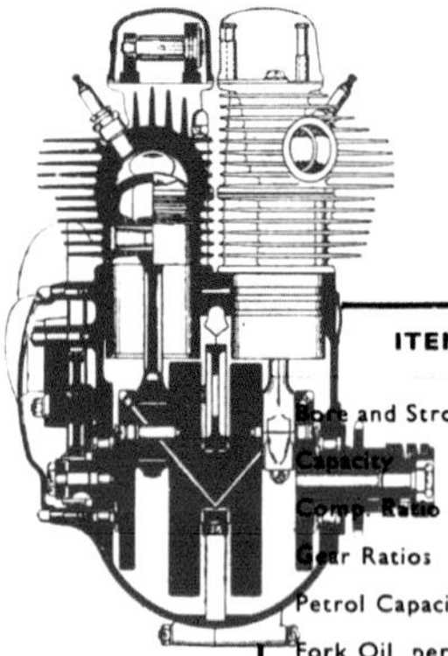

Matchless Data

ITEM	G3/L	G3/LS	G3/LC	G3/LCS	G80	G80/S	G80/C	G80C/S	G9
Bore and Stroke ...	69 × 93 mm.	69 × 93 mm.	69 × 93 mm.	69 × 93 mm.	82.5 × 93 mm.	82.5 × 93 mm.	82.5 × 93 mm.	82.5 × 93 mm.	66 × 72.8 mm.
Capacity	347 c.c.	347 c.c.	347 c.c.	347 c.c.	498 c.c.	498 c.c.	498 c.c.	498 c.c.	498 c.c.
Comp. Ratio ...	6.35 : 1	6.35 : 1	6.35 : 1	6.35 : 1	5.9 : 1	5.9 : 1	5.9 : 1	5.9 : 1	7 : 1
Gear Ratios	15.4, 9.9, 7.6 & 5.8 : 1	15.4, 9.9, 7.6 & 5.8 : 1	20.4, 13.6, 9.7 & 6.6 : 1	17.3, 11.2, 8.6 & 6.6 : 1	13.3, 8.5, 6.5 & 5.0 : 1	13.3, 8.5, 6.5 & 5.0 : 1	18.3, 11.8, 8.4 & 5.8 : 1	15.4, 9.9, 7.6 & 5.8 : 1	13.9, 8.9, 6.9 & 5.3 : 1
Petrol Capacity ...	3 G./13.6 L.	3 G./13.6 L.	2¼ G./10.2 L.	2¼ G./10.2 L.	3 G./13.6 L.	3 G./13.6 L.	2¼ G./10.2 L.	2¼ G./10.2 L.	3 G./13.6 L.
Fork Oil per Leg SAE 20.	185 c.c.	185 c.c.	185 c.c.	185 c.c.	185 c.c.	185 c.c.	185 c.c.	185 c.c.	185 c.c.
Suspension Oil per Leg SAE 20 ...	85 c.c.	85 c.c.	85 c.c.	85 c.c.	85 c.c.	85 c.c.	85 c.c.	85 c.c.	85 c.c.
Main Jet	150	150	150	150	180	180	180	180	180
Needle Jet	.105	.105	.105	.105	.105	.105	.105	.105	.105
Throttle Slide ...	6/4	6/4	6/4	6/4	29/4	29/4	29/4	29/4	6/4
Ignition Advance ...	½" (39°)	½" (39°)	½" (39°)	½" (39°)	½" (39°)	½" (39°)	½" (39°)	½" (39°)	⅜" (39°)
Primary Chain ...	½" × 5/16"	½" × 5/16"	½" × 5/16"	½" × 5/16"	½" × 5/16"	½" × 5/16"	½" × 5/16"	½" × 5/16"	½" × 5/16"
Rear Chain	⅝" × ⅜"	⅝" × ⅜"	⅝" × ⅜"	⅝" × ⅜"	⅝" × ⅜"	⅝" × ⅜"	⅝" × ⅜"	⅝" × ⅜"	⅝" × ⅜"
Dynamo Chain ...	⅜" × .225	⅜" × .225	⅜" × .225	⅜" × .225	⅜" × .225	⅜" × .225	⅜" × .225	⅜" × .225	—
Wheelbase	54"	55¼"	53"	55¼"	54"	55¼"	53"	55¼"	55¼"
Ground Clearance ...	5½"	5½"	6½"	6½"	5½"	5½"	6½"	6½"	5½"
Saddle Height ...	30"	31"	32½"	32½"	30"	31"	32½"	32½"	31½"
Weight	342 lbs.	368 lbs.	295 lbs.	321 lbs.	350 lbs.	380 lbs.	298 lbs.	324 lbs.	405 lbs.
Length	85"	86¼"	82"	85¼"	85"	86¼"	82"	85¼"	86¼"
Width	29½"	29½"	29½"	29½"	29½"	29½"	29½"	29½"	29½"

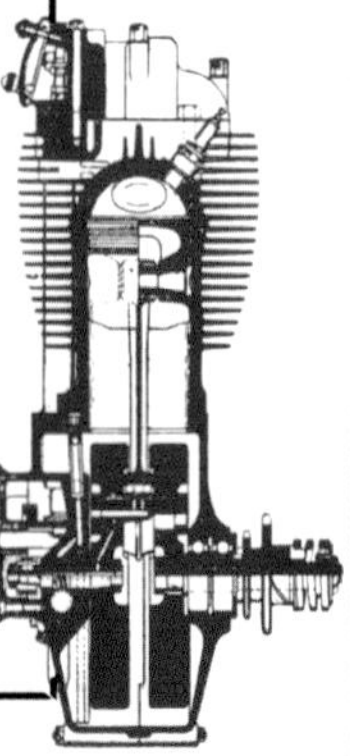

Beneath the large winged M that looked down on the 1953 show stand, visitors were treated to a police version of the G9 twin with radio transmitting and receiving equipment, the Super Clubman ridden by Bob Manns as a member of Britain's victorious ISDT team, and the new G45 500cc twin-cylinder racer. Scrambles and trials singles were also on display, the latter featuring a new lightweight welded-up frame. Besides these specialist machines there was a selection of road-going 500 twins and singles – all featuring the new alloy full-width front hubs, as well as small twin pilot lights on each side of the headlamp.

This 500 single is something of an oddity in that it has a chromium tank with red panels whilst all home-market models had black enamelled tanks with the exception of G9 twins. In the past this finish had been an option for export models so, although no mention is made in this brochure, it was likely the case for 1955 as well.

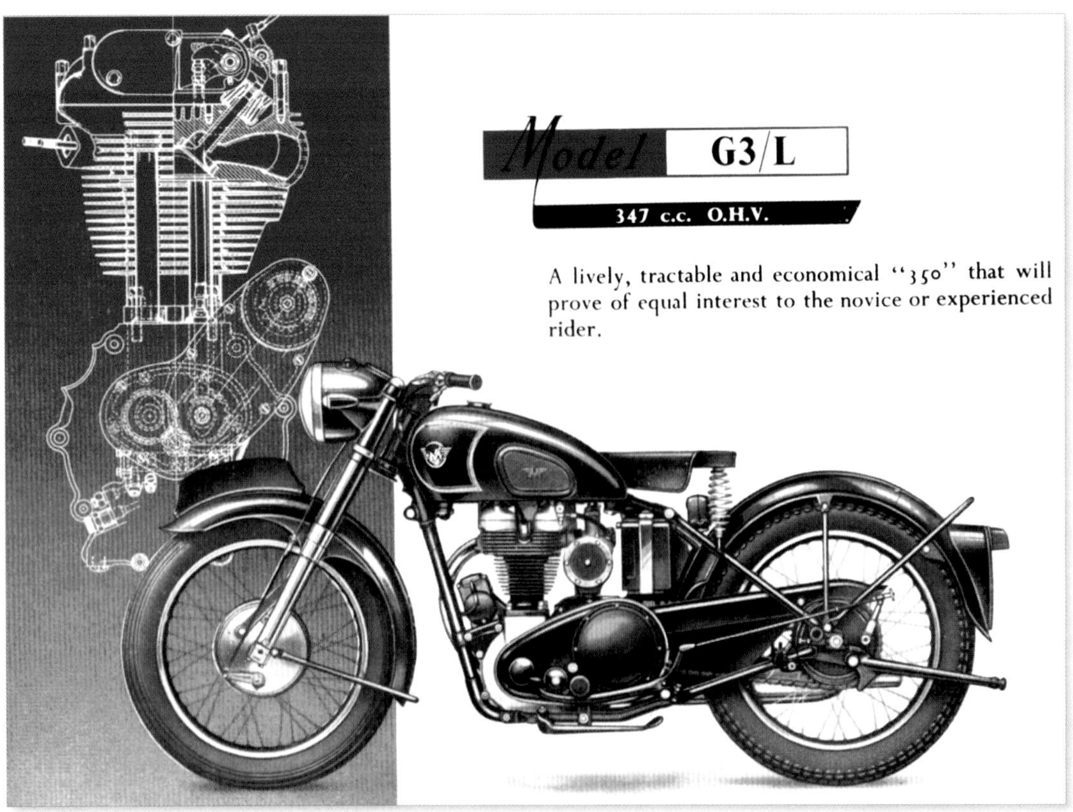

This would be the last year for the rigid-framed singles that had, since the advent of swinging-arm versions, taken on the guise of economy models. But they too boasted full-widths hubs and the new style of front mudguard.

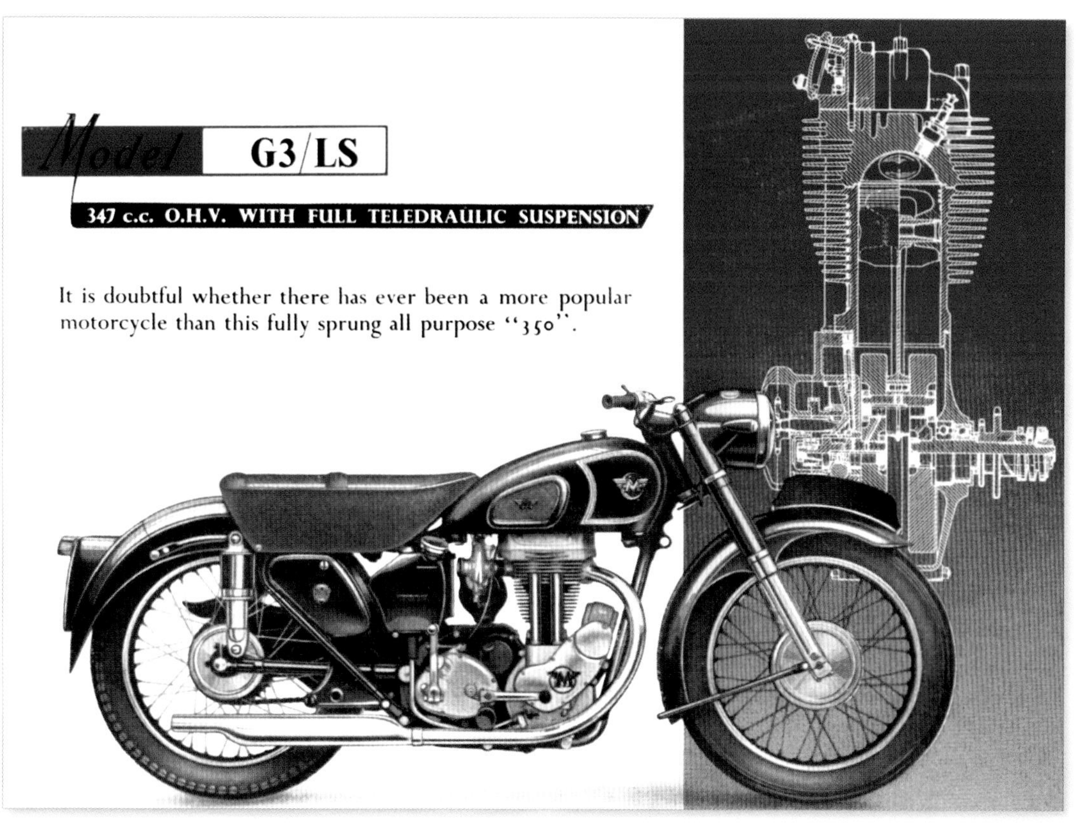

A rotating magnet magneto with automatic advance and retard had been introduced the previous season for the G80 and G80S, necessitating a bulge in the upper part of the aluminium timing cover; these components were now also employed on G3/L and G3/LSs.

The Matchless 500cc centre-main-bearing twin in road-going (right) and racing G45 (below) forms.

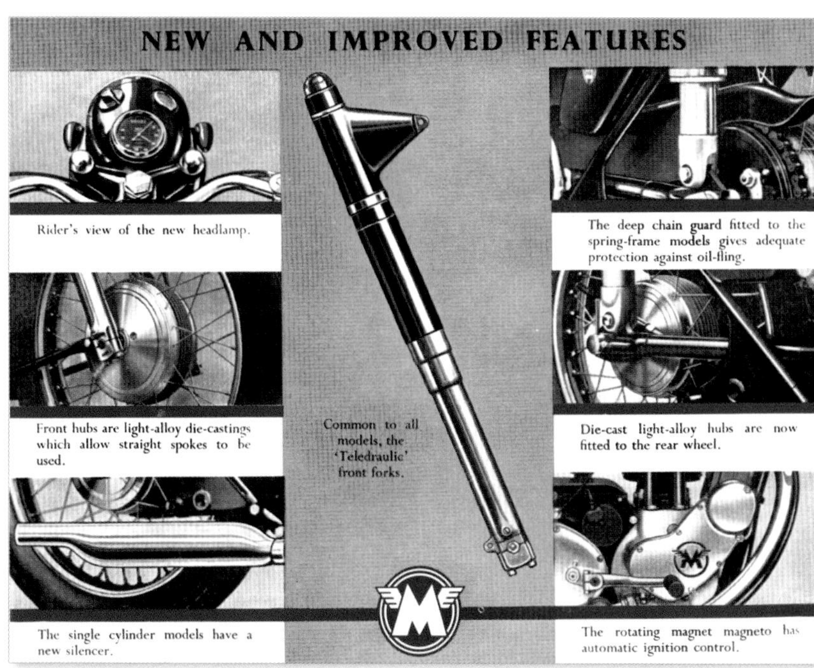

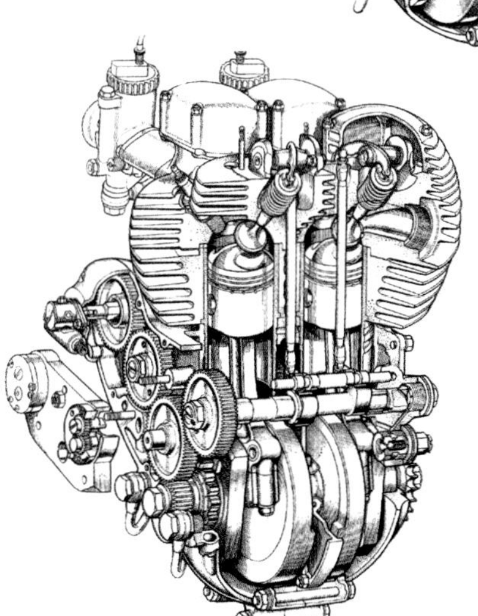

One of the main advantages of the full-width hub was that it allowed the use of straight spokes in the building of the wheels. To facilitate clutch maintenance a detachable cover for this component had been introduced the previous season.

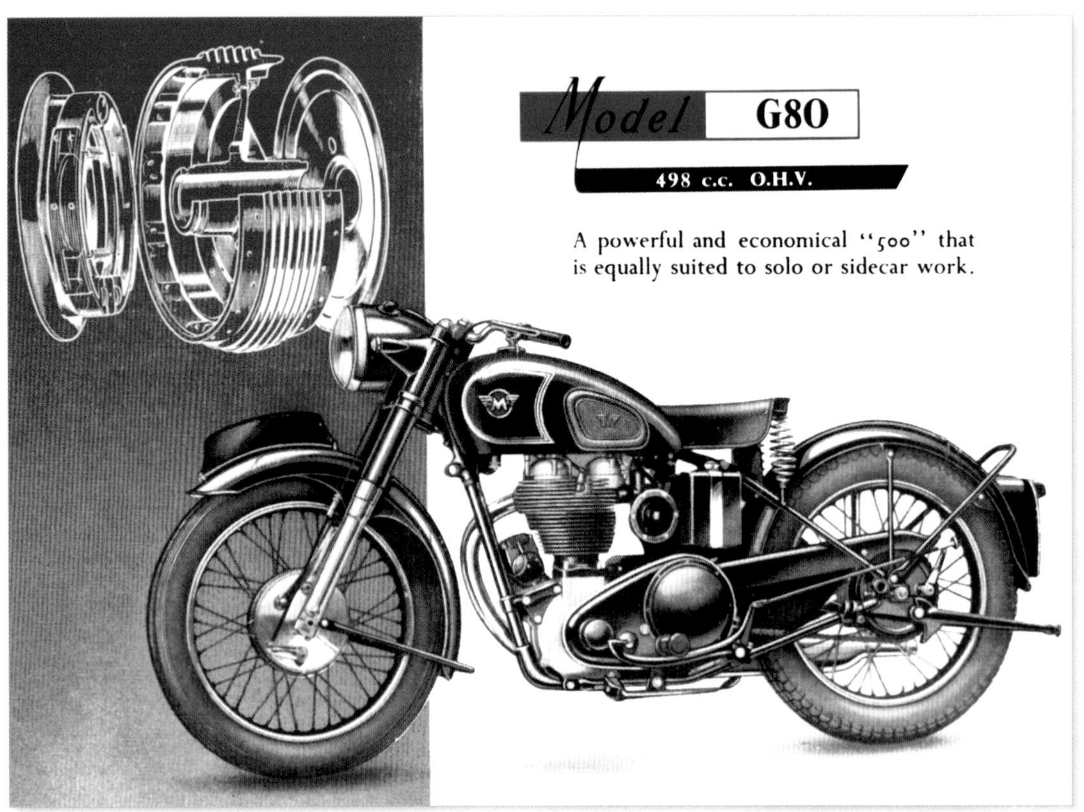

Despite being pricier than its G80 stablemate, the G80S had for some time been outselling it.

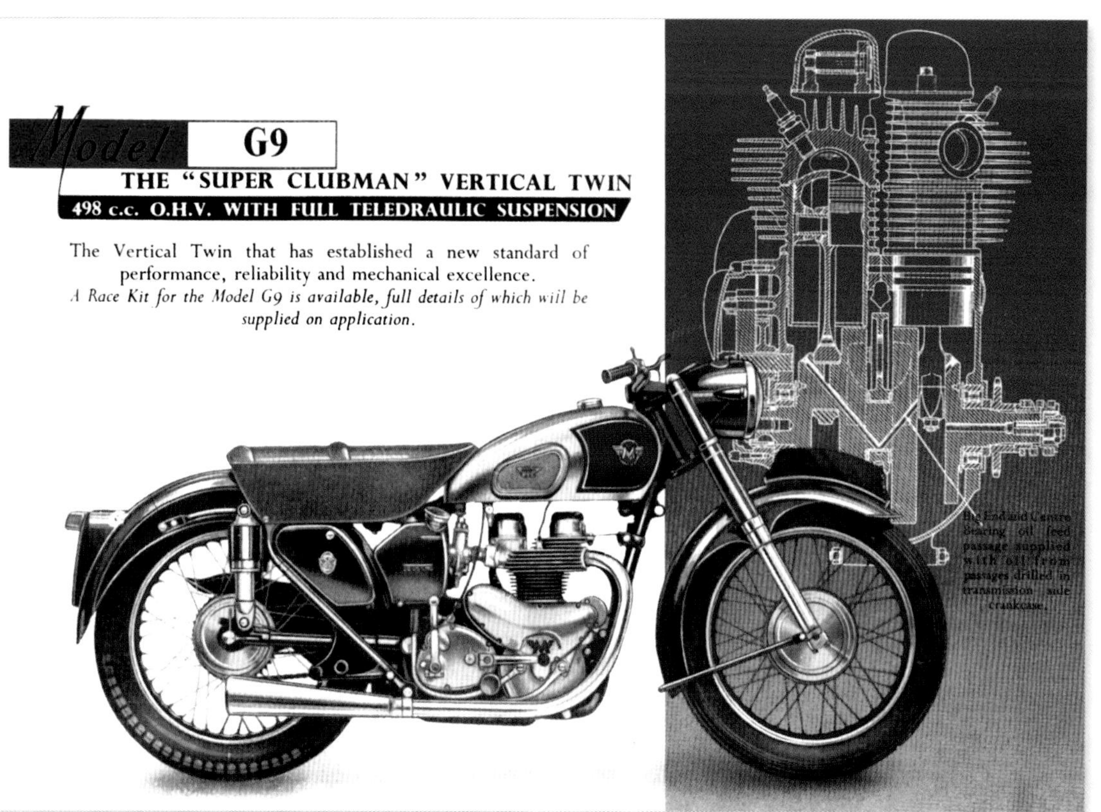

AMC twins were unusual amongst British twins in that they featured three main bearings as well as individual barrels and heads for each cylinder.

Models and specifications for 1955.

	G3/L	G3/LS	G3/LC	G3/LCS	G80	G80S	G80C	G80CS	G9
Engine	347 c.c. (69×93 mm) o.h.v. single				498 c.c. (82·5×93 mm.) o.h.v. single				498 c.c. 66×72·8mm. o.h.v. twin
Compression Ratio	6·5 or 7·5			7·5	6·3 or 7·3			7·3	7·0 or 8·0
Power—b.h.p. and r.p.m.	18 at 5750			24 at 6000	24·4 at 5500			30 at 5600	29 at 6800
Carburettor. Choke size	1 1/16″			1 1/16″	1 5/32″			1 3/16″	1″
Main jet size	210			300	260			340	240
Throttle slide No. ...	3			5	3			7	4
Sparking plug type—K.L.G. ...	FE80				FE80				FE80
Gear ratios 1st—2nd	15·4—9·9		21·1—16·1	17·4—11·2	13·3—8·5		18·6—14·1	15·4—9·9	13·9—8·9
3rd—top	7·6—5·8		10·4—6·6	8·6—6·6	6·5—5·0		9·1—5·8	7·6—5·8	6·9—5·25
Tyre size. Front	3·25×19″		2·75×21″	3·00×21″	3·25×19″		2·75×21″	3·00×21″	3·25×19″
Rear	3·25×19″		4·00×19″		3·50×19″		4·00×19″		3·50×19″
Brake diameter and width ...	7×7/8″				7×7/8″				7×7/8″
Ignition timing b.t.d.c.	39° or 1/2″				39° or 1/2″				39° or 3/8″
Valve timing: Inlet opens b.t.d.c. ...	36°			59°	18°			59°	35°
Inlet closes a.b.d.c. ...	51°			69°	69°			69°	65°
Exhaust opens b.b.d.c.	50°			74°	50°			74°	65°
Exhaust closes a.t.d.c.	30°			48°	30°			48°	35°
Primary chain	1/2×0·305″				1/2×0·305″				1/2×0·305″
Rear chain	5/8×3/8″				5/8×3/8″				5/8×3/8″
Dynamo and Magneto chain ...	3/8×0·225″				3/8×0·225″				—
Petrol consumption. m.p.g. at 40 m.p.h.	85		—	—	80		—	—	75
Weight—pounds	344	375	293	321	354	387	296	324	394
Wheelbase—inches	54	55¼	53	55¼	54	55¼	53	55¼	55¼
Seat height—inches	30	31½	32½	32½	30	31½	32	32½	31½
Ground clearance—inches ...	5½	5½	6½	6½	5½	5½	6½	6½	5½
Overall length—inches	85	86¼	82	85¼	85	86¼	82	85¼	86¼
height—inches	41	41½	43	43	41	41½	43	43	41½
width—inches	28				28				28

Models

G3/LC

347 c.c. O.H.V.

G80C

498 c.c. O.H.V.

The successes achieved by Matchless Competition Models in Open and Club events during the 1954 Season emphasise, once again, that these specially designed models admirably fulfil the function for which they are intended.

For obvious reasons these Competition Models differ from the Standard Models in many respects.

Both the rigid and spring frame versions are fitted with a high level exhaust system, trials tyres and security bolts, extra heavy wheel spokes and wide rims, light alloy cylinder barrel, Lucas waterproof magneto with manual ignition control, 2¼-gallon light-alloy petrol tank, folding kick-starter, steel crankcase shield and polished light alloy mudguards. The rigid frame fitted to the Models G3/LC and G8OC is of all-welded construction and provides a high ground clearance and a wheelbase of 53 inches. The waterproof saddle is adjustable for height and the gearbox has the essential wide ratios. Tyre sizes are: front, 2.75 x 21 inch; rear, 4.00 x 19 inch.

The all-welded 14-gauge lightweight rigid frame used for these machines had been introduced for the 1954 season and at the same time even more suitable gear ratios for trials had been installed in the C-model gearboxes – one set for 350s and another for the 500s.

A *Matchless* spring frame, with special *Teledraulic* rear suspension units and stronger fork springs, is fitted to the Models G3/LCS and G8OCS. The frame is of normal construction and provides a standard wheel base but is strengthened at several points and permits a high ground clearance to be obtained. In addition, the Specification includes a Twinseat of new design, robust footrests, racing cams, a high, compression piston, and an Amal T.T.10 Carburettor. Tyre sizes are: front, 3.00 x 21 inch; rear, 4.00 x 21 inch.

OPTIONAL EQUIPMENT

3¾ gallon steel petrol tank, standard or wide ratio gears, wheels as fitted to standard Models.

OPTIONAL EXTRAS

Electric lighting equipment with quickly detachable headlamp, exhaust pipe extension, Dunlop 'knobbly' tyres.

MODEL G45

A 500 c.c. o.h.v. racing vertical twin specifically designed for International road races. Full details will be supplied on application.

Models

G3/LCS

347 c.c. O.H.V.

G80CS

498 c.c. O.H.V.

The latest Super Clubman streaks across the cover of this '56 brochure, one of many given out by James Wooldridge and Son who were, perhaps, Launceston's longest-established garage businesses, James having begun trading just prior to the First War.

The entire existing range had undergone a facelift in the form of large matching pannier oil tank and toolbox assemblies – the latter also housing the battery, a VC unit and horn. In fact, the oil tank had a detachable pressed-steel cover, of the same shape, attached by a pair of cheese-headed screws either side of the M motif – the artist, however, neglected to portray this feature in any of the machines in this brochure.

Underneath the skin there was a redesigned frame, having a vertical seat post with large malleable lug at its lower end that housed the self-lubricating porous bronze pivot bushes for the swinging arm. This lug was extended downwards and was sandwiched between the rear of the engine cradle members and these in turn by the rear loop – the whole locked by a through bolt. The triangular pillion footrest brackets, first seen the previous season, now took the form of a stronger single wrapped plate construction that was bored and brazed in place.

The restyled 500cc G9 Super Clubman.

The rigid trials frame had at last been done away with and replaced by this special lightweight structure unique to this Matchless and AJS's 16MC. Other competition models (the 500cc G80C and scrambles G3/LCS and G80CS) were not featured in this year's brochure.

BRIEF SPECIFICATION
498 c.c. O.H.V. vertical twin cylinder engine, deeply finned light-alloy cylinders and cylinder heads, forged steel crankshaft, twin camshafts, push rod operated valves, two G.P. Amal carburettors, Lucas racing magneto. Each engine develops not less than 48 b.h.p. on 82 octane petrol. Welded duplex cradle frame, 4-speed close-ratio gearbox, 8¼ inch brakes, aluminium-alloy rims, magnesium-alloy hubs, 6-gallon petrol and 1-gallon light-alloy oil tanks, full *Teledraulic* suspension, forged light-alloy fork sliders, light-alloy mudguards, 19 × 3.00 inch front tyre, 19 × 3.25 inch rear tyre, racing Dunlop tyres.

Designed to conform to the road racing requirements of the F.I.M., the 1956 Model G45 incorporates the many improvements evolved as a result of the use of similar machines by works riders in 1955 races.

The first of AMC's G9 twin-based racers was entered for the 1951 Senior Manx GP and to not a few people's surprise Robin Sherry finished in fourth place behind three Nortons, but in front of many more. For a rolling chassis and cycle parts the organisation had to look no further than AJS's 7R, and into this had gone the developed twin with generously finned aluminium heads and barrels – the combination to be marketed as the G45. Derek Farrant's victory in the 1952 Senior Manx was just two months before it was to be officially presented to the public at the 1952 Motor Cycle Show. Derek was lucky to say the least, but one swallow does not a summer make. Although it was to enjoy limited production its early promise never translated into another Island victory. By the time it became included in the company's sales brochure it had been uprated with a forged steel crankshaft.

MODEL	G3/LC Trials	G3/LS Single 350	G9 Twin 500	G11 Twin 600	G80S Single 500
Engine: o.h.v. single	347 c.c. (69×93 mm.)		—		498 c.c. (82·5×93 mm.)
o.h.v. twin	—		498 c.c. (66×72·8 mm.)	592 c.c. (72×72·8 mm.)	—
Compression ratio	6·5	7·5 or 6·5	8·0 or 7·0	7·5 or 6·5	7·3 or 6·3
Power b.h.p.	18 at 5750 r.p.m.	19 at 5750 r.p.m.	30 at 6800 r.p.m.	32 at 6700 r.p.m.	25·5 at 5500 r.p.m.
Carburettor: Choke size	1 1/16″		1″	1″	1 5/32″
Main jet size	210		240	270	260
Throttle slide No. ...	3	3½	4	4	3½
Valve timing: Inlet opens	26° before t.d.c.	36° before t.d.c.	35° before t.d.c.		18° before t.d.c.
Inlet closes	53° after b.d.c.	51° after b.d.c.	65° after b.d.c.		69° after b.d.c.
Exhaust opens ...	64° before b.d.c.	50° before b.d.c.	65° before b.d.c.		50° before b.d.c.
Exhaust closes ...	25° after t.d.c.	30° after t.d.c.	35° after t.d.c.		30° after t.d.c.
Ignition timing	39° or ½″ before t.d.c.		39° or ½″ before t.d.c.		39° or ½″ before t.d.c.
Gear ratios: 1st—2nd—3rd—4th ...	21·0—16·0—10·3—6·6	15·4—9·9—7·6—5·8	13·9—8·9—6·9—5·25		13·3—8·5—6·5—5·0
Brakes: front and rear	7″ diam. × ⅞″ wide		7″ diam. × ⅞″ wide		7″ diam. × ⅞″ wide
Tyres: front	2·75″ × 21″	3·25″ × 19″	3·25″ × 19″		3·25″ × 19″
rear	4·00″ × 19″	3.25″ × 19″	3·50″ × 19″		3·50″ × 19″
Rear Chain	⅝″ pitch × 0·380″ width		⅝″ pitch × 0·380″ width		⅝″ pitch × 0·380″ width
Primary Chain	½″ pitch × 0·305″ width		½″ pitch × 0·305″ width		½″ pitch × 0·305″ width
Dynamo and Magneto Chain ...	⅜″ pitch × 0·225″ width		—		⅜″ pitch × 0·225″ width
Petrol consumption at 40 m.p.h. ...	—	85 m.p.g.	75 m.p.g.	72 m.p.g.	80 m.p.g.
Wheelbase	54″	55¼″	55¼		55¼″
Seat height	32½″	31½″	31½″		31½″
Ground clearance	6½″	5½″	5½″		5½″
Overall length	83″	86¼″	86¼″		86¼″
height	43″	41½″	41½″		41½″
width	28″	28″	28″		28″
Weight	320 lb.	375 lb.	394 lb.	396 lb.	387 lb.

Road machine range and specs for 1956.

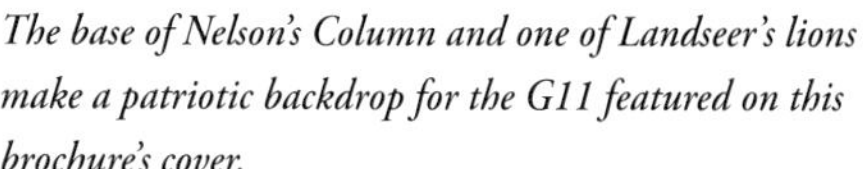
The base of Nelson's Column and one of Landseer's lions make a patriotic backdrop for the G11 featured on this brochure's cover.

At a quick glance the '57 G3/LS, and G80S too for that matter, were all but unchanged with just the slimmer Girling rear suspension units to tell them apart from the previous year's jampot versions. There was a brand-new AMC-developed and manufactured gearbox, however; and look – the screws securing the oil tank's cover are now shown, and there's a different transfer between them too.

In addition to the new gearbox and improved rear suspension units the G9 'Super Clubman' now had its tank finished in the same manner as the G11 excepting that the base colour was black with centres of the chromium plated wheel rims to match.

The new heavyweight four-speed gearbox of AMC design and manufacture, with statically and dynamically balanced three-bearing twin-cylinder crankshaft. Quickly detachable rear wheel incorporating cushioned rubber drive. Waterproof rotating magnet single-cylinder magneto.

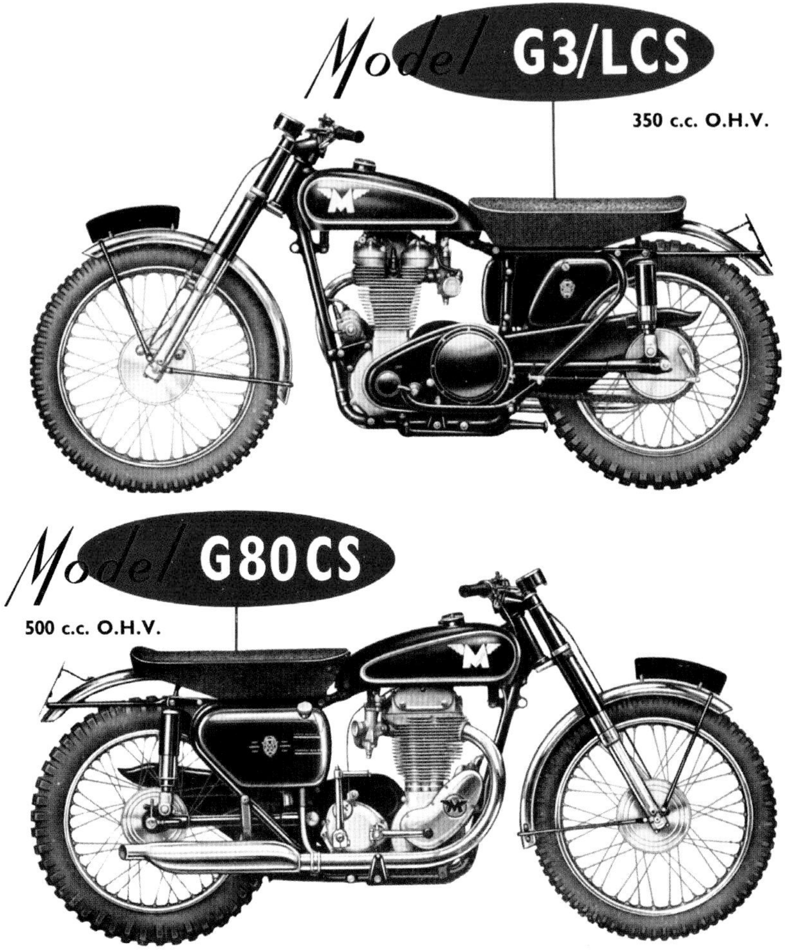

Both 350 and 500 scramblers were back for '57 in much-improved form, in particular the G80CS that now had a special Phil Walker-designed short-stroke oversquare (86x85.5mm) motor that it shared with its AJS equivalent. The AMC gearbox in the 350 had special ratios of its own, whilst the 500 had the same ratios as the road-going G3/LS.

Trials bike had been further improved with updated rear suspension units and minor frame alterations to suit.

In the following respects the model G3/LC differs from the standard models.

The redesigned frame is of welded construction and provides much increased ground clearance and a wheelbase of 53 inches. The waterproof saddle is adjustable and the gear box has the essential wide ratios, with a folding kick-starter. Lucas waterproof magneto with manual ignition control, small capacity light alloy fuel tank, crankcase shield, polished alloy mudguards with tubular steel stays. Extra heavy straight wheel spokes and Dunlop Trials tyres.

Tyre sizes are: Front 2·75 × 21 inch—Rear 4·00 × 19 inch.

The cylinder barrel is light alloy with an iron liner and is retained by through bolts, upswept exhaust system is fitted.

OPTIONAL EXTRA

Electric lighting equipment and quickly detachable head-lamp.

THESE models have been designed to meet the demands of the most discriminating riders who realise that success can only be assured by choosing machines specially designed and built for the job. From the technical specification it will be apparent that these models include all the features that are so essential in the exacting sport:

SPECIFICATION

Engine
348 c.c. capacity—Bore 72 mm., stroke 85·5 mm. 497 c.c. capacity—Bore 86 mm., stroke 85·5 mm. Special features are racing cams, twin camshafts, Duralumin push rods, hairpin valve springs and fully enclosed valve gear, steel flywheels, high tensile steel connecting rod, large diameter crankpin and a caged roller big end bearing, high compression racing piston, light alloy cylinder head and barrel. A double acting reciprocating oil pump operating a dry sump lubrication system is employed.

Ignition
Lucas racing type waterproof magneto with manual control.

Carburettor
Large bore Amal 'Monobloc'.

Frame
Strengthened Duplex cradle with swinging arm suspension. All joints are brazed.

Forks
'Teledraulic' with extra strong springs and oil damping.

Gear Box
Entirely new and of Matchless design and manufacture. Heavyweight 4-speed positive foot control and dry multiplate clutch incorporating efficient rubber shock absorber.

Transmission
Oil bath primary chaincase and fully protective guard for final drive chain.

Wheels
Fitted with wide rims, full-width light alloy hubs straight extra heavy spokes and adjustable taper roller bearings.

Brakes
7 inch diameter and machined for accuracy after assembly.

Mudguards
Front and rear are of polished light alloy. Tubular steel stays.

Tyres
Dunlop 'knobbly'. Security bolts are fitted to both wheels.

Seat
Comfortable racing twinseat of Vynide covered Dunlopillo.

Handlebars
Fully adjustable for height and angle.

Tanks
2-gallon capacity light alloy fuel tank. Half-gallon steel oil tank.

Footrests
Forged steel of immense strength.

Finish
Polished light alloy and chromium plate. All ferrous surfaces bonderized prior to black stove enamelling.

Equipment
Steel crankcase shield. Speedometer. Prop stand. Modified spring up centre stand and light alloy number plates.

Optional Equipment
3¾-gallon petrol tank. Standard gear ratios. Standard wheels and tyres. Low compression piston.

Optional Extras
Quickly detachable electric lamps.

Vertical twin cylinder engine of 498 c.c. capacity, light alloy cylinders and cylinder heads, twin camshafts, push rod operated valves. Two Amal Grand Prix carburettors, Lucas racing magneto. Maximum power is developed at 7,100—7,200 r.p.m. (not less than 50 b.h.p. on 82 octane petrol).

Fully sprung duplex cradle frame, light alloy mudguards and tanks. Magnesium alloy wheel hubs, straight spokes and $8\frac{1}{4}$ inch brakes.

3·50 × 19 inch rear and 3·00 × 19 inch front wheels. Dunlop racing tyres. Smith's rev. counter; two-piece adjustable handlebars. Quick action filler caps. Fully equipped for use in races under F.I.M. Regulations.

Claimed power was up for the latest G45 but, although it enjoyed some successes at venues around the world other than on the Isle of Man, it was forever destined to play second fiddle to the Manx Norton. Burman racing gearboxes hitherto employed in both 7Rs and G45s had magnesium alloy casings and this practice continued.

MODEL	G3/LC	G3/LS	G80S	G9	G11	G3/LCS	G80CS
No. of cylinders	1	1	1	2	2	1	1
Bore/stroke mm.	69 × 93		82·5 × 93	66 × 72·8	72 × 72·8	72 × 85·5	86 × 85·5
Capacity c.c.	347		498	498	592	348	497
Compression ratio	6·5	7·5 or 6·5	7·3 or 6·3	8·0 or 7·0	7· or 6·75	9·9	8·7
Carburettor: Amal	Monobloc 376/5		Monobloc 389/1	Monobloc 376/6	Monobloc 376/78	Monobloc 389/18	Monobloc 389/12
Choke size (inches)	$1\frac{1}{16}$		$1\frac{5}{32}$	1	$1\frac{1}{16}$	$1\frac{1}{8}$	1
Throttle slide No.	3	$3\frac{1}{2}$	$3\frac{1}{2}$	4	4	3	
Main Jet No.	210		260	220	280	270	440
Gear ratios: top, 3rd, 2nd, 1st	6·5, 9·6, 15·5, 21·3	5·8, 7·8, 10·3, 15·5	5·0, 6·8, 8·9, 13·4	5·25, 7·1, 9·3, 14·0		6·5, 8·8, 11·5, 17·4	5·8, 7·8, 10·3, 15·5
Tyres: rear (inches) ...	4·00 × 19	3·25 × 19	3·50 × 19	3·50 × 19		4·00 × 19	
front (inches)	2·75 × 21	3·25 × 19	3·25 × 19	3·25 × 19		3·00 × 21	
Brake dimensions (inches) ...	$7 \times \frac{7}{8}$		$7 \times \frac{7}{8}$	$7 \times \frac{7}{8}$		$7 \times \frac{7}{8}$	
Chains: front (inches) ...	$\frac{1}{2} \times 0·305$		$\frac{1}{2} \times 0·305$	$\frac{1}{2} \times 0·305$		$\frac{1}{2} \times 0·305$	
rear (inches) ...	$\frac{5}{8} \times 0·380$		$\frac{5}{8} \times 0·380$	$\frac{5}{8} \times 0·380$		$\frac{5}{8} \times 0·380$	
Petrol tank capacity (galls.) ...	2	$3\frac{3}{4}$	$3\frac{3}{4}$	$3\frac{3}{4}$		2	
Oil tank capacity (pints) ...	4	4	4	4		4	
Overall length (inches) ...	83	$86\frac{1}{4}$	$86\frac{1}{4}$	$86\frac{1}{4}$		$85\frac{1}{4}$	
„ width „ ...	28	28	28	28		28	
„ height „ ...	43	$41\frac{1}{2}$	$41\frac{1}{2}$	$41\frac{1}{2}$		43	
Ground clearance (inches) ...	$6\frac{1}{2}$	$5\frac{1}{2}$	$5\frac{1}{2}$	$5\frac{1}{2}$		$6\frac{1}{2}$	
Seat Height (inches)	$32\frac{1}{2}$	$31\frac{1}{2}$	$31\frac{1}{2}$	$31\frac{1}{2}$		$32\frac{1}{2}$	
Wheelbase (inches)	54	$55\frac{1}{4}$	$55\frac{1}{4}$	$55\frac{1}{4}$		$55\frac{1}{4}$	
Weight (lbs.)	320	375	387	394	396	326	329

Road, Trials and Scrambles range for 1957.

The '58 brochure's cover focused on the cleaner appearance of both G3/LS (depicted here) and G80S motors due to the changeover from magneto to coil ignition – a relatively small symmetrical contact breaker cover having replaced the magneto drive's aluminium casing. The engine/gearbox plate also no longer housed a dynamo, as charging was taken care of by an alternator driven by the drive-side mainshaft. Competition singles retained magneto ignition and consequently their engine casings were unchanged.

MATCHLESS
1958

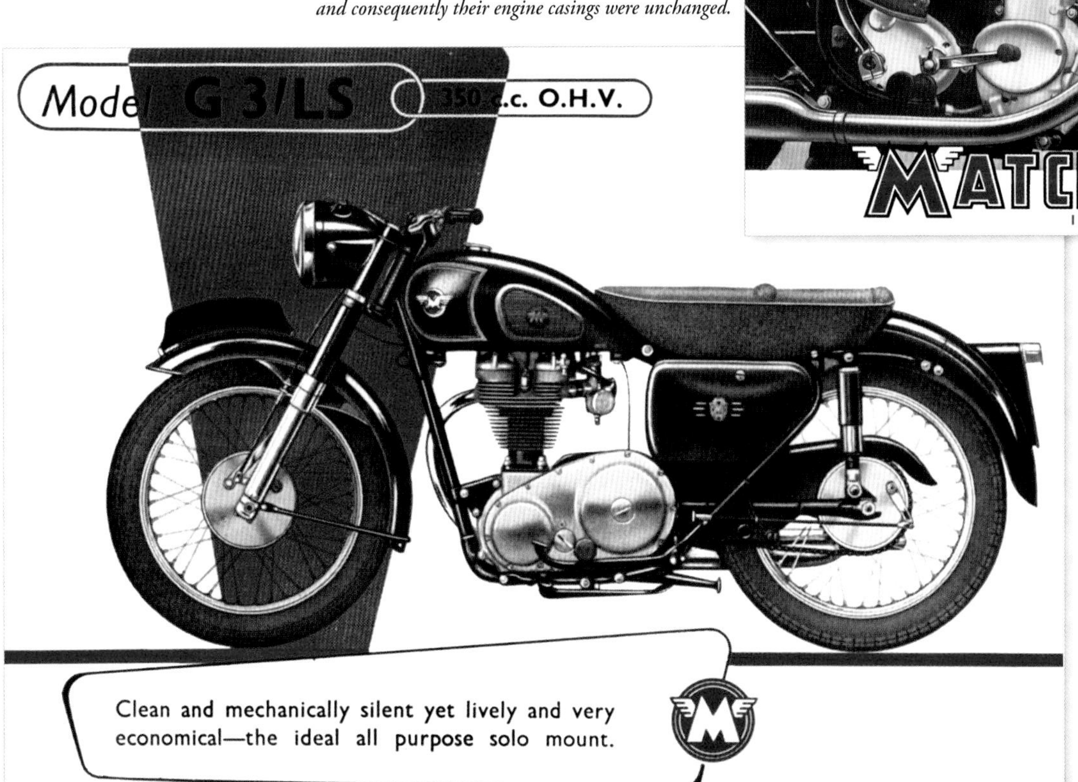

From the drive side, both 350 and 500 singles looked a little less cluttered around the engine without a magneto. The aluminium primary chain case was much less prone to leakage than the pressed-steel version it replaced.

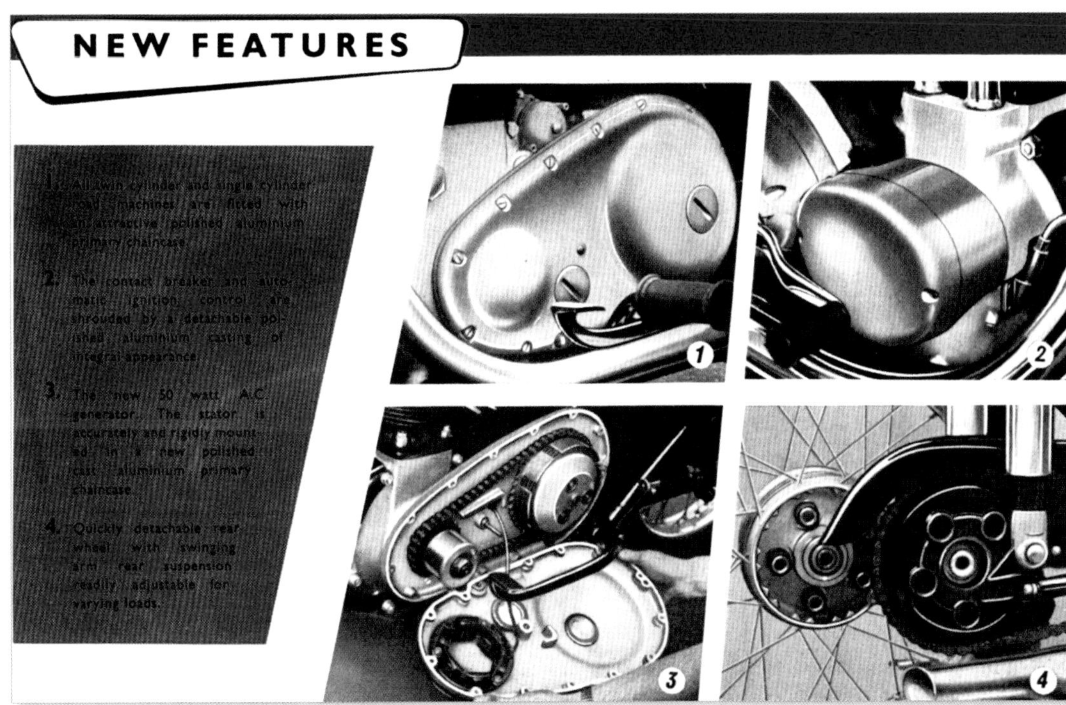
NEW FEATURES

1. All twin cylinder and single cylinder road machines are fitted with an attractive polished aluminium primary chaincase.
2. The contact breaker and automatic ignition control are shrouded by a detachable polished aluminium casting of integral appearance.
3. The new 50 watt A.C. generator. The stator is accurately and rigidly mounted in a new polished cast aluminium primary chaincase.
4. Quickly detachable rear wheel with swinging arm rear suspension readily adjustable for varying loads.

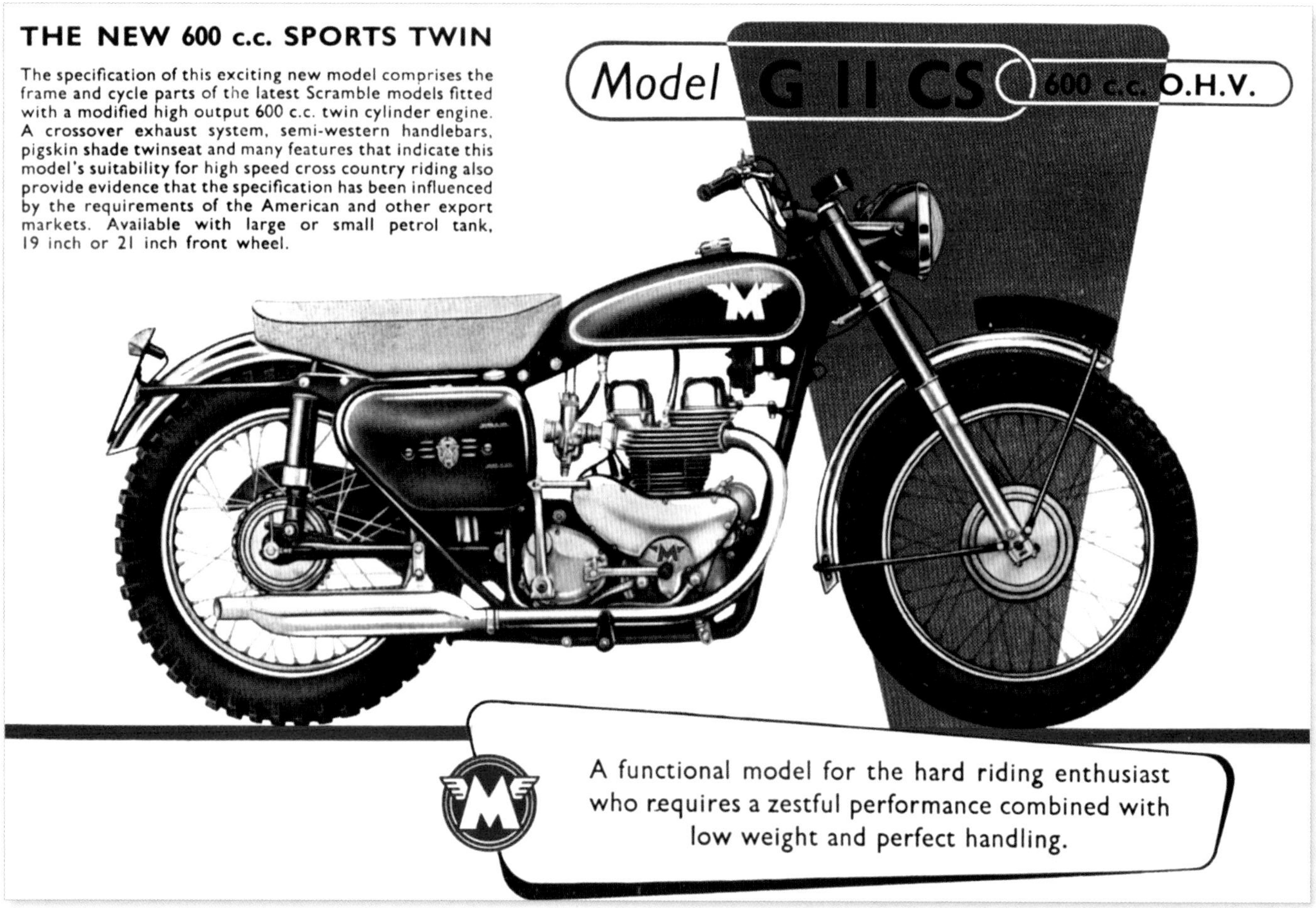

THE NEW 600 c.c. SPORTS TWIN

The specification of this exciting new model comprises the frame and cycle parts of the latest Scramble models fitted with a modified high output 600 c.c. twin cylinder engine. A crossover exhaust system, semi-western handlebars, pigskin shade twinseat and many features that indicate this model's suitability for high speed cross country riding also provide evidence that the specification has been influenced by the requirements of the American and other export markets. Available with large or small petrol tank, 19 inch or 21 inch front wheel.

Model G 11 CS 600 c.c. O.H.V.

A functional model for the hard riding enthusiast who requires a zestful performance combined with low weight and perfect handling.

AJS's publicity for its version, the 30CS, was a little more to the point, stating that it had been 'Designed primarily for the North American market', rather than the text in this brochure where it is simply 'influenced by'. Its compression ratio hike from the standard G11's 6.75 or 7.4 to a heady 8.5 signified it would have some additional poke too – but how many, if any, were sold for UK consumption, I wonder?

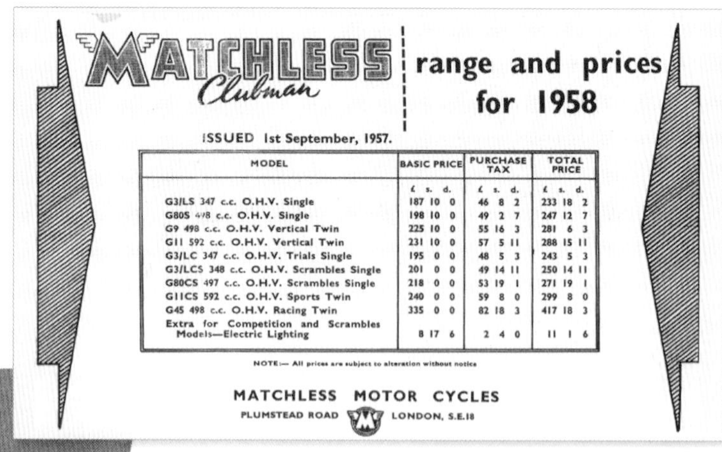

MATCHLESS Clubman

range and prices for 1958

ISSUED 1st September, 1957.

MODEL	BASIC PRICE	PURCHASE TAX	TOTAL PRICE
	£ s. d.	£ s. d.	£ s. d.
G3/LS 347 c.c. O.H.V. Single	187 10 0	46 8 2	233 18 2
G80S 498 c.c. O.H.V. Single	198 10 0	49 2 7	247 12 7
G9 498 c.c. O.H.V. Vertical Twin	225 10 0	55 16 3	281 6 3
G11 592 c.c. O.H.V. Vertical Twin	231 10 0	57 5 11	288 15 11
G3/LC 347 c.c. O.H.V. Trials Single	195 0 0	48 5 3	243 5 3
G3/LCS 348 c.c. O.H.V. Scrambles Single	201 0 0	49 14 11	250 14 11
G80CS 497 c.c. O.H.V. Scrambles Single	218 0 0	53 19 1	271 19 1
G11CS 592 c.c. O.H.V. Sports Twin	240 0 0	59 8 0	299 8 0
G45 498 c.c. O.H.V. Racing Twin	335 0 0	82 18 3	417 18 3
Extra for Competition and Scrambles Models—Electric Lighting	8 17 6	2 4 0	11 1 6

NOTE:— All prices are subject to alteration without notice

MATCHLESS MOTOR CYCLES

PLUMSTEAD ROAD LONDON, S.E.18

Although both the G9 and G11 twins (this is the latter) were still fitted with magneto ignition and a dynamo for charging they too benefitted from an aluminium primary chain case.

They also popped what I would take to be a US-spec (or very near) G80CS in this year's brochure.

MODEL	G9	G11	G11CS	G3LS	G3LC	G3LCS	G80CS	G80S
Capacity c.c.	498	592		347		348	497	498
Engine: type	O.H.V.	O.H.V.		O.H.V.		O.H.V.	O.H.V.	O.H.V.
Bore/Stroke mm.	66×72·8	72×72·8		69×93		72×85·5	86×85·5	82·5×93
Compression ratio	8·0 or 7·0	7·4 or 6·75	8·5	7·5 or 6·5	6·5	9·9	8·7	7·3 or 6·3
No. of cylinders	2	2	2	1	1	1	1	1
Gear ratio: Top	5·25	5·0	5·0	5·8	6·5	6·5	5·8	5·0
Third	7·1	6·8	6·8	7·8	9·6	8·8	7·8	6·8
Second	9·3	8·9	8·9	10·3	15·5	11·5	10·3	8·9
First	14·0	13·4	13·4	15·5	21·3	17·4	15·5	13·4
Rear chain	⅝″×0·360″	⅝″×0·380″	⅝″×0·380″		⅝″×0·380″		⅝″×0·380″	
Front chain	½″×0·305″	½″×0·305″	½″×0·305″		½″×0·305″		½″×0·305″	
Tyres: Front	3·25″×19″	3·25″×19″	3·50″×19″ or 3·00″×21″	3·25″×19″	2·75″×21″	3·00″×21″		3·25″×19″
Rear	3·50″×19″	3·50″×19″	4·00″×19″	3·25″×19″	4·00″×19″	4·00″×19″		3·50″×19″
Carburettor: Amal	Monobloc 376/6	Monobloc 376/78	Monobloc 376/78	Monobloc 376/5	Monobloc 376/59T	Monobloc 389/18	Monobloc 389/12	Monobloc 389/1
Choke size	1″	1 1/16″	1 1/16″	1 1/16″	1 1/16″	1⅛″	1 3/16″	1 5/32″
Main Jet No.	220	280	280	210	210	270	440	260
Throttle slide No.	4	3½	4	3½	3	3	3	3½
Brakes: Front and rear	7″×⅞″		7″×⅞″		7″×⅞″		7″×⅞″	
Petrol tank capacity (galls.) ...	3¾	3¾	2	3¾	2	2	2	3¾
Oil tank capacity (pints) ...	4	4	4	4	4	4	4	4
Weight (lbs.)	394	396	380	375	320	326	329	387
Length	86¼″	86¼″	85¼″	86¼″	83″	85¼″		86¼″
Width	28″	28″	28″	28″	28″	23″	28″	28″
Height	41½″	41½″	43″	41½″	43″	43″	43″	41½″
Clearance	5½″	5½″	6½″	5½″	10″	6½″	6½″	5½″
Wheelbase	55¼″	55¼″	55¼″	55¼″	54″	55¼″	55¼″	55¼″
Seat height	31½″	31″½	32½″	31½″	32½″	32½″	32½″	31½″

Road bike specifications for 1958.

Alone amongst the large manufacturers in having nothing but two-strokes in its 250cc-and-under portfolio, AMC's remedy was this 250 to be marketed as either an AJS or a Matchless. The Matchless edition naturally shared its ultra-short stroke (70x65mm) unit-construction motor with AJS and, like the latter, was available in road or scrambles trim – known simply as the G2 and G2CS. The former, like BSA's C15 Star, and Royal Enfield's 250s come to that, had 17in road wheels.

MODEL G2 250 c.c.

ENGINE
High efficiency O.H.V. single cylinder. Die cast aluminium cylinder head. Stellite tipped valves operated by twin cams, lever followers, Duralumin pushrods and hairpin valve springs. Dry sump lubrication from 2½ pint reservoir and positive feed by duplex plunger pump to all moving parts including caged roller big end bearing and wire wound piston. 7.8:1 compression ratio. 70 mm. bore. 65 mm. stroke. 248 c.c. capacity.

GEAR BOX
Mounted direct on the rear of the crankcase and incorporating primary chain adjustment. Positive stop gearchange, folding kickstarter. Gear ratios 6.89, 8.96, 12.75 and 20.12. Multi plate clutch with vane type shock absorber.

ELECTRICAL EQUIPMENT
High output A.C. generator, accessible contact breaker and automatic ignition control, 6" headlamp with lighting, ignition and emergency ignition switches. Enclosed battery, rectifier etc. Combined dipper switch and horn button.

CARBURETTOR
1 1/16" Amal Monobloc (Enclosed air cleaner extra).

FRAME
1½" dia. single tube from head lug to rear of gearbox. Pressed steel under channel enclosing centre stand operating mechanism. Swinging arm rear frame with large pivot bearing. Oil damped telescopic forks and rear suspension units.

WHEELS
Journal ball bearings, full width hubs, 3.25" x 17" tyres front and rear.

TRANSMISSION GUARD
A normal deep section chainguard is standard equipment but full rear chain enclosure is an optional extra.

BRAKES
6" internal expanding with cast drums.

TWINSEAT
Foam rubber, Vynide covered and piped in red.

FINISH
Frame and deep section mudguards, etc., black stoved enamel, petrol tank Cardinal red with silver lines. Attractive plastic badge and rubber kneegrips. Rims, adjustable handlebars, exhaust systems etc., heavily chromium plated.

I'd love to have seen the look on everyone's faces, including their own, had Adrian and Carol turned up at the Ace Café on the North Circular dressed as they are here whilst apparently engaged upon an Alpine tour.

Unusually for a UK-market scrambler the G2CS had 19in wheels front and rear and also the same 2¾-gallon petrol tank as the road model. But that it was intended as a serious class contender was evidenced by its 10:1 compression against G2's 7.8. It also had heavy-duty forks, hubs and suspension units, as well as a strengthened frame.

FULL 1959 PROGRAMME

For your guidance . . .

Both 250cc. models are finished in black with hand lined cardinal red petrol tanks and polished engine covers.
All standard road models of 350cc. and upwards are finished in black and chromium with hand lining.
The Sportstwins are fitted with polished aluminium mudguards and cardinal red tanks and tool box. Chromium plated fork covers, etc. are available as an optional extra.
All road models are fitted with deep section one piece mudguards of new and pleasing design.
New large capacity petrol tanks are included in the specification of all road twins.
An optional two-tone finish in Arctic white and black with chromium plated tank panels is available for all standard models at small extra charge.
Quickly detachable wheels and chromium plated tank panels are available as optional extras on all standard models and are included in the specification of all de-luxe twin cylinder models.
The Sportstwins are the only Competition models fitted with electric lighting as standard. The CS. model is equipped with a quickly detachable headlamp and the CSR. model with the normal large headlamp.

In standard trim the G3 and its larger brother the G80 soberly continued on their way in black, but the brochure also offered them, at extra cost, with chromium-plated tank panel and red beading instead of hand lining. For the extrovert, however, there was an option, also at further cost, of Arctic White tank, mudguards etc, with chromium tank panels – or with the petrol tank in Arctic White and Black (or maybe Red as well?) with chromium separating strip.

Mechanically the same as the previous season, the G9 did, however, have a larger 4¼-gallon tank and, like all road-going singles and twins, restyled mudguards. The standard G9 came in Black but there were other options listed. The machine depicted here is the G9 De Luxe with optional extra two-tone finish. See illustration of tanks with available finishes.

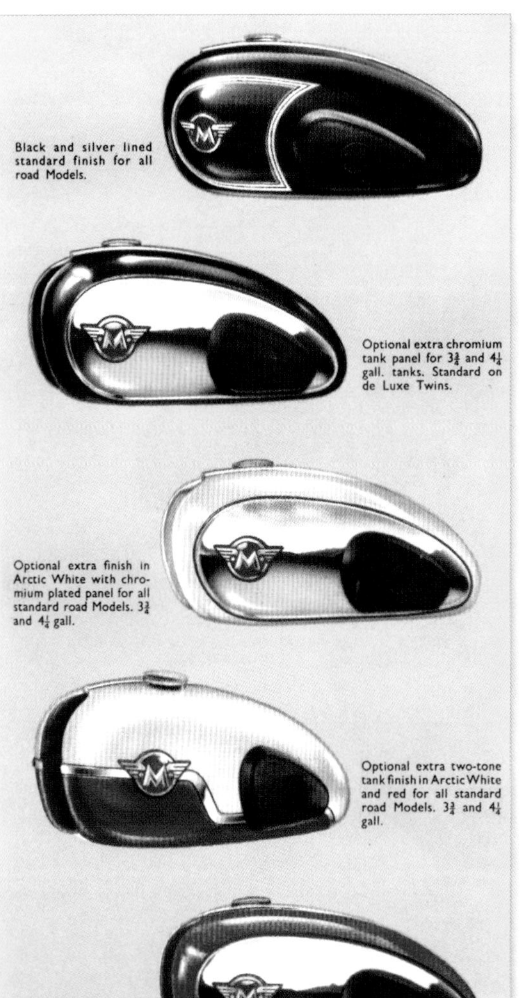

The manufacturer captioned this as a G12 De Luxe but I'm not so sure – you'd have to see it from the other side to tell for certain. The De Luxes (whether G12 or G9) had a magneto and dynamo whilst the normal G12 had coil ignition, so if its one of them there'd be no dynamo and a bulge in the primary chain cover to accommodate the alternator.

FINISH

The standard finish is three coats of high quality stoved black enamel on Bonderized base. Various engine, hub, fork and gearbox castings in aluminium are polished. The exhaust system, wheel rims, handlebars and various controls etc., are heavily chromium plated. Optional finishes on road models at a small extra cost are — Arctic White tank, mudguards etc., with chromium plated tank panels and black plastic beading.

As above but with the petrol tank in Arctic White and black with a chromium plated separating strip.

The standard black finish but with chromium plated tank panels and red beading instead of hand lining. Chromium plated tank panels are fitted as standard to the De Luxe Twins.

Factory customisation by Matchless, 1959 style. But the listed finish applications are a little misleading, with an Arctic White and Red tank illustrated but no mention of it in the text, whilst an Arctic White and Black tank is not pictured! So – using this key – I'll leave it to you to navigate your way through the model and colour options.

New for '59 were a pair of super sports Matchless twins honestly described as being suitable for sports class racing and high-speed road work. Along with the identical AJS version, the G12CSR was certainly a fast machine and a challenge to the quickest of the other manufacturers' big twins but the fastest, as its manufacturers suggested? That could be the topic of a long discussion. There was also an identically kitted-out 500 version (right) – the G9CSR. Both had a degree of tuning with a higher (8.5:1) compression ratio and were also fitted with magneto ignition and a 60-watt dynamo.

For British and European events of this nature – read motocross or scrambles – there was the G80CS, but as in the previous year's brochure it was depicted in US trim. You could still buy a 350 scrambler but it was no longer known as the G3/LCS – rather the G3CS.

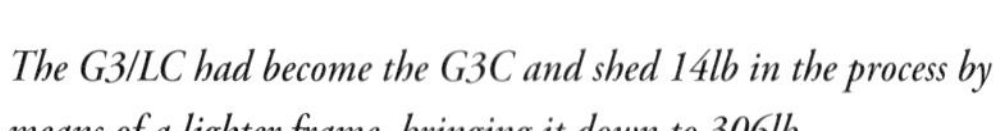

The G3/LC had become the G3C and shed 14lb in the process by means of a lighter frame, bringing it down to 306lb.

Last season's G11 had been dropped and replaced with this 650cc version. There was also a 500cc G9CS – by way of description the brochure judged them to be for 'cross country speed events'. Yes – but not in the UK.

For 1960 the G3, along with other road machines, was built around a much-improved frame with twin front down-tubes. Our rider Ken – he even looks like a Ken, don't you think – is just explaining to Liz that she's right, it isn't simply the new-type G3 with duplex frame but rather a special one because he splashed out the extra to have the petrol tank in Cardinal Red and Arctic White with a polished separating strip.

An option for both the new unit-construction G5, as well as its smaller relation, was a black fuel tank with silver lining. Extras, for both models, included fully-enclosed rear chain, safety bars, luggage carrier, luggage panniers and side stand. Tanks could also be finished in Red with chrome sides or Red and Arctic white.

All 500 and 650 twins, excepting the G12CS, now had a slightly larger 4½-gallon fuel tank. The 500 G9CS had been discontinued due to lack of demand – US buyers clamouring for more cc (the G12CS) rather than less.

650 c.c. SPORTSTWIN MODELS G12CS AND G12CSR

The CS. Sportstwin is intended for cross country speed events and the CSR version for high speed road work or Sports model racing.

ENGINE
Of similar basic design and dimensions to the standard engine, the tuned high compression engine fitted to the Sportstwins incorporates the redesigned big port cylinder heads and crossover single outlet exhaust system. A separate dynamo and magneto is fitted and the headlamp on the CS Model is of the 7" quickly detachable type.

TRANSMISSION
As for standard twins but with special alloy steel gear box internals.

FRAME
New and immensely strong twin tube incorporating extra steering trail. Now fitted with integral pillion footrest lugs. High lift centre stand.

FORKS AND SUSPENSION
Heavyweight Teledraulic with special springs and damping. Long action rear suspension units.

SEAT
Deep section racing type with reinforced steel base.

MUDGUARDS
Polished aluminium with strengthening plates and light gauge tubular steel stays.

ELECTRICAL EQUIPMENT
See engine.
Flexible centre point mounting for voltage control unit.

CARBURETTOR
Amal monobloc. 1⅛" bore.

HANDLEBARS
Standard, Semi-Western or Sports.

UNDERSHIELD
Heavy gauge sheet steel.

WHEELS, BRAKES AND TYRES
MODEL G12CSR: Standard.
MODEL G12CS: Standard front wheel with 3.25" × 19" Trials Universal Tyre.
4.00" × 19" rear wheel with knobbly tyre on WM.3 rim, extra heavy spokes, heat treated alloy steel spindle.

TANKS
MODEL G12CSR: 4½ gallon with chromium plated panels.
MODEL G12CS: 2 gallon Competition type.
Both with new 3-point mounting.
Modified 5 pint oil tank with shield.

FINISH
Black stoved enamel, chromium plated rims, exhaust system, etc., polished engine covers, primary chaincase, fork sliders, mudguards, etc.
Cardinal red tank with silver hand-lining on CS. Model.
Cardinal red tank with chromium plated panels on CSR. Model.

OPTIONAL EQUIPMENT
Standard tyres, wheels, petrol tank, engine sprocket, suspension, etc., where applicable.

OPTIONAL EXTRAS
Q-D rear wheel, air cleaner. Competition tank with integral chromium plated side panels, or 3 gallon competition tank, rev counter.

ENGINE
86 m.m. bore × 85.5 m.m. stroke. 497 c.c. capacity. Steel disc flywheels drilled for balance, special forged steel connecting rod, large roller big end bearing with Duralumin cage, extra roller timing-side main bearing, integral push rod tunnels in deeply finned light alloy cylinder, new big bore racing type cylinder head retained by invisible through bolts from crankcase, 1⅜" bore Grand Prix racing Amal carburettor, waterproof magneto, cast aluminium primary chaincase incorporating A.C. generator when lighting specified, H.C. racing piston.
For the 1960 season the Model G80CS is listed to a bare racing specification. The oil tank has been moved to the drive side to provide room for the G.P. carburettor and a large cylindrical air cleaner. Room exists for a small exposed battery on the timing side when lighting is required.

HANDLEBARS
Wide Scrambles type.

OPTIONAL EQUIPMENT
As for Sportstwins.

OPTIONAL EXTRAS
Electric lighting, silencer, road number plates, Q-D rear wheel, stop light, pillion footrests, red and chromium petrol tank, 4½ gallon petrol tank, rev counter, etc.

This shows the new frame used for the traditional big singles, with the exception of the G3C, as well as 500 and 650 twins; also the new style of dual seat. Standard G9s and G12s had coil ignition whilst the De Luxe and sports variants continued with the magneto/dynamo set-up.

The **MODEL G9**

66 m.m. × 72.5 m.m. 498 c.c. capacity. Vertical Twin.

The 500 c.c. G9 is intended to appeal to the knowledgeable enthusiast who requires a high quality twin cylinder model, capable of over 90 m.p.h., with economy and reliability, but without complication and at the lowest possible cost.

500 c.c. O.H.C. RACING MODEL G50

ENGINE

90 m.m. × 78 m.m. 496 c.c. capacity.

Magnesium crankcase, timing cover, cam box castings, steel disc flywheels, robust forged steel connecting rod, large diameter 2-piece crankpin, Duralumin caged roller big end bearing, single chain-driven camshaft, forged steel roller cam followers on needle roller bearings, eccentric rocker spindle valve adjustment, duplex hairpin valve springs, light alloy cylinder and cylinder heads, shrunk in valve seats, twin gear oil pumps.

G-P Amal carburettor, Lucas racing magneto, manual ignition control.

Four-speed racing gear box and multi-plate clutch.

Lightweight duplex cradle frame of welded construction, one piece welded swinging arm, journal bearing magnesium hubs with alloy iron brake liners, straight spokes, light alloy rims and 3.00″ × 19″ front and 3.50″ × 19″ rear racing tyres.

Five gallon light alloy petrol tank, 7 pint oil tank, glass fibre racing seat shell with foam rubber and Vynide covering.

Glass fibre number plate and rev counter mounting with Perspex screen.

Rev counter, steering damper and racing number plates supplied.

The **MODEL G50**

90 m.m. × 78 m.m. 496 c.c. capacity. Overhead Camshaft. Racing Single.

The limited number of G50's produced are indivudally built in the Works Racing Department. Each engine is run in on the bench and power tested to a predetermined figure before being accepted for installation.

Supplied to the current F.I.M. racing specification and ready for immediate use in International events.

Had AMC started production and development of the 500cc version of the 7R at the same time as it was introduced, rather than ten years later, the bigger Manx Nortons might not have had quite so much their own way. Instead the company went up a bit of a blind alley with the G45 and switched to the G50 late in the day. Never quite as fast as Senior Manxes, a well-ridden G50, with its slightly lighter weight, greater engine flexibility and the nimbleness of a 7R, could more than hold its own on twisty sections of a track.

	248 c.c. SINGLE	248 c.c. SINGLE	348 c.c. SINGLE	347 c.c. SINGLE	347 c.c. SINGLE	498 c.c. SINGLE	498 c.c. SINGLE	498 c.c. TWIN	646 c.c. TWIN	646 c.c. TWIN	646 c.c. TWIN	646 c.c. TWIN	496 c.c. SINGLE
MODEL	G2	G2CS	G5	G3	G3C	G80	G80CS	G9	G12	G12 De Luxe	G12CS	G12CSR	G50
BORE and STROKE	70 × 65	70 × 65	72 × 85.5	69 × 93	69 × 93	82.5 × 93	86 × 85.5	66 × 72.5	72 × 79.3	72 × 79.3	72 × 79.3	72 × 79.3	90 × 78
COMPRESSION RATIO	7.8	10.0	7.4	6.5 or 7.5	6.5	6.5 or 7.3	8.7	7.0 or 8.0	7.5	7.5	8.5	8.5	10.6
MAGNETO or COIL	C	C	C	C	M	C	M	C	C	M	M	M	M
IGNITION TIMING	36°	32°	34°	39°	39°	39°	37°	35°	35°	35°	34°	34°	33.5°
AMAL CARBURETTOR CHOKE dia. ins.	1-1/16	1-1/16	1-1/8	1-1/16	1-1/16	1-5/32	1-3/8	1	1-1/8	1-1/8	1-1/8	1-1/8	1-3/8
MAIN JET	180	190	220	210	210	260	350	220	400	400	430	410	420
SPARKING PLUG LONG REACH K.L.G.	FE80	FE220	FE80	FE80	FE80	FE80	FE220	FE80	FE80	FE80	FE220	FE80	E/258/2
DYNAMO or ALTERNATOR	A	A	A	A	D	A	A	A	A	D	D	D	—
GEAR RATIO 1st	20.12	21.62	18.66	14.85	21.00	12.86	14.85	13.42	12.23	12.23	13.42	12.23	7.16
„ „ 2nd	12.75	16.55	11.82	9.85	15.80	8.53	9.85	8.93	8.13	8.13	8.93	8.13	5.34
„ „ 3rd	8.95	11.63	8.30	7.08	10.10	6.13	7.08	6.40	5.83	5.83	6.40	5.83	4.42
„ „ Top	6.89	8.95	6.39	5.80	6.48	5.02	5.80	5.25	4.78	4.78	5.25	4.78	4.02
TYRE Front	3.25 × 17	3.00 × 19	3.25 × 18	3.25 × 19	2.75 × 21	3.25 × 19	3.00 × 21	3.25 × 19	3.25 × 19	3.25 × 19	3.00 × 21	3.25 × 19	3.00 × 19
„ Rear	3.25 × 17	3.50 × 19	3.25 × 18	3.25 × 19	4.00 × 19	3.50 × 19	4.00 × 19	3.50 × 19	3.50 × 19	3.50 × 19	4.00 × 19	3.50 × 19	3.50 × 19
TYRE PRESSURE lbs/sq. inch Front	22	As required	21	20	As required	21	As required	22	22	22	As required	22	22
„ „ „ Rear	22	As required	22	22	As required	24	As required	25	25	25	As required	25	24
ENGINE OIL Above 50°F	S.A.E. 50	S.A.E. 50	S.A.E. 50	S.A.E. 50	S.A.E. 50	S.A.E. 50	S.A.E. 50	S.A.E. 50	S.A.E. 50	S.A.E. 50	S.A.E. 50	S.A.E. 50	CASTOR
„ „ 32°F to 50°F	S.A.E. 30	S.A.E. 30	S.A.E. 30	S.A.E. 30	S.A.E. 30	S.A.E. 30	S.A.E. 30	S.A.E. 30	S.A.E. 30	S.A.E. 30	S.A.E. 30	S.A.E. 30	CASTOR
„ „ Below 32°F	S.A.E. 20	S.A.E. 20	S.A.E. 20	S.A.E. 20	S.A.E. 20	S.A.E. 20	S.A.E. 20	S.A.E. 20	S.A.E. 20	S.A.E. 20	S.A.E. 20	S.A.E. 20	CASTOR
WHEELBASE	53″	53.75″	53.75″	55.25″	53.75″	55.25″	55.25″	55.25″	55.25″	55.25″	55.25″	55.25″	55″
SEAT HEIGHT	29″	32″	29.5″	31″	32.5″	31″	32.5″	31″	31″	31″	32.5″	31″	31″
GROUND CLEARANCE	5.5″	7.25″	6″	5.5″	10″	5.5″	6.5″	5.5″	5.5″	5.5″	6.5″	5.5″	6.75″

For 1961 the range was all but unchanged.

Magnificent
MATCHLESS
MOTOR CYCLES
1962

Built at the same Belfast shipyard as the Titanic: during her early years SS Canberra was P&O's flagship on the Great Britain-to-Australia run that carried so many emigrants. She'd entered service just a few months before our couple bought their 650 Majestic, but by the way they are looking longingly as the great ship passes they'd willingly trade their Matchless for a new life down under.

For those who wanted to stand out amongst other Monitor owners there was the optional extra of the whole machine being finished in Tartan Red with white mudguards and tank flash.

MONITOR
250 c.c. MODEL G2

Making the utmost use of every gallon of petrol but equipped, designed and very capable of man-size transport for two, the cleanly styled Monitor provides low budget, high performance motor cycling at its best.

MONITOR SPORTS
250 c.c. MODEL G2S

Powered by a delightfully clean and vibrationless engine the model G2S is a joy to the discriminating rider who appreciates the positive steering, superb road-holding and scintillating performance provided by this elegant sports edition of the Monitor.

Prospective owners may have thought they'd get the bike pictured in the brochure but when they placed their order they'd have been told that the chromium mudguards and rear chain guard were optional extras.

Perhaps to attract a more machismo breed of customer, the humble G5 was renamed the Matador. Sadly, had true macho man read The Motor Cycle*'s test of one before visiting his local dealer he'd have probably not found the prospect of 75 flat out with 'high frequency vibration through handlebar and footrests' at anything over 60mph too alluring, and gone for something else.*

MATADOR
350 c.c. MODEL G5

With the same classic good looks of the Monitor but designed for the rider who demands even more power, the Matador's added torque allied to its light weight and excellent handling produce an outstandingly popular machine.

MERCURY
350 c.c. MODEL G3

Known and respected the world over, the G3 for 1962 has an all-new short stroke motor with greatly increased power output. The duplex frame, large dual-seat and generously proportioned brakes provide luxurious and superbly safe motor cycling.

The revamped shorter-stroke (74x81mm) motor with 8.5:1 compression, which, although lacking little of the tractability of the old unit, had more power at higher revs. This allowed a fraction over 70mph in third gear before valve-bounce set in and 78mph in top, coupled with a reasonable 80mpg at 50mph.

To whom a 'sporting' version of the G3 would appeal totally defeats me – especially when I tell you that it was mechanically identical to its touring brother, and to add insult to injury even the chrome mudguards were an optional extra. If it alone had been given the new short-stroke motor it would have been a different matter.

MERCURY SPORTS
350 c.c. MODEL G3S
Steering superlatively well and with brakes to match its enhanced performance, the exhilarating Mercury Sports is made to measure for the man in a hurry.

From either side a Major and Mercury, apart from the former having a bulkier head and barrel, could be identical twins. By paying a bit more you could have either of them in Tartan Red with White mudguards and a QD wheel.

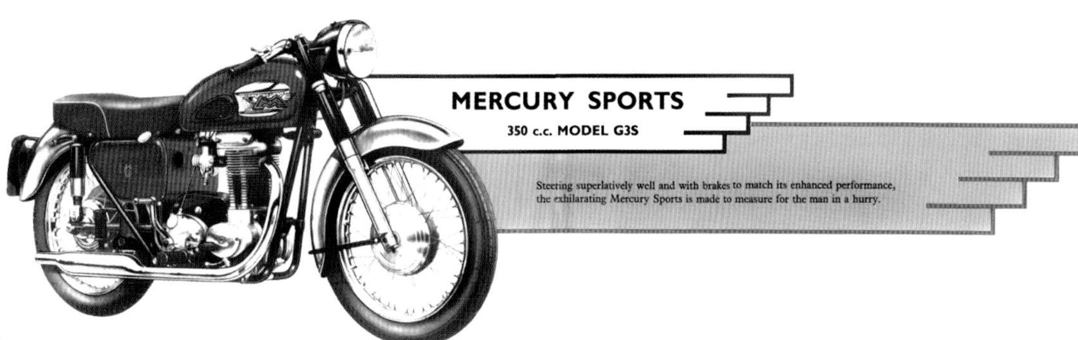

MAJOR
500 c.c. MODEL G80
Exemplifying all that is best in the British tradition of large capacity single cylinder motor cycles. Immaculately finished and possessing the ability to devour distance in a most unobtrusive manner, the model G80 represents an extremely sound investment.

Pounds, dollars and rupees; but how many found a home in India? I'd like to think anyone would prefer the standard black finish; however, this one's in the optional Tartan Red with White Mudguards, but what colour is the seat? It looks like grey; which would be bad, but white could be worse. To paint up its wares like cheap clowns in order to compete with the increasing numbers of brightly-painted Japanese bikes that were reaching Great Britain would achieve nothing – as time, before too long, would tell.

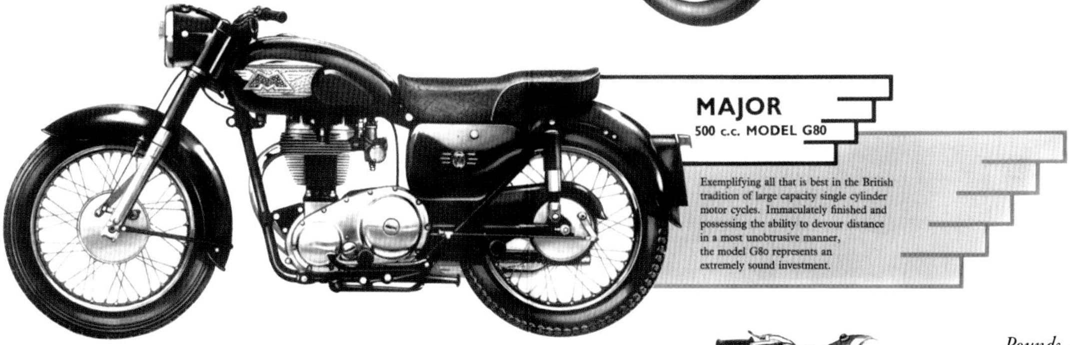

MAJESTIC
650 c.c. MODEL G12
Striking in style, power, performance and dependability, the luxurious G12 is unrivalled for both solo or sidecar use, whilst the man who demands value for every pound, dollar or rupee, cannot fail to be satisfied.

Despite its nasty tank badge the 650 CSR was still a genuinely sporting mount.

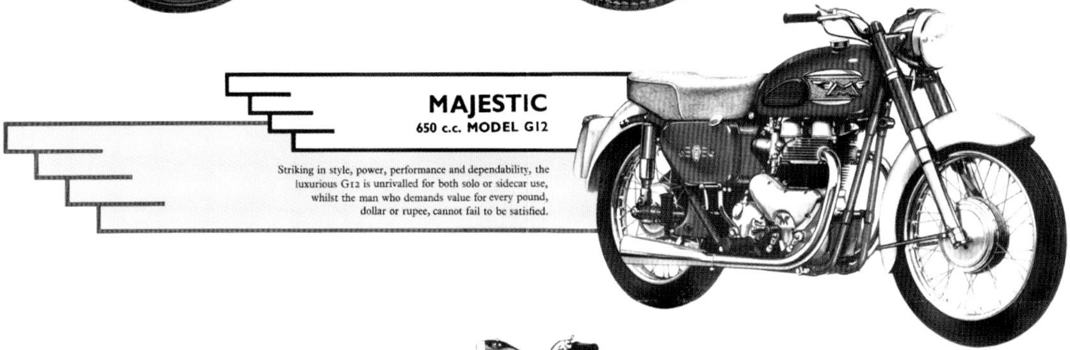

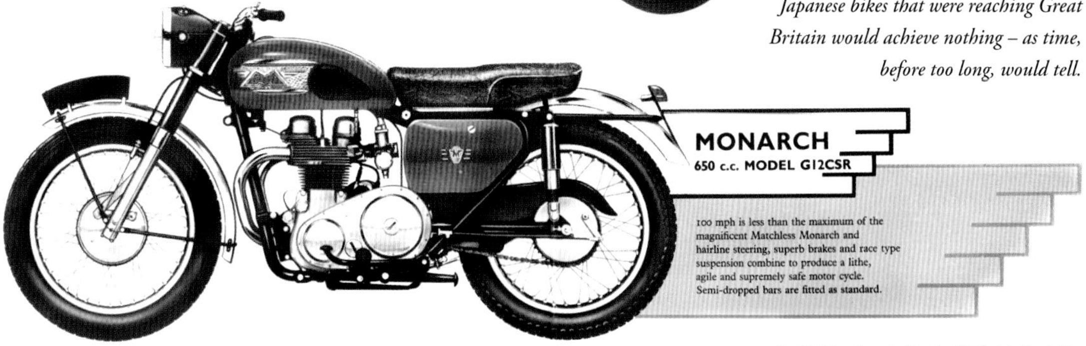

MONARCH
650 c.c. MODEL G12CSR
100 mph is less than the maximum of the magnificent Matchless Monarch and hairline steering, superb brakes and race type suspension combine to produce a lithe, agile and supremely safe motor cycle. Semi-dropped bars are fitted as standard.

In 1963 a heroic Senior TT ride by Mike Duff would end with his G50 first of the British singles, behind Hailwood, Hartle and Read on Italian four-cylinder machines. The following year Mike Hailwood and his MV triumphed once again but Fred Stevens and Derek Woodman took third and fourth places with Matchless's racer. The 1965 Senior was wet, and although Hailwood won for the third year slippery conditions brought the speeds right down; beaten by Joe Dunphy's Manx Norton, Duff's G50 was third.

500 c.c. MODEL G50
50
A team of three G50's won the Manufacturers Team Prize in the 1961 Isle of Man Senior T.T.

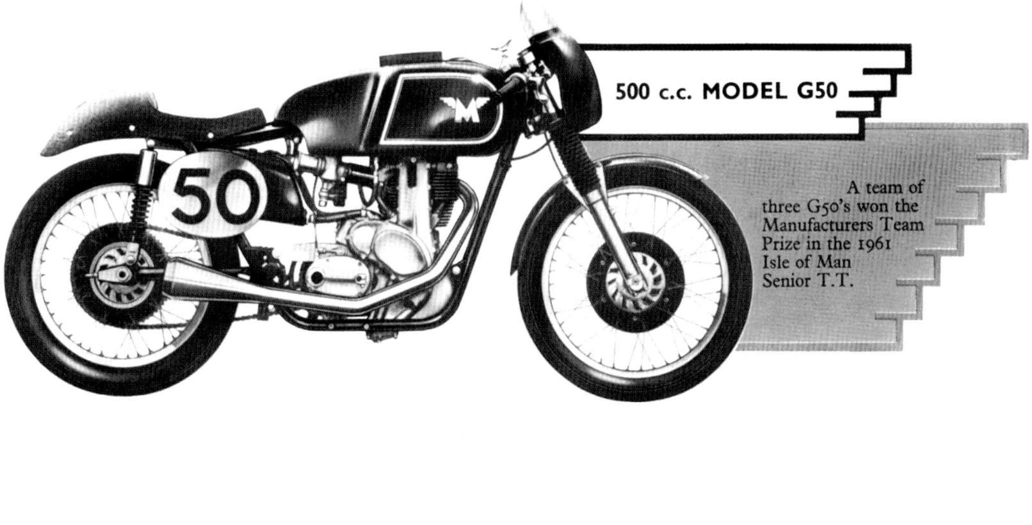

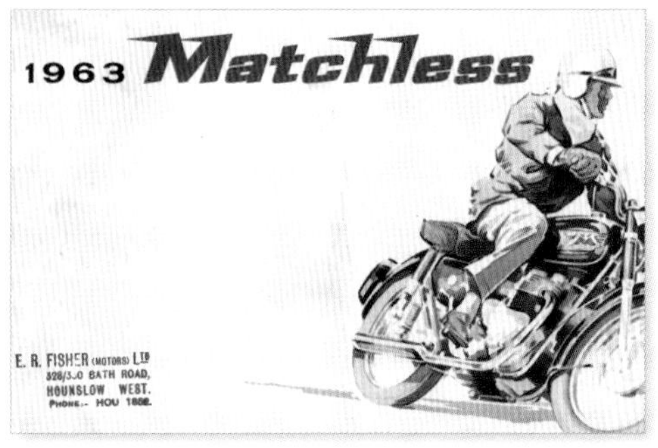

You can still visit ER Fisher on Bath Road, Hounslow but you'll be arranging insurance through the company, not buying a motorcycle – let alone an all-black Majestic like this.

With AMC's empire going into decline the sports 650s put on a brave face.

The 350 c.c. MERCURY and 500 c.c. MAJOR

Apart from the engines, almost everything on these two models is new for 1963. Smaller wheels, larger brakes in new hubs, new mudguards, shorter rear sub-frame, better silencers, streamlined oil tank and toolbox, smarter petrol tank with knee recesses, and a lower and more comfortable riding position.
Both these machines are renowned for their ruggedness and reliability, but other notable features are the Mercury's snappy performance and the Major's sheer slogging power at low engine speeds.

(500 c.c. Model G80 Major)

SPECIFICATION

ENGINE:
Model 16. 348 c.c. o.h.v. single (74 mm. x 81 mm.).
Model 18. 498 c.c. o.h.v. single (82.6 mm. x 93 mm.).
Light alloy cylinder head with cast-in valve seats: stellite tipped valves: duplex hairpin valve springs: built-up rockers: hiduminium pushrods: mushroom type cam followers: separate camwheels: built-up crankshaft supported by ball journal and plain bearings: triple row caged roller big-end bearing: forged steel connecting rod: reciprocating plunger oil pump: ignition by battery and coil.

GEARBOX: Separate from engine for adjustment of primary drive. 4 speed, positive foot change, driven through multi-plate clutch incorporating vane type shock absorber.

FORKS: Heavy duty Teledraulic forks, two-way oil-damped with multi-rate springs: alloy sliders and chromed extensions.

FRAME: Twin tube duplex cradle of brazed and bolted construction: integral sidecar lugs: rear sub-frame loops are short and pivoted rear fork braced for rigidity: rear suspension by Girling adjustable units.

LIGHTING: 6 volt, 60 watt, crankshaft mounted alternator: 11 a.h. battery: 7" headlamp: combined rear and stop lights.

WHEELS: 18" diameter with Dunlop tyres.

BRAKES: 7" diameter: light alloy full width hubs.

TWINSEAT: Two level foam rubber with waterproof covering.

COLOUR FINISH: All black, with usual parts chromium plated. Red tanks and toolbox optional.

OPTIONAL: Upswept handlebars: sidecar gears and suspension.

OPTIONAL EXTRAS: Chrome mudguards and chainguard: fully enclosed rear chaincase: air cleaner: steering damper: steering lock: safety bars: luggage carrier: luggage panniers.

Not much change for these two except a more modern design of silencer as well as a more curvaceous oil tank and toolboxes. Whoever came up with the bright idea of red with white mudguards had their knuckles rapped, however, and relative normality had returned to colour choices.

The 650 c.c. Model G12 MAJESTIC

Described by the Press as "all the best in British' Big Bike 'tradition", the Majestic's keynote is undoubtedly versatility. Featuring the same redesigned cycle parts as the single cylinder models, and the same detail refinements, such as the new stoplight switch and the larger number plate for seven digit registration marks, this 650 c.c. twin has many technical features unique in motor cycle design.
Road test reports, listing, apart from performance figures, these features are available for the Majestic in both solo and sidecar forms.

Majestics had been given the same makeover – including the banishment of inappropriate mudguard colouring.

SPECIFICATION

ENGINE: 646 c.c. o.h.v. vertical twin (72 mm. bore and 79.3 mm. stroke). Both the cylinder barrels and the heads are separate for ease of maintenance. Barrels are deeply spigotted into crankcase for rigidity.
Light alloy cylinder heads with cast-in valve seats: stellite tipped valves: multi-rate coil type valve springs: one-piece rockers adjustable by eccentric spindles, which are mounted between pillars integral with heads: hiduminium pushrods: lever cam followers with Delchrome pads: separate camshafts mounted fore and aft of engine: one-piece, three bearing crankshaft supported by two large diameter roller bearings and a plain centre bearing: indium flashed lead bronze big-end bearings: forged alloy connecting rods: forged alloy pistons: two new high capacity gear-type oil-pumps driven by camshafts: ignition by battery and coil.

GEARBOX: Separate from engine for primary drive adjustment: 4 speeds, positive foot change, driven through multi-plate clutch incorporating vane type shock absorber.

FORKS: Heavy duty Teledraulic forks: two-way oil damped: multi-rate coil springs: alloy sliders and chromed extensions.

FRAME: Twin tube duplex cradle of brazed and bolted construction: integral sidecar lugs: pivoted rear fork controlled by Girling adjustable units.

LIGHTING: 6 volt, 60 watt, crankshaft mounted alternator: 11 a.h. battery: 7" headlamp: combined rear and stop lights.

WHEELS: 18" diameter with 3.25" front and 3.50" rear Dunlop tyres.

TWINSEAT: Two level foam rubber with waterproof covering.

COLOUR FINISH: All black, with usual parts chrome plated. Red tanks and toolbox optional.

OPTIONAL: Upswept handlebars: sidecar gears and suspension: siamezed exhaust.

OPTIONAL EXTRAS: Magneto ignition: steering damper: fully enclosed rear chaincase: air cleaner: steering lock: safety bars: luggage carrier: luggage panniers.

Sad but true. Matchless and the rest of AMC certainly were going places – one place: downhill. They'd need more than a lightning flash on the tank of this Majestic 650, and the Norton brakes, to save the show.

This was the second season for the Monitor in this form, but now it was simply the Super Sports and the G2CSR prefix employed in '63 had been dropped.

ENGINE. Highly tuned 248 c.c. o.h.v. single (70 mm. bore x 65 m.m. stroke): Deeply finned light alloy cylinder head with cast-in valve seats: large bore carburettor and a long inlet tract allied to a large diameter inlet valve provides the necessary gas flow to allow full use of the engine's potential: heavy poundage duplex hairpin valve springs: built-up rockers housed in detachable light alloy rocker box: hiduminium push-rods with hardened steel end-cups: lever type cam followers: both cams on single shaft: built-up crankshaft with steel flywheels and two-piece crankpin, supported by roller, ball and plain main bearings: duralumin caged roller big-end bearing: high tensile steel connecting rod: forged alloy piston with three rings: cast- iron barrel: crankshaft driven reciprocating plunger oil-pump: ignition by battery and coil, with an independent emergency start circuit.

GEARBOX. Separate from engine, and clamped to crankcase by two flexible steel straps. Engine side covers give appearance of unit construction. Four speeds operated by positive selector mechanism. Driven through multi-plate clutch incorporating rubber vane shock absorber. Duplex primary chain adjusted by rotation of gearbox within clamping straps. Folding kickstarter.

FRAME. Brazed and bolted construction: Single front down tube, continuous single top and saddle tube, pressed steel engine under-channel: short triangulared rear sub-frame for rigidity: large lug at base of saddle tube houses lubricated pivot bush for rear swinging fork.

REAR SUSPENSION. Swinging fork: off-side arm pressed on, and welded to, heat treated steel pivot shaft: drive-side arm cottered to shaft: tube ends pinched and welded for wheel spindle slots. Fork movement controlled by adjustable Girling hydraulic units.

FORKS. Competition type "Teledraulic" forks, with progressive two-way oil damping: large diameter heat-treated tubular steel stanchions: multi-rate springs: light alloy sliders with chromed steel extension.

WHEELS. 17" diameter chrome plated steel rims: heavy duty spokes. Fitted with 3.25" Dunlop high hysteresis tyres.

HUBS & BRAKES. Full width light alloy front hub with cast-in 6" diameter drum: 1⅜" wide linings and shoes mounted on webbed light alloy brake plate. Full width rear hub with 6" diameter brake drum and integral sprocket bolted to hub.

LIGHTING. 6 volt. 54 watt, crankshaft mounted alternator; 11 a.h battery: 6" headlamp: combined rear and stoplight with integral reflector.

TWINSEAT. Two level touring seat: pressed steel base: foam rubber padding: waterproof Vynide covering.

PETROL TANK. 3.25 gallon pressed steel completely rubber mounted.

OIL TANK. Cast alloy container bolted up to crankcase side and separate from flywheel compartment.

HANDLEBARS. Fully adjustable, as are the control levers. Upswept handlebars optional.

DIMENSIONS. Seat height 29.5": ground clearance 6.5": weight 307 lbs.

COLOUR FINISH. Jet black primarily: petrol tank chrome plated and polychromatic red: accessory covers polychromatic red: mudguards, chainguard, wheels, rims, exhaust system, etc., chrome plated: engine cover, primary chaincase: gearbox cover, fork sliders, cylinder head fin extremities etc., are highly polished.

OPTIONAL EXTRA. Range of Dolphin fairings.

1964's TOP SPORTING LIGHTWEIGHT

MEET THE MATCHLESS 350 c.c. MERCURY AND 500 c.c. MAJOR

MERCURY A snappy performer with a low, comfortable riding position. Robust, reliable, easy on fuel consumption, you'll get many miles of enjoyable motor cycling behind the Mercury's handlebars.

MAJOR For sheer slogging power at low engine speeds, you'll have to go a long way to find a machine that compares with the Major. A rugged dependable performer, here's the ideal bike for touring the countryside in comfort.

ENGINE. Model G3. 348 c.c. o.h.v. single (72 mm. bore x 85.5 mm. stroke) Model G80. 497 c.c. o.h.v. single (86 mm. bore x 85.5 mm. stroke) Light alloy cylinder head with cast-in valve seats: chrome plated, stellite tipped valves: exhaust valve lifter fitted: duplex hairpin valve springs: built-up rockers housed in detachable light alloy rocker box separate inspection cover: hiduminium pushrods with hardened steel end-cups: mushroom type cam followers: separate cam wheels: built-up crankshaft, with individually balanced steel fly wheels and two-piece crankpin, supported by ball, roller and plain main bearings: duralumin caged roller big-end bearing with improved direct oil feed: high tensile steel connecting rod: forged alloy piston: cast iron cylinder barrel with integral pushrod tunnels: new gear type oil pump driven off timing side crankshaft: ignition by battery and coil with independent emergency start circuit.

GEARBOX. Separate four speed box: light alloy shell and covers: wide tooth heavy duty pinions: multi-plate clutch with integral rubber vane shock absorber: primary drive housed in cast alloy oil bath.

LIGHTING. 6 volt. 60 watt crankshaft mounted alternator: 11 a.h. battery: 7" headlamp: combined rear and stoplight with integral reflector.

DIMENSIONS. Seat height 29.5": ground clearance 5.5": weight 394 lbs.

COLOUR FINISH. All black and chrome. Polychromatic red is optional for petrol tank, oil tank and toolbox.

OPTIONAL. Sidecar specification—special forks, gears and suspension.

OPTIONAL EXTRAS. Range of dolphin fairings. Full enclosed rear chaincase. Air cleaner. Steering damper. Front and rear safety bars.

CYCLE PARTS as 650 c.c. Swift.

Nary a word about the Norton brakes but the whole thing was getting so sloppy that they forgot which name and badge applied to what – citing the cycle parts as attributable to AJS's Swift whereas they meant Matchless's Monarch. But Swift and Monarch were the same anyway, bar the badges and colours, so what the hell!

MATCHLESS 650 c.c. MONARCH

Specification is similar in many respects to the standard 650 c.c. twin but, with the following alterations.

ENGINE. Highly tuned with 8.5:1 compression ratio. Magneto ignition.

MUDGUARDS. Chrome plated steel blades.

COLOUR FINISH. Black frame, fork covers, etc., with polychromatic red and chrome petrol tank, and polychromatic red oil tank and toolbox.

OPTIONAL EXTRAS. Range of Dolphin fairings. Speedkit comprising twin carburettors, h.c. pistons and special camshafts. Rev-counter. Steering damper. A racing magneto and separate exhaust system can be fitted if the speedkit is supplied as original equipment.

No longer with the exciting G12CSR prefix, the Monarch was simply that and was looking ever more tarty and less sporty despite improved brakes from the AMC parts bin out of Norton.

The 350 trials bike had been known as the Maestro for the past two seasons but was now equipped with the short-stroke (72x85.5mm) motor that had been first used in works machines. The G80CS had become the Marksman and for the past year had the option of a 12:1 piston so that 'you can race with an engine identical to those used by works riders'.

Matchless
350cc. G3 MERCURY
500cc. G80 MAJOR

Just black and chrome for these now and, thank goodness, the frightful tank badging has gone and been replaced by this fairly unobtrusive but tacky item. Believe me when I tell you it looks better in this illustration than real life. The 650 Monarch, too, was just in black and identically badged. Remaining on the optional extra list, surrounded by Dolphin fairings, and safety bars, was magneto ignition.

Matchless
650cc. G12CSR MONARCH

Sharing a common brochure with Norton and AJS meant that some models were given precedence on each page – hence there was a large illustration of AJS's Hurricane with a tiny Monarch tucked away in a corner and the text serving for both.

SPEED . . . SAFETY . . . HANDLING EASE . . . A.M.C.'s winning formula—translated here into two exceptional twins. Stepped-up speed—yours with the optional extra speed-kit, which does not affect the low down flexibility of the motor's pulling power.
Safety—summed-up by top-rate roadholding and braking, goes hand in hand with steering light enough to ensure complete handling ease.

SPECIFICATION
Specification is similar in many respects to the standard 650cc twin, but, with the following alterations.
Engine. Highly tuned with 8.5:1 compression ratio, Magneto ignition.
Mudguards. Chrome plated steel blades.
Colour Finish. Black frame, fork covers etc. with cherry red (A.J.S. blue) and chrome petrol tank and cherry red (A.J.S. blue) oil tank and toolbox.
Optional Extras. Range of Dolphin fairings. Speedkit comprising twin carburettors, h.c.pistons and special camshafts. Rev-Counter. Steering Damper. A racing magneto and separate exhaust system can be fitted if the speedkit is supplied as original equipment.

Matchless
500cc. Model G80 CS
"MARKSMAN"

Engine. 497cc (86mm x 85.5mm) all alloy o.h.v. single developed solely for scrambling.
1⅜" choke diameter Amal Grand Prix carburettor: alloy cylinder head with cast-in valve seats, and central plug: 1⅞" dia. open exhaust pipe: chrome plated, stellite tipped valves: exhaust valve lifter fitted: racing duplex hairpin valve springs: built up rockers housed in detachable light alloy rocker box: separate inspection cover: hiduminium push-rods with hardened steel end cups: mushroom type cam followers: special high lift cams (type HS) on separate pinions: built up crankshaft (individually balanced) with steel flywheels and two piece crankpin (alloy steel centre pin with hardened steel sleeve) supported by two-ball journal, one roller and one plain, main bearings: duralumin caged single row roller big-end bearing: forged steel connecting rod with pressed in hardened liner: alloy piston (standard C.R.8.7: 1): alloy cylinder barrel with low friction iron liner: gear-type oil pump driven by timing side of crankshaft: manually controlled Lucas waterproof competition magneto (breather pipe terminates under petrol tank), driven by chain: alloy timing chest: level high exhaust pipe.
Gearbox. Separate medium-close ratio four speed gearbox: alloy shell: wide tooth heavy duty pinions: special multi-plate clutch: single primary chain housed in cast alloy oil-bath: rubber vane shock absorber integral with clutch: foot operated gear pedal: folding kickstarter.
Frame. Brazed and bolted construction: twin tube duplex cradle: single top and saddle tubes: two large diameter looped tubes, welded together by cross-bracing struts, form rear sub-frame: large robust lug at base of seat tube houses self lubricating pivot bush for rear swinging fork.
Rear Suspension. Large braced malleable lug into which two heavy duty large diameter tubes are brazed, form a very rigid swinging fork assembly: large diameter heat-treated steel pivot shaft pressed into lug: fork movement controlled by fully adjustable oil damped units.
Forks. Heavy duty 'Teledraulic' forks, designed specially for scrambling; give extra long movement and precise progressive two-way damping: multi-rate springs: large diameter heat-treated tubular steel stanchions: alloy sliders: rubber gaiters: forged steel handlebar lug and fork crown: crown pinch-bolts act as steering lock stops.
Mudguards. Polished alloy blades, with tubular steel stays.
Wheels. 19" diameter chrome plated steel rims fitted with 3.00" front and 4.00" rear tyres: heavy gauge spokes.
Hubs and Brakes. Slim alloy front hub with cast-in 7" diameter brake drum: wider shoes and linings mounted on webbed light alloy back plate: two ball journals support hub on high tensile steel spindle. Alloy rear hub mounted on taper roller bearings: one piece brake drum and rear sprocket bolted up to hub.
Twinseat. Single level competition seat: pressed steel base: foam rubber filling: waterproof Vynide covering.
Petrol Tank. Two gallon pressed steel completely rubber mounted: mounting at front by expanding rubber bushes: at rear by rubber bands: tank rests on foam rubber pads.
Oil Tank. 4.5 pint pressed steel tank bolted up to rear sub-frame.
Air Filter. (Standard fitting) Flat "works" pattern mounted on offside, and up to rear sub-frame. Concertina shaped felt and guaze element.
Handlebars. Fully adjustable with adjustable ball ended controls.
Dimensions. Seat height 32": wheelbase 55.25": ground clearance 6½": Handlebar width 32": weight 345-lbs.

Matchless 750cc. Model G15

SPECIFICATION
Engine. 750cc o.h.v. vertical twin (73mm bore x 89mm stroke): alloy cylinder head: parallel induction tracts with large diameter inlet valves: forged steel rockers: alloy pushrods: iron alloy tappets: single high performance camshaft: built up forged steel crankshaft with large diameter central iron flywheel: plain big end bearings: two piece connecting rods: alloy pistons: cast iron cylinder: gear type oil pump: carburetion by twin Amal Monoblocs: ignition by Magneto with automatic advance and retard.
Transmission. Separate four speed gearbox: wide tooth heavy duty pinions: driven through five plate clutch: primary chain housed in cast alloy oil-bath.
Frame. Brazed and bolted construction: twin tube duplex cradle: rear sub-frame loops are short and swinging fork braced for rigidity: rear suspension is controlled by fully adjustable oil-damped Girling units.
Forks. "Roadholder" forks with built in thief proof lock: two way oil damping: large diameter heat treated tubular steel stanchions: alloy sliders with chromed steel extensions.
Wheels. Large diameter alloy hubs: front brake drum cast into hub: one piece rear drum and sprocket separate from hub: ball journal bearings. Brake sizes—8" x 1¼" front, 7" x 1¼" rear. Tyres 3.50 x 18 and 4.00 x 18.
Lighting. 12 volt crankshaft mounted alternator: two 6 volt batteries mounted in series: Zener Diode: 7" headlamp; 50w/40w head bulb: combined rear and stop light with integral reflector.
Tanks. 4 gallon petrol tank completely rubber mounted: single two level tap: 4 pint oil tank.
Colours. All black and chrome.

"Its performance will see off most other roadsters. Yes, it's a man's mount," eulogised The Motor Cycle *in their Autumn 1964 test. All very good until you delve into their findings further where, under the heading 'Sure Footed', we read that 'for unhurried touring, the roadholding was steady and precise, but high speed on bumpy bends caused slight head-shaking and rear-end-twitters'.*

So with this restriction on 'scratching' they're going to tell us that it was so blindingly fast nothing much would even get a whiff of its exhaust fumes? Wrong. Despite it being capable of a 14.3-second quarter-mile sprint I can think of several machines of a lesser capacity that would have no trouble holding off this 'man's machine' on the road, in particular one giving away 250cc, and from AMC too, that would motor steadily past it and away.

It was not too thrifty on fuel either, drinking a pint of petrol every 5½ minutes at 60mph – or a gallon every 44 miles. By the summer of '65 a CSR version arrived, with twin carbs, rear sets, swept-back exhausts and alloy mudguards. It could reach 114mph and cover the standing ¼ mile in 13.8sec.

NORMAN

The 1950 B2 was little changed since its introduction. Available either with battery or direct lighting this is the latter, cheaper version. It was finished in maroon.

Upon returning to their home town of Ashford in Kent after serving in the First World War, brothers Fred and Charles Norman recommenced the trades they were familiar with by establishing the Kent Plating and Enamelling company – reputedly in a garden shed. Be that as it may, their metal finishing business prospered to the extent that further staff were taken on and the building of bicycle frames began to be undertaken.

As one can well imagine, the accommodation offered by the 'shed' was soon insufficient so a move was made to more substantial premises in nearby Victoria Road, where the production of complete bicycles for the trade became possible. Unlike all too many small manufacturers the brothers' firm not only weathered the recession but as the country emerged from it was doing well enough to have a factory built just around the corner in Beaver Road – their relocation there, in 1935, coinciding with a change of name to Norman Cycles Ltd.

Now a manufacturer in its own right with a 40,000sq.ft factory turning out upwards of 1,500 cycles a week – from the Club Racer to tandems – the idea of adding small motorcycles to its range of products was very appealing. Motive power was not a problem, as Villiers was only too happy to add the firm to its list of existing clients, and by 1938 98cc Norman Motobyks and 122cc Lightweights started to leave the Ashford factory.

A little over a year later Britain was at war, but for the meanwhile production continued and even could be said to have expanded due to the acquisition of a licence to build Rudge Auto-Cycles; but by 1941 manufacture was curtailed and, it is reputed, the factory mothballed. Despite finding no record of war work I find it hard to believe that it was not put to some good use, but either way it narrowly escaped being razed to the ground in March 1943 when some bombs intended for Ashford's railway works fell on Beaver Road and flattened a nearby school (the pupils had made it to the shelters).

Post-war motorcycle production carried on more or less where it had left off albeit with less Rudge – Norman's own pedal-assisted 98cc taking on a derivation of its name by being marketed as the Autocycle.

For the 1948 Show there were three new models – the Model C (a revamped Autocycle with the latest Villiers 2F) and the B1 and B2, also powered by Villiers of 122 and 197c; both had lightweight rigid frames and the firm's own design of telescopic forks but neither offered anything out of the ordinary. The following year the gap between Model C and B1 was filled by introducing the 98cc two-speed ultra-lightweight Model D. And at the 1952 show, Norman announced a fresh pair of 197s – the Competition and the B2S, the latter with spring frame.

By this time the company was a subsidiary of the huge Tube Investments group, which had acquired Norman around 1950 along with other cycle manufacturers such as Philips and Hercules. In 1956 TI set up the British Cycle Corporation to control the Midlands cycle makers it owned – but Norman, for the meanwhile, was left to carry on independently.

Factory riders had had some successes in the Scottish Six Days Trial, and as a result the rigid-framed B2C and later springer versions enjoyed a certain amount of popularity, particularly in the South East, but never to the extent of similar machinery available from the likes of Greeves or James. Extending the range to include a 250 twin at the end of 1954 brought about a three-year flirtation with British Anzani but otherwise Norman would remain faithful to Villiers for all Ashford-manufactured machines, from 250 down to the 50cc. The 50 went into Nippy and Lido mopeds when, after having first sold the Nippy under the Norman name with Sachs engine, the firm took over tooling and rights from the European manufacturer to produce them in house. The Ashford factory also played a part in the development of Armstrong leading-link forks and, as well as fitting them to its own machines from 1954, manufactured later improved versions for its own consumption as well as Cotton's.

By the late '50s the abandonment of Anzani's unloved twin and adoption of Villiers's superior and better-performing 2T encouraged Norman to bring out a sports 250 that, somewhat surprisingly, turned out to have competition potential when one entered by Canterbury dealer Ray Hallet finished second in the 1959 Thruxton 500 miles race. This did wonders for the marque's hitherto rather staid image and the resulting popularity of the B3 Sports encouraged the design of a new frame for the twins and introduction of the B4 Sports and Roadsters for 1961.

Sadly, however, the Ashford factory had but a few more months to live. The previous year TI had not only taken over Raleigh Industries but also given over control of all of its subsidiary cycle companies – Norman included. A decision had quickly been taken to close the Sun, Hercules, Phillips and Norman factories, with any future manufacturing to take place at one or other of Raleigh's plants. Fortunately for the Norman brothers this came at a time when they were ready to retire and the Ashford factory closed its doors for the last time at the end of August 1961. Moped and B4 production was moved up to the Midlands and carried on for a while in a desultory fashion whilst the singles were axed along with the projected B5, which had been under development with duplex frame and Italian Mival 250 OHC motor. The last of the B4s were made towards the end of 1962; Raleighised Nippys and Lidos made by Motobecane in France lived on for a little while, and then that was that.

The B2C had been introduced in the autumn of 1952 with a three-speed gearbox – this is the updated version of a year later with four speeds.

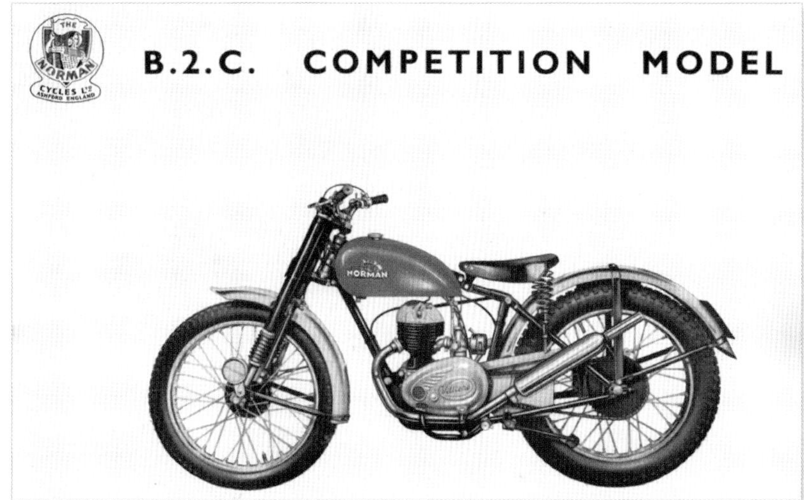

ENGINE
Villiers 197 c.c. 2-stroke 7E Competition Engine is fitted to this machine and incorporates foot change and 4-speed gearbox with kick starter in Unit Construction.

FRAME
The Norman Competition frame has been specially designed for Competition Work and allows for the engine to be offset to give the extra chain clearance necessary with the Universal Competition tyre. It is of tubular construction brazed and bolted and built with Reynolds 'A' quality tubing.

FORKS
The telescopic forks have been designed specially for the Competition Model and an arrangement of springs is incorporated giving an easy action fork, coupled with complete rigidness over the very roughest trials going.

FOOTRESTS
These are forged from EN.8Q steel and are adjustable radially over 360°. Provision is also made for 3 alternative fitting positions. This, combined with the adjustable saddle mounting allows for a riding position to suit any rider.

WHEELS
The front wheel is fitted with Dunlop 21″ WM1 Rim and the rear with a 19″ WM2 rim. The Tyres are by Dunlop, the front 21″ x 2.75″ and the rear 19″ x 4.00″. 5″ internal expanding brakes are fitted to both wheels. Security bolts are fitted both front and rear.

HUBS
These have been designed especially for the Competition Model. Both front and rear are fitted with journal race bearings, and the speedometer drive is incorporated inside the rear brake drum.

MUDGUARDS
Both front and rear mudguards are of 5″ ribbed section and are constructed of light alloy. The stays have both strength and rigidity having been specially designed for this machine.

SADDLE
This is by Dunlop having the well known Drilastic top and provision is made for the adjustment both at the nose and back.

TRANSMISSION
Is by "RENOLD" Roller Chain throughout with primary chain running in an oilbath. The main driving chain is protected by a light alloy competition chainguard.

STAND
The normal type stand has been dispensed with on the Competition Model, a side prop stand being fitted as standard.

HANDLEBARS
These are a "special bend" designed solely for Competition Work and they are adjustable radially.

PETROL TANK
This is of special design to suit the Competition frame and has a capacity of 1¾ gallon.

EQUIPMENT
This includes the usual tool kit, inflator, bulb horn and Competition number plate. Lighting equipment is not fitted to this model.

GEAR
Special gearing for Competition Work utilising a 50T rear hub sprocket giving 1st 22·6, 2nd 15·0, 3rd 8·4, top 6·5. A wide range of sprockets between 44T and 54T can be substituted to special order.

FINISH
The finish is in Norman colours of black and maroon. The mudguards are polished aluminium and all usual parts are chromium plated.

CARBURETTOR
The Villiers engine can be fitted with AMAL or Villiers Carburettor as required.

Also available with Armstrong Link Action Oil Damped Forks.

For the this fine machine Norman collaborated with Cyclemaster to produce what was almost certainly the feeblest moped one could buy in 1954 – its 32cc giving away 16cc to even Vincent's Firefly. To be fair to the Ashford concern, it had little to do with the thing other than make the bicycle that, the brochure pointed out, could be bought for £16, and very probably a preferable option to the entire package for £44.

Quite conventional in other respects, the rear of the 1953/4 sprung-frame B2S had a slightly unusual appearance on account of some peculiar tube work to support the silencer, and inordinately long adjustable suspension units. The first had three-speed gearboxes but four-speeds were introduced for the 1954 season.

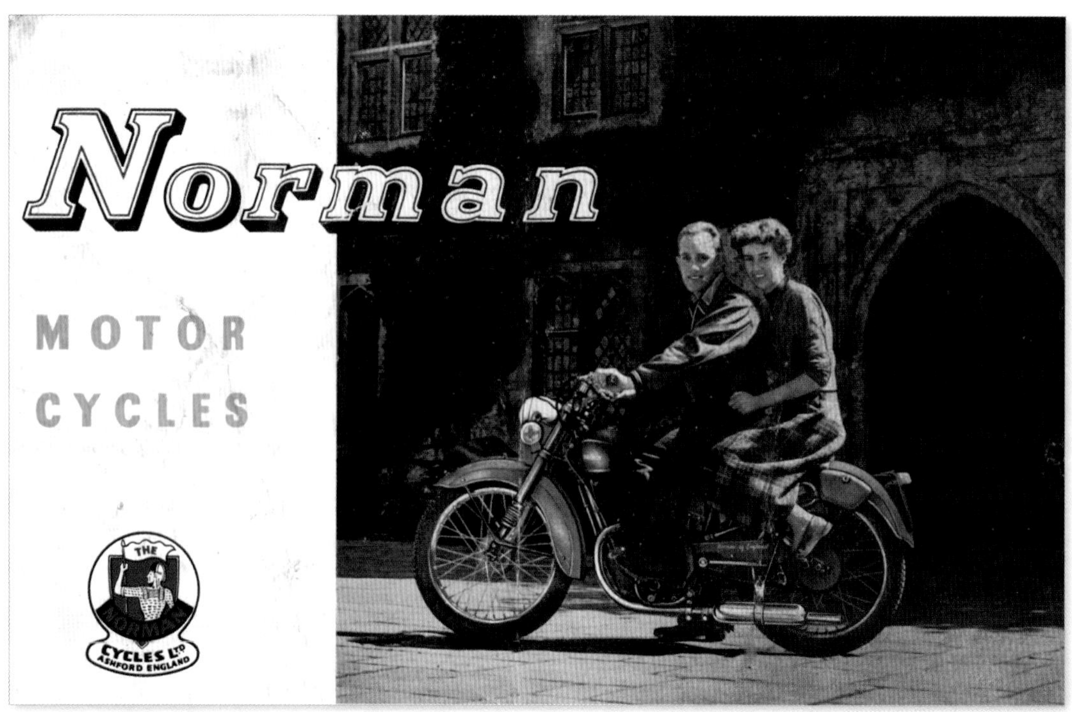

This once-pristine brochure was handed to a young man at the 1954 Motor Cycle Show as he gazed in wonder at the medieval castle that dominated Norman's stand. Feigning interest in the motorcycles rather than a construction that owed more to a Disney film set than Earls Court he asked the representative to jot down all the prices with, he couldn't fail to notice, one of the new Parker Jotters. Unlike the majority of this book's brochure cover stars who go by names pulled out of a hat, this is Norman employee and member of its works trials team Gerry Mills astride a B1/S with his future wife Rosemarie on the pillion.

ENGINE: Villiers 2 stroke 150 c.c. 30C Unit. Footchange 3-speed gearbox. **FRAME:** Norman "Cantilever" Spring Frame employs dual spring boxes, providing both main and overload springing. Built throughout with best quality steel tubing and brazed to ensure complete rigidity. **FORKS:** "Built for the job" telescopic forks employing an arrangement of springs which will deal adequately with all normal and overloads. **FOOTRESTS:** Are forged steel and fully adjustable radially through 360 degrees, fitted with rubbers. Fold up Pillion Footrests fitted as standard. **WHEELS:** Dunlop 19″ WM1 Rims and fitted with Dunlop 19″ x 3″ tyres. Both have 5″ internal expanding brakes. **HUBS:** Front and rear have been specially designed to suit the spring frame. Journal race bearings which need no adjustment are used and lubrication by packing with grease annually is all the attention needed. **MUDGUARDS:** Front and Rear are fully valanced and adequately stayed. **SADDLE:** Is a soft top dual seat of finest quality fitted to built on sub-frame. **TRANSMISSION:** "RENOLD" roller chain throughout, the Primary running in an oil bath whilst the main driving chain is protected by an efficient heavy gauge pressed steel guard. **STAND:** Central spring up stand constructed of special section steel tubing is fitted, of all welded construction with extra wide base. **HANDLEBARS:** Are specially designed and ensure a maximum of comfort and control, fully adjustable radially, all chromium plated. **PETROL TANK:** 2¼ gallons capacity, fitted with knee grips and large filler cap. **EQUIPMENT:** Standard equipment includes, inflator, horn, tool boxes and tools. **B.I.S.** has direct lighting with 5″ headlamp incorporating dipper switch and streamlined rear lamp. **B.I.S. De Luxe** has Rectified Lighting with 6″ Headlamp, Switch, Ammeter and "Stop" light. Lucas Battery and Carrier are standard on this model. **FINISH:** Frame and forks etc., "SPRA-GRANODISED" and enamelled black. Tank enamelled maroon. MID GREEN POLYCHROMATIC FINISH Extra.

Why Norman used different frame combinations for each 1954 model beats me, but here's the B1/S, which took a leaf out of Vincent's book with a cantilever rear. It had first appeared the previous year as a 125cc with Villiers 13D unit. Most manufacturers of the period Bonderised their frames prior to painting but Spra-Granodised is a new one on me. Norman had long been in the metal finishing business so was the company using a superior process for the same job?

ENGINE: Villiers two stroke 197 c.c. 8E three speed or 8E four speed unit. **FRAME:** Norman Cantilever Spring frame employs two rate adjustable spring boxes which permits two rates of springing for solo or a pillion passenger. Built throughout with best quality steel tubing and brazed to ensure complete rigidity. **FORKS:** Designed specially for the Norman Spring frame are the Armstrong link action oil damped forks. These have proved on test to be a great advance over the usual type of telescopic fork and give a very comfortable ride over the roughest of going combined with perfect steering. **FOOTRESTS:** Forged steel and fully adjustable radially through 360 degrees, fitted with rubbers. Fold up Pillion Footrests fitted as standard. **WHEELS:** Dunlop 19″ WMI Rims fitted with Dunlop 19″ x 3″ tyres. Both have 5″ internal expanding brakes. **HUBS:** Front and rear have been specially designed to suit the spring frame. Journal race bearings which need no adjustment are used, lubrication by packing with grease annually is all the attention needed. **MUDGUARDS:** Front and Rear are fully valanced and adequately stayed. **SADDLE:** Is a soft top dual seat of finest quality fitted to built on sub-frame. **TRANSMISSION:** "RENOLD" roller chain throughout, the Primary running in an oil bath whilst the main driving chain is protected by an efficient heavy gauge pressed steel guard. **STAND:** Central spring up stand constructed of special section steel tubing is fitted, of all welded construction with extra wide base. **HANDLEBARS:** Have been specially designed and ensure a maximum of comfort and control, fully adjustable radially, all chromium plated. **PETROL TANK:** 2¼ gallons capacity, fitted with knee grips and large filler cap. **EQUIPMENT:** Standard Equipment includes—Inflator, horn, tool box and tools. **B.2.S.** has direct lighting with 5″ head lamp incorporating dipper switch and streamlined rear lamp. **B.2.S. De Luxe** has rectified lighting with 6″ Headlamp, Switch, Ammeter and "Stop" light. Lucas Battery and Carrier are standard on this model. **FINISH:** Frame and forks etc. "SPRA-GRANODISED" and enamelled black. Tank enamelled maroon.
MID GREEN POLYCHROMATIC FINISH Extra.

The Armstrong forks employed on the latest B2/S dictated a higher-mounted mudguard with deep valancing. I suspect that owners may have had trouble with the ungainly tubular silencer bracket so the single bolt that previously secured it at the top had been augmented by two and it had been rotated to almost vertical – still an ugly contrivance that looked like an afterthought, however. Even worse: if the road surface was other than billiard table-smooth any pillion passenger would have had a dreadful time as their footrests were attached to the pivoted fork.

For Norman's first foray into the over-197 class it elected to use British Anzani's outboard-derived disc-valve two-stroke. Most certainly not performers they were, however, particularly smooth, even compared to other contemporarty twins of their genre. On Armstrong front fork models the front brake plate was fully floating to prevent torque reaction rendering the suspension all but inoperative under heavy braking. Although the frames of the T/S and B2/S differed they both look like what is commonly referred to as swinging-arm; however, their manufacturer called them 'Norman Cantilever spring frames'. A neater silencer bracket was employed on the T/S.

A DE LUXE LIGHTWEIGHT TWIN
The Ideal Touring Model. Superb road holding qualities.

T/S
242 c.c.

ENGINE British Anzani Uni-Twin fitted with four speed gearbox and kick start in unit construction ; flywheel magneto and electrical generator. **FRAME**: Norman Canti-lever spring frame employing Armstrong automatic two rate oil damped spring units. **FORKS**: Designed specially for the Norman Spring frame are the Armstrong link action oil damped forks. These have proved on test to be a great advance over the usual type of telescopic fork and give a very comfortable ride over the roughest of going combined with perfect steering. **FOOT-RESTS**: Forged steel and have full radial adjustment of 360 degrees. Cylindrical rubber pads are fitted for maximum comfort. **WHEELS**: Both wheels are built with Dunlop 19" WM1 rims and fitted with Dunlop 19" x 3" tyres. Both wheels have 5" internal expanding brakes. **HUBS**: Both hubs employ journal raced bearings which need no adjustment in use. The front hub is provided with knock out spindle for instant removal and the front brake anchor plate is arranged to float on a special bearing to ensure maximum efficiency. **MUDGUARDS**: Both guards are fully valanced and adequately stayed. **DUAL SEAT**: New and improved pattern utilising a soft top, finest quality covering and mounted on a spring mattress base. **TRANSMISSION**: Renolds chain throughout, the Primary chain running in an oil bath. **STAND**: Central spring up stand constructed of oval section tubing and adequately stayed. **HANDLEBARS**: Designed with a special bend to ensure maximum comfort and control. Fully adjustable radially and chromium plated. **PETROL TANK**: 2¼ gallons capacity fitted with specially shaped knee grips and extra large filler cap. **EQUIPMENT**: Standard equipment includes—Inflator, electric horn, tool box and battery carrier, complete set of tools. Pillion footrests are built in the rear sub frame. **LIGHTING**: The Lighting equipment is to de luxe specification employing rectifier and Lucas battery. 6" head lamp fitted with switch, ammeter and built-in speedometer. Stop light and dipper switch are standard. **FINISH**: "SPRA-GRANODISED" and enamelled black. Petrol tank enamelled maroon, lined gold. Mid Green Polychromatic finish extra.

ENGINE: Villiers 197 c.c. 2-stroke 7E Competition Engine incorporates foot change and 4-speed gearbox, special kick start in Unit Construction. **FRAME**: Norman Competition frame allows the engine to be offset to give the extra chain clearance necessary with the Universal Competition tyre. Is of tubular construction brazed and bolted, built with Reynolds 'A' quality tubing. **FORKS**: Telescopic, designed specially for the Competition Model, an arrangement of springs incorporated gives an easy action fork, coupled with complete rigidness over the very roughest trials going. **FOOTRESTS**: Forged from EN.8Q steel adjustable radially over 360°. Provision is made for 3 alternative positions. This, with the adjustable saddle mounting allows for a position to suit any rider. **WHEELS**: Dunlop, front 21" WM1 Rim, rear 19" WM2 Rim. Tyres Dunlop, front 21" x 2·75" rear 19" x 4·00". 5" internal expanding brakes fitted to both wheels. Security bolts fitted to front and rear. **HUBS**: Designed especially for the Competition Model. Both front and rear fitted with journal race bearings, speedometer drive incorporated inside rear brake drum. **MUDGUARDS**: Both of 5" ribbon section constructed of light alloy. Stays have strength and rigidity are specially designed for this machine. **SADDLE**: Dunlop Drilastic top, adjustment at nose and back. **TRANSMISSION**: "RENOLD" Roller chain throughout, primary chain running in an oilbath. The main driving chain protected by a light alloy chainguard. **STAND**: A side prop stand is fitted as standard. **HANDLEBARS**: "Special competition bend" designed solely for Competition Work they are adjustable radially. **PETROL TANK**: Of special design to suit the Competition frame, capacity 1¾ gallon. **EQUIPMENT**: Includes tool kit, inflator, bulb horn and Competition number plate. Lighting equipment is not fitted to this model. **GEAR**: Special gearing for Competition Work utilising a 50T rear hub sprocket giving 1st 22·6, 2nd 15·0, 3rd 8·4, top 6·5. A wide range of sprockets between 44T and 54T can be substituted to special order. **FINISH**: Is in Norman colours of Black and Maroon. Mudguards polished aluminium and all usual parts chromium plated. **CARBURETTOR**: AMAL or VILLIERS as required.

Norman's two-stroke trials machines enjoyed a good deal of success.

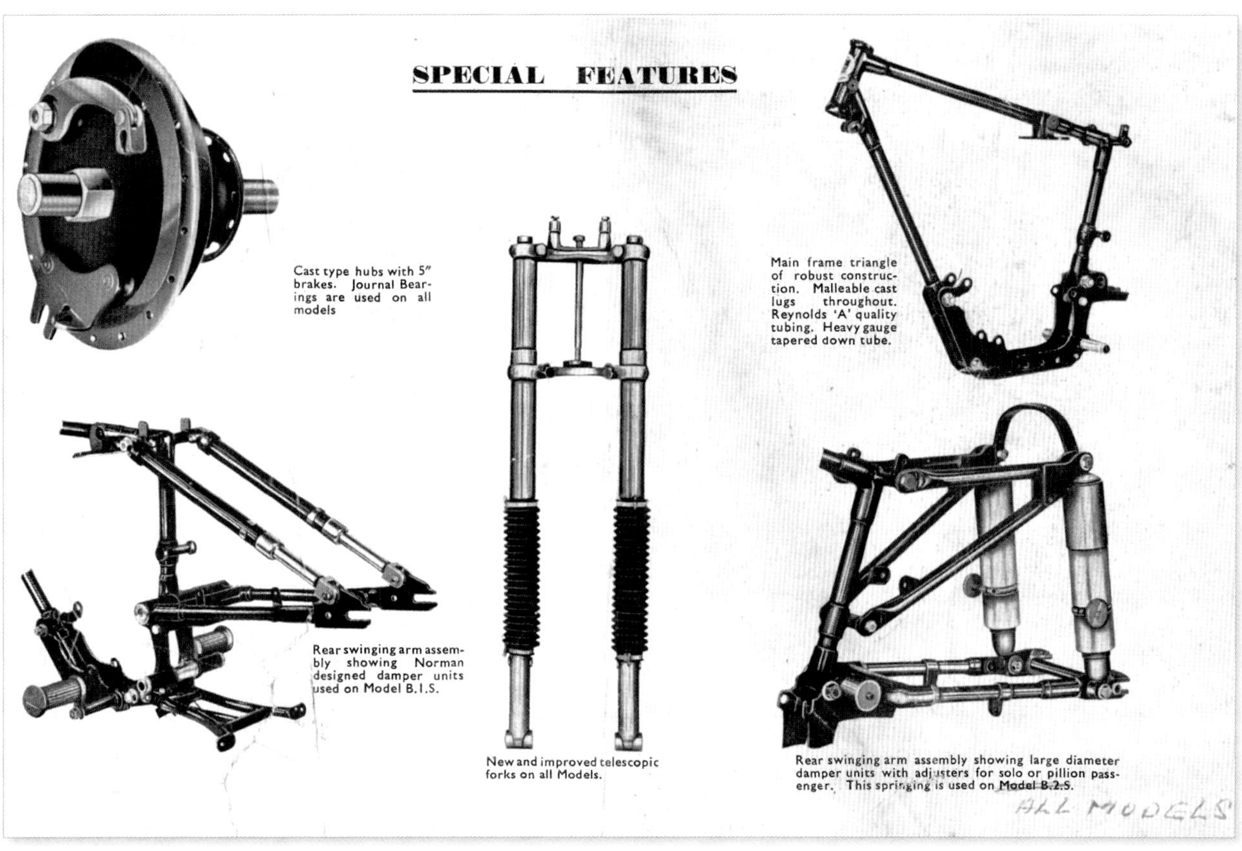

Cantilever or swinging-arm, Norman elected to refer to them as the latter here, and our anonymous rep from 60 years ago even conscientiously corrected a printing mistake for what he took to be a prospective customer.

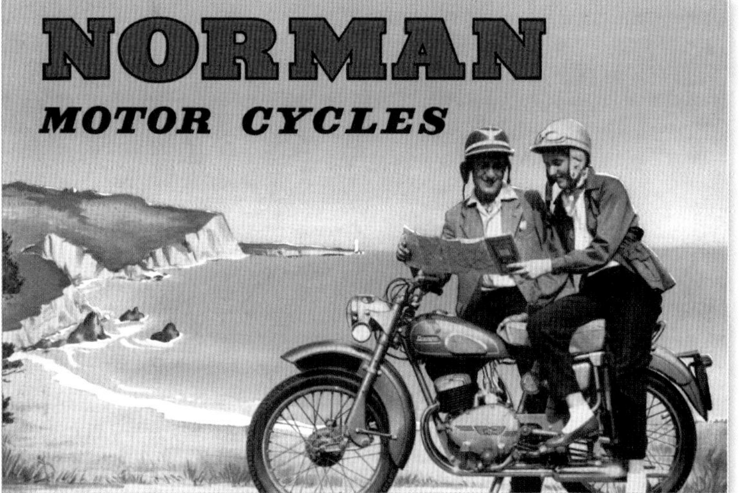

For 1956 the B2/S could be had with either a Villiers 8E three-speed unit or 9E with four speeds. Colour scheme of Mid Green Polychromatic was unchanged.

At a quick glance the 1956 T/S was very much the same as the previous year but could be distinguished by such details as a different headlamp and its updated British Anzani power unit, which featured enlarged finning to barrels and cylinder heads. Good to see that Norman insisted on Valerie wearing something rather more sensible to accompany Graham to the seaside than the impossible outfits chosen by some other manufacturers for their brochure scenarios.

Was it common sense or customer feedback that led to the adoption of a single frame design for 1956? No coincidence, I'm pretty sure, that it was the very one (from the previous year's T/S) that meant the end of oscillating pillion footrests and about a foot of tube to act as a bracket to secure the silencer. The B1/S had now been given Armstrong forks too – note the unusual front frame down-tube mounting for the tyre pump employed on the B1/S and B2/S.

B1/S 150 cc

SPECIFICATION

ENGINE: Villiers two stroke 150 c.c. 30c. three speed unit. **FRAME:** Norman Cantilever Spring frame employs two rate automatic spring boxes which permits two rates of springing for solo or a pillion passenger. Built throughout with best quality steel tubing and brazed to ensure complete rigidity. **FORKS:** Designed specially for the Norman Spring frame are the Armstrong link action oil damped forks. These have proved on test to be a great advance over the usual type of telescopic fork and give a very comfortable ride over the roughest of going combined with perfect steering. **FOOTRESTS:** Forged steel and fully adjustable radially through 360 degrees, fitted with rubbers. Fold up Pillion Footrests fitted as standard. **WHEELS:** Dunlop 19″ WMI Rims fitted with Dunlop 19″x 3″ tyres. Both have 5″ internal expanding brakes. **HUBS:** Front and rear have been specially designed to suit the spring frame. Journal race bearings which need no adjustment are used, lubrication by packing with grease annually is all the attention needed. **MUDGUARDS:** Front and Rear are fully valanced and adequately stayed. **SADDLE:** Is a soft top dual seat of finest quality fitted to built on sub-frame. **TRANSMISSION:** "RENOLD" roller chain throughout, the Primary running in an oil bath whilst the main driving chain is protected by an efficient heavy gauge pressed steel guard. **STAND:** Central spring-up stand constructed of special section steel tubing is fitted, of all welded construction with extra wide base. **HANDLEBARS:** Have been specially designed and ensure a maximum of comfort and control, fully adjustable radially, all chromium plated. **PETROL TANK:** 2¼ gallons capacity, fitted with knee grips and large filler cap.

EQUIPMENT: Standard Equipment includes—Inflator, horn, tool box and tools.

B.I.S. has direct lighting with 5″ head lamp incorporating dipper switch and streamlined rear lamp.

B.I.S. De Luxe has rectified lighting with 6″ Headlamp, Switch, Ammeter and "Stop" light. Lucas Battery and Carrier are standard on this model.

FINISH: Frame and forks etc. "SPRA-GRANODISED."

COLOUR: MID GREEN POLYCHROMATIC.

COMPETITION MODEL B2/C

SPECIFICATION

ENGINE: Villiers 197 c.c. 2-stroke 9E Competition Engine, incorporating 4-speed gearbox with foot operation and kick starter in Unit Construction. **CARBURETTOR:** This instrument is by Villiers and is standard on this machine. **FRAME:** The Norman Competition frame allows for the engine to be offset to give the extra chain clearance necessary with the Universal Competition tyre. It is of tubular construction, brazed and bolted and built with Reynolds 'A' quality tubing. The well known Norman canti-lever rear springing is incorporated and makes use of Armstrong two rate Automatic rear suspension units. **FORKS:** The Competition version of the well-known Armstrong bottom link oil damped forks are used on this model. This type of fork has been well tried and has proved ideal for Competition work. **FOOTRESTS:** These are forged from EN.8Q steel and are adjustable radially over 360 degrees. Provision is made for three alternative positions. This, with the adjustable saddle mounting allows for a position to suit any rider. **WHEELS:** These are built with Dunlop rims utilising a 21″ WMI Rim for the front wheel and a 19″ WM2 rim for the rear. Tyres are Dunlop, front 21″ x 2·75″, rear 19″ x 4″. 5″ internal expanding hub brakes are fitted to both wheels. Security bolts are fitted to both front and rear. **HUBS:** Designed especially for the Competition Model. Both front and rear fitted with journal race bearings. **MUDGUARDS:** Both of 5″ ribbed section and constructed of light alloy. Stays have both strength and rigidity and are specially designed for this machine. **SADDLE:** Dunlop Drilastic top, adjustment at the nose and back. **TRANSMISSION:** "RENOLD" Roller chain throughout, primary chain running in an oilbath. The main driving chain protected by a light alloy chainguard. **STAND:** A side prop stand is fitted as standard. **HANDLEBARS:** "Special Competition bend" designed for Competition work, they are adjustable radially.

PETROL TANK: Of special design to suit the Competition frame with a capacity of 1¾ gallon.

EQUIPMENT: Includes tool kit, inflator, bulb horn and Competition number plate. Smith Chronometric speedometer driven from the engine gearbox. Lighting equipment is not fitted to this model.

GEARS: Special gearing for Competition work utilising a 56T rear hub sprocket giving the following gear ratios—1st. 25·6; 2nd. 14·58; 3rd. 9·57; top 7·05. A range of sprockets between 50T and 58T are available and can be substituted to special order.

FINISH: In Norman colours of Black and Maroon. Mudguards polished aluminium and all usual parts chromium plated.

By 1956, although still designated the B2/C, Norman's trials mount now boasted a swinging-arm frame with Armstrong rear suspension units and front forks.

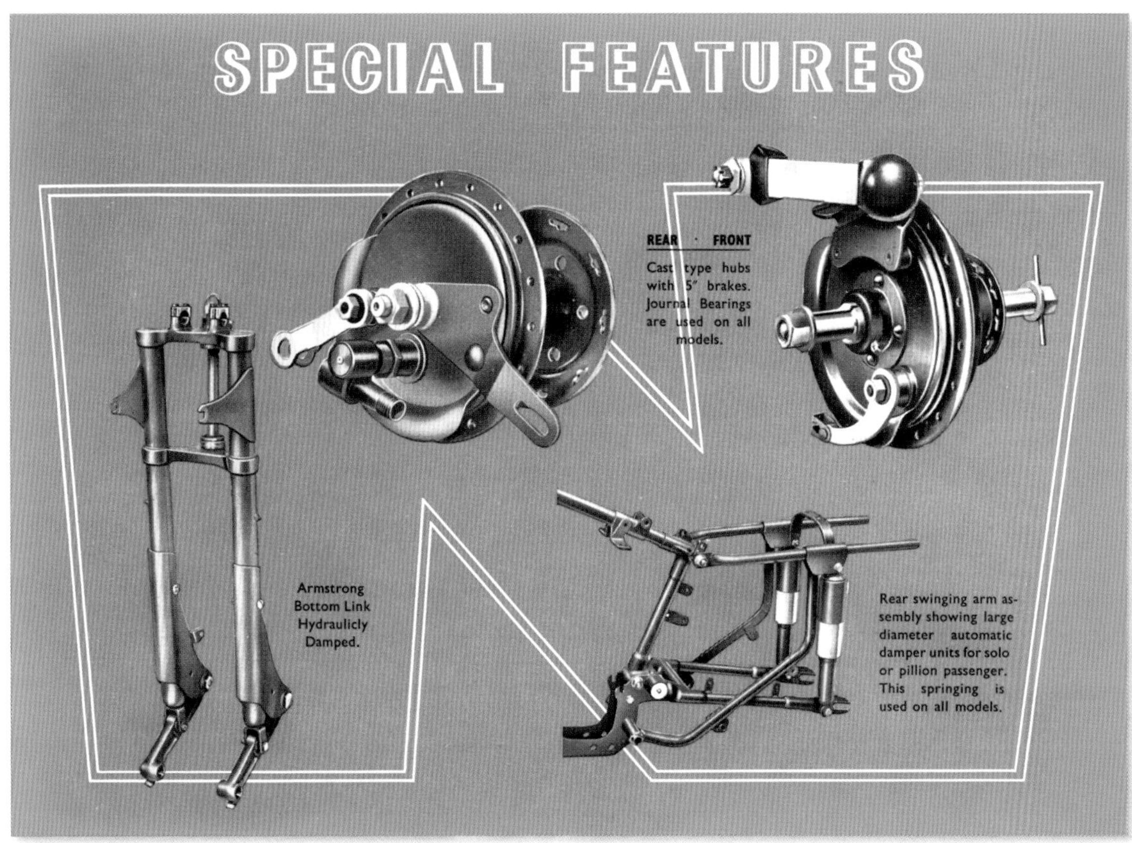

Norman had a hand in the development of Armstrong leading-link forks and later on would manufacture an improved version, as well as supplying them to other manufacturers. This is the updated version.

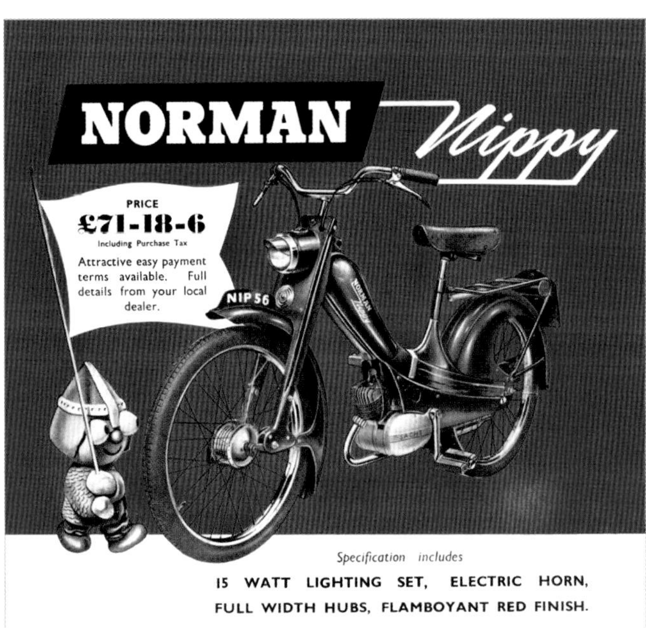

Naughty Norman? In spite of it being on its stand at the 1955 show the Sachs-engined Nippy was Norman in name only – being simply a rebadged German Capri made in Holland under licence from the West German Achilles company. Later on, when the latter got into trouble, Norman acquired tooling and rights to manufacture an updated rear-sprung Nippy and the rather ritzy Lido, both of which were fitted with Villiers 3K moped units.

This is a 1958 B2/S but from the start of the 1957 season the B1/S, B2/S and T/S roadsters featured these pressed-steel side panels. For 1958 the twin was given a Villiers 2T in place of the British Anzani and renamed the B/3; it also had a larger 3¼-gallon fuel tank and 6in full-width front hub whereas the rest of the range retained the 5in unit. All were finished in two-tone Dark Blue Metallic and Light Blue enamel with the dual seat covered in Blue leather cloth.

Fittingly the firm's last brochure was published the year that Fred and Charles Norman retired and, as though determined to go out in style, the cover featured the new B4 Sports Twin. Its nearest direct competitor would have been Cotton's Double Gloster, as many components were the same. Pricewise too there was little difference – the Norman being just £1 cheaper.

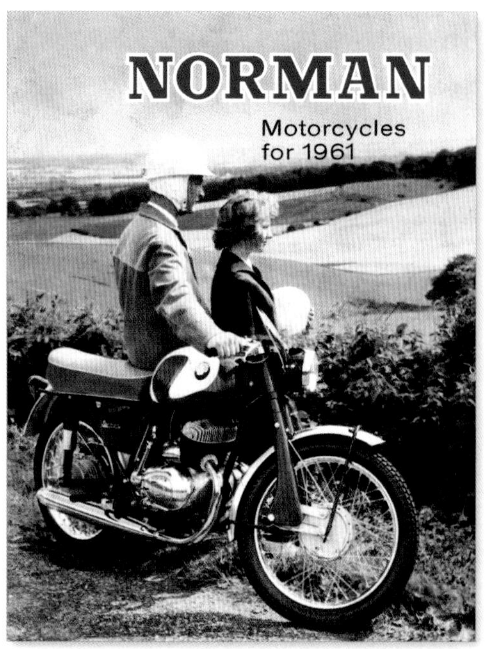

For 1959, sports versions of both B2/S and B3 were introduced. With drop handlebars, fly screen, polished aluminium mudguards, competition-type footrests, smaller fuel tank with knee recesses and chromium flash, plus the option of racing alloy rims, they had an attractive specification and were finished in Black with Red tank. The 197 and 250 roadsters were finished in either Black or Dark Metallic Blue, whilst the B1/S retained the same colours as the previous two seasons and up until the end of 1960 when it was dropped from the range.

What would prove to be the last of the B2Ss in De Luxe trim in Black (Dark Metallic Blue was still an alternative).

NORMAN

MOTOR CYCLE PRICES – SEASON 1961

(operative as from October 20th, 1960)

MODEL	RETAIL £	s.	d.	PURCHASE TAX £	s.	d.	TOTAL £	s.	d.
B 4 SPORTS 250 c.c. TWIN VILLIERS 2 T High Compression Engine 4-speed De Luxe, Red	159	3	6	32	16	6	192	0	0
B 4 ROADSTER 250 c.c. TWIN VILLIERS 2 T 4-speed De Luxe. Cypress Green or Black	159	3	6	32	16	6	192	0	0
B 4 C TRIALS 200 c.c. VILLIERS 9 E 4 Single Cylinder	142	12	0	29	8	0	172	0	0
B 4 C TRIALS 250 c.c. VILLIERS 32 A Single Cylinder	145	1	6	29	18	6	175	0	0
B 4 C SCRAMBLER 250 c.c. VILLIERS 34 A Single Cylinder	153	7	6	31	12	6	185	0	0
B 2 S ROADSTER 200 c.c. VILLIERS 9 E 3-speed. Standard., Blue or Black	123	16	6	25	10	9	149	7	3
B 2 S/DL ROADSTER or SPORTS 200 c.c. VILLIERS 9 E. 3-speed De Luxe. Roadster Blue or Black. Sports Red	129	6	9	26	13	6	156	0	3
B 2 S/DL ROADSTER or SPORTS 200 c.c. VILLIERS 9 E. 4-speed De Luxe. Roadster Blue or Black., Sports Red	135	1	3	27	17	3	162	18	6
Lighting Set on B 4 C Trials Models	2	16	0		11	6	3	7	6
Light Alloy Racing Rims on Model B 4 Sports	7	10	4	1	11	0	9	1	4

All above models (except B 4 C Scrambler) are fitted with Smiths Non-Trip Speedometer

B2S/DL 200 c.c. Sports model
A proved successful 200 c.c. Sports Model. Exceptional value. Full specification. **No extras.**

The Sports 197 remained all but unaltered for its swansong year too – still with a three-speed gearbox as an option, although I cannot imagine that many buyers didn't stump up the extra seven quid-or-so for four speeds.

B4 250 c.c. Roadster model
Completely re-designed frame and swinging arm. New Italian styled petrol tank. New type tool boxes and steel fairings. Superbly finished. Comprehensive specification. **No extras.**

The B4 replaced the B3 and was more than a new model in name only, with brand-new frame, tank and rear enclosure. It also had full-width 6in hubs back and front. This one is the Cypress Green Lustre edition.

B4 250 c.c. Twin Sports model
An entirely new 250 c.c. Sports model, incorporating 3¾ gallon capacity Italian styled tank. A real thoroughbred. High Compression engine fitted to this model. Superbly finished. Comprehensive specification. **No extras.**

Very stylish – and without any rear enclosure there was more of the new design of frame on show. All the racy bits and pieces were standard, including the shapely Italianesque fuel tank, but if you wanted alloy wheel rims to make it really look the business they were a little less than a tenner.

B4C 200 or 250 c.c. Trials model
An entirely re-designed Competition model. Many new features. May be fitted with 200 c.c. engine or 250 c.c. single. An extremely robust and functional machine.

With the larger 32A-engined version only £3 more than the 9E I would doubt the firm sold too many of the latter. There was a B4C Scrambler too but that was fitted with the more powerful Villiers 34A engine and had more substantial mudguard stays, different gear ratios and, I trust, a larger seat – whether trails or scrambles they were to special order only.

MODEL	ENGINE	FRAME	FORKS	TANK	WHEELS	FINISH
B 4 SPORTS	Villiers 2T, 249 c.c. Twin Sports Engine. Unit 4 Speed Gearbox. High Compression Head. Clutch case, magneto cover and carburetter cover are polished as standard.	Norman frame, with new design sub-frame and swinging arm.	The well proved Norman Armstrong leading link oil damped forks.	This is an Italian style tank of pleasing appearance, with knee recesses, quick action filler cap. It holds 3¾ gallons of petrol and provides a reserve mileage of 10 miles.	19in. diameter wheels are fitted as an aid to good handling with 2.75in. front and 3in. rear Dunlop Universal tyres. Both brakes are of 6in. full width design. The front hub is fitted with a 'floating' brake plate to improve suspension under braking conditions.	Frame and fork "Spra-Granodised" Enamelled Ruby Red Epinamel with Ivory Tank Panels. be fitted to order.
B 4 ROADSTER	Villiers 2T, 249 c.c. Twin, Engine. Unit 4 Speed Gearbox. Clutch Case, Magneto cover and Carburetter cover are polished as standard.	New Norman frame, with new design sub-frame and swinging arm.	The well proved Norman Armstrong leading link oil damped forks.	New large capacity tank holding 3¼ gallons giving a reserve mileage of 10 miles.	19in. diameter front and rear with 3in. Dunlop Universal tyres. Both brakes are 6in. full width design. The front hub is fitted with a 'floating' brake plate to improve suspension under braking conditions.	Frame and Fork "Spra-Granodised" Enamelled Cypress Green Lustre Hi-Gloss or Black.
B 2 S/DL SPORTS	Villiers 9E, 197 c.c. Single Cylinder Engine. Gear Unit, 3 Speed or 4 Speed.	Norman Cantilever.	Norman Armstrong leading link.	2½ gallon, 10 miles reserve. This tank has knee recesses.	19in. diameter front and rear, both brakes 5in. 'Full-Width'. 2.75in. Dunlop Universal tyre fitted to the front wheel and 3in. Dunlop Universal tyre fitted to the rear wheel.	Frame and Fork "Spra-Granodised" Enamelled Ruby Red Epinamel.
B 2 S & B 2 S/DL ROADSTER	Villiers 9E, 197 c.c. Single Cylinder Engine. Gear Unit. 3 Speed or 4 Speed.	Norman Cantilever.	Norman Armstrong leading link.	3¼ gallons capacity, 10 miles reserve.	19in. diameter front and rear. Both brakes 5in. 'full-width'. 3in. Dunlop tyres.	Frame and Forks "Spra-Granodised" Enamelled Hi-Gloss Black, or Dark Metallic Blue.
B 4 C TRIALS	Villiers Mark 32A, 246 c.c. single cylinder engine. Unit 4 Speed Gearbox or 9E4, 197 c.c. Competition single cylinder. Unit 4 Speed Gearbox.	New Norman design frame and swinging arm.	Norman Armstrong leading link oil damped.	Special slim design. 1¾ gallon capacity.	Front 21in., rear 19in., both use 6in. full width hubs. Front tyre—2.75in. Dunlop Trials Universal. Rear tyre—4in. Dunlop Trials Universal.	Frame and Forks "Spra-Granodised" Enamelled Black with Red Tank.
B 4 C SCRAMBLER	Villiers Mark 34A 250 c.c. Engine. Unit 4-Speed Gearbox.	Norman frame with new design sub-frame and swinging arm.	Norman Armstrong leading link oil damped.	Special slim design. 1¾ gallon capacity.	21in. front wheel, 19in. rear wheel. 6in. 'Full Width' hubs front and rear. Front tyre 2.75in. Dunlop Sports. Rear tyre 3.5in. Dunlop Sports.	Frame and Forks "Spra-Granodised" Enamelled Black with Red Tank.

NORTON

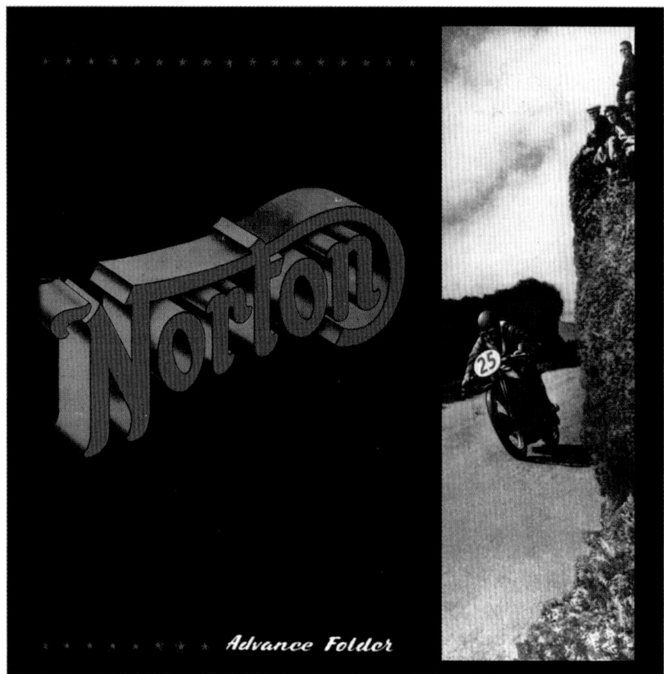

Somewhat satanic perhaps but the minute hostilities ceased, Norton rushed this out – no racing as yet but past glories hadn't been forgotten.

The rear cover speaks for itself, and a number of the outfits including those at the top left are the Big Fours with the driven sidecar wheel. Fitted with no differential of any kind, a legend persists that if used on tarmac they were treacherous on corners – exhibiting a lethal tendency to go straight on. Whether true or not the very few that I have seen all had had their driveshaft cut off short of the outer universal joint.

Having commenced his working life as an apprentice toolmaker in the jewellery trade James Lansdowne Norton, who was born in 1869, had come to the decision that he was better suited to become an engineer – this later borne out when he became one of the founders of the Institution of Automobile Engineers.

Hampered periodically by periods of ill health he had nevertheless started his own company in 1898, which specialised in the manufacture of components and fittings for the cycle trade, and thereafter making complete cycles. In 1902 he built his first motorised cycle – engagingly christened the Energette, it was powered by a French Clement engine of a little under 150cc and soon went into production with either direct belt-drive or chain-cum-belt via a two-speed gearbox.

Soon his machines became simply Nortons, using engines by Peugeot – except in 1907 when the Energette title was reintroduced in conjunction with a small Moto Reve V-twin powered machine. Of greater significance that same year, however, was Rem Fowler's victory at the helm of a Peugeot-engined Norton in the twin-cylinder class of the very first Tourist Trophy race held on the Isle of Man – outrunning his rivals but not the two fastest singles in their class.

The following year the Energette was replaced by a 2hp single named the Nortonette but this was to be short-lived as by now the firm had begun to manufacture its own engines – the first of which went into what would turn out to be the long-lived side-valve Big Four that would be produced for nigh on 50 years. Indifferent health notwithstanding, Norton himself rode in three TTs, from 1909 to 1911 but finished in none, in spite of fielding one his new 79x100mm 490c side-valve singles that would become the TT model in the last of them – a machine that would later become the 16H and would enjoy similar longevity to the Big Four.

A gifted engineer if not successful racer he most certainly was, but Pa Norton, so named on account of his prematurely-aged appearance, was no businessman and despite the introduction of such worthwhile machines his company was fast heading for bankruptcy. The axe fell over the winter of 1912 but due to the intervention of accessories manufacturer Robert Shelley, who was one Norton's main suppliers (and thus creditors) as well as a personal friend, the firm had a fresh start in 1913 as Norton Motors Ltd. Shelley appointed himself and Pa Norton as joint directors with another business associate, Charles Vandervell of the CAV electrical company as chairman; but it was Bill Mansell's employment as production manager that ensured racing would play a prominent part in the marque's future.

Enlisting the services of renowned tuner and racer Daniel O'Donovan, who happened also to be Shelley's brother-in-law, a programme of development, racing and record breaking with the existing TT model as a basis ensued, which culminated in the BS and BRS (Brooklands Special and Brooklands Road Special) models being added to the firm's range in 1914.

Motorcycle production continued during the first years of the war with the emphasis increasingly on export, and in 1916 a Colonial version of the 633cc Big Four, which by now featured a three-speed gearbox and all-chain drive, was introduced. Government contracts for machines, such as were enjoyed by the likes of Triumph and Douglas, failed to come Norton's way but a military-model Big Four was produced with batches sent, for instance, to Russia.

Post-war the Big Four (model 1), along with three direct-belt-drive sports machines (models 7, 8 and 9) were joined by a more civilized version of the last with chain drive and three speeds. The model 16 – or 3½ TT as it was referred to in the 1920 brochure – was dearer by far (at £132 against £98 for the basic TT) and considered the last word in sports 490 Nortons. That year the firm made a move to Bracebridge Street and racing on the Isle of Man was resumed, where out a field of 27 machines in the Senior TT, 13 were Nortons. Eight completed the course and although it was Tommy de la Hay's day on a Sunbeam, with another third, Nortons were second, fourth, seventh, eighth, tenth, 11th, 13th and 14th – one of their riders being a certain Graham Walker, in his first TT, in that 13th spot.

In search of greater performance than even the Wizard O'Donovan could extract from a side-valve motor, Norton came up with a pushrod inclined-valve OHV top end for the 79x100 motor in 1922 and, given the model number 18 and title Speedy, this became the firm's fastest road machine and racer – the difference between the two at the time being negligible.

Bested by Sunbeam in 1922 and Douglas in '23's Senior it all came good for Norton the next year with TT star and previous winner Alec Bennett riding for the company. The sidecar event was Norton's too, and overwhelmingly so, as Tucker's Norton finished half-

You could have bought an ex-WD considerably cheaper and no doubt got one with little or no delay but it would have had the old semi-diamond frame whereas the post-war model was built upon a cradle frame. For some reason the front brake had reverted to being on the right as it had been immediately pre-war whereas WD machines were on the left.

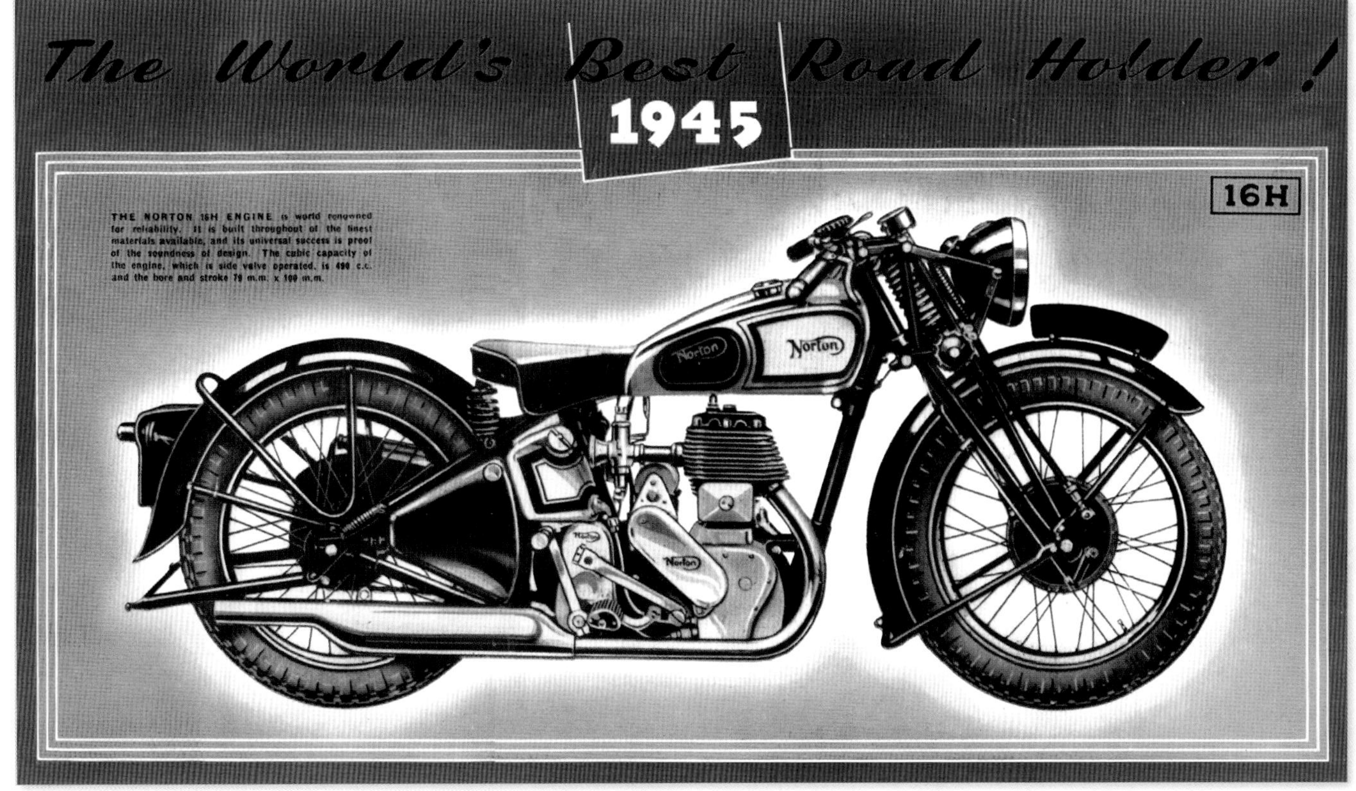

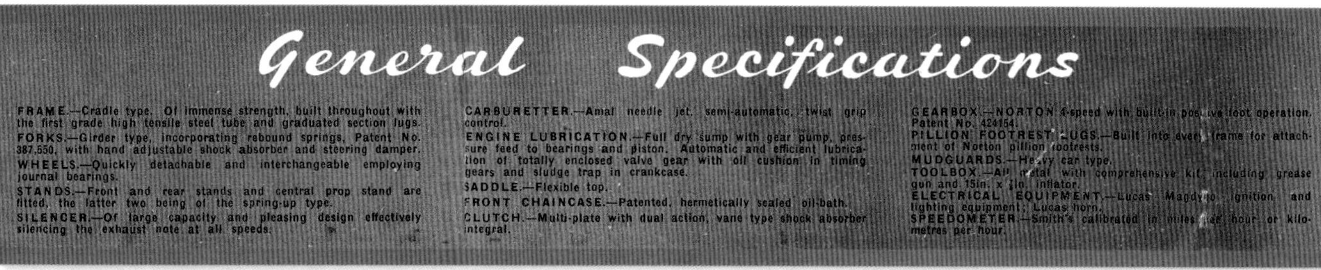

General Specifications

FRAME.—Cradle type. Of immense strength, built throughout with the first grade high tensile steel tube and graduated section lugs.

FORKS.—Girder type, incorporating rebound springs, Patent No. 387,550, with hand adjustable shock absorber and steering damper.

WHEELS.—Quickly detachable and interchangeable employing journal bearings.

STANDS.—Front and rear stands and central prop stand are fitted, the latter two being of the spring-up type.

SILENCER.—Of large capacity and pleasing design effectively silencing the exhaust note at all speeds.

CARBURETTER.—Amal needle jet, semi-automatic, twist grip control.

ENGINE LUBRICATION.—Full dry sump with gear pump, pressure feed to bearings and piston. Automatic and efficient lubrication of totally enclosed valve gear with oil cushion in timing gears and sludge trap in crankcase.

SADDLE.—Flexible top.

FRONT CHAINCASE.—Patented, hermetically sealed oil-bath.

CLUTCH.—Multi-plate with dual action, vane type shock absorber integral.

GEARBOX.—NORTON 4-speed with built-in positive foot operation. Patent No. 424154.

PILLION FOOTREST LUGS.—Built into every frame for attachment of Norton pillion footrests.

MUDGUARDS.—Heavy car type.

TOOLBOX.—All metal with comprehensive kit, including grease gun and 15in. x ⅞in. inflator.

ELECTRICAL EQUIPMENT.—Lucas Magdyno ignition and lighting equipment; Lucas horn.

SPEEDOMETER.—Smith's calibrated in miles per hour or kilometres per hour.

When the overhead-valve Model 18 had been introduced in the early 1920s it had been the firm's most sporting production model, so it was shades of the past when it featured as top dog of the immediate post-war two-model range. A major change had taken place, however, in that it now had the full cradle frame previously reserved for ES2 and camshaft models.

an-hour ahead of Harry Reed on one of his DOTs.

After a further prolonged period of deteriorating health, but with the succour of having at long last having seen a machine of his once more victorious on the Island – as well as in several GPs on the Continent – Pa Norton died in 1925. That year's Senior TT was HRD's, however, with Howard Davies himself the winner; Bennett on the highest-placed Norton was third behind an AJS.

During the following year the company was floated on the stock market, and as a consequence it was reformed as Norton Motors (1926) Ltd. The 633cc Big Four was now also available with a four-speed gearbox and fully-enclosed rear chain case; known as the Model 14 it was priced at just £5 more than the three-speed. New also was the Model 19, an enlarged 588cc version of the Model 18, arrived at by combining the 490's 79mm bore with the 633's 120mm stroke. It was also available as the Model 24 with four speeds, but in that form its purpose was that of a powerful tourer rather than an out-and-out sports – the latter role being the 18's, and 19's; or for racing the higher-specification pushrod OHV 490cc that would be catalogued as the Model 25 the next season. Dublin-born Stanley Woods was new to the Norton team for 1926, and whilst Alec Bennett failed to finish it was the Irishman who clocked up his second Island victory on one of these, his first having been the Junior on a Cotton in 1923.

No less than ten models, all based around the existing range, as well as a selection of sidecars, were catalogued for 1927; but in order to keep abreast of other manufacturers' developments the firm's chief designer Walter Moore had come up with a 79x100 bore and stroke OHC motor. Debuted that summer on the Isle of Man, Alec Bennett beat all comers with the new cradle-framed machine; meanwhile, Stanley Woods made the fastest lap before retiring. The CS1, standing simply for camshaft one, along with a new sporting pushrod OHV 490 named the ES2, went on the market for 1928 – both with the same triple rear stay cradle frame, saddle tank and cycle parts.

For the TT there was a 350 OHC machine, the CJ, but despite the factory now having riders of the calibre of Woods, Craig, Guthrie, Hunt (Norton would lose Bennett whilst gaining Jimmy Simpson in 1929) neither the Junior nor Senior brought success –

Wood's fifth in the '28 Senior and Hunt's fourth in '29 a disappointing tally.

Continental GPs were similarly blighted, largely due to the camshaft motor failing to fulfil its early promise, but the departure of Moore to NSU in 1929, taking his engine design with him, resulted in what would prove to be a vastly improved engine being drawn up by his successor Arthur Carroll. Made available to the public in 1931 it also enjoyed a startlingly successful maiden racing season – winning no less than 14 international road races, including Junior and Senior TTs, Dutch TT and the French, German and Belgian GPs. To celebrate those achievements with a similar machine for the public, the Model 30 and 40 (500 and 350cc) International were introduced for 1932 – both of which featured a four-speed positive stop-change gearbox whilst the rest of the firm's range, including the CS1 and CJ, retained a three-speed with hand-change as standard.

At the same time the long rangy look of the first of the saddle tank machines, which had replaced the lean flat-tankers, had given way to a more cobby appearance – largely due to new frames that gave a shorter wheelbase, along with a shorter fuel tank that went with them.

Weathering the depression without resorting to cut-price or small-capacity models as had some other manufacturers, Norton's range had remained much the same and would continue to be, if periodically modernised. The addition of a 350 pushrod OHV in 1933, fashionable twin-port options for this and its larger relation, and the availability of any model in trials trim from 1936 on, were the main model innovations during the '30s.

That decade was truly the marque's golden years as far as racing was concerned, however, and on the Continent and even further afield Nortons were more often than not highly placed or the winners. In the TT alone, of the 16 Junior and Senior events between 1932 and '39 no less than 12 were won by Carroll-engined Nortons; just the '38 and '39 Junior were taken by Stanley Woods on a Velocette, whilst he rode a Moto Guzzi to victory in the '35 Senior and the '39 was a one-two for BMW's supercharged twins.

Plunger suspension was introduced on works racers for 1936, and by 1938 as an extra for all Internationals. The camshaft engine, especially the racing version, was steadily developed too, gaining hairpin valve springs as well as an increasing amount of aluminium and magnesium alloy components, with twin camshafts appearing for the first time in practice for the 1936 TT. Stanley Woods's double Junior and Senior TT wins in 1933 had been his last for the Bracebridge Street concern, and thereafter its top riders were Jimmie Guthrie and Freddy Frith. Between the two of them they shared the remainder of firm's later-'30s TT successes with the exception of the 1938 Senior, which was won by Harold Daniell whose Norton career carried on post-war with Senior victories in 1947 and '49.

World War Two saw the factory fully occupied, with munitions production taking a second place to War Department contracts for its side-valve singles. Over 100,000 16Hs, Big Fours and sidecar outfits had left the works by the time peace returned in 1945.

Although telescopic forks and plunger rear suspension were to have been fitted to some 1940 models these features had been put on hold for the meanwhile, and so the 16Hs and Model 18s that comprised the initial post-war range were in essentially pre-war form. By 1947 ten models were listed and all had telescopic forks, whilst a plunger frame was employed for ES2s, Internationals and Manx racers.

For the latter, although unexpectedly trounced by a hopped-up Triumph twin (that would go into production as the GP the following year) in the 1946 Manx GP, there had been a return to the status quo enjoyed prior to 1939. From 1947 to '54, Manx Nortons won every Senior TT – and the Junior too, once they had got the better of Velocette's ageing KTTs, from 1950 to '53. This was the era of the legendary Geoff Duke, who notched up two Seniors and two Juniors, including a double in 1951; and then, after Duke had switched to Gilera, the brilliant Rhodesian Ray Amm, who won Senior and Junior in 1953, followed by the controversial foreshortened Senior in '54.

By that time, despite constant improvements overseen by Joe Craig (who had been responsible for the twin-cam head) the adoption of the McCandless brothers Featherbed frame (in 1950), and the freer-revving short-stroke (86x 85.5mm) 500 motor (1953), the single-cylinder Manx was increasingly unable to match the speed of the Italian fours, and there was no money for a multi of the company's own. It was the end of an era.

Norton ceased to mount a works team, Amm moved on to ride for MV in Italy, and Craig retired. This was by no means the end of the Manx as a highly-effective race machine though, and its successes continued to be legion on national and international levels – proof of which was its glorious last hurrah on the Isle of Man in 1961 when Phil Read won the Junior and Mike Hailwood the Senior.

Without Norton's road machines there would have been no racing, however, and the 1948 show had seen the introduction of the first of the vertical twins, the Model 7 – a 500 from the drawing board of Bert Hopwood, in years to come it would be progressively

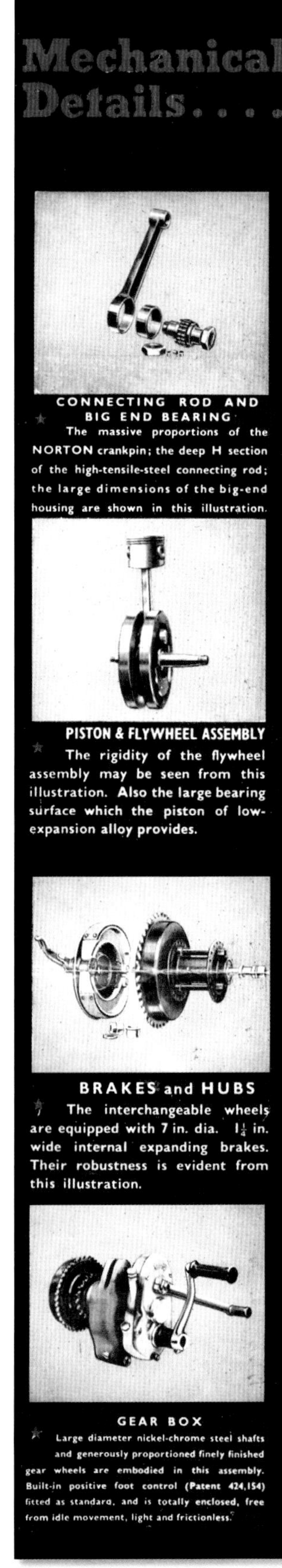

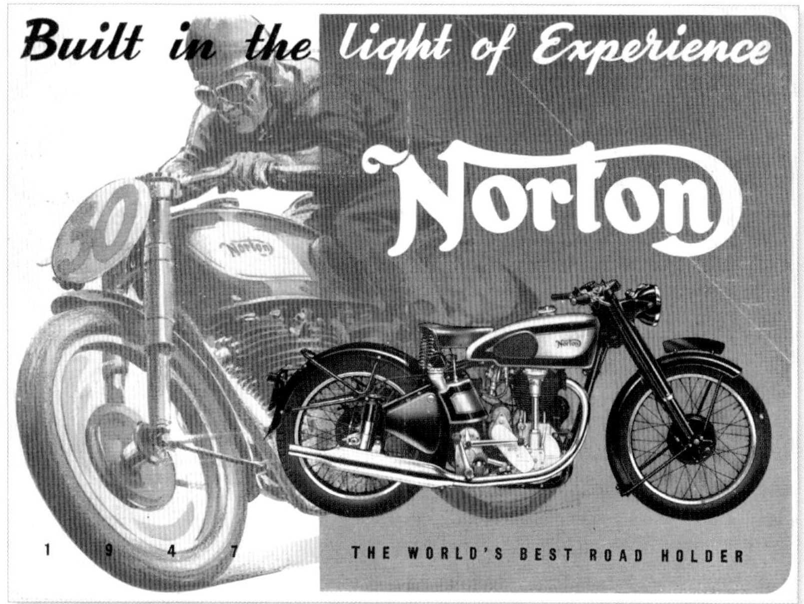

By the autumn of 1946 it was time to publish the next season's brochure and the company was very much back on track in more ways than one.

enlarged, first to a 600, then 650, 750 and on to just over 825cc in the 1970s, as well as being developed as a production-based racer.

Up until 1951 they had the firm's plunger frame but at that year's show an export-only version with the race-bred Featherbed frame was announced as the Dominator 88. It would not be available on the home market until the 1953 season, by which time Model 7s and ES2s had been modernised with a swinging-arm version of their plunger cradle frame.

All was not well with the company's finances, however, and with shareholders deserting what they perceived to be a sinking ship Associated Motor Cycles stepped in to become the new owner. For a short while Bracebridge Street was left to carry on as it was, but casualties came at the close of the 1954 season. Gone were the long-running side-valve singles and the Model 18, along with the trials 500T; in their place the OHV Model 19 was reintroduced with either a rigid (1955 only) or swinging-arm frame. By 1956 the International, which had a 'Featherbed' frame since 1953, was relegated to special order-only status, but a larger 600 Dominator (the 99) had been added to the catalogue, perhaps as some kind of recompense, which the reintroduction of the 350 single (Model 50) most certainly was not.

In 1958 the Nomad, a twin-carb 600 twin in single down-tube, swinging arm frame, was introduced for the US off-road market. But for 1959 Norton, which had scarcely ever made a bad motorcycle, brought out one that was pretty close. Anxious to annex some of the burgeoning learner 250 market, its Jubilee, unfortunately named to celebrate the marque's diamond anniversary, was, apart from an all-new twin-cylinder engine, nothing more than a parts-bin conglomeration of other AMC products. Hardly something with which to celebrate a long and at times glorious history. On a more positive note, the remaining 350 and 500 singles now had the Dominators' Featherbed frames.

The big twins had a makeover for 1960 with a new frame – the soon-to-be nicknamed slimline, with Model 50s and ES2s following the same route a year later. Although a fraction wider aft of the headstock, the spacing of the twin top-tubes was nipped in towards their rear to increase rider comfort and facilitate the fitting of Jubilee-inspired and fashionable rear enclosure to newly-introduced de luxe Dominators. At the 1960 show the public were treated, or rather subjected, to the Navigator, a 350 variant of the Jubilee – both of which could be had with or without faired-in hindquarters.

Stateside, the Nomad, which by then was made as a 500 or 600, was dropped and in 1961 its place was taken by the first of Norton's 650s – the twin-carb Manxman. This preceded Super Sports versions of the 88s and 99s, also with twin carbs, for home and export later on in the year; and then 650 Dominators, from Standard to SS, for 1962. There were calls from the US importers for an even bigger motor, however, so the 650's bore was increased by 5mm to create the 750 Atlas, which was exclusively for export until it began to appear on the home market at the end of '64.

By then Nortons were being manufactured in London due to AMC having closed the Birmingham factory the previous year, as part of a cost-cutting

Both the 16H and Big Four had first seen the light of day prior to the First World War and gone on to see active service in the Second. Different machines by far from their spindly long-wheelbase forebears, they had, however, stuck to the same engine dimensions throughout. By now on all Nortons were fitted with the telescopic forks that the company had begun developing in the late 1930s.

and rationalisation programme. Production had been transferred down to the Woolwich plant, the Manx had been axed, the race shop was no more and few employees had migrated south – the bad times were about to get worse.

Prior to the Atlas reaching the British, dealers had just five models to work with in 1964, including the 400 Electra – something of a lemon that had been built for the US market to try and beat the Honda 305 at its own game. It hadn't, so there were plenty to try and unload on the Brits – who were also embracing all manner of excitingly trendy motorcycles from the Orient with some considerable gusto. There were some bright spots such as the P11 desert racer for the US (an Atlas engine in Matchless GC80S frame) but they were tempered by irrationally introduced last-ditch stand models such as the so-called Mk2 Model 50s and ES2s (AMC singles with a Norton badge) in 1965.

AMC was by that time in terminal decline, and when the end came in 1966 it was acquired by Manganese Bronze Holdings, whose chairman Dennis Poore saw Norton, with its image and relatively healthy exports to the US, as the most viable of its brands. Reformed as Norton-Villiers the new company made Atlases and Atlas-engined P11s, along with some badged as AJS and Matchless, until 1968 when all were dropped to make way for the Norton Commando.

Utilising the same engine, this featured a brand-new isolastic frame with large-diameter single top-tube and a fully rubber-mounted power unit that was designed to smooth out the vibratory big twin. Initially its main components, such as engines and frames, were produced at various locations, with assembly taking place at Plumstead. When this closed due to a compulsory purchase order in the summer of 1969, government funding was obtained for a new assembly line at Andover in Hampshire, whilst much

of the manufacturing would take place at Villiers's old Wolverhampton factory. Despite initial teething troubles the Commando was awarded the Machine of the Year accolade by the *Motor Cycle News* five times in a row and enjoyed worldwide success.

Government intervention of a more serious nature came into play during 1972 when as a condition of the rescue of the terminally ill BSA-Triumph Group they insisted on a merger with Norton-Villiers: thus the disastrous Norton Villiers Triumph combine was created.

Early in 1973 the 850 (actually 828cc) Commando was introduced but industrial unrest, due to redundancies at Andover, followed. Then in 1974 the government subsidies that had created the whole NVT behemoth were withdrawn; only to be reinstated by the incoming Labour government, providing troubles with Triumph were resolved.

The following year Norton's range was cut back to just two models, and then in the summer the government refused to renew the group's export credits and demanded repayment of a large loan. Large-scale

The ES2 was back and although, unlike the Model 18, it had a cradle frame in the 1930s it now came with plunger rear suspension as standard (whereas it has been introduced as an optional extra for 1939). Motor Cycling *did 1,500 miles on one in the autumn of '46, and mightily impressed they were by 'the manner in which normal bumps or potholes simply melted beneath the wheels when travelling at 45mph or more'... 'bumpy corners could be taken at speeds up to 70mph without a waver'. OHV Norton singles have a reputation for being good on fuel and this one lived up to it, returning just under 80mpg on a run. Top speed was perhaps a little below what might be expected at 77mph; but this was achieved at well below 5,000rpm, so it probably ran out of puff on the pool petrol of the day as it was timed at just under 60 in second gear at getting-on-for 6,500rpm a little earlier. Standard finish was black with chromium tanks coach-lined in red and black, the petrol tank having silver side panels with Norton transfer.*

During the 1930s there had been several 'camshaft' models – for instance the 1938 catalogue listed the CJ (350cc), CS1 (500cc), Model 40 International (500cc), Model 30 International (350cc), International to Racing Specification (350 or 500cc). Now, strictly speaking, the International was a sports machine and if you wanted a Norton racer you bought a Manx. However, the Clubmans TT, which precluded out-and-out racing machines, was inaugurated in 1947. A popular innovation for the clubmen and the clubs whose aegis they would be entering under, whilst manufacturers had mixed feelings – some for, some against. It was little surprise when Norton Internationals proved a popular choice but some were of pre-war vintage – like the Lancefield-prepared 1939 Inter that romped away with the Senior event and the 350 that Denis Parkinson led the Junior with from start to finish. Both riders successfully gambled the disadvantage of girder to Roadholder forks against the advantages of the quicker pre-war aluminium version of the camshaft motor.

redundancies followed at NVT's various locations but the group's total demise was averted by the government's involvement once more – the outcome being the formation of NVT Engineering Ltd with a workforce of 300. The Wolverhampton factory had ended up in the hands of the official receiver, however, and under his control Commandos continued to be made there until a purchaser could be found for the site – thereafter a tiny number were assembled at Andover in the early part of 1978.

This was in effect the end of the marque's pure bloodline stretching back to its inception but the name

From 1931 until the war Norton had won every Senior TT, apart from 1935 when Stanley Woods's Moto Guzzi outran the Bracebridge Street machines and in 1939 when a pair of supercharged BMWs were simply too fast. When racing returned to the Island once more in 1947 supercharging had been banned and the Senior TT was once again the preserve of the 500 Model 30 Nortons, although their Model 40s had to give best to Velocette's MkVIII KTTs in the Junior race.

Many of you will be familiar with the looks of Norton's well-known 500T trials bike but perhaps not so the first of them. Born out of ES2-based machines that had been used in the 1939 ISDT it had gone into limited production, fitted with girder forks, for favoured riders from 1946. Works machines were equipped with the new telescopics, however, and it was in this form that they were eventually catalogued and became available to the general public for the 1947 season. They proved to be uncompetitive when up against the equivalent BSA and AMC competition 350s and 500s, so successes were few and far between.

lived on when a Wankel-engined project, which had been inherited from BSA, was sold by the receiver and went into production as a Norton – most seeing service with the police and other such bodies.

The name was also traded to other individuals, and Nortons of varying designs and a variety of power units were produced in more than one country.

In 2008 UK businessman Stuart Garner bought the rights to the name and relaunched Norton, once again based in the Midlands but this time at Donington Park. The manufacture of a 961cc parallel-twin ensued, and in 2013 Donington Hall was purchased as the company's corporate headquarters with a 45,000sq.ft factory subsequently being built to the rear.

Currently, various sports twins are in production, there is an active race programme and a 1200cc V4 is under development.

It was common practice for some manufacturers to catalogue sidecars, and in the late 1930s Norton had a range of four including this Model 'G'. The firm didn't make a suggestion as to which of the motorcycles would go best with it but the Big Four was the official sidecar machine – even though the bike hitched to the 1946 Model 'G' in this picture is an OHV machine.

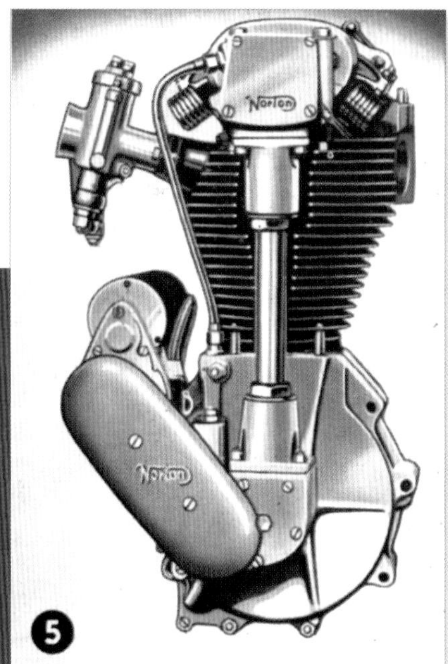

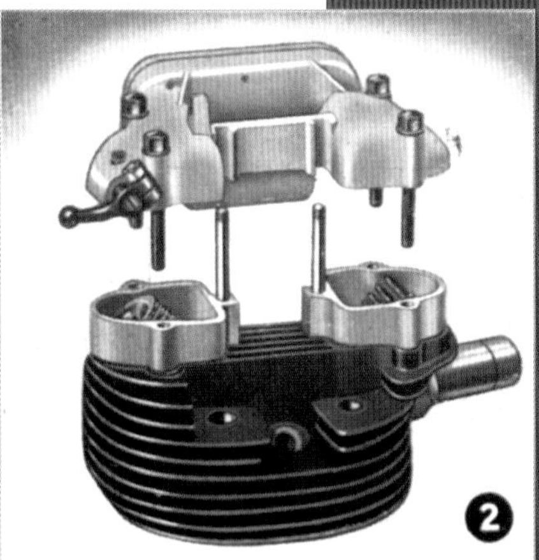

THE FEATURES THAT COUNT

1. **O.H.V. PUSH ROD ENGINE.** As will be seen, the valve gear is totally enclosed. It is automatically lubricated. By means of positive lubrication, large bearing surfaces and ground timing-gear teeth, silence in operation is ensured.

2. **OVERHEAD CYLINDER HEAD AND ROCKER BOX.** An extremely neat method of valve enclosure is employed. The rockers are carried in a one-piece aluminium casting which is rigidly attached to the cylinder head at six points. The generous finning of the cylinder head will be observed.

3. **GEARBOX.** The improved appearance of the re-designed gearbox is apparent from this illustration. The generously proportioned gears and shafts remain as before, but the ease of gear changing has been still further increased.

4. **TELESCOPIC FORKS.** "ROADHOLDER" telescopic forks, incorporating liquid damping, Patent No. 557,982, here illustrated, giving positive steering, improved braking and supreme comfort, will be fitted as standard on all models.

5. **INTERNATIONAL MODEL ENGINE.** Renowned the world over for high speed and wonderful reliability, its performance is unsurpassed. The universal successes obtained with this particular type of engine are an indication of the soundness of design.

6. **THE SPRING FRAME.** The spring frame is standard on International and E.S.2 Models. The mechanism is totally enclosed, consisting of a stationary hardened steel rod on which the patent alloy fork end slides. Balanced top and bottom springs are employed, the whole being enclosed in telescopic tubes.

NORTON MOTORS Ltd.

BRACEBRIDGE STREET
BIRMINGHAM, 6

1947 SEASON

Model 16H	...	£125 0 0	plus Purchase Tax	£33 15 0
,, No. 1 (Big 4)		£128 5 0	,, ,, ,,	£34 12 6
,, 18	...	£130 0 0	,, ,, ,,	£35 2 0
,, ES2	...	£142 0 0	,, ,, ,,	£38 6 9
,, 30	...	£181 0 0	,, ,, ,,	£48 17 5
,, 40	...	£174 0 0	,, ,, ,,	£46 19 7
,, 30M	...	£235 0 0	,, ,, ,,	£63 9 0
,, 40M	...	£235 0 0	,, ,, ,,	£63 9 0
(Models 30M and 40M are to racing specification and incorporate aluminium alloy heads and barrels),				
,, 350T	...	£135 0 0	plus Purchase Tax	£36 9 0
,, 500T	...	£135 0 0	,, ,, ,,	£36 9 0
(Machines to trials specification).				
Model 'G' Sidecar		£40 0 0	plus Purchase Tax	£10 16 0

Extra for SMITH Speedometer £4 plus Purchase Tax £1/1/8.

An ES2 was used for the cover of the 1949 brochure. The artist neglected to include the deeper valancing for the front mudguard abaft of the front forks that was a feature of this model since its inception in late '46, however. Accompanying text tells us that, "The saddle position of the ES2 has been lowered, to give an altogether more comfortable riding position." Contradictory to this, however, The Motor Cycle *had this to say about the latest ES2's seating: "The saddle height, 31in, is greater than average."*

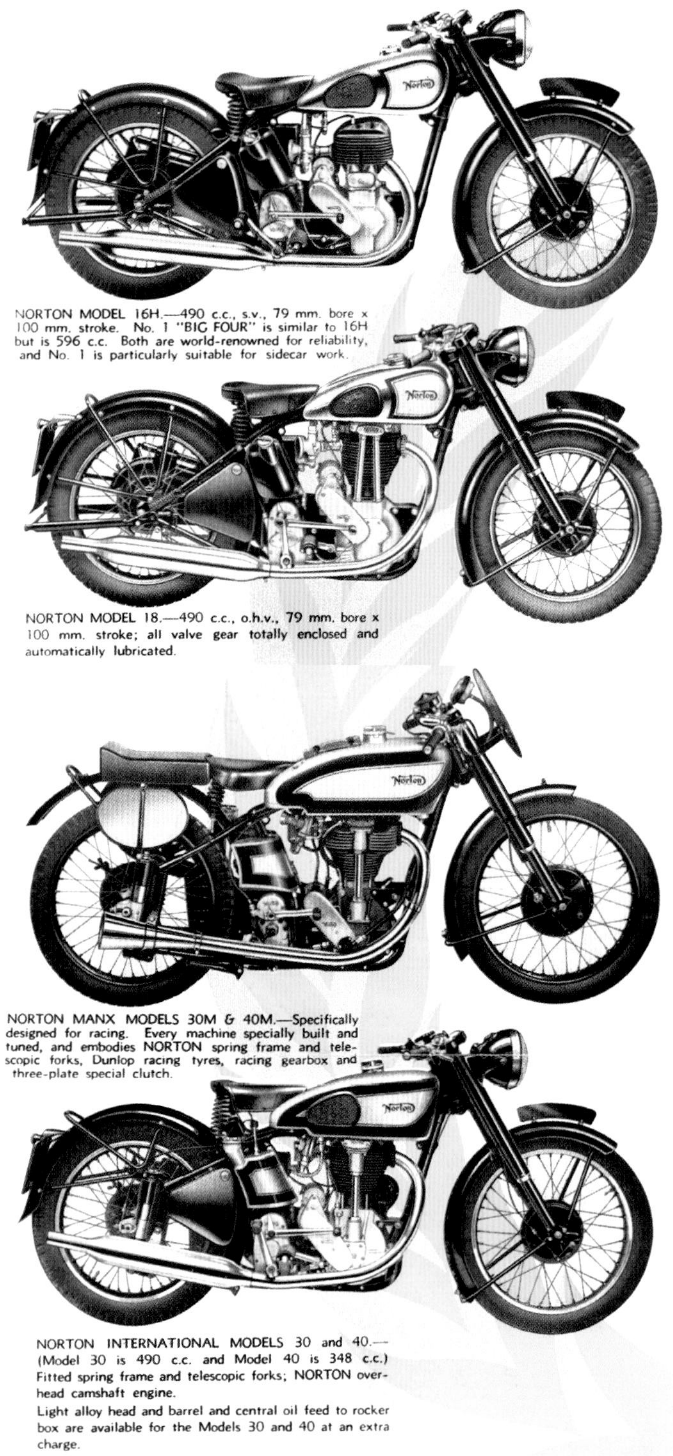

NORTON MODEL 16H.—490 c.c., s.v., 79 mm. bore x 100 mm. stroke. No. 1 "BIG FOUR" is similar to 16H but is 596 c.c. Both are world-renowned for reliability, and No. 1 is particularly suitable for sidecar work.

NORTON MODEL 18.—490 c.c., o.h.v., 79 mm. bore x 100 mm. stroke; all valve gear totally enclosed and automatically lubricated.

NORTON MANX MODELS 30M & 40M.—Specifically designed for racing. Every machine specially built and tuned, and embodies NORTON spring frame and telescopic forks, Dunlop racing tyres, racing gearbox and three-plate special clutch.

NORTON INTERNATIONAL MODELS 30 and 40.—(Model 30 is 490 c.c. and Model 40 is 348 c.c.) Fitted spring frame and telescopic forks; NORTON overhead camshaft engine.
Light alloy head and barrel and central oil feed to rocker box are available for the Models 30 and 40 at an extra charge.

Oil tanks were now in black on all but camshaft models but both side-valve and pushrod OHV engines had been improved. The 16H's power had shot up to around 15bhp courtesy of some modification to the valve gear, including flat-base tappets operated directly by the cams (with full enclosure), along with an aluminium cylinder head and more extensive finning to keep the whole lot cool. With its newfound urge The Motor Cycle *found one to be capable of 73mph, with 70 available in third and a standing-start quarter-mile in 20 seconds. Pushrod OHV engines had been redesigned in the same way, with crankcase rockers being done away with and cams now bearing directly on flat-base tappets, which in turn acted upon light alloy pushrods.* The Motor Cycle *extracted 78mph in top, 74 in third and a standing-start quarter-mile in 18.6 seconds.*

Internationals had been out of luck in the 1948 IOM Clubmans races, with a KSS Velo taking the Junior and a Vincent HRD the Senior (machines up to 1000cc were eligible at the time). Although 1949 saw the first win by BSA's Gold Star in the Junior it also saw the emergence of a new star rider in the form of Geoff Duke, whose Norton left a pack of Triumphs along with other Inters and also-rans in its wake. Almost two years earlier, The Motor Cycle *and* Motor Cycling *tested a pair of Model 30 Internationals, the results of which were published on the same day – 3 July 1947. Both machines were ostensibly the same and in full road-going trim.* The Motor Cycle*'s machine was registered HOE 63 and it recorded 80mph in third gear and 86 in top, with the standing-start quarter-mile covered in 16.4 seconds.* Motor Cycling, *on the other hand, took HOE 445 to the Isle of Man during TT week. Various staff members had a thrash on it, including Phil Heath who had been runner-up in the previous year's Clubmans on a Vincent, but no mention was made of who was aboard during its timed runs. Nevertheless, it recorded no less than 83mph in second, with 91 coming up in third and 97 in top. Both machines were early models with Brooklands-type silencer, both were on Castrol R and both had identical gear ratios, so what was it: rider ability, weather conditions (nothing untoward was mentioned) or just chance?*

New for the 1948 Earls Court Motor Cycle show was the Bert Hopwood-designed 500cc Model 7 Dominator twin that had been several years in the making. The machine displayed at the show had its carburettor bolted straight to the cast-iron cylinder head, with integral common inlet tract, but some redesign had taken place by the time Motor Cycling *were lent the pilot production model. The head now had individual inlets and an aluminium manifold giving separate feeds to each cylinder from the single carburettor. The question on everybody's lips at Earls Court had been, "What'll she do?" so the magazine's staff were happy to provide the answers: 85 in third and 95 in top with the rider 'lying down to it' as effectively as he was able with the standard footrests.*

The NORTON Twin is introduced to the public as a leader of multi cylinder contemporary design.

It has already earned its reputation. Designed on the basis of experience it has been tried and proved under the most exacting conditions, and is a conception of several years of research and development. No other machine offered to the public embodies such a large number of unique features.

Its road-holding qualities and its smooth urging power are to be experienced to be appreciated. It is a worthy addition to the unapproachable range of machines.

PETROL TANK. Entirely new registered design, combining a shapely contour to fit the rider. Large capacity but narrow riding position, with built-in oil gauge and shapely resilient knee-grips. Handsomely finished in heavy chrome with suitable panelling. Capacity 3¾ gall.

OIL TANK. Entirely new type of improved lines. Capacity 7 pints.

SADDLE. Large flexible top, forward pivotal mounting and adjustable for height, giving low and exceptionally comfortable riding position.

FRONT CHAINCASE. Fully patented (Patent No. 406599) NORTON design with single bolt fixing, hermetically sealed.

CLUTCH. Multi-plate with special "Ferodo" inserts. Dual action vane type shock absorber.

GEARBOX. Entirely new four speed design with novel short movement, positive stop foot change mechanism. The whole mechanism is completely enclosed with accessible adjustment points. An extremely handsome gear-box, Patent No. 424154.

STAND. Central prop stand fitted.

SILENCERS. Pleasing in appearance, heavily chrome-plated, giving a remarkable degree of silence without excessive loss of power.

HANDLEBARS. Of clean design and adjustable for rake.

PILLION FOOTREST lugs built-in for attachment of NORTON pillion footrests.

MUDGUARDS. Entirely new contour with handsome, generous section, affording excellent weather protection. Rear mudguard instantly detachable from seat stays with concealed stay fitting points enabling the utmost cleanliness to be achieved.

ENGINE.
The NORTON Parallel Twin Engine, Prov. Patent Nos. 20200/47, 20201/47, 20202/47, has a bore and stroke of 66 m/m x 73 m/m, capacity 499 c.c.

Fully patented cylinder head and valve operation, totally enclosed and positively lubricated. This layout provides an unusually efficient inlet port, enabling cooling air to pass between inlet and exhaust valves in addition to the spaces between the combustion chambers. Cylinder head and rocker chamber are cast integral, eliminating unnecessary joints. Geometrically correct fixed centre chain drive to single high-camshaft, with built-in adequately ported mechanical breather. Toughened alloy steel crankshaft of utmost rigidity, mounted on generous ball and roller journal bearings. Dry sump lubrication system with valveless gear pump, and massive foolproof pressure relief valve, totally eliminating cylinder lubrication bias. Patented hollow car-type semi-barrel cast iron tappets of unique design, operating direct in cylinder with chilled glass-hard rubbing surface, eliminating all noise and wear. Push rods operating inside cast-in cavities and the rocker gear oil drains are built-in, thus eliminating all potentially leaky joints.

The R.R. 56 light alloy forged connecting rods and caps are of immense stiffness and have steel backed micro-babbit bearings which are easily replaced when necessary. Automatic advance magneto with extremely silent chain drive and separate 45-watt output dynamo, with silent fibre gear drive of generous proportions and with built-in slipping clutch. AMAL needle jet carburettor, semi-automatic with twist-grip control.

SPECIFICATION:

Stroke 72.6 m/m, Bore 66 m/m — Capacity 497 c.c.
Compression ratio 6¾

Gear Ratios: SOLO — Top 5.00, Third 6.05, Second 8.85, Bottom 14.9

Primary Chain: Renold ½in. pitch x .305in. wide.
Rear Chain: Renold ⅝in. pitch x .25in. wide.
Brake dimension: Front and Rear 7in. x 1¼in

TYRES: Front, .300 x 21 Dunlop Ribbed. Rear, .350 x 19 Dunlop triple stud.

PETROL TANK CAPACITY 3¾ gall. OIL TANK CAPACITY 7 pints.

FRAME of immensely rigid cradle construction, built with high tensile steel tube with graduated section lugs. The famous NORTON rear sprung suspension is fitted standard.

FORKS. Fully patented "Road-Holder" telescopic design (Patent No. 557982) hydraulically damped and automatically lubricated. This fork has been tried and proved in the most strenuous International Road Races over many years.

WHEELS. Brakes of exceptional power and smoothness with journal bearings of generous capacity. Chrome plated rims with enamelled centres and suitably lined.

Light alloy head and barrel are available at an extra charge.

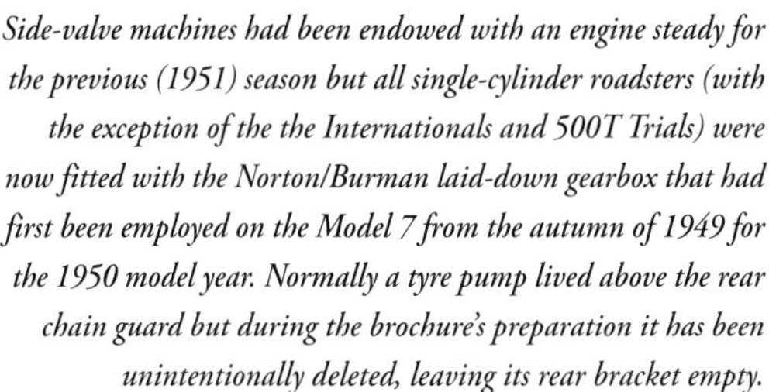
Side-valve machines had been endowed with an engine steady for the previous (1951) season but all single-cylinder roadsters (with the exception of the the Internationals and 500T Trials) were now fitted with the Norton/Burman laid-down gearbox that had first been employed on the Model 7 from the autumn of 1949 for the 1950 model year. Normally a tyre pump lived above the rear chain guard but during the brochure's preparation it has been unintentionally deleted, leaving its rear bracket empty.

BIG 4 The Big 4 is world renowned for reliability. It is built throughout of the finest materials available, and its universal success is proof of the soundness of design. The machine is ideally suited to sidecar work. The side valve engine has a capacity of 596 c.c. and a bore and stroke of 82 mm. × 113 mm.

MODEL 16H. The Model 16H machine is to the same specification as the Big 4, with the exception that the side valve engine has a capacity of 490 c.c. Bore and stroke 79 mm. × 100 mm.

At the end of 1948 Norton had unveiled an entirely new competition model, the 500T. Evolved with input from the McCandless brothers it was based on a WD-type open frame into which was fitted the pushrod 500 motor equipped with an Al-fin barrel and aluminium head. Weight saving was a primary consideration and the resulting 53in-wheelbase machine tipped the scales at almost dead on 300lb. In those days many a motorcycle racer and not a few racing drivers would take to trials riding during the winter months, and Norton's recently-signed star rider Geoff Duke also rode a 500T for the factory – winning the 1950 Victory Trial on one. In production until the end of 1954, they were fitted with an 8in front brake for their last season.

E.S.2 MODEL E.S.2. An overhead valve engine is employed, push rod operated. The whole of the valve gear is totally enclosed, and automatically lubricated. Large bearing surfaces and ground timing gear teeth ensure silent operation. The engine has a bore and stroke of 79 mm. × 100 mm. giving a capacity of 490 c.c. The Norton spring frame is fitted as standard specification.

MODEL 18. The Model 18 machine is to exactly the same specification as the Model E.S.2 with the exception that a rigid frame is fitted.

500 T

ENGINE. 490 c.c. (79 × 100) O.H.V. with light alloy cylinder head and barrel. Compression ratio 6 : 1. Totally enclosed and automatically lubricated valve mechanism, dry sump lubrication. B.T.H. magneto, Amal carburettor, KLG. waterproof sparking plug.

TRANSMISSION. Wide ratio, four speed, positive stop foot operated gearbox giving ratios of 5·5, 8·1, 13·15 and 18·1 with 20 tooth engine sprocket and 16 tooth gearbox axle sprocket. Multi plate, Ferodo lined clutch with vane type shock absorbers Primary chain housed in hermetically sealed oil bath chaincase. Folding kickstarter.

FRAME. Light triangulated construction, with crankcase shield. Side prop and rear stands, narrow light alloy mudguards and small type Dunlop saddle. Roadholder telescopic forks giving 100° total lock.

WHEELS. Front, 2.75 × 21 (WM. 1—21), rear, 4.00 × 19 (WM. 3—19) high tensile rims. 7″ diameter. Brakes with light alloy plates and finger adjustment.

TANKS. Petrol 2½ gallons capacity. Three point rubber mounting with single bolt fixing, finished in dull chrome plating, suitably lined. Separate narrow type oil tank of 3½ pints capacity.

INTERNATIONAL MODEL 30. The Model 30 employs the world renowned NORTON overhead camshaft engine. The universal success obtained with this particular type of engine is an indication of the soundness of design. The bore and stroke is 79 mm. × 100 mm. and the capacity is 490 c.c. The NORTON spring frame is employed as standard specification.
MODEL 40. This machine is to the same specification as the Model 30, with the exception that the engine capacity is 348 c.c. Bore and stroke 71 mm. × 88 mm.
The Models 30 and 40 are available with light alloy head and barrel, with central oil feed to rocker box, at an extra charge.

Although the 1952 International continued virtually unchanged, even retaining the old Sturmey Archer-derived Norton gearbox manufactured by Burman, various types of fuel tank could be fitted according to the customer's wishes. This one had the 'bolt through' type that is sometimes mistaken for an out-and-out racing fitment; usually they were painted but I have come across tanks that were originally chromium-plated.

DOMINATOR MODEL 7 "DOMINATOR." The NORTON twin has already proved itself to be worthy of inclusion in the "UNAPPROACHABLE" NORTON range. The Machine was designed following several years of research and development. No other machine offered to the public embodies such a large number of unique features. Its road-holding qualities and smooth surging power are to be experienced to be appreciated. The petrol tank is of outstanding design, having a capacity of 3¾ gallons. The NORTON parallel twin engine, Prov. Patent Nos. 20200/47, 20201/47 and 20202/47, has a bore and stroke of 66 mm. × 72.6 mm., giving a capacity of 497 c.c.

" The NORTON 497 c.c. parallel-twin engine in the Dominator sets a new criterion in its class."
—" The Motor Cycle."

To many motorcyclists the words Dommy or Dominator conjure up Norton's Featherbed models from the mid to late '50s or '60s, so it is easy to forget that they started here.

TABULATED SPECIFICATIONS

MODELS	16H	Big 4	18	ES.2	30	40	500T	No. 7 Twin
Bore and Stroke . .	79 × 100mm.	82 × 113mm.	79 × 100mm.	79 × 100mm.	79 × 100mm.	71 × 88mm.	79 × 100mm.	66 × 72·6
Cylinder capacity	490 c.c.	596 c.c.	490 c.c.	490 c.c.	490 c.c.	348 c.c.	490 c.c.	497 c.c.
Compression ratio	4·9	4·5	6·6	6·6	7·2	7·3	6	6·7
Valves	S.V.	S.V.	O.H.V.	O.H.V.	O.H.C.	O.H.C.	O.H.V.	O.H.V.
Gear ratios—top	4·9	5·46	4·64	4·64	4·64	5·16	5·5	5
,, ,, third	5·93	6·62	5·64	5·64	5·1	5·67	8·1	6·05
,, ,, second	8·67	9·66	8·24	8·24	6·18	6·85	13·15	8·85
,, ,, bottom	14·6	16·2	13·84	13·84	10·8	10·02	18·2	14·88
Saddle height	28″	28″	28″	30″	30″	30″	32″	30″
Wheel base	54½″	54½″	54½″	54½″	54½″	54½″	53″	54½″
Overall length	84½″	84½″	84½″	84½″	84½″	84½″	82″	84½″
,, width	28″	28″	28″	28″	28″	28″	28″	28″
Ground clearance	5½″	5½″	5½″	6½″	5½″	5½″	7¼″	5½″
Weight	367 lbs.	373 lbs.	374 lbs.	379 lbs.	395 lbs.	388 lbs.	300 lbs.	413 lbs.
Petrol tank capacity	3½ galls.	3½ galls.	3½ galls.	3½ galls.	3¾ galls.	3¾ galls.	2½ galls.	3¾ galls.
Oil tank capacity	4 pts.	4 pts.	4 pts.	4 pts.	6 pts.	6 pts.	3½ pts.	7 pts.
Tyre size—front	3·25 × 19	3·25 × 19	3·25 × 19	3·25 × 19	3·00 × 21	3·00 × 21	2·75 × 21	3·00 × 21
,, ,, rear	3·25 × 19	3·25 × 19	3·25 × 19	3·25 × 19	3·25 × 20	3·25 × 20	4·00 × 19	3·50 × 19
Brake dimensions	7″ DIAMETER × 1¼″ WIDE FRONT AND REAR				7″ DIAMETER × 1¼″ WIDE FRONT AND REAR			
Chains	½″ PITCH × ·305″ WIDE FRONT. ⅜″ PITCH × ¼″ WIDE REAR.				½″ PITCH × ·305″ WIDE FRONT. ⅜″ PITCH × ¼″ WIDE REAR.			

MANX 30 · MANX 40

SPECIFICATION

ENGINE: **Model 30M**—Bore 79.62 mm., stroke 100 mm., capacity 499 c.c.
Model 40M—Bore 71 mm., stroke 88 mm., capacity 348 c.c.
Cylinder Barrel and Head light alloy. Twin overhead camshaft valve operation. Forged light alloy piston. Forged H section steel connecting rod with double row roller bearing big end. Magnesium alloy crankcase. Lucas racing magneto, Amal T.T. type Carburetter.

TRANSMISSION: Primary Chain ½"×.305". Rear Chain ⅝"×¼". Lubrication to both chains by jet feed from main oil tank. Four speed "Norton" gearbox with remotely mounted positive foot operation.

RATIOS: Model 30M with 23T engine sprocket—4.64, 5.1, 6.18, 8.22–1. Model 40M with 18T engine sprocket—5.16, 5.67, 6.85, 9.12–1. 5 Plate Clutch with Ferodo inserts.

FRAME: Patented duplex loop tubular construction with cross-over tubes on steering head. All joints bronze welded. Swinging arm rear suspension with rubber pivot suspension, oil damper.
Norton telescopic Road-Holder Forks.

WHEELS: Alloy Rims, magnesium hubs front and rear. Brakes 8" dia. front, 7" dia. rear.
Front ribbed 3.00"×19", rear studded 3.50"×19".
Light alloy rubber mounted racing mudguards.

TANKS: Light alloy petrol tank having capacity of 5½ gallons, secured by central strap. Light alloy oil tank, capacity one gallon, quick action filler caps.

REV. COUNTER: Smiths 8,000 r.p.m. rev. counter fitted on fork lug, driven by cambox bevel shaft extension.
Sponge rubber racing seat with back rest.

OTHER EQUIPMENT: Wire gauze fly screen.
Racing number plates.
Megaphone exhaust.

An insignificant flyer was printed for potential customers of the swinging-arm-framed Manx that was now available as an over-the-counter racer, but its best advertisement was a rapidly-accruing track record that any one of them would have likely already been familiar with.

1952

	Retail Price	Purchase Tax
Model 18 ...	£158 0 0	£43 17 9
Model E.S.2 ...	£172 10 0	£47 18 4
Model 16H ...	£153 0 0	£42 10 0
Model Big 4 ...	£156 10 0	£43 9 5
Model No. 7 ...	£192 0 0	£53 6 8
Model 30 Int. ...	£219 0 0	£60 16 8
Model 40 Int. ...	£211 0 0	£58 12 3
Model 30M ...	£336 0 0	£93 6 8
Model 40M ...	£336 0 0	£93 6 8
Model 500 T. ...	£164 0 0	£45 11 1

PRICES INCLUDE SPEEDOMETER

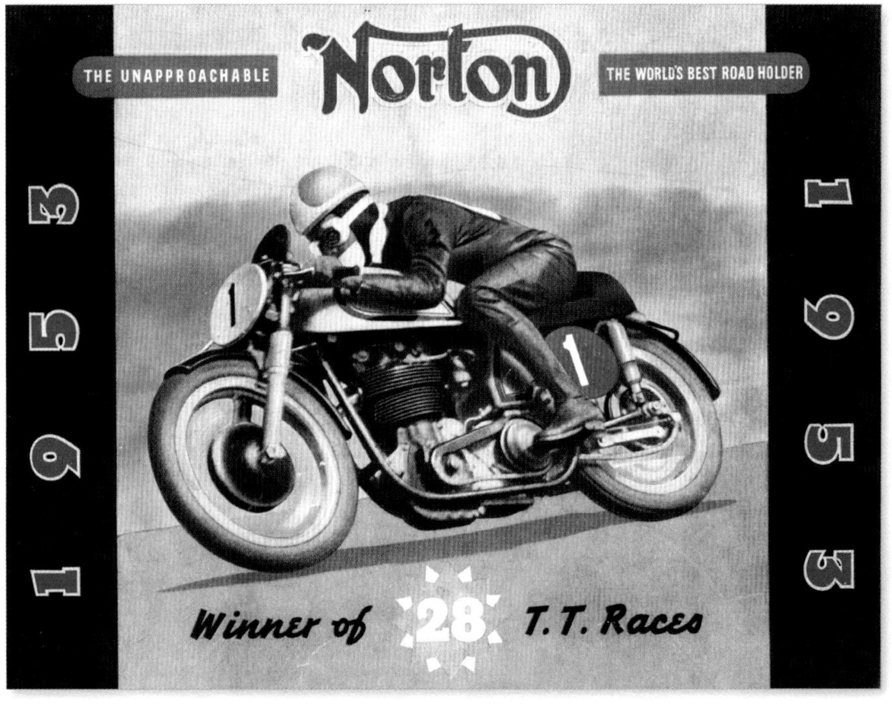

A twin-overhead-camshaft Manx with the McCandless-designed Featherbed frame on the cover and the firm's very numerous 1952 racing successes celebrated on a centre page spread. Whether they rode a Big Four combination or aspired to one of the new Dominators, owners and enthusiasts alike were more than aware of the firm's racing heritage.

BIG 4

A dual seat for the old side-valvers. Ace Norton tuner Steve Lancefield delighted in using a Big Four that he had mildly breathed upon for solo road work, but as the model was intended for sidecar duties let's see what Motor Cycling *made of one combined with a Canterbury Viking double-adult on a heavyweight chassis in 1953. Admitting that it was the first side-valve he had ridden since the war, the tester then proceeded to press on by 'Galloping the outfit probably more briskly than the private owner might care to do' (Lancefield excepted). He took it up to 52mph in third and then built up to 61 in top, 'the big engine unperturbed and with a deep-toned chortle coming from the carburettor intake'. Fuel consumption worked out at about 50mpg but, pressing on once more, 'a fast run back to the office heading into the teeth of a gale' brought it down below 40.*

The Model 18 retained its rigid frame but for the ES2 had a reworked version of the plunger frame with swinging-arm or pivoted-fork (call it what you will) rear suspension. This was the year that traditional tubular silencers gave way to these pear-shaped units. Some people like the look of them, some don't – I'm not sure, but they are certainly distinctive.

Sharing a frame with the ES2 meant that other parts were common to both machines. This year Nortons featured a new headlamp with pre-focus light unit and underslung pilot light – the latter a necessity, as it couldn't be incorporated with the headlight. Ammeter and light switch were no longer atop the headlamp and had been relocated to the dashboard that bridged the top of the fork legs. Since the 1949 season this carried the speedometer but was now enlarged to accommodate the additional functions.

Although it no longer featured in the sales brochure the International had received a new lease of life by being given an alloy head and barrel as standard, coupled with the 'laydown' gearbox and mounted in a Featherbed frame. At a few shillings over £269 for the 350 Model 40 and £279 for the 500 Model 30 each was about £25 more than the respective Gold Star Clubman, and a one-two-three in the 1953 Senior Clubmans TT was a glorious finale before the Small Heath singles annexed the race.

At the 1951 show rumours proved to be true, and exhibited on stand 72 had been the new Dominator De Luxe (Model 88) – the 500 twin engine housed in what was, to all intents and purposes, the same frame as the all-conquering Manx Norton's. Finished in polychromatic grey the show bikes attracted enormous attention but UK residents could only wish as, for the meanwhile at any rate, they were for export only.

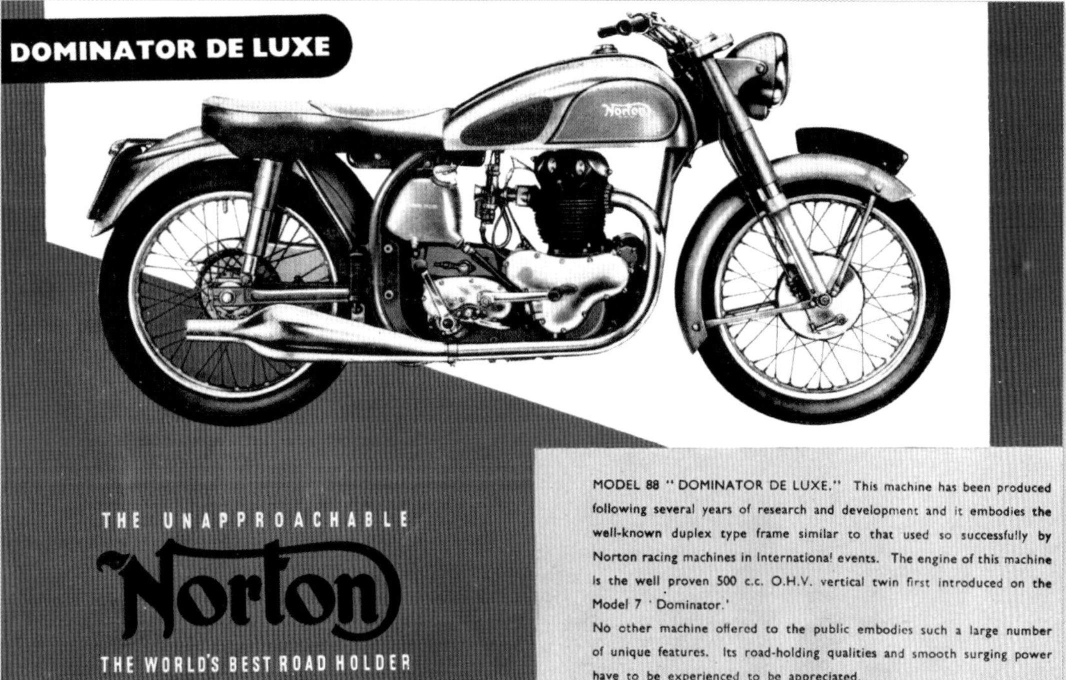

By the time that they became available on the UK market the original deeply-valanced front mudguards, mounted in an ungainly fashion on the upper part of the forks, had been done away with in favour of a more abbreviated pattern with stays bolted to the base of the forks. The latter were the short Roadholder variety – the first time these had been employed on road-going Nortons – while other models had long Roadholders.

MODELS	16H	Big 4	18	ES.2	500T	No. 7 Twin	88 Twin	MODELS
Bore and Stroke ..	79×100mm.	82×113mm.	79×100mm.	79×100mm.	79×100mm.	66×72·6	66×72·6	Bore and Stroke
Cylinder capacity ..	490 c.c.	596 c.c.	490 c.c.	490 c.c.	490 c.c.	497 c.c.	497 c.c.	Cylinder capacity
Compression ratio ..	4·9	4·5	6·16	6·16	6	6·7	6·7	Compression ratio
Valves	S.V.	S.V.	O.H.V.	O.H.V.	O.H.V.	O.H.V.	O.H.V.	Valves
Gear ratios—top .. ,, ,, third .. ,, ,, second ,, ,, bottom	5 6·05 8·85 14·88	5·6 6·78 9·9 16·6	4·75 5·75 8·4 14·2	4·75 5·75 8·4 14·2	5·5 8·1 13·15 18·2	5 6·05 8·85 14·88	5 6·05 8·85 14·88	Gear ratios—top ,, ,, third ,, ,, second ,, ,, bottom
Saddle height ..	29″	29″	29″	31″	32″	31″	31″	Saddle height
Wheel base	54½″	54½″	54½″	54½″	53″	54½″	55½″	Wheel base
Overall length ..	84½″	84½″	84½″	84½″	82″	84½″	84″	Overall length
,, width.. ..	28″	28″	28″	28″	28″	28″	26″	,, width
Ground clearance ..	5½″	5½″	5½″	6½″	7¼″	5½″	6¾″	Ground clearance
Weight	367 lbs.	373 lbs.	374 lbs.	379 lbs.	300 lbs.	413 lbs.	393 lbs.	Weight
Petrol tank capacity ..	3½ galls.	3½ galls.	3½ galls.	3½ galls.	2½ galls.	3¾ galls.	3½ galls.	Petrol tank capacity
Oil tank capacity ..	4 pts.	4 pts.	4 pts.	4 pts.	3½ pts.	4 pts.	4½ pts.	Oil tank capacity
Tyre size—front .. ,, ,, rear ..	3·25×19 3·25×19	3·25×19 3·25×19	3·25×19 3·25×19	3·25×19 3·25×19	2·75×21 4·00×19	3·25×19 3·50×19	3·00×19 3·50×19	Tyre size—front ,, ,, rear
Brake dimensions ..	7″ DIAMETER × 1¼″ WIDE FRONT AND REAR							Brake dimensions
Chains	½″ PITCH × ·305″ WIDE FRONT. ⅝″ PITCH × ¼″ WIDE REAR.							Chains

Apart from the larger front brake the ES2 was unchanged from the previous season, as was the rigid-framed Model 18.

Worlds apart! But (virtually) the same chassis. A Manx streaks past cheering onlookers during a fantasy race and a genteel couple go for a spin on a Dominator 88 – I love her Wee Willie Winkie hat.

Another update for the Norton family's pensioners in the form of the newly-introduced 8in single-sided front brake. At the end of the season their obituary would put them on record as being the longest-running model, in continuous production, of any British motorcycle.

Norton SUCCESSES

Brave Rhodesian Ray Amm's riding style was at times lurid but upon Geoff Duke's decampment to Gilera he became Norton's number one rider for the 1953 season. World championship wins were to elude him that year but a historic double in the Isle of Man brought him world acclaim. Accompanied everywhere by his wife Jill they are pictured here in the brochure's annual celebratory spread – after his wins in the Junior (left) and Senior (right). In '54 he was second in the World Championship to Duke and then successfully wooed by MV Augusta to challenge Gilera and his ex-teammate; but during his first race for the Italian company, at Imola, he left Jill with his habitual, "I'll see you at the end of the race, or if not in the next world," for the last time.

The shapely tank of the Model 7 Dominator, complete with the new circular plastic badges now fitted to all road-going machines, was depicted on the cover of the 1955 brochure. Barclay Motors is still in Bury St Edmunds but discontinued the motorcycle side of its business many years ago.

Dominators were now fitted with aluminium cylinder heads and Amal monobloc carbs – all Nortons, with the exception of Internationals (which had Amal TTs), now being equipped with the latter.

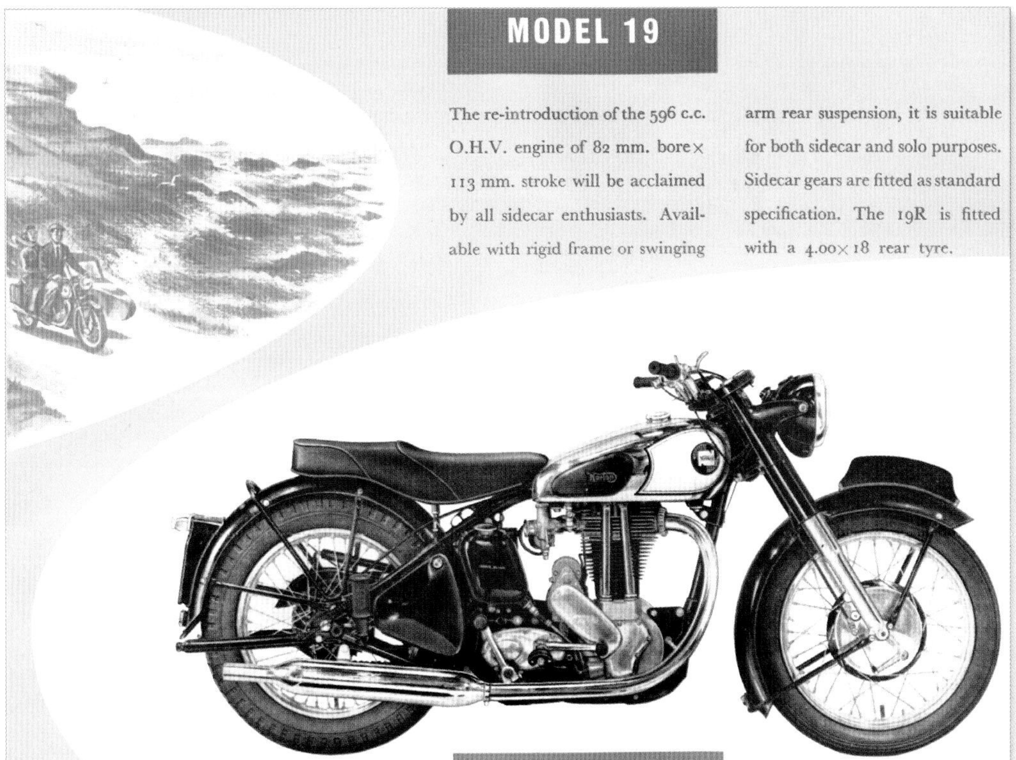

MODEL 19

The re-introduction of the 596 c.c. O.H.V. engine of 82 mm. bore × 113 mm. stroke will be acclaimed by all sidecar enthusiasts. Available with rigid frame or swinging arm rear suspension, it is suitable for both sidecar and solo purposes. Sidecar gears are fitted as standard specification. The 19R is fitted with a 4.00 × 18 rear tyre.

To replace the big side-valves Norton brought back a modernised version of the old Model 19, which had last been made in the 1930s. Back then it had shared the same frame as the Model 18 and this time around it did the same; except in 19R form it took the place of the now-discontinued 18, utilising its rigid cradle frame and cycle parts. There was also the more expensive 19S that was built into the current swinging-arm ES2 frame but had slightly higher overall gear ratios.

All 1955 models now had a boxed-in rear number plate incorporating a larger Lucas 777 lamp, as well as a circular reflector at the tip of the rear mudguard. Updates for the ES2, and other non-Featherbed swinging-arm models, included a fuller rear mudguard with rear stays to suit, the latest adjustable Armstrong rear suspension units and tyre pump carried on the offside rear frame tube, as well as different dual seat and handlebars. The 596cc 19S could be distinguished fairly readily from an ES2 such as this on account of its taller motor but both had aluminium cylinder heads.

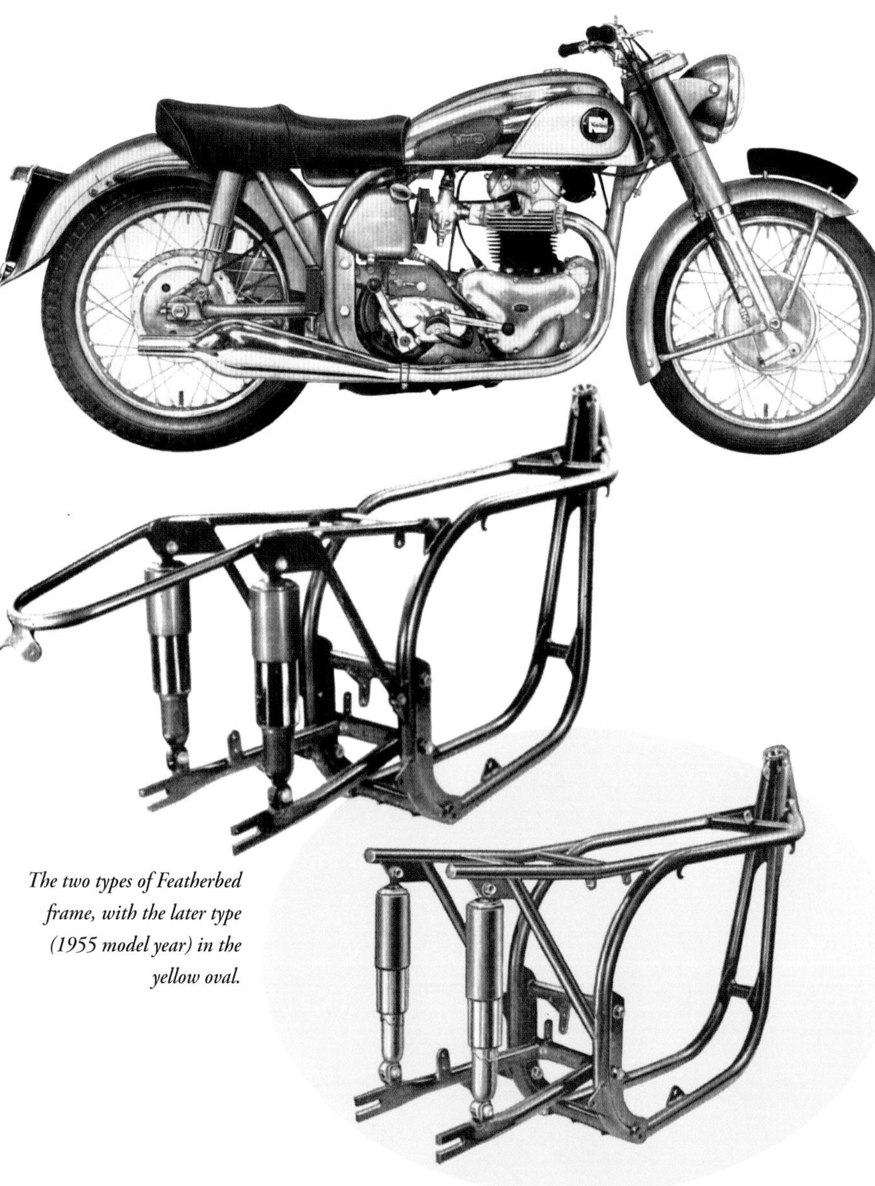

You will find it hard to discern in the 1955 brochure's illustration on account of the pillion footrest and seat base, but from now onwards Featherbed frames had their rear subframes welded integrally with the main duplex frame, as opposed to being bolted on as before. Upper frame tubes also terminated just aft of suspension mountings rather than carrying on with a dropped loop around the rear mudguard, and suspension-mount bracing tubes had also been increased in diameter from ¾in to 1in. The rear mudguard was also of a slightly different pattern, with deeper valancing and bolt-on tubular rear supports. The other major innovation this year was the introduction of full-width alloy hubs for the 7in rear and 8in front brakes. There were also other minor differences such as bayonet filler caps for oil and petrol tanks, as well as a redesigned dual seat.

The two types of Featherbed frame, with the later type (1955 model year) in the yellow oval.

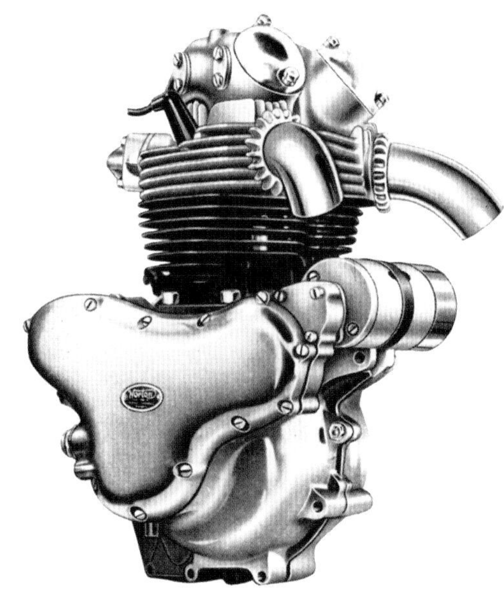

MODELS	19R	19S	ES.2	No. 7 Twin	88 Twin	MODELS
Bore and Stroke ..	82 × 113mm	82 × 113mm	79 × 100mm	66 × 72·6	66 × 72·6	Bore and Stroke
Cylinder capacity ..	596 c.c.	596 c.c.	490 c.c.	497 c.c.	497 c.c.	Cylinder capacity
Compression ratio ..	6·2	6·2	6·8	6·8	6·8	Compression ratio
Valves	O.H.V.	O.H.V.	O.H.V.	O.H.V.	O.H.V.	Valves
Gear ratios—top .. „ „ third .. „ „ second .. „ „ bottom	5·28 6·38 9·34 15·67	4·52 5·47 8 13·4	4·75 5·75 8·4 14·2	5 6·05 8·85 14·88	5 6·05 8·85 14·88	Gear ratios — top „ „ third „ „ second „ „ bottom
Saddle height ..	29″	31″	31″	31″	31″	Saddle height
Wheel base ..	54½″	54½″	54½″	54½″	55½″	Wheel base
Overall length .. „ width ..	84½″ 28″	84½″ 28″	84½″ 28″	84½″ 28″	85½″ 25″	Overall length „ width
Ground clearance ..	5½″	6½″	6½″	5½″	6¾″	Ground clearance
Weight	367 lbs.	372 lbs.	369 lbs.	400 lbs.	380 lbs.	Weight
Petrol tank capacity	2¾ galls.	2¾ galls.	2¾ galls.	3¾ galls.	3½ galls.	Petrol tank capacity
Oil tank capacity ..	4 pts.	4 pts.	4 pts.	4 pts.	4½ pts.	Oil tank capacity
Tyre size—front .. „ „ rear ..	3·25 × 19 4·00 × 18	3·25 × 19 3·25 × 19	3·25 × 19 3·25 × 19	3·25 × 19 3·50 × 19	3·00 × 19 3·50 × 19	Tyre size—front „ „ rear
Brake dimensions ..	FRONT—8″ dia. × 1¼″ wide.			REAR—7″ dia. × 1¼″ wide		Brake dimensions
Chains	½″ PITCH × ·305″ WIDE FRONT			⅝″ PITCH × ¼″ WIDE REAR		Chains

Now fitted with a light alloy cylinder head of improved design, the twin cylinder engine fitted to models 7 and 88, also employs an entirely new Amal carburetter, resulting in enhanced performance and economy of operation. The basic design remains unaltered. The widely spaced exhaust valves ensuring adequate cooling area and accessible adjustment are retained, together with the sturdy built up crankshaft with its in-built central sludge trap and light alloy connecting rods. A large readily detachable filter serving also as a drain plug is fitted into the base of the sump, effectively preventing grit, etc., from being re-circulated through the engine.

This 1956 brochure was one of many given out by Clement Garreau over the years. The company had been and importer of British motorcycles and cycles since well before World War Two and was a mecca for Anglophile Parisian motorcyclists to the end of the era covered this book and beyond. Last time I passed by, although no longer displaying Nortons, Matchless and AJSs in each of the large windows on three floors, I was surprised to see the outside of the building almost untouched since the '60s. It's on the corner of Rue Montauban and Rue Robert Lindet, very near the Porte de Versailles off the Peripherique, if anyone wants to see for themselves.

Introducing . . .

THE 1956 NORTON MACHINES

The NORTON record of achievement . . . the fame and reputation of the name . . . is known far and wide: it stands as a beacon in a world of progress and advancement. The world's best road holder. For the most fastidious rider there is a pride of ownership with NORTON, incomparable pleasure, and thousands of miles of perfect and sufficient service. Only the best quality material and equipment is used in the building of the 'Unapproachable' . . . coupled with faultless design and attention to detail. Quality inspection at all stages of manufacture — cost is always a secondary consideration — here are the secrets of NORTON perfection: the reason for the constant reliability that gives every NORTON owner confidence and satisfaction. The 1956 NORTON range of models are the best modern craftsmanship can produce . . . complete with numerous refinements . . . with enhanced performance . . . with traditional NORTON road-holding and all the attributes that have made the name NORTON famous throughout the world. There is a new 350 c.c. model single and a 600 c.c. Twin introduced for the first time, both with a sparkling performance. New details include: engines of higher compression ratio to take full advantage of modern fuels: high lift cams: softer front springing: improved riding position: increased steering lock: better mudguarding: full width hubs on all models: adjustable rear damping suspension units: modified rear chain adjustment: battery enclosure and styling of matching shape with re-designed oil tank. There are numerous other features which modern technique and fashion demand. Every detail has had prolonged tests on road and track. Over 150,000 miles has been covered by staff testers proving 1956 models. Positive hair-line steering; road-holding that is unsurpassed; brakes that are smooth and efficient; everything to harmonise with the amazing engine performance—rapid acceleration—the smooth surge of power—all the qualities appropriate and acceptable to a discerning motor cycling public.

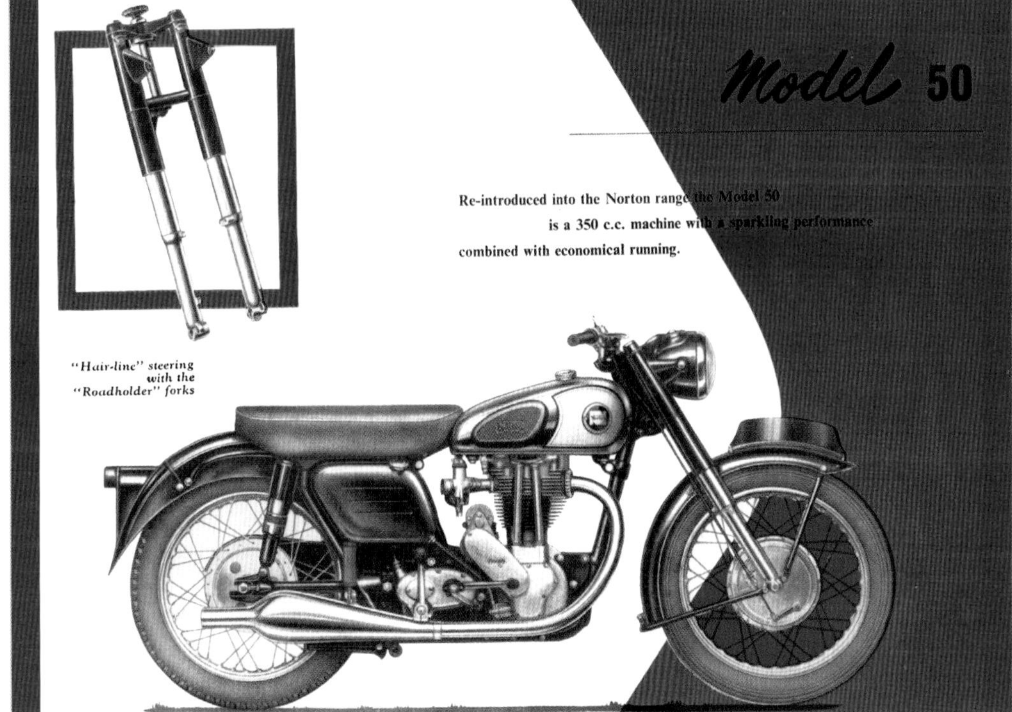

Discontinued upon the onset of World War Two, Norton's smallest single was once again available but it would have to wait until 1959 to acquire the Featherbed frame. Like the recently introduced Model 19, it retained the same bore and stroke as it had in the 1930s

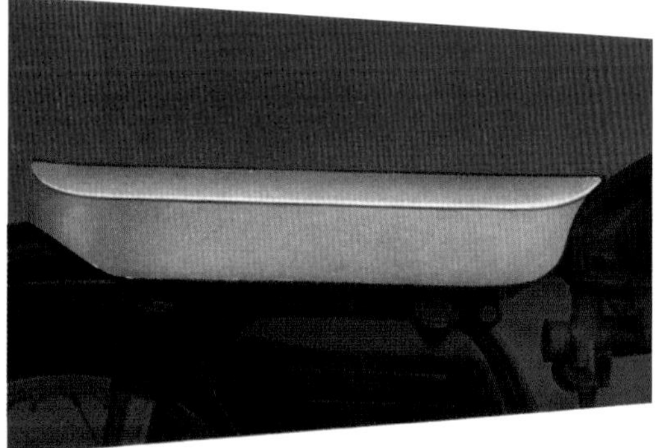

Re-designed dual seat fitted to Models 50, ES2 and 19S

Model 19S

The very successful Model 19S has the same specification as the Model ES2 but with 596 c.c. O.H.V. engine. A delightful sidecar machine or fast touring solo mount.

The demand for any kind of motorcycle with an unsprung rear end, for sidecar use or whatever, had shrunk to infinitesimal so the 19R had been quietly dropped within a year of it carrying on where the 16H and Big Four had left off, leaving just the swinging-arm-framed 19 in the range. The Motor Cycle *put one that had to drag a vast Canterbury Carmobile around with it to test at the beginning of the year – in spite of the view expressed by some that it was nothing short of cruelty to harness it to such a behemoth. Even when the bike was heavily loaded the oil in the tank was often found to be only warm after a couple of hours on the road. Speed tests were taken with just rider and one passenger, during which about 63mph was found to be its maximum, with 22.8 seconds needed for the quarter-mile sprint.*

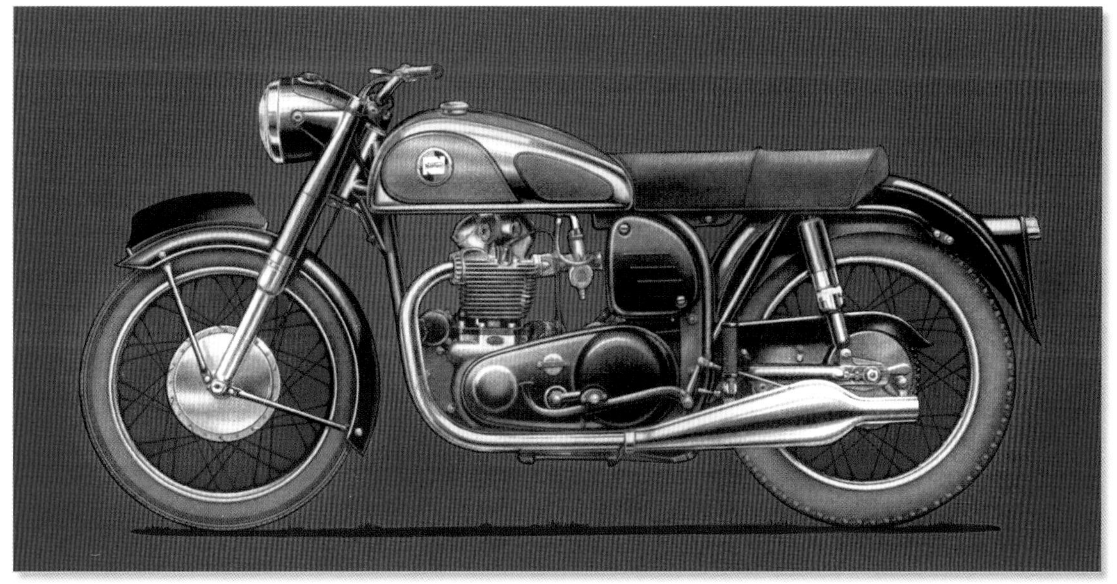

Changes to the 88 for 1956 included a new headlamp that carried instrumentation and switches, as well as a pre-focus headlight with integral pilot light, thus doing away with fork-top dashboard and underslung auxiliary lamp. Upper fork sleeves had a differently-shaped headlamp bracket, oil tank capacity remained four pints but had been redesigned, and the battery was now housed in a matching container on the nearside. Tools were carried in a tray under the seat on these Featherbed models. By now the 88 was a more sporting proposition – equipped with an aluminium cylinder head, the so-called Daytona camshaft and a compression ratio of 7.8:1. Early the following year one of the latest models with AMC gearbox and barrel silencers was lent to The Motor Cycle *and they managed 92mph one way, with a mean of 90 and 85 possible in third gear. The standing-start quarter-mile took 16.7 seconds and a steady 50mph would yield 68mpg, with 60mph dropping it to 60mpg.*

Model 99

Apart from the 99's internal dimensions of 68x82mm bore and stroke as opposed to the 88's 66x72.6mm, there was nothing apart from serial numbers to tell the two apart. Prior to this season Norton twins had carried a small oval maker's plate on the timing cover but now this had been transferred to the mouth of the crankcase on the drive side and a small circular facsimile of the tank badge was affixed to the timing cover. Engine number prefix for the 500cc 88 was 122 and for the 600cc 99 was 14 – it was stamped on the top of the drive-side crankcase. Throughout the period covered by this book, engine and frame numbers matched, with the latter being stamped on the drive-side vertical gusset above the swinging-arm pivot on Featherbed models. A wintertime test undertaken by Motor Cycling *of the updated '57 model with AMC gearbox and barrel silencers proved it to be just capable of passing the magic 100 mark – 101mph, with 92 possible in third gear. More surprising, however, was its economy. The factory had told them that 100mpg was a possibility, but with extreme care this was exceeded by 10 per cent, whilst give-and-take riding returned very nearly 80mpg.*

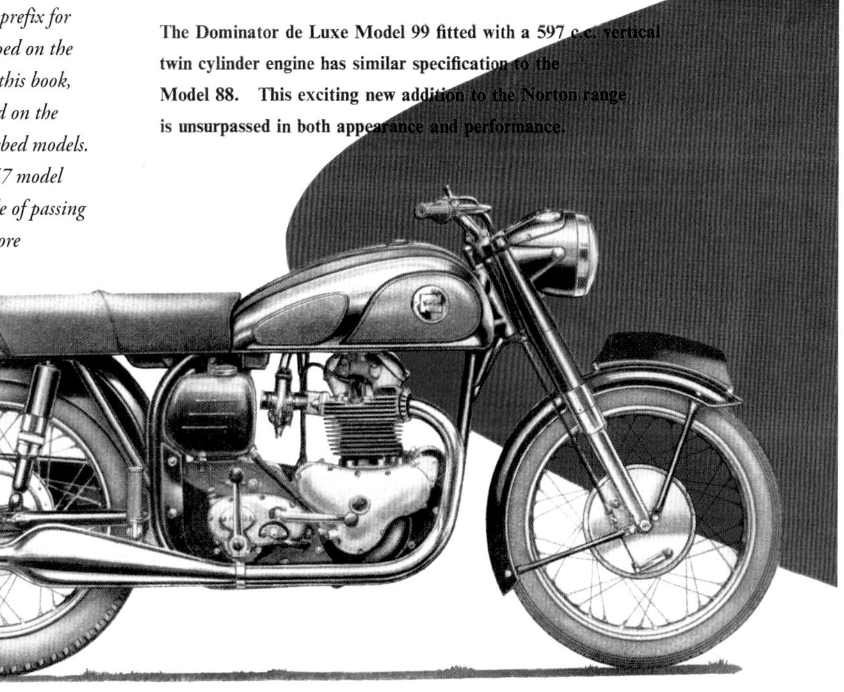

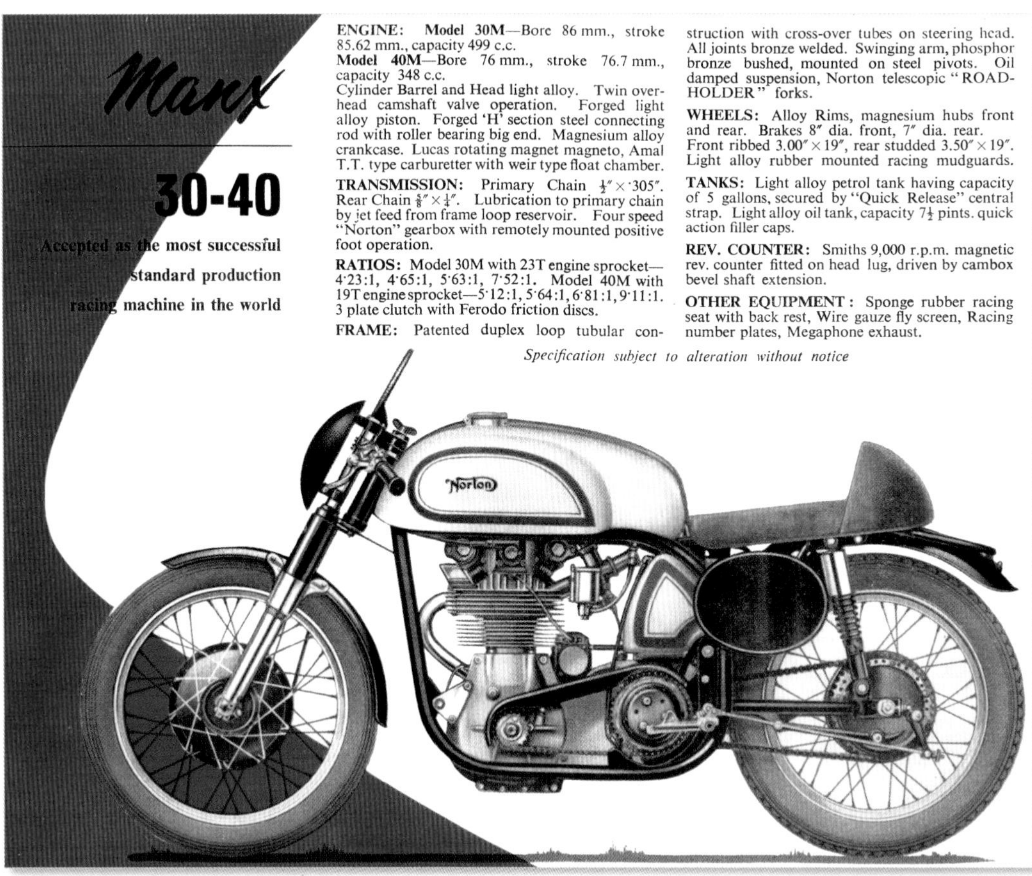

Manx

30-40

Accepted as the most successful standard production racing machine in the world

ENGINE: **Model 30M**—Bore 86 mm., stroke 85.62 mm., capacity 499 c.c.
Model 40M—Bore 76 mm., stroke 76.7 mm., capacity 348 c.c.
Cylinder Barrel and Head light alloy. Twin overhead camshaft valve operation. Forged light alloy piston. Forged 'H' section steel connecting rod with roller bearing big end. Magnesium alloy crankcase. Lucas rotating magnet magneto, Amal T.T. type carburetter with weir type float chamber.

TRANSMISSION: Primary Chain ½″ × ·305″. Rear Chain ⅝″ × ¼″. Lubrication to primary chain by jet feed from frame loop reservoir. Four speed "Norton" gearbox with remotely mounted positive foot operation.

RATIOS: Model 30M with 23T engine sprocket—4·23:1, 4·65:1, 5·63:1, 7·52:1. Model 40M with 19T engine sprocket—5·12:1, 5·64:1, 6·81:1, 9·11:1. 3 plate clutch with Ferodo friction discs.

FRAME: Patented duplex loop tubular construction with cross-over tubes on steering head. All joints bronze welded. Swinging arm, phosphor bronze bushed, mounted on steel pivots. Oil damped suspension, Norton telescopic "ROADHOLDER" forks.

WHEELS: Alloy Rims, magnesium hubs front and rear. Brakes 8″ dia. front, 7″ dia. rear. Front ribbed 3.00″ × 19″, rear studded 3.50″ × 19″. Light alloy rubber mounted racing mudguards.

TANKS: Light alloy petrol tank having capacity of 5 gallons, secured by "Quick Release" central strap. Light alloy oil tank, capacity 7½ pints. quick action filler caps.

REV. COUNTER: Smiths 9,000 r.p.m. magnetic rev. counter fitted on head lug, driven by cambox bevel shaft extension.

OTHER EQUIPMENT: Sponge rubber racing seat with back rest, Wire gauze fly screen, Racing number plates, Megaphone exhaust.

Specification subject to alteration without notice

The International was by special order only and had, since the changeover from plunger frame to Featherbed, ceased to appear in the company's sales brochures, but in time for the '56 season the Manx re-joined the over-the-counter range. Norton's last Isle of Man victory had been in 1954 when Ray Amm trounced Gilera-mounted Geoff Duke in the 1954 Senior but it was still by far and away the best prospect for a 'private' if he wanted to get in the money.

MODELS	50	E.S.2	19S	88	99	30M	40M	MODELS
Bore and Stroke (m/m)	71 × 88	79 × 100	82 × 113	66 × 72.6	68 × 82	86 × 85.62	76 × 76.7	Bore and Stroke (m/m)
Cylinder Capacity	348 c.c.	490 c.c.	596 c.c.	497 c.c.	597 c.c.	499 c.c.	348 c.c.	Cylinder Capacity
Compression Ratio	7.3	7.1	6.4	7.8	7.4	9.45	9.45	Compression Ratio
Valves	O.H.V.	O.H.V.	O.H.V.	O.H.V.	O.H.V.	Dble.O.H.C.	Dble.O.H.C.	Valves
Gear Ratio. Top " " Third " " Second " " Bottom	5.29 6.4 9.36 15.7	4.75 5.75 8.41 14.11	5 6.05 Side 8.85 Car 14.85	4.75 5.75 8.41 14.11	4.53 5.48 8.03 13.42	4.23 4.65 5.63 7.52	5.12 5.64 6.81 9.11	Gear Ratio. Top " " Third " " Second " " Bottom
Saddle Height	31″	31″	31″	31″	31″	30″	30″	Saddle Height
Wheel Base	56″	56″	56″	55½″	55½″	55″	55″	Wheel Base
Overall Length " Width	86″ 29″	86″ 29″	86″ 29″	85½″ 26½″	85½″ 26½″	80½″ 22″	80½″ 22″	Overall Length " Width
Ground Clearance	6½″	6½″	6½″	6¾″	6¾″	5½″	5½″	Ground Clearance
Weight	382	389	393	390	395	313	307	Weight
Petrol Tank Capacity	3 Gal.	3 Gal.	3 Gal.	3½ Gal.	3½ Gal.	5 Gal.	5 Gal.	Petrol Tank Capacity
Oil Tank Working Capacity	4 Pts.	4 Pts.	4 Pts.	4½ Pts.	4½ Pts.	7½ Pts.	7½ Pts.	Oil Tank Working Cap.
Tyre Size—Front " " —Rear	3.25 × 19 3.25 × 19	3.25 × 19 3.25 × 19	3.25 × 19 3.25 × 19	3.00 × 19 3.50 × 19	3.00 × 19 3.50 × 19	3.00 × 19 3.50 × 19	3.00 × 19 3.50 × 19	Tyre Size—Front " " —Rear
Brake Dimensions	Front 8″ dia. × 1¼″ wide. Rear 7″ dia. × 1¼″ wide.					Front 8″ dia. × 1½″ wide. Rear 7″ dia. × 1½″ wide.		Brake Dimensions
Chains	½″ Pitch × .305″ wide front. ⅝″ Pitch × ¼″ wide rear.					½″ Pitch × .305 wide front. ⅝″ Pitch × ¼″ wide rear		Chains

De Havilland's Comet had made history as the world's first commercial jet airliner, but after a series of airframe failures caused tragic accidents BOAC voluntarily grounded its fleet early in 1954. Between then and the autumn of 1958, when the airline resumed service with brand-new Comet 4s, only one of these aircraft was flown carrying BOAC livery. The first occasion was at the 1954 Farnborough Air Show when the only Comet 3 to be completed (G-ANLO) was demonstrated. During December the following year the same aeroplane, once again in BOAC colours, became the first jet airliner to circumnavigate the globe. The artist chose this aircraft as a backdrop for the Model 99 on the cover of the 1958 brochure. Coil ignition in conjunction with an alternator had been introduced for the 88s and 99s, and the enlarged bulge on the primary chain case was to accommodate the stator.

The laydown gearbox had been replaced by this updated AMC version (below) on all models at the commencement of the 1957 season, and a new cylinder head with additional finning had also been phased in on the singles. At the same time, this type of tubular silencer was introduced, and petrol tanks (whatever the road model) had separate chromium-plated side panels surrounded by plastic beading and inset badge.

The Model 7 had been dropped at the close of the 1956 season and replaced by the 77 for '57. Primarily thought of as a sidecar machine by the maker, one attached to a Swallow Jet 80 was an appropriate test of its capabilities. The Jet was a fibreglass-bodied sports single-seater and The Motor Cycle *summed up the ensemble thus: "A zestful and elegant outfit for the owner requiring super-sports performance and first class handling." This translated into mean maximum speeds of 72mph in third and 70 in top with rider, passenger and some luggage – the outfit proving to be over-geared for the strong headwinds encountered. With the same load it could do a quarter-mile sprint in 20.5 seconds and return 52mpg at a steady 50.*

Drive side of the ES2, which shared the Model 50 and 19S's cycle parts. The 1957 season had seen a change from Armstrong to these Girling rear suspension units.

A dual purpose twin of high performance, embodying the main characteristics of the 600 c.c. Model 99 but with magneto ignition, dynamo lighting and cradle frame. Attractive polychromatic grey finish. Sidecar specification available to order.

MODEL 77

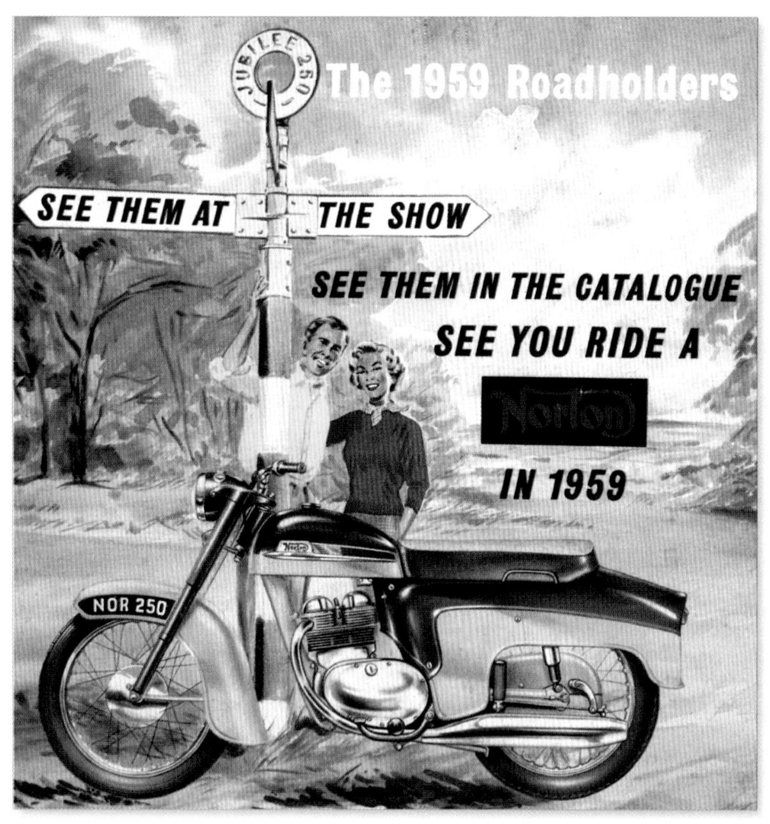

Norton had always steered well clear of the small-to-medium-capacity market but that had all changed by the 1958 show, where its classy big bikes played second fiddle to the unveiling of an uncharacteristic newcomer. It would be several months, however, before production got under way and it became generally available.

Simple and positive valve adjustment provided by eccentric rocker spindles.

By the time that David and Maureen took delivery of the bike they'd fallen in love with at the Earls Court show it was getting on for eight months later. There were three batches of 300 bikes built. Theirs was one of the third batch made – the last of which was completed on 22 June 1959. The love affair soured shortly after its running-in period was completed, however, when David was cautiously letting the revs build up in the gears – and the crankshaft snapped. The fact that the local dealer told them that he'd heard of three others doing the same thing was of little cheer, and when the replacement did the same they decided upon a separation (from the Jubilee). Too late they heard that someone at the factory had got things screwed up and a large amount of the cranks had been made of the wrong type of iron and that it was all now sorted out.

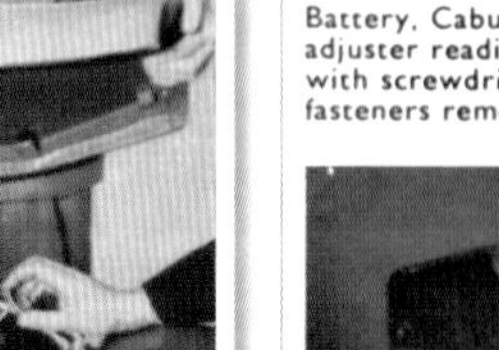

The rubber cushioned "Spring-on" dualseat is removed to show the compact Tool Tray; also the combined dip stick and oil filler cap.

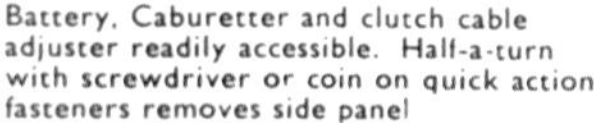

Battery, Caburetter and clutch cable adjuster readily accessible. Half-a-turn with screwdriver or coin on quick action fasteners removes side panel

The rigid "one piece" crankshaft illustrated contributes in no small measure to the smooth power of this outstanding unit.

The rear wheel is easily withdrawn when the quickly detachable rear number plate has been removed.

Engine, gearbox and rear enclosure apart (the enclosure made by an affiliated company, Clarendon Pressings), the remainder of the Jubilee – or rather the frame, forks and wheels – consisted of nothing more exciting than those from the Francis-Barnett Cruiser. Nothing wrong with that relative to its original application but for Motor Cycling *to end their first appraisal of one by stating that 'the newcomer to the Bracebridge Street range adds to the stature of the Norton concern' was, even taking into account the mollifying journalese of the day, fairly fatuous. In the course of their deliberations they found it to have a not-at-all-unreasonable top speed of some 75mph, but by taking its hugely oversquare (60x44mm) engine up to 8,600 rpm (52mph) in second they must have been unknowingly within a whisker of discovering an as-yet-unknown manufacturing defect.*

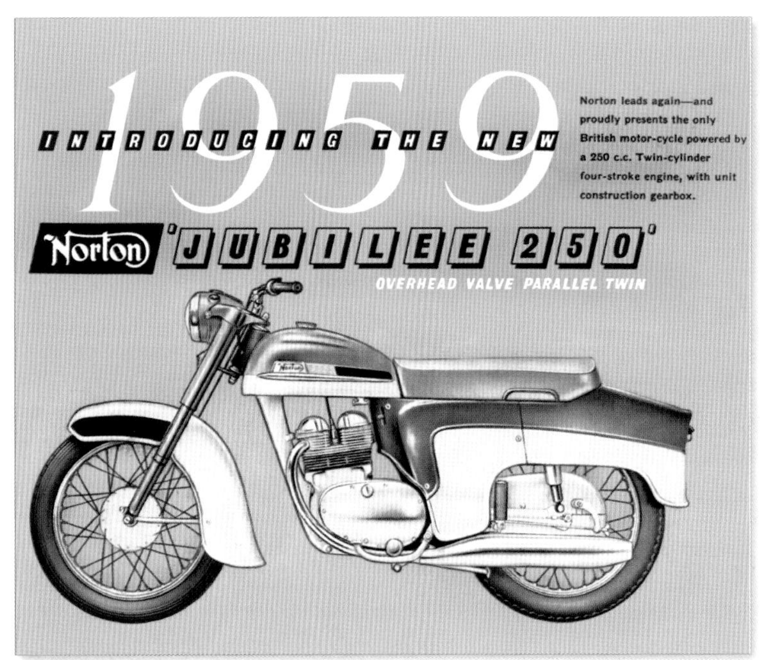

Prior to this Norton seldom made reference to colour schemes in sales material, and up until relatively recently it had been unnecessary, as traditionally the firm's products had been finished in black with silver tanks, or tank panels coach-lined in black and red. I owned a bog-standard one of these in this colour many years ago, and a very nice little bike it was too – providing you remembered it was no performer… The battle I had to make headway against a strong headwind whilst crossing the Severn Bridge on a trip to west Wales is well remembered. Looking at Motor Cycling*'s contemporary test, however, my bike may have been a little below par, as they managed 66mph in third gear at 5,850rpm and just under 75 in top at nearly 900rpm less, along with the quarter-mile dash in just short of 20 seconds and about 90mpg. They're quite rare now as all too often they fell victim to those in search of raw material for Tritons or other concoctions.*

The ES2 was now the largest single in the range. Clearly seen in the illustration is the more robust pivoted fork incorporating rear lugs that had been introduced in 1957 for the entire range.

Alternators, in conjunction with coil ignition, had been introduced for the 88 and 99 in 1957 but by now the entire range was equipped with this system. As the alternator is located outboard of the main shaft sprocket a more commodious bulge in the tin primary chain case was a consequence.

SOME OF THE NORTON **SUCCESSES** IN **1958**

GREAT BRITAIN
I.O.M. Tourist Trophy Races.
350 c.c. class—13 in first 14 places.
500 c.c. class— 8 in first 9 places.

AUSTRALIA
New South Wales T.T. Mount Druitt.
350 c.c., 500 c.c. and Unlimited classes—1st & 2nd.
Queensland T.T. Brisbane.
350 c.c. & 500 c.c. classes—1st, 2nd & 3rd.

AUSTRIA
Austrian Grand Prix.
350 c.c. class—1st & 2nd.

CZECHOSLOVAKIA
Piestany Race Meeting.
350 c.c. & 500 c.c. classes—1st & 2nd.

FRANCE
French Grand Prix.
350 c.c. class—1st & 2nd.
500 c.c. class—1st to 6th inclusive.

IRELAND
North West "200".
350 c.c. & 500 c.c. classes—1st, 2nd & 3rd.

SOUTH AFRICA
Port Elizabeth "200".
350 c.c. class—1st & 3rd.
500 c.c. class—1st, 2nd & 3rd.

SWEDEN
Swedish Grand Prix.
350 c.c. class—1st to 7th inclusive.
500 c.c. class—1st & 3rd.

Manx 30/40

The most successful standard production racing machine in the world.

Basically identical, both engines employ bevel-driven twin overhead camshafts, light alloy heads and barrels and high tensile steel connecting rods. A compression ratio suitable for international racing fuels is standard. Lucas rotating magnet magneto and Amal G.P. weir type carburetters are used.

TRANSMISSION : Close ratio 4-speed gearbox ; 3-plate clutch, primary chain oil carried in frame.

SUSPENSION: "Roadholder" telescopic forks with clip-on handlebars. Pivoted fork rear suspension with hydraulically damped shock absorber units.

WHEELS : Light alloy hubs, rims and brake shoes ; two leading shoe type front brake.

TANKS : Light alloy with quick action caps.

FRAME : Double loop, all welded, equipped to carry fairings.

OTHER EQUIPMENT : 8,000 r.p.m. revolution counter ; fly screen ; megaphone ; light alloy guards ; steering damper ; ball-ended brake and clutch levers.

FINISH : Black and Silver enamel with chromium plating.

Models	Bore and Stroke (m/m.)	Cylinder Capacity	Compression Ratio	Gear Ratio	Weight	Petrol Tank Capacity	Oil Tank Working Capacity	Tyre Size	Brake Dimensions
30M	86 × 85·6	499 c.c.	10·07	Top 4·23 2nd 5·63 3rd 4·65 Bot. 7·52	313	5 Gal.	7½ pts.	F.3·00 × 19 R.3·50 × 19	Front: 8″ dia. × 1¾″ wide
40M	76 × 76·7	348 c.c.	10·15	Top 5·12 2nd 6·81 3rd 5·64 Bot. 9·11	307	5 Gal.	7½ pts.	F.3·00 × 19 R.3·50 × 19	Rear: 7″ dia. × 1¾″ wide

I hate to correct Norton's annual tally of successes but, as far as the 1958 Isle of Man TT races were concerned, in the Junior it had 12 bikes in the first 14 (Surtees won on an MV and Bob Brown was 14th on an AJS 7R). The Senior was a different story, however: Surtees won again with an MV but with the exception of Dickie Dale's BMW in 12th spot it was a solid phalanx of Nortons right down to 21st place. The fuel tank depicted is a smaller capacity than the regular five-gallon variety.

Anxious to show that it too was encompassing the fashion for skirts and bright colours, Norton's 1960 brochure showcased its new slimline Dominator so attired. All a matter of personal taste, I know, but I much prefer the look of the 1954-59 wideline Dominators; in contrast, a good friend and fellow Norton owner, based on their performance in the Thruxton 500 race, would have a circa-'64 slimline 650SS like a shot. On the other hand, we both agree that machine depicted here would look better by far denuded of its tinware. I have a feeling that we are not alone in this viewpoint, so survivors that have remained clothed are a rarity.

Haute couture from the house of Norton by Clarendon Pressing and Welding Co, 1960.

This famous race-bred frame is a high quality, high grade steel tube, all-welded duplex loop construction, liberally gusseted at the rear for optimum rigidity of the swinging arm. Note the unique head construction giving rigidity in all planes, one of the main reasons for the wonderful steering characteristics of Norton. The rear fork ends are solid forged for maximum strength.

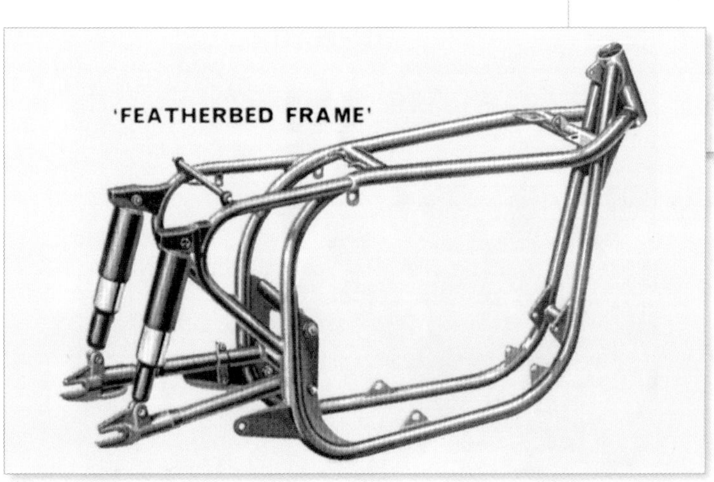

Left is the so-called slimline version of the Featherbed frame introduced for the 1960 season – in fact, at its widest point it was marginally wider than its wideline forebear. Above is the variety upon which the rear enclosure models are built, with additional brackets and rear loop necessary to facilitate its attachment. Manx models continued in their use of the racing version of the wideline, however.

Fortunately, fulsome bodywork was not obligatory but the standard slimline-framed 88s and 99s had a very different look from the previous season's models.

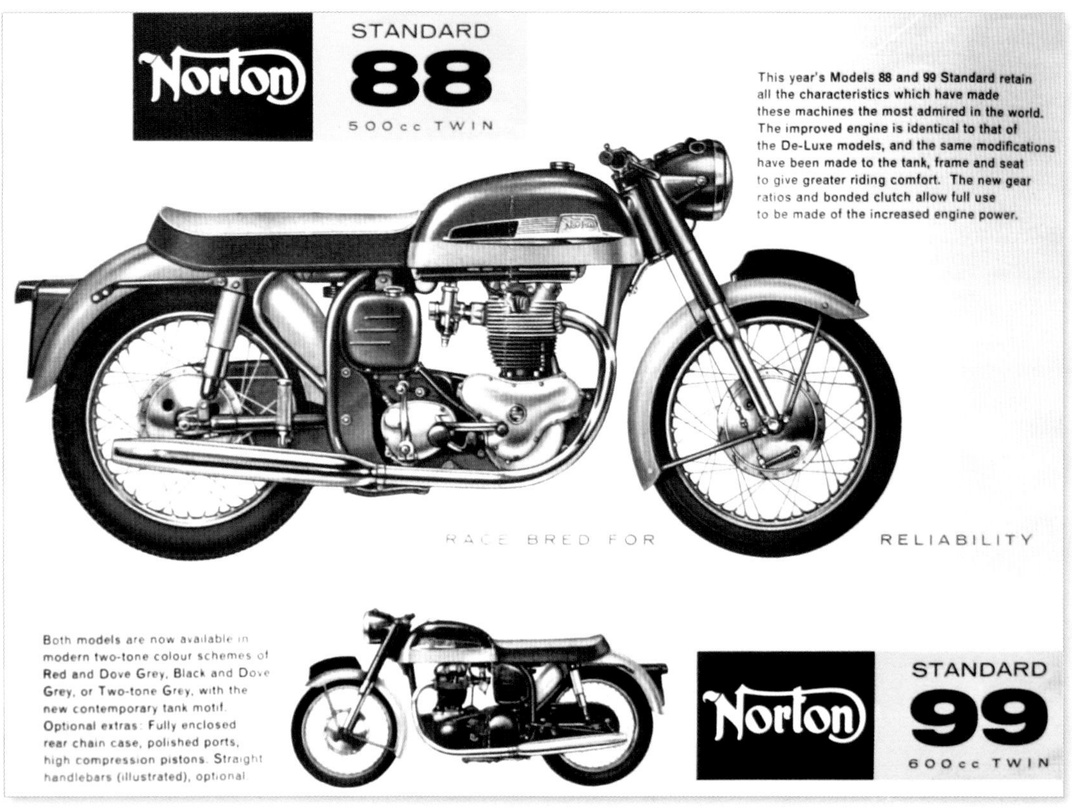

I sincerely hope it wasn't this model that had been selected by the Design Centre; but then many of us stand back aghast at what is sometimes considered worthy of the annual Turner Prize. Our rather wobbly and apprehensive-looking rider is wearing the same shoes and plaid socks as the gent on the brochure's cover, so has he changed suits or was the footwear standard issue?

Cover model for this brochure looks far more assured on his Blue-and-Dove Grey 99 De Luxe than last year's – and is suitably dressed too. The artwork is somehow reminiscent of Frank Wootton's but without his signature, so consider it to be the work of another artist.

Two years on from its announcement and the Jubilee had been given what the factory described as 'restyled' front forks, a 7in headlamp and quick-action fastener for the dual seat. On the mechanical front there was an improved ignition contact breaker allowing for individual cylinder timing and, no doubt to alleviate the public's concerns as to the bottom end fragility, the brochure mentioned that the crankshaft was of nodular iron. Would that have meant anything to the average sales prospect, however? There were now, by popular demand, two models – the existing version became the De Luxe and was joined by a Standard version with less-enveloping panels. It was described as 'essentially a machine for the enthusiast… Lighter mudguards and light styling panels combine to give a sporting appearance'. The De Luxe came in Blue and Dove Grey whilst the Standard came in Red and Dove Grey.

Following their policy of progressive development, Norton introduce with pride this brilliant newcomer to the range. The Norton Navigator with its twin cylinder, four stroke, engine-gearbox unit of 349 c.c. capacity, provides smooth, effortless power by virtue of its unique design and dimensions. It has a forged steel crankshaft and mono-bloc cylinder barrel. An outstanding feature of the Norton Navigator is the 'Roadholder' front forks incorporating 8 inch diameter brake, which adds superb handling and fatigue free steering to the powerful performance of this magnificent machine.
Available in Standard or De-Luxe form.
The Standard model, illustrated on the left, is finished in Blue and Dove Grey. The De-Luxe model, illustrated above, is in Black and Dove Grey.

New for 1961 was the Navigator. I should have thought that anyone who started their motorcycling career on a Jubilee would have been all too keen to move on to pastures new once they'd passed their test; but Norton must have thought otherwise when its bigger brother was put into production. Elsewhere in the brochure we're told that 'this modern machine has been given all the superb handling attributes of the Norton Dominators'. What, with the Francis-Barnett-sourced frame? I don't think so!

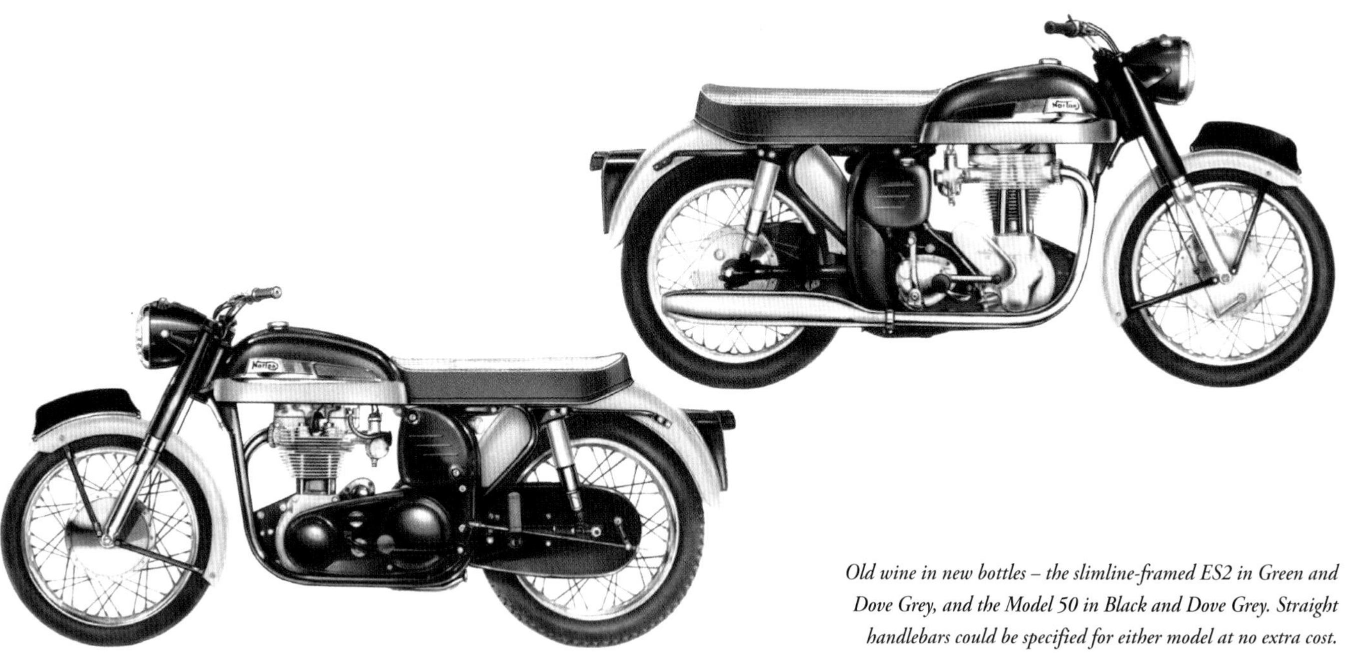

Old wine in new bottles – the slimline-framed ES2 in Green and Dove Grey, and the Model 50 in Black and Dove Grey. Straight handlebars could be specified for either model at no extra cost.

Smaller in engine capacity but with all the attributes of the Dominator 99, the Dominator 88 is a favourite with all experts who want high average speeds over long distances with comfort and absolute reliability.

Like the Model 99, the Dominator 88 is available in Standard or De-Luxe form. The 88 Standard is finished in Green and Dove Grey, the De-Luxe in Red and Dove Grey. Straight handlebars are available. An optional extra is the totally enclosed rear chain case. Compression ratios are now 8·5—1.

Basically identical, both engines employ bevel-driven twin overhead camshafts, light alloy heads and barrels, and high tensile steel connecting rods. A compression ratio suitable for international racing fuels is standard. Modifications to tappets and pistons have been made. Lucas rotating magnet magneto and Amal weir type carburettors are used.

SUSPENSION: 'Roadholder' telescopic forks with improved handlebar fixing, pivoted fork rear suspension with hydraulically damped shock absorber units.

FRAME: Double loop, all welded, equipped to carry fairings.

TRANSMISSION: Close ratio 4 speed gearbox; 3-plate clutch, primary chain oil carried in frame.

WHEELS: Serrated wheelrims; light alloy hubs, rims and brake shoes; two leading shoe type front brake.

TANKS: Light alloy with quick action caps.

OTHER EQUIPMENT: 9,000 r.p.m. revolution counter, fly screen, improved megaphone, light alloy guards, steering damper, ball-ended brake and clutch levers.

FINISH: Black and silver enamel with chromium plating.

Models	Bore and Stroke (m/m.)	Cylinder Capacity	Com-pression Ratio	Gear Ratio	Weight	Petrol Tank Capacity	Oil Tank Working Capacity	Tyre Size	Brake Dimensions
30M	86 × 85·6	499 c.c.	11 to 1	Top 4·23 2nd 5·63 3rd 4·65 Bot. 7·52	313	5 Gal.	7½ pts.	F.3·00 × 19 R.3·50 × 19	Front: 8″ dia. × 1¾ wide
40M	76 × 76·7	348 c.c.	11 to 1	Top 5·12 2nd 6·81 3rd 5·64 Bot. 9·11	307	5 Gal.	7½ pts.	F.3·00 × 19 R.3·50 × 19	Rear: 7″ dia. × 1¾″ wide

This was no idle boast as, even though the factory had long-since ceased fielding its own machines, the Manx was still more than capable of holding its own in international competition. The 1960 Senior TT may have been dominated by Surtees and Hartle on works MVs but behind them it was Norton, Norton, Norton – from Mike Hailwood in third place down to Roy Ingram in 12th. In '61 the sole MV retired and Hailwood's Manx took the Senior, with three more behind him and places thereafter divided between yet more Nortons and a few Matchless G50s. In the Junior, Gary Hocking and the 350 MV were bested by the young Phil Read and his Manx, with others third and fourth.

MODEL	JUBILEE STANDARD	JUBILEE DE-LUXE	NAVIGATOR STANDARD	NAVIGATOR DE-LUXE	50	E.S.2	88 STANDARD	88 DE-LUXE	99 STANDARD	99 DE-LUXE
CAPACITY C.C.	249	249	349	349	348	490	497	497	597	597
ENGINE TYPE	O.H.V.	O.H.V.	O.H.V.	O.H.V.	O.H.V.	O.H.V.	O.H.V.	O.H.V.	O.H.V.	O.H.V.
BORE AND STROKE M/M	60 × 44	60 × 44	63 × 56	63 × 56	71 × 88	79 × 100	66 × 72·6	66 × 72·6	68 × 82	68 × 82
COMPRESSION RATIO	8·75	8·75	8·75	8·75	7·3	7·1	8·5	8·5	8·25	8·25
NO. OF CYLINDERS	2	2	2	2	1	1	2	2	2	2
GEAR RATIO: TOP	6·76	6·76	5·72	5·72	5·59	4·75	5·0	5·0	4·75	4·75
THIRD	8·8	8·8	7·44	7·44	6·8	5·8	6·1	6·1	5·8	5·8
SECOND	12·5	12·5	10·6	10·6	9·5	8·08	8·5	8·5	8·08	8·08
FIRST	19·7	19·7	16·7	16·7	14·28	12·16	12·75	12·75	12·16	12·16
REAR CHAIN	½″ × ·305″	½″ × ·305″	½″ × ·305″	½″ × ·305″	⅝″ × ¼″	⅝″ × ¼″	⅝″ × ¼″	⅝″ × ¼″	⅝″ × ¼″	⅝″ × ¼″
FRONT CHAIN	⅜″ DUPLEX	⅜″ DUPLEX	⅜″ DUPLEX	⅜″ DUPLEX	½″ × ·305″	½″ × ·305″	½″ × ·305″	½″ × ·305″	½″ × ·305″	½″ × ·305″
TYRES: FRONT	3·25 × 18	3·25 × 18	3·00 × 19	3·00 × 19	3·00 × 19	3·00 × 19	3·00 × 19	3·00 × 19	3·00 × 19	3·00 × 19
REAR	3·25 × 18	3·25 × 18	3·25 × 18	3·25 × 18	3·50 × 19	3·50 × 19	3·50 × 19	3·50 × 19	3·50 × 19	3·50 × 19
CARBURETTOR: AMAL.	MONOBLOC 375	MONOBLOC 375/36	MONOBLOC 375	MONOBLOC 375	MONOBLOC 376/68	MONOBLOC 376/17	MONOBLOC 376/66	MONOBLOC 376/247	MONOBLOC 376/67	MONOBLOC 376/248
CHOKE SIZE	25/32″	25/32″	⅞″	⅞″	1″	1 1/16″	1″	1″	1 1/16″	1 1/16″
MAIN JET NO.	130	130	170	170	210	270	240	240	250	250
THROTTLE SLIDE NO.	3½	3½	3½	3½	3½	4	3½	3½	3	3
BRAKES: FRONT	6″ dia. × 1″	6″ dia. × 1″	8″ dia. × 1¼″	8″ dia. × 1¼″	8″ dia. × 1¼″	8″ dia. × 1¼″	8″ dia. × 1¼″	8″ dia. × 1¼″	8″ dia. × 1¼″	8″ dia. × 1¼″
REAR	6″ dia. × 1″	6″ dia. × 1″	6″ dia. × 1″	6″ dia. × 1″	7″ dia. × 1¼″	7″ dia. × 1¼″	7″ dia. × 1¼″	7″ dia. × 1¼″	7″ dia. × 1¼″	7″ dia. × 1¼″
PETROL TANK CAPACITY	3 GALLS.	3 GALLS.	3 GALLS.	3 GALLS.	3⅝ GALLS.	3⅝ GALLS.	3⅝ GALLS.	3⅝ GALLS.	3⅝ GALLS.	3⅝ GALLS.
OIL TANK CAPACITY	3½ PTS.	3½ PTS.	3½ PTS.	3½ PTS.	4½ PTS.	4½ PTS.	4½ PTS.	4 PTS.	4½ PTS.	4 PTS.
WEIGHT (LBS.)	320 LBS.	325 LBS.	330 LBS.	335 LBS.	377 LBS.	384 LBS.	390 LBS.	395 LBS.	395 LBS.	400 LBS.
OVERALL LENGTH	80″	81″	80″	81″	85″	85″	85″	85″	85″	85″
OVERALL WIDTH	26″	26″	26″	26″	27″	27″	27″	27″	27″	27″
SEAT HEIGHT	29″	29″	29″	29″	31″	31″	31″	31″	31″	31″
GROUND CLEARANCE	5½″	5½″	5½″	5½″	6¼″	6¼″	6¼″	6¼″	6¼″	6¼″
WHEELBASE	52½″	52½″	51½″	51½″	55½″	55½″	55½″	55½″	55½″	55½″

Totally enclosed rear chain case is available on all models as an optional extra.
Sidecar specification is available on all models except the 250 c.c. and 350 c.c. twins.

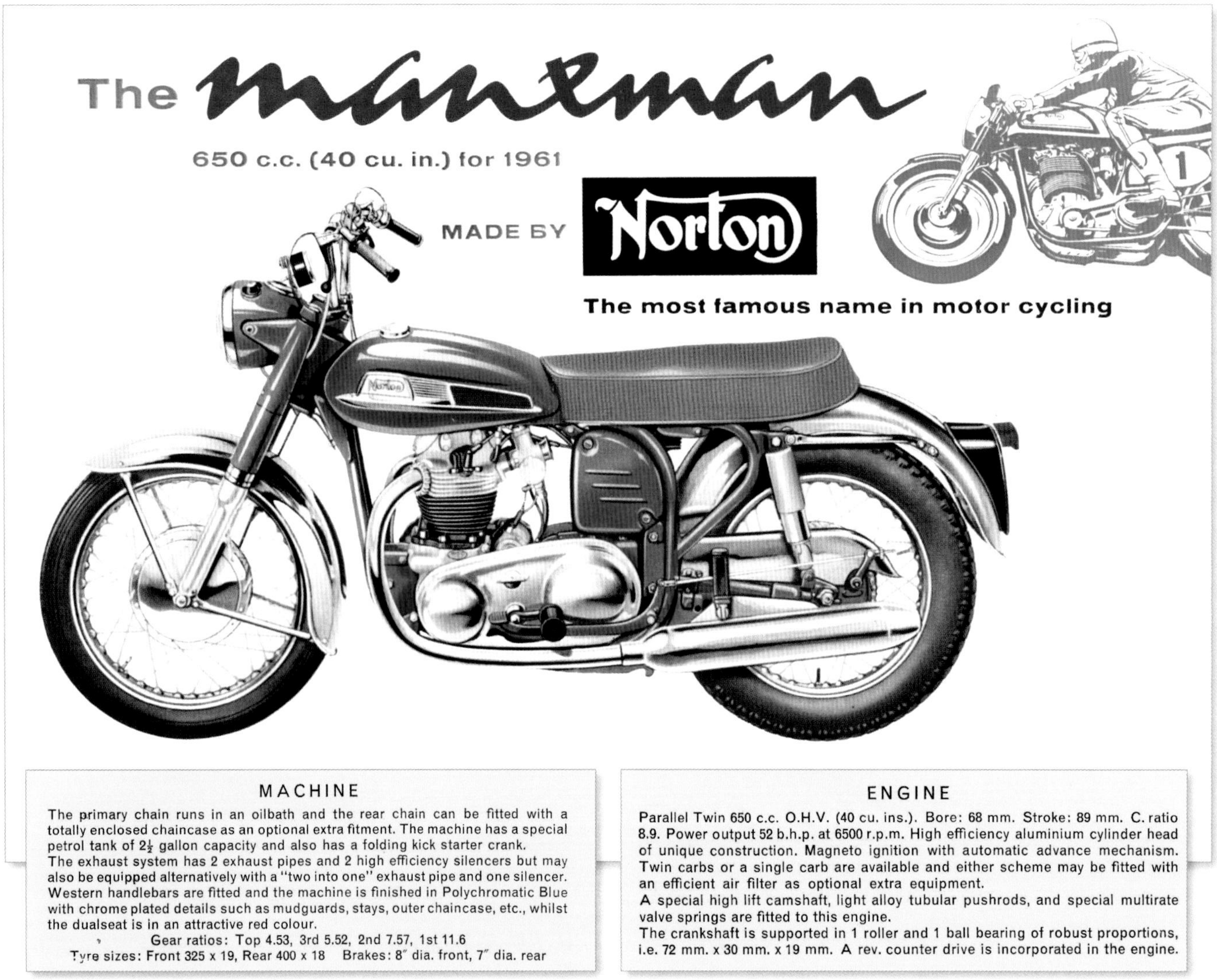

The Manxman

650 c.c. (40 cu. in.) for 1961

MADE BY Norton

The most famous name in motor cycling

MACHINE

The primary chain runs in an oilbath and the rear chain can be fitted with a totally enclosed chaincase as an optional extra fitment. The machine has a special petrol tank of 2½ gallon capacity and also has a folding kick starter crank.
The exhaust system has 2 exhaust pipes and 2 high efficiency silencers but may also be equipped alternatively with a "two into one" exhaust pipe and one silencer. Western handlebars are fitted and the machine is finished in Polychromatic Blue with chrome plated details such as mudguards, stays, outer chaincase, etc., whilst the dualseat is in an attractive red colour.
Gear ratios: Top 4.53, 3rd 5.52, 2nd 7.57, 1st 11.6
Tyre sizes: Front 325 x 19, Rear 400 x 18 Brakes: 8" dia. front, 7" dia. rear

ENGINE

Parallel Twin 650 c.c. O.H.V. (40 cu. ins.). Bore: 68 mm. Stroke: 89 mm. C. ratio 8.9. Power output 52 b.h.p. at 6500 r.p.m. High efficiency aluminium cylinder head of unique construction. Magneto ignition with automatic advance mechanism. Twin carbs or a single carb are available and either scheme may be fitted with an efficient air filter as optional extra equipment.
A special high lift camshaft, light alloy tubular pushrods, and special multirate valve springs are fitted to this engine.
The crankshaft is supported in 1 roller and 1 ball bearing of robust proportions, i.e. 72 mm. x 30 mm. x 19 mm. A rev. counter drive is incorporated in the engine.

During the latter part of 1960, as a result of pressure from US importer Berliner, Norton began production of a 650 version of the 99 twin (a capacity of 647cc was arrived at by increasing the stroke of the 597cc 99's engine by 7mm). Christened, also at Berliner's behest, with the evocative name of Manxman, its looks were, however, far removed from the racing Nortons that had won acclaim on the island. Only ever an export model, it was nevertheless the precursor to the 650 and in particular the twin-carb 650SS that would be introduced for the UK and Europe a year later. Interestingly, Norton claimed 49bhp for the latter but 52 for the Manxman – both with the same engine and carb configuration. All Manxmen were finished in Polychromatic Blue, and after perhaps 100 had been produced this was extended to include the rear number plate box. The Manxman also featured specially-manufactured silencers that were unique to this model.

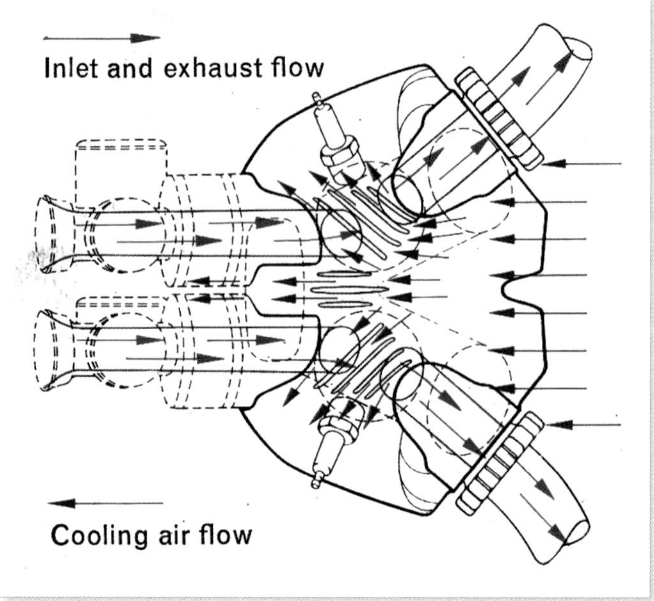

ENGINE. 647 c.c. vertical twin, O.H.V. with bore and stroke of 68 × 89. New type cylinder head with parallel inlet tracts and wide splayed exhaust ports for extra performance and increased cooling. Special multi-rate valve springs; light alloy tubular push rods; new high performance camshaft; high compression (8·9 to 1) solid skirt pistons; crankshaft assembly based on the very successful 88/99 components but with larger diameter journals and greater flywheel effect. Twin exhaust pipes with specially tuned silencers. Ignition/Lighting system incorporating an emergency start device.
GEARBOX. 4 speed; positive foot change driven through a heavy duty multi-plate clutch with bonded friction plates and vane-type shock absorbers.
FORKS. "Roadholder" forks, 2-way damping, hydraulically controlled single rate springs housed within large diameter main tubes.
FRAME. "Featherbed" frame famed for road holding and stability. Tubular, duplex welded construction with great lateral rigidity and torsional resistance. Swinging arm 2-way damped, pivoting on bonded rubber bushes.
BRAKES. Front, 8″ × 1¼″. Rear, 7″ × 1¼″. Smooth, powerful, non-fade. Full width light weight polished alloy hubs.
LIGHTING. 6 volt, 60 watt, crankshaft mounted alternator; 13 A.H. battery; 8″ head-lamp incorporating 120 m.p.h. speedometer, ammeter and lighting/ignition switch. Combined rear/stop lamp with built-in reflector.
TWIN SEAT. Comfortable, slim, foam rubber cushion with waterproof covering. Quickly detachable for access to tool tray.
WHEELS. Quickly detachable rear wheel. Tyres: Front, Avon 3.00 × 19; Rear, 3.50 × 19 G.P.
OPTIONAL EQUIPMENT. Straight handlebars. Sidecar specification.
OPTIONAL EXTRAS. Enclosed rear chain case. Chrome guards (Standard model only).
COLOUR FINISH.
De-Luxe: two-tone, Blue and Dove Grey
Standard: single tone, Norton Grey.

Built originally for the export market where they have proved tremendously successful, these fabulous 650's are now offered to the British rider in Standard or De-Luxe trim. The surging power of the vertical twin engine is coupled with roadholding and steering characteristics which Norton alone, with their vast experience of fast and safe machines, can produce. This is a machine for the experienced rider who insists upon the very best in motor cycles.

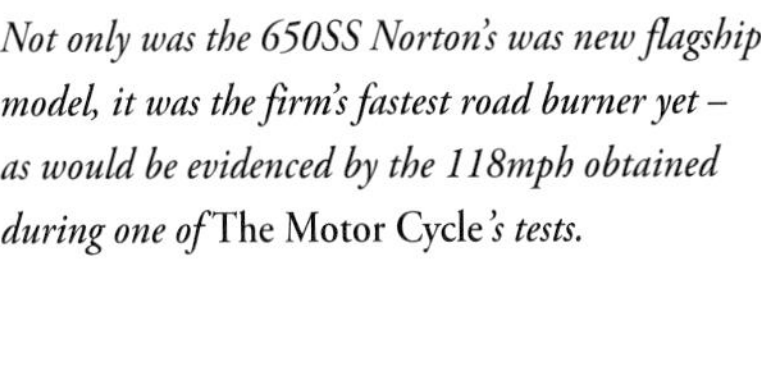
Not only was the 650SS Norton's was new flagship model, it was the firm's fastest road burner yet – as would be evidenced by the 118mph obtained during one of The Motor Cycle*'s tests.*

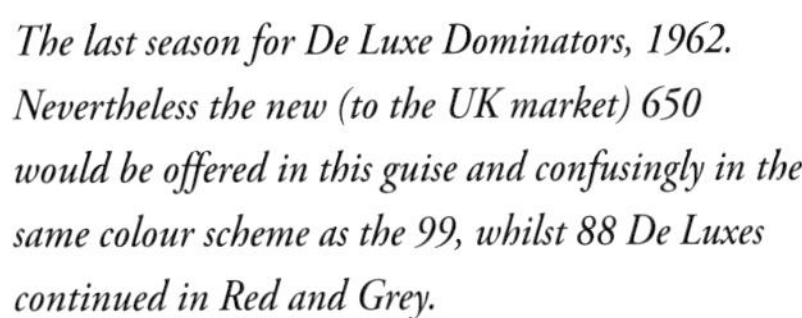
The last season for De Luxe Dominators, 1962. Nevertheless the new (to the UK market) 650 would be offered in this guise and confusingly in the same colour scheme as the 99, whilst 88 De Luxes continued in Red and Grey.

Packing tremendous power, yet wonderfully docile in traffic, the Dominator 650 is a joy to ride. "Featherbed" frame and "Roadholder" forks give to this machine roadholding, steering and general handling attributes unequalled in any other machine. Its reliability is founded upon more than fifty years of successful racing experience. The riding comfort and good looks of the Dominator 650 are in keeping with the magnificent performance of this fine machine. Smooth, graceful, powerful, with stylish two-tone finish this is a machine you will be most proud to own.

Dominator 650

650 c.c. Vertical Twin

Specially designed for the rider who wants extra performance, these really powerful machines have been produced to give, not only high performance but also the highest degree of safety. For high speed cruising and motor-way travel, or production machine racing, these Sports Specials are the tops.

ENGINE. 647 c.c. O.H.V. vertical twin with basic specification similar to the 650 c.c. machines but with twin carburettors incorporating special balance system in induction tracts to facilitate low speed running. Magneto ignition with automatic advance and retard mechanism. Maximum power is developed at 6,800 r.p.m. giving 49 b.h.p.
GEARBOX. 4 speed positive foot change with heavy duty, multi-plate clutch as fitted to all 650 c.c. machines.
FORKS. "Roadholder" forks; straight handlebars and racing-type ball ended levers.
FRAME. Racebred "Featherbed" frame, famous for its safe roadholding qualities and extreme rigidity.
BRAKES. Front, 8″ × 1¼″. Rear, 7″ × 1¼″. Very powerful, non-fade.
LIGHTING. Crankshaft mounted alternator for lighting only: 13 A.H. battery; powerful, adjustable, 8″ headlamp with 150 m.p.h. speedometer and lighting switch in headlamp shell. Combined rear/stop lamp with built-in reflector.
TYRES. Avon 3.00 × 19 front, 3.50 × 19 G.P. rear tyre. Q.D. rear wheel.
OPTIONAL EQUIPMENT. 2 into 1 exhaust pipes.
OPTIONAL EXTRAS. Folding kick start. Rev. counter. Chrome guards. Fully enclosed rear chain case.
COLOUR FINISH. All black with silver tank.

SPORTS SPECIALS

Norton 88/99

500 c.c. and 600 c.c. Vertical Twins

88 SPORTS SPECIAL

497 c.c. vertical twin, O.H.V. with basic specification similar to the Model 88 Standard but using twin carburettors; new type cylinder head as fitted to the 650's; multi-rate valve springs; light alloy push rods; high performance camshaft; high compression pistons of 9·5 to 1. Manually operated magneto ignition. Low output, crankshaft mounted alternator for lighting only. Straight handlebars with racing-type, ball ended levers. Quickly detachable rear wheel; Avon G.P. tyre on rear wheel.

OPTIONAL EQUIPMENT. 2 into 1 exhaust pipes.

OPTIONAL EXTRAS. Folding kickstart. Rev. counter. Chrome guards. Fully enclosed rear chain case.

COLOUR FINISH. Smart two-tone finish in Green and Dove Grey.

99 SPORTS SPECIAL

597 c.c. vertical twin, O.H.V., similar in general specification to the Model 99 Standard, but with twin carburettors; special valve springs; high performance camshaft; light alloy push rods; polished ports. Compression ratio, 8·25 to 1. Straight handlebars with racing-type ball ended levers. A machine capable of sustained high average speeds.

Quickly detachable rear wheel. Tyres: Front, Avon 3.00 × 19; Rear, 3.50 × 19 G.P.

OPTIONAL EQUIPMENT. 2 into 1 exhaust pipes.

OPTIONAL EXTRAS. Folding kickstart. Rev. counter. Chrome guards. Fully enclosed rear chain case.

COLOUR FINISH. Stylish, two-tone finish in Grey and Dove Grey.

Both 650 and 500 versions proved highly successful in production racing, with a Sid Lawton-prepared 650SS winning the Thruxton 500 outright three years in succession, whilst the 88SS did the same in the 500cc class. As well as winning the Silverstone 1,000 miles Production Touring Machine Race the big bike also won the coveted Machine of the Year Award.

QD rear wheels were nothing new to Nortons but single-piece rear mudguards had been introduced at the same time as the slimline-framed bikes. Tyre is the Avon GP, fitted as standard to the new SS models.

INSTRUMENT GROUP

This typical arrangement of the instruments for the Sports Specials shows the optional 8,000 r.p.m. rev. counter resiliently mounted in a bracket attached to the top of the fork leg. The whole group is easily visible in all riding positions.

Norton's adherence to this headlamp with inset speedo made for an awkwardly-mounted optional rev counter, giving it very much the appearance of an afterthought – which I suppose in some respects it was.

ENGINE. Both engines are of basically similar design employing bevel driven double overhead camshafts; light alloy heads; "Alfin" barrels; electron crankcases; high tensile steel connecting rods and crankshafts; and forged light alloy pistons. The compression ratio of 11 to 1 is suitable for International racing fuels. "Lucas" rotating magnet magnetos and "Amal" G.P. type carburettors are fitted.

TRANSMISSION. Close ratio four speed gearbox together with a three-plate clutch employing bonded inserts; primary chain oil is carried in the frame tube.

FRAME. Double loop, bronze welded "Reynolds" 531 tube Brackets are fitted for the attachment of a fairing.

SUSPENSION. "Roadholder" telescopic front forks employing hydraulic damping; swinging fork rear controlled by "Girling" suspension units.

WHEELS. Light alloy serrated rims, electron hubs, brake plates and shoes. The new front brake is a "twin" type employing two leading shoes on both sides. The surface area is 71½ sq. in. and large air scoops are fitted.

TANKS. Light alloy, rubber mounted, with quick action filler caps.

FINISH. Black and silver enamel with chromium plating.

Models	Bore and Stroke (mm.)	Cylinder Capacity	Compression Ratio	Gear Ratio	Weight	Petrol Tank Capacity	Oil Tank Working Capacity	Tyre Size	Brake Dimensions
30M	86×85·6	499 c.c.	11 to 1	Top 4·23 2nd 5·63 3rd 4·65 Bot. 7·52	313	5 Gal.	7½ pts.	F.3·00×19 R.3·50×19	Front: Double 7″×1⅝″ wide
40M	76×76·7	348 c.c.	11 to 1	Top 5·12 2nd 6·81 3rd 5·64 Bot. 9·11	307	5 Gal.	7½ pts.	F.3·00×19 R.3·50×19	Rear: 7″ dia.×1¾″ wide

Improvements for the 1962 Manx included a completely new twin front brake and redesigned oil tank.

MODEL	JUBILEE STANDARD	JUBILEE DE-LUXE	NAVIGATOR STANDARD	NAVIGATOR DE-LUXE	MODEL 50	MODEL E.S.2
CAPACITY c.c.	249	249	349	349	348	490
ENGINE TYPE	O.H.V.	O.H.V.	O.H.V.	O.H.V.	O.H.V.	O.H.V.
BORE STROKE	60×44	60×44	63×56	63×56	71×88	79×100
COMPRESSION RATIO	8·75	8·75	8·5	8·5	7·3	7·1
No. OF CYLINDERS	2	2	2	2	1	1
GEAR RATIO: TOP	6·76	6·76	5·72	5·72	5·59	4·75
" " THIRD	8·8	8·8	7·44	7·44	6·8	5·8
" " SECOND	12·5	12·5	10·6	10·6	9·5	8·08
" " FIRST	19·7	19·7	16·7	16·7	14·28	12·16
REAR CHAIN	½″×·305″	½″×·305″	½″×·305″	½″×·305″	⅝″×¼″	⅝″×¼″
FRONT CHAIN	⅜″ DUPLEX	⅜″ DUPLEX	⅜″ DUPLEX	⅜″ DUPLEX	½″×·305″	½″×·305″
TYRES: FRONT	3·00×18	3·25×18	3·00×19	3·00×19	3·00×19	3·00×19
REAR	3·25×18	3·25×18	3·25×18	3·25×18	3·50×19	3·50×19
CARB: AMAL	MONOBLOC	MONOBLOC	MONOBLOC	MONOBLOC	MONOBLOC	MONOBLOC
" TYPE	375/43	375/36	375/48	375/47	376/68	376/17
CHOKE SIZE	25/32″	25/32″	⅞″	⅞″	1″	1 1/16″
MAIN JET No.	130	130	170	170	210	270
THROTTLE SLIDE No.	3½	3½	3½	3½	3½	4
BRAKES: FRONT	6″ dia.×1″	6″ dia.×1″	8″ dia.×1¼″	8″ dia.×1¼″	8″ dia.×1¼″	8″ dia.×1¼″
REAR	6″ dia.×1″	6″ dia.×1″	6″ dia.×1″	6″ dia.×1″	7″ dia.×1¼″	7″ dia.×1¼″
PETROL TANK	3 GALLS.	3 GALLS.	3 GALLS.	3 GALLS.	3⅝ GALLS.	3⅝ GALLS.
OIL TANK	3½ PTS.	3½ PTS.	3½ PTS.	3½ PTS.	4½ PTS.	4½ PTS.
WEIGHT	320 LBS.	325 LBS.	330 LBS.	335 LBS.	377 LBS.	384 LBS.
OVERALL LENGTH	80″	81″	80″	81″	85″	85″
OVERALL WIDTH	26″	26″	26″	26″	27″	27″
SEAT HEIGHT	29″	29″	29″	29″	31″	31″
GROUND CLEARANCE	5½″	5½″	5½″	5½″	6¼″	6¼″
WHEELBASE	52½″	52½″	51½″	51½″	55½″	55½″

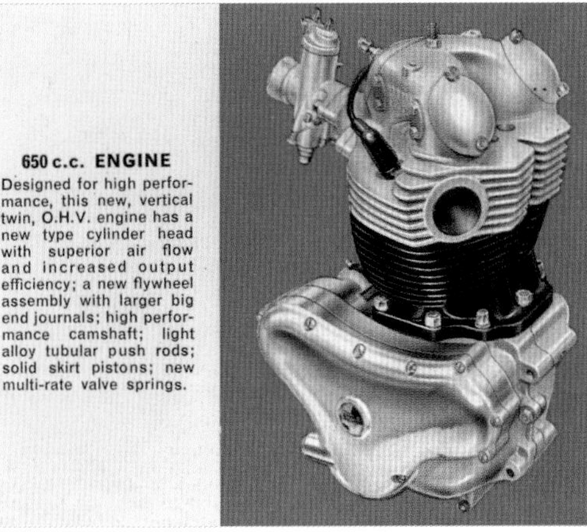

650 c.c. ENGINE

Designed for high performance, this new, vertical twin, O.H.V. engine has a new type cylinder head with superior air flow and increased output efficiency; a new flywheel assembly with larger big end journals; high performance camshaft; light alloy tubular push rods; solid skirt pistons; new multi-rate valve springs.

650 c.c. CRANK ASSEMBLY

This new assembly is of the same patented design as the very successful 88/99 components but with larger diameter journals of 1¾" and a wider flywheel which gives greater flywheel effect. This well proved design is unique in that the crankshaft tapers in hollow section, from large to small, in perfect stress harmony.

NORTON 1962 RANGE PRICE LIST

EFFECTIVE FROM 1st SEPTEMBER, 1961

MODEL	RETAIL PRICE £ s. d.	PURCHASE TAX £ s. d.	TOTAL PRICE INCLUDING PURCHASE TAX £ s. d.	COLOUR FINISH
Jubilee 250 Standard	176 0 0	38 14 5	214 14 5	Red/Grey
Jubilee De Luxe	182 10 0	40 3 0	222 13 0	Blue/Grey
Navigator 350 Standard	191 10 0	42 2 7	233 12 7	Blue/Grey
Navigator De Luxe	198 0 0	43 11 2	241 11 2	Black/Grey
50	200 0 0	44 0 0	244 0 0	Black/Grey
E.S.2	205 0 0	45 2 0	250 2 0	Green/Grey
88 Standard	233 10 0	51 7 5	284 17 5	Green/Grey
88 De Luxe	238 0 0	52 7 2	290 7 2	Red/Grey
88 Sports Special	241 0 0	53 0 5	294 0 5	Green/Grey
99 Standard	238 10 0	52 9 5	290 19 5	Grey/Grey
99 De Luxe	243 10 0	53 11 5	297 1 5	Blue/Grey
99 Sports Special	246 0 0	54 2 5	300 2 5	Grey/Grey
650 c.c. Standard	240 10 0	52 18 2	293 8 2	Norton Grey
650 De Luxe	245 10 0	54 0 2	299 10 2	Blue/Grey
650 Sports Special	255 0 0	56 2 0	311 2 0	Black/Silver Tank

OPTIONAL EXTRAS

OPTIONAL EXTRA EQUIPMENT	RETAIL PRICE £ s. d.	PURCHASE TAX £ s. d.	TOTAL PRICE INCLUDING PURCHASE TAX £ s. d.
Rear Chaincase — All models	2 10 0	11 0	3 1 0
Chrome Mudguards — All Standard models	3 5 0	14 4	3 19 4
Rev. Counter — Sports Special models only	5 15 0	1 5 4	7 0 4

MODEL	88 STANDARD	88 DE-LUXE	88 SPORTS	99 STANDARD	99 DE-LUXE	99 SPORTS	650 STANDARD	650 DE-LUXE	650 SPORTS
CAPACITY c.c.	497	497	497	597	597	597	647	647	647
ENGINE TYPE	O.H.V.	O.H.V.	O.H.V.	O.H.V.	O.H.V.	O.H.V.	O.H.V.	O.H.V.	O.H.V.
BORE STROKE	66 × 72·6	66 × 72·6	66 × 72·6	68 × 82	68 × 82	68 × 82	68 × 89	68 × 89	68 × 89
COMPRESSION RATIO	8·5	8·5	9·5	8·25	8·25	8·25	8·9	8·9	8·9
No. OF CYLINDERS	2	2	2	2	2	2	2	2	2
GEAR RATIO: TOP	5·0	5·0	5·0	4·75	4·75	4·75	4·53	4·53	4·53
" " THIRD	6·1	6·1	6·1	5·8	5·8	5·8	5·52	5·52	5·52
" " SECOND	8·5	8·5	8·5	8·08	8·08	8·08	7·57	7·57	7·57
" " FIRST	12·75	12·75	12·75	12·16	12·16	12·16	11·6	11·6	11·6
REAR CHAIN	⅝" × ¼"	⅝" × ¼"	⅝" × ¼"	⅝" × ¼"	⅝" × ¼"	⅝" × ¼"	⅝" × ¼"	⅝" × ¼"	⅝" × ¼"
FRONT CHAIN	½" × ·305"	½" × ·305"	½" × ·305"	½" × ·305"	½" × ·305"	½" × ·305"	½" × ·305"	½" × ·305"	½" × ·305"
TYRES: FRONT	3·00 × 19	3·00 × 19	3·00 × 19	3·00 × 19	3·00 × 19	3·00 × 19	3·00 × 19	3·00 × 19	3·00 × 19
REAR	3·50 × 19	3·50 × 19	3·50 × 19GP	3·50 × 19	3·50 × 19	3·50 × 19	3·50 × 19GP	3·50 × 19GP	3·50 × 19GP
CARB: AMAL	MONOBLOC	MONOBLOC	TWO MONOBLOCS	MONOBLOC	MONOBLOC	TWO MONOBLOCS	MONOBLOC	MONOBLOC	TWO MONOBLOCS
" TYPE	376/66	376/247	376/288 + 9	376/67	376/248	376/220	389/71	389/72	376/288 + 9
CHOKE SIZE	1"	1"	1 1/16"	1 1/16"	1 1/16"	1 1/16"	1⅛"	1⅛"	1 1/16"
MAIN JET No.	240	240	250	250	250	250	320	320	250
THROTTLE SLIDE No.	3½	3½	3½	3	3	3	3	3	3½
BRAKES: FRONT	8" dia. × 1¼"	8" dia. × 1¼"	8" dia. × 1¼"	8" dia. × 1¼"	8" dia. × 1¼"	8" dia. × 1¼"	8" dia. × 1¼"	8" dia. × 1¼"	8" dia. × 1¼"
REAR	7" dia. × 1¼"	7" dia. × 1¼"	7" dia. × 1¼"	7" dia. × 1¼"	7" dia. × 1¼"	7" dia. × 1¼"	7" dia. × 1¼"	7" dia. × 1¼"	7" dia. × 1¼"
PETROL TANK	3⅝ GALLS.	3⅝ GALLS.	3⅝ GALLS.	3⅝ GALLS.	3⅝ GALLS.	3⅝ GALLS.	3⅝ GALLS.	3⅝ GALLS.	3⅝ GALLS.
OIL TANK	4½ PTS.	4 PTS.	4½ PTS.	4½ PTS.	4 PTS.	4½ PTS.	4½ PTS.	4 PTS.	4½ PTS.
WEIGHT	390 LBS.	395 LBS.	390 LBS.	395 LBS.	400 LBS.	395 LBS.	398 LBS.	403 LBS.	398 LBS.
OVERALL LENGTH	85"	85"	85"	85"	85"	85"	85"	85"	85"
OVERALL WIDTH	27"	27"	26"	27"	27"	26"	27"	27"	26"
SEAT HEIGHT	31"	31"	31"	31"	31"	31"	31"	31"	31"
GROUND CLEARANCE	6¾"	6¼"	6¼"	6¼"	6¼"	6¼"	6¼"	6¼"	6¼"
WHEELBASE	55½"	55½"	55½"	55½"	55½"	55½"	55½"	55½"	55½"

Sidecar Specification, which is available on all models except 250 c.c. and 350 c.c. Twins includes:— Heavier rate front fork springs, crown and column of different angle for trail variation, heavier duty shock absorbers, engine sprocket of reduced size.

For 1963, standard finish for the Standard Jubilee was this Flamboyant Burgundy and Black but an alternative was Red and Dove Grey. The De Luxe version was in Off White and Black, with Blue and Dove Grey as an option. You could have straight handlebars if you wished on either model, as well as a fully-enclosed rear chain case, but that would cost you a bit more. Chromium mudguards were an optional extra too, but only on the Standard Jubilee.

A 650SS ridden by Phil Read and Brian Setchell had won the 1962 Thruxton 500 mile race but, as this was surely to celebrate the event, wouldn't it have been better if the artist had depicted the machine's correct racing number and one of its riders' actual helmet colours? The Read/Setchell partnership went on to win the '63 race and then in '64 Setchell, this time partnered by Derek Woodman, won again to make it a hat-trick for the 650SS.

The Standard Navigator was finished in Polychromatic Blue and Black with the option of Blue and Dove Grey – it could also be had with chromium mudguards and a totally-enclosed rear chain case. The De Luxe was in Black and Dove Grey. Straight handlebars were an option for both models.

As you may have noticed, starting with 1960-season bikes, Norton had been chopping and changing between barrel silencers with offset inlet and those with central inlet, which had been introduced that year on the new Dominators. In 1961 Dominators alone still had these and the same for 1962, except that the SS variants had offset inlet type. In '63 it got complicated with Jubilees and Navigators now having the type you see here, whilst Model 50s, ES2s, Standard Dominator 650s, 650SSs and 88SSs had the offset variety.

Nice-looking machine. The 1963 Standard 650 Dominator in Polychromatic Blue and Black. Sidecar specification, straight bars, chromium mudguards and enclosed chain case all optional.

Another good-looking bike – and fast too for a 500 – as Motor Cycling *found out when they managed to record 111mph at MIRA with an early example a couple of years earlier. Granted this was with a light tailwind but it proved capable of lapping the track at just under 98mph and could be wound up to 90-plus in third gear – at the same time returning nearly 80mpg at a steady 50, or 62mpg at 70. As for handling and braking? "Road-holding was – Norton. Handling was truly superlative on bends or straights, bumpy or smooth, fast or slow… Braking was faultless. In power the stoppers were fully equal to the requirements of a sports mount driven to the limit." From the autumn of '63 Sports Specials would be equipped with 12-volt electrics.*

ENGINE. 497 c.c. vertical twin, O.H.V. with basic specification similar to the Model 88 Standard but using twin carburettors; new type cylinder head as fitted to the 650's; multi-rate valve springs; light alloy push rods; high performance camshaft; high compression pistons of 9·5 to 1. Magneto ignition with Automatic Advance and retard.

FORKS. "Roadholder" forks; straight handlebars with racing type, ball ended levers.

FRAME. Racebred "Featherbed" frame giving maximum roadholding and stability.

BRAKES. Front, 8″ × 1¼″. Rear 7″ × 1¼″.

LIGHTING. Low output crankshaft mounted alternator for lighting only. Adjustable headlamp. Combined rear/stop lamp.

WHEELS. Quickly detachable rear wheel with Avon G.P. tyre 3·50 × 19. Front tyre, 3·00 × 19.

OPTIONAL EXTRAS. Folding kickstart. Rev. counter. Chrome guards. Fully enclosed rear chain case.

COLOUR FINISH. All black with silver tank.

At the instigation of the US importer, Berliner Motor Corporation, New Jersey, Norton made its best attempt yet to emulate Far Eastern rivals with the new ES 400 Electra – albeit little more than a bored-out (by 3mm) Navigator with a heavyweight rear hub and a few electrical gizmos. The most notable of which was electric starting – but when The Motor Cycle *tested one at the tail end of '63 they found this feature worked best when the motor was hot. On cold mornings a few prods with the kick-start were advisable – in spite of 12 volts and a reduction in compression ratio from the Navigator's. It was no speed machine either, with a light tailwind necessary for them to record a best one-way of 83mph, with 56 in third and 78 in top being the norm. The handlebar-tip flashing indicators, however, were a thoroughly good and practical innovation – in spite of the necessity to release the twist grip to operate the right-hand unit.*

1st again...with press-button starting!

The NEW NORTON ES400

400cc high camshaft twin

1. STARTING POWER. The willing electric starter gives you power at the touch of a button. Everyone who's ever been stalled in heavy traffic, held up while getting back to neutral and unfolding the kick starter will want push button starting. Now you just pull in the clutch, press the button and away!

2. GOING POWER. Minimum reciprocating weight – maximum efficiency, that's the power magic of the ES400. Short piston stroke, high camshaft, light racing type valve gear – it all adds up to a high revving power plant smooth as a jet turbine, that simply thrives on high speed cruising, and gives exhilarating acceleration.

3. HOLDING POWER. The ES400 is above all a Norton. Road holding and handling are of the highest order; the big 'Road Holder' forks make sure of that. This is a motor cycle that you can rely on under the most arduous conditions.

4. STOPPING POWER. The massive brakes will pull you up like a giant's hand. As fitted to the 500 c.c. SS and the 650 c.c. SS machines which have swept the board in Europe's long distance races for the past two years, they are housed in brightly polished hubs with deep cooling fins.

5. LIGHTING POWER. A full 12-volt lighting system means that the ES400 is just as happy by night as by day. The big headlamp with its 50/40 w. bulb throws out a wide powerful beam, lighting the road hundreds of yards ahead.

6. PLUS COMFORT. Settle on to the luxurious twin seat, the ES400 fits you as though 'tailor made'. The seat height; the set of the handle bars; the placing of the controls; the smooth suspension, all combine to make the ES400 the most comfortable motor cycle. Try one for yourself!

LIGHTWEIGHT TWIN ENGINE

This outstanding lightweight vertical twin engine is famous in 250 c.c. and 350 c.c. form as the smooth and flexible power plant of Norton Jubilee and Navigator models. For 1964 extensive development has led to a 400 c.c. version with electric self-starter which which powers the new model ES400. The performance of all 3 engines is a tribute to the basic design construction. The high camshafts permit super light valve gear giving smooth, turbine-like, high-revving characteristics. Simple and positive valve adjustment is provided by eccentric rocker spindles. The whole unit is elegantly finished with bright polished, timing side covers, primary chaincase and rocker covers. Kick-start and gear-change levers are in durable, bright chrome plate finish.

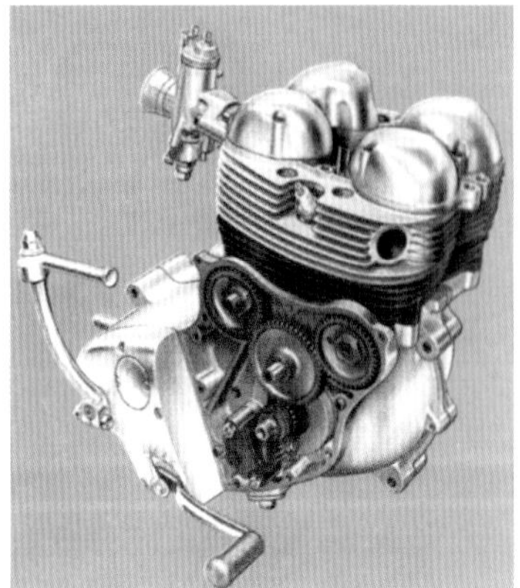

By 1964, and now just a part of AMC, the range was down to just five models. Having peaked in 1962 with 15 (17 if you count the two Manxes), it had been reduced to ten (or 12 with Manxes) for 1963.

	250 Jubilee	350 Navigator	ES 400	500 SS	650 SS
Capacity c.c.	249	349	384	497	647
Bore x Stroke	60 x 44	63 x 56	66 x 56	66 x 72·6	68 x 89
Compression Ratio	8·75 : 1	8·5 : 1	7·9 : 1	9·5 : 1	8·9 : 1
Amal Carburettor Choke Size	25/32″	7/8″	7/8″	1 1/16″	1 1/16″
Rear Chain	1/2″ x ·305″	1/2″ x ·305″	1/2″ x ·305″	5/8″ x 1/4″	5/8″ x 1/4″
Front Chain	3/8″ Duplex	3/8″ Duplex	3/8″ Duplex	1/2″ x ·305″	1/2″ x ·305″
Tyres Front	3·00 x 18	3·00 x 19	3·00 x 19	3·00 x 19	3·00 x 19
Rear	3·25 x 18	3·25 x 18	3·25 x 18	3·50 x 19GP	3.50 x 19GP
Brakes Front	6″ dia x 1″	8″ dia 1 1/4″	8″ dia x 1 1/4″	8″ dia x 1 1/4″	8″ dia x 1 1/4″
Rear	6″ dia x 1″	7″ dia x 1 1/4″	7″ dia x 1 1/4″	7″ dia x 1 1/4″	7″ dia x 1 1/4″
Petrol Tank	3 galls.	3 galls.	3 galls.	3 5/8 galls.	3 5/8 galls.
Oil Tank	3 1/2 pts.	3 1/2 pts.	3 1/2 pts.	4 1/2 pts.	4 1/2 pts.
Seat Height	29″	29″	29″	31″	31″
Ground Clearance	5 1/2″	5 1/2″	5 1/2″	6 1/4″	6 1/4″
Wheel Base	52 1/2″	51 1/2″	51 1/2″	51 1/2″	51 1/2″

It was 1965 and the marque no longer had its own brochure – sharing this and a good deal more of its components with its AMC brethren. Catalogued models had risen to eight, however, with the reintroduction of two oldies and the inclusion of the Atlas.

The Jubilee was still around, but only in one colour and no chromium mudguard option, with just an enclosed rear chain case remaining on the list of extras.

The Navigator, but no chromium mudguards either.

Goodness knows how, but Motor Cycle News *managed a 15.75-second quarter-mile with an Electra and the brochure was quick to quote them. They also persuaded an Electra to exceed* The Motor Cycle*'s top speed by 5mph, as well as well as having better luck with starting: "Not even cold and damp weather prevented the motor firing at a touch on that little red button." Joy oh joy, you could have chrome mudguards on this one and, what is more, they were standard to boot.*

A flood of requests, both from home and overseas, prompted the return of these large capacity singles into the Norton range.
Rated with the best on performance, reliability and economy, both machines have the confident power of well-proved engines. Backed by the use of an established frame and the famous 'Roadholder' forks, these Nortons ride the road . . . hold the road . . . handle like a Norton . . .

Norton 350cc. Model 50 Mk II
500cc. Model ES2 Mk II

What a travesty. It shouldn't need me to explain what AMC had come up with in answer to the 'flood of requests'. One thing is for certain, however – this was most certainly not what had been requested as, if they'd wanted a Matchless G3 or a G80, they wouldn't have asked for a Norton Model 50 or ES2. As for calling these things MkIIs… My foot!

Fortunately for Norton's good name the 88 and 650 Sports Specials had been retained and there was also the 750 Atlas. First produced for – and marketed by – Joe Berliner in the United States it had taken its name from the family of intercontinental ballistic missiles.

Engine. 745cc o.h.v. vertical twin (73mm bore x 89mm stroke). Alloy cylinder head with integral rocker box: parallel induction tracts with large diameter inlet valves: forged steel rockers: alloy push-rods: large diameter tappets: single chain-driven camshaft: built-up forged steel crankshaft with large diameter central iron flywheel: plain big-end bearings: 2-piece connecting rods: alloy pistons (c.r. 7.6:1): one-piece cast-iron cylinder block: crankshaft driven gear type oil pump: carburation by twin Amal Monoblocs: ignition by magneto, with automatic advance and retard.
Frame. The famous Norton 'Featherbed' with its race-bred handling and road-holding.
Forks. 'Roadholders' with built-in thief-proof lock: progressive two-way oil-damping: single rate springs housed within heat treated tubular steel stanchions: alloy sliders with chromed steel extensions.

OEC

Having made a name for himself as a racing cyclist during the last years of the 19th century, Frederick Osborne decided to see how he might fare if an engine was added to the equation. History does not relate how he got on, so we must assume that the combination of a lightweight frame and proprietary large-ish single-cylinder motor, which he put together in 1901, was not an unqualified success.

He next cropped up in 1919 when, together with Frederick Wood, they founded the Osborn Engineering Company and, shortly after it became vacant, took over a recently-shut-down aircraft factory at Gosport in Hampshire. Their intention was to manufacture motorcycles under the brand name OEC.

At some point the firm was dubbed Odd Engineering Company (or Contraptions) and very likely this sprang from one of its early endeavours – the OEC Blackburne Sidecar Taxi, with large saloon body and a steering wheel instead of handlebars. This was by no means the only oddity that the two men came up with, and their patented Duplex Steering of 1927 was a precursor to devices such as the water-cooled single-cylinder Tinkler and another that almost defies brief description: a conventional front end with Duplex steering and 500cc side-valve engine terminating in an articulated bogie with a pair of wheels in tandem, shod with balloon tyres and demountable rubber tracks. Having said that, however, the vast majority of OEC's output consisted of fairly straightforward machines powered by Villiers, JAP or Blackburne engines housed in rigid duplex or semi-duplex frames with conventional girder forks.

OEC also found a champion in moneyed racing motorcyclist Claude Temple, who became involved in the firm financially – as it did in the rebuilding and building of some of his record-breaking machines. In 1926 Temple set a new motorcycle speed record of 121.3mph at Arpajon, France on his Temple-Anzani, which had become OEC-Temple-Anzani. He next

Now operating at the Atlanta Works, Stamshaw Road, Portsmouth the post-war range was, sensibly, but a shadow of the firm's former extravagances. The OEC 125s and 197s, whatever the specification, had the name Atlanta.

Over 20 years leadership in the Lightweight field

1928 O.E.C. introduced their (then completely revolutionary) system of rear suspension.

1930 Rear springing was standardised throughout the complete range of O.E.C. models. The world's maximum speed record was captured by J. S. Wright at 150.74 m.p.h. on an O.E.C.-J.A.P.

1933 O.E.C. introduced the first medium priced 250 cc. rear sprung machine. In the same year, the first 125 cc. model with rear springing and all-welded frame was launched by O.E.C.

1937 The Department of Scientific and Industrial Research commissioned O.E.C. to produce motor cycle combinations of special design for the purpose of testing road surfaces.

1939 The famous O.E.C. Commodore became the first motor cycle ever to be fitted with twin Girling brakes front and rear.

1948 Post-war production began with the introduction of a new sidecar and the Villiers-powered Lightweight with all-welded frame.

1949 The O.E.C. Competition model scored successes in the Cotswold Scramble, Blandford Road Races, the British Championship Scramble, etc.

1950-51 The perfect rear sprung Lightweight.

Amidst the short resumé of what were considered the firm's high points it was a great shame that it continued to promulgate the false record claim of 1930 (described on the next page) – more worthy by far to have put that naughtiness to bed and spoken about the record that the OEC-Temple-JAP did *establish, however briefly, in the same year.*

ENGINE
125 cc. or 197 cc. Villiers two-stroke: single port type with deflectorless piston; ball and roller bearings throughout.

GEAR BOX
Unit construction; engine drive by chain totally enclosed in aluminium oil-bath; single plate clutch; three speeds; gear ratios (125 cc. model) 7.55, 10.57, 20.0; (197 cc. model) 5.33, 7.46, 14.2; folding kick starter; foot-operated gear lever.

LIGHTING
Rectifier lighting; charging a "Lucas" battery from the flywheel generator; full capacity headlamp beam at all speeds; 6½" headlamp with ammeter; "stop" light in tail lamp.

IGNITION
By flywheel magneto of robust design; fully enclosed and waterproof.

CARBURETTOR
Villiers automatic, with efficient air filter and easy starting device; twist grip throttle control.

FRAME
All steel; specially designed loop-type frame of English steel throughout; scientifically welded, without castings or lugs. This method of construction, employed by O.E.C. for many years, combines great strength with low weight. Black enamel finish.

SADDLE
"Lycett" multi-spring seat.

FORKS
O.E.C. telescopic type of proved design; load and rebound taken by compression springs; black enamel finish.

WHEELS
Chromium plated rims; rustless spokes; "Dunlop" tyres (125 cc. model) 2.75 x 19; (197 cc.) 3.00 x 19; internal expanding brakes (front) 4", (rear) 5".

TANK
Welded steel for petroil mixture; capacity 2¼ gallons; enamelled polychromatic silver.

EXHAUST
Low level exhaust pipe; large capacity silencer of maximum efficiency; chromium plated.

MUDGUARDS
5" wide dome section type front and rear; enamelled polychromatic silver.

HANDLEBARS
Adjustable sports type with normal controls and twist-grip throttle.

EQUIPMENT
Electric horn; rear "stop" light; central stand; tool box; tool kit; tyre inflator; licence holder.

WEIGHT
Tank empty (125 cc. model) 180 lbs. (197 cc. model) 190 lbs.

We may be compelled by circumstances beyond our control to vary the above specification from time to time without notice.

For the standard 1952 models just a rigid loop frame and a pair of very ordinary telescopic forks.

had the firm build a machine from scratch with a supercharged JAP V-twin featuring Duplex steering, and with it Joe Wright retook the record from Brough-Superior, also at Arpajon, by covering the two-way kilometre at an average of 137.23. Hardly had this been ratified before BMW's star Ernst Henne nudged it a fraction of a mile-an-hour higher, encouraging Temple and Wright to seek out a long straight road in Southern Ireland where they might unleash the OEC-Temple-JAP. Some record books will tell you that they were successful, leaving the record at just over 150mph, and in a way they were – but using another machine. With the OEC misbehaving, as it often did, Temple had substituted his old Zenith-JAP at the last minute. Zenith didn't need the publicity (as the company was going out of business) but OEC did, so a large white lie was perpetrated and the latter's bike went on display as the record-breaker.

Not that it did the Gosport firm much good in the long run, as the official receiver was shortly to come calling; the factory, adjoining houses and all plant and equipment was auctioned off in the November of 1931.

Before long, however, and almost certainly with financial aid from national and local dealers Glanfield Lawrence, OEC was back in business at new premises at Highbury Street, Portsmouth. There, throughout the 1930s, the company produced an almost bewildering variety of machines – nearly all of which featured the variety of pivoted-fork rear suspension the firm had patented a few years earlier, and either girder or Duplex front forks. Engines ranged from large JAP V-twins to small Villiers two-strokes, but in between the majority originated from AJS or Matchless.

In 1933 OEC built some racers with Rudge engines for the TT but had no more luck than normal on the Island, with none reaching the finish. The firm's best result had been in 1924 with an eighth place in the Junior, but retirements blighted the majority of the 16 races entered between 1922 and 1935.

Seemingly still unable to resist acting upon Fred Wood's occasional flights of fancy the company returned to eccentricity by unleashing the Whitwood Monocar onto the unsuspecting public during 1934. More ridiculous in many ways than his earlier designs, this one was in effect a small two-wheeled open touring car that accommodated two people in tandem. With a tubular frame, the company's Duplex steering and powered by a range of engines – from a small two-stroke to a large V-twin – it was in effect a motorcycle with a steering wheel. However, as you couldn't put your feet down to keep it upright when at rest, it was equipped with a pair of ineffective-looking stabiliser wheels. To whet your appetite I'll tempt you with one or two extracts from its brochure: "The long-desired car on two wheels... Safer than any vehicle on the roads today and easier to drive... Brings the joy of luxurious private road travel to all classes." How many were sold I can't tell you but I've never set eyes on one or likely ever will. However, the thing was catalogued from 1934 until 1936.

I've never ridden one of the Duplex OECs either, but from period reports on the experience it is clear that directional stability was outstanding: *Motor Cycling* in June 1928 wrote, "Over bad going one can plough through liquid mud, over pot holes,

125 c.c. Villiers Mk. 10D engine ; ball and roller bearings throughout ; flat top piston ; light alloy cylinder head.
Gear Box. Unit construction with engine ; totally enclosed primary drive in aluminium oil bath ; gear ratios 7.55, 10.57, 20.0.
Carburettor. Villiers, with air filter and strangler.
Ignition. Flywheel magneto, fully enclosed.
Lighting. Rectifier lighting, charging a Lucas battery from flywheel generator.
Frame and Forks. Loop frame with rear suspension ; welded construction throughout ; telescopic front forks.
Fuel Tank. Welded steel tank with large filter cap ; capacity 2½ gallons.
Wheels. Rustless spokes ; 19″ rims ; " Dunlop " tyres 2.75 x 19″; internal expanding brakes.
Finish. Black and polychromatic silver ; stove enamelled.

This is the 1952 SS 1 – designating rectifier lighting with battery, spring frame and 125cc. The SS 2 had the same specs other than a 197cc 6E Villiers. Models with rigid frame and rectifier lighting were the S 1 and S 2 respectively. For those who wanted to save money by having simple direct lighting there were the rigid-framed D 1 and D 2 or, a little bit pricier, the sprung-framed SD 1 and SD 2.

rocks, ruts, tree-stumps and everything else in a way that simply cannot be done with any conventional machine." Or how about *Motor Sport* of June 1928? –"You can ride along hands off and punch as hard as you can either end of the bars and simply nothing happens, the bus just 'shivers' and goes straight on." The latter feat, however unlikely it sounds, was quite possible due to system's steering geometry, which imparted a powerful self-centring action that was well nigh impossible to overcome – the front of machine rising if the handlebars were forced to either side. This, coupled with an almost laughably bad steering lock and an odd appearance, were peculiarities to be borne by the everyday owner-rider; but one might ponder on why it was not further refined and adopted more widely if it was so very fool-proof.

A little more conventional than the Monocar, but still odd, was the Duplex-steered Atlanta Duo – a low-slung motorcycle with even lower seating for two between the wheels, made possible by its steeply-canted and forward-mounted engine. It was proudly exhibited on OEC's Motor Cycle Show stand but the public were unenthusiastic.

By the time that war was declared OEC had reined itself in and offered a three-model range with the 500 Commodore as the flagship. All had girder forks as standard with Duplex steering as an option – but how the company loved that word: the 1939 Matchless Clubman-engined Commander was advertised as having duplex Girling braking.

Portsmouth's naval dockyard (and other naval and military establishments) became prime targets for Nazi bombers when large raids got under way in the summer of 1940; and outside of London the city was amongst the most heavily bombed of any in England – suffering nearly 70 air raids, including three of Blitz proportions, over the ensuing years. Situated as it was just to the south of the docks, the OEC factory was in a high-risk area and luck ran out during the first Blitz on 10 January 1941, when Highbury Street was repeatedly hit and the works decimated.

Salvaging what little it could and taking new premises at the top of Stamshaw Road, the company first carried out engineering and fabrication work before recommencing motorcycle manufacture in the late 1940s. Content, this time around, to stick almost exclusively to Villiers-engined lightweights, it remained amongst the less successful firms similarly employed.

Its sole digression from two-strokery came about in the autumn of 1951 with the idea that the same feeble 250 side-valve that powered Brockhouse's Indian Brave would be a worthwhile addition to its wares. It wasn't, of course, but as the inaptly-named Apollo it lasted as long as long as the firm's motorcycle production, which withered and died out by the end of 1954. There is a small memorial, however, insomuch as the Stamshaw Road site of its last factory is still, as of 2015, known as the Atlanta Works and a neighbouring property Osborn House.

The O.E.C. method of rear suspension is unique in the lightweight field. Of welded construction throughout, the rear frame unit is complete in itself, and is bolted to the main frame.

The rear fork is of 1⅛″ dia. steel tubing, pivoted on a fixed ⅞″ dia. spindle. The special fibre bushes used for bearings require the minimum of lubrication and attention. Phosphorbronze washers take the side thrust.

The looped sub-frame to which the rear fork is mounted is of ¾″ dia. tubing. To this lugs are welded to provide anchorage for the top spring housing. The spring units are a pair of telescopic tubes with a variable rate spring secured at each end, controlling both load and rebound action. Movement is smooth and progressive through approximately 2″ range.

By now the system of rear suspension devised in the late 1920s had been abandoned in favour of this. As far as I can see it is swinging-arm by any other name; but if it wasn't then yes, it was unique. Besides, whilst OEC may have been at the forefront of springer lightweights it was by no means alone – James and Tandon, to name two others.

125 cc. Engine. Bore 50 mm. x 62 mm.; stroke develops 4.9 b.h.p. at 4,400 r.p.m.

197 cc. Engine. Bore 59 mm. x 72 mm.; stroke develops 7.5 b.h.p. at 4,000 r.p.m.

Frame and Forks. Special competition type, with high ground clearance and saddle.

125 cc & 197 cc MODELS

Ground Clearance. 7½″.

Saddle Height. 31″.

Handlebars. ⅞″ dia.; 30″ wide; chromium plated; clip-on controls.

Wheels. Chromium plated 19″ rims; rustless spokes; "Dunlop" Universal tyres, 2.75 front and 3.25 rear.

Mudguards. Polished aluminium alloy; tubular stays.

Exhaust. Designed for maximum efficiency and ease of maintenance.

There was no sprung-frame option for the competition models, which were designated the C 1 (125cc) and C 2 (197cc).

The Brockhouse-powered Apollo.

In 1953, at what would prove to be OEC's last stand at the Motor Cycle Show, they had some fresh machinery, including the ST3 Competition 197cc with square-tube frame, swinging-arm suspension and this system of crossover final drive that ensured constant rear chain tension. The road-going ST2 version had the same type of frame and suspension but its drive chains all on one side. Also on the stand were examples of the lesser SS1 with round-tube frames, with 125s and 197s plus the 250cc Brockhouse-engined Apollo.

the new **OEC**

Sidecar

FOR LARGER MOTOR CYCLES

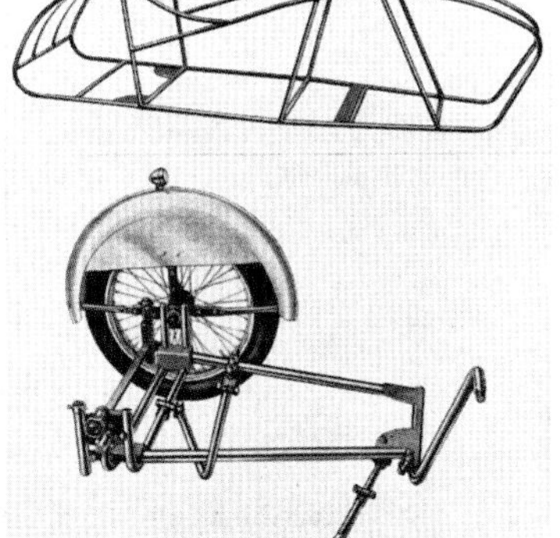

The O.E.C. sidecar is new: new in design, and new in construction. With its proved road holding and suspension, it offers a new standard of sidecar comfort.

The chassis is an all-welded tubular structure of the simplest kind. It is extremely strong and, due to the absence of heavy castings, is very much lighter than a comparable chassis of orthodox construction. The body is almost entirely of metal. Light gauge steel tubing is employed to make a completely welded frame unit which is panelled with aluminium-alloy sheet. This lightweight construction makes possible a body with increased interior space, giving much greater comfort to the passenger.

The suspension leaves nothing to be desired. At the rear, enclosed coil springs and plunger (much after the style of the famous O.E.C. motor cycle rear springing) provide a type of underslung suspension with an extremely low centre of gravity. The front of the body is rubber-mounted directly to the chassis thus controlling all pitching and swaying of the front, and minimising vibration.

Manufacturers of suitable machinery to hitch them to, such as BSA and Norton, catalogued their own sidecars – so not only was OEC vying for their business, it was more especially that of specialist makers such as Watsonian and Canterbury. Efforts amounted to little, however, as within a year-or-so the company would be out of business.

PANTHER

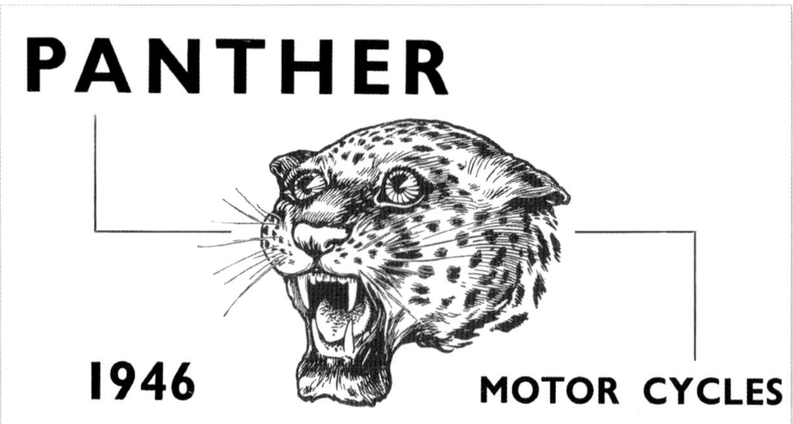

"Day and Night, throughout six long years, we have devoted all our energies and resources to winning the War. Some of Britain's finest weapons contain parts which we have manufactured, and we are now better trained and better equipped to build Motor Cycles than ever before," read the introduction to the first post-war brochure.

Commencing with a feature that would become synonymous with his firm's motorcycles, Joah Phelon, in partnership with his nephew Harry Rayner, designed and built a machine in 1900, patenting this feature – the utilisation of a sloping single-cylinder engine as a frame front down-tube – at the same time. A lack of finance and the death of Harry Rayner in a motoring accident led to an arrangement with Humber to manufacture it under licence, but by 1904 Joah had a fresh partner named Richard Moore and, with royalty disputes also a factor, set up as Phelon and Moore at Cleckheaton in Yorkshire.

Early plans were for a three-wheeler fore-car but they were soon abandoned in favour of motorcycles. From the first, P&M (as they were known) remained faithful to Phelon's original concept of a sloping engine forming a stressed member of the frame and fully chain-driven – but by now with two-speeds, worked by friction clutches and twin primary chains, which had been intended for the three-wheeler. This system dictated the deletion of pedals, and so the P&M became the first British motorcycle to rely on engine power alone, rather than varying degrees of pedal assistance – an innovation that attracted derision until its four-stroke 300cc power unit alone was found to be well up to the job. A foot-operated gear-change was also a novelty embodied in early products but this soon gave way to a tank-side lever operating the gears via chain and sprockets, and kick-starting was introduced in 1912.

By this time an engine of 499cc had been standardised, and P&Ms took part in the first ISDT in 1913, as well as other long-distance trials – the reputation thus gained resulting in worthwhile government contracts for the supply of large quantities of similar machines to the Royal Flying Corps during the forthcoming hostilities. A four-speed 770cc V-twin was under development at the time the Great War began but it was catalogued for just 1915 before being dropped due to prevailing conditions – its gearbox, however, reappeared in a new single of some 550cc that was introduced late in 1922. Named the Panther, as would be all subsequent P&Ms, it was a sporting machine with low riding position but was the last side-valve engine machine that the firm would make, and was superseded by an OHV version with Granville Bradshaw-designed motor for 1924.

Webb forks and a saddle tank were introduced the following year, and at the 1926 show a minor sensation was caused by the introduction of the 250cc transverse-twin Panthette with four-speed car-type gearbox, also from Bradshaw's drawing board; but sales failed to live up to early interest and it was dropped after perhaps 200 had found customers over a year or so. During this period Panthers put in appearances on the Isle of Man with a trio of machines fielded in 1925 and '26 for the Senior TT. None lasted the course, however, apart from one ridden by Tom Frederick, which surprised the pundits by coming fourth; and in spite of – or because of – this flash in the pan, a TT Special with valves angled at 90 degrees and a guaranteed speed of 90mph was brought out for 1927.

These vagaries done with, the firm fell into line with a number of other manufacturers by calling upon Villiers to supply the power units for more economy-minded products that were added to the 1928 catalogue – a prudent move with the slump oncoming. The following year, with sidecar use very much in mind, the 600cc '100' made its first appearance, the firm seemingly unaffected by the recent death of its founder Joah Phelon.

Twin headlamps, one of which the rider could swivel by means of a handlebar control, were an attention-getter for a while on the big Panthers a couple of years later – a novelty that was of less use in practice than theory! The first of the Red Panthers was introduced in 1932, a 250 overhead-valve single, with a 350 version added in 1933 – the smaller model later achieving a little notoriety on account of it being, for a while at least, the cheapest new machine you could buy due to a factory arrangement with South London dealers Pride and Clarke, who put them out for a few shillings under £30.

The mid '30s-onwards saw the larger Panthers used for some newsworthy endurance activities that proved their ruggedness, such as the exploits of intrepid Misses Wallach and Blenkiron, who rode from London to Cape Town on a 600 Redwing sidecar outfit complete with a trailer; or the solo that completed a well-publicised 10,000-mile marathon on English soil.

World War Two resulted in a suspension of motorcycle output whilst the factory fulfilled engineering contracts for the government, followed by an all-but-unchanged resumption for the Cleckheaton manufacturer. In common with some other makes it hung on to girder forks for a while but they soon gave way to proprietary Dowty Oleomatics.

At the end of 1949, the days of the 'sloper' (60 and 70) 250s and 350s ended with the introduction of vertical cylinders – the new models, which also boasted cradle frames, becoming the 65 and 75 with a competition version in either capacity. The first of the rear-sprung Panthers appeared in 1953 and a swinging-arm frame was coupled with the firm's own telescopic forks on all models, with a rigid frame version of the 100 remaining current for traditionalists.

By the mid 1950s, despite their upgrades, the smaller four-strokes were rapidly dating and lacked a following such as was enjoyed by the firm's even more dated big slopers, so to boost sales what was perceived as a trendy range of Villiers-powered lightweights was introduced at the '56 show.

Sales of these were becoming increasingly important as the gradual decline in the popularity of the motorcycle and sidecar was gathering momentum, even though enough stalwarts remained to ensure the continuance of Panther's 594cc 100, and even its enlargement to the 645cc 120 model 1959.

A while before this the firm had hit upon the idea of importing French Terrot scooters to generate additional income, but when sales failed to live up to expectations it embarked upon what would turn out to be a less-than-fortuitous foray into manufacturing

P & M Panthers continued more or less where they had left off before the war, seeing no immediate necessity to alter the basic concepts that they had adhered to since the 1920s even though changes were in the pipeline. Although this is the Model 60 there was a visually all but identical Model 70 with a bore of 71mm that brought it up to 348cc. It also had a 4-speed Burman gearbox with slightly higher overall ratios that gave it a (manufacturer's) top speed of 75 and a 100-mpg fuel consumption.

Specification of 1946 Model 60 PANTHER

These machines are the modern de-luxe editions of the famous Models 20 and 30 Red Panthers. The outstanding efficiency and economy of these engines are known throughout the world and many thousands of enthusiastic owners have testified to the qualities of these two models.

ENGINE Panther design and manufacture throughout. 60 mm. bore × 88 mm. stroke, 248 c.c. Compression ratio 6·5. Long full-skirted piston with two compression rings and oil control ring. Double-row roller big-end. Engine shafts carried on roller journal and phosphor-bronze bearings. Valve gear fully enclosed and pressure lubricated. All-gear drive to pump and dynamo. Contact breaker driven from camshaft and in a very accessible position on timing cover. Semi-dry sump incorporated in crankcase ensures quick circulation of oil from cold and external cleanliness. Downdraught carburettor.

FRAME Constructed of straight high carbon steel tubes throughout with forged steel lugs. Central spring-up stand. Pillion footrest attachments incorporated.

FORKS Webb girder pattern. Damper adjustable from the saddle.

TANK 2½ gallons petrol capacity, streamline. Finished in royal blue with eggshell-blue panel, lined in gold. Embossed Panther name-plates in red and chromium.

GEAR Burman 3-speed gears with enclosed foot control. Ratios 5·9, 9·5, 15·5. 3-plate clutch with cork inserts running in oil.

TRANSMISSION Spring cam shock absorber on engine shaft. Gear box and rear spindle are adjusted by twin cams so that correct alignment of the chain drive is maintained under all conditions. The primary chain is enclosed in an oil bath case and the rear chain has an effective cover.

WHEELS AND BRAKES Heavy duty rims with 26″ × 3·25″ tyres. Journal ball bearings, non-adjustable in both hubs. Rear brake 6″ diameter, rod operated. Front brake 6″ diameter.

SILENCER Burgess absorption silencer of latest cylindrical pattern.

IGNITION AND LIGHTING 36 watt dynamo. Contact breaker on timing case driven by camshaft at half-engine speed gives remarkably easy starting. Coil fully protected under tank. 13 amp. hour accumulator. 7″ headlamp with fluted glass 18/18 Diplite main bulb. Rear lamp of modern design.

SADDLE Terry spring seat.

HANDLEBARS 1″ diameter chromium bar with adjustable controls.

FINISH Black with heavy gold lining throughout.

WEIGHT 280 lbs.

WHEELBASE 53″

OVERALL LENGTH 82″

PETROL CONSUMPTION 110 m.p.g.

OIL CONSUMPTION 2,500 m.p.g.

SPEED 65 m.p.h.

one of its own. Despite reducing manufacturing costs by getting together with other scooter-minded manufacturers Sun and Dayton, the Panther Princess, which hit the market in 1959, made little headway against the by-then firmly-entrenched Italian makes and was largely responsible for the firm's path towards the official receiver, who was called in during 1962.

Remarkably, especially as by this time the sidecar market had all but evaporated due to the affordability and popularity of the Mini and other relatively cheap small family cars, it carried on and outlived this book's dateline. With a much-reduced range, along with other engineering work to try and make ends meet, the books still didn't balance, even though the scooter had been discontinued in '64.

By 1966 there was just the electric-start 35 Villiers 2T twin along with the 120 de luxe, each leaving the factory in penny numbers for another couple of years. In 1968, although it had no interest in the motorcycle side of the business, Samuel Birkett, a local (Heckmondwike) manufacturer of valves and engineering fittings, acquired P&M, itself becoming part of Imperial Metal Industries ten years later

The marathon referred to was widely advertised by Panther stalwart and dealer Frank Leach, later briefly a manufacturer in his own right (see FLM), who doubtless gained a good number of sales for his Leeds dealership on the back of it. It was however undertaken by a team of four riders who took it in turns to slog up and down between North London and Leeds for 10,000 miles at an average speed of over 40 including stops. In 1939 the Model 100 was known as the Redwing and had a smaller triangular shaped toolbox and unvalanced rear mudguard but was otherwise as the one illustrated here.

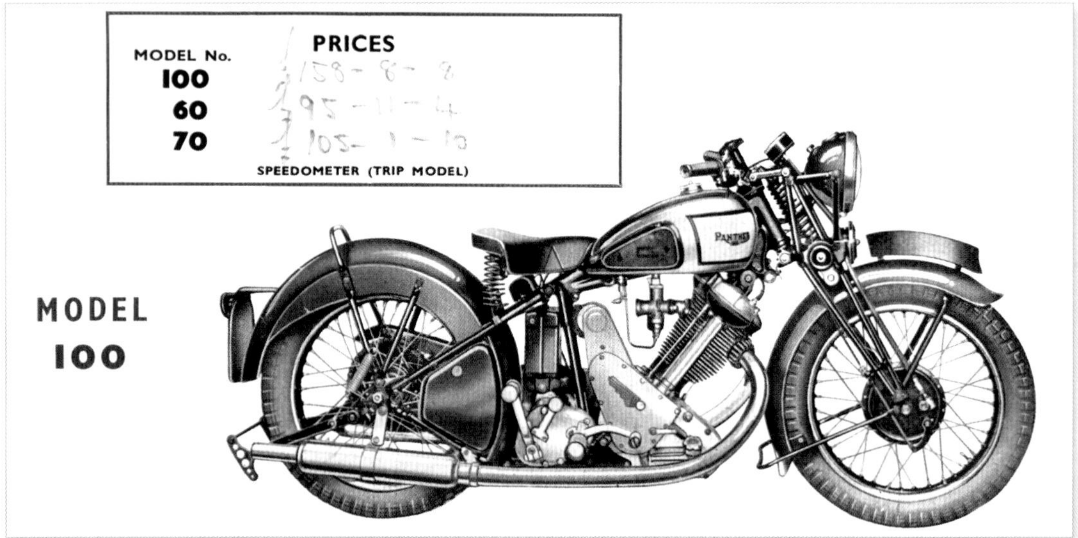

This great machine has been developed to its present stage of perfection over a great many years. This model has an enormously strong construction and has recently become known as the marathon model, having completed under A.C.U. observation in March, 1939, the greatest test to which a motor cycle has ever been subject. It was run continuously day and night over a distance of 10,000 miles. This distance was covered in just over ten days and the machine was still in perfect condition.

Its supremacy as a side-car machine was also strikingly demonstrated by gaining the award for the best side-car performance in the Scottish Six Days' Trial—the severest organised competitive test held in the British Isles.

ENGINE Panther design and manufacture throughout. O.H.V., 87 mm. bore × 100 mm. stroke. 598 c.c. Compression ratio 6·5.

Slipper piston with two compression rings and oil control ring for improved cold starting. Double-row roller big-end. Engine shafts carried on widely spaced ball and roller journals. Valve gear fully enclosed and pressure lubricated. All-gear drive to pump and magneto. Gears precision-cut in 60-ton nickel chrome steel. Semi-dry sump incorporated with crankcase ensures quick oil circulation from cold and external cleanliness. Crankcase adequately ventilated. Oil capacity half a gallon. Half compression device ensures easy starting.

FRAME Cantilever frame of high carbon steel tubes with forged steel lugs. Sidecar and pillion footrest attachments incorporated. Roller rear stand.

FORKS Panther-Webb girder fork with phosphor-bronze bushes and ground spindles. Four-plate damper is anchored in rubber and is self-aligning and adjustable from the saddle. Steering damper.

TANK Streamline chromium tank, panelled cream and lined red and black. Embossed Panther name-plates in red and chromium. Hinged filler cap and twin petrol taps fitted with filter. Capacity 3¼ gallons.

GEAR Burman 4-speed with fully enclosed operation. Footstarter and foot control are fully adjustable to suit individual riding position. Clutch fitted with Neoprene inserts and running in oil. Ratios, solo: 4·3, 5·8, 7·3 and 11·5.

TRANSMISSION Shock absorber built into rear hub. Positive central adjustment of gear in both directions for primary drive. Rear spindle adjusted by twin cams so that correct alignment of the chain drive is maintained under all conditions. Primary chain ½" × ·305" in cast aluminium oil bath. Rear chain ⅝" × ⅜", automatically oiled by adjustable feed.

SILENCERS Twin Burgess absorption silencers of latest cylindrical pattern.

WHEELS AND BRAKES Heavy duty rims with 26" × 3·25 tyres. Journal bearings, non-adjustable in both hubs. Rear brake 8" diameter, rod operated. Front brake 7" diameter.

IGNITION AND LIGHTING Latest type Lucas magneto-driven through Panther quick detachable coupling. 36 watt dynamo driven by silent duplex chain fully enclosed. 7" dia. headlamp with fluted glass. 24/24 Diplite main bulb. Latest pattern rear lamp. 13 amp. hour accumulator.

HANDLEBARS Rubber mounted, chromium-plated bars with fully adjustable controls.

SADDLE Terry spring seat.

FINISH Black with red lines. Rims chromium-plated with black centres lined red.

WEIGHT 385 lbs. including standard equipment.

WHEELBASE 54"

OVERALL LENGTH 83"

WIDTH OVER HANDLEBARS 29"

SPEED Solo, 85 m.p.h. Sidecar, 65 m.p.h.

PETROL CONSUMPTION Solo, 90 m.p.g. Sidecar, 60 m.p.g.

OIL CONSUMPTION 2,000 m.p.g.

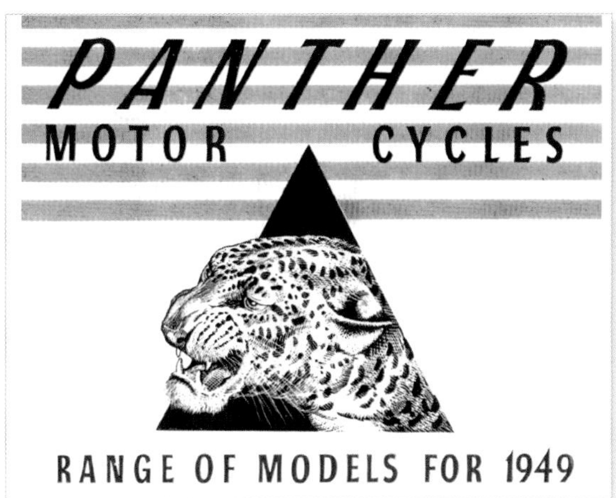

Although both 65 and 75 engines had the same appearance this is the 350cc version with Lucas K.1F auto advance magneto: the 250 had coil ignition. Tappets were accessed for adjustment by undoing the two nuts at the base of the pushrod tunnel and sliding the lower portion up to expose them.

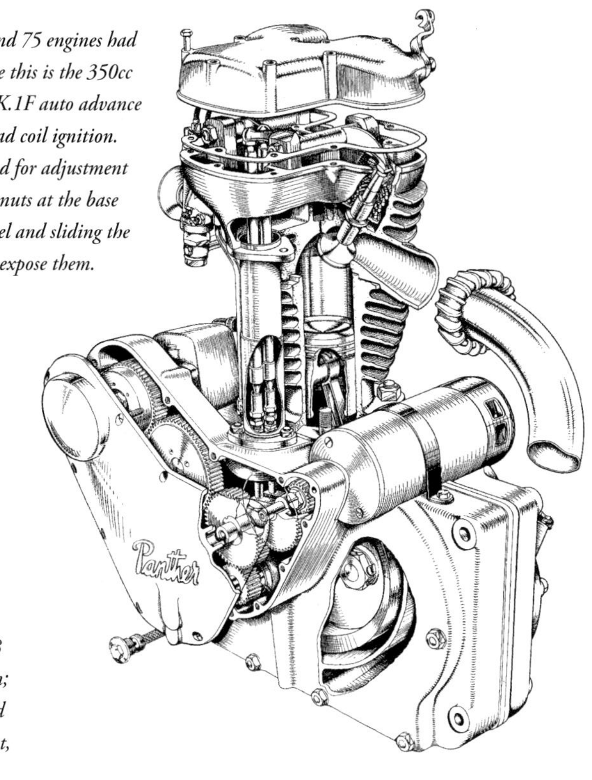

'The Panther is built by engineering craftsmen in the West Riding of Yorkshire where mechanical ability is handed down from father to son and only the highest standards of workmanship are recognised'.

Dowty Oleomatic forks had been introduced on all models for 1947 but in the September of 1948 new engines for the smaller Panthers were introduced along with a cradle frame to mount them in; the 250 becoming the 65 and the 350 the 75. Dimensions such as bore and stroke were unchanged but the barrel and head surmounted an entirely different set of castings as well as standing upright, giving them quite a different appearance.

SPECIFICATION OF THE 1949 MODEL 65 PANTHER

ENGINE. 60 M.M. bore x 88 M.M. stroke 248 c.c. O.H.V. Compression ratio 6·5 to 1. Non-slap Hepolite piston with two compression rings and oil control ring. Double row roller big-end. Lead-bronze bearings to crankshaft with pressure oil feeds. All gear drive to valveless oil pump, dynamo and contact breaker. Valve gear fully enclosed and pressure lubricated. Accessible tappet adjustment at base of push rods. High tensile steel connecting rod.

LUBRICATION. Semi-dry sump incorporated with crankcase ensures quick oil circulation from cold and external cleanliness. Large oil filter extremely accessible at base of sump. Sump capacity $2\frac{1}{2}$ pints.

FRAME. Full cradle type constructed of straight tubes throughout of high carbon steel with forged steel lugs. Steering head $6\frac{1}{4}$″ long.

FORKS. Dowty Oleomatic giving progressive air springing with oil damping. Instant adjustment for any weight of rider or riding conditions—solo or pillion.

TRANSMISSION. Spring cam shock absorber on engine shaft. Front chain fully enclosed in oil bath chaincase. Rear chain protected by effective guard. Rear wheel spindle is adjusted by twin cams so that correct alignment of the chain is maintained under all conditions.

GEARBOX. New type Burman fully enclosed 3 speed positive stop foot control. Ratio 6·05, 10 and 16 to 1. 3 plate clutch with cork inserts running in oil.

ELECTRICAL EQUIPMENT. 40 watt dynamo mounted in front and contact breaker with automatic advance and retard mounted behind engine, both accessible. Coil fully protected under tank. Large headlamp with ammeter and switch in body. Latest pattern domed fluted lamp glass giving powerful long-range wide angle beam.

TANK. Capacity $2\frac{7}{8}$ gallons. Fitted with two taps, one for reserve, rubber mounted and with embossed Panther nameplates.

WHEELS AND BRAKES. Heavy duty rims, rustless spokes. Non-adjustable journal ball bearings in both hubs. Rear brake $6\frac{1}{2}$″ and front 6″.

STAND. Central spring up.

FINISH. Frame, mudguards, wheels, chain cases, rims and forks finished black. Tank finished in royal blue with eggshell blue panel, lined in gold.

WEIGHT. (Dry) 304 lbs.

WHEELBASE. 54″.

OVERALL LENGTH. 83″.

PETROL CONSUMPTION. 110 M.P.G.

OIL CONSUMPTION. 2,500 M.P.G.

SPEED. 65 M.P.H.

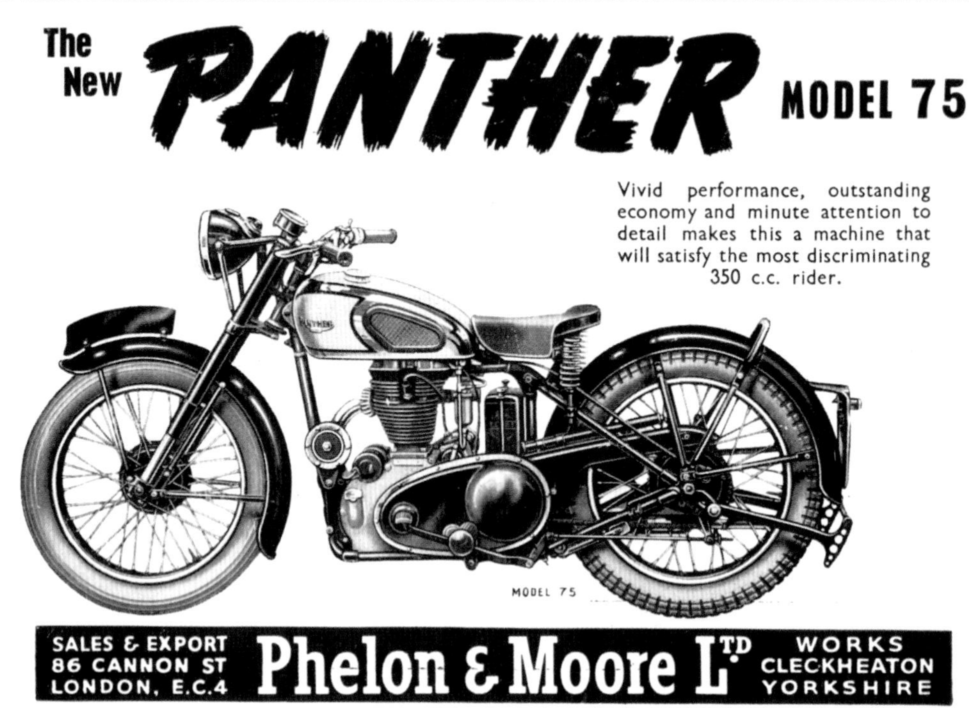

This kind of fuel consumption (90mpg) from a large capacity engine, providing it was achieved at a reasonable average speed, harked back to the kind of figures achieved by the likes of Norton singles way before the war.

SPECIFICATION OF THE 1949 MODEL 100 PANTHER

ENGINE. 87 M.M. bore x 100 M.M. stroke 598 c.c. O.H.V. Compression ratio 6·5 to 1. Hepolite slipper piston with two compression rings and oil control ring for improved cold starting. Double row roller big-end. Engine shafts carried on widely spaced ball and roller journals. Valve gear fully enclosed and pressure lubricated. All gear drive to pump and magneto. Gears precision-cut in 60 ton nickel chrome steel. Half compression device ensures easy starting. Two-port exhaust gives exceptional quietness and cool running.

LUBRICATION. Semi-dry sump incorporated with crankcase ensures quick oil circulation from cold, and external cleanliness. Crankcase adequately ventilated and heavily finned to ensure oil does not overheat. Oil capacity half a gallon.

FRAME. Cantilever frame of high carbon steel tubes with forged steel lugs. An unusual feature of this frame is that the engine forms an integral part. Originally introduced by us many years ago this strong and rigid construction has proved capable of standing up to the most arduous conditions of solo or sidecar work and is practically unbreakable. Sidecar lugs are incorporated for attachment of the sidecar to the left or right hand side.

FORKS. Heavy duty Dowty Oleomatic Telescopics giving progressive air springing with oil damping. Individual adjustment to any weight of rider or riding conditions—solo, pillion or sidecar. Sliding members reversible for correct solo or sidecar steering, wheel lugs forward for sidecar and backwards for solo. Adjustable friction type steering damper.

TRANSMISSION. Shock absorber built into rear hub. Front chain fully enclosed in oil-bath polished aluminium chaincase. Rear chain protected by effective guard. Rear spindle adjusted by twin cams so that correct alignment of the chain drive is maintained under all conditions. Adjustable oil feed to back chain from primary chaincase.

GEARBOX. Heavyweight Burman Type BA 4 speed positive stop foot control. Solo ratios: 4·3, 5·8, 7·3 and 11·5 to 1. Sidecar ratios: 5·1, 6·4, 8·7 and 13·7 to 1. Footstart and foot change levers fully adjustable. Clutch fitted Neoprene inserts and running in oil.

ELECTRICAL Magneto driven through Panther quickly detachable coupling. 40 watt dynamo driven by silent duplex chain fully enclosed Automatic advance and retard within timing case. Large headlamp with ammeter and switch in body. Latest type domed fluted lamp glass giving long-range wide angle beam.

TANK. Streamlined tank fitted two taps, one for reserve, rubber mounted and with embossed Panther nameplates and kneegrips. Capacity 3 gallons.

WHEELS AND BRAKES. Heavy duty rims and rustless spokes. Non-adjustable journal bearings to hubs. Rear brake 8″ diameter, rod operated. Front brake 7″ diameter.

STANDS. Roller rear stand and tubular front stand.

FINISH. Frame, mudguards, rear chain case and forks finished black, gold lined. Wheel rims chromium plated with black centres lined red. Chromium plated tank with cream panels, lined red and black.

WEIGHT. 385 lbs.

WHEELCASE. 54″.

OVERALL LENGTH. 83″.

WIDTH OVER HANDLEBARS. 29″.

PETROL CONSUMPTION. Solo, 90 M.P.G., Sidecar, 60 M.P.G.

OIL CONSUMPTION. 2,000 M.P.G.

SPEED. Solo, 85 M.P.H.; Sidecar, 60 M.P.H.

When ordering the buyer should specify whether the machine is for solo or sidecar use so that the machine is supplied with the correct fork setting and gear ratios to give maximum efficiency.

STROUD MARK II

250/350 c.c. OHV

Putting up a good record all over the world as a trials and scramble machine, these motorcycles are produced specially for selected individuals for competition work, and are not offered as ordinary road machines.

As a result of experience gained in the last few years, we offer the Mark II with several modifications, and we ask riders who are genuinely interested in using these machines to write to us direct for any further information they require.

The specification includes 1½ gallon tank, waterproof saddle, low level upswept exhaust pipe, Lucas "Wading" magneto with manual control, crankcase shield and twin petroflex fuel pipes. The finish is chromium tank panelled cream, lined red and black, chromium rims centered cream lined red, and polished aluminium alloy mudguards. Dynamo and lighting equipment including quick detachable headlamp is available as an extra.

It's a **PANTHER** for 1951!

Model	65	65 de Luxe	75	100	Stroud 250	Stroud 350
Bore and Stroke	60m.m. × 88m.m.	60m.m. × 88m.m.	71m.m. × 88m.m.	87m.m. × 100m.m.	60m.m. × 88m.m.	71m.m. × 88m.m.
Comp. Ratio	6·5	6·5	6·5	6·5	6·5	6·5
Ignition	Lucas Coil	Lucas Coil	Lucas Magneto	Lucas Magneto	Lucas Magneto	Lucas Magneto
Capacities Petrol	2⅞ gals.	2⅞ gals.	2⅞ gals.	3 gals.	1½ gals.	1½ gals.
Capacities Oil	2½ pints	2½ pints	2½ pints	4 pints	2½ pints	2½ pints
Chains Front	½″ × ·305″ × ·335″	½″ × ·305″ × ·335″	½″ × ·305″ × ·335″	½″ × ·305″ × ·335″	½″ × ·305″ × ·335″	½″ × ·305″ × ·335″
Chains Rear	½″ × ·305″ × ·335″	½″ × ·305″ × ·335″	½″ × ·305″ × ·335″	⅝″ × ⅜″	⅝″ × ·308″ × ·4	⅝″ × ·308″ × ·4
Gear Ratios 1	15·94	15·67	14·05	Solo 11·98 Side-car 13·61	24·00	21·75
Gear Ratios 2	9·78	10·34	9·25	7·04 8·00	15·5	14·00
Gear Ratios 3	6·04	7·52	6·73	5·65 6·42	9·5	8·75
Top		5·88	5·26	4.49 5·10	7·25	6·75
Tyres Front	Dunlop Ribbed 26 × 3·25	Dunlop Ribbed 26 × 3·25	Dunlop Ribbed 26 × 3·25	Dunlop Ribbed 26 × 3·25	Dunlop Universal 21 × 2·75	Dunlop Universal 21 × 2·75
Tyres Rear	Dunlop Universal 26 × 3·25	Dunlop Universal 26 × 3·25	Dunlop Universal 26 × 3·25	Dunlop Universal 26 × 3·50	Dunlop Universal 19 × 4·00	Dunlop Universal 19 × 4·00
Brakes Front	6″	6″	6″	7″	6″	6″
Brakes Rear	6½″	6½″	6½″	8″	8″	8″
Weight Dry	304 lbs.	306 lbs.	314 lbs.	385 lbs.	273 lbs.	273 lbs.
Wheel Base	54″	54″	54″	54″	54″	54″
Overall Length	83″	83″	83″	83″	83″	83″

During 1949, after extended testing by factory riders, Competition versions of both 250 and 350 Panther became available to the public; known as the 'Stroud' they had 4-speed gearboxes with trials ratios as standard. This is the improved 1951 version. By 1953 the 1½-gallon fuel tank was finished in Polychromatic Blue with cream side panels; but more significantly they were equipped with alloy barrels and heads.

This was the second season for sprung versions of the 65 and 75 but the first for the 100.

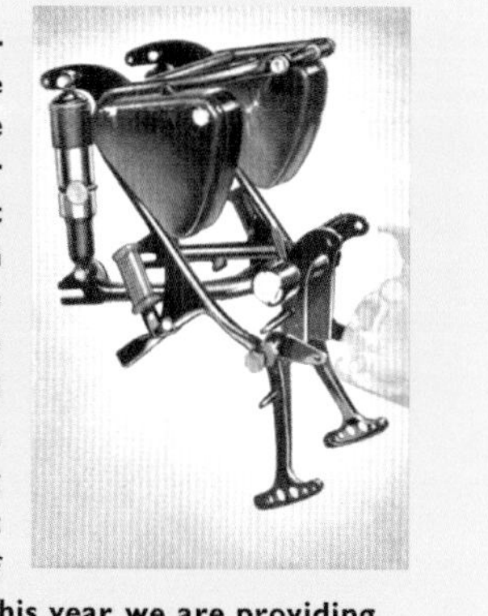

Our Company has been manufacturing Motorcycles since 1901, almost as long as any other in the industry, and far longer than most. During that time our policy has remained constant, to provide our customers with Motorcycles that give them the finest value for every pound they spend. We stick to certain classes of machines and concentrate, by a ceaseless programme of testing and modification, on keeping Panther at the top of the Tree. This year we are providing perfected suspension, both front and rear right through the range.

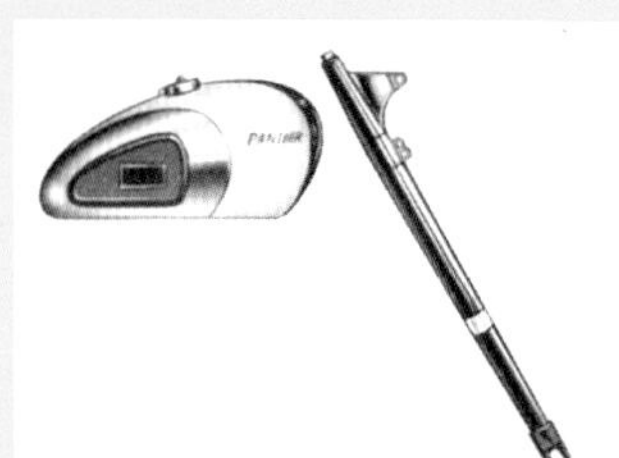

In their 1951 brochure P & M told us that they had made their first motorcycles in 1904. Now, three years later, they tell us they've been making them since 1901. By the time they came to publish the 1959 edition it had crept back to 1900. So which is it? If you count the earliest Phelon and Raynor machine then the latter is correct but Phelon and Moore's did not appear until 1904. This is the rear sub frame for the newly available swinging arm version of the 100, by the way.

A swinging arm frame version of the 65 had been introduced for the 1953 season but the rigid version continued to be listed for those who preferred it or wanted to save £20 or so. Both models had the same main frame but, whilst the forks on the latter were still by Dowty, the springer had Panther's own, as did the rest of the range.

MODEL 65
SPRING FRAME

The de Luxe 250 with the finest specification available anywhere to-day. There is no longer any need for 250 riders to do without any of the refinements enjoyed by riders of larger capacity machines. Full chrome finish, magneto and dual seat are available as extras.

The 'Stroud' itself had been dropped from the catalogue but this 'Stroud' type motor was used for the 75s. It had an alloy head and was unusual in that it had no cam followers and the camshaft acted directly on the base of the tappets.

MODEL 75
SPRING FRAME

Fitted with the new Stroud engine this machine retains its position as the finest 350 c.c. sports machine available. In the equipment is a new silencer, and an aluminium brake cover plate. Petrol tank 3 gallons capacity, chrome plated, panelled blue lined gold, mudguards and chaincase blue, wheels chrome centred, blue lined gold. Dual seat available as an extra.

The 350's sprung frame was quite different from that of the 250 as can be seen here. The cheaper rigid version was finished in the same colours.

MODEL 100 SPRING FRAME

This famous machine is now offered fitted with a swinging arm spring frame. Full provision has been made for sidecar fixing, and a specially designed dual seat is offered as an extra.

Despite the opportunity of greater comfort offered by the new model there was still a large hard core of sidecar men who preferred an unsprung rear end. All rigid models had the option of a dual seat as an extra but also featured the older type rear mudguards devoid of valancing: those on the 100 being in black with gold coach lining. I don't know if you will be able to make it out or not but a feature of the big Panthers was a little decompression lever located on the timing cover, just forward of the gear lever.

MODEL		65 Rigid	65 Springer	75 Rigid	75 Springer	100 Rigid	100 Springer
Bore and Stroke		60×88 mm.	60×88 mm.	71×88 mm.	71×88 mm.	87×100 mm.	87×100 mm.
Compression Ratio		6.5 : 1	6.5 : 1	6.5 : 1	6.5 : 1	6.5 : 1	6.5 : 1
Ignition		Lucas Coil	Lucas Coil	Lucas Magneto	Lucas Magneto	Lucas Magdyno	Lucas Magdyno
Capacities :	Petrol ...	$2\frac{7}{8}$ gals.	$2\frac{7}{8}$ gals.	$3\frac{1}{4}$ gals.	$3\frac{1}{4}$ gals.	4 gals.	4 gals.
	Oil ...	$2\frac{1}{2}$ pts.	$2\frac{1}{2}$ pts.	$2\frac{1}{2}$ pts.	$2\frac{1}{2}$ pts.	4 pts.	4 pts.
Chains :	Front ...	$\frac{1}{2}''\times.305''\times.335''$	$\frac{1}{2}''\times.305''\times.335''$	$\frac{1}{2}''\times.305''\times.335''$	$\frac{1}{2}''\times.305''\times.335''$	$\frac{1}{2}''\times.305''\times.335''$	$\frac{1}{2}''\times.305''\times.335''$
	Rear ...	$\frac{1}{2}''\times.305''\times.335''$	$\frac{1}{2}''\times.305''\times.335''$	$\frac{1}{2}''\times.305''\times.335''$	$\frac{1}{2}''\times.305''\times.335''$	$\frac{5}{8}''\times\frac{3}{8}''$	$\frac{5}{8}''\times\frac{3}{8}''$
Gear Ratios :	1st ...	15.70	15.70	14.04	14.04	Solo 11.98 Side-car 13.62	Solo 11.98 Side-car 13.62
	2nd ...	10.40	10.40	9.26	9.26	7.05 8.00	7.05 8.00
	3rd ...	7.54	7.54	6.73	6.73	5.66 6.43	5.66 6.43
	Top ...	5.88	5.88	5.26	5.26	4.49 5.1	4.49 5.1
Tyres :	Front ...	Dunlop 19×3.25	Dunlop 19×3.25	Dunlop 19×3.25	Dunlop 19×3.25	Dunlop 19×3.25	Dunlop 19×3.25
	Rear ...	Dunlop 19×3.25	Dunlop 19×3.25	Dunlop 19×3.25	Dunlop 19×3.25	Dunlop 19×3.50	Dunlop 19×3.50
Brakes :	Front ...	6" Dia.×1"	6" Dia.× 1"	6" Dia.×1"	6" Dia.×1"	7" Dia.×$1\frac{1}{4}$"	7" Dia.×$1\frac{1}{4}$"
	Rear ...	6" Dia.×1"	6" Dia. × 1"	6" Dia.×1"	6" Dia.×1"	8" Dia.×1"	8" Dia.×1"
Weight, Dry		312 lbs.	330 lbs.	314 lbs.	330 lbs.	406 lbs.	426 lbs.
Wheel Base		54"	56"	54"	56"	54"	56"
Overall Width		29"	29"	29"	29"	30"	30"
Overall Length		83"	85"	83"	85"	85"	85"
Ground Clearance		6"	8"	6"	8"	6"	7"
Saddle Height		29"	30"	29"	30"	29"	30"

We reserve the right to modify or deviate from the printed specifications in this list.

EXTRAS

Dualseats (all Models) 69/-, Pillion Footrests 12/10 per pair, Leg Shields 67/2, Air Cleaners - Model 100 24/-, Models 65/75 31/2, Chrome Rims Models 65 36/-, Chrome Tank Model 65 48/-, Magneto Ignition Models 65 144/-. All prices include Purch. Tax.

SIDECARS

All the leading sidecar manufacturers supply sidecars with the correct fittings for the Panther Model 100. Models 65 and 75 are designed for solo work only.

A happy family with the very latest Model 100 Springer de luxe on the brochure's cover, but who ever would have imagined that P & M would market as many two-strokes as four-strokes.

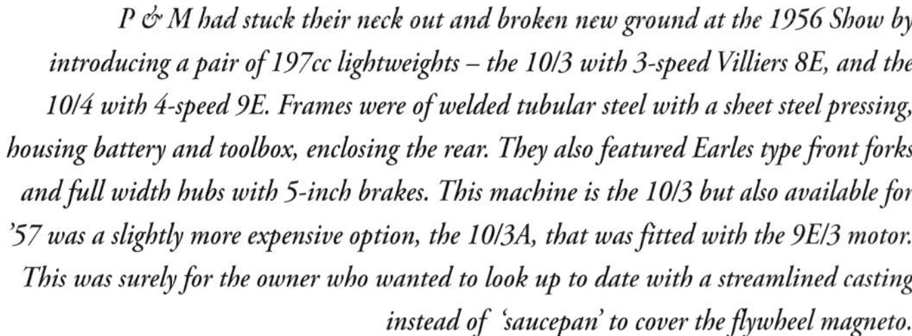

P & M had stuck their neck out and broken new ground at the 1956 Show by introducing a pair of 197cc lightweights – the 10/3 with 3-speed Villiers 8E, and the 10/4 with 4-speed 9E. Frames were of welded tubular steel with a sheet steel pressing, housing battery and toolbox, enclosing the rear. They also featured Earles type front forks and full width hubs with 5-inch brakes. This machine is the 10/3 but also available for '57 was a slightly more expensive option, the 10/3A, that was fitted with the 9E/3 motor. This was surely for the owner who wanted to look up to date with a streamlined casting instead of 'saucepan' to cover the flywheel magneto.

The introduction of these two now gave marque loyalists no fewer than three different 250s to choose from. Above is the model 25 with 247cc Villiers single and to its right is the 35 with 249 Villiers twin. All two strokes were finished in Maroon with silver painted wheel rims.

model 65

Standard finish, chrome and maroon—lined gold, with crimson and gold tank nameplate. Burman 4-speed gearbox, Armstrong rear suspension, Lucas electrical equipment. A full sized machine with great economy and ease of handling. Specification includes box type air filter and prop stand. Magneto, full width 7-in. alloy front hub and dualseat are available as extras.

model 75

One of the liveliest and smartest 350's on the road to-day. Finished in Sherwood Green and Chrome with gold lining. The 3-gallon tank has a new chrome panel and the latest crimson and gold " Panther " nameplate. The standard specification includes box type air filter, Lucas separate gear driven magneto and dynamo, and the latest streamlined headlamp with quickly removable instrument panel. Full width alloy front hub and prop stand are standard. Dualseat is extra.

It's not pictured in the brochure but the traditionalist could still opt for the good old 100 in unsprung guise.

model 100

Springer Standard

A new version of the famous Model 100 at a highly competitive price. The finish is all enamel in a real maroon colour, lined gold with the red and gold " Panther " name-plate. This machine is fitted with the single port version of the Model 100 engine and has orthodox, i.e., not full width brakes front and rear. An air filter, dualseat and pillion foot rests are included as standard.

model 100

Springer de luxe

The great sidecar machine. Specification includes black chrome and gold enamel with dualseat, air cleaner and pillion footrests as standard. It also includes the 8-in. by 1½-in. full width alloy quickly detachable and interchangeable hubs and brakes front and rear. This machine is also available in a rigid frame version, but with brakes similar to the standard Model 100 Springer.

Here's the rear end of the 100 Springer de luxe; but for a firm so proud of their engineering heritage there's a niggling error in its accompanying caption! 'A heavily finned alloy casting with cast in Meanite (sic) brake drum of 8" x 1½" dimensions. Drive through six steel and rubber bushes. Single 'knock-out' spindle. Front and rear wheels are quickly and easily interchangeable'. The variety of cast iron used for the brake drum they were referring to is Meehanite!

Whoever proof-read this brochure's spec sheet failed to notice that a model 76 was listed. There was no such thing as the 4-stroke 350 was a 75.

MODEL:	10/3	M10/3A	10/4	25	35	65 Springer	76 Springer	100 Rigid	Standard 100 Springer	De Luxe 100 Springer
Bore and Stroke	59 × 72 mm.	59 × 72 mm.	59 × 72 mm.	66 × 72 mm.	50 × 63·5 (twin)	60 × 88 mm.	71 × 88 mm.	87 × 100 mm.	87 × 100 mm.	87 × 100 mm.
Compression Ratio	7·25 : 1	7·25 : 1	7·25 : 1	7·25 : 1	8·2 : 1	6·5 : 1	6·7 : 1	6·5 : 1	6·5 : 1	6·5 : 1
Ignition	Flywheel mag.	Flywheel mag.	Flywheel mag.	Villiers coil	Villiers coil	Lucas coil	Lucas Magneto	Lucas Magdyno	Lucas Magdyno	Lucas Magdyno
Capacities: Petrol / Oil	2½ gallons Petroil	2½ gallons Petroil	2½ gallons Petroil	2½ gallons Petroil	2½ gallons Petroil	2⅞ gallons 2½ pints	3 gallons 2½ pints	4 gallons 4 pints	4 gallons 4 pints	4 gallons 4 pints
Chains: Front	66 pitches Renolds 110038	66 pitches Renolds 110038	58 pitches Renolds 110038	60 pitches Renolds 110038	60 pitches Renolds 110038	½" × ·305" × ·335"	½" × ·305" × ·335"	½" × ·305" × ·335"	½" × ·305" × ·335"	½" × ·305" × ·335"
Rear	Renolds 110046 119 pitches	Renolds 110046 119 pitches	Renolds 110046 121 pitches	Renolds 110046 121 pitches	Renolds 110046 121 pitches	½" × ·305" × ·335"	½" × ·305" × ·335"	⅝" × ⅜"	⅝" × ⅜"	⅝" × ⅜"
Gear Ratios:								*solo* *sidecar*	*solo* *sidecar*	*solo* *sidecar*
1st	13·21	13·21	18·25	19·0	19·0	17·70	14·04	12.44 13·50	12·44 13·50	12·44 13·50
2nd	7·87	7·87	11·05	11·79	11·79	10·40	9·26	7·33 7·94	7·33 7·94	7·33 7·94
3rd	——	——	7·90	8·19	8·19	7·54	6·73	6·16 6·37	6·16 6·37	6·16 6·37
Top	5·88	5·88	6·22	6·21	6·21	5·88	5·26	4·67 5·06	4·67 5·06	4·67 5·06
Tyres: Front	Dunlop 18 × 3·25	Dunlop 18 × 3·25	Dunlop 18 × 3·25	Dunlop 18 × 3·25	Dunlop 18 × 3·25	Dunlop 19 × 3·25	Dunlop 19 × 3·25	Dunlop 19 × 3·25	Dunlop 19 × 3·25	Dunlop 19 × 3·50
Rear	Dunlop 18 × 3·25	Dunlop 18 × 3·25	Dunlop 18 × 3·25	Dunlop 18 × 3·25	Dunlop 18 × 3·25	Dunlop 19 × 3·25	Dunlop 19 × 3·25	Dunlop 19 × 3·50	Dunlop 19 × 3·50	Dunlop 19 × 3·50
Brakes: Front	5" dia. × ⅞"	5" dia. × ⅞"	5" dia. × ⅞"	6" dia. × 1"	6" dia. × 1"	6" dia. × 1"	7" dia. × 1⅛"	7" dia. × 1⅛"	7" dia. × 1⅛"	8" dia. × 1½"
Rear	5" dia. × ⅞"	5" dia. × ⅞"	5" dia. × ⅞"	6" dia. × 1"	6" dia. × 1"	6" dia. × 1"	6" dia. × 1"	8" dia. × 1"	8" dia. × 1"	8" dia. × 1½"
Weight—Dry	235 lbs.	235 lbs.	245 lbs.	280 lbs.	290 lbs.	330 lbs.	340 lbs.	406 lbs.	426 lbs.	426 lbs.
Wheel Base	52½"	52½"	52½"	52½"	52½"	56"	56"	54"	56"	56"
Overall Width	26"	26"	26"	26"	26"	29"	29"	30"	30"	30"
Overall Length	78"	78"	78"	78"	78"	85"	85"	85"	86"	86"
Ground Clearance	6"	6"	6"	6"	6"	8"	8"	6"	7"	7"
Saddle Height	28½"	28½"	28½"	28½"	28½"	30"	30"	29"	30"	30"

It made little sense to have both 250 single and 250 twin in their two-stroke range so the single had been dropped and there was now a Sports version of the twin with higher compression engine (up to 8.7 to 1 from 8.2) and a 7-inch front brake. Very fetching it must have been in Sea Mist Grey with chromium tank panel and what they described as a 'Hide-coloured dual seat trimmed in red', whatever that signifies. The machine pictured here however is the Model 45 sports with 324cc Villiers 3T. This also has a 7-inch front brake but is finished in Italian Red with chromium tank panel and a more plausibly described 'hide covered dual seat'.

Whatever next? Panther Scooters? A good deal of this brochure is taken up by their 'All-British Scooter with the Continental line! The beautiful Panther Princess': but as this is a motorcycle book we won't go there – except to say that it proved to be a really bad move.

Not at all sure that I like this one little bit: but anyway here you are – the Model 50 Grand Sports. If nothing else, with those whopping 8in brakes, its probably got the biggest set of stoppers of any two-stroke prior to the coming of the Japanese racers of the following decade.

With the rigid 100 now dropped from their catalogue they'd bored and stroked the 100's engine from 87mm by 100mm to 88mm by 106mm to create the model 120.

To go with either the 100 or 120 was 'For the First Time ever – a sidecar chassis "Built to Match" a Panther'. Special features included complete interchangeability of all wheels, Armstrong suspension unit identical to those fitted to the rear of the bike and provision for attaching a trailer tow bar. Yes some sidecarists did tow a trailer or even a small caravan, believe it or not.

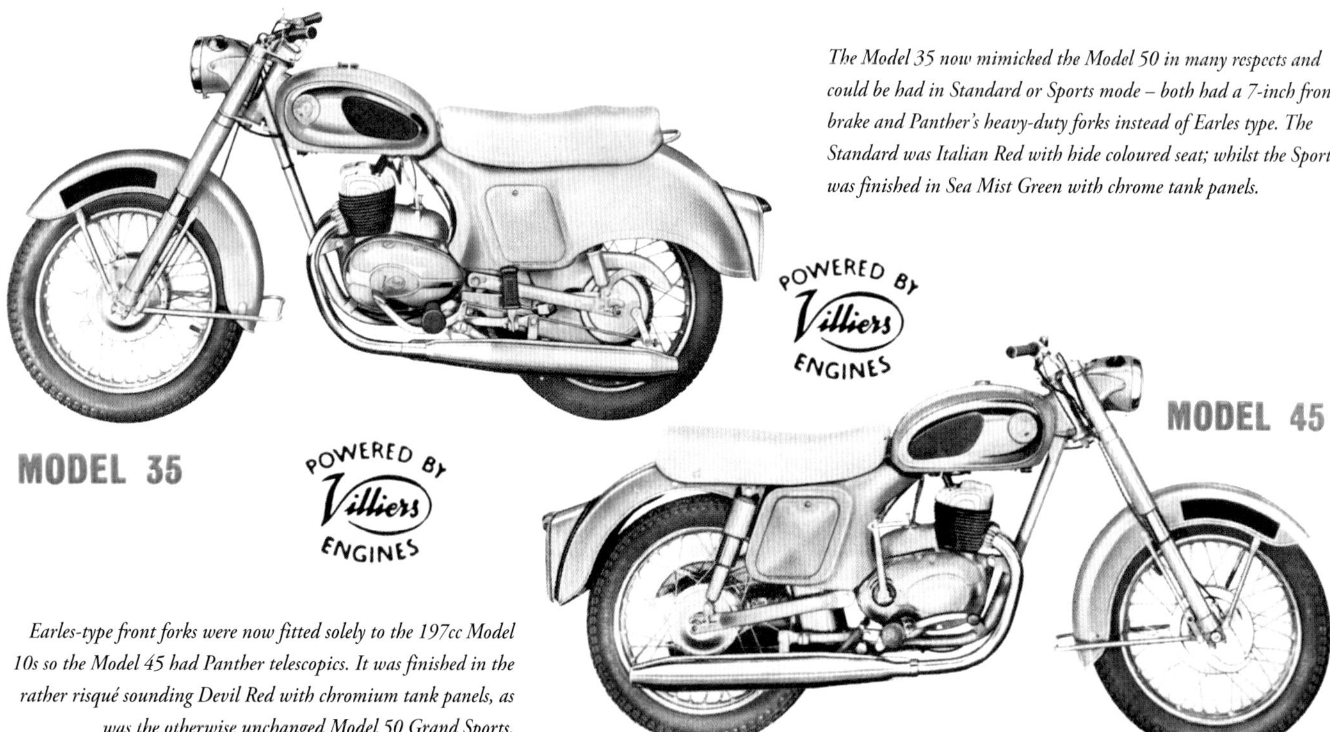

The Model 35 now mimicked the Model 50 in many respects and could be had in Standard or Sports mode – both had a 7-inch front brake and Panther's heavy-duty forks instead of Earles type. The Standard was Italian Red with hide coloured seat; whilst the Sports was finished in Sea Mist Green with chrome tank panels.

Earles-type front forks were now fitted solely to the 197cc Model 10s so the Model 45 had Panther telescopics. It was finished in the rather risqué sounding Devil Red with chromium tank panels, as was the otherwise unchanged Model 50 Grand Sports.

No mention of the unmentionable Panther Princess scooter on the cover of this brochure or within, but the damage wreaked by the firm's entry to the scooter market had already been done.

MODEL:	Bore and Stroke	Compression Ratio	Ignition	Capacities: Petrol, Oil	Chains: Front Rear	Gear Ratios: 1, 2, 3, Top	Tyres: Front Rear	Brakes: Front Rear	Weight —Dry	Wheel Base	Overall Width	Overall Length	Ground Cl'ce	Saddle Height
10/3	59 × 72 mm.	7·25 : 1	Flywheel mag.	2½ gallons Petroil	66 pitches Renolds 110038 Renolds 110046 119 pitches	14·96 7·86 — 5·87	Dunlop 18 × 3·25 Dunlop 18 × 3·25	5" dia. × ⅞" 5" dia. × ⅞"	235 lbs.	52½"	26"	78"	6"	28½"
10/3A	59 × 72 mm.	7·25 : 1	Flywheel mag.	2½ gallons Petroil	66 pitches Renolds 110038 Renolds 110046 119 pitches	15·83 8·32 — 6·21	Dunlop 18 × 3·25 Dunlop 18 × 3·25	5" dia. × ⅞" 5" dia. × ⅞"	235 lbs.	52½"	26"	78"	6"	28½"
10/4	59 × 72 mm.	7·25 : 1	Flywheel mag.	2½ gallons Petroil	58 pitches Renolds 110038 Renolds 110046 121 pitches	18·25 11·05 7·90 6·22	Dunlop 18 × 3·25 Dunlop 18 × 3·25	5" dia. × ⅞" 5" dia. × ⅞"	245 lbs.	52½"	26"	78"	6"	28½"
35	50 × 63·5 (twin)	8·2 : 1	Villiers coil	2½ gallons Petroil	60 pitches Renolds 110038 Renolds 110046 121 pitches	19·0 11·79 8·19 6·21	Dunlop 18 × 3·25 Dunlop 18 × 3·25	6" dia. × 1" 6" dia. × 1"	290 lbs.	52½"	26"	78"	6"	28½"
35 Sports	50 × 63·5 (twin)	8·7 : 1	Villiers coil	2½ gallons Petroil	60 pitches Renolds 110038 Renolds 110046 121 pitches	19·0 11·79 8·19 6·21	Dunlop 18 × 3·25 Dunlop 18 × 3·25	7" dia. × 1" 6" dia. × 1"	290 lbs.	52½"	26"	78"	6"	28½"
45 Sports	57 × 63·5 mm.	8·0 : 1	Villiers coil	2½ gallons Petroil	60 pitches Renolds 110038 Renolds 110046 121 pitches	18·0 11·0 7·8 5·9	Dunlop 18 × 3·25 Dunlop 18 × 3·25	7" dia. × 1" 6" dia. × 1"	309 lbs.	52½"	26"	78"	6"	28½"
50 Sports	57 × 63·5 mm.	8·0 : 1	Villiers coil	2½ gallons Petroil	60 pitches Renolds 110038 Renolds 110046 122 pitches	18·0 11·0 7·8 5·9	Dunlop 18 × 3·25 Dunlop 18 × 3·25	8" dia. × 1¼" 8" dia. × 1¼"	333 lbs.	52½"	26"	78"	6"	28½"
65 Springer	60 × 88 mm.	6·5 : 1	Lucas coil	2¾ gallons 2½ pints	½" × ·305" × ·335" ½" × ·305" × ·335"	17·70 10·40 7·54 5·88	Dunlop 19 × 3·25 Dunlop 19 × 3·25	6" dia. × 1" 6" dia. × 1"	330 lbs.	56"	29"	82"	8"	30"
75 Springer	71 × 88 mm.	6·7 : 1	Lucas Magneto	3 gallons 2½ pints	½" × ·305" × ·335" ½" × ·305" × ·335"	14·04 9·26 6·73 5·26	Dunlop 19 × 3·25 Dunlop 19 × 3·25	7" dia. × 1⅛" 6" dia. × 1"	340 lbs.	56"	29"	85"	8"	30"
Standard 100 Springer	87 × 100 mm.	6·5 : 1	Lucas Magdyno	4 gallons 4 pints	½" × ·305" × ·335" ⅝" × ⅜"	*solo* / *side-car* 12·44 13·50 7·33 7·94 6·16 6·37 4·67 5·06	Dunlop 19 × 3·25 Dunlop 19 × 3·50	7" dia. × 1⅛" 8" dia. × 1"	426 lbs.	56"	30"	86"	7"	30"
De Luxe 100 Springer	87 × 100 mm.	6·5 : 1	Lucas Magdyno	4 gallons 4 pints	½" × ·305" × ·335" ⅝" × ⅜"	*solo* / *side-car* 12·44 13·50 7·33 7·94 6·16 6·37 4·67 5·06	Dunlop 19 × 3·50 Dunlop 19 × 3·50	8" dia. × 1½" 8" dia. × 1½"	426 lbs.	56"	30"	86"	7"	30"
120 Springer	88 × 106 mm.	6·5 : 1	Lucas Magdyno	4 gallons 4 pints	½" × ·305" × ·335" ⅝" × ⅜"	*solo* / *side-car* 12·44 13·50 7·33 7·94 6·16 6·37 4·67 5·06	Dunlop 19 × 3·50 Dunlop 19 × 3·50	8" dia. × 1½" 8" dia. × 1½"	426 lbs.	56"	30"	86"	7"	30"

WE RESERVE THE RIGHT TO MODIFY OR DEVIATE FROM THE PRINTED SPECIFICATIONS IN THIS LIST

EXTRAS

Models 10/3, 10/3A, 10/4, 35, 35 Sports.—Legshields, Windscreen, Luggage Carrier (only).

Model 65 (only)—Magneto Ignition, Full Width Hub, 7" dia. Brake.

Models 65, 75 and all Models 100—Legshields, Windscreen, Panniers (Frames, Bags and Carrier complete)

Model 50 Grand Sports—Sports Windscreen.

ROYAL ENFIELD

Acquired by Albert Eadie and RW Smith in the early 1890s, the Eadie Manufacturing Company was the new title of a renamed business started some 40 years earlier by George Townsend at Redditch in Worcestershire to manufacture sewing needles, since progressing to gun components and bicycles.

Shortly after Eadie and Smith had taken over the business, a large contract to supply rifle parts was landed with the Royal Small Arms Factory; and to mark this prestigious association their bicycles from then on were known as Enfields (the location of the RSAF), with a fresh firm known as the Enfield Manufacturing Company set up to manufacture them.

A year later, in 1893, the machines were rebranded as Royal Enfields, again in celebration of their tie-in with the large munitions factory – and with some justification advertised as being 'Made like a gun', a motto that would stick.

A further name change, to the New Enfield Cycle Co, took place in 1896 and then a year later to the Enfield Cycle Co Ltd, which just two years hence would build its first motorised vehicle – a quadricycle powered by one of Count De Dion's single-cylinder engines that were readily available by that time. A similarly-engined tricycle followed, and by the time that the firm turned its hand to producing motorcycles in 1902, three- and four-wheelers were well established.

The first of the two-wheelers was, however, nothing more than one of the firm's bicycles with a 1.5hp single-cylinder proprietary motor mounted forward of the headstock, with direct drive to the rear wheel effected by nothing more sophisticated than a figure-of-eight belt – a primitive design that gave way the following year to one with the motor mounted in conventional motorcycle fashion and with countershaft chain-drive. Within a short while singles were ousted in favour of small-capacity V-twins with, for the main part, Peugeot powerplants, as it would be some time before the company constructed its own engines.

Motorcars had by now joined the Redditch factory's portfolio but in 1906 an offshoot company, the Enfield Autocar Co Ltd was established and took over production of a range that was headed by a four-

Predictors for use with Bofors Anti-Aircraft Guns.

Oil Motors for operating Bofors Guns; Ships' Stabilizers; Searchlight Control; for Fuse-setting, etc.

Diesel-engined 5.6 K.V.A. Generator Sets for Wireless Transmitting and Receiving Stations.

Petrol-driven Generator Sets ranging from 80 watts to 3000 watts.

Electrically-driven Generator Sets for testing Aeroplane and Radar Equipment.

Gyroscopic Sights for Oerlikon and other Guns.

Resetter Boxes for Gun Sights.

Anti-vibration Mountings for Gun Sights.

Armour-piercing Shot for 40 m.m. Anti-tank Guns.

Petrol-driven Pump Units for operating the Gun Turrets of Tanks.

Straight-line Cams for use in Precision Instruments.

Self-synchronising Equipment for 40 m.m. Guns.

Lag-compensating and Self-sectoring Equipment for Gun Sights.

Tubular Crates for enclosing Motor Cycles to be dropped by Parachute.

Justifiably proud of its contribution to the war effort, Royal Enfield quite straightforwardly set out an immediate course of action, as well as itemising some of its wartime products.

Royal Enfield

"MADE LIKE A GUN"

MODEL R.E. 125 c.c. Two-Stroke

ENGINE	125 c.c. two-stroke single cylinder. Bore and stroke, 53·79×55 m.m. Piston of heat treated aluminium alloy with two compression rings and fully floating gudgeon pin. **Detachable aluminium alloy cylinder head.**
CARBURETTOR	Needle jet type with air cleaner.
IGNITION AND LIGHTING SET	Specially designed flywheel magneto; 6 volts, 27 watt output. Gives adequate driving light even at low engine speeds.
FRAME	Best quality steel tubing. Front fork with pressed steel blades and rubber suspension.
GEARBOX	**Unit construction with engine.** Three-speed with hand control. Ratios: 7·6, 12·3 and 22·3 to 1.
TRANSMISSION	**Roller chains, front one enclosed in oil-bath case.**
WHEELS	Royal Enfield hubs with deep-groove, non-adjustable journal bearings. Brakes, 4in. front, 5in. rear. Dunlop Tyres, 2·50-19in.
FINISH	Best quality black enamel. Bright parts chromium plated. Tank black with frosted silver motif.
SPEEDOMETER	Smith's "Lightweight" Chronometric Speedometer. Extra charge.
LEGSHIELDS	Can be supplied at an extra charge.

These little machines, in their War guise, have been used in Airborne and Parachute landings on various Fronts and also in other directions by H.M. Forces. Their light weight and general handiness make it possible for them to perform duties quite beyond the capabilities of the heavier machines.

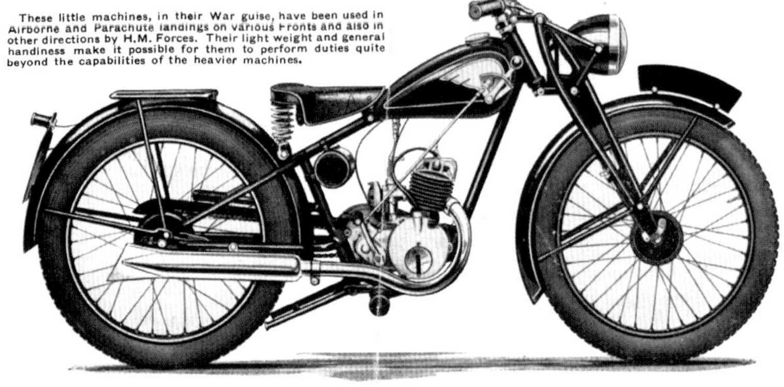

Emanating from the DKW-influenced Royal Baby that had debuted at Holland's Rotterdam show in 1939, the military Flying Flea had proved to be everything that the specifically-designed Welbike wasn't – apart from collapsible. They were used in conjunction with airborne and waterborne operations, with their light weight giving them good cross-country capabilities for general communications duties. The civilian version was almost identical and a really honest little machine.

cylinder of just under six litres. Financial difficulties for the car arm arrived in 1908, which were resolved with a takeover by Alldays, as well as a move to Birmingham where the company continued as Enfields – and subsequently Enfield-Alldays – until 1925.

With cars out of the way, fresh impetus was put into the firm's motorcycles and, as well as some mild competition work (this resulting in a fifth place in the 1911 Junior TT for one of the V-twins), the design and manufacture of the company's own engines was commenced. By 1914 an in-house 3hp V-twin was in production and the introduction of a 225cc two-stroke impending, but it was a 770cc JAP twin that powered the largest Enfield. Further visits to the Isle of Man had produced mediocre results until, with the First World War just weeks away, the company very nearly pulled off a victory in the Junior. Frank Walker headed the field for a while on a TT-twin before first one then another accident dropped him down the leader board; but having remounted he finished third – sadly crashing after crossing the line and succumbing to his injuries a few days later.

Ideal as a sidecar machine, the Royal Enfield JAP was taken up by the War Department and built in quantities as a light ambulance (or more commonly a machine gun carrier) whilst the company's smaller-capacity machines were ordered by the Russian government. Experimentation at this time resulted in a three-cylinder two-stroke of something under 700cc, as well as an 850cc side-valve four, but neither went any further and peace saw the resumption of single and big-twin models – the largest of which was the 976cc Vickers-Wolseley-engined machine that was brought to the market in 1921.

The '20s saw an expansion of the singles range that, utilising Royal Enfield's own or JAP engines, encompassed such diversities as the two-stroke Ladies Model and a 500 OHV twin-port at the very end of the decade – the best TT result coming shortly before with a second place in the 1928 lightweight event.

The depression years were weathered more successfully than many manufacturers, as the company had accrued sufficient reserves to absorb current trading deficits. In 1931, to run with the times, the Cycar 150cc two-stroke with pressed-steel frame and total enclosure of its mechanicals was introduced. That same year Albert Eadie died, followed two years later by his fellow founder – the latter being succeeded by his son Major Frank Smith, who had been with the company since the war.

It was at this time that Royal Enfield brought out the first of its sports overhead-valve Bullets. Available in 250, 350 or 500 form the engines were slopers like the rest of the firm's singles but the largest had an exotic four-valve head. The model's early years were punctuated by changes such as a reduction in valves to three (twin inlets and a single exhaust), the reinstatement of four, vertical engines from 1936 and the withdrawal of the 350 for a while; but these sports Enfields, in one guise or another, were to become the longest-lasting model in motorcycling history.

In 1933 the V-twin's capacity increased to 1140cc for export but home-market customers would have to wait until 1937 to get one. They were treated to another tiddler to take advantage of the 15-shilling-a-year road tax the following year, however, with a miniature of the larger sloper OHVs – the 148cc Model T. If nothing else the company seemed to thrive on variety, and so it continued until the war with a large range including economy lightweights, tourers, sports and competition mounts, and large V-twins that coped with sidecar work so well.

Having products that, with minimal modification, government departments deemed fit for military use

Royal Enfield

"MADE LIKE A GUN"

Model J. 499 c.c. Overhead Valve

ENGINE - - 499 c.c. single cylinder. Bore and stroke 84×90 m.m. **Valves, rocker gear and push rods totally enclosed and automatically lubricated High compression piston** of heat-treated aluminium alloy, form-turned oval, enabling close clearances to be used without risk of seizure. Light alloy connecting rod. Detachable cylinder head. Timing gear running in oil bath.

LUBRICATION - Royal Enfield dry-sump system, entirely automatic and positive in action, oil compartment integral with crank-case. Oil fed direct to the big-end and to the rear of the cylinder as well as being positively pumped to the rocker gear and timing gear.

CARBURETTOR - AMAL, with twist grip control.

IGNITION AND LIGHTING SET - Lucas 6-volt Magdyno with automatic voltage control. Electric horn. Dynamo gear-driven from engine.

FRAME - - - Of cradle type, combining great strength and rigidity with moderate weight. Built of finest quality steel tubing.

FRONT FORK - **Telescopic fork of Royal Enfield design,** with hydraulic damping and exceptionally long enclosed springs, giving perfect steering and shock-absorbing qualities. Lubrication is entirely automatic and requires no attention.

TRANSMISSION - **Roller chains, front one enclosed in oil-bath case.** Four-speed gearbox with positive foot change and **special device for easily finding neutral**. Enfield patent cush drive in rear hub. Gear ratios: 5; 6·5; 9 and 13·9 to 1.

WHEELS - - Royal Enfield hubs with non-adjustable deep-groove journal bearings. Brakes, 6 in. front and rear, with finger adjustment. Dunlop tyres, 3·25-19 in. front; 3·50-19 in. rear. **Special design rear hub which enables an inner tube to be changed without removing the wheel.**

MUDGUARDS - Efficient wide mudguards. Rear guard quickly detachable for access to wheel.

FINISH - - - Best quality black enamel. Bright parts chromium plated. Tank chromium plated and panelled in frosted aluminium.

SPEEDOMETER - Smith's Chronometric Speedometer. Extra charge.

MODEL G.

346 c.c. Overhead Valve

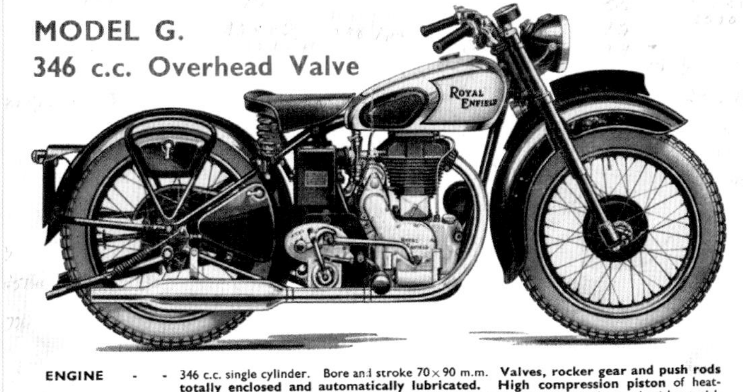

ENGINE - - 346 c.c. single cylinder. Bore and stroke 70×90 m.m. **Valves, rocker gear and push rods totally enclosed and automatically lubricated. High compression piston** of heat-treated aluminium alloy, form-turned oval, enabling close clearances to be used without risk of seizure. Light alloy connecting rod. Detachable cylinder head. Timing gear running in oil bath.

LUBRICATION - Royal Enfield dry-sump system, entirely automatic and positive in action, oil compartment integral with crankcase. Oil fed direct to the big-end and to the rear of the cylinder as well as being positively pumped to the rocker gear and timing gear.

CARBURETTOR - AMAL, with twist grip control.

IGNITION AND LIGHTING SET - Lucas 6-volt Magdyno with automatic voltage control. Electric horn. Dynamo gear-driven from engine.

FRAME - - - Of cradle type, combining great strength and rigidity with moderate weight. Built of finest quality steel tubing.

FRONT FORK - **Telescopic fork of Royal Enfield design,** with hydraulic damping and exceptionally long enclosed springs, giving perfect steering and shock-absorbing qualities. Lubrication is entirely automatic and requires no attention.

TRANSMISSION - **Roller chains, front one enclosed in oil-bath case.** Four-speed gearbox with positive foot change and **special device for easily finding neutral.** Enfield patent cush drive in rear hub. Gear ratios: 5·5; 7·2, [illegible] and 15·3 to 1.

WHEELS - - Royal Enfield hubs with non-adjustable deep-groove journal bearings. Brakes, 6 in., front and rear, with finger adjustment. Dunlop tyres, 3·25-19 in. **Special design rear hub which enables an inner tube to be changed without removing the wheel.**

MUDGUARDS - Efficient wide mudguards. Rear guard quickly detachable for access to wheel.

FINISH - - - Best quality black enamel. Bright parts chromium plated. Tank chromium plated and panelled in frosted aluminium.

SPEEDOMETER - Smith's Chronometric Speedometer. Extra charge.

Royal Enfield

"MADE LIKE A GUN"

Enfield's pre-war Model G had also seen active service, as the WD/G – albeit in small numbers compared with the side-valve WD/C and later on its OHV derivative, the WD/CO. Although the WD/CO remained in civilianised production for a limited period it was not catalogued, so the rejuvenated G, complete with up-to-the minute telescopic forks, along with the similarly-treated J led the way in true post-war production.

ensured that the factory was kept busy with motorcycle production for the duration of the war – so large numbers of OHV machines of 350cc, side-valves from 250 to 570cc, and perhaps most especially the recently-introduced 125 Flying Fleas saw active service. With the Redditch factory at risk of air raids, a shadow factory was established in the Westwood Quarry near Bradford on Avon, Wiltshire, a vast underground complex in which museums' collections of art and antiquities were also housed for safe keeping at this period. In the subterranean limestone caverns, as well as at Redditch, motorcycles, vast amounts of ordnance (such as gun control systems and precision engineering) was carried out – with the Westwood facility remaining in use and in fact outlasting the parent Redditch factory, finally closing in 1970.

The immediate post-war range consisted of late-1930s' 350 Model Gs and 500 Model Js revamped with telescopic forks, plus a civilianised version of the Flea; but towards the end of 1948 the company was at the forefront of frame design when it unveiled its 500 twin and re-introduced the Bullet – both boasting pivoted-fork rear suspension.

Machines with this frame enjoyed a good deal of success in both international and national trials, and it was probably this that brought the Bullet to the attention of the Indian government. Anxious to equip border patrols with simple, reliable and rugged machines they placed an initial order for several hundred 350 Bullets. With the situation on-going a liaison was formed with Madras Motors to assemble Royal Enfield's single under licence, and from this Enfield India sprung in 1955. At first all components were manufactured in England but by the late '50s tooling had been sent out to India to produce its own, and by the early '60s the firm was self-sufficient – continuing to this day with the manufacture of traditional 'British' singles at the Chennai factory, now known as Royal Enfields since purchase of the name in the mid 1990s.

By 1955 the company's home-market range consisted of 700 and 500 twins, 500 and 350 Bullets, and the 250 Clipper, as well as the 150 two-stroke Ensign that had superseded the Flea, and it was at this time that the company entered into an additional export agreement. By coincidence it also involved Indians but on this

Just two machines on the cover of a 1948 home-market brochure signified that one of the three that had made up Enfield's range since the war was no longer included – the 500 Model J, which since 1947 had been available with twin-port head and twin exhausts, was for the meantime for export only.

occasion it was a tie-up with Brockhouse of Southport, Lancashire, which still owned Indian Motorcycles but whose manufacturing efforts with the lacklustre Indian Brave had ceased. Jockeyed by the American publisher Floyd Clymer, Enfields were to be painted red, badged as Indians and sold as such in the US – but few fell for this ridiculous piece of badge-engineering, and thankfully after five years the terms of the agreement came to an end. Clymer, however, wasn't one to throw in the towel and continued to handle the marque in the US, but under its own name, until the late 1960s.

None of the above fazed RE's model policy too much, and the company entered the '60s with nothing much more of note than the befairinged Airflows as attention-getters in the recent past, and increasingly-sporting 250s for the present. In 1962 the Smith dynasty came to an abrupt end with the death of Major Frank, and the company was taken over by E&HP Smith, a Midlands engineering and machine tool-making conglomerate. At first the future appeared rosy with every indication that a programme of modernisation would breathe new life into what was for the most part a dated range; the hiring of ex-champion road-racer Geoff Duke as a consultant boded well.

In search of the prestige garnered by competition success a two-stroke 250 racer, the GP5, was developed, as well as a two-stroke off-roader but although the former in particular showed promise, economies sought at a time of falling road machine sales brought about an early demise.

The final flowering of the sporting 250s was the rather good Continental GT, a true little café racer, but despite this and the introduction of a Villiers 250 two-stroke Turbo Twin, as well as the big 750 Interceptor now being available worldwide, Royal Enfield was slithering down the same slippery slope of decline as other British makers. Its owner E&HP Smith was, we must suppose, a realist, and after continuing with a severely pared-back range closed the Redditch factory and sold the Enfield Cycle Co to Norton-Villiers, retaining Enfield Precision engineers, which still operated out of the Wiltshire limestone caverns. It was there, under contract from Norton-Villiers, that Interceptor engines continued to be made – the complete machines almost exclusively destined for Floyd Clymer's US enterprise. But 1970

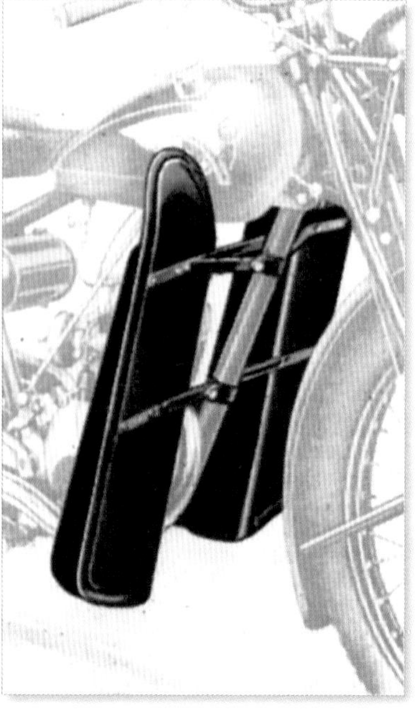

The 125 RE retained its 'rubber band' suspension for the pressed-steel front forks but a few small alterations had been made, as you will see by comparing it with the immediately post-war version on page 388. It was also now finished in Maroon with frosted silver tank motif and wheel rims; handlebars as well as the exhaust system were chromium-plated. Although this machine is fitted with a speedo driven from the front hub it was in fact an optional extra, as were these pressed-steel leg shields.

saw it all end with the closure of the Bradford-on-Avon facility and Clymer's death.

Well, not quite all. In fact, a couple of hundred-or-so engines were left over and a deal with the Rickman brothers resulted in the Interceptor-engined Rickman Enfield before the field was left clear for the marque to carry on in spirit (and eventually in name) halfway to the other side of the world from where it had begun.

Due to it now being regarded as the economy or basic Royal Enfield four-stroke, changes to the Model G were confined to such trivia as the means of securing the tool box. There was, however, the option of a high-level exhaust system but a speedo or leg shields cost extra.

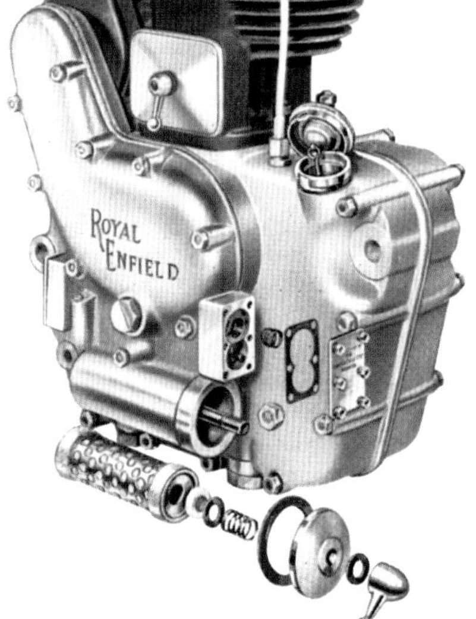

TELESCOPIC FRONT FORK

The ROYAL ENFIELD Patent Telescopic Fork has particularly long flexible springs combined with oil damping which is light in the normal position but becomes progressively more effective at either end of the fork's movement. The result is perfect steering and road-holding under all conditions. The generous bearings are automatically lubricated by the oil in the fork and virtually no attention is required over long periods.

DETACHABLE REAR MUDGUARD

AND TWO-PIECE REAR SPINDLE

This feature is of great assistance when dealing with punctures which, experience has shown, nearly always occur in the rear tyre. By loosening only four nuts the entire mudguard can be lifted away, as shown, giving access to practically the whole of the tyre without removing the wheel from the frame. An additional refinement consists of a two-piece rear spindle with a detachable distance piece. Removal of this enables the inner tube to be withdrawn and replaced without disturbing the wheel.

NEUTRAL FINDER

This device removes the one objection ever raised against the modern positive stop foot gear control—the difficulty sometimes experienced in finding "neutral." A small additional lever is provided which enables "neutral" to be positively selected from second, third or top gear. All that has to be done is to press the neutral finder lever firmly against its stop with the heel when the normal "neutral" will be selected ready to engage first gear again when the rider wishes to move off.

LUBRICATION SYSTEM

The lubrication system employed on ROYAL ENFIELD four-stroke engines is self-contained, efficient and reliable. The oil is carried in a compartment cast round the crankcase, thus eliminating connecting pipes and ensuring the full rate of circulation immediately after starting up. The circulation is controlled by two simple low speed oscillating plunger pumps. Oil is fed through a large felt filter to the big-end bearing and also to the rear wall of the cylinder, the overhead rocker gear and the timing gear being finally collected and returned to the tank.

Royal Enfield's very effective cush drive hub had been around since the 1920s and was employed by other manufacturers such as Brough Superior and Norton – my 1927 Model 18 has one.

CUSH DRIVE

This distinctive feature is largely responsible for the smoothness always associated with ROYAL ENFIELD Motor Cycles. Extremely simple and effective, the rubber blocks smooth out chain snatch and add considerably to the life of both chains and tyres as well as contributing largely to the rider's comfort and enjoyment.

The reasons for the Model G's demotion were contained in this fold-out prospectus, which was handed out by Hammants, who had been in the cycle and motorcycle trade at Bell Street, Henley-on-Thames since shortly after World War One.

Royal Enfield's first production swinging-arm frame laid bare, along with telescopic forks. Interestingly, although adhering to the same principles, it differed in many respects from AMC's sprung frame that hit the market at the same time.

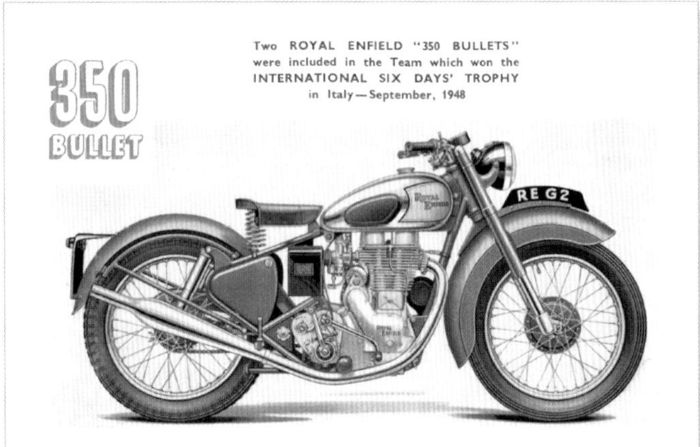

In the early-to-mid 1930s Enfield's 500cc Bullets were very serious sporting machines, and so it was appropriate that the name was revived for this model with its immediate cachet of having been part of the successful British ISDT team. Its lineage stretched back to the '30s and through to the Model G but despite them featuring a now somewhat archaic floating big-end bush, RE saw no reason the change it. Power output of the Bullet was quoted as 19bhp at 5,750rpm as opposed to 15bhp at 5,400rpm for the Model G. Both Bullet and 500 Twin were finished in Lustrous silver-grey enamel with frosted silver panels on the chromium-plated fuel tank.

As well as sharing a first with AMC as regards swinging-arm frames the two manufacturers had something else in common: their new 500cc vertical twins had separate heads and barrels for each cylinder. Moreover the heads were of aluminium whilst BSA, Triumph and Norton twins were all of iron. Aside from this the AMC shared its machine's oiling and ignition arrangements with the others, whilst Enfield had its oil reservoir in the crankcases and its ignition by coil and distributor. There surely was a good reason but why didn't the firm locate the ignition/lighting switch and ammeter in the headlamp like the Bullet rather than down by the rider's right calf?

ENGINE: 346 c.c. single cylinder, O.H.V. Bore and stroke, 70×90 mm. Light alloy cylinder head of entirely new design with wide angle valves and cast-in inserts for valve seats and sparking plug. Piston of heat treated aluminium alloy, form-turned oval, enabling close clearances to be used without risk of seizure. Light alloy connecting rod. Timing gear running in oil bath.

IGNITION AND LIGHTING SET: Lucas 6-volt Magdyno with automatic voltage control. Dynamo gear-driven from engine. Electric horn.
Alternative Equipment:—Racing magneto (no lights, bulb horn).

GEAR RATIOS: Standard ratios: 5·67; 7·37; 10·2 and 15·8 to 1. Special wide ratio for Trials or close ratio for Scrambles can be supplied to order.

EXHAUST SYSTEM: Downswept pipe with up-turned silencer of new taper design giving pleasantly quiet exhaust note with maximum power. High level system or straight-through pipe supplied to order.

TYRES: Dunlop Universal 3·25–19in. front and rear. 3·00–21in. front and 4·00–19in. rear tyres optional on machines to Trials specification.

GROUND CLEARANCE: Approximately 7in. with rider normally seated.

MUDGUARDS: Light narrow guards giving ample tyre clearance.

SPEEDOMETER: Smiths Chronometric Speedometer.

PRICE ... ... **£135** Plus **£36. 9s. 0d.** Purchase Tax.

SPEEDOMETER EXTRA ... ... **£4.** Plus **£1. 1s. 7d.** Purchase Tax.

ENGINE: 496 c.c. vertical twin cylinder, O.H.V. Bore and stroke, 64×77 mm. Separate cylinders, with light alloy heads, having cast-in inserts for valve seats and sparking plugs. Massive one-piece crankshaft integral with central flywheel. Light alloy connecting rods. Pistons of heat treated aluminium alloy, form-turned oval. Two chain-driven high level camshafts operating valves through large diameter flat base tappets and short push rods.

IGNITION AND LIGHTING SET: Lucas 3½in. 50 watt dyno-distributor with automatic voltage control. Battery and coil ignition with automatic advance and retard mechanism. Switches, control unit, cut-out, warning light and ammeter mounted in switch box carried on seat tube. Electric horn.

GEAR RATIOS: Standard ratios: 5·1; 6·6; 9·2 and 14·2 to 1.

EXHAUST SYSTEM: Twin exhaust pipes with two efficient silencers giving a pleasant note combined with maximum power.

TYRES: Front, 3·25-19in. Dunlop ribbed.
Rear, 3·50-19in. Dunlop Universal.

SPEEDOMETER: Smiths Chronometric speedometer with 120 m.p.h. dial and coloured segments showing r.p.m. in each gear.

PRICE ... ... **£155** Plus **£41. 17s. 0d.** Purchase Tax.

SPEEDOMETER EXTRA ... ... **£4.** Plus **£1. 1s. 7d.** Purchase Tax.

Lucky chap! He must have managed to get an advance issue of one of the very latest Bullets – for that is what he's on. Enfield had a habit of signifying the model by its registration plate in the publicity material at this time so, although I've not seen it in print, did the factory perhaps refer to the Bullet as the G2?

BSA announced that it was the world's largest motorcycle manufacturer, Triumph the best motorcycle in the world, but Royal Enfield trumped them both on the cover of the 1950 brochure.

The Flea had been updated with a pair of 'Enfield exclusive telescopic forks' and Maroon had given way to Lustrous silver-grey enamel for the paintwork. There was a complete set of tools in the under-saddle cylindrical container and a Smiths chronometric speedo was thrown in for the price of £73 17s 8d. The factory claimed that a full 1¾-gallon tank would carry the rider for more than 250 miles and that it would do up to 50mph.

The J2 was off the export-only list now, so anyone could buy what, in simple terms, was in effect a big bore (84x90mm) version of the G with flashy (but pointless as it had only one exhaust valve) twin-port head and corresponding exhausts. As a further sop to Mr Flash, as though he'd go for one of these, there was a Smiths 120mph speedo – but a pair of the optional extra leg shields would have rather spoiled the effect. Finish for both J2 and G were Black enamel with chromium-plated tank panelled in frosted silver with blue-and-red lining.

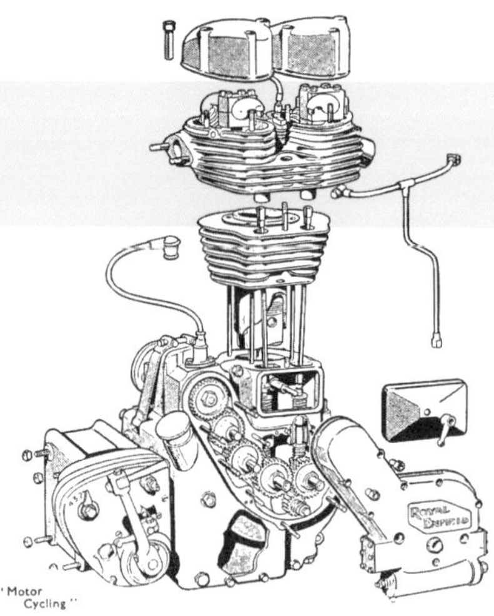

350 BULLET—TRIALS MODEL

Developed by successful experience in One Day Reliability Trials and in the International Six Days, this Model is specially suitable wherever difficult cross-country conditions are encountered. Based on the standard "350 Bullet" it has the following modifications to the specification :—

IGNITION. Racing magneto gear driven. No lights. Bulb horn.

GEARBOX. Special wide ratios : 7·6; 10·65; 16·3 and 22·8 to 1. Folding kickstarter. No neutral finder.

EXHAUST SYSTEM. High level system.

TYRES. Dunlop Universal. 3·00–21 in. front. 4·00–19 in. rear. Security bolts fitted.

GROUND CLEARANCE. Approximately 7 in. with rider seated.

MUDGUARDS. Chromium plated light narrow guards giving ample tyre clearance.

EQUIPMENT. One toolbox with tool kit. Crankcase shield. Mudguard pad. Carburetter intake shield in lieu of air filter.

SPECIFICATION

350 BULLET—SCRAMBLES MODEL

In its special "Scramble" form the "350 Bullet" has already given a good account of itself in many events on grass, sand and road circuits. High compression pistons suitable for petrol, petrol-benzol or alcohol fuels are available, as well as special racing cams. The specification is similar to that of the standard "350 Bullet" with the following modifications :—

ENGINE. Fitted with high compression piston to order. $7\frac{1}{2}$ to 1 for petrol ; $8\frac{1}{2}$ to 1 for petrol-benzol ; 11 to 1 for alcohol fuel.

IGNITION. Racing magneto gear driven. No lights or horn.

GEARBOX. Standard ratios : 7·08; 9·2; 12·7 and 19·7 to 1. Special close ratios (to order) : 7·08; 9·2; 11·8 and 15·4 to 1. Folding kick-starter. No neutral finder.

EXHAUST SYSTEM. Straight through open exhaust pipe.

TYRES. Dunlop Sports, 3·00–21 in. front ; 4·00–19 in. rear. Security bolts fitted.

GROUND CLEARANCE. Approximately 7 in. with rider seated.

MUDGUARDS. Chromium plated light narrow guards, giving ample tyre clearance.

EQUIPMENT. Crankcase shield. Mudguard pad. Tool kit. Carburetter intake shield in lieu of air filter.

Both Bullet and 500 Twin had been given a cast-aluminium fork head that carried the speedo, as well as restyled upper fork sleeve/headlamp bracket; there was also a slightly less ponderous-looking front guard to help alleviate its awkwardness– always a problem, as Norton would find out with the first of the Dominators, when mounted in this way rather than by stays or brackets to the bottom section of the forks. When The Motor Cycle *tested one in the spring of 1950 it was early days for swinging-arm machines and so without many yardsticks to judge them by their observation that 'no praise is too high for the steering and road-holding' should be taken in context. For something with sporting pretentions it wasn't especially fast – its best figures of 68mph in third and 73 in top being about the same as BSA's touring B31. Acceleration was pretty much the same too, with both doing a test quarter-mile in 20.4 seconds. General fuel economy was a little worse, however, with the Bullet managing 80mpg at a steady 50mph to the BSA's 90mpg.*

The 496cc twin had a bore and stroke of 64mm by 77mm, the same as their 248cc 'S' model single upon which certain aspects of it were based, and like all British vertical twins I can quickly recall had aluminium connecting rods – Enfield's being of Hiduminium RR56 in case you are technically minded. In the same manner as the Bentley designed Lagonda V-12 engine there were no bearing inserts, the con rods' machined big ends running directly on the crankpins.

They'd had a go at repositioning the ammeter and switches but the former was still unreadable by the rider – the switch, it has to be said, was far better off facing forward and inboard to prevent the possibility of the rider's leg interfering with the key, bending it or, worst of all, breaking it off. "Corners and bends could be taken stylishly at speed, the wheels hugging the chosen line in the highest confidence-instilling manner," wrote The Motor Cycle *at the end of 1950. Conversely they then commented that 'the footrests were not sufficiently high from the road and were often grounded during fast cornering or when the machine was being turned in narrow lanes' – definitely not conducive to stylish cornering! It was good in a straight line, however, with a standing quarter-mile in 16.2 seconds, and had a reasonable top speed of 85mph with 75 possible in third – all at an average fuel consumption of about 60mpg.*

AIR CLEANER

On all ROYAL ENFIELD motor cycles (except the "Trials" and "Scrambles" Bullets) the air entering the carburetter is passed through an air cleaner. This ensures long life for the cylinder and piston, a fact which is proved by users' experience in all parts of the world. The air cleaner on each model is sufficiently large to ensure that it does not cause any loss in speed or power or increase in petrol consumption.

No mention of any new models on the cover of the September '52 brochure; but there were three this season, including the 500 Bullet speeding down this slope with Maureen hanging on for dear life behind nonchalant David in his Harris tweed jacket and old school tie.

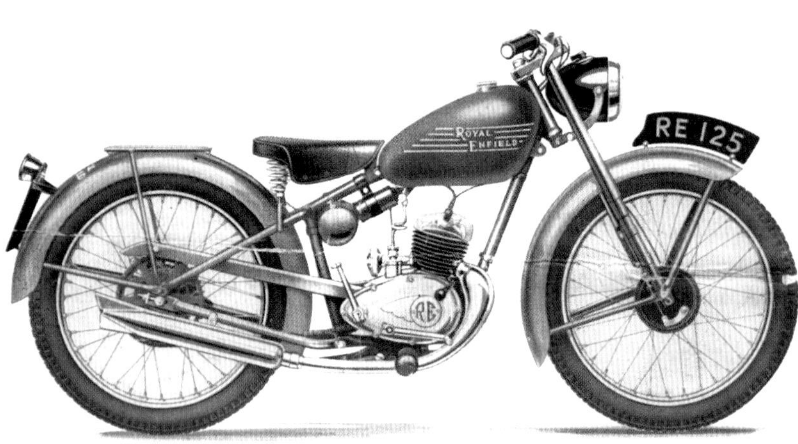

The Prince of Lightweights, as the factory now dubbed the Flea, had been given a radical makeover for the 1951 season. Its frame had been redesigned and was now of all-welded construction, handlebars now mounted forward of the steering axis, and the engine, although of the same bore and stroke, was completely revised. The lower half was enclosed by a set of four 'streamlined' die-castings and now featured a cross-over drive and foot change for the three-speed gearbox. Transfer porting had been improved and power was said to up from 2¾ to 4½bhp; there was a new Miller generator and ignition system too. It was still in Lustrous silver-grey enamel but with 'attractive new tank transfer of modern design'. The factory's sometime claim of up to 250 miles to a tankful of petroil was put into context by The Motor Cycle*'s testers when they found that this was possible, but at a steady 20mph; a more normal 40 yielding a still-creditable 116mpg. Top speed was 47 and it would do 37mph in second.*

Old G for Gertie had been given a mild update with the cast-aluminium fork crown and, at last, its front mudguard (and the rest of the range's too) was mounted on the bottom section of the forks, which in turn allowed it to have a more pleasing shape. Yes I do know about unsprung weight and all that but the difference and effect is negligible with machines of this nature. Finish was now a la Henry Ford – black. The twin-exhaust J2 had been given the same treatment and colour scheme, and we mustn't forget the 'attractive metal tank motif in chromium, red and gold' for the pair of them.

Looking uncommonly as though it has some kind of form of plunger suspension with exposed springs, Enfield's new Ensign, as the caption tells us, actually had a swinging arm. For the meanwhile Enfield's two tiddlers would be produced side-by-side but the new 150 would shortly entirely replace the long-running 125.

At last! They'd seen sense and transferred the ammeter and switchgear up to the headlamp. Note the revised cylinder head with direct oil feed for rocker gear.

When the new 500 Bullet was put through its paces by The Motor Cycle *in the summer of '53 their summary spoke of 'good low-speed torque and excellent handling qualities' as well as an 'effortless loping gait on part throttle openings'. 'Reasonably good fuel economy' translated into 74mpg at 50mph or 60mpg at 60; but what they failed to point out was that its top speed of 78 was, if anything, less than a Bullet of 20 years earlier. The big Bullet was finished in polychromatic Copper Beech.*

ENGINE : 692 c.c. O.H.V. vertical Twin. High efficiency cylinder heads fitted on separate cylinders. R.R.56 light alloy connecting rods. Massive one-piece crankshaft. Chain-driven high level camshafts. Lubrication of all working parts ensured by the well-known Royal Enfield Dry-sump system, which incorporates a large capacity felt oil filter. **CARBURETTER :** Amal, with air filter. **GEARBOX :** Four-speed foot-controlled with positive neutral finder. **WHEELS :** Front, 3·25-19in. Dunlop ribbed tyre. Rear, 3·50-19in. Dunlop Universal tyre. **BRAKES :** Front, Dual 6in. diameter, giving maximum stopping power combined with smoothness. Rear, 7in. diameter, incorporating cush drive. **FINISH :** Distinctive Copper Beech polychromatic enamel with bright parts heavily chromium plated. Attractive metal tank motif in chromium, red and gold. For sidecar use a front fork with reduced trail, stronger springs and a steering damper is fitted. For sidecar gear ratios, see technical data on back page. When ordering, please specify whether machine is intended for Solo or Sidecar use.

The Dualseat and Pannier set illustrated above, are available as extras, see separate leaflets.

Meteor 700

The introduction of the Meteor elevated Royal Enfield to the top of the capacity table for British vertical twins for a good few years.

Royal Enfield had been the first of many manufacturers to break away from the traditional rigid frame for trials machines and their format was further honed for 1953.

350 Bullet (Trials)

This versatile machine is now available to an improved and modified specification for trials use. The following are deviations from Standard Specification :—

ENGINE : Light alloy cylinder barrel. Small bore carburetter and heavier flywheels. 6 : 1 compression ratio. **IGNITION :** Lucas wader magneto. No lighting set. Bulb horn. **GEARBOX :** Special ratios: 7·1, 9·95, 15·25 and 21·3 to 1. **EXHAUST SYSTEM :** Small bore high level. **WHEELS :** Front, 3·00-21in. Trials Universal tyre. Rear, 4·00-19in. Trials Universal tyre. Security bolts fitted. **MUDGUARDS :** Narrow section light alloy guards. Pad fitted to rear. **PETROL TANK :** Approximately 2-gallons capacity. **EQUIPMENT :** One toolbox with kit. Small air filter to carburetter. **GROUND CLEARANCE :** Approximately 7in. with rider seated. A robust shield is fitted to the crankcase.

	Meteor 700	500 Twin	500 Bullet	350 Bullet	Ensign	Model J2	Model G	Model RE	[illegible]
Bore and Stroke mm.	70×90	64×77	84×90	70×90	56×60	84×90	70×90	53·79 ×55	[illegible]
Cubic Capacity c.c.	692	496	499	346	148	499	346	125	[illegible]
Compression Ratio	6½ to 1	6½ to 1	6¼ to 1	6½ to 1	6½ to 1	5½ to 1	6 to 1	5½ to 1	[illegible]
Gear Ratios ... (Std. Solo)	4·47 5·8 8·05 12·4 : 1	5 6·5 9 13·9 : 1	4·91 6·4 8·85 13·65 : 1	5·67 7·37 10·2 15·8 : 1	6·95 11·3 20·35 : 1 —	5·1 6·6 9·2 14·2 : 1	5·6 7·3 10·1 15·6 : 1	7·55 12·3 22·1 : 1 —	[illegible]
Gear Ratios (Sidecar)	5·03 6·53 9·05 13·95 : 1		5·72 7·45 10·3 15·9 : 1			5·95 7·7 10·7 16·6 : 1			[illegible]
Petrol Tank Capacity Imp. Gals.	4 gals. (18 litres)	3¼ gals. (15 litres)	3¼ gals. (15 litres)	3¼ gals. (15 litres)	2 gals. (9 litres)	2¾ gals. (12½ litres)	2¾ gals. (12½ litres)	1¾ gals. (8 litres)	[illegible]
Oil Tank Capacity	4 pints	4 pints	4 pints	4 pints	—	4 pints	4 pints	—	[illegible]
Approx. Max. Speed m.p.h.	95-100	85-90	85-90	75-80	50-55	80-85	70-75	45-50	[illegible]
Approx. Petrol Consumption m.p.g.	55-60	65-70	70-75	75-80	110-120	70-75	75-80	120-150	[illegible]
Weight ... lb.	405	390	379	350	155	395	370	140	[illegible]
Wheelbase	4ft. 6in.	4ft. 6in.	4ft. 6in.	4ft. 6in.	4ft. 0in.	4ft. 6½in.	4ft. 5½in.	4ft. 0in.	[illegible]
Saddle Height ...	29½in.	29½in.	29½in.	29½in.	28in.	28½in.	29in.	28in.	[illegible]
Ground Clearance ...	5½in.	5½in.	6¼in.	6¼in.	6in.	4¾in.	5¼in.	5¾in.	[illegible]
Overall Width ...	2ft. 4in.	2ft. 4in.	2ft. 4in.	2ft. 4in.	2ft. 1½in.	2ft. 4in.	2ft. 4in.	2ft. 1½in.	[illegible]

The bike that wasn't! Not a mention of it in September 1952's brochure excepting the rear cover's data sheet, right-hand column, before being obscured I can just make out Model S, 64x77, 248 etc. So it's the obscure reintroduction, with telescopic forks added, of the pre-war Model S that was made and exported in limited numbers in the early '50s. It would officially be inaugurated into the UK Standard range consisting of the old rigid G and J at the end of 1953 but for now it was destined to be in limbo.

Since they'd first competed in the ISDT with springer machines in 1948, Royal Enfields had amassed no less than 26 Gold Medals and won the Manufacturer's Team Prize on three occasions (1949, 1951 and 1953) using both singles and twins.

The victorious ROYAL ENFIELD 1953 Team: Johnny Brittain (Trophy), Don Evans (Vase A) and Jack Stocker (Trophy), all mounted on "500 Twins."

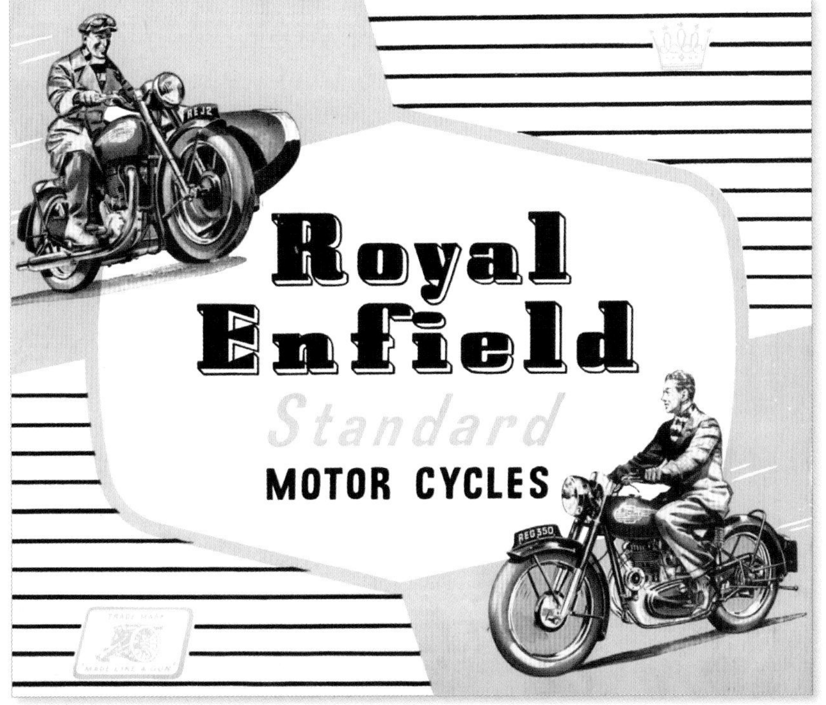

November 1953's brochure for utility machines now included the S – the three were black, black and black.

TECHNICAL DATA

	Model "G"	Model "J2"	Model "S"
Bore and Stroke (m.m.)	70×90	84×90	64×77
Cubic Capacity (c.c.) ...	346	499	248
Compression Ratio ...	6 to 1	5½ to 1	6½ to 1
Gear Ratios (Solo) ...	5·6 7·3 10·1 15·6 : 1	5·1 6·6 9·2 14·2 : 1	6·25 8·45 13·1 18·5 : 1
Gear Ratios (Sidecar) ...	—	5·95 7·7 10·7 16·6 : 1	—
Petrol Tank Capacity (Imp. Gals.)	2¾ (12½ litres)	2¾ (12½ litres)	2¾ (12½ litres)
Oil Tank Capacity (Pints)	4	4	4
Approx. Maximum Speed (m.p.h.)	70–75	80–85	60–65
Approx. Petrol Consumption (m.p.g.)	75–80	70–75	95–100
Weight (lbs.)	370	395	336
Wheelbase (inches) ...	53½	54½	53½
Saddle Height (inches) ...	29	28½	29
Ground Clearance (inches)	5¼	4¾	5¼
Overall Width (inches)	28	28	28

248 c.c. O.H.V.

Model "S"

Engine: 248 c.c. o.h.v. single cylinder. Dry sump lubrication incorporating large capacity oil filter. **Frame and Forks:** Robust brazed frame of chrome molybdenum tubing. Self-lubricating hydraulically damped telescopic forks with aluminium facia panel. **Transmission:** 4-speed foot-operated gearbox. Multi-plate clutch. Primary drive by $\frac{3}{8}$-in. pitch chain running in oil. Final drive by $\frac{5}{8}$-in. pitch. **Carburettor:** Amal carburettor with air cleaner. **Wheels:** Dunlop 3·00–19-in. ribbed front tyre. Dunlop 3·00–19-in. Universal rear tyre. The rear hub incorporates the Enfield patented cush drive which absorbs all transmission shocks. Powerful internal expanding hub brakes. **Electrical Equipment:** Miller 6-volt 45-watt output generator with automatic voltage control. Coil ignition. **Equipment:** Smith's chronometric illuminated speedometer, inflator and tool kit. **Finish:** Durable black enamel. Bright parts heavily chromium plated. Attractive tank motif of modern design.

Royal Enfield

By the look of them this couple are merely passers-by who've come across an apparently abandoned Meteor 700 and are now gazing intently at what the owner or owners are up to in the field. Another idyllic scenario courtesy of British motorcycle manufacturers' brochures – Royal Enfield, spring frame range, 1954.

The latest Ensign was still in polychromatic Copper Beech but had one or two insignificant alterations such as the headlamp mounting and also a suitably scaled-down version of the current tank badge.

For those that could stretch their finances to afford it the new swinging-arm Clipper was a far more attractive proposition than the S. The company hadn't even seen fit to include the latter in September '53's price list but it was just £138 basic against the Clipper's £162, so the by the time purchase tax was added the difference would have been the not-inconsiderable sum of £28.

Engine : 248 c.c. o.h.v. single cylinder. Dry sump lubrication incorporating large-capacity oil filter. **Frame and Fork :** Robust swinging-arm spring frame of chrome molybdenum tubing with hydraulic damping. Self-lubricating hydraulically-damped telescopic forks incorporating the new "Casquette" fork head. **Transmission :** 4-speed foot-operated gearbox. Multi-plate clutch. Primary drive, ½-in. pitch chain enclosed in oilbath case, final drive by ½-in. pitch chain. **Carburettor:** Amal carburettor fitted with oil-wetted air filter. **Wheels :** Patented cush drive incorporated in rear hub eliminates all transmission shocks. Dunlop 3·00-in. ribbed front, and studded rear tyres. Powerful internal expanding hub brakes. **Electrical Equipment :** A.C. Generator and rectifier giving 6-volt 60-watt output, enclosed in primary chain case. Electric horn. Headlamp and light switch mounted in "Casquette" fork head. **Equipment :** Smith's Chronometric illuminated speedometer. Centre stand, inflator and tool kit. **Finish :** Distinctive olive green enamel. Bright parts heavily chromium plated or polished aluminium. Attractive metal tank motif of modern design.

Royal Enfield

"Made like a Gun"

Motor Cycle Prices

MODEL	Retail Price	Purchase Tax	Total
SPRING FRAME MODELS	£ s. d.	£ s. d.	£ s. d.
"Ensign" 148 c.c. Two stroke ...	78 0 0	15 12 0	93 12 0
"250 Clipper" 248 c.c. O.H.V. ...	135 0 0	27 0 0	162 0 0
"350 Bullet" 346 c.c. O.H.V. ...	155 0 0	31 0 0	186 0 0
"500 Bullet" 499 c.c. O.H.V. ...	170 0 0	34 0 0	204 0 0
"500 Twin" 496 c.c. O.H.V. ...	185 0 0	37 0 0	222 0 0
"Meteor 700" 692 c.c. O.H.V. ...	195 0 0	39 0 0	234 0 0
STANDARD MODELS	£ s. d.	£ s. d.	£ s. d.
Model G. 346 c.c. O.H.V. ...	135 0 0	27 0 0	162 0 0
Model J.2. 499 c.c. O.H.V. ...	145 0 0	29 0 0	174 0 0
EXTRA EQUIPMENT	£ s. d.	£ s. d.	£ s. d.
Legshields ("Ensign")	1 17 6	*	1 17 6
Pillion Seat and Footrests ("Ensign") ...	1 19 6	*	1 19 6
Legshields (Other Models)	1 19 6	*	1 19 6
Dual Seat on Four stroke Models	3 10 0	14 0	4 4 0
Pannier Set on Spring Frame Models	5 10 0	1 2 0	6 12 0
Sidecar Forks, Gear and Steering Damper on Model J.2., "500 Bullet" and "Meteor 700"	1 17 6	7 6	2 5 0

1st September, 1953. *Tax Free—Supplied separately.

Engine: 346 c.c. o.h.v. single cylinder. Aluminium alloy cylinder head. R.R.56 light alloy connecting rod. Dry sump lubrication incorporating large-capacity oil filter. **Frame and Forks :** Robust swinging-arm spring frame of chrome molybdenum tubing with hydraulic damping. Self-lubricating hydraulically damped telescopic forks incorporating the new "Casquette" fork head. **Transmission :** Four-speed foot-operated gearbox incorporating positive neutral finder. Multi-plate clutch. Primary drive by Duplex chain enclosed in oilbath case. Final drive by ⅝-in. chain. **Carburettor :** Amal carburettor fitted with oil-wetted air filter. **Wheels :** Patented cush drive incorporated in rear hub eliminates all transmission shocks. Dunlop 3·25-in. ribbed front and studded rear tyres. Powerful internal expanding hub brakes. **Electrical Equipment :** Lucas 60-watt output magdyno. Automatic voltage control. Electric horn. Headlamp, two pilot lamps and lighting switch mounted in "Casquette" fork head. Combined stop and rear light. **Equipment :** Smith's Chronometric illuminated speedometer. Centre stand, prop stand. Pillion footrests. Inflator and tool kit. **Finish :** Silver-grey polychromatic enamel. Bright parts heavily chromium plated or polished aluminium. Attractive metal tank motif of modern design.

The Bullet now had a conventional-looking exhaust system whereas it had previously been tilted upwards towards the rear, competition-style – the '53 model even having had a curious silencer with angled tailpipe to render its last few inches horizontal. The Casquette fork head, as well as providing a neat mounting for instruments and switches, was Enfield's convenient answer to the problem manufacturers were facing at this time as to the location of pilot lights.

Spring Frame
692 c.c. O.H.V.

"Meteor 700"

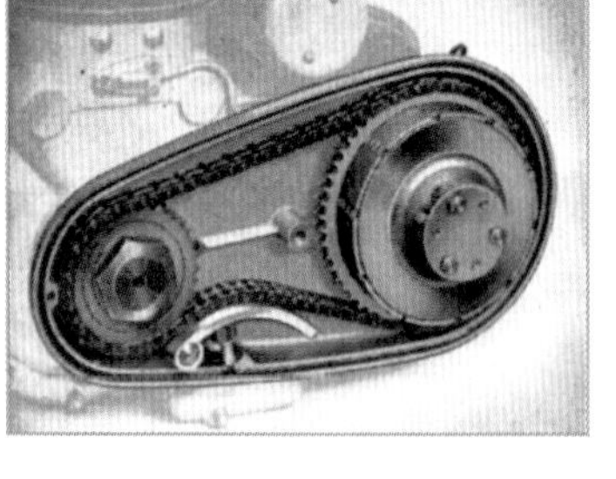

Although Meteors were invariably illustrated at this time with panniers and dual seat they were optional extras. Twins and big singles had duplex primary drive in conjunction with this tensioner running in a cast-aluminium oil bath casing.

Engine : 692 c.c. o.h.v. vertical twin cylinder. Separate cylinder heads fitted on deep-finned cylinders. R.R. 56 light alloy connecting rods. Massive one-piece crankshaft. Chain-driven high-level camshafts. Dry sump lubrication incorporating large-capacity oil filter. **Frame and Forks :** Robust swinging arm spring frame of chrome molybdenum tubing with hydraulic damping. Self lubricating hydraulically damped telescopic forks incorporating the new "Casquette" fork head. **Transmission :** 4-speed foot-operated gearbox incorporating positive neutral finder. Multi-plate clutch. Primary drive by Duplex chain enclosed in oilbath case. Final drive by ⅝-in. chain. **Carburettor :** Amal carburettor fitted with oil-wetted air filter. **Wheels :** Patented cush drive incorporated in rear hub eliminates all transmission shocks. Dunlop 3·25-in. ribbed front and 3·50-in. studded rear tyres. Powerful dual front brake. **Electrical Equipment :** Lucas 6-volt 75-watt dynamo lighting and ignition. Automatic voltage control. Headlamp, two pilot lamps and lighting switch mounted in "Casquette" fork head. Combined stop and rear light. Electric horn. **Equipment :** Smith's chronometric illuminated speedometer. Centre stand, prop stand. Pillion footrests. Inflator and tool kit. **Finish :** Copper beech polychromatic enamel. Bright parts heavily chromium plated or polished aluminium. Attractive metal tank motif of modern design.

For sidecar use a front fork with reduced trail, stronger springs and a steering damper is fitted. For sidecar gear ratios, see Technical Data on back page. When ordering, please specify whether machine is intended for Solo or Sidecar use.

The Dual Seat and Pannier Set illustrated above are available as extras; see separate leaflets.

	"Meteor 700"	"500 Twin"	"500 Bullet"	"350 Bullet"	"250 Clipper"	"150 Ensign"
Bore and Stroke (m.m.)	70×90	64×77	84×90	70×90	64×77	56×60
Cubic Capacity (c.c.)	692	496	499	346	248	148
Compression Ratio	6½ to 1	6½ to 1	6½ to 1	6½ to 1	6½ to 1	6½ to 1
Gear Ratios (Solo)	4·47 5·8 8·05 12·4 : 1	5 6·5 9 13·9 : 1	4·91 6·4 8·85 13·65 : 1	5·67 7·37 10·2 15·8 : 1	6·25 8·45 13·1 18·5 : 1	6·95 11·3 20·35 : 1
Gear Ratios (Sidecar)	5·03 6·53 9·05 13·95 : 1	—	5·72 7·45 10·3 15·9 : 1	—	—	—
Petrol Tank Capacity (Imp. Gals.) ...	4 (18 litres)	3¼ (15 litres)	3¼ (15 litres)	3¼ (15 litres)	3¼ (15 litres)	2 (9 litres)
Oil Tank Capacity (Pints)	4	4	4	4	4	—
Approx. Maximum Speeds (m.p.h.) ...	95–100	85–90	85–90	75–80	60–65	50–55
Approx. Petrol Consumption (m.p.g.) ...	55–60	65–70	70–75	75–80	95–100	110–120
Weight (lbs.)	405	390	370	350	330	155
Wheelbase (inches)	54	54	54	54	54	48
Saddle Height (inches)	29½	29½	29½	29½	29½	28
Ground Clearances (inches)	5½	5½	6¼	6¼	6	6
Overall Width (inches)	28	28	28	28	28	25½

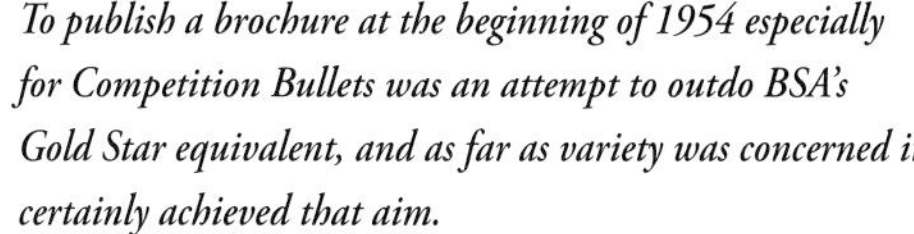

To publish a brochure at the beginning of 1954 especially for Competition Bullets was an attempt to outdo BSA's Gold Star equivalent, and as far as variety was concerned it certainly achieved that aim.

TRIALS MODEL

Six years previously, three prototype Bullets had been entered in the Colmore Cup Trial and from these the highly-successful ISDT bikes had stemmed. Up until that point it had been de rigueur for trials mounts to have unspring frames but the Redditch factory's Bullets showed the way forward, and over the years factory rider Johnny Britain had a great deal of success with them.

Engine: 350 or 500 c.c. The Bullet engines fitted to the Trials machines are specially tuned to meet the requirements of the trials rider, having low compression pistons, small bore carburetters and heavier flywheels than standard. The engines are also fitted with an efficient air filter and Lucas "Wader" magneto. **Gearbox:** Special ratios—"350": 7·1, 9·95, 15·25 and 21·3 to 1. "500": 6·06, 8·5, 13·03 and 18·2 to 1. **Wheels:** Front—2·75—21in. Dunlop Trials Universal tyre. One security bolt. Rear—4·00—19in. Dunlop Trials Universal tyre. Two security bolts. Special light hubs to both front and rear wheels. **Frame and Fork:** Very light yet immensely strong construction incorporating the well known Royal Enfield hydraulically damped suspension on both front and rear. The ground clearance is approximately 7in. when the rider is seated. **Equipment:** Light alloy mudguards. Small capacity petrol tank. Air cleaner. Engine undershield. One toolbox with tools. Pad on rear mudguard. Prop stand in addition to centre stand. Upswept high level exhaust system. **Finish:** "500": Polychromatic "Copper Beech." "350": Polychromatic Silver Grey. Bright parts heavily chromium plated.

SCRAMBLER

Engine: 346 or 499 c.c. Single Cylinder. Extremely robust and rigid crankcase and crankshaft assembly. Heavy duty mainshaft ball bearings. Large oil circulation. Aluminium alloy cylinder head with shrunk-in valve seats. Aluminium alloy cylinder barrel with austenetic iron liner. Compression ratios available—"350": 7·5, 8·5 or 10·5 to 1. "500": 7·25, 8 or 9·5 to 1. Lucas "Wader" type magneto. Polished cylinder head, flywheels, etc. **Gearbox:** Fitted with kickstarter. Improved heavy duty clutch. Primary drive by Duplex ⅜in. pitch chain running in oil. Final drive by ⅝in. pitch chain. Gear ratios—"500": 6·06, 7·9, 10·1 and 16·8 to 1. "350": 7·08, 9·2, 12·7, 19·7 to 1. For alternative available ratios see chart. **Wheels:** Front—3·00—21in. Dunlop Sports tyre. One security bolt. Rear—4·00—19in. Dunlop Sports tyre. Two security bolts. 7in. brake. **Suspension:** Front—new Royal Enfield telescopic fork with improved hydraulic damping. Rear—swinging arm type with suspension units incorporating improved hydraulic damping. **Equipment:** Light alloy mudguards. Small capacity petrol tank. Dual seat. Engine undershield. Steering damper. Straight through upswept exhaust pipe. Air cleaner. **Finish:** "500": Polychromatic "Copper Beech." "350": Polychromatic Silver Grey. Bright parts heavily chromium plated.

Enfield's scrambler should perhaps have enjoyed more success than it did but at that time BSA and AMC's big singles were virtually omnipotent and used by the majority of star riders.

Engine: 346 or 499 c.c. Single Cylinder. Extremely rigid and robust crankcase and crankshaft assembly. Heavy duty mainshaft ball bearings. Large oil circulation. Aluminium alloy cylinder head with shrunk-in valve seats. Aluminium alloy cylinder barrel with austenetic iron liner. Racing valve timing. Lightened flywheels. Amal 10 G.P. racing carburetter. Lucas racing magneto. Compression ratios available—"350": 7·5, 8·5 or 10·5 to 1. "500": 7·25, 8 or 9·5 to 1. Polished cylinder head, flywheels, etc. **Gearbox:** No kickstarter. Heavy duty clutch. Primary drive by ⅜in. pitch Duplex chain running in oil. Final drive by ⅝in. pitch chain. Normal close gear ratios—"500": 4·91, 5·35, 6·28 and 8·1 to 1. "350": 5·72, 6·75, 8·01, 10·3 to 1. For alternative available ratios, see chart. **Wheels:** Front—3·00—19in. Dunlop Ribbed Racing tyre. One security bolt. Dual 6in. front brakes. Rear—3·50—19in. Dunlop Road Racing tyre. One security bolt. 7in. brake. Steel rims standard. Light alloy rims fitted as extra. **Suspension:** Front—new Royal Enfield telescopic fork with improved hydraulic damping. Rear—swinging arm type with suspension units incorporating improved hydraulic damping. **Equipment:** Light alloy mudguards. Small capacity petrol tank. Dual seat. Rear mounted. Footrests, gear and brake operation. Steering damper. Straight through exhaust pipe. Revolution counter fitted as extra. **Finish:** "500": Polychromatic "Copper Beech." "350": Polychromatic Silver Grey. Bright parts heavily chromium plated.

TECHNICAL DATA

	Bore & Stroke	Petrol Tank Capacity	Oil Tank Capacity	Weight	Wheelbase	Ground Clearance
"350" Scrambles	70×90 mm.	2 gallons	4 pints	320 lbs.	54 inches	7 inches
"500" Scrambles	84×90 mm.	2 gallons	4 pints	328 lbs.	54 inches	7 inches
"350" Racer	70×90 mm.	2 gallons	4 pints	305 lbs.	54 inches	6¼ inches
"500" Racer	84×90 mm.	2 gallons	4 pints	315 lbs.	54 inches	6¼ inches
"350" Trials	70×90 mm.	2 gallons	4 pints	320 lbs.	54 inches	7 inches
"500" Trials	84×90 mm.	2 gallons	4 pints	328 lbs.	54 inches	7 inches

The following gear ratios are available:

With kickstarter:

No. 12 ... ... 1, 1·4, 2·15, 3·3
No. 14 ... ... 1, 1·4, 1·98, 3·3
No. 16 ... ... 1, 1·3, 1·67, 2·14

Racing close ratio, no kickstarter:

No. 1 ... ... 1, 1·09, 1·28, 1·65
No. 3 ... ... 1, 1·18, 1·4, 1·8
No. 5 ... ... 1, 1·18, 1·4, 2·13

In addition the following sprockets can be supplied:

Model	Engine Sprocket	Countershaft Sprocket
"350 Bullet"	20 or 25	14, 15, 16, 17, 18, 19.
"500 Bullet"	25 or 29	14, 15, 16, 17, 18, 19, 20, 21.

The reasoning behind the marketing of the Bullet as an out-and-out racer, especially as late as this, is difficult to fathom. Obviously it would provide no competition for a camshaft AJS 7R or Manx Nortons, so were Enfield's directors hoping to humble BSA's production-based Gold Star road racing model? If one uses the Junior Clubmans TT as a guide, in which neither ran in out-and-out racing trim, the records are not encouraging: 1949 saw five Bullets entered and four finishing, in 28th, 42nd, 44th and 54th places – with Enfield employee and future TT winner Bill Lomas on the fifth completing just one lap, over a minute slower than the eventual winner, before expiring (might it have been the big end bearing?). Over the next three years a total of five were entered and just one managed to complete more than a single lap – finally finishing 60th. On all four occasions a plunger ZB Gold Star was the outright winner; as was a swinging-arm DB in 1955 when Enfield Bullets brought Isle of Man adventures to a close with a solitary entry and retirement.

Jenny looks distinctly reluctant as Colin and John suggest she goes for a spin around the block on the back of the latter's new 1955-model Meteor 700 with dual front brakes. Besides, they were a stuffy pair who liked the current hits by Vera Lynn or Winifred Atwell, and she was on her way to the coffee bar where she could listen to more exciting stuff like Shake, Rattle and Roll by Bill Haley or Sh-boom by the Crew Cuts.

Enclosed rear springs for the Ensign rendered the appearance of its rear end a little less cranky.

The Clipper had received a minimal facelift, including the new ovular air filter, but for a bit extra the customer could specify Rich Deep Maroon or Polychromatic Silver-Grey as an alternative to the standard Olive Green.

DUAL SEAT

Specially designed to ensure the comfort of rider and passenger, and to blend with the lines of the machine. Constructed with a deep, luxurious Dunlopillo cushion on a shaped metal base, and covered with weather-resisting Vynide plastic.

DUAL FRONT BRAKE

All Bullet and Twin cylinder machines are now equipped with dual front brakes, which give absolute stability during hard braking combined with tremendous power and long life.

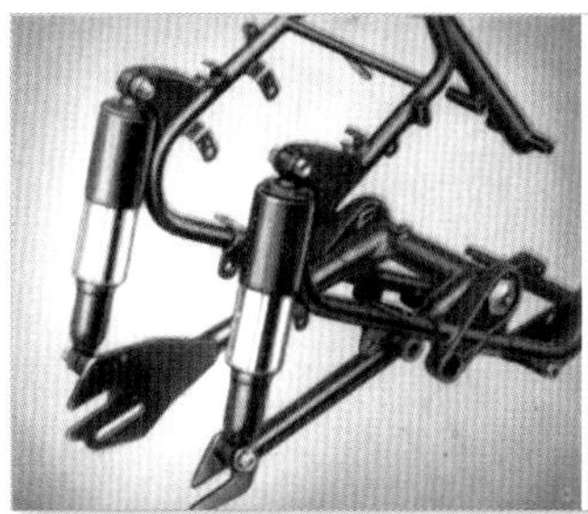

SPRING FRAME

The ROYAL ENFIELD spring frame is of the scientifically-correct swinging-arm type with hydraulic movement control and ensures maximum comfort and perfect road holding under all conditions.

AIR FILTER

This efficient unit ensures that only clean air enters the carburettor. As a result, wear of the cylinder, piston, piston rings and valve guides is reduced to a minimum.

Bullets and twins now had a redesigned rear section of frame, dual front brakes and, not before time, dual seats were fitted at no extra cost. The 350, here, was finished in Silver-Grey Polychromatic but you could also have it in Rich Deep Maroon or Olive Green. The 500 came in Rich Deep Maroon with the other two as an option. If you wanted to use it for hauling a sidecar a front fork with reduced trail, stronger springs and a steering damper was recommended, as it was for any Enfield.

Rich Dark Maroon was the standard colour for the Meteor 700 but you could also have one in Olive Green or Silver Grey Polychromatic. The 500 Twin, on the other hand, came in Silver Grey Polychromatic with either of the other two to choice. The pannier illustrations had been abandoned but they were still available to order and at extra cost.

TECHNICAL DATA 1955 Models

	"Meteor" 700"	"500 Twin"	"500 Bullet"	"350 Bullet"	"250 Clipper"	"150 Ensign"
Bore and Stroke (m.m.)	70×90	64×77	84×90	70×90	64×77	56×60
Cubic Capacity (c.c.)...	692	496	499	346	248	148
Compression Ratio	7·25 to 1	6·5 to 1	6·5 to 1	7·25 to 1	6·5 to 1	6·5 to 1
Gear Ratios (Solo)	4·47 5·8 8·05 12·4 : 1	5 6·5 9 13·9 : 1	4·91 6·4 8·85 13·65 : 1	5·67 7·37 10·2 15·8 : 1	6·25 8·45 13·1 18·5 : 1	6·95 12·0 21·7 : 1 —
Gear Ratios (Sidecar)	5·03 6·53 9·05 13·95 : 1	—	5·72 7·45 10·3 15·9 : 1	—	—	—
Petrol Tank Capacity (Imp. Gals.) ...	4	3¼	3¼	3¼	3¼	2
Oil Tank Capacity (Pints)	4	4	4	4	4	—
Approx. Maximum Speeds (m.p.h.) ...	95–100	85–90	85–90	75–80	60–65	50–55
Approx. Petrol Consumption (m.p.g.) ...	55–60	65–70	70–75	75–80	95–100	110–120
Weight (lbs.)	405	390	370	350	330	155
Wheelbase (inches)	54	54	54	54	54	48
Saddle Height (inches)	29½	29½	29½	29½	29½	28
Ground Clearances (inches)	5½	5½	6¼	6¼	6	6
Overall Width (inches)	28	28	28	28	28	25½

THE ENFIELD CYCLE CO. LTD.

The new Super Meteors, as well as 500 Twins and Bullets, had a redesigned frame with no seat pillar, as well as a one-piece battery and air filter case. The 500 Twins stuck to coil ignition but Meteors and Bullets had rotating magnet magnetos and all had a mainshaft-driven alternator in the primary chain case. Tank badges were now the fashionable 3D plastic variety and a QD rear wheel with full-width hub was an optional extra.

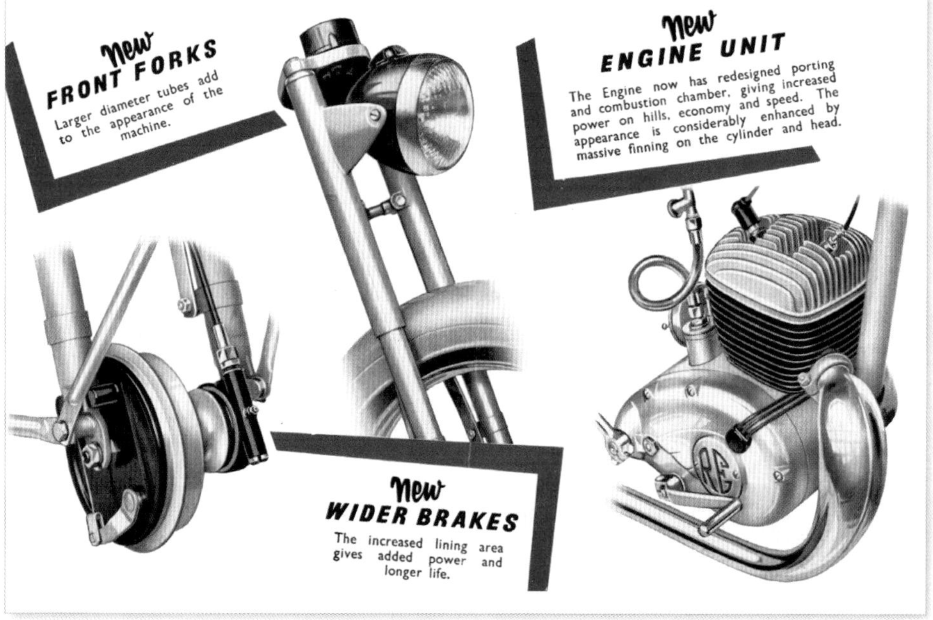

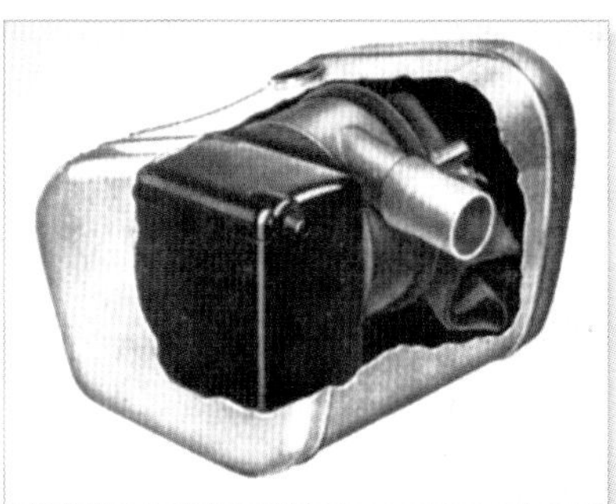

Battery and Air Filter Compact:

The battery, air cleaner and toolbox are compacted in one pleasing unit with easily removable covers on each side.

Rear Suspension:

Royal Enfield rear suspension has proved its worth for many years in international competitions all over the world and the latest type ensures maximum comfort and perfect road holding under all conditions.

In the absence of detailed data we'll have to take the company's word about the Ensign's engine and brake improvements but you'll no doubt notice that the factory captions accompanying the improved forks and engine were overly concerned with their enhanced appearance. Of course it did look more modern and colour was changed to Light Surf Green too.

By comparing this spec with the old model we find that top gear ratio is the same whilst bottom and second a little lower, claimed consumption a smidgeon improved, and seat height 1in lower; but the little blighter had put on 3lb in weight. In fact The Motor Cycle *were unable to extract more than 51mph from the machine they tested. But if you were prepared to ride at 20mph on a level road it'd do 200 miles to a gallon of petroil – or, more realistically, 168mpg at 30mph or 98 at 40.*

ROYAL ENFIELD ENSIGN II	
Bore and Stroke (m.m.)	56×60
Cubic Capacity (c.c.)	148
Compression Ratio	6·5 to 1
B.H.P. and R.P.M.	6 at 4750 r.p.m.
Gear Ratios (Solo)	6·95 12·0 21·7
Petrol Tank Capacity (Imp. Gals.)	2
Approx. Maximum Speed m.p.h.	55
Approx. Petrol Consumption m.p.g.	120-130
Weight (lbs.)	158
Wheelbase (inches)	48
Seat Height (inches)	27
Ground Clearance (inches)	6
Overall Width (inches)	25½

It's September 1956 and Jenny, who now rides a bike herself and is crazy about Elvis Presley – who's got three records in the top 20 – has been captured by the artist whilst on a Mediterranean publicity trip with the latest model. As well as sporting a brand-new frame and engine, the Crusader 250 was the first British bike to feature stylish aluminium castings that encapsulated the bottom half of the engine, gearbox and generator as well as a reservoir for the oil.

Engine-Gear Unit: 248 c.c. O.H.V. single cylinder engine, 70 m.m. bore, 64·5 m.m. stroke, short RR.56 light alloy connecting rod, split shell white metal big end bearing, working direct on massive one piece Meehanite iron crankshaft.

The crankshaft is carried on large diameter ball and roller bearings.

The 70 m.m. bore enables large valves to be used; these are push rod operated and the camshaft driven by chain.

Lubrication is full dry sump by high speed oscillating plunger pumps which give a rapid oil circulation. A large capacity filter is incorporated in the system.

The four speed gearbox, oil bath and A.C. generator are all housed in the streamlined engine-gear "bloc."

Frame and Forks: Completely new frame, with swinging arm rear suspension and hydraulic damping; all main tubes are constructed of chrome molybdenum tubing. Front forks automatically lubricated and damped.

Transmission: Four speed foot operated gearbox, primary drive by $\frac{3}{8}$" pitch chain enclosed and lubricated. Final drive by $\frac{1}{2}$" pitch chain fully enclosed in chaincase.

Carburettor: Amal "Monobloc" with efficient fabric type air filter.

Wheels: Front fitted with full width hub and 17"×3·25" Dunlop ribbed tyre. Rear quickly detachable with full width hub and 17"×3·25" Dunlop studded tyre. The rear sprocket incorporates the well known ROYAL ENFIELD cush drive.

Electrical Equipment: Lucas A.C. generator and rectifier giving 6 volt 60 watt output. Coil ignition. The ignition switch has an emergency start position. Electric horn. Headlamp, twin pilot lights, ammeter and light switch mounted in Casquette fork head.

Equipment: Smith's chronometric illuminated speedometer. Easy lift centre stand, inflator and tool kit.

Finish: Light surf green. Bright parts polished aluminium or heavy chromium plate. Optional finishes, maroon or black enamel.

The full width front hub and 17" wheel are enclosed in a beautifully styled front mudguard.

By loosening two bolts, the whole rear mudguard assembly and dual seat may be lifted clear of the machine.

Here's a Crusader equipped with the optional-extra leg shields and panniers all set for the Grand Tour. The ignition key is all set for trouble too, as the company returned to bad old habits with the switch's placement.

Bore and Stroke (m.m.)	70×64½	Weight (lb.)	312
Cubic Capacity (c.c.)	248	Approx. Petrol Consumption m.p.g.—Solo	100
Compression Ratio	7·3 to 1	Wheelbase (inches)	52
Max. B.H.P. and R.P.M. ..	13 at 5,750	Brake diameter and width (inches) Front ... ... / Rear	6×1 / 6×1
Gear Ratios—Solo	5·8 / 7·83 / 10·44 / 16·97		
Petrol Tank Capacity (Imp. Gals.)	3	Seat Height (inches)	29
Oil Tank Capacity (pints) ...	3	Ground Clearance (inches) ...	5½
Approx. Maximum Speed m.p.h. —Solo	70	Overall width (inches) ...	24½

The artist depicted the latest Super Meteor pretty much as it was apart from the fuel tank, which had chrome panels on this year's models. His rigging of the dinghy is a little less proficient, however.

Introduced the previous year, the 350 Clipper was something of a retrograde step – reintroducing the iron-head Model G motor. It had a Clipper 250-type frame but ignition and charging by magdyno rather than its smaller brethren's coil/AC generator and rectifier setup. It was finished in Olive Green enamel whilst the 250 was in Rich Deep Maroon.

The previous year's Bullets with redesigned frames now featured chrome tank panels and full-width hubs with QD rear wheels were standard issue. Whether 350 or 500 they were finished in Rich Deep Maroon. Bullet scramblers had been updated to resemble the works machines – renamed Moto Cross they had the new frame, full-width front hub and Amal TT carb.

Twins, large and less large, were both in Rich Deep Maroon but the large (Super Meteor) had a rotating magnet magneto whilst the less large (500 Twin) had coil ignition, along with side-mounted switch.

Quickly Detachable Rear Wheel :

Embodying full width polished light alloy hub and the famou~ Royal Enfield cush drive, the rear wheel may be easily removed after the withdrawal of one bolt, leaving the rear sprocket and chain in situ.

	"SUPER METEOR"	"500 TWIN"	"500 BULLET"	"350 BULLET"	"350 CLIPPER"	"250 CLIPPER"	"CRUSADER 250"	"150 ENSIGN II"
Bore and Stroke (m.m.)	70 × 90	64 × 77	84 × 90	70 × 90	70 × 90	64 × 77	70 × 64·5	56 × 60
Cubic Capacity (c.c.)	692	496	499	346	346	248	248	148
Compression Ratio	7·25 to 1	7·5 to 1	6·5 to 1	7·25 to 1	6·5 to 1	6·5 to 1	7·3 to 1	6·5 to 1
Max. B.H.P. and R.P.M.	40 at 5500	27 at 6000	25 at 5250	19 at 6000	15 at 5500	11 at 5500	13 at 5750	6 at 4750
Gear Ratios—Solo	4·33 5·63 7·87 12·05	5·15 6·7 9·35 14·3	4·91 6·4 8·85 13·65	5·72 7·45 10·35 15·9	5·6 7·3 10 15·6	6·25 8·45 13·1 18·5	5·8 7·83 10·44 16·97	6·95 12·0 21·7
Gear Ratios—Sidecar	4·88 6·34 8·85 13·55		5·72 7·45 10·35 15·9					
Petrol Tank Capacity (Imp. gallons) ... Oil Tank Capacity (pints)	4 4	3¼ 4	3¼ 4	3¼ 4	3¼ 4	3¼ 4	3 3	2 —
Approx. Max. Speed m.p.h.—Solo ... " " " " —Sidecar ...	100 75–80	85–90	85–90 70–75	75–80	70–75	60–65	70	55
Weight (lbs.)	410	390	370	350	362	330	312	158 165 (with rectifier)
Approx. Petrol Consumption m.p.g.— Solo ... Sidecar ...	55–60 50–55	70–75	70–75 60–65	80–85	80–85	95–100	100	120–130
Wheelbase (inches)	54	54	54	54	54	54	52	48
Brake diameter and width (inches)— Front ... Rear ...	6 × 1 Dual. 7 × 1	6 × 1 Dual. 7 × 1	6 × 1 Dual. 7 × 1	6 × 1 Dual. 6 × 1	6 × 1 6 × 1	6 × 1 6 × 1	6 × 1 6 × 1	5 × 1 5 × 1
Seat Height (inches)	31	31	31	31	29½	29½	29	27
Ground Clearance (inches)	5½	5½	5½	5½	6	6	5½	6
Overall Width (inches)	28	28	28	28	28	28	24½	25½

The 1958 Crusader powers around a bend on a country road, virtually unchanged from last year's model other than a more up-to-date barrel silencer, repositioned horn and restyled dual seat with white piping. As for listed colour schemes, despite this cover illustration, they were Black or the following two-tone finishes: Black/Polychromatic Burgundy; Black/Polychromatic Wedgewood Blue or Black/Polychromatic Silver Grey. With a competition career encompassing scrambles to road racing that stretched back to the 1930s, Freddie Hawken was particularly proud of his TT rides, and for many years in his showroom had the 7R he finished on twice.

If customers were thinking the Ensign III represented exciting improvements over the still-current Ensign II they were in for a disappointment – it even came in the same colours of Light Surf Green or Black. So what was the point? A battery and generator rather than the II's direct lighting.

ENGINE-GEAR UNIT : 148 c.c. two-stroke engine and gear unit of modern streamlined design. The new aluminium alloy cylinder head and cast-iron cylinder barrel give much-improved performance and economy. Robust crankshaft carried by four main journal ball bearings. Roller bearing big-end. Foot-operated 3-speed gear. Totally enclosed primary drive running in oil. The improved engine speed clutch gives smooth, silky pick-up, positive drive and very light operation. High output flywheel generator. Full-sized ignition coil, which ensures certain starting under all conditions.

FRAME AND FORKS : Frame constructed of chrome-molybdenum tubing, utilising full swinging-arm type rear suspension. Self-lubricating telescopic forks. Streamlined cast aluminium casquette encloses the new headlamp which houses the speedometer, switch and ammeter.

CARBURETTER : Amal needle type with oil-wetted air cleaner.

WHEELS : Fitted with $2{\cdot}75 \times 19$-in. Dunlop tyres, final drive by $\frac{1}{2}$-in. pitch chain. Powerful brakes on both wheels.

LIGHTING SYSTEM : A.C. rectified current supplies an 8 amp. hour wet battery which operates the lamps and electric horn.

EQUIPMENT : Lightweight chronometric, illuminated speedometer, electric horn, centre stand, dual seat and pillion footrests, inflator and tool kit.

FINISH : Light Surf Green or Black. Bright parts heavily chromium plated or polished aluminium.

The 250 Clippers were no more, the 350 now had the same frame as Bullets, its motor had been uprated to be more Bulletlike, and now gave out a claimed 16.5hp instead of 15. It retained its iron head, however, and had been swapped from magneto to coil ignition. Colour was now Black.

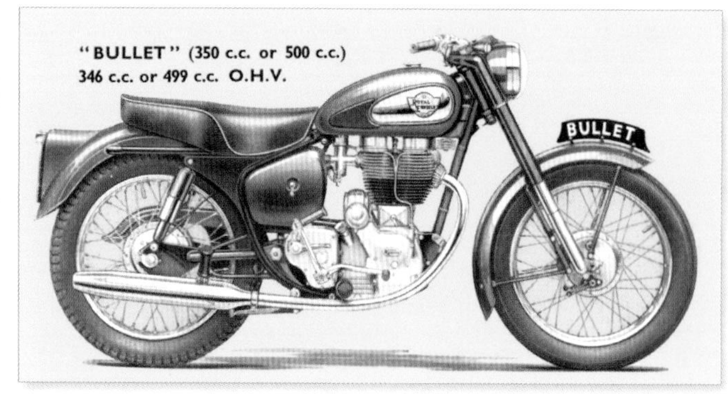

Bullets and twins had the new-style dual seat and silencers. This is the 500, for which the manufacturer claimed 25hp; the 350 giving 19hp. They were finished in Black as standard with the option of these two-tone colour schemes – Black/Polychromatic Burgundy; Black/Polychromatic Wedgewood Blue and Black/Polychromatic Silver Grey.

With space travel on everyone's minds, Enfield launched the new 500 twin in spring '58 rather than wait for autumn. Not only did it have Crusader styling, its motor shared its bore and stroke dimensions. You could have it in Black but many opted for two-tone with frame and forks in Black with tanks, battery/toolbox and mudguards in either Polychromatic Burgundy, Poly Wedgewood Blue or Poly Silver Grey.

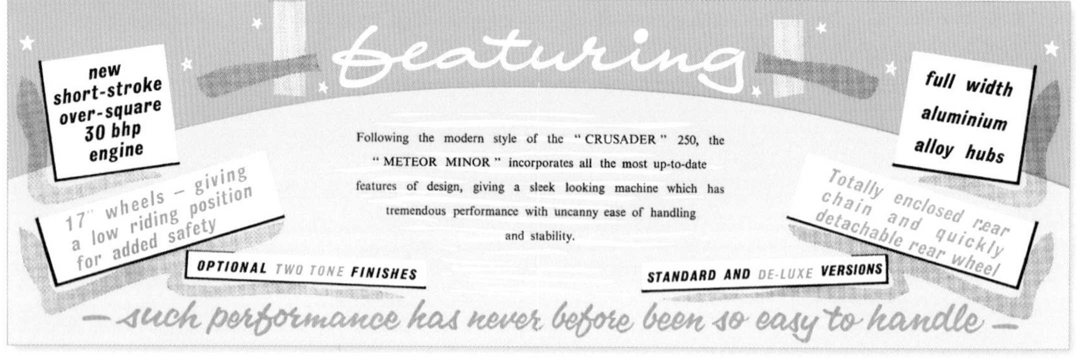

Bore and Stroke (mm.)	70 x 64.5	Approx. Maximum Speed ...	90—95
Cubic Capacity (c.c.)	496	Weight (lbs.)	388
Compression Ratio	8 : 1	Approx. Petrol Consumption (m.p.g.)	70—75
Max. B.H.P. and R.P.M.	30 at 6,250	Wheelbase (inches)	53
Gear Ratios—Solo	4.67 6.08 8.42 13.00	Brake diameter and width (inches) Front (de-luxe) ... ... Rear	 7 x 1½ 7 x 1
		Seat Height (inches)	29
Petrol Tank Capacity (Imp. Gals.)...	3	Ground Clearance (inches) ...	5½
Oil Tank Capacity (pints) ...	4	Overall width (inches)	26

The Standard Meteor Minor was finished in Black and, believe or not, had a Terry spring seat saddle specified, although I can't imagine many leaving the showrooms without the optional dual seat. It also had a 6in front brake – only the De Luxe having the new full-width 7in. With a strong following wind The Motor Cycle *managed to extract 97mph out of one (89 two ways) and at 50mph it would return 75 miles for a gallon of fuel, or 58mpg at a steady 60mph. The pronouncement was that it was a 'compact and sprightly twin'.*

rusader 250

Airflow

REA 250

Royal Enfield

Looks— Superb "airflow" styling gives beautifully smooth lines and flowing curves, to please the most aesthetic eye.

Performance— This beauty is also functional—improvements of approximately 20 per cent. in fuel consumption and 8 per cent. in maximum speed, result from the streamlined contours, with the rider normally seated. Engine cooling too is more efficient than on the orthodox style motorcycle, because of the special design of the air duct.

Protection— You're "out of the weather" riding the "Airflow" ! The elements flow past on either side and overhead, leaving you warm and dry. No more cold hands or splashed legs ! No need to "dress like a diver."

Construction— The shield section of the "Airflow" and the front mudguard are moulded from glass reinforced plastic—light, yet extremely tough. It's most practical too because in the unlikely event of damage it's so easy and cheap to repair.

Another of Enfield's surprises was the first of what would grow to be the Airflow range. Colours were as for the regular Crusader but with this fairing they claimed 65-to-70mph and 115-to-120 mpg. The Motor Cycle*'s February 1958 figures were 65mph (highest one-way 69mph), and 120mpg at a steady 40mph or 99mpg at 50. Wilemans Motors, who gave out this brochure, were established in the late 1930s. As far as I am aware, at the time of writing they sell spares for classic motorcycles.*

TECHNICAL DATA

CONSTELLATION

Bore and Stroke (mm.)	70×90	Approx. Max. Speed (M.P.H.)	110
Cubic Capacity (c.c.)	692	Approx. Petrol Con. (M.P.G.)	50/55
Compression Ratio	8·5 to 1	Weight (lbs.)	403
B.H.P. and R.P.M.	50 at 6,250	Wheelbase (inches)	54
Gear Ratios	4·44, 5·77 7·99, 12·35	Seat Height (inches)	31
Petrol Tank Capacity (Imp. Gallons)	4½	Brake diameter and width (ins.) Front Rear	6×1 Dual 7×1
		Ground Clearance (inches)	5½
Oil Tank Capacity (Pints)	4	Overall Width (inches)	25½

Russia may have beaten the rest of the world into outer space with the Sputnik at the end of 1957 but Royal Enfield wasn't to be outdone, and the Constellation was the second of its space-age-themed bikes to be released onto the British market for spring and summer buyers. With supreme honesty the company resisted the temptation to call it new as it was already available in the US. And anyway, in reality, it was a Super Meteor, revamped and given considerably more power.

In the company of Enfield's Jack Booker, who wanted to test out an Airflow Meteor Minor at speed, Motor Cycling*'s Bernal Osborne took a Constellation to Belgium in the spring of '58. Early one morning in pretty much ideal conditions he repeatedly traversed a suitable stretch of road at increasing velocities until he managed to record a fraction more than 115mph over a quarter-mile and 95 in third whilst accelerating. Quite apart from this the pair put in some fast average speeds over the entire trip, the whole of which resulted in the Constellation returning almost exactly 50mpg.*

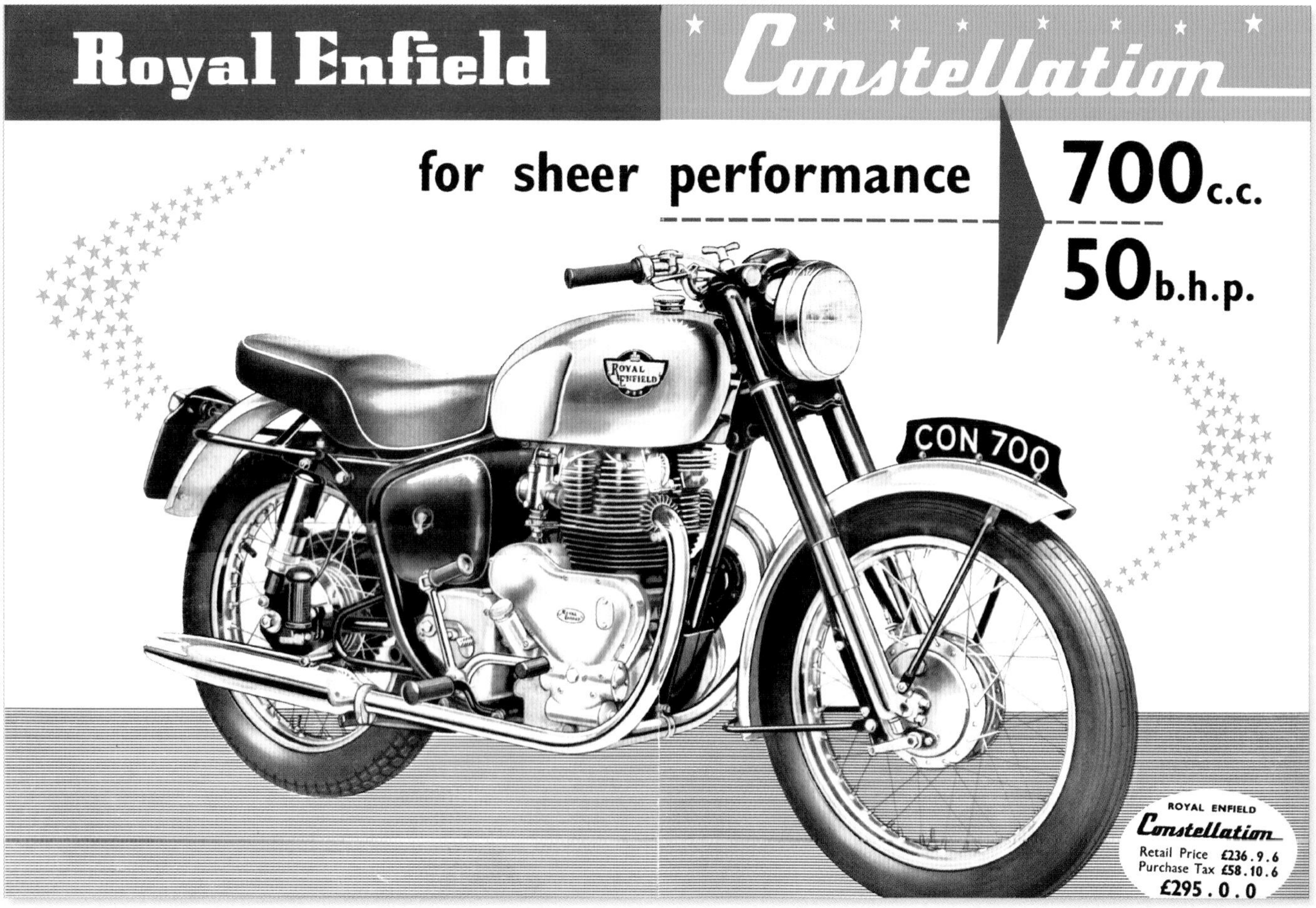

Royal Enfield Constellation

for sheer performance 700c.c. 50b.h.p.

CON 700

ROYAL ENFIELD Constellation
Retail Price £236.9.6
Purchase Tax £58.10.6
£295.0.0

What else to feature on the cover of the autumn 1958 brochure's cover than one of the new '59-model Airflows, its riders enjoying a sinuous mountain road and the dramatic scenery.

Other manufacturers' 150 two-strokes had been running around with conventional swinging-arm suspension for some while, so it was not before time that Enfield offered this as a slightly pricier version of the Ensign III; and a smart little thing it was in two-tone Black and Cherry Red.

The 250 Clipper was back as a low-cost alternative to the Crusader, now with the same mechanicals except for an iron head (as had the Crusader Airflow) and an insignificantly lower compression (7.5:1 against 8:1) but, to my mind, a far more attractive front mudguard. Although more soberly finished, Clippers were Black/Cherry Red; Crusaders were Black/Polychromatic Burgundy or Black/Polychromatic Peacock Blue.

What else to feature on the cover of the autumn 1958 brochure's cover than one of the new '59-model Airflows, its riders enjoying a sinuous mountain road and the dramatic scenery.

With this, Enfield unashamedly entered the 250 sports market and within a few years would be acknowledged as its leader – as far as British bikes were concerned. Its horsepower increase over the standard Crusader was achieved at greater revs (up from 5,750 to 6,250rpm) and Motor Cycling *were certainly impressed with WNP 852 during their spring 1959 test. Dubbing it 'Britain's fastest quarter-litre roadster' they spoke of 'speeds in the neighbourhood of 80mph, handling and road-holding to near-racing standards, good brakes and excellent fuel consumption'. In hard figures this meant 78mph in top, 67 in third and 98mpg at 50mph.*

Bullets had been given the same brash persona as the Crusader Sports and Constellation. The factory was now claiming 80-to-85mph for the 350 and an optimistic 95-to-100mph for the 500.

Although it was not featured in the main brochure Royal Enfield still offered a workmanlike and efficient trials version of the 350 Bullet. The Works Replica had an aluminium top end and was marketed with the slogan 'Now you can win too'.

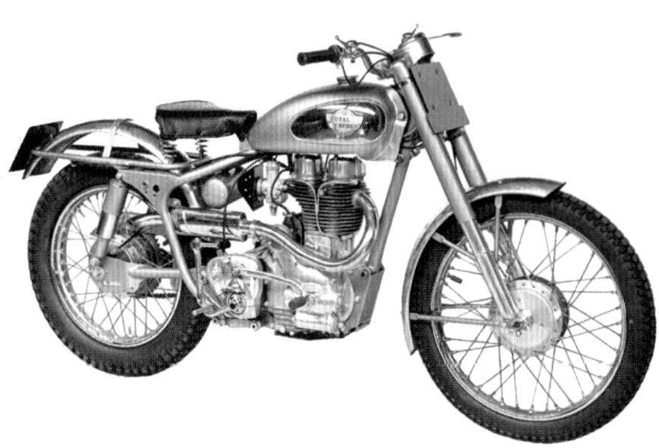

BULLET 350 & 500

These popular machines have a background of Competition successes second to none and in their 1959 form have still more efficient engines with redesigned cams, larger bore carburetters and inlet ports, etc. The 500 c.c. model has a completely new and redesigned cylinder head with downdraught carburetter and larger inlet valve (see illustration). The machines have been restyled with large capacity chromium plated petrol tanks, chromium plated mudguards and new exhaust system. The two new Bullets are handsome fast road machines, which any owner may be proud to possess.

Despite Bob McIntyre and Derek Powell being runners-up to Mike Hailwood's Triumph 110 in the Thruxton 500 the previous year with one, the 1959 brochure had relegated the Super Meteor to being 'ideal for heavy-duty sidecar work' – whilst at the same time assuring the possible customer that it 'has flashing acceleration up to a maximum speed, in the region of 100mph'. This, the Constellation, was now the flagship model. The promise of a top speed of around 115mph was helped by the employment of an Amal TT carb along with other engine upgrades to elevate it from the now-humbled Super Meteor.

COLOUR SCHEMES. The following two-colour finishes are available :

Black/Polychromatic Burgundy, with optional Black/Polychromatic Peacock Blue

"Constellation." "Meteor Minor De Luxe." "Crusader 250."
"Super Meteor." "350 and 500 Bullets." "Crusader Sports."

Black/Cherry Red

"150 Prince." "350 Clipper."
"250 Clipper." "Meteor Minor Standard."

Black or Surf Green

"Ensign III"

The tank, mudguards, compact covers, chain covers and mudguards are finished in the appropriate coloured enamel.

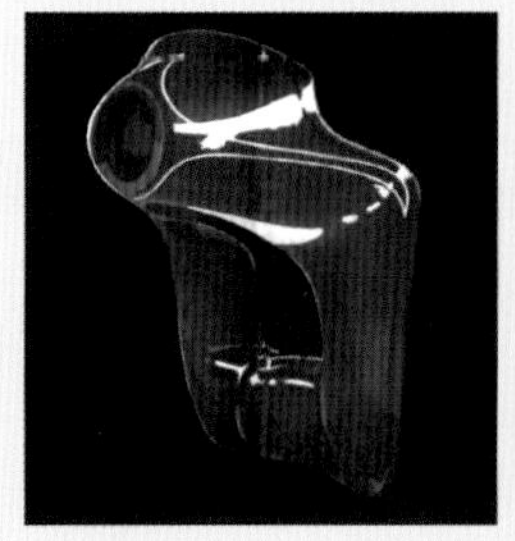

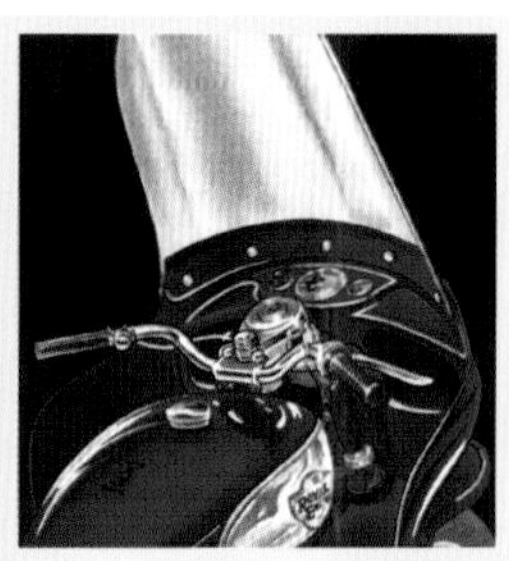

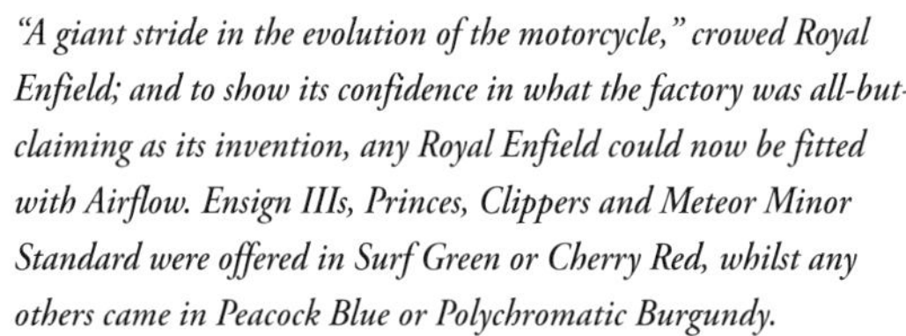

"A giant stride in the evolution of the motorcycle," crowed Royal Enfield; and to show its confidence in what the factory was all-but-claiming as its invention, any Royal Enfield could now be fitted with Airflow. Ensign IIIs, Princes, Clippers and Meteor Minor Standard were offered in Surf Green or Cherry Red, whilst any others came in Peacock Blue or Polychromatic Burgundy.

As a further aid to selling Airflows this fun little thing above was a publicity hand-out. You simply dialled up the various models. Frankly it was eccentric enough to include the Prince but stopped short of including the Ensign III in spite of it too being on the Airflow menu. If anyone can furnish me with irrefutable proof that they, or a direct relation of theirs, bought an Ensign III Airflow new I will be happy to refund to them what they paid for this book.

Specs for1959.

Facts	ENSIGN	PRINCE	250 CLIPPER	CRUSADER 250	CRUSADER SPORTS	350 CLIPPER	350 BULLET	500 BULLET	METEOR MINOR	SUPER METEOR	CONSTELLATION
Engine type	Two-stroke	Two-stroke	Four-stroke	Four-stroke	Four-stroke	Four-stroke	Four-stroke	Four-stroke	Four-stroke	Four-stroke	Four-stroke
Number of cylinders	1	1	1 o.h.v.	1 o.h.v.	1 o.h.v.	1 o.h.v.	1 o.h.v.	1 o.h.v.	2 o.h.v.	2 o.h.v.	2 o.h.v.
Cylinder head	Light alloy	Light alloy	Cast iron	Light alloy†	Light alloy	Cast iron	Light alloy	Light alloy	Light alloy	Light alloy	Light alloy
Cubic capacity (c.c.m.) ...	148	148	248	248	248	346	346	499	496	692	692
Bore and stroke (mm.) ...	56×60	56×60	70×64·5	70×64·5	70×64·5	70×90	70×90	84×90	70×64·5	70×90	70×90
Compression ratio	6·5 to 1	6·5 to 1	7·5 to 1	8 to 1	8·5 to 1	6·75 to 1	7·75 to 1	7·25 to 1	8 to 1	7·25 to 1	8 to 1
B.H.P.×R.P.M.	6 at 4,750	6 at 4,750	13½ at 5,750	13½ at 5,750	17 at 6,250	16·5 at 5,500	20 at 5,750	27 at 5,750	30 at 6,250	40 at 5,500	50 at 6,250
Carburetter	Amal with air cleaner	Amal with air cleaner	Amal	Amal with air cleaner	Amal	Amal	Amal with air cleaner	Amal	Amal with air cleaner	Amal with air cleaner	Amal T.T.
Ignition lighting	Miller A.C. battery	Miller A.C. battery	Lucas A.C. coil	Lucas A.C. coil	Lucas A.C. coil	Lucas A.C. coil	Lucas A.C. magneto	Lucas A.C. magneto	Lucas A.C. coil	Lucas A.C. coil	Lucas A.C. magneto
Primary drive chain	⅜″ pitch	⅜″ pitch	⅜″ pitch	⅜″ pitch	⅜″ pitch	⅜″ p. Duplex	⅜″ p. Duplex	⅜″ p. Duplex	⅜″ p. Duplex	⅜″ p. Duplex	⅜″ p. Duplex
Final drive chain	½″ pitch	½″ pitch	½″ pitch	½″ pitch	½″ pitch	⅝″ pitch	⅝″ pitch	⅝″ pitch	⅝″ pitch	⅝″ pitch	⅝″ pitch
Rear Suspension	Pivoted fork	Pivoted fork hydraulically damped	Pivoted fork hydraulically damped	Pivoted fork hydraulically damped	Pivoted fork hydraulically damped	Pivoted fork hydraulically damped	Pivoted fork hydraulically damped	Pivoted fork hydraulically damped	Pivoted fork hydraulically damped	Pivoted fork hydraulically damped	Pivoted fork hydraulically damped
Front fork	Telescopic automatic lubrication	Telescopic automatic lubrication	Telescopic hydraulically damped	Telescopic hydraulically damped	Telescopic hydraulically damped	Telescopic hydraulically damped	Telescopic hydraulically damped	Telescopic hydraulically damped	Telescopic hydraulically damped	Telescopic hydraulically damped	Telescopic hydraulically damped
Hubs : Front ... ... Rear	Standard Standard	Full width Full width	Light alloy full width standard	Light alloy full width Q.D.	Light alloy full width Q.D.	Light alloy full width standard	Light alloy full width Q.D.	Light alloy full width Q.D.	Light alloy full width *	Light alloy full width Q.D.	Light alloy full width Q.D.
Gear ratios	6·95, 12·0 21·7	6·95, 12·0 21·7	5·8, 7·83 10·44, 16·97	5·8, 7·83 10·44, 16·97	5·8, 7·83 10·44, 16·97	5·67, 7·37 10·2, 15·8	5·72, 7·45 10·35, 15·9	4·91, 6·4 8·85, 13·65	4·67, 6·08 8·42, 13·00	4·44, 6·04 8·16, 12·35	4·44, 6·04 8·16, 12·35
Approx. maximum speed (m.p.h.)	55	55	70	70	75–80	70–75	80–85	95–100	90–95	100	110–115
Approx. petrol consumption (m.p.g.)	120	120	100	100	95	80–85	80–85	70–75	70–75	55–60	50–55
Petrol tank capacity (gallons)	2	3	3	3	3¾	3¼	3¾	4¼	3¼	4	4¼
Oil tank capacity (pints) ...	—	—	3	3	3	4	4	4	4	4	4
Tyre sizes : Front—Dunlop ribbed ... Rear—Dunlop studded ...	2·75×19 2·75×19	2·75×19 2·75×19	3·25×17 3·25×17	3·25×17 3·25×17	3·25×17 3·25×17	3·25×19 3·25×19	3·25×17 3·25×17	3·25×19 3·50×19	3·25×17 3·50×17	3·25×19 3·50×19	3·25×19 3·50×19
Brake diameter and width : Front (ins.) ... ... Rear (ins.)	5×1 5×1	5×1 5×1	6×1 6×1	6×1 6×1	7×1½ 6×1	6×1 7×1	7×1½ 7×1	6×1 dual 7×1	De Luxe 7×1½ 7×1	6×1 dual 7×1	6×1 dual 7×1
Seat height (ins.)	27	28½	29	29	29	31	30	31	29	31	31
Wheelbase (ins.)	48	48	52	52	52	54	54	54	52	54	54
Overall width (ins.)	25½	25½	25½	25½	25½	25½	27½	27½	27	26½	26½
Ground clearance (ins.) ...	6	6	5½	5½	5½	6½	6	5½	5½	5½	5½
Weight (lbs.)	168	200	305	305	305	362	367	375	388	410	403

With a grin like a Cheshire cat, Dave heads his Meteor Minor Airflow south on a deserted French A-road, blissfully unaware he's on the wrong side of the road… No flies in his teeth with that screen, however, and Rona's well out of the wind too.

BSA could still just about get away with it with the 125 Bantam in 1961, but to close a deal on a new plunger Ensign III (Airflowed or otherwise) would have been a task that even the most resolute salesman would pale at the thought of, so it had been dropped. If you wanted an RE 150 it'd have to be a Prince from now on.

The Clipper continued as second best to the Crusader but to my eyes the former, ranked by its maker as a mere utility machine, was increasingly the more attractive – first on account of its front mudguard and secondly its colour scheme. As for any difference in performance, they both had the same gear ratios and I'm sure one would ever notice the lack of half a horsepower.

Not quite correct: the 1960 Thruxton 500 was won by an AJS 650, whereas this was referring to 250 class honours.

250 Clipper

The 250 Clipper, basically similar to the Crusader, has the same high standard of safety and stability, which is the result of the low seating position and 17 inch wheels. Exceptional economy in running and low initial cost make the 250 Clipper an outstanding utility machine. **Finish**—Black/Mist Grey.

Providing you didn't mind 4hp less at the end of the throttle cable than the 350 Bullet the Clipper was indeed good value, being about ten per cent cheaper.

Enfield's 700s now featured a restyled rear mudguard and faired hindquarters.

TECHNICAL DATA	METEOR MINOR DE LUXE	METEOR MINOR SPORTS	SUPER METEOR	CONSTELLATION
Engine type	Four-stroke	Four-stroke	Four-stroke	Four-stroke
Number of Cylinders	2 o.h.v.	2 o.h.v.	2 o.h.v.	2 o.h.v.
Cylinder head	Light alloy	Light alloy	Light alloy	Light alloy
Cubic capacity (c.c.)	496	496	692	692
Bore and stroke (mm.)	70×64·5	70×64·5	70×90	70×90
Compression ratio	8 to 1	8 to 1	7·25 to 1	8 to 1
B.H.P.×R.P.M.	30 at 6,250	33 at 6,500	40 at 5,500	51 at 6,250
Carburetter	Amal Monobloc	Amal Monobloc	Amal Monobloc	Two Amal Monoblocs
Lighting and charging set	Lucas A.C. Rectifier	Lucas A.C. Rectifier	Lucas A.C. Rectifier	Lucas A.C. Rectifier
Ignition	D.C. Coil	D.C. Coil	D.C. Coil	Magneto
Primary drive chain	⅜" duplex	⅜" duplex	⅜" duplex	⅜" duplex
Final drive chain	⅝" pitch	⅝" pitch	⅝" pitch	⅝" pitch
Rear suspension	Pivoted fork hydraulic damping	Pivoted fork hydraulic damping	Pivoted fork hydraulic damping	Pivoted fork hydraulic damping
Front fork	Telescopic automatic lubrication	Telescopic automatic lubrication	Telescopic hydraulic damping	Telescopic hydraulic damping
Hubs:				
Front	Light alloy full width	Light alloy full width	Light alloy full width	Light alloy full width
Rear	Q.D.	Standard	Q.D.	Q.D.
Gear ratios (solo)	4·67, 6·37, 8·6, 13·00	4·67, 6·37, 8·6, 13·00	4·44, 6·05, 8·19, 12·35	4·44, 6·05, 8·19, 12·35
Tyre sizes:				
Front, Dunlop ribbed (ins.) ...	3·25×17	3·25×17	3·25×19	3·25×19
Rear, Dunlop studded (ins.) ...	3·50×17	3·50×17	3·50×19	3·50×19
M.P.H. per 1,000 r.p.m. in top gear ...	15·2	15·2	17·5	17·5
Approx. maximum speed (m.p.h.) ...	90–95	95–100	100	110–115
Approx. petrol consumption (m.p.g.)	70–75	70–75	55–60	50–55
Petrol tank capacity (gallons) ...	3¾	3¾	4¼	4¼
Oil tank capacity (pints)	4	4	4	4
Gearbox oil capacity (pints)	¾	¾	¾	¾
Brake diameter and width:				
Front (ins.)	7×1½	7×1½	6×1 dual	6×1 dual
Rear (ins.)	7×1	7×1	7×1	7×1
Seat height approx. (ins.)	30	30	31	31
Wheelbase (ins.)	54	54	54	54
Overall width (ins.)	25½	26	26	26
Ground clearance (ins.)	5½	5½	5½	5½
Weight (lbs.)	388	388	410	403
Equipment	Stop light Prop stand Air cleaner	—	Stop light Prop stand Air cleaner	Stop light Prop stand

One of the fastest production roadster motorcycles available today. The highly developed engine with special cams, high compression pistons, machined induction tracts, special valves, valve springs, etc., gives a maximum speed of approximately 115 m.p.h. The twin carburettors give improved power particularly at the lower end and middle of the speed range. The new attractively styled rear mudguard/dual seat assembly gives much improved protection for both rider and passenger, and at the same time adds to the already attractive lines of the Constellation. **Finish**—Black/Polychromatic Blue or Black/Polychromatic Burgundy.

Twin Amal Monoblocs had replaced a single TT on Constellations. They were just as fast but owners were not too sure that the much-vaunted dual front brake was up to the job of hauling the thing down from ton-plus velocities.

Royal Enfield MOTOR CYCLES

Prices of 1961 Models

MODEL	Basic Retail £	s.	d.	Purchase Tax £	s.	d.	Retail Inc. Purchase Tax £	s.	d.
"Prince" 148 c.c. Two stroke	103	2	2	21	5	4	124	7	6
"250 Clipper" 248 c.c. O.H.V.	157	2	0	32	8	0	189	10	0
"Crusader" 248 c.c. O.H.V.	173	13	7	35	16	5	209	10	0
"Crusader Sports" 248 c.c. O.H.V. ...	181	17	4	37	10	2	219	7	6
"350 Clipper" 346 c.c. O.H.V.	182	5	7	37	11	11	219	17	6
"350 Bullet" 346 c.c. O.H.V.	198	15	11	41	0	1	239	16	0
"500 Bullet" 499 c.c. O.H.V.	208	3	9	42	18	9	251	2	6
"Meteor Minor Sports" 496 c.c. O.H.V.	210	19	3	43	10	3	254	9	6
"Meteor Minor" De Luxe 496 c.c. O.H.V.	216	19	6	44	15	0	261	14	6
"Super Meteor" Solo or Sidecar 692 c.c. O.H.V.	232	2	6	47	17	6	280	0	0
"Constellation" 692 c.c. O.H.V. ...	248	5	10	51	4	2	299	10	0

EXTRA EQUIPMENT

(Prices when supplied as original equipment on new machines)

	£	s.	d.	£	s.	d.	£	s.	d.
Legshields—All models	3	13	6		*		3	13	6
"Airflow" Prince	20	4	9	4	3	6	24	8	3
"Airflow" 4-stroke models up to 500 c.c.	21	2	2	4	7	1	25	9	3
"Airflow" Super Meteor and Constellation	25	9	3	5	5	0	30	14	3
Pannier Set (4-stroke models only) ...	7	16	8	1	12	4	9	9	0
Air Cleaner 4 stroke models where not standard	1	8	2		5	10	1	14	0
Prop Stand 4 stroke models where not standard	1	13	2		6	10	2	0	0
Total rear chain enclosure on 4-stroke models where not standard	4	5	0		17	6	5	2	6
Close Ratio Gears "Crusader Sports" and "Constellation"	1	2	0		4	6	1	6	6
Rev. Counter "Constellation" and "Crusader Sports"	5	14	3	1	3	6	6	17	9
Pillion Footrests 4 stroke models where not standard		17	5		3	7	1	1	0
Q.D. Rear Wheel 4 stroke models where not standard	3	10	6		14	6	4	5	0

*Tax Free—Supplied separately

The Prince bowed out at the end of 1962, its final season being spent in a livery of Burgundy and Cream.

Enfield's new super sports 250 sped across the 1962 brochure cover, its rider looking a bit of a twit with half a grapefruit on his head.

Both the Crusader and Crusader Sports now had the curvaceous rear mudguard styling introduced the previous year on the largest Enfields. Crusaders were in Burgundy and Cream whilst the Sports version could be had in Black/Polychromatic Burgundy or Black/Peacock Blue.

The 350 and 500 Bullets shared the same colour options as the Crusader Sport, as well as the rear mudguard treatment and two-tone grey/black dual seats. The 350 Clippers were now finished in Burgundy/Cream and retained the old style of dual seat and silencer.

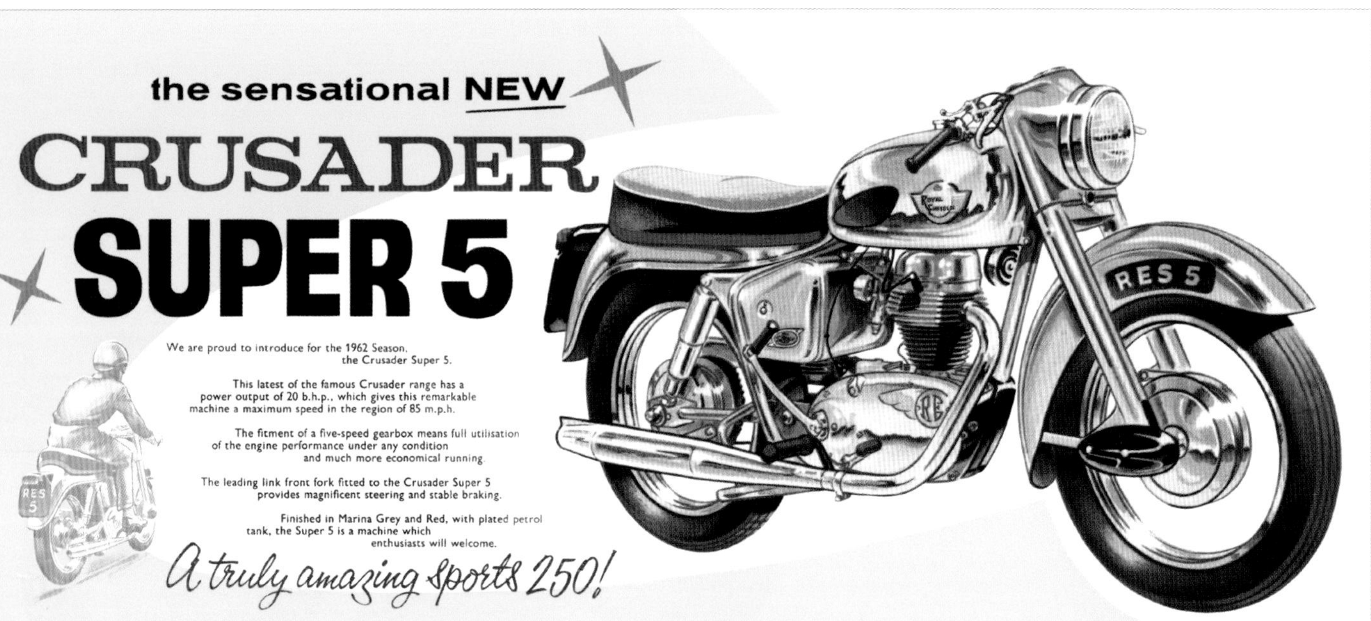

TECHNICAL DATA	CRUSADER SUPER 5
Engine type	Four-stroke
Number of Cylinders	1 o.h.v.
Cylinder head	Light alloy
Cubic capacity (c.c.)	248
Bore and stroke (mm.)	70×64·5
Compression ratio	9·75 to 1
B.H.P.×R.P.M.	20 at 7,500
Carburetter	Amal Monobloc
Lighting and charging set	Lucas A.C. Rectifier
Ignition	D.C. Coil
Primary drive chain	⅜″ pitch
Final drive chain	½″ pitch
Rear suspension	Pivoted fork hydraulic damping
Front fork	Leading link hydraulic damping
Hubs:	
Front	Light alloy full width
Rear	Q.D.
Gear ratios (solo)	6·02, 7·52, 9·57, 12·82, 17·4
Tyre sizes:	
**Front, Dunlop ribbed (ins.) ...	3·25×17
Rear, Dunlop studded (ins.) ...	3·25×17
M.P.H. per 1,000 r.p.m. in top gear ...	11·54
Approx. maximum speed (m.p.h.) ...	80–85
Approx. petrol consumption (m.p.g.)	90
Petrol tank capacity (gallons) ...	3¾
Oil tank capacity (pints)	3
Gearbox oil capacity (pints)	¾
Brake diameter and width:	
Front (ins.)	7×1½
Rear (ins.)	6×1
Seat Height approx. (ins.)	29½
Wheelbase (ins.)	52
Overall width (ins.)	26
Ground clearance (ins.)	5½
Weight (lbs.)	308

Other manufacturers contrived to make distinctly pedestrian 250s appear sporting whereas Enfield, with the Super 5, had introduced a genuine sports bike – and with no less than five gears – that didn't. Blinded by its own enthusiasm RE reckoned the machine to have 'sleek sporting style'… Oh dear. Leading-link forks can look less than elegant but they'd set a new benchmark and topped it with a lumpy LE Velocette-like front mudguard before icing it with a plethora of red coach lines.

To most young men the 33hp Meteor Minor Sports was the more desirable of Enfield's 500 twins, and at £260 all-in was £6 10s cheaper than the 30hp De Luxe version. As an alternative to this Sports finish of Black/Polychromatic Burgundy one could choose Peacock Blue for the few coloured parts. The De Luxe came in Burgundy/Cream.

Full enclosure of the rear chain is standard on Crusader 250 and Meteor Minor de Luxe machines and available as an extra on all other four-stroke models. It greatly increases the life of the rear chain and adds to the cleanliness of the machine.

The rear of a Peacock Blue Constellation with optional fully-enclosed chain. This type of finned silencer was fitted, as a general rule, to Enfields other than those classed as economy versions.

SUPER METEOR

This machine is unrivalled in the big twin class. Its engine characteristics, with very high torque at relatively low engine speed, make it ideal for all-round sidecar work. As a solo machine the Super Meteor is extremely flexible and has vivid acceleration up to its maximum speed, which is in the region of 100 m.p.h. Finish—Burgundy/Cream.

CONSTELLATION

One of the fastest production roadster motorcycles available today. The highly developed engine with special cams, high compression pistons, machined induction tracts, special valves, valve springs, etc., gives a maximum speed of approximately 115 m.p.h. The twin carburettors give improved power, particularly at the lower end and middle of the speed range. The attractively styled rear mudguard/dual seat assembly gives much improved protection for both rider and passenger, and at the same time adds to the already attractive lines of the Constellation. Finish—Black/Polychromatic Peacock Blue or Black/Polychromatic Burgundy.

This would be the final year for the Constellation in its super sports guise as the following season it would be shorn of 10 horsepower and given a more fully valanced, painted front mudguard. This relegating it, as the Super Meteor had been earlier when the Constellation had first appeared, to a more utilitarian role and 'ideal for heavy-duty sidecar work'. Its fate was sealed by fitment of sidecar gearing as standard.

Royal Enfield
MOTORCYCLES
RE 250
1963 for your pleasure!

Generally speaking, Enfield's 250s, like this chap's Crusader Sports, were pretty oil-tight but he's taken a bit of a chance with his whites – in so much of a hurry to make his woodland assignation after the cricket match that all he'd changed was his shirt.

The Leading Link Front Fork fitted to the Crusader Super 5 provides, with its complete hydraulic control, magnificent steering and absolutely stable braking.

This year the Super 5 had been plastered in chrome, the voluminous front mudguard had gone and the company had rather coyly attempted to make the forks look like normal telescopics. It would have been better if they'd been thrown away at the end of the '62 season rather than the end of this. Was there stock to get rid of?

The Continental 250 was much more on target! A fashionable and sexy Italian-style fuel tank, air scoop on its 7in front brake, five-speed 'box, racing screen, matching Smiths chronometric rev counter and speedo, and Ace bars. Not so sure about the chequered fork tops but I'd have very likely thought they were the business back in the day. It was made in this form for just the 1963 season.

Enfield's trials Crusader wasn't a big seller and for the '64 season someone came up with the idea to export a variant to Australia for sheep and cattle farmers. The Wallaby had lower gearing, a higher ground clearance and a front wheel of the same diameter as the rear, shod with 3.50 trials tyre. Despite being equipped with a basic lighting set it was strictly utilitarian, with plating restricted to the handlebars and the rim of the tiny ISDT-type headlight; even the wheel rims were painted. Apart from a red tank and mudguards, all other painted parts were black.

Offering the De Luxe Meteor with less poke at a higher price hadn't paid off, so it was gone and a shimmering gold Sports was what you rode out of the showroom if you wanted a new 500 Enfield twin in '63.

At long last the old guard had been put out to grass. The 350 Clipper and 500 Bullet were no more, whilst the 350 Bullet lived on but had been Crusaderised. It retained the long-standing bore and stroke of 70x90mm, however, but had found either 1 or 1½ extra horsepower depending on whether this brochure's caption or data sheet was correct.

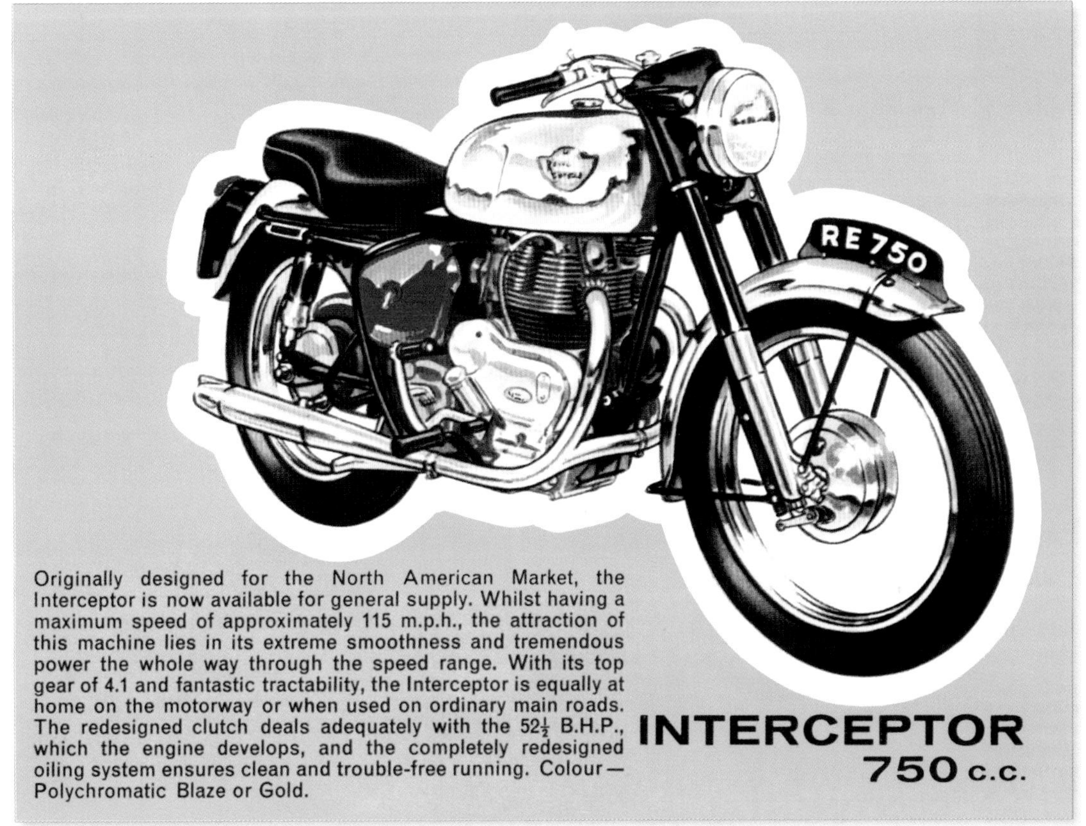

Although firmly based upon the Constellation's 70x90mm 692cc twin, the 71x93mm 736cc Interceptor's motor was very much improved and also extremely well balanced, allowing it to produce its peak power at 6,000rpm.

Geoff was either too much of a gentleman or too modest to point out that he'd actually won six world championships – three on Nortons and three on Gileras. He was working with Enfield on the development of a two-stroke racer that, like the 4T-engined Turbo Twin he was astride, would also, initially, be powered by Villiers before the assistance of Hermann Meier was sought to enable the firm to put together an engine of its own. The Turbo Twin's 'firm springing and low centre of gravity make bend-swinging a pleasure,' wrote The Motor Cycle *after they'd tested one in the autumn of '63. They also liked the 'utter smoothness of both engine and transmission', the combination of Villiers's 4T and Enfield's cush-drive rear hub resulting in 'something akin to electric propulsion'. Mean top speed was 68mph, with 70 reached one way; petroil disappeared at a rate of a gallon every 76 miles at a steady 40mph or every 52 miles at 60mph.*

Exclusive to Royal Enfield "250" owners, this race-tailored aerodynamically designed fairing gives weather protection and increased performance, together with a truly sporting and fashionable appearance.

Easily fitted in a very short time the "Sportsflow" is supplied in matching colours for your model. Also available in white.

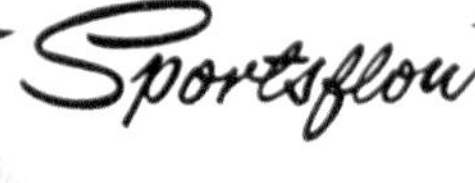

CONTINENTAL DE LUXE:

Five speed gearbox as standard, a power unit developing 20 B.H.P. Magnificent steering, superb brakes and a distinctive sporting appearance puts the Continental top of its class.
FINISH: Polychromatic Blaze or Hi-Fi Blue, with chromium plated petrol tank, mudguards, etc.

STANDARD MODEL:

Available less rev. counter and flyscreen, with Polychromatic enamelled Blue or Blaze petrol tank and mudguards.

CONTINENTAL

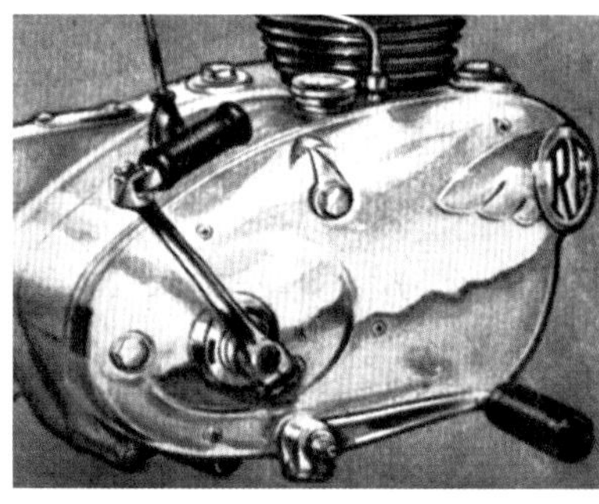

On all four-stroke Royal Enfield machines the oil tank is cast integrally with the engine. This permits rapid warming up and circulation of the oil in the full dry sump lubricating system and reduces to the minimum the number of oil pipes and joints which might cause oil leakage.

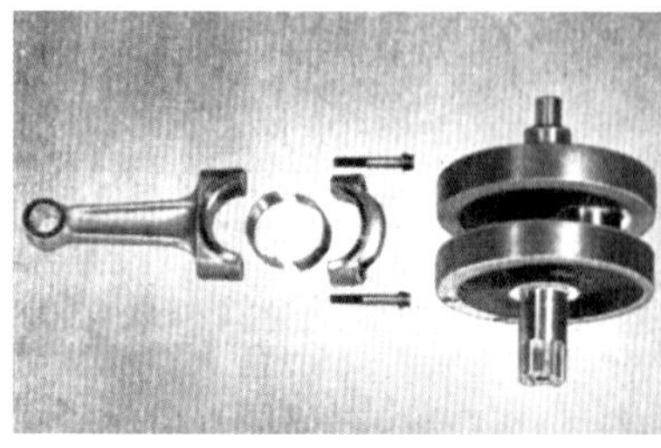

A spheroidal Graphite cast iron one piece crankshaft ensures absolute accuracy and alignment in manufacture and in servicing. Long big end life is assured by the use of white metal lined shell bearings running direct on the crankshaft, oil being fed to the bearing by a high pressure oil pump.

For 1964 the Continental had been given a Crusader fuel tank. There was even a downmarket model with painted tank, shorn of its screen, with a chromium blanking plate in place of its 8,000rpm rev counter.

INTERCEPTOR

Finned silencers were out this year for the entire range and the Bullet tank and mudguards were painted in Flame and Cream – as were the 250 Clipper's.

The most expensive Enfield now came with 12-volt electrics but if you were happy with 6-volt then there was the slightly cheaper Standard model. Both had either Polychromatic Blaze or Hi-Fi Blue panels but the tank and mudguards of the cheaper model were enamelled in Polychromatic Silver rather than being chromium-plated.

TECHNICAL DATA

	TURBO TWIN	250 CLIPPER	CRUSADER SPORTS	CONTINENTAL	350 BULLET	INTERCEPTOR
Engine type	Two stroke	Four stroke	Four stroke	Four stroke	Four stroke	* Four stroke
No. of Cylinders	Twin	1 o.h.v.	1 o.h.v.	1 o.h.v.	1 o.h.v.	2 o.h.v.
Cylinder head	Light alloy	Light alloy	Light alloy	Light alloy	Light alloy	Light alloy
Cubic capacity	248	248	248	248	346	736
Bore and stroke	50 x 63·5	70 x 64·5	70 x 64·5	70 x 64·5	70 x 90	71 x 93
Compression ratio	8·7 to 1	9 to 1	9 to 1	9 to 1	7·5 to 1	8 to 1
B.H.P. x R.P.M.	17 at 6,000	14½ at 5,750	17 at 7,250	20 at 7,500	22 at 6,500	52½ at 6,000
Carburettor	Villiers S25	Amal Monobloc	Amal Monobloc	Amal Monobloc	Amal Monobloc	Two Amal Monoblocs
Lighting and charging set	A.C. rectified Villiers/Lucas	Lucas A.C. Rectifier	Lucas A.C. Rectifier	Lucas A.C. Rectifier	Lucas A.C. Rectifier	Lucas A.C. Rectifier 6 or 12 volt
Ignition	Villiers energy transfer	D.C. Coil	D.C. Coil	D.C. Coil	D.C. Coil	Magneto
Primary drive chain	⅜" pitch	⅜" pitch	⅜" pitch	⅜" pitch	⅜" pitch	⅜" duplex
Final drive chain	½" pitch	½" pitch	½" pitch	½" pitch	½" pitch	⅝" pitch
Rear suspension:	Pivoted Fork Hydraulic damping	Pivoted Fork Hydraulic damping	Pivoted Fork Hydraulic damping	Pivoted Fork Hydraulic damping	Pivoted Fork Hydraulic damping	Pivoted Fork Hydraulic damping
Front Fork:	Telescopic Automatic lubrication	Telescopic Automatic lubrication	Telescopic Automatic lubrication	Telescopic Automatic lubrication	Telescopic Automatic lubrication	Telescopic Hydraulic damping
Hubs: Front	Light alloy full width	Light alloy full width	Light alloy full width	Light alloy full width	Light alloy full width	Light alloy full width
Hubs: Rear	Standard	Standard	Q.D.	Q.D.	Q.D.	Q.D.
Gear ratios	5·85, 7·75, 11·12, 17·9	6·14, 7·8, 11·05, 18·0	6·14, 7·8, 11·05, 18·0	6·02, 7·52, 9·57, 12·82, 17·4	5·15, 6·57, 9·27, 15·1	4·22, 5·72, 7·8, 11·75
Tyre sizes: Front	3·25 x 17	3·25 x 17	3·25 x 17	3·25 x 17	3·25 x 17	3·25 x 19
Tyre sizes: Rear	3·25 x 17	3·25 x 17	3·25 x 17	3·25 x 17	3·25 x 17	3·50 x 19
M.P.H. per 1,000 r.p.m. in top gear	11·8	11·3	11·3	11·54	13·65	18·4
Approx. maximum speed (m.p.h.)	75	75	75 – 80	80 – 85	85	110 – 115
Approx. petrol consumption (m.p.g.)	80 – 85	100	95	90	80 – 85	55
Petrol tank capacity (galls.)	3½	3¾	3½	3½	3¾	4¼
Oil tank capacity (pints)	—	3	3	3	3	4
Gearbox oil capacity (pints)	½	¾	¾	¾	¾	¾
Brake dia. and width: Front (ins.)	6 x 1	6 x 1	7 x 1½	7 x 1½	7 x 1½	6 x 1 dual
Brake dia. and width: Rear (ins.)	6 x 1	6 x 1	6 x 1	6 x 1	6 x 1	7 x 1
Seat height approx. (ins.)	29½	29	29½	29½	29½	31
Wheelbase (ins.)	52	52	52	52	52	54
Overall width (ins.)	25½	25½	26	26	26	26
Ground Clearance (ins.)	5½	5½	5½	5½	5½	5½
Weight (lbs.)	298	300	305	305	310	410

At £206 the Turbo Twin was the cheapest bike in Redditch's repertoire, with the £215 Sports a mere £3-or-so more than the least-expensive four-stroke, the Clipper. With a multitude of established and popular two-strokes by other manufacturers already on the market it is hard to see a reason for the TT's existence, but desperation leads to strange decisions.

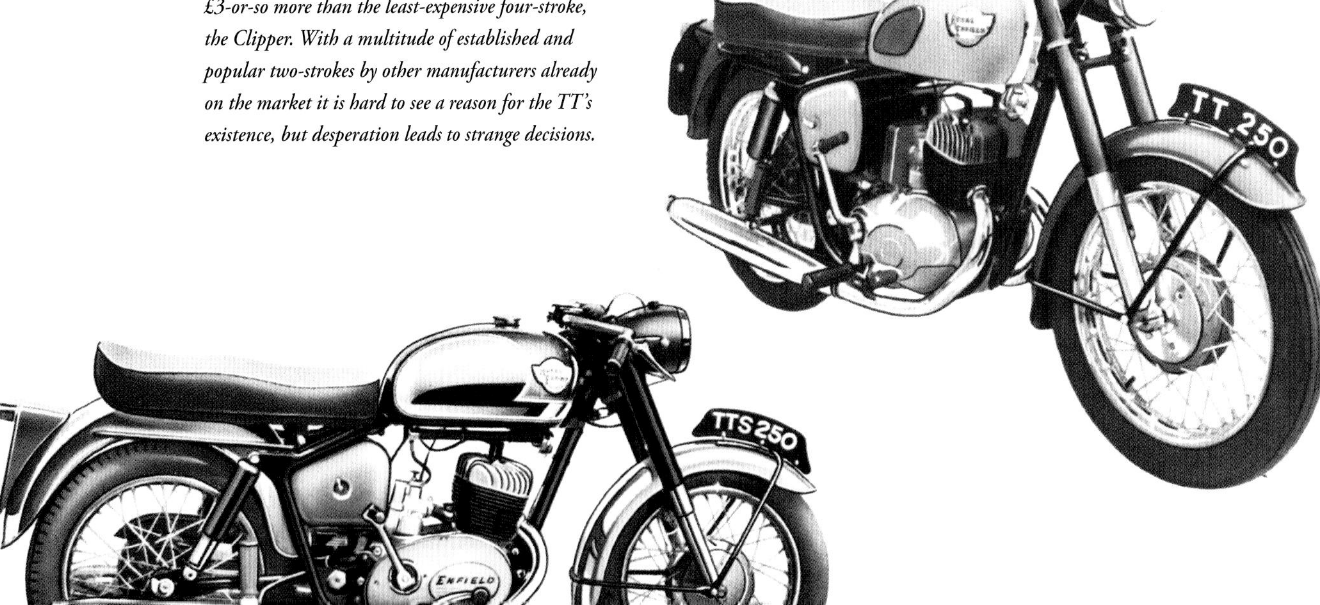

The latest version of the Continental 250 had fork gaiters and the suggestion of a racing seat. Colours were as in '64, other than White now being introduced as the standard finish; very sensibly, the ridiculous Standard version had been dropped. No doubt with high hopes for the GP5 250 racing machine, there was a racer ghosting across in the background – shame the Continental resembled their two-stroke racer in no way whatsoever.

TURBO TWIN and TURBO TWIN SPORTS

Engine type	Two stroke
No. of Cylinders	Twin
Cylinder head	Light alloy
Cubic capacity	248
Bore and stroke	50 ×63·5
Compression ratio	8·7 to 1
B.H.P. x R.P.M.	17 and 6,000
Carburettor	Villiers S25
Lighting and charging set	A.C. rectified Villiers/Lucas
Ignition	Villiers energy transfer
Primary drive chain	⅜" pitch
Final drive chain	½" pitch
Rear suspension:	Pivoted Fork Hydraulic damping
Front Fork:	Telescopic Automatic lubrication
Hubs: Front	Light alloy full width
Rear	Standard
Gear ratios	5·85, 7·75, 11·12, 17·9
Tyre sizes: Front	3·25 ×17
Rear	3·25 ×17
M.P.H. per 1,000 r.p.m. in top gear	11·8
Approx. maximum speed (m.p.h.)	75
Approx. petrol consumption (m.p.g.)	80 – 85
Petrol tank capacity (galls.)	3½
Oil tank capacity (pints)	—
Gearbox oil capacity (pints)	½
Brake dia. and width	
Front (ins.)	6 ×1
Rear (ins.)	6 ×1
Seat height approx. (ins.)	29½
Wheelbase (ins.)	52
Overall width (ins.)	25½
Ground Clearance (ins.)	5½
Weight (lbs.)	298

Complete with electric horn, inflator, toolkit, speedometer and centre stand.

Standard Finish: Flame/Cream
Sports Finish: Flame only.
Chromium plated petrol tank and mudguards.
Sports-type handlebars.

The Crusader Sports. "Get astride it and you'll realise why it is the most successful sports machine ever"… From Redditch, perhaps, Geoff; but 'ever' is an all-inclusive word that could well have raised the hackles of some Triumph, BSA or Norton owners, to name but a few.

Geoff Duke says . . .

"*A luxury sports model with smooth clean lines, the Olympic utilises the fabulous leading-link type front fork which provide such magnificent steering and stability.*"

Engine type	Four stroke
No. of Cylinders	1 o.h.v.
Cylinder head	Light alloy
Cubic capacity	248
Bore and stroke	70 × 64·5
Compression ratio	9 to 1
B.H.P. x R.P.M.	14½ at 5,750
Carburettor	Amal Monobloc
Lighting and charging set	Lucas A.C. Rectifier
Ignition	D.C. Coil
Primary drive chain	⅜" pitch
Final drive chain	½" pitch
Rear suspension:	Pivoted Fork Hydraulic damping
Front Fork:	Leading link Hydraulic damping
Hubs: Front	Light alloy full width
Rear	Standard
Gear ratios	6·14, 7·8, 11·05, 18·0
Tyre sizes: Front	3·25 × 17
Rear	3·25 × 17
M.P.H. per 1,000 r.p.m. in top gear	11·3
Approx. maximum speed (m.p.h.)	75
Approx. petrol consumption (m.p.g.)	100
Petrol tank capacity (galls.)	3½
Oil tank capacity (pints)	3
Gearbox oil capacity (pints)	¾
Brake dia. and width	
Front (ins.)	7 × 1½
Rear (ins.)	6 × 1
Seat height approx. (ins.)	29½
Wheelbase (ins.)	52
Overall width (ins.)	26
Ground Clearance (ins.)	5½
Weight (lbs.)	305

Complete with electric horn, inflator, toolkit, speedometer and centre stand.

Finish: Polychromatic Blaze and Silver or Hi-Fi Blue and Silver

Sorry Geoff, I know you were getting consultancy fees of some kind, but if the Crusader Super 5's forks were that good why on earth weren't they fitted to all Enfield 250s? And for the thing to be renamed the Olympic was, if nothing else, sad. Japan had hosted the '64 games and it was their Hondas, Suzukis and Yamahas that were kicking sand in the eyes of the British bike industry.

Engine type	Four stroke
No. of Cylinders	1 o.h.v.
Cylinder head	Light alloy
Cubic capacity	248
Bore and stroke	70 × 64·5
Compression ratio	9 to 1
B.H.P. x R.P.M.	17 at 7,250
Carburettor	Amal Monobloc
Lighting and charging set	Lucas A.C. Rectifier
Ignition	D.C. Coil
Primary drive chain	⅜" pitch
Final drive chain	½" pitch
Rear suspension:	Pivoted Fork Hydraulic damping
Front Fork:	Telescopic Automatic lubrication
Hubs: Front	Light alloy full width
Rear	Q.D.
Gear ratios	6·14, 7·8, 11·05, 18·0
Tyre sizes: Front	3·25 × 17
Rear	3·25 × 17
M.P.H. per 1,000 r.p.m. in top gear	11·3
Approx. maximum speed (m.p.h.)	75 – 80
Approx. petrol consumption (m.p.g.)	95
Petrol tank capacity (galls.)	3½
Oil tank capacity (pints)	3
Gearbox oil capacity (pints)	¾
Brake dia. and width	
Front (ins.)	7 × 1½
Rear (ins.)	6 × 1
Seat height approx. (ins.)	29½
Wheelbase (ins.)	52
Overall width (ins.)	26
Ground Clearance (ins.)	5½
Weight (lbs.)	305

Complete with electric Horn, inflator, toolkit, speedometer and centre stand.

Finish: Polychromatic Blaze or Hi-Fi Blue with chromium plated petrol tank, mudguards, etc.

If I remember correctly, part of the GT's launch included a run from Lands End to John O'Groats in under 24 hours, which seemed rather tame for such a machine, even though we knew its bark was worse than its bite. Nevertheless it was an able and good-looking little café racer that has stood the test of time better than many of its contemporaries.

Continental 'GT' 250 cc

- ✱ Race proved Fibreglass petrol tank!
- ✱ Race styled dual seat!
- ✱ Clip-on handlebars!
- ✱ Sporty-style exhaust pipe!
- ✱ Polished front brake hub flanges!
- ✱ Polished aluminium mudguards!
- ✱ Chromed rear springs!

GT 90

CONTINENTAL G.T.

Engine type	Four stroke
No. of Cylinders	1 o.h.v.
Cylinder head	Light alloy
Cubic capacity	248
Bore and stroke	70 x 64·5
Compression ratio	9 to 1
B.H.P. x R.P.M.	20 at 7,500
Carburettor	Amal Monobloc
Lighting and charging set	Lucas A.C. Rectifier
Ignition	D.C. Coil
Primary drive chain	⅜" pitch
Final drive chain	½" pitch
Rear suspension:	Pivoted Fork Hydraulic damping
Front Fork:	Telescopic Automatic lubrication
Hubs: Front	Light alloy full width
Rear	Q.D.
Gear ratios (5-speed)	6·02, 7·52, 9·57 12·82, 17·4
Tyre sizes: Front	3·25 x 17
Rear	3·25 x 17
M.P.H. per 1,000 r.p.m. in top gear	11·54
Approx. maximum speed (m.p.h.)	80 – 85
Approx. petrol consumption (m.p.g.)	90
Petrol tank capacity (galls.)	3½
Oil tank capacity (pints)	3
Gearbox oil capacity (pints)	¾
Brake dia. and width	
Front (ins.)	7 x 1½
Rear (ins.)	6 x 1
Seat height approx. (ins.)	29½
Wheelbase (ins.)	52
Overall width (ins.)	26
Ground Clearance (ins.)	5½
Weight (lbs.)	300

Geoff Duke says . . .

"This is a really super version of the 'Continental' which will delight the young enthusiast with its sporty looks and traditional 'Continental' performance."

RE 750

Geoff Duke says . . .

"You're right out in front on the Motorways on this big, smooth, high-performance machine, with its breath-taking power and amazing flexibility. The special sidecar version is a must for sidecar enthusiasts."

The new Interceptor's wheelbase had grown by 3in, and a separate headlamp and fork-top fascia replaced the Casquette that had been synonymous with the bigger Enfields for the last ten years.

SCOTT

Contrary to the majority of would-be motorcycle manufacturers, Yorkshire-born Alfred Angas Scott was drawn to the two-stroke engine as a power source from the outset – later asserting that it was on account of its greater frequency of power strokes to revolutions and his grounding in steam engines.

Before commencing as a manufacturer, however, he spent several years experimenting with engines of his own design that were fitted into small boats and at least one bicycle, which met with varying degrees of success. By 1904 he considered he had come up with the ideal and patented his designs for a vertical twin two-stroke, at which time he set about formulating a suitable frame and running gear to house it – the results being patented in due course too.

With no immediate means of making complete machines himself, he reached an agreement with local Bradford motor manufacturer Jowett to make half a dozen-or-so whilst he took steps to set up and equip suitable premises of his own. This done, the newly-formed Scott Engineering Company took over production during 1908 and before long Scott himself was putting his own machines to the test – competing with success at hillclimbs such as Sutton Bank, Newnham and Wass Bank. So successful was he, in fact, that for a while, as a result of protestations, the ACU imposed a punishing handicap on his machines. If it hadn't been for these early performances Scott's motorcycles, with their partially water-cooled engines mounted low in his unique open frame, might have been dismissed as oddities, despite having chain drive, two speeds and a kick-starter; but as it was, when one turned up for the 1909 Senior TT those in the know took notice. Although fast it failed to finish but the following year two were entered and both lasted the course, finishing ninth and 24th.

By 1912 the twin-cylinder engine had been further developed and now featured water cooling to barrels as well as the cylinder heads, and had been enlarged to just over 530cc – in which form it proved to have to legs of the rest of the field on the Isle of Man, winning the Senior that year and again in 1913.

Come World War One, although proven on the racetrack, Scott's two-stroke-engined machines were not considered suitable for general military purposes, so the firm failed to garner MOD contracts of any importance. Nevertheless, it did manufacture a number of sidecar outfits, some mounting Lewis machine-guns with others to act as ammunition carriers, which served on the front as mobile gun units. From these came the idea for what Alfred Scott considered a superior three-wheeler gun carrier, with triangulated tubular frame, rack-and-pinion steering with wheel, and shaft final drive; but the Ministry didn't want them. Instead he decided they would make practical little two-seater passenger cars. Putting them into production had to wait until after the war, however, and to that end Scott left the company he had founded in 1917 and set up the Scott Autocar Company, still in Bradford, with production of his brainchild commencing in 1921.

Scott failed to take a stand at the first post-war Motor Cycle Show but you could order one of the latest models at what was virtually the local dealership. Unlike Scott, however, Earnshaws is still very much in business and still to be found on Manchester Road.

Unfortunately the public viewed his Sociable, as he'd named it, much less favourably, and by the time that the last of the 200-or-so that were made had been disposed of (at a heavily discounted price) just over three years later he called it a day.

Sadly, he was to die in 1923 when, whilst pursuing his hobby of potholing, a particularly cold and wet subterranean expedition led to him contracting pneumonia.

Meanwhile his old firm had continued to manufacture its characteristic open-framed motorcycles: introducing the sporting Squirrel for 1921 and then the even more sporting Super Squirrel with hub brakes and three speeds in 1924. Next came the Flying Squirrels with a more conventional, if heavier, duplex frame layout with long or TT-type fuel tank, as well as three speeds as standard; nevertheless, so many customers preferred the lighter open-frame two-speeders that they continued to be made until the 1933.

Although the firm would never repeat its pre-war successes on the Isle of Man, Scotts had continued to compete, and third and fourth in 1922's Senior, second in 1924, fifth in 1925 and third in 1928 were praiseworthy performances for such a small firm – in spite of the fact that there had been hopes of a better result in the last of these due to it being the racing debut of the new long-stroke motor. In search of better high-speed performance the firm's chief designer Harry Shackleton had revised the port timing by the simple expedient of lengthening the stroke by just over 3mm (68.25 to 71.4mm), and encouraged by the results next set about redesigning the motor's bottom end. Due to concerns over the structural integrity of the original design's crankpins, which were outrigged from the flywheel, motors with built up crankshafts were constructed for the 1930 Senior TT but potentially catastrophic vibration led to the retirement of all three entries – it would be the marque's last Isle of Man appearance.

Despite, or perhaps because of, being in increasingly dire financial straights a 300cc single-cylinder air-cooled (two-stroke) Lightweight Squirrel was added to the range, which consisted of Super, Sports and Flying Squirrels, TT Replica and Speedway Special in 1929; but neither did it sell in any quantities nor did it save the firm from going into voluntary liquidation in 1931.

Fresh finance from a farmer-cum-entrepreneur named Reginald Vinter got the company going again, if not properly on its feet, and reorganisation led to

THE Scott FLYING SQUIRREL

The world-famous Scott Flying Squirrel again appears in the characteristic bold unconventional design. To-day the Scott stands alone as the only break-away from the orthodox which has stood the test of time.

1949

Scott

Continuous development and improvement have resulted in the new Flying Squirrel which maintains the same high quality of material and thoroughness of workmanship as its predecessors.

EQUIPMENT

IGNITION and LIGHTING. All machines are fitted with Lucas 6v.-70w. Dynamo Lighting, with constant Dynamo Voltage Control. Distributor and coil ignition.

ELECTRIC HORN. High frequency electric horn.

SPEEDOMETER. 80 m.p.h. Internally illuminated.

TRANSMISSION. Large shock absorber built into rear hub.

PRIMARY CHAIN. ½in. pitch by ·305in. wide.

REAR CHAIN. ⅝in. pitch by .38in. wide.

Primary Chain lubricated by means of adjustable drip feed from oil tank.

SILENCER and EXHAUST PIPE. Two in one exhaust pipe fitted with efficient silencer. Chromium plated and of attractive appearance.

STANDS. Front and central "roll-on" type.

SADDLE. Flexible top. Mounted direct on frame.

TOOLS. Full complement of tools in neat metal case. Repair outfit and inflator.

FINISH. Chromium plate and finest black enamel. All steel parts "Bonderised" to ensure adhesion and thorough rust-proofing.

"We do not claim that the Scott is a utility machine – it is a thoroughbred. Treat it as such and you will get the maximum pleasure from your Scotting. You can use the Scott as a hack – you could do the same with a Derby winner – let's leave it at that," read one of the brochure's slogans. As far as suggestions that the oiling system should be switched to petroil, the company had certainly done the latter but Dowty Oleomatic forks had replaced Brampton girders.

some improvement in production methods, as well as the machines themselves, such as the adoption of aluminium cylinder heads. Lessons had not been learnt, however, and at the 1934 show the company exhibited its pièce de résistance in the form of the 3S, a 986cc three-cylinder water-cooled two-stroke that, despite being a novel and somewhat splendid machine, unfortunately had every hallmark of a potential white elephant before it even turned a wheel. Designed by Scott's William Cull, who also came up with an air-cooled in-line two-stroke twin to be offered as a power unit for that piece of 1930s' aeronautical idiocy the Flying Flea, it sold in penny numbers (reputedly eight) but was listed until 1936 along with the current 498 and 596cc Flying Squirrels. By the outbreak of the Second World War spring fames were available as an optional extra, and in the event you wanted something superior to one of the Squirrels there was the 596cc Clubman's Special with a claimed 33hp and 85/90mph maximum speed.

Motorcycle production then lapsed for the duration while the works turned its hands towards the national cause by undertaking precision engineering, including components and generator motors for Kerrison Predictors used in conjunction with Bofors guns.

A snapshot of the firm's immediate post-war activities results from an account by one of *Motor Cycling*'s staff, who was lent a pre-production prototype when he visited the factory in the summer of 1946. In essence very much as the '39 Squirrel it did, however, have full-width cast-aluminium hubs: the front housing twin 6in brakes with pulley balancer for the cables and the rear an 8in with integral cush drive. In search of improved steering, its rake had been altered and the girder forks were now by Brampton. As an existing Scott owner himself he may have been biased, but upon returning the machine after a week and getting on for 1,000 miles he was impressed on all counts other than Scott's adherence to the traditional method of engine

SCOTT MOTOR CYCLES, 1949 MODEL

RETAIL PRICES FOR GREAT BRITAIN & NORTHERN IRELAND.

TYPE.	RETAIL PRICE.	PURCHASE TAX	TOTAL
596 cc Flying Squirrel	£194-10-0	£52-10-3	£247-0-3
Speedometer extra.	£ 4 -0-0	£ 1 -1-8	£ 5-1-8

1. All retail sales are subject to the Guarantee published in the Company's literature and the prices quoted on this list are for delivery Free of Charge at Dealer's premises.

2. The prices quoted here operate on and after 1st November 1948, and all previous lists are cancelled.

3. The Company reserves the right to revise prices without prior notice and Purchase Tax is also subject to revision.

THE SCOTT MOTOR CYCLE CO.

SALTAIRE, SHIPLEY, YORKS.

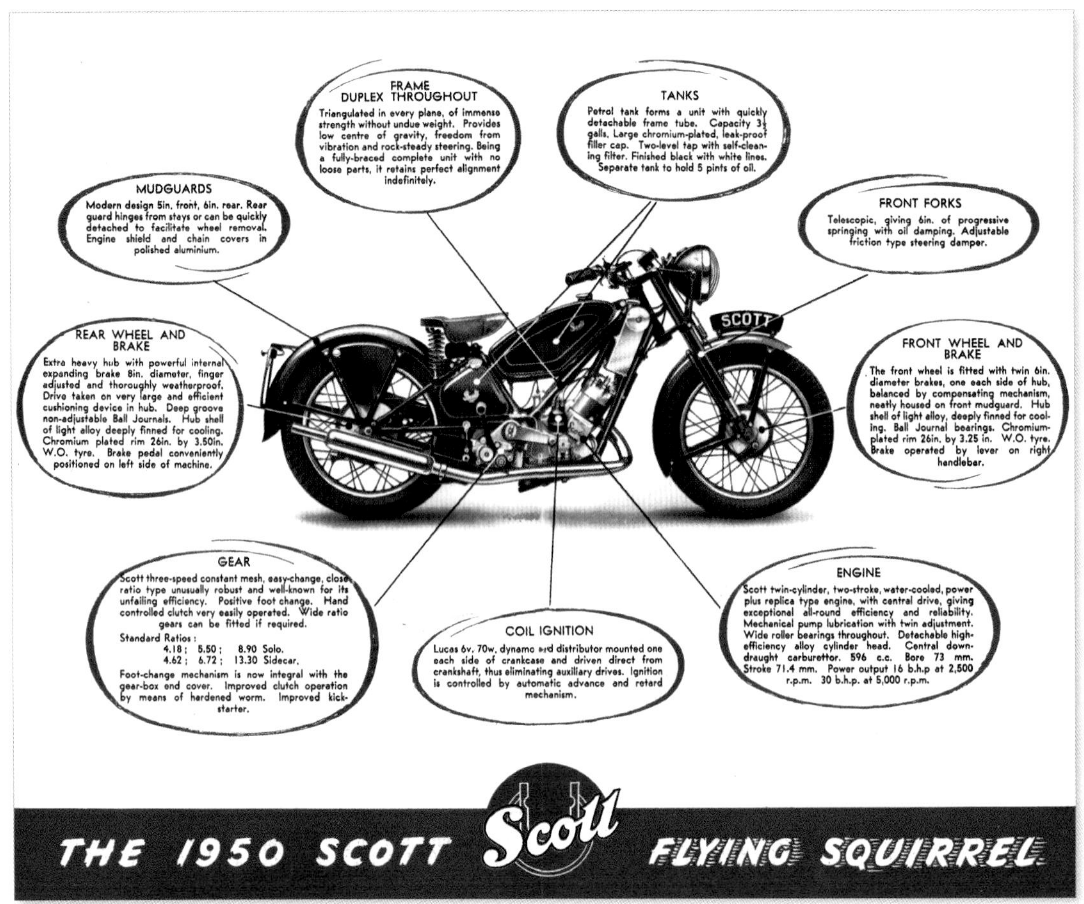

Nothing new for 1950, but production was shortly to cease and time was now fast running out for the company in its present guise.

lubrication by adjustable pumps: "Please would they use petroil lubrication on the '47, or, at the latest, the '48 machines, or else provide some means of adjusting the oil pump settings from the saddle?"

Alas, he found that that eccentricities were also afoot, with Cull admitting that what he described as a 'design that would undoubtedly make two-stroke history' had been filed away and was unlikely ever to go into production; meanwhile, Vinter was keen for him to experience the on-going experiments with the three-cylinder two-stroke apropos its use, or another larger version, in cars.

To this end Scott's MD wooed William Lyons, for some extraordinary reason hoping that he would find the idea of Jaguars powered by a Scott six-cylinder an attractive one – a pipedream doomed from its inception, if for no other reason due to the Coventry car manufacturer being on the verge of introducing its own twin-cam six.

Time and money spent on dead-end projects, along with disappointing sales of the modernised Squirrels, were in themselves debilitating enough, but it was then discovered that Mr Vinter had been appropriating funds received from government contracts for his own and the company's use. Awarded a prison term for his wrongdoing, Reginald was out of the way but the company's demise was all but inevitable and it went into voluntary liquidation in 1950.

A reprieve from oblivion came, however, and Scott enthusiast Matt Holder's company Aerco Jig and Tool Company acquired the name and assets – recommencing limited production at the St Mary's Road, Birmingham, works. By the mid '50s, with modernisation of the Squirrel increasingly overdue, the larger-capacity version was repackaged with a duplex swinging-arm frame and long-travel telescopic forks. This was to have been followed by a sporting 500 named the Swift but plans changed, and for the remainder of Scott's life in Holder's hands a few Squirrels were produced each year up until the late 1960s when he decided to call it a day.

In the early 1970s something of a revival was enacted by George Silk, who commenced building Scott engines into modern running gear with Spondon frames; but when supplies became exhausted and permission to use the Scott name for engines of his own manufacture was withheld by Matt Holder he went on to develop his own 700cc two-stroke twin. The Silk 700, in various guises, was made from 1975 until 1979 and around 100 were produced.

FRAME : Exceptionally strong welded cradle fitted with swinging arm rear suspension controlled by Girling or Armstrong Spring Units adjustable for spring tension.

ENGINE : Scott twin-cylinder ; two stroke water cooled power-plus T.T. Replica engine with central drive, giving exceptional efficiency, smoothness and reliability ; mechanical oil pump ; new die-cast alloy cylinder head with increased water capacity ; wide roller bearings throughout.

GEARBOX : Scott three-speed constant mesh, close ratio (wide ratio supplied to order) ; positive foot-change.

WHEELS : Front wheel fitted with twin 7″ x 1⅛″ brakes in die-cast alloy hub, 3.25 x 19 ; ribbed tyre. Rear wheel fitted with powerful 8″ x 1⅜″ brake in die-cast hub, 3.50 x 19 tyre ; chrome plated rims.

FRONT FORKS : Telescopic, giving 6 inch of progressive springing, with oil damping adjustable friction type steering damper.

A rider whose garb owed more to the 1920s or '30s was chosen to model the latest evocation of the Squirrel on the cover of the 1956 sales pamphlet, but the artwork was a good deal more fluid and atmospheric than that in the sales literature of many larger manufacturers.

Its up to the minute swinging-arm frame did little to disguise the fact that this was a Scott with its own particular looks and manner of going – and it still had just three speeds in its gearbox.

LIGHTING AND IGNITION

Headlamp fitted with sealed beam unit, with ammeter, switch and 120 m.p.h. trip speedometer fitted in casing ; combined stop and tail light ; coil ignition with 6 volt alternator dynamo and distributor, mounted one each side of crankcase, driven from crankshaft automatic advance and retard mechanism.

Some features of the 1956 Flying Squirrel.

THE "SUPERIOR"

A Boon and a

Blessing to Man

Cyc-Auto

MADE IN ENGLAND

Its slogan was something of a misnomer as by all accounts it was a feeble thing and its worm drive inclined to wear itself out, but the Cyc-Auto, the brainchild of one Wallington Butt, lays claim to being the first British autocycle. Introduced in 1934 it became the property of Scott in 1938 but from 1953 was manufactured by Winsmith – the Scott title, however, being retained.

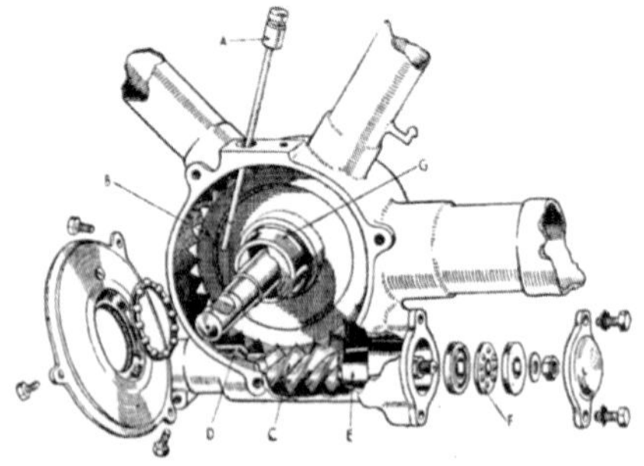

A - Oil Level Dipstick
B - Worm Wheel
C - Worm Shaft
D - Front Bush
E - Thrust Race Housing
F - Thrust Race
G - Worm Wheel Centre Inner Race

The Scott 98 c.c. engine is the heart of the Cyc-Auto and is now manufactured by **Winsmith (Finchley) Ltd.**

The component parts used are of the highest grade material; accuracy and precision in production ensures maximum performance and reliability with the minimum of attention.

Bore 50 m.m. by 50 m.m. Cylinder of Patented design with Transfer Ports directed towards the semi-spherical detachable aluminium cylinder head, Cylinder is chromidium cast-iron, with ample finning to ensure efficient cooling; decompressor valve for easy starting. Piston of special heat-treated aluminium alloy with Aero type tapered rings.

SUN

Having commenced in business as brass founders and metal workers, the Birmingham firm of James Parkes & Son had specialised in lamps and associated products, but by the mid-1880s had added cycle fittings and then frames to its repertoire. This soon necessitated a move to larger premises in Aston Brook Street, Aston, followed by a change of name to Sun Cycle Fittings Co in 1887 – the title prompted by the manufacture of incandescent lamps. As time went on the cycling side took increased precedence so the final years of the 19th century saw the firm begin to produce complete bicycles. In 1907 the firm became the Sun Cycle and Fittings Company Ltd.

From there it was a logical progression to think of motorised two-wheelers, and in 1911 the firm had branched out into this field with a Precision-engined machine. The following year it began a relationship with Villiers and pioneered the use of the recently-developed Villiers two-stroke engine, with the 269cc Sun-Villiers – a move that was to have far-reaching and long-lasting influence on the British motorcycle industry.

Further models followed, and during the First World War a quantity of machines were supplied to French and Russian forces but other war work took precedence and motorcycle production ceased.

In addition to Precision and Villiers engines the company had used V-twin and single JAPs, as well as another two-stroke made by a neighbouring firm named VTS, which it now owned. The first of the post-war models, the Sun-Vitesse, was thus fitted with one of these engines – a rotary valve two-stroke with a capacity of 250cc designed by VTS's founder John Duffey.

Like many makers, Sun decided to have a go at the Tourist Trophy races, and at the first attempt, in 1921, was rewarded by ninth and tenth places in the 250 class of the Junior. The following year the Lightweights had a race all to themselves and the young Gus Kuhn took a Sun to 12th place, with another 13th. But competition was not pursued and for the reminder of the decade the firm built a range of utilitarian machines with its own, Villiers and Blackburn engines.

197 c.c. CHALLENGER DE LUXE

Frame: Heavily built Lugged frame, rear springing with centre spring up stand. **Forks:** Telescopic Double spring action, with armour chrome sliding members, forged steel centre brackets. **Engine:** Villiers 197 c.c. Series (6E) Roller bearing to Big end, Ball bearing supporting mainshaft. Light alloy cylinder Head. Petroil lubrication. **Carburettor:** Villiers, with our filter and strangler twist grip control. **Transmission:** ½" main drive with Three-quarter chain cover. **Mudguards:** Extra wide 2½" chain line. Tubular stays. **Wheels:** Dunlop 19 × 3.00. **Brakes:** 5" × ¾" Internal expanding front and rear. **Tank:** Saddle type, twin petrol outlet, capacity 2¼-galls. **Lighting:** Lucas Battery charged from fly wheel generator 6" Head Lamp 24W main bulb. Electric Horn. **Speedometer:** Smiths 65 m.p.h. **Carrier:** Extra strong tubular carrier. **Finish:** Sun Bright maroon on Bonderized frame, all bright parts chromium plated, wheels silver.

Petrol consumption over 100 m.p.g. Road Tax: 37/6 per annum.

Top of the Sun-produced range in 1951 was the new three-speed 197 Challenger De Luxe.

By the early 1930s, having found its bicycles more readily saleable during the slump, the decision was taken to discontinue the manufacture of motorcycles and concentrate efforts on pedal-powered transportation. Had it not have been for the war the end the '30s would have seen the introduction of a Sun autocycle but events put it on hold, and instead the next few years were devoted to fulfilling government contracts for steelwork, fittings and rivets – around a million of them per day. The projected autocycle, Villiers-powered, finally went into production in 1946 and

Introduced for the 1950 season, the 122 had a rigid frame but it now had a plunger rear and was a De Luxe. Front forks on this and the Challenger were Metal Profiles components. Believe it or not, one of these was entered for the 1951 Ultra lightweight TT by Paddy Johnston, who brought it home 16th and last of the finishers. An Island stalwart, it was the last of his 32 TTs. He'd started out riding a New Imperial in 1922 but had most frequently ridden Cottons – runner-up in the lightweight on one in 1925 and winning in 1926. His Sun, however, averaged just 48mph to the winner Cromie McCandless's 74 on a Mondial.

122 c.c. MODEL DE LUXE

Frame: Sun Lug Built. Damper action rear springing with forged steel spring box housing—centre spring-up stand. **Forks:** De Luxe Telescopic double spring action—with armour chrome sliding members. Forged Steel centre brackets. **Engine:** Villiers M.K (10d) 122 c.c. Light Alloy Cylinder Head. Ball bearing supporting mainshafts. Petroil lubrication. **Carburettor:** Villiers, with air filter-strangler—Twist grip controls. **Gear Box:** 3-speed with foot change, cork inset clutch running in oil. **Transmission:** ½" Chain with Three-quarter chain cover to prevent dirt contacting chain. **Ignition:** Flywheel Magneto (Villiers). **Lighting:** Lucas Battery charged from fly-wheel generator. 6" Head Lamp. Electric Horn. **Speedometer:** Smith's 65 m.p.h. **Mudguards:** Extra wide. 2½" chain line to give extra clearance. **Tyres:** Dunlop 19 × 3.00. **Carrier:** Large tubular extra strong. **Brakes:** British Hub 5" internal expanding rear and front. **Tank:** Saddle Type twin petrol outlet, capacity 2¼-galls. **Finish:** Bonderized and enamelled. Sun Bright Maroon, all bright parts chromium plated. Wheels Silver. **Special Features:** Front and Rear springing as used so successfully in many competitions.

Petrol consumption over 100 m.p.g. Road Tax 37/6 per annum.

98 c.c. MODEL DE LUXE

Frame: Brazed Lugged Frame, spring-up centre stand. **Forks:** Tubular centre spring link action adjustable. **Engine:** Villiers 98 c.c. (Series I.F) Roller bearing big end Ball bearing mainshaft. Light alloy Cylinder Head. Petroil lubrication. **Carburettor:** Villiers—air filter. Twist grip throttle control. **Gear Box:** Two-speed change operated by Handlebar Lever, cork inset clutch running in oil. **Drive:** ½" driving chain with chain cover. **Ignition:** Villiers Flywheel Magneto. **Lighting:** Direct large head lamp 18w. main bulb. **Tyres:** Dunlop 19 × 2.50. **Brakes:** British Hub 4" Internal expanding. **Tool Box:** Extra large triangular fitted to rear stay. **Carrier:** Large strong. **Mudguards** Extra wide. **Tank:** Saddle type, twin outlet, capacity 1¾-galls. **Finish:** Bonderized and enamelled Sun Maroon, and spray varnished. All bright parts chromium plated, Wheels Silver.

Petrol consumption over 150 m.p.g. Road Tax 17/6d. per annum.

The little 98cc two-speed didn't run to telescopic forks, but as tiddlers went it was one of the best of the bunch.

was made until a tentative return to the world of fully-fledged motorcycles began at the 1948 Motor Cycle Show, where the company took a stand on the central aisle. There, amongst the various Sun bicycles, was the Villiers-powered 98cc Autocycle but beside it, also with a Villiers 98, was a proper little two-speed motorbike with rigid frame and girder-type central spring forks.

The following year Sun was back and sprung a last-minute surprise with the unveiling of a 122cc machine with a rigid frame and spindly-looking telescopic front forks, which *The Motor Cycle* described as 'one of the best finished machines on display'.

By the mid '50s Sun's range had grown to encompass swinging-arm-framed road machines up to 250cc, with a 197 for the competition rider, and plans were afoot to enter the scooter market. During 1958, shortly after these reached fruition in the form of the 98cc Geni, the Parkes family accepted a takeover bid from Tube Investments, which wanted to add the bicycle side of the business to its British Cycle Corporation. With Fred Parkes carrying on as chairman, larger-capacity Wasp scooters joined the Geni but motorcycles were phased out at the end of 1959 to clear the way for increased scooter production.

In 1960 TI took over Raleigh Cycles and the following year Sun's long-running Aston Brook Street factory shut down – with scooter production set to move elsewhere. It never happened, but bicycle manufacture was from thereon undertaken by Carlton Cycles at Worksop, another part of the TI/Raleigh Group, and Sun-branded bicycles continued to be built until the mid 1980s.

SUN
Lightweight
MOTOR CYCLES

BEFORE YOUR VERY EYES—

We make no apology for using this expression because illustrated for you to see is our latest range of "Light-weights", noted for quality in design and materials—The outstanding successes of the Challenger Competition model go to prove this, and in its first year in the most important Competitions, this Motor Cycle has been singularly successful—Every Competition model is hand built in our Development Department, this means yours also if you choose wisely.

"SUN" VILLIERS 1st 1912—1st 1954

By 1954 the company was rightfully able to boast of some success with its recently-introduced competition model. Although this is not he, Ted Breffitt had gained a coveted first class award in the 1953 Scottish Six Days Trial with one.

98 c.c. Mk. II

The MkII 98 had the latest 4F Villiers but otherwise was altered from its predecessor in small details such as the positioning of the tyre pump, which was now clipped to the front down-tube rather than atop the chain guard as it had been previously.

200 c.c. COMPETITION MODEL

Frame: Specially built rigid with Cast Lugs and 10×12 Tapered Body Tubes, clearance from ground 8". **Forks:** Specially built with additional rake and special rubber recoil buffer. **Footrests:** Extra strong and of special design. **Wheels:** Front 2.75×21, Rear 4.00×19 Rims, Chromium Plated. **Stand:** Detachable Prop. **Mudguards:** Aluminium with Centre Steel Strip. **Tank:** Capacity $2\frac{1}{4}$-gallons. **Saddle:** Special Mounting. A Cushion Seat can be supplied as extra. **Finish:** Bright Maroon.
VILLIERS SPECIALLY TUNED ENGINE AND CARBURETTOR.

THIS MODEL SUPPLIED IN THESE MODELS:—
- Mk. I. Standard Engine with 3-speed Gearbox.
- Mk. III. Specially tuned with 3-speed Gearbox.
- Mk. IV. Specially tuned with Competition 4-speed Gearbox.

A direct lighting set was an optional extra but unless an owner wanted the machine to double as a ride-to-work job it would have been an unlikely choice. Although not mentioned in this brochure, some factory publicity referred to and illustrated a raised air filter beneath the saddle – achieved by inserting a long U-shaped tube between carburettor and standard air filter, the latter then facing forwards just behind the forward lug for the saddle subframe.

Sun's 1954 Challenger had been brought right up to date with a swinging-arm frame – the previous MkII had plunger rear suspension. Optional extras included a four-speed gearbox, leg shields, chromium-plated tank, and a carrier. Generally a good looking machine, other than the gap beneath the seat that could have been neatly filled with a tool box rather than perching one behind the suspension unit.

200 c.c. CHALLENGER DE LUXE Mk. III

Frame: Heavily Built Lugged Frame — Swinging Rear Fork Arm Suspension, using Armstrong shock absorbers, centre stand. **Forks:** Telescopic double spring action, with rubber cushion return shock absorber. **Carrier:** This can be fitted as extra charge, and is capable of carrying two large weekend cases. **Engine:** Villiers 200 c.c., Roller Bearings to big end, Ball Bearing to supporting mainshaft — Light Alloy Cylinder Head and 3-speed Gearbox, etc., etc. **Lubrication:** Petrol Oil system. **Carburettor:** Latest type Villiers — Twist Grip control. **Transmission:** ½" Main drive with Three-quarter chain cover. **Mudguards:** Extra wide, centre ribbed with strong tubular stays. **Wheels:** Dunlop 19×3.00. **Brakes:** Internal Expanding front and rear. **Tank:** Saddle type, capacity 2¼-galls.—Maroon panelled and chromium, maroon metal nameplate. **Lighting:** Lucas large capacity Battery charged from Flywheel Generator, 6" Head Lamp and large Rear Stop Light. **Speedometer:** 65 m.p.h. **Saddle:** Spring Seat. **Finish:** Bright Maroon, Tank lined Gold or panelled and Chromium Plated extra. Wheels Chromium Plated.

*Latex Cushion Co. Twin Seat Extra. Carrier can be supplied as extra.

It's strange how smaller manufacturers needlessly complicated matters. In this case, two utterly different frames for machines of similar capacity.

225 c.c. "SUN" AVENGER

Engine: 225 c.c. IH Villiers with enclosed Carburetter and Flywheel; 4-speed Gearbox; foot control Kick Start. **Frame:** Specially designed, giving exceptional strength with lightness; single front taper gauge down tube, with twin tube cradle housing for the Engine; Twin Seat Tubes to Swinging Arm Pivot eliminating Side Sway; additional supporting fixed Stay from Bracket to Spring Box. **Forks:** Bulged taper main members and Armour Chromium Plated Sliding members; telescopic action, fitted with double spring and rubber buffer return damper; forged steel front forkends. **Tank:** 2½ gallons capacity. **Mudguards:** Large Valence with Tubular Stays. **Wheels:** Chromium Plated, fitted with Dunlop 3.25×19 Tyres. **Brakes:** Extra large pattern with cable direct control on the rear. **Lighting:** Lucas large capacity Battery, charged from Flywheel Generator; Locking device for ignition — key supplied; 6" Head Lamp with Ammeter. **Twin Seat:** Latex Rubber. **Footrests** for passenger. **Speedometer:** 65 m.p.h. **Finish:** Black Enamel with Chromium Plated parts; Tank lined with elegant Gold Plated and Enamel Nameplate; Tank can be supplied with Chromium Plated Panels as illustrated as extra.

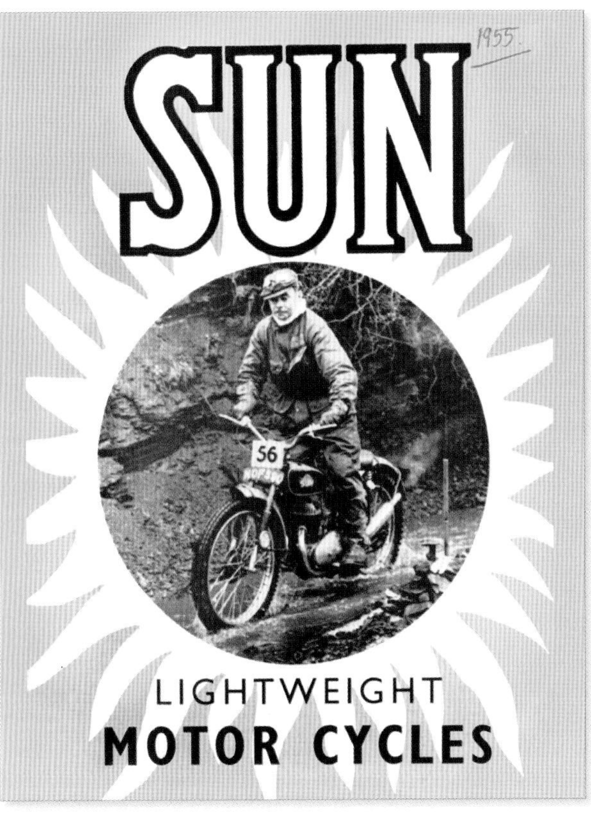

Sun's 1955 brochure cover featured the same rider and machine as '54's but the firm claimed an additional 50 trials and scrambles awards in the interim.

Instead of a 125cc option for the Challenger MkIII there was now this. Apart from the engine, its manufacturer said, it was largely as the larger-capacity MkIV. A little confusing but I expect you get the general idea, as well as noticing the differences such as mudguard stays and the exhaust that has the downward kink used for previous year's Challengers. The saddle too – although the 197 MkIV listed the dual seat as an extra, so we must presume it had a sprung saddle as standard. As I said – confusing.

The 98 carried on with little or no material change but did at last have a name.

SUN *Challenger MkIV* SUN *Cyclone*

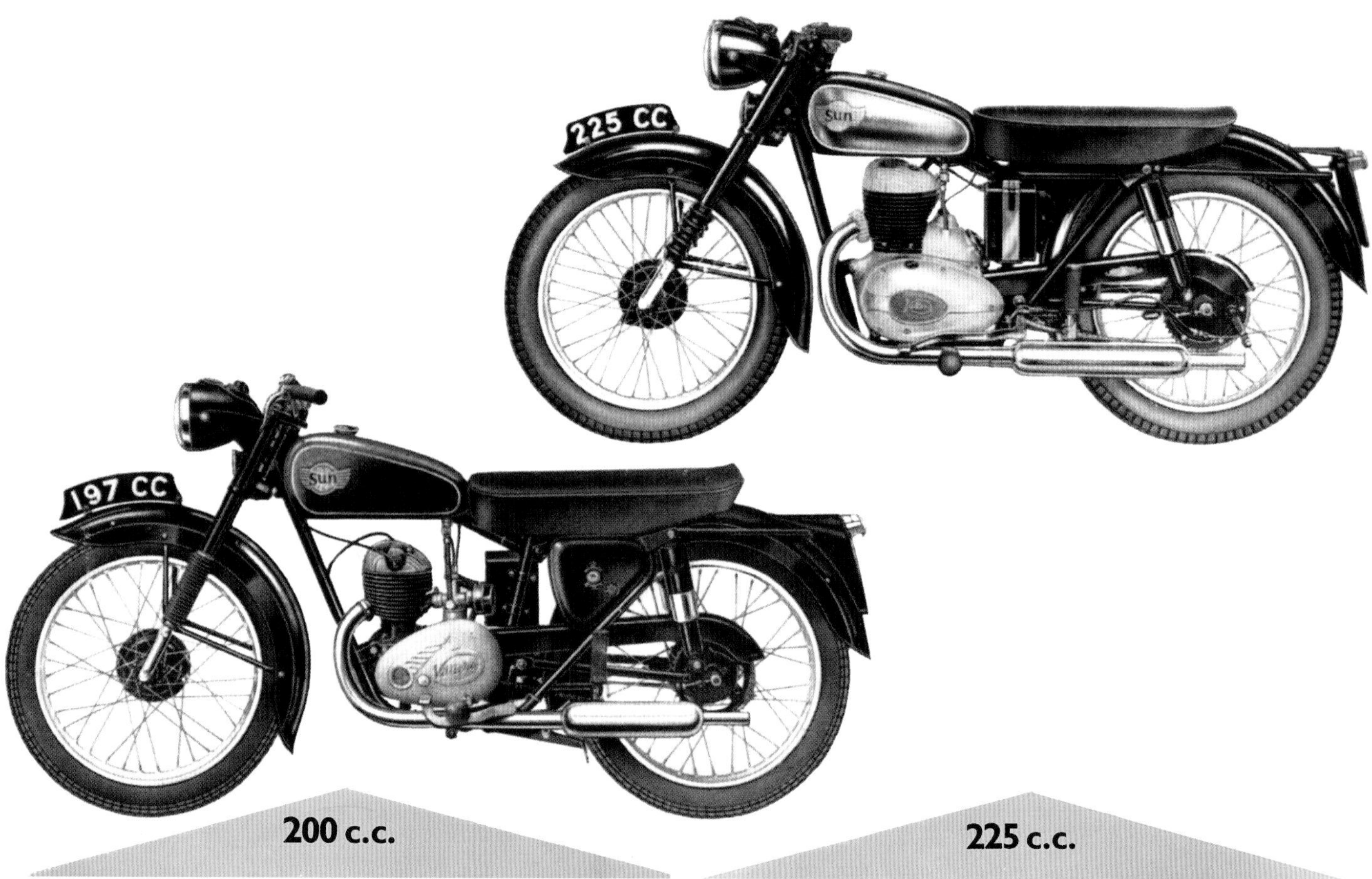

Frame: Heavily Built Lugged Frame — Swinging Rear Fork Arm Suspension using Armstrong shock absorbers, centre stand. **Forks:** Telescopic double spring action with rubber cushion return shock absorber. **Carrier:** This can be fitted as extra charge, and is capable of carrying two large week-end cases. **Engine:** Villiers 200 c.c. Roller Bearings to big-end, Ball Bearing to supporting mainshaft — Light Alloy Cylinder Head and Three-speed Gearbox, etc., etc. **Lubrication:** Petrol Oil system. **Carburettor:** Latest type Villiers — twist Grip control. **Transmission:** ½″ main drive with three-quarter chain cover. **Mudguards:** Large valance. Front and rear fitted with tubular stays. **Wheels:** Dunlop 19×3.00. Rims Chromium Plated. **Brakes:** Internal expanding front and rear. **Tank:** Saddle Type. Capacity 2½-gallons —Maroon panelled and Chromium Plated extra.

*Latex cushion Twin-seat Extra. Carrier supplied as extra.

£123 - 0 - 0 3-speed Including P.T.

Engine: 225 c.c. 1H Villiers with enclosed Carburettor and Flywheel; 4-speed Gearbox; foot control Kick Start. **Frame:** Specially designed, giving exceptional strength with lightness; single front taper gauge down tube, with twin tube cradle housing for the Engine; Twin Seat Tubes to Swinging Arm Pivot eliminating side sway; additional supporting fixed Stay from Bracket to Spring Box. **Forks:** Bulged taper main members and Armour Chromium Plated Sliding members; telescopic action, fitted with double spring and rubber buffer return damper; forged steel front forkends. **Tank:** 2½ gallons capacity. **Mudguards:** Large Valance Front and Rear with Tubular Stays. **Wheels:** Chromium Plated, fitted with Dunlop 3.25×19 Tyres. **Brakes:** Extra large pattern with cable direct control on Rear. **Lighting:** Lucas large capacity Battery charged from Flywheel Generator; Lucas rear stop light; Locking device for ignition — Key supplied; 6″ Head Lamp with Ammeter. **Twin Seat:** Specially designed Latex Cushion. **Footrests** for Passenger. **Speedometer:** 65 m.p.h. **Finish** Black Enamel with Chromium Plated parts; Tank lined with elegant Gold Plated and Enamel Nameplate. Tank can be supplied with Chromium Plated Panels as illustrated as extra.

£150 - 0 - 0 Including P.T.

Mudguards with deep valancing for all road models apart from the Hornet for 1955, whereas these had previously only been fitted to the 225 Avenger. I see they've put a suitably-shaped tool box where it should have been on the Challenger MkIII and the run of the exhaust is much more graceful too.

Last year's Avenger had become the Cyclone but otherwise the maker was happy to leave it as it was. Shortly after the '54 Show Motor Cycling *were lent POP 159 and, as the weather was generally wet and miserable, were pleased to find that its mudguards were particularly efficient. Not so pleasurable was the over-noisy exhaust and irregular firing, however – the latter traced to its maker sending it out with an over-rich petrol/oil mix. Once this was sorted, performance tests returned a max of a whisker under 60mph and 53 in third gear, with average petroil consumption of 90-to-95mpg.*

OVER 200 AWARDS

50 AWARDS in scrambles and trials during last season

THE SUN CYCLE & FITTINGS CO. LTD.
ASTON BROOK STREET, BIRMINGHAM, ENGLAND

SUN *Scrambler*

200 c.c.

This Trials model has been extraordinary successful during the past season gaining a big number of First-class Awards, including the Scottish Six Days. We guarantee every model is built by hand in our Development Department.
Frame: Heavily built lugged Frame — clearance from ground 8″. Swinging Rear Arm suspension using Armstrong shock absorbers. **Forks:** Specially designed Earles Pattern. **Footrests:** Extra strong of special design. **Wheels:** Front 2.75 × 21. Rear 4.00 × 19. **Rims:** Chromium Plated. **Stand:** Detachable Prop; **Mudguards:** Aluminium with strong Tubular Stays. **Tank:** Capacity $2\frac{1}{4}$ gallons. **Saddle:** Special mounting. **H.M.F.** Special Competition Seat can be fitted as an extra. **Finish:** Sun Maroon all bright parts Chromium Plated.

£142 - 16 - 0 Including P.T.
Complete with special engine and 4-speed gearbox.

200c.c. Trials Model Produced with rigid frame, standard engine **£120 - 0 - 0**
Specially tuned 4-speed engine for Trials Model - - **£10 - 16 - 0**

From the heading you might think this is the Scrambler but it's very obviously a swinging-arm-frame version of the Trials bike, which for 1955 did have Earles forks. Elsewhere in the brochure the Scrambler is listed as an 'entirely new model' so must we presume that it was as this illustration with the substitution of scrambles tyres, exhaust, handlebars and seat, and the removal of bulb horn and number plates?

Engine: 250 c.c. Twin, Villiers 2T 4-speed. **Frame:** This has been specially constructed for this very powerful Twin Motor—Entirely new silencing system is employed. Silencers having been specially designed for use with this engine. **Forks:** Heavy pattern Armstrong with leading link action and oil damped shock absorbers. **Rear Suspension:** By Swinging Arm and Armstrong shock absorbers. **Wheels:** Built up with Dunlop Chromium Plated Rims, Large equal flanged Aluminium Centre Hubs, Wheels fitted, ribbed front and universal rear Dunlop Tyres 3.00×19″. **Tank:** Steel welded, capacity 2¾-gallons. **Mudguards:** Specially designed, all-weather type eliminating all Mudguard Stays and special Side Valance is used similar to the "Sun" Wasp for protection from water and dirt on pillion riders' legs. **Lighting:** 6″ Lucas Headlamp fitted with Ammeter and Rear Stop Light—Charged from Flywheel Generator. Electric Horn. **Toolboxes:** And Battery enclosed. **Twin Seat:** Designed and made for this model by Latex Cushion Company using Dunlopillo rubber seating. Footrests are supplied for passenger. **Speedometer:** 80 m.p.h. is supplied and this Motor is capable of 70 m.p.h. plus with its extraordinary acceleration. The whole Motor Cycle is designed to cope with this engine's performance. **Finish:** Colour Quaker Grey with two-tone finish to the Tank and to the Boxes, Chromium Plated panel Tank optional extra. 'This really is Britain's Premier Lightweight.'

Cover girl for 1957 was Sun's brand-new flagship Overlander that was powered by, Sun assured potential customers, 'the very latest 250cc Twin described as the most fantastic engine produced for 1957'.

The Challenger soldiered on in its latest form with rather less gawky headlamp arrangements, horn now mounted forward of the tool box and remodelled dual seat amongst other bits and pieces. The separate 150cc IA had been dropped and instead a smaller engine option was for export only.

This model is retained for another year with only slight modifications. **Engine:** Villiers 8.E. 3-speed Kickstart 197 c.c. Roller Bearings to big-end. Light Alloy detachable Cylinder Head. **Carburettor:** Villiers. **Lubrication** by petrol oil system. The oil measure being fitted to the petrol filler cap four measures to one gallon. **Frame:** Heavily built, lug type frame with Swinging Arm. **Rear Suspension:** Using Armstrong heavy shock absorbers. **Forks:** Telescopic double spring action with rubber cushion return shock absorber. **Mudguards:** Heavy duty, all-weather pattern with Side Valances and Tubular Stays. **Wheels:** Dunlop Chromium Plated Rims, 5″ Internal Expanding Brakes, fitted with Dunlop Tyres 19×3.00. **Tank:** Steel welded, capacity 2¾-gallons. **Lighting:** Lucas 6″ Headlamp and Rear Light charged through flywheel generator to large capacity battery. Carrier can be fitted to this model if desired. **Finish:** Maroon.

150 c.c. Engine can be fitted and is a special Export model.

This model is introduced this year because of the popularity of the Villiers 8.E. Engine with 3-speed Gear. The frame however is entirely new and is of up-to-date design.

Engine: Villiers 8.E. 3-speed 197 c.c. Roller bearings to big-end. Light Alloy detachable Cylinder Head. **Carburettor:** Villiers. **Lubrication** by petrol oil system. The oil measure being fitted to the petrol filler cap four measures to one gallon. **Frame:** Entirely new design with enclosed Battery and Toolbox. **Forks:** Telescopic double action spring fitted with rubber cushion return shock absorber. **Rear Suspension:** Swinging Arm with large Armstrong Shock Absorbers. **Wheels:** Dunlop Chromium Plated Rims built up with 5″ British Hub Company's Brakes, fitted with Dunlop 19×3.00 Tyres. **Mudguards:** Large all-weather with Side Valances. **Twin Seat:** Made by Latex Cushion Co., with Dunlopillo seating. **Tank:** Steel welded, 2¾-gallon capacity. **Lighting:** 6″ Lucas Headlamp and rear Stop Light, large capacity, Lucas Battery charged from flywheel generator. **Colour:** Quaker Grey with two-tone panel, Tank in Grey and Mushroom, also all Maroon. Carrier can be supplied to fit this model optional extra.

Personally I prefer the look of the Challenger, which to my eyes also appears more business-like. I wonder if Sun also had doubts – otherwise why not drop the older model if this was such an advantageous up-to-date design?

sun WASP 200

Engine: 200 c.c. Villiers 9E 4-speed. **Frame:** Tubular lugged and brazed. **Forks:** Designed by Armstrong with leading link action and oil damped Shock Absorber. **Rear Suspension:** Swinging Arm with Armstrong Shock Absorbers. —All-weather protection Mudguards—Mudguard Stays entirely eliminated. Twin toolboxes and battery enclosed, electric Horn inserted in toolboxes—Special side valances designed for protection of pillion passenger's legs from water dripping off mudguard valance, this is an important feature. **Tank:** Steel welded, capacity $2\frac{3}{4}$ gallons. Wheels Chromium Plated, Dunlop Rims, built with full width Aluminium Centre Hubs with Journal Bearings—Tyres, Dunlop 19×3.00. **Lighting:** Lucas large capacity battery, charged from flywheel generator, 6″ Headlamp fitted with Ammeter and stop light fitted to Rear Number Plate **Twin Seat:** Specially designed made for this model by Latex Cushion Co., using Dunlopillo rubber seating—Pillion Foot-Rests are fitted—Speedometer 80 m.p.h. drive from engine gearbox. **Finish:** The whole machine enamelled in Quaker Grey with two-tone Tank, finished in Quaker Grey and panel in Mushroom, Toolboxes also in Mushroom, making a very attractive contrast finish. Chromium Plated panels on tank is optional extra.

Sun's most prestigious 197, this one with full-width hubs and leading-link forks like the Overlander. But what a mélange of styles produced for 1957, seemingly unable to take a definitive step one way or t'other. The firm was a little muddled in its grasp of entomology too: the 98cc tiddler was still current as the Hornet (now finished in Sax (sic) blue), whilst anyone knows that one of those is a larger and more intimidating proposition than a mere wasp.

sun CYCLONE

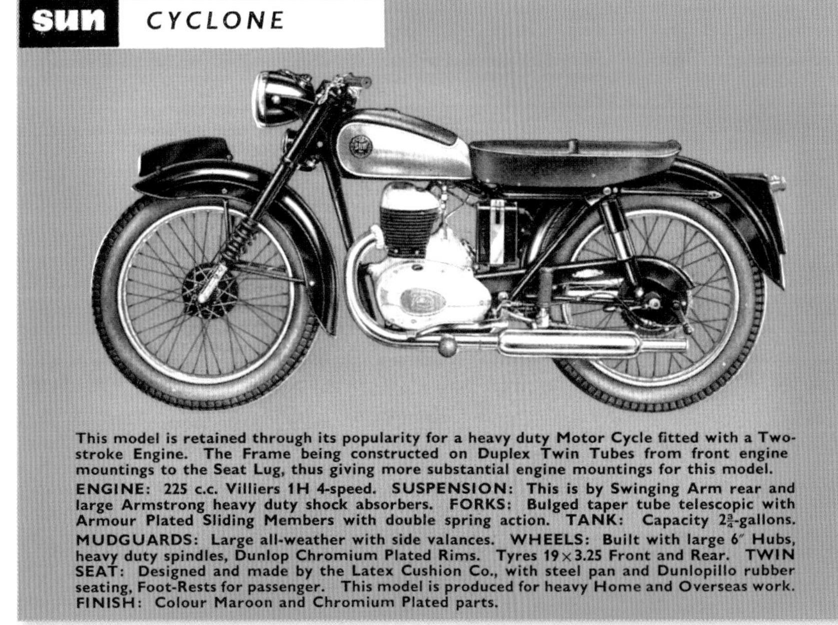

The Cyclone was another retained model but had now taken on the role of heavyweight. Little changed but seat and tank differed from its previous incarnation.

sun COMPETITION

Still depicted in trials trim but Sun had addressed the frame's weak point – a common Achilles heel of other tubular-framed lightweight competition machines at that time, as I personally experienced. Full-width alloy brakes were specified but single-sided are shown, so I don't know what was going on there – maybe they were for the scrambles-kitted version but as this brochure carries no list of options and only the Trials version appears in the price list (£159 10s all in) it's only a guess.

This model has been altered very considerably for 1957. Frame having been made suitable for both Trials and Scrambles, which has a supporting strut from the top tube to the front down tube, thus strengthening frame across the head.

Engine fitted is the very latest type of 9.E.4-speed, which has recently been developed for competition work with a heavier flywheel and raised induction pipe, this giving amazing new power output. We guarantee every model is produced in our Development Department and so receives the attention to detail so necessary in competition Motor Cycles.

Forks: These are of the latest Armstrong Trials pattern which have been so successful since introduced a few months ago. **Mudguards:** Are Alloy with supporting steel strip for added strength and quickly detachable Rear Tubular Stays. **Saddle:** Dunlop Trials. **Tank:** Special, $2\frac{1}{4}$-gallons capacity. **Brakes:** Latest type, full width Alloy Centre, Foot Rests, double fixing extra strong. **Tyres:** Front 2.75×21, Rear 4.00×19. **Wheels:** Security Bolts are fitted as standard. **Finish:** Maroon enamelled and Chromium Plated parts.

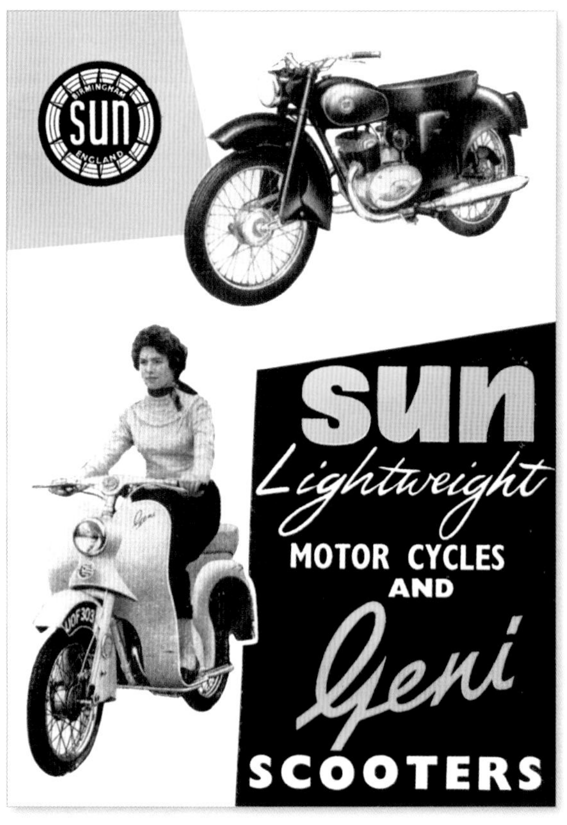

Sun's 1958/9 brochures would be the last to include motorcycles, with the depleted range of just two allotted less space than the Geni and Wasp scooters. The latter was available as a 150 or 175; both with Seba electric starting for the Villiers engines.

The SUN WASP 200 c.c.

It was a sleeker version of the Wasp's 1957 styling that had been chosen to grace the latest version, as well as the Overlander.

Engine: 200 c.c. Villiers 9E 3-speed. **Frame:** Tubular lugged and brazed. **Forks:** Designed by Armstrong with leading link and oil damped Shock Absorber. **Rear Suspension:** Swinging Arm with Armstrong Shock Absorbers.—All weather protection Mudguards.—Mudguard stays entirely eliminated.—Twin toolboxes and battery enclosed, electric horn inserted in toolboxes. **Rear Body Pressing:** Rear of machine completely enclosed with one pressing eliminating the rear mudguard giving complete weather protection to pillion passenger. In addition a valanced splash guard is also fitted underneath rear body pressing. **Tank:** Steel welded, capacity 2¾ gallons. Wheels chromium plated, Dunlop rims, built with full width Aluminium Centre Hubs with journal bearings.—Tyres, Dunlop 19×3.00. **Lighting:** Lucas large capacity battery, charged from flywheel generator, 6″ Headlamp fitted with Ammeter and stop light fitted to Rear Number Plate. **Twin Seat:** Specially designed, made for this model by Latex Cushion Co. using Dunlopillo rubber seating. Pillion foot-rests are fitted—Speedometer 80 m.p.h. drive from engine gearbox. **Finish:** Italian Red, tank lined out. Chromium Plated tank panels as an optional extra.

OVERLANDER TWIN 250 c.c.

Engine: Villiers Twin 250 c.c. 4-speed foot operated control. **Frame:** Specially constructed so that Mudguards do not require stays. This also applies to the front fork, and the design obviously overcomes the annoyance of mudguard rattles. **Forks:** Designed by Armstrong, with leading link action, and oil damped Shock Absorbers. **Rear Suspension:** Pivoted Swinging Arm oil damped Shock Absorbers. **Silencers:** Latest type Villiers, and specially designed for the engine. **Rear Body Pressing:** Rear of machine completely enclosed with one pressing eliminating the rear mudguard giving complete weather protection to the pillion passenger. In addition a valanced splash guard is also fitted underneath rear body pressing. **Battery Toolbox:** These are enclosed in twin cases, with the electric horn inserted in the Toolbox. **Tank:** Capacity 2¾ gallons. **Wheels:** Chromium plated rims fitted with large flange aluminium centre hubs. **Brakes:** 6″ diameter front and rear. Tyres 3.00×19. **Lighting:** 6″ Headlamp with fitted Ammeter and rear stoplight. Battery charged from flywheel generator. **Electric Horn: Twin Seat:** Designed and made by Messrs. Latex Cushion Co., using Dunlopillo and rubber. **Footrests:** For pillion passenger, fitted as standard. **Speedometer:** 80 m.p.h. **Note:** Larger brakes are now fitted to cope with the increased performance and acceleration of this engine. **Colour:** Italian Red, tank lined out. Chromium plated tank panels as optional extra.

In view of what was shortly to transpire, this introduction is somewhat poignant: "The Overlander Twin is retained, as indeed it must be. This 250cc two-stroke is the motorcycle of the future..." The machine tested by Motor Cycling *in the spring of '58 was finished in Silver Blue with deeper Blue, Gold-lined tank top, and like other non-competition Suns had deeply-valanced mudguards. Its Armstrong forks and rear suspension units afforded excellent handling and the generous (10in) ground clearance was, the manufacturer said, with an eye on export markets. The 'lively acceleration' enthused about was obtained by spinning the motor to 6,900 (43mph in 10 seconds from rest) but from there it took a further 34 seconds to reach its terminal velocity of 69mph. At 40 it would return 90mpg, but hold a steady 50mph and that came down to 68mpg.*

SUNBEAM

With origins stretching back to the black japanware so beloved of the Victorians it is easy to see why Sunbeams were renowned for the quality of their black finish. Apprenticed as a teenager to the Jeddo Works of Wolverhampton (manufacturer of tinplate and japanwares), John Marston set up on his own account once he had served his time in 1859.

Before long the quality of Marston's domestic wares had become a byword, and when his former employee Edward Perry died in 1871 he was in a position to incorporate his firm, with the two becoming John Marston and Company Ltd. By the early 1880s his Paul Street works boasted a workforce of some 150, so upon detecting a gradual slackening in trade and with a sizeable workforce to keep busy, his thoughts turned to the possibility of a fresh enterprise – and being an avid cyclist he alighted upon that trade.

Commencing with a cycle built for himself by his works foreman, the original plan had been to produce tricycles but, he reasoned, the latest up-to-the minute safety machines would have a much broader appeal. From the outset these bicycles were finely made and, legend has it, came to be named Sunbeams on account of Marston's wife commenting upon the sun's reflections from the original's lustrous black finish. Be that as it may, in 1888 the name Sunbeam was duly registered and the Paul Street works henceforth known as Sunbeamland.

Competing as it had to with a multitude of other emergent manufacturers, the growth of the make was at first steady but the machines' quality and the optional fitment of Carter's fully-enclosed chain cases to touring models made them a popular mount for the gentry and their ladies. So much so that by the mid 1890s there was a London showroom and several depots, the firm's name had been streamlined to simply John Marston Ltd, and all but its racing machines featured Little Oil Bath chain cases – a slogan and feature that would remain integral to the marque for very many years.

As a result of a fact-finding trip to the United States by Marston's son Charles the decision was taken to manufacture the company's own pedals and other cycle parts, so another tinplate works was purchased, in Wolverhampton's Villiers Street, and Villiers Cycle Components Co set up there in 1898. This ultimately became Villiers Engineering, maker and supplier of two-stroke engines employed by many of the motorcycle manufacturers covered in this book.

By the following year experimentation with motor vehicles had begun, and in 1901 the Sunbeam-Mabley (part named after its designer) was put on the market. This quaint vehicle lasted until 1904, by which time more advanced motorcars had been made, including one with six cylinders, the domestic metalware side of the business had been disposed of, and in its place the motor radiator manufacture begun – Marston radiators going on to enjoy a long and multifaceted career. The formation of the Sunbeam Motor Car Company Ltd in 1905 saw the car manufacturing side of John Marston's growing empire now carried out at the Moorfield Works adjacent to Villiers Street, with subsidiary factories elsewhere in Wolverhampton.

Contrary to other bicycle-turned-motor manufacturers who progressed through motorcycles to cars, John Marston did the opposite and was in his mid-seventies when his firm put its first motorcycle into production. Designed by Harry Stevens of nearby AJS, motorcycles were made at the Paul Street works and, powered by a 2.75hp single-cylinder side-valve engine, featured all-chain drive with, naturally, the Little Oil Bath enclosure for the rear. During the time

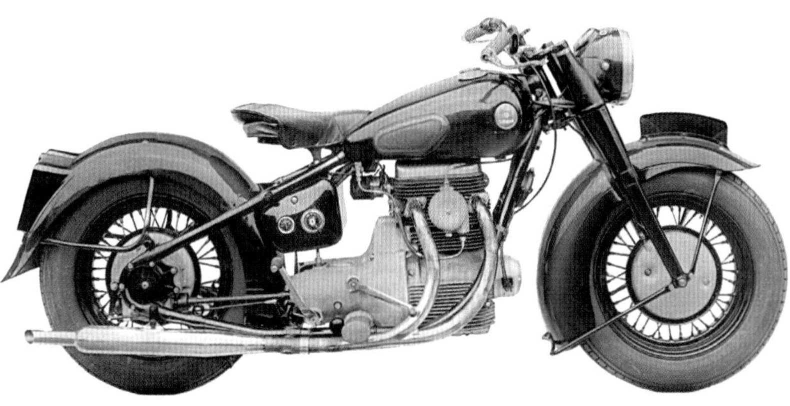

That BMW's R75 influenced Erling Poppe's formulation of the Sunbeam S7 is abundantly clear in this factory photograph of a pre-production prototype in which certain aspects are uncannily like the German military machine. Its power unit, however, emanated from exploratory work done by BSA in the early 1930s on a fore-and-aft OHC twin. Further BMW influence was also evident – in this case the pre-war R66 – in the finalised spring-frame version that went on sale.

In the spring of 1946 Motor Cycling*'s editor Graham Walker, accompanied by his son Captain Murray Walker (lately commander of a Sherman tank and much later a motor racing commentator), took this prototype of the Sports S7 to be evaluated by Sunbeam's legendary speed merchant and record breaker from the '20s, George Dance. Although apparently the veteran racer had not so much as sat astride a motorcycle for over 15 years he happily sped over a fast stretch of road and through a series of S-bends at 80-plus – exclaiming, "It's champion!" upon his return. Walker, himself an ex-Norton, Sunbeam and Rudge works rider, then had a serious go along the straight where he managed 86mph one-way and 91 on the return with an adverse side-wind. A few days later the machine's designer called him to say that under more ideal conditions and after some adjustments it had achieved 94mph with 'more to come'. Be that as it may, the Sports never reached production – the possibly detrimental effect of its overabundance of power on the transmission sometimes being cited as the reason.*

that remained before the outbreak of the First World War progress was rapid and a larger 3½hp single was introduced, and then a V-twin with 770cc JAP motor – both with three-speed gearboxes and enclosed all-chain drive. A team of three of the 3½s was entered for the 1914 Senior TT and Howard Davies, later to be the manufacturer of HRDs, put in a stirring maiden performance for himself and the marque to tie for second place with an Indian – his teammates finishing 11th and 13th.

The years of conflict brought plentiful contracts from Allied Governments for the supply of military bicycles and both single- and twin-cylinder motorcycles, the latter in sidecar form undertaking various roles from gun carrier to stretcher bearer – their all-chain-drive standing up well to this kind of work. With the war nearing its end the company should have been able to look forward to a prosperous future as a result of continuously full order books but early in 1918, in quick succession, John Marston's eldest son died, and then John himself, followed by his wife – these sad events leaving his surviving son Charles with a considerable amount of death duties to settle. The knock-on effect was a series of disposals that ended in 1920 with Sunbeam cars (which also now was a volume producer of aero engines) amalgamating with Darracq and becoming part of STD (Sunbeam, Talbot, Darracq), whilst Sunbeam bicycles and motorcycles (John Marston Ltd) were bought by Kynoch, part of the conglomerate of explosives manufacturer Nobel Industries – organisations that were understandably well-placed financially after years of war.

These machinations had no adverse effect on the business of producing motorcycles, however, and under the direction of the firm's chief engineer/designer John Greenwood, who had joined the company prior to the war, both singles and V-twins had soon returned to full civilian production.

The company was also quick to renew its competition activities, and Tommy de la Hay won the first post-war Senior TT at a record speed of over 51mph, with top rider George Dance putting in a lap not far short of 56mph before he was forced to retire. Sunbeam's crack riders Dance, de la Hay and Alec Bennett were up against some very stiff opposition the following year, and Bennett's fourth place behind an AJS and two Indians was all they could manage on the Island. But Bennett took the French GP on the new Longstroke racer – this 77x105.5mm motor, in both side- and later overhead-valve form, generally acknowledged to be the best and destined to remain current until the Second World War. In 1922 Bennett scored the first of his five TT wins but unfortunately for Sunbeam it would be his sole for the firm, as the following year he was aboard a Douglas before swopping to Norton for 1924, a move that brought him his second victory.

Further successes on the Island eluded Sunbeam for the meanwhile, despite its motors now having pushrod overhead-valve and, in 1925, a brief flirtation with OHC. But on the Continent it was a different story: with Sunbeams almost certainly the most popular British machine amongst the racing fraternity, a large number of GPs, other events and championships were won by competition versions of the 500cc Model 9. At home, too, the marque was kept in the public eye by George Dance and de la Hay, whose performances in sprints and speed events became legendary.

It all came good in the TT in 1928 when, after two years of being trounced by principal rival Norton, Charlie Dodson won the Senior at over 62mph (and again in 1929 when he averaged just over 10mph more), with Bennett, now back with Sunbeam, second. That year also saw ownership of the company change hands once more when Nobel became part of the giant Imperial Chemical Industries combine – a move that would have both beneficial and detrimental effects on the marque. Having the might of ICI behind it, the company was able to weather the depression but rationalisation and subsequent economies of production resulted in the range being reduced to just four models for 1931 – a new cheaper 350 OHV (the

Model 10); a fresh version of the 500 Model 6 side-valve now named the Lion after ICI's trademark; Model 9; and the Road Racing Model 90.

Despite adverse trading conditions this had increased to eight models by 1934. Consisting of a 250 OHV Longstroke, 350 OHV Model 8, 500 and 600cc Lions, 500 and 600cc Model 9s and a pair of racers, the 250 Little 95 and 500cc 95, they were the last machines presided over by John Greenwood as he retired that year. The racers, however, had hardly moved with the times so little success came their way, and with the business running at a loss it would be the last time that it sent machines to the Isle of Man – concentrating instead on fielding a trials team that yielded awards and publicity far more economically.

By 1937 ICI was tiring of what was perceived as a lame dog amongst its group of companies and so was happy to dispose of Sunbeam motorcycles, and cycles, to Matchless's Collier brothers, who were putting together Amalgamated Motor Cycles. No immediate changes were made but by 1938 production of the existing range had been moved down to Woolwich, whilst new models were prepared for the following season. Utilising many components common to other AMC (now Associated Motor Cycles) machines, they were equipped with either the old Lion engine or a brand-new AMC-designed high-camshaft OHV in four capacities of approximately 250, 350, 500 and 600cc, with sports and competition versions catalogued. Shortly before the impending war a rear suspension option was announced for the larger of the high-camshaft models and this, a pivoted fork controlled by boxed plungers, was carried on to the 1940 range but production was soon curtailed as Matchless's G3 had been taken up by the War Department and the remainder of the workforce was needed for the manufacture of aircraft components.

Had BSA not purchased the Sunbeam name in 1943 the marque might never have been resurrected, but afterwards its rebirth was supposedly set in motion by deliberations in the wartime motorcycle press as to the ideal machine of the future. Grasping the nettle, so to speak, BSA engaged the Austrian-born designer Erling Poppe, who set about his task using elements of BMW's military R75 and pre-war R66 as a source of inspiration. The end result, although clearly influenced by the German machines, was very different if only on account of its in-line twin-cylinder overhead-cam motor. Initial tests revealed chronic vibration and concerns regarding the strength and possible longevity of the worm final drive but the former was quelled by substantial rubber mountings – unfortunately after a quantity of export machines had been returned as unrideable – and the production version of the latter proved to be sufficiently robust in practice.

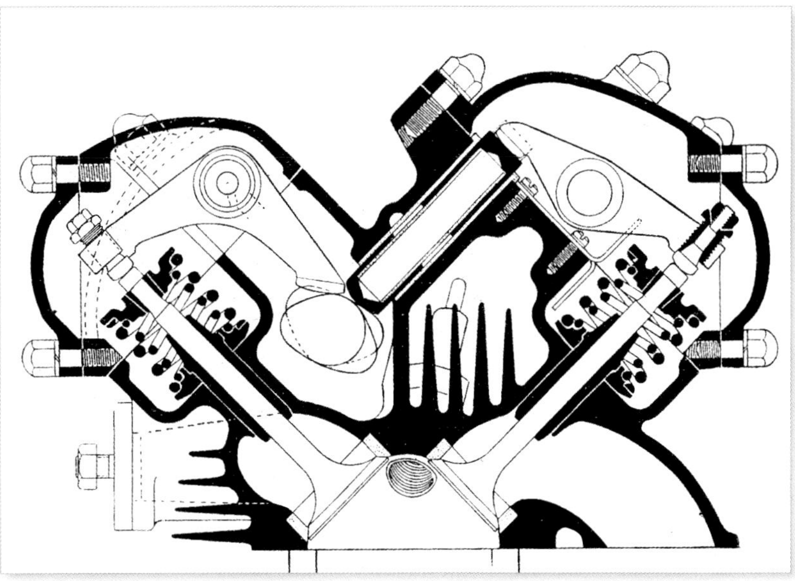

The cylinder head and valve configuration that was largely responsible for the performance of the Sports – the 90-degree valve angle in the fully-hemispherical head was facilitated by right-angle inlet rockers and the exhaust rockers' activation by short pushrods. Valve clearance adjustment was accessed by way of removable side covers. In addition to this special head the Sports had a larger 1in choke carb (standard was 15/16th), 8:1 compression (standard was 7:1), a hotter camshaft and lightened flywheel. The cylinder head employed on production S7s had a squish-type head with 22-degree valve inclination.

The bulky-looking shaft-drive 500cc S7 – standing on 16in wheels shod with balloon tyres – was introduced to the market in 1946, its undamped forks conspiring with the podgy Dunlops to produce handling that was less than confidence-inspiring. Unleashed upon a slightly bemused public who didn't know quite what to make of such a beast it sold in not great but sufficient numbers (with most going for export) for an improved, more conventional and mildly sporting version to be introduced at the 1948 Motor Cycle Show. The latest S7 De Luxe was indeed an improvement and its cohort, the new S8 (as well as being normalised with BSA front forks and wheel from the A7 or B series, an 18in rear and a conventional saddle) was some ten per cent cheaper and about the same amount faster.

Never huge sellers, something over 7,600 S7s (the majority being the improved De Luxe) and a little over 8,500 S8s finally reached the public but by 1956 sales had dropped to such an extent that production ceased – with unsold machines remaining current into the following season.

The Sunbeam name then lay fallow until BSA decided to enter the scooter market with a 250cc four-stroke twin and a 175cc two-stroke single; marketed as either Triumphs or BSA Sunbeams they were produced from 1959 until 1965.

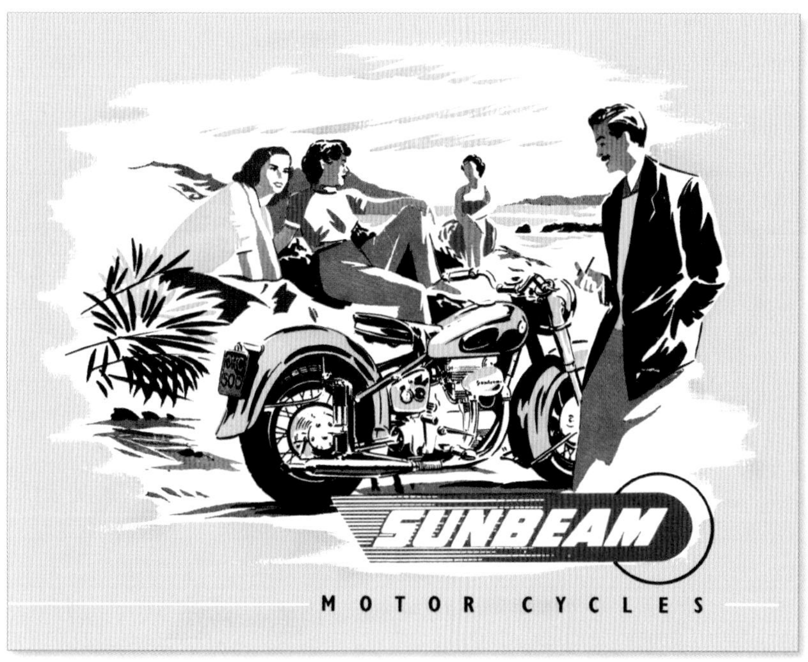

The 1952 brochure's cover presents a choice of feminine company for the chap; but who's wearing the trousers and is it his S7, or one of theirs? An S7, even in its improved De Luxe form, would have been an unusual choice for one of these beachside belles, and if it's his he'll be leaving by himself as he was too mean (or lacked sufficient foresight) to splash out on a pillion seat (£1 16s) or a pair of pillion footrests (16s 10d).

SUNBEAM

MOTOR CYCLE PRICE LIST

from September 1st, 1953

Model		Retail Price £	s.	d.	Purchase Tax £	s.	d.	Total Retail £	s.	d.
S7	500 c.c. O.H.C. Twin	220	0	0	44	0	0	264	0	0
S8	500 c.c. O.H.C. Twin	200	0	0	40	0	0	240	0	0
EXTRAS—ALL MODELS										
Pillion Seat		1	10	0		6	0	1	16	0
Pillion Footrests			14	0		2	10		16	10
Colour Finish—Grey on S8		3	0	0		12	0	3	12	0
SUNBEAM SIDECARS										
Model S22/50	De Luxe Tourer	64	10	0	12	10	0	77	0	0
Model S23/52	Family Model	70	10	0	13	13	3	84	3	3

This is the 1952 S7, which had benefitted from numerous improvements, not least of which was some damping for the forks, since The Motor Cycle*'s test of a '48 model – so one has to view their praise of its handling as 'rose-tinted journalese'. Despite its same somewhat ponderous looks imparted by large-section tyres and fulsome mudguards the latest model was a distinct improvement; but back to those 1948 testers who assured their readers that, "Traffic work was a sheer delight. The low-speed handling is good, the engine idles and pulls sweetly and smoothly, and mechanical and exhaust quietness is impressive... The machine is comfortable over the most neglected of cobbled and rippled surfaces." Road-holding too was found to be 'first-class' with 'light and positive steering'. Although a maximum of only 72mph was recorded it proved to capable of 'cruising effortlessly and tirelessly at around the 65 mph mark'. Fuel consumption was 66mpg at a steady 50mph but only 2 less at 60mph.*

Classed as a sports machine, I would put the S8 down more as a fast tourer, but either way Motor Cycling*'s staff were full of praise for it in their 1950 test, summing up by remarking that, "It had given us some of the most pleasant motorcycling experienced since post-war road tests were started." Pleasurably 'free from undue noise, unnecessary dirt and tinkering', their small concern was its fuel consumption, in those days of rationing, with 69mpg returned at a steady 50mph or 45mpg at 70mph. Speeds in the gears were 58, 72 and 80mph but during their test of a similar machine at the end of 1949* The Motor Cycle *recorded 58, 80 and 83mph.*

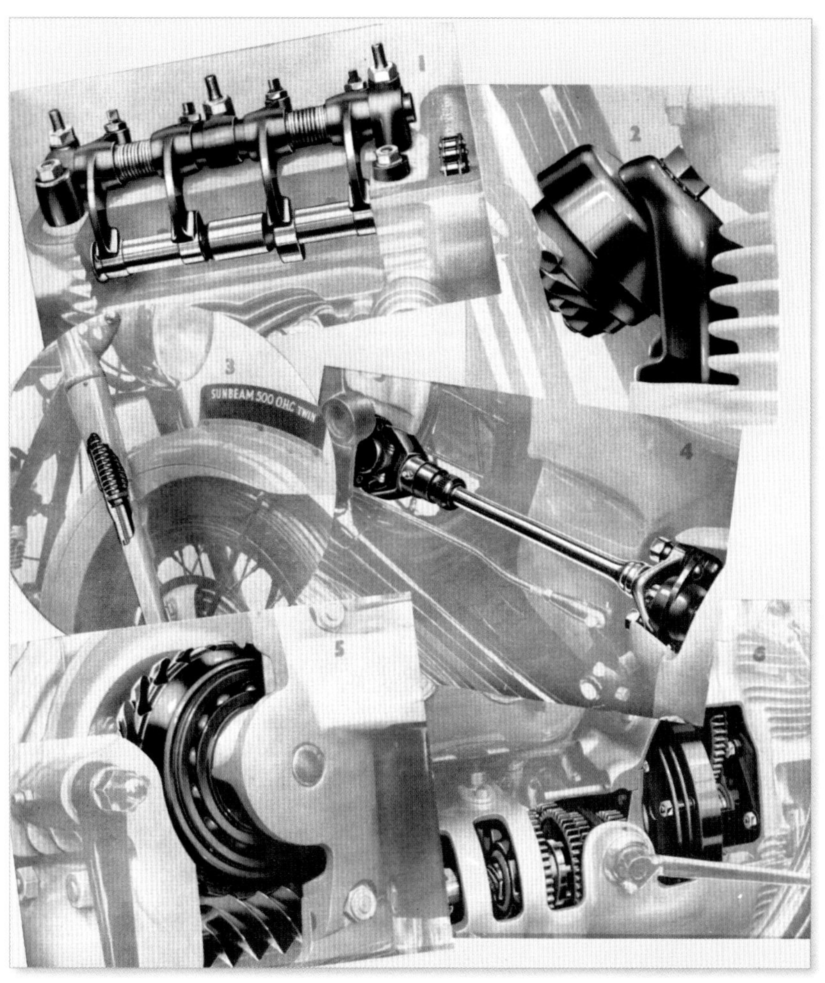

Traditional English values for the cover of 1954's export brochure with St Paul's Cathedral, a double-decker London bus and, of course, a Sunbeam S7.

Whilst Sunbeam's S7 had front forks and brake all of its own, that of the S8 had been sourced from its parent firm BSA – the 7in stopper doing duty on the 350/500 touring singles and A7. Also clearly visible in this view of the S8 is the Lucas dynamo driven from the front of the aluminium in-line twin's crankshaft, as well as the car-type sump with a marginal capacity of just three pints. The 7's silencer was also an aluminium casting.

FEATURES

1 The chain driven overhead camshaft is mounted on plain bearings of generous dimensions, pressure fed direct from the oil pump.

2 A smooth flow of power from the engine is ensured by its rubber mountings, the upper one being shown in the illustration. They are both oil and petrol proof.

3 Superb steering is provided by the telescopic front forks fitted with automatic progressive hydraulic damping.

4 Shaft drive is now accepted as the ideal form of power transmission. The Sunbeam design is of sturdy construction and incorporates a needle roller universal joint at the rear.

5 The worm reduction gear is of robust proportions, requires little maintenance, and is unaffected by the removal of the rear wheel.

6 A four-speed gearbox and a single plate dry clutch are in unit construction with the engine.

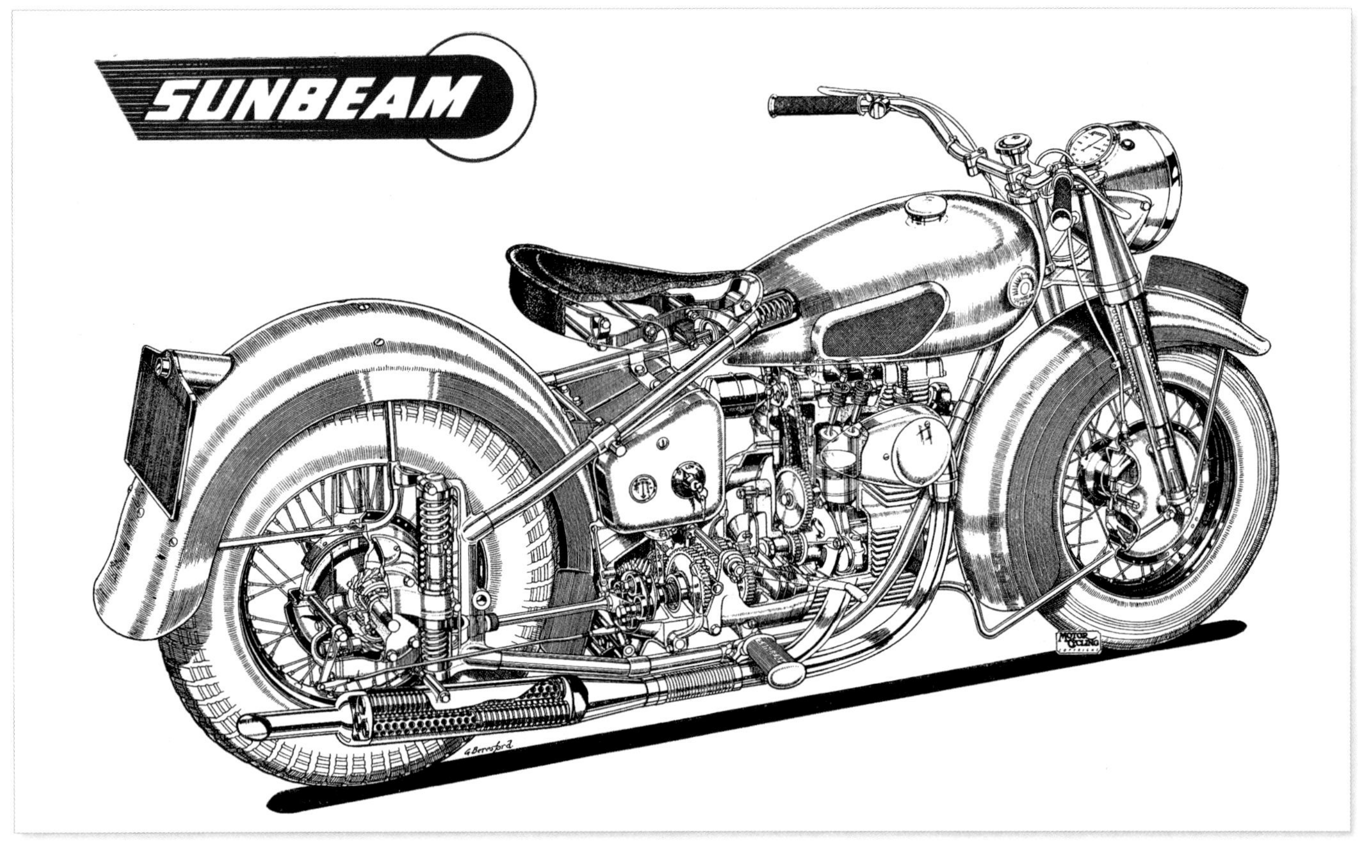

George Beresford was one of the masters of the cutaway drawing, his work often appearing in Motor Cycling, *and here is his exposé of the S7. Its mildly inclined valves, chain-driven overhead camshaft and distributor drive can clearly be seen plus internals of gearbox and rear hub. Both S7 and S8 had a flexible insert between exhaust pipe and silencer as, although rubber mountings isolated the rider and rest of the machine from the motor's vibrationary activities, they were still there. Front and rear wheels of the S7 were interchangeable.*

SUNBEAM 500c.c. OVERHEAD CAMSHAFT TWIN

General Specification

POWER UNIT: Fully floating power unit, mounted on rubber, with high frequency vibration damper.

ENGINE: Unit construction vertical twin, 2¾ in. bore × 2½ in. stroke; crankcase and cylinders in one-piece aluminium alloy casting and detachable 'Brivadium' cylinder liners; one-piece aluminium alloy cylinder head; overhead camshaft drive by chain with automatic tensioner; totally-enclosed and specially lubricated cam and rocker gear; light alloy connecting rods with special 'Vandervell' plain shell big-end bearings; crankshaft main bearings—front, deep-groove ball; rear, 'Glacier' plain shell white metal; Amal carburetter; Vokes (oil dip) air cleaner.

LUBRICATION: Car type engine lubrication; separate oil supply for gearbox and rear drive; other parts by grease gun.

TRANSMISSION: Direct drive from engine through single plate car-type dry clutch to gearbox; four speeds with positive stop foot gear change; shaft drive to rear wheel from gearbox layshaft through one shock absorber and one needle bearing universal joint; final drive from shaft to rear wheel by totally enclosed worm gear; gear ratios: solo 5.3, 6.5, 9.0 and 14.5 to 1; sidecar 6.13, 7.4, 10.3, 16.6 to 1.

FRAME: Tubular duplex cradle; telescopic front forks with automatic hydraulic damping; rear suspension by totally enclosed plunger springs; rubber mounted petrol tank (capacity three gallons with half gallon reserve); easy action central stand; integral frame lugs for L.H. or R.H. sidecar attachment. Domed and valanced mudguards, rear hinged.

CONTROLS: Twist grip throttle, front brake and horn button on right bar; clutch and dip switch on left bar. Handlebar and footrests adjustable to suit rider.

EQUIPMENT: Dunlop tyres; Lucas 6 volt 60 watt dynamo lighting set with compensated voltage control; 8 in. headlamp with built-in speedometer, ignition and oil warning lights; new style rear number plate with combined stop and tail lights; coil ignition with automatic advance. Coil, cut-out, switch, ammeter and spare bulb holder in offside box protected from weather; battery in rubber buffers in nearside box. Electric horn; spring seat saddle; metal toolbox complete with toolkit; tyre inflator; licence holder; folding prop stand. Saddle type pillion seat and folding pillion footrests extra.

	Model S7	*Model S8*
SILENCER:	Absorption type, chromium plated.	Baffle type, cast aluminium.
WHEELS:	Instantly detachable and interchangeable.	Instantly detachable.
TYRES:	Front: 4.50—16 ribbed. Rear: 4.75—16 studded.	Front: 3.25—19 studded. Rear: 4.00—18 studded.
BRAKES:	8 in. diameter.	Front: 7 in. diameter. Rear: 8 in. diameter.
SADDLE:	Spring cradle mounting, adjustable for rider's weight.	Three-point attachment.
FINISH:	Mistgreen with black frame and chromium plated handlebar, exhaust system, etc.	Black lustre with chromium plated handlebar, exhaust pipes, etc. Alternative colour, silver grey.

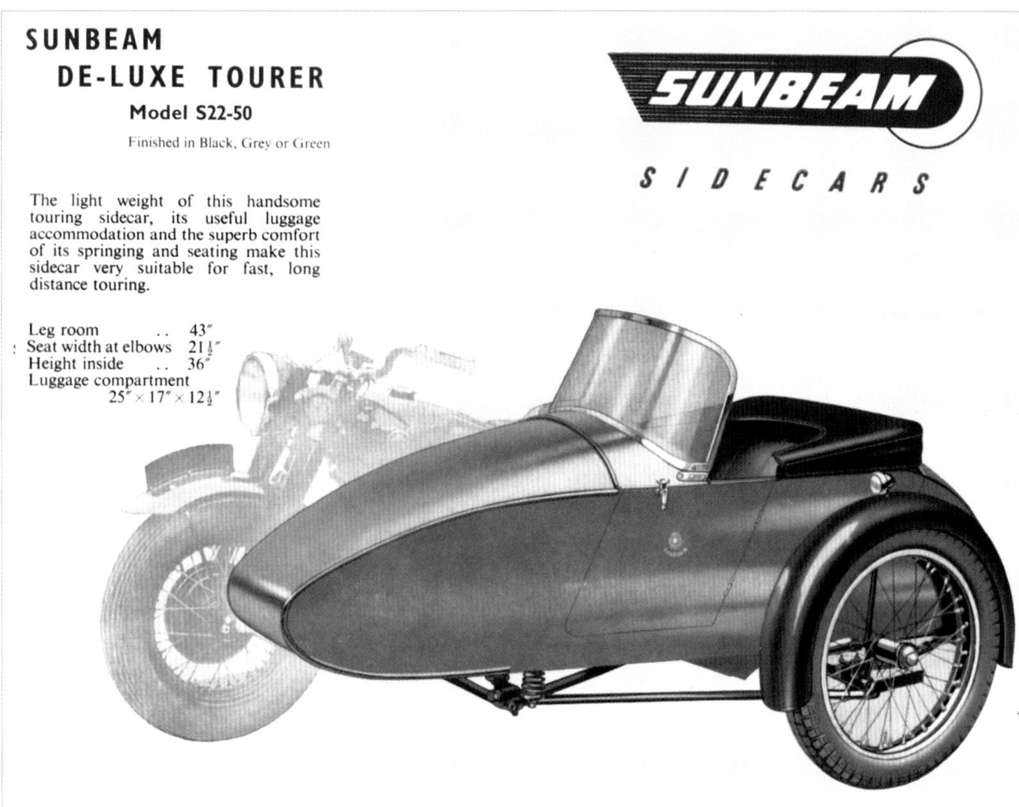

On occasions publicity material was prone to exaggeration but this was indeed a handsome ensemble and, as Motor Cycling *tested a virtually identical outfit (the sidecar being the earlier 21/50 single-seater) in 1953, here are a few of their findings: starting from cold took several kicks with the ignition off and then two or three more with it on, but when warm the merest 'dab on the pedal would bring the engine into subdued life' (contrary to all other reports, which remarked on ease of starting even when cold). Clutch was light, gears selected easily and steering was first-class, whilst acceleration in the gears was ample for negotiating traffic and the cruising speed was high enough for long-distance trips to be undertaken. Importantly, flexibility proved to be outstanding, with 10mph or less easily held in top gear. Maximum speeds in the gears proved to be 49mph in second, 59 in third, with just another couple of mph attained in top with the engine spinning at 4,900rpm; to obtain the second-gear maximum the tester had taken it to a heady 6,570rpm. It required 34ft to bring the outfit to a halt from 30mph, and at a steady 40mph it would return 64mpg, or 48mpg at 50mph.*

SUNBEAM
SINGLE SEAT SALOON
Model S22-54
Finished in Black

The comfort, smart appearance and many practical features of this single seat saloon side-car makes it ideal for year round transport. The luggage compartment is fitted with a lock and the lid at the rear hinges down to form a platform.

Leg room .. .. 48″
Seat width at elbows .. .. .. 21″
Height inside .. .. 34″
Luggage compartment .. 22″ × 20″ × 18″

SUNBEAM
FAMILY SIDECAR
Model S23-52
Finished in Black

Here's the sidecar for the family man. It provides saloon car comfort for an adult and child. It is completely weatherproof. The top of the body hinges towards the machine for easy access.

Leg room .. .. 50″
Seat width at elbows .. 20½″
Height inside .. .. 28″

Compared with some other sidecars of the period, the Busmar double-adult to name but one, Sunbeam's were good looking, if a trifle 1930s in appearance.

TANDON

With the exception of its telescopic forks, which had knurled adjusters at the top of each leg, Tandon's 122cc Milemaster could easily have been mistaken for a machine from an earlier age. One has to wonder how its bolt-up-cum-clamp-up method of frame construction would have withstood the rigours of what passed for roads in third-world countries – especially as it might have been expected to transport two or more persons plus the family pig on the carrier.

As the processes that would set India free from its years of British Colonial rule drew to a conclusion and preparations were being made for the handover of power to the two new countries of India and Pakistan in the summer of 1947, a middle-aged Indian gentleman living in England was making plans of his own.

Very soon, he reasoned, the vast population of his native land would be crying out for a range of Western products, especially those that gave increased mobility via cheap personal transportation – to wit small motorcycles. Besides, the watchword in post-war Britain was export, export, export, and attached to this were all manner of government incentives so, with no grounding in the motorcycle industry that I am aware of, he made the decision to become both manufacturer and exporter. Finance was raised and before long Devdutt Tandon was in business as Tandon Motors Ltd, with a Ludgate Hill, EC4 address and a stand booked at Earls Court in November.

Grandiosely christened the Milemaster, the first Tandon was a rather crude little affair; but as the intention was to send the majority of production to India and other far-flung countries CKD (completely knocked down) for assembly by un- or semi-skilled labour its very crudeness could be considered an attribute. The method of construction also allowed for its manufacturers to operate with very basic tooling and equipment – anything specialised such as castings or sheet metalwork being subcontracted and components bought in.

The duplex-type cradle frame consisted of straight tubes assembled with clamp-type cast alloy lugs and steering head. An engine had presented no problem and, like other manufacturers such as James, Tandon was able to call upon Villiers for a supply of Villiers Mk9Ds; this pre-war design's twin exhausts and hand-change, coupled with the Milemaster's angular fuel tank, gave it something of a vintage appearance.

Devdutt Tandon's aspirations to becoming a major exporter were given a fillip when pictures of India's Prime Minister Nehru astride one of his machines appeared in the British and Indian press, but neither India nor other emerging nations came knocking. Things might have worked out differently had Tandon established a network of dealerships and advertised widely but finances were tight, so he was faced with job of selling a prematurely dated-looking machine on the UK market – a market that was already well catered for by large manufacturers such as James and Royal Enfield, with BSA's Bantam freshly arrived on the scene.

Not to be outdone, Devdutt stuck at it and the MkII or Superglid was brought to the 1949 show, bringing the range up to two, and by the time the 197cc Superglid Supreme was announced a new factory just north of Watford was operational.

Over the ensuing years the range was enlarged to include competition models, first a trials and then a scrambler, and even twins powered by British Anzani, but the marque never really caught the public's imagination. The workforce was a jolly lot by all accounts, however, as they would periodically break into song – encouraged by their boss to chant 'wonderful, wonderful Devdutt Tandon' to the tune of 'wonderful, wonderful Copenhagen' from the Danny

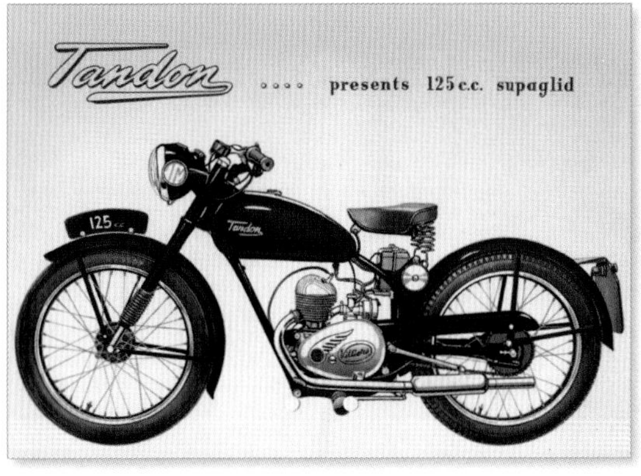

The Supaglid was a much more up-to-date-looking proposition than the Milemaster but just look at the rear of the frame – it incorporates Tandon's 'famous swinging-arm rubber controlled suspension'. The rear forks extend forward of their pivot and this section acts in a downward direction, compressing a rubber cartridge retained above a plate beneath the engine/gearbox unit. All very well, but definitely no pillion riders with the rear mudguard joggling up and down; I also wonder about structural rigidity. Both motorcycle magazines tested the same polychromatic blue 125 Supaglid De Luxe during the summer of 1950 and Motor Cycling *in particular were full of praise for its suspension: "London tramlines and subsiding manhole covers disappear beneath the wheels with no further intimation of their presence than a slight jar."* The Motor Cycle*, on the other hand, found the 'brakes disappointing – neither being up to the required standard'. Both agreed on its top speed, however, as 48mph. Early in '51* The Motor Cycle *borrowed one of the first 197cc Supaglid Supremes, describing it as 'a powerful lightweight with outstandingly good suspension'. They then brought a smile to my face when they continued by commenting that 'on full fork depression the front number plate fouled the headlamp rim...the result was a shattered headlamp glass', further suggesting that 'this fault could easily be remedied by repositioning the plate'. Quality control, Devdutt! The brakes, they weren't quite so keen on: "They lacked power and there was a disconcerting sponginess," things going from bad to worse when the front cable nipple pulled off. Speed-wise they got it up to 49mph in second and 55 in top. At a steady 30mph it returned 98 miles for a gallon of petrol, whilst they managed to get 136mpg out of the little 122cc Supaglid at the same speed a few months earlier.*

ENGINE Villiers 122 c.c. (50 x 62 mm.) single cylinder two-stroke with three speed gear box in unit. Flat crown, die cast, aluminium-alloy piston. Roller bearing big end, ball bearing supported main shafts. Detachable light-alloy cylinder head with half pear-shaped combustion chamber Petroil lubrication.

ENGINE SPROCKET 18 teeth.

MINIMUM NON-SNATCH SPEED 11 m.p.h. in top gear.

GEAR RATIOS

Top	7.55 — 1
Second	10.57 — 1
First	20.08 — 1

CARBURETTER Villiers type ¾ single lever.

IGNITION Fully advanced 5/32" before T.D.C.

FINAL DRIVE CHAIN ½" Renold chain No. 110044.

TYRES DUNLOP

Front ins.	3.00 x 19
Rear ins.	3.00 x 19

SADDLE HEIGHT 28"

WHEELBASE 50"

GROUND CLEARANCE 6¾"

WEIGHT 178 lbs. (dry).

PETROL TANK 2½ gallons.

SUPAGLID SPECIFICATION

ENGINE Villiers 122 c.c. Model 10D.

TRANSMISSION Primary chain in cast aluminium oil bath case with polished motif. Rear chain protected on top run.

PETROL TANK All-steel welded streamline design.

FRAME Welded full cradle type with large diameter tubes.

FRONT FORKS Tandon telescopic pattern with 5" of movement.

REAR SUSPENSION Tandon famous Supaglid swinging arm rubber controlled suspension.

BRAKES 4" front, and 5" rear.

HANDLEBARS Chrome plated ⅞" dia. with adjustable brake and clutch levers and quick action twist grip.

MUDGUARDS 4" section with welded on stays to prevent rusting, and to provide smooth surface.

WHEELS AND TYRES Plated rims and rustless spokes. Dunlop tyres ribbed front and studded rear.

TOOL BOX Large capacity in tank top with plated top cover plate retained with one knurled screw.

EQUIPMENT Villiers AC generator with Westalite rectifier and large diameter Lucas streamlined headlamp incorporating AC/DC switch. Lucas electric horn. Smiths 65 m.p.h. chronometric speedometer internally illuminated.

FINISH Frame, forks, tank, etc., stove enamelled in polychromatic blue or maroon, also in black. Wheel centres enamelled and lined to match. All bolts and nuts, etc., cadmium plated. Exhaust pipe silencer, etc., chrome plated. Highest quality materials and finish throughout.

The Kangaroo, dare I suggest so named on account of its undamped suspension, was first introduced with a 125 Villiers and Tandon's rubber-cushioned rear end but for 1953 it had been endowed with swinging-arm. Mind you, if looks were everything it wouldn't have been a winner, in spite of the fact that the frame geometry could allow a much lower seat in line with modern machines.

Kaye film that was very popular at the time. This little tale, by the way, I got directly from my friend Cyril Ayton, staff writer for *The Motor Cycle* during the 1950s and then long-time editor of *Motorcycle Sport*, who assured me that it is absolutely true.

By 1955, however, although there was a range of half-a-dozen-or-more Tandons to choose from, the firm's creditors had reached a frame of mind that judged Devdutt to be anything but wonderful and proceedings were begun that culminated in the ultimate demise of his firm.

The Imp (left) had been introduced as a replacement for the Milemaster at the 1952 show and had been powered by a 125 Villiers. The vee formed by the rear of the frame of the smaller-capacity model had a shallower radius than that of the 1955 version below.

150c.c. IMP

ENGINE :	Villiers 150 c.c. Model 30C Petroil Lubrication 16-1.
GEARBOX :	In unit with engine, internal ratios, 1st 2.66-1, 2nd 1.4-1, 3rd 1-1.
FRAME :	Bronze welded throughout. Single loop frame constructed from "Kromo" tube by Accles & Pollock Ltd.
FRONT FORKS :	Constructed from Reynolds "531" tube, 5in. total movement, springs controlling impact and rebound.
WHEELS AND TYRES :	3.00 x 19in. Dunlop tyres, front and rear. Rims: Chromium-plated, 5in. hubs front and rear.
MUDGUARDS :	5in. section with bolted-on stays.
SPEEDOMETER :	Smiths' 65 m.p.h.
LIGHTING :	Direct lighting set with parking battery.
HORN :	A.C. electric horn.
EXHAUST PIPE :	Low level with barrel-type silencer giving excellent performance with quietness—all chromium-plated.
FINISH :	Beige stove enamel. Bright parts chromium-plated. Also black and chromium.
PETROL TANK :	1½ gallon capacity.
DIMENSIONS :	Wheel Base, 49in.; Ground Clearance, 6½in.; Saddle Height, 25in.; Weight, 140 lb.

TM

Tandon

TANDON MOTORS LTD.
29, LUDGATE HILL
LONDON, E.C.4

Motor Cycles of Distinction

1955

Works:- Colne Way, By-Pass Road, WATFORD

Devdutt's last throw of the dice was on the table with this brochure.

197 c.c. IMP SUPREME

ENGINE :	Villiers 197 c.c. Model 8E Petroil Lubrication 16-1.
GEARBOX :	In unit with engine, internal ratios, 1st 2.66-1, 2nd 1.4-1, top 1-1. Overall ratios: 1st 15.6-1, 2nd 8.2-1, top 5.9-1.
FRAME :	Bronze welded throughout. Single loop frame constructed from Reynolds " 531 " tube. Braced mainframe with subframe carrying rear suspension.
SUSPENSION :	Front—Constructed from Reynolds " 531 " tube, 5in. total movement. Springs controlling impact and rebound. Rear—Swinging arm controlled by telescopic Hydraulic Damped units attached to subframe.
WHEELS AND TYRES:	Front—3.00 x 19in. Dunlop tyre. 5in. hub brake. Rear—3.00 x 19in. Dunlop tyre. 5in. hub brake. Rims: Chromium-plated.
MUDGUARDS :	5in. section with bolted-on stays.
SPEEDOMETER :	Smiths' 80 m.p.h. trip.
LIGHTING :	5in. diameter Villiers headlamp. Lucas rear lamp, direct lighting.
HORN :	A.C. electric horn.
EXHAUST PIPE :	Low level with barrel-type silencer giving excellent performance with quietness—all chromium-plated.
FINISH :	Beige stove enamel. Bright parts chromium-plated. Also black and chromium.
PETROL TANK :	1¾ gallon capacity.
DIMENSIONS :	Wheel Base, 49in.; Ground Clearance, 7in.; Saddle Height, 27in.; Weight, 176 lb.

What's this: a sensible suspension system in a substantial-looking frame? In fact the Imp Supreme had been introduced in this form at the '52 show – so much for the 'famous rubber controlled' business. A rather nice feature of many Tandons was a longitudinal compartment in the top of the tank, beneath a chrome cover, that held a tyre pump and tools. Another peculiarity was that on some models the tail pipe was blanked off and the exhaust exited through a slot in the underside of the silencer – in order, the manufacturer explained, to stop the two-stroke's necessarily oily exhaust gases getting on the rear tyre.

ENGINE—GEARBOX :	Villiers 197 c.c. Model 8E4. Petroil Lubrication 16-1. Four speed gearbox in unit with engine.
FRAME :	Welded throughout, large diameter Reynolds " 531 " tubing.
SUSPENSION :	Telescopic front forks. Springs controlling impact and rebound. Pivoted fork rear suspension controlled by Armstrong two-rate hydraulic damped spring units.
WHEELS AND TYRES :	Front and rear both Dunlop 3.00 x 19in. Rims: Chromium-plated.
SEAT :	Tandon Duplex, also pillion foot rests.
MUDGUARDS :	Fully valanced front and rear, also large valanced chain guard.
SPEEDOMETER :	Smiths' 80 m.p.h. built in the headlamp.
LIGHTING :	Lucas rectifier set.
HORN :	H.F. electric horn.
EXHAUST SYSTEM :	Low level with barrel type silencer.
FINISH :	Beige stove enamel, bright parts chromium-plated, also black and chromium.
PETROL TANK :	2¼ gallons. Beige finish with Red Flash, also Black finish with Ivory Flash.
DIMENSIONS :	Wheel Base, 49in.; Ground Clearance, 6½in.; Saddle Height, 30in.; Weight, 201 lb.

Here's the Imp Supreme De Luxe with a larger petrol tank, flashier colour options and an 8E4 Villiers. Armstrong front forks were an option on this model. Motor Cycling *tested one so equipped, and very complimentary on its characteristics they were too – with the traditional Tandon good steering unaffected. Main-road cruising was in the order of 45-to-50mph and top speed 56mph. A gallon of petroil was consumed every 124 miles at a steady 30mph and every 97 miles at 50mph.*

197c.c. SCRAMBLER

ENGINE—GEARBOX:	Tuned Villiers 197 c.c. Model 7E Petroil Lubrication. Four speed gearbox in unit with engine. Extra tuning, £5.
FRAME:	Bronze welded throughout; constructed of Reynolds "531" tubing.
SUSPENSION:	Tandon patent pivoted fork front suspension with Armstrong hydraulically damped spring units. Pivoted fork near suspension controlled by Armstrong hydraulically damped spring units. Constructed throughout of Reynolds "531" tubing.
WHEELS AND TYRES:	Dunlop Competition Wheels and Tyres—Front, 3.00 x 19in.; Rear, 3.25 x 19in. Chromium-plated rims. Heavy Duty Competition Hubs with Journal Bearings.
SEAT:	H.M.F. Racing.
MUDGUARDS:	Front, fully sprung, 4in. aluminium. Rear, 5in. aluminium. Three racing number plates situated in usual positions.
EXHAUST SYSTEM:	Tuned open pipe.
FINISH:	Beige frame and forks; usual bright parts chromium- and cadmium-plated.
PETROL TANK:	2 gallons. Chromium plated with Red Flash.
DIMENSIONS:	Wheel Base, 49in.; Ground Clearance, 8½in.; Weight, 212 lb.

Tandon

Leads again

These Records Will Endure

Ist. To introduce 125 c.c. Motor Cycles with Telescopic Front Forks.

Ist. To introduce 125 c.c. machines with Pivoted Fork Rear Suspension.

Ist. To produce Motor Cycles in Polychromatic Stove Enamelled Finish.

Ist. To introduce a Featherweight Modern Duplex Spring Frame.

Ist. To use "KROMO" Tubing on all production machines.

Ist. To offer 197 c.c. Motor Cycles with Telescopic Front Forks and Hydraulically controlled Pivoted Fork Rear Suspension for £90.

Ist. To introduce a Lightweight "Scrambler" Motor Cycle with Hydraulically controlled Pivoted Front Fork and Rear Suspension.

Ist. To incorporate hydraulically controlled bottom link forks.

By Tandon standards the 1955 scrambler looked quite a business-like machine. Although there was never an extensive factory competition programme there was one works rider in the form of John Babb, who enjoyed a certain degree of success after he had altered the weight distribution of his machine by repositioning its engine more to the rear of the frame.

I could be wrong but methinks some of these claims are questionable…It would be interesting to see what answers knowledgeable vintage club members came up with if these were put to them as questions. For all I know, Tandon may have been a pioneer in the use of Accles and Pollock's Kromo tubing on motorcycles but it had most certainly been a favourite of bicycle manufacturers since the 1930s due to its air hardening properties (its strength increases when brazed, unlike other tubes such as Reynolds 531 that weakens and was not imbued with this quality until relatively recently). Another poser is why, if aware of Kromo's properties and proclaiming its use, had the company switched to 531 tubing for the frames of the current range?

225c.c. MONARCH

ENGINE—GEARBOX :	Villiers 225 c.c. Model 1H Petroil Lubrication. Four speed gearbox in unit with engine.
FRAME :	Bronze welded throughout. Constructed from Reynolds " 531 " tubing.
SUSPENSION :	Armstrong hydraulically controlled front forks. Pivoted fork rear suspension controlled by Armstrong two-rate hydraulically damped spring units.
WHEELS AND TYRES :	Front and rear both Dunlop 3.00 x 19in. Rims: Chromium-plated. Fitted with 6in. alloy full width hubs front and rear.
SEAT :	Dual shaped seat, foam rubber cushioned. Pillion foot rests.
MUDGUARDS :	Fully valanced front and rear, also double valanced chain guard.
SPEEDOMETER :	Smiths' 80 m.p.h. built in the headlamp.
LIGHTING :	Rectifier lighting with Lucas battery and electric horn.
EXHAUST PIPE :	Low level with barrel type silencer, all chromium-plated.
FINISH :	Beige stove enamel, bright parts chromium-plated, also black and chromium.
PETROL TANK :	2¼ gallons. Beige finish with Red Flash, also Black finish with Ivory Flash.
DIMENSIONS :	Wheel Base, 49in.; Ground Clearance, 7in.; Weight, 262 lb.

Hedging its bets by using both Villiers and British Anzani to power the twins? The 10bhp Villiers 1H was the more widely used of the two, being employed in Francis-Barnetts, Suns and Ambassadors. Ambassador's 225 Villiers-powered machine was called the Supreme, whilst Tandon also had a Supreme but with a 250 British Anzani.

250c.c. TWIN SUPREME
325c.c. VISCOUNT

ENGINE—GEARBOX :	British Anzani Twin Two-Stroke with Rotary Inlet Valves. Petroil Lubrication. Four speed gearbox in unit with engine.
FRAME :	Bronze welded throughout. Constructed of Reynolds " 531 " tubing.
SUSPENSION :	Armstrong fully hydraulically controlled front forks. Pivoted fork rear suspension controlled by Armstrong two-rate hydraulically damped spring units.
WHEELS AND TYRES :	Front and rear both 3.00 x 19in. Rims: Chromium-plated. Fitted with 6in. alloy full width hubs front and rear.
MUDGUARDS :	Fully valanced front and rear. Also double valanced chain guard.
SPEEDOMETER :	Smiths' 80 m.p.h. built into headlamp.
LIGHTING :	Rectified lighting with Lucas battery and electric horn.
EXHAUST PIPES :	Low level, chromium-plated, with barrel type silencers.
FINISH :	Beige stove enamel, bright parts chromium-plated. Also black and chromium.
PETROL TANK :	2¼ gallons. Beige finish with Red Flash, also Black finish with Ivory Flash.
DIMENSIONS :	Wheel Base, 50in.; Ground Clearance, 7in.; Weight, 262 lb.
SEAT :	Dual shaped seat, foam rubber cushioned.

Although British Anzani twins were not taken up by many manufacturers Greeves did, and its 250 Fleetwings and 325 Fleetmasters were direct competitors of this duo. The Fleetwing couldn't manage to pass the 60mph barrier, so I wonder what the 1955Twin Supreme was capable of, especially as Greeves's Fleetmaster romped away to 73mph whilst Tandon's Viscount could only manage 70mph in Motor Cycling*'s hands. They did, however, stress that this Tandon, named apparently after the record-breaking Viscount airliner, was designed to be a 'powerful touring motor cycle' and that there was a 'total lack of vibration at touring speeds'. "Cornering at all speeds was first class," they went on to say, and overall fuel consumption bettered the 100mpg mark. In slight variance to the brochure they quoted the colour schemes as beige and red or black and ivory.*

TRIUMPH

Triumph's 1947 brochure featured the Victory Parade of 8 June 1946, during which King George VI and Queen Elizabeth (standing on the dais) and assembled VIPs were treated to a cohort of Metropolitan police riding slowly past on Speed Twins.

Having journeyed from his home town of Nuremberg in Germany to Coventry in England, young Siegfried Bettmann, who at the age of 20 already had a good command of English as well as being fluent in several other languages, found that his multilingual status made him much in demand as a translator. Employed initially by Kelly's Directories he soon moved on to the White Sewing Machine Company – firstly in its export office and then in the field as a sales representative in northern Europe.

Drawing on this experience he was encouraged to set up a London-based import/export agency on his own account, its prime interests being the handling of German-made sewing machines and bicycles made in Birmingham by William Andrews, which he marketed as Triumphs. Trading for the first year under the title of S Bettmann & Co, such was the success of the cycle side of his fledgling business that in 1886 he altered it to the more alluring Triumph Cycle Company. In 1887, underwritten in part by the Dunlop Tyre Company, which was anxious to promote its newfangled pneumatic tyres, his expanding business was registered as Triumph Co Ltd and he was joined by another young German named Mauritz Schulte, who also hailed from Nuremberg.

The following year, with some family money behind them and Schulte keen for them to manufacture their own bicycles, a modest ex-textile factory in Much Park Street, Coventry, was acquired – the firm relinquishing its London headquarters and relocating there when production commenced.

In 1896 further premises on nearby Priory Street were found, and the pair also established a subsidiary cycle factory in their home town of Nuremberg. For a good number of years the Triumph Werke Nürnberg's products echoed those of the English factory but subsequent to 1913 the two diverged and TWN, as it was then known, would go on to operate as a separate entity. In 1956 it was merged with office equipment and motorcycle manufacturer Adler, the whole shortly becoming part of Max Grundig's empire, and motorcycle production, which had commenced in 1903, terminated.

Back to England and the mid 1890s: at Triumph's Coventry factory, Mauritz Schulte, with thoughts of trying to obtain a licence to manufacture them, had acquired a Munich-made Hildebrand & Wolfmuller – the world's first production motorcycle. His ambitions in that direction came to nought, as did the partners' later talks with Beeston Humber along the same lines. But the seed was sown and in 1902 they began to make their own.

In common with most early motorcycles Triumph's first was based around a bicycle (the firm's own) and employed a proprietary engine, in this case a 2¼hp Minerva, one of the best on the market at the time. Attached to the front down-tube, the engine had a direct belt drive on the opposite side to the pedalling gear, as was the convention at the time. Over the next couple of years an encouraging number of similar machines found customers, latterly with either JAP or Fafnir engines, but in 1905 Triumph brought out a 3hp machine with a proprietary engine carrying its own name cast on its crankcase mounted within the frame, designed most probably by the works manager Charles Hathaway. It was not an unqualified success, as its twin front down-tube frame was prone to breakage so a fresh one with single down-tube was introduced. Anxious to be in the forefront of progress, various innovations were effected for 1906, such as magneto ignition for the engines and the company's own design of rocking front forks with a pair of horizontal springs – changed to a single spring in 1912.

Encouraged no doubt by rider Frank Hulbert's success at the Dashwood Hill Climb the previous year, there was a strong Triumph presence with the new 3½hp machines in the single-cylinder class of the inaugural Isle of Man motorcycle TT races. Two of them lasted the distance, with Jack Marshall second to Charlie Collier's Matchless and Frank Hulbert third; two retired.

Further expansion occurred in 1907, with the majority of production now taking place at the enlarged Priory Street factory, with the Park Street premises used for cycle and sidecar manufacture as well as servicing.

The following year no less than eight of the 15 singles entries were Triumphs and the redoubtable Collier brothers were back hungry for another Matchless victory. This time it was Jack Marshall who led Charlie Collier at the finish, with all the remaining ten finishers being Triumph-mounted other than a Chater Lea and Brown sixth and ninth. Harry Collier's year was 1909 – his Matchless besting an Indian, with a Triumph third – whilst 1910 was a Matchless double, with Charlie Collier first and Harry second; Triumphs were behind them in third and fourth places. In 1912 Haswell's Triumph got the better of both Collier brothers, who were third and fourth in what was now the Senior event, but all were outrun by Applebee's speedy Scott two-stroke twin.

To celebrate the marque's Isle of Man forays, TT roadsters and TT racers were catalogued alongside the firm's other 3½hps, which included the Free-engine model with a clutch in the rear hub. All were highly regarded and none other than BSA looked to them for inspiration when deciding to join the ranks of motorcycle manufacturers – Triumph's engines in particular being robust and reliable.

For 1913, having experimented with various methods of gearing for a while, the Model C featuring Sturmey Archer's three-speed hub was introduced. Experimentation with a vertical twin side-valve motor of some 600cc based upon the Belgian-made Bercley had also been taking place but various factors conspired against it going into production; nevertheless it proved to be a presage of the future.

Something a little less adventurous that did come

At first glance the 1947 350cc 3T appears to be nothing more than a small-capacity version of Triumph's Speed Twin on account of them sharing the same running gear; but its power unit was very different and had been developed for use in the 3TW at the outset of the war. Supposedly the first batch was crated and awaiting delivery in the Coventry factory on the night of 14 November 1940 when the city, including its cathedral and nearby Triumph works, was devastated by German bombers. Although this spelt the end of the 3TW its engine, another Edward Turner design, was resurrected post-war. Differing from his already-successful 500 twin in many respects (notably rocker boxes incorporated in the cylinder head casting and one-piece connecting rods running on a built-up crankshaft) it would have a limited lifespan. All unplated parts were finished in Black enamel with tank panels, mudguards and wheel rim centres lined in Ivory.

The bike that never was. Or was it? By telling you this machine never went into production I risk sod's law producing a previously-unheard-of cache of the blighters; but I'll stick to my guns and reiterate that it didn't. There was presumably at least one prototype, however, and if this illustration is a depiction of the same then it was fitted with Triumph's newly introduced optional spring-wheel rear suspension. Intended, and listed, finishes were a chromium-plated tank with Silver Sheen panels lined in Blue. Wheel rims were chromium-plated with Silver Sheen centres bordered by Blue lines and the mudguards were also to be finished in Silver Sheen with a black centre strip.

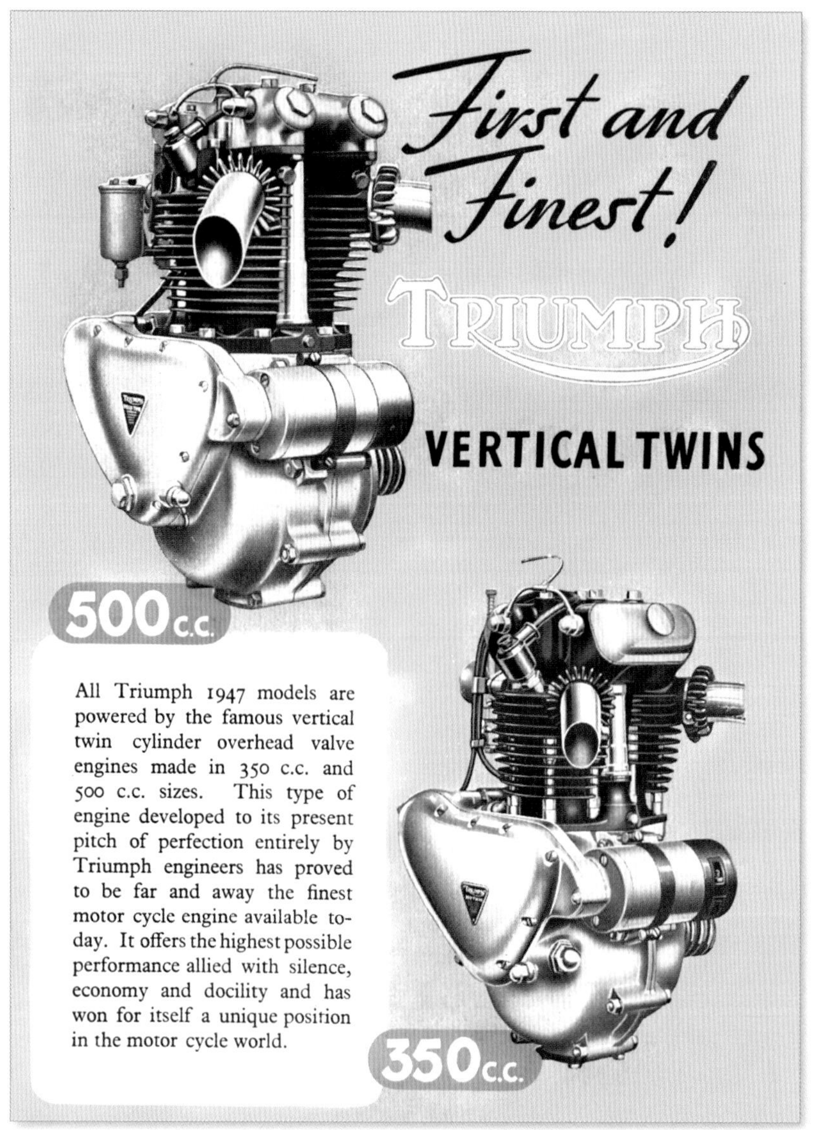

Unlike the 350 the 500 twin was based around a two-piece crankshaft flange bolted to the central flywheel with Hiduminium connecting rods fitted with car-type white metal big ends. However, as can be seen here, the differences between the two types of Triumph twin engines were more than just cylinder head and crankshaft design.

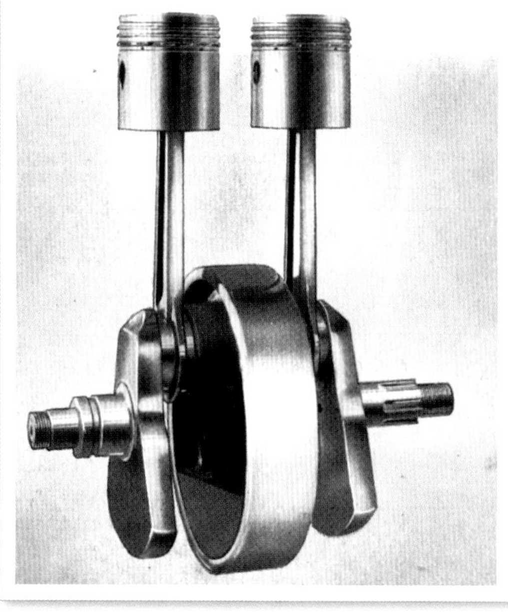

349 cc. O.H.V. vertical twin cylinder. Bore and stroke 55 mm. × 73.4 mm. Valve gear fully enclosed; rocker box integral with cylinder head. Patented crankshaft of rigid construction (see photograph of crankshaft assembly below). Connecting rods of high tensile alloy steel. Dry sump lubrication with positive feed to big ends and valve gear. Oil from rocker box drained without external piping. Automatic advance magneto and accessible separate dynamo, all-gear driven. Amal Carburetter, with Triumph patented quick action twist grip control.

Specification of the 3T and Tiger 85 motor. Flywheel/crankshaft assembly was secured by cotter pins.

to fruition that year was the 225cc single-cylinder two-stroke, two-speed LW Junior – affectionately known as the Baby it was intended to appeal to novices and women riders, as well as the more experienced, and would remain in production right up until the early '20s with its capacity increased to 250cc post-war. A version named the Knirps ('Nipper') was made by TWN in Germany and it also ended up being built under licence and marketed in the USA by Excelsior motorcycles of Chicago.

Come 1914 and Bettmann was to all intents and purposes very well established. Not only was his own company going from strength to strength but he had recently bought into the Standard Motor Co and become its chairman. Within the community he was also president of Coventry's Chamber of Commerce, and the year before had been elected as the city's mayor – the first non-British subject to be so honoured. Storm clouds were gathering, however, and upon the declaration of war such was the anti-German feeling that, in addition to having to register as German-born with the Home Office, he was ousted from his position at Standard and then forced to resign his mayorship.

Had he not fulfilled an urgent request to supply 100 motorcycles at short notice to the BEF for immediate shipment to France in the early days of the war and also defused local antagonism by bringing English directors on to Triumph's board, things might have gone very differently. In the event, and as his company was one of the few in a position to be able manufacture the quantities of machines that could be required by the allied armed forces, the initial order was followed by others in quick succession.

By 1915 the Model H, which drew on the firm's existing 550cc models but had a conventional Sturmey

Archer three-speed gearbox coupled with chain primary and belt final drive, had passed all trials and was pouring out of the Priory Road factory at a rate of several hundred a week. Quickly earning the nickname Trusty due to their faithful and uncomplaining qualities (and also borrowed from the firm's pre-war advertisements), some 30,000 were supplied to branches of the armed forces by the time of the Armistice in November 1918. This number, added to machines supplied before its introduction and amounts of Babies that were used for lighter duties, surely dispelling any stigma attached to the founder of Triumph's country of birth.

The officer who had made that fortuitous phone call in the early days of the war had been Staff Captain (later Colonel) Claude Holbrook of vehicle procurement, and as a result of their dealings he and Bettmann had become friends; so when Schulte (who by that time was general manager) left after a disagreement about future policies in 1919 Holbrook was asked to take his place. Somewhat ironically the cause of the rift between Bettmann and Schulte had been the latter's insistence that car manufacture should replace bicycles, and once Holbrook had taken his place he successfully argued that a similar modus operandi was indeed the way forward.

As a result, in 1921 the premises of the short-lived Dawson Car Company over on Clay Street were bought, along with all fixtures and fittings. Having had no car manufacturing experience whatsoever, Triumph turned to Lea-Francis, whose design department came up with what was launched as the Triumph 10/20 in 1923. Later supplemented by 13 and 15hp models it had the distinction of being the first British car to feature hydraulic brakes; as recompense for its input Lea-Francis was paid a royalty for every one sold.

In 1927, with sights on Austin's Seven, Triumph brought out its own Super 7. But it lacked the Austin's magic and its superior specification was let down by lesser quality – Longbridge's baby attracting more customers in a single year than Triumph's did in its entire seven-year lifespan.

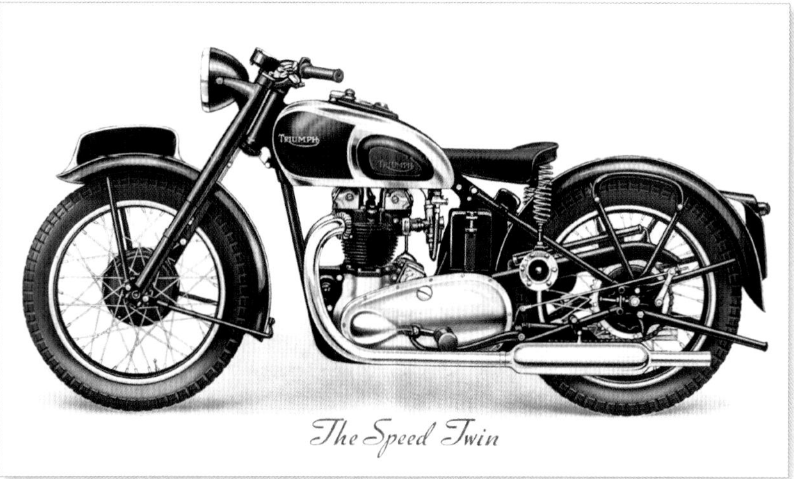

Unveiled in the summer of 1937 and available to the public for the 1938 season the Speed Twin had been an immediate success, and when production resumed after the war in the new Meriden factory Edward Turner was sufficiently comfortable with the rightness of his original design for it to continue very much as it had been conceived. Understandably, girder forks had given way to Triumph's own telescopics whilst another easily visible change was the repositioning of the dynamo to forward of the motor – this necessitating modified bottom end castings and a drive from the exhaust cam gear. To allow the engine to breathe more efficiently there was now a timed rotary valve driven by the inlet cam, and the original external return pipes from the rocker feeds had gone – excess oil now draining downwards via the pushrod tubes. Frame, forks and other cycle parts were in Amaranth (dark red) whilst the chrome-plated tank had Red panels lined in Gold.

The Tiger 100, which had been added to the range for the 1939 season, mirrored its more touring 5T stablemate in all its essentials, including cadmium-plated nuts and bolts throughout, other than its finish and engine tune. The latter was catalogued to be 'specially tuned and assembled with high compression pistons of silicon low expansion alloy', whilst 'the cylinder heads, ports and all moving parts are highly polished'. Finish was as for the stillborn Tiger 85 with Silver Sheen panels lined in blue for the chromium-plated four-gallon tank, Silver Sheen mudguards with Black centre strip and chromium-plated wheel rim centres in Silver Sheen bordered by Blue lines. The machine illustrated here has the standard rear wheel but the T100, in common with all other Triumphs, could now be had with the manufacturer's newly introduced spring wheel – more often referred to as a sprung hub. FNX 963 was so equipped when Motor Cycling *tested it in the summer of 1947, and they were most impressed with its performance, road-holding and braking – assisted, they reasoned, by its optional sprung hub. "Capable of cruising at speeds beyond the safety limit of modern British roads," [nothing changes] it would do 67mph in second, 88 in third and 95 in top; overall fuel consumption worked out at around 70mpg.*

The instrument panel let into a recess on the top of the petrol tank housed an oil pressure gauge, ammeter, lighting switch and lamp.

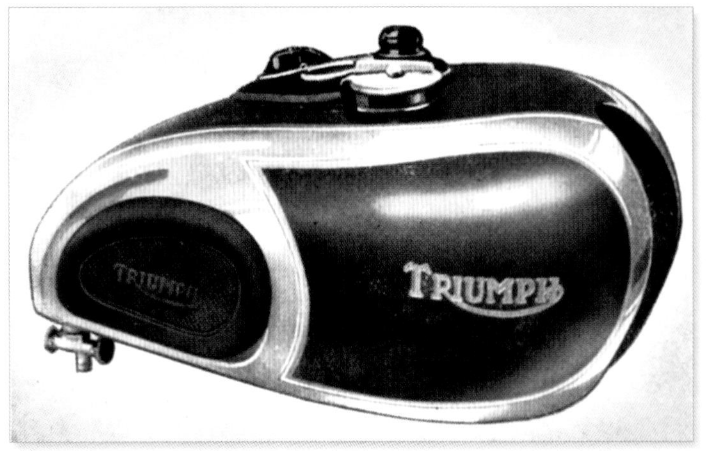

A move upmarket was made in the '30s with a range of four- and six-cylinder Coventry Climax-powered cars having sporting pretensions, but competition guru Donald Healey, who had come close to winning the Monte Carlo Rally with one in 1934, set Triumph on a path that would contribute to its undoing. By that time the firm's technical director, he oversaw Triumph's crib of Alfa Romeo's supercharged twin-cam straight-eight – Healey did the Monte twice in one but due to the company's financial position the plug was pulled and it never went into production. So dire was the state of affairs that Triumph's motorcycles side was sold; but three years later, in the summer of 1939, the Triumph Motor Company as it had been known as since 1930, went into receivership. During the latter part of World War Two it was acquired by the Standard Motor Company, which formed a subsidiary named the Triumph Motor Company (1945) Ltd.

TRIUMPH

Springing - FRONT & REAR

For 1947 the emphasis is on springing—better springing, better roadholding, more comfort. The introduction of the Triumph telescopic fork marked a big step forward in this direction and its many advantages have been acclaimed by thousands of riders. Now we are proud to introduce the Triumph Spring Wheel which provides the answer to the problems of rear wheel springing with a degree of simplicity and efficiency never before approached in this all-important phase of motor cycle design.

TRIUMPH
TELESCOPIC FORKS

Hydraulically damped these forks permit over six inches of wheel movement and provide the highest possible standard of comfort, steering and roadholding. There are no adjustments of any kind to be made by the rider and maintenance is reduced to checking the oil level every 10,000 miles.

TRIUMPH
SPRING WHEEL
PATENT No. 524885

This remarkable springing system is enclosed in a massive aluminium alloy hub shell to which is attached the powerful eight inch diameter rear brake. The Spring Wheel is mounted in the frame in exactly the same way as a normal wheel and adds a mere three per cent. to the total weight of the machine. At the same time it reduces the total unsprung weight to little more than the weight of the rims and tyres. This remarkably low figure explains the exceptional roadholding and control at high speed which is such a feature of the rear-sprung Triumph twin. The pillion passenger enjoys the same degree of comfort as the rider.

Triumph's own slender front forks were a little on the flimsy side, which could lead to slightly wayward handling at speed, but over the ensuing years they would be improved. Edward Turner's 'sprung hub' provided about 2in of travel and was surprisingly effective for its day; however, by the '60s it was seen as an oddity and woe betide any amateur mechanic who pulled one to bits without recourse to the maker's book of words. If I remember correctly its cast-alloy side plate even carried an appropriate warning.

	3T	T85	5T	T100
Bore and stroke mm.	55 × 73.4	55 × 73.4	63 × 80	63 × 80
Cylinder capacity	349	349	498	498
Compression ratio	7 : 1	8 : 1	7 : 1	8 : 1
Engine Sprocket No. of teeth solo	19	19	22	22
Gear ratios:				
Top solo	5.8	5.8	5.0	5.0
Third	6.95	6.95	6.0	6.0
Second	10.0	10.0	8.65	8.65
First	14.7	14.7	12.7	12.7
Top s/c	—	—	5.8	5.8
Third	—	—	6.95	6.95
Second	—	—	10.0	10.0
First	—	—	14.7	14.7
Front chain size	½″ × .305″ all models			
Rear chain size	⅝″ × ⅜″ all models			
Tyres – Dunlop front	19 × 3.25	19 × 3.25	19 × 3.25	19 × 3.25
rear	19 × 3.25	19 × 3.25	19 × 3.50	19 × 3.50
Saddle height	28½″	28½″	29½″	29½″
Wheelbase (static)	53¼″	53¼″	55″	55″
Overall length	82½″	82½″	84″	84″
Overall width	28½″	28½	28½″	28½″
Ground clearance	6″	6″	6″	6″
Weight lbs.	335	335	364	364
Petrol Tanks capacity galls.	3⅛	3⅛	4	4
Oil Tank capacity galls.	¾	¾	¾	1

TRIUMPH

REVISED

RETAIL PRICES

for

Great Britain & Northern Ireland

SEASON 1947

MODEL	RETAIL PRICE	PURCHASE TAX	TOTAL PRICE
TIGER "100" ... 500 c.c. O.H.V.	£152 0 0	£41 0 10	£193 0 10
SPEED TWIN ... 500 c.c. O.H.V.	£142 0 0	£38 6 10	£180 6 10
3T. DE LUXE ... 350 c.c. O.H.V.	£128 0 0	£34 11 3	£162 11 3
SPEEDOMETER . (EXTRA all Models)	£4 0 0	£1 1 8	£5 1 8

The above prices operate on and after 21st April, 1947 & all previous lists are cancelled.

THE COMPANY RESERVES THE RIGHT TO REVISE PRICES WITHOUT PRIOR NOTICE AND PURCHASE TAX ALSO IS SUBJECT TO REVISION.

All retail sales are subject to the guarantee given to Triumph Dealers and the conditions and terms of business published in the Company's catalogue.

TRIUMPH ENGINEERING Co. Ltd. Meriden Works, Allesley, Coventry

Although the mysterious Tiger 85's specifications were listed there was no mention of it in this 1947 price list, as it was never unleashed upon the buying public. Due in part to shortages of raw materials, it had been sacrificed to concentrate on the firm's established Tiger 100.

And on it went to an ignominious demise in 1984, with the trademark presently the property of BMW.

Returning to Triumph, motorcycles and the immediate post-war boom: the Model H continued to be made for the civilian market until 1923 but, although the firm had yet to find someone of the calibre of chief designer Charles Hathaway (he had died during the war) an improved and more expensive version with all-chain drive was put on the market in 1920. Fitted with a three-speed gearbox of the firm's own design, the clutch incorporated a spring drive to reduce snatch for those used to belt-drive and it was named the SD on account of this device. From it sprang the overhead-valve Model R with exotic four-valve head. A modified SD with this type of valve gear and devised by Major Frank Halford, who worked with Harry Ricardo, had showed remarkable form when raced by its originator so Triumph, keen to update its ageing side-valve racers, put a similar machine into production. Enormously disappointed by its TT debut (where the company's own old side-valves proved faster) Triumph returned in 1922 when a rather brave Walter Brandish managed to jockey an R to finish second to the winning Sunbeam – the last victory for a side-valve. Even as a roadster, any attempt to use the R's not-altogether-remarkable performance was fraught due to tricky handling imparted by its SD parentage; nevertheless the Riccy is (on account of its motor) revered by some enthusiasts and remained catalogued as Triumph's most sporting offering until 1927. A rather better sports OHV Triumph, with just two valves but an entirely new frame, had been designed by Vic Horseman back in 1924 and this was put into production in 1927, marketed as the TT until 1929.

Almost without a doubt Triumph's best machine of the mid '20s, as well as being the one that brought the firm back from the financial brink once the post-war boom had subsided, was the utilitarian Model P. Launched at the 1924 show and priced at just a few shillings over £42, it was incredible value for a full-blown quality 500, and although the profit on each must have been infinitesimal, sales of approaching 50,000 in its lifespan of less than three years made it a resounding success. An improved version designated the Model N followed in 1927 and then, the first of the saddle-tank Triumphs, the N De Luxe for 1928. The spiritual successor to the popular Baby also proved a ready seller: current from 1927 to '30 and with a side-valve 277cc motor, it was first known as the Model W and then, with the newly-fashionable saddle tank, as the WS for 1929 and '30. An entirely

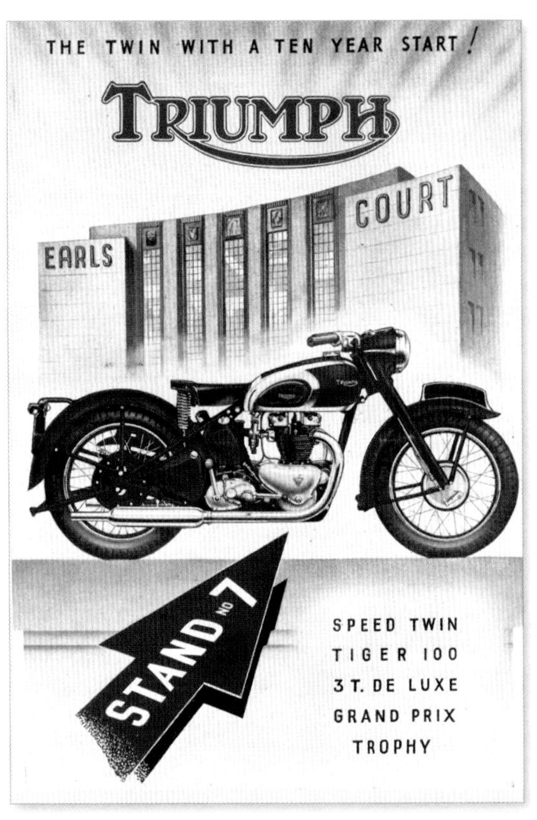

In the lead up to the inaugural post-war Motor Cycle Show of 1948, with the other major British manufacturers about to unveil 500 twins, Triumph put out a reminder that the company had pre-empted the lot of them by treading the same path over ten years before; and to rub it in put no less than 19 vertical twins on the stand. New for Triumph, however, would be the competition Trophy that had been developed from the successful ISDT machines. It had a shorter frame than other 500s in the range, the main part of which was shared with the military TWR side-valve, and Allan Jeffries's actual Six Days machine would be on the stand. Also mentioned in this flyer was the GP racing model – both it and the Trophy having aluminium head and barrels originally designed for the company's World War Two aircraft generator sets.

new range of side-valve and OHV machines was introduced at the end of 1928: the C models all featured recirculating engine lubrication and generous 7in brakes front and rear. The larger side-valve 550cc CSD lasted until 1932 and the larger OHV, the 497cc CTT, was current from 1930 to '31 – the depression by that time slowing sales dramatically.

By that time Triumph had responded to the international situation by reverting to two-stroke power, courtesy of Messrs Villiers, for some basic economy transport with the 174cc Model X of 1930 – supplemented by the even-more-frugal 148cc Model Z for 1932 to take advantage of the government's newly introduced lower tax rate for sub-150s. If you fancied something even smaller you could have bought a 98cc Gloria in 1932 and '33 – made by Triumph but marketed under the same name as the firm's Gloria sidecars, it was joined by a 147cc version for 1933 only.

Slopers were all the rage at this time so, in spite of adverse trading conditions, Triumph had responded to this latest fad with a range to suit various pockets, designed by Arthur Sykes. Starting with an OHV 250, the firm's first machine of this capacity, there were 350s with side- and overhead-valves and a 500 OHV – or if you were able to afford it, one of the top-of-the-range 500 or 550cc Silent Scouts.

Next were the X lightweights of 1933 and '34 – initially launched with a jewel-like 147cc OHV motor it was supplemented by a larger-bore 174cc edition for 1934 along with a cut-price £25 10s version with twin-port Villiers engine. These little four-strokes were unusual in that their inclined engines had horizontal finning and the Villiers-powered XV/1 would be Triumph's last two-stroke motorcycle.

A year or so earlier Ariel's chief designer Val Page had left the troubled company in the run up to its change of ownership and come to Triumph to take over the design department. Page had been the architect of Ariel's major revamp in the mid '20s along with the excellent singles that would see the firm through the next 30 years, and so was more than qualified – the results of his work being evident in the new range of Triumphs introduced in the late summer of 1933 for the 1934 season.

Heading the list and of great interest, but unappetisingly titled the 6/1, was a hefty 649cc OHV vertical twin primarily intended for sidecar work – to Page therefore the honour of designing the first of that configuration that Triumph would put into production, and would in a short while become inseparable from. The remainder, also unexcitingly identified numerically, were singles prefixed 2/1 and 2/5 for 249cc; 3/1, 3/2 and 3/5 for 343cc; 5/1 for 549cc; and 5/2, 5/3, 5/4 and 4/5 for 493cc – all being OHV except the 3/1 and 5/1. All were conventional and well-engineered, with the OHV models boasting fashionable twin-port heads, but to add to their dreary nomenclature they featured somewhat ungainly duplex frames and had a somehow dowdy overall appearance.

The following season there was little change other than a couple of additions to the catalogue – a cheaper 250 and the 5/10 that was excitingly listed as a racer! The factory had entered three of these in the 1934 Senior TT but all failed to finish. For 1936 the range was trimmed back and there were improvements throughout, such as a lighter frame and enclosed valve gear for the smaller OHV models.

The old regime was about to end, however. By this time Claude Holbrook had taken over as chairman from Siegfried Bettmann and Triumph was in dire straits financially, with the motorcar arm of the business being the main culprit. It was no secret that he had little interest in the wellbeing of its motorcycles (or for that matter bicycles) so both were sold off in an ill-starred attempt to save Triumph cars. Bicycles went to Raleigh whilst the canny Jack Sangster bought the motorcycle operation early in 1936 for some £50,000 – its trading name henceforth becoming the Triumph Engineering Co Ltd.

Val Page had moved on to BSA and in his place Sangster appointed 35-year-old Edward Turner, whom he also made General Manager, with added incentives such as a small percentage of any forthcoming profits and shares in the company.

Setting to work immediately, and ably abetted by Bert Hopwood, three interim new models that would set the timbre for Triumph's future were rushed through in time for the spring. With high-level exhausts, along with a good deal of polished alloy and chrome set off by silver tank panels lined in blue, they were in fact nothing more than customised versions of the existing valve-in-head 250, 350 and 500s, but marketing them as Tiger 70s, 80s and 90s was a masterstroke that stated power and speed.

By the time that the 1937 brochure was printed in October '36 there had been time to do the job properly, and the Tigers sported brand-new single-down-tube frames and forks with revised versions of Page's engines allied to a new positive-stop four-speed gearbox. These features also applied to the De Luxe models that complemented each Tiger as well as the 3S (343cc) and brand-new 6S (597cc) side-valve model – the 6/1 vertical twin having been quietly dropped. If any enthusiasts wondered why, despite it having brought Triumph the Maudes Trophy in 1933, a peek behind the scenes at the factory would have likely told them one of the reasons: work was afoot to launch an entirely new model, and for the meanwhile the current range adequately filled the average motorcyclist's requirements. As if to prove it a trio of Tigers, one of each capacity, successfully bid for the Maudes Trophy in March.

Launched in the autumn of 1937, Edward Turner could have little imagined what the consequences would be when he brought his Speed Twin into the world, its coming simply heralded by the company's 1938 brochure thus: "Founded on well tried Triumph practice this machine incorporates an entirely new 498cc OHV vertical twin-cylinder power unit which marks a milestone in motorcycle progress and combines a startling performance with extreme docility and silence." A milestone indeed, as Turner's twin would win universal acceptance for this configuration and, as soon as they were able, it would adopted by rival makers – but that would be ten years down the road.

Deservedly taking its place at the head of Triumph's otherwise unchanged range it was priced at £75 to the Tiger 90's £70 and was turned out in what would become the model's traditional Amaranth Red with a plentiful amount of chrome.

Sangster's wisdom in appointing Turner and

To justify its price ticket of £270 against £154 for one of the new Trophies, or £152 for a Tiger 100, Triumph's over-the-counter racer, the GP, in addition to an aluminium top end, had a specially built and tuned engine featuring roller-bearing crank and twin Amal carbs. There was also a special oversize 8in front brake, large-capacity oil tank, aluminium wheel rims and mudguards, rev counter and other fitments that would allow the owner to head straight for the racetrack. Although what could be termed as the prototype had won the 1946 Manx Grand Prix in the hands of Ernie Lyons, the machines that went on sale in 1948 failed to be consistent front-runners in major international competition, even though there were successes such as Ken Mudford's victory in the 1950 New Zealand TT and Ron Coates's win at Daytona in the 100-mile amateur race the same year. On the Isle of Man, however, fifth and sixth in 1949 proved to be a high point, with Syd Jensen's fifth giving him 11th place in the 500 World Championship; but this small success garnered the GP's only points of the season. In less prestigious events, especially on slower twisty tracks where their impressive low-down acceleration counted, they gave many an up-and-coming racer his first taste of success, however, and something over 200 of them were sold.

The 1949 brochure's cover, with a Speed Twin-mounted rider in an idyllic Alpine vista, would remain a pleasant dream for most; but despite currency restrictions, petrol rationing and other impedimenta a surprising amount of intrepid British motorcyclists did make it over to Continental Europe. Once there and away from areas devastated by the recent war there was much to gladden the tourist's heart, and those on Triumph's twin found it coped pretty well with the appalling fuel that was 'on tap' in some countries too.

Turner's many talents, not least of which was his innate flair for styling, had in two short years brought the marque to the fore by catching the public's attention, firstly with the Tigers and now the Speed Twin. Sales were on the up, so to capitalise and hold interest, what better way than a super sports version of the vertical twin? Rather more than simply a customised Speed Twin its frame was endowed with a greater steering head angle, the front forks had marginally longer lower links and it had a finned front brake drum. The engine had a higher compression, with polished internals and even an optional bronze cylinder head if you splashed out an extra £5; plus each one was put on a dynamometer and your new machine came with a test card signed by the chief tester. Large-capacity petrol and oil tanks gave a business-like appearance as well as being practical; and specially-designed silencers could be transformed into megaphones by removing the tail section complete with baffles. Favourable conditions could find a crouched rider able to justify his mount's title with the needle of its 120mph speedo ('supplied as standard unless otherwise ordered. £2 15s extra') hovering around the 100 mark.

One of the stars of the 1938 show, this Tiger 100 was an alternative to the Speed Twin rather than intended to overshadow it, and as well as becoming Triumph's priciest model at £80 (£95 5s if a customer went for competition specification, bronze head and 120mph speedo with 5in dial) it replaced the 500 single-cylinder 90. The factory avowed in the brochure that it had 'long held the view that for sports use the OHV single of over 350cc is an obsolete type' – a statement that some might have good reason to question both then and in the future!

Due to concerns of structural integrity the barrel/crankcase union had been uprated from six to eight studs for the latest vertical twins, and to fall in line with the 100 all Tigers now had silver sheen mudguards with black stripe. The rest of the range remained as it had been other than the addition of a 497cc side-valve, the 5S.

Concerns notwithstanding, a few weeks before one of the earlier Speed Twins, specially prepared and kitted out with an Arnott supercharger, had lapped Brooklands at a fraction over 118mph – a class record that Triumph added to those already held for 350 and 750cc, and one that was to stand in perpetuity.

In order to promote the touring and sporting qualities of the Speed Twins and Tiger 100s Triumph decided to have another shot at the Maudes Trophy, and in February 1939 a pair of them, selected at random from dealers' showrooms, completed getting on for 2,000 road miles, followed by six hours circulating the Brooklands track. With other manufacturers yet to run it was months before the results were known, and by that time the victory had little significance as Britain was once more at war. All summer, Europe had been teetering on the brink,

Tubular side handles for lifting the machine onto its rear stand would continue to be fitted to the 3T alone, despite it also having the same rear number plate, with handhold incorporated, as fitted to Speed Twins and Tiger 100s. Finish was as before with painted parts in Black and mudguards and wheel centres lined in Ivory.

New for 1949 was the stylish headlamp nacelle that would remain a hallmark of Triumphs for over a decade; and as it housed the instruments and switches the tank-top dashboard that had been a feature of Triumphs since the 1930s had been done away with. As a tank-top luggage rack had become available as an optional extra, all tanks were manufactured with four blind tapped holes to allow its fitment – these being plugged with small rubber grommets on machines such as this in standard trim.

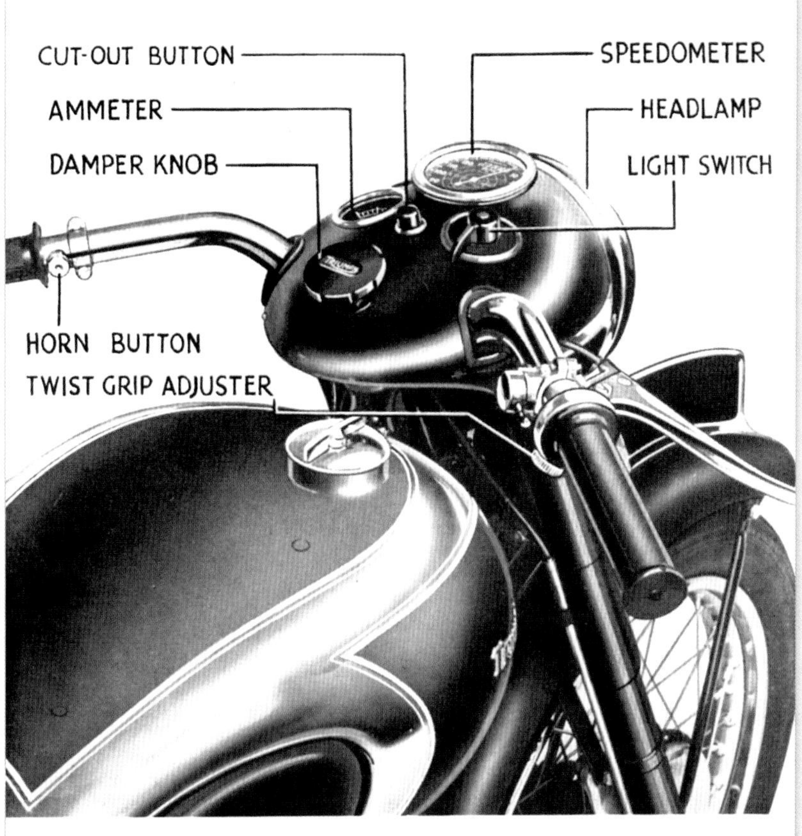

but early in July a personal tragedy overtook Edward Turner when his wife was killed in a car accident. Accustomed to spending time in the USA, it was there that he journeyed on compassionate leave. Whilst in California he met with a lawyer named Bill Johnson, who the following year, with Turner's blessing, established his West Coast distributorship.

Back in England, although a limited amount of machines – including 1940 models – went for export, Triumph was once again called upon to supply motorcycles for the services. The peacetime 3S was militarised into the 3SW, the 5S into the 5SW and overhead-valve 3H into the 3HW, as a Turner-designed lightweight 350 OHV vertical twin especially for military use was still under development. Certainly it was up and running, with several under evaluation, when the centre of Coventry was pulverised and the Triumph factory destroyed in a bombing raid on the night of 14 November 1940. But I am not so sure that production had begun and that the first batch were crated and awaiting collection when the Luftwaffe's explosive and incendiary bombs rained down upon the Dale Street factory.

Whatever the case, it was the end of the HW. But with typical wartime resourcefulness, what serviceable plant and equipment remained was salvaged, along with any repairable motorcycles and a limited output of just the single-cylinder 350cc military machines recommenced as soon as was feasible in temporary premises at The Cape, Warwick. Meanwhile, although Sangster favoured rebuilding in Coventry, Turner had overridden him due to the possibility of further air raids; so land on the outskirts of the village of nearby Meriden had been acquired and a large new factory was going up on the site – production being in full swing by the summer of 1942. This enabled large-scale production of Triumph's military 350s to recommence, and production to begin of aircraft

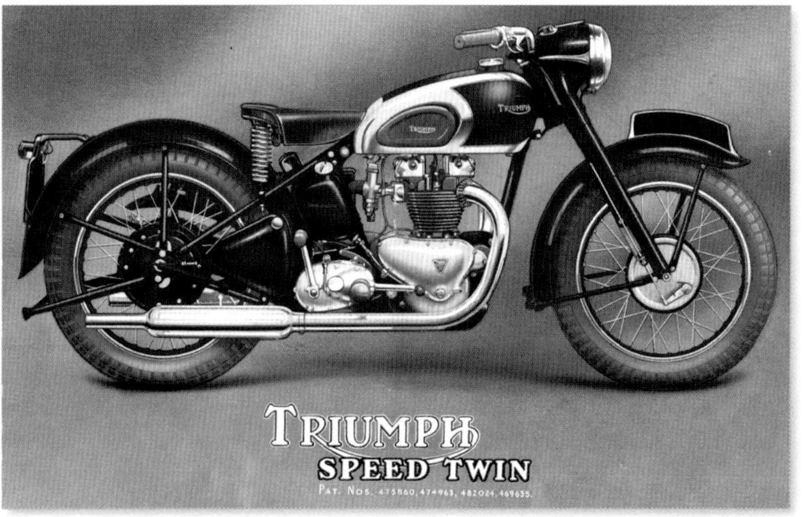

You'll have trouble spotting it in this illustration but as there was no longer an oil pressure gauge, with its attendant feed pipe leading from the oil pressure relief valve at the front of the timing case, an external oil pressure indicator button was fitted to a modified version of the valve in its place. Another innovation for 1949 models was the fitting of an air cleaner as standard for road-going models.

Some features highlighted in the 1949 brochure.

generator sets, which Turner had designed utilising a lightweight version of his vertical twins; spare capacity was employed in the manufacture of large quantities of aircraft parts and components for other military vehicles.

Around this time an on-going disagreement concerning patents and royalties between Sangster and Turner erupted and the latter was given his marching orders – whereupon an almost immediate overture from BSA's James Leek resulted in him being given the post of technical director. There, amongst other tasks, he began work on the design of a 500cc side-valve vertical twin specifically for the military, whilst back at Meriden, Bert Hopwood, who was now in charge of design, had been instructed to come up with a similar machine that could be a direct competitor to BSA's for government contracts. In the event, Hopwood's machine was up and running before Turner's, as he was able to utilise existing twin components; but it was summarily scrapped and the BSA failed to meet the War Department's criteria. The Triumph, however, with revisions by Turner and post-war running gear, would go into production as the TRW in 1948 after being given NATO approval, and be supplied to armed forces at home and abroad.

His and Sangster's differences settled, or conveniently swept under the carpet, Edward Turner rejoined Triumph in autumn 1943 and by the following year, with the war now going the way of the Allies, he was once more managing director.

Initial plans for the recommencement of civilian production included a 350 single but Turner chose

MODEL	3T	5T	T100
Engine : Type	O.H.V.	O.H.V.	O.H.V.
No. of cylinders	2	2	2
Bore and stroke, mm.	55 × 73·4	63 × 80	63 × 80
Cylinder capacity	349	498	498
Compression ratio	6·3 : 1	7 : 1	7·8 : 1
Engine sprocket, number of teeth solo	19	22	22
R.P.M. at 10 m.p.h. in top gear	750	646	646
Gear ratios :			
Top, solo	5·8	5·0	5·0
Third ,,	6·95	6·0	6·0
Second ,,	10·0	8·65	8·65
First ,,	14·7	12·7	12·7
Top, sidecar	—	5·8	5·8
Third ,,	—	6·95	6·95
Second ,,	—	10·0	10·0
First ,,	—	14·7	14·7
Carburetter main jet	120	140	150*
,, slide	5/4	6/3½	6/3½
,, needle jet	107	107	107
Ignition fully advanced	†11/32″	3/8″	3/8″
Front chain size	½″ × ·305″ all models		
Rear chain size	⅝″ × ⅜″ all models		
Tyres—Dunlop, front, ins.	3·25—19	3·25—19	3·25—19
rear, ins.	3·25—19	3·50—19	3·50—19
Saddle Height	28½″	29½″	29½″
Wheelbase (static)	53¼″	55″	55″
Overall length	82½″	84″	84″
Overall width	28½″	28½″	28½″
Ground clearance	6″	6″	6″
Weight, lbs. (dry)	325	365	365
Petrol tank capacity, galls.	3	4	4
Oil tank capacity, galls.	¾	¾	¾

† 9/32″ with low octane fuel * 160 without air cleaner

to concentrate on twins alone so, apart from the repurchase and sale of scores of ex-WD machines that were reconditioned and taken out of their military drab, Meriden's workforce would be turned over to them once civilian production got under way in earnest in 1946.

With Turner's twins-only policy Triumph stood out from other manufacturers, which for the most part were struggling to update and re-release pre-war models; there was also no question of anything other than telescopic front forks post-war, even though Turner's first design was flawed and had to be modified by his chief development engineer Freddie Clarke. After looking closely at Dowty's sprung aircraft wheels Turner had also designed his sprung hub and intended to introduce it on the firm's 1940 models, but it had been put on hold and at first offered as an option in 1946.

That year, in spite of Edward Turner's well-known aversion to racing (but conveniently whilst he was on one of his sojourns in the United States) a sprung-hub T100 fitted with one of his wartime lightweight generator engines was entered for the Manx Grand Prix. Ridden by Irishman Ernie Lyons it was not an official works entry (despite being prepared at Meriden by Freddie Clarke and others) but in the pouring rain he surprised not a few people by finishing over two minutes ahead of second-placed Ken Bills on a Manx Norton. When Turner heard, he was apparently not amused but relented and put on a celebration dinner.

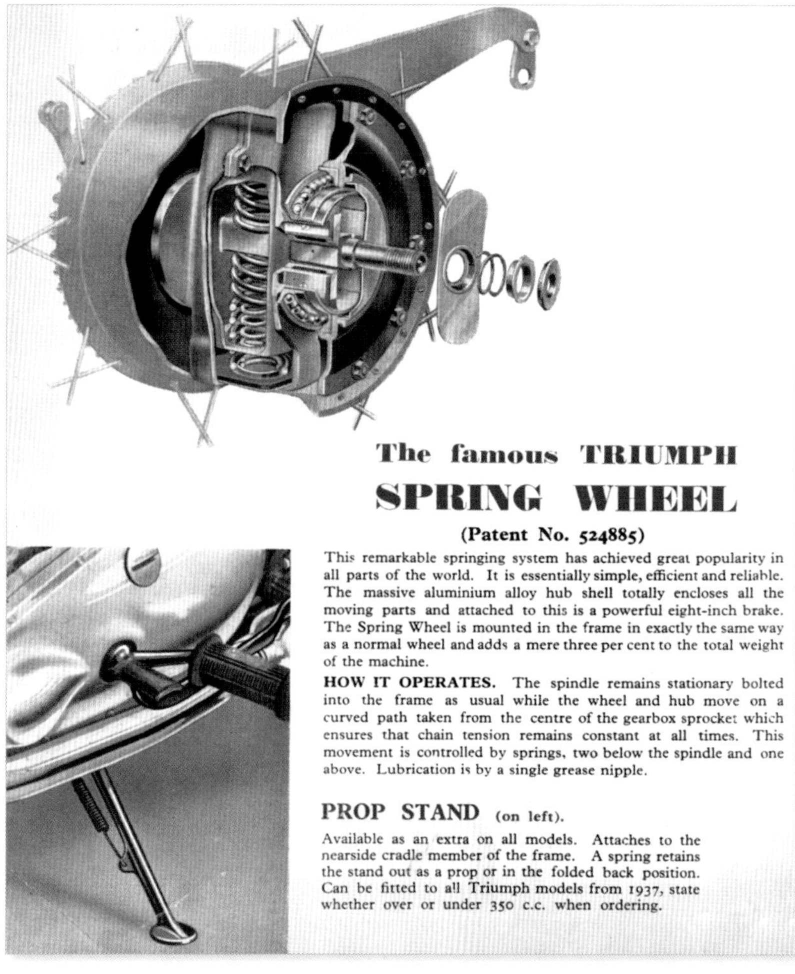

Even though the Tiger 100 in the 1949 brochure was equipped with a sprung hub, if you wanted one it would cost you an extra £15. One of the five 100s on the firm's stand was rigged up to show the advantages of this device – a revolving eccentric drum beneath the rear wheel replicating road surface undulations that the hub would easily cope with.

Preferred mode of dress for the sporting rider – 1949 season! Dispatch rider boots over long woollen socks (turned over) with leather gauntlets to warm and protect the hands – all, likely, ex-WD. Long double-breasted and belted leather coat, the proper motorcycling variety normally having a single vent and small internal leather straps for the rider to fasten it around his thighs. The ensemble completed with scarf and cap of choice with a pair of RAF MkVIII or similar goggles. From this angle you can see the slots at the base of the headlamp nacelle, behind which the horn was mounted rather than on the nearside rear frame stay as it had often been of yore.

He then, although still anti-racing, sanctioned replicas of the winning machine to be made for sale as the GP in 1948 and introduced at that year's Motor Cycle Show, along with the competition Trophy, which also used the generator-type aluminium head and barrels. A trio of prototypes had won the manufacturers' trophy in the 1948 ISDT, so to name the model had been easy; but further team awards in '49, '50 and '51 demonstrated that their success had been no mere one-off.

That same show, the first since the war, was notable in that Britain's other major motorcycle manufacturers had all followed Triumph's lead and each had a vertical twin on display. BSA had been the first with the A7 in 1946, but amongst this year's newcomers was Norton's 500cc Model 7 – designed by Bert Hopwood who was now with BSA but had worked for the Bracebridge Street concern for a short while after leaving Triumph in 1947.

In time each marque's twin would gain its own adherents and each would introduce twins of greater capacity, some better than others, but for many the very word went hand in hand with Triumph, which had started the ball rolling and for many years would manufacture no other type of motorcycle.

One that it didn't was the 3TU. Shortly before the war Jack Sangster had acquired the remnants of the bankrupt New Imperial motorcycle company and, with the intention of re-launching the brand, had Edward Turner design a 200cc OHV single with three-speed gearbox. Although it was never to see the light of day elements of this machine, including its disc wheels and voluminous mudguards, were reused several years later in the prototypical Triumph 3TU economy twin – inherent sense dictating that was as far as it went.

New for 1950 was the 650cc Thunderbird, named after a mythical American Indian bird and aimed directly at the US, where Johnson Motors's now-well-established Pasadena-based distributorship was shifting a good proportion of Triumph's output through its network of dealerships but had nevertheless been crying out for more cubic inches. Hungry for an even larger share of the American market, Triumph next set up a distributorship of its own, leaving JoMo with the 19 states west of Texas. Based in Baltimore and headed by British-born Denis McCormack, TriCor, as it was named, proved a roaring success, with Triumph sales to the US up over 150 per cent in the first year.

Having sold Ariel during the latter stages of the war to BSA, Jack Sangster next managed to put together a deal for Triumph; and in 1951, the same year that the firm's long-retired founder Siegfried Bettmann died, it was consummated. For around £2,500,000 the buyer got Triumph, but not TriCor, whilst Sangster received a seat on BSA's board and Turner perhaps some £250,000 for patent rights and other considerations, as well as remaining at Meriden's helm. Furthermore, in five years' time Sangster would ascend to be the Chairman of BSA and upon so doing would appoint Turner as managing director of the entire group's motorcycle and car divisions.

With Triumph now part of what was indubitably the world's largest motorcycle manufacturing group there were little, if any, signs of the union, and the two major names continued for all the world as if they were still rivals, which paradoxically they still were – even to the extent of their foreign distributors: BSA having Rich Child (BSA Inc from 1954) for eastern states and Hap Alzina in the west, whilst Triumph had TriCor and JoMo. The ensuing years saw Triumph's Thunderbird and BSA's equivalent the Golden Flash (both having been introduced at the same time) spawn more powerful variants; but the Triumph's combination of good looks and slick marketing imbued Meriden's 650s with greater charisma and often the transatlantic sales edge – irrespective of certain other factors. Why, for instance, when BSA had come out with the excellent duplex swinging-arm frame in 1952 did Triumph wait

By opening up the outside of the 1950 brochure one has an artist's rendition of what I take to be yacht racing on the Solent with the Isle of Wight and Needles in the background. One of the new Thunderbirds is making its way past the sailing club and across the rear cover but it is the spectating couple's Speed Twin that takes pride of place on the front.

two years before it too began to switch to the same method of rear suspension, and then combine it with a much inferior frame? To have looked in-house for the solution and used BSA's would have compromised the firm's individual persona; but to spend the next dozen-or-so years moving from one structurally questionable design to the next, rather than sitting down and designing a fresh one using known parameters, seems to defy all logic – except that of Triumph's brimming order books. Late though they may have been to convert to pivoted-fork rear suspension and whatever their failings, the 1954 Tiger 100 and fast new Tiger 110 were exceptionally good-looking motorcycles and the public loved them.

So were the inter-company politics, combined with Edward Turner's well-known authoritarianism that kept the marques very distinct from each other, so very wrong?

These conditions also dictated that when Triumph introduced lightweights into the range (the 150cc Terrier at the end of 1952 and the 200cc Cub a year later) they bore no resemblance to BSA's Bantams – or for that matter to the C series 250s – so ancillaries from outside suppliers aside, the products of Small Heath and Meriden Triumphs had nothing in common.

By the mid '50s the entire range had converted to swinging-arm frames – the Speed Twin, Trophy and Thunderbird in'55 and finally the Cub (Terriers had been dropped) in '57. A large proportion of the TR5 Trophies were now going to Johnson Motors due to the popularity of desert racing, and in response to the call for more grunt the 650cc TR6 with the latest aluminium-headed T110 motor was introduced in 1956.

Performance and far more of it was what airline pilot Stormy Mangham and ace tuner Jack Wilson had in mind when, that same year, they built a very special machine at Fort Worth, Texas – their simple wish that it could be the fastest thing on two wheels. Named the Devil's Arrow, powered by either a methanol-burning Triumph 500 or 650, and to be ridden by flat track racer Johnny Allen, they took it to Utah and the Bonneville Salt Flats where, now known as the Texas Ceegar on account of its streamlined fibreglass shell, it did just that. On 31 August 31 with a Tiger 100 motor AMA officials recorded it though the traps at a whisker over 198mph. And then on 6 September and using the 650 it was timed at 214.4mph – an absolute world record. Or it would have been if the FIM, whose observers were present, had not denied it on a technicality.

The magic had worked, however, and even Edward Turner (who apparently knew nothing of what had been going on, even though members of his staff had given technical assistance) admitted that Triumph gained far more publicity as a result of the AMA record refuted by the FIM than if it had been ratified.

Just over two years later, amidst the short-lived fashion for rear enclosure and fuller mud-guarding, the Triumph Bonneville came into being at the behest of the US distributors and as a last-minute addition to the 1959 range. Despite its evocative title the T120 was not far removed from the current T110 with optional twin carbs; so although it was mercifully spared the indignities of a rear skirt (the T110 was to get one the following year) a dual-carb-equipped TR6 Trophy cut more of a dash. With sales failing to take off on either side of the Atlantic its maker effected something of a makeover later on in the season by offering an alternative to its none-too-macho pastel colour scheme, which was correctly seen as a part of the problem – for the UK only at first, as the backlog

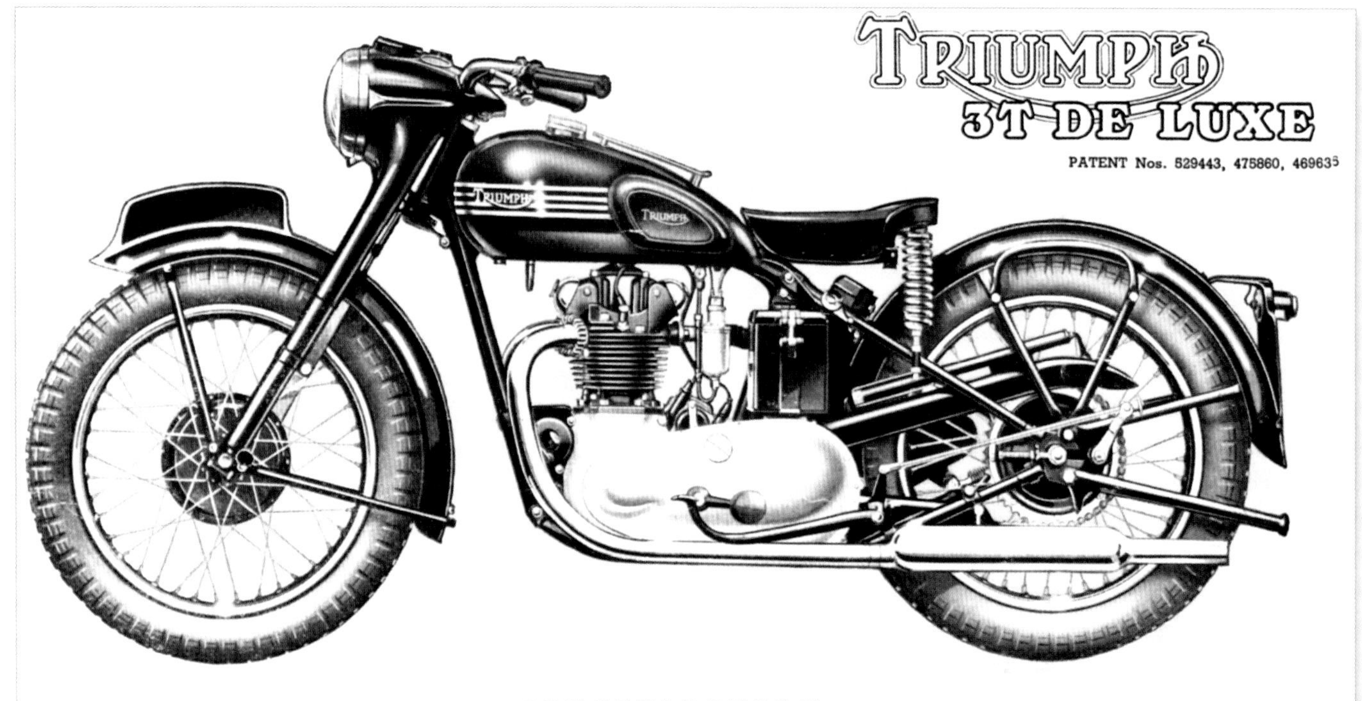

In common with other models in the 1950 range a 60-watt dynamo was now fitted to the 3T in place of a 40-watt unit and correspondingly the Lucas MCR1 voltage control regulator was superseded by an MCR2 – now mounted on its side beneath the seat rather than upright. Also beneath the seat – and clipped to the nearside rear frame tube on all models with headlamp nacelle since its introduction – was the magneto advance and retard lever.

of unsold machines in US showrooms could have otherwise worsened.

New for 1960 was a duplex frame for Triumph's 650s, with the Bonneville version now much more as it had been envisaged with abbreviated mudguards, twin 'clocks' and a separate headlamp conspiring to give it a leaner, lither look.

By now Triumph's smaller twins were all unit-construction – a development begun with the reintroduction of a 350 (the Twenty One) in 1957, continued with the Speed Twin for 1959, and now the T100. Of no relevance in this book but it should be mentioned that 1959 had seen the debut of a Triumph scooter, the Turner-designed Tigress with 250cc twin-cylinder four-stroke motor. Made until 1965 it was supplemented by the 100cc two-stroke Tina in 1962, which remained current until 1970.

To many, the last of the pre-unit Bonnies in 1962 were the best of all – weight pared a fraction, and with a new crank assembly (for the other 650s as well) that was further altered during the season, improving torque and reducing the vibration that had been a bugbear of the model since its inception.

Others, however, would have it that the unit-construction Bonnies, along with their 650 siblings, were the best of the bunch on account, if for no other reason, of their brand-new and vastly improved frame. Triumph had at last grasped the nettle, coincidentally the year that Edward Turner stepped down as CEO of the BSA group, and tackled the big twin's frame issues, if not those of the smaller.

Whichever the preference, the Bonneville was – and still remains for most – the 'it' bike of the '60s. Archetypical Triumph good looks, invigoratingly fast point-to-point and king of the coffee bar racers; but how did it do on the track when pitted against its contemporaries? Given that Edward Turner eschewed the manufacture of purpose-built factory racers (the production-based GP along with race accessories for the likes of the Tiger 100 being exceptions), not too badly at all.

Starting with the Tiger 100, Alan Jefferies had been runner-up in the inaugural Senior Clubmans TT in 1947 and then again two years later. Ace Triumph pilot Ivan Wicksteed would have won the 1950 event had his petrol tank not split on the last lap, but Brian Hargreaves did the following year; and in '55 a pair came second and third. Later on, in 1962, Don Burnett won the Daytona 200 miles race in Florida on a modified T100; and then wins in '66 and '67, with Doug Hele-developed machines, resulted in Daytona-titled T100s being added to the range.

Just a few months before the Bonneville's introduction, Thruxton's first 500-mile production race had been won by a T110 in the hands of Dan Shorey and a youthful Mike Hailwood. But although new Bonnevilles were second to a BMW R69 in 1959, and then second, third and fourth to an AJS CSR in 1960, it was not until the following year that Triumph had a winner.

The following three years proved to be a benefit for a Syd Lawton-prepared Norton 650SS coupled with some rather good riders, and when a T120 tasted victory once more the event had moved temporarily to Castle Combe in Wiltshire – Dave Degens being one of its riders who trounced the second-place A65 BSA. A little prematurely, or perhaps with a degree a clairvoyance, Triumph had added a Thruxton Bonneville to the range for the '65 season; but anyhow Degens and Rex Butcher beat all-comers at the following year's 500, now held at Brands Hatch, with another T120 second. Bonnevilles were first and second again in '67, the same year as John Hartle won the Production TT with one – perhaps the model's most well-known victory.

After one of the latest Tiger 100s had won in '68 the Bonneville scored its fifth and last 500 Mile win in 1969 with a one-two-three – after which Norton Commandos had it pretty much all their own way until 1974, with the exception of 1971 when a Triumph Trident beat one of BSA's triples.

These successes, however, represented an infinitesimal, if very British, part of the marque's competition achievements around the globe – from the little T20 Cub's prowess in trials to the Trophy's in events such as California's Big Bear Run. For years the Meriden marque combined good looks with enough performance, or more, to envelope a large swathe of the market: the 200cc Cub or Trials Cub for learner or National Trials winner; the 350cc Twenty One or Tiger 90, a gentle tourer or boy racer; the 500cc Speed Twin or Tiger 100 for everyday or clubman; and the 650s for fast touring, desert racing or being an ultimate road burner. Heroes and anti-heroes such as Marlon Brando, James Dean, Steve McQueen, Bob Dylan and Clint Eastwood, all of whom owned Triumphs or were portrayed as such on film, also added immeasurably to their allure and did sales no harm.

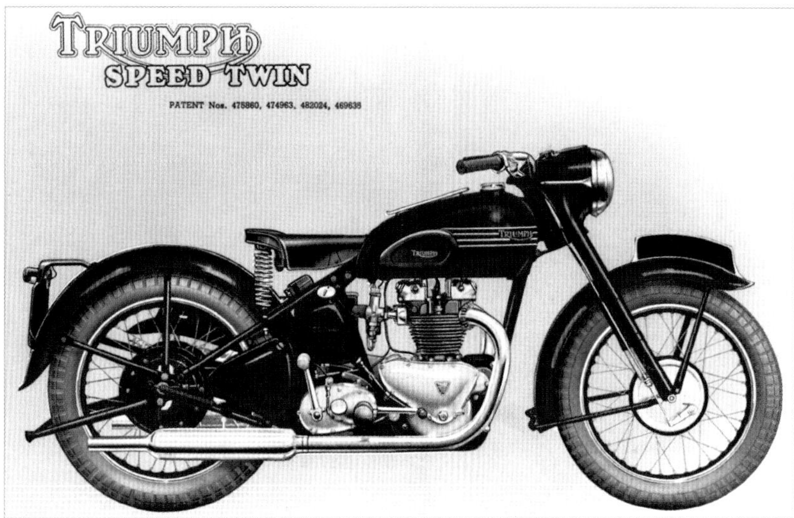

500 c.c. OHV "SPEED TWIN"

"The Speed Twin—forerunner of every other vertical twin in production to-day."
—The Motor Cycle, 29/9/49.

ENGINE: Vertical twin cylinder with two gear driven camshafts. Bore 63 mm. Stroke 80 mm. Capacity 498 c.c. Overhead valves. Totally enclosed and positively lubricated valve gear. High tensile aluminium alloy crankcase of great rigidity. "H" section connecting rods in RR56 hiduminium alloy with patented plain big-ends. Patented crankshaft mounted on massive ball and roller bearings with central flywheel. Full dry-sump lubrication, plunger type pumps with positive feeds to big-ends and valve gear. Pressure indicator on timing cover. Auto-advance magneto and separate dynamo, all gear-driven. Amal carburetter, Triumph quick-action twist grip.

TRANSMISSION: Primary chain in polished cast aluminium oil-bath case. Rear chain positively lubricated and protected on both runs.

FOUR-SPEED GEARBOX: Entirely new Triumph design. Four speeds with large diameter shafts and gears of hardened nickel and nickel-chrome steel. Special dogs for easy changing. Positive stop footchange fully enclosed. Integral speedometer drive. Large diameter multiplate clutch.

PETROL TANK: All-steel welded streamline design. Quick opening plated filler cap. Two-way tap with reserve. Plated parcel grid on tank top.

OIL TANK: All-steel welded design with accessible filters, drain plug and separate vent. Screw-down leak-proof alloy filler cap.

FRAME: Brazed full cradle type with large diameter tapered front down tube and incorporating lugs for sidecar either side.

FRONT FORKS: Famous Triumph telescopic pattern with six inches of hydraulically-damped movement. Fuller details, page three.

BRAKES: Triumph design of exceptional power. Polished front brake anchor plate. Finest quality linings, finger adjustment back and front.

HANDLEBAR: Triumph design. Quick-action twist grip with finger adjustment friction control. Integral horn push. Adjustable plated clutch and brake levers.

MUDGUARDS: Wide "D" section with streamline stays. Completely detachable rear guard for rear wheel accessibility. Rear number plate with centrally mounted lamp and lifting handle.

WHEELS AND TYRES: Triumph design wheels with heavy-duty dull chromium plated spokes. Dunlop tyres.

TOOLBOX: All-steel large capacity with quick release fastener. Complete set good quality tools and greasegun.

NACELLE: Unique Triumph design instrument panel. All instruments rubber mounted, illuminated and readily accessible. Fuller details, page three.

EQUIPMENT: Lucas 6 volt 60 watt dynamo with full ball-bearing armature. Powerful built-in headlamp with adjustable rim. Triumph design rubber kneegrips. Adjustable de Luxe saddle. Smiths 120 m.p.h. chronometric speedometer with r.p.m. scale and internal illumination. Electric horn. Tyre inflator.

AIR CLEANER: Triumph design patented Vokes air cleaner, mounted behind the battery, neat and efficient. See page three for fuller details.

FINISH: Frame, forks, etc., in amarenth (dark red) lacquer. Petrol tank with new chromium motif. Wheels, chromium plated with red hubs and rim centres (lined gold). All bolts and nuts cadmium plated. Highest quality materials throughout.

New style of tank was the most noticeable change to the 5T for 1950 but engine and gearbox had come in for a good deal of improvement. As it would also now have to cope with the greater torque of Triumph's new 650 the 'box had been redesigned to incorporate more robust internals, including a driven layshaft with integral top gear pinion instead of the floating type employed previously. Other alterations included the repositioning of the speedo drive from rear to front of the gearbox. Part-way through the season an improved MkII version of the sprung rear hub was introduced to obviate trouble that some owners had experienced with fractured springs.

The 1950 T100 echoed the changes made to the 5T except that its engine had a higher compression and a degree of internal polishing – its colour scheme too, like that of the 5T, remained as in previous seasons.

By the mid '60s, although most of us who were around at that time did not notice, it had all begun to collapse around the company's ears – as I briefly related earlier in this book when covering the rise and fall of BSA, which had been intertwined with Triumph since the early 1950s.

Jack Sangster had retired in 1961 and Edward Turner stepped down as CEO of the BSA group two years later, retaining a seat on the board until 1967. New chairman Harry Sturgeon had come up through the ranks of BSA, and with Triumph's godfather no longer in charge set about the rationalisation of the entire group, with modernisation and unification as the main goals. What Turner saw as Meriden's demotion to a subsidiary rather than a co-owned but separate entity did not amuse him but there was little he could do about it; and even he must have realised that the status quo could not continue. Sturgeon's reign was brief, as he unexpectedly died in 1967 – too soon to see the disastrous research and development facility he had set in motion established at Umberslade Hall. But to his credit he did implement some worthwhile changes, as well as being an avid supporter of competition as a means to good publicity. Even so, the group – indeed the entire British motorcycle industry – was in terminal decline, the oft-blamed Japanese invasion being largely but by no means entirely at fault. Nor was the much-reviled Lionel Jofeh, who took the late Sturgeon's place – although it might be hard to find anyone who recalled his activities with anything but rancour.

Throughout these troubled times Triumph's sales remained buoyant but they would soon be dragged down with the firm's floundering parent, in spite of (or because of) measures taken at Meriden to take Triumph into the future.

Back in 1962 Doug Hele and Bert Hopwood had formulated a 750cc pushrod OHV triple. With a prototype up and running by 1965 it would very likely have gone into production in 1967 had not BSA insisted on its own version – with a sloping engine in a different frame, and both unattractively restyled at the behest of the group's notorious Umberslade Hall. When it finally appeared in the summer of '68 it was soon overshadowed and vastly outsold by Honda's CB750 – despite early publicity accrued for the vital US market at Daytona, and much later the Vetter-customised X75 Hurricane. Later still there was more publicity through the successful racing exploits of the Doug Hele-developed, Rob North-framed triples but by that time it was far too late. Too late, also, was the 350cc twin-cam twin designed by Edward Turner in his retirement to compete in the immensely popular 350 market, and brought to fruition by Hopwood and Hele. Unveiled in the November of 1970 as the Triumph Bandit, at the same time as the rest of the range that had been 'trendified' by the cretins of Umberslade Hall, it would be killed off prior to production.

As the new year unfolded, gloom descended, with profit warnings from Jofeh turning out to be optimistic and the reality far worse – by July he was ousted, albeit replete with a large and undeserved golden handshake. In a desperate search for money,

The new 6T Thunderbird was in direct response to requests, nay demands, for more cubic inches from across the Atlantic; but it had been given its baptism of fire at the Montlhéry track in France where three of them averaged over 92mph for 500 miles, did a final lap at 100mph, and were then ridden back to the Meriden factory. A special colour named Thunder Blue had been formulated for the model and all painted parts (with the exception of gold lining bordering the wheel centres) were so finished.

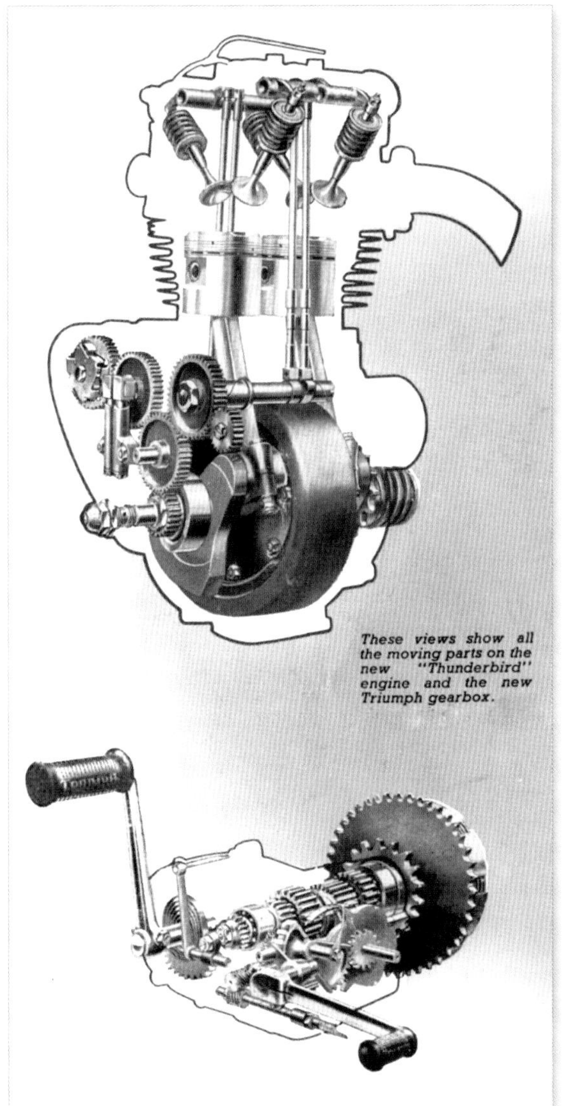

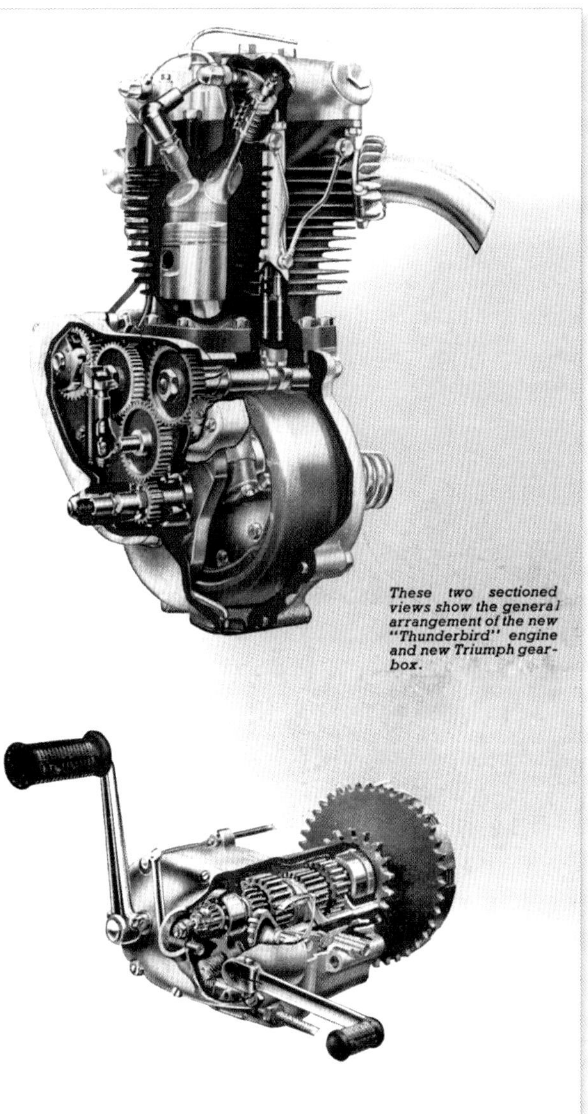

Due to the 650's larger bore, internal drain for the oil returning from the rockers was no longer feasible, so external pipes were provided and reintroduced for the 500s – the latter having had them up until just post-war.

hefty price increases were made but only served to further alert the general public to the fact that all was not right 'at mill'. Then news of a possible takeover by a group of venture capitalists calling themselves Vision Enterprises, followed by their rapid withdrawal (once they'd ascertained that the entire group wasn't quite as ripe and juicy a plum for the picking as they'd hoped) merely engendered further despair. One has to wonder, however, what their decision would have been if it had been only Triumph up for grabs.

As the year progressed various subsidiaries within the group were sold off, and then in the autumn its financial advisors strongly recommended that the only chance of salvation lay with the closure of BSA's Small Heath complex; and for motorcycle production to be amalgamated at Meriden, with a much reduced range of BSAs and Triumphs for 1972. In the event, in spite of large-scale redundancies throughout the group, both plants remained open for the meanwhile but by the end of the year matters had deteriorated still further and to such an extent that the group's new chairman Lord Shawcross sought government assistance. The upshot was that in a little over six months what remained of the BSA non-motorcycle subsidiaries were sold to Dennis Poore's Manganese Bronze holdings for a bargain price, whilst BSA and Triumph motorcycles became the property of his Norton-Villiers combine – the resulting amalgam to be known as Norton Villiers Triumph and to have Poore as its chairman. The choice to retain the Triumph name rather than BSA was perhaps of sustenance to Edward Turner in his last days, as he died quietly in his sleep that August.

In September, and like a bolt from the blue, Poore announced that contrary to what had been understood the Meriden factory would close the following February with nearly 70 per cent of its employees (of

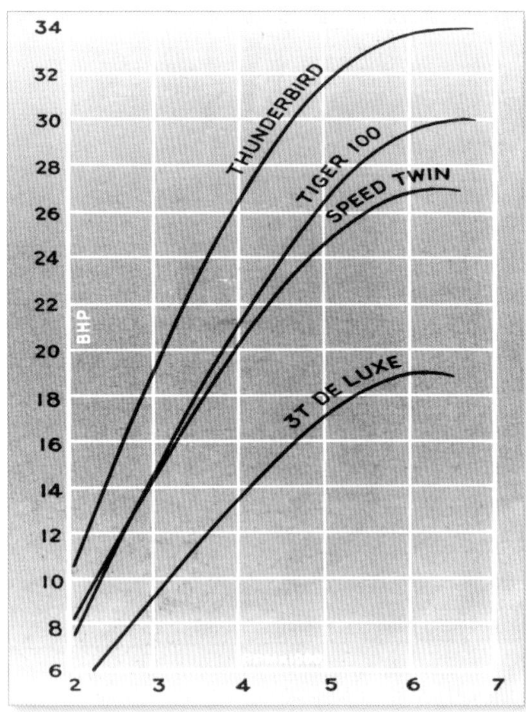

Triumph were sufficiently happy with the power produced by their twins that they included this chart in their 1950 brochure.

MODEL	3T	5T	T100	6T
Engine: Type	O.H.V.	O.H.V.	O.H.V.	O.H.V.
No. of cylinders	2	2	2	2
Bore and stroke, mm.	55 × 73·4	63 × 80	63 × 80	71 × 82
Cylinder capacity, c.cm.	349	498	498	649
Compression ratio	6·3 : 1	7 : 1	7·8 : 1	7 : 1
Engine sprocket, teeth solo	19	22	22	24
R.P.M. 10 m.p.h., top gear	750	646	646	580
Gear ratios:				
Top solo	5·8	5·0	5·0	4·57
Third solo	6·90	5·95	5·95	5·45
Second solo	9·8	8·45	8·45	7·75
First solo	14·13	12·2	12·2	11·2
Top, sidecar	—	5·8	5·8	5 24
Third, sidecar	—	6·90	6·90	6·24
Second, sidecar	—	9·8	9·8	8·85
First, sidecar	—	14·13	14·13	12·8
Carburetter, main jet	120	140	150*	‡170
,, slide	5/4	6/3½	6/3½	6 3½
,, needle jet	107	107	107	107
Ignition, fully advanced ins. (*mm.*)	†11/32″(*9*)	3/8″ (*9.5*)	3/8 (*9.5*)	3/8″ (*9.5*)
Front chain size		½″ × ·305″	all models	
Rear chain size		5/8″ × 3/8″	all models	
Tyres—Dunlop, front, ins.	3·25—19	3·25—19	3·25—19	3·25—19
,, ,, rear, ins.	3·25—19	3·50—19	3·50—19	3·50—19
Saddle Height, ins. (*cm.*)	28½″ (*72*)	29½″ (*75*)	29½″ (*75*)	29½″ (*75*)
Wheelbase, ins. (*cm.*) ...	53¼″ (*135*)	55″ (*140*)	55″ (*140*)	55″ (*140*)
Overall Length, ins. (*cm.*)	82½″ (*209*)	84″ (*214*)	84″ (*214*)	84″ (*214*)
Overall Width, ins. (*cm.*)	28½″ (*72*)	28½″ (*72*)	28½″ (*72*)	28½″ (*72*)
Ground Clearance, ins. (*cm.*)	6″ (*15.2*)	6″ (*15.2*)	6″ (*15.2*)	6″ (*15.2*)
Dry Weight, lbs. (*kilos*)	325 (*147*)	365 (*165.5*)	365 (*165.5*)	370 (*168*)
Petrol Tanks, galls (*litres*)	3½ (*16*)	4 (*18*)	4 (*18*)	4 (*18*)
Oil Tank, pints (*litres*) ...	6 (*3.4*)	6 (*3.4*)	6 (*3.4*)	6 (*3.4*)

†9/32″ (*7.2 mm.*) with low octane fuel. *160 without air cleaner.
‡190 without air cleaner.

some 4,500) being made redundant; future production would take place at the much larger Small Heath site, with its large proportion of immigrant workers. To Triumph's fiercely loyal and committed workforce this was unthinkable and demonstrations led to their occupation of the factory in a sit-in that was to last for 18 months.

Matters were finally resolved with the assistance of the newly-elected Labour government's trade and industry secretary Tony Benn, whose liaison between all parties resulted in the formation of the Meriden Motorcycle Co-operative that would operate through a company registered as Synova Motors Ltd. Thus the remaining 200-or-so workers resumed work for a company controlled by themselves and financially backed by the taxpayer, with Norton Villiers Triumph handling marketing and sales of the entire output.

This continued until the collapse of NVT in 1977, whereupon the cooperative bought the marketing rights with the help of further government loans – shortly becoming Triumph Motorcycles (Meriden) Ltd. Although the Trident had ceased to be manufactured in 1975 and production consisted of a pair of 750cc twins, the Tiger and Bonneville, US sales were good; but by the end of the decade this vital market had waned – largely due to the strength of the pound.

Despite a large part of Triumph's accrued debts to the government being written off and contracts for the supply of police motorcycles to emergent African countries, the cooperative's ten years ended in bankruptcy towards the end of August 1983.

And there it could have ended had it not been for John Bloor, owner of Bloor Homes, who had initially been interested in the factory site for development and ended up buying not only that but the firm's name and manufacturing rights from the official receiver. With the continuation of what by that time was Britain's longest-established motorcycle manufacturer in mind, Bonneville Coventry Ltd was formed; and while Bloor made his plans he granted the rights to build Bonnevilles and Tigers to Devon businessman Les Harris. They were made at Newton Abbott from 1985 until 1988, by which time Harris concentrated on the design and manufacture of his own Matchless motorcycles.

By that time Bloor was well on the way to commencing manufacture on his own account, and not only had prototype models been built but the construction of a brand-new factory was under way at Hinckley in Leicestershire.

The rest is another story, but suffice to say, after the setback of a disastrous factory fire in 2002 and a subsequent rebuild, output reached nearly over 45,000 in 2010. Since the marque's rebirth a multiplicity of two-, three- and four-cylinder models have been introduced – from traditional air-cooled twins like the 865cc Thruxton to the liquid-cooled three-cylinder 2,294cc Rocket III. With the first in 2002, factories have also been built in Thailand and more recently in India. Ironically, perhaps, Triumph's old Meriden site ended up covered by Bloor homes but by so doing its owner ensured the marque's renaissance and hopefully longevity.

Forecourt fashion parade by Triumph for 1952; but I do hope the young lady on the pillion of the Thunderbird is not planning to go too far dressed like that – bare legs and peekaboo toe shoes too. And please note that even motorcyclists received courteous service, and often from a smartly-dressed forecourt attendant, when they stopped for fuel back in those days – no waiting around in a queue whilst the minutes tick by as the person in front buys lottery tickets, crisps and other such 'essentials' with a credit card.

Wherever you look on a Triumph you will fina small exclusive items designed to give the superior service and satisfaction for which the Triumph is famed. For instance :

(1) Highly polished front brake anchor plate, primary chain case, timing cover and gearbox end-cover for better appearance and ease of cleaning.

(2) Plated streamline beading on front number plate banishes dangerous and rust collecting sharp edges.

(3) Twist grip friction can be adjusted instantly—while you are riding if necessary.

(4) Brake adjustment is a minute's work, without tools.

(5) A drain plug in the oil tank makes oil changing a simple job.

(6) Easily seen, trouble-free oil pressure indicator on the timing cover.

(7) Chainguards to **both** runs of rear chain.

(8) Footrests, handlebars, brake pedal and gear change pedal easily adjustable to suit all riding positions.

(9) Battery conveniently located for easy topping up.

(10) Attractive design rear number plate with lifting handle combined.

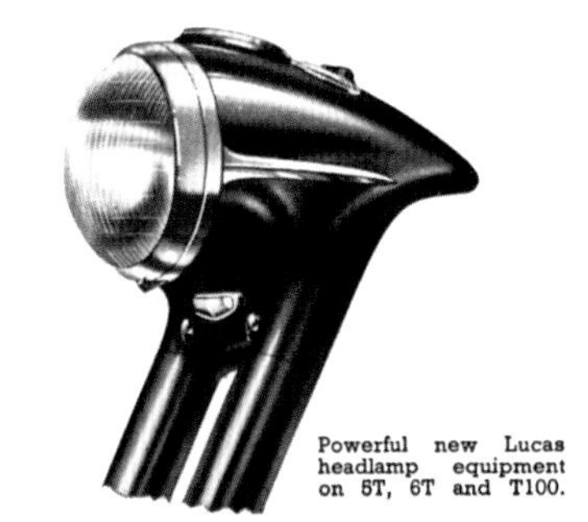

Powerful new Lucas headlamp equipment on 5T, 6T and T100.

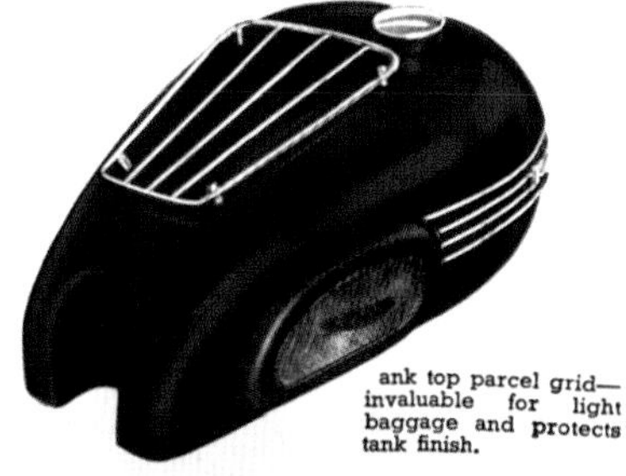

ank top parcel grid—invaluable for light baggage and protects tank finish.

Detachable rear mudguard for easy tyre repair (on 5T, 6T and T100).

The 3T had been dropped at the end of the 1951 season so henceforth the Speed Twin took on the role of Triumph's basic model; but together with both the T100 and 6T it had a new type of frame that incorporated an extra lug with lozenge-shaped aperture in the seat tube: this to facilitate the fitment of a more efficient (Vokes) air filter. Also common to these models was the introduction of a larger headlamp nacelle, now with a 7in sealed beam unit and a pilot light in place of slots for a horn. Also, talking of electrics, it was at this time that Triumph changed from negative to positive earth.

In 1949 and '50 Triumph T100-mounted riders had come home second in the Senior Clubmans TT. What's more, had Ivan Wicksteed not been sidelined with a split fuel tank on the last lap, when he had a three-minute lead, in 1950 he'd have likely won. The advent of the 1951 model with aluminium head and barrels (the latter with particularly closely-pitched fins) as well as the possibility of incorporating at least some of the goodies from the factory race kit, brought the prospect of outright victory even closer – or did it? Once again Wicksteed led the Senior, but lost out on the last lap when his main rival on a Norton put on a spurt whilst he slowed and finished runner-up by 20 seconds (the number 29 bike in this illustration was third-place man John Draper in the same race). Finally, in 1952 it all came good and a young member of the Bradford and District MCC, Brian Hargreaves, led from the first lap to give the Tiger 100 its first, and what would prove to be its only, Clubmans victory at an average of 82.45mph.

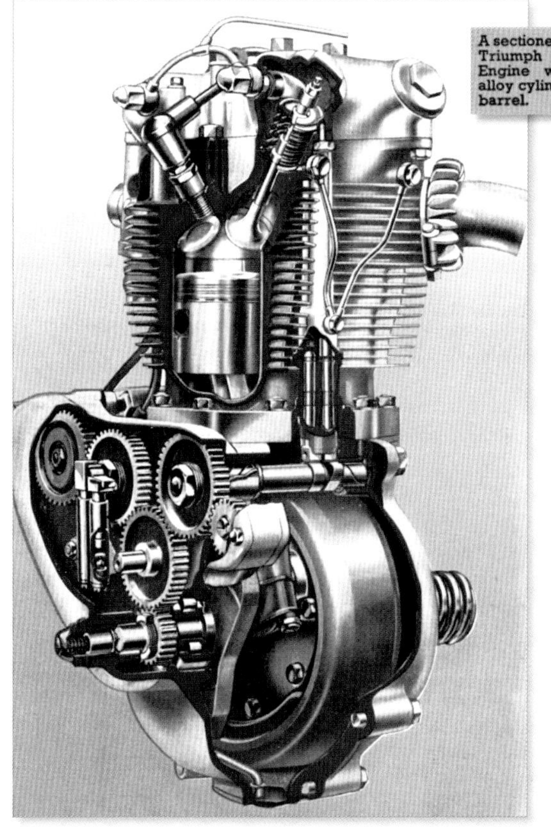

Now that the GP had gone out of production the Trophy (above and right) had the same close-finned aluminium head and barrel castings as the T100. Tank-top parcel grids had been standardised for 1951 and the TR5 was no exception. Sprung hub wheels on the other hand were still an optional extra and very few owners opted for one on Triumph's off-road competition machine; in general, an allegiance to an unsprung rear end for trials work was still strong.

Don't be misled! Thunder Blue had given way to Polychromatic Blue for the 1951 Thunderbird but this double-page spread from the 1952 brochure, although leaning slightly towards a darker version of the former, was neither one nor the other. They got some details right, however – such as the newly-introduced SU carburettor and special manifold that replaced the previously-employed Amal 276. Due to the shortage of nickel at this time Triumph, in common with other manufacturers, had cut down on the use of chrome plate, so components such as wheel rims were either painted body colour and silver or, this illustration imparted, simply body colour (either way with gold lining).

- ★ 650 c.c. O.H.V. Twin engine giving 34 B.H.P.
- ★ Triumph 4-speed gear-box with foot-operated change and heavy duty five-plate clutch.
- ★ S.U. automatically expanding choke type carburetter, giving outstanding performance, with economy of petrol. Specially developed for the Thunderbird.
- ★ New Lucas 7 inch high power "pre-focus" bulb type headlamp.
- ★ Beautifully finished in polychromatic blue lined in gold.

TECHNICAL INFORMATION

MODEL	5T	T100	6T	TR5
Engine : Type	O.H.V.	O.H.V.	O.H.V.	O.H.V.
No. of cylinders ...	2	2	2	2
Bore and stroke mm.	63 × 80	63 × 80	71 × 82	63 × 80
" " " ins.	2.48 × 3.15	2.48 × 3.15	2.79 × 3.23	2.48 × 3.15
Cylinder capacity c.cm.	498	498	649	498
" " ins.	30.50	30.50	40	30.50
Compression ratio ...	7 : 1	7.6 : 1	7 : 1	6 : 1
B.H.P. and R.P.M. (Low Octane Petrol) ...	27 at 6300	32 at 6500	34 at 6300	25 at 6000
	Solo S/C	Solo S/C	Solo S/C	Solo
Engine sprocket, teeth ...	22 19	22 19	24 21	21
R.P.M., 10 m.p.h. top gear	650	650	594	682
Gear ratios—	Solo S/C	Solo S/C	Solo S/C	Solo
Top	5.00 5.80	5.00 5.80	4.57 5.24	5.24
Third	5.95 6.90	5.95 6.90	5.45 6.24	7.46
Second	8.45 9.80	8.45 9.80	7.75 8.85	11.58
First	12.20 14.15	12.20 14.15	11.20 12.80	15.25
Carburetter main jet ...	140	160	S.U.	150
" slide ...	6/3½	6/3½	Needle	6/3½
" needle jet	107	107	M9	107
Ignition, fully advanced ins. (*mm.*)	⅜" (*9.5*)	⅜" (*9.5*)	⅜" (*9.5*)	⅜" (*9.5*)
Front chain size	½" × .305" all models			
Rear chain size	⅝" × ⅜" all models			
Tyres—Dunlop front				
Front ... ...ins.	3.25—19	3.25—19	3.25—19	3.00—20
Rear ... ...ins.	3.50—19	3.50—19	3.50—19	4.00—19
Saddle Height ins. (*cm*)	29½" (*75*)	31" (*79*)	29½" (*75*)	31" (*79*)
Wheelbase ins. (*cm*) ...	55" (*140*)	55" (*140*)	55" (*140*)	53" (*134*)
Overall length ins. (*cm*)	84" (*214*)	84" (*214*)	84" (*214*)	80" (*203*)
Overall width ins. (*cm*)	28½" (*72*)	28½" (*72*)	28½" (*72*)	29" (*74*)
Ground clearance ins. (*cm*) ...	6" (*15*)	6" (*15*)	6" (*15*)	6½" (*16*)
Dry weight, lbs. (*kilos*) ...	365 (*165.5*)	355 (*160*)	370 (*168*)	295 (*134*)
Petrol tanks, galls. (*litres*)	4 (*18*)	4 (*18*)	4 (*18*)	2½ (*11.35*)
Oil tank, pints (*litres*) ...	6 (*3.4*)	6 (*3.4*)	6 (*3.4*)	6 (*3.4*)

To convert miles per gallon into kilos per litre multiply by .354.
To convert kilos per litre into miles per gallon multiply by 2.825.

The '52 brochure's rear cover harked back to Triumph's successes during the previous season: Jim Alves third in the ACU National Trials Championship, with a 500, and a member of the victorious British team in the ISDT on a 650. And here's Ivan Wicksteed during the ride that should have ended with him winning the Senior Clubmans – this photo proving that his bike had the benefit of twin carbs from the factory race kit, and one or two other bits like cams too, I shouldn't wonder.

November 1952 and Triumph's prominent show stand once again featured this tank-badged portico for its wares. Chromium plate was still in short supply due to the on-going Korean War but even so this Thunderbird appears to have plated wheel rims.

For the 1953 export brochure cover Triumph decided upon this simplistic logo above a somewhat saturnine nocturnal Thunderbird rider. The father of the gentleman from whom I obtained this brochure was a good customer of Decat Motorcycles and went on to buy one of the first 1954 model swinging-arm Tiger 100s to be sold in Belgium.

Coil ignition and an alternator for the 1953 Speed Twin, so this meant a new type of transmission shock absorber, now within the clutch rather than on the engine shaft, a different primary chain case to accommodate the stator and rerouted nearside exhaust pipe to clear it. One of these, fitted with the optional 'twinseat' was put through its paces by The Motor Cycle *early in the year and particular attention was paid to the emergency starting facility in the event of a flat battery. Never a problem with a magneto, it could turn into a major one with coil ignition; but even after a night left in the open and with absolutely no juice in the battery it burbled into life at the first kick. With the emphasis on its attributes for touring its handling limits were not explored, and only the occasional bottoming of front and rear suspension was commented upon. Economy-wise it returned just over 60mpg at 50mph and 51 at 60mph. Flat out meant 83mph, with 76 available in third and the standing-start quarter-mile was covered in just 17.4 seconds.*

THE TRIUMPH A.C. LIGHTING-IGNITION UNIT

The introduction of this new lighting and ignition system on the Triumph Speed Twin marks a further step forward in progressive motorcycle design. The normal separate gear driven magneto and dynamo are replaced by a single alternator mounted on the crankshaft and enclosed in the primary chain case. This means a minimum loss of power in driving it, and generator bearings are eliminated altogether. A distributor and coil are fitted behind the engine and a rectifier is mounted above the air-cleaner. Lighting and Ignition switches are on the nacelle top. **Battery failure cannot affect engine starting as an "Emergency Start" position on the ignition switch diverts all the current produced by the alternator direct to the ignition circuit.** This new system offers simplicity with remarkable efficiency.

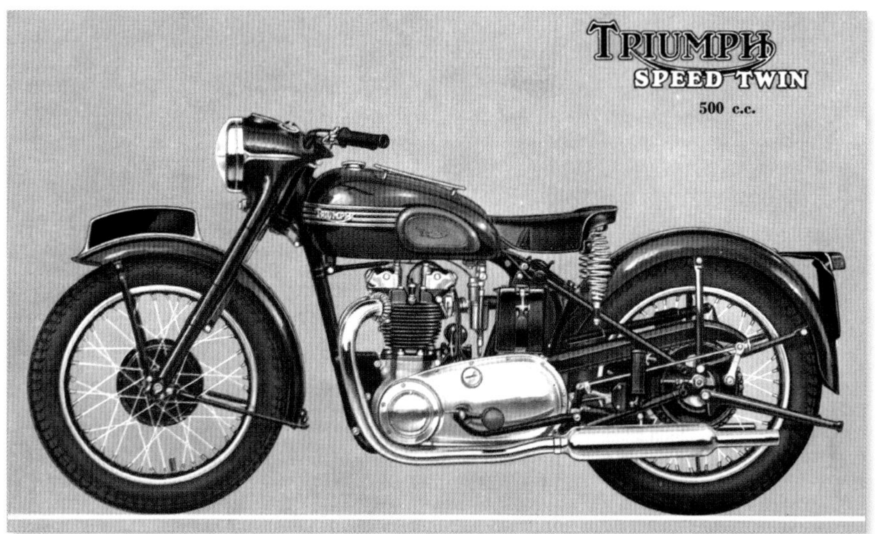

No visual changes for the T100 from the 1952 bikes but this allows you to view one from the nearside.

No doubt with an eye on repeating its Senior Clubmans success, Triumph came up with the T100C (C for Clubmans or Conversion depending on the source) for 1953. Ringwood Clubman and Bob Foster protégé Derek Powell took one over to the Island for the Senior together with a BB32 Gold Star for the Junior, winning the latter at just over 80mph. Practice for the Senior was wet but Powell was amongst the fastest and, as he had not long since won the Clubmans race at Eppynt high in the Brecon Beacons on the same machine, not to mention his Junior success on the BSA, he was amongst the favourites for the 500cc event. On the baking-hot race day, however, the better-handling Featherbed Inter Nortons had the legs of the Triumph with its indifferent handling – Powell visibly wrestling with it over patches of melting tarmac. His race average of 82.40mph was comparable to similarly-mounted Hargreaves the previous year but not enough – he came home fourth behind three Nortons, the fastest of which had covered the three laps at over 84mph.

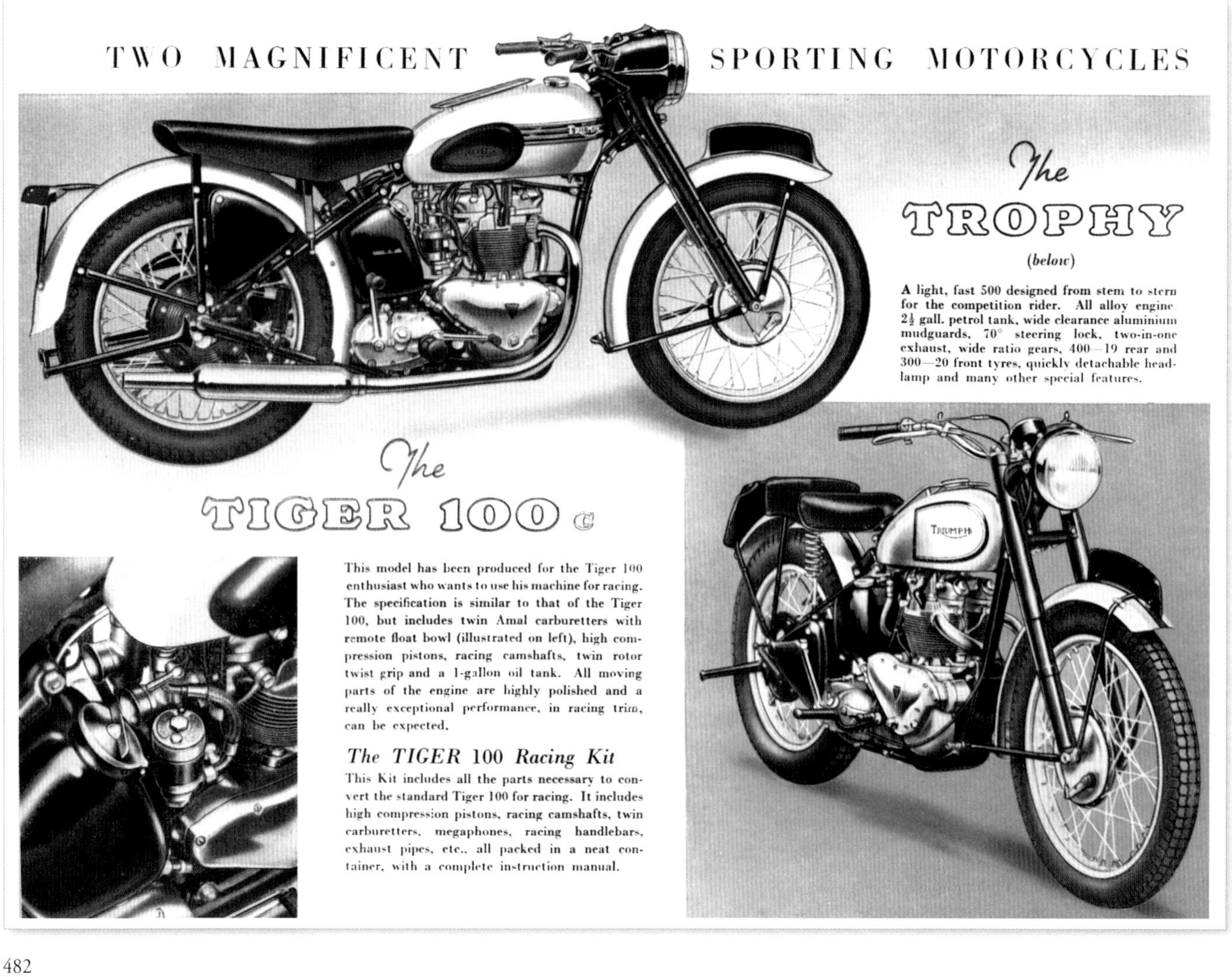

TWO MAGNIFICENT SPORTING MOTORCYCLES

The TROPHY

(below)

A light, fast 500 designed from stem to stern for the competition rider. All alloy engine, 2½ gall. petrol tank, wide clearance aluminium mudguards, 70° steering lock, two-in-one exhaust, wide ratio gears, 400—19 rear and 300—20 front tyres, quickly detachable headlamp and many other special features.

The TIGER 100 C

This model has been produced for the Tiger 100 enthusiast who wants to use his machine for racing. The specification is similar to that of the Tiger 100, but includes twin Amal carburetters with remote float bowl (illustrated on left), high compression pistons, racing camshafts, twin rotor twist grip and a 1-gallon oil tank. All moving parts of the engine are highly polished and a really exceptional performance, in racing trim, can be expected.

The TIGER 100 Racing Kit

This Kit includes all the parts necessary to convert the standard Tiger 100 for racing. It includes high compression pistons, racing camshafts, twin carburetters, megaphones, racing handlebars, exhaust pipes, etc., all packed in a neat container, with a complete instruction manual.

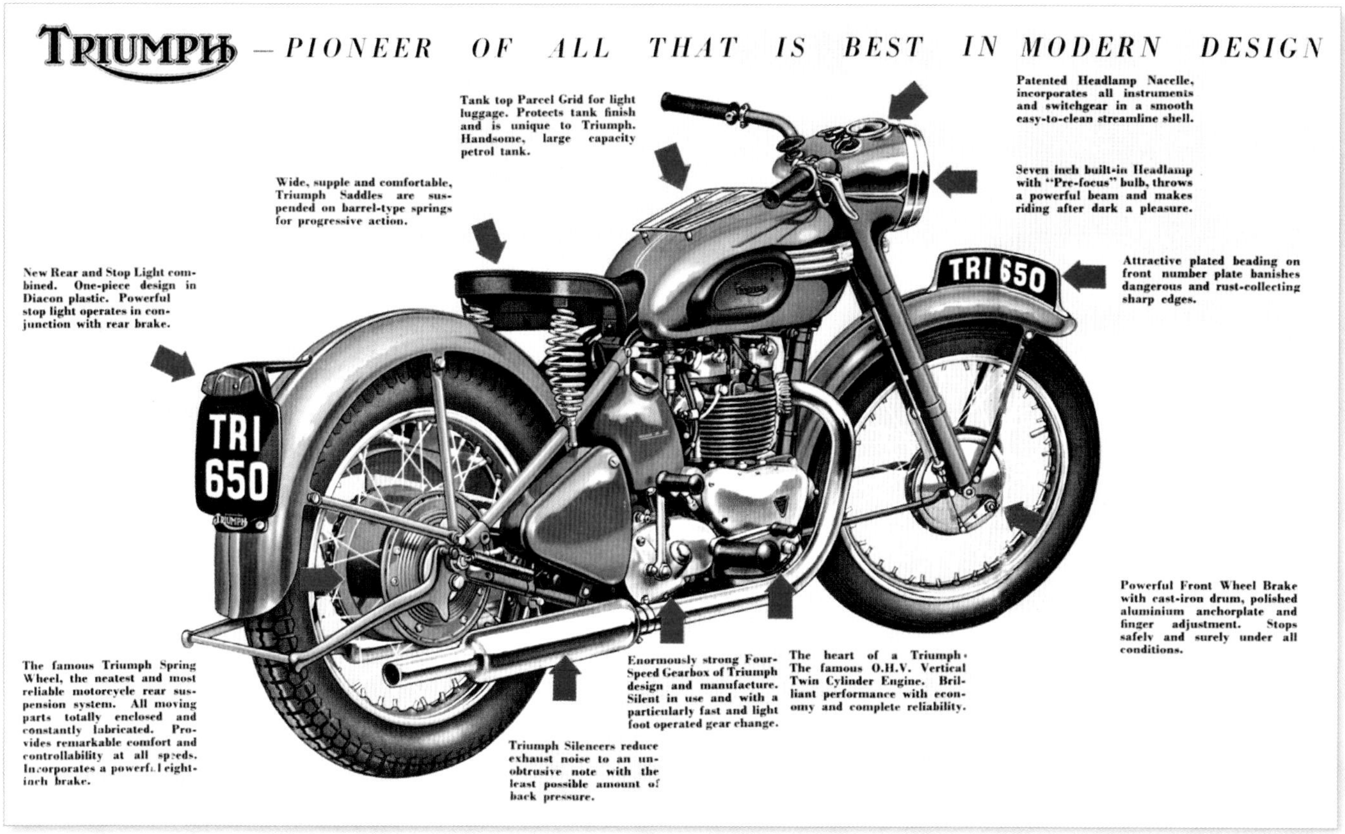

TRIUMPH — *PIONEER OF ALL THAT IS BEST IN MODERN DESIGN*

Tank top Parcel Grid for light luggage. Protects tank finish and is unique to Triumph. Handsome, large capacity petrol tank.

Patented Headlamp Nacelle, incorporates all instruments and switchgear in a smooth easy-to-clean streamline shell.

Wide, supple and comfortable, Triumph Saddles are suspended on barrel-type springs for progressive action.

Seven inch built-in Headlamp with "Pre-focus" bulb, throws a powerful beam and makes riding after dark a pleasure.

New Rear and Stop Light combined. One-piece design in Diacon plastic. Powerful stop light operates in conjunction with rear brake.

Attractive plated beading on front number plate banishes dangerous and rust-collecting sharp edges.

TRI 650

TRI 650

Powerful Front Wheel Brake with cast-iron drum, polished aluminium anchorplate and finger adjustment. Stops safely and surely under all conditions.

The famous Triumph Spring Wheel, the neatest and most reliable motorcycle rear suspension system. All moving parts totally enclosed and constantly lubricated. Provides remarkable comfort and controllability at all speeds. Incorporates a powerful eight-inch brake.

Enormously strong Four-Speed Gearbox of Triumph design and manufacture. Silent in use and with a particularly fast and light foot operated gear change.

The heart of a Triumph. The famous O.H.V. Vertical Twin Cylinder Engine. Brilliant performance with economy and complete reliability.

Triumph Silencers reduce exhaust noise to an unobtrusive note with the least possible amount of back pressure.

The Thunderbird from another angle in this '53 brochure double-page spread. There were just a very few internal mods such as a different type of transmission shock absorber – now incorporated in the clutch assembly rather than the engine shaft in the same way as the 5T. The latest Lucas (525) rear light, along with a number plate to suit, was now fitted to all Triumphs. Colour was still Polychromatic Blue and this illustration perhaps more accurately, if somewhat luridly, depicts it than some other factory publicity material of the time.

MODEL	Speed Twin (5T)	Tiger 100 (T100)	Tiger 100c (T100c)	Thunderbird (6T)	Trophy (TR5)
Engine : Type	O.H.V.	O.H.V.	O.H.V.	O.H.V.	O.H.V.
No. of cylinders	2	2	2	2	2
Bore/Stroke, mm.	63×80	63×80	63×80	71×82	63×80
,, ins.	2.48×3.15	2.48×3.15	2.48×3.15	2.79×3.23	2.48×3.15
Cyl. capacity, c.cm.	498	498	498	649	498
,, ins.	30.50	30.50	30.50	40	30.50
Compression ratio	7 : 1	7.6 : 1	8 : 1	7 : 1	6 : 1
B.H.P. and R.P.M. (Low Octane Fuel)	27 at 6300	32 at 6500	42 at 7000*	34 at 6300	25 at 6000
	Solo S/C	Solo S/C	Solo	Solo S/C	Solo
Engine sprocket, teeth ...	22 19	22 19	22	24 21	21
R.P.M., 10 m.p.h. : Top gear	650	650	650	594	682
Gear ratios :	Solo S/C	Solo S/C	Solo	Solo S/C	Solo
Top	5.00 5.80	5.00 5.80	5.00	4.57 5.24	5.24
Third	5.95 6.90	5.95 6.90	5.95	5.45 6.24	7.46
Second	8.45 9.80	8.45 9.80	8.45	7.75 8.85	11.58
First	12.20 14.15	12.20 14.15	12.20	11.20 12.80	15.25
Carburetters	Amal Type 6	Amal Type 6	Amal Type 6 (2)	S.U. MC2	Amal Type 6
Front chain size	½″ × .305″ all models				
Rear chain size	⅝″ × ⅜″ all models				
Tyres—Dunlop : Front, ins.	3.25—19	3.25—19	3.25—19	3.25—19	3.00—20
Rear, ins.	3.50—19	3.50—19	3.50—19	3.50—19	4.00—19
Brake diam., ins. (cm.) ...	7″ (17.78) front and rear ; 8″ (20.32) Spring Wheel				
Finish	Red	Silver/Blk	Silver/Blk	Poly/Blue	Silver/Blk
Seat height, ins. (cm.) ...	29½″ (75)	31″ (79)	31″ (79)	29½″ (75)	31″ (79)
Wheelbase, ins. (cm.) ...	55″ (140)	55″ (140)	55″ (140)	55″ (140)	53″ (134)
Length, ins. (cm.)	84″ (214)	84″ (214)	84″ (214)	84″ (214)	80″ (203)
Width, ins. (cm.)	28½″ (72)	28½″ (72)	28½″ (72)	28½″ (72)	29″ (74)
Clearance, ins. (cm.) ...	6″ (15)	6″ (15)	6″ (15)	6″ (15)	6½″ (16)
Weight, lbs. (kilos)	365 (165.5)	355 (160)	(364 165)	370 (168)	295 (134)
Petrol, galls. (litres)	4 (18)	4 (18)	4 (18)	4 (18)	2½ (11.3)
Oil, pints (litres)	6 (3.4)	6 (3.4)	8 (4.5)	6 (3.4)	6 (3.4)

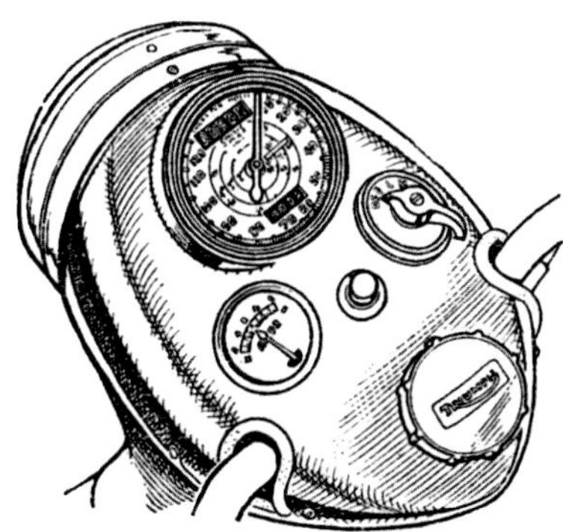

Triumph's headlamp nacelle mounted cluster featured a centrally mounted kill button for the magneto ignition.

It was 1954 – the year of The Wild One, *the cult movie in which the activities of Johnny Strabler and his Black Rebels Motorcycle Club left middle-aged Stateside cinema audiences shocked and mindful – could this happen in their town? So shocking, in fact, that even film censors across the Atlantic banned it in the UK until 1967, when it was finally released with an X certificate. Johnny, played by Marlon Brando, may have been the brooding star but right there with him and the object of his desire Kathie was his Polychromatic Blue Thunderbird kitted out with aftermarket high western bars and pannier bags. What a dramatic brochure cover a scene from this movie would have made, as to all intents and purposes it was the same machine that you could buy! However, even if it had been considered a good idea, which I'm sure it wouldn't have been, it was printed a couple of months before the movie's release and carried a picture of nice Nigel and sweet Sarah on a*

Interesting Triumph Features

CLUTCH SHAFT SHOCK ABSORBER
(*Below*)
Built into the clutch, this very efficient shock absorber transmits the drive through rubber pads located between vanes on the driving and driven members of the clutch centre. All models.

THE TRIUMPH SPRING FRAME
Fitted to the Tiger 100 and Tiger 110 models. A simple yet immensely strong design providing magnificent steering and road-holding even under the worst possible road or cross-country conditions. The springing is controlled by hydraulic dampers which can be adjusted to suit varying conditions of load.

THE TERRIER ENGINE/GEAR UNIT
This photograph shows the clean streamlined design of this modern engine/gear unit. The primary chain, clutch and A.C. Alternator are enclosed in the polished aluminium cover on the drive side. The cylinder head is die cast alloy with close pitch fins and all valve gear is totally enclosed and lubricated.

EXTRAS
PROP STAND. Retained by spring in both positions, out as a prop or folded back. Extra on Twin cylinder models.
TWINSEAT. Triumph design, of supple Latex foam covered with black waterproof Vynide. Steel base pan. Extra on Terrier, Speed Twin and Thunderbird (standard on Tiger 100 & 110).
PILLION FOOTRESTS. Folding type for all models. Rubber covered.
TWIN CARBURETTERS. Optional extra on Tiger 100 only.

RACING KIT
Includes all the parts necessary to convert the standard Tiger 100 for racing. High compression pistons, racing camshafts, twin carburetters, megaphones, racing handlebars, pipes, etc.

I don't think it's unfair to note that Triumph's early swinging-arm frames fell short of the structural integrity of those by BSA and in particular the Featherbed Norton.

MODEL	Terrier (T15)	Speed Twin (5T)	Thunderbird (6T)	Tiger 100 (T100)	Tiger 110 (T110)	Trophy (TR5)
Engine : Type ...	O.H.V.	O.H.V.	O.H.V.	O.H.V.	O.H.V.	O.H.V.
No. of cylinders ...	1	2	2	2	2	2
Bore/Stroke, mm. ...	57×58.5	63×80	71×82	63×80	71×82	63×80
„ ins. ...	2.24×2.3	2.48×3.15	2.79×3.23	2.48×3.15	2.79×3.23	2.48×3.15
Cyl. capacity, c.cm. ...	149	498	649	498	649	498
„ cu.ins.	9	30.50	40	30.50	40	30.50
Compression Ratio ...	7 : 1	7 : 1	7 : 1	7.6 : 1	8.5 : 1	6 : 1
B.H.P. and R.P.M. ...	8 at 6000	27 at 6300	34 at 6300	32 at 6500	42 at 6500	25 at 6000
		Solo S/C	Solo S/C			
Engine sprocket teeth	19	22 19	24 21	22	24	21
R.P.M., 10 m.p.h. :						
Top gear ...	1000	650	594	650	594	661
Gear ratios :						
		Solo S/C	Solo S/C			
Top	7.1	5.00 5.80	4.57 5.24	5.00	4.57	5.24
Third	9.4	5.95 6.90	5.45 6.24	5.95	5.45	7.46
Second	14.8	8.45 9.80	7.75 8.85	8.45	7.75	11.58
First	21.4	12.20 14.15	11.20 12.80	12.20	11.20	15.25
Carburetters	Amal	Amal 276	S.U. MC2	Amal 276	Amal 289	Amal 276
Front chain size ...	⅜×¼	½×.305	½×.305	½×.305	½×.305	½×.305
Rear chain size ...	½×.335	⅝×⅜	⅝×⅜	⅝×⅜	⅝×⅜	⅝×⅜
Tyres—Dunlop :						
Front, ins. ...	2.75×19	3.25×19	3.25×19	3.25×19	3.25×19	3.00×20
Rear, ins. ...	2.75×19	3.50×19	3.50×19	3.50×19	3.50×19	4.00×19
Brake diam., ins. (cm.)	5½ (13.97)	7 (17.78) front and rear ; 8 (20.32) Tiger models, front, and Spring Wheel.				
Finish	Red	Red	Poly/Blue	Blue/Blk.	Blue/Blk.	Blue/Blk.
Seat height, ins. (cm.)	28½ (71.8)	29½ (75)	29½ (75)	30½ (77.5)	30½ (77.5)	31 (79)
Wheelbase, ins. (cm.)	49 (124.5)	55 (140)	55 (140)	55¾ (141.6)	55¾ (141.6)	53 (134)
Length, ins. (cm.) ...	77 (195.5)	84 (214)	84 (214)	85½ (217)	85½ (217)	80 (203)
Width, ins. (cm.) ...	25 (63.5)	28½ (72)	28½ (72)	28½ (72)	28½ (72)	29 (74)
Clearance, ins. (cm.)	5 (12.7)	6 (15)	6 (15)	5 (12.7)	5 (12.7)	6½ (16)
Weight, lbs. (kilos.) ...	175 (79.4)	365 (165.5)	370 (168)	375 (170)	395 (179)	295 (134)
Petrol, galls. (litres) ...	2⅝ (11.9)	4 (18)	4 (18)	4 (18)	4 (18)	2½ (11.3)
Oil, pints (litres) ...	2½ (1.4)	6 (3.4)	6 (3.4)	6 (3.4)	6 (3.4)	6 (3.4)

During the 1920s Triumph had made the 250 two-stroke Baby and then in the '30s a range of various four-strokes from 150cc upwardss but had returned to the lightweight market with the introduction of the 150cc Terrier at the 1952 Earls Court Show. This is how it was depicted in the 1954 season brochure published in October 1953 with nary a mention of the 200cc version (the Cub) that was on the eve of release. From the outset it had a smaller version of the tapering silencers that were introduced on the firm's twins for 1954.

Patent Nos. 475860, 474963, 482024

This remarkable lightweight breaks fresh ground in many fields of design and provides all the accepted best features of a big motorcycle. Recognisable at once as a "little brother" to the famous Triumph twins, it is built to exactly the same standards of fine finish, quality and performance.

GENERAL SPECIFICATION

ENGINE. 150 c.c. high efficiency O.H.V. with die-cast alloy cylinder head, inclined large diameter valves, totally enclosed and lubricated valve gear. "H" section connecting rod with heavy duty big end bearing. Full dry sump lubrication with double plunger type oil pump. Highly polished timing cover. Plated exhaust pipe with barrel type silencer. Air cleaner.

FOUR SPEED GEARBOX. Built in unit with the engine in a polished and streamlined casing. Positive stop footchange. Multi-plate clutch with rubber pad type shock absorber. Primary chain in polished aluminium case.

FRAME. Unique Triumph design. Loop type tubular main frame, strong and light.

SUSPENSION. Triumph telescopic front forks. Double plunger type rear suspension.

BRAKES. Exceptionally powerful and smooth acting. Large diameter drums.

ELECTRICAL EQUIPMENT. Special A.C. Lighting-Ignition system with crankshaft mounted alternator. "Emergency Start" circuit. Large diameter headlamp in patent nacelle, integral with top of forks.

OTHER DETAILS. Large capacity fuel tanks; Smith's 70 m.p.h. speedometer; good quality tool kit; rubber knee grips.

The Terrier die cast alloy cylinder head.

5T and 6T

ENGINES. O.H.V. vertical twin cylinder with two gear-driven camshafts. "H" section RR56 alloy connecting rods with patented plain big ends. Central flywheel. Dry sump lubrication, plunger type pumps, pressure fed big ends and valve gear. Timing cover highly polished and fitted with oil pressure indicator. Patent air cleaner. New Triumph-Burgess barrel type silencers.

FOUR-SPEED GEARBOX. Triumph design and manufacture. Positive stop foot-change. Shafts and gears of finest nickel and nickel-chrome steel. Large diameter multi-plate clutch with rubber pad type shock absorber. Polished aluminium primary chaincase.

FUEL TANKS. All-steel welded tanks with quick release caps and accessible filters.

FRAMES. Brazed full cradle type with lugs for sidecar attachment either side. Front and rear stands.

SUSPENSION. Triumph design telescopic forks with hydraulic damping. Famous Spring Wheel rear suspension (extra).

BRAKES. Exceptionally powerful, with large diameter cast-iron drums. Finger adjusted. Controls adjustable for position.

WHEELS. Triumph design, with heavy duty dull-plated spokes. Dunlop tyres.

ELECTRICAL EQUIPMENT. Famous Triumph pioneered A.C. lighting-ignition set eliminating separate dynamo and magneto. Wide angle rear/stop light. Powerful Lucas 7" built in headlamp with combined reflector/front lens assembly, "pre-focus" bulb and adjustable rim. Separate parking light.

TOOLBOX. All steel, large capacity, with quick-release fastener. Complete set of good quality tools and grease gun.

MUDGUARDS. Efficient "D" shaped guards with central rib. Rear guard detachable for rear wheel accessibility.

NACELLE. Neat streamline shell ntegral with top of forks, encloses headlamp, instruments and switchgear. All instruments rubber mounted and internally illuminated.

SPEEDOMETER. Smiths 120 m.p.h. (or 180 km.p.h.) chronometric type with r.p.m. scale internal illumination and trip recorder.

OTHER DETAILS. Well sprung saddle; quick-action adjustable twist grip; integral horn push; comfortable adjustable handlebars; rubber knee grips; tank parcel grid.

For now the Speed Twin carried on much as before, although this season would be the solid frame's swansong; as it would also be for the Thunderbird, which had now acquired the same alternator electrics coupled with coil and distributor ignition as its 500cc counterpart. The sizable finned device under the saddle, by the way, was the then-current 4½in diameter Lucas rectifier. As a complete aside, many motorcyclists in the US averred a preference for black frames as on Tiger 100s rather than the red and blue parts of the 5Ts and 6Ts, and as a result of pressure from Stateside dealers the factory produced a number of all-black 6Ts that, although not catalogued as such, became known as Blackbirds – if you ever come across one in its original finish don't for heaven's sakes repaint it.

T100 and T110

ENGINE T100. 500 c.c. O.H.V. twin with two gear driven camshafts. High compression pistons, die cast alloy head and barrel with close pitch fins. Dry sump lubrication with pressure fed big ends and valve gear. Patented plain big ends. New massive crankshaft. Twin carburetters optional (extra). Racing Kit available.

ENGINE T110. 650 c.c. O.H.V. vertical twin with unique "shell moulded" cast iron head and barrel. High compression pistons, special camshafts. large bore carburetter, new heavier crankshaft, dry sump lubrication, pressure fed big ends and valve gear.

FOUR SPEED GEARBOX. Triumph design and manufacture. Heavy duty gears and shafts of finest quality nickel and nickel-chrome steel. Positive stop footchange. Multi-plate clutch with built-in rubber pad type shock absorber.

FUEL TANKS. All steel welded tanks with quick release caps and accessible filters. Oil tank in a streamlined "one piece" unit with air cleaner, battery and tool containers.

FRAME. Brazed cradle type frame with swinging fork rear suspension with hydraulic damping adjustable for varying loads.

FORKS. The famous Triumph telescopic pattern with long supple springs and hydraulic damping.

BRAKES. Powerful and smooth acting. New large diameter front brake with highly polished anchor plate. Cast iron drums.

WHEELS. Triumph design with dull plated spokes, Dunlop tyres and chromium plated rims. Fully valanced rear mudguard with side lifting handles. Q.D. rear wheel optional (extra).

ELECTRICAL EQUIPMENT. Powerful Lucas 7 in. built-in headlamp with combined reflector/front lens assembly, "pre-focus" bulb and adjustable rim. Separate parking light below. Lucas 6 volt 60 watt dynamo with full ball bearing armature, automatic voltage control and 12 a.h. battery. Wide angle rear/stop light. Gear driven magneto.

NACELLE. Triumph Patent 647670. Neat streamlined shell integral with top of forks, encloses headlamp, instruments and switchgear. All instruments rubber mounted and internally illuminated.

SPEEDOMETER. Smith's 120 m.p.h. (or 180 k.p.h.) chronometric type with r.p.m. scale internal illumination and trip recorder.

OTHER DETAILS. Complete set of good quality tools and greasegun; new "Two-Level" Twinseat, latex foam covered with black waterproof Vynide; adjustable tension twist grip; tank top parcel grid.

The world's most famous sporting 500 in a new and even more attractive form. Entirely new frame with " High Movement " hydraulically damped rear suspension giving the finest possible steering and roadholding. All alloy engine well known for its remarkable performance.

One would have thought that Triumph's marketing department would have insisted on one of these, or perhaps more especially the new Tiger 110, to front the 1954 brochure. This year's Tiger 100 was much more than just old wine in a new bottle, as in addition to the swinging-arm frame, at the heart of its motor was the stiffer crank with larger-diameter journals and bearings designed for the Tiger 110 (you can quickly tell the difference between small and large crank motors by feeling for a small bulge under the timing case – if there is one it's the latter). In order to fit engine and gearbox into the swinging-arm frame, space between the two had been reduced, which dictated a correspondingly shorter primary chain and shorter aluminium chain case. Centre stands were employed on the new swinging-arm models – this innovation introduced on the other twins for the following season when they too were endowed with sprung frames. There was no 100C version of the new machine but twin carbs and a race kit were still catalogued.

The Triumph "Tiger 110" offers the enthusiast everything he wants in a sports motorcycle. Up-to-the-minute in every detail of its specification, it combines superb suspension with an engine designed to produce the highest possible power output in a smooth and effortless manner.

I do believe that both this and the preceding artwork of the Tiger 100 are somewhat awry and could well mislead. Perhaps the illustrator produced these before the new models' specification was finalised, simply got it wrong, or there was an intention to build as you see them. Either way I'm 99 per cent certain that the old 7in front brake was not employed on production swinging-arm 100s or the new 110 – both being equipped with the first type of 8in from the start. Early production dual seats, however, were of a similar shape to this, and were all black – white piping came later. Both the 100 and 110 had their petrol tank and mudguards finished in Blue Sheen with the remainder in Black, as well as the mudguards' raised centre lines – the Tiger 100 is depicted in silver, however, so had the original intention to differentiate the two models been thus?

The Terrier had been joined by the Cub during the later part of 1953, and for 1954 the pair had a brochure of their own. Had it not have been for their different colours (Amaranth Red for the Terrier and Blue Sheen/Black for the Cub) and the high-level exhaust fitted to the new arrival for its first season, one would have been hard-pressed to tell them apart because they shared cycle parts, including the flawed frame design with swan-necked and unsupported headstock. This undesirable feature would be retained even when the original plunger frame was superseded by one with pivoted-fork rear suspension and necessitated the petrol tank acting as an essential part of the structure.

★ **200 c.c. HIGH EFFICIENCY O.H.V.**

★ **FULL DRY SUMP LUBRICATION**

★ **UNIT CONSTRUCTION ENGINE/GEARBOX**

★ **4-SPEED FOOT OPERATED GEARBOX**

★ **TELESCOPIC FORKS AND SPRING FRAME**

Edward Turner's diminutive overhead-valve single was designed from the first to have coil ignition, and its closely coupled four-speed gearbox with shared castings made it a very compact unit.

	TERRIER	TIGER CUB
Engine: Type	O.H.V.	O.H.V.
No. of Cylinders	1	1
Bore/Stroke, m.m.	57 × 58.5	63 × 64
,, ,, ins.	2.24 × 2.3	2.48 × 2.52
Cyl. capacity, c.cm.... ...	149	199 c.c.
,, ,, cu. ins. ...	9	12
Compression ratio	7 : 1	7 : 1
Engine sprocket, teeth ...	19	19
R.P.M., 10 m.p.h. top gear...	1000	900
GEAR RATIOS:		
Top	7.1	6.7
Third	9.3	8.8
Second	14.6	13.8
First	21.2	20.0
Carburetter	Amal	Amal
Front chain size	⅜″ × ¼″	⅜″ × ¼″
Rear chain size	½″ × .335	½″ × .335
Tyres—Dunlop	2.75 × 19	3.00 × 19
Brake diam., ins. (cm.) ...	5½ (14)	5½ (14)
Finish	Amaranth Red	Blue Sheen/Black
Seat height, ins. (cm.) ...	28½ (71.8)	30 (76.2)
Wheelbase, ins. (cm.) ...	49 (124.5)	49 (124.5)
Length, ins. (cm.)	77 (195.5)	77 (195.5)
Width, ins. (cm.)	25 (63.5)	25 (63.5)
Clearance, ins. (cm.) ...	5 (12.7)	5 (12.7)
Weight, lbs. (kilos)	175 (79.4)	182 (82.5)
Petrol, galls (litres)	2⅝ (11.92)	2⅝ (11.92)
Oil, pints (litres)	2½ (1.4)	2½ (1.4)

RETAIL PRICES FOR GREAT BRITAIN & NORTHERN IRELAND

MOTORCYCLES

ALL retail sales are subject to the Guarantee published in the Company's current catalogue and the prices quoted on this list are for delivery Free of Charge at Dealer's premises. The prices quoted here operate on and after 1st September, 1953, and all previous lists are cancelled. The Company reserves the right to revise prices without prior notice and Purchase Tax also is subject to revision.

1st SEPTEMBER, 1953

	MODEL	BASIC RETAIL	PURCHASE TAX	TOTAL RETAIL
T15	TERRIER 150 c.c. O.H.V.	£98 0 0	£19 12 0	£117 12 0
T20	TIGER CUB 200 c.c. O.H.V.	£106 0 0	£21 4 0	£127 4 0
5T	SPEED TWIN 500 c.c. O.H.V. Twin	£159 0 0	£31 16 0	£190 16 0
6T	THUNDERBIRD 650 c.c. O.H.V. Twin	£167 0 0	£33 8 0	£200 8 0
TR5	TROPHY 500 c.c. O.H.V. Twin	£175 0 0	£35 0 0	£210 0 0
T100	TIGER 100 500 c.c. O.H.V. Twin	£190 0 0	£38 0 0	£228 0 0
T110	TIGER 110 650 c.c. O.H.V. Twin	£200 0 0	£40 0 0	£240 0 0

EXTRAS
(when ordered with the machine)

SPRING WHEEL (5T, 6T, TR5)	£16 0 0	£3 4 0	£19 4 0
TWINSEAT (T15, 5T, 6T)	£1 15 0	7 0	£2 2 0
TWIN CARBURETTERS (T100 only)	£5 0 0	£1 0 0	£6 0 0
Q.D. WHEEL (T100, T110 only)	£3 0 0	12 0	£3 12 0
PROP STAND (All Twins)	15 6	3 2	18 8
PILLION FOOTRESTS (All Models)	16 0	3 3	19 3

TWINSEAT STANDARD ON T20, T100 and T110.

TRIUMPH ENGINEERING CO. LTD., Meriden Works, Allesley, COVENTRY.

This abbreviated sales folder was produced for France and French speakers in Belgium and Luxembourg.

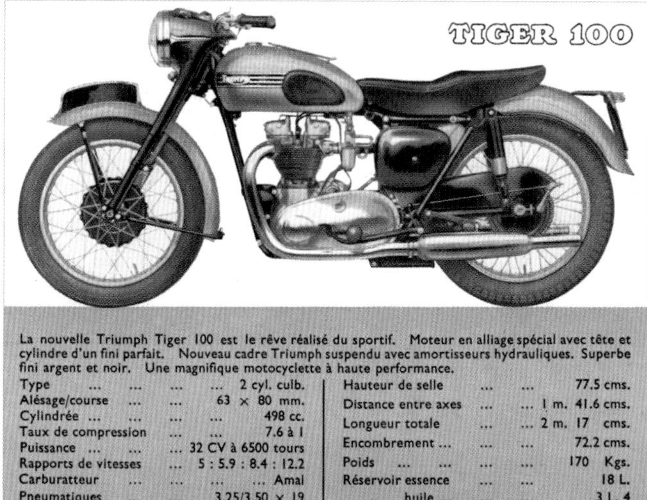

La nouvelle Triumph Tiger 100 est le rêve réalisé du sportif. Moteur en alliage spécial avec tête et cylindre d'un fini parfait. Nouveau cadre Triumph suspendu avec amortisseurs hydrauliques. Superbe fini argent et noir. Une magnifique motocyclette à haute performance.

Type	2 cyl. culb.	Hauteur de selle	77.5 cms.
Alésage/course	63 × 80 mm.	Distance entre axes	1 m. 41.6 cms.
Cylindrée	498 cc.	Longueur totale	2 m. 17 cms.
Taux de compression	7.6 à 1	Encombrement	72.2 cms.
Puissance	32 CV à 6500 tours	Poids	170 Kgs.
Rapports de vitesses ...	5 : 5.9 : 8.4 : 12.2	Réservoir essence	18 L.
Carburatteur	Amal	„ huile	3 L. 4
Pneumatiques	3.25/3.50 × 19		

The entire range was lined up for the covers of the 1955 brochure that was published the previous September.

A semi-cutaway of the Tiger 110 was chosen to illustrate some of the range's features, as well as to give the layman an idea of what went on inside.

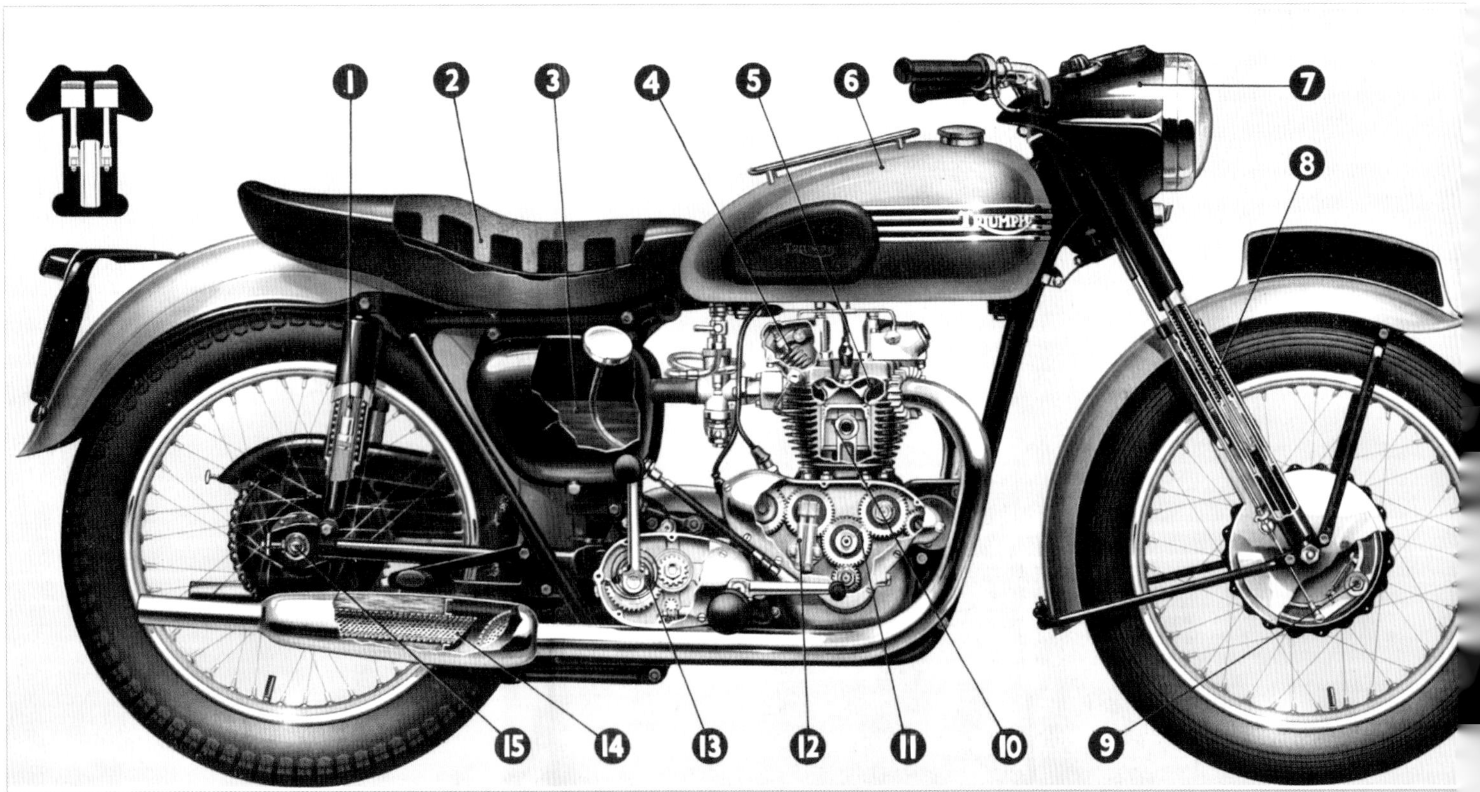

To bring them into line with their sporting counterparts both Speed Twin and Thunderbird were now manufactured with the same swinging-arm frames and associated running gear – including shorter chain cases, which now had a restyled and one-piece outer shell with either the legend Speed Twin or Thunderbird in counter-relief. The Speed Twin's motor had also been uprated and now featured the same beefier bottom end as its siblings plus an additional update with the adoption of the 6T's crankcases, with cylinder barrels to match towards the end of the model year. As for colours, both 5T and 6T continued to be finished in Amaranth Red and Polychromatic Blue respectively.

Sprung-frame Tigers had a very impressive 8in front brake with finned drum and cast-aluminium back plate featuring an air scoop along with a smaller warm-air exit slot. Initially, and for at least the first model year, the cast-iron drum incorporated distinctive sprocket-like flanges for the spokes but a few instances of owners experiencing fractures led to the design being altered to an appropriately drilled continuous flange. A factory-prepared T100 equipped with the improved brake was ridden in the 1955 Clubmans TT by Motor Cycling*'s John Griffiths, who finished down in 13th place at an average speed of 63.55mph. Considering its state of tune (9.5 pistons, special cams, twin carbs, close-ratio gears, etc) and the performance figures that were taken afterwards, it is surprising he didn't do better – his lap times, however, were around a minute slower around the short Clypse course than the winner Eddie Dow and his Gold Star. As far as I'm aware, Dow's DBD 34 was not evaluated after the event, and nor were the second and third-place T00s, but for the record Griffiths' Tiger 100 was timed at a noteworthy 93mph in second gear, 108 in third and 116 in top – and it still returned between 65 and 70mpg at a steady 50mph if you could restrain yourself.*

POPULAR FEATURES OF TRIUMPH DESIGN

1. Swinging Arm rear suspension with hydraulic damping readily adjustable for varying loads.
2. Triumph "Two Level" Twinseat. Soft latex foam covered with black waterproof Vynide. Specially shaped steel base rigidly mounted. The ideal seat solo or with passenger.
3. Combined unit exclusive to Triumph —incorporating oil tank, air cleaner, battery and tool box. Smooth full width exterior, easy to clean and neat in appearance.
4. Fully enclosed overhead valve gear lubricated under pressure. Alloy rocker boxes with accessible threaded valve covers for easy tappet inspection.
5. The famous Triumph hemispherical cylinder heads with large diameter inclined valves. Remarkable performance proves the outstanding efficiency of this design.
6. Shapely 4 gallon Petrol Tank with plated quick release filler. Useful tank top luggage grid. Chromium styling bands and rubber knee grips.
7. Triumph Nacelle (Patent No. 647670) encloses headlamp unit in neat streamlined shell integral with top of forks. All switchgear and instruments rubber mounted.
8. Triumph Telescopic Forks, long action with hydraulic damping. Ensure a comfortable ride and accurate steering at all speeds.
9. The Triumph Front Brake has always been renowned for its power, smoothness and safe operation. Large diameter cast iron drum with polished alloy anchor plate. Finger adjustment.
10. Alloy full skirted pistons with internal strengthening ribs. Two scraper and one oil control rings. "H" section connecting rods of RR56 alloy with massive plain big-end bearings.
11. Drives to the camshafts, magneto and dynamo are by a selectively assembled train of gearwheels. Accuracy in manufacture ensures silent operation and complete reliability.
12. The specially designed double plunger type oil pump driven from the inlet camshaft spindle delivers, under pressure, a constant supply of oil to the engine bearings and overhead valve gear, returning it subsequently to the oil tank.
13. The famous Triumph 4 speed Gearbox with positive foot operated gearchange. Multi-plate clutch with cork inserts operating in oil, sweet in action and light to handle. Polished alloy outer cover. Rubber pad type shock absorber in clutch.
14. Exclusive to Triumph, barrel shaped silencers heavily chromium plated. Particularly efficient in use, providing a very subdued but pleasing exhaust note.
15. The Triumph Q.D. Rear Wheel ends the bogey of difficult wheel removal. The wheel can be extracted by withdrawal of the spindle leaving the rear brake and chain untouched.

EXTRAS

PROP STAND. Retained by spring, out as a prop or folded back. For all models.

PILLION FOOTRESTS. For all models. Folding type, rubber covered.

TWIN CARBURETTERS. For Tiger 100 only.

QUICKLY DETACHABLE REAR WHEEL. For 5T, 6T, T100, T110, TR5.

TWINSEAT for "Terrier".

One of these was the first high-powered 'modern' machine I rode; it was eight years old and I was only seven years older. I can still remember the anticipation, acceleration, speed and exhilaration, coupled with unease as it gently squirmed while weaving its way through a series of fast bends. "Yes they do that," said its owner when I handed it back to him, "You get used to it." I never really did, even when I owned a 10,000-mile-from-new '56 model about ten years later. Despite the shortcomings, or perhaps because of them, I still rate an early T110 as an exciting and satisfying machine to ride hard and far; and 60-plus years ago there was little quicker (in a straight line). In the autumn of 1954 Motor Cycling *recorded these figures – a two-way top speed of 113mph (117 with standard 200 carb jet replaced with a 220), 93 in third and 70 in second. Fuel consumption was almost as impressive, with over 90mpg achievable by keeping it under 50mph and nearly 70mpg overall. Finally, to counter my memories of their handling, the men from* Motor Cycling *remarked upon its 'hair-line cornering and good navigational qualities'.*

Wishful thinking indeed – especially when you consider the handling characteristics of those old sprung-frame Triumphs!

By 1955 there was no denying the fact that trials and off-road competition machinery with solid rear ends had finally become outmoded for most purposes, so the Trophy was revamped with a sprung frame. After cutting his Triumph teeth on a second-hand T110 James Dean traded it in for a brand-new one of these (TR5 59196) from Ted Evans Motorcycles of Culver City, CA during the making of Rebel Without a Cause.

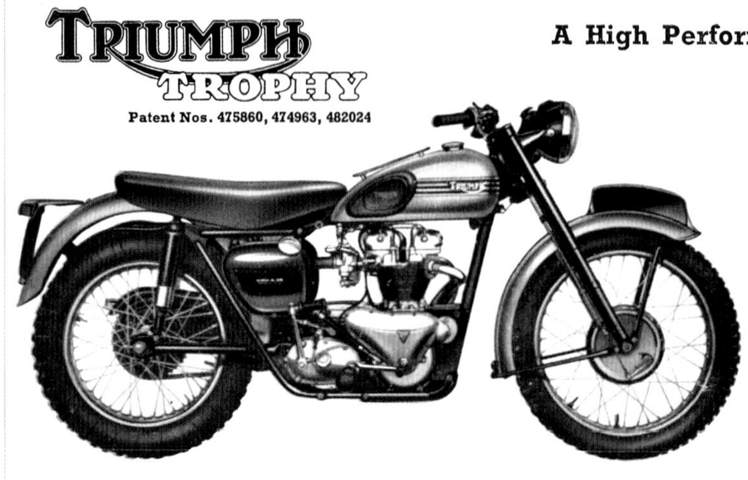

A High Performance Model for the Competition Enthusiast

A new model, of high performance, designed to be readily adaptable to most forms of motorcycle competition. Its specification includes many practical features which will appeal instantly to the really experienced competition rider.

SPECIFICATION

ENGINE. O.H.V. high compression vertical twin with die-cast alloy head and barrel, two gear-driven camshafts, "H" section RR56 alloy connecting rods, plain big ends, and central flywheel. Dry sump lubrication, pressure-fed big ends and valve gear. Air cleaner. Upswept two-in-one exhaust pipe with silencer.

FOUR - SPEED GEARBOX. Positive foot-change, large diameter multi - plate clutch with rubber pad type shock absorber.

FRAME. Brazed cradle type frame with swinging arm rear suspension with hydraulic damping adjustable for varying loads.

FORKS. The famous Triumph telescopic pattern with long supple springs and hydraulic damping.

FUEL TANKS. All-steel welded with quick-release caps and accessible filters.

BRAKES. Large diameter cast iron drums, polished front anchor plate, finger adjustment.

ELECTRICAL EQUIPMENT. Powerful headlamp with quickly detachable harness. Lucas 6 volt 60 watt dynamo, automatic voltage control. Lucas gear-driven "Wader" type magneto.

OTHER DETAILS. 120 m.p.h. (or 180 km.p.h.) Smiths Speedometer; Triumph Twinseat; twist grip with adjustable tension; shell blue sheen and black finish.

TECHNICAL SPECIFICATIONS *ALL MODELS*

MODEL	Terrier (T15)	Tiger Cub (T20)	Speed Twin (5T)	Thunder-bird (6T)	Tiger 100 (T100)	Tiger 110 (T110)	Trophy (TR5)
Engine : Type ...	O.H.V.	O.H.V.	O.H.V.	O.H.V.	O.H.V.	O.H.V.	O.H.V.
No. of Cylinders ...	1	1	2	2	2	2	2
Bore/Stroke, mm. ...	57 × 58.5	63 × 64	63 × 80	71 × 82	63 × 80	71 × 82	63 × 80
„ „ ins. ...	2.24 × 2.3	2.48 × 2.52	2.48 × 3.15	2.79 × 3.23	2.48 × 3.15	2.79 × 3.23	2.48 × 3.15
Cyl. capacity, c.c.m.	149	199	498	649	498	649	498
„ „ cu. ins.	9	12	30.50	40	30.50	40	30.50
Compression Ratio ...	7 : 1	7 : 1	7 : 1	7 : 1	8 : 1	8.5 : 1	8 : 1
B.H.P. & R.P.M. ...	8 at 6000	10 at 6000	27 at 6300	34 at 6300	32 at 6500	42 at 6500	33 at 6500
Eng. sprocket teeth...	19	19	Solo 22 S/C 19	Solo 24 S/C 21	Solo 22 S/C 19	Solo 24 S/C 21	21
R.P.M., 10 m.p.h. : Top Gear	1000	900	650 755	594 680	650 755	594 680	680
Gear Ratios : Top	7.1	6.7	Solo 5.00 S/C 5.80	Solo 4.57 S/C 5.24	Solo 5.00 S/C 5.80	Solo 4.57 S/C 5.24	5.24
Third	9.4	8.8	5.95 6.90	5.45 6.24	5.95 6.90	5.45 6.24	6.24
Second	14.8	13.8	8.45 9.80	7.75 8.85	8.45 9.80	7.75 8.85	8.85
First	21.4	20.0	12.20 14.15	11.20 12.80	12.20 14.15	11.20 12.80	12.80
Carburetters ...	Amal.	Amal.	Amal.376/25	S.U. MC2	Amal. 276	Amal. 289	Amal. 276
Front chain size ...	⅜ × ¼	⅜ × ¼	½ × .305	½ × .305	½ × .305	½ × .305	½ × .305
Rear chain size ...	½ × .335	½ × .335	⅝ × ⅜	⅝ × ⅜	⅝ × ⅜	⅝ × ⅜	⅝ × ⅜
Tyres—Dunlop : Front, ins. ...	2.75 × 19	3.00 × 19	3.25 × 19	3.25 × 19	3.25 × 19	3.25 × 19	3.00 × 20
Rear, ins. ...	2.75 × 19	3.00 × 19	3.50 × 19	3.50 × 19	3.50 × 19	3.50 × 19	4.00 × 18
Brake diam. : ins. (cm.)	5½ (13.97)	5½ (13.97)	7 (17.78)	7 (17.78)	8 (20.32) Front 7 (17.78) Rear		7 (17.78)
Finish	Red	Blue/Blk.	Red	Poly/Blue	Blue/Blk.	Blue/Blk.	Blue/Blk.
Seat height, ins. (cm.)	28½ (71.8)	30 (76.2)	30½ (77.5)	30½ (77.5)	30½ (77.5)	30½ (77.5)	30½ (77.5)
Wheelbase, ins. (cm.)	49 (124.5)	49 (124.5)	55¾ (141.6)	55¾ (141.6)	55¾ (141.6)	55¾ (141.6)	55¾ (141.6)
Length, ins. (cm.) ...	77 (195.5)	77 (195.5)	85½ (217)	85½ (217)	85½ (217)	85½ (217)	85½ (217)
Width, ins. (cm.) ...	25 (63.5)	25 (63.5)	23½ (72)	28½ (72)	28½ (72)	28½ (72)	28½ (72)
Clearance, ins. (cm.)	5 (12.7)	5 (12.7)	5 (12.7)	5 (12.7)	5 (12.7)	5 (12.7)	5 (12.7)
Weight, lbs. (kilos) ...	185 (84)	193 (88)	380 (173)	385 (175)	375 (170)	395 (179)	365 (166)
Petrol, galls. (litres) ..	2⅝ (11.9)	2⅝ (11.9)	4 (18)	4 (18)	4 (18)	4 (18)	3 (13.5)
Oil, pints (litres) ...	2½ (1.4)	2½ (1.4)	6 (3.4)	6 (3.4)	6 (3.4)	6 (3.4)	6 (3.4)

To convert miles per gallon into kilos per litre, multiply by .354
To convert kilos per litre into miles per gallon, multiply by 2.825

Catalogue published September 1954

TELEPHONES COVENTRY 60221 MERIDEN 331

MOTOR CYCLES

TELEGRAMS "TRUSTY" COVENTRY

MERIDEN WORKS ALLESLEY COVENTRY

TRIUMPH ENGINEERING COMPANY LIMITED

OUR REF YOUR REF

November, 1953.

TO ALL DISTRIBUTORS AND DEALERS.

1954 LITERATURE.

Dear Sirs,

We have pleasure in enclosing samples of Triumph literature for the 1954 Season. You will note that the catalogue is once again in full colour and as supplies obviously must be limited to a certain extent, with such an expensive production, we must ask you to use some discretion in distributing it. Bulk supplies will be available shortly and will be despatched to you in the normal way. No application is necessary.

The Tiger Cub folder is not likely to be available in any quantity as this model will be incorporated in later editions of the main catalogue.

Yours faithfully,
for: TRIUMPH ENGINEERING COMPANY LIMITED,

(I.G. Davies),
Publicity Manager.

Highest placed Triumph in th e 1954 Clubman's Senior was this Tiger 100 which Tom Owens rode to 4th position.

Triumph's crack rider Jim Alves took a class award with trials-modified single in the 1954 Scottish Six Day Trial.

A competitor rushes this T110 through a bend during an event in continental Europe.

Quite different personas for the 1956 season's little singles imparted by the adoption of 16in wheels for the Cub; Motor Cycling *conducted what they claimed was the first post-war test of a single-cylinder Triumph with one. They liked the 'substantial appearance' and softer ride imparted by the 3.25-section tyres and 'handling the machine at touring speeds in the region of 50mph on patches of neglected road surface produced no marked difficulty' sounds like just the bike for the UK's current unkempt, potholed highways! The little four-stroke was quite happy to buzz up to 6,000rpm, at which point the manufacturer claimed an output of 10hp and* Motor Cycling*'s man in the saddle was doing 67mph – with nearly 70 possible downhill. A standing-start quarter-mile consumed 20 seconds, and if you stuck rigorously to 30mph the tiny feline would reward you with nearly 140mpg. Push that up to 50, however, and its economy was not that much better than the figure they'd coaxed from a carefully-driven T110 a few months earlier.*

"One day, when we're…." dream Steve and Carol as they gaze upon what had arisen from the ruins of Coventry's blitz-damaged Broadgate a good while before Triumph's 1956 brochure was published. Sixty years on and the buildings are virtually unchanged but the one on the left is a Travelodge whilst Primark occupies the ground floor retail space of the glass-fronted edifice. The statue of Lady Godiva atop her trusty steed, however, has been repositioned on more than one occasion since its erection in 1949.

TWO HIGH PERFORMANCE O.H.V. LIGHTWEIGHTS

The Triumph " Terrier " and " Tiger Cub " have firmly established themselves as the performance leaders in their respective classes. Embodying all the best features of a big motorcycle—four stroke O.H.V. engine, dry sump lubrication, four-speed gearbox, etc., these sparkling lightweights are easy and safe to ride and are really economical. The " Tiger Cub " offered now to a " de-luxe " specification will further enhance its popularity in the lightweight field.

T15 and T20 GENERAL SPECIFICATION

ENGINES. T15 150 c.c. : T20 200 c.c. : Advanced O.H.V. design with die-cast alloy cylinder head, inclined large diameter valves and totally enclosed and lubricated valve gear. " H " section connecting rod with heavy duty plain big end. Dry sump lubrication with double plunger type oil pump. Highly polished timing cover. Chromium-plated exhaust pipe with efficient barrel type silencer. Air cleaner.

FOUR-SPEED GEARBOX. Robust design built in unit with the engine in a polished streamlined casing. Positive foot-operated gear-change. Multiplate clutch with Neolangite linings and rubber pad type shock absorber. Polished aluminium case for primary chain.

TRIUMPH SPEED TWIN

Patent Nos. 475860, 474963, 482024

5T and 6T GENERAL SPECIFICATION

ENGINES. 5T 500 c.c. : 6T 650 c.c. : Vertical twin cylinder O.H.V. with two gear-driven camshafts. Central flywheel. "H" section RR56 alloy connecting rods with patented plain big ends. Dry sump lubrication, high capacity plunger type pump, pressure-fed big ends and valve gear. Oil pressure indicator. Patent air cleaner. Efficient silencers.

FOUR-SPEED GEARBOX. Positive stop footchange. Large diameter multi-plate clutch with Neolangite linings, rubber pad type shock absorber.

FUEL TANKS. All-steel welded tanks with quick-release caps and accessible filters.

FRAME. Brazed cradle type frame with swinging arm rear suspension with adjustable hydraulic damping.

FORKS. Triumph telescopic forks, hydraulic damping.

BRAKES. Large diameter cast iron drums. Finger adjustment.

WHEELS. Triumph design, with plated spokes and rims.

ELECTRICAL EQUIPMENT. Triumph pioneered A.C. Lighting-Ignition system with emergency start circuit. Wide angle rear/stop light. Powerful Lucas 7-in. built-in headlamp with combined reflector/front lens assembly, "pre-focus" bulb and adjustable rim.

TOOLBOX. Combined with the oil tank, air cleaner and battery container in a "one piece" unit.

MUDGUARDS. Efficient "D" shaped guards with central rib.

NACELLE (Patented). Neat streamline shell integral with top of forks, enclosing headlamp, rubber-mounted instruments and switch-gear.

SPEEDOMETER. Smiths 120 m.p.h. (or 180 km.p.h.) chronometric type with trip recorder.

OTHER DETAILS. Finish : 5T amaranth red ; 6T polychromatic "crystal grey" ; quick-action adjustable twist grip ; rubber knee grips ; tank parcel grid.

Anxious to show the international appeal of their wares Triumph took us around the world this year, and the artwork of the Speed Twin was given a photographic backdrop of Lake Mary, near Flagstaff in Arizona, along with a mention that this model was in use by 80 police forces worldwide. The Motor Cycle *had to be content with London and its environs, however, when they tested a similar model in 1955, summing it up as 'a gentlemanly machine to ride – comfortable, tractable and quiet'. No heroics were attempted and they found that 'on bends and corners of every type it could be heeled over gracefully and with the minimum of effort' but elsewhere mentioned that bumpy surfaces taken at high speed induced 'slight tendency' for the front end of the machine to waver and the forks to bottom when braking heavily. Third gear was good for over 75mph and top 85, with very nearly 80mpg possible if you stuck to 50mph.*

RETAIL PRICES FOR GREAT BRITAIN & NORTHERN IRELAND

MOTORCYCLES

ALL retail sales are subject to the Guarantee published in the Company's current catalogue and the prices quoted on this list are for delivery Free of Charge at Dealer's premises. The prices quoted here operate on and after 9th January, 1956, and all previous lists are cancelled. The Company reserves the right to revise prices without prior notice and Purchase Tax also is subject to revision.

9th JANUARY, 1956

	MODEL	BASIC RETAIL	PURCHASE TAX	TOTAL RETAIL
T15	TERRIER 150 c.c. O.H.V.	£105 0 0	£25 4 0	£130 4 0
T20	TIGER CUB 200 c.c. O.H.V.	£113 0 0	£27 2 5	£140 2 5
5T	SPEED TWIN 500 c.c. O.H.V. Twin	£190 0 0	£45 12 0	£235 12 0
6T	THUNDERBIRD 650 c.c. O.H.V. Twin	£197 10 0	£47 8 0	£244 18 0
T100	TIGER 100 500 c.c. O.H.V. Twin	£206 0 0	£49 8 10	£255 8 10
T110	TIGER 110 650 c.c. O.H.V. Twin	£214 0 0	£51 7 3	£265 7 3
TR5	TROPHY 500 c.c. O.H.V. Twin	£208 0 0	£49 18 5	£257 18 5
TR6	TROPHY 650 c.c. O.H.V. Twin	£216 0 0	£51 16 10	£267 16 10

EXTRAS
(when ordered with the machine)

Q.D. REAR WHEEL (Twins only)	£3 0 0	14 5	£3 14 5
TWIN CARBURETTERS (T100 only)	£5 0 0	£1 4 0	£6 4 0
TWINSEAT (T15)	£2 10 0	12 0	£3 2 0
PROP STAND	15 6	3 9	19 3
PILLION FOOTRESTS	16 0	3 11	19 11

The men from Meriden's world tour next alighted at Copenhagen and its Little Mermaid. This, 1956, was the last year for the Tigers' Shell Blue finish, and this year the wheels had plain chromium rims rather than blue centres as they had in '54 and '55. Mudguards, however, still had a central black stripe edged with thin white lines. Triumph's iron-engined sports twins had always been inclined to run rather hot, and to address this T110s and TR6s now sported an aluminium head (known as the Delta on account of its splayed exhaust ports: as well as improved cooling its design also incorporated oil ways so that external drainage pipes were done away with).

TRIUMPH
TIGER 110

Patent Nos. 475860, 474963, 482024

The Little Mermaid watching over the shipping in busy Copenhagen Harbour, Denmark.

Off to Australia for the Thunderbird, and although this was ten years-or-so before we were treated to the televised adventures of Skippy, however unlikely, I'd like to think one of these 'roos is he. Anyhow, the 1956 version was very attractively finished in Polychromatic Crystal Grey and retained its SU carburettor, whilst by now the remainder of Triumph's twins had gone over from the long-standing separate float chamber Amals to the same manufacturer's newly-introduced Monobloc.

TRIUMPH
TIGER 100

Patent Nos. 475860, 474963, 482024

IN the Speed Twin and Thunderbird models, the discriminating rider has the choice of two motorcycles with world-wide reputations for zestful performance and easy handling. The Speed Twin, used by eighty police forces, is fast, smooth, and tractable while the 650 c.c. engine of the Thunderbird provides that extra power demanded by some riders and is of course ideal for heavy sidecar work.

TRIUMPH
Thunderbird

Patent Nos. 475860, 474963, 482024

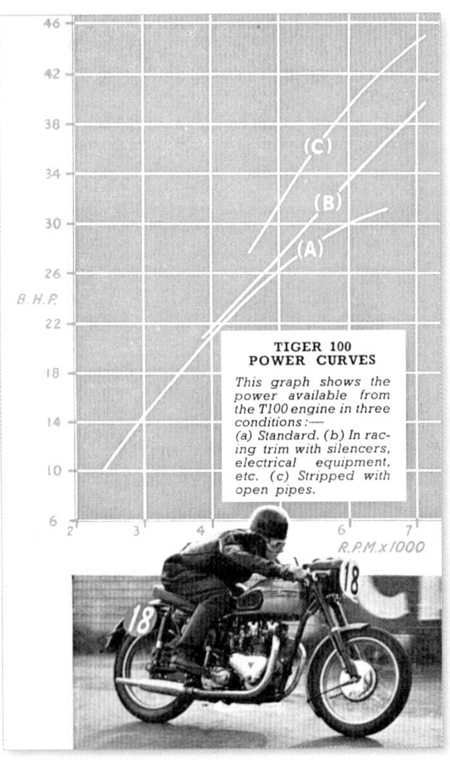

The 1956 brochure offered twin carbs as an option for the T100 along with the simple line: 'racing conversion parts available'; judging by this graph they must have been pretty comprehensive. With a claimed power output of 40-odd-horsepower, even in B trim, the T100 should have made a formidable production racer but in the very last (1956) Clubmans TT the best of them was seventh, with a couple more trailing in 19th and 20th – and nothing else other than all-but-omnipotent Gold Stars in the top 20. The best of the Triumphs was admittedly two years old but it had been completely overhauled at the factory and brought up to date with a special cylinder head and race tuning. Years later its owner remembered seeing 120mph on the Sulby straight with full road equipment (obligatory that year) but also that 'the handling was terrible'. Incidentally, the winner Bernard Codd (BSA DBD34) averaged 86.33mph, whilst John Thurlstone's T100 did 80.65mph.

Twin petrol tanks' welded central seam was now covered by a chrome strip and tank-top grid altered to four bars in order to blend stylistically.

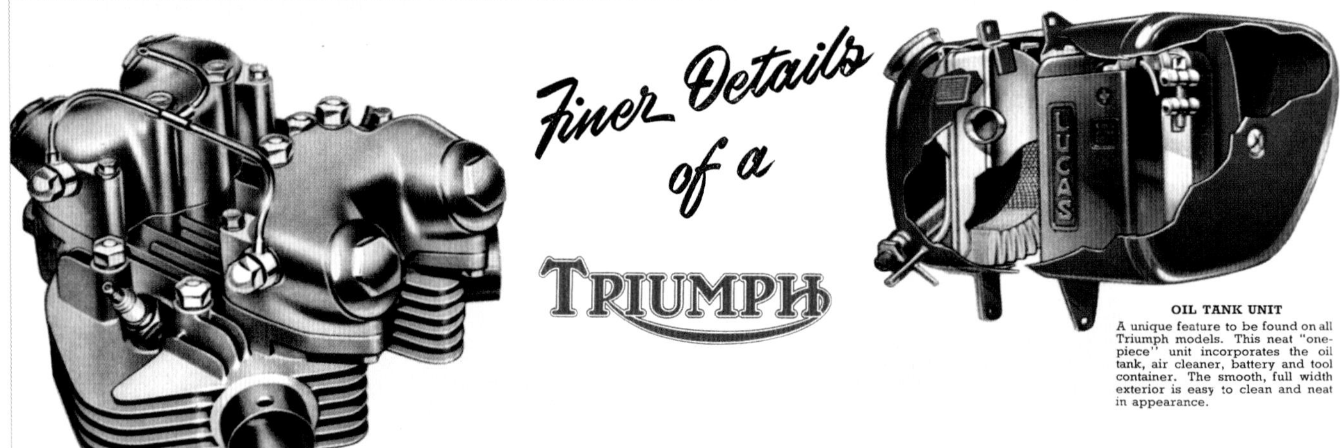

OIL TANK UNIT
A unique feature to be found on all Triumph models. This neat "one-piece" unit incorporates the oil tank, air cleaner, battery and tool container. The smooth, full width exterior is easy to clean and neat in appearance.

LIGHT ALLOY CYLINDER HEAD
This entirely new design has many points of technical interest. Die cast in light alloy, it effects a considerable saving in weight. It incorporates cast-in passages to promote cooling air flow between the cylinder heads and by eliminating external pipes the risk of oil leaks is avoided. The heads are of the usual Triumph hemispherical type with large diameter valves and totally enclosed and positively lubricated valve gear. This head is fitted to the T110 and TR6 models.

PETROL TANK
Of ample capacity to enable long distances to be covered between refills, the handsome Triumph petrol tank is of all-welded design with a quick-release plated filler cap, useful parcel grid and large rubber knee grips. Chromium name bands and a central chromium bead add distinction. TR5 and TR6, 3 gallon capacity, all other twins 4 gallon.

OTHER VALUABLE TRIUMPH FEATURES

- Efficient suspension front and rear on all models.
- Twin cylinder engine big-end bearings are fitted with easily replaceable thin wall bearing shells.
- The Triumph Nacelle (Patent No. 647670) enclosing headlamp unit. Neat streamlined shell integral with top of forks. All switchgear and instruments rubber mounted.
- Powerful brakes incorporating non-distorting cast iron drums of ample diameter and finest quality linings.
- Dry sump lubrication on all engines, lightweights and twins. Efficient double plunger type oil pump ensures adequate lubrication of all moving parts.
- 4 speed Gearboxes on all models, with short action foot-change and smooth multiplate clutch with Neolangite linings. The clutch also includes a most efficient rubber pad type shock absorber.
- A.C. Lighting-Ignition system on 5T, 6T and lightweights. This system, pioneered by Triumph, is esssentially simple and completely reliable. A single crankshaft mounted alternator replaces the separate dynamo and magneto with their attendant drives and provides current for both ignition and lighting. In the unlikely event of battery failure, an emergency circuit enables the engine to be started in the usual way.
- The Triumph Quickly Detachable Rear Wheel (optional extra on all twins) enables the wheel to be extracted instantly, leaving the rear brake and chain untouched.

EXTRAS

PROP STAND. Retained by spring, out as a prop or folded back. For all models.

PILLION FOOTRESTS. For all models. Folding type, rubber covered.

TWIN CARBURETTERS. For Tiger 100 only.

QUICKLY DETACHABLE REAR WHEEL. For 5T, 6T, T100, T110, TR5, TR6.

TWINSEAT for "Terrier".

Largely in response to ambitious US West Coast distributor Bill Johnson of Pasadena, who was anxious to be able to fulfil demand for ever-more-powerful off-road machinery due to the popularity of desert racing, the Trophy was now also available as a 650 powered by the latest T110 motor with Delta head. From this view the fuel tank looked the same as those fitted to other twins in the range but was narrower and of three-gallon capacity rather than their four. Also note that the artist depicted this 650 version correctly with 'aluminium' barrels as although they were iron (as the T110's) those employed in Trophy motors were painted silver; were it a TR5 with aluminium T100-type motor the fins would have been more numerous and closer set. A revolution counter, driven from the exhaust camshaft via a modified timing cover, was an optional extra from now on.

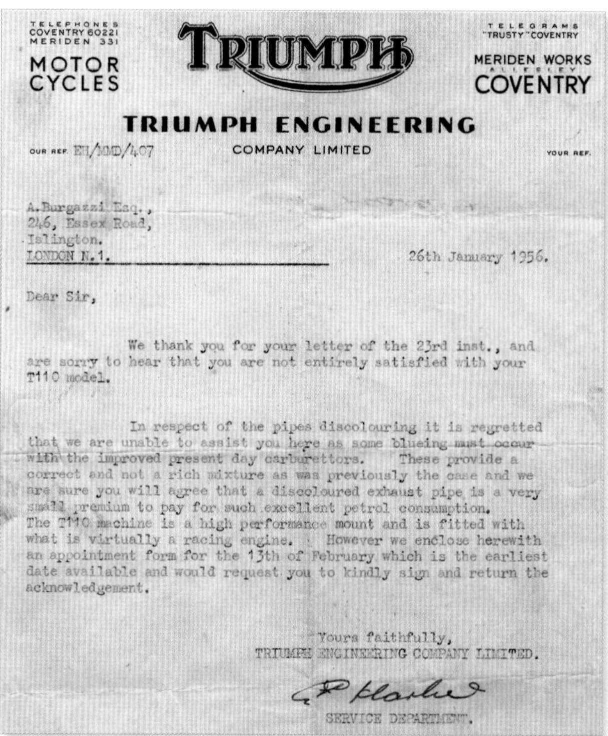

TELEPHONES COVENTRY 60221 MERIDEN 331 — MOTOR CYCLES

TRIUMPH

TELEGRAMS "TRUSTY" COVENTRY — MERIDEN WORKS ALLESLEY COVENTRY

TRIUMPH ENGINEERING COMPANY LIMITED

OUR REF. EH/MMD/407 — YOUR REF.

A. Burgazzi Esq.,
246, Essex Road,
Islington.
LONDON N.1.

26th January 1956.

Dear Sir,

We thank you for your letter of the 23rd inst., and are sorry to hear that you are not entirely satisfied with your T110 model.

In respect of the pipes discolouring it is regretted that we are unable to assist you here as some blueing must occur with the improved present day carburettors. These provide a correct and not a rich mixture as was previously the case and we are sure you will agree that a discoloured exhaust pipe is a very small premium to pay for such excellent petrol consumption.
The T110 machine is a high performance mount and is fitted with what is virtually a racing engine. However we enclose herewith an appointment form for the 13th of February which is the earliest date available and would request you to kindly sign and return the acknowledgement.

Yours faithfully,
TRIUMPH ENGINEERING COMPANY LIMITED.

SERVICE DEPARTMENT.

MODEL	Terrier (T15)	Tiger Cub (T20)	Speed Twin (5T)	Thunder-bird (6T)	Tiger 100 (T100)	Tiger 110 (T110)	Trophy (TR5)	Trophy (TR6)
Engine : Type	O.H.V.	O.H.V.	O.H.V.	O.H.V.	O.H.V.	O.H.V.	O.H.V.	O.H.V.
No. of Cylinders	1	1	2	2	2	2	2	2
Bore/Stroke, mm.	57 × 58.5	63 × 64	63 × 80	71 × 82	63 × 80	71 × 82	63 × 80	71 × 82
,, ,, ins.	2.24 × 2.3	2.48 × 2.52	2.48 × 3.15	2.79 × 3.23	2.48 × 3.15	2.79 × 3.23	2.48 × 3.15	2.79 × 3.23
Cyl. capacity, c.c.m. ...	149	199	498	649	498	649	498	649
,, ,, cu. ins. ...	9	12	30.5	40	30.5	40	30.5	40
Compression Ratio	7 : 1	7 : 1	7 : 1	7 : 1	8 : 1	8.5 : 1	8 : 1	8.5 : 1
B.H.P. & R.P.M.	8 at 6000	10 at 6000	27 at 6300	34 at 6300	32 at 6500	42 at 6500	33 at 6500	42 at 6500
			Solo S/C	Solo S/C	Solo S/C	Solo S/C		
Engine sprocket : teeth ...	19	18	22 19	24 21	22 19	24 21	21	24
Clutch ,, ,, ...	48	36	18 18	18 18	18 18	18 18	18	18
Gearbox ,, ,, ...	17	17	43 43	43 43	43 43	43 43	43	43
Rear wheel ,, ,, ...	48	54	46 46	46 46	46 46	46 46	46	46
R.P.M., 10 m.p.h. : Top Gear	1000	940	650 755	594 680	650 755	594 680	680	594
Gear Ratios :								
Top	7.1	6.35	5.00 5.80	4.57 5.24	5.00 5.80	4.57 5.24	5.24	4.57
Third	9.4	8.35	5.95 6.90	5.45 6.24	5.95 6.90	5.45 6.24	6.24	5.45
Second	14.8	13.08	8.45 9.80	7.75 8.85	8.45 9.80	7.75 8.85	8.85	7.75
First	21.4	18.95	12.20 14.15	11.20 12.80	12.20 14.15	11.20 12.80	12.80	11.20
Carburetter	Amal 332/2	Amal 332/3	Amal 376/25	S U. 590	Amal 376/35	Amal 376/40	Amal 376/35	Amal 376/40
Front chain size	⅜ × ¼	½ × .205	½ × .305	½ × .305	½ × .305	½ × .305	½ × .305	½ × .305
Rear chain size	½ × .205	½ × .205	⅝ × ⅜	⅝ × ⅜	⅝ × ⅜	⅝ × ⅜	⅝ × ⅜	⅝ × ⅜
Tyres—Dunlop :								
Front, ins.	2.75 × 19	3.25 × 16	3.25 × 19	3.25 × 19	3.25 × 19	3.25 × 19	3.00 × 20	3.00 × 20
Rear, ins.	2.75 × 19	3.25 × 16	3.50 × 19	3.50 × 19	3.50 × 19	3.50 × 19	4.00 × 18	4.00 × 18
Brake dia. : ins. (cm.) ...	5½ (13.97)	5½ (13.97)	7 (17.78)	7 (17.78)	8 (20.32) Front 7 (17.78) Rear		7 (17.78)	7 (17.78)
Finish	Red	Blue/Blk.	Red	Poly/Grey	Blue/Blk.	Blue/Blk.	Blue/Blk.	Blue/Blk.
Seat height, ins. (cm.) ...	28½ (71.8)	29½ (74.5)	30½ (77.5)	30½ (77.5)	30½ (77.5)	30½ (77.5)	30½ (77.5)	30½ (77.5)
Wheelbase, ins. (cm.) ...	49 (124.5)	49 (124.5)	55¾ (141.6)	55¾ (141.6)	55¾ (141.6)	55¾ (141.6)	55¾ (141.6)	55¾ (141.6)
Length, ins. (cm.)	77 (195.5)	77 (195.5)	85½ (217)	85½ (217)	85½ (217)	85½ (217)	85½ (217)	85½ (217)
Width, ins. (cm.)	25 (63.5)	25 (63.5)	28½ (72)	28½ (72)	28½ (72)	28½ (72)	28½ (72)	28½ (72)
Clearance, ins. (cm.) ...	5 (12.7)	4 (10.2)	5 (12.7)	5 (12.7)	5 (12.7)	5 (12.7)	5 (12.7)	5 (12.7)
Weight, lbs. (kilos)	185 (84)	205 (94.1)	380 (173)	385 (175)	375 (170)	395 (179)	365 (166)	370 (168)
Petrol, galls. (litres)	2⅝ (11.9)	3 (13.5)	4 (18)	4 (18)	4 (18)	4 (18)	3 (13.5)	3 (13.5)
Oil, pints (litres)	2¾ (1.55)	2¾ (1.55)	6 (3.4)	6 (3.4)	6 (3.4)	6 (3.4)	6 (3.4)	6 (3.4)

Triumph's mid-1950s Tigers were exceptionally good looking machines from any angle.

What else to focus on for the 1957 brochure other than the new-style tank badge – a feature that placed Triumph firmly in the motorcycle forefront of the burgeoning rock and roll age.

A splayed-port twin-carb head was a new option for the Tiger 100, whilst Speed Twins, Thunderbirds and the 500 Trophy now had a full-width front hub with 7in brake. The Cub had not been forgotten and now boasted a swinging-arm frame.

With the updating of the Cub and introduction of a supplementary competition version, the T20C – which would later be known as the Trials Cub in the UK, and as the Mountain Cub in the US (from 1964) – the little 150 Terrier had been quietly dropped. Whether by accident or design the Cub still carried the old type of tank badging – most probably, I would guess, because the company simply had not got around to producing the necessary patterns for a more petite version of that employed on the firm's twins.

TIGER CUB

The sleek o.h.v. four stroke Tiger Cub with its clean, efficient dry sump lubrication, provides a performance comparable with much larger, heavier and more costly machines. Every feature of the big machine is included in the Cub—o.h.v. engine, 4 speed unit gearbox, swinging-arm rear suspension with hydraulic damping, and large powerful brakes. It is safe and easy to ride and handles particularly well. Beautifully finished in silver grey and black with all chrome wheels.

T20C illustrated on the left, is a competition model based on that ridden so successfully in the 1956 I.S.D.T. by K. Heanes. It will appeal immediately as an efficient mount for the job, light in weight, with ample power and superb handling characteristics.

Now simply referred to as Red in the brochure, the Speed Twin was still turned out in Amaranth, giving Triumph's hardy perennial the aura of timelessness. It was not bereft of annual improvements and updating, however, and for 1957 it meant a full-width front hub, fuller rear chain guard and new petrol tank of the same four-gallon capacity with, of course, the latest tank badging – the chain guard, tank and badging being common to all twins except TR5s and TR6s, which had a smaller (three-gallon) tank. Fork ends and wheel location for all twins had been improved too, and their lower extremities now featured bolt-up caps, with a spindle to suit, rather than the previous arrangement where the spindle screwed into the base of the right leg with a clamped split hole on the left.

This is a standard Tiger 100 with 8:1 compression pistons that its makers rated at 32bhp, but for the speed merchant with a little more cash to spend the new splayed-port aluminium cylinder head fitted with twin Amal Monoblocs was an optional extra. Tiger 100 and 110 retained the impressive single-sided 8in front brake for one more season but were now finished in Silver Grey and Black like this one – with Ivory, Blue and Black an alternative if you were prepared to spend a bit extra.

A '57 Tiger 110 in its optional livery of Ivory, Blue and Black – the thinking behind the horizontal chrome strips to the front and rear of Triumph's tank now being apparent as they served to delineate the two-tone colour scheme when employed.

The '57 Thunderbird in Gold and Black was a very handsome machine but US customers could opt for Aztec Red and Black if they so wished – either way the mudguards had a broad black centre line edged in white or gold respectively.

For 1957 the 650 Trophy, illustrated, was given the single-sided 8in brake that up until then had been fitted to only Tiger 100s and 110s, whilst the 500 version made do with the 7in hitherto employed on both machines. Front wheel size was reduced from 20 to 19in but the rear was unchanged at 18in. Tank was of the same style as the other latest Triumphs but of a reduced width, which gave it a capacity of three gallons.

The Triumph "Trophy" model, available with a choice of 500 c.c. or 650 c.c. engines, is a sporting mount with a world-wide reputation. In events where speed and stamina of the highest order are vital—like the I.S.D.T. in Europe and the big Enduros in U.S.A.—the "Trophy" has an enviable record, its reliability being almost legendary! It is easily adaptable to most forms of motorcycle sport and has a specification which includes all those features demanded by the sporting rider, features which have been tested and proved in active competition. "Trials" specification available for TR5 if required.

TECHNICAL SPECIFICATION

MODEL	Tiger Cub (T20C)	Tiger Cub (T20)	Speed Twin (5T)		Thunder-bird (6T)		Tiger 100 (T100)		Tiger 110 (T110)		Trophy (TR5)	Trophy (TR6)
Engine Type	O.H.V.	O.H.V.	O.H.V.		O.H.V.		O.H.V.		O.H.V.		O.H.V.	O.H.V.
No. of Cylinders	1	1	2		2		2		2		2	2
Bore/Stroke, mm.	63 × 64	63 × 64	63 × 80		71 × 82		63 × 80		71 × 82		63 × 80	71 × 82
Bore/Stroke, ins.	2.48 × 2.52	2.48 × 2.52	2.48 × 3.15		2.79 × 3.23		2.48 × 3.15		2.79 × 3.23		2.48 × 3.15	2.79 × 3.23
Cyl. capacity, c.c.m.	199	199	498		649		498		649		498	649
Cyl. capacity, cu. ins.	12	12	30.5		40		30.5		40		30.5	40
Compression Ratio	7 : 1	7 : 1	7 : 1		7 : 1		8 : 1		8 : 1		8 : 1	8 : 1
B.H.P. & R.P.M.	10 at 6000	10 at 6000	27 at 6300		34 at 6300		32 at 6500		40 at 6500		33 at 6500	40 at 6500
			Solo	S/C	Solo	S/C	Solo	S/C	Solo	S/C		
Engine sprocket teeth	18	18	22	19	24	21	22	19	24	21	21	24
Clutch sprocket teeth	36	36	43	43	43	43	43	43	43	43	43	43
Gearbox sprocket teeth	10	17	18	18	18	18	18	18	18	18	18	18
Rear wheel	54	54	46	46	46	46	46	46	46	46	46	46
R.P.M., 10 m.p.h.:												
Top Gear	900	940	650	755	594	680	650	755	594	680	680	594
Gear Ratios:												
Top	6.7	6.35	5.00	5.80	4.57	5.24	5.00	5.80	4.57	5.24	5.24	4.57
Third	8.8	8.35	5.95	6.90	5.45	6.24	5.95	6.90	5.45	6.24	6.24	5.45
Second	13.8	13.08	8.45	9.80	7.75	8.85	8.45	9.80	7.75	8.85	8.85	7.75
First	20.0	18.95	12.20	14.15	11.20	12.80	12.20	14.15	11.20	12.80	12.80	11.20
Carburetter	Amal 332/3	Amal 332/3	Amal 376/25		S.U.603		Amal 376/35		Amal 376/40		Amal 376/35	Amal 376/40
Front Chain size	½ × .205	½ × .205	½ × .305		½ × .305		½ × .305		½ × .305		½ × .305	½ × .305
Rear Chain size	½ × .205	½ × .205	⅝ × ⅜		⅝ × ⅜		⅝ × ⅜		⅝ × ⅜		⅝ × ⅜	⅝ × ⅜
Tyres—Dunlop:												
Front, ins.	3.00 × 19	3.25 × 16	3.25 × 19		3.25 × 19		3.25 × 19		3.25 × 19		3.25 × 19	3.25 × 19
Rear, ins.	3.50 × 18	3.25 × 16	3.50 × 19		3.50 × 19		3.50 × 19		3.50 × 19		4.00 × 18	4.00 × 18
Brake dia., ins. (cm.)	5½ (13.97)	5½ (13.97)	7 (17.78)		7 (17.78)		8 (20.32 F.) 7 (17.78 R.)		8 (20.32 F.) 7 (17.78 R.)		7 (17.78)	8 (20.32 F.) 7 (17.78 R.)
Finish	Grey/Blk.	Grey/Blk.	Red		Gold/Blk.		Grey/Blk.		Grey/Blk.		Grey/Blk.	Grey/Blk.
Seat height, ins. (cm.)	30 (76.2)	28½ (72)	30½ (77.5)		30½ (77.5)		30½ (77.5)		30½ (77.5)		30½ (77.5)	30½ (77.5)
Wheelbase, ins. (cm.)	49 (124.5)	49 (124.5)	55¾ (141.6)		55¾ (141.6)		55¾ (141.6)		55¾ (141.6)		55¾ (141.6)	55¾ (141.6)
Length, ins. (cm.)	77 (195.5)	77 (195.5)	85½ (217)		85½ (217)		85½ (217)		85½ (217)		85½ (217)	85½ (217)
Width, ins. (cm.)	25 (63.5)	25 (63.5)	28½ (72)		28½ (72)		28½ (72)		28½ (72)		28½ (72)	28½ (72)
Clearance, ins. (cm.)	6 (15.24)	4½ (11.9)	5 (12.7)		5 (12.7)		5 (12.7)		5 (12.7)		5 (12.7)	5 (12.7)
Weight, lbs. (kilos)	205 (92)	215 (98)	395 (179)		395 (179)		385 (175)		390 (177)		375 (170)	380 (173)
Petrol, galls. (litres)	3 (13.5)	3 (13.5)	4 (18)		4 (18)		4 (18)		4 (18)		3 (13.5)	3 (13.5)
Oil, pints (litres)	2¾ (1.55)	2¾ (1.55)	5 (2.8)		5 (2.8)		5 (2.8)		5 (2.8)		5 (2.8)	5 (2.8)

This Catalogue published October, 1956

TRIUMPH ENGINEERING COMPANY LIMITED

MERIDEN WORKS · ALLESLEY · COVENTRY . ENGLAND

Telephone: Coventry 60221 *Telegrams: "Trusty, Coventry"*

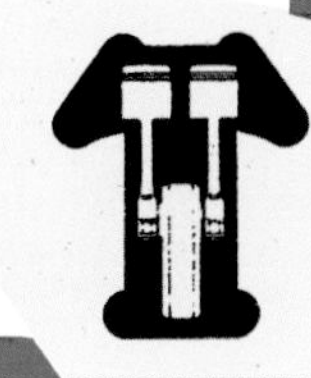

"Any Triumph is a passport to the endless pleasures of motorcycling", enthused the 1957 brochure. For the police, too, if their force was so equipped.

"Look, isn't that Lady Docker over there?" exclaims Alan, having spotted the lady getting out of a posh Daimler to ask the way, turning his back on the brand-new 1958-model Twenty One in the process. "I shouldn't think so," replies Lesley, "her husband doesn't own the company any more". She was quite right: Sir Bernard Docker had been removed from his chairmanship of BSA, which also owned Daimler and, since 1952, Triumph, during 1956 when the couple's extravagances hit the headlines once too often. Triumph's Twenty One was so named to celebrate Edward Turner's vertical twin's 21st birthday, but conveniently for the US market it was also its engine capacity in cubic inches.

MODEL TWENTY-ONE

ENGINE
Vertical twin cylinder o.h.v. 348 c.c. with two camshafts driven by gears. Pushrod operated overhead valves in an advanced design alloy cylinder head. High Duty iron cylinder block. Dry sump lubrication with plunger type pump. Steel connecting rods with plain big-ends. A.C. lighting-ignition system with crankshaft mounted alternator and emergency start circuit. Oil pressure indicator. Silent Duplex primary chain in polished aluminium oil-bath. Efficient air cleaner.

GEARBOX
Four speeds with positive foot operation and gear position indicator. Built in unit with engine. Heavy duty shafts and gears of hardened nickel and nickel-chrome steel. Multiplate clutch with Neolangite linings and rubber block shock absorber. Folding kickstarter.

FUEL TANKS
Large capacity tank with parcel grid. Oil tank under twinseat within rear enclosure. Quick release filler caps with integral dipstick on oil tank cap. Rubber knee grips.

FORKS
Telescopic pattern with hydraulic damping. Steering damper. Front wheel stand.

FRAME
Completely new design, heavy duty brazed cradle type frame with swinging arm rear suspension, hydraulically damped. "Easylift" centre stand. Provision for padlocking steering head against theft.

NACELLE (Patent No. 647670)
Integral with top of forks enclosing headlamp unit, 120 m.p.h. (180 Km.p.h.) speedometer, ammeter and switchgear. All instruments internally illuminated and rubber mounted.

BRAKES
Full width front hub heavily finned, incorporating powerful 7 inch brake. Same diameter rear brake. Cast-iron drums, finger adjustment front and rear.

WHEELS AND MUDGUARDS
Special Triumph design with plated rims and spokes. Front mudguard of generous proportions. Stylish rear enclosure.

LIGHTING EQUIPMENT
Powerful seven inch headlamp has a combined reflector/front lens assembly, "pre-focus" bulb and adjustable rim. Wide angle rear/stop light with integral reflex reflector.

TWINSEAT ASSEMBLY
Latex foam cushioned seat, covered in black "Vynide" completely waterproof. The seat is hinged and when lifted reveals the air cleaner, 12 a.h. battery, coil, rectifier, oil tank and filler (with integral dipstick) and tools in moulded compartments in rubber container. The seat release knob is removable as an anti-theft device. (See illustration below).

HANDLEBAR
Chrome plated bar with quick action twistgrip adjustable for friction. Integral dipswitch/horn button. Adjustable plated levers with built-in cable adjusters.

FINISH
Shell Blue Sheen with Black frame.

EXTRAS (21)
Pillion footrests. Prop Stand.

For its return to the 350cc market Triumph introduced the Twenty One in the Spring of '57 – unmistakably a Triumph Twin but with a difference. Its Edward Turner-designed motor (with aluminium head and iron barrels) was in unit with the gearbox, following the ground broken by the firm's little singles. It was also given a frame that drew heavily on that of the Cub, having a low top-tube that swept up to the headstock – this necessitating the fuel tank, with internal bracing bar, to act as a stressed member in order to impart some integrity to the whole. Rear enclosure was becoming fashionable and this was Meriden's version in pressed steel with complementarily styled front mudguard. Also, following the adoption of smaller wheels for the Cub, the Twenty One was endowed with a pair of 17s. The first 100-or-so Twenty Ones were finished in Silver Grey but thereafter they were turned out in Blue Sheen as per the brochure's specifications. Most, if not all, '57 machines were devoid of a tank-top luggage grid, and the Easylift main stand came later.

This is the TRIUMPH "TWENTY-ONE," a sleek new 350 twin—new from end to end. As modern as the day, yet designed with all that skill, beauty and exciting performance that is so traditionally Triumph — performance which combines turbine-like smoothness with quite exceptional mechanical silence. A truly modern motorcycle for modern motorcyclists.

★ SMOOTH ★ SILENT ★ CLEAN

By the time the 1958 brochure was printed Triumph had got around to depicting the T20 Cub with its own version of the marque's tank badge but the T20C retained the old type. It had, however, been rendered more 'competition' by the fitment of fork gaiters.

T20C (Illustrated on the left). Designed expressly for sporting riders, the T20C will perform efficiently as a competition mount, being light in weight with ample power and superb handling characteristics.

Owners who did not find Turner's slick-shift to their liking soon found a simple way to convert the mechanism to manual mode. It certainly wasn't to everyone's taste but today is an intriguing facet of late-1950s' Triumph ownership.

THE TRIUMPH "SLICKSHIFT" GEARCHANGE

All Triumph 500 c.c. and 650 c.c. twins are now fitted with automatic clutch operation. Movement of the gearchange pedal releases the clutch and enables gearchanging to be carried out with this one action only. The handlebar clutch lever is retained and over-rides the auto mechanism if used. Quicker, easier gearchanging results from this interesting new development.

For the 1958 Speed Twin and its stablemates there were fuller mudguards, with the rear now being a one-piece pressing rather than with applied valances as before, and for the front a single stay. There was also a pure piece of bling in the form of space-age faux finning embossed upon the chromium embellisher for the full-width front hub. Of far more interest, however, was the introduction of Triumph's slick-shift gearbox, an invention of Edward Turner's, which facilitated clutchless gear changes – if so desired. A good idea on the drawing board, perhaps, but in practice the system was unloved by the majority of riders. Of little importance but the side-saddle belle and her consort were snapped in Pakistan.

The '58 season brought an enlarged full-width front hub with 8in brake for 500 and 650 Tigers, whilst exhaust pipe diameter on all twins had been reduced from 1¾ to 1½in. Standard paintwork was Silver Grey and Black but Black and Ivory was an optional extra for both the T100 and T110. The Tiger 100 alone could be had with a twin-carb head, according to the brochure, but other optional extras and applicable to all twins were a steering lock, prop stand, pillion footrests and QD rear wheel.

Either of Triumph's Tigers still looked striking, and perhaps particularly so in the optional Ivory and Black finish, but the new full-width front stopper was somehow less characterful. No matter: a teenage Mike Hailwood partnered by Dan Shorey won the inaugural Thruxton 500-mile race (which had replaced the nine-hour event) after a long battle with Bob McIntyre and Derek Powell on an Enfield Super Meteor. What is more, although the sales brochure would have it otherwise, I think I'm right in telling you that there was also a twin-carb variant of the improved Delta cylinder head (there had been problems with cracking) – a foretaste of what was shortly to come.

The Thunderbird in Gold and Black still looked very good but in my eyes the more fulsome mudguards introduced for this season on all twins except the Trophies were rather less attractive. The slick-shift gearbox was easily recognisable by the oval alloy plate with two retaining screws, situated midway between kick-start and gear pedal on the gearbox end cover.

Full width hubs for the Trophy now – 7in for the 500 and 8in for the 650.

MODEL	Tiger Cub (T20C)	Tiger Cub (T20)	Twenty One (21)	Speed Twin (5T)	Thunder-bird (6T)	Tiger 100 (T100)	Tiger 110 (T110)	Trophy (TR5)	Trophy (TR6)
Engine Type	O.H.V.	O.H.V.	O.H.V.	O.H.V.	O.H.V.	O.H.V.	O.H.V.	O.H.V.	O.H.V.
No. of Cylinders	1	1	2	2	2	2	2	2	2
Bore/Stroke, mm.	63 × 64	63 × 64	58.25 × 65 5	63 × 80	71 × 82	63 × 80	71 × 82	63 × 80	71 × 82
Bore/Stroke, ins.	2.48 × 2.52	2.48 × 2.52	2.3 × 2.6	2.48 × 3.15	2.79 × 3.23	2.48 × 3.15	2.79 × 3.23	2.48 × 3.15	2.79 × 3.23
Capacity, c.c.m.	199	199	348	498	649	498	649	498	649
Capacity, cu. ins.	12	12	21.23	30.5	40	30.5	40	30.5	40
Compression Ratio	7 : 1	7 : 1	7.5 : 1	7 : 1	7 : 1	8 : 1	8 : 1	8 : 1	8 : 1
B.H.P. and R.P.M.	10 at 6000	10 at 6000	18.5 at 6500	27 at 6300	34 at 6300	32 at 6500	40 at 6500	33 at 6500	40 at 6500
				Solo S/C	Solo S/C	Solo S/C	Solo S/C		
Eng. sprocket teeth	19	19	26	22 19	24 21	22 19	24 21	21	24
Clutch sprocket teeth	48	48	58	43 43	43 43	43 43	43 43	43	43
Gearbox sprocket teeth	16	18	18	18 18	18 18	18 18	18 18	18	18
Rear wheel	46	46	43	46 46	46 46	46 46	46 46	46	46
R.P.M., 10 m.p.h. : Top Gear	965	940	760	650 755	594 680	650 755	594 680	680	594
Gear Ratios :									
Top	7.2	6.45	5.31	5.00 5.80	4.57 5.24	5.00 5.80	4.57 5.24	5.24	4.57
Third	9.4	8.38	6.30	5.95 6.90	5.45 6.24	5.95 6.90	5.45 6.24	6.24	5.45
Second	14.4	12.9	9.32	8.45 9.80	7.75 8.85	8.45 9.80	7.75 8.85	8.85	7.75
First	21.6	19.35	13.00	12.20 14.15	11.20 12.80	12.20 14.15	11.20 12.80	12.80	11.20
Carburetter	Amal 332/3	Amal 332/3	Amal 375/25	Amal 376/25	S.U. 603	Amal 376/35	Amal 376/40	Amal 376/35	Amal 376/40
Front Chain size	⅜ Duplex	⅜ Duplex	⅜ Duplex	½ × .305	½ × .305	½ × .305	½ × .305	½ × .305	½ × .305
Rear Chain size	½ × .205	½ × .205	⅝ × ⅜	⅝ × ⅜	⅝ × ⅜	⅝ × ⅜	⅝ × ⅜	⅝ × ⅜	⅝ × ⅜
Tyres—Dunlop :									
Front, ins.	3.00 × 19	3.25 × 16	3.25 × 17	3.25 × 19	3.25 × 19	3.25 × 19	3.25 × 19	3.25 × 19	3.25 × 19
Rear, ins.	3.50 × 18	3.25 × 16	3.25 × 17	3.50 × 19	3.50 × 19	3.50 × 19	3.50 × 19	4.00 × 18	4.00 × 18
Brake dia., ins. (cm.)	5½ (13.97)	5½ (13.97)	7 (17.78)	7 (17.78)	7 (17.78)	8 (20.32 F.) 7 (17.78 R.)	8 (20.32 F.) 7(17.78 R.)	7 (17.78)	8 (20.32 F.) 7 (17.78 R.)
Finish	Grey/Blk.	Grey/Blk.	Blue/Blk.	Red	Gold/Blk.	Grey/Blk.	Grey/Blk.	Grey/Blk.	Grey/Blk.
Seat height ins. (cm.)	30 (76.2)	28½ (72)	28½ (72.4)	30½ (77.5)	30½ (77.5)	30½ (77.5)	30½ (77.5)	30½ (77.5)	30½ (77.5)
Wheelbase ins. (cm.)	49 (124.5)	49 (124.5)	51¾ (131.4)	55¾ (141.6)	55¾ (141.6)	55¾ (141.6)	55¾ (141.6)	55¾ (141.6)	55¾ (141.6)
Length, ins. (cm.)	77 (195.5)	77 (195.5)	80 (203)	85½ (217)	85½ (217)	85½ (217)	85½ (217)	85½ (217)	85½ (217)
Width, ins. (cm.)	25 (63.5)	25 (63.5)	26 (66)	28½ (72)	28½ (72)	28½ (72)	28½ (72)	28½ (72)	28½ (72)
Clearance, ins. (cm.)	6 (15.24)	4½ (11.9)	5 (12.7)	5 (12.7)	5 (12.7)	5 (12.7)	5 (12.7)	5 (12.7)	5 (12.7)
Weight, lbs. (kilos)	205 (92)	215 (98)	340 (154.4)	395 (179)	395 (179)	385 (175)	390 (177)	375 (170)	380 (173)
Petrol, galls. (litres)	2⅝ (11.9)	3 (13.5)	3½ (16)	4 (18)	4 (18)	4 (18)	4 (18)	3 (13.5)	3 (13.5)
Oil, pints (litres)	2¾ (1.55)	2¾ (1.55)	5 (2.8)	5 (2.8)	5 (2.8)	5 (2.8)	5 (2.8)	5 (2.8)	5 (2.8)

To many, and in particular many Americans, Triumph increasingly stood for performance – but upon picking up the 1959 brochure you might not have thought so, with a rosy-cheeked chap in a violet V-neck (and just beginning to carry a little too much avoirdupois) ambling across its cover on one of the new unit-construction Speed Twins.

With the drive side outer cover removed you can see the Cub's compact design and crankshaft-mounted alternator. Duplex primary chain was an innovation for this season.

TRIUMPH
TIGER CUB **200 cc**

In concentrating on the Cub's fashionable semi rear enclosure and trying to get the Zenith carb (now fitted in place of an Amal) correct, as well as enlarged finning for the motor, the artist went a little awry with its fuel tank and positioning of its correct new-type badge.

With its brilliant performance the Triumph "Tiger Cub" is the popular choice of the lightweight enthusiast today. He appreciates the lively four-stroke o.h.v. engine with its simple dry-sump lubrication system and four-speed gearbox built in unit. He likes, too, the clean design throughout, which is so typically Triumph. As for economy of running and value for money, the "Cub" is really on its own.

For the sporting rider the T20C (on right) follows the general specification of the standard model but includes certain items such as larger wheels and upswept pipe which make it easily adaptable for competitive riding.

To celebrate the Speed Twin's 21st birthday a new version was introduced to the public at the 1958 show; and it was no coincidence that it bore more than a passing resemblance to the Twenty One, or 3TA as it had become known. Now designated the 5TA the new Speed Twin was in effect a large-bore 3TA, complete with its poorly thought-out frame, having an oversquare (69x65.5mm) engine (the Twenty One/3TA's dimensions were 58.25x65.5mm), with alloy head and one-piece crankshaft, in unit with the four-speed gearbox – its connecting rods, however, were of alloy whereas the 3TA's were steel. But what a way to repay the faithful and long-serving Speed Twin by foisting this travesty of a frame design upon it for its 21st! Pillion footrests, prop stand and QD rear wheel were all optional extras on 3 and 5TAs.

Stateside distributors' publicity got a little carried away by referring to the smaller touring twins as Streamliners, and although they described the Speed Twin and Twenty One's colours differently the former was certainly not this garish.

A new one-piece forged crankshaft for all twins with flywheel bolted radially to the crank. Full-width hubs at the front – 7in for Twenty Ones, Speed Twins and Thunderbirds, with 8in for Tiger 100s and 110s.

Personally I find the '59 Thunderbird in Charcoal and Black a most handsome machine.

No doubt to appeal to the US market, where it was sold as the Trophybird, the Trophy was turned out with Aztec Red and Ivory fuel tank and mudguards, with the rest in Black. This would be the last season for the TR5 version, as the 63 x 80mm bore/stroke 500 twins fitted to this and the Tiger 100 would be discontinued – and the latter henceforth made with the short-stroke unit-construction motor. Although no longer catalogued there were something over 100 TR5s produced this year, including some 25 Daytona-spec versions with twin carbs, 3134 race cams and so on.

When the 1959 brochure went to press in October '58 the Tiger 110 was, disregarding the Trophy, Triumph's ultimate road-burner; but decisions had been taken that would, within a few months, demote it to an also-ran. With twin carbs an increasingly demanded option for both T110 and Trophy in the US the way forward was surely a super sporting model that offered them as standard; and in conjunction with West and East Coast distributors, Johnson Motors and Tricor, the go-ahead had been given for just such a machine in the late summer.

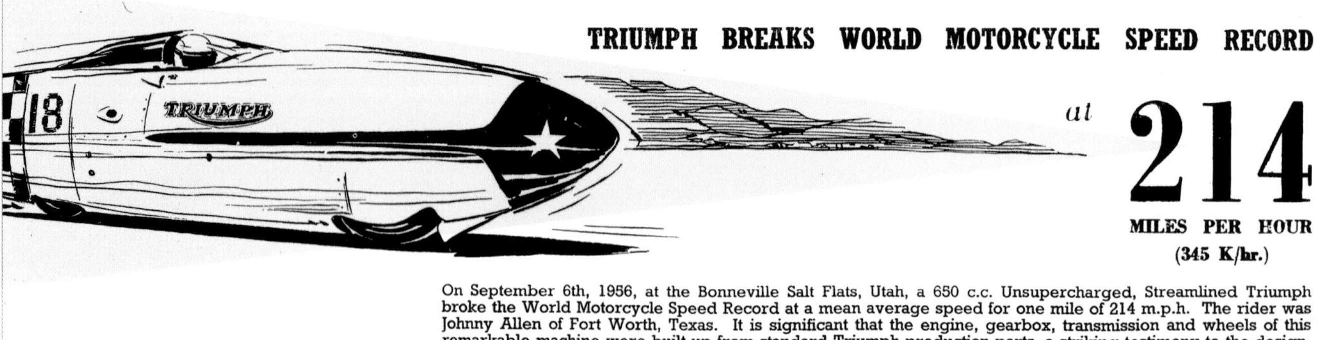

Harking back to the speed records taken at Utah's salt flats two years earlier, Triumph's new and fastest road burner would be called the Bonneville. Ready in time to take its place on Triumph's spacious show stand in November it was, however, accorded no dramatic special treatment other than the bike itself and a carefully-sectioned example of its engine for the mechanically-minded to ponder upon what went on within to give it 46hp. Arranged amongst the other exhibits, which included the Hailwood/Shorey Thruxton-winning T110, it appeared to be at risk of being eclipsed by the Speed Twin's limelight-hogging 21st birthday celebrations.

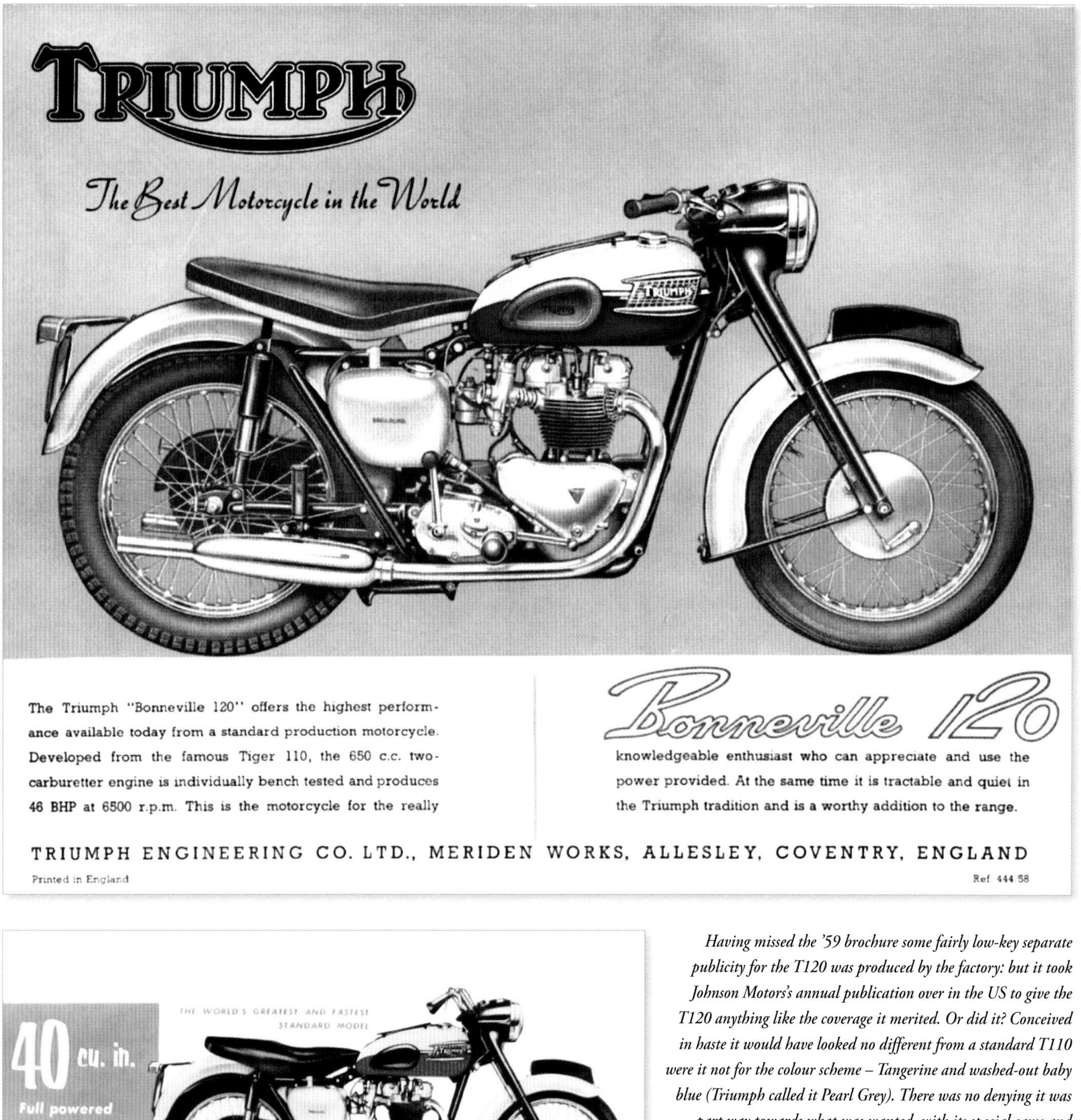

TRIUMPH
The Best Motorcycle in the World
The Triumph "Bonneville 120" offers the highest performance available today from a standard production motorcycle. Developed from the famous Tiger 110, the 650 c.c. two-carburetter engine is individually bench tested and produces 46 BHP at 6500 r.p.m. This is the motorcycle for the really
Bonneville 120
knowledgeable enthusiast who can appreciate and use the power provided. At the same time it is tractable and quiet in the Triumph tradition and is a worthy addition to the range.
TRIUMPH ENGINEERING CO. LTD., MERIDEN WORKS, ALLESLEY, COVENTRY, ENGLAND
Printed in England
Ref. 444/58

THE WORLD'S GREATEST AND FASTEST STANDARD MODEL
40 cu. in.
Full powered High performance range
NEW
BONNEVILLE
T120
SUPER SPORTS
Lightning-fast, supremely powerful, unexcelled in performance

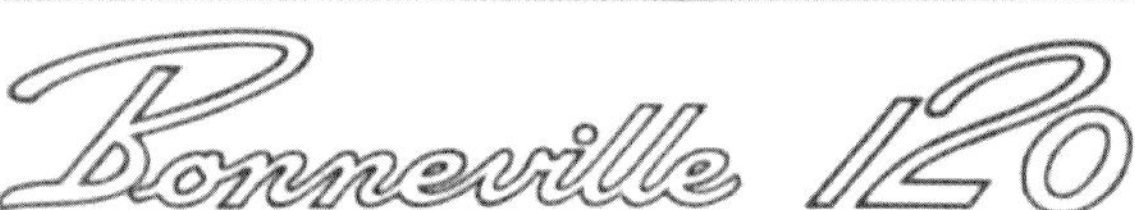

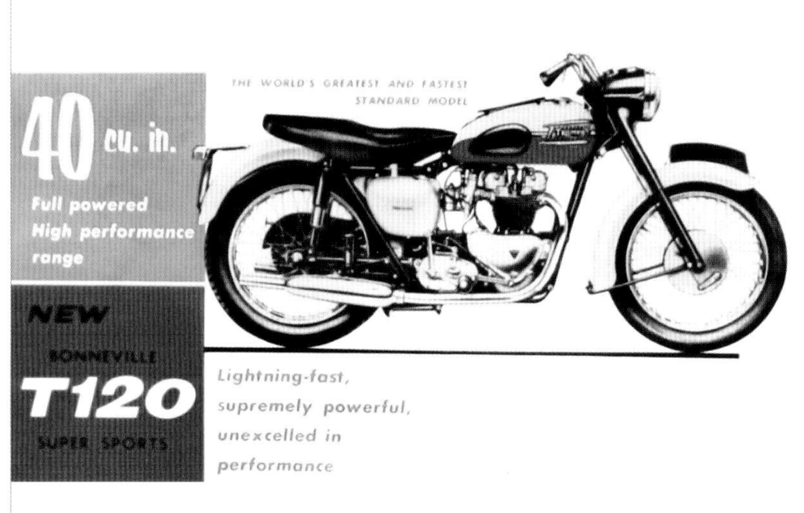

Having missed the '59 brochure some fairly low-key separate publicity for the T120 was produced by the factory: but it took Johnson Motors's annual publication over in the US to give the T120 anything like the coverage it merited. Or did it? Conceived in haste it would have looked no different from a standard T110 were it not for the colour scheme – Tangerine and washed-out baby blue (Triumph called it Pearl Grey). There was no denying it was part way towards what was wanted, with its special cams and cut-down Amal Monoblocs served by a GP remote float chamber, but horsepower wasn't the whole story – it had to look like a racer too; and as for the colour scheme, that could have killed it stone dead. As it was, many Stateside customers preferred to leave their dealership aboard a Trophy with twin carbs, leaving the 'tangerine dreams' where they were on the showroom floor. Late in the season the factory got the message and Tangerine became Royal Blue, which harmonised well with Pearl Grey, but mindful of the hard-to-shift backlog across the Atlantic they were only released onto the UK and general export market for the meanwhile.

MODEL	Tiger Cub (T20)	Tiger Cub (T20C)	Twenty-One (3TA)	Speed Twin (5TA)	Tiger 100 (T100)	Thunder-bird (6T)	Tiger 110 (T110)	Trophy (TR6)
Engine Type	O.H.V.	O.H.V.	O.H.V.	O.H.V.	O.H.V.	O.H.V.	O.H.V.	O.H.V.
No. of Cylinders	1	1	2	2	2	2	2	2
Bore/Stroke, mm.	63 × 64	63 × 64	58.25 × 65.5	69 × 65.5	63 × 80	71 × 82	71 × 82	71 × 82
Bore/Stroke, ins.	2.48 × 2.52	2.48 × 2.52	2.3 × 2.6	2.72 × 2.6	2.48 × 3.15	2.79 × 3.23	2.79 × 3.23	2.79 × 3.23
Capacity, c.c.m.	199	199	348	490	498	649	649	649
Capacity, cu. ins.	12	12	21.23	29.8	30.5	40	40	40
Compression Ratio	7 : 1	7 : 1	7.5 : 1	7 :1	8 : 1	7 : 1	8 : 1	8 : 1
B.H.P. and R.P.M.	10 at 6000	10 at 6000	18.5 at 6500	27 at 6500	32 at 6500 Solo S/C	34 at 6300 Solo S/C	40 at 6500 Solo S/C	40 at 6500
Eng. sprocket teeth	19	19	26	26	22 19	24 21	24 21	24
Clutch sprocket teeth	48	48	58	58	43 43	43 43	43 43	43
Gearbox sprocket teeth	18	16	18	20	18 18	18 18	18 18	18
Rear wheel	46	46	43	43	46 46	46 46	46 46	46
R.P.M., 10 m.p.h.: Top Gear	940	965	760	670	650 755	594 680	594 680	594
Gear Ratios:								
Top	6.45	7.2	5.31	4.80	5.00 5.80	4.57 5.24	4.57 5.24	4.57
Third	8.38	9.4	6.30	5.62	5.95 6.90	5.45 6.24	5.45 6.24	5.45
Second	12.9	14.4	9.32	8.35	8.45 9.80	7.75 8.85	7.75 8.85	7.75
First	19.35	21.6	13.00	11.56	12.20 14.15	11.20 12.80	11.20 12.80	11.20
Carburetter	Zenith 17MX	Zenith 17MX	Amal 375/25	Amal 375/3	Amal 376/35	Amal 376/210	Amal 376/40	Amal 376/40
Front Chain size	⅜ Duplex	⅜ Duplex	⅜ Duplex	⅜ Duplex	½ × .305	½ × .305	½ × .305	½ × .305
Rear Chain size	½ × .205	½ × .205	⅝ × ⅜	⅝ × ⅜	⅝ × ⅜	⅝ × ⅜	⅝ × ⅜	⅝ × ⅜
Tyres—Dunlop:								
Front, ins.	3.25 × 16	3.00 × 19	3.25 × 17	3.25 × 17	3.25 × 19	3.25 × 19	3.25 × 19	3.25 × 19
Rear, ins.	3.25 × 16	3.50 × 18	3.25 × 17	3.50 × 17	3.50 × 19	3.50 × 19	3.50 × 19	4.00 × 18
Brake dia., ins. (cm.)	5½ (13.97)	5½ (13.97)	7 (17.78)	7 (17.78)	8 (20.32 F.) 7 (17.78 R.)	7 (17.78)	8 (20.32 F.) 7 (17.78 R.)	8 (20.32 F.) 7 (17.78 R.)
Finish	Grey/Blk.	Grey/Blk.	Blue/Blk.	Amaranth Red	Grey/Blk. *	Charcoal/ Blk.	Grey/Blk. *	Aztec Red/ Ivory
Seat height ins. (cm.)	28½ (72)	30 (76.2)	28½ (72.4)	28½ (72.4)	30½ (77.5)	30½ (77.5)	30½ (77.5)	30½ (77.5)
Wheelbase ins. (cm.)	49 (124.5)	49 (124.5)	51¾ (131.4)	51¾ (131.4)	55¾ (141.6)	55¾ (141.6)	55¾ (141.6)	55¾ (141.6)
Length, ins. (cm.)	77 (195.5)	77 (195.5)	80 (203)	80 (203)	85½ (217)	85½ (217)	85½ (217)	85½ (217)
Width, ins. (cm.)	25 (63.5)	25 (63.5)	26 (66)	26 (66)	28½ (72)	28½ (72)	28½ (72)	28½ (72)
Clearance, ins. (cm.)	4½ (11.9)	6 (15.24)	5(12.7)	5 (12.7)	5 (12.7)	5 (12.7)	5 (12.7)	5 (12.7)
Weight, lbs. (kilos)	215 (98)	205 (92)	345 (156.3)	350 (159)	385 (175)	395 (179)	390 (177)	380 (173)
Petrol, galls. (litres)	3 (13.5)	2⅝ (11.9)	3½ (16)	3½ (16)	4 (18)	4 (18)	4 (18)	3 (13.5)
Oil pints (litres)	2¾ (1.55)	2¾ (1.55)	5 (2.8)	5 (2.8)	5 (2.8)	5 (2.8)	5 (2.8)	5 (2.8)

* Two tone Ivory/ Black Optional extra.

CUBS SWEEP THE "SCOTTISH"

The most arduous event in the British trials calendar is the famous Scottish Six Days' Trial, a thousand miles of rocky mountainous tracks in the Highlands. Held first in 1909—and won by a Triumph—the 1959 event marked the Golden Jubilee—and it was again won by a Triumph, a Tiger Cub. Tiger Cubs in fact finished first, fourth and seventh, winning the Premier Award (Best Solo), the Manufacturers' Team Award and the 200 c.c. class—a clean sweep. The winning rider was Roy Peplow and his team mates were Ray Sayer and Arthur Ratcliffe. The latter is here seen negotiating the notorious Loch Eild path while the ultimate winner, Peplow, on the right, watches him intently.

Photo coverage of an inspiring event sadly made an uninspiring cover for 1960's brochure but within there was a multitude of changes – some for the worse and some for the better. Chapmans of Norwich were still selling Triumphs from their Duke Street premises in the 1970s.

TIGER CUB T20S 200cc

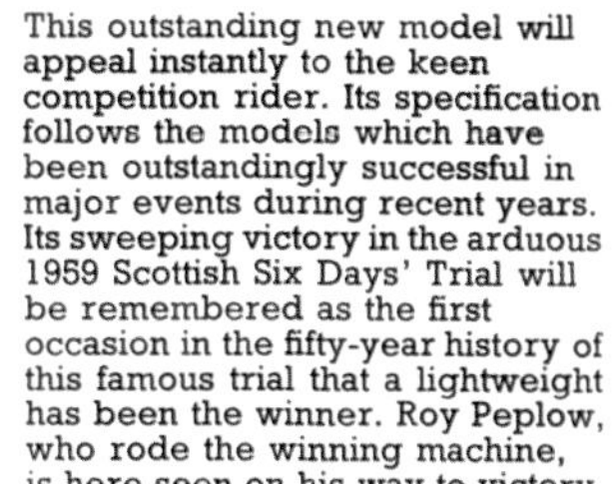
This outstanding new model will appeal instantly to the keen competition rider. Its specification follows the models which have been outstandingly successful in major events during recent years. Its sweeping victory in the arduous 1959 Scottish Six Days' Trial will be remembered as the first occasion in the fifty-year history of this famous trial that a lightweight has been the winner. Roy Peplow, who rode the winning machine, is here seen on his way to victory.

This year the artist had got the standard Cub's details pretty well correct, as well as making a good job of the new T20S competition version. The latter was now more specialised and had energy-transfer ignition with direct lighting so it could be run without a battery, and the headlamp was quickly detachable. Forks were of heavier design, with larger-diameter stanchion tubes and full hydraulic damping. Alternative specifications were also available to special order to meet specific competition requirements. Standard Cub was finished in Silver Grey and Black whilst the T20S was Azure Blue and Ivory with Black frame and cycle parts.

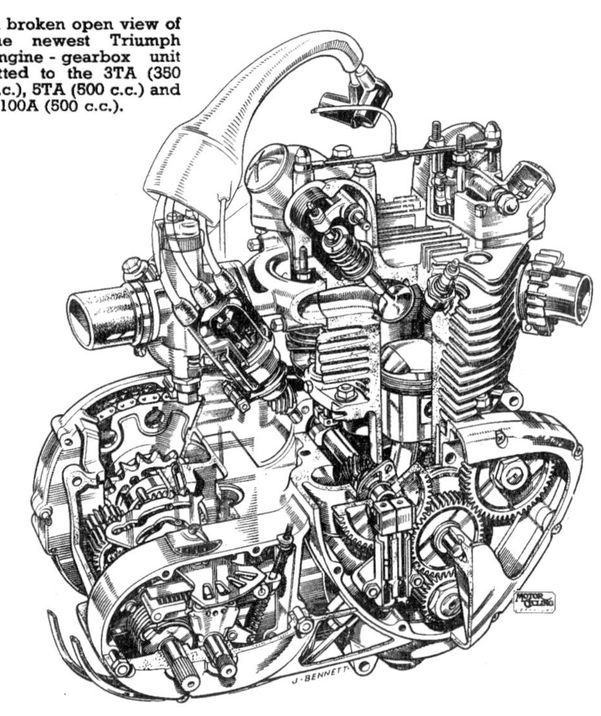

For 1960 the Speed Twin's long-running finish of Amaranth Red had been altered to Ruby Red, whilst the Twenty One's colour scheme, which had been Blue with Black frame, was now listed as Shell Blue with Black frame. Both had a new type of hinged seat, without pillion passenger sissy strap, over their comprehensively-equipped tool compartment. Front hub chrome embellishers on all models were no longer embossed with radial finning.

How the mighty Tiger 100 had fallen – in appearance, at any rate – looking for all the world like a humble 3TA or 5TA, even down to the 17in wheels and complete with unit-construction engine and 'box. Fortunately the poor thing was allowed to retain a modicum of pride, as its motor boasted an extra 5hp (32 at 7,000rpm) over the Speed Twin's 27hp at 6,500rpm. For some reason, however, it weighed more (I can't think why but there must be a simple answer) at 365lb against 350lb.

Not before time, Triumph had taken steps to address the matter of its whippy swinging-arm frames and for the 1960 season all four 650s featured a new duplex frame. It certainly looked more substantial despite retaining a bolt-on rear section but had one major new flaw, as well as retaining the one that had contributed more than anything to the previous design's sometimes wayward behaviour. The latter could easily have been eradicated during the redesign by providing a better location for the swinging arm than the single down-tube but it hadn't. More serious was the lack of structural integrity surrounding the headstock; and it took numerous frame breakages and at least one fatal accident for the factory to modify the design to incorporate reinforcement in the form of a subsidiary tube that formed a triangulation between the rear of the top rail and upper part of the down-tubes. Machines that had been sold prior to that, regardless of whether or not their frames had fractured, could be updated but the 1960 brochure had been in print for some time, so this Charcoal Grey Thunderbird's duplex frame was depicted in its original form.

These two pictures, one from the 1960 brochure (published in October '59) and the other from the 1961 (published October '60) were intended to demonstrate the new type of rubber-mounted petrol tank with securing strap but also well illustrated the first flawed duplex frame construction and the factory's solution. Nothing was mentioned about the frame's serious shortcomings but the pictorial evidence was clear enough.

TIGER 110 650 cc

Patent Nos. 475860, 474963, 482024

The most exciting of all road-going motorcycles, the Tiger 110 offers performance plus, with first-class roadholding and braking. Features of the specification include an alloy cylinder head with special pistons and camshafts, a duplex cradle frame and semi-enclosure of the rear wheel in the now familiar Triumph pattern. This is one of the most popular of all Triumph models as its smooth effortless performance is quite unique and appeals strongly to the keen rider.

Not too much of an insult for the T-bird to be given Twenty One/Speed Twin tinware but to inflict it on what had so recently been the company's flagship road-burner was reprehensible. The buying public thought so too, particularly in the United States, but the dislike for what was sneeringly referred to as Triumph's 'bathtub' styling was universal and over the years, whether it be Speed Twin or Tiger, the offensive metalwork would very often be stripped off and discarded. However, as is the often-perverse way of the world, that which was held in little regard when new has attained desirability with the passing of years.

The 1960 Bonneville was everything, or almost everything, it should have been in the first place, with optional paired speedo and rev counter (standard for the US), separate chrome headlamp, slenderer mudguards and fork gaiters, along with this year's restyled dual seat successfully conspiring to give it looks in keeping with its performance. Unfortunately Triumph's duplex frame, even in improved form, did not really do any of the 650s, and most especially the T120, justice. True the twin-tube frame gave the bike superior road manners to its predecessor, partially due to a reduction in fork rake and a consequently shorter wheelbase, but the additional stiffness amplified the 46hp motor's vibration, making the Bonnie's capacity for high speeds somewhat academic if you wanted to maintain them with any degree of comfort.

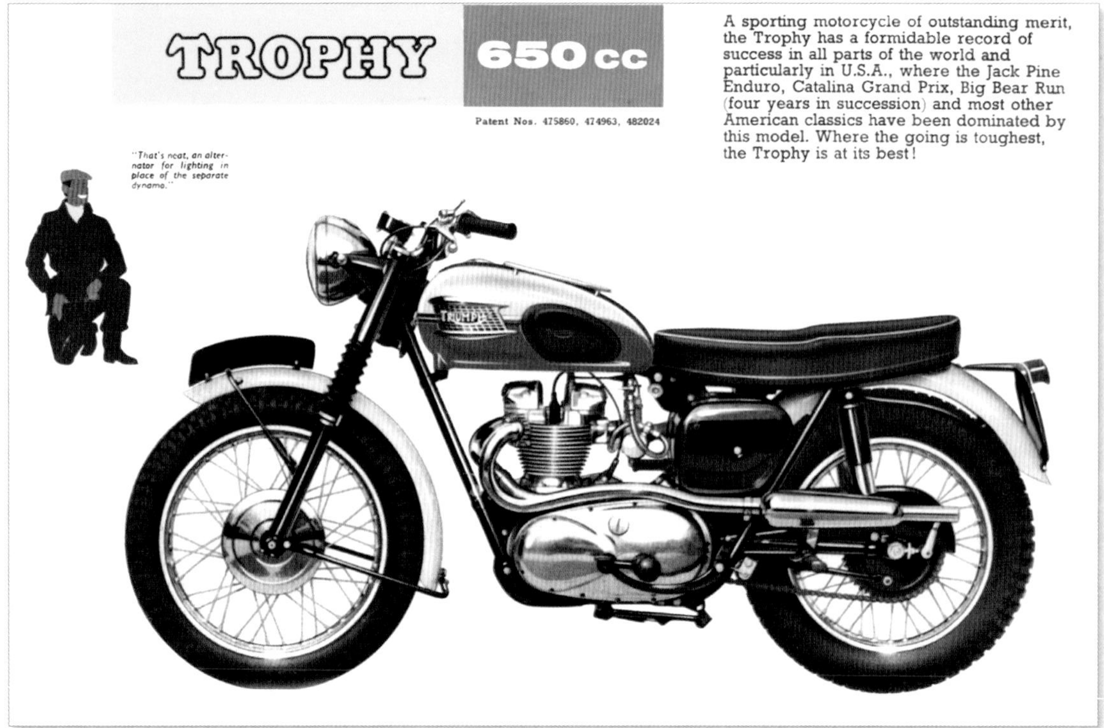

The Trophy and Bonneville had become more closely entwined with the latter's fresh persona and this year, although magneto ignition was retained, both were equipped with alternators. Colour and carbs apart, matters had become a little complicated with the availability of the Trophy in two guises – the TR6A and TR6B. This is the latter, shod with Dunlop Trials Universal on the front wheel and Dunlop Sports on the rear, whilst the TR6A had twin low-level pipes, normally a rev counter, and a Dunlop ribbed front tyre with K70 Universal on the rear.

MODEL	Tiger Cub (T20)	Tiger Cub (T20S)	Twenty-One (3TA)	Speed Twin (5TA)	Tiger 100 (T100A)	Thunder-bird (6T)	Tiger 110 (T110)	Trophy (TR6)	Bonneville 120 (T120)
ENGINE TYPE	O.H.V.	O.H.V.	O.H.V.	O.H.V.	O.H.V.	O.H.V.	O.H.V.	O.H.V.	O.H.V.
No. of Cylinders	1	1	2	2	2	2	2	2	2
Bore/Stroke, mm.	63×64	63×64	58.25×65.5	69×65.5	69×65.5	71×82	71×82	71×82	71×82
Bore/Stroke, ins.	2.48×2.52	2.48×2.52	2.3×2.6	2.72×2.6	2.72×2.6	2.79×3.23	2.79×3.23	2.79×3.23	2.79×3.23
Capacity, cu. cms.	199	199	348	490	490	649	649	649	649
Capacity, cu. ins.	12	12	21.23	29.8	29.8	40	40	40	40
Compression Ratio	7 : 1	7 : 1	7.5 : 1	7 : 1	9 : 1	7 : 1	8 : 1	8 : 1	8.5 : 1
B.H.P. and R.P.M.	10 @ 6,000	10 @ 6,000	18.5 @ 6,500	27 @ 6,500	32 @ 7,000	34 @ 6,300	40 @ 6,500	40 @ 6,500	46 @ 6,500
Engine sprocket teeth									
Solo	19	19	26	26	26	23	23	22	22
Sidecar	—	—	—	—	—	20	20	—	19
Clutch sprocket teeth	48	48	58	58	58	43	43	43	43
Gearbox sprocket teeth	17	17	18	20	20	18	18	18	18
Rear wheel teeth	46	54	43	43	43	43	43	43	43
R.P.M., 10 m.p.h.:									
Top Gear	980	1,075	760	670	670	597	597	608	608
						Solo S/car	Solo S/car		Solo S/car
Gear Ratios—Top	6.84	8.0	5.33	4.80	4.80	4.46 5.12	4.46 5.12	4.66	4.66 5.40
,, ,, —Third	9.04	11.6	6.32	5.69	5.69	5.30 6.1	5.30 6.1	5.55	5.55 6.42
,, ,, —Second	14.05	18.1	9.37	8.44	8.44	7.55 8.7	7.55 8.7	7.88	7.88 9.13
,, ,, —First	20.30	26.3	12.96	11.66	11.66	10.9 12.5	10.9 12.5	11.38	11.38 13.2
Carburetter—Make	Zenith	Zenith	Amal	Amal	Amal	Amal	Amal	Amal	Amal-Twin
,, —Type	18MXZ C17	18MXZ C18	375/32	375/35	375/35	376/246	376/244	376/40	376/233
Front Chain Size	⅜" Duplex	⅜" Duplex	⅜" Duplex	⅜" Duplex	⅜" Duplex	½"×.305"	½"×.305"	½"×.305"	½"×.305"
Rear Chain Size	½"×.205	½"×.205	⅝"×⅜"	⅝"×⅜"	⅝"×⅜"	⅝"×⅜"	⅝"×⅜"	⅝"×⅜"	⅝"×⅜"
Tyres—Dunlop:									
Front, ins.	3.25×17	3.00×19	3.25×17	3.25×17	3.25×17	3.25×18	3.25×18	3.25×19	3.25×19
Rear, ins.	3.25×17	3.50×18	3.25×17	3.50×17	3.50×17	3.50×18	3.50×18	4.00×18	3.50×19
Brake dia., ins. (cms.)	5½" (13.97)	5½" (13.97)	7" (17.78)	7" (17.78)	7" (17.78)	7" (17.78)	8" F (20.32) 7" R (17.78)	8" F (20.32) 7" R (17.78)	8" F (20.32) 7" R (17.78)
Finish	Grey/Black	Ivory/Blue	Shell Blue/Black	Red	Black/Ivory	Charcoal Grey	Black/Ivory	Ivory/Aztec Red	Grey/Blue
Seat height, ins.(cms.)	29" (73.7)	30" (76.2)	29¼" (74.5)	29¼" (74.5)	29¼" (74.5)	30" (76.2)	30" (76.2)	30½" (77.5)	30½" (77.5)
Wheelbase, ins. (cms.)	49" (125.5)	49" (125.5)	51¾" (131.4)	51¾" (131.4)	51¾" (131.4)	54½" (138.5)	54½" (138.5)	54½" (138.5)	54½" (138.5)
Length, ins. (cms.)	77" (195.5)	77" (195.5)	80" (203)	80" (203)	80" (203)	83" (211)	83" (211)	85½" (217)	85½" (217)
Width, ins. (cms.)	25" (63.5)	25" (63.5)	26" (66)	26" (66)	26" (66)	28½" (72)	28½" (72)	28½" (72)	28½" (72)
Clearance, ins. (cms.)	5" (12.7)	6" (15.2)	5" (12.7)	5" (12.7)	5" (12.7)	5" (12.7)	5" (12.7)	5" (12.7)	5" (12.7)
Weight, lbs. (kilos)	220 (99.7)	210 (95)	345 (156.3)	350 (159)	363 (165)	392 (177)	390 (176)	393 (178)	393 (178)
Petrol, galls. (litres)	3 (13.5)	2⅝ (11.9)	3½ (16)	3½ (16)	3½ (16)	4 (18)	4 (18)	3 (13.5)	4 (18)
Oil, pints (litres)	2¾ (1.55)	2¾ (1.55)	5 (2.8)	5 (2.8)	5 (2.8)	5 (2.8)	5 (2.8)	5 (2.8)	5 (2.8)

Hinged twinseat featured on all twins excepting TR6 and T120. Easily detachable rubber-mounted tank on all 650 c.c. twins.

"Come on, watch me, not the flippin' seagulls" – pleads Chris, eager to give the girls a display of his riding skills and his Kingfisher Blue and Silver T110's speed on North Devon's Westward Ho! beach for the 1961 brochure's cover. The long gone and all but forgotten garage's stamp from Wadebridge in neighbouring North Cornwall is a reminder of the days when most towns of this size could boast of one or maybe two motor cycle dealers.

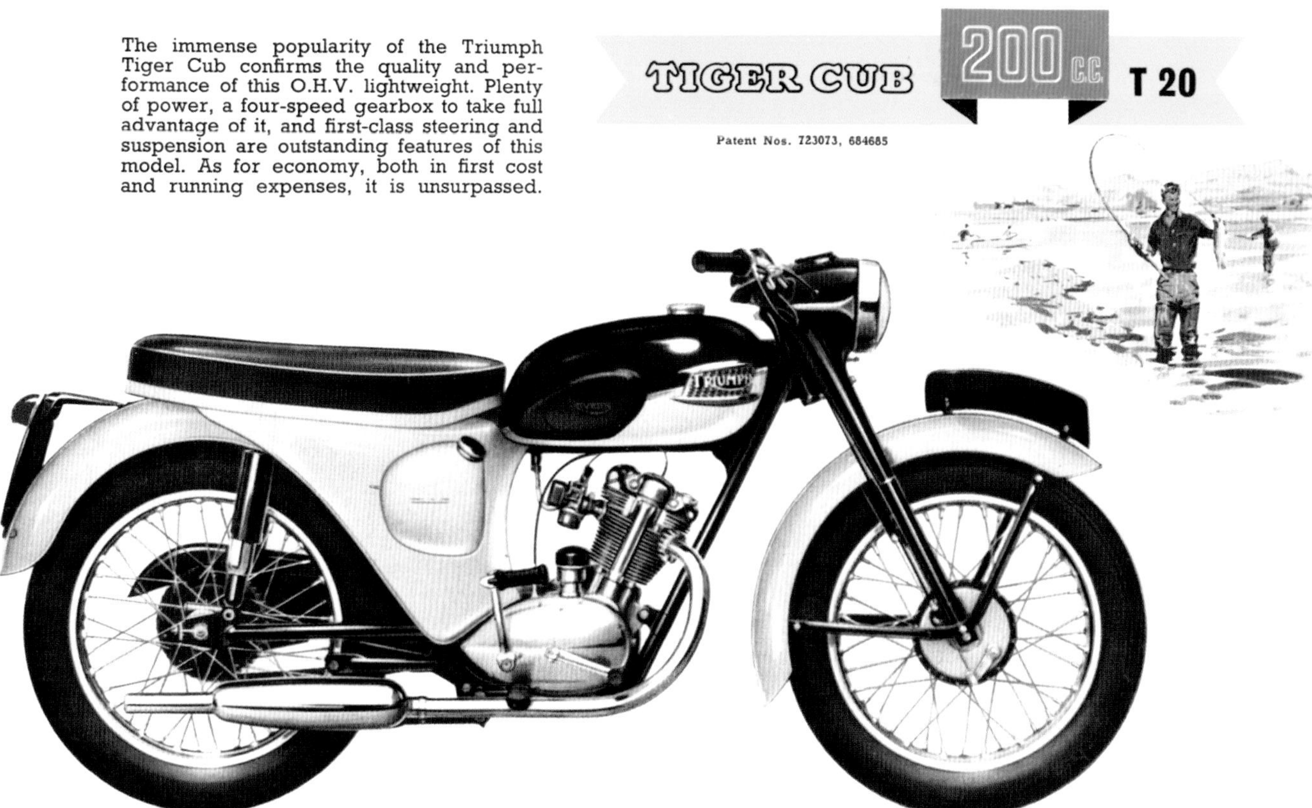

The T20 had been brought into line with its larger brethren this season with eye catching two-tone paintwork.

Alternative Cubs to the T20 were becoming more specialised, with a T20S/L (high performance model) and T20T for trials now catalogued. The T20S/L was fitted with an Amal Monobloc carb whilst the T20T and T20 soldiered on with the tricky-to-tune Zenith until the end of the season.

TIGER 100 500 c.c. T 100A

Patent Nos. 475860, 723073, 684685

A light, easily handled 500 twin bearing a name synonymous with high performance —the Triumph Tiger 100. High compression pistons, special camshafts and many unique features — allied to modern appearance and first class handling, underline the special appeal of this model to the sporting rider.

The 3TA and 5TA carried on all but unchanged (2,995 Twenty Ones and 1,495 Speed Twins including 18 for the police left the factory in 1961) but the T100A was now turned out in Black and Silver and had, according to factory figures, another 2hp wrung out of its motor to bring it up to 34 at the same 7,000rpm as last year. For export only, the majority going to the US, were the TR5AC and TR5AR. The former had a small competition fuel tank, 19in front and 18in rear wheels shod with Dunlop Trials, wide-ratio gears, siamesed exhaust with upswept silencer and energy transfer ignition with no battery but a QD headlamp; the AR, although similar in most respects, had road tyres, a standard gearbox, standard fuel tank and twin low-level exhausts. Colour scheme for both was Kingfisher Blue over Silver Sheen with Black frame and cycle parts. Production numbers in 1961 were 1,006 (T100A), 665 (TR5AC) and 462 (TR5AR).

As 'bathtub' Triumphs go, Black and Silver was in my opinion the most attractive colour scheme and this year you could chose between a 500 or 650 in this finish. If you went for a 1961 Thunderbird the company had uprated the front brake to the same 8in, now with fully-floating shoes, as employed on the T110 and T120. It had also been uprated with the T110's aluminium cylinder head; this increasing its compression ratio but not, according to factory data, its power output.

Sleek, modern twin cylinder OHV Engine-gearbox unit as fitted to "C" range models (350/500 c.c.).

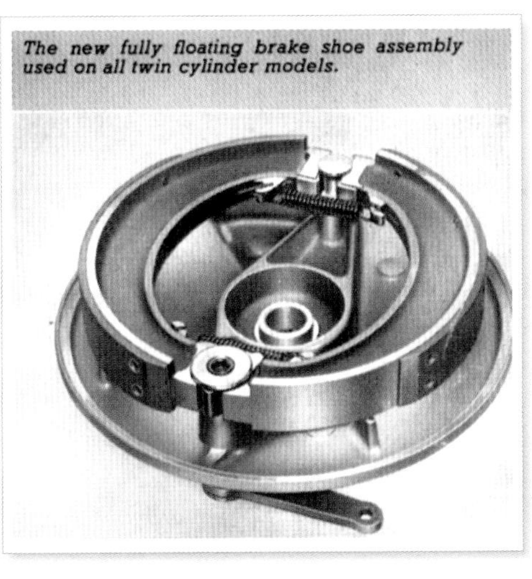

The new fully floating brake shoe assembly used on all twin cylinder models.

For 1961 the Bonneville became available as the T120R or the T120C. The former was the standard road version as depicted here whilst the 120C was the street scrambler with high pipes for the US market. Amongst Triumph aficionados opinions are divided as to which is the most desirable Bonneville but many would agree that as far as looks go the last of the pre-unit machines from '61/'62 in Sky Blue and Silver Sheen take it – the Blue applied over the Silver on tank top and mudguard's strip, each edged with a gold line, giving it a subtle lustre. Mechanical and other improvements included a new cylinder head casting (also for the other 650s) with integral pillars between the outer cylinder fins to stop high-frequency ringing, needle roller bearing for the gearbox layshaft and a larger 4.00-section rear tyre. The Motor Cycle *tested 717 BWD in the early summer and disposed of the machine's shortcomings thus: "Vibration was not absent, but was never excessive… High-speed handling was of a kind which some car people call 'interesting' – on really fast corners there was a certain amount of unauthorised rear wheel movement." It was the following, however, that better encapsulated what a T120 was all about: "With exceptional top-end performance goes extraordinary vigour and tractability at low and medium engine speeds – a combination which makes it perhaps the fastest point-to-point roadster produced in Britain today." Feeling that its timed lap speed at MIRA of 108mph could be improved upon they later tested the very same machine, now fitted with the optional (£15 11s 6d extra) chopped Monoblocs and remote float chamber, and they were right: 116.5mph with rider prone, as he had been for the previous test. What is more, with the engine now able to rev to its full 7,500 rpm the ton was attainable in third gear. Economy wasn't really an issue but somewhat surprisingly it was found to do 80 miles to a gallon at a steady 50mph, and 64mpg overall.*

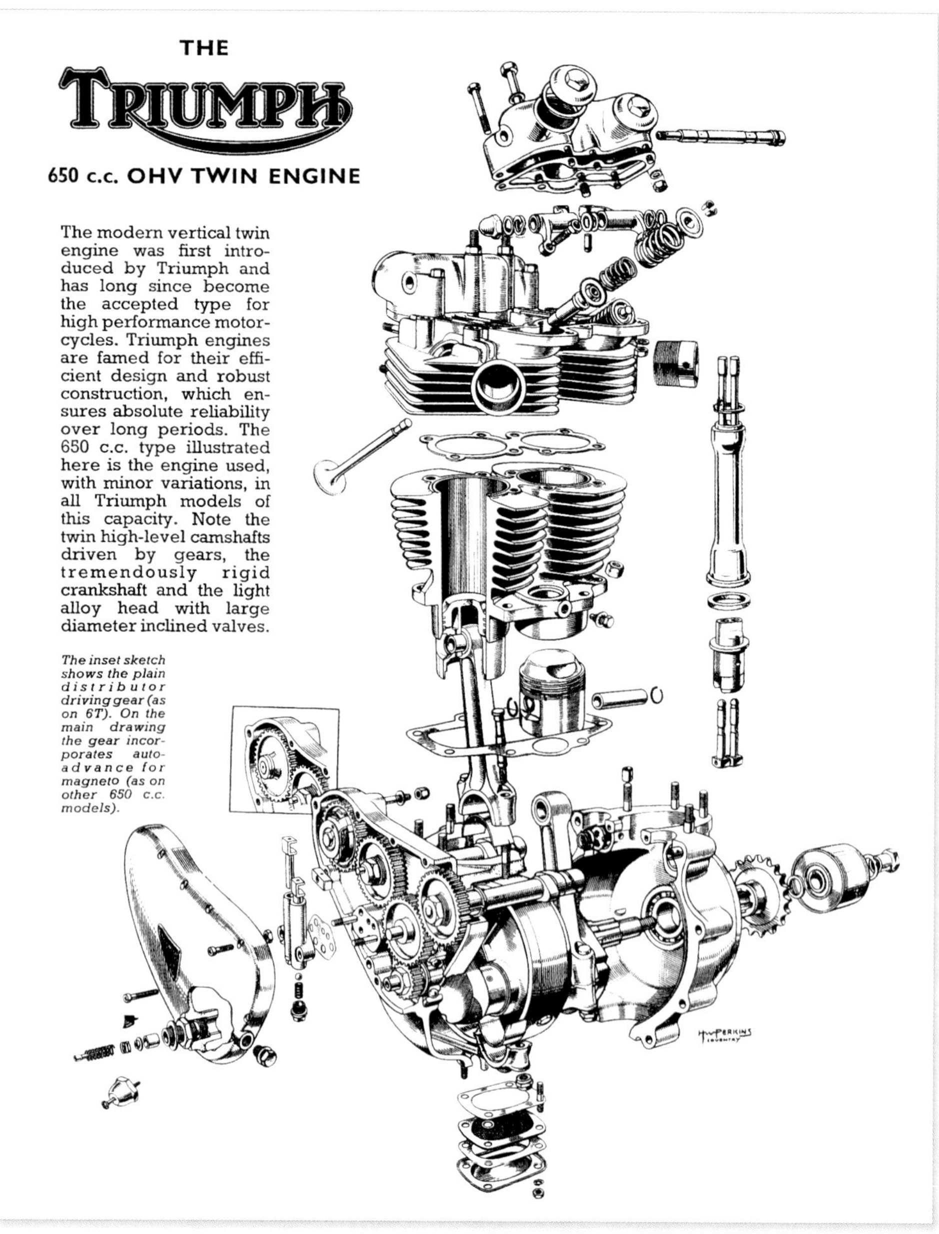

Bonneville 120 650 c.c. T 120 R

Patent Nos. 475860, 469635, 684685

STAR FEATURES ON YOUR TRIUMPH

- ★ All gearboxes on 650 c.c. models have layshafts running in needle roller bearings at each end to ensure complete reliability under all conditions.
- ★ All Triumph silencers are made in an exclusive barrel shape, are heavily chrome plated and emit a very subdued exhaust note.
- ★ All twin cylinder models can be supplied with a quickly detachable rear wheel as an optional extra. This enables the wheel to be removed by withdrawing the spindle and without disturbing the chain or brake.
- ★ All models have swinging fork rear suspension controlled by hydraulic dampers which are readily adjustable to suit varying conditions of load.
- ★ All twin cylinder engine big-end bearings are fitted with easily replaceable thin wall bearing shells.
- ★ All models are equipped with crankshaft mounted alternators to supply electrical requirements. These units are simple, silent and completely reliable.
- ★ All models, single and twin cylinder, are fitted with light alloy cylinder heads. The hemispherical shaped combustion chambers and large diameter valves ensure efficiency of the highest order.

MODEL	Tiger Cub (T20)	Tiger Cub (T20S/L)	Tiger Cub (T20T)	Twenty-one (3TA)	Speed Twin (5TA)	Tiger 100 (T100A)	Thunderbird (6T)	Tiger 110 (T110)	Bonneville 120 (T120R)
Engine Type	O.H.V.	O.H.V.	O.H.V.	O.H.V.	O.H.V.	O.H.V.	O.H.V.	O.H.V.	O.H.V.
Number of Cylinders ...	1	1	1	2	2	2	2	2	2
Bore/Stroke, mm. ...	63×64	63×64	63×64	58.25×65.5	69×65.5	69×65.5	71×82	71×82	71×82
Bore/Stroke, ins.	2.48×2.52	2.48×2.52	2.48×2.52	2.3×2.6	2.72×2.6	2.72×2.6	2.79×3.23	2.79×3.23	2.79×3.23
Capacity, cu. cms. ...	199	199	199	348	490	490	649	649	649
Capacity, cu. ins. ...	12	12	12	21.23	29.8	29.8	40	40	40
Compression ratio ...	7 : 1	9 : 1	7 : 1	7.5 : 1	7 : 1	9 : 1	7.5 : 1	8.5 : 1	8.5 : 1
B.H.P. and R.P.M. ...	10 @ 6,000	14.5 @ 6,500	10 @ 6,000	18.5 @ 6,500	27 @ 6,500	34 @ 7,000	34 @ 6,300	40 @ 6,500	46 @ 6,500
Engine Sprocket Teeth—									
Solo	19	19	19	26	26	26	22	22	21
Sidecar	—	—	—	—	—	—	20	20	19
Clutch Sprocket Teeth ...	48	48	48	58	58	58	43	43	43
Gearbox Sprocket Teeth	17	17	16	18	19	19	18	18	18
Rear Sprocket Teeth ...	46	48	54	43	43	43	43	43	43
R.P.M. 10 M.P.H. Top Gear	985	960	1,150	742	702	702	625	625	638
							Solo / S/C	Solo / S/C	Solo / S/C
Gear Ratios—Top ...	6.84	7.13	8.55	5.33	5.05	5.05	4.67 / 5.12	4.67 / 5.12	4.88 / 5.40
„ „ —Third ...	9.04	8.56	12.4	6.32	6.0	6.0	5.55 / 6.1	5.55 / 6.1	5.81 / 6.42
„ „ —Second ...	14.05	13.37	19.4	9.37	8.88	8.88	7.88 / 8.7	7.88 / 8.7	8.25 / 9.13
„ „ —First ...	20.40	19.8	28.1	12.96	12.28	12.28	11.4 / 12.5	11.4 / 12.5	11.92 / 13.2
Carburetter—Make ...	Zenith	Amal	Zenith	Amal	Amal	Amal	Amal	Amal	Twin Amal
Carburetter—Type ...	18MXZ C17	375/317	18MXZ C18	375/32	375/35	376/273	376/255	376/40	376/257
Front Chain Size ...	3/8" Duplex	3/8" Duplex	3/8" Duplex	3/8" Duplex	3/8" Duplex	3/8" Duplex	1/2×.305"	1/2×.305"	1/2×.305"
Rear Chain Size	1/2×.205"	1/2×.205"	1/2×.205"	5/8"×3/8"	5/8"×3/8"	5/8"×3/8"	5/8"×3/8"	5/8"×3/8"	5/8"×3/8"
Tyres—Front, ins. ...	3.25×17	3.00×19	3.00×19	3.25×17	3.25×17	3.25×17	3.25×18	3.25×18	3.25×19
„ —Rear, ins. ...	3.25×17	3.50×18	3.50×18	3.50×17	3.50×17	3.50×17	3.50×18	3.50×18	4.00×18
Brake Diameter–ins. (cms.)	5½" (13.97)	5½" (13.97)	5½" (13.97)	7" (17.78)	7" (17.78)	7" (17.78)	8" F (20.32) 7" R (17.78)	8" F (20.32) 7" R (17.78)	8" F (20.32) 7" R (17.78)
Finish	Black/ Silver	Ruby Red/Silver	Ruby Red/Silver	Shell Blue Sheen	Ruby Red	Black/ Silver	Black/ Silver	Kingfisher Blue/Silver	Sky Blue/ Silver
Seat Height —ins. ...	29"	30"	30"	29¼"	29¼"	29¼"	30"	30"	30½"
„ „ —cms. ...	(73.7)	(76.2)	(76.2)	(74.5)	(74.5)	(74.5)	(76.2)	(76.2)	(77.5)
Wheelbase—ins. ...	49"	49"	49"	52¾"	52¾"	52¾"	54¾"	54¾"	55¼"
„ „ —cms. ...	(124.5)	(124.5)	(124.5)	(134)	(134)	(134)	(139)	(139)	(140.3)
Length—ins.	77"	77"	77"	81"	81"	81"	83¼"	83¼"	86¼"
„ —cms.	(195.5)	(195.5)	(195.5)	(206)	(206)	(206)	(212)	(212)	(219)
Width—ins.	25"	25"	25"	26"	26"	26"	28½"	28½"	28½"
„ —cms.	(63.5)	(63.5)	(63.5)	(66)	(66)	(66)	(72)	(72)	(72)
Clearance, —ins.... ...	5"	6"	6"	5"	5"	5"	5"	5"	5"
„ —cms. ...	(12.7)	(15.2)	(15.2)	(12.7)	(12.7)	(12.7)	(12.7)	(12.7)	(12.7)
Weight—lbs.	220	210	210	345	350	363	392	390	393
„ —kilos	(99.7)	(95)	(95)	(156.3)	(159)	(165)	(177)	(176)	(178)
Petrol—Galls.	3	2⅝	2⅝	3½	3½	3½	4	4	3
„ —Litres	(13.5)	(11.9)	(11.9)	(16)	(16)	(16)	(18)	(18)	(13.5)
Oil—Pints	2¾	2¾	2¾	5	5	5	5	5	5
„ —Litres	(1.55)	(1.55)	(1.55)	(2.8)	(2.8)	(2.8)	(2.8)	(2.8)	(2.8)

Commercial and sometime staff artist for The Motor Cycle *Bernard Wragg's distinctive style captured the latest Tiger 100 for the cover of Triumph's 1962 brochure.*

Last year's T20S/L Sports Cub had been re-designated as the T20S/S but was almost identical apart from its finish now being described as Burgundy Red and Silver Grey rather than Ruby Red and Silver, which knowing a little about Triumph's modus operandi, could well mean the same thing. Cub seats, however, now had a grey top panel and the T20S/S had, according to the factory's data sheet, put on a little weight (210lb to 223lb). On the technical front, all Cubs had an improved oil pump. The Trials Cub as a distinct model had been discontinued but the T20S/S could be had with a low-compression engine, high-level exhaust (for which a bracket was already provided on the frame), competition tyres and such like.

"An ideal fast light sports 500"

says **JOHN GILES**

– famous Triumph trials and scrambles star, winner of the 1961 Experts Grand National and countless events in U.K. and on the Continent. Gold Medal winner in 1961 International Six Days Trial riding a Tiger 100S S. Member of British Trophy Team.

What more could any potential customer need than a personal endorsement from the father of Triumph's range of twins, and for many years the guiding force behind the firm.

"It is a far cry from my original Triumph 'Speed Twin' of twenty years ago to the sleek twins and sporting lightweights described in this latest catalogue, but having been more than intimately connected with every Triumph development in the ensuing period, I know that this fine new range will further enhance the reputation enjoyed by Triumph throughout the world."

Edward Turner, M.I.Mech.E.,
Managing Director of Triumph and the Automotive Group of The Birmingham Small Arms Co. Ltd.

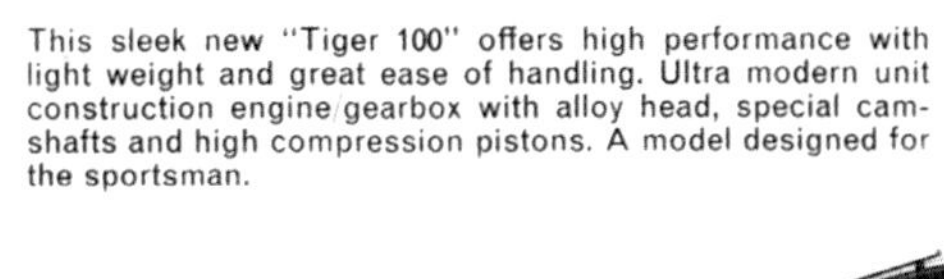

This sleek new "Tiger 100" offers high performance with light weight and great ease of handling. Ultra modern unit construction engine/gearbox with alloy head, special camshafts and high compression pistons. A model designed for the sportsman.

Bathtub 3TA and 5TAs carried on much as before other than updates such as the newly-introduced duo-tone dual seat, but the Tiger 100A had given way to the more sportingly-styled T100S/S – its general demeanour, assisted more than somewhat by a return to proper-sized wheels (19in at the front and 18in for the rear), being very much on Bonneville lines apart from the abbreviated rear enclosure. For the US market there were updated versions of the previous season's models, now designated the T100S/R and the T100S/C – the latter having a very limited production of just 13 machines, whilst the S/R ran to 424 and the UK's T100S/S 1,470. All were turned out in Kingfisher Blue and Silver Sheen.

"We had a wonderful ride on the 120 to win the Thruxton 500 mile race" say JOHN HOLDER and TONY GODFREY

For sheer performance the Triumph "Bonneville 120" is without equal as a standard production fully equipped road going motorcycle. This is proved by the spectacular results of the Thruxton International 500 Mile Race where this model swept the board. Two carburetters, special camshafts, alloy head, duplex frame and many other features make the Bonneville the choice of the really experienced rider who can use the power with skill and discretion.

Not advertised as such at the time but the '62 Bonneville would be the last of the pre-units, and arguably the best of them. Continuing efforts to reduce the vibration that plagued Triumph's most powerful twin had led to the introduction of a new flywheel late the previous season, and then a modified crankshaft – the end result producing a balance factor of 85 per cent that reduced, but not eliminated, the T120's characteristic vibratory tendencies. Both T120 and TR6 now incorporated rubber bushings in their oil tank mounts. For those who wanted to upgrade their Bonnie a list of special equipment for production racing was available from its manufacturer.

THRUXTON 500 MILE RACE

Outright winner of this arduous International Race for standard production motorcycles was a Triumph "Bonneville" ridden by Tony Godfrey and John Holder. Above is a fine view of Holder at speed on the winning machine. Other "Bonnevilles" filled 2nd, 4th, 5th and 6th places in the multicylinder class.

Triumphs may not have been renowned for their road-holding properties but in order to stay ahead of the second-place Norton Dominator 88 the winners of the 1961 Thruxton 500 laid their machine well into the corners, by the look of its silencers. In fourth place, behind a Velocette Venom, was another Bonneville co-ridden by the factory's chief tester Percy Tait. Shame the publicity department chose to rewrite history to the firm's glorification – they should have inserted the word 'large' before multi-cylinder, as the second-place (500cc) Norton was also, of course, a multi-cylinder.

—famous American cross-country star who has scored most of his innumerable successes in major U.S. events on Triumph Trophy models.

TROPHY 650 c.c. TR6S/S

Patent Nos. 475860, 469635, 684685

This fine sporting motorcycle is a firm favourite throughout the world and its specification includes every refinement demanded by the enthusiast. 40 B.H.P. engine, 2 into 1 exhaust, heavy duty competition type forks, duplex frame, rubber mounted fuel tanks and many other items which ensure success under the most arduous conditions.

The Trophy's looks and specifications were now Bonneville but without the twin carbs and other tweaks that gave the latter an extra 6hp. Bud Ekins was also a Triumph dealer but is perhaps best remembered for being a good friend and motorcycling buddy of Steve McQueen – standing in for the actor on occasions to perform stunt work. It was he, for instance, who did the famous jump scene, on a Triumph thinly disguised as a Nazi Wehrmacht machine, towards the end of the 1963 film The Great Escape.

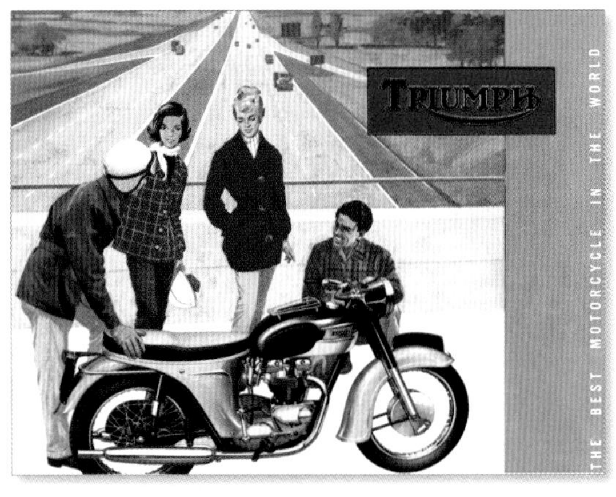

"There's only room on the pillion for one of you if we're going to see what she'll do on the motorway," says John; but whilst blonde Jenny looks undecided I think Suzette's up for it, don't you? This or something similar was the storyline in the scenario dreamt up for the 1963 brochure's cover, the intention being to promote the larger Triumphs as being more than capable of devouring motorway miles with ease. In addition to the new frame and unit-construction motor the '63 Thunderbird had also been brought up to date with the latest style of 'bikini' rear enclosure, but retained a fulsome front mudguard.

The standard Cub's nacelle-mounted gear position indicator had been done away with in favour of a plunger rising and falling through the top face of the gearbox. Less convenient for the rider but cheaper for the manufacturer, no doubt. Finish was now Flame and Silver Grey. All Cubs had the new ignition set-up with contact-breaker assembly located in the timing cover, as well as a pair of finned rocker covers.

TIGER 90
350 CC

An entirely new sports 350 c.c. twin with a specification similar to the well-known 500 c.c. model Tiger 100. With a brilliant performance, smooth, fast and easy to handle, this interesting addition to the Triumph range will undoubtedly prove a popular model with the rider who prefers a 350 and can appreciate the "plus" performance of this new model.

This is the 1963 T20S/H Sports Cub in Burgundy Red and Silver, which now had the option of a rev counter added to the existing extras such as prop stand, pillion rests and steering lock. Also available were the Cub Scrambler and Trials Cub – the latter being a popular choice of mount for some well-thought-of riders, many of whom would elect to fit more robust Alpha bottom ends. Long known as the little machine's weakest link, if one discounted its frame, the factory had uprated from a plain to ball main bearing in 1960 and a sturdier big end for '63.

Fifteen years after aborting its first 350 sports twin, the Tiger 85, Triumph decided the time was ripe to bring another to the market, the Tiger 90. To make it more than simply a sporty-looking Twenty One with abbreviated weather equipment and 18in (as opposed to 17in) wheels, its manufacturer had boosted the engine's power to 27hp by way of larger valves, sports camshaft and a compression ratio hike from 7.5 to 9:1. The Motor Cycle *liked it too: "An attractive sports model which will leave you solvent after you've paid the insurance premium; has the creditable top speed of 90mph; takes a shade under two seconds longer to cover the quarter-mile from rest than that status symbol of the four-wheel fraternity, the E-Type Jaguar. That, in a nutshell, is the 348cc Triumph Tiger 90." No Bonneville, perhaps, but some of its looks, with 'light, positive cog-swapping' and 'effortless, all-day 75mph cruising' and, as they emphasised, without the 650's insurance costs. As the saying goes, 'what you gain on the roundabouts, you lose on the swings' and in this case it was the extra money you spent on petrol – in most circumstances it used more than its larger, faster relation. The Alaskan White finish was enhanced with Gold mudguard centres lined in Black. A rev counter was listed as an optional extra for both Tigers, along with QD rear wheel, steering lock, prop stand and pillion footrests. Just under 850 T90s were produced this year, two of which came first and second in the 350 class of the Bemsee 1,000-mile race, and 25 special T90S/Cs were produced at the request of Johnson Motors.*

Designed down to the last detail for the sporting rider who demands the highest performance with light weight and ease of handling—the 500 c.c. Tiger 100 has proved its worth in many tough competitive events. Winner of the classic 1962 Daytona 200 mile race in the United States at record speed and gold medal winner in the 1961 and 1962 International Six Days' Trials.

TIGER 100

500 CC

Both Tiger 90 and 100 (with the exception of some export models) now had their ignition timing driven off the exhaust camshaft with condensers and points accessed via a chrome cover on the timing case. Although the petrol tank continued to act as a stressed member, with internal strengthening beam, it was a different design with space on the underside for the twin ignition coils (T100S/R and T100S/Cs destined for the US generally had a smaller tank with four-point mounting and a frame brace). The 'bikini' rear enclosure had been restyled to extend around the seat base and incorporate a styling flash but was still none too popular. Home-market T100S/S was finished in Regal Purple over Silver with Black pin-striping and, with less than 350 manufactured, is now something of a rarity.

TRIUMPH SETS A NEW WORLD SPEED RECORD AT 224 M.P.H.

(Subject to confirmation by F.I.M.)

On the 5th September, 1962, at the Bonneville Salt Flats, Utah, a new motorcycle world speed record of 224.57 m.p.h. (360 k.p.h.) for the flying kilo was achieved by a 650 c.c. TRIUMPH streamliner ridden by Bill Johnson of California.

The engine used was a standard production type 650 c.c. Triumph twin as used in the Bonneville 120 model—a striking testimony to the quality and performance of this engine.

New double contact breaker unit fitted neatly in the timing cover and driven off the camshaft.

Ignition points were relocated thus on all models other than Twenty Ones, Speed Twins and some export models.

The exploits of Triumph-engined machines on Utah's salt flats several years earlier had given rise to the Bonneville T120, so it was natural that its power unit should be used to try for further records.

A new frame, as well as integral crankcase and gearbox (unit construction) characterised the 1963 Bonneville and its 650 siblings. With handling a priority Triumph's ex-Norton development engineer Doug Hele had spent much time on the former and the combination of a vastly-improved rear fork pivot and altered steering geometry had done wonders, as journalist/racer Vic Willoughby found when he had tested the prototype (8 EAC) late in '62. "Several times when flat out I hit patchy road repairs without a waiver," he wrote; and as for its acceleration he merely commented that, "Pick up is legalised violence." No timing was done but he found that sitting upright, "The job would hum along with the speedo needle a notch or two beyond the 100 mark," and that, "whenever I shifted my boots to the pillion rests and chinned the tank-top luggage grid another ten knots were rung up on the dial." The '63 T120s and T90s were turned out in Alaskan White with Gold central mudguard stripes lined in Black.

Offering the ultimate in road performance, the famous 650 c.c. Bonneville 120 is the choice of the really skilful and experienced rider. Specification includes new unit construction twin carburetter engine, completely new frame, new twin coil ignition system, duplex primary chain and a considerable reduction in overall weight, for safe and easy handling.

Triumph's take on their new unit-construction 650 speaks for itself.

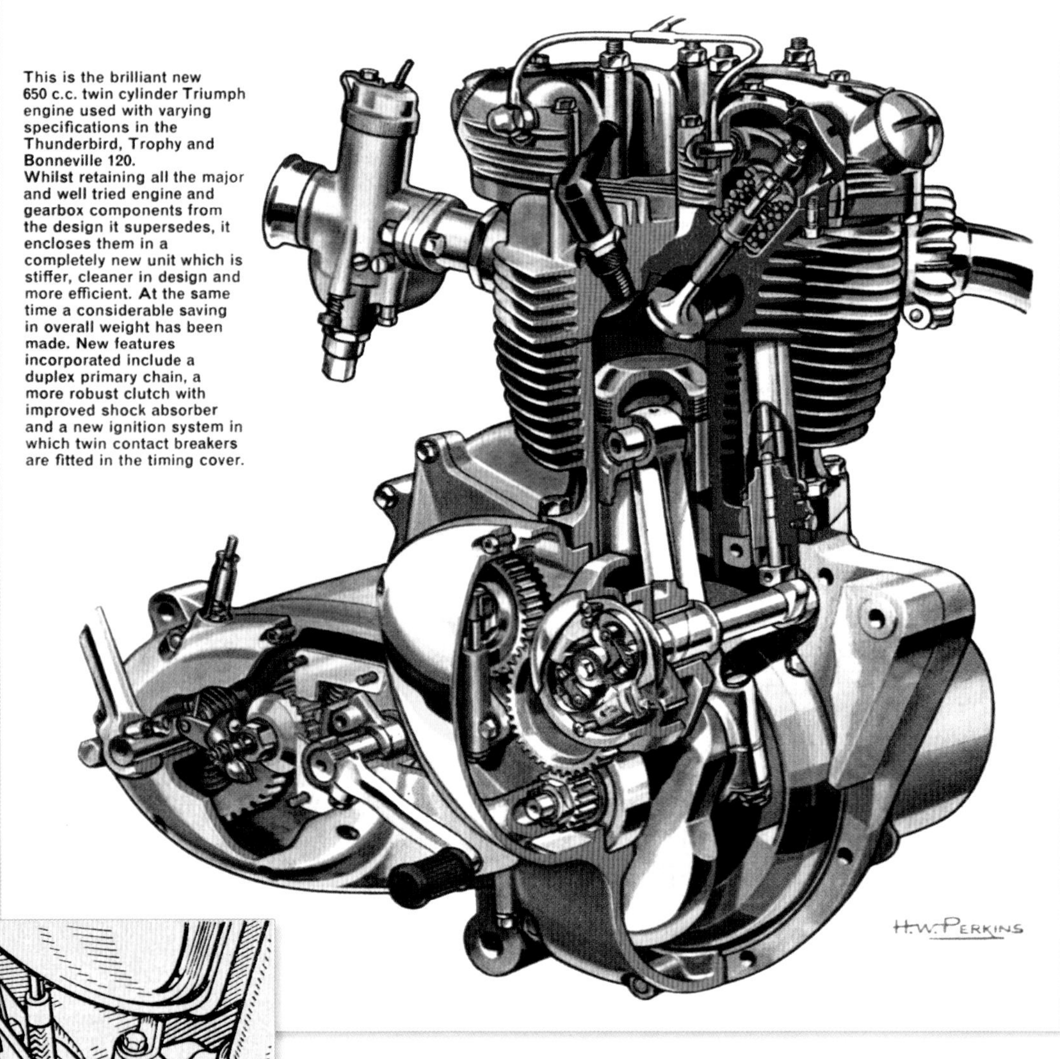

New frame on all 650's. The swinging arm runs on large diameter bronze bushes and is rigidly mounted at the back of the engine unit as well as at the seat tube.

The Trophy continued to be tantamount to a single-carb Bonneville, and looked like one too apart from its Regal Purple over Silver finish, whilst the Bonneville was Alaskan White (note, the upper colour on Trophy and Thunderbird fuel tanks now swept down below the knee grips). It also retained a 19in front wheel this season, whereas the Bonneville's had been reduced to 18in.

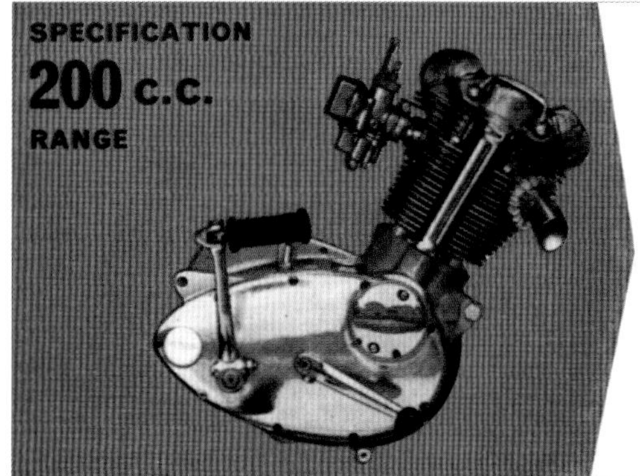

ENGINE. High-performance single cylinder o.h.v. with die-cast alloy cylinder head and finned rocker box caps inclined valves. "H" section connecting rod with plain big-end. Dry sump lubrication. Efficient barrel type silencer. Air cleaner.

FOUR SPEED GEARBOX. In unit with engine. Multiplate clutch with cork sheet linings and rubber torsion shock absorber. Positive stop footchange. Duplex primary chain.

FORKS. Triumph telescopic type giving comfortable ride and accurate steering. Heavy duty competition type on T20S/H.

FRAME. Strong loop type frame. Swinging fork rear suspension with hydraulic damping. Provision for anti-theft lock.

BRAKES. Very efficient smooth-acting brakes with large diameter drums and finger adjustment.

WHEELS. Triumph design with plated spokes and rims. Efficient mudguards front and rear. Stylish rear enclosure panels. (T20 only).

FUEL TANKS. All-steel welded petrol tank, chrome motif. Ample capacity oil tank. Quick release caps and accessible filters.

ELECTRICAL EQUIPMENT. A.C./D.C. lighting-ignition system with crankshaft-mounted alternator and emergency start circuit. Contact breaker mounted in timing cover. Powerful head and rear lamps.

TOOLBOX. All steel with kit of good quality tools and inflator.

NACELLE. T20 only (Patent No. 647670). Neat streamlined shell encloses headlamp, instruments and socket connected switchgear.

SPEEDOMETER. Smiths 80 m.p.h. (140 Km.p.h.) speedometer with anti-vibration mountings.

OTHER DETAILS. Finish T20 Flame/Silver Grey. T20S/H Burgundy Red/Silver Grey. Smooth action twistgrip, rubber knee grips. "Vynide" covered cushioned twinseat.

EXTRAS. Pillion footrests. Prop stand. Steering lock. Tachometer (T20 S/H).

ENGINE. Advanced design vertical twin cylinder o.h.v. with two camshafts driven by gears. Pushrod operated overhead valves in a light alloy cylinder head. High duty iron cylinder block. Dry sump lubrication with plunger type pump. Steel connecting rods with plain bearing big-ends. A.C./D.C. lighting-ignition system with crankshaft mounted alternator and emergency start circuit. Oil pressure indicator. Twin contact breaker unit mounted in timing cover (T90 and T100S/S only). Silent Duplex primary chain in polished aluminium oil-bath with tensioner. Air cleaner.

GEARBOX. Four speed with positive stop foot operation built-in unit with engine. Heavy duty shafts and gears of hardened nickel-chrome steel, multiplate clutch with cork sheet linings and rubber torsion shock absorber.

FUEL TANKS. All steel welded petrol tank with parcel grid. Oil tank under twinseat. Provision for reserve.

FRAME. Heavy duty brazed cradle type frame with swinging fork rear suspension, hydraulically damped "Easylift" centre stand.

NACELLE. (3TA 5TA only) integral with top of forks enclosing headlamp unit, 120 m.p.h. (180 Km.p.h.) speedometer, ammeter and switchgear.

BRAKES. Full width front hub heavily finned, incorporating powerful 7 in. brake. Fully floating shoes, finger adjustment.

WHEELS AND MUDGUARDS. Triumph design wheels with plated rims and spokes. Stylish rear enclosure on 3TA and 5TA which incorporates provision for mounting panniers. Sports semi rear enclosure on T90 and T100S/S.

LIGHTING EQUIPMENT. Powerful 7 in. headlamp has a combined reflector/front lens assembly, "pre-focus" bulb and adjustable rim. Wide angle rear/stop lighting with integral reflex reflector.

TWINSEAT ASSEMBLY. Cushioned seat, covered in waterproof black grey "Vynide". Seat is hinged and covers the 12 a.h. battery, rectifier, oil tank and filler, and tools.

HANDLEBAR. Chrome-plated bar with smooth action twistgrip adjustable for friction. Integral dipswitch/horn button. Adjustable levers with built-in cable adjusters.

FINISH. 3TA: Shell Blue Sheen or Silver Bronze. T90: Alaskan White. 5TA: Ruby Red. T100S/S: Regal Purple and Silver.

EXTRAS. Pillion footrests. Prop stand. Quickly detachable rear wheel. Steering lock. Tachometer (T90—T100 S/S).

ENGINE. 650 c.c. o.h.v. vertical twin with two gear driven camshafts. Light alloy cylinder head, cast-iron barrel, high compression pistons large bore carburetter. Splayed port head with two carburetters on T120. Finned rocker boxes. One-piece forged crankshaft with bolt-on central flywheel. "H" section RR56 alloy connecting rods with plain bearing big-ends. Dry sump lubrication with plunger type pump and pressure indicator. Twin coil ignition. Oil bath primary chaincase. Air cleaner (not T120).

GEARBOX. Built in unit with engine. Shafts and gears of hardened nickel and nickel-chrome steel. Needle roller layshaft bearings. Positive stop footchange. Multiplate clutch with indestructible cork sheet linings and rubber torsion shock absorber. Accessible filler and level plugs.

FRAME. Brazed cradle type frame with single large diameter front down tube and swinging fork suspension, hydraulically damped and adjustable for varying loads, "Easylift" centre stand. Provision for anti-theft lock. Front wheel stand.

FORKS. Triumph design telescopic pattern with hydraulic two-way damping and steering damper.

NACELLE. 6T only (Patent No. 647670) integral with top of forks enclosing headlamp, instruments and switchgear.

FUEL TANK. Large capacity all-steel welded petrol tank mounted on rubber and easily detached. Quick release fillers. Provision for reserve. Plated parcel grid.

BRAKES. Front: Full width finned hub, 8 in. diam. Rear: 7 in. diam. drum integral with sprocket. Fully floating shoes.

WHEELS AND MUDGUARDS. Triumph design wheels with plated spokes and rims semi rear enclosure, 6T only.

LIGHTING EQUIPMENT. Lucas alternator crankshaft mounted. 12 a.h. battery, powerful headlamp (quickly detachable when nacelle not fitted) with combined reflector/front lens assembly, "pre-focus" bulb and adjustable rim. Wide angle rear/stop light with combined reflector.

SPEEDOMETER. Smiths 120 m.p.h. (180 Km.p.h.) Chronometric type with R.P.M. scale and trip recorder. (140 m.p.h. 240 Km.p.h. on Bonneville 120).

HANDLEBAR. Chromium-plated with smooth action twistgrip and adjustable friction control. Integral horn push. Adjustable levers with built-in cable adjusters.

FINISH. 6T: Black/Silver. TR6: Regal Purple/Silver. T120: Alaskan White.

EXTRAS. Prop stand. Pillion footrests. Quickly detachable rear wheel. Steering lock.

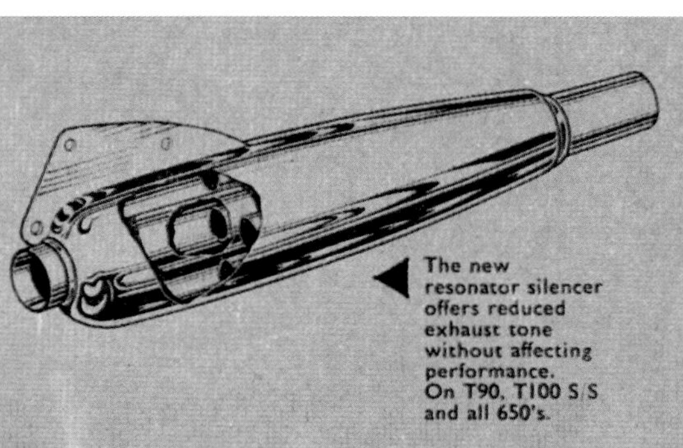

The new resonator silencer offers reduced exhaust tone without affecting performance. On T90, T100 S/S and all 650's.

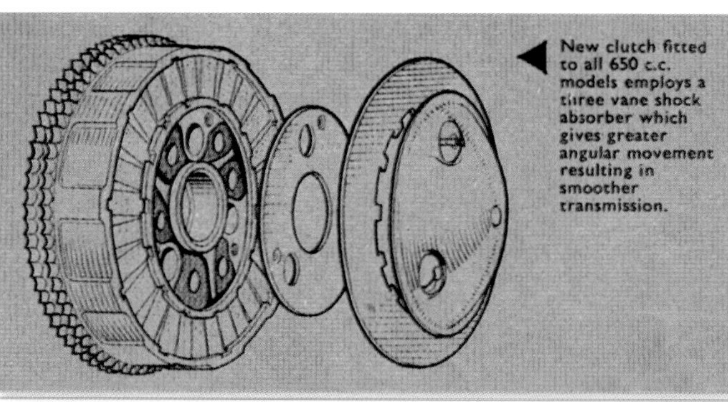

New clutch fitted to all 650 c.c. models employs a three vane shock absorber which gives greater angular movement resulting in smoother transmission.

MODEL	Tiger Cub (T20)	Sports Cub (T20S/H)	Twenty-one (3TA)	Tiger 90 (T90)	Speed Twin (5TA)	Tiger 100 (T100S/S)	Thunderbird (6T)	Trophy (TR6)	Bonneville 120 (T120)
Engine Type	O.H.V.	O.H.V.	O.H.V.	O.H.V.	O.H.V.	O.H.V.	O.H.V.	O.H.V.	O.H.V.
Number of Cylinders	1	1	2	2	2	2	2	2	2
Bore/Stroke, mm.	63 × 64	63 × 64	58.25 × 65.5	58.25 × 65.5	69 × 65.5	69 × 65.5	71 × 82	71 × 82	71 × 82
Bore/Stroke, ins.	2.48 × 2.52	2.48 × 2.52	2.29 × 2.58	2.29 × 2.58	2.72 × 2.58	2.72 × 2.58	2.79 × 3.23	2.79 × 3.23	2.79 × 3.23
Capacity, cu. cms.	199	199	349	349	490	490	649	649	649
Capacity, cu. ins.	12.2	12.2	21.2	21.2	30	30	40	40	40
Compression ratio	7:1	9:1	7.5:1	9:1	7:1	9:1	7.5:1	8.5:1	8.5:1
B.H.P. and R.P.M.	10@6,000	14.5@6,500	18.5@6,500	27@7,500	27@6,500	34@7,000	34@6,300	40@6,500	46@6,500
Engine Sprocket Teeth—Solo	19	19	26	26	26	26	29	29	29
Clutch Sprocket Teeth	48	48	58	58	58	58	58	58	58
Gearbox Sprocket Teeth	17	17	18	17	19	18	20	19	19
Sidecar (G/Box Sprocket)	—	—	—	—	—	—	18	17	17
Rear Sprocket Teeth	46	48	43	46	43	46	46	46	46
R.P.M. 10 M.P.H. Top Gear	985	960	742	810	702	763	616	630	648
							Solo / S/C	Solo / S/C	Solo / S/C
Gear Ratios—Top	6.84	7.13	5.33	6.04	5.05	5.70	4.60 / 5.11	4.84 / 5.41	4.84 / 5.41
„ „ —Third	9.04	8.56	6.32	7.15	6.0	6.75	5.47 / 6.08	5.76 / 6.44	5.76 / 6.44
„ „ —Second	14.05	13.37	9.37	9.80	8.88	9.26	7.77 / 8.64	8.17 / 9.15	8.17 / 9.15
„ „ —First	20.40	19.8	12.96	14.67	12.28	13.86	11.43 / 12.48	11.81 / 13.40	11.81 / 13.40
Carburetter—Make	Amal	Amal	Amal	Amal	Amal	Amal	Amal	Amal	Twin Amal
Carburetter—Type	32/1	376/272	375/62	376/300	375/35	376/273	376/285	376/40	376/286–287
Front Chain Size	⅜″ × .225″ × .25″ Duplex	⅜″ × .225″ × .25″ Duplex	⅜″ × .225″ × .25″ Duplex	⅜″ × .225″ × .25″ Duplex	⅜″ × .225″ × .25″ Duplex	⅜″ × .225″ × .25″ Duplex	⅜″ × .225″ × .25″ Duplex	⅜″ × .225″ × .25″ Duplex	⅜″ × .225″ × .25″ Duplex
Rear Chain Size	½″ × .205″ × .335″	½″ × .205″ × .335″	⅝″ × ⅜″ × .40″	⅝″ × ⅜″ × .40″	⅝″ × ⅜″ × .40″	⅝″ × ⅜″ × .40″	⅝″ × ⅜″ × .40″	⅝″ × ⅜″	⅝″ × ⅜″
Dunlop Tyres—Front, ins.	3.25 × 17	3.00 × 19	3.25 × 17	3.25 × 18	3.25 × 17	3.25 × 18	3.25 × 18	3.25 × 19	3.25 × 18
„ „ —Rear, ins.	3.25 × 17	3.50 × 18	3.50 × 17	3.50 × 18	3.50 × 17	3.50 × 18	3.50 × 18	4.00 × 18	3.50 × 18
Brake Diameter-ins. (cms.)	5½″ (13.97)	5½″ (13.97)	7″ (17.78)	7″ (17.78)	7″ (17.78)	7″ (17.78)	8″ F (20.32) 7″ R (17.78)	8″ F (20.32) 7″ R (17.78)	8″ F (20.32) 7″ R (17.78)
Finish	Flame/ Silver Grey	Burgundy Red/Silver Grey	Shell Blue or Silver/ Bronze	Alaskan White	Ruby Red	Regal Purple/ Silver	Black/ Silver	Regal Purple/ Silver	Alaskan White
Seat Height—ins.	29″	30″	29¼″	30″	29¼″	30″	30″	30½″	30½″
„ „ —cms.	(73.7)	(76.2)	(74.5)	(76.2)	(74.5)	(76.2)	(76.2)	(77.5)	(77.5)
Wheelbase—ins.	49″	50″	52¾″	53½″	52¾″	53½″	55″	55½″	55″
„ —cms.	(124.5)	(124.5)	(134)	(136)	(134)	(136)	(139.6)	(141)	(139.6)
Length—ins.	77″	78½″	81″	82¼″	81″	84¼″	84″	84½″	84″
„ —cms.	(195.5)	(199.3)	(206)	(209)	(206)	(213.9)	(213.5)	(214.5)	(213.5)
Width—ins.	25″	26″	27″	26½″	27″	26½″	27½″	27″	27″
„ —cms.	(63.5)	(66)	(68.5)	(67.3)	(68.5)	(67.3)	(70)	(68.5)	(68.5)
Clearance—ins.	5″	8¼″	5″	7.5″	5″	7.5″	5″	5″	5″
„ —cms.	(12.7)	(21)	(12.7)	(19)	(12.7)	(19)	(12.7)	(12.7)	(12.7)
Weight—lbs.	215	223	340	336	341	336	369	363	363
„ —kilos	(94)	(101)	(154.6)	(152.8)	(155)	(152.8)	(167)	(165)	(165)
Petrol—Galls.	3	3	3	3	3	3	4	4	4
„ —Litres	(13.5)	(13.5)	(13.5)	(13.5)	(13.5)	(13.5)	(18)	(18)	(18)
Oil—Pints	2¾	2¾	5	5	5	5	5	5	5
„ —Litres	(1.55)	(1.55)	(2.8)	(2.8)	(2.8)	(2.8)	(2.8)	(2.8)	(2.8)

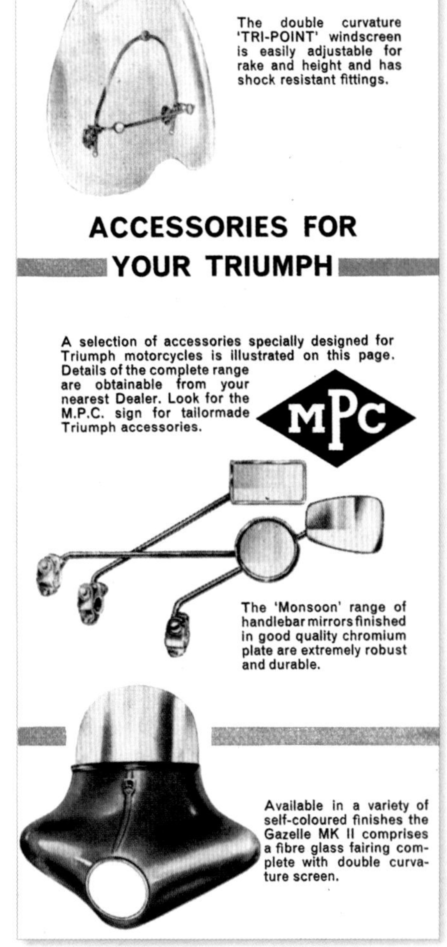

Just in case the racy look wasn't for you, and you wanted to spoil the looks of your Triumph, the brochure offered some tacky bolt-ons courtesy of MPC.

In the 1963 International Six Days' Trial in Czechoslovakia the Triumph team won three gold medals and a manufacturers team award. All the Triumph works riders were chosen for the British teams and finished without loss of marks in this, the most arduous event in the competitions calendar. Another notable gold medal winner was the famous American rider, Bud Ekins, on his favourite mount—the Triumph Trophy.

RIDERS AND MACHINES

K. Heanes	**Triumph 650 c.c.**	**Trophy TR6**
J. Giles	**Triumph 500 c.c.**	**Tiger 100**
R. Peplow	**Triumph 350 c.c.**	**Tiger 90**

Triumph was justifiably proud of its riders' achievements in the International Six Days Trial; not all, as you can see, were riding the big 650 Trophy. The Trials Cub was also a frequent award winner in major trials such as the Scottish Six Days and the West of England, ridden by the likes of Ray Sayer, Scott Ellis, John Giles and Roy Peplow.

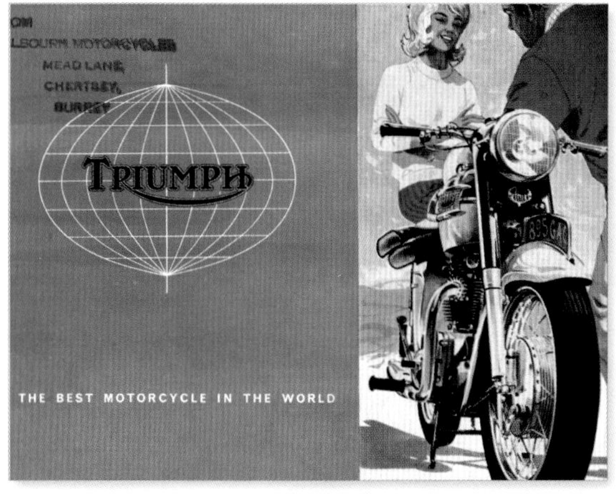

Still with vivid memories of the direct-lighting Bantam she'd owned and the undersized aftermarket headlamp on his ratty old T110, Prue was delighted when Steve came back from their local dealer on one of the new 1964 Thunderbirds with 12-volt electrics. Chertsey's Kilbourn Motorcycles is now long gone but back in the day was an enthusiastic dealership that even sponsored some racing, including a Tiger 100 in that year's Thruxton 500.

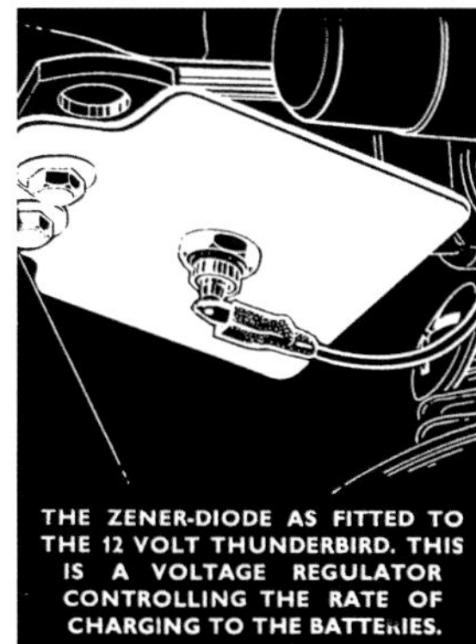

Cubs, whether the Sports (shown here, now featuring an extended chain guard), Standard, Trials or Scrambles were now turned out in Hi-Fi Scarlet over Silver. They also had been given tougher crankpins and oil pump drive pinions. At the behest of JoMo in California, who were anxious to be able to offer an alternative to the increasingly popular small-capacity Jap off-roaders, the Mountain Cub had been introduced. The T20M, as it was designated, was essentially a Trials Cub with the Sports's higher compression and more powerful motor.

The trusty 350 and 500 tourers, whilst retaining full swept front mudguards, now looked a little more sprightly due to the adoption of 'bikinis'. UK colours were Silver Beige for the 3TA and Black over Silver for the 5TA – the latter forsaking the tradition of red. Both continued in the use of a stressed fuel tank with internal brace whilst the (home-market) sports models began to be fitted with the four-point-mounting type in conjunction with frame brace later in the season. This system had been employed on US and other export models since 1961 but would be standardised for 1965.

For its second season the Tiger 90 continued to ape the Bonneville in colour if not performance – hence its sobriquet Baby Bonnie. I'm not too sure our chap on his Baby quite trusts his girlfriend, however, as he's keeping an eye on what she's up to with the clog-wearing, pipe-smoking, tulip-selling, stop-me-and-buy-one Dutchman. Optional extras for T90 and T100S/S included a rev counter. Both this and the standard speedometer on all Triumph twins were now magnetic – taking the place of the more complex and expensive chronometric type previously employed.

TIGER 90

350 c.c.

A sporting 350 c.c. twin which has already established itself after only one season as a new favourite in the Triumph range. Based on the well-known 500 c.c. Tiger 100, the Tiger 90 embodies a sporting specification already well tried and proved in the 1963 International Six Days' Trial where it won a gold medal and was 350 c.c. Class Winner in the 1963 1000 Km production machine race at Oulton Park. A 350 with power 'plus' performance to match superb road holding.

Like the 90 the '64 Tiger 100 S/S looked the better for having had its 'bikini' removed: the side panels fitted in its place being of less effete appearance and more in line with contemporary taste. Lighting and ignition switches, which had hitherto been mounted on the nearside front of the enclosure were now similarly located on the corresponding side panel. With the new forks came a revised mounting for the front stays of the sports models' blade front mudguard by way of lugs high on the front of the sliders.

TIGER 100

500 c.c.

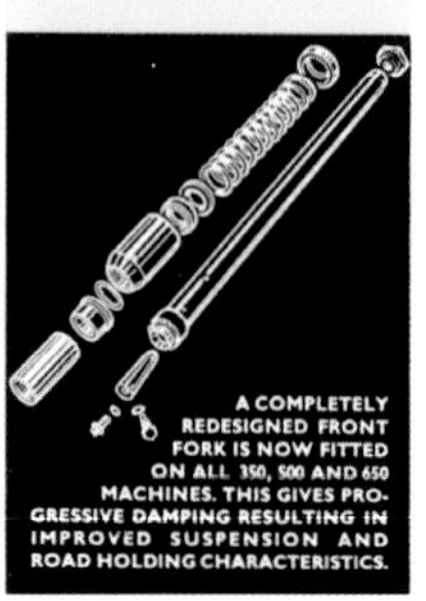

Winner of the 500 c.c. class in the 1963 Thruxton 500 mile Production machine race and gaining gold medal honours in the International Six Days' Trial for the past three years, the Tiger 100 has more than proved itself in these tough marathon endurance tests. Produced especially for the sporting rider who demands the ultimate in performance from a 500 c.c. machine.

Double gold medal winner in the gruelling 1963 International Six Days' Trial, proving ground for the world's best sports machines, the Trophy has an unequalled reputation for speed and stamina under any conditions. The powerful alloy head engine offers effortless and reliable high performance. The Trophy is a consistent winner in the toughest American long distance enduros.

Welsh Three Days' Trial		
Premier Award	John Giles	Trophy TR6
Gold Medal	Ken Heanes	Trophy TR6
Gold Medal	Roy Peplow	Tiger 90
Silver Medal	Ray Sayer	Tiger 100
Manufacturers Team Award	John Giles	Trophy TR6
	Ken Heanes	Trophy TR6
	Roy Peplow	Tiger 90
Army Three Days' Trial		
Premier Award	John Giles	Trophy TR6
Manufacturers Team Award	John Giles	Trophy TR6
	Ken Heanes	Trophy TR6
	Roy Peplow	Tiger 90
International Six Days' Trial		
Gold Medal	Roy Peplow	Tiger 90
Gold Medal	Ray Sayer	Tiger 90
Gold Medal	John Giles	Trophy TR6
Gold Medal	Ken Heanes	Trophy TR6
*Gold Medal	Dave Ekins	Tiger 100
*Gold Medal	Cliff Coleman	Trophy TR6
*Silver Medal	John Steen	Tiger 100
Manufacturers Team Award	Roy Peplow	Tiger 90
	John Giles	Trophy TR6
	Ken Heanes	Trophy TR6

*U.S.A. Vase 'A' Team Members.

As well as bettering its tally of Gold Medals in 1963's ISDT the Trophy enjoyed numerous other successes in 1964 – from long distance events in the UK to Enduros in the US. Triumph riders' participation in the '64 ISDT was not so much famous on account of those who were victorious but more for those who fell by the wayside, however. Since his return from the previous year's event Bud Ekins had got together some likeminded individuals consisting of himself, his brother Dave, his good friend Steve McQueen, Cliff Coleman and John Steen, who were keen to have a serious crack at the Silver Vase category of the arduous European marathon. With finance largely supplied by McQueen, the five made their way over to East Germany via the Meriden factory where they picked up the machines that they'd be riding. Ironically, on the third of the event's five days, seasoned off-road competitor Bud brushed a bridge, and although he finished the day it was found he had broken leg so did not restart on Thursday. Wednesday also proved to be Barbour-clad Steve's undoing after a series of prangs left his machine too badly damaged to continue. After collecting the SC Trophy (registration number BNX 822B) from the factory he took it to Comerfords, Thames Ditton, workshops where he participated in its preparation: it was finished in Hi-Fi Scarlet over Silver just like the bike in the brochure.

After a single season of Alaskan White the Bonneville and its 350cc pretender the Tiger 90 had been given a simple and effective facelift by finishing the upper portion of the tank in Gold of the same hue as the mudguard stripes. Prior to the 1966 season T120s were illustrated in sales literature with just a speedometer, as a matching rev counter was an optional extra. Curiously, however, unlike the T90s and 100s, it was not listed in the brochure.

AGAIN TRIUMPH EXTENDS THE LEAD IN THE HIGH PERFORMANCE GROUP OF MOTORCYCLES WITH THE TWIN CARBURETTER 650 c.c. BONNEVILLE 120. OFFERING THE HIGHEST POSSIBLE PERFORMANCE FROM A STANDARD PRODUCTION MOTORCYCLE AND FEATURING, AS OTHER TWIN CYLINDER MODELS, THE NEW FRONT FORK ARRANGEMENT WITH EXCEPTIONAL SUSPENSION AND DAMPING, THIS MODEL IS THE CHOICE OF THE MOST EXPERIENCED RIDERS. A 650 c.c. BONNEVILLE ENGINE HOLDS THE CURRENT WORLD SPEED RECORD OF 224.57 m.p.h. FOR TWO-WHEELED MACHINES, A PROUD TITLE WHICH IS UNDERLINED BY THE NUMEROUS SUCCESSES WHICH THE BONNEVILLE HAS ACHIEVED THROUGHOUT THE WORLD.

Tiger Cub (T20)	Sports Cub (T20S/H)	Twenty-one (3TA)	Tiger 90 (T90)	Speed Twin (5TA)	Tiger 100 (T100S/S)	Thunderbird (6T)	Trophy (TR6)	Bonneville 120 (T120)
O.H.V.	O.H.V.	O.H.V.	O.H.V.	O.H.V.	O.H.V.	O.H.V.	O.H.V.	O.H.V.
1	1	2	2	2	2	2	2	2
63 × 64	63 × 64	58.25 × 65.5	58.25 × 65.5	69 × 65.5	69 × 65.5	71 × 82	71 × 82	71 × 82
2.48 × 2.52	2.48 × 2.52	2.29 × 2.58	2.29 × 2.58	2.72 × 2.58	2.72 × 2.58	2.79 × 3.23	2.79 × 3.23	2.79 × 3.23
199	199	349	349	490	490	649	649	649
12.2	12.2	21.2	21.2	30	30	40	40	40
7:1	9:1	7.5:1	9:1	7:1	9:1	7.5:1	8.5:1	8.5:1
10@6,000	14.5@6,500	18.5@6,500	27@7,500	27@6,500	34@7,000	34@6,300	40@6,500	46@6,500
19	19	26	26	26	26	29	29	29
48	48	58	58	58	58	58	58	58
17	17	19	17	20	18	20	19	19
—	—	—	—	—	—	18	17	17
46	48	46	46	46	46	46	46	46
986	955	749	808	711	763	616	634	649
						Solo S/C	Solo S/C	Solo S/C
6.84	7.13	5.40	6.04	5.13	5.70	4.60 5.11	4.84 5.41	4.84 5.41
9.04	8.56	6.59	7.36	6.26	6.95	5.47 6.08	5.76 6.44	5.76 6.44
14.05	13.37	8.69	9.71	8.26	9.18	7.77 8.64	8.17 9.15	8.17 9.15
20.40	19.8	13.40	14.96	12.71	14.14	11.43 12.48	11.81 13.40	11.81 13.40
Amal 32/1	Amal 376/272	Amal 375/62	Amal 376/300	Amal 375/35	Amal 376/273	Amal 376/303	Amal 389/97	Twin Amal 389/203
⅜″ × .225″ × .25″ Duplex	⅜″ × .225″ × .25″ Duplex	⅜″ × .225″ × .25″ Duplex	⅜″ × .225″ × .25″ Duplex	⅜″ × .225″ × .25″ Duplex	⅜″ × .225″ × .25″ Duplex	⅜″ × .225″ × .25″ Duplex	⅜″ × .225″ × .25″ Duplex	⅜″ × .225″ × .25″ Duplex
½″ × .205″ × .335″	½″ × .205″ × .335″	⅝″ × ⅜″ × .40″	⅝″ × ⅜″ × .40″	⅝″ × ⅜″ × .40″	⅝″ × ⅜″ × .40″	⅝″ × ⅜″ × .40″	⅝″ × ⅜″	⅝″ × ⅜″
3.25 × 17 3.25 × 17	3.00 × 19 3.50 × 18	3.25 × 17 3.50 × 17	3.25 × 18 3.50 × 18	3.25 × 17 3.50 × 17	3.25 × 18 3.50 × 18	3.25 × 18 3.50 × 18	3.25 × 19 4.00 × 18	3.25 × 18 3.50 × 18
5½″ (13.97)	5½″ (13.97)	7″ (17.78)	7″ (17.78)	7″ (17.78)	7″ (17.78)	8″ F (20.32) 7″ R (17.78)	8″ F (20.32) 7″ R (17.78)	8″ F (20.32) 7″ R (17.78)
Hi-Fi Scarlet/ Silver	Hi-Fi Scarlet/ Silver	Silver Beige	Gold/ Alaskan White	Black/ Silver	Hi-Fi Scarlet/ Silver	Black/ Silver	Hi-Fi Scarlet/ Silver	Gold/ Alaskan White
29″ (73.7)	30″ (76.2)	29¼″ (74.5)	30″ (76.2)	29¼″ (74.5)	30″ (76.2)	30″ (76.2)	30½″ (77.5)	30½″ (77.5)
49″ (124.5)	50″ (127)	52¾″ (134)	53½″ (136)	52¾″ (134)	53½″ (136)	55″ (139.6)	55½″ (141)	55″ (139.6)
77″ (195.5)	78½″ (199.3)	81″ (206)	83¼″ (211.5)	81″ (206)	83¼″ (211.5)	84″ (213.5)	84½″ (214.5)	84″ (213.5)
25″ (63.5)	26″ (66)	27″ (68.5)	26½″ (67.3)	27″ (68.5)	26½″ (67.3)	27½″ (70)	27″ (68.5)	27″ (68.5)
5″ (12.7)	8¼″ (21)	5″ (12.7)	7.5″ (19)	5″ (12.7)	7.5″ (19)	5″ (12.7)	7⅛″ (18.1)	5″ (12.7)
215 (94)	223 (101)	340 (154.6)	336 (152.8)	341 (155)	336 (152.8)	369 (167)	363 (165)	363 (165)
3 (13.5)	3 (13.5)	3 (13.5)	3 (13.5)	3 (13.5)	3 (13.5)	4 (18)	4 (18)	4 (18)
2¾ (1.55)	2¾ (1.55)	5 (2.8)	5 (2.8)	5 (2.8)	5 (2.8)	5 (2.8)	5 (2.8)	5 (2.8)

Some trendy artwork for the cover of the 1965 season's brochure and it looks like Steve and Prue are still together, he more elegantly casual and she more sophisticated than last year. But it looks like he's thinking of yet another Triumph or perhaps even gone ahead and bought it. Although it could almost be either one of the latest Burnished Gold and White Tiger 100s or a Trophy that they're admiring I'll plump for the former, as the lack of finning on the rocker box and what looks to be a 7in front brake point to it being a Tiger.

A simple seasonal facelift for Twenty Ones and Speed Twins with a sportier front mudguard. But under the skin, or to be more precise the tank, the frame brace and four-point mounting was officially standardised, even though it had been fitted to a good number of 1964 machines and on US models since 1961.

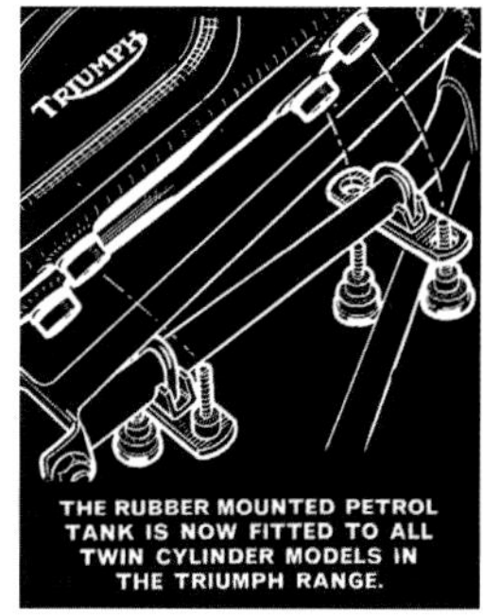

Whilst attention was drawn to the tank mountings the frame's reinforcement, although illustrated, was not mentioned.

The continuing appeal of the Tiger 90 lay in its visual similarity to the Bonneville coupled with lower cost of insurance; but its reputation as a good performer (for a British 350) was in jeopardy with 250cc Japanese machines going just as well. One was still good enough for the Reverend Bill Shergold, 'ton-up vicar' and leader of the legendary 59 Club, however – buying KPD 403C brand-new from Comerfords this year. Finish for both T90 and T120 was Pacific Blue over Silver with Blue central stripes for mudguards and Gold pin-striping.

With the Tiger 100 and Trophy looking so similar to the casual observer it's as well to illustrate them one above the other (Tiger 100 top), so the main visual differences between Triumph's little-and-large twins of this period will be more obvious. To point you in the right direction I'll suggest frames, front brakes, front wheels, petrol tanks, gearbox, primary chain case and top end of motors; but there's much more. The observations above also apply to the Tiger 90s and Bonnevilles but the latter's twin carbs, unless some wag had stuck a pair on his 350 twin, rather gave the game away.

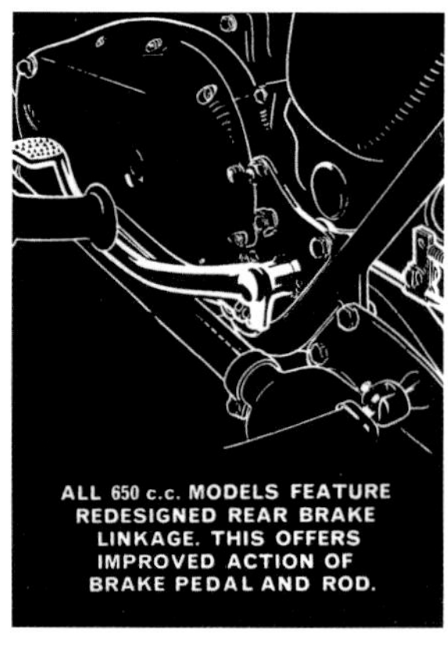

The Bonneville remained Triumph's flagship machine and good value at 'only' £43 more than its little pretender the Tiger 90, but it is all too easy to forget how much that sum represented 50-plus years ago. Rounding down prices to the nearest pound its £326 was also very competitive against other British 650 sportsters, with BSA's Lightning at £341, AJS's Hurricane or Matchless's Monarch at £342 apiece, with Norton's 650SS the dearest at £351. Not in the brochure but shown at the '64 show and available to special order was a 650 that topped the lot, however – the Thruxton Bonneville Production Racer listed at £357 9s 3d. Since Triumph's 1961 success the 500 had been bested each year by a 650SS Norton but upon the relocation of the event to Castle Combe for 1965, and then to Brands Hatch for '66 and '67, Bonnevilles enjoyed three consecutive victories.

In common with its smaller-capacity touring stablemates the T-bird was given a more sporting front mudguard for 1965 and, like Triumph's other 650s, had improved rear brake actuation.

RETAIL PRICES FOR GREAT BRITAIN & NORTHERN IRELAND

TRIUMPH

All retail prices are subject to the Guarantee published in the Company's current catalogue and the prices quoted on this list are for Delivery Free of Charge at Dealer's premises. The prices quoted here operate on and after 2nd March, 1964, and all previous lists are cancelled. The Company reserves the right to revise prices without prior notice and Purchase Tax also is subject to revision.

	MODEL	BASIC RETAIL	PURCHASE TAX	TOTAL RETAIL
T20	TIGER CUB 200 c.c. O.H.V.	£143 0 0	£27 15 11	**£170 15 11**
T20S/H	SPORTS CUB 200 c.c. O.H.V.	£158 0 0	£30 14 3	**£188 14 3**
TR20	TRIALS CUB 200 c.c. O.H.V.	£167 10 0	£32 11 2	**£200 1 2**
3TA	TWENTY-ONE 350 c.c. O.H.V. Twin	£234 0 0	£45 9 8	**£279 9 8**
T90	TIGER 90 350 c.c. O.H.V. Twin	£237 0 0	£46 1 5	**£283 1 5**
5TA	SPEED TWIN 500 c.c. O.H.V. Twin	£237 0 0	£46 1 5	**£283 1 5**
T100	TIGER 100 500 c.c. O.H.V. Twin	£240 0 0	£46 13 0	**£286 13 0**
6T	THUNDERBIRD 650 c.c. O.H.V. Twin	£258 0 0	£50 3 0	**£308 3 0**
TR6	TROPHY 650 c.c. O.H.V. Twin	£268 10 0	£52 3 10	**£320 13 10**
T120	BONNEVILLE 650 c.c. O.H.V. Twin	£273 10 0	£53 3 3	**£326 13 3**

EXTRAS
(When supplied with machine)

Q.D. REAR WHEEL	£3 18 9	15 4	**£4 14 1**
PROP STAND	£1 1 9	4 3	**£1 6 0**
PILLION FOOTRESTS	£1 1 0	4 1	**£1 5 1**
STEERING LOCK (200 c.c. and 650 c.c. Models)	14 3	2 10	**17 1**
TACHOMETER ASSEMBLY (T20S/H TR6 T120 T90 T100)	£6 17 0	£1 6 8	**£8 3 8**

TRIUMPH ENGINEERING CO. LTD.
MERIDEN WORKS · ALLESLEY · COVENTRY

Although this publicity material was a joint effort between JoMo and TriCor it did note that machines to Western specifications could vary from those shown. With a racer on the cover the inference could have been Triumph's efforts to dominate the USA's premier event the Daytona 200, which, apart from Don Burnet's victory in '62, had for years been the happy hunting ground of Harley Davidson's highly-tuned side-valve 750s whilst British contenders, with their overhead-valve motors, could field nothing larger than 500cc. Their day was coming, however, and 1966 and '67 would see back-to-back victories for the Meriden marque.

The TT Special had been brought out at the behest of Johnson Motors for 1963 and that first year boasted a heady 12:1 compression ratio. It was reduced to 11.2:1 for '64 but with 1³⁄₁₆in Amals 52hp was claimed. Upswept straight-through pipes were replaced by shorter low-level straight-throughs for '65. Another special US Bonneville was the T120/C or Competition Sports. First introduced in pre-unit form for 1961 they continued into the unit-construction era until 1965. More popular in the Eastern states, they were in the same state of tune as the regular Bonneville but featured upswept exhausts with small silencers, a crankcase shield and Dunlop trials tyres.

As well as the standard T20 these two were available in the US and the short-lived lemon, the Junior Cub, was still listed. Intended for beginners it was identical to the T20 but featured a smaller Zenith carb that restricted its power to just under 5hp. Launched in 1961, when it found about a dozen customers, it perversely remained on the books in the US despite no further sales having taken place.

Apart from western handlebars and a lack of front number plate the S/R's looks differed little from the home-market 100 but with the S/C the spirit of the old 500 Trophies lived on.

"Geared to the pace of space age life," read the preamble to Triumph's October 1965 brochure. So having undertaken a good deal of restyling for the '66 season, including the badge, plus the publication's theme of modernity and the future, why on earth did Triumph's advertising department imagine that this intent-looking chap on the cover, whose mode of dress and helmet was more '50s or sensible, would fill potential purchasers with anticipation? And the bike? With just a speedo it's surely a Tiger 90, but then his mum wouldn't want him on anything bigger.

The T20S/H Sports Cub (top) carried on much as before with basically the same frame design as had been used since the Cub's Terrier ancestor. Its low top-tube rising in swan-neck fashion to the headstock created an area of questionable structural integrity; a failing that the manufacturer had chosen to address by incorporating bracing within the petrol tank rather than at source. It did the job, however, as witness the Trials Cub's successes in trials over many seasons, even though the scrambles version was not well thought of (Sports Cub frames had a bracket on the offside for the high-level exhaust, as they were common to the off-road models).

Big news on the Cub front, however, concerned the regular T20s. For the 1966 season, in pursuit of an economy that in my mind turned out to do the little things a great favour, they began to be built with BSA Bantam frames – remember, BSA had owned Triumph since the early '50s. Turned out with the Bantam's undeniably superior frame, larger wheels, smaller petrol and larger oil tanks, chrome headlamp, and denuded of their rear enclosures, I quite liked the way they looked – some aspects of which were slightly reminiscent of the then-current small Ducatis. Cub buffs, however, then and now, generally feel differently, I suspect.

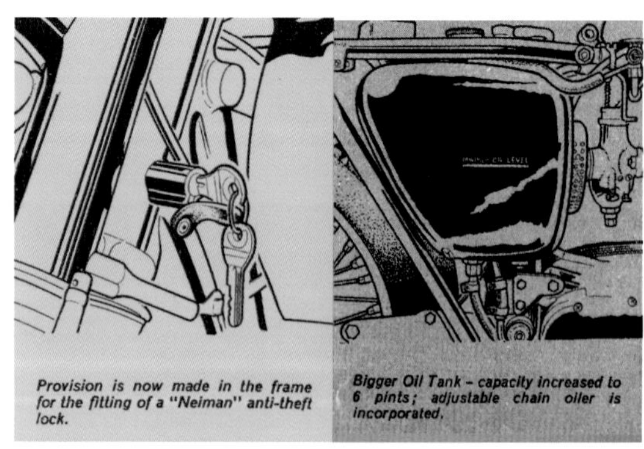

With all this space-age stuff it looked as though publicity had got a bit muddled – there were BSA Rockets, not Triumph. That aside, rear enclosures for Twenty Ones and Speed Twins were now a thing of the past, although nacelles remained; but the bikes themselves would soon be gone too, as this is their last year – production terminating in June 1966. In common with other Triumph twins they now had larger six-pint oil tanks with provision for chain oiling; also throughout the twin range the electrics were now 12-volt – at first with twin six-volt batteries and late on in the season a single 12. Trivia lovers may notice the different front mudguard bracket this year but you won't see that the rear guard was modified on account of the oil tank, or the location of the anti-theft lock, for that matter. The 3TAs were turned out in Pacific Blue and White whilst 5TAs continued with Black and Silver.

This is a home-market Tiger 100S/S but matters overseas were slightly complicated when the T100SR and T100SC models were superseded by T100S and T100Cs early (around November 1965) in the '66 season. Why Triumph hadn't sorted out the inadequacies of its frames properly years before with a total redesign beats me, but if the old adage 'if it looks wrong it is wrong' is to be heeded then 350/500 twin variety were definitely wrong 'uns. Various methods of bolstering up the headstock/top-tube area had been employed and the latest fix was to weld the previously-bolted-up bracing tube in place. To counter these comments it should be noted that Triumphs with this type of frame, from 200cc Cubs to 500cc T100s, sold in their thousands and competition versions excelled in various branches of motorcycle sport.

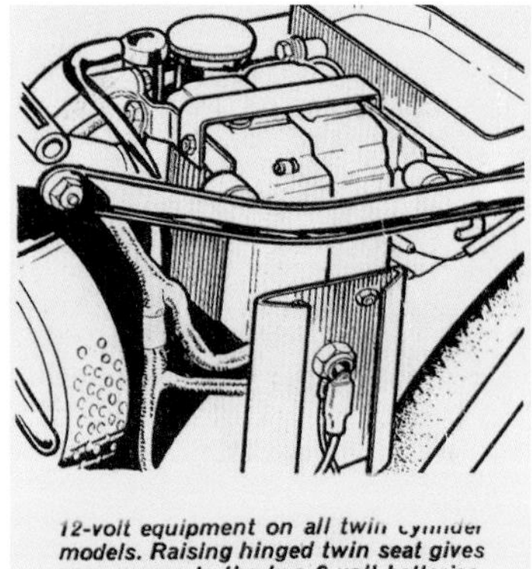

Batteries (firstly twin six-volt and later single 12) were carried thus on all twins, and those without headlamp nacelles (Tigers 90 and 100, Bonneville and Trophy) had their switchgear mounted in the nearside side panel. And here is the brochure's rose-tinted 1965 vision of future road systems. We wish! Fifty years on, despite grandiose governmental pronouncements, what happened?

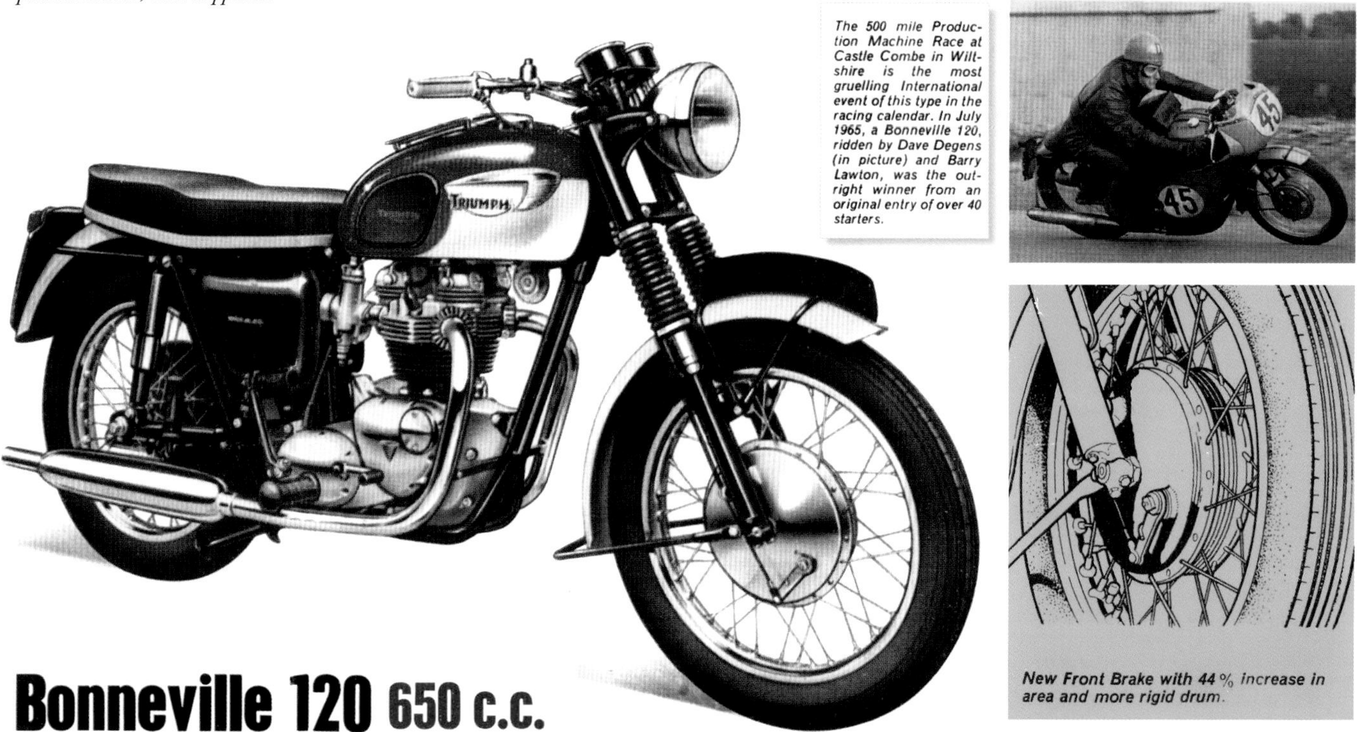

The Bonneville was still top of the range – and a race winner too – but something of the magic of the earlier versions was missing, and the colour scheme didn't help.

Manufactured and marketed as a sports rather than an out-and-out competition mount for several years, by now the big Trophy was still a capable machine in the right kind of event, especially in the US where the 'desert sled' was a popular mount for all-out racing or riding over the inhospitable scrubby wastelands of California and allied Western states. The days of big British cross-country irons were rapidly drawing to a close, however, as two- and four-stroke dirt bikes of lighter weight and equal or more performance from Scandinavia, mainland Europe and Japan took over – Ken Heanes persevering with increasingly uncompetitive Cheney-Triumphs until the early '70s, by which time over in the US even the 'King of Cool' had forsaken his Triumphs for Husqvarnas.

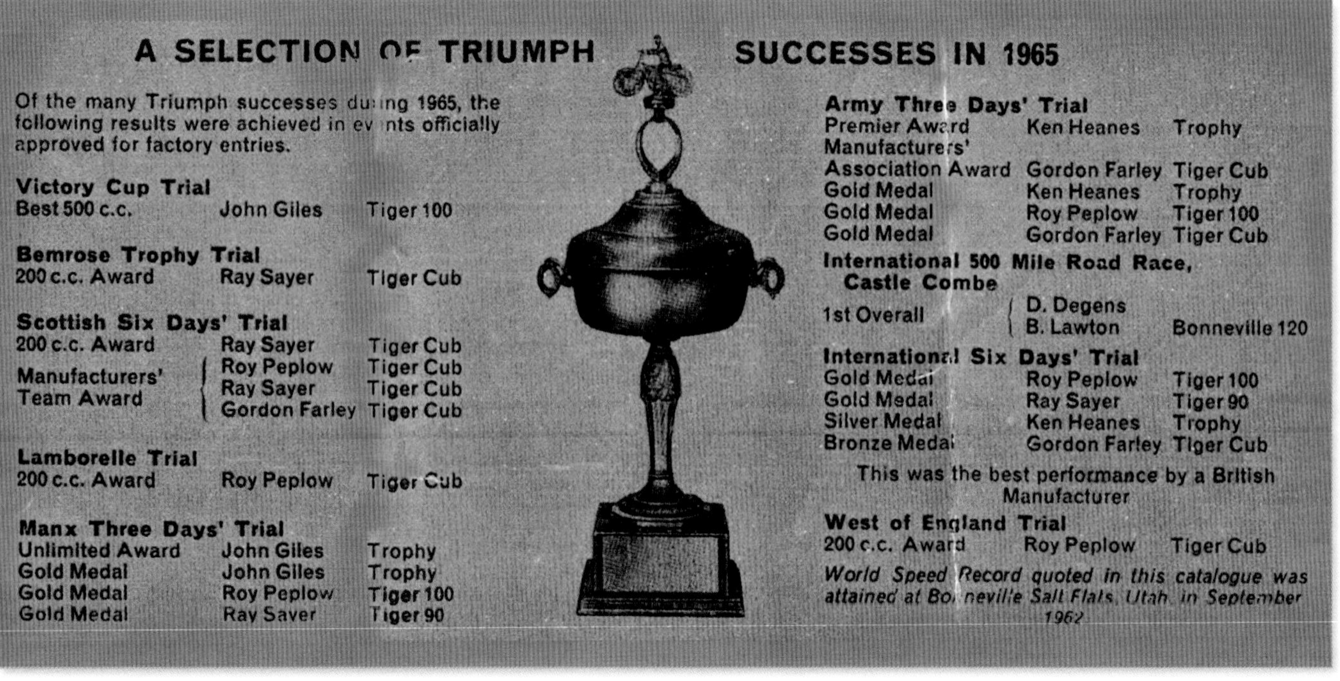

A SELECTION OF TRIUMPH SUCCESSES IN 1965

Of the many Triumph successes during 1965, the following results were achieved in events officially approved for factory entries.

Victory Cup Trial

Best 500 c.c.	John Giles	Tiger 100

Bemrose Trophy Trial

200 c.c. Award	Ray Sayer	Tiger Cub

Scottish Six Days' Trial

200 c.c. Award	Ray Sayer	Tiger Cub
Manufacturers' Team Award	Roy Peplow	Tiger Cub
	Ray Sayer	Tiger Cub
	Gordon Farley	Tiger Cub

Lamborelle Trial

200 c.c. Award	Roy Peplow	Tiger Cub

Manx Three Days' Trial

Unlimited Award	John Giles	Trophy
Gold Medal	John Giles	Trophy
Gold Medal	Roy Peplow	Tiger 100
Gold Medal	Ray Sayer	Tiger 90

Army Three Days' Trial

Premier Award	Ken Heanes	Trophy
Manufacturers' Association Award	Gordon Farley	Tiger Cub
Gold Medal	Ken Heanes	Trophy
Gold Medal	Roy Peplow	Tiger 100
Gold Medal	Gordon Farley	Tiger Cub

International 500 Mile Road Race, Castle Combe

1st Overall	D. Degens B. Lawton	Bonneville 120

International Six Days' Trial

Gold Medal	Roy Peplow	Tiger 100
Gold Medal	Ray Sayer	Tiger 90
Silver Medal	Ken Heanes	Trophy
Bronze Medal	Gordon Farley	Tiger Cub

This was the best performance by a British Manufacturer

West of England Trial

200 c.c. Award	Roy Peplow	Tiger Cub

World Speed Record quoted in this catalogue was attained at Bonneville Salt Flats, Utah, in September 1962

Thunderbird 650 c.c.

MODEL	Tiger Cub (T20)	Sports Cub (T20S/H)	Twenty-one (3TA)	Tiger 90 (T90)	Speed Twin (5TA)	Tiger 100 (T100S/S)	Thunderbird (6T)	Trophy (TR6)	Bonneville 120 (T120)
Engine Type	O.H.V.	O.H.V.	O.H.V.	O.H.V.	O.H.V.	O.H.V.	O.H.V.	O.H.V.	O.H.V.
Number of Cylinders	1	1	2	2	2	2	2	2	2
Bore/Stroke, mm.	63 × 64	63 × 64	58·25 × 65·5	58·25 × 65·5	69 × 65·5	69 × 65·5	71 × 82	71 × 82	71 × 82
Bore/Stroke, ins.	2·48 × 2·52	2·48 × 2·52	2·29 × 2·58	2·29 × 2·58	2·72 × 2·58	2·72 × 2·58	2·79 × 3·23	2·79 × 3·23	2·79 × 3·23
Capacity, cu. cms.	199	199	349	349	490	490	649	649	649
Capacity, cu. ins.	12·2	12·2	21·2	21·2	30	30	40	40	40
Compression ratio	7:1	9:1	7·5:1	9:1	7:1	9:1	7·5:1	8·5:1	9:1
B.H.P. and R.P.M.	10@6,000	14·5@6,500	18·5@6,500	27@7,500	27@6,500	34@7,000	37@6,700	40@6,500	47@6,700
Engine Sprocket Teeth—Solo	19	19	26	26	26	26	29	29	29
Clutch Sprocket Teeth	48	48	58	58	58	58	58	58	58
Gearbox Sprocket Teeth	17	17	17	17	19	18	20	19	19
Sidecar (G/box Sprocket)	—	—	—	—	—	—	18	17	17
Rear Sprocket Teeth	47	48	46	46	46	46	46	46	46
R.P.M. 10 M.P.H. Top Gear	1006	955	808	808	723	763	616	634	649
							Solo / S/C	Solo / S/C	Solo / S/C
Gear Ratios—Top	6·98	7·13	6·04	6·04	5·4	5·70	4·60 / 5·11	4·84 / 5·41	4·84 / 5·41
,, ,, —Third	9·23	8·56	7·36	7·36	6·6	6·95	5·47 / 6·08	5·76 / 6·44	5·76 / 6·44
,, ,, —Second	14·34	13·37	9·71	9·71	8·7	9·18	7·77 / 8·64	8·17 / 9·15	8·17 / 9·15
,, ,, —First	20·82	19·8	14·96	14·96	13·4	14·09	11·43 / 12·48	11·81 / 13·40	11·81 / 13·40
Carburettor—Make	Amal	Amal	Amal	Amal	Amal	Amal	Amal	Amal	Twin Amal
Carburettor—Type		376/272	375/62	376/300	375/35	376/273	376/303	389/97	389/203
Front Chain Size	⅜" × ·225" × ·25" Duplex	⅜" × ·225" × ·25" Duplex	⅜" × ·225" × ·25" Duplex	⅜" × ·225" × ·25" Duplex	⅜" × ·225" × ·25" Duplex	⅜" × ·225" × ·25" Duplex	⅜" × ·225" × ·25" Duplex	⅜" × ·225 × ·25" Duplex	⅜" × ·225" × ·25" Duplex
Rear Chain Size	½" × ·205" × ·335"	½" × ·205" × ·335"	⅝" × ⅜" × ·40"	⅝" × ⅜" × ·40"	⅝" × ⅜" × ·40"	⅝" × ⅜" × ·40"	⅝" × ⅜" × ·40"	⅝" × ⅜"	⅝" × ⅜"
Tyres—Front, ins.	3·25 × 18	3·00 × 19	3·25 × 18	3·25 × 18	3·25 × 18	3·25 × 18	3·25 × 18	3·25 × 19	3·25 × 18
,, —Rear, ins.	3·25 × 18	3·50 × 18	3·50 × 18	3·50 × 18	3·50 × 18	3·50 × 18	3·50 × 18	4·00 × 18	3·50 × 18
Brake Diameter-ins. (cms.)	5½" (13·97)	5½" (13·97)	7" (17·78)	7" (17·78)	7" (17·78)	7" (17·78)	8" F.(20·32) 7" R.(17·78)	8" F.(20·32) 7" R.(17·78)	8" F.(20.32) 7" R.(17·78)
Finish	Pacific Blue/White	Metallic Blue/White	Pacific Blue/White	Grenadier Red/White	Black/Silver	Sherbourne Green/White	Black/Silver	Pacific Blue/White	Grenadier Red/White
Seat Height—ins.	31"	30"	30"	30"	30"	30"	30"	30½"	30½"
,, ,, —cms.	(78·7)	(76·2)	(76·2)	(76·2)	(76·2)	(76·2)	(76·2)	(77·5)	(77·5)
Wheelbase—ins.	51⅛"	50"	53½"	53½"	53½"	53½"	55"	55½"	55"
,, ,, —cms.	(130)	(127)	(136)	(136)	(136)	(136)	(139·6)	(141)	(139·6)
Length—ins.	79⅜"	78½"	83¼"	83¼"	83¼"	83¼"	84"	84½"	84"
,, —cms.	(201·5)	(199·3)	(211·5)	(211·5)	(211·5)	(211·5)	(213·5)	(214·5)	(213·5)
Width—ins.	27¾"	26"	27"	26½"	27"	26½"	27"	27"	27"
,, —cms.	(70·5)	(66)	(68·5)	(67·3)	(68·5)	(67·3)	(68·5)	(68·5)	(68·5)
Clearance—ins.	5½"	8¼"	6"	6"	6"	6"	5"	7⅛"	5"
,, —cms.	(14)	(21)	(15·2)	(15·2)	(15·2)	(15·2)	(12·7)	(18·1)	(12·7)
Weight—lbs.	220	223	341	337	341	337	369	365	365
,, —kilos	(99·8)	(101)	(154·7)	(152·8)	(154·7)	(152·8)	(167)	(165·5)	(165·5)
Petrol—Galls.	2	3	3	3	3	3	4	4	4
,, —Litres	(9)	(13·5)	(13·5)	(13·5)	(13·5)	(13·5)	(18)	(18)	(18)
Oil—Pints	4	2¾	6	6	6	6	6	6	6
,, —Litres	(2·27)	(1·55)	(3·35)	(3·35)	(3·35)	(3·35)	(3·35)	(3·35)	(3·35)

As well as signalling the end of the smaller touring twins this season would be the last for the good old Thunderbird too. For its swansong it had been, thankfully, stripped of its bikini and given the same new 8in front brake as the other 650s, as well as being fitted with the improved front mudguard stay. Its tank was of course adorned with the new badges, which somehow suited its colour scheme more than its more brightly-painted brethren, thus allowing it to live out its twilight year with some grace.

VELOCETTE

Like almost all other manufacturers Velocette's initial post-war range was all but unchanged from 1939. Perhaps the firm selected the MAC for this 1947 brochure cover as some 2,000 in military trim had been supplied to the War Department during recent hostilities.

By the time that the Goodman family – father and sons – put their Velocette two-stroke motorcycles into production shortly after the end of the First World War, their Anglicisation was complete.

This venture had commenced many years earlier when Johan Gutgemann, born in 1857 in the small Rhineland town of Oberwinter, had moved to England – making his new home in the Midlands, where he met and later married the daughter of a prominent Shropshire family. By 1885 he had joined forces with the owner of a firm named Isaac Taylor and Co, which before diversifying into other products had apparently specialised in the manufacture of patent medicines. Under Johan's reign the company began to become involved in the bicycle industry with a shop near the jewellery quarter of Birmingham; meanwhile, he came to be known as John Taylor. By 1896, however, he had moved on, and in association with William Gue set up a firm trading as Taylor Gue Ltd, manufacturer of bicycles and associated parts, with workshops in Peel Street not far from Winson Green Prison.

In common with many other bicycle manufacturers the company became slowly but surely drawn into the realm of motorised transport, in this case largely due to John's eldest son Percy, who was working on a redesign of the Belgian Kelcom motorcycle engine for the London-based firm of Ormond. A completely new frame and running gear was needed, and not only was Taylor Gue contracted to make it but before long – at the end of 1904 – had taken over the company itself.

From there the logical step was to commence manufacturing a machine of the firm's own, and in 1905, even though young Percy had been lured over to Wolseley Motors and sent to India to promote the marque, it was advertising a lightweight motorcycle named the Veloce. The genesis of the Veloce unfortunately coincided with a downturn in the market that brought down Taylor Gue, but undismayed, and almost immediately, John Taylor found financial backing and formed Veloce Ltd – maker of components to the cycle industry, roller skates, rickshaws or anything similar.

Two years later Percy was back from India and, joined by his younger brother Eugene and with help from their father, set up New Veloce Ltd, which they hoped would soon be manufacturing a car of his design for the colonies. Although a running prototype saw the light of day it went no further, and henceforth the company built engines for Veloce, which recommenced motorcycle production in 1910, not long after which John Taylor was granted his long-wished-for British citizenship.

In 1912 Percy came up with an overhead-inlet-valve motor of some 275cc that featured a unit-construction two-speed gearbox with foot change, and a Veloce so-equipped was entered for the 1913 Junior TT. Ridden by Cyril Pullin it finished 22nd.

Next off Percy's drawing board was a little two-stroke of just over 200cc, which went into a loop-frame lightweight with either single or two speeds. Finished all in black with the word Velocette on its tank (on account of it being a small Veloce), it went on sale in 1914 along with an open-frame ladies' version. For the first two years of the war the company continued to make this alongside its four-stroke machines, but from 1916 production was curtailed and the works were subcontracted to engineering for firms such as Rolls-Royce. During the latter part of the war Johan

Gutgemann's transformation was completed, and by the process of deed poll John Taylor became John Goodman.

When civilian work was allowed once more the two-stroke went back into production, and in 1920 a move was made to new premises in Victoria Road, Aston. Over the next few years all manner of improvements were incorporated, such as mechanical lubrication and three speeds and, not before time, a clutch in 1922. Four were entered in the 250cc class of the 1921 Junior TT and, although one failed to finish the others came third, fifth and seventh. The following year there was a separate lightweight race, and one was placed third behind a Levis and a Rex-Acme.

Percy Goodman next embarked upon the design of an engine that was to bring the family company almost immediate and long-lasting success. Very definitely conceived with performance in mind, it had inclined overhead valves activated by an overhead camshaft driven by a shaft and bevels – its bore and stroke of 74x81mm giving it a capacity of 349cc.

Brought to the market late in 1925, a pair of machines had already run that year's Junior TT and both failed to finish, but by the following year the Goodmans were confident enough in their new K model, as it was designated, to enlist the services of two-times Senior TT winner Alec Bennett (with a Sunbeam in 1922 and a Norton in 1924).

Averaging over 66mph for the seven-lap race, Bennett finished over ten minutes ahead of his nearest rival, Jimmy Simpson on an AJS, and the newly inaugurated team prize was also won due to the fifth and ninth places by the other cammy Velos. Also in 1926, upon the dissolution of the Humphries and Dawes partnership, Velocette took the opportunity to make what would turn out to be its final move by relocating to the OK factory at York Road, Hall Green, Birmingham. Dawes left to become a cycle manufacturer whilst Humphries carried on, renaming the firm OK-Supreme.

The 1927 Junior TT was something of a disappointment due to the retirement of Bennett but designer/rider Harold Willis, who would shortly be responsible for Velocette introducing the positive-stop gear-change for motorcycles, came second to Freddie Dixon's HRD.

For a short while the camshaft 350s, available in either sporting or touring guise, were the only machines produced by the company, but in 1928 two-strokes, discontinued two years earlier, were reintroduced. That year Bennett gave the marque another Junior TT victory, with Willis runner-up once more and newcomer Freddie Hicks fifth.

The final year of the 1920s sadly saw the death of John Goodman but also the company's most overwhelming Junior result so far, with no less than six machines in the top ten. This time Hicks was the winner whilst a camshaft AJS was runner-up and Bennett third. The future looked rosy indeed, and a replica of the racing KSS – the KKT – was now marketed complete with Willis's ingenious gear-change.

Within a few months, however, the Wall Street Crash had taken place and Great Britain's economy was heading rapidly for the rocks. Nevertheless a redesigned and generally more robust two-stroke christened the GTP was introduced in 1930 and a cheaper camshaft model with twin-port head and coil ignition was

MODEL MOV

Complete with electric lighting, high frequency horn, licence holder, and trip speedometer with illuminated dial.

SPECIFICATION

LIGHTING. Dynamo 6-volt with voltage control. Accumulator 13-ampere hour. Headlamp dia. 8¼" (21.0 cm.) with dip-light. parking light, rear light and illuminated speedometer dial.
ENGINE. Velocette single port push-rod 248 c.c. Bore 68 mm., stroke 68¼ mm. Compression ratio 6½ to 1. Totally enclosed valve gear including valve stems.
LUBRICATION. Dry sump system. Constant circulation of oil by gear pump with the ½ gallon (2.27 litres) oil tank under the saddle. Primary chain is enclosed in an oil bath chain case. Gearbox is filled with oil and other parts lubricated by grease gun.
CARBURETTER. Controlled by quick action thin twist grip and fitted with starting and slow running throttle stop. Air lever on handlebar.
IGNITION. Magneto with flange fixing, gear driven, Automatic timing.
GEARBOX. Velocette 4-speed. Twin top. Gears controlled by foot gear lever ; gear change mechanism is enclosed in the gearbox. Kickstarter has folding crank. Clutch—three plates. Handcontrol lever on handlebar. Extra strong clutch cable 2.8 mm. dia.
GEAR RATIOS. 19 T sprocket. Top, 6.3 ; 3rd, 8.4 ; 2nd, 11.1 ; 1st, 16.1.
FRAME. Very sturdy. All joints are brazed, making a very rigid construction.
FRONT FORKS. Bronze bushed, ground spindles. Hand adjustable shock absorber and steering damper.
PETROL TANK. Capacity 2½ gallons (11.35 litres).
BRAKES. 6" dia. (15.23 cm.) with hand adjustments. Provision is made for keeping mud from both the front and rear brakes.
WHEELS. Detachable rear wheel. The wheel itself is mounted on two self contained journal bearings and can be quickly removed, leaving the brake shoes, drum, sprockets and chain in position.
RIMS. WM 2-19.
TYRES. 3.25 × 19.
SADDLE. Flexible top adjustable fixing.
STANDS. Rear stand is provided, but for ordinary use a prop stand is fitted. Usual type of front stand is also fitted.
FOOTRESTS. Steel forgings, rubber covered and adjustable.
SILENCER. Chromium plated, large capacity with integral fishtail.
MUDGUARDS. Ribbed round section 6" (12.7 cm.) wide. Detachable rear portion. Tubular stays.
TOOLKIT. Complete for all running adjustments, carried in large all-metal tool box with spare room. Also grease gun and inflator.
GROUND CLEARANCE. 5" (12.7 cm.) Crankcase is protected by the lower part of the frame.
HEIGHT TO TOP OF SADDLE. 27½" (70 cm.)
WHEELBASE. 52¼ (132.8 cm.)
WEIGHT COMPLETE. 280 lb. (127 kg.)
WIDTH OVER HANDLEBARS. 27½" (70 cm.)
SPEED. 65 m.p.h. (104.5 k.p.h.)
FINISH. Black and chromium. Tank, black and gold.

The GTP two-stroke had seen very limited production immediately after the war but by the time this brochure was printed in late 1946 it had been discontinued, so if you wanted a 250 Velo there was no longer a choice. With its short stroke the pushrod overhead-valve MOV was a willing performer and, size for size, it proved to be the most responsive to tuning of the M-series machines.

MODEL MAC Complete with electric lighting, high frequency horn, licence holder, and trip speedometer with illuminated dial.

SPECIFICATION

LIGHTING. Dynamo 6-volt with voltage control. Accumulator 13-ampere hour. Headlamp dia. 8¼" (21.0 cm.) with dip-light, parking light, rear light and illuminated speedometer dial.
ENGINE. Velocette single port push-rod 349 c.c. Bore 68 mm., stroke 96 mm. Compression ratio 6 to 1. Totally enclosed valve gear including valve stems.
LUBRICATION. Dry sump system. Constant circulation of oil by gear pump with the ½ gallon (2.27 litres) oil tank under the saddle. Primary chain is enclosed in an oil bath chain case. Gearbox is filled with oil and other parts lubricated by grease gun.
CARBURETTER. Controlled by quick action thin twist grip and fitted with starting and slow running throttle stop. Air lever on handlebar.
IGNITION. Magneto with flange fixing, gear driven. Automatic timing.
GEARBOX. Velocette 4-speed twin top. Gears controlled by foot gear lever ; gear change mechanism is enclosed in the gearbox. Kickstarter has folding crank. Clutch—seven plates. Hand control lever on handlebar. Extra strong clutch cable 2.8 mm. dia.
GEAR RATIOS. 19 T sprocket. Top, 5.5 ; 3rd, 7.3 ; 2nd, 9.6 ; 1st, 14.1.
FRAME. Very sturdy. All joints are brazed, making a very rigid construction.
FRONT FORK. Bronze bushed, ground spindles. Hand adjustable shock absorber and steering damper.
PETROL TANK. Capacity 2½ gallons (11.35 litres).
BRAKES. 6" dia. (15.23 cm.) with hand adjustments. Provision is made for keeping mud from both the front and rear brakes.
WHEELS. Detachable rear wheel. The wheel itself is mounted on two self-contained journal bearings, and can be quickly removed leaving the brake shoes, drum, sprocket and chain in position.
RIMS. WM 2-19.
TYRES. 3.25 × 19.
SADDLE. Flexible top, adjustable fixing.
STANDS. Rear stand is provided, but for ordinary use a prop stand is fitted. Usual type of front stand is also fitted.
FOOTRESTS. Steel forgings, rubber covered and adjustable.
SILENCER. Chromium plated, large capacity with integral fishtail.
MUDGUARDS. Ribbed round section 6" (12.7 cm.) wide. Detachable rear portion. Tubular stays.
TOOLKIT. Complete for all running adjustments, carried in large all-metal tool box with spare room. Also grease gun and inflator.
GROUND CLEARANCE. 5" (12.7 cm.) Crankcase is protected by the lower part of the frame.
HEIGHT TO TOP OF SADDLE. 27½" (70 cm.)
WHEELBASE. 52¼" (132.8 cm.)
WEIGHT COMPLETE. 285 lb. (130 kg.)
WIDTH OVER HANDLEBARS. 27½" (70 cm.)
SPEED. 70 m.p.h. (112.5 k.p.h.)
FINISH. Black and chromium. Tank, black and gold.

Fine Quality and Lasting Finish

Once again the inimitable Velocette is available, allowing those to whom fine quality is important to discriminate in favour of this famous make.

During the war years our already unique facilities for precision engineering were augmented with some of the finest machine tools in the world. With this capacity we were selected to manufacture special equipment calling for absolute accuracy and the finest limits. To-day these valuable resources are concentrated on producing the post-war Velocette which emerges an even finer motor cycle.

Superfine quality and a lasting finish, characteristic of pre-war Velocettes, again distinguish the post-war models as among the finest of their type.

At first glance the 1947 MAC is almost identical to the MSS. There were, however, many distinguishing features.

marketed as the KTP. In reality it was little cheaper to produce and its head robbed it of power so, after dallying with a 350cc side-valve, a high-camshaft four-stroke single that would be far cheaper to build than the costly Ks was planned. The first of what would become the M-series had a capacity of 250cc and was introduced for 1933 as the MOV; within a year it was joined by the 350cc MAC, then a year later by the 500cc MSS.

By this time, in an attempt to break Norton's stranglehold on the larger classes of the Tourist Trophy races, Velocette had come up with a 500cc racer and the KTT 350 was in its Mk V form. Although they managed excellent results, as high as second in both Senior and Junior races, outright victory was to elude them until a Mk VII KTT won the Junior in 1938 and a Mk VIII in 1939.

During those last years of peace Charles Udall, who had joined the firm some ten years earlier and headed the design department, together with Australian Phil Irving had come up with a pair of extraordinarily advanced machines. Both were vertical twins with twin contra-rotating crankshafts coupled by gears, and both had shaft drive but there the similarity ended. Irving was mainly concerned with a road-going machine of some 600cc with pushrod OHV mounted in a frame with stressed-skin rear that housed adjustable swinging-fork suspension. Udall's baby, on the other hand, was a 500cc supercharged OHC vertical-twin racer that the Goodmans hoped would finally win them the coveted Senior TT. The latter made it to the Isle of Man where it ran in just one practice session before being returned unraced to Hall Green, as it was obviously not race-ready. Within all too short a time Great Britain was at war and the two prototypes would remain just that whilst the factory became immersed in essential war work.

A MAC was evaluated by the War Department and suitably-modified versions ordered. Designated the MDD it was, however, produced in penny numbers compared with the military machines made by concerns such as BSA and Norton – the government considering that the factory's facilities were better employed on other contracts. Thus a large amount of specialised engineering work was carried out for the Castle Bromwich and other shadow factories, whilst the enamelling department was kept busy finishing the likes of steel helmets and similar products.

For a considerable time the Goodman brothers had yearned to make a machine that was truly a motorcycle for everyman and it now began to come to fruition in a strange way. Charles Udall was convalescing at home after severe appendicitis, and seizing upon his enforced sabbatical from war work, had his drafting equipment delivered to his home, where he drew up what would become the Velocette LE.

After a lengthy gestation period it would be launched at the first post-war show; and although its unconventional looks prevented it from widespread popularity amongst the motorcycling public its uptake by around 50 of the UK's police forces helped it to become the company's best-selling model ever – if not the hoped-for money-spinner due to its high tooling costs. No speed machine with its diminutive 150cc (enlarged to 192cc in 1951) side-valve horizontally-opposed motor, three-speed gearbox and shaft drive, it would, however, waft its rider along with barely a burble from its exhaust, and was a far more pleasant machine (and advanced for its time) than its looks might suggest.

Meanwhile Velocette's post-war singles recommenced where they had left off before hostilities, with the pushrod overhead-valve MOV, MAC and MSS, the overhead-cam KSS and even the two-stroke GTP, the last being discontinued almost immediately and before it had time to make it into the '46 sales brochure. The 250 MOV and 500 MSS lasted until 1948 when they were discontinued to concentrate on the new LE – the MOV forever and the MSS temporarily.

Velocette's racing department had suffered a setback with the death of Harold Willis in the summer of 1939 but as soon as was practicable the KTT Mk VIII, also virtually in pre-war form, was made available to a lucky few privateers. For a while it was the very best 350 racer that money could buy – as witness its three Junior TT wins from 1947 to '49. There were 500 versions as well, and Eugene Goodman's son Peter made joint-fastest lap on the way to finishing third behind two Nortons in the '47 Senior. He was also fourth in the Junior that year but his promising career as a racer came to an end when, through no fault of his own, he was badly injured at a small meeting in Eastern France a few weeks later. Although he recovered he never raced again, and his parents thereafter all but eschewed racing, leaving Percy Goodman's son Bertie to head that side of the business.

Drawing upon the Willis-designed twin-cam motor that had been campaigned in 1936, and which Ted Mellors had used to win that year's European 350 Championship, Bertie came up with an improved version for the 1949 season. Probably half-a-dozen 350s and a couple of 500s were built and financed as quasi-works entries by Nigel Spring, Dennis Mansell and Dick Wilkins to contest the 350 class of the first World Championship of 1949. Freddie Frith had won the Junior TT the previous year on a Spring-sponsored KTT, and by winning every round of the new series – as well as the Junior TT – on one of Spring's twin-cams he became the first 350 World Champion. The following year, with Frith now past 40 and having retired, Bob Foster was the most experienced Velo rider; although he failed to finish the Junior TT he too took the 350 Championship using a Wilkins-backed dohc KTT.

The following year Velocette ran its own factory team managed by Bertie Goodman but the KTT had had its day, and although some success came its way the advantage of Norton's Featherbed frame with Geoff Duke aboard was insurmountable. Nevertheless, until that point the KTT Velos from the family-run Black Country factory, with their pre-war sprung frame and girder forks, enjoyed a magnificent run before being bested by more modern designs.

Dowty Oleomatic front forks had been introduced on the road machines in late 1948 and fitted to the works racers for 1951/2 but at least one rider insisted on girders being fitted, as he claimed the newfangled forks did not work in harmony with the Dowty

MODEL MSS Complete with electric lighting, high frequency horn, licence holder, and trip speedometer with illuminated dial.

SPECIFICATION

LIGHTING. Dynamo 6-volt with voltage control. Accumulator 13-ampere hour. Headlamp dia. 8¼" (21.0 cm.) with dip light, parking light, rear light and illuminated speedometer dial.

ENGINE. Velocette single port short push-rod 495 c.c. Bore 81 mm., stroke 96 mm. Compression ratio 6 to 1. Totally enclosed valve gear including valve stems.

LUBRICATION. Dry Sump system. Constant circulation of oil by gear pump with ½ gallon (2.27 litres) oil tank under the saddle. Primary chain is enclosed in an oil bath chain case. Gearbox filled with oil and other parts lubricated by greese gun.

CARBURETTER. Controlled by quick action thin twist grip and fitted with starting and slow running throttle stop. Air lever on handlebar.

IGNITION. Magneto with flange fixing, gear driven. Automatic timing.

GEARBOX. Velocette 4-speed, twin top. Gears controlled by foot gear lever ; gear change mechanism is enclosed in the gearbox. Kickstarter has folding crank. Clutch—7 plates with fabric inserts. Hand control lever on handlebar. Extra strong clutch cable 2.8 mm. dia.

GEAR RATIOS. Solo 18 T sprocket. Top, 4.9 to 1 ; 3rd, 5.9 ; 2nd, 7.7 ; 1st, 11.2. Sidecar 17 T sprocket. Top, 5.1 to 1 ; 3rd, 6.2 ; 2nd, 8.2 ; 1st, 11.8.

FRAME. Cradle type, very rigid and strong. All joints are brazed. Lugs are provided for sidecar attachment on either side of the machine.

FRONT FORK. Bronze bushed, ground spindles. Hand adjustable shock absorber and steering damper.

PETROL TANK. Capacity 3½ gallons (15.9 litres). Special 3 point fixing.

BRAKES. 7" (17.7 cm.) dia. with hand adjusters. Provision is made for keeping mud from both front and rear brakes.

WHEELS. Detachable rear wheel. The wheel itself is mounted on two self-contained journal bearings and can be quickly removed, leaving the brake shoes, drum, sprocket and chain in position.

TYRES. 3.50 × 19 front, 4.00 × 19 rear.

RIMS. WM 3-19.

SADDLE. Flexible top, adjustable fixing.

STANDS. Rear stand is provided, but for ordinary use a prop stand is fitted. Usual type of front stand is also fitted.

FOOTRESTS. Steel forgings, rubber covered and adjustable.

SILENCER. Chromium plated, large capacity with integral fishtail.

MUDGUARDS. Ribbed round section 6" (15.25 cm.) wide. Detachable rear portion and tubular rear stays.

TOOLKIT. Complete for all running adjustments, carried in large all-metal tool box with spare room. Also grease gun and inflator.

GROUND CLEARANCE. 4¾" (12.05 cm.) Crankcase is protected by the lower part of the frame.

HEIGHT TO TOP OF SADDLE. 28" (71 cm.)

WIDTH OVER HANDLEBARS. 27½" (59.8 cm.)

WHEELBASE. 55" (140 cm.)

WEIGHT UNLADEN. 340 lb. (155 kg.)

SPEED. Solo 75/80 m.p.h. (120/128 k.p.h.) With light sports sidecar and passenger, 65 m.p.h. (105 k.p.h.)

FINISH. Black and chromium. Tank black and gold.

Despite the kudos attached to the ownership of a KSS, if it was out-and-out speed you wanted the MSS – as well as being a fine fast touring machine – offered greater possibilities, as the legendary Burt Munro demonstrated by clocking over 130mph and a circa-12½-second standing quarter-mile on his highly-modified example.

MODEL KSS Complete with electric lighting, high Frequency horn, licence holder and trip speedometer with illuminated Dial

The camshaft Velocette was manufactured to very high standards and had never been an economic proposition for its maker. Nevertheless it reappeared in the post-war range.

SPECIFICATION OF MODEL KSS.

LIGHTING. Dynamo 6-volt with voltage control. Accumulator 13-ampere hour. Headlamp dia. 8¼" (21.0 cm.) with dip-light, parking light, rear light and illuminated speedometer dial.
ENGINE. Velocette single port overhead camshaft 348 c.c. Bore 74 mm., stroke 81 mm. Compression ratio 7.6 to 1 with plates under the cylinder or with plates removed 8.4 to 1. Rocker box cast in one piece with the head in aluminium alloy, with inserted valve seats. Valves and rocker gear totally enclosed and automatically lubricated. Accessible tappet adjustment by means of eccentrically mounted rocker spindles.
LUBRICATION. Dry sump system. Constant circulation of oil by gear pump, with ½ gallon (2.27 litres) oil tank under the saddle. Primary chain is enclosed in an oil bath chain case. Gearbox is filled with oil and other parts lubricated by grease gun.
CARBURETTER. Controlled by quick action thin twist grip and fitted with starting and slow running throttle stop. Air lever on handlebar.
IGNITION. Magneto with flange fixing. Controlled by lever from handlebar.
GEARBOX. Velocette 4-speed, twin top. Gears controlled by foot gear lever; gear change mechanism is enclosed in the gearbox. Kickstarter has folding crank. Clutch—7 plates with fabric inserts. Hand control lever on handlebar. Extra strong clutch cable 2.8 mm. dia.
GEAR RATIOS. 17 T sprocket. Top, 5.6; 3rd, 6.8; 2nd, 9.0; 1st, 13.0.
FRAME. Cradle type, very rigid and strong. All joints are brazed. Lugs are provided for sidecar attachment on either side of the machine.
FRONT FORKS. Bronze bushed, ground spindles. Hand adjustable shock absorber and steering damper.
PETROL TANK. Capacity 3½ gallons (15.9 litres) special 3 point fixing.
BRAKES. 7" (17.7 cm.) dia. with hand adjusters. Provision is made for keeping mud from both front and rear brakes.
WHEELS. Detachable rear wheel. The wheel itself is mounted on two self-contained journal bearings and can be quickly removed, leaving the brake shoes, drum, sprocket and chain in position.
TYRES. 300 × 21 front and 3.25 × 20 rear.
RIMS. WM 1-21 front and WM 2-20 rear.
SADDLE. Flexible top, adjustable fixing.
STANDS. Rear stand is provided, but for ordinary use a prop stand is fitted. Usual type of front stand is also fitted.
FOOTRESTS. Steel forgings, rubber covered and adjustable.
SILENCER. Chromium plated, large capacity with integral fishtail.
TOOLKIT. Complete for all running adjustments, carried in large all-metal tool box with spare room. Also grease gun and inflator.
GROUND CLEARANCE. 4½" (11.42 cm.) Crankcase is protected by the lower part of the frame.
HEIGHT TO TOP OF SADDLE. 28" (71 cm.)
WIDTH OVER HANDLEBARS. 27½" (69.8 cm.)
WHEELBASE. 55" (140 cm.)
WEIGHT UNLADEN. 340 lb. (155 kg.)
SPEED. Solo 70/75 m.p.h. (112/120 k.p.h.)
FINISH. Black and chromium. Tank black and gold.

rear suspension units that had always been fitted to sprung-frame KTTs. When the export-only option of a sprung frame was announced for the pushrod singles at the 1952 show the Dowty phase had passed, and suspension front and rear was by conventional springs and hydraulic dampers - this frame, with its unconventional adjustable rear settings, doing duty for the rest of Velocette's life.

In 1952 the MAC's engine had been revamped with alloy head and barrel, as well as hairpin valve springs, but when the MSS was reintroduced two years later its motor, as well as having these attributes, now had a square bore and stroke ratio of 86x86mm. Swinging-arm frames were now standard and, largely on demand from the US, a scrambles machine was introduced in 1955.

That autumn the first of the sports pushrod 350s and 500s were announced in the form of the Viper and Venom. Initially little more than lightly breathed-upon, their abbreviated chrome mudguards and chromed tank singled them out from their more humble brethren. Over the years, however, a range of options such as aluminium rims, racing magneto, TT carburettor, close-ratio gears and a rev counter enabled one of the 500s so equipped to top the ton. Ample proof was recorded in March 1961 when a specially-prepared Venom Clubman with Avon fairing averaged 100.05mph for 24 hours at France's Montlhéry track – one of the team of eight riders included Bertie Goodman, who after the death of his father Percy in October 1953, had taken over as MD of the firm but still revelled in high-speed motorcycling. At the time of writing, the record still stands.

Completely new for the 1956 show, or nearly so on account of the engine dimensions and other features it shared with the 192cc LE, was the Valiant – a

New for '48 were Dowty Oleo-matic front forks, born of the Dowty Oleo undercarriage strut for aircraft. The system's first motorcycle application, almost certainly at the suggestion of Harold Willis, had been for the rear suspension units on pre-war Velocette works racers – later going into production on the Mk VIII KTTs. Good seals were imperative as the legs were pumpued up to, and had to hold, around 40psi. Damping was by oil.

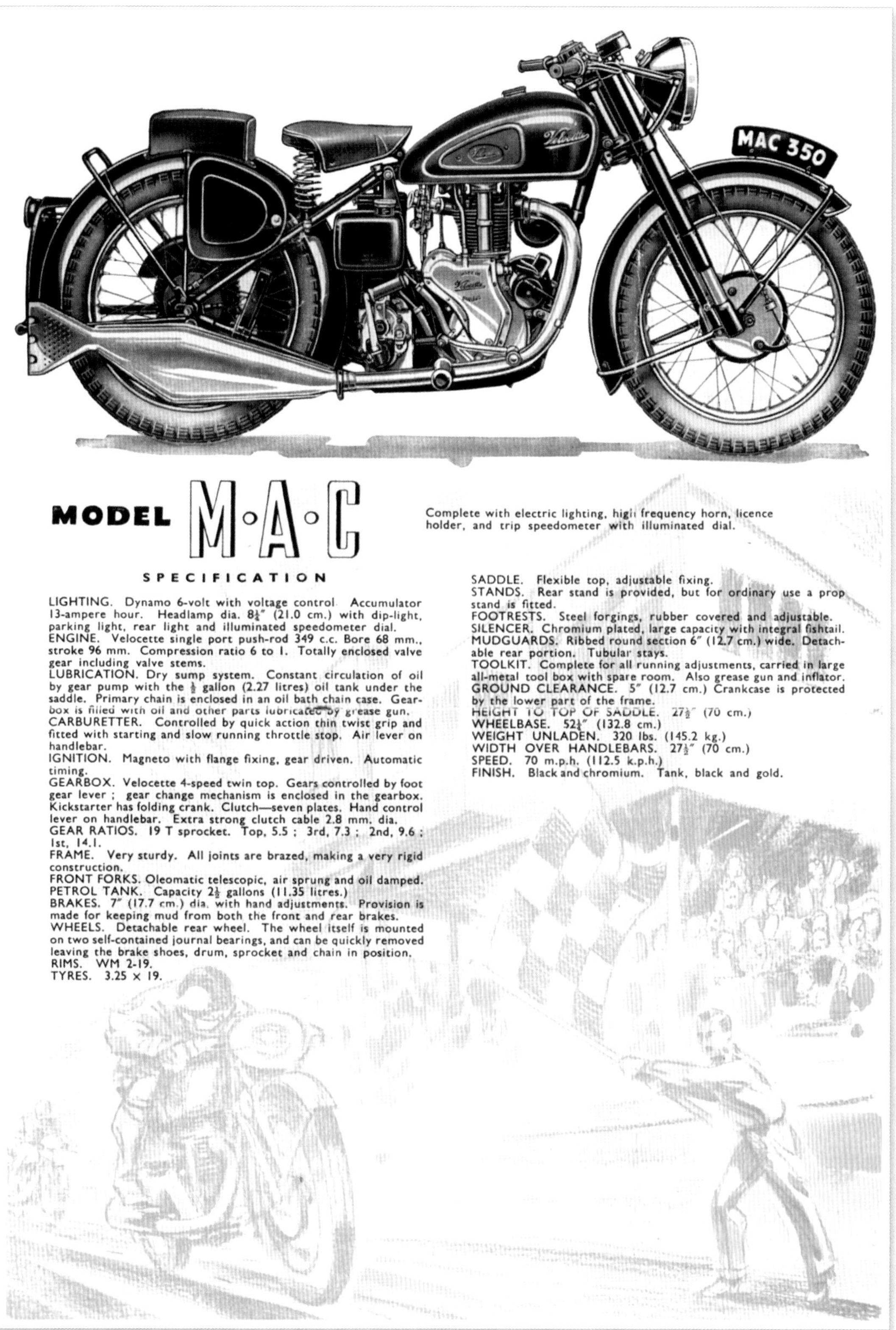

MODEL M·A·C

Complete with electric lighting, high frequency horn, licence holder, and trip speedometer with illuminated dial.

SPECIFICATION

LIGHTING. Dynamo 6-volt with voltage control. Accumulator 13-ampere hour. Headlamp dia. 8¼" (21.0 cm.) with dip-light, parking light, rear light and illuminated speedometer dial.
ENGINE. Velocette single port push-rod 349 c.c. Bore 68 mm., stroke 96 mm. Compression ratio 6 to 1. Totally enclosed valve gear including valve stems.
LUBRICATION. Dry sump system. Constant circulation of oil by gear pump with the ½ gallon (2.27 litres) oil tank under the saddle. Primary chain is enclosed in an oil bath chain case. Gearbox is filled with oil and other parts lubricated by grease gun.
CARBURETTER. Controlled by quick action thin twist grip and fitted with starting and slow running throttle stop. Air lever on handlebar.
IGNITION. Magneto with flange fixing, gear driven. Automatic timing.
GEARBOX. Velocette 4-speed twin top. Gears controlled by foot gear lever ; gear change mechanism is enclosed in the gearbox. Kickstarter has folding crank. Clutch—seven plates. Hand control lever on handlebar. Extra strong clutch cable 2.8 mm. dia.
GEAR RATIOS. 19 T sprocket. Top, 5.5 ; 3rd, 7.3 ; 2nd, 9.6 ; 1st, 14.1.
FRAME. Very sturdy. All joints are brazed, making a very rigid construction.
FRONT FORKS. Oleomatic telescopic, air sprung and oil damped.
PETROL TANK. Capacity 2½ gallons (11.35 litres.)
BRAKES. 7" (17.7 cm.) dia. with hand adjustments. Provision is made for keeping mud from both the front and rear brakes.
WHEELS. Detachable rear wheel. The wheel itself is mounted on two self-contained journal bearings, and can be quickly removed leaving the brake shoes, drum, sprocket and chain in position.
RIMS. WM 2-19.
TYRES. 3.25 × 19.
SADDLE. Flexible top, adjustable fixing.
STANDS. Rear stand is provided, but for ordinary use a prop stand is fitted.
FOOTRESTS. Steel forgings, rubber covered and adjustable.
SILENCER. Chromium plated, large capacity with integral fishtail.
MUDGUARDS. Ribbed round section 6" (12.7 cm.) wide. Detachable rear portion. Tubular stays.
TOOLKIT. Complete for all running adjustments, carried in large all-metal tool box with spare room. Also grease gun and inflator.
GROUND CLEARANCE. 5" (12.7 cm.) Crankcase is protected by the lower part of the frame.
HEIGHT TO TOP OF SADDLE. 27½" (70 cm.)
WHEELBASE. 52¼" (132.8 cm.)
WEIGHT UNLADEN. 320 lbs. (145.2 kg.)
WIDTH OVER HANDLEBARS. 27½" (70 cm.)
SPEED. 70 m.p.h. (112.5 k.p.h.)
FINISH. Black and chromium. Tank, black and gold.

Opinions differ as to which of the early post-war Velocettes was the nicest but those I have spoken with more often than not cite the little MAC, like this 1949 model, as the one they remember with the most affection.

horizontally-opposed OHV air-cooled twin. Handling was what one would expect from a Velocette but its engine lacked the smoothness of its stablemate and its performance was none too sparkling. Furthermore its advanced specifications made it expensive for a sub-200 machine so, in spite of remaining in production until 1964, it was never a best-seller.

In 1960, the year that the long-running MAC came

As well as Dowty Oleomatic forks, 1949 Mac and MSS machines had other minor differences from the previous year, such as less fully valanced front mudguards.

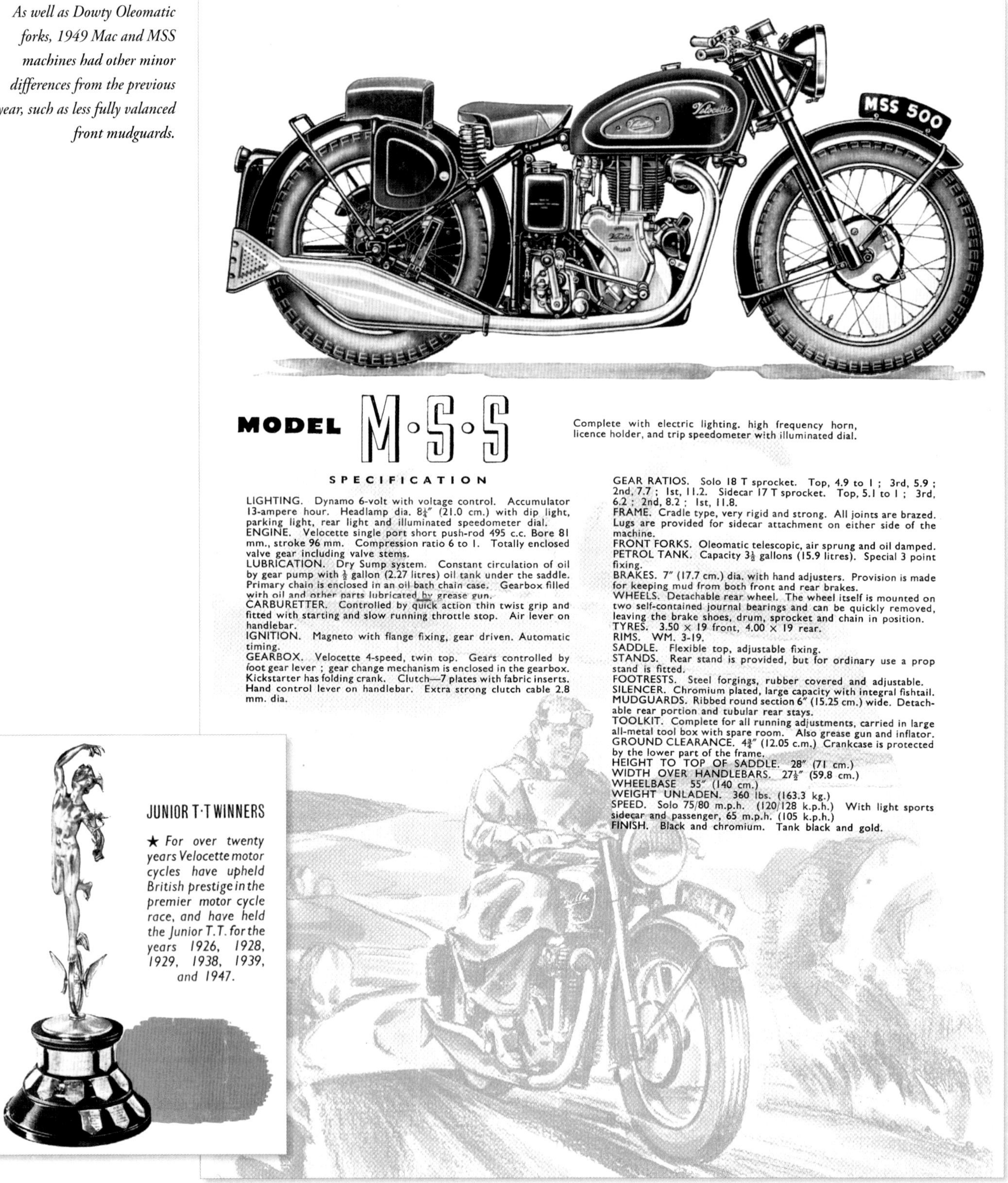

MODEL M·S·S

Complete with electric lighting. high frequency horn, licence holder, and trip speedometer with illuminated dial.

SPECIFICATION

LIGHTING. Dynamo 6-volt with voltage control. Accumulator 13-ampere hour. Headlamp dia. 8¼" (21.0 cm.) with dip light, parking light, rear light and illuminated speedometer dial.
ENGINE. Velocette single port short push-rod 495 c.c. Bore 81 mm., stroke 96 mm. Compression ratio 6 to 1. Totally enclosed valve gear including valve stems.
LUBRICATION. Dry Sump system. Constant circulation of oil by gear pump with ½ gallon (2.27 litres) oil tank under the saddle. Primary chain is enclosed in an oil bath chain case. Gearbox filled with oil and other parts lubricated by grease gun.
CARBURETTER. Controlled by quick action thin twist grip and fitted with starting and slow running throttle stop. Air lever on handlebar.
IGNITION. Magneto with flange fixing, gear driven. Automatic timing.
GEARBOX. Velocette 4-speed, twin top. Gears controlled by foot gear lever ; gear change mechanism is enclosed in the gearbox. Kickstarter has folding crank. Clutch—7 plates with fabric inserts. Hand control lever on handlebar. Extra strong clutch cable 2.8 mm. dia.
GEAR RATIOS. Solo 18 T sprocket. Top, 4.9 to 1 ; 3rd, 5.9 ; 2nd, 7.7 ; 1st, 11.2. Sidecar 17 T sprocket. Top, 5.1 to 1 ; 3rd, 6.2 ; 2nd, 8.2 ; 1st, 11.8.
FRAME. Cradle type, very rigid and strong. All joints are brazed. Lugs are provided for sidecar attachment on either side of the machine.
FRONT FORKS. Oleomatic telescopic, air sprung and oil damped.
PETROL TANK. Capacity 3½ gallons (15.9 litres). Special 3 point fixing.
BRAKES. 7" (17.7 cm.) dia. with hand adjusters. Provision is made for keeping mud from both front and rear brakes.
WHEELS. Detachable rear wheel. The wheel itself is mounted on two self-contained journal bearings and can be quickly removed, leaving the brake shoes, drum, sprocket and chain in position.
TYRES. 3.50 × 19 front, 4.00 × 19 rear.
RIMS. WM. 3-19.
SADDLE. Flexible top, adjustable fixing.
STANDS. Rear stand is provided, but for ordinary use a prop stand is fitted.
FOOTRESTS. Steel forgings, rubber covered and adjustable.
SILENCER. Chromium plated, large capacity with integral fishtail.
MUDGUARDS. Ribbed round section 6" (15.25 cm.) wide. Detachable rear portion and tubular rear stays.
TOOLKIT. Complete for all running adjustments, carried in large all-metal tool box with spare room. Also grease gun and inflator.
GROUND CLEARANCE. 4¾" (12.05 c.m.) Crankcase is protected by the lower part of the frame.
HEIGHT TO TOP OF SADDLE. 28" (71 cm.)
WIDTH OVER HANDLEBARS. 27½" (59.8 cm.)
WHEELBASE 55" (140 cm.)
WEIGHT UNLADEN. 360 lbs. (163.3 kg.)
SPEED. Solo 75/80 m.p.h. (120/128 k.p.h.) With light sports sidecar and passenger, 65 m.p.h. (105 k.p.h.)
FINISH. Black and chromium. Tank black and gold.

JUNIOR T·T WINNERS

★ For over twenty years Velocette motor cycles have upheld British prestige in the premier motor cycle race, and have held the Junior T.T. for the years 1926, 1928, 1929, 1938, 1939, and 1947.

There would be two more shields engraved with the word Velocette added to the base of this trophy after further victories in 1948 and 1949.

to the end of the line, Velocette tried its hand at the scooter market with the Viceroy. Powered by a 250cc horizontally-opposed two-stroke twin, it had larger wheels than the norm and handling a bit above par, but it didn't catch on and after four years they called it a day, with a mere 700-odd having found buyers.

Even less popular was the Vogue, which debuted at the 1962 show. At first glance it appeared as though

Velocette had taken a leaf out of Ariel's book and added twin headlights to the Leader; but under the skin was the combination of a hefty tubular spine frame and the mechanicals of the Mk III LE – a recipe that resulted in rather good road-holding and rather poor performance. The net result of the whole was sales that averaged little more than one a week over its six-year lifespan.

Apart from doing the company's finances no good these peccadilloes were fortunate insomuch as they discouraged Velocette from deviating again from what it did best – building high-quality, honest-to-goodness (and by that time old-fashioned) singles in the sporting tradition.

With the demise of the Clubmans TT in 1956 the annual endurance race held at Thruxton airfield circuit in Hampshire had taken on its mantle, and the early events were dominated by BSA Gold Stars; meanwhile Velocettes were all too often dogged by bad luck. From 1960 to '63, Norton 88s won the 500 class with a Venom in second place on all three occasions, and again in 1963 – this time to a Triumph T100. Finally, in 1964 – the last time that the event was held at Thruxton – Velocette achieved its ambition and Venoms finished first, second and third in their class, following with a win at the new 500-mile venue, Silverstone, the following year, and then at Brands Hatch in 1966.

Thus was born the magnificent Velocette Thruxton that enraptured Velo enthusiasts along with the wider public, many of whom by that time saw the large British single as something of an anachronism, at the 1964 Motorcycle Show. Over the next seven years just over 1,000 would be produced, and in 1967 a pair came first and second in the inaugural 500cc Production TT on the Isle of Man.

With the passing of the '60s the firm's other singles gradually came to the end of their lives, the Viper in 1968 and the Venom in 1970. At this time, however, a strange and unfortunate twist to what would be the last days of the company came about in the form of an arrangement with the American publisher and owner of the Indian motorcycle name, Floyd Clymer. Using a combination of Italian cycle parts along with an Italjet-made frame and Venom engine and gearbox, the Indian Velo, finished in bilious colour schemes of Clymer's choice, was to be marketed by Indian dealerships in the States. Unsurprisingly they proved next-to-impossible to sell and something over 100 had found homes when Clymer's death in 1970 brought the curtain down on these ill-conceived and expensive hybrids.

The Thruxton remained in production until the end came in 1971 when the old firm, thankfully spared the indignities and machinations of takeovers and government meddling, quietly declared itself insolvent and was wound up.

SPECIFICATION OF MODEL KSS

LIGHTING. Dynamo 6-volt with voltage control. Accumulator 13-ampere hour. Headlamp dia. 8¼" (21 0 cm.) with dip-light, parking light, rear light and illuminated speedometer dial.
ENGINE. Velocette single port overhead camshaft 348 c.c. Bore 74 mm., stroke 81 mm. Compression ratio 7.6 to 1 with plates under the cylinder or with plates removed 8.4 to 1. Rocker box cast in one piece with the head in aluminium alloy, with inserted valve seats. Valves and rocker gear totally enclosed and automatically lubricated. Accessible tappet adjustment by means of eccentrically mounted rocker spindles.
LUBRICATION. Dry sump system. Constant circulation of oil by gear pump, with ½ gallon (2.27 litres) oil tank under the saddle. Primary chain is enclosed in an oil bath chain case. Gearbox is filled with oil and other parts lubricated by grease gun.
CARBURETTER. Controlled by quick action thin twist grip and fitted with starting and slow running throttle stop. Air lever on handlebar.
IGNITION. Magneto with flange fixing. Controlled by lever from handlebar.
GEARBOX. Velocette 4-speed, twin top. Gears controlled by foot gear lever ; gear change mechanism is enclosed in the gearbox. Kickstarter has folding crank. Clutch—7 plates with fabric inserts. Hand control lever on handlebar. Extra strong clutch cable 2.8 mm. dia.
GEAR RATIOS. 17 T sprocket. Top 5.6.; 3rd, 6.8 ; 2nd, 9.0 ; 1st, 13.0.
FRAME. Cradle type, very rigid and strong. All joints are brazed. Lugs are provided for sidecar attachment on either side of the machine.
FRONT FORKS. Oleomatic telescopic, air sprung and oil damped.
PETROL TANK. Capacity 3½ gallons (15.9 litres) special 3 point fixing.
BRAKES. 7" (17.7 cm.) dia. with hand adjusters. Provision is made for keeping mud from both front and rear brakes.
WHEELS. Detachable rear wheel. The wheel itself is mounted on two self-contained journal bearings and can be quickly removed, leaving the brake shoes, drum, sprocket and chain in position.
TYRES. 300 × 21 front and 3.25 × 20 rear.
RIMS. WM 1-21 front and WM 2-20 rear.
SADDLE. Flexible top, adjustable fixing.
STANDS. Rear stand is provided, but for ordinary use a prop stand is fitted.
FOOTRESTS. Steel forgings, rubber covered and adjustable.
SILENCER. Chromium plated, large capacity with integral fishtail.
TOOLKIT. Complete for all running adjustments, carried in large all-metal tool box with spare room. Also grease gun and inflator.
GROUND CLEARANCE. 4½" (11.42 cm.) Crankcase is protected by the lower part of the frame.
HEIGHT TO TOP OF SADDLE. 28" (71 cm.)
WIDTH OVER HANDLEBARS. 27½" (69.8 cm.)
WHEELBASE. 55" (140 cm.)
WEIGHT UNLADEN. 360 lbs. (163.3 kg.)
SPEED. Solo 70/75 m.p.h. (112/120 k p.h.)
FINISH. Black and chromium. Tank black and gold.

The Mk II KSS had replaced the Mk I for 1936 and here it is in its final 1949 form with the Dowty forks that had replaced the Webb girders for the last year of production. The cost of its engine was the biggest factor by far that led to its demise, as the majority of the cycle parts were the same as the MSS. Although it didn't feature in the factory sales literature the KTT Mk VIII was available as an over-the-counter racer in the same way as the Norton Manx; and if you contacted the factory it would send you Roneoed specifications along with a picture. This shows how far removed from one another the two cammy Velos had become since their bloodline had begun to diverge with the creation of the KTT version of the KSS in 1929. The KTT outlived its road-going relation, and by the time that the last were made in 1950 around 240 had been produced.

The autumn 1948 launch brochure for the LE had one of the pre-production machines placed beside a couple admiring the Mawddach Estuary with Barmouth Railway Bridge in the distance. Conceived in the dark days of World War Two, Eugene Goodman's long-held dream of a motorcycle for all men was at last released for sale to the public. In almost clandestine fashion it was designed by Charles Udall, with reference to preliminary sketches by Phil Irving and Eugene's notes, whilst he was at home convalescing from severe appendicitis during 1942. Although the factory was flat out with government contracts time was 'stolen' to construct a prototype, which was up and running by 1944. Registered FON 598 it was used as a development hack for several years, and upgraded accordingly, before being sold to Motor Cycling's *Bernal Osborne.*

Engine.	149 c.c. Bore 44 m/m., Stroke 49 m/m., horizontally opposed twin cylinder, four stroke, side valve. Water cooled by thermo syphon system, with radiator mounted forward of the engine.
Ignition.	By coil with automatic advance. Coil contact breaker and distributor housed inside generator casing at front of engine.
Carburetter.	Twist grip controlled and fitted with easy starting control. An air cleaner is mounted between the two elements of the radiator. A petrol filter also is fitted and is quickly detachable for cleaning.
Lubrication.	Constant circulation of oil by gear pump from pressed steel sump beneath engine. Dip stick for checking oil level. Capacity of sump, 1¼ pints. Gearbox and final drive casings filled to levels.
Gear Box.	Three speed, controlled by gate change hand lever.
Gear Ratios.	Top, 7—1; Second, 13—1; First, 21—1.
Transmission.	Transmission by enclosed universal joint and shaft to Zerol bevel gears driving rear wheel.
Starting.	By upward pull on accessible hand lever. Operation of starting lever automatically raises stand.
Lighting.	Special 6 volt, 30 watt generator mounted on front of engine, feeding 13 A.H. accumulator. Headlamp of 6 in. diameter with 24 watt bulb and 3 watt parking light. Dip switch on left handle bar.
Frame.	Light, rigid steel pressing, incorporating rear mudguard, battery box, tool box (with tool roll and kit of tools) and (mounted underneath) petrol tank of 1¼ gallons capacity.
Suspension.	By coil springs front and rear. Front enclosed in telescopic forks; rear adjustable for varying loads.
Saddle.	Pan seat with soft rubber pad, water-proof cover and coil springs.
Wheels.	Quickly detachable, with aluminium alloy rims and 19 in. × 3 in. tyres.
Brakes.	5 in. diameter front and rear. Front operated by lever on handlebar; rear by pedal.
Mudguards.	Of entirely new design, giving complete protection.
Legshields.	Aluminium alloy with top panels, containing lighting and ignition switches, speedometer and carrying tyre inflator.
Footboards.	Rubber covered, shaped to provide alternative foot positions.
Horn.	6 volt, high frequency with press button on handiebar.
Speedometer.	Mounted on panel on legshields; driven from gearbox.
Licence Holder.	Fitted in front number plate.
Stand.	Double sided prop stand, automatically raised by starting lever.
Finish.	Silver-grey, black and chromium.

Full of anticipation for the coming success of the 'everyman's lightweight', Velocette put no less than ten of them, all finished in silver, on the 1948 show stand. Also on display were a pair of KTTs and a pair of MACs – the MOV and MSS having been dropped to free up production space for the newcomer and the KSS on economic grounds. The adjustable rear suspension, shaft drive, and associated stressed sheet steel frame had been a feature of Phil Irving's pre-war vertical twin Model O prototype. As first envisaged the footboards had been flat but they were soon altered to this stepped pattern to better accommodate a pillion passenger.

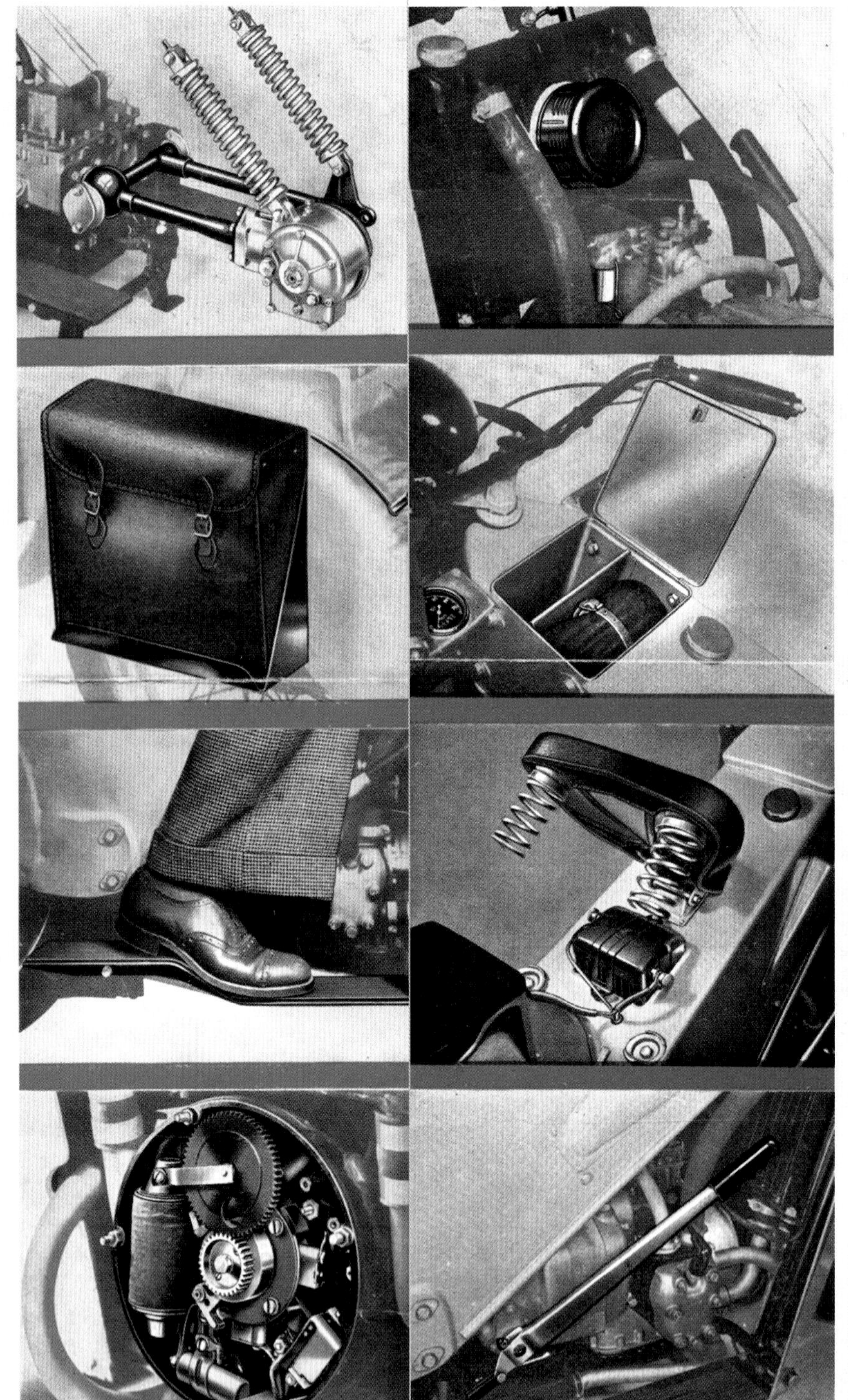

Rear Suspension and Shaft Drive.

The shaft drive completely enclosed, eliminates the dirt, noise and frequent adjustment inseparable from chain drive. In conjunction with the simple rear suspension, it offers a degree of luxury and long life never attained previously in a machine of this class.

Suspension Adjustment and Panniers.

To be able, instantly, to adjust the rear suspension to suit the load carried, is a point, the value of which is obvious. The built-in pannier bags solve all the problems of the tourist or the shopper. Luggage is carried without risk of damage, thanks to the suspension.

Natural Foot Position.

Long Foot Boards, having two levels, permit a change of foot position which is most desirable on long runs. Again, the short rider is made comfortable and the tall rider is not cramped.

B.T.H. Generator.

Lighting and ignition are attended to by a really robust generator mounted at the front of the engine. The contact breaker is readily accessible, automatic ignition control is included and provision is made for starting the engine should the battery become exhausted through negligence.

Air Cleaner.

An efficient air cleaner with a large filtering area is fitted neatly behind the radiator. A vent pipe from the crankcase is taken into the air filter, thereby preventing dust entering the engine crankcase.

Tool Box.

Where they are most accessible, the tools are kept in a capacious box which does not spill them to the floor when the lid is opened. A separate compartment is provided for spares or other items.

Battery.

Completely insulated from shock and shielded from the weather, the battery is made instantly accessible by hingeing the saddle forward. The saddle springs are released from their cups by a quick turn of the wrist.

Hand Starter.

No engine is easier to start than this. The unique hand starter is an unmixed boon and removes all the drudgery and difficulty associated with kick starters. Operation of the starter automatically lifts the stand.

With a good number of LEs now in circulation the most often voiced criticism had been its lack of power, so the original 149cc version was superseded by the introduction of the 192cc Mk II in the autumn of 1951. The increased capacity was achieved by enlarging the bore to 50mm. Otherwise its specification was unaltered, with the exception of a slight drop in top gear ratio from 7:1 to 7.25:1.

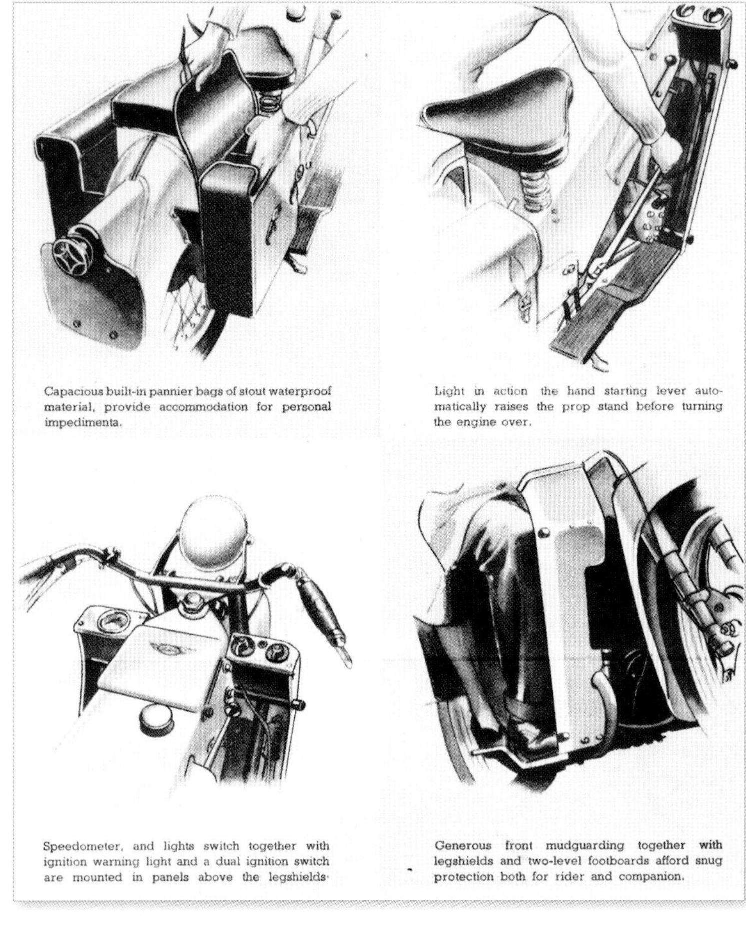

Pillion work, even in hilly country is well catered for by that extra power output of the '200' engine. The rear suspension is adjustable for riding weight.

The subframe carrying the engine, transmission, rear suspension forks, stand, footboards and radiator.

Yes, either of these two gents could easily have used an LE for commuting – but nowadays? Their equivalent would more likely be about the climb into some executive motor or squeezed into unsuitably skin-tight Lycra and about to do the cycling thing.

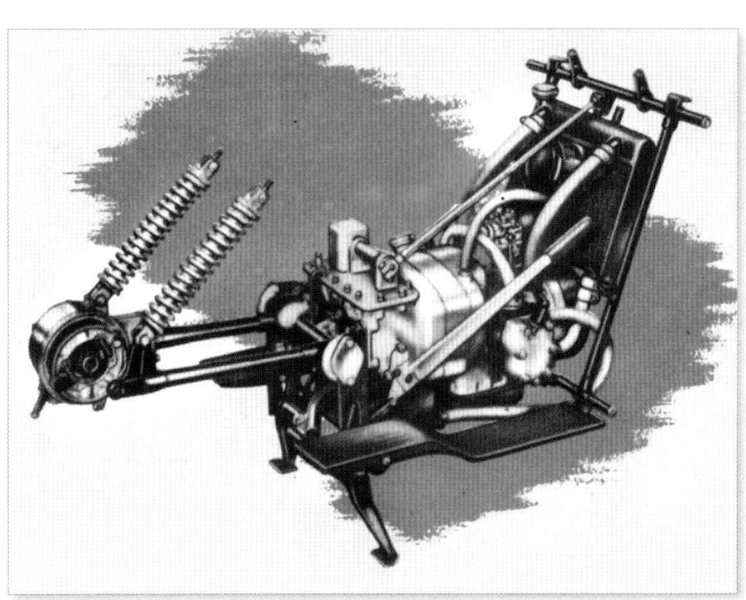

Visitors to the 1951 Earls Court Show could have been excused for thinking that the 350s on the Velocette stand had a completely new short-stroke motor with aluminium head and barrel. The MAC's bore and stroke remained at 68x96mm, however – it was just that the redesigned cylinder head and shorter pushrod tube gave that impression. The timing cover had been cleaned up too and no longer carried the maker's name. Pressurised Dowty front forks had been replaced by units of rather more conventional Velocette design that incorporated headlamp mounts on the top fork sleeves.

If you lived in Great Britain, Velocette's 1952 show stand was a bit of a tease, as prominently displayed were the very latest 350 MAC machines with swinging-arm frames that sales staff and factory publicity maintained were closely based on that of the late lamented and very much revered KTT Mk VIII. I'd hate to get into an argument with marque cognoscenti over this but would comment that, whilst the seat tube and swinging-arm assembly were KTT-based much of the rest was very different. Be that as it may the new model was quite obviously a desirable addition to the range and would be keenly sought after – in vain. And here was the catch – the new model was for export only. You didn't believe it? Then consult the price lists: "LE –£173 15s 7d; MAC – £191 0s 7d; MAC Springer – for export only." So, unless you could pull some serious strings or were prepared to buy abroad and import, if you wanted a new MAC it would have had to be a hard tail.

The aluminium MAC engine had replaced the previous type a year ago in the rigid-framed machines but the combination of the motor and gearbox with this casing was for the new swinging-arm-frame machines.

With the new frame came completely different tanks, rear mudguard and seat, to name a few things. But it was the reasoning behind the seat that the sales material went to some pains to explain: "Since ladies predominate as pillionists, they will appreciate the stepped rear seat which enables them to look over instead of into those broad shoulders of the man at the helm." By the way, and please note, at first this type of silencer was specified for the spring-frame MAC.

And, spring unit aside, here's what 'the man at the helm' would see if he glanced down, but with the speedo nudging 70mph would the pillion passenger (lady or otherwise) still be wanting to look over 'those broad shoulders'? Besides, the conditions would have to be very favourable for a MAC to do this with two up.

Some like the looks of Velocette's swinging-arm frame with adjustable rear suspension and some do not but – I have to admit that I am one of the latter – it works very well in practice.

Out of the 24 machines displayed on Velocette's 1953 show stand six were a completely new model. For 1954 and by popular demand the 500 MSS was back – an old name but with a new engine and in the new, to the UK market, sprung frame. This was the last year that handlebars of the singles were finished in black enamel – the following season they would be chromium plated. Sales material published for the US market featured chromium-plated American-style handlebars. The absolute stickler for original finishes should note that spokes were also black-enamelled until the end of the season, whereafter they were plated.

Rather than being a larger bore (81x98mm) 495cc version of the MAC's (68x96mm) motor, as it had been before, the new MSS was a short-stroke unit with dimensions of 86x86mm, which displaced 499cc. In the future it would prove capable of considerable development but for the meanwhile it was no flyer, as The Motor Cycle *found out. Valve float announced its top speed in third to be 71mph and in top it could just persuade the speedo needle past the 80 mark, with a gallon of fuel disappearing every 72 miles at a steady 50mph or every 52 miles at 60.*

THE MSS ENGINE

Engine and gearbox are in close and rigid assembly. The O.H.V. power unit has an aluminium alloy head and barrel with iron liner. Hairpin valve springs are fitted and valve gear is totally enclosed.

Full enclosure of the gearchange mechanism will be noted. A smooth operating four-plate clutch transmits the drive.

Several years ago I owned a Liverpool-registered example of this machine that was virtually one-owner. Apart from the paint on the petrol tank, a later-type dual seat and a replacement front mudguard it was completely original. It did everything I asked of it but was somehow unexciting. In retrospect, however, I failed to appreciate its more important qualities – chief of which was simply its honest good quality. Exactly what the manufacturer claimed.

SPECIFICATION MAC and MSS Models

ENGINE. Velocette single cylinder, overhead valves.

CARBURETTER. Amal needle type, controlled by quick action thin twist grip and having a starting and slow running throttle stop. A separate air control lever is fitted on the handlebar

AIR CLEANER. A large oil-wetted air filter is housed between the oil tank and the accumulator. The filter element can be cleaned and re-oiled.

IGNITION. Gear driven, flange mounted magneto with automatic timing control.

LUBRICATION. Dry sump system with constant circulation by gear pump from ½ gallon (2.27 litres) oil tank. A large replaceable filter element in the tank ensures that all dirt is removed from the oil. An oil bath case encloses the primary chain, and the gearbox is lubricated by oil. Grease gun lubrication is used for other parts.

GEARBOX. Velocette, foot operated, four-speed with all gear change mechanism enclosed in the box. The kickstarter has a folding footpiece and the box is fitted with a multi-plate clutch.

FRAME. Velocette, swinging arm type with patented adjustment for rear suspension struts to cater for all loading conditions. Suspension struts are spring controlled and hydraulically damped.

FRONT FORKS. Velocette telescopic. Spring controlled and hydraulically damped.

PETROL TANK. Black with gold lines. 3 gallons (13.6 litres) capacity.

BRAKES. 7″ (17.7 cm.) diameter front and rear ; each with hand adjustment and special provision for excluding mud and water.

WHEELS. Rims WM.2-19 with 3.25″ x 19″ tyres. Mounted on journal ball bearings. Rear wheel, which is quickly detachable, leaves the brake assembly and chain in place.

SADDLE. Special two level dual seat giving a low seating position for the rider whilst allowing a comfortable seat for the passenger.

LIGHTING. 6-volt dynamo with automatic voltage control. Accumulator 13 ampere hour. Headlamp 7″ (17.7 cm.) diameter with dip-light and parking light. Rear lamp incorporates a stop light. The speedometer dial is illuminated.

MUDGUARDS. Round section 6″ (15.2 cm.) wide with central rib. Rear guard is deeply valanced and has a detachable rear portion. The tubular stays of the rear guard form convenient lifting handles.

STANDS. A central stand is fitted but for normal purposes a prop stand is provided.

FOOTRESTS. Steel forgings rubber covered and adjustable.

SILENCER. Large capacity with integral fishtail.

TOOLKIT. Complete for all running adjustments, carried in neatly mounted metal box. Grease gun and tyre inflator.

FINISH. Black and chrome ; Tank black and gold.

GROUND CLEARANCE. At normal loaded position 5½″ (14 cm.).

SADDLE HEIGHT. At normal loaded position 30½″ (77.5 cm.).

WHEEL BASE. 53¾″ (136.5 cm.).

WIDTH OVER HANDLEBARS. 27½; (70 cm.).

DETAILED SPECIFICATION

MAC MODEL

ENGINE. 349 c.c., 68 mm. bore x 96 mm. stroke. Compression ratio 6¾ to 1. Overhead valves and rocker gear totally enclosed in aluminium alloy cylinder head with one piece cover. Cylinder barrel has iron liner with aluminium alloy fins cast on.

GEAR RATIOS. With the standard 21-tooth gearbox sprocket : Top 5.5, third 7.3, second 9.6, first 14.00.

WEIGHT UNLADEN. 355 lbs. (161 kg.).

SPEED. 70 m.p.h. (112 k.p.h.) approx.

MSS MODEL

ENGINE. 499 c.c., 86 mm. bore x 86 mm. stroke. Compression ratio 6¾ to 1. Overhead valves and rocker gear totally enclosed in one piece aluminium alloy rocker box. Hairpin valve springs. Cylinder barrel has iron liner with aluminium alloy fins cast on. Alloy head.

GEAR RATIOS. With the standard 18-tooth gearbox sprocket : Top 4.87, third 5.86, second 7.74, first 11.18.

WEIGHT UNLADEN. 375 lbs. (170.6 kg.).

SPEED. 80 m.p.h. (128 k.p.h.) approx.

Once it became available on the home market for 1954 the sprung-frame MAC was given the traditional fishtail silencer. Rear suspension units were also of a slightly different type with aluminium covers. I trust you've also noticed that a rectangular oil tank transfer came into use at this time and sidecar lugs now featured on MAC frames. For those who wanted a cheaper version or simply preferred a solid rear end the unsprung frame model was still listed.

In 1953 Velocette's motivated US West Coast distributor Lou Branch prepared a couple of the new spring-framed MACs (one de-stroked to a 250) for experienced Californian off-road racer John McLaughlin to ride in that year's Catalina Island races. Not only did the 250 win the lightweight race but the nimble 350 got the better of the entire field to take the main event. The following year Branch was sent one of the first of the MSS scramblers, and with it Jim Johnson gave the marque its Catalina double by winning the Grand Prix. These victories attracted a following for the scramblers in the US but they never really caught on with the top British riders in the same way as the big-single BSA and AMC scramblers.

BASED on the MSS 500, the new Velocette Scrambler is specially designed for its purpose. The engine has a high compression piston giving a C.R. of 8.75 to 1, special cams and cylinder holding-down bolts of increased diameter are employed. Hand controlled magneto ignition is fitted. The Amal racing carburetter has a choke diameter of $1\frac{5}{32}''$. Petrol tank capacity reduced to $2\frac{1}{2}$ gallons. The telescopic front forks are hydraulically damped in both directions. Competition tyres of 3.00″ x 21″ and 4.00″ x 19″ are provided. The rear wheel has six stud drive with 60 tooth sprocket. A substantial undershield protects the engine and gearbox.

Velocette Equipment

Listed as an extra but designed and manufactured by Velocette for the MAC and MSS models, this useful twin pannier equipment will appeal to the tourist and every-day rider alike. Apart from this special feature both models are fully equipped with dual-seat, pillion footrests, lighting, horn, speedometer and licence holder as standard.

Electrics were by Miller and up until the end of the '54 season this rather attractive rear light was fitted, after which it was superseded by a more up-to-date-looking (and probably cheaper) unit with moulded Perspex cover.

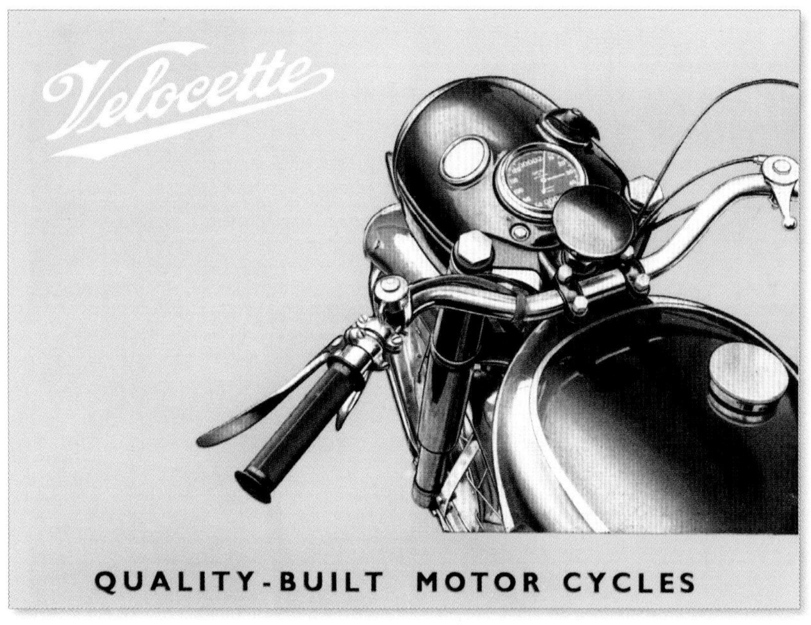

The transition from 1955 to '56 seasons saw an expanded range that included out-and-out sporting models once more – the road versions of which were equipped with this headlamp cowl that carried the instruments and switches. And here's a real piece of trivia: the petrol filler was now on the right-hand side of the tank top.

THE Silent L.E.

Horizontally opposed water-cooled 192 c.c. two cylinder engine. Plain bearings throughout, pressure fed through a full flow filter. Pistons fitted with chromium plated top rings for increased cylinder life. Air and petrol filters embodied in Amal carburettor. Fully selective three-speed gearbox controlled by gate change hand lever. Transmission by enclosed universal joint and shaft to bevel gears driving rear wheel. Starting by hand lever. Lighting by 6 volt generator mounted on front of engine crankshaft feeding accumulator through full wave rectifier with an additional switch position for emergency starting. Ignition has automatic advance and retard. 6″ diameter headlamp. Suspension by coil springs front and rear—the rear being adjustable for varying loads. Separate saddle and pillion seat standard. Dualseat (as illustrated) extra. Quickly detachable wheels. Mudguards and legshields give complete weather protection. Switch, ammeter and gearbox-driven speedometer in legshield top panels. Pressed steel frame encloses toolbox, quickly removable battery and petrol tank. A double sided prop-stand is fitted.

For those with no sporting pretentions whatsoever, and of course the police force whose predilection for the little beasts engendered their nickname of Noddy Bikes, the LE was still on the books. I'll wager that most of you will remember them in the standard finish of silver grey or maybe even Dove-grey/Grey, as here, but by this time there was a range of other finishes.

New streamlined metal panniers, supplied as extras L.E. model.

L.E. MODEL

Dual Seat.

Two colour finish.

Pannier Sets. Leathercloth type in black or colours complete with metal frames, fixing pins, etc.

Pannier Sets. Leathercloth type with extra large pannier bag and frame on off-side only.

Pannier Sets. Streamlined steel type.

Conversion Set for fitting foot brake pedal on off-side for disabled riders.

Oil gauge, pipe, and panel, etc.

Auxiliary petrol can with bracket, etc., used in conjunction with leathercloth type panniers only. Left or right hand fitting.

Full protection for nether garments, coloured legshields are standard L.E. model.

What a wonderfully old-fashioned description. We know what they meant but 'nether garments' could also refer to one's underclothes.

With its rear suspension units set in a more upright position and fitted with the newly-optional less-ungainly dual seat the 1956 MAC took on a rather different look – more cobby, perhaps? There had been a departure (for four-strokes) from the traditional Henry Ford-like 'any colour as long as it's black' (in this case black with gold lining) too: you could also have your MAC in Green with gold-lined tank. Circular 'Diacon' tank badges came mid-1956 for the MAC and its larger brother.

MAC '350' O.H.V.

Velocette single cylinder 349 c.c. overhead valve engine with aluminium alloy head enclosing valves and rocker gear. $\frac{15}{16}$″ Amal Mono-bloc carburettor. Lubrication by dry sump system incorporating full flow oil filter. Magneto has automatic advance and retard. Velocette four-speed gearbox, foot operated, with completely enclosed mechanism and folding footpiece kick starter. Primary chain fully enclosed in oil bath. Rear chain adequately guarded. Velocette telescopic spring front fork oil damped. Rear suspension is by swinging arm and adjustable for load by Velocette patented adjustment using oil damped spring suspension. Quickly detachable wheels with chromium plated rims. One-level or two-level Dualseat, covered to match machine. 7″ diameter brakes with hand adjustment. Prop and central low-lift stands are fitted. Lighting by 7½″ Miller headlamp from current supplied to accumulator by silent "V"-belt-driven Miller AVC dynamo. Speedometer illuminated.

THE NEW *Viper* '350' SPORTS O.H.V.

Velocette high performance sports type single cylinder 349 c.c. overhead valve engine. Aluminium cylinder head fully enclosing valves, hairpin valve springs and rocker gear. Dry sump lubrication with large renewable oil filter. Main bearings and big-end bearing similar to the 500 c.c. models, taking care of the greater stresses arising through increased performance. Down-draught Amal Mono-bloc 1″ carburettor. Magneto automatic advance and retard. Fully enclosed primary chain driving Velocette four-speed foot controlled close ratio gearbox. Final drive by adequately guarded chain. Velocette telescopic oil damped spring front fork. Rear, by swinging arm, fully adjustable for load by Velocette patented adjustment with oil damped spring suspension. Both wheels have full width aluminium alloy hubs. Rims chromium plated. Front wheel with ribbed tyre. One-level Dualseat covered to match machine. Mudguards and stays chromium-plated—rear stays form lifting handles. Central low-lift stand and prop stand. 7½″ Miller headlamp carried in streamlined cowl also housing illuminated speedometer, switch and ammeter. Current provided by separate voltage regulated dynamo driven by enclosed silent "V"-belt feeding an accessibly mounted accumulator.

The Viper was much more than a dressed-up MAC and is not to be confused with some other manufacturers' 'sports' derivations of standard models. Its motor, although of identical cubic capacity to its touring relative, was a special small-bore (72mm) version of the MSS/Venom unit with a compression ratio of 8.5:1. Standard finish was black with chromium-plated, panelled and gold-lined tank and having three-dimensional 'Diacon' badges. A green tank in an identical style was an alternative. This illustration presents something of a puzzle, to me at any rate, as you will see that the tank has gold Velocette script transfers rather than the 'Diacon' embellishments that were introduced with the Viper and Venom for the 1956 season but presumably after this brouchure had been finalised. Certainly the machine tested by Motor Cycling *in the early part of 1956 had the tank that I'd expect on a Viper and mightily were they impressed – their only criticisms amounting to slight oil leaks from the engine and none automatically fed to the rear chain. Performance-wise they managed a mean top speed of a fraction under 91mph at 6,500rpm and 82 in third gear at 7,200rpm. But its tractability in top was if anything more impressive, with as little as a non-snatch 12mph achievable. Its economy was also outstanding and day-to-day riding returned 85-or-more miles to a gallon of fuel.*

New streamlined headlamp cowl with instruments and switch, Viper and Venom.

Quickly detachable front wheel, 7½″ brake, full-width hub, Viper and Venom.

Quickly detachable rear wheel with full-width hub, Viper and Venom. The adjustable springing is common to all models and is an exclusive Velocette feature.

THE NEW *Venom* '500' SPORTS O.H.V.

The Venom is a companion model to the Viper but has a higher performance. Velocette engine similar to the Viper in most details but of 499 c.c. with Amal Mono-bloc $1\frac{1}{8}''$ carburettor. Like the Viper the timing gears are fine pitch helical cut, giving exceptionally long life and freedom from noise, and the magneto is also flange mounted and provided with automatic advance mechanism. The foot change gearbox is of Velocette manufacture, having four speeds with completely enclosed operating mechanism. Close ratio gears are used, and as on the Viper the gearbox assembly is carried between the rear engine plates, giving a rigid mounting and bringing the gearbox into a close and compact unit with the engine. The front fork is a Velocette telescopic spring type with oil damping. As on all other Velocette models the rear fork springing is infinitely adjustable between the 'light' and 'hard' positions to take care of varying loads—an exclusive Velocette feature. Mudguards, stands and the Dualseat are all the same as on the Viper, and the new headlamp cowl is also fitted. The front guard carries a new style number plate. The new full-width aluminium alloy hubs are fitted and the front tyre has a ribbed tread. The electrical equipment is as on the Viper.

From a few feet, apart from the top end of the motor, the larger-capacity Venom looked identical to the Viper, but I've included this illustration as it shows the drive side. Clearly visible is the forward-mounted dynamo drive's pressed-steel cover and also the Velocette peculiarity of having the drive sprocket mounted outboard of the clutch with, naturally, chain guard to suit. The outboard drive sprocket was common to all Velos and the forward-mounted dynamo to just the single cylinders, bar competition machines. Standard finish for the Venom was Black in the same style as the Viper but in this case Dove-grey (Beige) was the alternative. The following were listed as optional extras for both Viper and Venom: air cleaner, American-style handlebars, exhaust pipe extension, sodium-cooled exhaust valve.

THE *Scrambler* '500' O.H.V.

Overhead valve 499 c.c. engine developed from well tried MSS. Timing and compression ratio gives maximum performance with open exhaust system, and in conjunction with racing type Amal carburettor, the characteristics of engine are eminently suitable for scrambles and similar competitions. In other mechanical details engine is similar to MSS. Every Scrambler engine is individually tested. Crankcase protected by undershield. Velocette four-speed gearbox has close ratios and with the special driving sprocket and 60-tooth rear chain wheel, provide low overall ratios for scramble work. Rear hub and brake drum have a six-stud wheel mounting for extra loads. Front fork has modified damping giving control on shock and recoil; sliders are protected from mud, by special gaiters. Rear swinging arm of standard Velocette design with spring units specially developed, and adjustable for varying conditions. Wheels have competition tyres fitted with security bolts, larger diameter front wheel gives increased ground clearance. Mudguards finished polished aluminium with large tyre clearance; front arranged to prevent mud clogging the wheel. Dualseat of special one-level type.

With little or no factory support or development the 'names' would tend to avoid Velocette's scramblers so it's difficult to judge them fairly, but I suspect that it would have been the running gear and/or gearbox rather than the motor that would have been lacking over the rough. From the factory they came in black with plated and panelled tank, recessed at the front for increased steering lock, plus Scrambles or American upswept handlebars to choice and pads on the footrests to stop the rider's feet slipping (which I'm pretty sure would have been removed or replaced by any serious rider, as plain steel was de rigueur).

THE *Endurance* **'500' O.H.V.**

This machine, originally listed at the special request of customers in the United States of America for "Enduro" competitions, is similar in many respects to the Scrambler. Scrambler engine, but is not specially bench tested. Standard MSS magneto, carburettor and silencer. A short extension pipe can be supplied for use if the silencer is removed so that the effective length of the exhaust pipe can be made up to the Scrambler open pipe length. MSS type gearbox and clutch in conjunction with standard sprockets, and three-stud rear hub. Wheels and tyres, undershield, mudguards and stays are Scrambler type. Included in the specification is a $7\frac{1}{2}''$ Miller headlamp, battery, and "V"-belt-driven dynamo. Registration number plates are fitted and the rear one carries a rear lamp. The petrol tank, as with Scrambler, is a special small capacity type with the recessed front. A standard front fork is used and the frame has lugs for sidecar attachment.

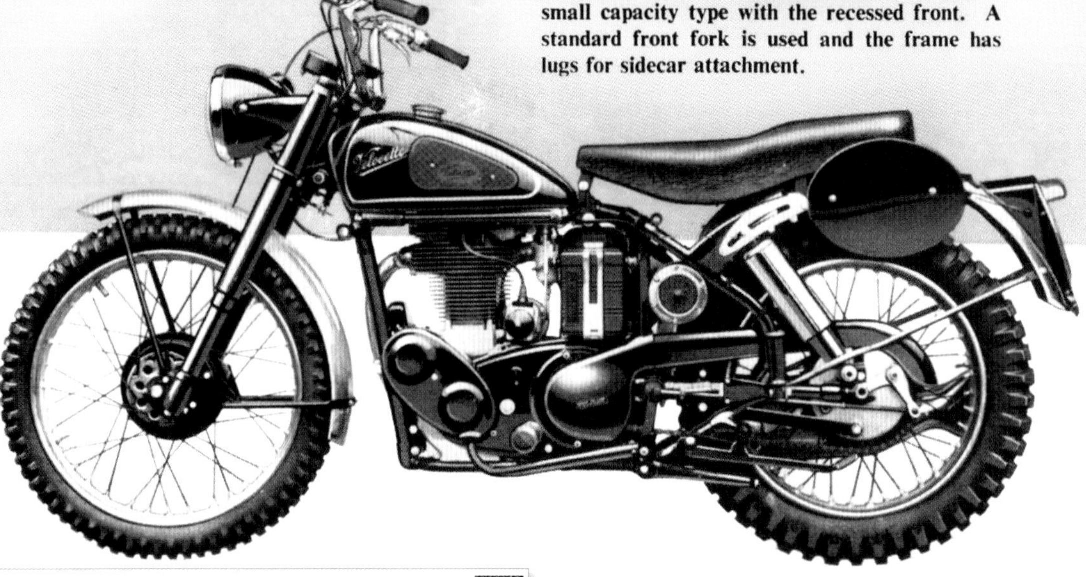

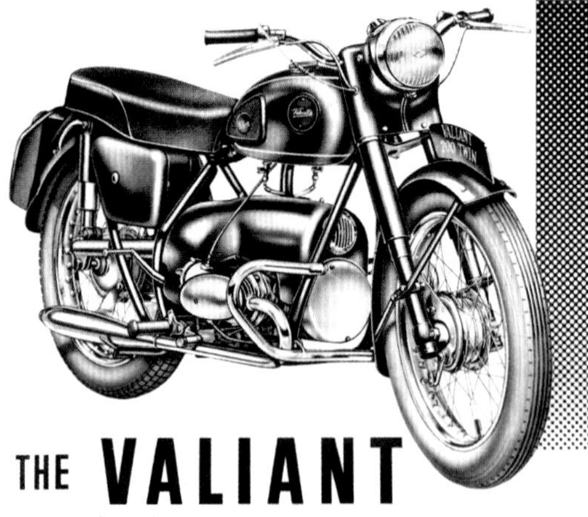

THE VALIANT

. . . a great Velocette lightweight! Features unbeatable—horizontally opposed O.H.V. twin engine 192 c.c., twin Monobloc carburettors, four-speed constant-mesh foot-controlled gearbox; the full spec. is a joy to read! Looks unparalleled—sleekly styled engine cowling, choice of two superb finishes—black or green enamel: performance unbounded, economy unexcelled, reliability unswerving!

a quality-built Lightweight by **Velocette**

I wonder how many of these, if any at all, found homes in the UK, as they didn't suit any of the established motorcycling disciplines. Had green-laning been as popular as it is today, however, it might well have been a different story. They were finished in black or Dove-grey (Beige) with gold-lined tank, with any of the following as optional extras: pillion footrests, air cleaner, chromium-plated petrol tank, BTH BKH magneto, stop light and switch (surely this would have come with the standard lighting set?).

Announced at the 1956 show, Velocette's brand-new lightweight had been on the market for some nine months by the time that Motor Cycling *published their test findings which, in the manner of the day, were inclined to the non-committal. Praise indeed, however, that the writer should end by saying that 'the little model provided the most interesting and stimulating 1,000 miles experienced by the tester for a very long time'. Their figures? Maximum speed 67.6mph. Fuel consumption at a steady 50mph: 98mpg. It was just as much of an oddball of a machine as their other little twin in many ways, as well as sharing its cubic capacity and shaft drive. Its engine was a considerably reworked version of the latter with pushrod overhead valves, air-cooling and a beefier bottom end, whilst its duplex frame with pivoted-fork suspension was an entirely new design, even though the forks came straight from the LE.*

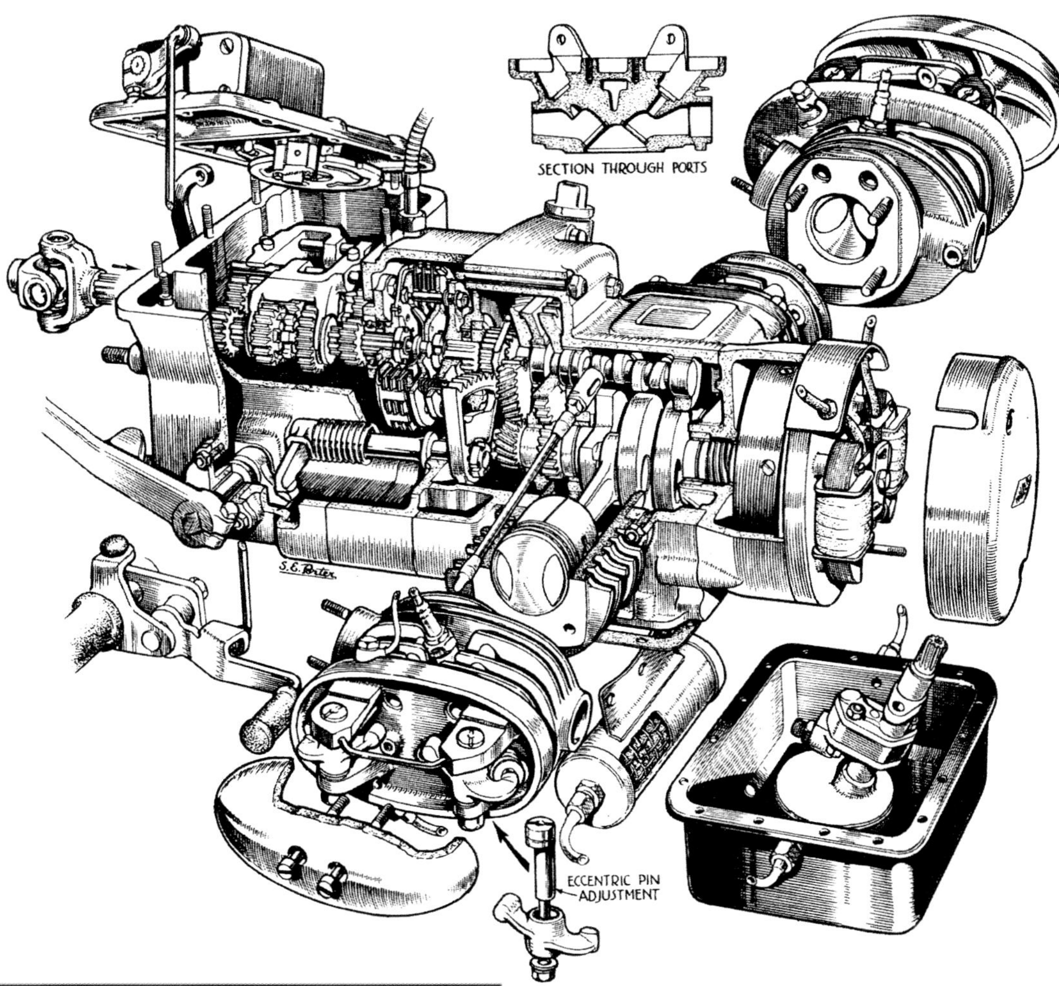

The overhead-valve, flat-twin Valiant motor.

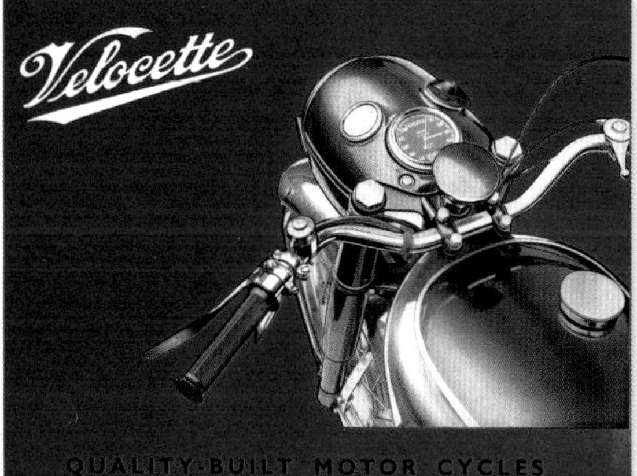

Part-way through 1957, as the new models became established, the factory issued a second brochure and further optional extras became available. The majority of the freshly-introduced options were, as you can see, aimed at Viper and Venom owners or prospective purchasers who wanted to make their mounts even more sporting or perhaps, although the word was not mentioned, even indulge in a little racing at clubman level. On the more pedestrian front and not mentioned here, the little LE had yet another colour option of Polychromatic-green/Grey but this was an extra rather than an option.

OPTIONAL EQUIPMENT SINGLE CYLINDER MODELS.

§All enamelled petrol tank.
Two-level dual seat.
Sidecar gear ratios and sidecar front fork springs.
Choice of colour.
Choice of gear ratios ("Standard" or "Close").
"Reversed" gear operating cam plate.

EXTRAS AND ACCESSORIES. SINGLE CYLINDER MODELS.

Air cleaner 350 c.c.
Air cleaner 500 c.c.
American † or English style handlebar.
Carrier (for use with Velocette panniers).
*Chromium plated panelled petrol tank.
Exhaust pipe extension.
*Full width hubs and brake assembly.
Miller type D6 50 W dynamo.
Pannier frames and bags.
*Pillion footrests and bolts, etc.
Safety bar (polished chromium plated).
*Stop light and switch.

AND THE FOLLOWING SPECIAL RACING EQUIPMENT.

Light alloy wheel rims.
Modified oil tank breather.
‡Racing magneto with hand control.
Racing saddle.
Rear mounted footrests, brake, and gear control pedals.
Silencer and exhaust pipe.
Sodium cooled or Nimonic 80 exhaust valve.
Reinforced drive side rear engine plate.
**Tachometer (rev. counter) with drive from special timing cover.
T.T. or G.P. type carburetter.
T.T. Close internal gear ratios.
Top 1 to 1; 3rd, 1.098 to 1; 2nd, 1.444 to 1; 1st, 1.9 to 1.
‡Two-way front fork damping.

EXTRAS & ACCESSORIES

L.E. MODEL

Auxiliary petrol can with bracket, etc. For fitting to leather cloth type pannier frames. Left or right hand fitting.

Conversion set for fitting brake pedal to right hand side. For disabled riders.

Dualseat.

Luggage grid.

Oil pressure gauge, pipe, and special panel.

Pannier sets. Leather cloth type in black or colours, complete with metal frames and fixing pins.

Pannier sets. Leather cloth type with extra large pannier bag and frame on right hand side only.

Pannier sets. Streamlined steel type. In standard grey or colours.

§Standard on MAC and MSS.
**Standard on Viper and Venom.*
‡Standard on Scramblers.
†Standard on Endurance.
***Can only be fitted if hand controlled magneto is used.*

Both MAC and MSS now had the headlamp cowl that had debuted on the sports models a few months earlier. Both also had the newer style of tank with 'Diacon' badges and knee-grips positioned slightly more to the rear. The anomaly of the Viper and Venom tanks was continued with this publication, as both were depicted with the older-style knee-grip position and Velocette script transfer, whilst the description once again alluded to those 'Diacon' badges in no uncertain manner. Colour choices were unchanged – Black or Green for the MAC, and Black or Dove-grey (Beige) for the MSS.

MAC '350' O.H.V.

Velocette single cylinder 349 c.c. overhead valve engine with aluminium alloy head enclosing valves and rocker gear. Amal Monobloc carburetter. Lubrication by dry sump system incorporating full flow renewable fabric filter. Magneto has automatic advance and retard. Velocette four-speed gearbox, foot operated, with completely enclosed mechanism and folding kick starter. Primary chain fully enclosed in oil bath. Rear chain adequately guarded. Velocette telescopic spring front fork—oil damped. Rear suspension by swinging arm, and adjustable for load by Velocette patented adjustment using oil damped spring suspension. Quickly detachable wheels with chromium plated rims. One-level or two-level Dualseat. 7" brakes with simple adjustment. Prop and central stands are standard equipment. 7½" Miller headlamp carried in streamlined cowl which also houses illuminated speedometer, the lighting switch and ammeter. Separate voltage regulated dynamo driven by "V" belt charges accessibly mounted battery.

MSS '500' O.H.V.

Velocette "square" single cylinder overhead valve engine of 499 c.c. with aluminium alloy cylinder head enclosing hairpin valve springs, valves and rocker gear. Alloy jacketed cylinder. Amal Monobloc carburetter. Dry sump lubrication with full flow renewable fabric filter. Magneto has automatic advance and retard. Velocette four-speed foot operated gearbox with fully enclosed mechanism, kick starter having folding foot-piece. Primary chain enclosed in oil bath and rear chain adequately guarded. Velocette telescopic oil damped spring front fork. Stronger springs for sidecar available. Rear suspension by swinging arm, adjustable for load by Velocette patented system using oil damped suspension. Quickly detachable wheels with chromium plated rims. One-level or two-level Dualseat. 7" diameter brakes with simple adjustment. Prop and central stands included. Headlamp cowl and speedometer as on MAC. 6 volt. "V" belt driven dynamo with automatic voltage regulator. Accessibly mounted battery.

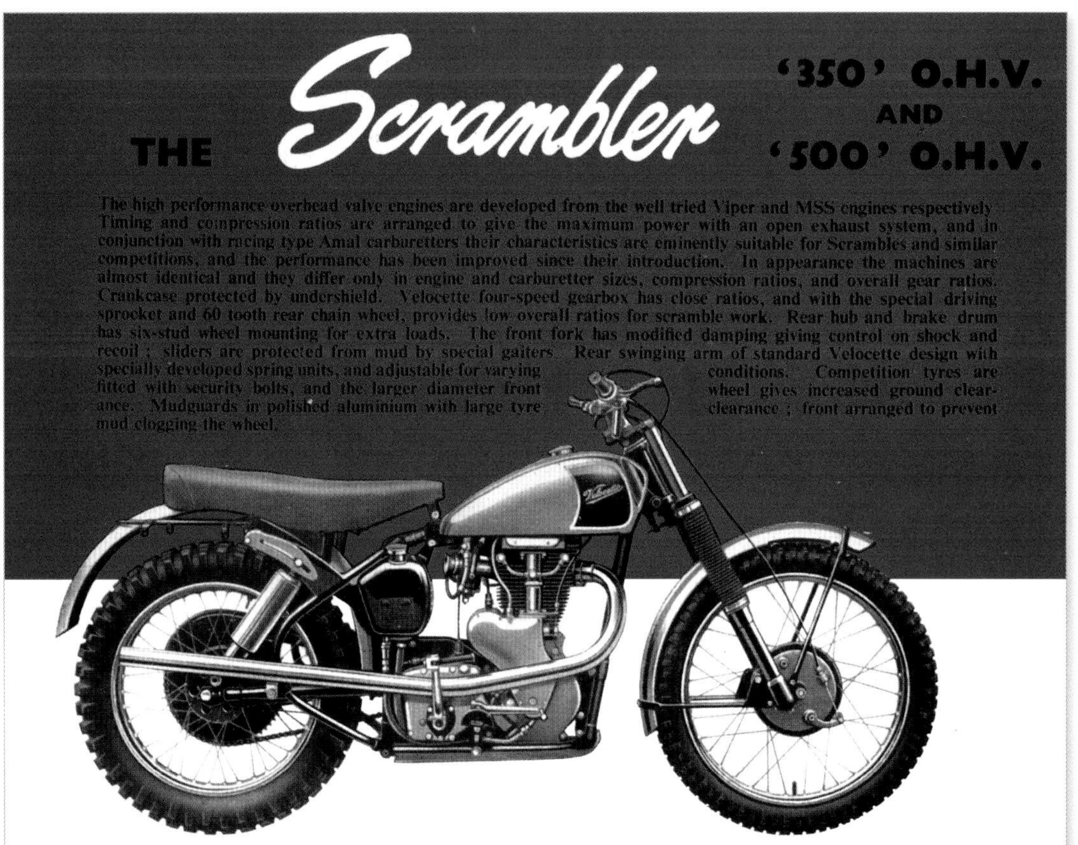

A mid-season addition to the range was the Viper-powered scrambler.

MODEL	L.E.	MAC	MSS	VIPER	VENOM	350 SCRAMBLER	500 SCRAMBLER	ENDURANCE
ENGINE : Type	Side-valve Twin	O.H.V. Single	O.H.V. Single	O.H.V. Single	O.H.V. Single	O.H.V. Single	O.H.V. Single	O.H.V. Single
Bore and Stroke	50 x 49 mm. 1.968 x 1.929 ins.	68 x 96 mm. 2.677 x 3.779 ins.	86 x 86 mm. 3.385 x 3.385 ins.	72 x 86 mm. 2.83 x 3.385 ins.	86 x 86 mm. 3.385 x 3.385 ins.	72 x 86 mm. 2.834 x 3.385 ins.	86 x 86 mm. 3,385 x 3.385 ins.	86 x 86 mm. 3.385 x 3.385 ins.
Cylinder Capacity	11.7 cu.ins. 192 cc.	21.29 cu.ins. 349 cc.	30.45 cu.ins. 499 cc.	21.29 cu.ins. 349 cc.	30.45 cu.ins. 499 cc.	21.29 cu.ins. 349 cc.	30.45 cu.ins. 499 cc.	30.45 cu.ins. 499 cc.
Compression Ratio	7 to 1	6.75 to 1	6.75 to 1	8.5 to 1	8 to 1	9.3 to 1	8.75 to 1	8 to 1
Brake h.p. and r.p.m.	8 at 5,000 r.p.m.	15 at 5,500 r.p.m.	23 at 5,000 r.p.m.	27 at 6,800 r.p.m.	36 at 5,700 r.p.m.	29 at 7,000 r.p.m.	40 at 5,700 r.p.m.	36 at 5,700 r.p.m.
Carburettor ...	Amal Monobloc	Amal Monobloc	Amal Monobloc	Amal Monobloc	Amal Monobloc	Amal T 10TT9	Amal 10TT9	Amal Monobloc
Magneto ...	—	Lucas KIF with auto adv.	Lucas KIF with auto adv.	Lucas KIF with auto adv.	Lucas KIF with auto adv.	B.T.H. hand controlled	B.T.H. hand controlled	Lucas KIF with auto adv.
Generator ...	Miller AC4.42 watt	Miller DVR 36 watt	Miller DVR 36 watt	Miller DVR 36 watt	Miller DVR 36 watt	None	None	Miller DVR 36 watt
Gen. Drive ...	Flywheel	"V" Belt	"V" Belt	"V" Belt	"V" Belt	None	None	"V" Belt
GEARBOX Overall Ratios, 4th	—	5.5 to 1	Solo 4.87 Sidecar 5.5	5.5	4.87	7.85 to 1	7.2 to 1	4.87
3rd	7.25	7.3 to 1	Solo 6.52 Sidecar 7.32	6.64	5.87	9.5 to 1	8.58 to 1	5.87
2nd	10.85	9.6 to 1	Solo 8.57 Sidecar 9.625	8.73	7.74	12.46 to 1	11.41 to 1	7.74
1st	20.4	14 to 1	Solo 12.4 Sidecar 13.91	12.62	11.2	17.9 to 1	16.65 to 1	11.2
Final Dve. Sprocket	None Shaft drive	21 driver 55 driven	18 driver 46 driven	21 driver 55 driven	18 driver 46 driven	16 driver 60 driven	16 driver 60 driven	18 driver 46 driven
CHAINS. Primary	None Shaft drive	.5 x .305 in. 67 Pitches	.5 x .305 in. 68 Pitches	.5 x .305 in. 67 Pitches	.5 x .305 in. 68 Pitches	.5 x .305 in. 67 Pitches	.5 x .305 in. 68 Pitches	.5 x .305 in. 68 Pitches
Rear ...	None Shaft drive	.5 x .305 in. 124 Pitches	.625 x .380 in. 101 Pitches	.5 x .305 in. 124 Pitches	.625 x .380 in. 101 Pitches	.625 x .380 in. 108 Pitches	.625 x .380 in. 108 Pitches	.625 x .380 in. 101 Fitches
RIMS. Front ...	WM2 x 18 ins.	WM2 x 19 ins.	WM2 x 19 ins.	WM2 x 19 ins.	WM2 x 19 ins.	WM1 x 21 ins.	WM1 x 21 ins.	WM1 x 21 ins.
Rear ...	WM2 x 18 ins.	WM2 x 19 ins.	WM2 x 19 ins.	WM2 x 19 ins.	WM2 x 19 ins.	WM3 x 19 ins.	WM3 x 19 ins.	WM3 x 19 ins.
TYRES. Front ...	3.25 x 18 ins. Ribbed	3.25 x 19 ins.	3.25 x 19 ins.	3.25 x 19 ins. Ribbed	3.25 x 19 ins. Ribbed	3 x 21 ins. Com.	3 x 21 ins. Com.	3 x 21 ins. Com.
Rear ...	3.25 x 18 ins.	3.25 x 19 ins.	3.25 x 19 ins.	3.25 x 19 ins.	3.25 x 19 ins.	4 x 19 ins. Com.	4 x 19 ins.Com.	4 x 19 ins. Com.
BRAKES. Front ...	5 in. dia. Area 9.25 sq. ins.	7 in. dia. Area 10.75 sq. ins.	7 in. dia. Area 10.75 sq. ins.	7.5 in. dia. Area 23 sq. ins.	7.5 in. dia. Area 23 sq. ins.	7 in. dia. Area 10.75 sq. ins.	7 in. dia. Area 10.75 sq. ins.	7 in. dia. Area 10.75 sq. ins.
Rear ...	5 in. dia. Area 9. 5 sq. ins.	7 in. dia. Area 10.75 sq. ins.	7 in. dia. Area 10.75 sq. ins.	7 in. dia. Area 10.75 sq. ins.	7 in. dia. Area 10.75 sq. ins.	7 in. dia. Area 10.75 sq. ins.	7 in. dia. Area 10.75 sq. ins.	7 in. dia. Area 10.75 sq. ins.
LENGTH OVERALL	92 ins. 209 cms.	84 ins. 213 cms.	84 ins. 213 cms.	84 ins. 213 cms.	84 ins. 213 cms.	89 ins. 226 cms.	89 ins. 226 cms.	89 ins. 226 cms.
WIDTH OVERALL	26 ins. 66 cms.	27.5 ins. 70 cms.	27.5 ins. 70 cms.	27 5 ins. 70 cms.	27.5 ins. 70 cms.	34.5 ins. 89 cms.	34.5 ins. 89 cms.	30 ins. 76 cms.
HEIGHT OVERALL	39 ins. 99 cms.	40 ins. 102 cms.	40 ins. 102 cms.	39 ins. 99 cms.	39 ins. 99 cms.	43 ins. 109 cms.	43 ins. 109 cms.	44.5 ins. 113 cms.
WEIGHT UNLADEN	250 lbs. 113.3 kilos	355 lbs. 161 kilos	375 lbs. 170 kilos	370 lbs. 168 kilos	375 lbs. 170 kilos	335 lbs. 152 kilos	335 lbs. 152 kilos	375 lbs. 170 kilos
WHEELBASE Normally loaded	51.25 ins. 131.8 cms.	53,75 ins. 136.5 cms.	53.75 ins. 136.5 cms.	53.75 ins. 136.5 cms.	53.75 ins. 136.5 cms.	53,75 ins. 136.5 cms.	53.75 ins. 136.5 cms.	53.75 ins. 136.5 cms
GRD. CLEARANCE Normally loaded	4.5 ins. 11.4 cms.	5.5 ins. 14 cms.	5.5 ins. 14 cms.	5.5 ins. 14 cms.	5.5 ins. 14 cms.	6.5 ins. 16.5 cms.	6.5 ins. 16.5 cms.	6.5 ins. 16.5 cms.
SEAT HEIGHT Normally loaded	28 ins. 71 cms.	30.5 ins. 77.5 cms.	30.5 ins. 77.5 cms.	30.5 ins. 77.5 cms.	30.5 ins. 77.5 cms.	33 ins. 83.8 cms.	33 ins. 83.8 cms.	33 ins. 83.8 cms.
FUEL TANK CAPACITY	1.625 galls. Imp. 1.95 U.S. galls. 7.4 litres	3 galls. Imp. 3.6 U.S. galls. 13.6 litres	3 galls. Imp. 3.6 U.S. galls. 13.6 litres	3 galls. Imp. 3.6 U.S. galls. 13.6 litres	3 galls. Imp. 3.6 U.S. galls. 13.6 litres	2.5 galls. Imp. 3 U.S. galls. 11.35 litres	2.5 galls. Imp. 3 U.S. galls. 11.35 litres	2.5 galls. Imp. 3 U.S. galls. 11.35 litres
ENGINE OIL CAPACITY	.25 gall Imp. .3 U.S. gall 1.14 litres	.5 gall. Imp. .6 U.S. gall. 2.27 litres	.5 gall. Imp. .6 U.S. gall. 2.27 litres	.5 gall. Imp. .6 U.S. gall. 2.27 litres	.5 gall. Imp. .6 U.S gall. 2.27 litres	.5 gall. Imp. 6 U.S. gall. 2.27 litres	.5 gall. Imp. .6 U.S gall. 2.27 itres	.5 gall. Imp. .6 U.S. gall. 2.27 litres

THE SILENT L.E.

MARK III

This machine, used by over 30 police forces in the country, has set and maintained a standard that is unsurpassed for silence, cleanliness, and ease of maintenance, now has a foot controlled four-speed gearbox and pedal "press" starting. High average speeds are possible solo or with passenger without fuss or fatigue and the extra ratio makes hill climbing faster and easier.

Quickly adjustable rear springing takes care of differing loads. Other features include car-type all-plain-bearing engine with renewable oil filter. Provision for fitting oil gauge. Emergency starting position for ignition. 6 volt 13 A.H. unspillable battery. Switch and instruments carried in headlamp. Quickly detachable wheels with chromium-plated rims and large tyres for extra comfort and road holding. Non-lift central stand for effortless parking. Dual seat as illustrated—extra.

Standard finish in Silver Grey. Also available in "two-colour" finishes. Blue/Grey, Willow Green/Grey, or Polychromatic-green/Grey, as an extra (as illustrated). Other parts are finished in Black and Chrome.

MODEL	LE MARK III	VALIANT	VALIANT "VEE-LINE"
ENGINE—Type	S.V., water cooled, horizontal opposed twin	O.H.V., air cooled horizontal opposed twin	O.H.V., air cooled horizontal opposed twin
Bore and Stroke	50 x 49 mm. (1.968 x 1.929 ins.)	50 x 49 mm. (1.968 x 1.929 mm.)	50 x 49 mm. (1.968 x 1.929in.)
Capacity (swept volume)	192 c.c. (11.7 cu. in.)	192 c.c. (11.7 cu. in.)	192 c.c. (11.7 cu. in.)
Compression Ratio	7 to 1	7.8 to 1	7.9 to 1
Brake Horse-power	8 b.h.p. at 5,000 r.p.m.	12 b.h.p. at 7,000 r.p.m.	12 b.h.p. at 7,000 r.p.m.
Carburettor	Amal Monobloc	Two Amal Monobloc	Two Amal Monoblocs
Ignition	Battery and coil	Battery and coil	Battery and coil
Generator	Miller type AC4 flywheel altnr. 6v. 42 w. output	Miller type AC4 flywheel altnr. 6v. 42w. output	Miller type AC4 flywheel altnr. 6v. 42w. output
Generator Drive	—	—	—
GEARBOX	Velo. 4-spd. foot control	Velo. 4-spd. foot control	Velo. 4-spd. foot control
Gear Ratios (overall) Top	7.25 to 1	7.25 to 1	7.25 to 1
Third	9.82 to 1	9.82 to 1	9.82 to 1
Second	13.3 to 1	13.3 to 1	13.3 to 1
First	20.4 to 1	20.4 to 1	20.4 to 1
TRANSMISSION			
Sprockets... Engine	Shaft and spiral bevel	Shaft and spiral bevel	Shaft and spiral bevel
Clutch	—	—	—
Gearbox	—	—	—
Rear Wheel	—	—	—
Chains... Primary	—	—	—
Rear	—	—	—
WHEELS			
Rims Front	WM2 x 18in.	WM2 x 18in.	WM2 x 18in.
Rear	WM2 x 18in.	WM2 x 18in.	WM2 x 18in.
Tyres Front	3.25 x 18in. Ribbed	3.25 x 18in. Ribbed	3.25 x 18in. Ribbed
Rear	3.25 x 18in. Studded	3.25 x 18in. Studded	3.25 x 18in. Studded
BRAKES—Drum diameter and width and			
Lining Area Front	5in. x 1in. (9.25 sq. in.)	5in. x 1in. (9.25 sq. in.)	5in. x 1in. (9.25 sq. in.)
Rear	5in. x 1in. (9.25 sq. in.)	5in. x 1in. (9.25 sq. in.)	5in. x 1in. (9.25 sq. in.)
CAPACITIES			
Water	2.5 Imp. pts. (1.42 litres, 3 U.S. pts.)	—	—
Engine Oil	1.75 Imp. pts. (1 litre, 2.1 U.S. pts.)	1.75 Imp. pts. (1 litre, 2.1 U.S. pts.)	1.75 Imp. pts. (1 litre, 2.1 U.S. pts.)
Fuel Tank	1.625 Imp. galls. (7.4 litres, 1.95 U.S. gall.)	3 Imp. galls. (13.6 litres, 3.6 U.S. gall.)	3 Imp. gall. (13.6 litres, 3.6 U.S. gall.)
PRINCIPAL DIMENSIONS			
Length Overall	82in. (209 cms.)	79in. (200.6 cms.)	79in. (200.6 cms.)
Width Overall	25.5in. (72.39 cms.)	25.5in. (72.39 cms.)	25.5in. (72.39 cms.)
Height Overall	38in. (96.5 cms.)	38in. (96.5 cms.)	58in. (147 cms.)
Wheelbase (in static loaded position)	51.25in. (130.17 cms.)	51.25in. (130.17 cms.)	51.25in. (130.17 cms.)
Ground Clearance (in static loaded position)	4.5in. (11.4 cms.)	6in. (15.24 cms.)	6in. (15.24 cms.)
Seat Height (in static loaded position)	28in. (71 cms.)	29in. (73.66 cms.)	29in. (73.66 cms.)
UNLADEN WEIGHT	263 lbs. (119 kilos)	255 lbs. (115.67 kilos)	273.5 lb. (124 kilos)

The LE in its latest (1959) form had a four-speed gearbox with foot-change and what its maker referred to as 'pedal "press" starting'. In accepted motorcycle parlance the latter meant kick-starter – the long lever that operated the stand and brought the motor to life having been done away with. Otherwise it looked very much as it had done for the last ten years. 'Enhanced performance in the latest version of a quiet and docile lightweight' was Motor Cycling*'s test overview, and although top speed would hardly be the criterion it managed 56mph, with 50 possible in third. A steady 40mph returned 94mpg but if you were content with 30mph you could squeeze another 15 miles out of a gallon.*

EXTRAS AND ACCESSORIES

L.E. AND VALIANT MODELS

- *Auxiliary petrol can with bracket, etc. For fitting behind left-hand pannier frame.
  Stop light and switch.
- *Dualseat.
- *Luggage grid.
- *Oil pressure gauge, pipe and special panel.
- *Pannier sets. Leather cloth type with metal frames and fixing pins.
- *Pannier sets. Leather cloth type with extra large pannier bag and frame on right-hand side only.
- †Pillion footrests with fixing plates, etc.
- †Chromium plated safety bar.
- †Left-hand matching tool box.
- Windscreen : Feridax or Olicana.

*L.E. only. †Valiant only.

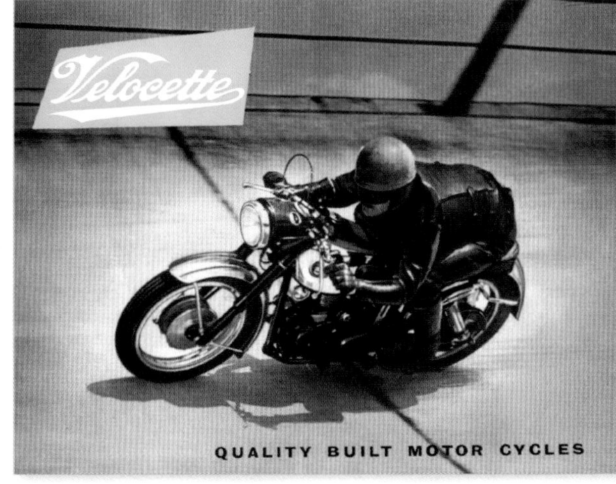

I've a sneaking suspicion that it's none other than Velocette's managing director thrashing this Venom around MIRA's banking, as he delighted in personally carrying out high-speed testing at this venue. As you can see it was kitted out with light-alloy wheel rims, rear set footrests and a tachometer.

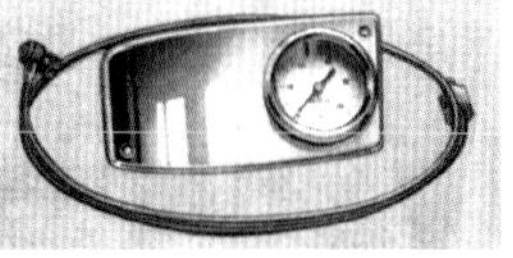

Sports and tuning accessories and extras were strictly for the singles but LEs and Valiants had a range all to themselves.

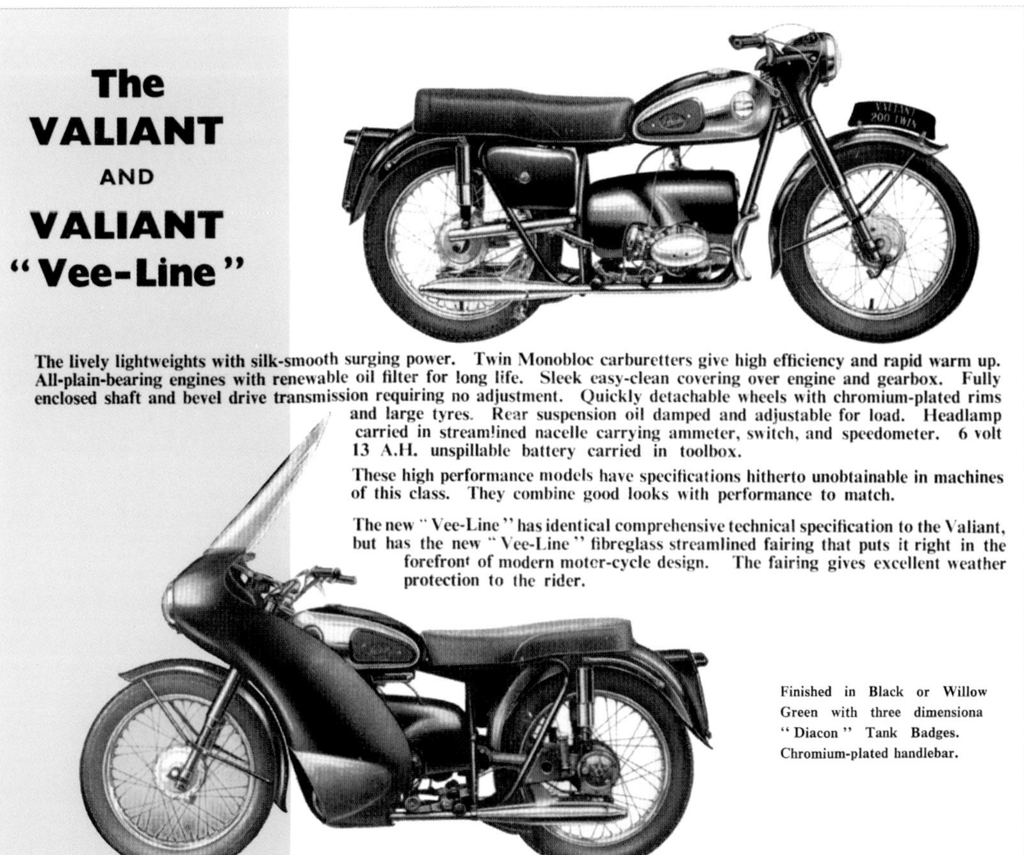

The VALIANT AND VALIANT "Vee-Line"

The lively lightweights with silk-smooth surging power. Twin Monobloc carburetters give high efficiency and rapid warm up. All-plain-bearing engines with renewable oil filter for long life. Sleek easy-clean covering over engine and gearbox. Fully enclosed shaft and bevel drive transmission requiring no adjustment. Quickly detachable wheels with chromium-plated rims and large tyres. Rear suspension oil damped and adjustable for load. Headlamp carried in streamlined nacelle carrying ammeter, switch, and speedometer. 6 volt 13 A.H. unspillable battery carried in toolbox.

These high performance models have specifications hitherto unobtainable in machines of this class. They combine good looks with performance to match.

The new "Vee-Line" has identical comprehensive technical specification to the Valiant, but has the new "Vee-Line" fibreglass streamlined fairing that puts it right in the forefront of modern motor-cycle design. The fairing gives excellent weather protection to the rider.

Finished in Black or Willow Green with three dimensiona "Diacon" Tank Badges. Chromium-plated handlebar.

In the '60s some used to light-heartedly refer to the Valiant as being 'like a little BMW' on account of its engine and shaft drive but any similarity was probably coincidental. I did have a go on one once but it was just a trip up and down the road, so conclusions would not be fair; however, although it was uncannily smooth (compared with the single I had in daily use) it was at the same time a gutless wonder and I never felt the need to seek out a lengthier relationship. As the factory bumf said, 'silk-smooth', but 'surging power' emphatically no. Disappointing performance, complexity and unconventional looks, but probably most of all its relatively high price, were some of the reasons it never sold well, but nevertheless it was produced until 1963.

The VIPER '350' SPORTS O.H.V. AND VENOM '500' SPORTS O.H.V.

Two high performance sports models in the best Velocette tradition that handle superbly. Single cylinder overhead valve engines (Nimonic 80 exhaust) with aluminium alloy heads and jacketed barrels. Close-spaced main bearings and "whip-free" flywheel assemblies identical in both models. Dry sump lubrication, including large renewable filter. Automatic ignition control. Oil bath primary chain. Velocette four-speed, foot controlled close ratio gearbox (alternative ratios obtainable). Crankcase, gearbox, dynamo and battery enclosed in streamlined fibreglass fairing of sleek appearance, simplifying cleaning, and further improving performance. Rear swinging arm suspension and oil damped Velocette front fork—the former quickly adjustable for load. Full width alloy hubs with exceptionally powerful front brake, chromium-plated rims, ribbed front tyre. Sports type mudguards with tubular stays chromium-plated. Miller lighting equipment with 7½in. headlamp in streamlined cowl, stop light, and 6 volt automatically regulated dynamo with car type silent 'V' belt drive. These machines can be obtained fitted with racing equipment. Alternative sized driving sprockets are obtainable to alter overall gear ratios.

Standard finish in Black enamel, with bright Chromium plated tank, panelled and Gold lined (all enamelled optional), and having three-dimensional "Diacon" badges. Alternatively the model can be supplied in Willow Green. See page 9 for details of additional racing equipment.

In spite of the slightly staid looks imparted by their engine enclosure, both Viper and Venom could be had with a variety of well thought out racing parts.

The SCRAMBLER '350' O.H.V. AND '500' O.H.V.

Standard finish in Black with plated and panelled tank, giving increased steering lock and small turning circle. Footrests with pads to prevent the rider's feet slipping. Special Scrambler handlebar or American upswept to choice.

The high performance overhead valve engines are developed from the well tried Viper and Venom engines respectively. Timing and compression ratios are arranged to give the maximum power with an open exhaust system, and in conjunction with racing type Amal carburetters their characteristics are eminently suitable for Scrambles and similar competitions, and the performance has been improved since their introduction. In appearance the machines are almost identical and they differ only in engine and carburetter sizes, compression ratios, and overall gear ratios. Crankcase protected by undershield. Velocette four-speed gearbox has close ratios, and with the special driving sprocket and 60 tooth rear chain wheel, provides low overall ratios for scramble work. Rear hub and brake drum has six-stud wheel mounting for extra loads. The front fork has modified damping giving control on shock and recoil; sliders are protected from mud by special gaiters. Rear swinging arm of standard Velocette design with specially developed spring units. Competition tyres are fitted with security bolts. Mudguards in polished aluminium with large tyre clearance; front arranged to prevent mud clogging the wheel.

In an attempt to eradicate some of the scrambler's shortcomings the rear of the frame had been completely redesigned, with the result that, if nothing else, it no longer looked so much a modified road model as a purposeful competition machine. I find it odd that the specs, down to the dimensions and weight, had not altered one iota from the earlier models but they were released by the factory, so who am I to argue?

Enclosure of some kind or other was becoming fashionable by 1959 and Hall Green responded by equipping its big singles, MAC excepted, with these fibreglass cowlings. Some liked them and some did not, so after a while they became optional. Although this MSS had the old single-sided hub the Viper/Venom full-width variety was now an option on this and the MAC. Black, as ever, was the standard colour but for no extra charge you could have your MAC or MSS in Willow Green.

OPTIONAL EXTRAS

Prices when ordered to be supplied as original equipment only
(including allowance for standard component not fitted where applicable)
For Replacement Prices—see relevant Spares Price Lists

	Retail £ s. d.	Purchase Tax £ s. d.	Total £ s. d.
LE MODEL			
Dual Seat	3 3 0	13 0	3 16 0
Two-Colour finish—Blue/Grey, Green/Grey, Polychromatic Green/Grey	3 5 0	13 5	3 18 5
Pannier Sets in Grey (leathercloth type), complete with metal frames, fixing pins, etc.	2 12 5	10 10	3 3 3
Stop Light and Switch	10 0	2 1	12 1
VALIANT MODEL			
Stop Light and Switch	11 6	2 5	13 11
Chromium plated Petrol Tank	2 5 0	9 4	2 14 4
L/H additional Tool Box, to match up with standard box (complete with lid, etc.)	1 10 0	6 2	1 16 2
350 c.c. and 500 c.c. MODELS			
Air Cleaner	1 15 0	7 3	2 2 3
~~Steering Damper, Assembly complete~~	~~1 0 0~~	~~4 1~~	~~1 4 1~~
Stop Light and Switch (where not standard)	9 0	1 10	10 10
Chromium plated Petrol Tank (where not standard)	3 10 0	14 5	4 4 5
*B.T.H. Racing BKH.1.-type hand-controlled Magneto, complete	6 8 0	1 6 5	7 14 5
60-watt Dynamo	2 3 0	8 10	2 11 10
*T.T. Carburettor	6 12 0	1 7 3	7 19 3
Rear Mounted Footrests and Pedal Set	2 0 0	8 3	2 8 3
Clubmans Exhaust Pipe and Silencer	1 10 0	6 2	1 16 2
*††Reinforced Driving Side Engine Plate	2 0 0	8 3	2 8 3
T.T. Close-ratio Gears	10 0	2 1	12 1
Megaphone (for use with Clubmans exhaust pipe)	1 15 3	7 3	2 2 6
*Ball Ended Clutch and Brake Levers, per pair	8 0	1 8	9 8
*Racing type Petrol Taps	4 0	10	4 10
350 c.c. and 500 c.c. MODELS			
†Full width Hubs and Brake Units, per pair	9 15 0	2 0 2	11 15 2
Full width Hub and Brake Unit, FRONT only	5 12 6	1 3 2	6 15 8
Full width Hub and Brake Unit, REAR only...	4 2 6	17 1	4 19 7
Rev Counter, complete with all fittings	7 5 0	1 9 11	8 14 11
Alloy Rims (Viper and Venom Models), per pr.	8 10 0	1 15 1	10 5 1
*Two-way Damping for Front Forks	1 0 0	4 1	1 4 1

*Standard on Scrambler Models.
†Standard Equipment on Venom and Viper Models.

———o———

The April 1959 price list will, if nothing else, give readers unfamiliar with the good old British pounds, shillings and pence system of currency the chance to practise their mental arithmetic. To make it easy, forget the shillings and pence: pounds were the same (albeit worth a staggering amount less). It is, however, interesting to compare the price and note, compared with an LE or a Valiant, what an absolute bargain a Venom or a Viper was. What price some of the extras too? An Amal TT for £8! That's even allowing for the cost of the Monobloc you were no longer receiving.

Velocette

MOTOR CYCLES

	Retail £ s. d.	Purchase Tax £ s. d.	Total £ s. d.
192 c.c.			
LE MARK III Model, 4 Speed, Foot Start.... Foot Change. Spring Frame. Silver Grey.	162 10 0	33 10 4	196 0 4
"VALIANT" Model .... Spring Frame. Black or Green.	174 0 0	35 17 9	209 17 9
VALIANT "VEELINE" .... Spring Frame. With Fairing Black or Green.	191 10 0	39 9 11	230 19 11
350 c.c.			
MAC Model .... Spring Frame. Black.	192 10 0	39 14 1	232 4 1
"VIPER" SPORTS Model.... .... Spring Frame. Black and Chrome or Red/Black, or White/Black.	207 0 0	42 13 11	249 13 11
"SCRAMBLER" Model .... Spring Frame. Black	210 0 0	43 6 3	253 6 3
500 c.c.			
MSS Model .... Spring Frame. Black.	198 0 0	40 16 9	238 16 9
"VENOM" SPORTS Model .... Spring Frame. Black and Chrome or Red/Black, or White/Black.	214 0 0	44 2 9	258 2 9
"ENDURANCE" Model .... Spring Frame. Black.	207 0 0	42 13 11	249 13 11
"SCRAMBLER" Model .... Spring Frame. Black.	215 0 0	44 6 11	259 6 11

In order to spread the word it was common practice for manufacturers to place advertisements such as this in the motorcycling press. A few days after your postcard had gone off you would receive a current brochure, perhaps a road test, and a letter (mimeographed or original) on the company's headed notepaper thanking you for your consideration. Sales-wise this was partially flawed due to the amount requested by schoolboys. Clubman versions of the Viper and Venom were added to the range in the autumn of 1959. Shame they hadn't appeared on the scene a few years earlier when they might have given the Gold Stars a run for their money in the last of the Isle of Man Clubmans TTs. The Viper was priced at £273 6s 9d all-in and the Venom £281 15s 7d.

The VIPER
'CLUBMAN'
'350'

The VENON
'CLUBMAN'
'500'

Now for 1960 : the Clubman models are offered with suitable equipment for participation in sporting events. The specifications include Scrambler type piston and compression ratio, T.T. close ratio gears, T.T. type carburetter, racing type hand controlled magneto, rear-mounted footrests and pedals, reversed gear operating camplate, two-way damped front fork, steering damper, and a flexibly mounted petrol tank.

Tachometer (rev-meter), and light alloy rims are available as extras, and alternative sizes of driving sprockets can be obtained for changes of overall gearing.

Standard finish in Black with plated and panelled tank, Gold lined, with three-dimensional " Diacon " badges. Crankcase and Gearbox polished,

MODEL	VIPER "CLUBMAN"	VENOM "CLUBMAN"
ENGINE—Type	O.H.V., air cooled vertical single cylinder	O.H.V. air-cooled Vertical single cylinder
Bore and Stroke	72 x 86 mm. (2.834 x 3.385in.)	86 x 86 mm. (3.385 x 3.385 m.)
Capacity (swept volume)	349 c.c. (21.29 cu. in.	499 c.c. (30.45 cub. in.)
Compression Ratio	9.3 to 1	8.75 to 1
Brake Horse-power	29 b.h.p at 7,000 r.p.m.	38 b.h.p at 6,200 r.p.m.
Carburetter	Amal TT9	Amal 10TT9
Ignition	B.T.H. Racing Hand Controlled B.K.H.I.	B.T.H. Racing Hand on-trolled BKH1.
Generator	Miller Type DVR with Auto volt reg. 6v. 36w. output.	Miller type DVR with auto volt reg. 6v. 35w. output.
Generator Drive	Enclosed 'V' belt	Enclosed 'V' belt
GEARBOX	Velo. 4-spd. foot control	Velo. 4-spd. foot control
Gear Ratios (overall) Top	5.5 to 1	4.87 to 1
Third	6.03 to 1	5.35 to 1
Second	7.94 to 1	7.03 to 1
First	10.45 to 1	9.25 to 1
TRANSMISSION		
Sprockets Engine	.5in. pitch, 21 teeth	.5in. pitch, 23 teeth
Clutch	.5in. pitch, 44 teeth	.5in. pitch, 44 teeth
Gearbox	.5in. pitch, 21 teeth	.625in. pitch, 18 teeth
Rear Wheel	.5in. pitch, 55 teeth	.625in. pitch, 46 teeth
Chains Primary	.5in. x .305in., 67 pitches	.5in. x .305in., 68 pitches
Rear	.5in. x .305in., 124 pitches	.625in. x .380in., 101 pitches
WHEELS		
Rims Front	WM2 x 19in.	WM2 x 19in.
Rear	WM2 x 19in.	WM2 x 19in.
Tyres Front	3.25 x 19in. Ribbed	3.25 x 19in. Ribbed
Rear	3.25 x 19in. Studded	3.25 x 19in. Studded
BRAKES—Drum diameter and width and Lining Area Front	7.5in. x 1.5in. (23 sq. in.)	7.5in. x 1.5in. (23 sq. in.)
Rear	7in. x 1in. (10.75 sq. in.)	7in. x 1in. (10.75 sq. in.)
CAPACITIES		
Water	—	—
Engine Oil	.5 Imp. gall. (2.27 litres, .6 U.S. gall.)	.5 Imp. gall. (2.27 litres, .6 U.S. hall.)
Fuel Tank	3 Imp. gall. (13.6 litres, 3.6 U.S. galls.)	3 Imp. gall. (13.6 litres, 3.6 U.S. galls.)
PRINCIPAL DIMENSIONS		
Length Overall	84in. (213 cms.)	84in. (213 cms.)
Width Overall	27.5in. (70 cms.)	27.5in. (70 cms.)
Height Overall	39in. (99 cms.)	39in. (99 cms.)
Wheelbase (in static loaded position)	53.75in. (136.5 cms.)	53.75in. (136.5 cms.)
Ground Clearance (in static loaded position)	5.5in. (14 cms.)	5.5in. (14 cms.)
Seat Height (in static loaded position)	30.5in. (77.5 cms.)	30.5in. (77.5 cms.)
UNLADEN WEIGHT	380 lbs. (172 kilos)	385 lbs. (174 kilos)

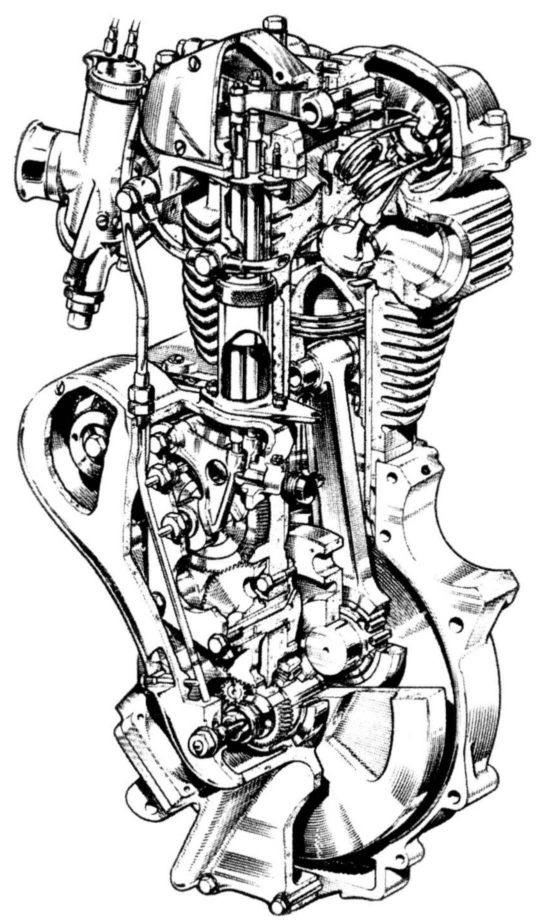

Despite the image having been used for previous brochures the 1961 edition's blue night time-like hue turned out to be a particularly apt choice as, with a bit of imagination, it could be Velocette's MD during the 2,000-odd miles he completed before declaring the prototype Venom Veeline ready to undertake something he and champion French motorcyclist Georges Monneret had planned.

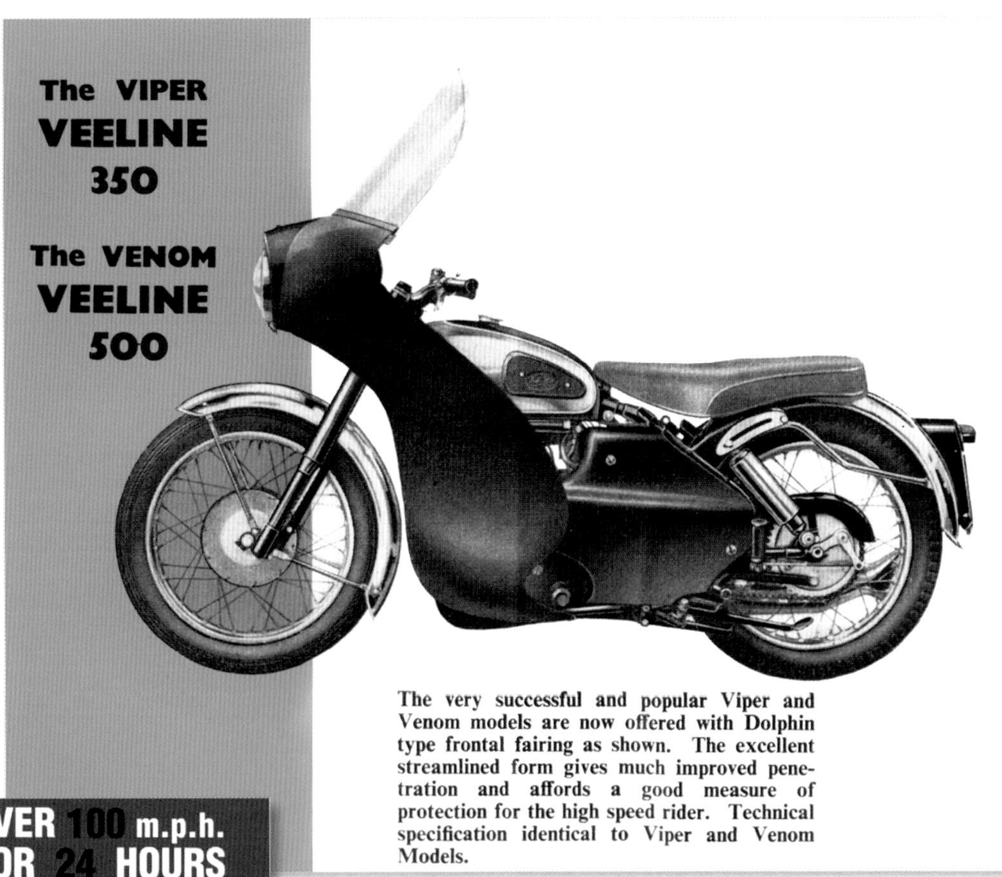

The Valiant Veeline had not proved to be a good seller but might be considered a precursor for these very civilised high-speed tourers that could also, if you were Bertie Goodman and others, be record breakers. Over the 24 hours of 17/18 March 1961 he, along with Motor Cycling*'s Bruce Main-Smith, Georges Monneret, his son Pierre and other French riders averaged 104.66mph for 12 hours and 100.05mph for the full 24 at the Montlhéry track to the south of Paris with the prototype Venom Veeline. It had been carefully assembled and nothing other than catalogued accessories used but had been stripped of lamps, primary chain case, and the screen abbreviated. With no allowance made for refuelling and tyre change stops – as well as one of over half-an-hour to repair the gear-change mechanism – the majority of laps had been covered at between 105 and 107mph.*

These super sports editions of the Viper and Venom models incorporate special racing equipment for participation in Clubman Type races. Specification includes high compression piston, Racing type carburettor. Racing type hand controlled magneto. Close ratio gears. Rear mounted footrests and pedals. Flexibly mounted re-designed petrol tank with increased capacity. The front fork has two-way damping and is fitted with a steering damper. Tachometer (rev. meter) and light alloy rims available extra. Also the two entirely new streamlined models with Dolphin type fairing : the Viper Clubman VeeLine and Venom Clubman VeeLine. Mechanical specification as above.

The latest Clubman petrol tank boosted capacity 4.25 gallons.

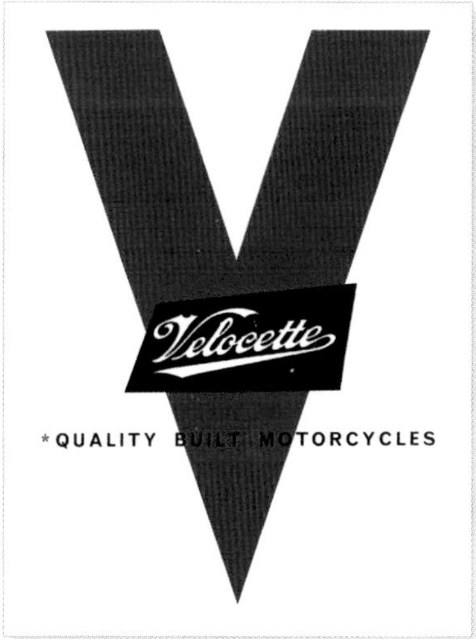

The 1963 season's wares were within this stark cover that simply stated what had become the firm's motto.

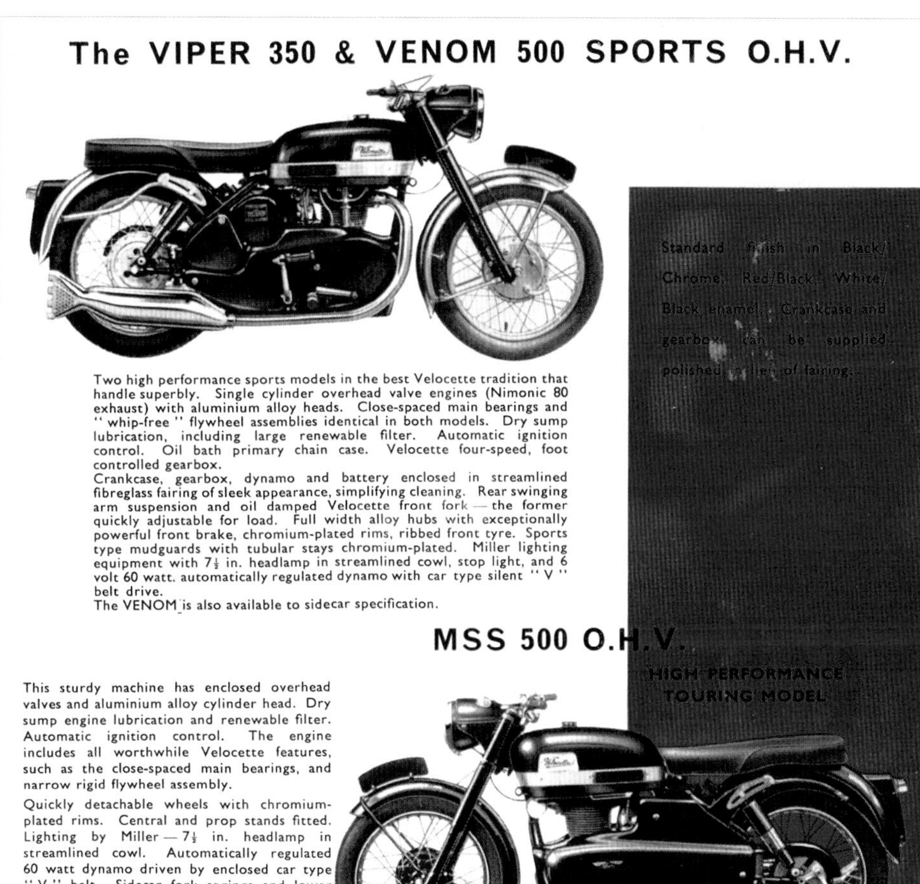

The long-running MAC had finally been discontinued in the late summer of 1960 but the MSS soldiered on. As it too had the larger tank and same choice of colour schemes there was little to tell the casual observer it wasn't one of its more exotic relations – especially if it was fitted with the optional extra full-width hubs.

The large tank and flatter dual seat had been standardised for all singles for the '63 season. Velocette's fairings were manufactured by Avon.

These super sports editions of the Viper and Venom models incorporate special racing equipment participation in Clubman Type races, Specification includes high compression piston. Racing type carburettor. Racing type hand controlled magneto. Rear mounted footrests and pedals. Flexibly mounted large capacity petrol tank. The front fork has two-way damping and is fitted with a steering damper. Tachometer (rev. meter) and light alloy rims available extra. Also the two streamlined models with Dolphin type fairing: the Viper Clubman VeeLine and Venom Clubman VeeLine. Mechanical specification as above.

Standard finish in Black/Chrome, Red/Black, White/Black enamel. Crankcase and Gearbox can be supplied polished in lieu of fairing.

L.E. VOGUE Acknowledged a magnificent model, based on the silent model LE, world approved by both Police and Public it reaches a new level in styling and sets new standards for performance, rider comfort, protection and all-round safety. The glass fibre non-rust all-weather body (styled by Mitchenall) has built in parcel pockets and provision for flashing indicators and matching glass fibre panniers. Twin headlamps give superb lighting and quickly removable side panels give easy access to engine and gearbox.

VIPER & VENOM SPECIAL 350 & 500 General specification as sports models but standard finish in pale blue enamel and anodised aluminium motif on petrol tank. Additional equipment and chrome plated wheel rims are available as extras. Has the same mechanical efficiency and outstanding performance as the more expensive versions.

Gives the opportunity of owning a quality built machine at a price well below the standard sports models.

Standard two-tone colour finishes in light stone/off white, blue/off white or grey/off white.

As chalk and cheese but the same under the skin. With the LE still a current model, if looking more than somewhat dated, those faithful to its many attributes but anxious for something more modern had their wishes granted with the unveiling of the Vogue at Earls court in November 1962.

Rather than specials these should have been termed as economy models, but that would not have made particularly come-hither advertising. The message was clear enough to anyone reading the specifications, but as The Motor Cycle *pointed out when they tested the Venom version, "Chromium-plated trimmings are all very well, but they never add performance." At a saving of £28 you still got the 'superb road-holding allied to exceptionally powerful brakes' and a timed one-way maximum of 95mph, with 85 (accompanied by valve float!) in third, was well up to par.*

Standard finish in pale blue enamel, the petrol tank having an attractive anodised aluminium motif.

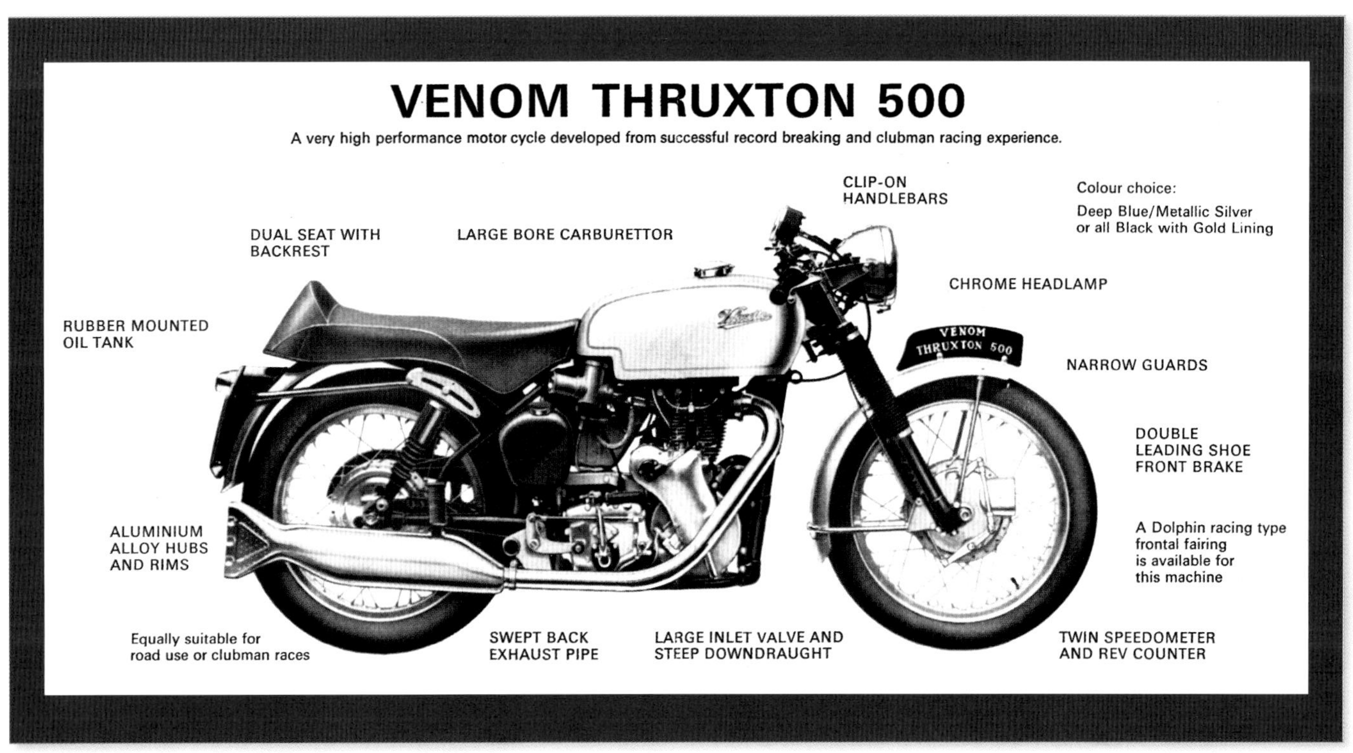

Early Thruxtons were finished in silver and blue but traditional black and gold soon became an option.

MODEL	VENOM THRUXTON 500
ENGINE—Type	O.H.V., air cooled vertical single cylinder
Bore and Stroke	86 x 86 mm. (3·385 x 3·385 in.)
Capacity (swept volume)	499 c.c. (30·45 cu. in.)
Compression Ratio	9 to 1
Brake Horse-power	41 b.h.p. at 6,200 r.p.m.
Carburettor	Amal
Ignition	Battery and Coil
Generator	6 volt with auto voltage regulator
GEARBOX	Velo. 4-spd. foot control
Gear Ratios (overall) Top	4·4 to 1
Third	5·3 to 1
Second	6·97 to 1
First	10·1 to 1
TRANSMISSION	
Sprockets Engine	·5 in. pitch, 23 teeth
Clutch	·5 in. pitch, 44 teeth
Gearbox	·625 in. pitch, 20 teeth
Rear Wheel	·625 in. pitch, 46 teeth
Chains Primary	·5 in. x ·305 in., 68 pitches
Rear	·625 x 380 in., 103 pitches
WHEELS	
Rims Front	WM2 x 19 in.
Rear	WM2 x 19 in.
Tyres Front	3·00 x 19 in. Ribbed
Rear	3·25 x 19 in. Studded
BRAKES—Drum diameter and width and Lining Area Front	7·5 in. x 1·5 in. (23 sq. in.)
Rear	7 in. x 1 in. (10·75 sq. in.)
CAPACITIES	
Engine Oil	·5 Imp. gall. (2·27 litres, ·6 U.S. gall.)
Fuel Tank	4·25 Imp. gall. (19·3 litres, 5·1 U.S. gall.)
PRINCIPLE DIMENSIONS	
Length Overall	84 in. (213 cms.)
Width Overall	27·5 in. (70 cms.)
Height Overall	39 in. (99 cms.)
Height Overall VeeLine Models	
Wheelbase (in static loaded position)	53·75 in. (136·5 cms.)
Ground Clearance " "	5·5 in. (14 cms.)
Seat Height " "	30·5 in. (77·5 cms.)
UNLADEN WEIGHT	375 lb. (170 kilos)

As November 1964 approached, Velocette aficionados eagerly awaited their annual visit to Earls Court, as word was out that on 'their' stand there would be something very special. Few were disappointed. Named after the Thruxton 500-mile race, which many saw as a continuation of the old Clubmans TT, it was a production version of the '64 500cc-class race winner – a Clubman Venom with one of the special cylinder heads that were now available. As conceived and produced the Thruxton was a wonderful reminder of days past amongst the throngs of flashy multi-cylinder sports bikes, but that remains its magic – a magic that enabled a pair of them to vanquish all other 500cc machines in the 1967 Isle of Man Production TT.

VINCENT

With the war in Europe won and Japanese capitulation within sight, reminders as to the firm's continued existence started to appear in the motorcycling press. In effect a cartoon, this depicts neither the pre-war A Rapide nor forthcoming Series B but does allude to the latter's 'frameless' construction and timing chest design.

Shame to say it, but I've ridden a Vincent twin on only one occasion. However, the afternoon I did was a memorable one as it took me out through the north-west suburbs of Buenos Aires, and if I had kept going would have led to what could be considered the marque's spiritual birthplace – for its creator Philip Conrad Vincent's family home was a large estancia in the Argentinian province of Cordoba. Not that I was thinking about the connection as I navigated my friend Rudolfo's wonderfully scruffy old Series B Rapide along the deeply textured and potholed roads through unfamiliar terrain; it only occurred to me later. Silly that I did at all, as the link was tenuous and young Vincent's life might very well have taken a different course had it not have been for his parents' desire to have him not only born in England but mainly educated there too.

Their decision, however, led to him being sent to Harrow school, where what would be his lifelong passion was awakened by a fellow pupil's stash of motorcycling magazines when the two of them were quarantined in the school sanatorium.

From there on it was only a matter of time before his father caved into his son's enthusiasm and sanctioned the purchase of a new but shop-soiled 'round tank' 250 BSA; but the reality did not live up to the dreams and it was soon gone in favour of an ABC. The little twin ran far more smoothly than the single but it did what all of its kin were prone to do and shed its valve gear at the slightest excuse, so young Vincent began thinking he might be able to do better, and within a couple of years, whilst up at Cambridge reading mechanical sciences, he put some of his ideas into practice and built his own machine.

Utilising a 350cc Swiss MAG motor, as well as various other proprietary components such as Enfield brakes, it featured a triangulated frame with his own design of cantilever rear suspension, which he duly took out a patent for, and went a considerable way to realising his ideals. Hugely encouraged by these endeavours and now determined to become a motorcycle manufacturer, he abandoned university and within a short while had fulfilled his goal.

He did so in 1928 by the simple expedient of buying, with financial help from his family, what remained of the recently-liquidated HRD motorcycle company from its new owner Ernie Humphries of OK Supreme, who had acquired it for the factory space. The material assets may have been negligible but the name came with a certain cachet due to its founder Howard Davies having won the 1925 Senior TT with one of his own JAP-engined creations shortly after he had commenced in business, and Freddie Dixon winning the Junior as recently as 1927.

Unfettered by tradition, premises were acquired in Stevenage, Hertfordshire, and at his father's behest a friend of his named Frank Walker was installed to manage the new enterprise. Established as it was in the last impoverished years of the 1920s, the fledging Vincent-HRD was lucky to survive, considering that yearly production had grown to only 35 machines by 1930. Survive it did, however, and the company benefitted greatly when it was joined by Phil Irving, a young Australian engineer who arrived in England after having literally hitched a lift from Melbourne on the pillion pad of a Vincent-HRD that was engaged upon a round-the-world tour.

Realising that the current triangulated frame was detrimental to sales, Vincent gave his new assistant the job of designing a more acceptable diamond pattern that nevertheless incorporated his patented rear suspension, and this was featured on the machines exhibited at the 1931 show. Sadly, motorcyclists of the period were wary of even properly-engineered rear suspension such as Vincent's, so the firm struggled with output nearing only 100 per annum by 1933 – the year that dual brakes were introduced front and rear, something that became a hallmark of the firm's motorcycles from then on.

The company had also put a small three-wheeled delivery van, with an advertised capacity of 2½cwt, on the market; powered firstly by a side-valve JAP and then a Villiers two-stroke. Goods were carried between the front wheels, which were steered by rack and pinion whilst its operator was provided with a car-type seat and steering wheel – goodness knows how many were made but within a couple of years-or-so it was dropped.

Since they had first been employed in 1931, Rudge Python motors had increasingly displaced JAPs as the power unit of choice for the majority of Vincent-HRDs but a factory team of three machines fitted with JA Prestwich's latest racing engine were sent over to the Isle of Man for the 1934 Senior. The resulting debacle caused by repeated engine failures in practice and the event proper side-lined all three, and that, coupled with Rudge's decision to suspend the supply of its engines to other manufacturers, persuaded Phil Vincent that from then on his firm would make its own.

The design was a joint effort between Vincent and Irving, and was a 500cc high-camshaft pushrod overhead-valve that incorporated some novel features in its valve operation and had a bore and stroke of 84x90mm – dimensions that would be retained throughout the life of the firm's big singles and forthcoming twins. Remarkably for such a small firm, the time between the new motor's conception and completion was short, so it was ready to make its debut in the machines that were unveiled to the public at the November show and would go on sale for the 1935 season alongside a water-cooled Villiers two-stroke and JAP-engined 500, which were in effect leftovers from the previous year. Although the sprung-frame was all but unchanged, the new Meteors (and pricier, more-sporting Comets) finally shrugged off any thoughts that Phil Vincent's operation was anything less than one of a full manufacturer. Final proof came in June when the even more highly tuned TT model won its right to the title, with Vincent-HRDs making up five

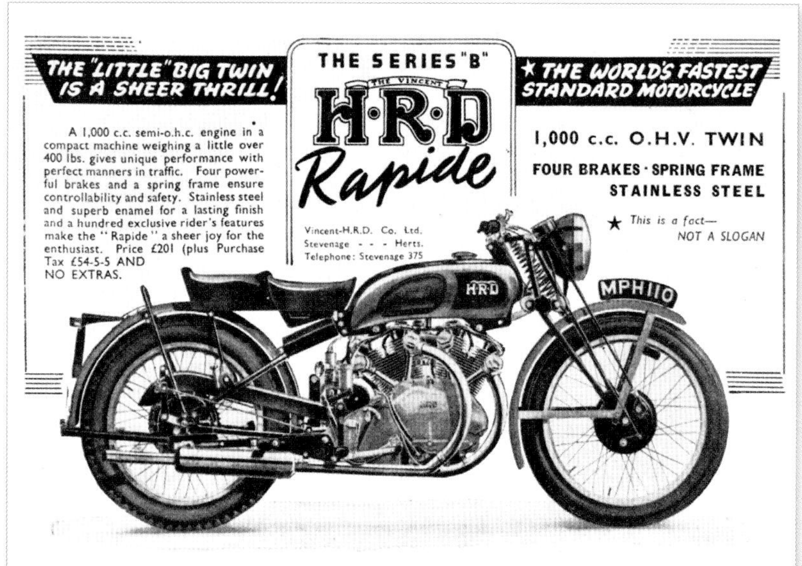

out of the 14 finishers in the Senior TT – a year that was particularly hotly contested by factory teams.

All models other than Vincent-HRDs with in-house motors were dispensed with for 1936, and a Comet Special and TT Replica (both with bronze-head semi-race engines) were added to the range while Phil Irving had been formulating something that would turn out to be very special. It had come to him that certain aspects of the existing 500 (499cc) single lent themselves to the creation of a 1000cc (998cc) V-twin and that its frame only needed lengthening by a few inches to accommodate it – and what a machine that would make!

Sure enough, by November plans had been transmuted into metal and Vincent-HRD's Series A Rapide was up, running, and in the flesh at the annual Motorcycle Show. The two Philips, Vincent and Irving, had created the fastest standard road machine on two – or even, arguably – four wheels.

Its true performance was somewhat academic due to the borderline ability of the Burman gearbox and clutch to cope with the power, despite both having been beefed up – suffice to say, however, that its top speed was 110mph or possibly more, as Brooklands laps of that figure were recorded. Engineering and performance of this nature did not come cheap, and the Series A sold for a little over £140 but, it should be said, compared with the far more agricultural Brough Superior SS100 at £155 (1939 prices) it could be considered quite reasonable. George Brough had an even more expensive product in the form of the £185 four-cylinder shaft-drive Dream, and all three had rear springing in one form or another, but the war saw the end of them as none were suitable for military duties – just under 80 Rapides having been made.

The Series B Rapide with its extensively redesigned engine and unit-construction gearbox, the whole forming a stressed member that took the place of the lower part of a conventional frame, was unveiled in the spring of 1946. But it was nearly six months before the very first production machines began to leave the factory. For the meanwhile advertising led potential customers both at home and overseas to believe that the sleek machine depicted was the one they would soon be able to buy. But it was not so. What in my eyes could have been the most attractive Vincent of all time, a more spindly version of what was truly to come, set off with that deliciously sexy tank, existed on paper alone.

Although miniscule in comparison to some other motorcycle factories, Vincent-HRD did its share towards the war effort by producing a multiplicity of components for aircraft such as de Havilland's Mosquito, as well as fuses and casings for landmines. In 1937 Phil Irving had left to work for Velocette (the company that had briefly employed him upon his first arrival in the UK) but in 1943 he was back at Stevenage in order to assist with the development of Vincent's own design of two-stroke engines – one version of which was intended for Uffa Fox's airborne lifeboats had it been ready before the war ended. His time was also put to other uses, however, as even prior to D-Day in mid 1944 work was afoot on the machine that would replace the Series A when peace finally came.

Abandoning a conventional frame, the Series B, as it would be named, was based around a redesigned 998cc V-twin in unit with a bolted-on gearbox of the firm's own manufacture – the whole forming the main stressed member. A fabricated box-section backbone incorporating the oil tank was bolted to a forged steering head and attached to the cylinder heads via brackets, whilst the rear frame was pivoted behind the gearbox with its spring units bolted to the rear of this upper frame member. The new machine, more compact than its predecessor and weighing some 450lb, was announced shortly before the war's end, and by the spring of 1946 had been enthusiastically evaluated by the press.

It was several months before deliveries commenced, however, as haphazard post-war availability of materials and other constraints such as out-dated and worn machine tools were a hindrance to production and would remain so for a good while. Aluminium, albeit of sometimes questionable quality, was plentiful whilst some varieties of steel were allocated according to export performance; absolute priority was therefore given to export sales – the very first of which appropriately was to the Argentine.

Phil Vincent carried out a good deal of testing himself, and early in 1947, when a gear pinion seized on the layshaft in the gearbox of the Rapide he was evaluating, he was thrown off. Gearboxes from then were suitably modified but he suffered severe head injuries and was unable to return to work for several months. It was during this time that a standard Rapide was transformed into what would turn out to be a very effective competition machine – known as Gunga Din, it would oft as not be ridden by one of its originators, factory test engineer and racer George Brown, and during its career won innumerable races and hillclimbs, as well as endurance and speed records. He would have won the 1948 Senior Clubmans TT had he not run out of fuel at Keppel Gate on his last lap when well in the lead. Two other Vincents came first and second but Brown's heroic push-in of over four miles to claim sixth place brought him a standing ovation.

The following year there was a separate class for 1000s and although it was a Vincent benefit his mount went down on one cylinder for much of the race, so he was the last of the finishers, in fifth place, and over half-an-hour behind an Ariel Square Four.

Back at work and encouraged by the performance obtained from the modified Rapide, PCV (as friends and associates called him) decided the time was right to introduce a super sports road machine, as well as an out-and-out racer that would be available on a limited basis. Thus the Vincent stand at Great Britain's first post-war (1948) motorcycle show had on display a racing Black Lightning at an eye watering £400 (all prices plus purchase tax). *Motor Cycling* magazine remarked that 'with its straight through pipes, Girdraulic forks and shining black enamel it is small wonder that throughout show week it was a constant attraction for visitors'. Nearby stood Gunga Din, recently returned from record-breaking in Belgium; Series B and C Black Shadows at £300 and £315 respectively; Series B and Series C Rapides at £250 and £265; plus a Series C Rapide with Blacknell sidecar. Also on the stand were a brace of the re-introduced single-cylinder models: a Series C Comet at £215 and a Series B Meteor at £195 – the distinguishing feature of B and C Series being Brampton front forks on the former and new Girdraulics on the latter.

Behind this impressive array of the most exotic and

The USA was where production would be encouraged to head for, and by the latter part of 1946 several dealerships were established. There was, however, a paucity of machines for them to sell and it would not be until early the following year that orders could begin to be fulfilled, even though Vincent Martin had had the third (numerically) Series B shipped to him at the beginning of October and Rod Coates the seventh shortly after.

expensive motorcycles at the show their manufacturer was finding it hard going, however. Despite a healthy order book, the trust that it had been hoped would be investing in the company (to fund modern machine tools and streamline production) had got cold feet. PCV's family money was by no means endless and finances were tight, so alternative sources of income such as outside engineering work were explored. To make matters worse, Vincent's lucrative trade with the Argentine came to an end when its government under Juan Peron terminated importation agreements.

For a while there were hopes of a liaison with Indian Motorcycles after PCV had visited the firm during one of his sales trips to the US. This would have involved the fitting of Rapide engines in place of Indian's own V-twin, and the project even got as far as Phil Irving overseeing the construction of a prototype at the Stevenage works – apparently finished in blue and dubbed a Vindian. There was talk of 200-odd machines per month being a possibility but it all fell apart when Indian was bought by the English Brockhouse concern, whose main aim was to take control of the countrywide dealerships that were also agents for various British marques. That done, Brockhouse made it clear that it would be happy to handle Vincents but had no interest in the proposed amalgams.

All of the foregoing and other factors – such as difficulty with a regular supply of the Girdraulic fork castings from the manufacturer – would shortly force the company into the hands of the official receivers but before this happened, at the end of 1949, Phil Irving left the company once more and returned to his native Australia.

A stroke of good fortune dictated that the appointed official, one EC Baillie, felt the firm had a future and he was largely instrumental in its continuation and subsequent prosperity – becoming a director in the process. By 1952 the company was enjoying a degree of profitability that had only been dreamt of in the past; and with average production running at some 250 machines per month it was renamed Vincent Engineers (Stevenage) Ltd during November. "Now that the company is engaged in the manufacture of aero engines, marine engines and many other precision products in addition to its range of world-famous motorcycles, it is felt that the new title indicates more clearly the company's wide range of activities," ran the press release.

The aero engines could have been a real money-spinner but, through no fault of their maker, cost too much time and produced little – if any – profit. Hoping for a long-lasting and lucrative Air Ministry contract, a specially adapted and uprated 60-plus-bhp version of the V-twin was developed to power a small radio-controlled aircraft built by ML Aviation, which would be used as a gunnery target. After many teething problems, including the necessity to change from carburation to fuel injection due to cutting out, and crashing during assisted take-off, the Picador (as it was named) was passed as fit for purpose; but dysfunctional remote controls and other ills brought the project to an end and left Vincent with a number of unwanted engines. Of no use for motorcycles, they were later sold off for a fraction of their cost – ironically, in the main bought to construct specials or for the components they contained that could be used to tune Vincent twins.

Vincent's 1947 brochure – at last the Series B was in regular production and available, even if export took precedence over the home market. The fastest perhaps, but over-the-counter racing models as suggested here were yet to come.

To demonstrate the firm's diversity, if nothing else, 'other precision products' included hydraulic pit props for mining – another idea that could have paid off very handsomely. Imagine a constant demand for Picadors as gunnery practice improved accuracy and droves of the little aircraft were shot down, or mile upon mile of subterranean mine workings shored up with Vincent pit props. Either could have brought in so much money, but didn't.

Seemingly undismayed, Phil Vincent forged ahead, and his stand at the 1953 show featured no less than 23 machines. Incongruously rubbing shoulders with his B and C Series singles and twins were a selection of rather less aristocratic, but nevertheless Vincent badged, two-wheelers. The Firefly was a 45cc clip-on motor, the rights of which had been acquired by Vincent from its original manufacturer Miller; and on the stand there were several of the things variously attached to Sun cycles, a Philips, and a tandem, for goodness' sakes! Owners and would-be owners of big Vincents were not amused.

Completing the assemblage were three

As an engineer above all else, Philip Vincent chose to fill his sales literature with good, solid and exhaustive data to accompany these side views of the Series B Rapide. Verging on dour, as was a good deal of the company's advertising, it was nevertheless informative. "A connoisseur's machine with a colossal performance and many appealing features," was the totally appropriate sub-heading of the The Motor Cycle*'s 1947 road test. Speeds recorded in the gears were 56, 86 and 98mph, with 'not obtained' noted against top; but in the text there was talk of 114mph being reached on one occasion and the standing quarter-mile was covered in 15 seconds. The dual compensated brakes came in for much praise, and just 26ft was needed to bring the 476lb machine to a halt from 30mph. Fuel consumption was not a primary factor but it consumed a gallon of the inferior fuel of the period every 64 miles at 50mph, and 62 miles at 60mph.*

Specification

ENGINE.—Original and massive Vincent H.R.D. design and manufacture. 50 degree Vee Twin, rear cylinder offset 1¼ in. for improved cooling. Bore 84 m.m., Stroke 90 m.m.—998 c.c. Very massive ribbed crankcase cast in unit with oilbath chaincase and gearbox from DTD424 Aircraft Specification Aluminium Alloy. Four large-diameter main bearings. Forged high-tensile steel flywheels machined all over. Crankpin 1 9/16 in. dia. (37·7 m.m.) EN36 case-hardened steel. Side-by-side forged connecting rods, 65 ton steel; big end liners EN31 steel, hardened, ground and honed. 6 rows of 3 m.m. dia. × 5 m.m. long rollers in big ends. Rigid taper-bored ⅞ in. (22 m.m.) dia. gudgeon pins, fully floating, retained by circlips. Specialloid pistons with 2 pressure and 1 scraper ring. Replaceable cast-iron liners shrunk into aluminium cylinder jackets. Deeply finned cylinder heads cast in RR53B aluminium alloy and heat treated. Both exhaust ports face forwards. Inclined o.h. valves each with twin valve guides. Inlet valve 1·8 in. dia. (46 m.m.), of Silchrome steel; exhaust valve, 1·67 in. dia. (42·5 m.m.), of DTD49B steel. Valve seats shrunk in, inlet seat austenitic cast-iron, exhaust seat aluminium bronze. Entirely enclosed and lubricated o.h. rockers of straight rigid design forged from KE805 steel with contact faces hardened. Very accessible tappet adjustment. Totally enclosed and lubricated duplex helical valve springs. Stainless steel push-rod tubes. Two camshafts mounted high in timing case with push rods only 6 in. (152 m.m.) long. Mechanical rotary breather valve. Four 65-ton steel tubular bolts fasten each cylinder head direct to crankcase.

LUBRICATION.—Dry-sump system. A large double-acting rotary plunger pump, worm driven from timing side mainshaft, draws oil from 6-pint (3·4 litre) oil tank through gauze filter and large bore pipe, pumps it through a very large full-flow Tecalemit fabric filter and thence direct to big ends, camshaft bearings and rear of cylinder walls. Return oil is scraped from flywheels and pumped back to tank. Bye-pass jets from return pipe to tank lubricate valve gear.

CARBURETTORS.—Two vertical 1 1/16 in. (27 m.m.) Choke Amals operated by twist grip through a junction box. Simple adjusters for synchronising are provided. Separate air levers on handlebar. " Amal " air filters can be supplied as extras.

PRIMARY DRIVE.—By Triplex ⅜ in. pitch " Renold " Chain. Engine sprocket incorporates a multi-spring 3-lobe cam-type shock absorber of special design. The whole drive runs in oil and is enclosed in a polished aluminium case. Very simple and accessible external adjustment by means of a single adjusting screw.

CLUTCH.—Special Vincent H.R.D. design and manufacture. Patents applied for in Great Britain and abroad. A normal single-plate clutch provides the expanding pressure to work a pair of shoes in a high-duty cast-iron finned drum. Although incredibly light in operation this clutch will transmit great torque. It is housed outside the oil bath and protected from oil by special seals. Clutch is fully accessible without removing oil bath cover.

GEARBOX.—Vincent H.R.D. design, 4-speed constant mesh, made in our own factory. Very massive construction and highest quality materials endow it with great strength and long life. Ratios 3·5, 4·2, 5·5 and 9·1 to 1. All shafts supported by large-diameter ball bearings. Accessible oil filler with dip-stick. External indicator lever can be used to select neutral or change by hand.

STANDARD SPROCKET SIZES.—Engine 35T., Clutch 56T., Gearbox Final Drive 21T., Rear Wheel 46T. Ratios altered by changing rear wheel sprocket. Actual gearbox reduction ratios 1, 1·19, 1·55, 2·6 to 1.

KICKSTARTER.—Special design giving great leverage. Can be mounted on left hand side of the machine for extra charge when R.H. sidecar is fitted. Folding footpiece.

FINAL DRIVE.—By heavy ⅝ in. × ⅜ in. " Renold " chain with chain guard. Can be adjusted in less than 1 min. without tools.

FRAME.—Original Vincent H.R.D. design employing the massive engine-gear unit as the main central structure. An immensely strong forged-steel head-lug is bolted to a steel bracket fixed to the front cylinder head. The head is bolted to the front of the oil tank which stays it against the rear cylinder head. Long travel, 5½ in. (140 m.m.) movement, rear suspension is provided by the patented Vincent H.R.D. rear fork of rigid triangulated design, similar to those fitted to all earlier Vincent H.R.D. models. Adjustable friction shock absorbers are provided for rear springing. All necessary sidecar attachment points are provided.

FRONT FORKS.—Triangulated tubular girder, link type. This fork ensures the perfect tracking of both wheels which is essential for first-class handling and provides the finest steering in the world. Toughened steel spindles running in oil-impregnated bronze bearings eliminate the need for oiling and frequent adjustment. Shorter top links and stronger spring can be supplied for use with sidecar only.

IGNITION.—Gear-driven Lucas flange-mounted magneto with automatic advance ; protected by polished aluminium cowl.

LIGHTING SET.—Special Miller 6v. 50 watt voltage controlled, separate dynamo driven from primary chain. Sprocket easily detachable. Very accessible 13 a.h. Exide battery, fully sprung. Special 8 in. head lamp gives exceptional light. Stop light coupled to brakes. Lucas Altette horn. Large dynamo permits the use of extra lights without strain on the battery.

SEAT.—Specially designed by co-operation between our engineers and Messrs. Feridax Ltd. Great trouble has been taken to ensure that this exclusive Feridax Dual Seat of moulded Dunlopillo shall provide the maximum comfort for both rider and passenger. Rear end sprung by our Patented method, British Patent No. 424644. The very neat tool tray slides out of sight under this seat.

PETROL TANK.—Very handsome pressed steel design, Bonderized, enamelled black and hand lined with real gold leaf. Capacity 3¾ Imperial gallons, 4 American gallons (17 litres). Dropped rear end prevents water reaching tap outlet. Twin petrol taps, one for reserve. Quick-action filler cap.

PETROL AND OIL PIPES.—Brazed joints with flexible hose insertions to prevent fracture. ⅜ in. (7 m.m.) bore oil feed pipe to ensure easy flow in Arctic weather.

OIL TANK.—Forms part of frame. Very strong design. Capacity 6 pints (3·4 litres). Outlet union automatically shuts off oil when feed pipe is detached.

BRAKES.—The famous Vincent H.R.D. Duo Brakes. Two 7 in. (178 m.m.) dia. × ⅞ in. (22 m.m.) wide brakes on each wheel. Unquestionably the best brakes in the world, their balanced application gives equal braking stresses and thus eliminates tendency to "pull" or skid.

WHEELS.—Heavy gauge bright spokes and chromium plated Dunlop rims. Front rim WM1×20, rear rim WM2×19, S.K.F. large diameter taper roller bearings in hubs. Pull-out spindles and quick-release anchorages and brake-rods enable either wheel to be detached without tools in less than one minute. By fitting another sprocket to brake drum and reversing wheel the gear ratio can be changed in a few minutes, if need be, by the roadside. Both wheels are fitted with one security bolt and two balance weights.

TYRES.—Rear, Avon "Supreme" 26 in. × 3·50 in. studded tyre. Front, Avon "Speedster" 26 in. × 3·00 in. ribbed tyre. Both of natural rubber.

MUDGUARDS.—Special light alloy, highly polished. Enamelled tubular steel stays. Rear guard hinged for easy wheel removal.

STANDS.—Rear tubular stand. Twin prop stands, one either side, can also be swung down together to form front stand.

EXHAUST SYSTEM.—Two 1⅝ in. (41·5 m.m.) dia. steel exhaust pipes, secured to heads by finned nuts, join and run into a special "Carbjector" silencer. Whole system is chromium plated and gives a very subdued but pleasant note.

FOOTRESTS.—Exclusive Vincent H.R.D. design. Adjustable for length and angle. Gear-change and brake pedals move with footrests but are adjustable for position relative to them, and they are also reversible for a racing position. Built-in pillion footrests of forged steel are also adjustable, are fully sprung and can be used for a racing riding position. All four footrests can be folded.

HANDLEBARS.—The famous narrow straight Vincent H.R.D. bars which have been praised so highly by the technical experts. They give a remarkably comfortable riding position. Can be adjusted for wrist angle. Control levers of racing pattern are also adjustable.

FINISH.—All enamelled parts are Bonderized and finished in Pinchin Johnson's best cycle stoving enamel. Bright parts are mostly polished stainless steel or aluminium; others are chromium or cadmium plated.

SPEEDOMETER.—Smiths' "Chronometric" with total and trip recording and internal illuminator. Reads to 120 m.p.h. or 180 k.p.h. according to order. Driven from inside front brake drum for greater accuracy.

EQUIPMENT.—Includes tyre inflator, a complete set of high quality tools, grease-gun and tyre-levers.

POWER-WEIGHT RATIO.
10 lbs. per b.h.p. 4·5 kilos per b.h.p.
222 b.h.p. per ton. 220 b.h.p. per metric ton.

PETROL CONSUMPTION.
Average fast touring 50 to 60 m.p.g. (Imperial) 5 to 6 litres per 100 kilos.
Average fast touring 50 to 60 m.p.g. (American).

OIL CONSUMPTION.
About 1,500 m.p.g. 500 kilos per litre.

CRUISING SPEED.—Up to 85 m.p.h. 136 k.p.h.

MAXIMUM SPEED.—105 to 112 m.p.h. 168 to 180 k.p.h.

MINIMUM SPEED ON TOP.—18 m.p.h. 29 k.p.h.

MAXIMUM SAFE SPEEDS IN GEARS.
3rd ... 96 m.p.h. 154 k.p.h.
2nd ... 82 m.p.h. 130 k.p.h.
1st ... 50 m.p.h. 80 k.p.h.

ACCELERATION THROUGH GEARS.
0 — 30 m.p.h. (48 k.p.h.) — 1½ secs.
0 — 60 m.p.h. (96 k.p.h.) — 6 secs.
0 — 80 m.p.h. (128 k.p.h.) — 12 secs.
0 —100 m.p.h. (160 k.p.h.) — 24 secs.
Standing start ¼ mile (400 meters) in less than 15 secs.

DRY WEIGHT.—455 lbs. — 206 kilos.

LENGTH (Overall).—85½ in. — 2,175 m.m.

WHEELBASE.—56 in. — 1,420 m.m.

GROUND CLEARANCE.—6 in. — 150 m.m.

OVERALL HEIGHT.—39 in. — 1 meter.

WIDTH OVER HANDLEBARS. 25½ in. — 650 m.m.

TURNING CIRCLE (At tyres).
Under 16 ft. (5 meters) diameter of circle.

SHIPPING DIMENSIONS.
Assembled complete in closed case—handlebars detached.
Length ... ... 7 ft. 3½ in. — 2,220 m.m.
Width ... ... 17½ in. — 500 m.m.
Height ... ... 3 ft. 6½ in. — 1,080 m.m.
Approximate gross weight 6 cwts. — 305 kilos.

NSU-Vincents, which it was hoped would garner a lucrative portion of the lightweight market. Borne out of a recently-agreed collaboration between the two companies and Sir Lacey Vincent's (no relation) Layford Trading, which handled the German company's exports to the UK and Commonwealth, they would qualify for the Commonwealth Preferential Tariff providing they incorporated 51 per cent of British components, and to this end would be assembled at Stevenage. All finished in Vincent's traditional black livery they comprised a 250cc overhead-cam Max and two Foxes: a 123cc two-stoke and a 98cc OHV four-stroke.

The Max progressed no further than a single prototype but Foxes, based around NSU's frame and power unit did – although a total production in the low hundreds prevented them from becoming the hoped-for money-spinner. Another agreement that could have been fruitful gave Vincent the rights to market and service the rather good little NSU Quickly 49cc moped, as it soon won popularity and was becoming an excellent seller. But Vincent had only signed up for a year, and thereafter Layford reaped the benefits for itself.

Fireflies, Foxes, pit props et al aside, by 1954 there was a need to improve and modernise Vincent's own big twins and singles – despite, as ever, limited finances. Drawing on the findings of a questionnaire circulated amongst owners, as well as how he saw the way forward, Phil Vincent formulated the D Series. What he came up with was a range that heeded the requests of the faithful without swingeing retooling costs, and remained close to his own ideals – machines that looked very different but stayed essentially the same.

Calls for improvement in steering and road-holding, especially on uneven surfaces, as well as enhanced comfort, better weather protection for the long-distance rider and easier starting for all were issues that he was happy to address.

The combined upper frame member/oil reservoir was done away with, and in its place was a single tube with remote oil tank oil tank located in the rear skirt. He continued with a single, softer, rear spring/damper unit that gave greater rear suspension travel and softer springing for the Girdraulic forks. Starting gremlins were facilitated by a change from magneto to coil ignition. Additional comfort, whatever the weather, as well as radically altered (restyled) looks were achieved by voluminous, some might say stylish, fibreglass enclosures and fairings – finished all over in lustrous black.

Unveiled at the 1954 November show, the *Motor Cycle* spoke of the 'Stevenage firm's victory over bad weather', going on to say that, "The new models represent a big step forward in motorcycle development, both as regards the basic conception and in the use of light but strong glass-reinforced plastic material for the bodywork."

All of that was as it may have been, but for the

public it was one step too far. And rather than the new models taking the marque forward and into the future they presaged the end. By the following summer it was quite clear to Phil Vincent that it was unviable for motorcycle production to continue, and shortly before the Christmas of 1955 it was all over.

Not for Vincent Engineering, however, and for the next few years the company continued in business manufacturing, amongst other things, light engines and suchlike – the former employed in products such as the Rapier rotary mower made by Farmfitters Ltd of Gerrards Cross, Bucks.

But how the mighty may fall, and Vincent landed pretty much flat on its back with the peculiar fibreglass-bodied Amanda water scooter. If you've five minutes to spare, there's a period advertising film for them on the internet featuring ladies, children and inappropriately-dressed gentlemen having fun and frolics with a gaggle of Amandas…

By 1959 finances were such, and largely as a result of Amanda, that the company was bought out by Harper Engines, also of Stevenage, and PCV remained as a consultant for a while. This did not last, and within a few months, after a falling-out, he was sent on his way, and with what savings he had he purchased a small garage in Lincolnshire from which he also bought and sold cars as Vincent Motors.

But it was not a success, and he and his family sold up and moved to London where they lived in reduced circumstances – his wife working in the hotel trade to support them. For the remainder of his active life, apart from consultancy work and writing technical articles, he devoted himself to the design of rotary engines. Sadly, his health failed before they reached fruition and he died after prolonged illness in 1979.

A true visionary? Forty years after his enclosed motorcycles had failed to find favour this mode had become all but de rigueur amongst the very latest superbikes, and 40 years on from his water scooters Jet Skis were the preferred water-going toy of playboys and poseurs. So what of his long-cherished and fiercely-argued rotary engine concepts?

Visionary or not, Phil Vincent left us with the legacy of his fabulous motorcycles, the identity of which must rightfully rest with the surviving machines. But after Harper's tenure many years ago the trademark passed through various other hands before ending up in the USA with one Bernard Li, who announced the launch of Vincent Motors USA in 1998. Prototypes powered by a V-twin Honda engine were built but they came to nothing and Li was killed in a motorcycle accident ten years later. I sincerely hope it will not be resurrected once more in an attempt to give credence to some latter-day behemoth in billet and chrome.

An uncharacteristically lyrical teaser to attract prospects to the 1948 show stand where there would be seven models on display, from the basic Series B Meteor to the special-order Series C Black Lightning. Three would be Series B machines, consisting of the 500 single Meteor, Rapide and Black Shadow V-twin 1000s – all with HRD-Brampton girder forks. New for this year were C Series, which featured Vincent's own Girdraulic front forks, and there would be four of these on the stand: the Comet (500), the Rapide, the Black Shadow and the Black Lightning (1000 V-twins). What was intended to be a customer speedway engine with an amalgam of pre-war-type bottom end and post-war head and barrel was also displayed, but few were made.

This deliciously evocative brochure cover by the virtually unknown French artist Reyrolles was published in the late '40s even though the machine it loosely depicted was an earlier model with routing of the internal oilways visible on the timing cover. An unlikely-looking couple, however – the Vargas-like blonde's shoulder muscles bulging as she clings on for dear life to her abductor, and neither dressed for a fast ride in the countryside.

BY RE-INTRODUCING MODERNIZED VERSIONS OF THE

METEOR and COMET

Apart from the reduction of speed and acceleration to more normal levels due to their smaller 500 c.c. engines, these machines incorporate nearly every worth-while feature of the fabulous Rapides.

THE IDENTICAL FRAME AND FORKS, BRAKES AND Q.D. WHEELS, WONDERFUL STEERING, AND INSTANT STOPPING.

At least 80% of the parts are identical with those used in the famous twins — just think! These parts are designed to be safe at speeds up to 150 m.p.h.! ! The same cylinder head and barrel, valve gear, piston, con-rod, big-end, mainshafts and main bearings —— what a factor of safety! What life and reliability! What pride of ownership!

Are they cheap? Of course not! Vincent H.R.D. quality cannot be obtained at mass production prices.

Is the price reasonable? Definitely **YES**, particularly if you bear in mind the amazingly complete specification.

Delivery? Due to commence about March, 1949, but order yours immediately from your dealer, if you want one next year. The demand is already terrific.

THE SERIES "B"
THE VINCENT
H·R·D
Rapide

Made by the makers of —

★ **"THE WORLD'S FASTEST STANDARD MOTORCYCLE"**
and
★ **"THE WORLD'S FASTEST UNSUPERCHARGED MOTOR-CYCLE"**
★ **THESE ARE FACTS NOT SLOGANS**

THE VINCENT-H.R.D. COMPANY LTD., STEVENAGE, HERTS, ENGLAND.

Besides the manufacture of the existing twins, a good deal of the factory's time was taken up in 1948 by the development of the Girdraulic fork and the new Meteor and Comet singles. Whilst the pre-war twin had sprung from the single, the reverse was the case now – the two 500s looking for all the world like a V-twin shorn of its rear cylinder, which in effect they were, with many engine components interchangeable. The bargain basement, in Vincent terms that is, Meteor at just under £250 was equipped with Brampton forks, whilst the fitting of up-to-the minute Girdraulics to the Comet, as well as adding £25 to the price, signified that it (illustrated in this advertisement) was a Series C whilst the Meteor was a Series B.

Staunch believers always in the necessity of preserving absolute rigidity against all forms of lateral whip or twist in all components connecting the two wheels of a motor cycle, if perfect handling is to be expected at high speeds, we refused to join the general post-war stampede into new fork designs—we wanted time to consider all possible methods, weigh the pros and cons and strike the best balance—always with firm insistence on *lateral rigidity* for perfect steering and cornering.

As makers of *standard* models capable of 150 m.p.h., we have to exercise great care in fork design.

Fortunately we started with the considerable advantage of far greater experience in motor cycle springing, for we are the *only* well known makers *who have never built a rigid frame*.

During the last twenty years we have perfected our fully triangulated and completely whip-free spring frame and we did not intend to throw away this great advantage by using a parallel membered front fork, depending largely on the wheel spindle for any rigidity.

We therefore decided to retain the well proved girder principle for its inherent rigidity. We obtained a new high level in rigidity-weight ratio by using forged light alloy blades of tapered oval section and preserved the maximum of this rigidity by using one-piece forged links. The new fork is at least twice as rigid as the earlier tubular design.

The long soft action so popular in these days has been provided by mounting very long springs in telescopic cases between the bottom of the crown lug and the fork ends, but we have kept this action within the limits demanded by safety at high speeds. An ingenious eccentric action provides a variation of spring loading and fork trail to suit solo or sidecar use; this adjustment can be made in a few minutes without using any extra or different parts.

The other great improvement of modern fork design is also provided in the form of a two-way hydraulic shock-absorber, with hydraulic limit stops in both directions to eliminate metallic " bottoming," but with these important differences, vital differences to the thousands who live great distances from the factory or the dealer :—

1. The shock-absorber can be detached easily.

2. It weighs less than two pounds and is only eight inches long, so it can be sent by parcel post.

3. The machine can be ridden at reasonable speeds without the shock-absorber.

Now that simplifies service, doesn't it ?

To ensure long life and freedom from attention, large diameter ground high tensile steel spindles are used in conjunction with oil retaining bronze brushes. No oiling is required.

The forks have been arduously tested for many tens of thousands of miles, Rene Milhoux used them to establish two World Records with sidecar, and the Belgian Solo Record at over 143 m.p.h., they were fitted to Harold Taylor's outfit which put up a leading sidecar performance in the very stiff 1948 International Six-Days Trial. Yes, we have no hesitation in saying that the Girdraulic is the finest motor cycle fork ever made.

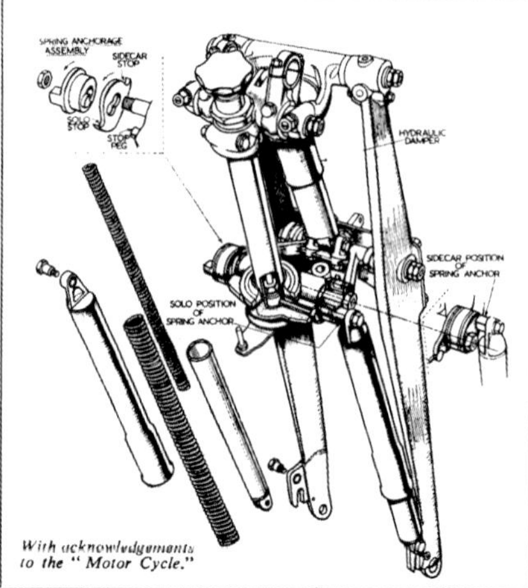

With acknowledgements to the " Motor Cycle."

Vincent went to a good deal of trouble to fully explain its new Girdraulic forks to potential customers. The simple alteration of fork trail for sidecar or solo use was an ingenious and thoroughly practical feature. Main alloy fork blades were made especially for Vincent by the Bristol Aircraft Company.

STAR PERFORMANCE · ABOUNDING IN EXCLUSIVE FEATURES

1000 c.c. Black Shadow Sports Rapide. Series C

1000 c.c. Black Lightning Racing Rapide. Series C

H·R·D

500 c.c. Standard Comet. Series C

1000 c.c. Standard Rapide. Series B

DESIGNED BY ENTHUSIASTS FOR THE DISCRIMINATING RIDER

H·R·D

A mix of Series C and B machines illustrated in the 1949 season sales material, the former having the new Girdraulic forks while the Series B Rapide at the lower right had HRD-Bramptons – a slightly altered post-war version of those that had been employed on Series A Rapides. Clearly visible too was the distinctive black finish of the Shadow and Lightning's primary chain case, crankcases, timing cover and other components.

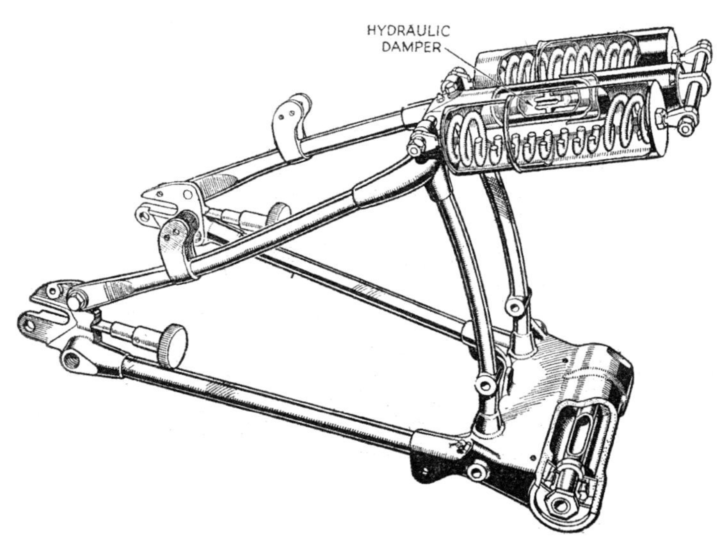

Rear suspension was on the same principle as that employed pre-war but the rear frame member had detail improvements and was now pivoted on taper roller bearings. This is the further-improved version with curved and slightly lengthened seat support lugs to give adequate clearance in the event that a large-section tyre was fitted, as introduced in 1949.

Up until the latter part of 1949 the name Vincent was displayed almost insignificantly above the initials HRD on the tank; meanwhile, HRD featured on the crankcase, timing cover, valve caps and primary case filler castings. From then on, reportedly due to concern of confusion between the British make and American Harley Davidson, tank finish and patterns were altered to simply Vincent.

Unveiled at the 1949 show was a single-cylinder racer. It was also offered with road equipment but due to pressure of work and other circumstances at the factory the model was available only sporadically, and at one point temporarily withdrawn. An Albion gearbox was fitted to the Grey Flash; it offered a greater choice of ratios than the Burman employed in the firm's other 500 singles. Up against pukka racers such as Norton's Manx they stood little chance, and their Senior TT record from 1950-to-52 lists six retirements and a 12th place by Ken Bills in 1950.

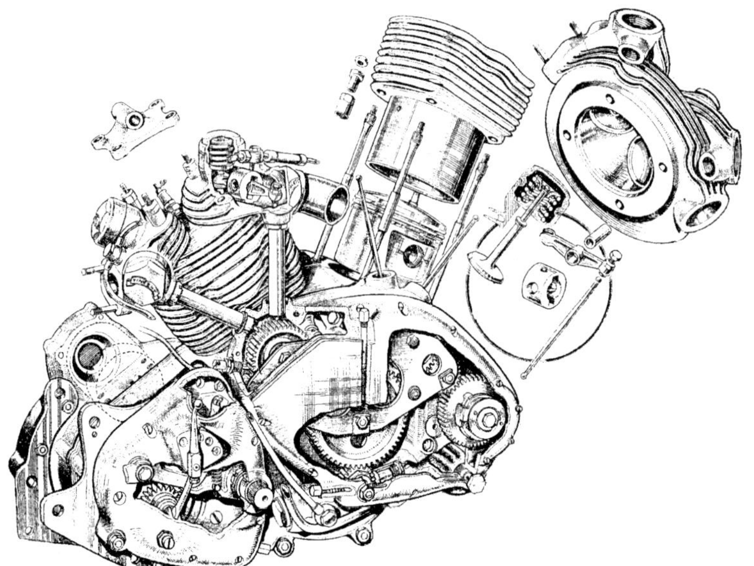

Ever since its first introduction towards the end of 1946 the post-war Rapide has been hard at work winning hundreds of races and other sporting events for its enthusiastic owners, in spite of the fact that it is only during the last few months that a racing version of this fascinating design has been available. We list below just a few of the brilliant successes achieved by these amazing machines all over the world. All these achievements have been put up by normal production models, frequently touring machines.

WORLD RECORDS

September 15th, 1948, Rene Milhoux at Jabbeke, in Belgium ;
Standing Start Kilometre Sidecar Record at 83·5 m.p.h.
Standing Start Mile Sidecar Record at 94 m.p.h.

NATIONAL RECORDS

September 13th, 1948, Roland R. Free at Bonneville, Utah, U.S.A.
AMERICAN Flying Mile Record at 150·313 m.p.h.
September 15th, 1948, Rene Milhoux at Jabbeke, in Belgium.
BELGIAN Flying Kilometre Record at 143·2 m.p.h.
January 25th, 1949, Jack Prime at Kingston, S.A.
AUSTRALIAN Sidecar Flying Mile Record at 102·53 m.p.h.
AUSTRALIAN Sidecar Standing Mile Record at 81·91 m.p.h.

RACES and SPEED EVENTS

1947

Jan. 1st.	Ballarat Grand Prix, Sidecar Class, 1st.
Jan. 27th.	Bonnie Vale Grand Prix, Sidecar Class, 1st.
March 23rd.	Flying Kilometre Trials, Belgium, 1st and 2nd.
April 8th.	Victorian T.T., Sidecar Class, 1st.
May 4th.	Czechoslovakia, Zlin Eight Race, 1st.
1st June.	Dinant Luxembourg-Dinant, 1st.
13th July.	Cinvald Hill Climb.
August 3rd.	Czechoslovakia, Prague Triangle Race, 1st.
Sept. 21st.	Santos Grand Prix, Brazil, 1st.
Oct. 12th	Rosamond Dry Lake, Speed Trials, Cal. U.S.A., 1st.
Oct. 12th.	Subida Da Montanha, Brazil, 1st, 2nd and 3rd.
Oct. 13th.	Canadian Hill Climb Championship, Open Class, 1st.
Oct. 19th.	Ratmalana Airport Races, Ceylon, Open Class, 1st.
Nov. 16th.	Sao Paulo Grand Prix, Brazil, Unlimited Class, 1st.
Nov. 16th.	Buckland Park Beach Races, South Australia, Sidecar Class, two 1sts.
Dec. 21st.	7th Brazilian Championship, Unlimited Class, 1st.
Dec. 26th.	South Australian Championship, Sidecar Class, 1st and 2nd.

1948

Jan. 1st.	Ballarat Grand Prix, Sidecar Class, 1st.
Feb. 29th.	Havana, Cuba, National Championship, 1st and 2nd.
March 23rd.	Flying Kilometre Trials, Belgium, Solo Class, 1st.
	Flying Kilometre Trials, Belgium, Sidecar Class, 1st.
March 27th.	Australian Sidecar T.T., Bathurst, 1st.
March 27th.	South Australian Sidecar Championship, 1st.
April 11th.	2nd International Circuit, Brazil, 1st and 2nd.
1st May.	Bukit Batok Hill Climb, Singapore, Unlimited Class, 1st.
June 27th.	Rosamond Dry Lake, Speed Trials, Cal., U.S.A., 61 c.i., 1st.
July 4th.	La Plata, Argentina, Unlimited Class, Road Race, 1st.
July 11th.	Cordoba, Argentina, Unlimited Class, Road Race, 1st.
August 28th.	Victorian Sidecar T.T., Australia, 1st.
August 29th.	Pennsylvania T.T., U.S.A., 1st.
Sept. 5th.	8th Brazilian Championship, 1st.
Sept. 7th.	Ribeirao Preto Circuit, Brazil, 1st, 2nd and 3rd.
Sept. 26th.	Rosamond Speed Trials, U.S.A. Stock Machine 61 c.i. Class, 1st, 2nd, 3rd, 4th and 5th.
Oct. 14th.	Parque Carrasco Circuit, Uruguay, 1st.
Oct.	Great Falls, Montana, U.S.A., Hill Climb, 1st.
Nov. 3rd.	Rafaela, Argentina, XII Hour Road Race, Unlimited Class, 1st, 2nd, 3rd, 4th and 5th.
Dec. 27th.	South Australian Championship, Sidecar Class, 1st, 2nd and 3rd.

1949

Jan. 1st.	Ballarat Grand Prix, Sidecar Class, 1st and 2nd.

The above represent but a small fraction of our lengthy list of successes, but they will serve to show the wonderful speed and stamina of our normal production machines, and their ability to perform magnificently in whatever part of the world they may find themselves.

The firm was justifiably proud of its competition successes, often in far-flung parts of the globe, but surprisingly no mention was made of the 1948 Clubmans TT – an event of far greater importance, especially to British enthusiasts, than some cited here. There had not been a single Stevenage machine in the inaugural 1947 event but for 1948 there were no less than 11 entered – the second greatest number of one make behind 16 Nortons. George Brown led from the start but was cruelly robbed of a certain victory when he ran out of fuel almost within sight of the finish and had to push in – finishing sixth. Other Vincent-HRDs, ridden by Daniels and Heath, were close behind him and finished first and second, however, with others fifth, sixth, eight and ninth; only one of the 11 failed to complete the course. The following over-500s had a class of their own, so it was a grand slam for Stevenage with just a solitary Ariel Square Four (of all things!) cheekily taking fourth place out of just five finishers – George Brown in last position on one cylinder and others having run out of fuel. The last year for the 1000 class was 1950, and understandably it was once again a Vincent benefit, with eight finishing out of 11 entries, and no Ariel to upset things this time.

Simply a flat cap and goggles, or at times only goggles, had been the headgear of Motor Cycling*'s Charles Markham when he put the prototype Black Shadow through its paces in the spring of 1948 (it was fitted with Brampton forks and registered JRO 102). Freely admitting he had never ridden so fast, he established a new benchmark top speed for a fully-equipped road machine of 122mph, with 110 coming up in third gear and 91mph in second. By 1950 the Black Shadow and all of Philip Conrad Vincent's other motorcycles carried his name alone on their tanks and elsewhere.*

Initially known as the Export Rapide, its specification was largely as a result of orders from Argentina's Peron government for police machines. Not only were the steel mudguards more durable, but large-section tyres coped better with the poor roads that prevailed both in towns and outlying districts. With his strong Argentinean connections, dual citizenship and an enthusiastic main agent, Phil Vincent was able to do good business and the 430-odd machines sold there ranked second to the USA as an export destination for his products.

Unveiled to the public at the 1948 show, the production Black Lightning had been preceded by a highly-modified Rapide known as Gunga Din raced by George Brown, as well as the racing Shadow made for John Edgar. The first Lightning built as such went to Vincent's Argentinean distributor Cimic early in 1949, and some 30 were produced in total.

BLACK LIGHTNING

MR. ROLLIE FREE BREAKS THE AMERICAN 1 MILE 5 MILES & 10 MILES RECORDS

at

Bonneville Salt Flats, Utah, September 11th, 1950

Confirmed by A.M.A.

In spite of very bad conditions of wet and bumpy salt, resulting in terrific wheelspin, the following high speeds were recorded by A.A.A. timing, the highest ever achieved on a motorcycle without the aid of streamlining or supercharging.

1 MILE	5 MILES	10 MILES
156.58 M.P.H.	154.46 M.P.H.	152.32 M.P.H.

This is a further proof that the machine that is

"ENTHUSIAST-DESIGNED AND BUILT FOR YOU"

The image of Rollie Free lying prone on a Vincent HRD at speed whilst clad in a pair of bathing trunks will be all too familiar to many motorcyclists – taken on 13 September 1948 at the Bonneville Salt Flats as he set a two-way average of 148.6mph, having stripped off all extraneous clothing in order to reduce wind resistance. The bike was specially built for John Edgar of California expressly for this purpose and is considered to be the prototype for the yet-to-be-named-and-announced Black Lightning, although built to B spec with Brampton forks. After Bonneville, Edgar took to riding it, at times furiously, around Hollywood, but after a night-time accident and some broken bones on his way home from a bar on Sunset Boulevard he decided to call it a day. Free later bought a Black Lightning for himself and it was this machine that he took to Bonneville in September 1950.

A small gathering of Vincents at Westmill in Hertfordshire, less than ten miles from the factory, for the 1952 brochure's cover; there was a Black Shadow outfit-owning family taking a picnic on the left, a Series C Rapide with more sporting Swallow Jet 80 sidecar on the right, and an unidentifiable machine heading down the street. Conway Motors was appointed as agent for HRD in 1934 and is still in business as a Vincent specialist to this day.

SERIES 'C' COMET MODEL

SERIES 'C' RAPIDE MODEL

Towards the end of 1950 The Motor Cycle *tested one of these (registration number MAR 292, in case it's still around) and typically found the steering heavy when first getting under way, but this transferred to 'road-holding which is a sheer delight, especially at high speeds'. Described as an 'uncompromising, high-speed, sporting single', it was found that its compression ratio of 6.8:1 necessitated a careful hand on the twist grip if pinking was to be avoided – the awful pool petrol of the period being the culprit. Starting, cold or hot, was usually a first-time affair, providing a lusty swing was given. Upward gear-changing was 'accomplished neatly and quietly' and downward changes 'as smartly as the controls could be operated'. Brakes were 'light, powerful and progressive', with the rear 'requiring slightly heavy pedal pressure' – this characteristic due to the small amount of leverage provided as part of the machine's design. It would cruise happily at 60mph with 'an absence of vibration', and when pushed was found to have maxima of 63, 78 and 84mph in the uppermost gears. At 50mph it was more economical than a Rapide, returning 79mpg, but maintain 60mph and the reverse was found, as it would only return 55mpg. As was often the case,* Motor Cycling *managed to extract a little more speed (88mph) when they tested one.*

As a good number of Vincents were hitched to sidecars in their youth it is interesting to see how the very same Series C with Swallow Jet 80 (registration LRO 644, as featured on this year's brochure cover) performed when put through its paces by The Motor Cycle. *Described only as a semi-sporting outfit by its manufacturer, the magazine's staff found, however, that it 'had few equals on the road – whether they were two-wheelers or four during the 1,000-odd miles they covered. In spite of a high bottom gear a standing quarter-mile was covered in 16.8 seconds with a terminal speed of 77mph; but they didn't tell us whether that was with or without a passenger. Best speeds in the gears were 72mph in second, 81 in third and 88 in top, and just over 36ft was needed to bring the thing to a halt on a wet road from 30mph. Petrol consumption worked out at 54mpg at a steady 50mph, and 46mpg at 60mph. The Swallow sidecar in Black and Silver complete with Black twill hood was a few shillings less than £90, tax included.*

SERIES 'C' RAPIDE TOURING MODEL

SERIES 'C' BLACK SHADOW MODEL

Although originally intended for the South American market the Touring Model was also a popular option for customers in the USA; so you will not be surprised when I tell you that a wider handlebar, which inevitably I suppose became known as the 'cowhorn' type, was an option. The regular colour for all post-war Vincent HRDs and Vincents was black enamel but a good number were supplied, almost exclusively to the American market, in Chinese Red. It was also not unknown for customers to request alternative finishes such as Black and Red or even Blue so a few bikes were turned out accordingly.

A magnet for schoolboys and adults alike was, and still is, Black Shadow's 5-inch Smiths 150mph speedometer prominently mounted atop its forks and at an angle just right for its rider. Early versions were housed in a bulky pressed steel drum but before long a shallow cast aluminium case was employed, as on the machine pictured here. Export customers could specify a kilometret speedo and this read up to a heady 240 kph.

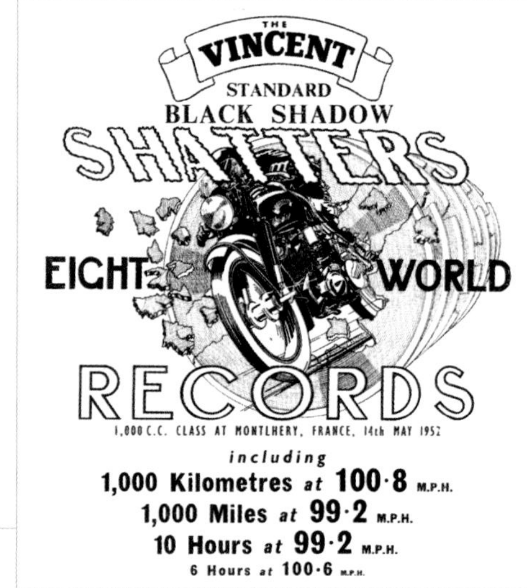

Several Vincents were taken to the Montlhéry track just outside Paris for the record attempts in May 1952. Special preparation for the intended record-breaker included 8:1 pistons, TT carbs, a five-gallon tank, Perspex fly screen and the removal of the front brakes. Riders included a young John Surtees who was a factory apprentice at that time, Phil Heath, renowned French racer Gustave LeFevre, and The Motor Cycle*'s sometime racing journalist Vic Willoughby. If a collapsed roller big end hadn't put an end to proceedings the endurance records might well have been of a longer duration, but as it was 18-year-old Surtees lapped the banked track at nigh on 130mph with one of the Lightnings that was in attendance.*

Performance Characteristics

Characteristic.	Black Lightning.	Black Shadow.	Standard Rapide.	Comet.	Units of measurement.
Power to Weight Ratio.	480	280	222	150	Brake-horse power per ton.
Dry weight.	380 172	458 207	455 206	390 176	Pounds. Kilogrammes.
Petrol Consumption.	— — —	55 to 65 50 to 60 5 to 6	55 to 65 50 to 60 5 to 6	75 to 80 70 to 75 4 to 5	Miles per Imp. Gall. " " Amer. " Litres per 100 Kilos.
Oil Consumption.	— —	1,500 500	1,500 500	2,000 650	Miles per gallon. Kilos per litre.
Cruising Speed.	— —	100 160	85 136	65 104	Miles per hour. Kilos " "
Maximum Speed.	150+ 240+	125 200	110 175	90 to 95 144 to 152	Miles per hour. Kilos " "

Characteristic.	Black Lightning.	Black Shadow.	Standard Rapide.	Comet.	Units of measurement.
Minimum speed in top gear.	— —	18 29	18 29	19 31	Miles per hour. Kilos " "
Maximum Safe Speeds in Indirect Gears.	According to Gearing.	110 85 65 175 136 104	96 80 50 154 127 80	77 55 38 123 88 60	3rd, 2nd, 1st } miles per hour. 3rd, 2nd, 1st } kilos per hour.
Acceleration through gears as recorded in "Motor Cycling" Road Tests.	Not yet tested.	3½ secs. 6½ " 10 " 21 " 31 " 44 "	1½ secs. 6 " 12 " 24 " 35 " —	3 secs. 9½ " 21 " — — —	0– 30 miles per hour. 0– 48 kilos " " 0– 60 miles " " 0– 96 kilos " " 0– 80 miles " " 0–128 kilos " " 0–100 miles " " 0–160 kilos " " 0–110 miles " " 0–175 kilos " " 0–120 miles " " 0–192 kilos " "

DIMENSIONS.

Ground Clearance 6 inches (150 m.m.).
Width over Handlebars 25½ inches (650 m.m.).

Wheelbase 56 inches (1,420 m.m.).
Length Overall 85½ inches (2,175 m.m.).

PRICES REDUCED

The constantly improving efficiency of our very modern factory has once again enabled us to offset the great rise in manufacturing costs and to make our contribution towards checking the vicious spiral of inflation. You can form some idea of this great achievement by comparing the current price of the Series "C" Rapide at £272 with the £142 for the Series "A" Rapide in 1937. An increase of *only* 89% for a machine of far better design, that is much more expensive to construct both as regards material and labour costs, in spite of the terrific increases in all prices since 1937.

The Comet, Rapide and Black Shadow continue to form the main planks of our programme, together with the Black Lightning which is available in limited quantities to special order. From time to time we introduce detail improvements to this well proven range of superb motorcycles and all models are notably quieter running than their equivalents of a year ago.
With the ending of another trading season we are pleased to be able to announce that, in spite of the difficulties caused by the closing of many markets, both number and value of Vincent motorcycles exported last season were a record by a substantial margin for the sixth year in succession. With the new reduced prices we look forward with every confidence to the establishment of new Export records in the coming year. Increasing Exports coupled with reduced material supplies will unfortunately mean severe curtailment of the number of machines available to the Home market, but we feel certain that our many friends will understand our difficulties if they have to wait longer than usual for their machines in the Spring and Summer of next year.

PRICES OPERATIVE FROM 1ST. SEPTEMBER 1952

BLACK SHADOW SERIES "C" -	**£305.0.0**	P.T. £84.14.5
RAPIDE SERIES "C" - - -	**£272.0.0**	P.T. £75.11.1
COMET SERIES "C" - - -	**£215.0.0**	P.T. £59.14.5

Lower prices but less availability for home-market buyers, despite an impressive show stand a couple of months later.

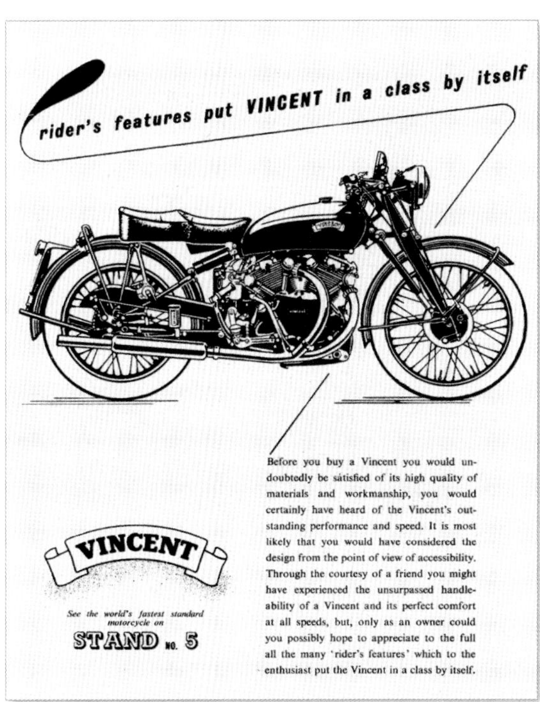

Advertising for their 1953 show stand gave no indication as to the Anglo-German wares that would be on offer.

Model and type	Engine dimension	C.R.	Approx b.h.p.	Suspension Front	Suspension Rear	Ignition and lighting	Gear ratios	Weight	Tyre size	Tank capacity	Wheelbase	Ground clearance	Saddle height	Br. lin. area	Basic price	Total, inc. P.T
								lb.	in.	gal.	in.	in.	in.	sq. in.	£ s. d.	£ s. d.
VINCENT.—Vincent Engineering (Stevenage) Ltd, Stevenage, Herts. Stand No. 5																
N.S.U.-Vincent "Fox" ..	50×50=98	7.2	6/6,500	LL	SF	FM, rect. ..	9.08, 12.82, 18.39, 28.6 ..	176	2.50×19	2¼	48	3¼	27½	—	104 –	124 16
N.S.U.-Vincent "Fox" ..	52×58=123	6.1	5/5,500	LL	SF	FM, rect. ..	8.17, 11.49, 16.54, 25.74 ..	180	2.50×19	2¼	48	3¼	27½	—	99 –	119 14
N.S.U.-Vincent "Lux" ..	62×66=198	6.1	8.6/5,250	LL	SF	D and C ..	6.86, 9.65, 13.9, 21.6 ..	320	3.25×19	3	52	6	30¾	—	—	—
N.S.U.-Vincent "Max" ..	69×66=247	7.4	18/6,750	LL	SF	D and C ..	6.78, 9.5, 13.73, 21.36 ..	342	3.25×19	3	52	6	30¾	—	190 –	228
"Comet"	84×90=499	6.8	28/5,800	GD	SF	Lucas M and Miller D	4.64, 5.94, 8.17, 12.4 ..	390	3×20 (fr.) 3.50×19 (r.)	3⅜	55¾	6	31	38.5	215 0 0	258 0 0
"Rapide"	84×90=998	6.45	45/5,500	GD	SF	Lucas M and Miller D	3.5, 4.2, 5.6, 9.1	455	3×20 (fr.) 3.50×19 (r.)	3⅝	56½	6	31	38.5	272 0 0	326 8 0
"Black Shadow" ..	84×90=998	7.3	55/5,700	GD	SF	Lucas M and Miller D	3.5, 4.2, 5.6, 9.1	458	3×20 (fr.) 3.50×19 (r.)	3⅜	56½	6	31	38.5	305 0 0	366 0 0
"Black Lightning" ..	84×90=998	Opt.	—	GD	SF	Lucas M ..	3.27, 3.89, 5.26, 6.77 (with 45-t. rear-wheel sprocket)	380	3×21 (fr.) 3.50×20 (r.)	3⅜	56½	6½	29	38.5	395 0 0	474 0 0

The "Rapide" and "Comet" are available also in touring trim with no change in prices.

VINCENT

SERIES 'C' TOURING RAPIDE SIDECAR MODEL

With the US being Vincent's largest export market (well over 1,000 machines during the company's post-war lifespan) advertising such as this was aimed specifically across the Atlantic.

As might be expected for this model there's a large rear sprocket fitted at the rear, so I'll quote a few facts and figures from a test carried out by Motor Cycling *in 1951 on a Rapide such as this, complete with Blacknell Sherwood child-adult sidecar (which was capable of accommodating a single adult and two children or two adults, providing one was on the tiny side). With several hundred pounds more to bring to a halt braking distances were understandably greater, with 49ft needed from 30mph, but the excess weight, thanks in part to the excellent Girdraulic forks, had little effect on the outfit's handling or ability to 'gobble up miles effortlessly'. With an empty sidecar it was timed at 88mph, achieving 83 in third and 71 in second in the process, but economy was most definitely not its strong point if one averaged '40 plus' on a journey, which would return you around 33mpg – better by far to stick to a steady 50mph and 46mpg.*

For some reason figures published in the '54 brochure no longer included maximum speeds; but that aside quite where, in the UK, you could have cruised your Shadow at 100mph I cannot immediately bring to mind.

Performance Characteristics

Characteristic.	Black Lightning.	Black Shadow.	Standard Rapide.	Comet.	Units of measurement.
Power to Weight Ratio.	480	280	222	150	Brake-horse power per ton.
Dry weight.	380 172	458 207	455 206	390 176	Pounds. Kilogrammes.
Approximate Petrol Consumption (Normal Touring Conditions).	— — —	55 to 65 50 to 60 5 to 6	55 to 65 50 to 60 5 to 6	75 to 80 70 to 75 4 to 5	Miles per Imp. Gall. " " Amer. " Litres per 100 km.
Approximate Oil Consumption.	— —	1,500 500	1,500 500	2,000 650	Miles per gallon. Km. per litre.
Cruising Speed.	— —	100 160	85 136	65 104	Miles per hour. Km. " "
Gearbox Ratios (Black Shadow on 7·2 Bottom Gear).	1, 1·19 1·61, 2·07	1, 1·19 1·61, 2·07	1, 1·19 1·61, 2·60	1, 1·26 1·69, 2·67	—

Characteristic.	Black Lightning.	Black Shadow.	Standard Rapide.	Comet.	Units of measurement.
Minimum speed in top gear.	— —	18 29	18 29	19 31	Miles per hour. km. " "
Maximum Safe Speeds in Indirect Gears (Black Shadow on 7·2 Bottom Gear).	According to Gearing.	110 85 65 175 136 104	96 80 50 154 127 80	77 55 38 123 88 60	3rd, 2nd, 1st } miles per hour. 3rd, 2nd, 1st } km. per hour.
Acceleration through gears as recorded in "Motor Cycling" Road Tests. (Black Shadow on 7·2 Bottom Gear.)	Not yet tested.	3½ secs. 6½ " 10 " 21 " 31 " 44 "	1½ secs. 6 " 12 " 24 " 35 " —	3 secs. 9½ " 21 " — — —	0– 30 miles per hour. 0– 48 km. " " 0– 60 miles " " 0– 96 km. " " 0– 80 miles " " 0–128 km. " " 0–100 miles " " 0–160 km. " " 0–110 miles " " 0–175 km. " " 0–120 miles " " 0–192 km. " "

DIMENSIONS.

Ground Clearance 6 inches (150 m.m.).
Width over Handlebars 25½ inches (650 m.m.).

Wheelbase 1000 c.c. models 56½ inches (1,433 m.m.) 500 c.c. models 55⅝ inches (1,414 m.m.)
Length Overall 85½ inches (2,175 m.m.).

Manufacturers reserve the right to effect alterations to the specifications without prior notice.

A Knight at the Roebuck.

VINCENT BLACK PRINCE

VINCENT BLACK KNIGHT

VINCENT VICTOR

VINCENT *Black Shadow*

VINCENT *Rapide*

VINCENT-
the 20th Century Knights of the Road

Dan 'My new Series "D" Black Shadow is terrific and the suspension, well . . .'
John 'Yes, I know, it's like floating on air. I have never enjoyed riding so much. I put in more miles now, on my Black Knight faster, and never feel tired.'
Dan 'Of course it's years ahead but then Vincents always have been . . .'
John 'That's true. We musn't forget they pioneered the spring frame too, back in the 20's, and have always something new round the corner.'

THE WORLD'S FASTEST AND SAFEST STANDARD MOTORCYCLES

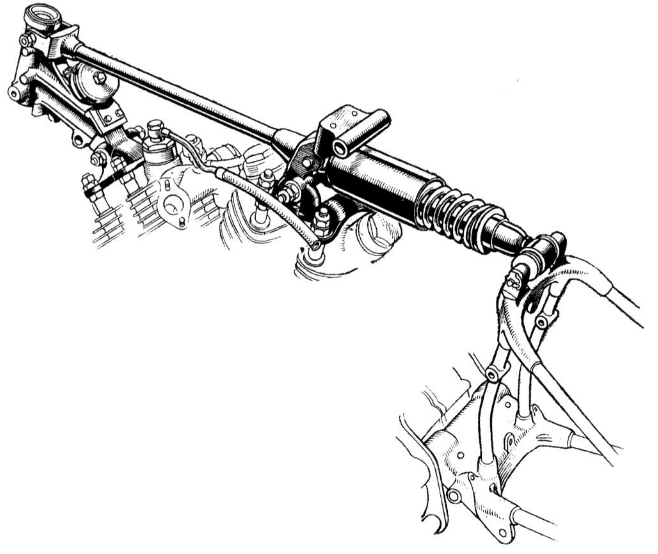

The Roebuck Inn on London Road, Stevenage was indeed a popular meeting place for Vincenteers of yore, and it's still open for business even though the parking arrangements are a little different nowadays. It was talk around the bar and a questionnaire published in the Vincent Owners' Club magazine that led to the introduction of the less overtly sporting Princes, Knights and Victors for 1955, but unfortunately what was attractive in theory was less so in practice and sales were very disappointing.

The Twentieth Century "Knights of the Road"

are years ahead of any other motor cycle, and give the ultimate in performance, road-holding, protection, safety and comfort.

The Black Prince, developed from the famous Black Shadow, combines racing performance and roadholding with the most luxurious touring equipment and docility for road work. The machine represents the last word in motor cycling for the discriminating rider and is the ideal model for sidecar work when maximum performance is required. The enclosure is also of advantage to those riders who like to take part in occasional sporting events.

The flagship of the new Series D range was the Shadow-derived Prince. Under the skin the new range differed considerably from Series Bs and Cs in that the fabricated upper frame member-cum-oil tank had given way to a single steel tube, with oil now carried in a separate tank located within the rear enclosure. In search of greater comfort a single Armstrong spring/damper unit with increased travel had taken the place of twin enclosed springs for the rear suspension, the rear frame member being altered accordingly. Either to reduce unsprung weight or for reasons of economy, there was now but a single rear brake.

Continuing the reputation of the Rapide, the Black Knight will appeal to those riders who require high performance in conjunction with fuel economy and maximum flexibility for touring, pillion riding or heavy sidecar work. The finest workmanship and materials ensure that this superbly engineered model will give lasting pride of ownership.

Model ... ... Type	"BLACK PRINCE" Series 'D'	"BLACK KNIGHT" Series 'D'	"VICTOR" Series 'D'
Engine (2S or 4S)	4	4	4
No. of Cylinders	2 (50°)	2 (50°)	1, inclined
Capacity ...	998 c.c.	998 c.c.	499 c.c.
Bore & Stroke (mm.)	84×90	84×90	84×90
Max. Power (bhp-rpm) ...	55@ 5700	45 @ 5300	28 @ 5800
Compression Ratio	7.3	6.45	6.8
Valve Position ...	o.h.	o.h.	o.h.
Carburettor Type	Amal "Monobloc" 389	Amal "Monobloc" 376	Amal "Monobloc" 389
Lubrication ..	Dry Sump	Dry Sump	Dry Sump
Ignition	Coil	Coil	Coil
Sparking Plug Size	14 mm.	14 mm.	14 mm.
Lighting	Lucas, F700 lamp.	Lucas, F700 lamp.	Lucas, F700 lamp.
Dynamo ...	60 Watt, A.V.C.	60 Watt, A.V.C.	60 Watt, A.V.C.
Battery Capacity	14 amp/hr.	14 amp/hr.	14 amp/hr.
No. of Speeds ...	4	4	4
Gearbox Make ...	Vincent	Vincent	Burman
Gearbox Control	Foot	Foot	Foot
Gear Ratios :			
Top	3.5	3.5	4.6
3rd	4.2	4.2	5.9
2nd	5.6	5.6	8.2
1st	9.1	9.1	12.4
Primary Drive ..	Chain, ⅜" Triplex	Chain, ⅜" Triplex	Chain, ½" × 5/16"
Final Drive ...	Chain, ⅝" × ⅜"	Chain, ⅝" × ⅜"	Chain, ⅝" × ⅜"
Frame	Tubular	Tubular	Tubular
Front Forks ..	"Girdraulic"	"Girdraulic"	"Girdraulic"
Rear Springing ...	Pivoted Fork	Pivoted Fork	Pivoted Fork
Stands	Front & Central lever operated	Front & Central lever operated	Front & Central lever operated
Brake Diameter...	7" (Ribbed)	7"	7"
Wheels	Q.D.	Q.D.	Q.D.
Wheel Base ...	56½"	56½"	55¾"
Ground Clearance	5"	5"	5"
Width	27"	27"	27"
Saddle Height ...	Dual Seat 31"	Dual Seat 31"	Dual Seat 31"
Overall Length ...	89"	89"	89"
Overall Height ...	44" (less screen)	44" (less screen)	44" (less screen)
Tyre Size, Front	3.50×19 } Avon	3.50×19 } Avon	3.50×19 } Avon
Tyre Size, Rear ...	4.00×18 } Avon	4.00×18 } Avon	4.00×18 } Avon
Petrol Tank Capacity ...	4 Imp. galls.	4 Imp. galls.	4 Imp. galls.
Oil Tank Capacity ...	5 pints	5 pints	5 pints
Dry Weight ...	460 lbs.	460 lbs.	390 lbs.
Finish	Black & Gold	Black & Gold	Black & Gold

Problems were encountered with the supply, quality and finish of the fibreglass mouldings; but mainly because of a distinct lack of customer enthusiasm, naked versions of the D Series were introduced – or rather the Rapide and Shadow were reintroduced in D Series form. Whilst the Princes and Knights were not to everyone's taste it is also true to say that their unclothed relations were, not least on account of their ungainly-looking dual seat, the least attractive of a marque renowned for the handsome appearance of its products.

The Vincent Victor, with the luxurious specification of the larger models, replaces the well-known Comet and sets new standards in the 500 c.c. class. The single cylinder engine maintains its reputation for smooth running, combined with fuel economy. The machine is equally suited for pillion riding and sidecar work.

The Series D Victor was intended to be a replacement for the discontinued Series C Comet but despite its appearance in the 1955 sales material just one was made – as was a solitary D Series Comet.

PLUS A POWERFUL
BUILT-IN LIGHTING
GENERATOR

Incorporated in the engine unit itself is a 9-watt A.C. generator which ensures powerful lighting at all running speeds.

From the sublime to the, almost, ridiculous. Having originally been patented, developed and marketed by Miller, a motorcycle electrical equipment manufacturer and supplier to Vincent, as merely a clip-on engine named the Miller Firefly, it was improved and manufactured by Vincent.

The Vincent/NSU Fox.

WOOLER

The Flying Banana had, according to some, resembled one from its inception: but it was reputedly Graham Walker, racing motorcyclist, journalist/editor of *Motor Cycling* magazine and father of motorsports commentator Murray, who nicknamed it thus during TT week in 1920 or '21. The odd but apt name stemmed from the unusual shape and (yellow) colour of its petrol tank, which enclosed and extended forward of the steering head and was to remain a feature of Wooler motorcycles throughout their spasmodic life. This was but a minor deviation from the norm compared with some others, however, as unconventionality went hand-in-hand with all the products of John Wooler's fertile brain.

Starting out in the manner he was destined to continue, his first machine's frame had a system of plunger springing front and rear – a real novelty in 1910 – but it was its engine that was downright eccentric: a single-cylinder horizontally-mounted two-stroke with double-acting piston that was persuaded to transfer the compressed mixture via an external pipe from rear to front chamber by means of a gudgeon pin that protruded through slots in the cylinder wall. I should leave you in suspense at this point but suffice to say that a pair of external connecting rods were harnessed at one end to the pin's extremities and the other to a crankshaft that, once the piston was whizzing backwards and forwards, imparted a revolving motion to an adjustable pulley that varied the belt final drive's ratio. Remarkably, after a partly finished example had been displayed at the 1911 show he managed to persuade (or perhaps pay) Wilkinson Sword, which already manufactured some motorcycles of its own, to go into production the following year – the machine to be known as the Wilkinson-Wooler. This arrangement was short-lived, however, and by the time the First World War was declared, Mr Wooler was producing some on his own account at a small works in North West London.

One must presume that over the next few years he turned over his facilities to the war effort, as no more motorcycles were made until 1919 when the two-stroke went back into production briefly. At the

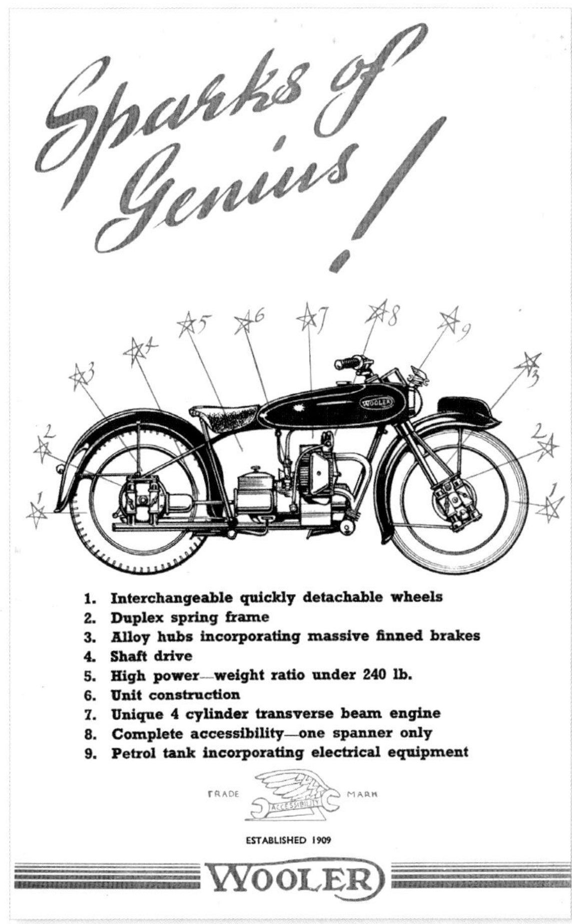

Both company logo and the machine's mascot on the cover of the 1948 brochure drew attention to the fact that just a single double-ended 2BA and ¼ BSF spanner was needed to dismantle a Wooler. To access the electrics within the tank, the forward cowling holding the speedometer and stylish oval domed headlamp with vertical divider was removed. 'Manufactured by Wooler & Sequerra Ltd' read the rear cover – but who was Sequerra? Try as I might I have been unable to come up with a definite answer, so I can only suggest that this was the name of a backer. Lest you have any doubts that this machine actually existed and was capable of moving under its own power I recommend that you look on the internet for video footage of the 'Wooler motorcycle'. This will produce a couple of short films for your enlightenment, one of which is entitled 'horizontal flyer' on account of it also featuring the brave Bob Berry on his Brough Superior at Pendine Sands. You will learn, as I did, there were apparently at least two working Woolers – WLF 49 and MMK 575. There was something very strange about their registration numbers, however, as WLF was first issued by London in January 1959, whilst my records would indicate that MMK was never used.

A Message from the Designer

As one who has both ridden, designed and manufactured Motor Cycles for the past forty years, it gives me great pleasure to present to the "fraternity" a machine in which, as a result of eight years research, I have endeavoured to embody all those features which go towards achieving a highly reliable, fast, touring machine.

I feel sure that you will gain as much pleasure from riding this machine as I have experienced whilst designing.

Yours,

John Wooler

I have no doubt whatsoever that John Wooler did indeed derive enormous pleasure from his work, even through the many trials and tribulations it must have involved. The problem was that whatever he turned his hand to ended up more as a fabulous design and engineering exercise than something that could ever be a commercial proposition.

Positively bristling with what would nowadays be heralded as 'exclusive features' the 1948 Wooler was viewed with fascination but little more. And those feeling for their chequebooks went elsewhere. At £200 (basic) it wasn't cheap, but a comparable competitor the Sunbeam S7 cost the same, or a 500 Vincent single was £195. All were far more pricey than the big manufacturers' 500 twins, which ranged from £142 for Triumph's Speed Twin to the brand-new Norton's £170. With a weight of 238lb the Wooler might, however, have established a record, which could well still stand, as the lightest production 500 ever – with two provisos: that the quoted figures were correct and that one is prepared to class it as a production machine.

1. **Single light alloy casting for engine**
2. **Simple exhaust union**
3. **Light alloy head**
4. **Wico Genimag**
5. **Unique exhaust system making use of frame tubes**

same time he announced his Wooler Mule cycle car – another oddity. Having the appearance of a three-wheeler it in fact had a pair of closely-set rear wheels and was powered by a horizontally-opposed rotary valve air-cooled four-stroke motor of a little over 1,000cc, which lurked behind a dummy radiator; a prototype or two were made and it ended there.

John Wooler may have been many things but he was certainly not work shy, and alongside the doomed Mule he was putting the finishing touches to his new motorcycle – a 350cc flat-twin IOE four-stroke mounted fore and aft in a sprung frame of the same design as his previous machines. This did go into production, and it was one of these with its trademark yellow tank that brought about Graham Walker's comment when he saw it during the TT. In fact, a Wooler competed on the Island in 1920 and '21 – retiring at its first attempt but future TT regular and Lightweight winner Frank Longman finished 34th out of 38 finishers in the second.

Sometime after the Wooler Motor Cycle Company (1919) Ltd's failure to take the Isle of Man by storm, and even though its machines now had three speeds and chain drive, money must have run short and production lapsed. Not for long, though, and after finance had been injected by wealthy railway contractor William Dederich, it recommenced with Wooler's name prefixed by his benefactor's on the company's letterhead. Henceforth various models came and went – a full OHV version of the twin, a 500 flat-twin and even an OHC single of similar capacity with rigid frame was experimented with. For a while the company was successful enough to subcontract manufacture to a firm of Croydon-based general engineers named Grigg that, as well building machines for others, made motorcycles of its own. It was not to last, however, and the mid-'20s slump saw the end of Grigg, and the Wooler brand fade quietly away.

As far as John Wooler was concerned, this was not the end of his motorcycles, just a lapse, while his engineering work and experiments continued –

the 12-piston, six-cylinder axial wobble-plate engine that he designed for aeronautical use during World War Two stands in the London Science Museum as a memorial to this.

Always in search of alternatives to the norm, he was concurrently working on a 500cc transverse four-cylinder beam engine and it was this that went into the machine that he exhibited at the first post-war Motor Cycle Show. 'Not only the engine but the whole general design is unconventional' commented *The Motor Cycle* in their show report and, although the machine was beautifully engineered and in many respects well thought out, its unconventionality more than anything proved to be its Achilles heel. John's son Roland was working alongside him in this venture, and despite all their efforts it was destined never to go into production, so just a few were hand-built for demonstrations and periodic outings at Earls Court over the next few years.

They didn't give up, however, and doggedly carried out a virtual redesign before commencing to build the new four-cylinder model. A stand was booked for the November 1954 Earls Court Show, and although two complete machines took their places on it their creator did not.

"Here is a Mecca for students of design… In all a most convincing display of the late John Wooler's ingenuity and determination to achieve a thoroughly practical and logical design," said *Motor Cycling* of stand 177 – those few words serving as a brief but apt obituary for the man who was never to know the fate of his last grand gesture.

Sadly it was almost a foregone conclusion that this too would fall on stony ground, and within a year-or-so son Roland had given up the unequal struggle and Wooler motorcycles were finally no more.

The Beam Principle
.......how it works

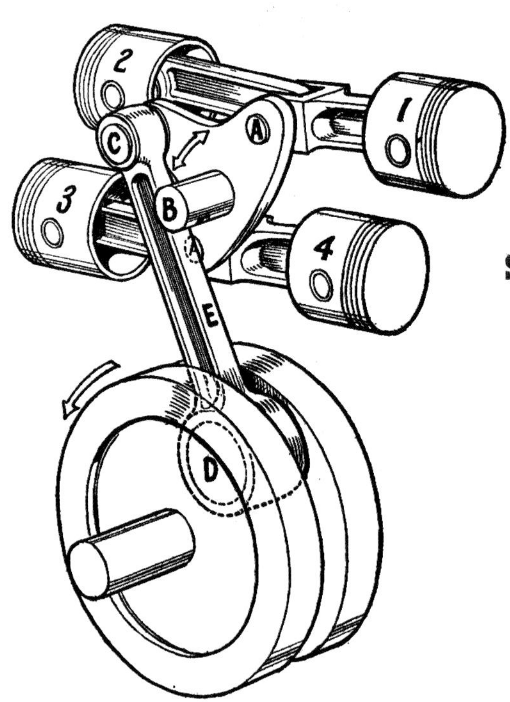

Some Advantages—

PERFECT BALANCE—	Freedom from Couple
GREATLY IMPROVED TORQUE—	Continuous power supplied to the master rod; unobtainable with a conventional layout
UNIFORM WEAR—	All bearing faces subjected to even loading
COMPACTNESS—	75% saving in overall length giving light weight and lower centre of gravity
IMPROVED COOLING—	Larger exposed surface area

The firing sequence of this engine is 1,2,3,4 and thus when No. 1 fires No. 2 is on the compression stroke and when No. 2 fires No. 3 is on its compression stroke and so on. Therefore, as No. 1 fires, the TRUNNION A rocks about point B thus causing point C to describe an arc downwards, which in turn revolves the crankshaft through 180° of its travel.

Piston No. 2 fires next in sequence and the reverse action takes place.

Pistons No. 3 and 4 then repeat the cycle of No's. 1 and 2.

The action at point C corresponds to that at the small end in a conventional single cylinder engine while point D is as per a normal crankshaft except that at all times the MASTER ROD E is transmitting a power stroke to the mainshaft.

Point B constitutes a fixed fulcrum through which the piston force is transmitted to the MASTER ROD.

● **ENGINE**	500cc. (50 × 63.75mm.) four-cylinder harmonic beam engine of patent design. Light alloy cylinder block fitted with steel liners. Coupling rods and master rod in RR. alloy with Meehanite bush in big end; plain bearings at coupling rod ends. Light alloy cylinder heads with patent ball joint rocker pivot.
● **CARBURETTOR**	Single SOLEX Carburettor. Twin AMAL supplied at an extra cost.
● **GEAR BOX**	Four Speed constant mesh, designed to form an integral part of the power unit and fitted with heel and toe control. Hand starter incorporated; single plate FERODO clutch of car type.
	RATIO'S :—SOLO Bottom 11.5 : 1 2nd 7.3 : 1 3rd 6.16 : 1 Top 5.0 : 1
● **TRANSMISSION**	SHAFT DRIVE incorporating a LAYRUB shock absorbing joint and a HARDY SPICER UNIVERSAL coupling, with E.N.V. spiral bevel pinion and Crown Wheel.
● **IGNITION**	WICO-PACY GENIMAG driven direct from the main shaft supplying A.C. current to the four LODGE plugs via a WICO distributor.
● **LUBRICATION**	Double purpose gear-driven pump maintaining a high pressure to all working parts except the pistons. A reservoir of half gallon capacity incorporated in a specially designed deep sump. Engine oil is used throughout, including gear box and bevel housing.
● **FRAME**	WOOLER PATENT straight tube design, bottom tubes carrying exhaust from the engine.
● **FORKS**	WOOLER PATENT design incorporating dual springing.
● **SUSPENSION**	WOOLER PATENT DUAL SPRINGING front and rear. Springs by TERRY.
● **STANDS**	FRONT and REAR independent legs.
● **WHEELS**	19″ × 3.25″ Designed to be quickly detachable and interchangeable. Light alloy hub fitted with straight spokes. DURAL rims supplied at extra cost.
● **BRAKES**	Patent light alloy finned hub of 7″ internal diameter fitted with steel liners and FERODO linings.
● **TYRES**	DUNLOP — 19″ × 3.25″
● **MUDGUARDS**	Specially designed to eliminate all exposed nuts and bolts. Rear end shaped to form number plate and to carry rear lamp.
● **HANDLEBARS**	WOOLER PATENT cluster control with single bolt fitting, embodying new type of smooth positive action twist grip for throttle and ignition control, as well as the horn push and cut out switch.
● **PETROL TANK**	Of light alloy embodying lighting, electrical fittings and speedometer. Fuel capacity 4¼ gallons.
● **SADDLES**	Made by BROOKS to our own design with totally enclosed springing.
● **LIGHTING**	Special wide beam front lamp built into the detachable tank nose. Rear lamp of our own design fitted directly to rear mudguard. Current from WICO GENIMAG via a rectifier and VARLEY battery. All connections made with the Wooler Patent spring terminal.
● **FINISH**	In black, chrome and polished aluminium with ivory and red lining. All enamelled parts pre-treated to ensure freedom from rust or corrosion, and only the highest quality materials used throughout.
● **WEIGHT**	238 lbs. — FULLY EQUIPPED.
● **PRICE**	£200 0s. 0d. (Excluding P.T.)
● **EXTRAS**	Speedometer, Pillion Seat and Footrests, Dural Rims.
● **SIDECAR**	Specially designed frame and sidecar chassis, which embodies the same springing system as employed on the solo model, is available for use on the WOOLER MOTOR CYCLE. All sidecar chassis' will leave our works correctly aligned and will require no additional adjustment.

Very ingenious and it worked, but had he asked, any other manufacturer or the average motorcyclist would have told Mr Wooler that this kind of thing was lost on Joe Public and was not what they wanted. Besides, no less an authority than Phil Vincent asserted that even good – let alone perfect – balance was an impossibility and that the forked ends to the light alloy links that coupled the pistons to the T-beam were a flawed design. Not to mention that the whole lot relied on a connecting rod-flywheel assembly sourced from a pre-war New Imperial 150!

1. Shaft Drive and Rear Springing.

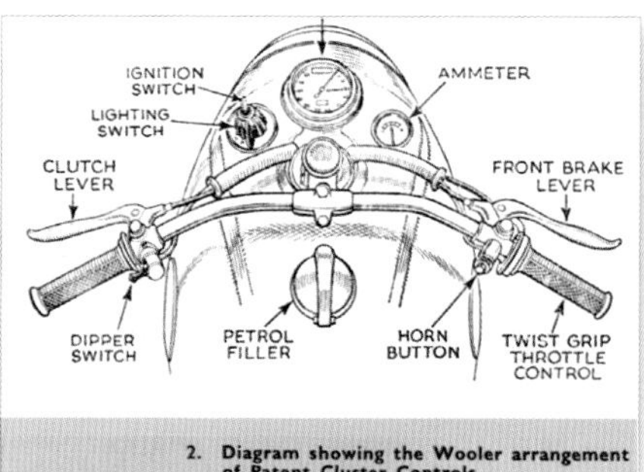

2. Diagram showing the Wooler arrangement of Patent Cluster Controls.

3. Front Wheel, showing Suspension System and Massive Brake Drum.

4. Rear Mudguard also used as Number Plate.

Aha! This Wooler's registration number checks out – YMU was issued by Middlesex in January 1953 and ran through until October the same year.

SPECIFICATION

ENGINE: 500 c.c. (50 × 63.5 mm.) FLAT FOUR cylinder. Light alloy cylinders with liners; cylinder heads, crankcase and sump in light alloy. Bearings: Vandervell thin wall for big ends; and three main bearings on crankshaft. Camshaft and timing gear drive by Renold 8 mm. Duplex chain.

CARBURETTOR: TWIN SOLEX.

GEARBOX: Four-speed constant mesh gearbox specially designed to run in engine oil. Designed so as to form an integral part of the power unit and incorporating a double-plate FERODO clutch of car type. Special design of easy light operating gear change. Ratios: Bottom 11.5 : 1; 2nd 7.3 : 1; 3rd 6.16 : 1; Top 5.0 : 1.

TRANSMISSION: SHAFT DRIVE to rear wheel incorporating a LAYRUB shock-absorbing joint and HARDY SPICER UNIVERSAL coupling with spiral bevel pinion and crown wheel.

IGNITION: LUCAS A.C. generator and distributor.

LUBRICATION: Gear-driven oil pump, maintaining a high pressure oil supply to all working parts. A reservoir of half-gallon capacity incorporated in a deep sump. Gearbox and Shaft Drive also lubricated with engine oil. Twin filters to ensure continuous purification of oil.

FRAME: WOOLER PATENT DUPLEX Frame with rear springing taking all road shocks and reactions. SPECIAL fabricated DUPLEX HEAD-LUG.

FORKS: WOOLER PATENT design Duplex steering stem and similar springing system to that used for the frame.

SUSPENSION: ORIGINAL WOOLER PATENT springing, front and rear, with compound springs set to automatically adjust for varying loads and speeds.

STANDS: Centrally positioned, easily operated, independent stands.

WHEELS: 19 in. by 3.25 in. detachable wheels of special design incorporating INTERCHANGEABILITY. Patent design Dural HUB fitted with straight spokes. Dural rims supplied at an extra charge.

BRAKES: Patent design of hubs of 7 in. internal diameter fitted with steel liner and FERODO brake linings.

TYRES: 19 in. × 3.25 in. by DUNLOP.

MUDGUARDS: Special design, eliminating all exposed nuts and bolts thus ensuring freedom from rusting, with the rear end of the guard being so shaped as to carry the registration number and rear lamp.

HANDLEBARS: WOOLER PATENT cluster controls with single bolt fitting, embodying positive action twist-grip for throttle and ignition control as well as horn push and cut-out switch.

PETROL TANK: Specially designed streamline tank embodying lighting and speedometer. Fuel capacity 3½ gallons.

SADDLE: Specially manufactured by WRIGHTS. Dual seats by FERIDEX.

LIGHTING: Special LUCAS lamp built into tank nose. Latest LUCAS rear lamp built into rear mudguard.

FINISH: In black and chrome. All enamelled parts pre-treated to ensure rust freedom with only really high quality materials used throughout.

WEIGHT: Complete machine weighs 355 lbs. when fully equipped.

EXTRAS: Pillion seat and footrests, dual seat, Dural rims, etc.

The swansong. John and his son Roland had done a huge amount of redesigning, not the least of which involved throwing the 'beams' out of the engine and rendering it considerably more conventional, but as you can see it was almost an entirely new machine. Although it was still beautifully engineered, the pair of them had decided that twin plunger suspension all round was superfluous and that single units were perfectly adequate. Gone too was the intricate system of seat springing, and now they made do with a pair of coil springs just like other manufacturers – although they couldn't resist saying that the pretty normal-looking seat was 'specially manufactured'. This time around any other involvement was specifically mentioned: 'Sole makers: Wooler & Partners Limited'. So, although (financial) partners might have been welcome I suspect father and son were carrying on in the garden shed, which was very likely the 'Research Department, West End Road, Ruislip' alluded to in this brochure.